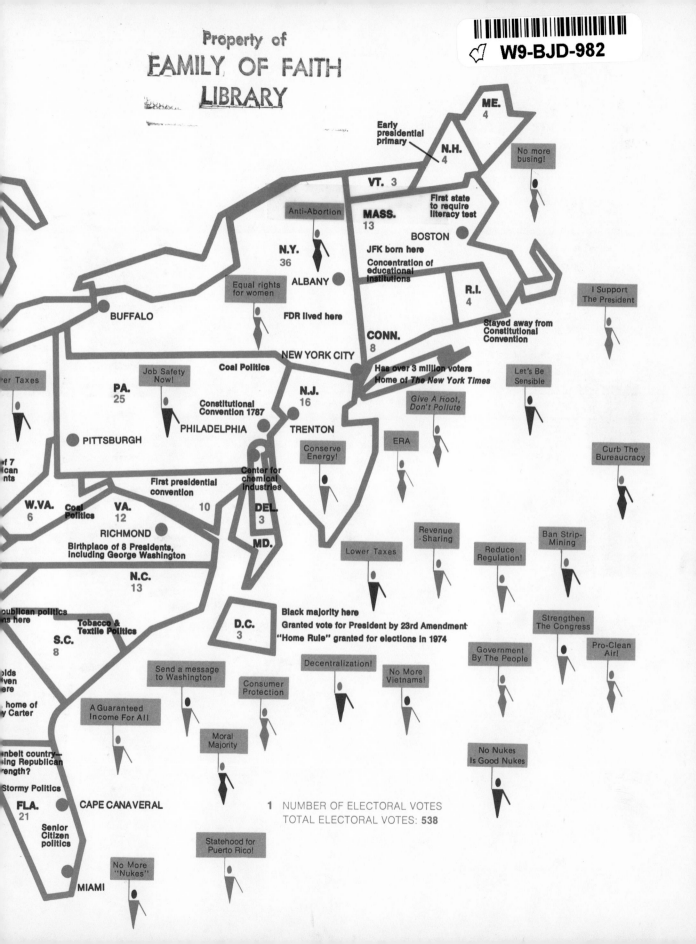

W9-BJD-982

ME. 4

Early presidential primary

N.H. 4

No more busing!

VT. 3

First state to require literacy test

MASS. 13

Anti-Abortion

N.Y. 36

ALBANY

BOSTON

JFK born here

Concentration of educational institutions

I Support The President

Equal rights for women

FDR lived here

R.I. 4

Stayed away from Constitutional Convention

BUFFALO

CONN. 8

Has over 3 million voters
Home of *The New York Times*

Let's Be Sensible

Coal Politics

NEW YORK CITY

er Taxes

Job Safety Now!

PA. 25

Constitutional Convention 1787

PHILADELPHIA

N.J. 16

TRENTON

Give A Hoot, Don't Pollute

Curb The Bureaucracy

PITTSBURGH

Conserve Energy!

ERA

of 7 can nts

Center for chemical industries

DEL. 3

Revenue -Sharing

Reduce Regulation!

Ban Strip- Mining

First presidential convention

10

W.VA. 6

Coal Politics

VA. 12

MD.

Lower Taxes

RICHMOND

Birthplace of 8 Presidents, including George Washington

N.C. 13

Strengthen The Congress

Pro-Clean Air!

ublican politics ns here

D.C. 3

Black majority here
Granted vote for President by 23rd Amendment
"Home Rule" granted for elections in 1974

Government By The People

Tobacco & Textile Politics

S.C. 8

Decentralization!

No More Vietnams!

olds ven ere

Send a message to Washington

Consumer Protection

home of y Carter

A Guaranteed Income For All

No Nukes Is Good Nukes

nbelt country— ing Republican rength?

Moral Majority

Stormy Politics

FLA. 21

CAPE CANAVERAL

1 NUMBER OF ELECTORAL VOTES
TOTAL ELECTORAL VOTES: **538**

Senior Citizen politics

Statehood for Puerto Rico!

No More "Nukes"

MIAMI

GOVERNMENT
BY THE PEOPLE

NATIONAL EDITION

TWELFTH ALTERNATE EDITION

GOVERNMENT BY THE PEOPLE

JAMES MAC GREGOR BURNS

Williams College

J. W. PELTASON

University of California, Irvine

THOMAS E. CRONIN

Colorado College

Prentice-Hall, Inc., Englewood Cliffs, New Jersey 07632

Library of Congress Cataloging in Publication Data

Burns, James MacGregor.
  Government by the people.

  Includes bibliographies and index.
    1. United States—Politics and government.
I. Peltason, J. W. (Jack Walter), (date)
II. Cronin, Thomas E.   III. Title.
JK274.B853   1985   320.973   84-26288
ISBN   0-13-361528-6

Acquisitions Editor: Stan Wakefield
Editorial/production supervision: Joyce Turner/Linda Benson
Interior design and cover design: Suzanne Behnke
Cover photo: James K. Clark
Manufacturing buyer: Barbara Kelly Kittle
Page Makeup: Meryl Poweski
Photo Research: Lorinda Morris/Photoquest

Printed in the United States of America
10 9 8 7 6 5 4 3 2 1

ISBN 0-13-361528-6 01

Prentice-Hall International, Inc., *London*
Prentice-Hall of Australia Pty. Limited, *Sydney*
Editora Prentice-Hall do Brasil, Ltda., *Rio de Janeiro*
Prentice-Hall Canada Inc., *Toronto*
Prentice-Hall Hispanoamericana, S.A., *Mexico*
Prentice-Hall of India Private Limited, *New Delhi*
Prentice-Hall of Japan, Inc., *Tokyo*
Prentice-Hall of Southeast Asia Pte. Ltd., *Singapore*
Whitehall Books Limited, *Wellington, New Zealand*

CONTENTS

AMERICAN FEDERALISM: PROBLEMS AND PROSPECTS 42

PART TWO/CIVIL LIBERTIES

FIRST AMENDMENT RIGHTS 67

EQUAL RIGHTS UNDER THE LAW 93

RIGHTS TO LIFE, LIBERTY, AND PROPERTY   123

PART THREE / THE PEOPLE IN POLITICS

GROUPS: THE POLITICS OF FACTION   151

MOVEMENTS: THE POLITICS OF CONFLICT   176

JUDGES: THE BALANCING BRANCH 373

BUREAUCRATS: THE REAL POWER? 403

PART FIVE/THE POLITICS OF NATIONAL POLICY

MAKING PUBLIC POLICY 433

PREFACE

Many people couldn't care less about politics and try to avoid it. But politics is all around us and affects almost every aspect of our lives. *Politics* is the process by which people live together, make decisions about how to meet their basic needs, solve common problems, organize for safety and security, even realize the "good life." Briefly put, politics is who gets what, when, and how? It is also the process of organizing, harnessing, and constraining public power. This involves both reconciling competing demands for governmental action and reconciling competing conceptions of the "good society" or "the public interest." *Government* seeks to resolve conflicts in a way that enhances a nation's values and purposes.

Your authors are political scientists. In the broadest sense *political science* is the study of politics and government. Political scientists study and try to understand how government structures get shaped and how government policies are made and enforced. What are the fundamental rules of the game? How are these rules changed? How do we think and behave politically? Who votes? Who has influence or "clout"? How does all this shape the final outcome—the policies that take money from us, give some back, shape our daily lives?

The challenge of political science, and the challenge in this book, is to explain why things political came to be and why they work as they do. Political ideas are powerful; they shape the way we see the world, and they shape our expectations and dreams. They also shape how we judge the political system's impact on our lives.

As political scientists we are interested in all aspects of American politics. We believe democracy flourishes when citizens enjoy basic freedoms, have a voice in how they are governed, and understand the workings of their government. We believe knowledge about American government is vitally important. *Knowledge* is knowing and understanding what is important—not just memorizing dates, details, and facts. But the road to knowledge must involve learning facts and gaining information. You will find plenty of information and description in the chapters that follow. We also provide interpretation and our own comments about what is important. In addition to teaching and conducting research, all three of us have worked in politics and government—including holding local office, running for Congress, lobbying, working in the White House, advising candidates, working in political parties and much more. However, you should form your own judgments and develop your own conclusions. Challenge what you read.

Nearly every aspect of the American political system is affected by and interconnected with other elements making up the whole system. Our book necessarily treats one aspect at a time. We take up and explore the Constitution in one chapter, elections in another, the media in another, Congress in yet another. In the real world these processes or institutions are not so neatly separated. They are constantly shaped by and interlocked with one another. Keep in mind, then, that we are discussing a highly dynamic system—not a static or unidimensional one.

Political scientists ultimately want to formulate theories about the why and the how and the "so what" of political life. Aristotle called the enterprise the "queen of sciences." He classified countries according to their political structures, making predictions about how varying structures would lead to different behavior. Machiavelli, another political theorist, examined political systems and forecast how rulers could best govern and how people would react to different styles of leadership. St. Thomas Aquinas, John Locke, Thomas Hobbes, and America's own James Madison were also political theorists and political philosophers. Two hundred years ago, in the summer of 1787 at Philadelphia, the persons who drafted the Constitution acted as political theoreticians as they attempted to mold theories into practical political institutions.

In the 1980s we continue to study and learn about the patterns of politics. Description yields understanding; understanding yields or can lead to explanation; explanation can lead to prediction; and predictions that work lead to theory. We continually search for the predictable–to discover, describe, and verify the basic "laws" of politics and governance. While political science in some ways is an ancient discipline, it is also in many ways a very young social science: Rigorous efforts to learn enough to allow us to explain and predict really began only in the past generation. Join us as we attempt to push the study of governance toward greater clarity and rigor.

New editions of this book require an infusion of fresh ideas and suggestions about the most recent research. We have asked several scholars for assistance and although they bear no responsibility for our interpretation they have all helped make this a better book. We thank Professor Diane L. Fowlkes who made major contributions to the redrafting, as well as the analysis, of Part Three chapters; and Timothy L. Wilkinson for research assistance and important revision suggestions in this edition. We thank Bruce Adams, Kathleen Murphy Beatty, Michael B. Binford, Curtis Cook, Tania Cronin, Randall Hubbard, David Kozak, Robert D. Loevy, David O'Brien, Austin Ranney, John Shockley, Carl Stenberg, and Marcia Whicker for especially helpful reviews and critiques of certain chapters. We also thank the scores of professors and students who have sent us their criticisms, ideas, and advice. We are in debt too, to Ann B. Armstrong for her excellent proofreading.

Talented professionals at Prentice-Hall helped enormously, especially our outstanding production editor, Joyce Turner; our political science editor, Stan Wakefield; our copy editor, Lois Goldrich; and Audrey Marshall, Marianne DiDomenico, Mary Helen Fitzgerald, Anita Duncan, Suzanne Behnke, Linda Benson, and Colette Conboy, who have helped in countless ways.

We call to your attention the excellent *Guide to Government by the People* by Raymond L. Lee and Dorothy A. Palmer, designed to give students an opportunity to participate more directly in the learning process. These authors have also prepared a valuable new edition of *Approaches to Teaching Government By the People*, available from Prentice-Hall to all teachers using this book. A new and much improved and expanded text manual and package for professors has been prepared by Professor Marcia L. Whicker of the University of South Carolina. A package of educational microcomputer learning programs has been specially prepared to accompany this new edition of *Government By The People*. These have been invented and designed by Professor Robert D. Loevy of Colorado College for both faculty and student use. We are pleased to be the first American government text, and one of the first texts in the country to provide this new and innovative learning feature; we believe it will be an important additional way for students to learn and think through for themselves many of the central features of the political system.

JAMES MACGREGOR BURNS
Williamstown, Mass.

J. W. PELTASON
Irvine, Calif.

THOMAS E. CRONIN
Colorado Springs, Colo.

February, 1985

P. S. Please point out any errors. Send us comments, suggestions, and alternative interpretations for future printings and editions. Address your letters to any one of us or all of us: c/o Political Science Editor, Prentice Hall, Inc., Englewood Cliffs, NJ. 07632

THE MAKING OF A REPUBLIC - 1787

1

Late in 1786 messengers rode into George Washington's plantation at Mt. Vernon with alarming news. Some farmers in western Massachusetts, crushed by debts and taxes, were rebelling against foreclosures, forcing judges out of their courtrooms, and turning debtors out of their jails. Washington was appalled. Ten years before, he had been leading Americans in a patriots' war against British redcoats. Now Americans were fighting Americans!

"What, gracious God, is man!" Washington exclaimed, that he should be so perfidious. "It is but the other day, that we were shedding our blood to obtain the Constitution of our choice." If government cannot check these disorders, he wrote to his friend James Madison, "what security has a man for life, liberty, or property?" It was obvious that without a stronger constitution, "thirteen Sovereignties pulling against each other, and all tugging at the federal head will soon bring ruin on the whole."

Not all Americans reacted as Washington did to the farmers' uprising, which came to be known as Shays's Rebellion. Some sided with the rebels. When Abigail Adams, wife of American minister John Adams in London, sent the news to Thomas Jefferson, minister in Paris, the Virginian replied: "I like a little rebellion now and then." Later Jefferson added, "The tree of liberty must be refreshed from time to time with the blood of patriots and tyrants. It is its natural manure."

At the time most informed Americans probably agreed much more with Washington than with Jefferson. They knew that their struggling little republic was surrounded by the big and hungry powers of Europe—Spain to the South, in Florida; the French to the West, in the Mississippi Valley; and the British to the North, in Canada. These Americans remembered that in 1776 the Declaration of Independence had proclaimed the unalienable rights of life, liberty, and the pursuit of happiness. But how, they asked, could these rights be protected in a small nation vulnerable to attack from outside, divided into thirteen independent states, and wracked by internal disorder?

Shays's Rebellion petered out after the farmers attacked an arsenal, and were cut down by cannon fire. It was not much of a rebellion, but it sent a stab of fear into the established leadership. It also acted as a catalyst, precipitating the decision to call a convention to meet in Philadelphia in the summer of 1787. Its purpose: to build a stronger national government that would truly be able to protect "life, liberty, and property."

WHAT KIND OF CONSTITUTION?

CREATING THE REPUBLIC

April, 1775	American Revolution begins at Lexington and Concord (Mass.)
June, 1775	George Washington assumes command of Continental forces
July, 1776	Declaration of Independence approved
Nov., 1777	Articles of Confederation, adopted by Continental Congress
March, 1781	Articles of Confederation, ratified by the states
Oct., 1782	British defeated at Yorktown
Mid-1783	Peace negotiations begin in Paris
Late 1783	British forces leave; General Washington retires
April, 1784	Congress ratifies Peace Treaty with British
Late 1786	Shays's Rebellion in western Massachusetts
May, 1787	Constitutional Convention begins in Philadelphia
Sept., 1787	Constitution for United States, adopted by Convention

Remember the Fourth of July, 1976? (Perhaps you were in your early teens.) This was the 200th anniversary of the signing of the Declaration of Independence—the decisive political act in our struggle to gain independence from Great Britain. It was the 200th birthday of that great tribute (penned by Adams and Jefferson, among others) to "life, liberty and the pursuit of happiness." Who can forget the wonderful pageantry in 1976—the old sailing ships in the harbor, the parades of carriages and stagecoaches, the bursting fireworks in the "best Fourth of July ever."

Soon we will be celebrating another 200th birthday: that of the Constitution of the United States. This occasion may call for hard thought rather than fireworks. For the great charter of 1787 is a "living constitution," that centrally influences "who gets what, when and how" in American society today; hence, it is still a subject of controversy. Then too, the Constitution—and our whole constitutional system—is a most complex affair, and we ought to understand what we celebrate. It might also be helpful for younger persons today, who will typically live until the mid-twenty-first century, to evaluate how a great instrument of government invented for the eighteenth century can meet the enormous pressures and crises we can expect to arise in the future.

This and virtually all the following chapters, will deal with key aspects of these problems, for a constitutional system embraces the whole range of laws, institutions, politics, and procedures that make up our political universe today. But two elements of the Constitution of 1787 are so crucial, they need to be highlighted at the very start: the *division* of powers between the national and state governments, and the *separation* of powers among the legislative, executive, and judicial branches.

By *division of powers* we mean federalism. Virtually all nations divide power between the central government and regional governments. What is unique about federalism is that power is not granted by the central government to the states, and hence cannot be withdrawn from them. Rather, a constitution divides the powers—delegating some to the national government and reserving others to the states. This arrangement seems to work most of the time, but will it hold up during the twenty-first century under intense pressures to centralize authority in the national government?

By *separation of powers* we mean more than allocating legislative powers to the Congress, executive powers to the president, and judicial powers to the Supreme Court and other federal courts. We also mean that each branch has constitutional and political *independence*, and thus there are *checks and balances* that allow the various branches to delay or block the actions of the other branches. This was the supreme creation of the framers in 1787. While the

Note: It took about 15 years for us to win Independence, form an interim government that tried to govern, fashion a "more perfect union" and actually get a three-branched government functioning.

concept was not new, the framers built the idea into a system of government so ingeniously that it has become a lasting and central part of our system. But again the question arises—Can a governmental system so divided and muscle-bound cope with the challenges that lie ahead?

Most other democracies operate on a principle quite different from checks and balances—that of majority rule, through a parliamentary system. Typically, if one party or a coalition of parties wins a majority of seats in parliament, that majority wins control of the government. This has been true, for example, of the (conservative) Thatcher government in Britain and the (socialist) Mitterand government in France. The victorious party, the majority party in the parliament, the cabinet, and the prime minister are fused together for joint decision and action, though of course there are many variations in practice.

Contrast the American system. It was carefully designed to delay or block majority action, for the framers, while they wanted energetic and competent government, did not want the "masses"—people like those led by Daniel Shays—to take control of the government. Thus, they fixed it so that it would not be enough for a majority "faction" to win control of the House of Representatives. Rather, such a faction must in a series of elections win control of the Senate and of the presidency—and perhaps ultimately of the Supreme Court. Further, countless antimajoritarian devices have been built into the system—for example, the right to filibuster bills to death in the Senate.

Is this the "government of the people, by the people, and for the people" that Lincoln celebrated in his Gettysburg address? Some critics contend that our constitutional system is fundamentally undemocratic, antimajoritarian, and antipopular. They argue further it was intentionally set up that way—that the framers were elitists who deliberately designed a system to protect their

Under the leadership of Daniel Shays, a group of farmers forcibly restrained the Massachusetts courts from foreclosing their mortgages. The uprising was known as Shays's Rebellion. *Culver.*

property. Defenders of the system reply that in the long run the people do control Congress, the presidency, and even the judiciary; the checks and balances merely cushion the impact of popular demands and passions. Moreover, they claim, the system protects minority rights—and minority rights are just as important as majority rule.[1]

Thus, there are some crucial questions involved in celebrating the birthday of the Constitution in the years immediately ahead. As we will note, these questions involve some of our most basic goals and values, including liberty, equality, and justice. We can hardly hope today to match the wisdom of the framers, one of the most talented groups of thinkers and doers in western history. But perhaps we can observe the bicentennial by trying to match their commitment to hard study and reasoned analysis. And a first step in analysis is careful definition of terms.

A Republic or a Democracy?

The American political system can be called either a constitutional republic or a constitutional democracy. Is there any real difference? Democracy comes from two Greek roots—*demos*, the people, and *kratis*, authority. The word was used by the Athenians to mean government by the many, as contrasted with government by the few (oligarchy) or by one (autocracy). At one time democracy meant only *direct* or *pure* democracy of the kind used in some Greek city-states, or in New England town meetings today, in which all citizens may take part in making laws. Today democracy is more likely to mean a representative democracy—or in Plato's term, a *republic*—in which the people do not actually make the laws or administer them but choose the people who do.

The founding fathers preferred the term *republic* to avoid any confusion with pure democracy. For them democracy meant mob rule, and demagogues appealing to the "masses."

Here we define democracy or republic to mean a system of government in which those who have the authority to make decisions (that have the force of law) acquire and retain this authority either directly or indirectly as the result of winning a free election in which the great majority of adult citizens are allowed to participate.

Ours is not only a democratic system, it is a *constitutional* one. While these two concepts are related, they are also different. Democracy refers to how

[1]For recent treatments of this question, see John Patrick Diggins, "Power and Authority in American History: The Case of Charles A. Beard and His Critics," *American Historical Review* (October 1981), pp. 701–30; and James MacGregor Burns, *The Vineyard of Liberty* (Knopf, 1982), chs. 1 and 2.

CONSTITUTIONAL
CHECKS ON PUBLIC
OFFICIALS

Written Constitution
Regular elections
Separation of powers
Federalism
Staggered terms of office
Judicial review
Minority rights
Right to petition for redress of
grievances
Impeachment process
Rule of law, making public
officials subject to criminal
prosecution
Freedom of the press to criticize
public officials

power is *acquired* and *retained*. Constitutionalism refers to how power is *limited*. A government can be constitutional without being democratic—as in seventeenth-century England. It can also be democratic without being constitutional, as in Athens at the time of Pericles. True, all governments have a constitution in the sense that there are agreed-upon ways by which governments proceed. In this sense both the Soviet Union and the People's Republic of China have constitutions. But the term constitutional government has come to have a more restricted meaning: government in which there are clearly recognized and regularly applied limits on the powers of those who govern. By this definition Great Britain, Canada, and the United States are constitutional democracies, but the Soviet Union is not, for there are few checks on the powers of Soviet rulers.

Our founding fathers created a system in which the first great safeguard against abuse of authority was to be reliance on the *people*—the democratic principle. But this was not to be the only safeguard. The framers established a variety of checks on the power of officeholders. These are recognized and routinely enforced limits on what public officials—even those elected by the people—may do.

In the chapters that follow we will look at our constitutional republic in greater detail. We will find that it is a complex system, difficult to describe. It is even harder to operate; constitutional republics such as ours exist in only a few nations. But to democrats—or, if you prefer—to republicans, it is a precious thing, precious because our system is committed to protecting and expanding liberty. That commitment rests on certain fundamental convictions.

Basic Premises of Democracy

First, democrats recognize the fundamental dignity and importance of the *individual*. This notion pervades all of democratic thought. It is woven into the writings of Thomas Jefferson, especially in the Declaration of Independence—*all men are endowed by their Creator with certain unalienable rights*. Individualism makes the person—rich or poor, black or white, male or female—the *central* measure of value. The state, the union, and the corporation are measured in terms of their usefulness to individuals. Not everyone, of course, believes in putting the individual first. Some believe in statism, considering the state or community supreme. Democrats, however, believe that the state, or even the community, is less important than the individuals who compose it.

Second, democrats recognize the right of each individual to be treated as a unique and inviolable human being. They do not insist that all are equal in talents or virtues; they do insist that one person's claim to life, liberty, and property must be recognized as much as another's. While this right raises difficult questions as to how equal rights can be secured, the *principle* of equality of right is clear.

Third, democrats are convinced that freedom is good in itself. *Liberty* or *freedom* (used interchangeably here) means that all individuals must have the opportunity to choose their own goals. The core of liberty is *self-determination*. Liberty is not simply the absence of external restraint on a person; it means the individual's power to act positively to reach his or her goals. Moreover, both history and reason suggest that individual liberty is the key to *social progress*. The greater people's freedom, the greater the chance of discovering better ways of life.

The basic values of democracy do not necessarily coexist happily with one another in a particular society. The concept of individualism may conflict with the older tradition of public virtue and collective welfare—of the citizen as a participant in the general welfare. Freedom as the *liberation* of the individual may conflict with freedom as the *alienation* of people from friends or communities. The concept of individual self-determination may conflict with that of collective decision making for the national welfare or for the public good. The right of a mill owner to run his factory as he pleases, as compared to the right of a millhand in that factory to join a union, or even to share in the running of the plant, illustrates this type of conflict in everyday life.

Liberty and Equality: Democratic Goals

Probably the single most powerful idea in American history has been that of liberty. It was for life, liberty, and the pursuit of happiness that independence was declared; it was to secure the blessings of liberty that the Constitution was drawn up and adopted. While there is no way to prove that liberty has been this powerful a concept for Americans, consider our patriotic anthems—it is to the "sweet land of liberty" that we sing. Or take a coin out of your pocket; that penny, nickel, dime, quarter, or half dollar proclaims not authority, security, or brotherhood, but *liberty*.

Liberty is a fuzzy as well as a compelling concept; much depends on how Americans define it as they make practical decisions. During the early decades of the republic, the American concept of liberty was essentially negative. The main aim of Jeffersonian democracy was to throw off the burdens of established governments, churches, and other institutions. These negative liberties were made explicit in the Bill of Rights of the Constitution, which granted free speech, free press, freedom of religion, and freedom of assembly. The main role of the Constitution was to remove governmental constraints on individual liberties.

During most of the nineteenth century, liberty as "freedom *from*" meshed with the dominant economic and social doctrine of laissez faire. Under this doctrine individuals must be free of governments that might stop them from reaching maximum efficiency and productivity. The state, it was argued, must intervene no more than is absolutely necessary to protect life and property. Further intervention, such as minimum wages, health protection, or even compulsory vaccination, is both immoral in theory and improper in fact. The idea is simple: the less governmental power, the more individual liberty.

But what was the meaning of liberty (or freedom, which is its equivalent) when not governments but other individuals—employers, lynch mobs, plantation owners, labor bosses—deprived persons of this right? Slavery forced Americans to rethink their ideas. "The world has never had a good definition of the word liberty," Abraham Lincoln said during the Civil War, "and the American people, just now, are in want of one. We all declare for liberty; but in using the same word we do not all mean the same thing. With some the word liberty may mean for each man to do as he pleases with himself, and the product of his labor; while with others the same word may mean for some men to do as they please with other men. . . ."[2] He used the example of the shepherd who drives the wolf from the sheep's throat: The sheep thanks the shepherd as his liberator, while the wolf denounces him as the destroyer of liberty.

With the coming of industrialization, urbanization, and agrarian and labor discontent; of unions, depressions, and social protest; and of leaders like William Jennings Bryan, Theodore Roosevelt, Robert La Follette, Eugene Debs, and Woodrow Wilson, liberty came to have far more positive meanings. Americans slowly came to understand that men and women, crowded more and more together, lived amid webs of all kinds—personal and private, institutional and psychological. To abolish one type of restraint (such as black slavery) might mean increasing another type of restraint (such as wage slavery). To cut down on governmental restraint of liberty might simply mean increasing private economic and social power. The question was not simply liberating

The signing of the Declaration of Independence, 1776. *Library of Congress.*

[2]Speech at Sanitary Fair, 1864.

6

people from *government*; it was how to use government to free people from *non*governmental curbs on liberty as well.

But what about the idea of *equality*, next to liberty probably the most vital concept in American thought. "All men are created equal and from that equal creation they derive rights inherent and unalienable, among which are the preservation of liberty and the pursuit of happiness." So read Jefferson's first draft of the Declaration, and the words indicate the primacy of the concept. Alexis de Tocqueville, James Bryce, Harold Laski, and other foreigners who investigated American democracy were struck by the strength of egalitarian thought and practice in both our political and social lives.

What did equality mean? What *kind* of equality? Economic, political, legal, social, or something else? Equality for *whom?* For blacks as well as whites? For children and teenagers as well as adults? Equality of *opportunity?*—almost all Americans said they wanted that—but also of *condition?* This last question was the toughest. Did equality of opportunity simply mean that everyone should have *the same place at the starting line?* Or did it mean that there should be an effort to equalize most or all the factors that during the course of a person's life might determine how well he or she fares socially or economically?

Herbert Hoover posed the issue when he said: "We, through free and universal education, provide the training of the runners; we give to them an equal start; we provide in government the umpire of fairness in the race. . . ."[3] Franklin D. Roosevelt sought to answer the question when he proclaimed first the Four Freedoms—freedom from *want* and *fear* as well as freedom of speech and religion—and later a "second Bill of Rights." Under this second bill of rights, he said, Americans now accepted the idea that a new basis of security and prosperity can be established for all, regardless of position, race, or creed. This meant good housing, health, jobs, and social security for all. The New Deal and its successor programs, in both their achievements and failures, have tried to advance the egalitarian intentions of the second bill of rights.

Thus, two concepts once seen as opposites have coalesced in a philosophy that calls for government to help broaden people's *social* and *economic* liberties, while it prevents other institutions (corporations or unions or landlords) from infringing on those liberties. At the same time, the government must prevent *itself* from interfering with liberty. This is no small task, and it is not always performed well—but the idea is exciting. It means that Americans, perhaps without being wholly conscious of it, have brought together the values of liberty and equality. No longer can one say flatly: "The more government, the less liberty"; but neither can one say the opposite.

Liberty and equality interlock and stimulate each other at some points; they are in a state of opposition, or at least tension, at other points. At still other points they do not relate to each other at all. Pushed too far, liberty becomes license and unbridled individualism; pushed too far, equality could mean leveling, a dull mediocrity, and even the erosion of liberty. Much of our political combat revolves around the question of how to strike a balance.

Democracy as Political Means

Some favor democracy not only because they believe it stands for goals such as liberty and equality, but also because they see it as the best way to govern a complex society. If those who admire democracy for the human ends it represents can be called principle democrats, those who see democracy as a tech-

---

[3]Herbert Hoover, *American Individualism* (Doubleday, Page, 1922), p. 9. This ancient debate continues: See two recent, highly influential books: John Rawls, A *Theory of Justice* (Harvard University Press, 1971); and Robert Nozick, *Anarchy, State and Utopia* (Basic Books, 1974).

nique of self-government can be called process democrats. Process democrats grant that democratic processes do not guarantee justice will be done, but they contend that the chances are better under "government by the people" than under any other system. It is important to note what is *not* included in the concept of democracy as a process for making decisions. Process democrats do not judge a democracy by its policy output. Their concern is with the *procedures* for making policy, and not with the rightness of the policy that is made.

Process democrats contend that government *by* the people usually will produce government *for* the people: They reject the notion that it is possible to define the public interest "scientifically." If one believes, as did Plato, that decisions about public policy are of the same nature as, say, a decision as to how to build a boat, then the best way to make policy is to turn everything over to a group of specialists or experts. Then, like Plato, one would favor a system that places authority in the hands of philosopher-kings or, in today's terms, in the hands of the "best and the brightest." Process democrats, on the other hand, take their stand with Aristotle, who argued that although an expert cook knows better than the nonexpert how to bake a cake, the person who eats it is the better judge of how it tastes.

Most Americans do not trust experts very much. As President Dwight Eisenhower stated in his farewell address: "Yet in holding scientific research and discovery in respect, as we should, we must also be alert to the equal and opposite danger that public policy could itself become the captive of a scientific-technological elite." Few democrats—especially process democrats—wish to shift the control of our destinies from voters and their elected leaders to some new priesthood of systems analysts.

Fundamental Democratic Processes

The crucial mechanism in all genuinely popular governments is a system of free, fair, and open elections. Democratic governments take many different forms, but democratic elections have at least four essential elements:

1. *All citizens should have equal voting power.* This does not mean that all must or will have equal political influence. Some persons, because of wealth, talent, or position, have much more power than others. How much extra influence key figures should be allowed to exercise in a democracy is one of the questions that faces democrats. But whether one is president or pick-and-shovel laborer, newspaper publisher or lettuce picker, each casts only one vote at the polls.

2. *Voters should have the right of access to facts, criticism, competing ideas, and the views of all candidates.* Here again, the extent to which different ideas actually receive equal attention is a problem because of the nature of the mass media, the special access of the president to television and the press, and the inability of many lower-income people to make their ideas known. Still, the principle of free competition of ideas during an election is essential.

3. *Citizens must be free to organize for political purposes.* Obviously, individuals can be more effective when they join with others in a party, a pressure group, a protest movement, or a demonstration.

4. *Elections are decided by majorities (or at least pluralities).* Those who get the most votes win, even if the winning side seems to be made up of idiots. The persons chosen by the majority take office. How much power the winners may then have over the losing minority is another problem, but there is no question that the winners take office and assume formal authority.

The American System: Democratic and Constitutional

The founding fathers believed in democracy both as a *principle* and as a *process*. Their genius lay in how they related the *goals* of democracy to its *methods*. If the Declaration of Independence was more concerned with *goals* such as liberty

"Gad, when I think of the power the people have . . . it just isn't fair." Copyright, 1983, *Los Angeles Times. Reprinted by permission.*

and equality, the Constitution focused more on the *processes* that could help realize these goals without sacrificing values such as controlled power, stability, continuity, due process, and balanced decision making. For two centuries American politicians, jurists, and other leaders have been enormously influenced by the resounding success of the revolutionaries of 1776 and 1787 in working out effective and durable political processes. The Watergate scandals were a dramatic warning, process democrats remind us, that to abuse democratic processes is to threaten both the means and the ends of a free people.

THE ORIGINS OF THE AMERICAN REPUBLIC

The American Revolution was conservative in several respects. Certainly, it had constitutional goals. Those who declared our independence from England did so reluctantly, and in the name of the English Constitution. They sought not to establish a new order but to restore the rights taken from them by the king.[4] As Alexis de Tocqueville, the perceptive nineteenth-century French visitor to the New World, observed: "The great advantage of the Americans is that they have arrived at a state of democracy without having to endure a democratic revolution. . . ."[5] De Tocqueville had not forgotten our war period, 1775–1781. He meant that the American Revolution was primarily a rebellion of colonies against an empire. But even in this respect, "the Americans [other than blacks] were not an oppressed people; they had no crushing imperial shackles to throw off. In fact, the Americans knew they were probably freer and less burdened with cumbersome feudal and hierarchical restraints than any part of mankind in the eighteenth century."[6] In the modern sense it was hardly a revolution; there were no sharp breaks with the past and no great social, economic, or political upheavals. Contrast the colonists' demand for the "rights of Englishmen" with the French demand for the "rights of man" in 1789. "Even the fact that Americans jettisoned a monarch and suddenly and without much internal debate adopted a republican government marked no great upheaval." Thomas Jefferson observed in the summer of 1777 that Americans "seem to have deposited the monarchical and taken up the republican government with as much ease as would have attended their throwing off an old and putting on a new suit of clothes."[7] As a result, the American Revolution did not open class wounds. The political system based on such revolution centered more on consensus than on conflict.

The New Governments

The destruction of English authority was the first step in establishing the American republic. The next was to create new state governments and to establish at least a limited central government under the Articles of Confederation.

Although the breaks with the past were not dramatic as compared to the French Revolution of a few years later (1789) or the Russian Revolution of this century (1917), the new governments were different from those they replaced. New state constitutions incorporated bills of rights, abolished most religious qualifica-

[4]See Martin Diamond, "The Revolution of Sober Expectations," *The American Revolution: Three Views* (American Brands, 1975), p. 57.

[5]*Democracy in America*, Vol. II, ed. F. Bowen (Sever and Francis, 1872), p. 13. For other statements of the same view, see Daniel J. Boorstin, *The Genius of American Politics* (University of Chicago Press, 1953), p. 68; and Louis Hartz, *The Liberal Tradition in America* (Harcourt, 1955).

[6]Gordon Wood, *The Creation of the American Republic, 1776-1787* (University of North Carolina Press, 1969), p. 3.

[7]Quoted by Wood, p. 92, Jefferson to Benjamin Franklin, August 2, 1777. In J. P. Boyd et al. (eds.), *Jefferson Papers*, Vol. II (Princeton University Press, 1950), p. 26.

tions, and liberalized property and taxpaying requirements for voting.[8] There were no kings. Power was concentrated in the legislatures. The governors and judges—officials who reminded Americans of royalty—lost influence. Governors were made dependent on the legislature for election, and the legislatures overrode judicial decisions and scolded judges whose rulings were unpopular. The legislative branch, later complained the writers of the *Federalist No. 48*, was drawing all power into its impetuous vortex. What about the central government? Having just fought a war against one central government, Americans were reluctant to create another. The Articles of Confederation, when finally approved by all the state legislatures in 1781, more or less legalized the arrangements under which the Continental Congress had assumed power in 1776. The Articles established only a fragile league of friendship, not a national government.

From 1777 to 1788 Americans made some progress under this system. But as we know from our history, the practical difficulties confronting the new nation would have tested the strongest government. The end of the war reduced the sense of urgency that had helped to unite the states, and conflicts among them were frequent. Within the states economic differences between creditors and debtors grew intense. There were foreign threats as well. The English, French, and Spanish surrounded the new nation, which—internally divided and lacking a strong central government—made a tempting prize.

As the problems mounted, many leaders, especially in New York, Virginia, Massachusetts, and Pennsylvania, became convinced that it would not be enough merely to revise the Articles of Confederation. To create a union strong enough to resist external threats, they needed to create a stronger central government with adequate powers. They therefore set out to establish a republican government that could be made to work by and for *ordinary people*.[9]

Although the need to give Congress authority to regulate commerce and collect a few taxes was increasingly recognized, many Americans were still suspicious of central government. But finally, in the late summer of 1786, under the leadership of Alexander Hamilton, those who favored a truly national government took advantage of a meeting at Annapolis, Maryland (on problems of trade and navigation, attended by delegates from five states) to issue a call for a "plenipotentiary Convention." Such a convention would have full authority to consider basic amendments to the Articles of Confederation. The delegates to the Annapolis Convention requested the legislatures of their states to appoint commissioners to meet at Philadelphia on the second Monday of May, 1787, "to devise such further provisions as shall appear to them necessary to render the Constitution of the Federal Government adequate to the exigencies of the Union."

For a short time all was quiet. Then in Western Massachusetts that fall and winter, the farmers rebelled under Shays and other leaders. This seriously disturbed Washington and other political leaders. The message seemed clear: Some kind of action must be taken to strengthen the machinery of government. Spurred on by Shays's Rebellion, seven states appointed commissioners to attend the Philadelphia Convention. Congress, apathetic and suspicious, finally issued a cautiously worded call to the states to appoint delegates for the "sole and express purpose of revising the Articles of Confederation." The cautious legislators specified that no recommendation would be effective unless approved

"You know, the idea of taxation with representation doesn't appeal to me very much either." *Drawing by Handelsman; © 1970 The New Yorker Magazine, Inc.*

[8]Elisha P. Douglass, *Rebels and Democrats* (University of North Carolina Press, 1955). See also R. R. Palmer, *The Age of the Democratic Revolution* (Princeton University Press, 1959), pp. 217-35; Chilton Williamson, *American Suffrage: From Property to Democracy, 1760-1860* (Princeton University Press, 1960), p. 92; Robert A. Rutland, *The Birth of the Bill of Rights, 1776-1791* (University of North Carolina Press, 1955); Richard Ashcraft, "Locke's State of Nature: Historical Fact or Moral Fiction?" *American Political Science Review* (September 1968), pp. 898-915; Samuel Eliot Morison, *The Oxford History of the American People* (Oxford University Press, 1965), p. 276; Hannah Arendt, *On Revolution* (Viking, 1963), p. 139.

[9]Wood, *American Republic, 1776–1787*, pp. 122, 612.

by Congress and confirmed by all the state legislatures, as provided by the Articles.

Eventually every state except Rhode Island appointed delegates. (The debtors and farmers who controlled the Rhode Island legislature rightly suspected that one of the major purposes of the proposed convention would be to limit the power of state legislatures to interfere with the rights of creditors.) Some of the delegates were bound by instructions only to consider amendments to the Articles of Confederation. Delaware went so far as to forbid its representatives to consider any proposal that would deny any state equal representation in Congress.

THE PHILADELPHIA CONVENTION—1787

The delegates who assembled in Philadelphia that summer were presented with a condition, not a theory. They had to establish a national government powerful enough to prevent the nation from dissolving. What these men did that summer continues to have a major impact on how we are governed. It also provides an outstanding lesson in political science.

The Delegates

Seventy-four delegates were appointed by the various states, but only fifty-five arrived in Philadelphia. Of these, approximately forty took a real part in the work of the convention. It was a distinguished gathering. Many of the most important men of the nation were there—successful merchants, planters, bankers and lawyers, and former and present governors and congressional representatives (thirty-nine of the delegates had served in Congress). As theorists, most had read widely in the classics of political science. As activists, most were interested in the practical task of constructing a national government.

The convention was as representative as most political gatherings at the time. Of course, there were no women or blacks. The delegates were mainly state or national leaders, for in the 1780s the ordinary person was not likely to participate in politics. (Even today farm laborers, factory workers, and truck drivers are seldom found in Congress, although a self-styled peanut farmer and a movie actor have made their way to the White House.) Although most of the leaders in attendance eventually supported the Constitution in the ratification debates, only eight of the fifty-six signers of the Declaration of Independence were present at the constitutional convention. Among those who did not come were Jefferson, Thomas Paine, Patrick Henry, Richard Henry Lee, Sam and John Adams, and John Hancock. Of the active participants at the convention, several men stand out as the prime movers.

Alexander Hamilton had been the engineer of the Annapolis Convention, and as early as 1778 he had been urging that the national government be made stronger. Hamilton had come to the United States from the West Indies and while still a student at Kings College (now Columbia University) had won national attention for his brilliant pamphlets in defense of the Revolutionary cause. During the war he served as General Washington's aide, and his experiences confirmed his distaste for a Congress so weak it could not even supply its troops with enough food or arms.

From Virginia came two of the leading delegates—General George Washington and James Madison. Although active in the movement to revise the Articles of Confederation, Washington had been extremely reluctant to attend the convention. He accepted only when persuaded that his prestige was needed for its success. He was selected unanimously to preside over the meetings. According to the records, he spoke only twice during the deliberations, but his influence was felt in the informal gatherings as well as during the sessions. The assumption that Washington would become the first president under the new constitution inspired confidence in it. James Madison was only thirty-six years old at the time of the convention, but he was one of the most learned members present. He had helped frame Virginia's first constitution and had served both in the Virginia Assembly and in Congress. Madison was also a leader of those who favored the establishment of a strong national government.

The Pennsylvania delegation included Benjamin Franklin and Gouverneur Morris. Franklin, at eighty-one, was the convention's oldest member and, as one of his fellow delegates said: "He is well known to be the greatest philosopher of the present age." Franklin enjoyed a world reputation unrivaled by that of any other American. Gouverneur Morris of Pennsylvania was more eloquent than brilliant. He addressed the convention more often than any other person. The elegance of the language of the Constitution is proof of his literary ability, since he was responsible for the final draft.

Luther Martin of Maryland, John Dickinson of Delaware, and William Paterson of New Jersey did not agree with a majority of the delegates, but they ably defended the position that all states should have equal representation.

The proceedings of the convention were kept secret. Delegates were forbidden to discuss the debates with outsiders, in order to encourage everyone to speak freely. It was feared that if a member publicly took a firm stand on an issue, it would be harder for him to change his mind after debate and discussion. Also, the members knew that if word of the inevitable disagreements got out, it would provide ammunition for the many enemies of the convention. There were critics of this secrecy rule, but without it agreement might have been impossible.

Benjamin Franklin. *New York Public Library.*

Consensus

The constitutional convention is usually discussed in terms of three famous compromises: the compromise between large and small states over representation in Congress, the compromise between North and South over the counting of slaves for taxation and representation, and the compromise between North and South over the regulation and taxation of foreign commerce. But this emphasis obscures the fact that there were many other important compromises and that on many of the more significant issues, most of the delegates were in agreement.

While a few delegates might have personally favored a limited monarchy, all supported republican government—and this was the only form of government seriously considered. It was the only form that would be acceptable to the nation. Equally important, all the delegates were constitutionalists who opposed arbitrary and unrestrained government, in whatever form.

The common philosophy accepted by most of the delegates was that of *balanced government*. They wanted to construct a national government in which no single interest would dominate. Because the delegates represented those alarmed by the tendencies of the farmers as an interest group to interfere with property, they were primarily concerned with balancing the government in the direction of protection for property and business. Most of them respected the remark of Elbridge Gerry (delegate from Massachusetts): "The evils we experience flow from the excess of democracy. The people do not want virtue, but are dupes of pretended patriots." Likewise, there was substantial agreement with Gouverneur Morris's statement that property was the "principal object of government."

Benjamin Franklin favored extending the right to vote to male nonproperty owners, but most of the delegates agreed that owners of land were the best guardians of liberty. James Madison voiced the fear that those without property, if given the right to vote, either would combine to deprive property owners of their rights or would become the "tools of demagogues." The delegates agreed in principle on restricted suffrage, but they differed over the kind and amount of property one must own in order to vote. Moreover, because the states were in the process of relaxing qualifications for the vote, the framers recognized they would jeopardize approval of the constitution if they made the federal franchise more restricted than the franchises within the states.[10] As a result, each state was left to determine the qualifications for electing members of the House of Representatives, the only branch of the national government in which the electorate was given a direct voice.

Within five days of its opening, the convention—with only Connecticut dissenting—voted to approve the Fourth Virginia Resolve, which stated that "a national government ought to be established consisting of a supreme legislative, executive, and judiciary." This decision to establish a national government resting on and exercising power over individuals would profoundly alter the nature of the central government and change it from a league of states to a national government.

Few dissented from proposals to give the new Congress all the powers of the old plus all other powers necessary to ensure that the harmony of the United States not be disrupted by the exercise of state legislation. The framers agreed a strong executive, which had been lacking under the Articles, was necessary to provide energy and direction. An independent judiciary was also accepted without much debate. Franklin favored a single-house national legislature, but most states had had two-chamber legislatures since colonial times, and the delegates were used to the system. Bicameralism—the principle of the two-house legislature—also expressed the delegates' belief in the need for balanced government. The upper house would represent the aristocracy and offset the more democratic lower house.

Conflict   There were serious differences among the various groups, especially between the representatives of the large states, who favored a strong national government (which they expected they could dominate), and the delegates from the small states, who were anxious to avoid being dominated. The Virginia delegation took the initiative. It had met during the delay before the convention and, as soon as the convention was organized, presented fifteen resolutions. These resolutions, the Virginia Plan, called for a strong central government. The legislature was to be composed of two chambers. The members of the lower house were to be elected by the voters. Those of the upper house were to be chosen by the lower chamber from nominees submitted by the state legislatures. Representation in both houses was to be on the basis of either wealth or numbers, thus giving the more populous and wealthy states—Virginia, Massachusetts, and Pennsylvania—a majority in the legislature.

The Congress thus created was to be given all the legislative power of its predecessor under the Articles of Confederation as well as the right "to legislate in all cases in which the separate States are incompetent." Furthermore, it was to have the authority to veto state legislation in conflict with the proposed constitution. The Virginia Plan also called for a national executive, to be chosen by the legislature, and a national judiciary with rather extensive jurisdiction. The national Supreme Court, along with the executive, was to have a qualified veto over acts of Congress.

For the first few weeks the Virginia Plan dominated the discussion. But by June 15 additional delegates from the small states had arrived, and they began to counterattack. They rallied around William Paterson of New Jersey, who presented a series of resolutions known as the New Jersey Plan. Paterson

[10]John P. Roche, "The Founding Fathers: A Reform Caucus in Action," *American Political Science Review* (December 1961), pp. 799–816, emphasizes the importance of such political considerations in the framers' deliberations.

did not question the need for a greatly strengthened central government, but he was concerned about how this strength would be used. The New Jersey Plan would give Congress the right to tax and regulate commerce and to coerce states, but it would retain a single-house legislature in which all states would have the same vote, regardless of size. The plan contained the germ of what eventually came to be a key provision of our Constitution—the *supremacy* clause. The national Supreme Court was to hear appeals from state judges, and the supremacy clause would require all the judges, state and national, to treat laws of the national government and the treaties of the United States as superior to the laws of each of the states.

Paterson maneuvered to force concessions from the larger states. He favored a strong central government, but not one the big states could control. Further, he raised the issue of practical politics: To adopt the Virginia Plan—which created a powerful national government dominated by Massachusetts, Virginia, and Pennsylvania and eliminated the states as important units of government—would guarantee defeat in the coming ratification struggle. But the large states resisted, and for a time the convention was deadlocked. The small states believed states should be represented equally in Congress, at least in the upper house. The large states insisted that representation in both houses be based on population or wealth and that national legislators be elected by the voters rather than by state legislatures. Finally, a Committee of Eleven was elected to devise a compromise. On July 5 it presented its proposals.

Because of the prominent role of the Connecticut delegation, this plan has since been known as the Connecticut Compromise. It called for an upper house in which each state would have an equal vote, but for a lower house in which representation would be based on population and in which all bills for raising or appropriating money would originate. This was a setback to the large states, who agreed to it only when the smaller states made it clear that this was their price for union. After equality of representation in the Senate was accepted, most objections to establishing a strong national government dissolved.

Slavery was already an issue in 1787. The southern states wanted slaves to be counted in determining representation in the House of Representatives. It was finally agreed that a slave should count as three-fifths of a free person, both in determining representation in the House and in apportioning direct taxes. Southerners were also fearful that a northern majority in Congress might discriminate against southern trade. They had some basis for this concern. John Jay, secretary of foreign affairs for the Confederation, had proposed a treaty with Great Britain that would have given advantages to northern merchants at the expense of southern exporters. To protect themselves the southern delegates insisted that a two-thirds majority be required in the Senate for ratification of treaties.

The delegates, of course, found other issues to argue about. Should the national government have lower courts, or would one federal Supreme Court be enough? This issue was resolved by postponing the decision; the Constitution states that there *shall* be one Supreme Court and that Congress *may* establish inferior courts. How should the president be selected? For a long time the convention accepted the idea that the president should be elected by Congress. But it was feared either that Congress would dominate the president, or vice versa. Election by the state legislatures was rejected, since these bodies were distrusted. Finally, the electoral college system was devised. This was perhaps the most novel and contrived contribution of the delegates; and today it is one of the most criticized provisions in the Constitution.[11]

Philadelphia Convention. *National Geographic Society Photographer. Courtesy U.S. Capitol Historical Society.*

[11]For studies on the early invention and establishment of the American presidency, see Charles Thach, *The Creation of the Presidency, 1775–1789* (Johns Hopkins Press, 1923), and Ralph Ketcham, *Presidents Above Party: The First American Presidency, 1789–1829* (University of North Carolina Press, 1984).

After three months the delegates stopped debating. On September 17, 1787, they assembled for the impressive ceremony of signing the document they were recommending to the nation. All but three of those still present signed; others, who opposed the general drift of the convention, had already left. Their work over, the delegates adjourned to the City Tavern to relax and celebrate a job well done.

The Framers— What Manner of Men?

"When my distinguished colleague refers to the will of the 'people,' does he mean his people or my 'people'?" *Drawing by Richter;* © *1976 The New Yorker Magazine, Inc.*

Were the delegates an inspired group of men who cast aside all thoughts of self-interest? Were they motivated by the desire to save the nation or by the desire to save themselves? Was the convention the inevitable result of the weaknesses of the Articles? Was it a carefully maneuvered coup on the part of certain elites? Was the difference between those who favored and those who opposed the Constitution mainly economic? Or was the difference mainly regional?

Students of history and government disagree on these and other questions. During the early part of our history, the members of the convention were the object of uncritical praise; the Constitution was the object of universal reverence. Early in the twentieth century a more critical attitude was inspired by J. Allen Smith and Charles A. Beard. Smith, in *The Spirit of American Government* (1911), painted the Constitution as the outgrowth of an antidemocratic reaction, almost a conspiracy, against the rule of majorities. Beard's thesis was that the Constitution represented the platform of the propertied groups who wanted to limit state legislatures and strengthen the national government as a means of protecting property. In his influential book *An Economic Interpretation of the Constitution* (1913), Beard described the economic holdings of the delegates and argued that the latter's support or opposition to the Constitution could best be explained in terms of their financial interests. He explicitly denied that he was charging the founding fathers with writing the Constitution for their personal benefit. Rather, he contended that men's political behavior reflects their broad economic interests.

Many, but not all, recent historical works have questioned the soundness of Beard's scholarship and challenged his interpretation. Some historians have pointed out that in 1787 there was no great propertyless mass in the United States.[12] Even the poor were interested in protecting property. The founding fathers, they argue, were too smart politically to think they could get away with a plan designed merely to protect their own wealth—even if that had been their motive.[13] Certainly, they were anxious to build a strong national government so that it could promote economic growth. Such a government would win the support of all classes of people.[14] These historians contend that the political differences over the merits of the Constitution, just like political arguments today, cut through economic class divisions. The struggle, it is argued, was between differing ideologies.[15]

Political scientist Martin Diamond takes issue with those who portray the Constitutional Convention as a reactionary attempt by aristocrats to curtail the brave democratic beginnings proclaimed in the Declaration of Independence. He calls this interpretation the "conventional wisdom of those who give academic and intellectual opinions to the nation." "The fact is," he writes, "the Declaration . . . is neutral on the questions of forms of government; any form is legitimate, provided it secures equal freedom and is instituted by popular con-

[12]Robert E. Brown, *Charles Beard and the Constitution* (Princeton University Press, 1956), pp. 197–98; Diggins, "Power and Authority in American History: The Case of Charles A. Beard and His Critics."

[13]Forrest McDonald, *We the People: The Economic Origins of the Constitution* (University of Chicago Press, 1958), pp. vii, 415.

[14]Gordon S. Wood, *The Convention and the Constitution* (St. Martin's Press, 1965), p. 31.

[15]Wood, *American Republic, 1776–1787*, pp. 484–85.

sent." It was the framers of our Constitution who gave us a democratic form of government. "Of course, the Founders," Diamond comments, "criticized the defects and dangers of democracy and did not waste much breath on the defects and dangers of the other forms of government. For a very good reason. They were not founding any other kind of government; they were establishing a democratic form, and it was the dangers peculiar to it against which all their efforts had to be bent."[16]

The various interpretations of the American Revolution and of the framing of the Constitution reflect changing styles of thought, with current political debates being read backward into our past. But the various interpretations also reflect the fact that "the American Revolution . . . was so complex and contained so many diverse and seemingly contradictory currents that it can support a wide variety of interpretations and may never be comprehended in full."[17]

Beard himself recognized that people are motivated by a complex of factors, both conscious and unconscious. Self-interest, economic or otherwise, and principles are inextricably mixed in human behavior. The founding fathers were neither gods for whom self-interest or economic considerations were of no importance, nor selfish elitists who thought only in terms of their own pocketbooks. They were, by and large, aristocrats fearful of the masses, but they were committed to an aristocracy of merit, of education, and of accomplishment—not of birth or wealth. The framers wanted to protect the nation from aggression abroad and dissension at home. While stability and strength were needed to protect their own interests, they were also needed to secure the unity and order necessary for the operation of a democracy.

TO ADOPT OR NOT TO ADOPT?

James Madison.

The delegates had gone far. They had not hesitated to disregard Congress's instruction about ratification or to ignore Article XIII of the Articles of Confederation. This article declared the Union to be perpetual and prohibited any alteration in the Articles unless agreed to by Congress and *by every one of the state legislatures*—a provision that had made it impossible to amend the Articles. But the convention delegates boldly declared that the Constitution should go into effect when ratified by *popularly elected conventions in nine states*. They had turned to this method of ratification for practical considerations and for reasons of principle. Not only were the delegates aware that there was little chance of securing approval of the new Constitution in all state legislatures, but many felt that the Constitution should be ratified by an authority higher than a legislature. A constitution based on popular approval would have a higher legal and moral status. The Articles of Confederation had been a compact of state governments, but the Constitution was to be a "union of people."[18]

Nevertheless, even this method of ratification would not be easy. The nation was not ready to adopt the Constitution without a thorough debate. The supporters of the new government, by cleverly appropriating the name Federalists, took some of the sting out of the charges that they were trying to destroy the states and establish an all-powerful central government. By calling their

[16]Martin Diamond, "The Declaration and the Constitution: Liberty, Democracy, and the Founders," *The Public Interest*, Vol. 41 (Fall 1975), pp. 40, 50, 52.

[17]Jack P. Greene, "The Reappraisal of the American Revolution in Recent Historical Literature," in Jack P. Greene (ed.), *The Reinterpretation of the American Revolution, 1763–1789* (Harper & Row, 1968), p. 2.

[18]Max Farrand (ed.), *The Records of the Federal Convention of 1787*, Vol. II (Yale University Press, 1911), pp.93, 476.

John Jay. *Culver.*

Alexander Hamilton.

opponents Antifederalists, they pointed up the negative character of the arguments of those who opposed ratification.

The split was in part geographical. The seaboard and city regions tended to be Federalist strongholds. The vast back-country regions from Maine through Georgia, inhabited by farmers and other relatively poor people, were areas in which the Antifederalists were strong. But, as in most political contests, no single factor completely accounted for the division between Federalists and Antifederalists. For example, in Virginia the leaders of both sides came from the same general social and economic class. New York City and Philadelphia strongly supported the Constitution, but so did predominantly rural New Jersey.

The great debate was conducted with pamphlets, papers, letters to the editor, and speeches. The issues were important, and the interest of those concerned intense; but the argument, in the main, was carried on in a quiet and calm manner. Out of the debate came a series of essays, known as *The Federalist*, written by Alexander Hamilton, James Madison, and John Jay to persuade the voters of New York to ratify the Constitution. The Federalist is still "widely regarded as the most profound single treatise on the Constitution ever written and as among the few masterly works in political science produced in all the centuries of history."[19] The great debate stands even today as an outstanding example of free people using the techniques of discussion and debate to determine the nature of their fundamental laws. (*Federalist No. 10* can be found in the appendix at the end of this text.)

The most telling criticism of the proposed Constitution made by the Antifederalists was its failure to include a bill of rights.[20] The Federalists argued that a bill of rights would be superfluous. The general government had only delegated powers, and there was no need to specify that Congress could not, for example, abridge freedom of the press. It had no power to regulate the press. Moreover, the Federalists argued, to guarantee *some* rights might be dangerous, because it would then be thought that rights *not* listed could be denied. The Constitution already protected some of the most important rights—trial by jury in federal criminal cases, for example. Hamilton and others also insisted that paper guarantees were weak reeds on which to depend for protection against governmental tyranny.

The Antifederalists were unconvinced. If some rights were protected, what could be the objection of providing constitutional protection for others? Without a bill of rights, what was to prevent Congress from using one of its delegated powers in such a manner that free speech would be abridged? If bills of rights were needed in state constitutions to limit state governments, why was one not needed in the national constitution to limit the national government? This was a government farther from the people and with a greater tendency, it was argued, to subvert natural rights. The Federalists, forced to concede, agreed to add a bill of rights if and when the new Constitution was approved.

The Politics of Ratification

The political strategy of the Federalists was to secure ratification in as many states as possible before the opposition had time to organize. The Antifederalists were handicapped. They lacked access to the newspapers, most of which supported ratification. Their main strength was in the rural areas, underrepresented in some state legislatures and difficult to arouse to political action. They needed time to perfect their organization and collect their strength. The Fed-

[19]Charles A. Beard and Mary R. Beard, *A Basic History of the United States* (New Home Library, 1944), p. 136.

[20]Rutland, *Birth of the Bill of Rights.* See also Alpheus T. Mason, *The States Rights Debates: Antifederalism and the Constitution* (Prentice-Hall, 1964), pp. 4, 66–97.

17

eralists, composed of a more closely knit group of leaders throughout the colonies, moved in a hurry.

In most of the small states, now satisfied by equal Senate representation, ratification was gained without difficulty. Delaware was the first state to ratify. The first large state to take action was Pennsylvania. The Federalists presented the Constitution to the state legislature immediately after the Philadelphia convention adjourned in September 1787. But the legislature was about to adjourn, and the Antifederalist minority felt that this was moving with too much haste (Congress had not even formally transmitted the document to the legislature for its consideration!). They wanted to postpone action until after the coming state elections, when they hoped to win a majority and so prevent calling a ratifying convention. When it became clear that the Federalists were going to move ahead, the Antifederalists left the legislative chamber. Since the legislature was now two members short of a quorum, business was brought to a standstill. But Philadelphia, the seat of the legislature, was a Federalist stronghold. The next morning two Antifederalists were roused from their quarters, carried into the legislative chamber, and forced to remain. The resolution calling for election of delegates to a ratifying convention was adopted.[21] Under the generalship of James Wilson, the Pennsylvania convention ratified by a vote of 46 to 23 in December 1787.

By early 1788 New Jersey, Connecticut, and Georgia had also ratified. The scene of battle then shifted to Massachusetts, a key state as well as a doubtful one. John Hancock and Samuel Adams had not declared themselves,

John Hancock.

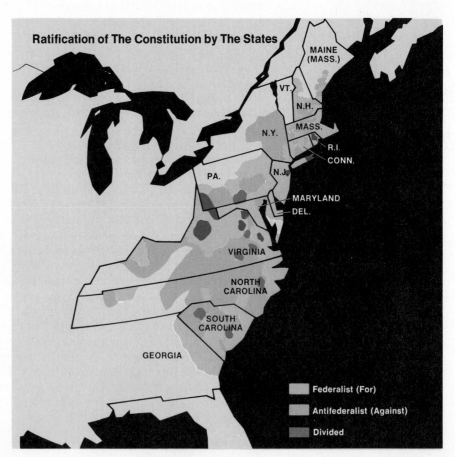

Ratification of The Constitution by The States

MAINE
(MASS.)

VT.

N.H.

N.Y.   MASS.

R.I.

CONN.

PA.   N.J.

MARYLAND

DEL.

VIRGINIA

NORTH
CAROLINA

SOUTH
CAROLINA

GEORGIA

Federalist (For)

Antifederalist (Against)

Divided

[21]Julius Goebel, Jr., *Antecedents and Beginnings to 1801* (Macmillan, 1971), p. 267.

Sam Adams.

Patrick Henry.

and these patriots of '76, with their great popular following, held the balance of power. The Federalists cleverly pointed out to Hancock that Washington would be the first president and that therefore the vice-president would undoubtedly be a New Englander. What citizen of New England was more distinguished than John Hancock? Whether or not this hint was effective, Hancock eventually came out for ratification. Adams was persuaded to vote for approval after securing a promise that a bill of rights would be forthcoming after adoption. Even so, Massachusetts ratified by a narrow margin (187 to 168).

By June 1788 Maryland, South Carolina, and New Hampshire had ratified; the nine states required to bring the Constitution into effect had been obtained. Still, neither Virginia nor New York had taken action, and without them the new Union would have little chance of success. Virginia was the most populous state and the home of many of the nation's outstanding leaders, and New York was important geographically.

The Virginia ratifying convention rivaled the constitutional convention in the caliber of its delegates. James Madison was the captain of the Federalist forces, and he had able lieutenants in Governor Randolph and in the young John Marshall. Patrick Henry, George Mason, and James Monroe within the convention, and Richard Henry Lee outside, led the opposition. Henry attacked the proposed government, point by point, with great eloquence; Madison turned back each attack quietly but cogently. At the critical juncture Washington sent a letter to the convention urging unqualified ratification. This tipped the scale, and Virginia ratified. News was rushed to New York.

The great landowners along the Hudson, unlike their southern planter friends, were opposed to the Constitution. They feared federal taxation of their holdings, and they did not want to abolish the profitable tax New York had been levying on the trade and commerce of other states. When the convention assembled, the Federalists were greatly outnumbered, but they were aided by the strategy and skill of Hamilton and by word of Virginia's ratification. New York approved by a margin of three votes. Although North Carolina and Rhode Island still remained outside the Union (the former ratified in November 1789, and the latter six months later), the new nation was created. In New York a few members of the old Congress assembled to issue the call for elections under the new Constitution—then Congress adjourned without setting a day for reconvening.

INTO THE THIRD CENTURY—AND SOME QUESTIONS

A constitution that is to endure must reflect the hard experiences and high hopes of the people for whom it is written. Those who framed our Constitution did not, of course, complete the task of constitution making. That process began long before the constitutional convention, and it continues still. Constitutions, even written ones, are growing and evolving organisms.

The completion of two centuries of self-government—a major accomplishment—*is* a time of national celebration. However, it is also appropriately a time of national questioning. The questions that are being asked have no easy answers. They are questions to which there is no single logical response, no answer that stems easily from an analysis of facts; they are basic questions that deal with value choices. The following questions may help stimulate your thinking as we proceed with a more detailed investigation of the operations of the American Republic:

1. Is the system sufficiently *open* to persons of all races, sexes, classes, and political views who wish to participate in making decisions?

2. Is the system sufficiently *responsive?* Is the leadership *accountable* to the voters?

3. Is the system sufficiently *representative?* This concept of "representation" is one of the most difficult in political science. Here we mean to focus not on whether those who govern precisely mirror divisions of class, race, interest, and region, but whether those who govern are sensitive to the needs and opinions of differing groups.

4. Is the system sufficiently *responsible?* Does the leadership keep in mind the long-term needs of the entire nation and not merely respond to the short-term demands of the most vocal or most prosperous special interests?

In considering these questions, we must remember that the framers did not favor a government in which the mass of people would participate directly, or which would be representative of or responsive to the people at large. Rather, they sought to control both the spirit of faction and the thrust of majorities. Their prime concern was how to fashion a viable, but limited, government. The framers had not seen a political party in the modern sense and would not have liked it if they had. They did not favor an arousing, mobilizing kind of leadership but preferred instead a stabilizing, balancing, magisterial leadership—the kind George Washington was expected to (and did) supply. Today we have *high-pressure politics* characterized by strongly organized groups and political action committees, potent and volatile public opinion dominated by opinion-making agencies, parties vying to mobilize nationwide majorities, and celebrity-leaders intimately covered by the media. How responsive are our political agencies to fast-moving changes in public attitudes and moods? Will our Constitution and the system it created be able to deal with the problems of our third century?

Following is a set of key questions about the constitutional system as it has developed and is working today. You might want to refer to this checklist as you read through the following chapters, where many of these questions will be discussed.

1. Too much—or too little—national power? Are the limits on the powers of the federal government realistic and enforceable, given the intense pressures on the government?

2. Does our form of federalism work? Does the Constitution provide for an efficient and realistic balance between national and state power?

3. Our individual liberties: Are they adequately protected in the Constitution?

4. Suspects' rights: Can representative government protect its citizens and yet uphold the rights of the criminally accused?

5. "All men are created equal": What kinds of equality are—and should be—protected by the Constitution, and by what means?

6. Women's rights: Are they adequately protected by the Constitution today?

7. Safeguarding minorities: Does the Constitution adequately protect the rights of blacks, native Americans, ethnics, and recent immigrants?

8. "Government by the people": Does the evolving constitutional system, including political parties and interest groups, strengthen fair and effective representation of the people?

9. Is the judicial branch too powerful? Are the federal courts exceeding their proper powers as interpreters of the Constitution?

10. Too many checks and balances? Does the constitutional separation of powers between the president and Congress create an ungovernable system, notably in economic policy?

11. Does the constitution look outward? Does the president possess adequate power—or too much power—over warmaking and foreign policy? Should Congress have more authority in this field?

12. Constitutional flexibility: Should we make changing our fundamental charter of government simpler and more democratic?

Adapted from Project 87, *this Constitution* (Sept., 1983), pp.4-8.

According to an old story, Benjamin Franklin was confronted by a woman as he left the last session of the constitutional convention in Philadelphia in September 1787.

"What kind of government have you given us, Dr. Franklin?" she asked, "a Republic or a Monarchy?"

"A Republic, Madam," he answered, "—if you can keep it."

SUMMARY

1. Our constitutional democracy is both a process for making decisions and a set of principles, namely, the importance of the individual, the uniqueness of each person, and the desirability of liberty. The process is one in which those who acquire power to make decisions do so as the result of winning a free and fair election. Most important, those defeated in one election are free to use all peaceful means to persuade voters to vote them into office at the next election.

2. Our constitutional democracy in its basic form rests on English institutions. After the American Revolution—a contained and conservative uprising—we operated under the Articles of Confederation, which gave us a loose league of states. But many leaders felt that it was necessary to create a national government with direct authority over individu-

als. They proposed such a form at the constitutional convention of 1787.

3. The constitutional convention is an outstanding example of a creative political act, as well as an outstanding example of creative political statecraft. The Constitution created was a medley of compromises and an ingenious balancing of interests. What the framers proposed was ratified by the states in special conventions after long debates in which those debating the Constitution demonstrated considerable political skill.

4. Two hundred years later we continue to live under the Constitution the framers proposed. But we must understand that system and constantly adapt it to changing conditions.

FURTHER READING

BERNARD BAILYN. *The Ideological Origins of the American Revolution* (Harvard University Press, 1967).

JAMES MACGREGOR BURNS. *The Vineyard of Liberty* (Knopf, 1982).

ALEXIS DE TOCQUEVILLE. *Democracy in America* (1830s). Several editions.

GEORGE J. GRAHAM, JR., and SCARLETT G. GRAHAM (eds.). *Founding Principles of American Government* (Indiana University Press, 1977).

ALEXANDER HAMILTON, JOHN JAY, and JAMES MADISON. *The Federalist* (1787–1788). Many editions.

J. ROLAND PENNOCK. *Democratic Political Theory* (Princeton University Press, 1979).

JACK N. RAKOVE. *The Beginnings of National Politics* (Knopf, 1979).

GORDON WOOD. *The Creation of the American Republic 1776–1789* (University of North Carolina Press, 1969).

THE LIVING CONSTITUTION

2

For a time some people were skeptical of the new Constitution. After watching merchants and mechanics march side by side in a parade celebrating ratification, a Bostonian remarked sourly: "It may serve to please children, but freemen will not be so easily gulled out of their liberties." On the other hand, a Philadelphian said that the procession in his city had "made such an impression on the minds of our young people that 'federal' and 'union' have now become part of the household words of every family in the city." This effect on youth was significant, for it was on the younger generation that hopes for the new government depended.

While only a few people liked all of the new Constitution, most people figured it was better than what they had. Moreover, it was a skinny document of only some 4300 words. It was a framework for governing—a document that would be acceptable to the states and that was often quite vague. Our founding politicians had high hopes that it would win adoption. Still, most of them would be surprised indeed to learn that nearly 200 years later we had not written another constitution, or two or three.

With the adoption of the Constitution came a return of prosperity. Markets for American goods were opening in Europe, and business was pulling out of its postwar slump. Such events seemed to justify Federalist claims that adoption of the Constitution would correct the nation's problems. Within a surprisingly short time the Constitution lost its partisan character; both Antifederalists and Federalists honored it. Politicians differed less and less over whether the Constitution was good; they now began to argue over what it meant.

As the Constitution won the support of Americans, it began to take on the aura of natural law: "The Fathers grew ever larger in stature as they receded from view; the era in which they lived and fought became a Golden Age; in that age there had been a fresh dawn for the world, and its men were giants against the sky;"[1]

Such adoration helped bring unity into the diversity of the new nation. Like the Crown in Britain, the Constitution became a *symbol* of national loyalty that evoked both emotional and rational support from all Americans, regardless of their differences. The framers' work became part of the American creed. It stood for liberty, equality before the law, limited government—indeed, for whatever anyone wanted to read into it.

But the Constitution is also a supreme and binding *law* that both grants and limits powers. "In framing a government which is to be administered by men over men," wrote James Madison in *The Federalist*, "the great difficulty lies in this: you must first enable the government to control the governed; and in the next place oblige it to control itself." The Constitution is both a *positive* instrument of government, enabling the governors to control the governed, and a *restraint* on government, enabling the ruled to check the rulers.

In what ways does the Constitution limit the power of the national government? In what ways does it create national power? How has it managed to serve both as a great symbol of national unity and as a somewhat adaptable and changing instrument of government?

CHECKING POWER WITH POWER

While it may seem strange to begin by stressing the ways in which the Constitution *limits* national power, we must keep in mind the dilemma the framers faced. They wanted a more effective national government, yet at the same time they were keenly aware that the people would not accept too much central control. They wanted a more *effective* government, but effectiveness was not as overriding a consideration as liberty. They wanted to ensure domestic tranquility and prevent future rebellions, but they also wanted to forestall the emergence of a home-grown George III. Accordingly, they allotted certain powers to the national government and reserved the rest for the states, establishing a system of federalism (the nature and problems of which will be taken up in Chapter 3). But even this was not enough. They felt they needed other ways to limit the national government.

The most important way to make public officials observe the constitutional limits on their powers is through *free elections:* The voters have the ability to throw out of office those who abuse power. But the framers were not willing to depend solely on such *political* controls, because they did not fully trust the people's judgment. Thomas Jefferson, a firm democrat, put it this way: "Free government is founded on jealousy, and not in confidence. . . . In questions of power, then, let no more be heard of confidence in man, but bind him down from mischief by the chains of the Constitution."[2] Even more important, the framers feared that a majority faction might use the new central government to deprive minorities of their rights. "A dependence on the people is, no doubt, the primary control on the government," Madison admitted,

---

[1]Max Lerner, *Ideas for the Ice Age* (Viking, 1941), pp. 241–42.

[2]Quoted in Alpheus T. Mason, *The Supreme Court: Palladium of Freedom* (University of Michigan Press, 1962), p. 10.

"but experience has taught mankind the necessity of auxiliary precautions." What were these "auxiliary precautions" against popular tyranny?

Separation of Powers

"And there are three branches of government, so that each branch has the other two to blame everything on." *Dunagin's People* by *Ralph Dunagin.* © News Group Chicago, Inc.—Courtesy of News America Syndicate.

The first step was the separation of powers; that is, allocating constitutional authority to each of the three branches of the national government. In *Federalist No. 47* James Madison wrote, "No political truth is certainly of greater intrinsic value, or is stamped with the authority of more enlightened patrons of liberty, than that . . . the accumulation of all powers, legislative, executive, and judiciary, in the same hands . . . may justly be pronounced the very definition of tyranny."

But logic alone does not account for the inclusion of this principle in our Constitution. This doctrine had been the general practice in the colonies for over a hundred years. Only during the Revolutionary period was authority concentrated in the hands of the legislature, and that experience confirmed the framers' belief in the merits of separation of powers. Many attributed the evils of state government and the lack of energy in the central government to the fact there was no strong executive to both check legislative abuses and give energy and direction to administration.

Still, separating power was not enough. There was always the danger—from the framers' point of view—that different officials with different powers might pool their authority and act together. Separation of powers by itself would not prevent government branches and officials from responding to the same pressures—for example, an overwhelming majority of the voters. If separating power was not enough, what else could be done?

Checks and Balances: Ambition to Counteract Ambition

The framers' answer was a system of checks and balances. "The great security against a gradual concentration of the several powers in the same department," wrote Madison, "consists in giving to those who administer each department the necessary constitutional means and personal motives to resist encroachment on the others. . . . Ambition must be made to counteract ambition."

Each branch is therefore given some role in the actions of the others. We have a "government of separated institutions *sharing* powers."[3] Thus, Congress enacts laws, but the president can veto them. The Supreme Court can declare unconstitutional laws passed by Congress and signed by the president, but the president appoints the justices with the Senate's approval. The president administers the laws, but Congress provides the money. The Senate and the House of Representatives have an absolute veto over each other in the enactment of a law, since bills must be approved by both houses.

Not only does each branch have some authority over the actions of the others, *but each is politically independent of the others.* The president is selected by electors (now popularly elected). Senators are now chosen by the voters in each state, and the members of the House by voters in their districts. And although federal judges are appointed by the president with the consent of the Senate, once in office they virtually hold terms for life.

The framers also ensured that a majority of the voters could win control over only part of the government at one time. A popular majority might take control of the House of Representatives in an off-year (that is, a nonpresidential) election, but the president, representing a previous popular majority, would still have two years to go. Further, senators are chosen for six-year terms, with only one-third being selected every two years.

[3]Richard E. Neustadt, *Presidential Power,* rev. ed. (Wiley, 1976), p. 101.

Finally, national courts were also provided. In fact, judges have become so important in our system of checks and balances that they deserve special attention.

JUDICIAL REVIEW AND THE "GUARDIANS OF THE CONSTITUTION"

It was not until some years after the Constitution was in operation that the judges asserted the power of judicial review—the power of a court of law to set aside an act of the legislature that in the opinion of the judges violates the Constitution. But from the beginning the judges were expected to be a check on the legislature and the groups represented by the legislative majority. "Independent judges," wrote Alexander Hamilton in *Federalist No. 78*, would be "an essential safeguard against the effects of occasional ill humors in society."

Judicial review is an American contribution to the art of government. If an English citizen or an American is thrown into prison without cause, either can appeal to the courts of his or her respective country for protection. But when Parliament passes a law, no English judge has the authority to declare it null and void because the judge believes it violates the English constitution: Parliament is the guardian of the English constitution. In the United States the courts, ultimately the Supreme Court, are the keepers of the constitutional conscience—not Congress and not the president. How did the judges get this tremendous responsibility?

Origins of Judicial Review

The Constitution itself says nothing about who should have the final word in disputes that might arise over its meaning. Whether the members of the Convention of 1787 intended to give the courts the power of judicial review is a question that has long been debated. There is little doubt that the framers intended the Supreme Court to have the power to declare *state* legislation unconstitutional, but whether they intended to give it the same power over *national* legislation is not clear. Edward S. Corwin, the outstanding authority on the American Constitution, concluded that unquestionably "the framers anticipated some sort of judicial review. . . . But it is equally without question that the ideas generally current in 1787 were far from presaging the present vast role of the court."[4] Why, then, did the framers not specifically provide for judicial review? Probably because they believed the power could readily be inferred from certain general provisions.

The Federalists—the men who wrote the Constitution and controlled the national government until 1801—generally supported the courts and favored judicial review. Their opponents, the Jeffersonian Republicans (after 1832 called Democrats), were less enthusiastic. In 1798 and 1799 Jefferson and Madison (the latter by this time had left the Federalist party) came very close in the Virginia and Kentucky Resolutions to arguing that the state legislatures—and not the Supreme Court—had the ultimate power to interpret the Constitution. These Resolutions even seemed to question whether the Supreme Court had the final authority to review *state* legislation, something about which there had been little doubt.

When the Jeffersonians defeated the Federalists in the elections of 1800, it was still undecided whether the Supreme Court would actually exercise the power of judicial review. "The idea was in the air, the ingredients to support a

[4]"The Constitution as Instrument and as Symbol," *American Political Science Review* (December 1936), p. 1078.

doctrine of judicial review were at hand, and a few precedents could even be cited"; nevertheless, judicial review was not an established power. Then in 1803 came *Marbury* v. *Madison*,[5] a case closely reflecting the political struggles between the Federalists and the Jeffersonians.

Marbury v. Madison

The elections of 1800 marked the rise to power of the Jeffersonian Republicans. President John Adams and his fellow Federalists did not take their defeat easily. Indeed, they were greatly alarmed at what they considered to be the "enthronement of the rabble." But there was nothing much they could do about it before leaving office—or was there? The Constitution gives the president, with the consent of the Senate, the power to appoint federal judges to hold office during "good behavior"—virtually for life. If the judiciary were manned by good Federalists, thought Adams and his followers, they could stave off the worst consequences of Jefferson's victory.

The Federalist lame-duck Congress created dozens of new federal judicial posts. By March 3, 1801, Adams had appointed, and the Senate had confirmed, Federalists to all these new positions. Adams signed the commissions and turned them over to John Marshall, the secretary of state, to be sealed and delivered. Marshall had just received his own commission as chief justice of the United States, but he was continuing to serve as secretary of state until Adams's term expired. Working right up to nine o'clock on the evening of March 3, Marshall sealed, but was unable to deliver, all the commissions. The important ones were taken care of, however, and only those for the justices of the peace for the District of Columbia were left undelivered. The newly appointed chief justice left the remaining commissions for his successor to deliver.

Jefferson was angered by this packing of the judiciary. When he discovered that some of the commissions had not been delivered, he told the new secretary of state, James Madison, to hold up seventeen of those still in his possession. Jefferson could see no reason why the District needed so many justices of the peace, especially Federalist justices.

Among the commissions that were not delivered was one for William Marbury. After waiting in vain, Marbury decided to seek action from the courts. Searching through the statute books, he came across Section 13 of the Judiciary Act of 1789, which authorized the Supreme Court "to issue writs of mandamus, in cases warranted by the principles and usages of law, to . . . persons holding office, under the authority of the United States." A writ of mandamus is a court order directing an official to perform a certain act. Delivering a commission is a ministerial act; the secretary of state is a person holding office under the authority of the United States. So, thought Marbury, why not ask the Supreme Court to issue a writ of mandamus to force Madison to deliver the commission? He and his companions went directly to the Supreme Court and, citing Section 13, they so asked.

What could Marshall do? If the Court issued the writ, Madison and Jefferson would probably ignore it. The Court would be powerless, and its prestige, already low, might suffer a fatal blow. On the other hand, by refusing to issue the writ, the judges would appear to support the Republican party's claim that the Court had no authority to interfere with the executive. Would Marshall issue the writ? Most people thought so; angry Republicans even talked of impeachment.

On February 24, 1803, the Supreme Court published its opinion. The first part was as expected. Marbury was entitled to his commission, said Marshall, and Madison should have delivered it to him; a writ of mandamus could

Chief Justice Marshall. *UPI.*

[5]1 Cranch 137 (1802).

be issued by the proper court against even so high an officer as the secretary of state.

Then came the surprise. Although Section 13 of the Judiciary Act seems to give the Supreme Court original jurisdiction in cases such as that in question, this section, said Marshall, is contrary to Article III of the Constitution, which gives the Supreme Court original jurisdiction *only* where an ambassador or other foreign minister is affected or in which a state is a party. While this is a case of original jurisdiction, Marbury is neither a state nor a foreign minister. If we follow Section 13, wrote Marshall, we have jurisdiction; if we follow the Constitution, we have no jurisdiction.

Marshall then stated the question in a more pointed way—namely: Should the Supreme Court enforce an unconstitutional law? Of course not, he concluded. The Constitution is the supreme and binding law, and the courts cannot enforce any action of Congress that conflicts with it.

The real question remained unanswered. Congress and the president had also read the Constitution, and according to their interpretation (which was also reasonable), Section 13 was compatible with Article III. Where did the Supreme Court get the right to say they were wrong? Why should the Supreme Court's interpretation of the Constitution be preferred to that of Congress and the president?

Paralleling Hamilton's argument in *Federalist No. 78*, Marshall reasoned that the Constitution is law; the judges—not legislators or executives—interpret law. Therefore, the judges should interpret the Constitution. "If two laws conflict with each other, the courts must decide on the operation of each," he said. Case dismissed.

Jefferson fumed. For one thing, Marshall had said that a court with the proper jurisdiction could issue a writ of mandamus even against the secretary of state. But there was little Jefferson could do about it, for there was not even a specific court order he could refuse to obey. Thus, in a single stroke Marshall had lectured the Republicans for failing to perform their duties and had gone a long way toward acquiring for the Supreme Court the power to review acts of Congress. And he had done it in a manner that made it difficult for the Republicans to retaliate.

Marbury v. *Madison* is a masterpiece of judicial strategy. Marshall went out of his way to declare Section 13 unconstitutional. He could have interpreted the section to mean that the Supreme Court could issue writs of mandamus in those cases in which it did have jurisdiction. He could have interpreted Article III to mean that Congress could add to, though not subtract from, the original jurisdiction the Constitution gives to the Supreme Court. He could have dismissed the case for want of jurisdiction without discussing Marbury's right to his commission. But none of these would have suited his purpose. Marshall was fearful for the Supreme Court's future; he felt that unless the Court spoke out, it would become subordinate to the president and Congress.

Marshall's decision, important as it was, did not by itself establish for the Supreme Court the power to review and declare unconstitutional acts of Congress. *Marbury* v. *Madison* could have meant that the Supreme Court had the right to interpret the scope of its *own* powers under Article III but that Congress and the president had the authority to interpret *their own powers* under Articles I and II, respectively. However, Marshall's decision has not been interpreted in this way (though it was not until the *Dred Scott* case in 1857 that another act of Congress was declared unconstitutional).[6] Had Marshall not spoken when he did, the Court might not have been able to assume the power of judicial

In 1857 the Supreme Court denied Dred Scott his freedom, ruling that slaves were property and protected as such, even in states which had outlawed slavery, by the Constitution. This decision declared the Missouri Compromise of 1820, an act of Congress, to be unconstitutional. *Library of Congress.*

---

[6]*Dred Scott* v. *Sandford*, 19 Howard 393 (1857).

review. The precedent had been created. Here we have a classic example of constitutional development through judicial interpretation. There is no specific authorization in the Constitution for the Court to declare congressional enactments null and void; yet today this practice is a vital part of our constitutional system.

Several important consequences followed from the acceptance of Marshall's argument that the judges are the official interpreters of the meaning of the Constitution. The most important is that even a law enacted by the Congress and approved by the president may, under many circumstances, be challenged by a single person. Through a lawsuit those who lack the clout to get a bill through Congress or who cannot influence a federal agency may secure a hearing before the courts. Litigation thus supplements, and at times takes precedence over, legislation as a way to make public policy.[7]

CHECKS AND BALANCES—DOES IT WORK?

YOU DECIDE !

Of the over 160 national constitutions in the world, the U.S. Constitution is the oldest and one of the most admired. A constitution cannot spell out everything and every successful constitution has compromises. Some things get left out, and some matters are viewed as less satisfactory a century later. Can you point to topics you believe should be in our Constitution that were left out? And topics that would best be deleted or modified? (The Constitution is available in the Appendix.)

(Answer/Discussion on the next page.)

Checks and Balances: Modifications

What if a majority of the people should get control of all branches of government and force through radical measures? The framers knew that if the great majority of the voters wanted to take a certain step, nothing could stop them. Nothing, that is, except despotic government, and they did not want that. The founding fathers reasoned that all they could do—and this was quite a lot—was to prevent, temporarily, full control by the popular majority.

It may seem surprising that the people did not object to these "auxiliary precautions," which often are barriers to action by a popular majority. But the Antifederalists were also deeply suspicious of officeholders and were even more anxious than the Federalists to see the power of national authorities defined and restrained.

Early Americans (and perhaps their descendants two centuries later) did not look on government as an instrument they could seize with their votes and use for their own purposes. Rather, they viewed it as something to be handcuffed, hemmed in, and rendered harmless. The separation of powers and the system of checks and balances were intended to make it difficult for a majority to gain control of the government. Equally important, they were intended to keep those who govern from exceeding their constitutional authority.

The framers, distrustful of both elites and the masses, deliberately built *inefficiency* into our political system; and almost 200 years after the ratification of the Constitution, Americans continue to debate whether it is desirable to maintain these limits under the vastly different conditions of the 1980s. Crucial questions remain: Are these checks necessary or sufficient to prevent abuses of political power? Is the greater danger that governments will not do the right things or that they will do the wrong things? Do these limitations work to prevent abuses, or do they make coherent governmental action for the general welfare difficult, if not impossible?

While fragmentation of political power remains, several developments have modified the way the system of checks and balances actually works.

1. *Rise (and fall) of national political parties.* Parties serve to a limited extent as unifying factors—at times drawing together the president, senators, representatives, and sometimes even judges behind common programs. But the parties, in turn, have been splintered and weakened by the necessity of working

[7]Karen Orren, "Standing to Sue: Interest Group Conflict in the Federal Courts," *American Political Science Review* (September 1976), pp. 723–41; J. W. Peltason, *Federal Courts in the Political Process* (Random House, 1955).

Most experts believe we should seldom change the Constitution. Some scholars and politicians think some changes might be considered:

☐ The right to privacy might be spelled out;

☐ The right to leave and return to the country is not set forth in the Constitution though we generally enjoy these rights;

☐ The provisions of the electoral college should be modified, especially the provision for election in the House of Representatives when no candidate achieves the needed 50 percent to win in the electoral college;

☐ A provision for a balanced budget;

☐ Some type of ERA measure;

☐ Clarification between the rights of individuals and the rights of groups;

☐ Clarification of the "establishment clause" in the First Amendment.

Perhaps by the end of this course you will add a few other subjects you would like to see added or altered. Undoubtedly, however, you will appreciate that changing the Constitution even in only minor ways is a complex and exceedingly delicate undertaking. It also always becomes a highly political endeavor.

through a system of fragmented governmental power, so that we have never developed strong, cohesive parties. With the decline in the 1970s of what little party structure we did have, parties are now making even less headway than in previous decades.

2. *Changes in electoral methods.* The framers wanted the president to be chosen by wise, independent men free from popular passions and hero worship. Almost from the beginning, however, presidential electors have pledged prior to elections to cast their vote for their party's presidential candidate. Further, senators, who were originally elected by state legislatures, are today chosen directly by the people.

3. *Establishment of agencies deliberately designed to exercise all three functions—legislative, executive, and judicial.* When the government began to regulate the economy, and detailed rules had to be made and judgments rendered on complex matters such as policing business practices or preventing energy shortages, it was difficult to assign responsibility to an agency without blending the powers to make and apply rules and to decide disputes.

4. *Changes in technology.* Atomic bombs, television, computers, instant communications—these and other alterations in our environment create conditions very different from those that existed two centuries ago. In some ways these new technologies have added to the powers of the president; in others they have given additional leverage to organized interests working through Congress; they have given greater independence and influence to nongovernmental agencies such as the press. Governmental power remains fragmented, but the system of checks and balances operates differently from the way it did in 1789, when there were no televised congressional investigating committee hearings, no FBI using electronic listening devices, no *New York Times* with a national constituency, no presidential press conferences, no live coverage of wars or of Americans being held hostage in foreign places.

5. *The emergence of the United States as a world power and the existence of recurrent crises.* Today crises and problems anywhere in the world become crises and problems for the United States, and vice versa. The need to deal with perpetual emergency has concentrated power in the hands of the chief executive and his immediate staff.

6. *The office of the president has sometimes served to impose some measure of national unity.* Drawing on constitutional, political, and emergency powers, the president has sometimes been able to overcome some of the restraints imposed by the Constitution on the exercise of cohesive governmental power—to the applause of some, and the alarm of others.

2–1

USE OF CHECKS AND BALANCES, 1789–1984

There have been more than 2410 Presidential vetoes of congressional acts.
Congress subsequently overrode about 95 of those vetoes.
The Supreme Court has ruled 100 congressional acts or parts of acts unconstitutional (and in 1983 their major ruling on legislative vetoes may affect as many as 200 provisions in various kinds of legislation).
The Senate has refused to confirm 27 nominees to the Supreme Court (out of 138 nominees).
Congress impeached 9 federal judges; of these, 4 were convicted. The Senate has also rejected at least 8 cabinet nominations. Many other cabinet and sub-cabinet levels appointments have withdrawn because of likely rejection by the Senate.

SOURCE: Adapted from information supplied by the Library of Congress.

A Study in Contrasts

Although many Americans question the usefulness and functions of our institutions, we tend to take the system of checks and balances for granted, considering it necessary for constitutional government. Like Madison, (and especially since Watergate), we view the amassing of power by any one branch of government as leading to tyranny. Yet it is quite possible for a government to be

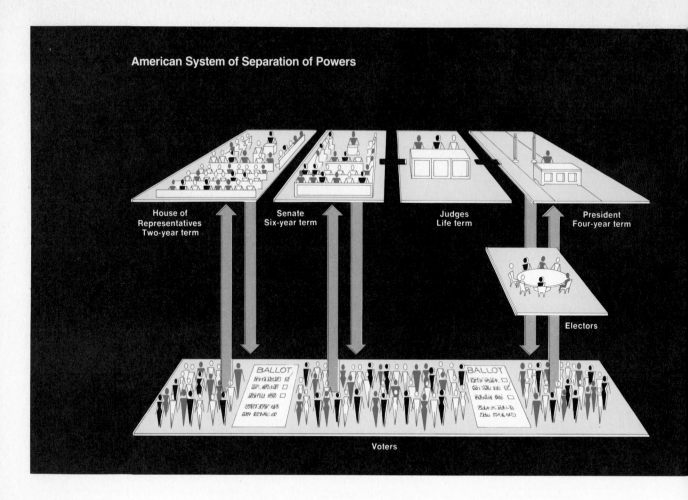

American System of Separation of Powers

House of
Representatives
Two-year term

Senate
Six-year term

Judges
Life term

President
Four-year term

Electors

BALLOT

BALLOT

Voters

constitutional without such an apparatus. Under the British system, voters elect members of Parliament from districts throughout the nation (much as we elect members of the House of Representatives). The members of the House of Commons have almost complete constitutional power: The leaders of the majority party serve as executive ministers, who collectively form the cabinet, with the prime minister as its head. When the executive officers lose the support of the majority in the Commons on a major issue, they must resign or call for new elections. Formerly the House of Lords could check the Commons, but now it is almost powerless. There is no high court with the power to declare acts of Parliament unconstitutional. The prime minister cannot veto them (though he or she may ask the Crown to dissolve Parliament and call for elections for members of the House of Commons). Needless to say, the English take their system as much for granted as we do our own.

The British system is based on *majority rule*—that is, a majority of the voters elects a majority of the legislators, who can put through the majority's program as long as the parliamentary majority stays together, at least until the next election. Our system usually depends on the agreement of many elements of society. The British system *concentrates* control and responsibility in the legislature; ours *diffuses* control and responsibility among several organs of government.

We have a written document called the Constitution; Britain has no such document. Yet both systems are constitutional in the sense that the rulers are subject to regular restraints. The limits our written Constitution and the con-

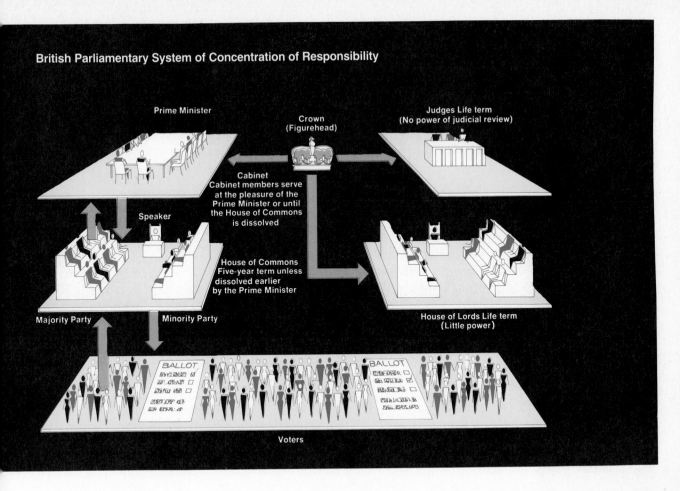

British Parliamentary System of Concentration of Responsibility

Prime Minister

Crown
(Figurehead)

Judges Life term
(No power of judicial review)

Cabinet
Cabinet members serve
at the pleasure of the
Prime Minister or until
the House of Commons
is dissolved

Speaker

House of Commons
Five-year term unless
dissolved earlier
by the Prime Minister

Majority Party   Minority Party

House of Lords Life term
(Little power)

BALLOT

BALLOT

Voters

ventions of the unwritten British constitution impose on all who exercise governmental power rest on underlying values, attitudes, and norms (rules).

THE CONSTITUTION AS AN INSTRUMENT OF GOVERNMENT

As careful as the founding fathers were to limit the powers they gave the national government, the main reason they had assembled in Philadelphia was to create a *stronger* national government. They had learned that weak central government, incapable of governing, is a danger to liberty. They wished to establish a national government within the framework of a federal system and with enough authority to meet the needs of all times. They made general grants of power, leaving the way open for succeeding generations to fill in the details and organize the structure of government in accordance with experience.

Hence, our formal, written Constitution is only the skeleton of our system. It is filled in by numerous rules that must be considered part of our constitutional system in its larger sense. In fact, it is primarily through changes in our *informal* Constitution that our system is kept up to date. These changes are to be found in certain basic statutes and historical practices of Congress, decisions of the Supreme Court, actions of the president, and customs and usages of the nation.

Congressional Elaboration

Because the framers gave Congress authority over many of the structural details of the national government, it is not necessary to amend the Constitution every time a change is needed: rather Congress can act from year to year. Examples of congressional elaboration appear in legislation such as the Judiciary Act of 1789, which laid the foundations of our national judicial system; in the laws establishing the organization and functions of all federal executive officials subordinate to the president; and in the rules of procedure, internal organization, and practices of Congress itself. (All these will be discussed in later chapters.)

IMPEACHMENT POWER—AN EXAMPLE OF CONGRESSIONAL ELABORATION One of the most dramatic examples of congressional elaboration is the use of the impeachment power. The constitutional language is sparse: It is up to Congress to give meaning to that language. Article I—the Legislative Article—says that the House of Representatives shall have the sole power of impeachment, and the Senate the sole power to try all impeachments. When sitting for that purpose, senators "shall be on oath or affirmation," with the chief justice of the United States presiding in the event the president is being tried. The article provides that conviction on impeachment charges requires the agreement of two-thirds of the senators present. Judgments shall extend no further than removal from office and disqualification from holding any office under the United States, but a person convicted shall also be liable to indictment, trial, judgment, and punishment according to the law. In Article II—the Executive Article—the Constitution provides that the "President, Vice-President, and all civil officers of the United States, shall be removed from Office on Impeachment for, and Conviction of, Treason, Bribery, or other high Crimes and Misdemeanors." The article also excepts cases of impeachment from the president's pardoning power. Article III—the Judicial Article—exempts cases of impeachment from the jury trial requirement.

Fortunately for the nation, impeachment has triggered few acute constitutional disputes. The House of Representatives has investigated about sixty-five persons for possible impeachment and has impeached twelve; the Senate has convicted four (all federal judges). One judge resigned after being impeached, and the charges against him were dropped. One president, Andrew Johnson, was impeached in 1868, but the Senate failed by one vote to muster the two-thirds necessary to support the charges. Another president, Richard Nixon, resigned in August 9, 1974, to avoid impeachment after the House Judiciary Committee recommended three articles of impeachment against him. The House did not press the matter further, but the articles of impeachment were submitted by the committee and "accepted" by the House.

The back of Richard Kleindienst as the former Attorney General testifies before the Senate Watergate Committee in August, 1973. *UPI.*

While congressional precedents have rejected the *broadest* view—that the Constitution authorizes removal of officers by impeachment because of *political* objections to officers or because of their unpopularity (a view that might have moved us more in the direction of a parliamentary type of government)—Congress has also rejected the *narrowest* construction—that the only impeachable offenses are those that involve violations of the criminal laws. Rather, the firmly established position is one that reflects a serious violation of constitutional responsibilities and a clear dereliction of duty.[8]

Presidential Practices

Although there has been no change in the formal constitutional powers of the president, that office is dramatically more important and more central today than it was in 1789. Among the more vigorous presidents, Washington, Jeffer-

---

[8]John R. Labovitz, *Presidential Impeachment* (Yale University Press, 1978).

son, Jackson, Lincoln, Theodore Roosevelt, Wilson, Franklin Roosevelt, and Harry Truman boldly exercised their political and constitutional powers, especially during times of national crisis. Such presidential practices have become important precedents, building the power and influence of the office. Even John Tyler made his contribution to constitutional elaboration. Upon becoming president through vice-presidential succession, Tyler established the precedent that under such circumstances the vice-president becomes the president, not merely the acting president.

Nuclear-age realities add force to the president's role as the nation's "final arbiter." Political scientist Richard Neustadt says: "When it comes to action risking war, technology has modified the Constitution: the President, perforce, becomes the only such man in the system capable of exercising judgment under the extraordinary limits now imposed by secrecy, complexity, and time."[9]

The presidency has also become the pivotal office for regulating the economy and protecting the general welfare. Plainly, the president has become a key legislator as well as the nation's chief executive.

Custom and Usage

Customs and usages have rounded out our governmental system. Presidential nominating conventions and other party activities are examples of constitutional usages. Although not specifically mentioned in the Constitution, these practices are fundamental to our system. In fact, it has been primarily through the development of national political parties and the extension of the suffrage within the states that our Constitution has become democratized. A broader electorate began to exercise control over the national government, and the presidential office was made more responsive to the people. In addition, the relationship between Congress and the president was altered. Further, through the growth of political parties, some constitutional blocks to popular rule were overcome.

Judicial Interpretation

Judicial interpretation of the Constitution, especially by the Supreme Court, has played an important part in keeping the constitutional system up to date. As social and economic conditions have changed and new national demands have developed, the Supreme Court has changed its interpretation of the Constitution to reflect these trends. In the words of Woodrow Wilson, "The Supreme Court is a constitutional convention in continuous session."

Because the Constitution is so flexible, and because it adapts easily to changing times, it does not require frequent formal amendment. The advantages of this flexibility may be appreciated when the national Constitution is compared with the rigid and often overly specific state constitutions. Many state constitutions, more like legal codes than basic charters, are so detailed that the hands of public officials are often tied. Such constitutions must be amended frequently or replaced every generation or so.

A Rigid or Flexible Constitution?

The idea of a constantly changing system disturbs many people. How, they argue, can you have a constitutional government when the Constitution is constantly being twisted by interpretation and changed by informal methods? This view fails to distinguish between two aspects of the Constitution. As an expression of *basic and timeless personal liberties*, the Constitution does not and should not change. For example, a government cannot destroy the right to free speech and still remain a constitutional government. In this sense the Constitution *is* timeless and unchanging.

But when we consider the Constitution as an *instrument of government* and *a positive grant of power*, we realize that if it does not grow with the nation

[9]Neustadt, *Presidential Power*, p. 280.

it serves, it will soon be pushed aside. The framers could not have conceived of the problems the government of more than 235 million citizens in an industrial nation would have to face in the 1980s. While the general purposes of government remain the same—to establish liberty, promote justice, ensure domestic tranquility, and provide for the common defense—the powers of government adequate to accomplish these purposes in 1787 are simply insufficient in the 1980s.

"We the people"—the people of today and tomorrow, not just the people of 1787—ordain and establish the Constitution. "The Constitution," wrote Jefferson, "belongs to the living and not to the dead." So firmly did he believe this that he proposed there might be a new constitution for every generation. But new constitutions have not been necessary, because in a less formal way each generation has taken part in the process of developing and changing the original Constitution. In fact, because of its remarkable adaptability, the Constitution has survived democratic and industrial revolutions, the turmoil of civil war, the tensions of major depressions, and the dislocations of world wars.

CHANGING THE LETTER OF THE CONSTITUTION

The framers knew that future experiences would call for changes in the text of the Constitution and that some means of formal amendment was necessary. In Article 5 of the Constitution, they gave this responsibility to Congress and to the states; the president has no formal authority over constitutional amendments. His veto power does not extend to them, although his political influence in getting amendments proposed by Congress and ratified by the states is often crucial. Nor may governors veto ratification of amendments by their respective legislatures or ratifying conventions. The Constitution vests ratification

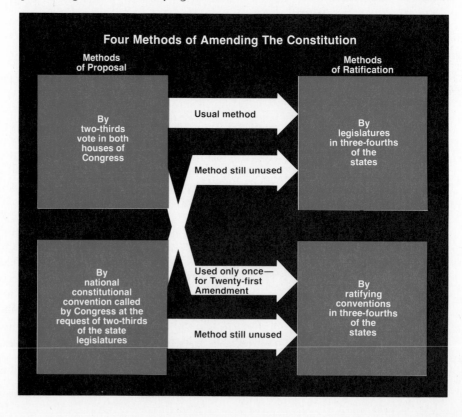

Four Methods of Amending The Constitution

Methods of Proposal		Methods of Ratification
By two-thirds vote in both houses of Congress	Usual method →	By legislatures in three-fourths of the states
	Method still unused →	
By national constitutional convention called by Congress at the request of two-thirds of the state legislatures	Used only once— for Twenty-first Amendment →	By ratifying conventions in three-fourths of the states
	Method still unused →	

in whichever body Congress designates—state *legislatures* or state ratifying *conventions*. The framers set up two ways to propose amendments and two ways to ratify them, and they saw to it that amendments could not be made by simple majorities. Each amendment must be both proposed and ratified.

PROPOSING AMENDMENTS

© News Group Chicago, Inc.— Courtesy of News America Syndicate.

The first method for proposing amendments—the only one that has been used so far—is by a two-thirds vote of both houses of Congress. Dozens of resolutions proposing amendments are introduced in every session. Over 10,000 have been introduced since 1789, a third of these during the last thirteen years. However, few make any headway. Currently before Congress are resolutions on equal rights for women, prayer in public schools, abortions, the electoral college, a six-year term for the president, balancing the federal budget, and restricting powers of federal courts, to mention just a few. Why has amending the Consitution recently become such a "popular frenzy"?[10] Interest groups unhappy with Supreme Court decisions seek to overturn them. Groups frustrated by their inability to get things done in Congress—balancing the budget, for example— seek an amendment, even if only for symbolic reasons. Scholars or interest-group representatives (not necessarily mutually exclusive categories) seek to change the procedures and process of government to make the system more responsive.

Although many seek to amend the Constitution, throughout our history Congress has proposed only thirty-three amendments (twenty-three, excluding the Bill of Rights). Most recently Congress almost proposed a Balanced Budget Amendment. This would require Congress each year to limit federal expenditures to an amount matching projected federal revenues unless Congress, by an extraordinary vote, declared an emergency. President Reagan strongly favored the amendment, and the Senate gave it the necessary two-thirds vote, but the Democratically controlled House defeated it. Some form of ERA II (see page 40) is likely to be proposed by Congress in the near future. One amendment—the District of Columbia Amendment (see pages 40–41)—is presently before the state legislatures for their consideration.

The second method for proposing amendments—calling a constitutional convention—has never been used. Whenever the legislatures in two-thirds of the states petition Congress to call such a convention to deal with a particular subject, "Congress shall call a Convention for proposing Amendments." "The Constitution's other Method"[11] presents some difficult questions. How long do state petitions remain alive? How should delegates be chosen? How should a convention be run? Recently Congress has considered proposals that would provide the answers to some of the questions. Most call on Congress to set the date and place for a convention whenever each chamber concludes that two-thirds of the state legislatures have petitioned about a particular subject closely enough in time to one another to reflect a "contemporaneous national request" for action. Under most proposals, each state would have as many delegates to the convention as it has representatives and senators in Congress. Finally—a crucial point—the convention would be limited to considering only the subject in the state legislative petitions and described in the congressional call for the conven-

[10]Gary L. McDowell, "On Meddling with The Constitution," *Journal of Contemporary Studies,* Institute of Contemporary Studies (Fall 1982).

[11]Ann Stuart Diamond, "A Convention for Proposing Amendments: The Constitution's Other Method," *Publius,* Vol. 11, No. 3–4 (Summer 1981), pp. 113–146; Wilbur Edel, "Amending The Constitution by Convention: Myths and Realities," *State Government,* Vol. 55 (1982), pp 51–56.

tion. (But does Congress have authority to limit what a constitutional convention might propose? Scholars are divided on this question.)[12]

Despite organized efforts to force Congress to call a constitutional convention (or else to propose the amendment itself), so far Congress has not acted. The closest we came to a convention was in the spring of 1967 when the thirty-third state legislature—only one short of the required number—petitioned Congress to call a convention to propose an amendment that would set aside a Supreme Court ruling that both chambers of a state legislature must be apportioned on the basis of population. Congress refused to propose an amendment, the thirty-fourth state never petitioned, and as the several state legislatures completed the process of reapportionment, pressures for this amendment abated.

Recently, Congress has received petitions for a convention to propose amendments to permit prayer in the public schools, to reverse Supreme Court decisions relating to abortions, and to deal with school busing, among other issues. But the most active campaign for a convention is that sponsored by the National Taxpayers Union in behalf of a Balanced Budget Amendment. At least thirty-two state legislatures have petitioned Congress on this issue. With the defeat in 1982 of the resolution that Congress itself propose such an amendment, the National Taxpayers Union has indicated that it will renew its efforts to secure the amendment via "The Second Method."

Why has Congress been so reluctant to call a convention? Members of Congress, and many other concerned citizens, are fearful of a "runaway convention" in which delegates would ignore the restraints imposed upon them and propose amendments on a variety of topics—perhaps even calling for a new form of government. Such fears are not new. In January 1789, James Madison expressed a strong preference that Congress should propose a Bill of Rights in the form of amendments rather than call for a second convention. He wrote: "The Congress who will be appointed to execute as well as to amend the Government, will probably be careful not to destroy or endanger it. A convention, on the other hand, meeting in the present ferment of parties, and containing perhaps insidious characters from different parts of America, would at least spread a general alarm, and be but too likely to turn everything into confusion and uncertainty."[13]

"First thing to do is toss out a lot of this stuff adopted by the previous convention." Copyright © 1979 by Herblock in The Washington Post.

Ratifying Amendments

After an amendment has been proposed, it must be ratified by the states. Again, two methods are provided—approval of the legislatures in three-fourths of the states, or approval of specially called ratifying conventions in three-fourths of the states. Congress determines which method shall be used. All amendments except one—the Twenty-first (to repeal the Eighteenth, the Prohibition Amendment)—have been submitted to the state legislatures for ratification. (In seven states an extraordinary majority of three-fifths or two-thirds of each chamber is necessary.)[14] While a state legislature may change its mind

[12]Frank J. Sorauf, "The Political Potential of an Amending Convention," in Kermit L. Hall, Harold M. Hyman, and Leon V. Sigal (eds.). The Constitutional Convention as an Amending Device. For Project '87 (American Political Science Association, 1981), pp. 113–130. Sorauf does not agree with these scholars but reviews their arguments and cites the literature. See also Bill Gaugush, "Principles Governing the Interpretation and Exercise of Article V Power." Western Political Quarterly, Vol. XXXV, No. 2 (June 1982), pp. 212–221, and response by C. Herman Pritchett, "Congress and Article V, Conventions" Western Political Quarterly, Vol. XXXV, No. 2 (June 1982), pp. 222–227.

[13]Letter to George Eve, quoted in Walter E. Dellinger, "The Recurring Question," Yale Law Journal, Vol. 88 (October 1979), p. 1979.

[14]Clement E. Vose, "When District of Columbia Representation Collides with the Constitutional Amendment Institution," Publius, Vol. 9 (Winter 1979), p. 114.

The Child Labor amendment, proposed in 1924, was ratified by only twenty-eight state legislatures, the last being in 1937. A reasonable time for ratification of the amendment has now passed. But as the result of Supreme Court decisions since 1937, the amendment is no longer needed to permit Congress to outlaw child labor. *Picture collection The New York Public Library and Museum of the City of New York.*

and ratify an amendment after it has voted against ratification, the weight of opinion is that once a state has ratified an amendment it cannot unratify it.[15]

Submission of amendments to legislatures rather than ratifying conventions permits the Constitution to be changed without any direct expression by the voters: The legislatures may have been elected before the proposed amendment was submitted to the states. In any event, state legislators are chosen because of their views on schools, taxation, or other matters, or because of their personal popularity. They are almost never elected because of their stand on a proposed constitutional amendment, although the candidates' positions on the ERA surfaced as a key issue in several state legislative elections.

Mechanics can make a difference. The decision to submit the Twenty-first Amendment to ratifying conventions came about because the "wets" rightly believed that repeal had a better chance of success with conventions than with the rural-dominated state legislatures. (For similar tactical reasons southern Democrats joined with eastern Republican conservatives in an unsuccessful effort to submit the Nineteenth Amendment, or Susan B. Anthony Amendment, as it was called, to ratifying conventions. Let the voters decide—the male voters, that is—they argued.)[16] Congress left it up to each state legislature to determine how the ratifying conventions would be organized and delegates elected. State delegates ran at-large on tickets in which they pledged to vote for or against repeal. As a result, when the convention in a state was called to order, the convention quickly ratified the decision the voters had already made. In effect, ratification was submitted to the voters.

[15]Samuel S. Freedman and Pamela J. Naughton, *ERA: May a State Change Its Vote* (Wayne State University Press, 1978).

[16]Alan P. Grimes, *Democracy and Amendments to the Constitution* (Lexington Books, 1978), p. 95; see also Clement E. Vose, *Constitutional Change* (Lexington Books, 1972), pp. 342–44, which focuses on amendment politics in the case of woman suffrage, child labor, and prohibition; Philip J. Martin, "Convention Ratification of Federal Constitutional Amendments," *Political Science Quarterly* (March 1967), p. 1.

Amendatory Power *cont.*

☐ The Twenty-third gave to the voters of the District of Columbia the right to vote for president and vice-president.

4. Amendments whose chief impact has been to *subtract from the power of the electorate.*

☐ The Twenty-second took from the electorate the right to elect any person to the office of president for more than two full terms.

5. Amendments *making structural changes in governmental machinery.*

☐ The Twelfth corrected deficiencies in the operation of the electoral college that were revealed by the development of a two-party national system.

☐ The Twentieth altered the calendar for congressional sessions and shortened the time between the election of presidents and their assumption of office.

☐ The Twenty-fifth provided procedures for filling vacancies in the vice-presidency and for determining whether presidents are unable to perform their duties.

The Fifteenth Amendment was ratified in 1870, but blacks were kept from voting in many southern states until Congress implemented that amendment by the Voting Rights Act of 1965. Here blacks lined up to register in Selma, Alabama, in January 1965 are stopped by local police officers at the main entrance. *UPI.*

A state must ratify proposed amendments within (what Congress considers) a reasonable time. The modern practice is for Congress to stipulate that an amendment will not become part of the Constitution unless ratified by the necessary number of states within seven years from the date of its submission. (In fact, ratification ordinarily takes place rather quickly; see Table 2–2). Sometimes Congress places the seven-year limitation in the text of the proposed amendment, sometimes in the enabling legislation that accompanies it. Where the limitations are placed can make a difference.

In the autumn of 1978 it appeared that the Equal Rights Amendment would fall three short of the necessary number of ratifying states prior to the expiration of the seven-year limit—that is, March 22, 1979. After an extended

2–2

THE 26 AMENDMENTS: HOW LONG THEY HAD TO WAIT

Here is the Length of Time Between Congressional Approval and Actual Ratification of Each of Today's 26 Amendments to the U.S. Constitution

AMENDMENT	TIME TO RATIFY	RATIFIED
1–10. Bill of rights	1 year, 2½ months	1791
11. Lawsuits against states	3 years, 10 months	1798
12. Presidential elections	8½ months	1804
13. Abolition of slavery	10½ months	1865
14. Civil rights	2 years, 1½ months	1868
15. Suffrage for all races	1 year, 1 month	1870
16. Income tax	3 years, 7½ months	1913
17. Senatorial elections	1 year, ½ month	1913
18. Prohibition	1 year, 1½ months	1919
19. Women's suffrage	1 year, 2½ months	1920
20. Terms of office	11 months	1933
21. Repeal of prohibition	9½ months	1933
22. Limit on presidential terms	3 years, 11½ months	1951
23. Washington, D.C., vote	9 months	1961
24. Abolition of poll taxes	1 year, 5½ months	1964
25. Presidential succession	1 year, 6½ months	1967
26. 18-year-old suffrage	4 months	1971

debate, and after voting down provisions that would have authorized legislatures to change their minds and rescind prior ratification, Congress—by a simple majority vote in both chambers—extended the time limit until June 30, 1982. This action was challenged by opponents of ERA; however, its defenders argue that the time limit was in the accompanying enabling legislation, not in the body of the proposed amendment, and is thus subject to congressional modification by simple majorities, since Congress determines what is a reasonable time. (The amendment failed, even with the extension, and thus made moot the pending court test of the extension's constitutionality.)

When Congress proposed an amendment to provide full congressional representation for the District of Columbia, it pointedly reverted to earlier practice and placed the seven-year limit in the text of the amendment. This suggests that (1) Congress wanted to preclude any possibility of extending the time limit for ratification of this amendment by a simple majority of both houses, and that (2) Congress sought to discourage proponents of unratified amendments from seeking extensions of time limits.

RATIFICATION POLITICS: ERA AND THE D.C. AMENDMENT

Until the submission of ERA and the D.C. Amendment, the only amendment since the Civil War that failed to be ratified was the Child Labor Amendment. While the existence of a political coalition sufficient to get an amendment through Congress ordinarily reflects sufficient strength in the nation to ensure ratification, the failure of the ERA and the D.C. Amendment makes it clear that this is not always the case.

ERA "had received overwhelming support in both houses of Congress. . . . Both major political parties had repeatedly supported the ERA in their national party platforms; not until 1980 did one party (the Republican) adopt a stance of neutrality. Every president from Truman to Carter [and many of their wives] had endorsed the amendment. And, by the end of the campaign for state ratification, more than 450 organizations with a total membership of over 50 million were on record in support of ERA."[17]

Soon after submission of the amendment in 1972, many legislatures quickly ratified—sometimes without hearings—and by overwhelming majorities. By the end of 1972 twenty-two states had ratified the amendment. "ERA was supported by a large majority nationwide, a large majority of the people in the unratified states, a large majority of housewives, a large majority of conservatives, and a large majority of religious fundamentalists."[18]

It appeared that ERA would soon become part of the Constitution. Then the opposition got organized under the articulate leadership of Phyllis Schlafly. Opponents argued that "women would not only be subject to the military draft but also assigned to combat duty. Full-time housewives and mothers would be forced to join the labor force. . . . Furthermore, women would no longer enjoy existing advantages under state domestic relations codes and under labor law."[19]

ERA became controversial. Legislatures were forced to hold hearings, floor debates became heated, and "with increasing frequency, legislators sought

[17]Janet K. Boles, "Building Support for the ERA: A Case of Too Much, Too Late," *P.S.*, Vol. XV (Fall 1982), p. 572.

[18]Mark R. Daniels, Robert Darcy, and Joseph W. Westphal, "The ERA Won—At Least in the Opinion Polls," *P.S.*, Vol. XV (Fall 1982), p. 583.

[19]Janet K. Boles, *The Politics of the Equal Rights Amendment* (Longmans, 1979), p. 4.

Women from all political parties have been involved in the long struggle for women's rights: from Abigail Scott Duniway's battles in Oregon in the 1880s to achieve the vote for women, to rallies a hundred years later for the Equal Rights amendment. *Oregon Historical Society and UPI.*

EQUAL RIGHTS FOR WOMEN AMENDMENT (ERA)

Proposed March 22, 1972. After heated debate in October 1978, Congress extended the time limit for its ratification until June 30, 1982. Nevertheless, it still failed to win ratification by the needed three-fourths of the state legislature.

Section 1.   Equality of rights under the law shall not be denied or abridged by the United States or by any State on account of sex.

Section 2.   The Congress shall have power to enforce by appropriate legislation, the provisions of this article.

Section 3.   This amendment shall take effect two years after date of ratification.

refuge in legislative procedure to delay or avoid entirely a public decision. . . ." Opposition to ratification arose chiefly in the same cluster of southern states that had opposed ratification of the Nineteenth Amendment. In Illinois a majority in each chamber voted for the proposal, but it failed to obtain the three-fourths majority required by the Illinois constitution.

As the opposition grew more active, proponents redoubled their efforts. The National Organization for Women, NOW, called for an economic boycott in nonratifying states, and many associations refused to hold their meetings in Chicago, Kansas City, Las Vegas, Miami, Atlanta, and New Orleans. In the 1980 presidential campaign President Reagan took an anti-ERA stand, and the campaign over ERA in the unratified states grew more intense. On March 22, 1982—the final deadline—the amendment was short of ratification by three state legislatures.

The framers intended that amending the Constitution should be difficult: The ERA ratification battle demonstrates how well they planned. But the defeat of ERA is hardly likely to end the struggle over this amendment.[20] NOW and the other groups that supported ERA emerged from the struggle with more members, more money, and a greater determination than ever to secure its passage.

The Proposed D.C. Amendment

Despite the fact it passed both chambers of Congress by big margins and with impressive bipartisan support, it appears that the District of Columbia Amendment will not be ratified. It is ratifiable until August 22, 1985, but as of 1984 only sixteen state legislatures had ratified. The amendment, proposed in 1978, would give to the 640,000 people of the District of Columbia two senators and the same number of representatives in the House of Representatives the area would have if it were a state (one under current law and with its present population). It would give the District three electoral votes (it has three under present arrangements), as well as a vote in the ratification of constitutional amendments. Finally, it would repeal the Twenty-third Amendment.

The coalition that pushed the D.C. Amendment through Congress has failed to maintain its cohesion during the ratification struggle. In many states it

[20]Margery L. Elfin, "Learning from Failures Present and Past"; Marian L. Palley, "Beyond the Deadline," both in *PS*, Vol. XV (Fall 1982), pp. 585–592.

is feared that the amendment will give additional strength to urban-based groups, especially blacks—a prospect that does not please state legislators from rural and small-town districts. Moreover, many proponents of the amendment have given up hope that it will be ratified and have turned their attention to persuading Congress to admit the District—except for a small portion that would remain the "seat of the Government of the United States"—to the Union as a state. Such an action would accomplish all that the District of Columbia amendment would do and more; but it would require only a simple majority vote of both houses of Congress to accomplish.

SUMMARY

1. Our Constitution both grants powers and limits them. The framers established a government to be operated by ordinary people; they did not anticipate Americans would be so special they could be trusted to operate without checks and balances. The framers were suspicious of people, especially of those having political power, so they separated and distributed the powers of the newly created national government in a variety of ways.

2. The framers were also concerned that the national government be strong enough to act to solve public problems. They wanted it to be responsive to the wishes of the people and to carry out those wishes—that is, the matured and refined wishes of the people. Thus, they gave the national government substantial grants of power. But these grants were made with such broad strokes that it has been possible for the national government and the constitutional system to remain flexible and adapt to changing conditions.

3. Although the American governmental system has its roots in English traditions, our separation of powers and

checks and balances system is different from the English system of concentrated responsibility. It is also different because our Supreme Court has the power of judicial review.

4. The system of checks and balances has been modified over time. The Constitution has been adapted to new conditions through congressional elaboration, modern presidential realities, custom and usage, and judicial interpretation.

5. Although adaptable, the Constitution itself needs to be altered from time to time, and the document provides for its own amendment. An amendment must be both proposed and ratified: proposed either by a two-thirds vote in each chamber of Congress or by a national convention called by Congress on petition of the legislatures in two-thirds of the states; ratified either by the legislatures in three-fourths of the states or by specially called ratifying conventions in three-fourths of the states. The Constitution has been formally amended twenty-six times.

FURTHER READING

JAMES BRYCE. *The American Commonwealth*, Vol. I and II (Macmillan, 1893).

CONGRESSIONAL RESEARCH SERVICE, LIBRARY OF CONGRESS. *The Constitution of the United States of America, Analysis and Interpretation* (U.S. Government Printing Office, 1972, with 1980 supplement, 1982).

ALEXIS DE TOCQUEVILLE. *Democracy in America*, Vols. I and II (Knopf, 1945, first published in 1835).

J. W. PELTASON. *Corwin & Peltason's Understanding the Constitution*, 9th ed. (Holt, Rinehart and Winston, 1981).

FORREST MCDONALD. A *Constitutional History of the United States* (Franklin Watts, 1982).

CLEMENT E. VOSE. *Constitutional Change* (Lexington Books, 1972).

AMERICAN FEDERALISM: PROBLEMS AND PROSPECTS

3

Talk to some people about federalism, or "intergovernmental relations"—the modern term—and you are likely to see their eyes glaze over. Yet in 1861 men and women fought and died for Virginia or Texas or for the Union (although it would be a mistake to think of the Civil War merely as a particularly heated debate over the principles of federalism). Federalism—the constitutional division of powers between the national and state governments—remains very much a part of our political life, affecting almost every political issue, as it has for almost two centuries.

Constitutionally speaking, our federal system consists only of the national government and the fifty states. "Cities are not," the Supreme Court recently reminded us, "sovereign entities." But in a practical sense we are a nation of more than 82,000 governmental units—from the national level down to the school board district. While this does not make for a tidy, efficient, easy-to-understand system, it does have its virtues.

Today almost everything is intergovernmentalized. Consider your college or university, whether public or independent. Half of the students are likely to be receiving some form of *federal* and *state* financial assistance to help pay their tuition, fees, room, and board. The college itself is chartered by the *state*. Most of the funds that pay for the teachers, staff, and buildings come from *state* appropriations or state bonds or from private gifts encouraged by *federal* tax laws, or a combination of *federal* and *state* and private sources. The research your faculty is doing, especially in the sciences, and the public service programs in which they are involved are likely to be supported by some *combination* of *federal*, *state*, and private—but tax deductible—dollars. The conditions under which students are admitted, how faculty and staff are appointed, how faculty and staff are evaluated and promoted, how your grades are posted and to whom they are reported—these questions involve *state* and *federal* regulations. The experimental animals on your campus are subject to supervision by *federal* and *state* inspectors. How the laboratories where your classes are held dispose of the chemicals you have used in your experiments are governed by *federal* and *state* laws. Such examples of "intergovernmentalization" are innumerable, affecting even such vital matters as your intercollegiate and intramural sports program.

The fact that ours is a federal system makes a lot of difference to us, even if we are not always aware that this is so. We need to ask: Is this system, established two hundred years ago, able to operate effectively now, or do we need to make some changes?

What is a federal system? The mere fact that we have both a national government and state governments does not make our system federal. What is important is that a *constitution* divides governmental powers between the central, or national, government and the constituent governments (called states in the United States), giving substantial functions to each. Neither the central nor the constituent government receives its powers from the other; both derive them from a common source, a constitution. This constitutional distribution of powers cannot be changed by the ordinary process of legislation—for example, by an act of either a national or state legislature. Finally, both levels of government operate through their own agents and exercise power directly over individuals. Among the countries that have a federal system of government are the United States, Canada, Switzerland, Mexico, and Australia.[1]

A **unitary,** as opposed to a federal, system of government is one in which a constitution vests all governmental power in the central government. The central government, if it so chooses, may delegate authority to constituent units, but what it delegates it may also take away. Britain, France, Israel, and the Philippines have this form of government. In the United States the relation between states and their local governments, such as counties and cities, is ordinarily of this sort.

A **confederation** may be defined as a government in which the constituent governments by constitutional compact create a central government but do not give it power to regulate the conduct of individuals. The central government makes regulations for the constituent governments, but it exists and operates only at their direction. The thirteen states under the Articles of Confederation operated in this manner.

It is unfortunate for our understanding of federalism that the founders of our Constitution used the term *federal* to describe what we now would call a confederate form of government. Moreover, today *federal* is frequently used as a synonym for *national:* People often refer to the government in Washington as "the federal government." But in fact, the states *and* the national government make up our federal system.

Numbers of Governments	
States	50
Counties	3,041
Municipalities	19,083
Townships	16,748
School Districts	15,032
Special Districts	28,733
	82,687

Source: 1982 Census of Governments, U.S. Dept. of Commerce.

WHY FEDERALISM?

We have a federal form of government in part because in 1787 there was really no other choice. Confederation had been found unsuccessful, and a unitary system was out because most of the people were too deeply attached to the state governments to permit the states to be subordinated to central rule.

[1]Ursula K. Hicks, *Federalism: Failure and Success, A Comparative Study* (Oxford University Press, 1979), for federalism around the world.

Confederation: 1781—1788

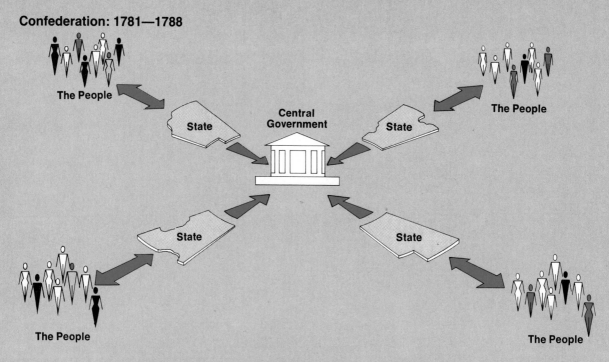

The Confederation was a union of states. The central government received power from the states and had no direct authority over the people.

—and Federation: 1789—

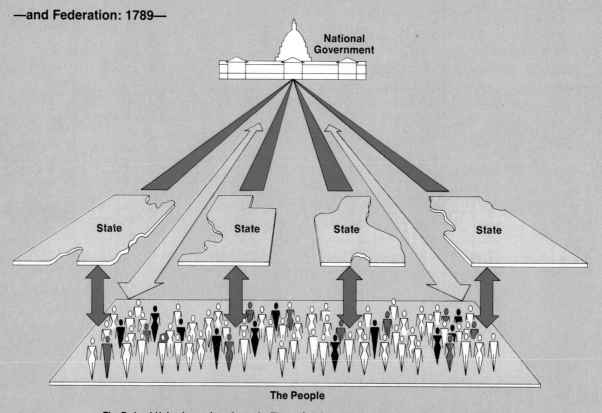

The Federal Union is a union of people. The national government and state governments receive power from the people and exercise authority directly over them.

The factors that led to the creation of our federal system in 1787, and that sustain it in the 1980s, should not be confused with the arguments for and against federalism. (We keep federalism largely because our political and electoral structure is decentralized enough to preserve the independence of the states in the face of the strong pressures toward central control.) Yet whatever the merits of their arguments, *all* insist that their actions will "strengthen the federal system."

Allows Unity Without Uniformity

"Step right up—everybody gets one star and part of a stripe." Copyright 1982 by Herblock in The Washington Post.

Even if a unitary state had been politically possible in 1787, it probably would not have been chosen. Federalism was and still is thought to be ideally suited to the needs of a heterogeneous people who are spread over a large continent, who are suspicious of concentrated power, and who desire unity but not uniformity.

Although in the rest of the world federal forms have not been notably successful in preventing tyranny, and many unitary governments are democratic, Americans tend to equate freedom and federalism. As Madison pointed out in *Federalist No. 10:* "(If) factious leaders . . . kindle a flame within their particular states," national leaders can check the spread of the "conflagration into other states." Shays's Rebellion was a dramatic example. Moreover, when one political party loses control of the national government, it is still likely to hold office in a number of states. It can then regroup, develop new policies and new leaders, and continue to challenge the party in power at the national level.

Such diffusion of power creates its own problems. For example, it makes it difficult for a national majority to carry out a program of action, and it permits those who control a state government to frustrate the consensus expressed through Congress and national agencies. To the founding fathers this was an advantage. They were more fearful that a single-interest national majority might capture the national government and attempt to suppress the interests of others than they were that minority interests might frustrate the national will. Of course—and this is a point often overlooked today—(but emphasized by Madison in *Federalist No. 10*) the size of the nation and the many interests within it are the greatest obstacles to the formation of a single-interest majority. Even if such a majority should form, the fact that it would have to work through a federal system would act as a check on it.

Another advantage of a federal system is that national politicians and parties do not have to iron out every difference on every issue in every state. Issues such as divorce and school dress codes are debated in state legislatures and city halls; there is no need to enforce a single national standard. Thus, it is easier to develop consensus on truly national problems.

Encourages Experimentation

According to conventional wisdom, federalism encourages experimentation. According to this wisdom, states serve as proving grounds. If they adopt programs that fail, the negative effects are limited; if programs succeed, they can be adopted by other states and by the national government. Georgia was the first state to permit eighteen-year-olds to vote. New York has been vigorous in its assault on water pollution; California has pioneered air pollution control programs. Also, many states altered their abortion laws before the Supreme Court acted (whether this is progress or regression, like so many questions of politics, depends upon one's values).

Some people doubt that federalism encourages experimentation. Federal Judge Skelly Wright asserts: "Mr. Justice Brandeis' [one of the most famous Supreme Court justices, who sat on the Court from 1916 to 1939] wonderful laboratory theory for state government experimentation has been shipwrecked

Everybody is against pollution, but how to prevent it and who should pay for the costs of avoiding it are subjects of intense political controversy. *Reynolds Aluminum and United Nations.*

on the contemporary fact of industrial mobility. No state dares impose sweeping new regulations on industry, for their imposition would drive away business concerns whose presence in the state opens up employment opportunities and accounts for vital tax resources."[2]

3–1

THE MOST POPULAR LEVEL OF GOVERNMENT?

LEVEL	From Which Level of Government Do You Feel You Get The Most For Your Money—Federal, State, or Local? (% U.S. Public)					
	1974	1976	1978	1980	1982	1984
Federal	29%	36%	35%	33%	35%	24%
Local	28	25	26	26	28	35
State	24	20	20	22	20	27
Don't know	19	19	19	19	17	14

SOURCE: Advisory Commission on Intergovernmental Relations.

Keeps Government Close to the People

Federalism, by providing numerous areas for decision making, involves many people and helps to keep government closer to the people. We have to be cautious, however, about the notion that state and local governments are necessarily "closer to the people" than the national government. True, more people are involved in local and state politics than in national affairs, and in recent years confidence in the ability of state governments has gone up while confidence in the ability of the national government has declined. But national affairs are more on the minds of most people than are state politics or even local politics. Fewer voters participate in state elections than in congressional and presidential elections. Still, states and their local units remain very much a part of the political life of those involved in public matters.

CONSTITUTIONAL STRUCTURE OF AMERICAN FEDERALISM

The formal constitutional framework of our federal system may be stated simply: The national government has only those powers, with the one important exception of foreign affairs, delegated to it by the Constitution. The states have all the powers not delegated to the central government except those denied to

[2]J. Skelly Wright, "The Federal Courts and the Nature and Quality of State Law," in S. I. Shuman (ed.), *The Future of Federalism* (Wayne State University Press, 1968), pp. 75–76.

them by the Constitution. But within the scope of its operations, the national government is supreme. Further, some powers are specifically denied to *both* the national and state governments; others are specifically denied *only* to the states; and still others are denied *only* to the national government.

Powers of the National Government

The Constitution, chiefly in the first three articles, delegates legislative, executive, and judicial powers to the national government. In addition to these express powers, the Constitution delegates to Congress those implied powers that may reasonably be inferred from the express powers. The constitutional basis for the implied powers of Congress is the necessary and proper clause (Article I, Section 8), which gives Congress the right "to make all Laws which shall be necessary and proper for carrying into Execution the foregoing powers, and all other powers vested . . . in the Government of the United States."

In the field of foreign affairs, the national government has inherent powers that do not depend on specific constitutional grants. The national government has the same authority in dealing with other nations as it would have if it were a unitary government. For example, the government of the United States may acquire territory by discovery and occupation, even though there is no specific clause in the Constitution allowing such acquisition. Even if the Constitution were silent about foreign affairs—which it is not—the national government would have the right to declare war, make treaties, and appoint and receive ambassadors.[3]

NATIONAL SUPREMACY CLAUSE Article VI states: "This Constitution, and the Laws of the United States which shall be made in Pursuance thereof; and all Treaties made . . . under the Authority of the United States, shall be the supreme Law of the Land; and the Judges in every state shall be bound thereby; any Thing in the Constitution or Laws of any State to the Contrary notwithstanding." All officials, state as well as national, are bound by constitutional oath to support the Constitution of the United States. States may not use their reserved powers to frustrate national policies. (Local units of government are agents of the states. What states cannot constitutionally do, local units cannot do either. In our discussion of the constitutional structure of federalism, local units are included in all references to the states.)

Federal tax dollars are often used to help state and local governments finance elementary school programs. *Salt River Project.*

Powers of the States

The Constitution reserves to the states all powers not granted to the national government, subject only to the limitations of the Constitution. Powers that are not by provision of the Constitution or by judicial interpretation given exclusively to the national government may be *concurrently* exercised by the states, as long as there is no conflict with national law. For example, the states have concurrent powers with the national government to levy taxes and to regulate commerce internal to each state.

These rather simple statements about the concurrent powers of the states and the national government conceal difficult constitutional questions: To illustrate a state may levy a tax on the same item as the national government. But a state cannot by a tax "unduly burden" a function of the national government or interfere with the operation of a national law or abridge the terms of a treaty of the United States. Who decides whether a state tax is an "undue burden" on a national function? Ultimately, the Supreme Court decides.

The issues are even more complicated as regards commerce. When Congress has not acted, the states may regulate those local aspects of interstate commerce which do not require uniform national treatment. But who decides what requires uniform national treatment? If Congress is silent, ultimately the

[3]*United States v. Curtiss-Wright Export Corporation*, 299 U.S. 304 (1936).

Interstate highways illustrate the need for federal coordination of state efforts. *UPI*.

Supreme Court decides. The Court has upheld state laws imposing speed limits on trains within city limits and requiring the elimination of grade crossings, but it has invalidated laws requiring trains to stop at every crossing.

What of state regulations designed to protect consumers from fraud, guard the public health, or collect a fair share of taxes from those who use state facilities? Again, if there is no clear congressional direction, the Supreme Court must decide whether such regulations are within the reserved powers of the state; whether they are overridden by, or come into conflict with, superior federal regulations; or whether they unduly burden interstate commerce. Thus, the Supreme Court has ruled that states and cities may not impose a curfew on jet takeoffs and landings at airports.

Constitutional Limits and Obligations

To make federalism work the Constitution imposes certain restraints on the national and state governments. States are prohibited from

1. Making treaties with foreign governments
2. Granting letters of Marque and Reprisal, that is, authorizing private persons to prey on the shipping and commerce of other nations
3. Coining money, issuing bills of credit, or making anything but gold and silver coin a tender in payment of debts

Nor may states without the consent of Congress

1. Tax imports or exports
2. Tax foreign ships
3. Keep troops or ships in time of peace (except for the state militia, now called the National Guard)
4. Enter into a compact with another state or a foreign nation
5. Engage in war, unless invaded or in such imminent danger as will not admit of delay (of course, an invasion of one state would be an invasion of the United States itself)

The national government, in turn, is required by the Constitution to refrain from exercising its powers in such a way as to interfere substantially with the ability of the states to perform their responsibilities. In recent decades it has been easier to make this generalization than to cite any specific examples. Since 1937 the Supreme Court, relying on the principle of national supremacy, has sustained every congressional act—except one—alleged to have prevented the states from carrying out their duties. The one exception was *National League*

CONSTITUTIONAL DISTRIBUTION OF POWERS

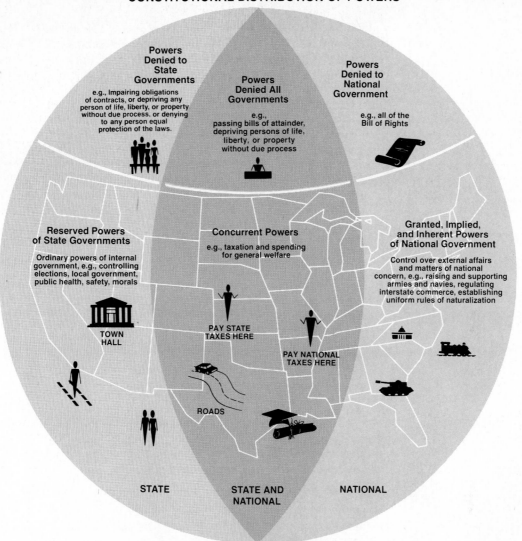

Powers Denied to State Governments
e.g., Impairing obligations of contracts, or depriving any person of life, liberty, or property without due process, or denying to any person equal protection of the laws.

Powers Denied All Governments
e.g., passing bills of attainder, depriving persons of life, liberty, or property without due process

Powers Denied to National Government
e.g., all of the Bill of Rights

Reserved Powers of State Governments
Ordinary powers of internal government, e.g., controlling elections, local government, public health, safety, morals

Concurrent Powers
e.g., taxation and spending for general welfare

Granted, Implied, and Inherent Powers of National Government
Control over external affairs and matters of national concern, e.g., raising and supporting armies and navies, regulating interstate commerce, establishing uniform rules of naturalization

TOWN HALL

PAY STATE TAXES HERE

PAY NATIONAL TAXES HERE

ROADS

STATE   STATE AND NATIONAL   NATIONAL

of Cities v. Usery (1976), when the Court ruled unconstitutional a 1974 amendment of the Fair Labor Standards Act extending federal minimum wage and maximum hours provisions to all state and local government employees.[4] Congress, said the Court, had sought to impair the states' ability to function effectively within a federal system.

While *National League of Cities* was hailed by some as reestablishing the doctrine of Dual Federalism, this has not been the case. Under this doctrine, which the Supreme Court espoused, off and on, until 1937, the national and state governments were viewed as equal sovereigns, each operating within its own restricted sphere, with the Supreme Court enforcing the boundary between the two levels. Rather, *National League of Cities* has been very narrowly construed by the Court. In fact, in 1983, although professing not to overrule this decision, the Supreme Court held by five to four that the national Age Discrimination in Employment Act could be applied to state and local employees.[5] This means that the national government can force state and local govern-

[4]426 U.S. 833 (1976).
[5]*Equal Employment Opportunity Commission v. Wyoming,* 75 L Ed 2d 18 (1983).

ments to keep on their payrolls persons that these governments think are too old to do their jobs.

While the scope of *National League of Cities* is limited at present, nevertheless it is available to be cited as a precedent by some future Supreme Court that thinks Congress has gone too far, impairing too much and too directly the ability of states to carry out their constitutionally granted and protected governmental functions.

The Constitution also requires the national government to guarantee to each state a **republican form of government**. The framers used the term to distinguish a republic from a monarchy on the one side, and from a pure, direct democracy on the other. The enforcement of this guarantee is a congressional responsibility.[6] When Congress permits the congressional delegation of a state to take their seats in Congress, Congress is in effect deciding that the state has a republican form of government.

In addition, the national government is obliged by the Constitution to protect the states against domestic insurrection. Congress has delegated authority to the president to send troops to put down insurrections at the request of the proper state authorities.[7]

Horizontal Federalism: Interstate Constitutional Relations

What obligations does the Constitution impose on the states in their dealings with one another? Three clauses, taken from the Articles of Confederation, require the states to give full faith and credit to one another's public acts, records, and judicial proceedings; to extend to one another's citizens the privileges and immunities of their own citizens; and to return persons who are fleeing from justice.

FULL FAITH AND CREDIT The **full faith and credit clause** is one of the most technical provisions of the Constitution. In general, it requires each state court to enforce civil judgments of other state courts and to accept their public records and acts as valid documents. (It does not require states to enforce the criminal laws of other states; in most cases, for one state to enforce the criminal laws of another would be unconstitutional.) The clause applies especially to noncriminal judicial proceedings.

INTERSTATE PRIVILEGES AND IMMUNITIES States must extend to citizens of other states the privileges and immunities granted to their own citizens, including the protection of the laws, the right to engage in peaceful occupations, access to the courts, and freedom from discriminatory taxes. Further, a state may not withhold political rights from United States citizens who move into the state by imposing unreasonable "durational residency" requirements.

EXTRADITION The Constitution asserts that a state shall deliver to proper officials criminals who have fled from another state when requested to do so by the government of the state from which the criminals have fled. Congress has supplemented this constitutional provision for **extradition** by making the governor of the state to which fugitives have fled the responsible agent for returning them. Despite the use of the word *shall*, the federal courts will not order governors to surrender (extradite) persons wanted in other states. Normally extradition is handled in a routine fashion. Further, Congress has made it a federal crime to flee from one state to another for the purpose of avoiding prosecution for a felony and has ordered the federal trial to take place in the state from which the person has fled.

[6]*Luther v. Borden*, 7 How. 1 (1849).
[7]*Ibid.*

EXAMPLES OF ACTIVITIES THAT DO NOT *DIRECTLY** INVOLVE BOTH NATIONAL AND STATE GOVERNMENTS

National Government Only:
Foreign policy making
Operating the Postal Service
Taxing and regulating foreign commerce
Funding and managing the space program

State and Local Governments Only:
Regulating marriages and divorces
Probating wills
Issuing birth certificates
Issuing death certificates

*The operative word is *directly*. If it were deleted, the above lists would be blank.

INTERSTATE COMPACTS   In addition to these three obligations, the Constitution also requires states to settle disputes with one another without the use of force. States may carry their legal arguments to the Supreme Court or may negotiate interstate compacts, which may also be used to establish interstate agencies and to solve joint problems. Before interstate compacts become effective, the approval of Congress is required. After a compact has been signed and approved by Congress, it becomes binding on all signatory states, and its terms are enforceable by the Supreme Court.

The Realities Today

This outline of the constitutional structure of federalism oversimplifies and—especially in terms of the division of powers between the national government and the states—even misleads. The basic law setting up the system has not changed, but the ways in which it has come to be applied have altered greatly.

As recently as the Great Depression of the 1930s, constitutional scholars and Supreme Court justices debated whether Congress had the authority to enact legislation dealing with agriculture, labor, education, housing, and welfare. Only a decade ago there were constitutional questions about the authority of Congress to legislate against racial discrimination. And it remains technically correct to state that Congress lacks any *general* grant of authority to do whatever it thinks necessary and proper in order to promote the general welfare or to preserve domestic tranquility. But as a result of the rise of a national economy, the growth of national demands on Washington, and the emergence of a world in which war could destroy us in a matter of minutes, our constitutional system has evolved to the point where the national government has authority to deal with almost every issue.

Today restraints on national power stem from constitutional provisions that protect the liberties of the people rather than from those relating to the powers of state governments. Still, despite the growth of national authority, states are vital and active governments backed by significant political forces.

TRIUMPH OF THE NATIONALIST INTERPRETATION

This summary of the constitutional construction of our federal system jumps over two hundred years of conflict and proclaims victory, at least for the moment, for the nationalist interpretation of that system. (The debate between those who favor national action and those in favor of state and local levels continues, but it does so generally outside the framework of constitutional principles.) This victory for the nationalists is a recent one. Throughout most of our history, there have been powerful groups in favor of states' rights interpretation.

The constitutional arguments revolving around federalism grew out of specific issues: whether the national government had the authority to outlaw slavery in the territories; whether states had the authority to operate racially segregated schools; whether Congress could regulate labor relations. While the debates were frequently phrased in constitutional language and appeals were made to the great principles of federalism, the real struggles were over who was to get what, where, and how, and who was to do what to whom.

Among those who favored the states' rights interpretation were Thomas Jefferson, John C. Calhoun, the Supreme Court from the 1920s to 1937, and more recently Ronald Reagan. Their position has been that the Constitution is an intergovernmental treaty among sovereign states which created the central government and gave it carefully limited authority. Because the national government is thus nothing more than an agent of the states, every one of its powers should be narrowly defined. Any doubt as to whether the states had given a particular function to the central government or reserved it for themselves should be resolved in favor of the states.

The states' righters hold that the national government should not be permitted to exercise its delegated powers in such a way as to interfere with activities reserved to the states. The Tenth Amendment, they claim, makes this clear: "The powers not delegated to the United States by the Constitution, nor prohibited by it to the States, are reserved to the States respectively, or to the people." They insist that the state governments are closer to the people and that therefore they reflect the people's wishes more accurately than does the national government. They maintain further that the national government is inherently heavy-handed and bureaucratic and that in order to preserve our federal system and our liberties, central authority must be kept under control.

The nationalist position, supported by Chief Justice John Marshall, Abraham Lincoln, Theodore Roosevelt, Franklin Roosevelt, and throughout most of our history by the Supreme Court, rejects the whole concept of the Constitution as an interstate compact. Rather, the Constitution is viewed as a *supreme law* established by the people. The national government is an agent of the *people*, not of the states, for it was the people who drew up the Constitution and created the national government. The sovereign people gave the national government sufficient power to accomplish the great objectives listed in the Preamble. They intended that the central government's powers should be liberally defined and that that government be denied authority only when the Constitution clearly prohibits it from acting.

The nationalists contend the national government is a government of all the people and that each state speaks for only some of the people. While the Tenth Amendment clearly reserves powers to the states, as Chief Justice Stone said: "The Tenth Amendment states but a truism that all is retained which has not been surrendered" (*United States* v. *Darby*, 1941).[8] The amendment does not deny the national government the right to exercise to the fullest extent all the powers given to it by the Constitution. The supremacy of the national government does, however, restrict the states; a government representing part of the people cannot be allowed to interfere with a government representing all of them.

McCulloch v. Maryland

In McCulloch v. Maryland (1819) the Supreme Court had the first of many chances to choose between these two interpretations of our federal system.[9] Maryland had levied a tax against the Baltimore branch of the Bank of the United States, a semipublic agency established by Congress. McCulloch, the cashier of the bank, refused to pay on the ground that a state could not tax an instrument of the national government. Maryland's attorneys responded that in the first place, the national government did not have the power to incorporate a bank—but even if it did, the state had the power to tax it.

Maryland was represented before the Court by some of the country's most distinguished lawyers, including Luther Martin, a delegate to the Constitutional Convention who had left early when it became apparent that a strong national government was in the making. Martin, basing his argument on the states' rights view of federalism, pointed out that the power to incorporate a bank is not expressly delegated to the national government. He contended that Article I, Section 8, Clause 18, which gives Congress the right to choose whatever means are necessary and proper to carry out its delegated powers, gives Congress only the power to choose those means and to pass those laws

"Sorry, but all my power's been turned back to the states." *Drawing by Lorenz; © 1981 The New Yorker Magazine, Inc.*

[8]312 U. S. 100 (1941).
[9]4 *Wheaton* 316 (1819).

absolutely essential to the execution of its expressly granted powers. Because a bank is not absolutely necessary to the exercise of any of its delegated powers, Congress has no authority to establish it.

As for Maryland's right to tax the bank, Martin's position was clear: The power to tax is one of the powers reserved to the states, which they may use as they see fit.

The national government was represented by equally distinguished counsel, chief among whom was Daniel Webster. Webster conceded that the power to create a bank is not one of the express powers of the national government. But the power to pass laws necessary and proper to carry out enumerated powers is expressly delegated to Congress, and this power should be interpreted to mean that Congress has authority to enact any legislation convenient and useful in carrying out delegated national powers. Therefore, Congress may incorporate a bank as an appropriate, convenient, and useful means of exercising the granted powers of collecting taxes, borrowing money, and caring for the property of the United States.

Webster contended that though the power to tax is reserved to the states, states cannot use their reserved powers to interfere with the operations of the national government. The Constitution leaves no room for doubt: In case of conflict between the national and state governments, the former is supreme.

Speaking for a unanimous Court, Marshall rejected every one of Maryland's contentions. He wrote: "We must never forget that it is a *constitution* we are expounding. . . . [A] constitution intended to endure for ages to come, and consequently, to be adapted to the various crises of human affairs." "The government of the Union," he continued, "is emphatically and truly a government of the people. In form and substance it emanates from them, its powers are granted to them, and are to be exercised directly on them. . . . It can never be to their interest and cannot be presumed to have been their intention, to clog and embarrass its execution, by withholding the most appropriate means." Marshall summarized his views on the powers of the national government in these now-famous words: "Let the end be legitimate, let it be within the scope of the Constitution, and all means which are appropriate, which are plainly adapted to that end, which are not prohibited, but consist with the letter and spirit of the Constitution, are constitutional."

Having thus established the doctrine of implied national powers, Marshall set forth the doctrine of national supremacy. No state, he said, can use its reserved taxing powers to tax a national instrument. "The power to tax involves the power to destroy. . . . If the right of the states to tax the means employed by the general government be conceded, the declaration that the Constitution, and the laws made in pursuance thereof, shall be the supreme law of the land, is empty and unmeaning declamation."

The long-range significance of *McCulloch* v. *Maryland* in providing support for the developing forces of nationalism can hardly be overstated. The arguments of the states' righters, if accepted, would have strapped the national government in a constitutional straitjacket and denied it powers needed to handle the problems of an expanding nation. In all probability the Constitution would have been replaced many years ago.

The Constitutional Basis of the Growth of the National Government

The formal constitutional powers of the national government are essentially the same today as they were in 1789. But the Supreme Court (building on Marshall's work in *McCulloch* v. *Maryland*), Congress, the president, and the people have taken advantage of the Constitution's flexibility to permit the national government to use whatever powers it needs to fight wars and depressions and to serve the needs of a modern industrial nation. The expansion of central government functions has rested on three major constitutional pillars.

THE WAR POWER The national government is responsible for protecting the nation from external aggression and, when necessary, for waging war. In today's world military strength depends not only on troops in the field but also on the ability to mobilize the nation's industry and to apply its scientific knowledge to the tasks of defense. The national government has the power to wage war and to do what is necessary and proper to wage it successfully. In these times this means the power to do almost anything that is not in direct conflict with constitutional guarantees.

THE POWER TO REGULATE INTERSTATE AND FOREIGN COMMERCE
Congressional authority extends to all commerce that affects more than one state and to all those activities, wherever they exist or whatever their nature, whose control is necessary and proper to regulate interstate and foreign commerce. The term *commerce* includes the production, buying, selling, and transporting of goods. The commerce clause packs a tremendous constitutional punch. In these few words the national government has been able to find justification for regulating a wide range of human activity and property. Today there are few aspects of our economy that do not affect commerce in more than one state.

The commerce clause can also be used to sustain legislation that goes beyond commercial matters. When the Supreme Court upheld the 1964 Civil Rights Act forbidding discrimination because of race, religion, or national origin in places of public accommodation, it said: "Congress' action in removing the disruptive effect which it found racial discrimination has on interstate travel is not invalidated because Congress was also legislating against what it considers to be moral wrongs." Discrimination restricts the flow of interstate commerce; interstate commerce was being used to support discrimination; therefore, Congress could legislate against the discrimination. Moreover, the law could be applied even to local places of public accommodation, since local incidents of discrimination have a substantial and harmful impact on interstate commerce. "If it is interstate commerce that feels the pinch, it does not matter how local the operation that applies the squeeze."[10]

THE POWER TO TAX AND SPEND Congress lacks constitutional authority to pass laws solely on the ground that the laws will promote the general welfare, but it may raise taxes and spend money for this purpose. This distinction between legislating and appropriating frequently makes little difference. Congress lacks constitutional power to regulate education or agriculture directly, but it does have the power to appropriate money to support education or to pay farmers subsidies. By attaching conditions to its grants of money, Congress may regulate what it cannot constitutionally directly control by law.

Because Congress puts up the money, it has a strong voice in determining how the money will be spent. By withholding or threatening to withhold funds, the national government can influence—or control—state operations and regulate individual conduct. In 1964, for example, Congress stipulated that federal funds should be withdrawn from any program in which any person was denied the benefits because of race, color, or national origin; subsequently the categories of sex and physical handicap were added.

These three constitutional powers—the war power, the power over interstate commerce, and most especially the power to tax and spend for the general welfare—have made possible a tremendous expansion of federal functions. If all the laws Congress has passed under these powers were wiped off the statute books, the size of the national government and the scope of its functions would shrink drastically.

Federal Air Traffic Controllers at work directing air commerce among the states. *UPI.*

---

[10]*Heart of Atlanta Motel v. United States,* 379 U.S. 241 (1964).

Today there are few doubts about the national government's constitutional authority to deal with issues affecting the nation, whether civil rights, speed limits on highways, or the kinds of holiday lights we may display. Nonetheless we may still argue about (1) whether Congress intended to regulate a subject completely—or was some of it to be left to state discretion—and (2) whether in the absence of congressional action, states may deal with subjects that affect commerce or people in other states.

While couched in terms of federalism, in reality such arguments reflect differences between various interests. The national and state governments are arenas in which and through which clashes take place between consumers and producers, workers and employers, airlines and railroads, and all the other contending groups that make up our political system. In these political battles judges, especially those on the Supreme Court, play a vital—but not exclusive—role.

The Role of the Federal Courts

Even today the Supreme Court occasionally questions whether Congress has exceeded its authority and invaded the reserved powers of the states. But judges spend much more time deciding whether the national Constitution, national laws, and national regulations preempt state actions.

The federal judges' authority to review the activities of state and local governments increased dramatically after the Civil War. The Thirteenth, Fourteenth, and Fifteenth Amendments (especially the Fourteenth), plus congressional legislation enacted to implement them, and the expansion of the habeas corpus jurisdiction of the federal district courts (see Chapter 29) ensure that almost every action by state and local officials can be challenged before a federal judge as a violation of the Constitution or of federal law. Although the aim of these amendments and of the implementing legislation is to protect the rights of people, they have fundamentally altered the nature of the relationship between state and local officials and federal courts.

Federal judges have become major expounders of the principles of federalism, and federal courts have become major forums in which to challenge the actions of state and local authorities. In judging the constitutionality of state and local measures, federal judges have, in effect, taken over the supervision of state prison systems, public hospitals, public schools, and other public facilities.

Other recent Supreme Court interventions in intergovernmental relations have especially jolted city officials. First, the Supreme Court opened federal courts to suits for damages against municipalities by persons who believe city officials have violated any of their federally protected rights—not just those guaranteed by the civil rights statutes—even when officials are acting contrary to city policies or ordinances.[11] As a result of these Section 1983 actions, as they are called, cities are now facing over four billion dollars worth of damages. In 1982 the Court sent further "shock waves through the nation's localities" when it opened federal courts to damage suits against city ordinances alleged to violate federal antitrust laws, even those relating to public health, safety, and welfare.[12] Many city officials agree with Justice Rehnquist, who wrote in dissent: "The Court's decision . . . will . . . impede, if not paralyze, local gov-

[11]*Maine* v. *Thiboutot,* 448 U.S. 1 (1980); *Owens* v. *City of Independence,* 448 U.S. 662 (1980). See Cynthia Cates Colella, "The Mandate, the Mayor, and the Menace of Liability," *Intergovernmental Perspective* (Fall 1981), pp. 15–25.

[12]*Community Communications* Co. v. *Boulder,* 445 U.S. 40 (1982). See George D. Brown, "The Courts and Grant Reform: A Time for Action," *Intergovernmental Perspective* (Fall 1981), pp. 6–14.

ernment's efforts to enact ordinances and regulations aimed at protecting public health, safety, and welfare, for fear of subjecting the local government to liability under the Sherman Act. . . ."

Stung by these judicial defeats, state and local governments have formed a privately funded State and Local Legal Defense Center. While a city's attorney is unlikely ever to have argued a case before the Supreme Court, lawyers representing those attacking the city are probably specialists from the American Civil Liberties Union, NAACP Legal Defense Fund, or from the office of the solicitor general of the United States, who often appear before the High Court. As a result, as Justice Powell has pointed out, the states and cities are often "outgunned." State and local officials hope that the new center will improve their record before the Court.[13]

While over the years the Court's decisions have favored national powers (including its own), few would deny the Supreme Court the power to review and set aside state actions. As Justice Holmes once remarked: "I do not think the United States would come to an end if we lost our power to declare an Act of Congress void. I do think the Union would be imperiled if we could not make that declaration as to the laws of the several States."[14]

Other Umpires (and Contestants) of the Federal System

Federal courts are not the only umpires of the federal system: Congress, too, has much to say about the distribution of functions and about whether federal or state standards will prevail. After Congress acts, the president and federal administrators approve the guidelines for grants, decide which projects to approve, and largely determine how federal standards will be applied.

It is one thing to get a law through Congress. It is another to impose national standards on state and local officials and the people they represent. The national law itself may well be ambiguous. Also, powerful local and state political factions often persuade Congress to build safeguards into the law to protect their interests. In the implementation battles the greater political power may be with state and local officials rather than with national enforcers.

FEDERALISM AND FEDERAL GRANTS

Federal-local partnership illustrates modern federalism. *Rapho/Photo Researchers.*

Today the "feds" are everywhere and into everything; but despite the expanding role of the federal government, the number of "feds" is about the same today as it was two decades ago. While state and local governments have gotten larger, the federal government has not. For Congress has chosen to use the states, the cities, the counties, the universities—and at times even private agencies—to administer the new programs, deliver the services, and carry out the federal mandates.

Congress has done this by using federal grants, of which there are four general types: categorical formula grants, project grants, block grants, and revenue sharing.

CATEGORICAL-FORMULA GRANTS Under these grants (which were virtually the only kind of grant available before the 1960s) Congress appropriates funds for specific purposes—welfare, school lunches, the building of airports and highways. The funds are allocated by formula. Each eligible unit seeking a grant has to put up some of its own money, agree to establish an appropriate agency to spend the funds, submit plans for advance approval, permit national

[13]Fred Barbash, *The Washington Post*, February 28, 1983, p. A 9.
[14]Oliver Wendell Holmes, Jr., *Collected Legal Papers* (Harcourt, 1920), pp. 295–96.

officials to inspect the completed work, and place employees who administer the grant under a merit system. Categorical grants permit Congress to determine with great precision on what the funds will be spent. Still, they leave to governors, state legislators, and state and local officials an active role in determining how the programs are carried out.

PROJECT GRANTS   These came into great prominence in the 1960s. Congress appropriates a certain sum, but the dollars are allocated to state and local units—and in some instances nongovernmental agencies—on the basis of applications from those who wish to participate.

BLOCK GRANTS   These grants have been promoted by the Advisory Commission on Intergovermental Relations (see Box) and tend to be favored by presidents—most especially by Nixon and Reagan. These are broad grants to states for certain prescribed activities—elementary and secondary education, social services, preventive health and health services—with only a few specific strings attached. However, we should not be misled into thinking that it is a simple matter for federal authorities to ignore their views on state and local communities.

REVENUE SHARING   General federal revenue funds are granted to state and local units of government to be used at their discretion, with only the most general conditions set. Under current law general revenue funds are available only for local governments—the state governments having been ousted from the program in 1980.

In 1964 Congress began to subject all federal grants, including to some extent general revenue sharing, to so-called *cross-cutting requirements*. The first and most famous of these holds that no person may be discriminated against in the use of federal funds because of race, color, national origin, sex, or handicapped status. Other cross-cutting requirements concern the environment, historical preservation, contract wage rates, access to governmental information, the care of experimental animals, the treatment of human subjects in research projects, and so on. There are over sixty such requirements.[15]

The Politics of Federal Grants

Arguments about the forms of federal aid involve more than considerations of efficiency. They reflect differences about what constitutes desirable public policy, where power should be located, and who will gain or lose by the various types of grants.

Supporters of the more generalized kinds of federal aid, such as block grants and revenue sharing, hope that their use will bring about a "transfer not simply of money but power."[16] Opponents say Congress and federal administrators are more likely to put the money where it is most needed, that is, largely in the big cities.

Presidents and governors tend to urge that categorical grants be consolidated into larger blocks. Congress and groups who benefit from existing programs are likely to resist, and most of the time to do so successfully. Consider the battle over libraries. "In 1969 the Administration proposed the consolidation of several narrow library grants. The Congress resisted, and the reason is simple. It can be expressed quantitatively: 99.99% of the public is not interested in

[15]Office of Management and Budget, *Managing Federal Assistance in the 1980's, Working Papers*, Vol. 1 (Government Printing Office, 1980).

[16]Richard P. Nathan et al., *Monetary Revenue Sharing* (The Brookings Institution, 1975), p. 10.

library grant reform. Of the .01 percent who are interested, all are librarians and oppose it."[17]

The debate about the form of grants is not just a dispute over whether state and local governments can be trusted to spend federal dollars wisely; it is also a debate about which state and local officials should be given control over the spending. Specialists who work for state and local governments often have more in common with specialists working for the national government than they do with their own governors or mayors or state legislators. These specialists (highway engineers, welfare administrators, educators) get together at meetings, read common journals, and jointly defend the independence of their programs from attempts by elected (national or state) officials to regulate them.[18]

These specialists may then join forces with their counterparts among the interest groups to create powerful "guilds,"[19] or issue networks of closely connected people who are knowledgeable about the complexities of specific federal aid programs. When they combine forces with specialists working for congressional committees, they create "iron triangles"—interest groups, congressional committee staffers, and federal bureaucrats (who in turn are connected to state and local bureaucrats)—of great effectiveness.

To counter the power of the specialists, governors, mayors, county supervisors, state legislators, and other officeholders have stepped up their own lobbying activities. Over thirty state governments have offices in Washington, many located in the "Hall of the States," an office building near Capitol Hill that also serves as the headquarters of the National Governors Association and the National Conference of State Legislatures. The National League of Cities has also become active. These "topcrats," as some call them, take an active interest in what goes on in Washington and are a political force to be reckoned with.

Federalism: Two Levels or Three?

Constitutionally speaking, the federal system consists only of the national government and the states. Nonetheless, with the urban crisis of the 1960s, the national government began in earnest to bypass the states and to provide *large-scale* direct federal aid to cities, counties, school districts, and other local units. In some ways Congress "became the city council of the nation," and the "president—acting very much like a Mayor"—started "taking on the meanest housekeeping concerns of daily existence."[20] There is now "virtually no function of local government from police to community arts promotion, for which there isn't a counterpart federal aid program."[21]

Governor Bruce Babbitt of Arizona has been one of several advocates for strengthening the states and decentralizing some of the functions of the national government. *Jerry Jacka Photography.*

Needless to say, governors and state legislators do not like to see federal funds go directly to city officials. However, this situation resulted—at least in part—from the belief that Congress and federal authorities are more likely than state officials to ensure that the "poor and the black, especially the latter" will get their fair share. Some federal programs even attempted to bypass City Hall and deal directly with agencies created especially to represent the poor. Democratic Governor Bruce Babbitt of Arizona contends Congress "ought to be worrying about arms control and defense instead of the potholes in the street. We just might have both an increased chance of survival and better streets."[22] On the other side, city officials, of course, favor such direct federal aid (however else the federal government provides money).

[17]Richard P. Nathan, "Special Revenue Sharing: Simple, Neat, and Correct," unpublished manuscript.

[18]Deil S. Wright, *Understanding Intergovernmental Relations*, 2nd ed. (Brooks-Cole, 1982).

[19]Harold Seidman, *Politics, Position and Power*, rev. ed. (Oxford University Press, 1980).

[20]From H. F. Graff, "Presidents Are Now Mayors," *The New York Times*, July 18, 1979, p. A-23.

[21]Neal R. Peirce, "The State of American Federalism," *Civic Review* (January 1980), p. 32.

[22]Bruce Babbitt, "States Rights for Liberals," *The New Republic*, January 24, 1981, p. 23.

Airports are built and operated through the combined efforts of the national, state, and local governments. *TWA.*

By the beginning of the 1980s the growth of federal-city programs had declined noticeably. The Reagan Administration's success in consolidating some categorical grants into block grants placed some of the funds in state rather than local hands, although Congress insisted upon some "pass-through" requirements that gave states no alternative but to deliver the federal funds to their cities.

Another factor strengthening the primacy of the federal-*state* link and reducing somewhat the importance of the federal-*city* link is that in some places the tensions between state and city officials are easing. Local authorities are finding that federal dollars bring federal controls that are in some way more burdensome than those imposed by their own state authorities. Within the states political forces are making state officials more responsive to city issues. Pollution, crime, poverty, unemployment, and other problems once thought to belong exclusively to cities have become suburban problems as well. Governors and state legislators are deeply concerned about these issues.

THE POLITICS OF FEDERALISM

Americans have always argued about the "proper" division of powers between central and local governments; and from time to time various governmental commissions and "experts" have tried to set definitive standards. But the experts discover, as did the founding fathers, that there are few objective standards. Rather, the problems involved are largely political. At one time or another northerners, southerners, businesspeople, farmers, workers, Federalists, Democrats, Whigs, and Republicans have championed "states' rights," but underlying their arguments have been issues such as slavery, labor-management relations, government regulation of business, civil rights, welfare politics, and so on.

In recent decades business groups have tended to support states' rights, and labor groups to oppose it. In the 1930s many businesspeople had little confidence in, and little influence over, the national government. Business interests found that state legislatures and state courts were more likely than their

59

Hot lunch program provided for by a combination of local, state, and federal aid. Some critics think the federal government has become too involved in local matters. Others disagree. *Wide World Photos.*

The Politics of National Growth

national counterparts to make decisions favored by business groups. On the other hand, labor leaders found national agencies more responsive to their needs. It is not surprising that while business groups were quick to defend the states against what they called the "federal octopus," labor leaders emphasized the need for national action and accused the states of being dominated by special interests.

A similar situation has existed with respect to racial issues. Fearing that national officials—responding to different political majorities—would work for racial integration, segregationists praised local governments, emphasized the dangers of overcentralization, and argued that the regulation of civil rights was not a proper function of the national government.

Today the politics of federalism is more complicated than it was in the past. Even in the area of civil rights,[23] the choice of action by national or state governments is more difficult. It is no longer safe to predict that the national government will be more favorable to the claims of minorities than most state or city governments.

On the whole, however, conservative ideology continues to favor state and local action, and liberal ideology to favor national action. But these "solid" positions have begun to crumble. Much of the talk nowadays—from all political perspectives—is anti-Washington.

Over the past 200 years there has been a steady drift of power to all governments, and most especially to the national government. "No one planned the growth . . . but everyone played a part in it."[24] How did this come about?

First, many of our problems became national in scope. Much that was local in 1789, in 1860, or even in 1930 is now national—even global. While state government could supervise the relations between a small merchant and his few employees, only the national government can supervise relations between an internationally organized industry and its thousands of employees organized in national unions. Big business, big agriculture, and big labor all add up to a big government.

As industrialization progressed, powerful interests made demands on the national government. First, business groups called on the government for aid in the form of tariffs, a national banking system, and subsidies to railroads, airlines, and the merchant marine. Farmers learned that the national government could give more aid than the states, and they too began to demand help. By the beginning of this century, urban groups in general, and organized labor in particular, pressed their claims.

The Great Depression of the 1930s stimulated extensive national action on issues such as relief, unemployment, and agricultural surpluses. World War II brought federal regulation of wages, prices, and employment, as well as national efforts to allocate resources, train manpower, and support engineering and inventions. After the war the national government helped veterans and inaugurated a vast system of support for university research. Moreover, the United States became the most powerful member of the free world and had to maintain substantial military forces, even during times of peace.

With the advance of the Great Society in the 1960s, and "with a style and grandeur that transformed the fiscal foundations of the republic, the federal government for 20 years poured out grants-in-aid to states and localities until

---

[23]Daniel J. Elazer, *American Federalism: A View from the States*, 2nd ed. (Crowell, 1972), p. 213.

[24]Advisory Commission on Intergovernmental Relations, *Restoring Confidence and Competence* (Advisory Commission on Intergovernmental Relations, 1981), p. 30.

scarcely a function remains at those levels that Washington doesn't own a piece of."[25]

City dwellers, including blacks who had migrated from the rural South to northern cities, began to seek federal funds for—at the very least—housing, education, and mass transportation. In 1960 there were fifty federal grant programs. By 1980 there were 500, costing over 80 billion dollars.

The growth of a national economy, and the creation of a national transportation and communications network, altered people's attitudes toward the national government. Prior to the Civil War the national government was viewed as a distant, even foreign, government. Today, in part because of television, most people identify as closely with Washington as they do with their state capitals.

While economic and social conditions do much to explain the expanded functions of the national government, they do not explain everything. In fact, members of Congress, presidents, federal judges, and federal administrators have actively promoted federal initiatives. Congress, in particular, has encouraged this trend. True, when there is widespread conflict about what to do— energy policy and social security reform are good examples—Congress waits for a national consensus and looks to presidents for leadership. But where an organized constituency wants something and there is no counterpressure, Congress, far "from being underresponsive . . . responds often to everyone, and with a vigour heretofore known only to exist among the offensive linemen of the Pittsburgh Steelers."[26]

Once established, federal programs generate groups who have vested interests in promoting, defending, and expanding the programs. Associations are formed; alliances are made. "In a word, the growth of government has created a constituency of, by, and for government."[27]

Yet the trend toward federal expansion, like most trends, has generated a counteraction, and by the beginning of the 1980s it encountered growing resistance from all points of the political spectrum. As national budget deficits began to mount, liberals and conservatives, Republicans and Democrats, began to argue that the expansion of the national government had gone too far. First the Carter Administration curtailed some federal programs. Then the Reagan Administration made its number one domestic priority limiting the role of the national government and reducing its scope.

3–2

WHICH OF THESE STATEMENTS COMES CLOSEST TO YOUR VIEW ABOUT GOVERNMENT POWER TODAY?

	Percent of U.S. Public			
	1982		1978	
	WHITES	NONWHITES	WHITES	NONWHITES
The federal government has:				
1. Too much power.	41	21	39	24
2. About the right amount.	18	15	17	23
3. Should use its power more vigorously.	28	45	36	36
4. No opinion.	13	19	7	16

SOURCE: Advisory Commission on Intergovernmental Relations, *Changing Public Attitudes on Governments and Taxes;* ACIR, 1982, p. 6.

---

[25]Walter Guzzardi, Jr., "Who Will Care for the Poor?" *Fortune,* June 28, 1982, p. 34.

[26]Cynthia Cates Colella, "The Creation, Care and Feeding of the Leviathan: Who and What Makes Government Grow," *Intergovernmental Perspective* (Fall 1979), p. 9.

[27]Aaron Wildavsky, "Bare Bones: Putting Flesh on the Skeleton of American Federalism," in *ACIR, The Future of Federalism in the 1980s* (1981), p. 79. Report and papers from the Conference on the Future of Federalism, Alexandria, Virginia, July 25–26, 1980. ACIR Publication M–126.

The War Among the States

TAX CAPACITY INDEX
Economic Ability to Raise
Revenue—from Most Able
to Least Able—1980
U. S. Average—100
Standard Deviation—15.7

Alaska	260
Wyoming	196
Nevada	154
Texas	124
California	117
Oklahoma	117
Colorado	113
Connecticut	112
Montana	112
Delaware	111
Washington D. C.	111
Kansas	109
Louisiana	109
Illinois	108
North Dakota	108
Hawaii	107
New Mexico	107
Iowa	105
New Jersey	105
Oregon	103
Washington	103
Minnesota	102
Florida	100
U. S. Average	100
Maryland	99
Michigan	97
Nebraska	97
New Hampshire	97
Ohio	97
Massachusetts	96
Virginia	95
Wisconsin	95
Missouri	94
West Virginia	94
Pennsylvania	93
Indiana	92
New York	90
South Dakota	90
Arizona	89
Idaho	87
Utah	86
Rhode Island	84
Vermont	84
Kentucky	83
Georgia	82
Maine	80
North Carolina	80
Arkansas	79
Tennessee	79
Alabama	76
South Carolina	75
Mississippi	69

Source: Advisory Commission on
Intergovernmental Relations.

The politics of federalism differs from state to state. Sunbelt states that produce fuel and other natural resources are more apt to elect "self-reliant" governors who do not want federal help than are the industrial states of the Northeast and Midwest that are facing industrial decline; the latter fear they are not getting a fair share of federal aid.

States vary tremendously in their economic ability to raise taxes as well as in their political willingness to do so. Alaska, with few people and much wealth, has almost four times the taxing capacity of Mississippi, which has many people and few mineral resources (see Box).[28]

Conflicts among the states go beyond disputes over allocations of federal funds. Tensions are growing as states with oil, coal, and natural gas increase their severance taxes on those products. Iowa has threatened to retaliate by taxing corn and soybeans, Massachusetts by taxing higher education. "We have on our hands the making of a Civil War, being fought with taxes instead of muskets," charges a spokesman for the Northeast-Midwest Institute.[29] He exaggerates, but he makes a point. The western states have other grievances. Many state officials would like to have more control over the vast tracts of western lands owned and managed by the federal government. Western state officials say national officials understand few of the region's unique problems.

In the words of Colorado Governor Richard Lamm: "Feelings of sectionalism and regionalism are the most intense of any time since the Civil War."[30]

Reprinted by permission: Tribune Company Syndicate, Inc.

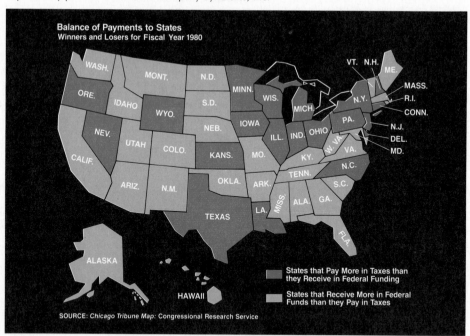

Balance of Payments to States
Winners and Losers for Fiscal Year 1980

■ States that Pay More in Taxes than they Receive in Federal Funding

□ States that Receive More in Federal Funds than they Pay in Taxes

SOURCE: *Chicago Tribune Map:* Congressional Research Service

[28]Robert B. Lucke, "Rich States—Poor States; Inequalities in our Federal System," *Intergovernmental Perspective* (Spring 1982), pp. 22–28.

[29]*Time,* August 24, 1981, p. 19.

[30]*The Denver Post,* September 23, 1979. See also Richard D. Lamm and Michael McCarthy, *The Angry West* (Houghton Mifflin, 1982).

New Federalism: What's So New About It?

Lyndon Johnson had his Creative Federalism, Richard Nixon his New Federalism, and Jimmy Carter his New Partnership. Before them Franklin D. Roosevelt had his Cooperative Federalism. We also have had Dual Federalism, Congressional Federalism, and Functional Federalism.[31] Subsequently Ronald Reagan gave us his version of New Federalism.

"My administration," said President Reagan, "is committed heart and soul to returning authority, responsibility and flexibility to state and local governments."[32] His dream, he said, was to stop the drift of power to Washington and "in a single stroke" to accomplish "a realignment that will end cumbersome administration and spiraling costs at the federal level while we ensure these programs will be more responsive to both the people they are meant to help and the people who pay for them."[33]

Many state governors applauded Reagan's proposals, although some Democratic governors, such as Hugh Carey—then Governor of New York—viewed Reagan's New Federalism as a "new feudalism."[34] Most mayors were critical. Fred Harrison, Mayor of Scotland Neck, North Carolina, and president of the National League of Cities, charged: "The proposal tilts much too strongly toward the states and leaves cities with virtually no security."[35] Many members of Congress, especially Democrats, and most beneficiaries of existing federal programs were actively opposed. Speaker Thomas P. O'Neill of the House of Representatives said: "It seems little more than a disguised attempt to balance the federal budget on the backs of American states and cities."[36]

Ultimately, even many of the governors who favored Reagan's offer to give more discretion to the states were not willing to support proposals that would mean such substantial reductions in federal funds. As a result, Reagan's proposal died amid the realities of the political system. Nevertheless, President Reagan's initiatives, although in grand design rejected by Congress, accelerated a trend first noticed in the Carter Administration and resulted in the first successful major assault in two decades on the expansion of federal programs.

Regardless of which party controls Washington, federal grants are not likely to grow at the same rate in the next decade as they did during the 1960–1980 period (see Table 3–3). Recognizing that the national government cannot regulate everything or solve all problems, both parties want to limit federal expenditures.

The underlying economic and social conditions that generated the demand for federal action have not substantially altered. On the contrary, in addition to traditional issues such as unemployment, inflation, and credit controls—which still require national action—the transformation from an industrial economy to one based on high-technology, service, and information has

[31]David B. Walker, *Toward a Functioning Federalism* (Winthrop, 1981), pp. 46–131.

[32]Ronald Reagan, *Federalism: The First Ten Months: A Report from the President* (Washington, D.C., November 1981), p. 1.

[33]Rochelle L. Stanfield, "A Neatly Wrapped Package With Explosives Inside," *National Journal*, February 17, 1982, p. 356.

[34]*The New York Times*, January 31, 1982.

[35]*Intergovernmental Perspective* (Summer 1982), p. 14.

[36]*National Journal*, February 27, 1982, p. 382. See also Brummond Aures, Jr., "City Mayors Yearn for the Old Federalism," *The New York Times*, June 24, 1981, E 5. For the views of a scholarly skeptic see David M. Kennedy, "The New Federalism: Battle the Tide of History." Paper presented at the American Enterprise Institute, December 9, 1982. For support of New Federalism in a paper presented at the same time by perhaps the most preeminent modern scholar of federalism, see Daniel J. Elazar, "Reagan's New Federalism and the American Federal Democracy."

3–3
HISTORICAL TREND OF FEDERAL GRANTS
(Dollar amounts in millions)

FISCAL YEARS	TOTAL GRANTS-IN-AID	|Federal Grants as a Percent of: BUDGET OUTLAYS TOTAL	DOMESTIC[1]	STATE AND LOCAL EXPENDITURES	GROSS NATIONAL PRODUCT
Five year intervals					
1950	$ 2,253	5.3%	8.8%	10.4%	0.9%
1955	3,207	4.7	12.1	10.1	0.8
1960	7,020	7.6	15.9	14.7	1.4
1965	10,904	9.2	16.5	15.3	1.7
1970	24,014	12.3	21.3	19.2	2.3
1975	49,834	15.4	21.5	23.0	3.3
Annually					
1976	59,093	16.2	21.9	24.2	3.5
1977	68,414	17.1	22.9	25.9	3.7
1978	77,889	17.4	23.1	26.8	3.7
1979	82,858	16.9	22.5	26.3	3.5
1980	91,472	15.9	21.2	26.2	3.6
1981	94,762	14.4	19.5	25.0	3.1
1982	88,194	12.1	16.6	22.1	2.9
1983 estimate	93,537	11.6	16.2	NA[2]	2.9
1984 estimate	95,926	11.3	16.3	NA	2.7
1985 estimate	99,162	10.8	16.0	NA	2.6
1986 estimate	102,468	10.4	15.7	NA	2.5

[1]Excludes outlays for the national defense and international affairs functions.
[2]NA: Not Available
SOURCE: Fiscal 1984 Budget

added countless new issues. Can workers displaced from our declining smoke-stack industries be retrained, or the human capital to support the postindustrial society be secured, without national action? Most people think not. Further, with one job in four in the United States generated by international markets, it seems essential that the national government continue to play an active role.

States have strengthened their governmental machinery during the last two decades, and they are more politically responsive than at any time in our history. But states—at least most of them—still lack the resources to undertake major programs such as cleaning up the air, building the highways, and repairing the bridges. Indeed, in the last decade many states have amended their constitutions to make it even more difficult to raise taxes. Faced with so many pressing national issues, it is unlikely that the national government will retreat to a pre-1930 posture or even a pre-1960 one.

Reforming the Intergovernmental System

Does the intergovernmental system—the way the present federal aid system works—need drastic revision? Some believe that it does: "The belief that the time is ripe for a more rational division of responsibilities among the federal, state and local governments crosses party lines and includes among its proponents individuals and organizations along a wide band of the political spectrum."[37] Many agree: "The current network of intergovernmental relations has become dangerously overloaded."[38]

[37]Claude Barfield, *Rethinking Federalism* (American Enterprise Institute, 1981), p. 58.

[38]Advisory Commission on Intergovernmental Relations, *An Agenda for American Federalism: Restoring Confidence and Competence* (Advisory Commission on Intergovernmental Relations, 1981), pp. 107–8: Donald H. Haider, "Intergovernmental Redirection," *The Annals*, Vol. 446 (March 1983), pp. 165–78.

Nevertheless, some observers disagree. One expert contends the present system works rather well, reflects political realities, and "needs incremental but not radical reform"[39] "The idea," he states, "of some tidy rearrangement where some functions belong to the central government, some to the states and some to local governments is attractive, but the world of government . . . is more complicated than that. . . . The 'Henny Penny' school tends to reach for simplistic . . . reforms of the governmental system that do not fit the values underlying the system."[40]

The Future of the States— Or "The More Things Change, the More They Stay the Same"

Predictions that states are about to disappear as meaningful governmental units are not new. Seeing state governments helpless during the Great Depression, one writer stated in 1933: "I do not predict that the states will go, but affirm that they have gone."[41] Thirty years later Senator Everett McKinley Dirkson from Illinois intoned that before too long, "the only people interested in state boundaries will be Rand-McNally."[42]

Still, in recent years states have reformed their governmental structures, taken on greater roles in funding education, launched programs to help distressed cities, and—despite new constitutional limitations—expanded their taxing bases. Also, we now have some excellent state governors.

The slow but steady expansion of the block grant as a means of delivering federal aid has also increased the role and expanded the discretion of state officials. This was demonstrated by their prompt action on retraining programs for the unemployed during the Great Recession of 1982. In sum, the constitutional and political durability of the states is secure and their powers of leadership increasingly noteworthy.

The Future of Federalism

"Not quite the building materials I was hoping for." Copyright 1981 by Herblock in The Washington Post.

The federal system remains firmly rooted in our political and constitutional systems, and we are not about to abolish it or modify it drastically. Yet while most Americans have strong abstract attachments to the federal system, most of their concerns are with more immediate problems—jobs, safety in the streets, equal rights, clean air, prices at the grocery store. In fact, most Americans are not much interested in the arguments of political scientists for or against block grants or for or against direct federal aid to cities. Rather, they are willing to use whatever governmental agencies or combinations of agencies they feel can best serve their needs and represent their interests. In the process, federal-state-local relations change, now as always. As de Tocqueville noted nearly a hundred and fifty years ago: "I have never been more struck by the good sense and the practical judgment of the Americans than the manner in which they elude the numberless difficulties resulting from the Federal Constitution."[43]

[39]Richard P. Nathan, quoted by Albert J. Davis and S. Kenneth Howard, *Intergovernmental Perspective* (Spring 1982), p. 13.

[40]Richard P. Nathan, "Reforming the Federal Grants-in-Aid System for States and Localities." Address delivered to the National Tax Association, Washington, D. C., May 18, 1981, p. 8, quoted by Barfield, *Rethinking Federalism*, p. 65.

[41]Luther Gulick, quoted by Terry Sanford in *Storm over the States*, (McGraw-Hill, 1967), p. 21.

[42]Also quoted by Sanford, *Storm over the States* p. 37.

[43]Alexis de Tocqueville, *Democracy in America*, Vol. 1 (Knopf, 1944), p. 167.

SUMMARY

1. Our federal constitutional system has evolved into something that is only slightly different in form but significantly different in fact from the one we began with. Whether or not we ever had a system in which it was possible to talk about neat divisions between the powers of the national and the state governments, it is certainly no longer accurate to do so.

2. To recognize that the national government has the constitutional authority to do whatever Congress thinks may be necessary and proper to do is not the same as saying that federalism is dead. Although during the last two centuries constitutional power has moved toward the national center, political power remains dispersed. States remain active and significant political communities.

3. Ideological bias in favor of either national or state action is likely to reflect concrete political objectives. In recent years the stand of conservatives in favor of states' rights and of liberals in favor of national action is no longer predictable. Shifting political issues continue to lead to shifting allegiances among the various levels of government.

4. The politics of federalism involves more than conflicts between the national government and the states. In recent years conflicts among various regions of the nation over the distribution of federal dollars have begun to heat up.

5. The drift toward increasing federal action has been fueled more by underlying economic and social changes than by concerns about federalism in the abstract, but we detect a vigorous trend toward the view that federalism as a political principle is worthy of being preserved.

6. The major instrument of federal intervention in recent decades has been the various kinds of grants-in-aid, of which the most prominent are categorical grants, project grants, block grants, and revenue sharing.

7. Today we no longer spend so much time debating the *law* of federalism. We have now moved to the *politics* of federalism. As now interpreted, the Constitution gives us the option to decide through the political process what we want to do, who is going to pay, and how we are going to get it done.

FURTHER READING

ADVISORY COMMISSION ON INTERGOVERNMENTAL RELATIONS. *An Agenda for American Federalism: Restoring Confidence and Competence* (1981). Final volume of an 11-volume study under the general title, *The Federal Role in the Federal System: The Dynamics of Growth*.

ADVISORY COMMISSION ON INTERGOVERNMENTAL RELATIONS. *Intergovernmental Perspective.* Published four times a year (U.S. Government Printing Office).

THE CENTER FOR THE STUDY OF FEDERALISM. *Publius: The Journal of Federalism.* Published quarterly (Temple University).

DANIEL J. ELAZAR. *American Federalism: A View from the States,* 2nd ed. (Crowell, 1972).

PARRIS N. GLENDENING and MAVIS MANN REEVES. *Pragmatic Federalism: An Intergovernmental View of American Government* (Palisades Publishers, 1977).

GEORGE E. HALE and MARIAN L. PALLEY. *The Politics of Federal Grants* (Congressional Quarterly Press, 1981).

ARNOLD M. HOWITT. *Managing Federalism* (Congressional Quarterly Press, 1984).

MICHAEL D. REAGAN and JOHN G. STANZONE. *The New Federalism,* 2nd ed. (Oxford University Press, 1981).

DAVID B. WALKER. *Toward a Functioning Federalism* (Winthrop, 1981).

DEIL S. WRIGHT. *Understanding Intergovernmental Relations,* 2nd ed. (Brooks-Cole, 1982).

FIRST AMENDMENT RIGHTS

4

"Congress shall make no law," declares the First Amendment, "respecting an establishment of religion, or prohibiting the free exercise thereof; or abridging the freedom of speech, or of the press; or the right of the people peaceably to assemble, and to petition the Government for a redress of grievances." Here are the fundamental supports of a free society—freedom of *conscience* and freedom of *expression*.

Although the framers drafted the Constitution, in a sense it was the people who drafted our basic charter of liberties. The Constitution drawn up at Philadelphia included no specific guarantee of the basic freedoms. The omission aroused suspicion and distrust among the people. In order to win ratification, the Federalists promised to correct this oversight. And in the very first session, the new Congress proposed amendments that were ratified by the end of 1791 and became part of the Constitution. These ten amendments are known as the Bill of Rights.

Note that the Bill of Rights concerns the *national* government. As John Marshall held in *Barron* v. *Baltimore* (1833), the Bill of Rights limits the national but not the state governments.[1] Why not the states? In the 1790s the people were confident they could control their own state officials, and most of the state constitutions already had bills of rights. It was the new and distant central government the people feared.

But as it turned out, those popular fears were largely misplaced. The national government, responsive to tens of millions of voters from a variety of races, creeds, religions, and economic groups, has shown less tendency to curtail civil liberties than have state and local governments. For the most part state judges have not used the bills of rights in their respective state constitutions

The Bill of Rights was set up for National gvmt.

[1]7 Peters 243 (1833).

to protect civil liberties. (However, as the Supreme Court under Chief Justice Burger retreated somewhat from the civil liberties stance of the Court under Chief Justice Warren, some state courts started to use state constitutions to provide more protection for some rights than current federal constitutional standards require.)[2]

With the adoption of the Fourteenth Amendment in 1868, which *does* apply to the states, some lawyers tried to persuade the justices of the Supreme Court to interpret the due process clause of this amendment to mean that whatever the Bill of Rights forbids the national government to do, the due process clause of the Fourteenth Amendment should forbid state and local governments to do. At least, they argued, freedom of speech should be included in the Fourteenth Amendment. For decades the Supreme Court refused to interpret the Fourteenth Amendment in this way. Then in 1925, in *Gitlow* v. *New York*, the Court announced: "For present purposes we may and do assume that freedom of speech and of press—which are protected by the First Amendment from abridgment by Congress—are among the fundamental personal rights and 'liberties' protected by the due process clause of the Fourteenth Amendment from impairment by the States."[3]

Gitlow v. *New York* was a major, revolutionary decision. For the first time the national Constitution provided protection for freedom of speech and of the press from abridgment by state and local governments. In the 1940s the other provisions of the First Amendment were brought within the protection of the Fourteenth Amendment. Today the First Amendment's restraints are applied to all those who exercise governmental authority—national, state, or local.

Virtually all Americans agree that governmental power should not be used to interfere with the freedoms of speech and conscience. Yet we seem frequently to be involved in quarrels about specific applications of these restraints. The trouble starts when we move from generalities to *specifics*. "All declare for liberty," wrote Justice Reed, "and proceed to disagree among themselves as to its true meaning."[4] In few areas are the problems more difficult to resolve and the differences more intense than in the realm of religious freedoms.

A WALL OF SEPARATION

The very first words of the First Amendment are emphatic: "Congress shall make no law respecting an establishment of religion."

Some have argued that this Establishment clause does not forbid governmental support for religion but simply prohibits *favoritism* toward a particular religion.[5] But the Supreme Court has consistently rejected this view. As Justice Powell said for the Court: "It is now firmly established that a law may be one 'respecting the establishment of religion' even though its consequence is not to promote a 'state religion,' and even though it does not aid one religion more than another but merely benefits all religions alike." On the other hand: "It is

[2]Justice William J. Brennan, "State Constitutions and the Protection of Individual Rights," *Harvard Law Review*, vol. 90 (1977), p. 489; *Pruneyard Shopping Center* v. *Robbins*, 447 U.S. 74 (1980).

[3]*Gitlow* v. *New York*, 268 U.S. 652 (1925).

[4]*Breard* v. *Alexandria*, 341 U.S. 622 (1951).

[5]Daniel Patrick Moynihan, "What Do You Do When the Supreme Court Is Wrong?" *The Public Interest*, Vol. 57 (Fall 1979), pp. 3–24; Walter Berns, *The First Amendment and the Future of American Democracy* (Basic Books, 1976), pp. 1–76; Paul J. Weber and Dennis A. Gilbert, *Private Churches and Public Money* (Greenwood Press, 1981).

In this and the next several chapters, we will be talking at some length about constitutional rules. As we have noted, to talk about the Constitution is to talk about Supreme Court decisions. Many of these decisions are cited in footnotes so that you can look them up if you wish. Two forms of citation are used here: (1) official Supreme Court Reports: For example, *Gitlow* v. *New York*, 268 U.S. 652 (1925), which means that this case can be found in the two hundred sixty-eighth volume of the United States Supreme Court Reports on page 652 and that it was decided in 1925. These reports are published by the United States Government Printing Office. (2) For more recent cases we cite the advance sheets of United States Supreme Court Reports published by the Lawyers Cooperative Publishing Company of Rochester, New York. Thus, *INS* v. *Chadha* is cited as 77 L Ed 2d 317 (1983) which means that this case can be found in volume 77 of the Lawyers' Edition, second series, on page 317 and that it was decided in 1983. For additional information about citations, see Keeping Informed in the Appendix at the back of this book.

Statutes can not advance or inhibit Religion [handwritten annotation]

Owner of a food store in New York State indicates his opposition to "blue laws," which would close supermarkets on Sundays. *Wide World.*

equally well established . . . that not every law that confers an 'indirect,' 'remote,' or 'incidental' benefit upon religious institutions is, for that reason alone, constitutionally invalid."[6]

Establishment clause cases are not easy: They stir deep feelings; and the justices are often divided among themselves. Jefferson's "wall of separation between church and state" has become "as winding as the famous serpentine wall" he designed for the University of Virginia.[7] The Supreme Court put forward in *Lemon* v. *Kurtzman* a three-part test to determine whether a statute violates the Establishment clause: First, it must have a secular legislative *purpose*; second, its primary *effect* must be one that neither advances nor inhibits religion; and finally, it must avoid "excessive government entanglement with religion." In other words, the Establishment clause is designed to prevent three main evils: "sponsorship, financial support, and active involvement of the sovereign in religious activity."[8]

Because of the Establishment clause, states—and of course their subdivisional governments such as school districts—may not introduce any kind of devotional exercises into the public school curriculum. Thus, devotional reading of the Bible, the recitation of the Lord's Prayer, and the posting of the Ten Commandments on the walls of classrooms are prohibited. The Supreme Court has not, as it is sometimes said, prohibited prayer in the public schools: It is not unconstitutional for people to pray in a school. What *is* unconstitutional is *the sponsorship or encouragement of prayer by public school authorities.*

What if school authorities merely provide a moment of silence? Several states have done so, and the issue will soon reach the Supreme Court. The Court will have to determine whether a state-required moment of silence reflects a secular legislative purpose, neither advances nor inhibits religion, and avoids excessive government entanglement with religion.

In 1984 Congress opened public high schools to student-run religious services by making it unlawful for any public high school that opens its facilities to student meetings and that receives federal financial aid "to discriminate against any students who wish to conduct a meeting . . . on the basis of religious, political, philosophical, or other content of speech at such meetings." The Supreme Court has already decided that a university that makes its facilities generally available to student activities does not violate the Establishment clause if it allows student groups to use facilities for worship.[9] On the contrary, if the university were to ban religious activities while allowing other kinds, it would violate the Free Exercise clause (see page 70). However, the Court pointedly noted that university students are young adults, less impressionable than younger students, and able to appreciate that the university's policy is one of neutrality. The Court may have to decide whether what Congress has done to open high schools to student-organized religious services—permissable under the Establishment clause at the collegiate level—is also permissable by that clause in high schools.

Other Court decisions include the following: A state may not prohibit the teaching of evolution or the use of books that discuss the Darwinian theory. School authorities may not permit religious instructors to come into public school buildings during the school day to provide religious instruction on a voluntary basis. States may not give churches the right to veto liquor licenses for establishments located within a 500-foot radius of the church, since "the

[6]*Committee for Public Education and Religious Liberty* v. *Nyquist*, 413 U.S. 756 (1973).

[7]Justice Jackson concurring in *Illinois ex rel McCollum* v. *Board of Education*, 333 U.S. 203 (1948).

[8]*Walz* v. *Tax Commission*, 397 U.S. 664 (1970); *Lemon* v. *Kurtzman*, 403 U.S. 602 (1971).

[9]*Widmar* v. *Vincent*, 454 U.S. 263 (1981).

States can not stop teaching of Evolution or Darwin Theory & They can't give church right to stop liquor store within 500 ft [handwritten annotation]

70

mere appearance of a joint exercise of legislative authority by Church and State provides a significant symbolic benefit to religion."[10]

On the other hand, the Constitution does not prevent the study of the Bible or of religion in public schools as part of a secular program of education. And Sunday closing laws—"blue laws," as they are called—are constitutional. Although these laws originally had a religious purpose, they now have a secular goal—providing a day of rest, recreation, and family togetherness.

Tax exemption for church property, along with an exemption for other kinds of nonprofit institutions, is constitutional. But a government may not impose certain reporting requirements upon organizations (such as The Unification Church) that solicit more than 50 percent of their funds from nonmembers, if at the same time it exempts the more traditional religions, which collect most of their funds from their own members. Such distinctions are not denominationally neutral, and hence they are not valid.

State legislatures and Congress may hire chaplains to open each day's legislative session, a practice which "has continued without interruption ever since the early session of Congress." If done in a public school, this practice would be unconstitutional. The difference is that legislators as adults are not "susceptible to religious indoctrination or peer pressure."[11]

One of the more troublesome areas involves attempts by many states to provide financial assistance to parochial schools. The Supreme Court has tried to draw a line between *permissible public aid to students*, including those in sectarian schools, and *impermissible public aid to religion*.

At the college level the problems are relatively simple. Tax funds may be used to construct buildings and operate educational programs at church-related schools, so long as the money is not directly spent on buildings used for religious purposes or used to teach religious subjects.

At the elementary and secondary level, the constitutional problems are much more complicated. Here the secular and religious parts of institutions and instruction are much more closely interwoven. Students are younger and more susceptible to indoctrination, and chances are greater that aid given to church-operated schools might seep over to aid for religion.

Some states have attempted to provide tax credits or deductions for those who send their children to private, largely church-affiliated schools. As long as the deductions or credits were made available *only* to parents of children attending nonpublic schools, the Supreme Court—by split votes—declared them unconstitutional.

Then in 1983, by a vote of five to four, the Supreme Court (*Mueller* v. *Oregon*) upheld a Minnesota provision allowing all taxpaying parents to deduct from their state income taxes what they paid, up to a certain amount, for tuition, textbooks, transportation, and other costs to send their children to school—public or private. Since parents sending children to public schools pay no tuition, most of these deductions benefit those sending children to private schools, 95 percent of which are sectarian. Nonetheless, the Court concluded that since Minnesota neutrally provided assistance to a broad spectrum of citizens, "no imprimatur of state approval can be deemed to have been conferred on any particular religion, or religion generally." The state was promoting a secular purpose of ensuring both a well-educated citizenry and the financial health of its private school system; no excessive government entanglement with religion was involved.[12]

[10]*Larkin* v. *Grendel's Den*, 459 U.S. 116 (1982).
[11]*Marsh* v. *Chambers*, 77 L Ed 2d 1019 (1983).
[12]77 L Ed 2d 721 (1983).

[Handwritten margin notes: "Sunday closings are constitutional" / "Draw line between public aid to students & public aid to religion" / "May deduct school costs from taxes"]

The Supreme Court has also approved using tax funds to provide students attending elementary and secondary church-operated schools (except those that deny admission because of race or religion) with textbooks, standardized tests, lunches, transportation to and from schools, diagnostic services for speech and hearing problems, and other kinds of remedial help—provided such services take place away from the "pervasively sectarian atmosphere of the church-related schools."[13] These schools may also be reimbursed for scoring state-required standardized tests.

Tax funds, however, may *not* be used to pay teachers' salaries in religious schools, to provide instructional equipment, to provide counseling for students inside such schools, to produce teacher-prepared tests, to repair facilities, or to transport students to and from field trips.

Why is it constitutional for state governments to pay for books but not for maps, for bus trips to schools but not for field trips from schools, for standardized tests but not for those prepared by teachers? The justices have argued that those on the "approved" side meet the three-part test, but those on the "forbidden" side fail one of the requirements. Transportation to and from school involves a routine trip that every student makes every day; it is unrelated to any aspect of the curriculum. Field trips, however, are controlled by teachers and are aids to instruction. Further, books and standardized tests can be evaluated much more easily than can maps or teacher-prepared tests, to ensure they are not designed to promote religion.[14]

"The court reached a decision on silent prayer in school . . . They ruled that a moment of silence is impossible." *Dunagin's People by Ralph Dunagin © 1983, Field Enterprises, Inc. Courtesy of Field Newspaper Syndicate.*

ALL PERSONS MAY WORSHIP IN THEIR OWN WAY

The Constitution not only forbids the establishment of religion, but it also forbids Congress and the states from passing any law "prohibiting the free exercise thereof." "The Court has struggled to find a neutral course between the two religion clauses, both of which are cast in absolute terms, and either of which, if expanded to a logical extreme, would tend to clash with the other."[15] A law that requires persons to do something that is contrary to the teachings of their religion interferes with their free exercise of religion. But to exempt them from the law because of their religious convictions may be to favor religion and offend the Establishment clause.

The right to hold any or no religious *belief* is one of our few absolute rights. One's religious beliefs are inviolable, and no government has authority to compel the acceptance of or to censor any creed. A state may not compel a religious belief nor deny persons any right or privilege because of their beliefs or lack of them. Religious oaths as a condition of public employment or as a prerequisite to running for public office are unconstitutional. In fact, the only time the Constitution mentions the word *religion* is to state: "No religious test shall ever be required as a Qualification to any Office or public Trust under the United States" (Article VI).

Although carefully protected, the right to *practice* one's religion has less protection than the right to hold particular beliefs: "It was never intended that the First Amendment . . . could be invoked as protection for the punishment of acts inimical to the peace, good order, and morals of society."[16] Religious convictions do not ordinarily exempt one from obeying otherwise valid and

[13]*Wolman v. Waters*, 433 U.S. 229 (1977).
[14]*Committee for Public Education v. Regan*, 444 U.S. 646 (1980).
[15]*Walz v. Tax Commission.*
[16]*Reynolds v. United States*, 98 U.S. 145 (1879).

The right to practice one's religion covers traditional as well as not so traditional religions. *UPI.*

nondiscriminatory laws. However, the Supreme Court will scrutinize laws that infringe on religious practices and insist upon some compelling public purpose. "Only those interests of the highest order and those not otherwise served can overbalance legitimate claims to the free exercise of religion."[17]

The Supreme Court has upheld laws forbidding the practice of polygamy as applied to Mormons; laws requiring vaccination of schoolchildren as applied to Christian Scientists; laws forbidding business activities on Sunday as applied to Orthodox Jews; the collection of social security taxes from the Amish, even though both the payment and receipt of social security benefits is forbidden by their faith; laws restricting where pamphlets and books may be sold in certain public facilities as applied to the Hari Krishna sect, even though the sale of such documents is part of their religious rituals; and Internal Revenue Service regulations denying tax exemption to religious schools that, in keeping with the teachings and practices of their religion, forbid interracial dating or admit only members of their own race. The Supreme Court pointedly wrote: "We deal only with religious schools, not with churches."[18]

On the other hand, a state may not require Jehovah's Witnesses (or anyone else, for that matter) to participate in a public school flag ceremony or to display material to which they object on state license plates. (The Supreme Court upheld the right of a Jehovah's Witness to cover up the New Hampshire state motto, "Live Free or Die," on his license plate.) Parents have a constitutional right to send their children to church-sponsored schools. In the face of three centuries of established Amish religious practices, the Court ruled that a state's compulsory school laws could not be applied to compel the Amish to send their children to school beyond the eighth grade: Through the eighth grade the interests of the state in ensuring that all children learn basic skills overbalances any religious convictions.

Along these same lines, states may not deny unemployment compensation to Sabbatarians who refuse to accept positions requiring them to work on Saturday; nor may they refuse to give such compensation to Jehovah's Witnesses who quit jobs for religious reasons. The Supreme Court has held that the payment of unemployment compensation to those who refuse employment for religious reasons but not to those who do so for nonreligious reasons "reflects nothing more than government neutrality in the face of religious differences." Justice Rehnquist in dissent charged the majority's opinion added "mud to the already muddied waters of First Amendment jurisprudence."[19]

What is a church? What is a religion? The Constitution provides no definitions, and the Supreme Court has been reluctant—understandably— to get into these questions. Clearly, "far-out" religions are entitled to the same constitutional protections as are the more traditional ones, but "only beliefs rooted in religion are protected by the Free Exercise Clause. . . ."[20] Cases involving the two religion clauses promise to become even more complicated as governmental actions continue to grow more pervasive and the number of nontraditional religious groups continues to grow.

[17]*Wisconsin v. Yoder,* 406 U.S. 205 (1972).

[18]*Bob Jones University v. United States,* 76 LEd 2d 157 (1983).

[19]*Thomas v. Review Board of Ind. Employment Service,* 450 U.S. 707 (1981).

[20]*Ibid.* See also Charles M. Whelan, "Governmental Attempts to Define Church and Religion," in Dean M. Kelley (ed.), *The Uneasy Boundary: Church and State, The Annals* (November 1979), p. 37.

Government by the people is based on every person's right to speak freely, to organize in groups, to question the decisions of the government, and to campaign openly against it. Only through free and uncensored expression of opinion can government be kept responsive to the electorate and governmental power transferred peacefully. Elections, separation of powers, and constitutional guarantees are meaningless unless all have the right to speak frankly and to hear and judge for themselves the worth of what others have to say.

Despite the fundamental importance of free speech to a democracy, some people seem to believe that speech should be free only for those who agree with them. Once we move to the level of specific questions or conflicts, there is a discouragingly low level of support for free speech. Not only do three Americans in four "draw a blank when asked if they know what the First Amendment . . . is or with what it deals," but almost 40 percent of the public would like to see strict curbs placed on newspapers.[21]

The Best Test of Truth

Free speech to get both side's ideas

The right to assemble and to protest is illustrated by antidraft participants in the early 1980s. *Catholics for a Free Choice.*

Ken Karp.

Believers in democracy insist on vigorous debate and the unlimited exchange of ideas; they are convinced that no group has a monopoly on truth. In the field of politics no group has the right to establish absolute standards of what is true and what is false. As Justice Holmes wrote: "The best test of truth is the power of thought to get itself accepted in the competition of the market."[22]

Free speech is not simply the personal right of individuals to have their say; it is also the right of the rest of us to hear them. John Stuart Mill, whose *Essay on Liberty* is the classic defense of free speech, put it this way: "The peculiar evil of silencing the expression of opinion, is that it is robbing the human race. . . . If the opinion is right, they are deprived of the opportunity of exchanging error for truth; if wrong, they lose, what is almost as great a benefit, the clearer perception and livelier impression of truth, produced by its collision with error."[23]

Freedom of speech is not merely freedom to express ideas that differ slightly from ours; it is, as the late Justice Jackson said, "freedom to differ as to things that touch the heart of the existing order."[24] Some people say they believe in free speech, but they draw the line at ideas they consider dangerous. What is a dangerous idea? Who decides? In the realm of political ideas, who can find an objective, eternally valid standard of right? The search for truth involves the possibility—even the inevitability—of error. The search cannot go on unless it proceeds freely in the minds and speech of all. This means, in the words of Justice Holmes, not only freedom of expression for those who agree with us "but freedom for the thought we hate."[25]

Despite the fact that the First Amendment denies Congress the power to pass any law abridging freedom of speech, the amendment has never been interpreted in such sweeping terms. Like almost all rights, the right to freedom of speech and of the press is limited.

[21]Results of Gallup Opinion Index reported in *Today*, April 25, 1980.

[22]*Abrams* v. *United States*, 250 U.S. 616 (1919), Justice Holmes in dissent.

[23]John Stuart Mill, "Essay on Liberty," in E. A. Burtt, *The English Philosophers from Bacon to Mill* (Modern Library, 1939), p. 961.

[24]*West Virginia State Board of Education* v. *Barnette*, 319 U.S. 624 (1943).

[25]For a thoughtful statement of a somewhat contrary point of view, see Walter Berns, *The First Amendment and the Future of American Democracy, op. cit.*

[handwritten margin notes: Anyone has right to believe as he wishes; Action is Restrained by Government; Obscene, seditious Speech not protected by const.]

In discussing the constitutional power of government to regulate speech, it is useful to distinguish among belief, speech, and action. At one extreme is the right to *believe* as one wishes, a right as absolute as any can be for people living in organized societies. Despite occasional deviations in practice, the traditional American view is that *thoughts* are inviolable. No government has the right to punish a person for beliefs or to interfere in any way with freedom of conscience.

At the other extreme is *action*, which is constantly restrained. We may *believe* it is all right to drive an automobile seventy-five miles an hour, but if we *do* so, we may be punished. Because one person's action directly affects the liberty and property of others, "the right to swing your arm ends where the other person's nose begins."

Speech stands somewhere between belief and action. It is not an absolute right, as is belief, but it is not as exposed to governmental restraint as is action. Speech that is obscene, libelous, or seditious, or that constitutes fighting words, is not entitled to constitutional protection, although there are many problems in distinguishing between what does and does not fit into these categories. (We will turn shortly to these problems.) All other speech is entitled to constitutional protection. But are there any limits?

Historical Constitutional Tests

While today the Supreme Court uses other language, the three great constitutional tests developed earlier in this century continue to reflect basic attitudes toward governmental regulation of speech. These are the bad tendency doctrine, the clear and present danger test, and the preferred position doctrine.

[handwritten margin note: Legislatures have power to outlaw speech]

THE BAD TENDENCY DOCTRINE This doctrine, stemming from the common law, has not had the support of the Supreme Court since *Gitlow* v. *New York* in 1925. It continues, however, to be the position of many, including (as late as 1982) some state courts.[26] According to the adherents of the bad tendency doctrine, legislatures and not courts have the primary responsibility to determine when speech should be outlawed. The Constitution, they contend, authorizes legislatures to forbid speech that has a tendency to lead to illegal action. Moreover, "the legislature cannot reasonably be required to measure the danger from every . . . utterance in the nice balance of a jeweler's scale. . . . It may, in the excercise of its judgment, suppress the threatened danger in its incipiency."[27]

Suppose a legislature, deciding that public utterances of abusive racial remarks are dangerous because such remarks often lead to violence, makes such remarks illegal. Those who hold to the bad tendency test would argue that this legislative action cannot be considered unreasonable and that therefore the law is constitutional.

[handwritten margin note: Outlaw speech that is clear & present danger]

THE CLEAR AND PRESENT DANGER TEST Justice Holmes announced this celebrated test in *Schenck* v. *United States*, when he wrote: "The question in every case is whether the words are used in circumstances and are of such a nature as to create a clear and present danger that they will bring about substantive evils that Congress has a right to prevent."[28] Furthermore, "no danger flowing from speech can be deemed clear and present," wrote Justice Brandeis concurring in *Whitney* v. *California*, "unless the incidence of the evil is so imminent that it may befall before there is opportunity for full discussion."[29]

[26]*Brown* v. *Hartlage*, 456 U.S. 45 (1982), where the Supreme Court reversed a decision of the Kentucky Court of Appeals based on the bad tendency doctrine.
[27]*Gitlow* v. *New York*.
[28]249 U.S. 47 (1919).
[29]274 U.S. 357 (1927).

Supporters of the clear and present danger doctrine agree that speech is not an absolute right. But they believe free speech to be so fundamental that no government should be allowed to restrict it unless it can be demonstrated that there is such a close connection between a speech and illegal action that the speech itself takes on the character of the action. (To shout fire falsely in a crowded theater is Holmes's famous example.) A government should not be allowed to interfere with speech unless it can prove that the particular speech in question presented an *immediate* danger of a major evil. For example, the speech clearly would have led to a riot, the destruction of property, the corruption of an election, or direct interference with recruiting of soldiers. Take our example above. Advocates of the clear and present danger test would argue that even though the legislature had made it illegal to use abusive racial remarks in public, judges should not permit the law to be applied unless the government presents convincing evidence that the particular remarks made by a particular individual clearly and presently might have led to a riot or to some serious evil.

THE PREFERRED POSITION DOCTRINE   This was the official view of the Supreme Court for a brief time during the 1940s. Those who take this view, such as Justice Black, come close to the position that freedom of expression—that is, the use of words and pictures—may *never* be curtailed. (The view does not mean that there is nothing left for judges to decide, for a line still must be drawn between speech and nonspeech.)

The preferred position interpretation of the First Amendment is that these freedoms have the highest priority in our constitutional hierarchy. Judges have a special duty to protect these freedoms and should be most skeptical about laws trespassing on them. Legislative majorities are free to experiment with and to adopt various schemes regulating our economic lives. But when they tamper with freedom of speech, they interfere with the channels of the political process. Only if the government can show that limitations on speech are absolutely

Justice Hugo Black, a member of the Court from 1937 to 1971, was a major champion of First Amendment rights. *UPI.*

MEMBERS OF THE SUPREME COURT SINCE 1946

Freedom of Speech has highest priority in Const.

Hugo L. Black	1937–1971	Roosevelt
Stanley F. Reed	1938–1957	Roosevelt
Felix Frankfurter	1939–1975	Roosevelt
William O. Douglas	1939–1975	Roosevelt
Francis W. Murphy	1940–1949	Roosevelt
Robert H. Jackson	1941–1954	Roosevelt
Wiley B. Rutledge	1943–1949	Roosevelt
Harold H. Burton	1945–1958	Truman
Frederick M. Vinson*	1946–1953	Truman
Tom C. Clark	1949–1967	Truman
Sherman Minton	1949–1956	Truman
Earl Warren*	1953–1969	Eisenhower
John Marshall Harlan	1953–1971	Eisenhower
William J. Brennan, Jr.	1956–	Eisenhower
Charles E. Wittaker	1957–1962	Eisenhower
Potter Stewart	1958–1981	Eisenhower
Byron R. White	1962–	Kennedy
Arthur J. Goldberg	1962–1965	Kennedy
Abe Fortas	1965–1969	Johnson
Thurgood Marshall	1967–	Johnson
Warren E. Burger*	1969–	Nixon
Harry A. Blackmun	1970–	Nixon
Lewis F. Powell, Jr.	1971–	Nixon
William H. Rehnquist	1971–	Nixon
John Paul Stevens	1975–	Ford
Sandra Day O'Connor	1981–	Reagan

*Chief Justices

necessary to avoid imminent and serious substantive evils are such limitations to be allowed.

If the preferred position doctrine is applied to our example of a law against abusive racial remarks, the law itself would be declared unconstitutional. Restraints on such abusive speech are not absolutely necessary to prevent riots. Whatever danger may come from such remarks does not justify a restriction on free comment. Moreover, supporters of the preferred position doctrine contend that the law, and not merely its application, violates the Constitution.

Current Tests

While the three historic doctrines discussed above provide the background for continuing debates on freedom of speech, today the Supreme Court is more apt to use the following tests (or doctrines, or rules of thumb) in measuring the limits of governmental power.

PRIOR RESTRAINT Of all forms of governmental interference with expression, judges are most suspicious of those that impose restraints prior to publication; these include licensing requirements before a speech can be made, a motion picture shown, or a newspaper published. The Supreme Court has specifically refused to declare all forms of prior censorship unconstitutional, but "a prior restraint on expression comes to this court with a 'heavy presumption' against its constitutionality. . . . The Government thus carries a heavy burden of showing justification for the enforcement of such a restraint."[30]

In *New York Times Company* v. *United States* (1971), the Supreme Court held that the government had not met this burden. The attorney general had secured from a lower court an injunction against the publication by several newspapers of parts of the *The Pentagon Papers*, a classified study of the government's decision-making process on Vietnam policy. Justices Black and Douglas took the view that the First Amendment forbids a court to impose, however briefly and for whatever reason, *any* prior restraint on a newspaper. But the prevailing view was that in this particular instance, especially without any congressional authorization, the attorney general had failed to show that the publication of these documents would cause immediate and specific damage to national security.[31]

Except as applied to motion pictures, the only examples in modern times of the Court's approval of prior restraints relate to the power of military commanders over military bases. The Court has refused to strike down military regulations prohibiting the distribution of publications on military bases without the prior written approval of military authorities. The Court has also said that the national government may screen what intelligence agents and ex-intelligence agents publish.

VAGUENESS Any law is unconstitutional if it "either forbids or requires the doing of an act in terms so vague that men of common intelligence must necessarily guess at its meaning and differ as to its application. . . ."[32] Laws touching First Amendment freedoms are required to meet an even more rigid standard. These laws must not allow those who administer them so much discretion that administrators could discriminate against those whose views they dislike. The laws must not be so vague that people are afraid to exercise pro-

Judges hard to hold up documents films.

YOU DECIDE !

In the Pentagon Papers case the government asserted a right to act without any specific congressional authorization. But in 1979, when federal executive officials learned that a magazine, *The Progressive,* was about to publish an article entitled "The H-Bomb Secret: How We Got It, Why We're Telling it," federal prosecutors acted pursuant to the Atomic Energy Act and went before a federal district judge to seek an injunction to prohibit the publication of this article. This act authorizes the federal government to enjoin the dissemination of restricted data concerning the design, manufacture, or use of atomic weapons. The district judge concluded that he could "find no plausible reason why the public needs to know the technical details about hydrogen bomb construction," and he issued a preliminary restraining order.

What do you think the Supreme Court would do with this example of prior restraint? And how would you have ruled?

(Answer/Discussion on the next page.)

---

[30]*Nebraska Press Assoc. v. Stuart*, 427 U.S. 539 (1976); see also Fred W. Friendly, *Minnesota Rag: The Dramatic Story of the Landmark Supreme Court Case That Gave New Meaning To Freedom of the Press* (Random House, 1981).

[31]403 U.S. 713 (1971).

[32]*Lanzetta v. New Jersey*, 306 U.S. 451 (1939).

Laws must be clear & exact

ANSWER/DISCUSSION

The courts refused to expedite the processing of this case. It never reached the Supreme Court because the government abandoned the effort to enjoin (that is, forbid) publication after the information in the article was published in other places.

Do you think the Supreme Court should have stepped in to see to it that there was a definitive judicial response to this action by the federal executives?

Do you think Congress should have passed a law making it an offense to publish information about how to build an H-Bomb?

Do you think the government was right in seeking this injunction?

Do you think the trial judge was right in issuing the preliminary injunction?

Do you think a newspaper or a magazine should publish anything it has a constitutional right to publish?

What does the above episode teach us about the ability of a free government in a free society to impose restrictions on the media?

Do you think the above episode might have a chilling effect on what other publishers might decide to publish in the future?

tected freedoms for fear of the law. Such vague and overbroad laws have a "chilling effect" on freedom of speech. The Supreme Court has struck down laws that condemn "sacrilegious" movies or publications of "criminal deeds of bloodshed or lust . . . . so massed as to become vehicles for inciting violent and depraved crimes."[33]

Laws can't be too broad

OVERBREADTH Closely related to the vagueness doctrine is the requirement that a statute relating to First Amendment freedoms cannot be so broad that it sweeps within its prohibitions protected speech as well as nonprotected activities; for example, a loyalty oath that endangers protected forms of association along with illegal activities. Since the very existence of overbroad statutes tends to repress protected speech, such statutes are often declared unconstitutional on their face.

Congress can not mess w/ 1st Amendment

LEAST DRASTIC MEANS Even for an important purpose, a legislature may not choose a law that impinges on First Amendment freedoms if there are other ways to handle the problem. To illustrate, a state may protect the public from unscrupulous lawyers, but it may not do so by forbidding organizations to make legal services available to their members, or by forbidding attorneys from advertising their fees for simple services. There are other ways to protect the public that do not impinge on the rights of freedom of association or speech.

But doctrines do not decide cases—judges do. Doctrines are judges' starting points; each case requires judges to weigh a variety of factors. *What* was said? *Where* was it said? *How* was it said? What was the *intent* of the person who said it? What were the *circumstances* in which it was said? *Which* government is attempting to regulate the speech—the city council that speaks for a few people, or the Congress that speaks for a wide variety of people? (Only a very few congressional enactments have ever been struck down because of conflict with the First Amendment.) *How* is the government attempting to regulate the speech? By prior censorship? By punishment after the speech? *Why* is the government attempting to regulate the speech? To protect the national security? To keep the streets clean? To protect the rights of unpopular religious minorities? To prevent criticism of those in power? These and scores of other considerations are involved in the never-ending process of determining what the Constitution permits and what it forbids.

FREEDOM OF THE PRESS

While street-corner meetings and public rallies are still important for communicating ideas and influencing public policies, today most of us rely on newspapers, television, radio, movies—the mass media—to find out what is happening in the world.

The Constitution speaks not merely of freedom of speech but also of freedom of the press. Until recently few thought to question whether the press has freedoms beyond those of other persons. It was assumed that freedom of speech is a synonym for freedom of the press—with the clause relating to speech protecting oral communications, and the phrase relating to the press embracing written ones. While this remains the dominant view, Chief Justice Burger has acknowledged that media representatives have a valid claim to function as "surrogates for the public and thus may be provided special seating and priority of

[33]*Winters v. New York*, 333 U.S. 507 (1948); *Burstyn v. Wilson*, 343 U.S. 495 (1952).

entry [at trials] so that they may report what people in attendance have seen and heard."[34] And although the First Amendment does not prohibit the application of general economic regulations to newspapers, the Supreme Court has been very careful to protect the press from special tax burdens, even when there is no evidence of any evil intent on the part of the taxing authorities.

Still, the prevailing view is: "The First Amendment does not 'belong' to any definable category of persons or entities; it belongs to all who exercise its freedoms."[35] Representatives of the press continue to argue otherwise. Moreover, they claim not merely the constitutional right to publish but also a right of access, the right to protect their sources, and a greater measure of security as regards search warrants for their files than applies to others. If they should prevail, the Court will have to determine who qualifies for whatever special benefits they claim.

Does the Press Have a Right to Know?

Courts have carefully protected reporters' right to publish information—no matter how they got it. But reporters, editors, and others have argued this is not enough. If the press is excluded from places where public business is being done, or denied access to information the government controls, it will not be able to perform its historic function of keeping the public informed.

The Supreme Court has refused to acknowledge a right to know, or a right of access. However, in 1980, in *Richmond Newspapers, Inc.* v. *Virginia*—which Justice Stevens called "a watershed case"—the Supreme Court ruled that the press, along with the public, does have a First Amendment right to attend criminal trials—more because such trials are public forums than because of a constitutional right to know.[36] Nonetheless, if the Court expands this right to other areas, *Richmond Newspapers* will, as the lawyer representing the American Society of Editors said, "rank right up there with some of the most significant First Amendment cases of the century."[37]

Although they have no constitutional obligation to do so, many states have adopted "sunshine laws" that require public agencies to open their meetings to the public and the press. Congress, too, has required many federal executive agencies to open various types of hearings and meetings of advisory groups to the public, and Congress holds most of its committee meetings in public. Federal and state courtroom trials are open, but judicial conferences are not.

By the Freedom of Information Act (1966, and amended in 1974), Congress has liberalized access to *nonclassified* government records. This act makes the records of federal agencies available on request, subject to certain exceptions, such as private financial transactions, personnel records, criminal investigation files, interoffice memoranda, and letters used in the internal decision-making process of the executive branches. The act requires federal agencies to move promptly on requests, and it gives persons a speedy judicial hearing if they are denied the information they seek. The burden is on the agency to explain any refusal to supply materials. Moreover, if the judge decides the government was wrong, the government has to pay the legal fees.

Executive Privilege

President Nixon and most presidents have claimed a constitutional right of executive privilege, which allows them to withhold information not only from

---

[34]*Richmond Newspapers, Inc.* v. *Virginia*, 448 U.S. 555 (1980). For a comprehensive history see David A. Anderson, "The Origins of the Press Clause," *UCLA Law Review*, Vol. 30 (February 1983), pp. 455–537.

[35]*First National Bank of Boston* v. *Bellotti*, 435 U.S. 765 (1978).

[36]448 U.S. 555 (1980); David M. O'Brien, *The Public's Right to Know: The Supreme Court and the First Amendment* (Praeger, 1981).

[37]Richard M. Schmidt, Jr., *The New York Times*, July 3, 1980.

President Nixon with his subpoenaed transcripts in his office following a nationwide television speech. *UPI.*

Prez is subject to subpoena

the press but even from Congress and the courts if, in the president's judgment, its release would jeopardize national security or interfere with the confidentiality of advice given to the president. There has been no suggestion by the courts that the press has any legal claim to materials the president wishes to withhold under executive privilege. But in the celebrated case of *United States v. Nixon* (1974), the Supreme Court ruled a president is subject to judicial subpoena for material relevant to a criminal prosecution.[38]

This historic decision—marking the first time the Supreme Court decided a matter directly involving the president as a party to a case—rejected the president's claim of absolute executive privilege and the idea that the president, rather than the judges, has the final say about what information to release and what to withhold. But the court fully recognized that a president does have a *limited* executive privilege.

If a president claims the privilege because disclosure would reveal military or diplomatic secrets, the courts would show "utmost deference" to such a decision. Even outside these areas the president's "singularly unique" role requires that great efforts be made to ensure that presidential communications are kept confidential. The trial judge was instructed to look at the subpoenaed materials in secret and to release to the prosecutor—and thus to the press and public—only the information the judge thought related to the trial. The other materials were returned to the president "restored to . . . privileged status."

Does the Press Have a Right to Withhold Information?

Press must give all info asked by court

Myron Farber, in dark shirt, *The New York Times* reporter who refused to turn over his notes during a murder trial, leaves the Bergen County jail after the New Jersey Supreme Court stayed his indefinite sentence pending an appeal of his contempt conviction. He was jailed on August 4, 1978. In January 1982 he was pardoned by Governor Byrne and the fines he and *The New York Times* had paid were remitted. *Wide World.*

Although many reporters have challenged the right of the government to withhold information, they claim a right to do so themselves, including the right to keep information from grand juries and legislative committees. Without this right, they argue, they cannot assure their sources of confidentiality and will not be able to get the information they need to keep the public informed. But the Supreme Court ruled in *Branzburg* v. *Hayes* (1972) that reporters, and presumably scholars, have no constitutional right to withhold information from juries.[39] Justice White, speaking for the Court, quoted from Jeremy Bentham: "Were the Prince of Wales, the Archbishop of Canterbury, and the Lord High Chancellor, to be passing by in the same coach, while a chimney-sweeper and a barrow-woman were in dispute about a halfpennyworth of apples, and the chimney-sweeper or the barrow-woman were to think proper to call upon them for their evidence, could they refuse it? No, most certainly." The Court concluded: " 'The public has a right to every man's evidence,' except for those persons protected by a constitutional, common-law, or statutory privilege." If any privilege is to be given to newspeople, said the Court, it should be done by act of Congress and of the states. The dissenting justices argued: "When neither the reporter nor his source can rely on the shield of confidentiality against unrestrained use of the grand jury's subpoena power, valuable information will not be published and the public dialogue will inevitably be impoverished."

Congress has not yet responded to the Supreme Court's suggestion that it should adopt a **shield law,** a law establishing the conditions under which newspaper people would be protected from having to respond to federal investigatory and judicial agencies. The attorney general has, however, issued guidelines limiting federal prosecutors' discretion in issuing subpoenas to newspersons. Most states have shield laws limiting state officials, and other states are considering their adoption.

[38]418 U.S. 683 (1974). See also Daniel N. Hoffman, *Governmental Secrecy and the Founding Fathers: A Study in Constitutional Controls* (Greenwood Press, 1981).

[39]408 U.S. 665 (1972).

**The Press and
Police Searches**

The press has not fared any better in its claim that the Constitution gives it special protection against police searches. Officers of the Santa Clara (California) County district attorney's office obtained a warrant to search through the files of the *Stanford Daily* for pictures of persons involved in a student takeover of the Stanford University Hospital. The newspaper argued that such searches jeopardized the ability of the press to gather, analyze, and disseminate news. It contended that materials could constitutionally be obtained from its files only by a subpoena issued by a judge after a hearing, not by a surprise search based on a warrant. A majority of the Supreme Court ruled otherwise.[40]

Following the Stanford decision Congress prohibited the issuance of search warrants to federal, state, and local police for searches of the "work products" of news organizations and others engaged in First Amendment activities, unless the persons involved (1) are suspected of a crime related to the materials they are holding or (2) there is reason to believe that the immediate seizure of the materials is necessary to prevent death or serious bodily injury. Those searched in violation of this act may sue for damages, but evidence otherwise admissible at a trial is not to be excluded from federal courts because it has been gathered in violation of the law (see page 135).

**Freedom of the Press
Versus Fair Trials**

When newspapers and television report in vivid details the facts of a crime, interview prosecutors and police, question witnesses, and hold press conferences for defendants and their attorneys, it may be difficult to hold a fair trial.

In England judges do not hesitate to punish newspapers that comment on pending criminal proceedings, and there are very strict rules as to what the media may report. In the United States the emphasis is on the side of free comment. The Supreme Court has even set aside contempt citations against editors who threatened judges with political reprisals unless these judges imposed a severe punishment on certain named defendants. But the Supreme Court has not been indifferent to the problems of protecting persons on trial from inflammatory publicity. Its remedies have been to order new trials or to instruct judges to impose sanctions on prosecutors and police, not on reporters.

Although defendants have a right to a public trial, they have no right to a private one. On the contrary, even if defendants want the judge to exclude the press and public from their trials, the judge must have a weighty reason for doing so. While states have no obligation to permit trials to be photographed or televised, they may do so if they wish. Further, defendants always have the right to present evidence demonstrating that televising their particular trials interfered with a fair hearing and deprived them of due process.

OTHER MEDIA

At the time the Constitution was written, "the press" referred to leaflets, newspapers, and books, but the Constitution also protects speech via the mails, motion pictures, radio, television, picketing, and certain kinds of symbolic conduct. Each form of communication entails special problems, resulting in different degrees of protection.

THE MAILS   Sixty years ago Justice Holmes wrote in dissent: "The United States may give up the Post Office when it sees fit, but while it carries it on, the use of the mails is almost as much a part of free speech as is the right to use our tongues."[41] In 1965 the Court adopted his views, striking down the

[40]*Zurcher v. Stanford Daily*, 436 U.S. 547 (1978).
[41]*Milwaukee Pub. Co. v. Burleson*, 255 U.S. 407 (1921).

first congressional act ever held to conflict with the First Amendment. That act directed the postmaster general to detain foreign mailings of "communist political propaganda" and to deliver these materials only upon the addressee's request. The Court has also set aside federal laws authorizing postal authorities to make administrative determinations of obscenity and to exclude such material from the mails, as well as a law prohibiting the mailing of unsolicited advertisements for contraceptives. "The level of discourse reaching a mailbox," said Justice Thurgood Marshall for the Court, "simply cannot be limited to that which would be suitable for a sandbox."[42]

While government censorship of the mails is unconstitutional, householder censorship is not. The Court has sustained a law that gives any householder the absolute right to ask the postmaster to order mailers to delete their names from all mailing lists and to refrain from sending any advertisements that householders in their sole discretion believe to be "erotically arousing or sexually provocative." It makes no constitutional difference if the householder includes in such a category a dry-goods catalogue. Moreover, Congress may forbid—and has forbidden—the use of mailboxes for any materials except those sent through the United States mails.

MOTION PICTURES   Films may be treated differently from books or newspapers. Prior censorship of films is not necessarily unconstitutional under all circumstances. However, laws calling for submission of films to a review board, or authorizing judges to issue restraining orders against showing motion pictures, are constitutional only if there is a prompt judicial hearing. The burden is on the government to prove to the court that the particular film in question is in fact obscene.

Today classification of films by the motion picture industry has largely replaced prior censorship. The Dallas Motion Picture Classification Board is the only local reviewing agency still in operation.[43]

RADIO AND TELEVISION   Television is increasingly the most important means for the distribution of news as well as the primary forum candidates use to appeal for votes. But "of all forms of communication, it is broadcasting that has received the most limited First Amendment protection."[44] Congress has established a system of commercial broadcasting, supplemented by the Corporation for Public Broadcasting that provides funds for public radio and television. The entire system is regulated by the Federal Communications Commission. Broadcasters use publicly owned airwaves, and they have no constitutional right to use these facilities without a license. The FCC grants licenses for limited periods and makes regulations for their use. Congress has specifically denied the commission authority to censor what is transmitted or to interfere with the right of free speech. The First Amendment would prevent such censorship if the FCC tried to impose it.

But the First Amendment does not prevent the FCC from imposing sanctions on stations that broadcast "filthy words"—even though such indecencies are not legally obscene—at least during periods when children are undoubtedly in the audience. (The FCC and the Supreme Court reserved decision on whether stations could be penalized for the use of indecent words as part of a live newscast.)

[42]Bolger v. Youngs Drug Product Corp, 77 L Ed 2d 469 (1983).
[43]Edward de Grazia and Roger K. Newman, Movies, Censors and the First Amendment (R.R. Bowker Co., 1983).
[44]Federal Communications Commission v. Pacifica Foundation, 438 U.S. 726 (1978).

The First Amendment does not prevent the FCC from refusing to renew a license if in its opinion a broadcaster has not served the public interest. Neither does the First Amendment prevent Congress and the FCC from adopting the fairness doctrine, which imposes on licensees an obligation to see that issues of public significance reflect differing viewpoints. Thus, if licensees make editorial statements or endorse candidates, they must give opponents an opportunity to respond. In the case of the candidates for public office, Congress has imposed an equal-time requirement, modified to make possible presidential debates between candidates of the major parties.

Do political parties, candidates for office, or interest groups have a right to radio or television time if they are willing to pay for it? This is a difficult issue that divides champions of free speech: It is hard to tell the good guys from the bad ones.

A unanimous Supreme Court concluded that governments could not force newspapers to accept advertisements or print replies from those they have criticized. Judges have had a much more difficult time finding the "right answer" to questions about broadcasting. Without too much trouble the justices concluded that the First Amendment does not prevent Congress from imposing on broadcast licensees an obligation to sell time to legally qualified federal candidates and from allowing the FCC to supervise how they do so. On the other hand, seven justices concluded (*Red Lion Broadcasting Co.* v. *Federal Communications Commission*) that neither the First Amendment nor the Federal Communications Act gives anybody the right to buy air time. The Court, however, could not muster a majority behind any single opinion. Chief Justice Burger noted that if broadcasters had to accept the offers of all who wished to buy air time, those with the most money would monopolize radio and television. He argued that although the First Amendment gives no one a right of access to broadcasting facilities, Congress or the FCC could provide such access. Justice Douglas, a long-time advocate of an expansive interpretation of the First Amendment, argued that refusal by broadcasters to accept paid political advertisements agreed to by the FCC violates the First Amendment rights of those who are denied access to television audiences.[45]

The coming of cable television, and technological developments such as satellite transmissions, are changing the nature of the problems involved. Many in the broadcasting industry and elsewhere are calling for a reassessment of the relationship between the FCC and the broadcasting industry. Some seek complete deregulation; some desire modification of the present system, especially as it relates to the fairness doctrine; and some would maintain the status quo.

HANDBILLS, SOUND TRUCKS, AND BILLBOARDS   Religious and political pamphlets, leaflets, and handbills are historic weapons in the defense of liberty, and their distribution is constitutionally protected. So, too, is the use of their modern counterparts, sound trucks and billboards. A state cannot restrain the passing out of leaflets merely to keep its streets clean; nor can it ban handbills that do not carry the name and address of the author. However, reasonable, content-neutral regulations as to where publications may be sold are permissible.

[45]*Red Lion Broadcasting Co.* v. *Federal Communications Commission*, 395 U.S. 367 (1969). See also Fred W. Friendly, *The Good Guys, the Bad Guys, and the First Amendment* (Random House, 1976), for a discussion of the fairness doctrine, its evolution and application; and Steven J. Simmons, *The Fairness Doctrine and the Media* (University of California Press, 1979). Also of interest is Irving R. Kaufman, "Reassessing the Fairness Doctrine: Should the First Amendment Apply Equally to the Print and Broadcast Media?" *The New York Times Magazine*, June 19, 1983, pp 18–20, for the views of a judge of the Court of Appeals for the Second Circuit.

Today, when so many people shop in privately owned and managed shopping malls, a delicate issue is raised as between the rights of private property owners and rights of free speech. Many customers don't like to be solicited—but shopping malls are wonderful places for candidates to meet and talk with potential voters, urge them to register, and give them literature. The Supreme Court has set some guidelines in this area (see page 88).

As for sound trucks, those that emit loud and raucous noises may be banned. Further, content-neutral regulations as to the time, place, and manner in which amplification devices may be used are acceptable. Billboards, too, are entitled to constitutional protection—those used for noncommercial purposes more so than those used for commercial reasons.

PICKETING   A state law forbidding all peaceful picketing would be an unconstitutional invasion of speech. However, "picketing involves elements of both speech and conduct, i.e., patrolling," and "because of this intermingling of protected and unprotected elements, picketing can be subject to controls that would not be constitutionally permissible in the case of pure speech.[46]

Even peaceful picketing can be restricted if it is conducted for an illegal purpose, such as to press an employer to practice racial or sex discrimination in the hiring of workers. For trade union picketing, however, federal regulations are so comprehensive that the power of states to interfere is much narrower than it might appear from First Amendment decisions.

COMMERCIAL SPEECH   While commercial speech is constitutionally protected, there are common sense differences between commercial and other kinds of speech. Thus, it is subject to much more regulation than the other varieties: Overbreadth analysis does not apply, nor perhaps the prohibition against prior restraint.

A law forbidding "false and misleading" commercial speech is constitutional, whereas a law forbidding false and misleading political speech clearly is not. In the realm of political debate, no one can say what is false and misleading. But an advertisement can be judged in that respect. Advertising on radio and television is subject to even greater regulation than advertising transmitted in print.

SYMBOLIC SPEECH   "We cannot accept the view," wrote former Chief Justice Earl Warren, "that an apparently limitless variety of conduct can be labeled speech whenever the person engaged in the conduct intends thereby to express an idea."[47] Or as Chief Justice Warren Burger wrote: "Conduct that the State police power can prohibit on a public street does not become automatically protected by the Constitution merely because the conduct is moved to . . . a 'live theatre' stage, any more than a 'live' performance of a man and woman locked in a sexual embrace at high noon in Times Square is protected by the Constitution merely because they simultaneously engaged in a political dialogue."[48]

Of course, the line between speech and conduct is not always clear. Deliberately burning a draft card in violation of a congressional regulation is not a constitutionally protected form of speech. Municipal police officers have no right to have long hair while serving on the police force. But on the other side of the line, although public school authorities can impose a reasonable dress

[46]*Food Employees v. Logan Plaza*, 391 U.S. 308 (1968).
[47]*United States v. O'Brien*, 391 U.S. 367 (1968).
[48]*Paris Adult Theatre I v. Slaton*, 413 U.S. 49 (1973).

code, they cannot—without evidence that the conduct would lead to disruption—forbid students to wear black armbands to school to protest political events such as the war in Vietnam.

LIBEL, OBSCENITY, AND FIGHTING WORDS

Official cannot collect unless it was said deliberately

As we noted at the beginning of this chapter, some kinds of speech are not entitled to constitutional protection. This does not mean that the constitutional issues relating to these kinds of speech are simple. On the contrary. How you prove libel, how you define obscenity, and how you determine which words are "fighting words" are hotly contested issues.

Libel

At one time newspaper publishers and editors had to take considerable care about what they wrote, for fear they might be prosecuted for libel by the government or sued for money damages by individuals. But through a progressive raising of constitutional standards, it has become more difficult to win a libel suit against a newspaper or magazine.

In *New York Times* v. *Sullivan*, one of the more important freedom of speech cases of recent years, the Supreme Court announced that *public officials or public figures* cannot collect damages for any comments made about them unless they can prove the comments were made with knowledge of their falsity or with reckless disregard for whether the comments were true or false—that is, unless they can prove the comments were made with "actual malice."[49]

To the anguish of newspeople, recent Supreme Court decisions permit more cases actually to go to trial. The Court has insisted that the question of "actual malice" be decided by the jury at the trial—not by the judge at a preliminary hearing. Moreover, in order to show malice, plaintiffs may question reporters and editors about the "editorial processes" that led to the offensive statement.[50]

Constitutional standards for libel charges brought by *private persons* are not so rigid. Such persons may collect damages without having to prove actual malice. They need only show that the charges made against them were false, that there was negligence on the part of the newspeople, and that as a result those libeled suffered damages. Moreover, one does not lose status as a private person and become a public figure—thus being held to the more rigid requirements for collecting libel damages—merely because of newspaper publicity; for example, for getting a divorce, for being accused of being a spy, or for being a scientist who receives federal grants and is accused by a senator of wasting taxpayers' money.

"I like Senator Goniff. Heck, I think he's one great guy. Right now, as I write this story, feeling great warmth and affection for the senator, it seems impossible that he bilked the people of his district out of $3 million." *Ed Stein. Reprinted by courtesy of Rocky Mountain News.*

Obscenity

Obscene publications are not entitled to constitutional protection, but the members of the Supreme Court, like everybody else, have had great difficulty in determining how obscenity is to be defined. Since 1957 there have been over eighty-five separate opinions written by Supreme Court justices. In *Miller* v. *California* (1973) the Court was finally able to assemble a majority opinion. Chief Justice Burger, speaking for five members of the Court, again stated that obscenity is not entitled to constitutional protection, and once again tried to clarify a constitutional definition of obscenity.

A work may be considered legally obscene provided: (1) the average person, applying contemporary standards of the particular community, would find

[49]376 U.S. 254 (1964).

[50]Fred Barbash, "Burger's Footnote Revises Libel Laws," *The Washington Post*, May 5, 1980, p. A–14. *Herbert* v. *Lando*, 441 U.S. 153 (1979).

that the work, taken as a whole, appeals to a prurient interest in sex; (2) it depicts or describes in a patently offensive way sexual conduct specifically defined by the applicable law or authoritatively construed; and (3) the work, taken as a whole, lacks serious literary, artistic, political, or scientific value.[51] The Chief Justice specifically rejected part of the previous test—the so-called *Memoirs* v. *Massachusetts* (1966) formula: No work should be judged obscene unless it is "utterly without redeeming social value."[52] The Chief Justice argued that such a test made it impossible for a state to outlaw hard-core pornography.

Under the current test the jury is to determine whether or not a work appeals to prurient interests and is patently offensive. It is to apply the standards of the community from which the jury comes, leaving open the possibility that a particular book or movie might be legally obscene in one community but not in another. The literary, artistic, political, or scientific value part of the test, on the other hand, is not limited by the values of a community and is a determination open to review by judges.

Did the *Miller* decision mean that local communities could ban whatever a prosecutor could persuade a jury was obscene? There were many who hoped so; there were many who feared so. They read *Miller* to mean that the Supreme Court would no longer review each book or movie in order to second-guess the decision of local authorities. But how far could the local community go? What if it decided to ban "Little Red Riding Hood"? After all, who really knows what went on in that bedroom?

A year after the *Miller* decision, the Supreme Court warned: "It would be a serious misreading of *Miller* to conclude that juries have unbridled discretion in determining what is patently offensive."[53] Appellate courts, said Justice Rehnquist speaking for the majority, should review jury determinations to ensure compliance with constitutional standards. And the Supreme Court itself, after such review, ruled that the movie *Carnal Knowledge* was not patently offensive, contrary to the conclusion of a jury in Albany, Georgia.

Obscenity, then, is not entitled to constitutional protection. But governments must proceed under laws that define specifically the kinds of sexual conduct forbidden in word or picture. Moreover, it cannot be made a crime for booksellers to offer an obscene book for sale; it must be shown that they did so knowingly. Otherwise, booksellers would tend to avoid placing on their shelves materials that some authorities might consider objectionable, and the public would be deprived of an opportunity to purchase anything except the "safe and sanitary." Nor can the mere private possession of obscene materials be made a crime.

States are primarily responsible for regulating obscene literature. But ever since Anthony Comstock started a national crusade against "smut" in the 1880s, Congress has been concerned with the subject. Congress has adopted, and the Supreme Court has upheld, laws forbidding the importing into the United States of pornographic materials or the sending of such materials through the mails or interstate commerce—even to willing adults, even transported by a person in a briefcase on an airline for private use.

What about "dirty books" and "X-rated movies" that fall short of the constitutional definition of obscenity? They are entitled to constitutional protection, but less protection than political speech; and they are subject to greater government regulation. The Supreme Court upheld a zoning ordinance forbidding "adult motion picture theaters" from being located within 1000 feet of two

[51]413 U.S. 15 (1973).
[52]*Memoirs* v. *Massachusetts*, 383 U.S. 413 (1966).
[53]*Jenkins* v. *Georgia*, 418 U.S. 153 (1974).

other such theaters. Justice Stevens wrote: "It is manifest that society's interest in protecting this type of expression is of a wholly different, and lesser, magnitude than the interest in untrammeled political debate. . . . The state may legitimately use the content of these materials as the basis for placing them in a different classification from other motion pictures."[54] Yet the small Borough of Mount Ephraim, New Jersey, went too far when it applied its zoning ban on live entertainment to prevent nude dancing in an adult book store. Said the Supreme Court: "Entertainment, as well as political and ideological speech, is protected by the Constitution," and "nude dancing is not without its First Amendment protections from official regulation."[55]

Sexually explicit materials either about minors or aimed at them are not protected by the First Amendment. State and local governments—provided they act under narrowly drawn statutes—can, for example, ban the knowing sale of "girly" magazines to minors, even if such materials would not be considered legally obscene if sold to adults. And they can make it a crime visually to depict sexual conduct by children, even if the depicted behavior would not be considered obscene if done by adults.

Censorship of films and books may be imposed by a variety of means other than formal action. In some cities a local group such as the Legion of Decency may put pressure on the authorities. Local police have been known to threaten booksellers with criminal prosecution if they persist in showing films or selling books of which some local people disapprove. Such a threat is often enough to compel exhibitors to stop showing the films or selling the books. Of course, any group is free to stay away from pictures or books that it dislikes, even to try to persuade others to stay away. What the Constitution forbids is the use of coercive powers of government in this regard.

A small business cleverly uses "First Amendment" in its name. *Stan Wakefield.*

FIGHTING WORDS There are certain well-defined and narrowly limited classes of speech "which by their very utterance inflict injury or tend to incite an immediate breach of peace that governments may constitutionally punish. . . ."[56] Fighting words must be limited to those that "have a direct tendency to cause acts of violence by the person to whom, individually, the remarks are addressed."[57] The mere fact that the words are abusive, harsh, or insulting is not sufficient. In fact, one close student of the Court has concluded that under Chief Justice Burger, fighting words have been so narrowly construed as to virtually eliminate the category.[58] For example, a four-letter word used in relation to the draft and worn on a sweater is not a fighting word, at least when it is not directed to any specific person.

RIGHT OF THE PEOPLE PEACEABLY TO ASSEMBLE, AND TO PETITION THE GOVERNMENT

"The right to assemble peaceably applies not only to meetings in private homes and meeting halls, but to gatherings held in public streets and parks, which since . . . time out of mind have been used for purposes of assembly . . . and discussing public questions."[59] In the winter of 1977 Frank Collins, "a racist

[54]*Young v. American Mini Theatres*, 427 U.S. 51 (1976).

[55]*Schad v. Borough of Mount Ephraim*, 452 U.S. 61 (1981).

[56]*Chaplinsky v. New Hampshire*, 315 U.S. 568 (1942).

[57]*Cohen v. California*, 403 U.S. 15 (1971).

[58]O'Brien, *The Public's Right to Know: The Supreme Court and the First Amendment*, p. 97.

[59]*Hague v. C.I.O.*, 307 U.S. 496 (1939).

and a fascist, a bigoted totalitarian, a self-avowed Nazi,"[60] threatened to lead his small band in a jack-booted march in brown shirts, carrying swastika regalia, through the streets of Skokie, Illinois. Skokie is a Chicago suburb where half the people are Jewish, some of them survivors of Hitler's extermination camps, and many of them with relatives who lost their lives in the Holocaust. Many people, including the officials of Skokie and a local judge, argued that Collins and his followers should not be allowed to march. They argued this would be like shouting "fire" in a crowded theater, and that to permit such a use of streets presented a clear and present danger of inciting people to violence. These same arguments were put forward to contend that Iranian followers of the Ayatollah Khomeini should not be allowed to protest publicly in Washington at a time when most Americans were angry about Khomeini's illegal and brutal treatment of innocent American hostages in Teheran. The right to assemble peaceably, they argued, should not be extended to Iranian aliens who were abusing this right to provoke Americans to violence. In both cases judicial authorities defended the rights of these unpopular minorities to demonstrate. (Collins never actually marched in Skokie, but he did march in another part of the Chicago area.) It also took judicial intervention in the 1960s to preserve for Martin Luther King, Jr., and his followers their right to demonstrate in the streets of southern cities in behalf of the rights of blacks.

These incidents present the classic free speech problem of the "heckler's veto." It is almost always easier to maintain order, and certainly politically more popular, by curbing public demonstrations of unpopular groups than by moving against those threatening violence against these groups. On the other hand, if police did not have the right to order a group to disperse, public order would be at the mercy of those who resort to street demonstrations just to create tensions and provoke street battles.

The Supreme Court has refused to give a categorical "yes" or "no" answer to the question, "Does the Constitution require police officers always to protect unpopular groups whose public demonstrations arouse others to violence or threats of it?" In 1951 in *Feiner* v. *New York*, the Court upheld the conviction for unlawful assembly of a sidewalk speaker who, on the orders of the only two police officers present, refused to move on after his provocative remarks aroused the crowd to anger.[61] The *Feiner* case has not been overruled, but since then the Supreme Court has emphasized the need for governments to act under more precisely drawn statutes than those of disturbing the peace and unlawful assembly. The Court has refused to sustain convictions of persons whose only offense has been to engage in peaceful but unpopular demonstrations.

It is clear, however, that the Constitution does not give a person the right to communicate "one's views at all times and places or in any manner that may be desired."[62] No one has the right deliberately to incite others to violence, to block traffic, or to hold parades or make speeches in public streets or on public sidewalks whenever he or she wishes. Governments may make reasonable time, place, and manner regulations, provided they are content-neutral. (Justice Stevens believes that the content neutral standard is of little help. He quipped: "Any student of history who has been reprimanded for talking about the World Series during a class discussion of the First Amendment knows that it is incorrect to state that a time, place, or manner restriction may not be based upon either the content or subject matter of speech.")[63]

Here, police protect a pro-Iran demonstrator in Los Angeles in November 1979. *UPI.*

---

[60]David M. Hamlin, "Swastikas & Survivors: Inside the Skokie-Nazi Free Speech Case," *The Civil Liberties Review* (March–April 1978).

[61]340 U.S. 315 (1951).

[62]*Heffron v. International Society for Krishna Consciousness,* 452 U.S. 298 (1981).

[63]*Consolidated Edison Company v. Public Service Commission of N. Y.,* 447 U.S. 530 (1980).

It is also true that "public places historically associated with the free exercise of expressive activities, such as streets, sidewalks, and parks, are considered, without more, to be 'public forums'." Courts will look closely at time, place, and manner regulations as they apply to these public forums to ensure that the law is being applied evenhandedly and that action is not taken "because of what is being said rather than how and where it is being said."[64]

What of public facilities, such as airports, libraries, courthouses, schools, and swimming pools, which are designed to serve as other than public forums? As long as persons assemble to use such facilities within the normal bounds of conduct, they may not be constitutionally restrained from doing so. However, if they attempt to interfere with programs or try to appropriate facilities—such as a university chancellor's office—for their own use, a state has authority to punish such activities.

What of private property? The right to assemble does not include a right to trespass on private property. A state may protect property owners against those who attempt to convert property to their own uses, even if they are doing so to express ideas. The spread of large, privately owned shopping malls, some of which cover many acres and are larger than some towns, present some difficult constitutional issues. The Supreme Court has set the following guidelines (*Pruneyard Shopping Center* v. *Robins*): Privately owned shopping malls and centers are not public streets and are not places of public assembly; no one has a constitutional right to use such a mall to hand out political leaflets, to picket for political purposes, or otherwise to exercise First Amendment freedoms. On the other hand, states and cities, if they wish, and to an extent still to be defined, may legally obligate the owners of such centers to permit their use for peaceful political purposes such as distributing handbills or getting people to sign petitions. In other words, although people have no constitutional right to engage in political action in a nonpublic shopping center, neither do the owners of such centers have a constitutional right to close them to political action in the face of reasonable state or local regulations providing access that does not interfere with their primary commercial purposes.[65]

Does the right of peaceful assembly and petition include the right to violate a law nonviolently but deliberately? We have no precise answer. But speaking in general terms, civil disobedience—even if peaceful—is not a protected right. When Dr. Martin Luther King, Jr. and his followers refused to comply with a state court's injunction forbidding them to parade in Birmingham without first securing a permit, the Supreme Court sustained their conviction, even though there was a serious doubt about the constitutionality of the injunction and the ordinance on which it was based. Justice Stewart, speaking for the five-man majority, said: "No man can be judge in his own case, however exalted his station, however righteous his motives, and irrespective of his race, color, politics, or religion." Persons are not "constitutionally free to ignore all the procedures of the law and carry their battles to the streets."[66] The four dissenting justices insisted that one does have a right to defy peacefully an obviously unconstitutional statute or injunction.

Freedom of Association

The right to organize for the peaceful promotion of political and other causes is not specifically mentioned in the Constitution, but "it is beyond debate that freedom to engage in association for the advancement of beliefs and ideas is an inseparable aspect of the 'liberty' assured by the Due Process clause of the Four-

[64]*United States* v. *Mary T. Grace*, 75 L Ed 2d 736 (1983).

[65]447 U.S. 74 (1980).

[66]*Walker* v. *Birmingham*, 388 U.S. 307 (1967).

[handwritten margin notes: Hatch Acts / Federal Employees Can not become involved in Political Leadership Roles]

teenth Amendment which embraces freedom of speech."[67] Many troublesome constitutional questions grow out of the conflict between the constitutional right to join political parties and the right of governments to regulate the conditions of public employment. Federal Hatch Acts (many states have similar laws) forbid most federal employees from actively campaigning or taking leadership roles in political parties, and these acts have been upheld by the Supreme Court as reasonable measures to ensure a neutral civil service and to free government employees from coercion in behalf of the party in power. The Supreme Court has even gone so far as to declare that under most circumstances the patronage system itself is unconstitutional.

Congress and many of the states have regulated the amount of money that candidates, parties, and interest groups can raise and spend for political purposes. But many of these regulations have come into conflict with the constitutional right of the people to petition the government for redress of grievances and to associate to promote political and social causes. The Court in *Buckely* v. *Valeo* sustained limits on the amount of money people may *contribute* to candidates and their campaign committees on the ground that such limits only marginally restrict contributors' ability to express political views.[68] But it has struck down limits on the amounts that may be contributed to associations formed to support or oppose ballot measures submitted to popular vote.

Limits on what people can *spend*, in contrast to what they can contribute, have fared even less well. Governments may not limit the amount of money people—including candidates—can spend directly on political matters. However, presidential candidates who accept federal funds for their campaigns may be limited in their spending as a condition of receiving such funds. (See page 12.)

The Supreme Court has somewhat reluctantly upheld requirements that *major* political parties maintain records and disclose information about contributions received and about how they have spent their funds. It has refused, however, to sanction the imposition of such requirements on minor parties if there is any evidence these disclosures might subject contributors to reprisal and thus impair the ability of the party to raise and spend funds.

SUBVERSIVE CONDUCT AND SEDITIOUS SPEECH

"If there is any fixed star in our constitutional constellation," Justice Jackson said, "it is that no official, high or petty, can prescribe what shall be orthodox in politics, nationalism, religion, or other matters of opinion. . . ."[69] Any group can champion whatever position it wishes: vegetarianism, feminism, sexism, communism, fascism, black nationalism, white supremacy, Zionism, anti-Semitism, Americanism. But what of those who are unwilling to abide by democratic methods, and who attempt through force or violence to impose their views on others? Here is a problem for a democratic government: How to protect itself against antidemocrats who are working to destroy the democratic system, while at the same time preserving constitutional freedoms and democratic procedures.

Traitors, Spies, Saboteurs, Revolutionaries

Laws aimed at acts of violence, espionage, sabotage, or treason in themselves raise no constitutional questions, nor do they infringe on protected constitutional liberties. However, they can be used to intimidate if they are loosely drawn or indiscriminately administered. The framers of the Constitution,

[67]NAACP v. *Alabama*, 357 U.S. 449 (1958).

[68]424 U.S. 1 (1976).

[69]*West Virginia State Board of Education v. Barnette*.

themselves considered traitors of the English Crown, knew the dangers of defining treason loosely. Accordingly, they carefully inserted a constitutional definition: Treason consists only of the overt acts of giving aid and comfort to the enemies of the United States or levying war against it. Further, in order to convict a person of treason, two witnesses to the overt treasonable acts must testify, or the defendant must confess, in open court.

The national government may also move against other conduct designed to subvert the democratic system. Congress, for example, has made it a crime to engage in espionage or sabotage, or to cross interstate boundaries or use the mails or interstate facilities to bomb buildings and schools. (This law was passed in 1960 and was aimed at the white segregationists who were alleged to have blown up black churches and to have used force to intimidate black leaders and their white allies.) It is also a crime to cross state lines or use interstate facilities with the intent to incite a riot (the so-called Rap Brown law passed in 1968, aimed at black militants who were alleged to foment riots), or to conspire to do any of the above.

More often than not, when the government prosecutes under such laws, the charge is conspiracy. It is easier to prove conspiracy than to sustain a charge against a named defendant that he or she has thrown a brick, planted a bomb, engaged in a riot, or committed an act of violence. But conspiracy charges, although long known to Anglo-American jurisprudence, are especially dangerous to civil liberties; they can be abused by prosecutors to intimidate the politically unpopular.

For the most part, the highly charged prosecutions of the late 1960s and the early 1970s against political radicals and black militants for allegedly engaging in, or conspiring to engage in, violent acts led to verdicts of not guilty, or reversals on appeal. To some this is evidence that our court system is strong and can be counted on to protect the innocent. To others it is evidence of the inability of the government to bring to justice those who should have been punished for their deeds. To still others it is evidence of how governments can use legal procedures to intimidate adherents of unpopular causes. For even if defendants are finally acquitted, the effort and expense of defending themselves in court have an intimidating impact on political dissenters. Historians, journalists, political scientists, and others will be debating the lessons of these trials for many years.

Demonstrators picket in front of the White House while awaiting the Supreme Court decision in the case of convicted spies Julius and Ethel Rosenberg. *UPI.*

Seditious Speech

It is one thing to punish persons for what they do; it is quite another to punish them for what they say. The story of the development of free government is in large measure the story of making this distinction clear. Until recent centuries seditious speech was so broadly defined that all criticism of those in power was considered criminal. As late as the eighteenth century in England, seditious speech was said to cover any publication intended to incite disaffection against the king or the government or to raise discontent among the people or to promote feelings of ill will between different classes.[70] And it made no difference if what was said was true. On the contrary, "the greater the truth the greater the libel." For if one charged the king's ministers with being corrupt, and in fact they were corrupt, such a charge would more likely cause discontent among the people than if it were false.

The adoption of the Constitution and the Bill of Rights did not result in

---

[70]Zechariah Chafee, Jr., "The Great Liberty: Freedom of Speech and Press," in Alfred H. Kelly (ed.), *Foundations of Freedom in the American Constitution* (Harper & Row, 1958), p. 79.

a quick, easy victory for those who wished to establish free speech in the United States.[71] In 1798, only seven years after the First Amendment had been ratified, Congress passed the first national sedition law. Those were perilous times for the young republic, for war with France seemed imminent. The Federalists, in control of both Congress and the presidency, persuaded themselves that national safety required some suppression of speech. The Sedition Act made it a crime to utter false, scandalous, or malicious statements intended to bring the government or any of its officers into disrepute or "to incite against them the hatred of the good people of the United States."[72] Popular reaction to the Sedition Act helped defeat the Federalists in the elections of 1800. They had failed to grasp the democratic idea that a person may criticize the government of the day, work for its downfall, and oppose its policies, but still be loyal to the nation.

THE SMITH ACT OF 1940

During World War I and the "Red scare" that followed it, there was a flurry of legislation and prosecutions aimed at seditious speech. Hundreds of people who expressed mildly radical ideas found themselves in trouble. Some went to jail.[73] But the first peacetime sedition law since the Sedition Act of 1798 was the Smith Act of 1940. The Smith Act forbids persons to advocate overthrow of the government with the intent to bring it about; to distribute, with disloyal intent, matter teaching or advising the overthrow of government by violence; and to organize knowingly or to help organize any group having such purposes.

In *Dennis* v. *United States* (1951) the Court agreed that the Smith Act could be applied to the leaders of the Communist party, who had been charged with conspiring to advocate the violent overthrow of the government.[74] But since then the Court has substantially modified its holding. Congress may not outlaw the mere advocacy of the abstract doctrine of violent overthrow: "The essential distinction is that those to whom the advocacy is addressed must be urged *to do* something now or in the future, rather than merely *to believe* in something."[75] Then the Supreme Court narrowed *Dennis* even further: Advocacy of the use of force may not be forbidden "except where such advocacy is directed to inciting or producing *imminent* lawless action and is likely to incite or produce such action."[76]

Seditious speech, if narrowly defined to cover only the advocacy of *immediate* and *concrete* acts of violence, is not constitutionally protected. Such narrow interpretation of antisedition laws means people are free to work for their political objectives so long as they abandon the use of force—or its specific and immediate advocacy—as a means of bringing it about.

[71]Leonard Levy, *Legacy of Suppression* (Harvard University Press, 1960), and *Freedom of the Press from Zenger to Jefferson* (Bobbs-Merrill, 1966).

[72]See James Morton Smith, *Freedom's Fetters: The Alien and Sedition Laws and American Civil Liberties* (Cornell University Press, 1956).

[73]The classic coverage of this episode is Zechariah Chafee, Jr., *Free Speech in the United States* (Harvard University Press, 1941). See also John P. Roche, *The Quest for the Dream* (Macmillan, 1963).

[74]341 U.S. 494.

[75]*Yates* v. *United States*, 354 U.S. 298 (1957).

[76]*Brandenburg* v. *Ohio*, 395 U.S. 444 (1969).

SUMMARY

1. First Amendment freedoms—freedom of religion, freedom from the establishment of religion, freedom of speech, freedom of press, freedom of assembly and petition, and freedom of association—are at the very heart of the democratic process.

2. Roughly since World War I, the Supreme Court has become the primary agency for giving meaning to these constitutional restraints. And since 1925 these constitutional limits have been applied not only to Congress but to all governmental agencies—national, state, and local.

3. Clashes about First Amendment freedoms are not profitably thought of as battles between the "good guys" and the "bad guys," or as dramas in which the judges at the last moment rush to the rescue of liberty. Rather, these are arguments over conflicting notions of what is good. Those who argue for restraint on First Amendment freedoms do so for a variety of reasons.

4. Over the years, the Supreme Court has taken a practical approach to First Amendment freedoms. It has refused to make them absolute rights above any kind of governmental regulation, direct or indirect, or to say that they must be preserved at whatever price. But the justices have recognized that a democratic society tampers with these freedoms at great peril. They have insisted upon compelling justification before permitting these rights to be limited. How compelling the justification is, in a free society, always will remain an open question.

FURTHER READING

Zechariah Chafee, Jr. *Free Speech in the United States* (Harvard University Press, 1941).

Bill F. Chamberlin and Charlene J. Brown (eds.). *The First Amendment Reconsidered: New Perspectives on the Meaning of Freedom of Speech and Press* (Longman, 1982).

Edward de Grazia and Roger K. Newman. *Movies, Censors and the First Amendment* (R.R. Bowker Co., 1983).

Ithiel de Sola Pool. *Technologies and Freedom* (Harvard University Press, 1983).

Franklyn S. Haiman. *Speech and Law in a Free Society* (University of Chicago, 1981).

Nat Hentoff. *The First Freedom: The Tumultuous History of Free Speech in America* (Delacorte, 1980).

John Stuart Mill. *Essay on Liberty*. First published in 1859, it is available in many editions, one of which is Edwin A. Buritt (ed.), *The English Philosophers* (Random House, 1939).

David M. O'Brien. *The Public's Right To Know: The Supreme Court and the First Amendment* (Praeger, 1981).

J. W. Peltason. *Understanding the Constitution* (Holt, Rinehart and Winston, 1982).

Ellis Sandoz. *Conceived in Liberty: American Individual Rights Today* (Duxbury Press, 1978).

Bernard Schwartz. *The Great Rights of Mankind: A History of the American Bill of Rights* (Oxford University Press, 1977).

EQUAL RIGHTS UNDER THE LAW

5

Consider again the ringing words of the Declaration of Independence: "We hold these truths to be self-evident, that all men are created equal, that they are endowed by their Creator with certain unalienable Rights, that among these are Life, Liberty, and the pursuit of Happiness. . . ." The Declaration does not talk about equality of white, Christian, or Anglo-Saxon men but of all men. (Undoubtedly, if the Declaration were to be written today, the framers would speak of persons rather than men.) This creed of individual dignity and equality is older than our Declaration of Independence; its roots go back at least as far as the teachings of Judaism and Christianity.

Certain liberties are essential to the operation of democratic government. But these liberties are not merely means of attaining self-government; they are ends in themselves. They do not exist to protect the government; the government exists to protect them. Long ago they were called natural rights; today we speak of human rights—but the belief is still the same: the primacy of people over government and the dignity and worth of each individual.

Today no problem is more compelling than that of ensuring all Americans their basic civil rights without discrimination because of race, religion, national origin, or sex. What should we do to protect civil rights and to extend opportunities for those who have been discriminated against? What we do—or fail to do—has significance beyond our national borders. People everywhere follow the treatment of our minorities with more than casual interest, especially since we call for human rights throughout the world.

Denial of equal rights not only negates the equality the Declaration of Independence asserts, it is also contrary to the guarantees of the Constitution. The Constitution provides two ways of protecting civil rights: It ensures that

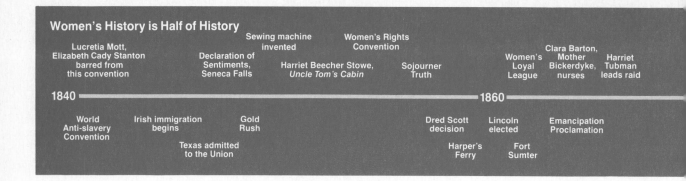

Women's History is Half of History

		Sewing machine invented		Women's Rights Convention				
Lucretia Mott, Elizabeth Cady Stanton barred from this convention	Declaration of Sentiments, Seneca Falls		Harriet Beecher Stowe, *Uncle Tom's Cabin*		Sojourner Truth		Women's Loyal League	Clara Barton, Mother Bickerdyke, nurses	Harriet Tubman leads raid

1840 ━━━━━━━━━━━━━━━━━━━━━━━━━━━━━━ **1860** ━

World Anti-slavery Convention	Irish immigration begins	Gold Rush			Dred Scott decision	Lincoln elected	Emancipation Proclamation
	Texas admitted to the Union				Harper's Ferry	Fort Sumter	

government itself imposes no discriminatory barriers; and it grants the national and state governments authority to protect civil rights against interference by private individuals. In this chapter we will be concerned with both problems.

TO SECURE EQUAL RIGHTS—AN OVERVIEW

In order to put into context the court decisions, laws, and other kinds of governmental actions relating to civil rights for women, blacks, Hispanics, and native Americans, it is useful to review the accelerating drive to make real the promises of the Declaration of Independence and the Constitution. For the human rights crusade is not just a series of legal decisions, laws, and constitutional amendments; it involves the entire social, economic, and political system. While the struggles of these groups are interwoven, they are not identical.

Women's Rights

Women suffragists demonstrating for the right to vote. *Culver.*

The struggle for equal rights for women has long been intertwined with the battle to secure such rights for blacks (and we shouldn't forget the obvious fact that half of black Americans are women). The Seneca Falls Women's Rights Convention (1848), which launched the women's movement, involved men and women who had long been active in the campaign to abolish slavery (see page 183). As the Civil War approached, women were urged to abandon their cause, at least temporarily, and devote all their energies to getting rid of slavery.[1] The Civil War brought the women's movement to a halt. The Fourteenth Amendment even introduced into the Constitution a provision that overtly discriminated against women: It provided that any state which kept *males* over twenty-one from voting should suffer a proportionate reduction of its representation in the House of Representatives. Women were no more successful with the Fifteenth Amendment.

For a time the Temperance Movement also diverted attention away from women's rights. But by the turn of the century, a vigorous campaign was under way for women's suffrage within the states. The first victories came in western states. Wyoming led the way. As a territory, Wyoming had given women the right to vote: It is said that when members of Congress in Washington grumbled about this "petticoat provision," the Wyoming legislatures replied that they would stay out of the Union a hundred years rather than come in without women's suffrage. Congress gave in and admitted Wyoming to the Union,

[1]These materials are based on Judith Hole and Ellen Levine, *Rebirth of Feminism* (Quadrangle, 1971). See also Ellen Carol DuBois, *Feminism and Suffrage: The Emergence of an Independent Women's Movement in America, 1848–1869* (Cornell University Press, 1978).

94

"Battle Hymn of the Republic," Julia Ward Howe	Equal Rights Association		Frances Willard, Women's Christian Temperance Movement	Clara Barton, Red Cross / Evaporated milk available	Radcliffe, Bryn Mawr	Mother Mary Jones, labor organizer	Emily Dickinson

═══════════════════════════════ 1880 ═══════════════════════════════

Lee surrenders to Grant / Lincoln assassinated	14th Amendments makes blacks citizens and adds the word "male" to the Constitution	15th Amendment— black male suffrage	Reconstruction / Custer, Little Big Horn		Civil Service reform	Transcontinental railroad completed

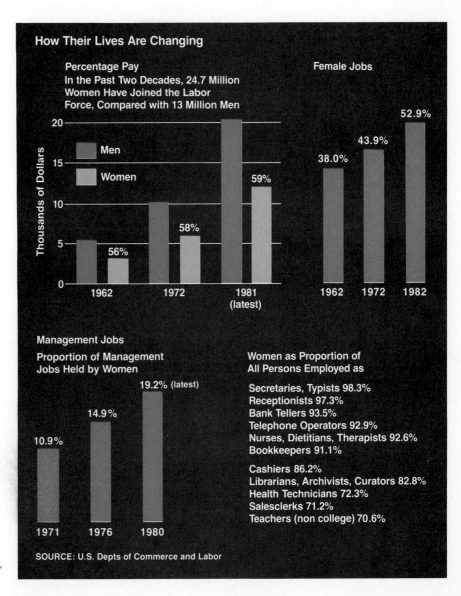

How Their Lives Are Changing

Percentage Pay
In the Past Two Decades, 24.7 Million Women Have Joined the Labor Force, Compared with 13 Million Men

Thousands of Dollars
Men
Women
56% 58% 59%
1962 1972 1981 (latest)

Female Jobs
38.0% 43.9% 52.9%
1962 1972 1982

Management Jobs
Proportion of Management Jobs Held by Women
10.9% 14.9% 19.2% (latest)
1971 1976 1980

Women as Proportion of All Persons Employed as

Secretaries, Typists 98.3%
Receptionists 97.3%
Bank Tellers 93.5%
Telephone Operators 92.9%
Nurses, Dietitians, Therapists 92.6%
Bookkeepers 91.1%

Cashiers 86.2%
Librarians, Archivists, Curators 82.8%
Health Technicians 72.3%
Salesclerks 71.2%
Teachers (non college) 70.6%

SOURCE: U.S. Depts of Commerce and Labor

From U.S. News & World Report, Inc., © Nov. 29, 1982.

95

International Council of Women	Ladies Home Journal	National American Woman Suffrage Association		Jane Addams— Hull House		Charlotte Perkins Gilman, Women and Economics	Women's Trade Union League	Brandeis brief— protective legislation
General Federation of Women's Clubs			Susan B. Anthony		Florence Kelly, reformer			

1900

	Samuel Gompers, American Federation of Labor	Immigration from Southern Europe		Progressive Era	Panama Canal begun
		Populists	Battle of Wounded Knee	Theodore Roosevelt	

women's suffrage and all. By the end of World War I, over half the states had granted women the right to vote in some or all elections.

To suffragists this state-by-state approach seemed slow and uncertain. They wanted a decisive victory—a constitutional amendment that would at one blow force all states to allow otherwise qualified women to vote. Then in 1920 Congress proposed the Nineteenth Amendment. Opposition to its adoption and ratification was intertwined with opposition to the rights of blacks. Many southerners opposed the amendment: Not only would it extend the franchise to black women, but also it might bring federal officials to investigate elections to ensure that the amendment was being obeyed, and would thereby call attention to how blacks were being kept from voting.[2]

Senator Vardman, Democrat from Mississippi, opposed the Nineteenth Amendment and called for "repeal of the Fifteenth, the modification of the Fourteenth . . ., making this a government by white men, of white men, for all men."[3] But opposition to women's suffrage was not limited to southerners. Senator Borah, a noted liberal Republican from Idaho, also opposed it, again on racial grounds: "There are 100,000 Japanese and Chinese women [in the Pacific states], and I have no particular desire to bestow suffrage upon them," he stated.[4]

With the ratification in 1920 of the Nineteenth Amendment, women won the right to vote. Still women were denied equal pay and equal rights, and they suffered numerous legal disabilities imposed by both national and state laws.

During the last several decades the struggle to secure the adoption of ERA has occupied much of the attention of the women's movement. But there are other goals. In Houston in November 1977 the National Commission on the Observance of International Women's Year—appointed by President Carter, presided over by Bella S. Abzug, and consisting of more than 2000 delegates— adopted a National Plan of Action.[5] This plan reflects the fact that the women's movement now involves more low-income women and pays more attention to their concerns.

With the emergence of the gender gap in the 1982 elections (see page 205), it is clear that the political clout of women is increasingly being mobilized behind issues that range from pay, through pensions, to peace.

[2]Alan P. Grimes, Democracy and the Amendments to the Constitution (D. C. Heath, 1979), pp. 90–91.

[3]Ibid.

[4]Ibid.

[5]The National Commission on the Observance of International Women's Year, An Official Report to the President, the Congress, and the People of the United States, The Spirit of Houston (Government Printing Office, 1978); Report of the National Commission on the Observance of International Women's Year, "To Form a More Perfect Union . . .," Justice for American Women (Government Printing Office, 1976).

| National Women's Party | Suffragists jailed for White House demonstration | Woman's Committee, National Council of Defense | | Women get the vote | League of Women Voters | Alice Paul introduces Equal Rights Amendment (ERA) | The Flapper | Margaret Mead, *Coming of Age in Samoa* | | Frances Perkins, Secretary of Labor | Frozen foods Introduced | Clare Booth Luce, *The Women* | Eleanor Roosevelt |

1920

| Woodrow Wilson | U.S. enters World War I | Treaty of Versailles | 19th Amendment ratified | Prohibition | | Herbert Hoover | Depression | | Stock market crash | FDR— New Deal |

The Struggle for Racial Justice

[handwritten margin notes: Freedmens Bureau Ed. for blacks; 13th, 14th, 15th amend adopted because of North Victory]

Americans have had a special confrontation with the problems of race—before, during, and after the Civil War. As a result of the northern victory, the Thirteenth, Fourteenth, and Fifteenth amendments became part of the Constitution. Congress also passed a series of civil rights laws to implement these constitutional provisions and established special programs such as the Freedmen's Bureau to provide educational and social services for the freed slaves.

Before these programs had a significant effect, the southern white male political community was restored to power. By 1877 Reconstruction was ending. Northern political leaders abandoned blacks to their fate at the hands of their former white masters. The president no longer concerned himself with the enforcement of civil rights laws, and Congress enacted no new ones. The Supreme Court either declared old laws unconstitutional or interpreted them so narrowly that they were ineffective. The Court also gave such a limited construction to the Thirteenth, Fourteenth, and Fifteenth amendments that they failed to accomplish their intended purpose of protecting the rights of blacks. By 1900 white supremacy was unchallenged in the South, where most blacks lived. Blacks were kept from voting; they were forced to accept menial jobs; and they were denied educational opportunities. In 1896 the Supreme Court, in *Plessy* v. *Ferguson*, gave constitutional sanction to governmentally imposed racial segregation.[6] Even if the Court had declared segregation unconstitutional, a decision so contrary to popular feeling and political realities would have had little impact. In 1896 blacks were lynched at an average of one every four days, and few whites raised a voice in protest.

During World War I blacks began to migrate to northern cities seeking educational opportunities and jobs. These trends were accelerated by the New Deal and World War II. And the South, through urbanization and industrialization, became more like the rest of the nation. As the migration of blacks out of the rural South into southern and northern cities shifted the racial composition of cities the black vote became important in national elections. While discrimination continued, there were also more jobs and more social gains. Above all, these changes created a black middle class opposed to segregation as a symbol of servitude and a cause of inequality. By the middle of the twentieth century, urban blacks were active and politically powerful citizens. There was a growing, persistent, and insistent demand for the abolition of color barriers.

Rosa Parks, a Montgomery seamstress, who on February 22, 1956, refused to give up a seat in front of the bus and started the modern civil rights movement. *UPI.*

[handwritten margin notes: White supremacy in South; Racial Segregation (Plessy v Ferguson)]

THE NATIONAL GOVERNMENT BEGINS TO RESPOND   Because of the special nature of the electoral college and the pattern of our political system, by the 1930s it became difficult for a person in the White House—or for one hoping to live there—to ignore the aspirations of blacks. The commitment of our presidents to the cause of equal protection became translated into the ap-

[6]163 U.S. 537

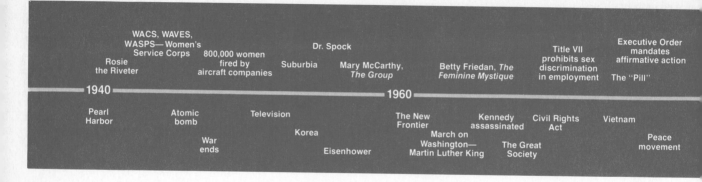

	WACS, WAVES, WASPS— Women's Service Corps	800,000 women fired by aircraft companies	Dr. Spock		Betty Friedan, *The Feminine Mystique*	Title VII prohibits sex discrimination in employment	Executive Order mandates affirmative action
Rosie the Riveter			Suburbia	Mary McCarthy, *The Group*			The "Pill"

◼ 1940 ◼◼◼◼◼◼◼◼◼◼◼◼◼◼◼◼◼◼◼◼◼◼◼◼◼◼◼◼◼◼◼◼◼◼◼ 1960 ◼

Pearl Harbor	Atomic bomb	Television		The New Frontier	Kennedy assassinated	Civil Rights Act	Vietnam
	War ends	Korea	Eisenhower	March on Washington— Martin Luther King	The Great Society		Peace movement

pointment of federal judges sympathetic to a broad construction of the Thirteenth, Fourteenth, and Fifteenth amendments.

In the 1930s blacks started to resort to lawsuits to secure their rights, especially to challenge the doctrine of segregation. They emphasized litigation because they had no alternative; they lacked the political power to make their demands effective before either state legislatures or Congress. By the 1950s civil rights litigation began to have an impact. Under the leadership of the Supreme Court, federal judges started to use the Fourteenth Amendment to reverse earlier decisions that rendered it and federal legislation ineffective. The Court outlawed all forms of governmentally imposed segregation and struck down most of the devices that had been used by state and local authorities to keep blacks from voting.[7] Presidents used their executive authority to fight segregation in the armed services and the federal bureaucracy, and they directed the Department of Justice to enforce whatever civil rights laws were available.

As the decade came to a close, the emerging national consensus in favor of governmental action to protect civil rights, and the growing political voice of blacks, began to have some impact on Congress. In 1957 Congress overrode a southern **filibuster** in the Senate and enacted the first federal civil rights laws since Reconstruction. During the 1950s the conflict was seen primarily as an attempt by the national government to compel southern state governments to stop segregating blacks into inferior schools, parks, libraries, houses, and jobs. Then came the summer of 1963.

A TURNING POINT A decade after the Supreme Court declared public school segregation unconstitutional, most black children in the South still attended segregated schools. In the North segregation in housing and education remained the established pattern in the cities. Most legal barriers in the path of equal rights had fallen. But most black Americans still could not buy a house where they wanted, secure the job they needed, find educational opportunities for their children, or walk on the streets without being insulted. What had once been thought of as a southern problem was recognized as a national problem. By 1963 the struggles in the courtrooms were being supplemented by a massive social, economic, and political movement.

The black revolt of 1963 did not come unannounced, and its immediate background was not the struggle to desegregate the schools. In one sense it began when the first black slave was educated three hundred years ago. Its more immediate origin was in 1955 in Montgomery, Alabama, when the black community boycotted city buses to protest segregation on them. The boycott

---

[7]For a general history of Supreme Court decisions affecting the constitutional rights of blacks, see Loren Miller, *The Petitioners* (Meridian Books, 1967); for a history of the political role of blacks, see Robert P. Turner, *Up to the Front Line: Blacks in the American Political System* (Kennikat Press, 1975).

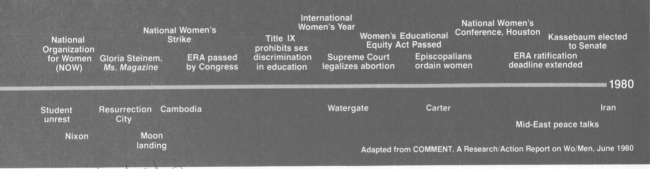

			International Women's Year		National Women's Conference, Houston	
National Organization for Women (NOW)	National Women's Strike		Title IX prohibits sex discrimination in education	Women's Educational Equity Act Passed		Kassebaum elected to Senate
	Gloria Steinem, *Ms. Magazine*	ERA passed by Congress		Supreme Court legalizes abortion	Episcopalians ordain women	ERA ratification deadline extended

1980

Student unrest	Resurrection City	Cambodia	Watergate	Carter		Iran
Nixon		Moon landing			Mid-East peace talks	

Adapted from COMMENT, A Research/Action Report on Wo/Men, June 1980

worked. Montgomery produced the first charismatic civil rights leader—Reverend Martin Luther King, Jr. Through his Southern Christian Leadership Conference and his doctrine of nonviolent resistance, King gave a new dimension to the struggle. By the early 1960s new organizational resources to support and sponsor sit-ins, freedom rides, live-ins, and mass demonstrations came into existence in almost every city.

The forces of social discontent exploded in the summer of 1963. It started with a demonstration in Birmingham, Alabama, which was countered by the use of fire hoses, police dogs, and mass arrests. It ended in a march in Washington, D.C., where over 200,000 people heard King speak. By the time the summer was over, there was hardly a city that had not had demonstrations, protests, or sit-ins; in many there was violence. This direct action had some effect: Civil rights ordinances were enacted in many cities, and more schools were desegregrated that fall than in any year since 1956. At the national level President Kennedy urged Congress to enact a comprehensive civil rights bill. Late in 1963 the nation's grief over the assassination of John Kennedy, who had become identified with civil rights goals, added political fuel to the drive for federal action.[8] President Johnson gave the civil rights legislation the highest priority. On July 2, 1964, after months of debate, he signed the Civil Rights Act of 1964 into law.

TWO SOCIETIES?   At the close of the 1960s the legal phases of the civil rights movement had about come to a close. But as "things got better," discontent grew. When blacks had been completely subjugated, they had lacked resources to defend themselves. But, as is true of almost all social revolutions, as conditions began to improve, demands became more and more insistent. Millions of impoverished black Americans, like the white Americans who came before them, demonstrated growing impatience with the discrimination that remained. This volatile situation gave way to racial violence and disorders. By 1965, the year of the Watts riots in Los Angeles, it was all too clear that disorders were becoming a part of the American scene. In 1966 and 1967 the disorders increased in scope and intensity; the Detroit riot in July 1967 was the worst such disturbance in modern American history. President Johnson appointed a special Advisory Commission on Civil Disorders to investigate the origins of the disorders and to recommend measures to prevent or contain such disasters in the future.

When the Commission (known as the Kerner Commission after its chairman, then Governor Otto Kerner of Illinois) issued its report, it said in stark,

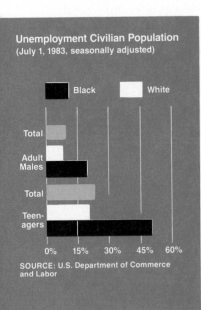

Unemployment Civilian Population
(July 1, 1983, seasonally adjusted)

■ Black   □ White

Total
Adult Males
Total
Teen-agers

0%   15%   30%   45%   60%

SOURCE: U.S. Department of Commerce and Labor

[8]For treatments of John F. Kennedy and civil rights policy, see Carl M. Brauer, *John F. Kennedy and the Second Reconstruction* (Columbia University Press, 1977). See also Joel D. Aberbach and Jack L. Walker, "The Meanings of Black Power," *American Political Science Review* (June 1970), pp. 367–88; and Harris Wofford, *Of Kennedy & Kings: Making Sense of the Sixties* (Farrar, Straus Giroux, 1980).

99

ERA Deadline
passed without
ratification

ERA
reintroduced
in Congress

First Woman
Supreme Court
justice appointed

1990

Martin Luther King, Jr., at the Lincoln Memorial, on August 28, 1963. *UPI.*

"I HAVE A DREAM. . ."

Five score years ago, a great American in whose symbolic shadow we stand, signed the Emancipation Proclamation. This momentous decree came as a great beacon light of hope to millions of Negro slaves who had been seared in the flames of withering injustice. It came as a joyous daybreak to end the long night of captivity.

But one hundred years later, we must face the tragic fact that the Negro is still not free. One hundred years later, the life of the Negro is still sadly crippled by the manacles of segregation and the chains of discrimination. One hundred years later, the Negro lives on a lonely island of poverty in the midst of a vast ocean of material prosperity. One hundred years later, the Negro is still languished in the corners of American society and finds himself an exile in his own land. So we have come here today to dramatize an appalling condition. . . .

. . . in spite of the difficulties and frustrations of the moment I still have a dream. It is a dream deeply rooted in the American dream.

I have a dream that one day this nation will rise up and live out the true meaning of its creed: "We hold these truths to be self-evident; that all men are created equal."

I have a dream that one day on the red hills of Georgia the sons of former slaves and the sons of former slaveowners will be able to sit down together at the table of brotherhood.

I have a dream that one day even the state of Mississippi, a desert state sweltering with the heat of injustice and oppression, will be transformed into an oasis of freedom and justice.

I have a dream that my four little children will one day live in a nation where they will not be judged by the color of their skin but by the content of their character. . . .

Martin Luther King, Jr., August 28, 1963, at the Lincoln Memorial, Washington D.C., speaking to 250,000 persons who participated in a "march for jobs and freedom."

clear language: "What white Americans have never fully understood—but what the Negro can never forget—is that white society is deeply implicated in the ghetto. *White institutions created it, white institutions maintain it, and white society condones it.*" The basic conclusion of the commission was that "our nation is moving toward two societies, one black, one white—separate and unequal" and that "only a commitment to national action on an unprecedented scale" could change this trend.

The commission made sweeping recommendations on jobs, education, housing, and improving the welfare system. But the Vietnam war, the partial calming down of racial tensions, and a growing skepticism about the effectiveness of governmental action have diverted attention from these recommendations, at least temporarily.

Today, legal barriers have been lowered, if not removed, by civil rights legislation, executive orders, and judicial decisions. Blacks can vote, get a

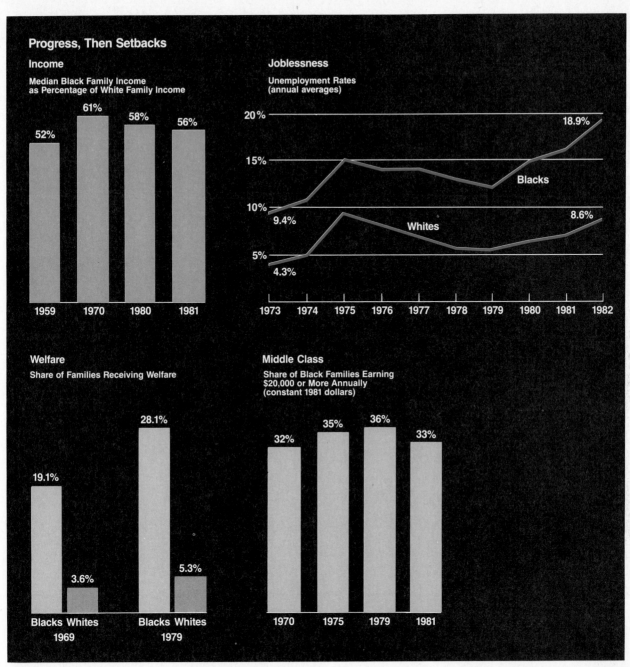

Progress, Then Setbacks

Income

Median Black Family Income as Percentage of White Family Income

- 1959: 52%
- 1970: 61%
- 1980: 58%
- 1981: 56%

Joblessness

Unemployment Rates (annual averages)

Blacks: 9.4% (1973) ... 18.9% (1982)

Whites: 4.3% (1973) ... 8.6% (1982)

1973 1974 1975 1976 1977 1978 1979 1980 1981 1982

Welfare

Share of Families Receiving Welfare

- 1969: Blacks 19.1%, Whites 3.6%
- 1979: Blacks 28.1%, Whites 5.3%

Middle Class

Share of Black Families Earning $20,000 or More Annually (constant 1981 dollars)

- 1970: 32%
- 1975: 35%
- 1979: 36%
- 1981: 33%

From U.S. News & World Report, Inc., © Jan. 31, 1983.

meal where they want, and stay at hotels, and thousands have entered the middle class. Although ways are still found to circumvent or obstruct the force of some civil rights laws, especially those that apply to housing, by and large the actions by governments in the 1960s did open the legal system and provide blacks with equal rights under the laws. Yet, said James Farmer, a civil rights activist: "They were victories largely for the middle class—those who could travel, entertain in restaurants and stay in hotels. Those victories did not change life conditions for the mass of blacks who are still poor."[9] Thirty percent of black families live below the poverty level—cut off from white society and alienated from the black middle class.

[9]James Farmer in Rochelle L. Stanfield, "Black Complaints Haven't Translated into Political Organization and Power," *National Journal*, June 14, 1980, p. 465.

Hispanics

Federico Peña was elected mayor of Denver in 1983—winning a majority of voter support in a city with only 18 percent Hispanics.

Hispanics "are among the world's most complex groupings of human beings. Most . . . are white, millions . . . are mestizos, nearly half a million in the United States are black or mulatto."[10] The largest subgroup are the more than 8 million Mexican Americans, often called Chicanos. A third of them are descended from citizens living in Mexican territory annexed to the United States in 1848. The rest have come to the United States in increasing numbers since 1920. Most live in Arizona, Texas, and California, but many are now in other parts of the nation. They are being joined by millions of "undocumented aliens" who cross our southern borders in search of jobs. The second largest group of Hispanics are the more than 2 million Puerto Ricans who reside on the mainland, primarily in the "barrios" of New York, Chicago, and other northern cities. They retain close ties with Puerto Rico and move back and forth from the island to the mainland. The politics of the Commonwealth of Puerto Rico as it debates whether to retain its special relationship with the United States, become a state, or become an independent nation are of great interest to Puerto Ricans living on the mainland. The third subgroup are about 800,000 persons who fled from Castro's Cuba early in the 1960s, with another wave of Cuban refugees in the 1980s. These Cubans live mainly in and around Miami and include a substantial number of well-educated, successful business people and professionals. The fourth group include a rapidly growing number of refugees from other nations in Central and South America who presently number around 2 million. This number is likely to grow as economic turmoil and political repression in that part of the world increase.

Today Hispanics are our fastest-growing minority: There are 16 million Hispanics in the country today as compared with about 27 million blacks. By the end of this century there could well be more than 40 million Hispanics living in the United States; Martinez is already our second most common surname.[11] We have the fourth largest Spanish-speaking population of any country in this hemisphere. New York is the fifth largest Spanish-speaking city in the world. Hispanic children make up 30 percent of New York's public school population, 58 percent of Los Angeles's, 60 percent of San Antonio's, and 35 percent of Hartford's.

To black power has been added brown power—sometimes as an ally, sometimes as an opponent. Yet not only do many Hispanics lack even the patronizing ties with the white power structure that provided some help for blacks—at least prior to the civil rights movement—but the English language of mainstream America is not their native one. Until recent decades in the

POPULATION PROJECTIONS (millions)			
Year	1980	2000	2020
Black	26.5	36.4	44.4
Hispanic	14.6	30.3	46.6

Source: Census Bureau.

STATE BY STATE
HERE ARE THE NINE
STATES WITH THE MOST
HISPANIC RESIDENTS:

State	1970	1980	Percent of Hispanics in USA
Calif.	2,369,292	4,544,331	31.1
Texas	1,840,648	2,985,824	20.4
N.Y.	1,351,982	1,659,300	11.4
Fla.	405,036	858,158	5.9
Ill.	393,204	635,602	4.4
N.J.	288,488	491,883	3.4
N.M.	308,340	477,222	3.3
Ariz.	264,770	440,701	3.0
Colo.	225,506	339,717	2.3

Source: Census Bureau, 1980.

[10]Valdes Y. Tapia, "Hispanics Need to Unite to End Their Exile at Home," *The Denver Post*, July 19, 1980.

[11]Ibid.

102

Schools must take steps to overcome language difference

Southwest, "no provision whatsoever was made for the education of Mexican-American children. When they were eventually allowed into the schools, they were segregated from Anglo children because of their language handicap. Considered by school authorities to be children of an inferior race, they were often punished for speaking Spanish, heard their names involuntarily Anglicized, and saw their cultural background systematically ignored in textbooks."[12]

Taking their cue from blacks, Hispanics are becoming increasingly active in politics, although they do not yet register or vote in significant numbers as compared to blacks. In Los Angeles County, home of 2 million Hispanics, there is not one Hispanic supervisor or school-board member. While Hispanics total 7 percent of the United States population, there are only six Hispanic members of the House of Representatives. However, things are beginning to change. There are now Hispanic mayors in San Antonio, Denver, Miami, and Tampa; and the number of Hispanics in leadership positions is growing. And increasingly active are the Mexican Legal Defense and Education Fund, the Puerto Rican Legal Defense and Education Fund, and the League of United Latin American Citizens (LULAC).

High on the Hispanic agenda is support for bilingual and bicultural education. In 1974 the Supreme Court in *Lau* v. *Nichols*, a case involving Chinese students in San Francisco, ruled that Title VI of the 1964 Civil Rights Act requires a school district to take steps to open instructional programs and overcome language difficulties whenever it has a substantial number of non-English-speaking students.[13] Many Hispanics actively support these programs, most especially those providing for instruction in Spanish. Not only do such programs assist Hispanic children in gaining an education, but they help preserve their heritage. Hispanics have also worked to amend civil rights laws to protect the rights of language minorities. Clearly, as the political position of Hispanics becomes more important in the years ahead, governments will be even more responsive to their claims.

HOW HISPANICS COMPARE

Here's a look at how whites, blacks, and Hispanics compare in income, age, and births.

Median Family Income	
White	$23,517
Black	13,266
Hispanic	16,401

Median Age	
White	31.5
Black	25
Hispanic	23

Birth Rate	
White	68.1
Black	84
Hispanic	107

(Births per 1,000 women 18–44)

Source: Population Reference Bureau, Census Bureau, 1983.

Native Americans

In 1978, over 2000 Indians paraded past the White House on their way to the Washington Monument. This climaxed a five-month trek, called the "Longest Walk," to protest discrimination. *UPI.*

There were 1,418,195 people who designated themselves as Indians in the 1980 census, of whom 680,000 live on or near a reservation and are enrolled as members of one of the 280 tribes within the continental United States or one of the 200 native Alaskan communities served by the Bureau of Indian Affairs. Indian tribes within the United States are wards of the nation. They are not states; nor are they nations possessed of the full attributes of sovereignty. Rather, they are a separate people with power to regulate their own internal affairs, subject to congressional supervision. Congress has special responsibilities to American Indians, or native Americans as many prefer to be called. Congress's power over the tribes precludes states from regulating or taxing them unless authorized by Congress.

By act of Congress, Indians are American citizens, and by act of the states in which they live, they have the right to vote. Off reservations they have the same rights as any other Americans. If they are enrolled members of a recognized tribe, they are entitled to certain benefits created by law and by treaty. These benefits are administered by the Bureau of Indian Affairs of the Department of the Interior. Moreover, Indians who belong to these federally recognized tribes have preference in employment within the Bureau, a preference the Supreme Court upheld as a grant not to a "discrete racial group, but, rather, as members of quasi-sovereign tribal entities. . . . As long as the special treatment for Indians can be tied rationally to the fulfillment of Congress's

---

[12] Alan Pifer, *Annual Report of the Carnegie Corporation of New York*, 1979, p. 16.
[13] 414 U.S. 563 (1974).

unique obligation toward the Indians, such legislative judgments will not be disturbed."[14]

As a result of the growing militancy of native Americans and a greater national awareness of the concerns of minorities, it has been realized that most Indians live in poverty. Some reservations lack adequate health care facilities, educational opportunities, decent housing, and jobs. Congress has started to compensate native Americans for past injustices and to provide more opportunities for the development of tribal economic independence. Judges are also showing a greater vigilance in the enforcement of Indian treaty rights.

EQUAL PROTECTION UNDER THE LAWS—
WHAT DOES IT MEAN?

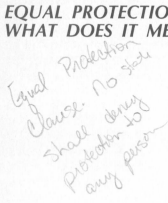

The Fourteenth Amendment declares: "No state [including any subdivision thereof] shall . . . deny to any person within its jurisdiction the equal protection of the laws." Although there is no **Equal Protection clause** limiting the national government, the Fifth Amendment's due process clause has been understood to impose the same restraints on the national government.

The Constitution does not prevent the government from making distinctions among people, for it could not legislate without doing so. What the Constitution forbids is *unreasonable* classifications. In general, a classification is unreasonable when there is no relation between the classes it creates and permissible governmental goals. For example, a law prohibiting redheads from voting would be unreasonable. On the other hand, laws denying to persons under eighteen the right to vote, to marry without the permission of their parents, or a license to drive a car seem to have some rationale (at least to most persons over eighteen).

One of the most troublesome constitutional issues is how to distinguish between a reasonable and an unreasonable classification. The Supreme Court has developed a variety of tests: **rational basis, suspect classifications,** almost-suspect classifications, and fundamental rights.

The Rational Basis Test

The traditional test to determine whether a law complies with the equal protection requirement places the burden of proof on those attacking it. If any facts justify a classification, it will be sustained: "It's enough that the state action be rationally based and free from invidious discrimination. . . . It does not offend the Constitution because the classification is not made with mathematical nicety or because in practice it results in some inequality."[15] For example, it was held that Illinois could exempt individuals from personal property taxes but impose such taxes on corporations.

Usually if the Supreme Court chooses to apply the rationality test, the law in question will be sustained. But occasionally a state law fails to meet even the minimal standards of this test—as when Alaska was told it could not give more from its oil fund surplus revenues to old-time citizens of the state than it gives to newcomers.

The Supreme Court's deference to the judgment of the legislatures in applying the rational basis test does not hold when a law is challenged as vio-

---

[14]*Morton v. Mancari,* 417 U.S. 535 (1974).

[15]*Dandridge v. Williams,* 397 U.S. 471 (1970).

Suspect Classifications

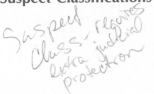

lating the equal protection clause in three situations: when a suspect classification is involved, when an almost-suspect classification is involved, and when a fundamental right is involved.

A suspect class, as outlined in *San Antonio School District* v. *Rodriguez*, is a class historically suffering disabilities, or subjected in the past to purposeful unequal treatment, or relegated by our society to a position of such political powerlessness as to require extraordinary judicial protection.[16]

Race and national origin are suspect classifications. So, too—probably—is religion, although there is no specific Supreme Court decision to this effect, probably because states have seldom classified persons according to religion.

When a law involves a suspect classification, the normal presumption of constitutionality is reversed. It is not sufficient that the law be a reasonable means to handle a particular problem. The Supreme Court must be persuaded both that there is a "compelling public interest" to justify such a classification and that there is no other, less restrictive way to accomplish this compelling public purpose.

AFFIRMATIVE ACTION AND SUSPECT CLASSES   Prior to 1954 when white majorities were using state power to segregate blacks and impose disabilities upon them, civil rights advocates cited with approval the words of the first Justice Harlan dissenting in *Plessy* v. *Ferguson:* "Our Constitution is color-blind and neither knows nor tolerates class among citizens."[17] While the Supreme Court itself seemed to be moving closer to Justice Harlan's view, it nevertheless sustained during World War II a national program forcing persons of Japanese ancestry, including American citizens, to move into what were called "relocation camps," but which were in fact prisons. (In 1983 a national commission characterized these actions as a "grave injustice" motivated by "race prejudice, war hysteria and a failure of political leadership."[18])

By 1954 Justice Harlan's views appeared to have triumphed. In *Brown* v. *Board of Education* (see page 110) the Court called racial classifications "odious to our system" and made it clear that race is a suspect class—probably an outlawed one. The Court has also established that although the Fourteenth Amendment was adopted to protect blacks, its provisions protect other minorities—as well as whites—from racial discrimination. The Court emphasized that the rights protected belong to each and every individual, not to the group to which he or she may belong.

Then in the 1960s came a new series of constitutional debates with some asserting that government neutrality is not enough: If governments and universities and employers merely stop discriminating against blacks, but change nothing else, blacks are still kept from equal participation in American life. They have been so handicapped by past discrimination that in the competition for openings in medical schools, or for skilled jobs, or for their share of government grants, they suffer disabilities not shared by whites.

What if governments, heeding these arguments, adopt, or require private employers and others to adopt, race-conscious remedies—popularly known as affirmative action programs by those who support them and as reverse discrimination by those who oppose them—that provide special help for minorities?

In January, 1983 three Japanese Americans who were jailed during World War II for resisting internment on the West Coast filed charges against the United States seeking damages and the overturn of their 1942 convictions. They claimed that the Army lied about possible security threats. Minour Yasui, Denver (center), said at a press conference, "I remember rattling in a stinking cell in Multnomah County Jail, Portland, Oregon. It could be justified if we can correct the injustices." The three include Fred Korematsu, Oakland, Ca. (1), and Gordon Hirabayashi, Seattle. *UPI.*

[16]411 U.S. 1 (1973).

[17]163 U.S. 537 (1896).

[18]Commission on Wartime Relocation and Internment of Civilians, quoted in *The New York Times*, June 17, 1983, p. 6.

Are these kinds of racial classifications also suspect? Are they unconstitutional? There has been no more hotly debated constitutional issue.[19]

The Supreme Court has faced these questions three times in recent years. Members of the Court are divided—as is the nation—as to whether race is a totally outlawed classification or whether it is one that can properly be taken into account to overcome past discrimination.

These perplexing issues were raised by Alan Bakke in what became one of the more celebrated cases of recent times. Bakke, a white male and a top student at Minnesota and Stanford universities, as well as a Vietnam war veteran, applied in both 1973 and 1974 to the medical school of the University of California at Davis. In each of those years the school admitted one hundred new students, eighty four in a general admissions program and sixteen in a special admissions program created for blacks, Chicanos, Asian Americans, and American Indians—groups who had been totally underrepresented there until the special admissions program was established.

Bakke's application was rejected in each year; but both times students with lower grade-point averages, test scores, and interview ratings were admitted under the special admissions program. After his second rejection Bakke went to the federal courts. He claimed he should be admitted to the school on the grounds that he had been excluded because of his race, contrary to the requirements of the Constitution and of Title VI of the Civil Rights Act of 1964 (see page 112).

In *University of California Regents* v. *Bakke* (1978), the Supreme Court declared unconstitutional the Davis plan.[20] But in an opinion by Justice Powell, which no other member of the Court completely shared, the Court also declared that affirmative action programs are not necessarily unconstitutional. In order to get a diversified student body, a state university may properly take race and ethnic background into account as *one* of several factors in choosing students. (However, the university's goal may not be to redress past misconduct by the society or to ensure that more minority members become doctors.) The problem with the California plan was that it created a category of admissions from which whites were excluded solely because of their race.

Thus, the Supreme Court—by a vote of five to four—resolved this highly charged case so that both Bakke and affirmative action won. Neither advocates nor opponents of affirmative action programs could claim a complete victory or a complete defeat. The debate on the merits and constitutionality of such programs continues.

In *Steelworkers* v. *Weber* (1979) the Court upheld the action of a private employer prompted by federal requirements to adopt a training program in which certain openings were reserved for blacks. *Weber* was debated in terms of the requirements of the Civil Rights Act of 1964 (see page 118) rather than of the Constitution, but the issues were similar to those raised by *Bakke*.[21]

In 1980 the Court came back to the same set of issues in *Fullilove* v. *Klutznick*. By a vote of six to three the Court upheld a provision in the Public Works Act of 1977 requiring that at least 10 percent of federal funds granted to local public works projects be used to procure services or supplies from minority

The Bakke decision aroused strong feeling across the country. *UPI.*

[19]Robert M. O'Neil, *Discrimination against Discrimination* (Indiana University Press, 1975), John C. Livingston, *Fair Game? Inequality and Affirmative Action* (W. H. Freeman, 1979), and Joel Dreyfus and Charles Lawrence, *The Bakke Case* (Harcourt Brace Jovanovich, 1979), in favor of such programs. Nathan Glazer, *Affirmative Discrimination* (Basic Books, 1976), and Alan H. Goldman, *Justice and Reverse Discrimination* (Princeton University Press, 1979), against. See also Allan P. Sindler, *Bakke, DeFunis, and Minority Admissions* (Longman, 1978).

[20]438 U.S. 265 (1978).

[21]443 U.S. 193 (1979).

business enterprises, defined as those owned by United States citizens "who are Negroes, Spanish-speaking, Orientals, Indians, Eskimos, and Aleuts."[22]

Chief Justice Burger and Justice Powell argued in *Fullilove* and *Bakke* that in a remedial context there is no requirement that governments "act in a wholly color-blind fashion." Although remedial programs that establish racial classifications should be subject to strict judicial scrutiny, they would uphold programs that create race-conscious remedies—provided the remedies are closely tailored to accomplish their goals. The judgment of Congress in this regard is to be given more weight than a similar judgment by a state legislature or state university. Congress is a coequal branch of the federal government and by the Fourteenth Amendment is granted the power "by appropriate legislation to enforce the provisions of this article."

Justices Marshall, Brennan, and Blackmun go even further. (They would have upheld the constitutionality of admissions programs by universities and colleges that set aside certain spaces for members of minorities.) These justices contend that although racial classifications designed for remedial purposes should be subject to a more rigorous review than the rational basis standard, such remedial uses of race should *not* be required to meet the strict scrutiny test of a compelling public need. They also distinguish classifications that create a preference for blacks and other minorities from those that create preferences for whites. The former are permissible some of the time; the latter are forbidden most, if not all, of the time. Whites, unlike blacks and other minorities, do not have the "traditional indicia" of a suspect class. They have not been systematically subjected to discrimination because of race or deliberately put into positions of political powerlessness.

In his *Bakke* opinion Justice Marshall, after stressing the fact that the very purpose of the Fourteenth Amendment was to protect blacks, wrote: "While I applaud the judgment of the Court that a university may consider race in its admissions process, it is more than a little ironic that, after several hundred years of race-based discrimination against Negroes, the Court is unwilling to hold that a race-based remedy for the discrimination is permissible." Justice Blackmun was somewhat less enthusiastic: "I yield to no one in my earnest hope that the time will come when an 'affirmative action' program is unnecessary and is, in truth, only a relic of the past. . . . [But] in order to get beyond racism, we must first take account of race. There is no other way."

THE CURRENT POSITION   Where do these Supreme Court decisions leave us with respect to race? The Court still firmly adheres "to the traditional view that racial classifications that stigmatize—because they are drawn on the presumption that one race is inferior to another or because they put the weight of government behind racial hatred and separatism"—are not only suspect, but outlawed.[23] A majority still adhere to the view that all practices and all programs that classify people by race or ethnic origin are suspect and should be subject to strict judicial scrutiny. However, where a race-conscious remedy is carefully created to help minorities overcome present effects of past discrimination, it may be constitutionally permissible, especially if the remedy has been adopted by Congress.

**Almost-suspect
Classifications:
Illegitimacy and Sex**

Some have argued that laws imposing disabilities on illegitimate children should be subject to the same severe tests as laws based on race. The Supreme Court has been unwilling to go that far. But in view of the long history of treating illegitimate children less favorably than legitimate ones, the Court has

SOME RECENT GOVERNMENTAL ACTIONS DECLARED UNCONSTITUTIONAL BY THE SUPREME COURT BECAUSE OF SEX DISCRIMINATION*

Provisions of social security laws providing benefits to families with unemployed fathers but not unemployed mothers

A state law giving sons child support from their fathers until they are twenty-one, but daughters only until they are eighteen

A state law prohibiting the sale of beer to males under twenty-one, but to females under eighteen

A state law providing that husbands, but not wives, may be required to pay alimony

A state law excluding males from enrolling in a professional nursing program, designed for women, offered by a public university

*The Constitution protects men as well as women from discrimination because of sex.

[22]448 U.S. 448 (1980).
[23]Justice Marshall in *Fullilove* v. *Klutznick*.

subjected laws dealing with illegitimate children to a level of scrutiny only slightly less exacting than those applied to suspect classifications such as race.

What of classifications based on sex? Not until 1971 was any classification based on sex declared unconstitutional. Prior to that time many laws that purported to provide special protection for women—such as one in Ohio forbidding any woman other than the wife or daughter of a tavern owner to serve as barmaid—were upheld. As Justice Brennan wrote for the Court in 1973: "There can be no doubt that our nation has had a long and unfortunate history of sex discrimination. Traditionally such discrimination was rationalized by an attitude of 'romantic paternalism' which, in practical effect put women, not on a pedestal, but in a cage."[24]

The majority view is that sex classifications, although not as suspect as those based on race, are subject to stricter testing than those relating to economic regulation. To sustain a classification based on sex, the burden is on the government to show that it serves "important governmental objectives" and is substantially related to these objectives. Treating women differently from men (or vice versa) is forbidden when supported by no more substantial justification than "archaic and overbroad generalizations," "old notions," and "the role-typing society has long imposed upon women."[25] And if the government's objective is "to protect members of one sex because they are presumed to suffer from an inherent handicap or to be innately inferior," that object itself is illegitimate.[26]

In recent years the Supreme Court has struck down almost every law brought before it alleged to discriminate against women. It has also sustained some said to discriminate against men. An Equal Rights Amendment would make sex classifications imposed by or sanctioned by governments totally unacceptable. Under the Equal Protection clause, classifications based on sex, although not suspect, require considerable justification before the Court will sustain them.

SOME RECENT GOVERNMENTAL ACTIONS ALLEGED TO BE UNCONSTITUTIONAL DISCRIMINATIONS AGAINST PERSONS BECAUSE OF SEX, BUT SUSTAINED BY THE SUPREME COURT

A state law granting a property tax exemption to widows but not to widowers

A naval regulation giving women thirteen years to be promoted or discharged, but giving male officers only nine years

A provision giving larger social security retirement benefits to women than to men

A federal law requiring registration for a possible draft for males but not for females

---

Is Poverty a Suspect Classification?

The Supreme Court has repeatedly been pressed to treat poverty as a suspect class, but it "has never held that financial need alone identifies a suspect class for purposes of equal protection analysis."[27] Thus, a state may rely on property taxes for funds for schools even if this means that those in "rich" districts attend schools where more is spent per pupil than those in poor districts. One of the more controversial recent cases had to do with the so-called Hyde Amendment to the Medicaid program, which Congress has adopted every year since 1976. Medicaid is a joint national-state program that reimburses the poor for certain medical costs. The Hyde Amendment, in the form considered by the Court, prohibited the use of any federal funds to pay for abortions except when the life of the mother would be endangered or for victims of rape or incest. As a result, poor women could get reimbursed for the costs of having children, but not for abortions, except in limited circumstances. In *Maher* v. *Roe* the Court ruled (by a vote of five to four) that since poverty is not a suspect classification, the appropriate constitutional test is whether the legislation is rationally related to a legitimate governmental objective. The majority concluded that the congressional provision bears a rational relationship to the government's legitimate interest in protecting the fetus.[28]

---

[24]*Frontiero* v. *Richardson*, 411 U.S. 677 (1973).
[25]*Califano* v. *Webster*, 430 U.S. 313 (1977).
[26]*Mississippi University of Women* v. *Hogan*, 458 U.S. 718 (1982).
[27]*San Antonio School District* v. *Rodriguez*, 411 U.S. 1 (1973).
[28]*Maher* v. *Roe* 432 U.S. 464 (1977).

Fundamental Rights   The Supreme Court subjects state regulations to especially close scrutiny when laws impinge on "fundamental rights." However, the justices are not too clear as to what makes a right fundamental. Justice Powell, in *San Antonio School District* v. *Rodriguez* (1973), explained that it is not the social importance of the right nor the justices' conclusions about the significance of the right that determines whether or not it is fundamental, but whether it *is explicitly or implicitly guaranteed by the Constitution*. Under this test the right to travel has been held to be fundamental, along with the right to vote and First Amendment rights such as the right to associate for the advancement of political beliefs. However, the rights to an education, or to housing or welfare benefits, or to have an abortion have not been held to be fundamental. Important as many feel these rights to be, they are not guaranteed by the Constitution. Nor are there any specific constitutional provisions protecting these rights from governmental regulation.

PROVING DISCRIMINATION

How can discrimination be proved? Does the fact that a law or a regulation has a differential impact on persons of different races by itself establish that it is unconstitutional? In one of its more important decisions of recent years, *Washington* v. *Davis* (1976), the Supreme Court stated: "The invidious quality of a law claimed to be racially discriminatory must ultimately be traced to a racially discriminatory *purpose*."[29] Or as the Court said in a later case: "The Fourteenth Amendment guarantees equal laws, not equal results."[30]

What does this mean in practical terms? It means city ordinances that permit only single-family residences and thus make low-cost housing projects impossible are not unconstitutional—even if their effect is to keep minorities from moving into a city—unless it can be shown that they were adopted with the intent to discriminate against minorities. It means also that a preference for veterans in public employment does not violate the equal protection clause, even though its effect is to keep many women from getting jobs: The distinction between veterans and nonveterans was not adopted deliberately to create a sex barrier.

Still, the fact that a law or governmental practice has a differential impact is not irrelevant. In a community where there are a large number of blacks or Hispanics, it would be considered suspicious if only a few of them were called for jury duty. Under such circumstances the burden of proof shifts to the state or city to demonstrate that it has not engaged in unconstitutional discriminatory conduct. Similarly, if a community with a past history of discrimination against black voters adopts new regulations which reduce the number of blacks eligible to vote, the burden of proof shifts to the state or city to demonstrate that it is not willfully discriminating.

It must also be understood that what is constitutional can be made illegal. (Things that are unconstitutional are always illegal, but that which is illegal may not always be unconstitutional.) Congress has by law made illegal, in many circumstances, the use of tests unrelated to job performance, if in fact such tests screen out members of one race or sex to a greater extent than another, regardless of the motives of the employers (see page 118).

"Treat people as equals and the first thing you know they believe they are." *Drawing by Mulligan;* © *1982. The New Yorker Magazine, Inc.*

[29]*Washington v. Davis*, 426 U.S. 229 (1976).
[30]*Personnel Administrator of Massachusetts v. Feeney*, 442 U.S. 256 (1979).

THE LIFE AND DEATH OF JIM CROW

Jim Crow
Laws -
Segregation

Laws requiring that blacks be segregated into separate public facilities date only from the end of the nineteenth century.[31] Prior to that time it was social custom and economic conditions, rather than law, that kept the two races apart. But by the end of that century, segregationists were urging the adoption of laws to make it a crime for members of the white and black races to use the same public facilities. Before long, southern states and cities had made it illegal for whites and blacks to ride in the same car on a train, attend the same theater, go to the same school, be born in the same hospital, or be buried in the same cemetery. Jim Crow laws, as they came to be called, soon blanketed southern life. How could these laws stand in the face of the equal protection clause?

Is Segregation Discrimination? *Plessy* v. *Ferguson*

In 1896 the Supreme Court, in *Plessy* v. *Ferguson*, endorsed the view that racial segregation did not constitute discrimination if equal accommodations were provided for the members of both races.[32] Even equal accommodations were not required except for public facilities and for a limited category of public utilities, such as trains and buses. Under this separate-but-equal formula, southern states, and some places in the North, enforced segregation in transportation, places of public accommodation, educational facilities, swimming pools, and parks. Although the *Plessy* decision required equality as the price for compulsory segregation, the "equal" part of the formula was meaningless. States segregated blacks into unequal facilities, and blacks lacked the political power to protest.

The passage of time did not lessen the inequality. In 1950, in all the segregated states, there were fourteen medical schools for whites, none for blacks; sixteen law schools for whites, five for blacks; fifteen engineering schools for whites, none for blacks; five dentistry schools for whites, none for blacks. Beginning in the late 1930s blacks started to file lawsuits challenging the doctrine. They cited facts to show that in practice, separate-but-equal always resulted in discrimination against blacks. However, the Supreme Court was not yet willing to upset the doctrine directly. Rather, it began to undermine it. The Court scrutinized each situation and in case after case ordered facilities to be equalized.

The 101st Division protecting students in Little Rock Central High after a Court Order to integrate in 1957. *UPI.*

The End of Separate but Equal: *Brown* v. *Board of Education*

Finally, in the spring of 1954, in *Brown* v. *Board of Education*, the Supreme Court reversed its 1896 holding as applied to public schools. It ruled "separate but equal" is a contradiction in terms. Segregation is itself discrimination.[33] A year later the Court ordered school boards to proceed with "all deliberate speed to desegregate public schools at the earliest practical date."[34]

In the years following the *Brown* decision, federal judges struck down a whole battery of schemes designed to evade the Court's ruling. Beginning in 1963 the Supreme Court gradually reversed its second Brown decision granting

Tuskegee Institute—a distinguished school then and now. *Library of Congress.*

[31]C. Vann Woodward, *The Strange Career of Jim Crow* (Oxford University Press, 1968).

[32]163 U.S. 537.

[33]347 U.S. 483 (1954). See also J. W. Peltason, *Fifty-eight Lonely Men: Southern Federal Judges and School Desegregation* (University of Illinois Press, 1971), p. 248.

[34]*Brown* v. *Board of Education*, 349 U.S. 294 (1955). For a comprehensive history of the events leading up to *Brown* v. *Board of Education*, see Richard Kluger, *Simple Justice* (Knopf, 1976). Earl Black, *Southern Governors and Civil Rights: Racial Segregation as a Campaign Issue in the Second Reconstruction* (Harvard University Press, 1977), shows response, reaction, and eventually neutralization of race as a political issue following the *Brown* decision.

separate but equal contradictory

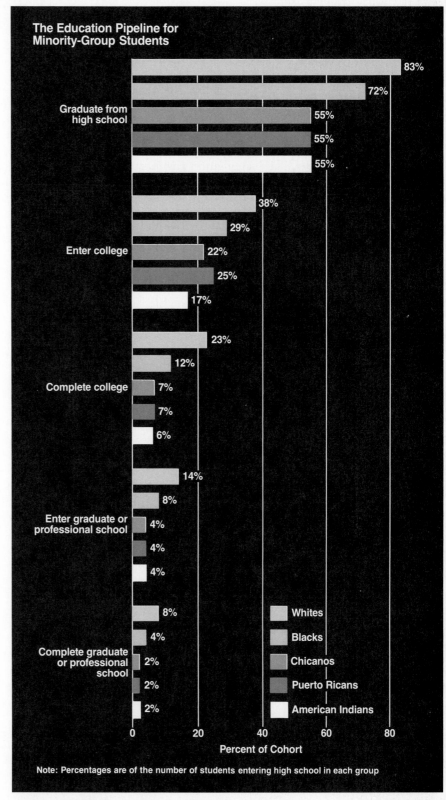

The Education Pipeline for Minority-Group Students

Graduate from high school
- 83%
- 72%
- 55%
- 55%
- 55%

Enter college
- 38%
- 29%
- 22%
- 25%
- 17%

Complete college
- 23%
- 12%
- 7%
- 7%
- 6%

Enter graduate or professional school
- 14%
- 8%
- 4%
- 4%
- 4%

Complete graduate or professional school
- 8%
- 4%
- 2%
- 2%
- 2%

Percent of Cohort

Whites
Blacks
Chicanos
Puerto Ricans
American Indians

Note: Percentages are of the number of students entering high school in each group

SOURCE: "Colleges Urged to Alter Tests, Grading for Benefit of Minority-Group Students," *Chronicle of High Education,* February 3, 1982, p. 11.

Minnie Jean Brown, one of the precipitators of the segregation battle in Little Rock, Arkansas. *UPI.*

Busing and Federal Courts

school districts time to prepare for desegregation. In 1969 the Court completed that reversal, stating: "Continued operation of racially segregated schools under the standard of 'all deliberate speed' is no longer constitutionally permissible. School districts must immediately terminate dual school systems based on race and operate only unitary school systems."[35]

Congress and the president increased their involvement in the battle against school segregation. Title VI of the Civil Rights Act stipulates that federal dollars—of major importance since the passage of the Elementary and Secondary Education Act of 1965—must be withdrawn from any school or institution of higher education that discriminates "on the ground of race, color, or national origin in any program or activity receiving federal financial assistance."[36] (The Education Act of 1972 adds sex to this list; other acts have added the handicapped, the aged, Vietnam veterans, and disabled veterans.) Title VI also imposes on schools a responsibility for taking affirmative action to ensure that persons in the protected categories are not denied access to any federally supported program or activity.

Half of all American students are bused to schools. Of these, less than 7 percent are bused to achieve school desegregation. Nonetheless, busing is one of the most hotly debated questions of our time.[37] If Congress reflects popular opinion, most people oppose busing to implement desegregation plans. Almost every year Congress adopts antibusing provisions. Moreover, the Reagan Administration has been more reluctant than its predecessors to pressure school districts to bus pupils in order to achieve desegregation.

The Supreme Court, however, has endorsed busing as one of the tools a federal judge may use to remedy the consequences of officially sanctioned— that is, de jure, or by law—segregation. On the other hand, it has refused to permit busing to overcome the effects of de facto segregation. In other words, if a judge finds that authorities have operated segregated schools in the past or by systematic and purposeful actions have caused segregation, he or she may order a school district to bus pupils. But judges may not order busing to overcome racial imbalances in schools not caused by official actions.[38]

The Court's decision in *Swann* v. *Charlotte-Macklenburg Board of Education* (1971) means that federal judges can act vigorously to integregate schools in those areas that prior to 1954 operated dual school systems, or outside those areas where the judges find official misconduct. Judges may also order other actions, such as remedial courses for black students, to help overcome the consequences of past official discrimination. Where schools are segregated only because of residential patterns, the authority of federal judges is much more limited.

In large metropolitan areas—partly as the result of white flight to the suburbs and private schools to escape court-ordered busing—many school districts in central cities are predominantly black. Where most of the students in a city are black, it is difficult to integrate schools by judicial decree, for the Supreme Court held in the first *Milliken* case that judges may not order cross-district busing unless it can be established that school district lines were drawn for the purpose of maintaining segregation, and that the suburban districts are also

An anti-busing demonstration in Cleveland, Ohio, 1979. *UPI.*

[35]*Alexander* v. *Board of Education*, 396 U.S. 19 (1969).

[36]Gary Orfield, *The Reconstruction of Southern Education: The Schools and the 1964 Civil Rights Act* (Wiley, 1969), p. 355.

[37]K. Arrington, *With All Deliberate Speed: 1954–19??* (U.S. Commission on Civil Rights, 1981); Gary Orfield, *Must We Bus? Segregated Schools and National Policy* (Brookings Institution, 1979); James Bolner and Robert Shenley, *Busing: The Political and Judicial Process* (Praeger, 1974).

[38]*Swann* v. *Charlotte-Macklenburg Board of Education*, 402 U.S. 1 (1971).

being operated in a discriminatory fashion. Justice Marshall, who dissented from this restrictive view of the power of federal judges to order cross-district busing, commented: "Unless our children begin to learn together, there is little hope that our people will ever learn to live together."[39]

BARRIERS TO VOTING

States determine suffrage qualifications for all elections, but they do so subject to a variety of constitutional restraints. Article I, Section 4, gives Congress the power to supersede state regulations as to the "times, places, and manner" of elections for federal officers—that is, for members of the House of Representatives, senators, and presidential electors. Congress has used this authority to set age qualifications and residency requirements to vote for presidential electors, a uniform day for all states to hold elections for members of Congress and presidential electors, and to give American citizens who reside outside the United States the right to vote for members of Congress and presidential electors in the state in which they previously lived.

The major limitations on the state's power to set suffrage qualifications, however, are contained in the Fourteenth and Fifteenth amendments (forbidding unreasonable qualifications and those based on race), the Nineteenth Amendment (forbidding qualifications based on sex), and the Twenty-sixth Amendment (forbidding states to deny citizens eighteen years of age or older the right to vote on account of age). These amendments also empower Congress to enact the laws necessary to enforce their provisions.

Getting Around the Fourteenth and Fifteenth Amendments

Despite fierce opposition to the Nineteenth Amendment, after its ratification there was no organized resistance to allowing all women in the North and *white* women in the South to exercise the rights secured for them. Not so in the case of the Fourteenth and Fifteenth amendments.

Right after the adoption of these two amendments, blacks were allowed to participate in the political life of the southern states only because the federal government insisted upon it. Until 1877 federal troops were stationed in the South. But as soon as southern Democrats regained control of state governments, they set out to keep blacks from voting. They used social pressure and threats of violence, and they organized secret societies like the Ku Klux Klan that engaged in terrorist activities such as threats, midnight shootings, burnings, and whippings. These measures "worked." But toward the end of the nineteenth century, for the first time since the Civil War, there were two strong political parties—the Democrats and the Populists—in many parts of the South. White supremacists were fearful that the parties might compete for the black vote and that the blacks might come to hold the balance of power. White supremacists also feared that the continued use of excessive force and fraud to disenfranchise blacks might cause the president and Congress to intervene.

Southern leaders reasoned that if they could pass laws that deprived blacks of the vote on grounds other than race, blacks would find it difficult to challenge the laws in the courts. Some whites protested that laws could be used against whites as well as blacks. But keeping poor whites from voting did not disturb the conservative leaders of the Democratic party, for they were often just as anxious to undermine white support for the Populist party as they were

U.S. Senator John Glenn campaigning with Harold Washington of Chicago. *Jacques M. Chenet/Newsweek.*

[39]*Milliken* v. *Bradley*, 418 U.S. 717 (1974). See also David L. Kirp, *Just Schools: The Idea of Racial Equality in American Education* (University of California Press, 1982); and Jeffrey A. Raffel, *The Politics of School Desegregation: The Metropolitan Remedy in Delaware* (Temple University Press, 1980).

to disenfranchise blacks: "The disenfranchisement movement of the 'nineties' gave the Southern states the most impressive system of obstacles between the voter and the ballot box known to the democratic world."[40]

In the 1940s the Supreme Court began to strike down one after another of the devices used to keep blacks from voting. In 1944 *(Smith* v. *Allwright)* the Court declared the "white primary" unconstitutional.[41] In 1960 it held that racial gerrymandering was contrary to the Fifteenth Amendment. The Twenty-fourth Amendment got rid of the poll tax in federal elections, and in 1966 the Court held that the Fourteenth Amendment forbade the tax as a condition in any election.

Those wishing to deny blacks the right to vote were forced to rely on registration requirements. On the surface these requirements appeared to be perfectly proper: It was the way they were administered that kept blacks from the polls. They were often applied by white election officers while white police stood guard, with white judges hearing appeals from decisions of registration officials. These officials often seized on the smallest error in an application blank as an excuse to disqualify a voter. In one parish in the state of Louisiana, after four white voters filed affidavits in which they challenged the legality of the registration of black voters on the grounds that these voters had made an "error in spilling" [sic] in their applications, registration officials struck 1300 out of approximately 1500 black voters from the polls.[42] In many southern areas literacy tests were administered by registration officials to discriminate against blacks. Some states, either as an additional requirement or as a substitute, required applicants to demonstrate to the satisfaction of election officials that they understood the national and state constitutions and, further, that they were persons of good character. Whites were often asked simple questions; blacks were asked questions that would baffle a Supreme Court justice. In Louisiana 49,603 illiterate white voters were able to persuade election officials they could understand the Constitution, but only two illiterate black voters were able to do so.

Ku Klux Klansmen salute their burning flag in a field near Greensboro, North Carolina. *UPI.*

Action by the National Government

For over twenty years federal courts, under the leadership of the Supreme Court, carefully scrutinized voting laws and procedures in cases brought before them. But this approach did not open the voting booth to blacks, especially those living in rural areas of the Deep South. Finally Congress began to act. At first the major responsibility was left with the courts: Civil rights statutes protecting the right to vote were strengthened. The Civil Rights Act of 1964 had hardly been enacted when events in Selma, Alabama, dramatized the inadequacy of depending on the courts to prevent racial barriers in polling places. A voter registration drive in that city led by Martin Luther King, Jr., produced arrests, marches on the state capitol, and the murder of two civil rights workers. But there was no major dent in the color bar at the polls. President Johnson, responding to events in Selma, made a dramatic address to the nation and to Congress calling for federal action to ensure that no person would be deprived of the right to vote in any election for any office because of color or race. Congress responded with the Voting Rights Act of 1965.[43]

Blacks—the newest power in Deep South politics—flock to the polls in Peachtree, Alabama. *UPI.*

[40]V. O. Key, Jr., *Southern Politics* (Knopf, 1949), p. 555. For a history of the rise and fall of black disenfranchisement, see Steven F. Lawson, *Black Ballots: Voting Rights in the South, 1944–1969* (Columbia University Press, 1976).

[41]321 U.S. 649 (1944).

[42]*Report of the United States Commission on Civil Rights* (Government Printing Office, 1959), pp. 103–104.

[43]David J. Garrow, *Protest at Selma: Martin Luther King and the Voting Rights Act of 1965* (Yale University Press, 1978).

HISPANIC BALLOT POWER

In States	Hispanic Share of Voting-Age Population
New Mexico	33.1%
Texas	17.7
California	16.1
Arizona	13.3
Colorado	9.8
Florida	8.5
New York	8.3
Hawaii	6.0
Nevada	5.8
New Jersey	5.7

Source: U.S. Dept. of Commerce.

BLACK BALLOT POWER

In States	Black Share of Voting-Age Population
Mississippi	31.0%
South Carolina	27.3
Louisiana	26.6
Georgia	24.3
Alabama	22.9
Maryland	20.8
North Carolina	20.3
Virginia	17.5
Delaware	14.2
Tennessee	14.2
U. S. Average	10.5

In Cities	
Washington, D.C.	65.8%
Atlanta	60.6
Detroit	58.3
Newark	55.1
Birmingham	50.6
Baltimore	50.4
New Orleans	48.9
Oakland	42.5
Memphis	42.0
Cleveland	41.1

Source: U.S. Dept. of Commerce, 1980.

THE VOTING RIGHTS ACT OF 1965 The adoption of this act—almost a century after the Fifteenth Amendment was ratified—finally made it possible for blacks to register and to vote in every district in the United States.

The act, whose constitutionality was upheld in *South Carolina* v. *Katzenbach*,[44] has been three times extended and strengthened by Congress—once in 1970, again in 1975, and most recently in 1982. This piece of legislation marks a major departure from earlier civil rights acts. Instead of depending solely on lawsuits brought by private citizens whose rights have been abridged, and on local officials to carry out their duties, the Voting Rights Act of 1965 authorizes direct action by federal officials to register voters, to see that they are allowed to vote, and to ensure that their ballots are honestly counted. It was unnecessary in most areas to appoint examiners, since the mere threat of sending them was enough in most instances. Nonetheless, as late as 1983 federal observers were still being sent into some places.

The act concentrates on states and political subdivisions, mostly but not exclusively in the South, with a long history of discrimination against blacks. It also covers areas that contain more than 10 percent of voting-age citizens belonging to language minorities—persons of Spanish heritage, Asian Americans, American Indians, and Alaskan natives.

As a result of the act, literacy tests are, in effect, set aside *everywhere*. In areas covered by the law, except those that are included only because of the presence of language minorities, the attorney general may call upon the Office of Personnel Management to appoint federal examiners to observe elections and if necessary to themselves register voters. If local election officials turn away any voter federal examiners find entitled to vote, the examiners may secure an order from a federal district court impounding all ballots until all persons entitled to vote are allowed to do so. The attorney general may also appoint poll watchers to ensure that the votes of all qualified persons are properly counted. In areas covered because of the presence of language minorities, bilingual election materials must be provided.

The act contains some unusual—and controversial—provisions designed to keep states from minimizing the effect of the voting power of blacks. No state or political subdivision covered by the act may make any change in its voting practices or laws, such as reapportioning a legislative body or changing from single-member districts to a multimember at-large election system—or even altering its boundaries—without prior clearance from the attorney general or from the United States District Court for the District of Columbia. (Note: Approval of the local federal district judge will not do. Congress did not want to entrust this responsibility to anyone who might be subject to local political pressures— even a federal judge.) A voting district may "bail out" from the prior clearance requirements for electoral changes if it proves to the District Court of the District of Columbia that it has had a clean voting rights record for the preceding ten years. Basically, the act forbids governments, subject to its provisions, from adopting or even maintaining procedures, *regardless of intent*, if such procedures result in the dilution of black voting power.

The Voting Rights Act does not guarantee, as Congress made clear, that "members of a protected class" have a "right to have members . . . elected in numbers equal to their proportion in the population." However, where blacks make up a substantial proportion of the population, the fact that few or none of them get elected because of some practice or procedure is part of the "totality of circumstances" judges may take into account to determine if there has been a violation of the act. These facts are also to be considered by the attorney

---

[44]383 U.S. 301 (1966).

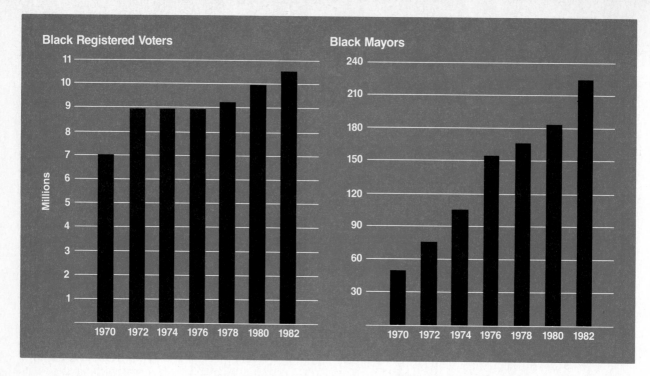

Black Registered Voters

Millions

11
10
9
8
7
6
5
4
3
2
1

1970 1972 1974 1976 1978 1980 1982

Black Mayors

240
210
180
150
120
90
60
30

1970 1972 1974 1976 1978 1980 1982

general in determining whether to allow any change in electoral practices or procedures.

The Voting Rights Act of 1965 has been effective. While blacks still do not use their voting power to the same extent as do whites, millions now participate in our political life. More than 5000 blacks hold national, state, or local office.[45] Although many of these offices are relatively minor, there are over 220 black mayors. In fact, the mayors of such key cities as Atlanta, Birmingham, Chicago, Detroit, Los Angeles, New Orleans, Philadelphia, and Washington, D.C., are black. There are blacks in all southern legislatures, and there are more blacks in the U.S. House of Representatives than at any time since Reconstruction.

The black vote is especially important where the political situation is not polarized around race—that is, where race is not so important that all whites vote only for white candidates and all blacks vote only for blacks. Except in areas where black voters outnumber whites, black voting power is likely to have its largest political impact where black votes can provide the margin of victory. As long as candidates believe they have a chance of getting enough black votes to win, or of keeping their opponent from getting enough votes to win, they will find it politically profitable to acknowledge the aspirations of black constituents.

BARRIERS TO PUBLIC ACCOMMODATIONS, JOBS, AND HOMES

An often overlooked point is that the Fourteenth Amendment applies only to *governmental* action, not to private discriminatory conduct. Moreover, our Constitution creates "a zone of privacy which precludes government from interfering with private clubs or groups. The associational rights which our system honors permit all-white, all-black, all-brown, and all-yellow clubs to be estab-

[45]Leonard A. Cole, *Blacks in Power: A Comparative Study of Black and White Elected Officials* (Princeton University Press, 1976).

lished. They also permit all-Catholic, all-Jewish, or all-agnostic clubs. . . . Government may not tell a man or a woman who his or her associates must be. The individual may be as selective as he desires."[46]

Does this mean the individual has a constitutional right to discriminate? No. "The Constitution places no value on discrimination," and it has never "been accorded affirmative constitutional protection."[47] Persons can be as prejudiced as they wish and dislike whomever they want: The government cannot regulate what people think or believe. But when individuals act outside their own homes, clubs, or close social circles and offer goods and services to the general public, they have no constitutional protection for discriminatory *conduct*. The power of state and local governments to act appropriately against discriminatory conduct has not been seriously questioned. Most states now ban racial, religious, national origin, or sex discrimination, most commonly in employment, places of public recreation and accommodation, housing, and education.

The proponents of the Fourteenth Amendment over a hundred years ago hoped it would authorize federal action against nongovernmental discrimination. But when in 1875 Congress made it a federal offense for any operator of a public conveyance, hotel, or theater to deny accommodations to any person because of race or color, the Supreme Court in the *Civil Rights Cases* invalidated this law on the ground that the Fourteenth Amendment does not give Congress authority to legislate against discrimination by private individuals.[48] What about the Thirteenth Amendment? Unlike the Fourteenth, it applies to private as well as governmental action. It empowers Congress to pass laws to prevent slavery or involuntary servitude. For a hundred years some people, including the first Justice Harlan, argued that the Thirteenth Amendment gives Congress authority to legislate against all the badges of slavery—that is, against racial discrimination in all its forms, regardless of source. But the Supreme Court interpreted the Thirteenth Amendment so narrowly that slavery meant only physical compulsion or peonage (a condition of compulsory servitude based on indebtedness of the worker to the employer).

Then, in *Jones* v. *Mayer Co.*, Justice Stewart—speaking for a seven-man majority—adopted the view of the first Justice Harlan (his grandson, the second Justice Harlan, dissented). The immediate question before the Court was the meaning and constitutionality of the Civil Rights Act of 1866 relating to the purchase of property. Justice Stewart stated that the Thirteenth Amendment became part of the Constitution so that Congress could have the power to remove the "badges of slavery" from the nation. "When racial discrimination," he wrote, "herds men into ghettos and makes their ability to buy property turn on the color of their skin, then it too is a relic of slavery. . . . At the very least, the freedom that Congress is empowered to secure under the Thirteenth Amendment includes the freedom to buy whatever a white man can buy, the right to live wherever a white man can live. If Congress cannot say that being a free man means at least this much, then the Thirteenth Amendment made a promise that the Nation cannot keep."[49]

The Supreme Court has extended *Jones* v. *Mayer*: It has ruled that the language of the Civil Rights Act of 1866 prohibiting racial discrimination in the making of contracts prevents employers from discriminating against employees because of race and prevents discrimination by private schools that open their doors to any child meeting the minimum qualifications. Congress clearly

[46]Justice Douglas dissenting in *Moose Lodge No. 107* v. *Irvis*, 407 U.S. 163 (1972).
[47]*Norwood* v. *Harrison*, 413 U.S. 455 (1973).
[48]*The Civil Rights Cases*, 109 U.S. 3 (1883).
[49]393 U.S. 409 (1968).

has the power under the Thirteenth Amendment to pass whatever legislation it thinks necessary to protect persons against disabilities imposed upon them because of race, whether the disabilities are imposed by private or state action.

The Thirteenth Amendment (and the Fourteenth) are not the only sources of national power to legislate against discrimination. The government may use, and has used, the power to tax and spend to prevent not merely racial discrimination but discrimination based on ethnic origin, sex, disability, and age. It may also use the power to regulate interstate commerce to do so, as it did in the most important and sweeping Civil Rights Act—that of 1964.

The Civil Rights Act of 1964, Title II: Places of Public Accommodation

Can not segregate

For the first time since Reconstruction, Congress authorized the massive use of federal authority to combat privately imposed racial discrimination. Title II forbids discrimination in places of accommodation and makes it a federal offense to discriminate against any customer or patron because of race, color, religion, or national origin. It applies to any inn, hotel, motel, or lodging establishment (except establishments with fewer than five rooms and occupied by the proprietor—in other words, small boardinghouses); to any restaurant or gasoline station that serves interstate travelers or serves food or products of which a substantial portion have moved in interstate commerce; and to any motion picture house, theater, concert hall, sports arena, or other place of entertainment that customarily presents films, performances, athletic teams, or other sources of entertainment that are moved in interstate commerce.

Title II has been vigorously enforced. Blacks organized programs to test it; the Department of Justice filed more than four hundred lawsuits; and within a few months after its adoption, the Supreme Court (*Heart of Atlanta Motel* v. *United States*) unanimously sustained its constitutionality.[50] As a result, most establishments, including those in the South, opened their doors to all customers.

The Civil Rights Act of 1964, Title VII: Employment

Can not deny employment because of color

The Constitution forbids *governments* to deny persons employment because of race, color, religion, or sex. In addition, under Title VII of the Civil Rights Act, Congress has now made it illegal for any employer or trade union in any industry that affects interstate commerce and employs fifteen or more people—and since 1972 any state or local agency such as a school or university—to discriminate in employment practices against any person because of race, color, national origin, religion, or sex. Other legislation makes it illegal to engage in these activities against those with physical handicaps, veterans, or persons between the ages of forty and seventy (see the Age Discrimination in Employment Act, page 121).

There are a few exceptions. Religious institutions such as parochial schools may use religious standards. Further, age, sex, or handicap may be considered where there are bona fide occupational qualifications necessary to the normal operation of a particular business or enterprise. The bona fide occupational qualification exception has been construed narrowly. Airlines may not specify that one must be a female or unmarried to serve as a flight attendant. Also, minimum height and weight requirements for prison guards are not permissible, although a state was allowed to deny women the right to serve as guards in a maximum security prison for males. States have also been allowed to compel the retirement of state police officers prior to age seventy.

Recent problems involve the use of employment practices such as employment tests or prior experience requirements that work to the disadvantage of blacks, Hispanics, women, and other protected groups. Title VII goes beyond constitutional standards. It forbids tests or practices, even if neutral on their face and adopted without intent to discriminate, that have a greater negative effect on persons of one race or sex. The only exceptions are for practices

"Thanks for coming in. It's such a relief to be able to deny someone a loan when there's no possibility of being charged with sex, race, age, or ethnic bias." *Drawing by Ed Fisher; © 1976 The New Yorker Magazine, Inc.*

[50]379 U.S. 421 (1964).

YOU DECIDE !

In 1970 New Springfield, a city of 200,000—of whom 40 percent are blacks and Hispanics—adopted an affirmative action program because at that time its police force of 80 persons was all white and all male. As a result of its affirmative action efforts, by 1984 its police force consisted of 50 white males, 15 black males, 3 black females, 2 white females, and 5 male Hispanics.

In 1984, because of a reduction in tax revenues, New Springfield had to reduce its police force and proposed to do so in accordance with the law of the state for civil servants—last hired, first fired. This would mean that of the eight persons to be laid off, all would be from minority groups or women.

Those threatened went to a federal district judge and argued that the proposed action would violate Titles VI and VII of the Civil Rights Act of 1964 and the Fourteenth Amendment. They asked the judge to order the city to lay off persons in such a manner that the percentage of minority and female officers would not fall below the level existing at the commencement of the layoffs. The city and the white male officers who would be laid off if the judge granted this request responded that (1) to lay off white males with more seniority than those retained would be to violate the state law and (2) to act against the men only because of their race and sex would be contrary to the Civil Rights Act of 1964 and the Constitution.

How would you decide if you were the judge?

How do you think the Supreme Court will decide? Remember what it has already said in *Bakke*, *Weber*, and *Fullilove*.

(Answer/Discussion on the next page.)

directly related to on-the-job performance and for seniority systems that give advantages to employees on the basis of their period of employment.

Title VII was passed to protect minorities and women. Nonetheless, employers who discriminate against white males also violate its provisions. Moreover, when Congress adopted Title VII, it stated that this provision should *not* be used "to require . . . any employer . . . to grant preferential treatment" to any individual or to any group on account of racial or sexual imbalance that might exist in the employer's workforce.

Despite this language the Supreme Court ruled in *Steelworkers* v. *Weber* that Title VII does not forbid an employer to give preference to blacks in a training program. This case developed from the action of the Kaiser Aluminum Company. At one point Kaiser had almost no blacks in its skilled craft labor force. Without saying that it had discriminated against black workers, Kaiser voluntarily adopted a training program in which at least 50 percent of the new trainees would have to be black, even if this meant giving preference to black employees with less seniority than white employees, until the ratio of black craftworkers in the Kaiser labor force was equal to the ratio of blacks in the local labor force. Title VII, said the Court, means that without a finding of past discrimination, the government cannot *force* a company to give blacks a racial preference. However, the Court took judicial notice of the fact that in the past blacks had been excluded from craft unions, and that under these circumstances Kaiser could *voluntarily* adopt an affirmative action plan without violating Title VII. The Court emphasized that the plan was to remain in force only until the effects of the past discrimination had been corrected.[51]

Title VII has several special features. Not only do aggrieved persons have a right of private action to sue for damages for themselves, but they can do so for other persons similarly situated—a so-called class action. In addition, Congress created the Equal Employment Opportunity Commission to enforce its provisions. The commission, consisting of five members appointed by the president with the consent of the Senate, works together with state authorities to try to bring about compliance with the act. It has authority to seek judicial enforcement of complaints against private employers: The attorney general prosecutes Title VII violations by public agencies.

Title VII is supplemented, indeed in some instances even supplanted, by presidential executive orders requiring all contractors of the federal government, including universities, to adopt and implement *affirmative action programs* to ensure a properly balanced labor force. Federal officials deny that these plans call for quotas, but they do call on contractors to establish timetables and goals; to follow open recruitment procedures; to keep records of applicants by race, sex, and national origin; and to explain why their labor force does not reflect the same proportion of persons in the covered categories as are found within the labor market pools. Failure of contractors to file and implement an approved affirmative action plan may lead to loss of federal contracts or grants.

How well have these affirmative action requirements worked? In the period between 1974 and 1980, the rate of minority employment among those employers doing business with the federal government—and thus subject to affirmative action requirements—grew 20 percent, but only 12 percent among companies covered only by Title VII. For women the rate of employment among government contractors grew by 15 percent as contrasted with 2 percent for other businesses.[52]

[51]443 U.S. 193 (1979).

[52]Unpublished Labor Department study reported by Robert Pear, *The New York Times*, June 19, 1983, p. 12.

119

Housing: The Civil Rights Acts of 1866 and 1968

ANSWER/DISCUSSION

Note: The plan to lay off workers in accord with the state law of last hired, first fired was not adopted with an *intent* to discriminate against women, blacks, and Hispanics, but the *effect* would be to cause them to lose their jobs. The reason they were last hired was that until recently the city's employment practices kept minorities and women from serving on its police force. On the other hand, to lay off white males with longer seniority would be to fire persons who were not themselves guilty of any discriminatory practices, although they might have benefited from them.

In 1984 in *Firefighters Union* v. *Statts* (8 Led 2d [1984]), the Supreme Court dealt with a similar situation. It announced that unless it can be shown that blacks have been the victims of discrimination as individuals and not just because of past discrimination against blacks in general, Title VII, which contains a provision protecting seniority systems, deprives federal courts of authority to order employers to disregard seniority systems in order to preserve the ratio of whites and blacks on a workforce or to protect more recently hired blacks from layoffs. The Court made it clear that it was not deciding what would have happened if a city itself had adopted a plan calling for layoffs that would preserve the racial composition of the force. The Court dealt only with layoffs, not initial hiring. The opinion did not reach constitutional issues, only the application of Title VII. However, the Court's opinion contains language that could be read to limit race-conscious remedies to instances where there is proof of victim-specific discrimination, and thus call into question the constitutionality of many affirmative action programs. What *Firefighters Union* v. *Statt* will come to mean is what members of Congress, voters, and judges will decide it means in the years ahead.

Fair housing is the last frontier of the civil rights crusade, the area in which progress is slowest and genuine change most remote. "Segregated housing contributes mightily to a vicious circle that also includes educational and employment discrimination. . . . Because of poor schools for many minorities, they cannot find well-paying jobs. Without such jobs they often cannot afford to live in nicer neighborhoods with decent housing. And because of their location in less desirable communities, good educational systems are less likely to be available."[53] As former Senator Birch Bayh pointed out, we face a "sordid endless chain of inequality." "That interlocking system of education, employment, and housing has been used to enslave a people by keeping them undereducated, jobless, and poor, as well as separately and substandardly housed."[54]

In 1948 the Supreme Court held in *Shelley* v. *Kraemer* that judges could no longer enforce racially restrictive covenants (a provision in a deed to real property restricting its sale).[55] In 1962 President Kennedy ordered federal housing authorities to cease making federal funds available to any project operated on a segregated basis. And as we have noted, in 1968 the Supreme Court interpreted the Civil Rights Act of 1866 to open federal courts to damage suits by those who had been denied the right to buy homes because of race. Despite all these actions, it was necessary for Congress to pass the Civil Rights Act of 1968 to ensure equal housing for black Americans.

The Civil Rights Act covers all housing offered for rent or sale *except* that owned by private individuals who own no more than three houses, who sell or rent these houses without the services of an agent, and who do not indicate any preference or discrimination in their advertising; dwellings that have no more than four separate living units, in which the owner maintains a residence ("Mrs. Murphy boardinghouses"); and religious organizations and private clubs housing their own members on a noncommercial basis.

For all other housing the Civil Rights Act forbids owners to refuse to sell or rent to any person because of race, color, religion, national origin, and—since 1974—sex. No discriminatory advertising is to be permitted. So-called blockbusting techniques—that is, attempts to persuade persons to sell or rent a dwelling by representing that blacks or other racial or religious groups are about to come into the neighborhood—are outlawed. Real estate brokers and lending institutions are also prohibited from discriminatory practices.

"The weakest links" in the act are those sections dealing with administration and enforcement. The act creates no new enforcement agency: Primary responsibility for enforcement falls upon those injured by a discriminatory housing practice. The injured party must file a complaint with the Secretary of the Department of Housing and Urban Affairs (HUD) or initiate a suit in a federal court. HUD's authority is limited. It can pursue a complaint only by "informal methods of conference, conciliation, and persuasion," and under many circumstances must first refer complaints to state and local civil rights agencies. If all this fails, HUD still can do nothing but refer the matter to the Department of Justice.

Former HUD Secretary Patricia Harris and the Leadership Conference on Civil Rights—a coalition of 165 national organizations—have urged Congress to give HUD authority to bring charges against alleged violators before administrative judges located within the department. While President Reagan would not go that far, he did propose that the attorney general be authorized to bring actions against offenders without having, as the law presently requires, first to find that a "pattern or practice of discrimination" exists. So far Congress has

[53]Charles M. Lamb, "Housing Discrimination and Segregation," *Catholic University Law Review*, Vol. 30 (Spring 1981), p. 370.

[54]Quoted in ibid., pp. 391–92.

[55]334 U.S. 1 (1948).

[handwritten annotations:] Department of Housing & Urban affairs

Can not refuse to sell or rent because of color

adopted neither President Reagan's proposals nor those of civil rights groups to strengthen the enforcement of the Housing Act of 1968.

Black leaders have given housing a lower priority than employment or education.[56] Ten years after the adoption of the Housing Act of 1968, 75 percent of blacks were still meeting discrimination whenever they sought to rent a home, 62 percent when they sought to buy one.[57]

But some progress has been made. The Department of Justice has filed, or joined in the filing, of some 350 cases, especially those involving large apartment complexes. The courts have built up "a formidable body of precedent that almost anyone who can prove discrimination, and has the determination and money to do so, can get the house he wants and even substantial damage awards."[58] Between 1970 and 1980 blacks slightly increased their share of the suburban population, and as of 1980, 26 percent of black families are in census tracts in which whites are in the majority. The percentage of blacks owning their own homes increased slightly during the decade, from 33 to 37 percent. But the basic and pervasive fact remains: Housing available to blacks is less adequate than that available to whites, and they have fewer choices. The efforts made so far are like "the dropping of a single vial of purifier into the Mississippi River."[59]

AGE DISCRIMINATION

Historically our laws and practices have commonly made distinctions based on age: to get a driver's license, to get married without parental consent, to attend schools, to buy alcoholic drinks, and so on. Many governmental institutions have age-specific programs: for senior citizens, for adult students, for midcareer persons. And the courts have not included age as one of the suspect or almost-suspect classifications requiring special justification. But Congress, responding to "Gray Power," is moving more and more to treat age as one of the protected categories.

The Age Discrimination in Employment Act of 1967 declared that governments and interstate employers could not discriminate on the basis of old age unless it can be convincingly demonstrated that age is related to proper job performance. As the law presently stands, there are no age limits for federal civil servants, and other sectors have an age limit of seventy. Congress is reconsidering and will likely "uncap" the retirement age for most employees, thus making it a federal offense for covered employers to require any person to retire just because of age. The legislation most likely to be adopted will still permit employers to limit initial appointments or promotions of workers after age seventy.

The Age Discrimination Act of 1975, as amended in 1978, also provides that no federal funds are to be given to any program or activity that denies to persons because of age the benefits of the program, or otherwise subjects such persons to age discrimination. Recipients of federal aid may take age into account in awarding programs *only* if age is a factor necessary to the operation of the program. (Presumably, a federally assisted kindergarten or nursery school program could establish some age limits.)

[56]Robert Reinhold, "Race Barriers in Housing Still High 11 Years after the Civil Rights Act," *The New York Times*, June 8, 1979.

[57]Jonathan Kaufman, "Black Mood," *The Wall Street Journal*, May 23, 1980.

[58]Reinhold, "Race Barriers."

[59]Ford Foundation letter, October 1, 1976.

The Equal Employment Opportunity Commission now handles complaints based on age. The number of age-based complaints is growing, and age discrimination cases now account for a quarter of the commission's work.

SUMMARY

1. The crusade for women's rights was born out of the struggle to abolish slavery. The fate of these two social movements has long been intertwined. Recently the struggle for equal rights under the law has been expanded to cover concerns for the rights of Hispanics and native Americans.

2. There is a close connection between what happens in our social and political life and what our courts decide about the meaning of the Constitution. The Supreme Court has played a prominent role in securing for blacks, women, Hispanics, and native Americans equal rights under the law. What happens in the country influences what the Court decides, and vice versa.

3. Progress in securing civil rights for blacks was a long time in coming. After the Civil War the national government briefly tried to secure for the freed slaves some measure of protection and to enforce the Thirteenth, Fourteenth, and Fifteenth amendments and the civil rights laws passed to implement them. But when the national government withdrew from the field in 1877, blacks were left to their own resources, and the rights granted by the Constitution became meaningless. After World War II the nation began to debate the proper role of the national and state governments in protecting civil rights. The Supreme Court reversed an 1896 decision and in *Brown* v. *Board of Education* announced that enforced racial segregation in public education was unconstitutional. Eventually Congress and the pres-

ident threw their weight behind a major effort to prevent racial segregation and discrimination against blacks.

4. The Supreme Court uses a three-tiered approach to evaluate the constitutionality of laws challenged as violating the equal protection clause. Laws touching economic concerns are sustained if they are rationally related to the accomplishment of a legitimate government goal. Laws that classify people because of sex or illegitimacy are sustained only if they meet the more rigorous test of serving important governmental objectives and are substantially related to the achievement of those objectives. The top or most stringent tier is used to review laws that touch fundamental rights or classify people because of race or ethnic origin. Such laws will be sustained only if the government can show a "compelling public interest."

5. After a long struggle women achieved the right to vote with the adoption of the Nineteenth Amendment in 1920. With the rebirth of the women's movement in the 1960s, federal courts began to interpret constitutional provisions to protect women against sex discrimination. Congress, the White House, and many state and local governments have amended laws and adopted programs to provide equal rights and opportunities for women.

6. Most recently older Americans have joined with Hispanics, native Americans, and others to secure legislative protection for their special concerns.

FURTHER READING

HARRY S. ASHMORE. *Hearts and Minds: The Anatomy of Racism from Roosevelt to Reagan* (McGraw-Hill, 1982).

RUSSEL LAWRENCE BARSH and JAMES YOUNGBLOOD HENDERSON. *The Road: Indian Tribes and Political Liberty* (University of California Press, 1980).

GEORGE H. BROWN, NAN L. ROSEN, and SUSAN T. HILL. *The Condition of Education for Hispanic Americans* (Government Printing Office, 1980).

First National Women's Conference. *The Spirit of Houston* (Government Printing Office, 1978).

RICHARD KLUGER. *Simple Justice* (Knopf, 1976).

Report on Indian Education, Final Report to the American *Policy Review Commission* (Government Printing Office, 1976).

ALLAN P. SINDLER. *Bakke, DeFunis, and Minority Admissions* (Longman, 1978).

We Mutually Pledge: A Report on the National Hispanic Leadership Conference, July 20–22, 1977 (The Dallas–Ft. Worth Spanish-Speaking Program Coordinators Council, 1977).

J. HARVIE WILKINSON, III. *From Brown to Bakke: The Supreme Court and School Integration: 1954–1978* (Oxford University Press, 1979).

RIGHTS TO LIFE, LIBERTY, AND PROPERTY

6

Public officials have great power. Under certain conditions they can seize our property, throw us in jail, and—in extreme circumstances—even take our lives. It is necessary to give great power to those who govern; it is also dangerous. It is so dangerous that to keep officials from becoming tyrants, we are unwilling to depend on the ballot box alone. We know that political controls mean little when a majority uses that power to deprive unpopular minorities of their rights. Because public power can be dangerous, we parcel it out in small chunks and surround it with restraints. No single official can decide to take our life, liberty, or property: Officials must act according to the rules. If they act outside the scope of their authority or contrary to the law, they have no claim to our obedience.

These are the precious rights of all who live under the American flag— rich or poor, young or old, black or white, man or woman, alien or citizen. The Constitution also confers some special rights on citizens and protects our right to become and to remain American citizens. Who belongs to the body politic? Who is an American?

Every nation has rules that determine nationality—that is, who is a member of, owes allegiance to, and is the subject of the nation-state. But in a democracy citizenship is something more than nationality, something more than merely being a subject. *Citizenship is an office* and, like other offices, carries with it certain powers and responsibilities. How citizenship is acquired and retained should therefore be a matter of considerable importance to everyone.

NATURALIZATION REQUIREMENTS

1. Being over eighteen, lawfully admitted for permanent residence, and residing in the United States for at least five years and in a state for at least six months.
2. Filing a petition of naturalization with a clerk of a court of record—federal or state—verified by two witnesses.
3. Being able to read, write, and speak English.
4. Possessing a good moral character.
5. Understanding and demonstrating an attachment to the history, principles, and form of government of the United States.
6. Demonstrating that one is well disposed toward the good order and happiness of the country.
7. Demonstrating that one does not now believe in, nor within the last ten years has ever believed in, advocated, or belonged to an organization that supports opposition to organized government, overthrow of government by violence, or the doctrines of world communism or any other form of totalitarianism.

It was not until 1868, with the adoption of the Fourteenth Amendment, that this basic right of membership in the body politic was given constitutional protection. The Fourteenth Amendment makes "all persons *born or naturalized* in the United States and subject to the jurisdiction thereof . . . citizens of the United States and of the State wherein they reside." All persons born in the United States, with the exception of children born to foreign ambassadors and ministers, are citizens of this country regardless of the citizenship of their parents. (Congress has defined the United States to include Puerto Rico, Guam, the Northern Marianas, and the Virgin Islands.) While the Fourteenth Amendment alone does not make members of Indian tribes citizens of the United States or of the state in which they live, Indians have been declared American citizens by act of Congress.

The Fourteenth Amendment confers citizenship according to the principle of jus soli—by place of birth. In addition, Congress has granted, under certain conditions, citizenship at birth according to the principle of jus sanguinis—by blood. A child born of an American living abroad becomes an American citizen at birth as long as the American parent has been present in the United States for ten years, five of which were spent in the country after age fourteen. Citizenship may also be acquired by naturalization, either collective or individual. The granting of citizenship to the people of the Northern Marianas in 1977 by an act of Congress was an example of collective naturalization. Individual naturalization requirements are determined by Congress. Today, with minor exceptions, nonenemy aliens over eighteen who have been lawfully admitted for permanent residence and who have resided in the United States for at least five years and in a state for at least six months are eligible for naturalization.

Any court of record (state or federal) in the U.S. can grant citizenship. The processing of the papers is a responsibility of the Immigration and Naturalization Service which makes the necessary investigations and a report to a judge. The final step is a hearing in open court. If the judge is satisfied that the applicant has met all the requirements, the applicant renounces allegiance to his or her former country and swears to support and defend the Constitution and laws of the United States against all enemies, as well as to bear arms in behalf of the United States when required to do so by law. Those whose religious beliefs prevent them from bearing arms are allowed to take an oath that if called to duty, they will serve in the armed forces as noncombatants or will perform work of national importance under civilian direction. The court then grants a certificate of naturalization.

Naturalized citizenship may be revoked by court order if the government can prove that it was secured by deception. In addition, citizenship, however acquired, may be voluntarily renounced. But Congress cannot order that citizenship be taken away from persons because of what they have done—for example, committed certain crimes, voted in a foreign election, or served in a foreign army. However, some actions, such as taking out citizenship in another country or swearing allegiance to another nation, may be taken into account as "highly persuasive evidence of a purpose to abandon citizenship." Even so, the government must prove by a predominance of the evidence that the citizen "not only voluntarily committed the expatriating act prescribed in the statute, but also intended to relinquish his citizenship."[1]

[1] *Vance v. Terrazas*, 444 U.S. 252 (1980).

jus soli - citizenship by place of birth
Jus sanguinis - by blood

Naturalization -

Rights of American Citizenship

An American citizen obtains state citizenship merely by residing in a state. (*Residence*, as used in the Fourteenth Amendment, means domicile, the place one calls home. The legal status of *domicile* should not be confused with the fact of physical presence. A person may be living in Washington, D.C., but be a citizen of California—that is, consider California home. Residence is primarily a question of intent.) It is from state citizenship that many of our most important rights flow.

The Supreme Court in the *Slaughter House Cases* (1873) carefully distinguished between the privileges of United States citizens and those of state citizens. It held that the only privileges attaching to national citizenship are those that "owe their existence to the Federal Government, its National Character, its Constitution, or its laws."[2] These privileges have never been completely specified, but they include the right to use the navigable waters of the United States; to assemble peacefully; to petition the national government for redress of grievances; to be protected by the national government on the high seas; to vote, if qualified to do so under state laws, and to have one's vote counted properly; and to travel throughout the United States.

THE RIGHT TO TRAVEL ABROAD This right is constitutionally protected, but while the right of interstate travel is virtually unqualified, the right to international travel can be regulated within the bounds of due process. Under current law it is unlawful (except as otherwise provided by the president, as has been done for travel to Mexico and Canada) for citizens to leave or enter the United States without a valid passport. The president, acting through the secretary of state, may refuse to grant or may revoke a passport if the holder's activities in foreign countries are causing or are likely to cause serious damage to our national security or to the foreign policy of the United States.

THE RIGHT TO LIVE IN THE UNITED STATES This right, which is not subject to any congressional limitation, is perhaps the most precious aspect of American citizenship. Aliens have no such right.

DUAL CITIZENSHIP

Since each nation has complete authority to decide for itself the question of nationality, it is possible for a person to be considered a citizen by two or more nations. Dual citizenship is not unusual, especially for persons from nations that do not recognize the right of the individual to choose his or her own nationality. (One of the issues of the War of 1812 was that England did not recognize that sailors born in England had abandoned their English citizenship on becoming naturalized American citizens.) Persons born abroad to American citizens may also be citizens of the nation in which they were born. Persons born in the United States of parents from a foreign nation may also be citizens of their parents' country.

Dual nationality carries negative as well as positive consequences; for example, you may be subject to national service obligations and taxes in both countries.

Rights of Aliens— Admission to the United States

Immigration law *annual ceiling 270,000; 20,000 from one nation*

Congress decides which aliens shall be admitted to the United States and under what conditions. By 1875 it began to restrict the entry of persons alleged to be "undesirable," such as prostitutes and revolutionaries. During World War I Congress for the first time set limits on the number of aliens who could be admitted each year. The Immigration Act of 1924 did the same, creating a national origin system that discriminated against immigrants from southern and southeastern Europe and Asia.

In 1965, after years of debate, a new immigration law was adopted. As amended in 1976 and 1980, the law sets an annual ceiling of 270,000—plus immediate relatives for permanent resident immigrants—of whom no more than 20,000 should be from one nation. Preference is given to family members of residents of the United States.

The 270,000 cap has many exceptions. Moreover, it has been supplemented by a series of ad hoc congressional measures designed to permit the entrance of large numbers of political refugees. In addition, the attorney general may employ "parole" discretion to permit the entrance of large numbers of persons.

In the Refugee Act of 1980, Congress tried to establish policies and procedures to deal with this growing problem. The normal flow of refugees was set

Albert Einstein and his daughter (right) and secretary (left) take the oath of citizenship in 1940. *UPI.*

[2]16 Wallace 36 (1873).

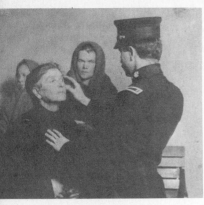

Ellis Island in New York harbor where immigrants were examined for diseases, before being allowed to enter the U.S. *Library of Congress.*

at 50,000 annually, but the president may request additional admissions for groups of "special humanitarian concern to the United States." The total number of refugees is determined each year by the president after consultations with Congress. (This is one of many provisions that will have to be reviewed as a result of the *Chada* decision—see Chapter 16). Since the act was adopted, the annual flow has been in excess of 150,000.

Refugees are defined as persons outside of their own country who have a well-founded fear of persecution in their own country based on race, religion, nationality, social class, or political opinion. In addition, the 1980 Act provides an elaborate system of review for those who request asylum in the United States. This process takes years, and it is difficult to expel any who claim this status.[3]

Some Americans want the United States to live up to its heritage as a haven for people fleeing religious and political persecution. (President Franklin Roosevelt is reputed to have opened his address to a convention of the Daughters of the American Revolution with the salutation: "Fellow immigrants and revolutionaries.") Others, however, question the wisdom of admitting refugees while so many Americans do not have jobs.

Undocumented Aliens

Even more controversial is the question of how to deal with the 3 to 6 million aliens who have illegally crossed our borders, most from Mexico but many from other nations in Central and South America.[4] There is no question about the constitutional power of national authorities to expel illegal aliens: "Over no

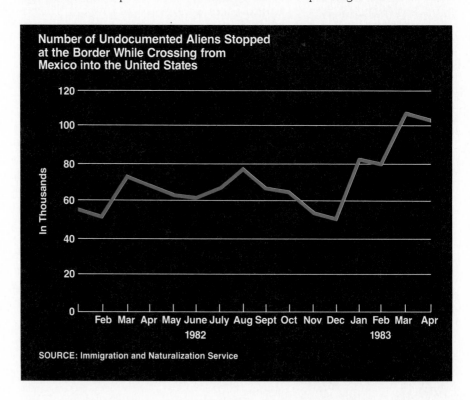

Number of Undocumented Aliens Stopped at the Border While Crossing from Mexico into the United States

In Thousands

	1982	1983
	Feb Mar Apr May June July Aug Sept Oct Nov Dec	Jan Feb Mar Apr

SOURCE: Immigration and Naturalization Service

---

[3]Arnold H. Leibowitz, "The Refugee Act of 1980: Problems and Congressional Concerns," *The Annals*, Vol. 467 (May 1983), pp. 163–71.

[4]George C. Kiser and Martha Woody Kiser (eds.), *Mexican Workers in the United States: Historical and Political Perspectives* (University of New Mexico Press, 1979).

conceivable subject is the legislative power of Congress more complete than it is over the admission of aliens."[5] But the problems here are of a different kind.

The Immigration and Naturalization Service does not have the money or staff to patrol the thousands of miles of our southern and northern borders. Moreover, it is even more difficult to track down these aliens inside the United States, round them up, and expel them in a fashion consistent with the practices and policies of a free society. Once here, undocumented aliens do not find it hard to become invisible, especially in our larger cities, or to find jobs. Some employers prefer to hire them, since they work for less money than those who are here lawfully.

New Departures: The Simpson-Mazzoli Bill?

These Mexican farm laborers are wading across the Rio Grande River at Juarez to seek farm jobs in Texas. *UPI.*

The related but separable problems of how to deal with undocumented aliens and how to handle political refugees has stimulated a national debate and much congressional attention. The discussions in the Congress about the Simpson-Mazzoli Bill (named after its chief sponsors in the Senate and the House, Senator Alan K. Simpson of Wyoming and Representative Romano Mazzoli of Kentucky) may result in a new law that will accomplish the following:

1. Set a more realistic cap on the total number of foreign-born persons allowed to enter the United States: 425,000 is the figure established by the Senate.
2. Streamline the asylum procedures.
3. Grant to most undocumented aliens who came to the United States by a specified date the right to become permanent resident aliens.
4. Fine employers who hire undocumented aliens, and require them to keep records, open to inspection by the INS.
5. Give the president the responsibility to develop a fraud-resistant social security card.

The last two provisions have stirred considerable debate. Hispanic groups fear that employers will hesitate to hire Hispanics. Employers worry that they will be required to keep costly records. Others are concerned about forcing back across the border persons whose desperate economic needs compel them to enter the United States in search of work. And clearly, the way we deal with undocumented workers will affect our relations with Mexico.

Rights of Aliens Inside the United States

While in the United States—no matter how they get here—aliens enjoy considerable constitutional protection. Most of the provisions of the Constitution speak of the rights of *persons*, not just of citizens. Congress and the states, for example, have no greater authority to interfere with an alien's freedom of religion than with that of citizens. State and local regulation of aliens is subject to "heightened" judicial scrutiny. In fact, the Supreme Court has ruled that states cannot keep children of undocumented aliens living within their boundaries from attending public schools free of charge (see page 400). It should also be noted that all aliens are "subject to the full range of obligations imposed by the states' civil and criminal laws."[6]

Congress has wide discretion in determining the grounds for deportation. Aliens may be deported for acts that were not grounds of banishment when they were performed, for such things as conviction of two crimes involving moral

[5]*Kleindienst* v. *Mandel*, 408 U.S. 753 (1972).
[6]Justice Brennan in *Plyler* v. *Doe*, 457 U.S. 202 (1982).

turpitude, for joining an organization that advocates revolution, or for engaging in activities that the attorney general believes to be "subversive to national security."

CONSTITUTIONAL PROTECTION OF PROPERTY

By *property rights* we mean the rights of an individual to own, use, rent, invest, or contract for property. Historically there has been a persistent emphasis on the close connection between liberty and ownership of property, between property and power. This emphasis has been reflected in American political thinking and American political institutions. A major purpose of the Constitution was to establish a government strong enough to protect each person's right to use and enjoy his or her property. At the same time the framers wanted a government so limited it could not endanger that right. They were disturbed by the efforts of some state legislatures in behalf of debtors at the expense of creditors. Therefore, in the Constitution they forbade states to make anything except gold or silver legal tender for the payment of debts or to pass any law "impairing the obligation of contracts."

The Contract Clause

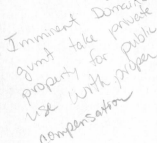

The contract clause was designed to prevent states from enacting legislation to extend the period during which debtors could meet their payments or otherwise get out of their contractual obligations. The framers had in mind an ordinary contract between private persons. However, beginning with Chief Justice John Marshall, the Supreme Court expanded the coverage of the clause to prevent states from altering in any way privileges previously conferred on a corporation.

In effect, the contract clause was used to protect vested property at the expense of the power of the states to guard the public welfare. Gradually, however, the Court began in the 1880s to restrict the coverage of the contract clause and to subject contracts to what in constitutional law is known as police powers—the power to protect the public health, safety, welfare, and morals. In *Home Building and Loan Association versus Blaisdell* (1934) the Supreme Court went so far as to hold that even contracts between individuals—the very ones the contract clause was intended to protect—could be modified by state law in order to avert social and economic catastrophe.[7] While the contract clause is still invoked occasionally to challenge a state regulation of property, it has ceased to be a significant limitation on governmental power.

Eminent Domain— What Happens When The Government Takes Our Property?

Both the national and the state governments have the power of eminent domain—that is, the power to take private property for public use—but the owner must be fairly compensated. This limitation was the first provision of the Bill of Rights to be incorporated within the Fourteenth Amendment (see page 144) and thus to be made applicable to the states.

What constitutes a "taking" for purposes of the Fifth Amendment? Ordinarily, but not always, the taking must be direct. The clause does not require compensation merely because government action may result in property loss, such as when a zoning regulation restricting a particular area to a single-family residential use lowers the value of a particular property.

Sometimes the courts will find that the government has "taken" property and owes compensation to its owners even when title is left in the hands of the owners. For example, if airplanes take off and land over property adjacent to airports in such a manner that the land is no longer suitable for its prior use

[7]290 U.S. 398 (1934).

(say, raising chickens), this taking will warrant compensation. A New York law permitting cable television companies to install equipment on apartment building roofs was also ruled to be a taking. "Just compensation" is not always easy to define. In case of dispute, the final decision is made by the courts.

Due Process

Perhaps the most difficult parts of the Constitution to understand are the clauses in the Fifth and Fourteenth amendments that forbid national and state governments to deny any person life, liberty, or property without due process of law. These **due process clauses** have resulted in more Supreme Court decisions than any other provisions in the Constitution, although the equal protection clause runs a close second. Even so, it is impossible to explain due process precisely. The Supreme Court itself has refused to give it a precise definition.

There are two kinds of due process—procedural and substantive. **Procedural due process** refers to the methods by which a law is enforced; but there are several ways in which a law itself, as enacted, may violate the procedural due process requirement.

First, the statute may be vague: "A statute which either forbids or requires the doing of an act in terms so vague that men of common intelligence must necessarily guess at its meaning and differ as to its application, violates the first essential of due process."[8] A vague statute fails to provide adequate warning and does not contain sufficient guidelines for law enforcement officials, juries, and courts (see Box in margin.)

A second way in which a law itself may violate procedural due process is by creating an improper presumption of guilt. Persons are presumed innocent; due process places the burden on the government to prove guilt beyond a reasonable doubt. This burden cannot be shifted, nor the standard of proof diminished by a statutory presumption of guilt. Thus, laws creating a presumption that all marijuana or cocaine in one's possession must have been obtained illegally have been declared unconstitutional. Still, the Court upheld such a presumption with respect to heroin, since little if any of it is made in this country, and virtually all of it is illegally imported. It is therefore not unreasonable to presume that a person who possesses heroin obtained it illegally.

Traditionally, however, procedural due process refers to the way in which a law is applied. To paraphrase Daniel Webster's famous definition, it requires a procedure that hears before it condemns, proceeds upon inquiry, and renders judgment only after a trial or some kind of hearing. Originally procedural due process was limited to criminal prosecutions, but it now applies to many different kinds of governmental proceedings. It is required, for instance, in juvenile hearings, disbarment proceedings, proceedings to determine eligibility for welfare payments or terminations of them, parole revocations, revocation of drivers' licenses, disciplinary proceedings in state universities and public schools, and even applications by parents to admit their minor children to state mental hospitals.

Procedural due process has taken on new importance with the expanded interpretation of the words *liberty* and *property*. The liberty that is protected by the due process clause is more than freedom from being thrown into jail; and the property that is secured goes beyond mere ownership of real estate, things, or money. Rather, liberty includes "the right of the individual to contract, to engage in any of the common occupations of life, to acquire useful knowledge, to marry, to establish a home and bring up children, to worship God according to the dictates of his own conscience, and generally to enjoy those common law privileges long recognized as essential to the orderly pursuit of happiness of

SOME STATUTES DECLARED VOID FOR VAGUENESS

A statute making it a crime to treat "contemptuously" the American flag.

A vagrancy ordinance classifying vagrants as "rogues and vagabonds," "dissolute persons who go about begging," "common night walkers," and so on.

An ordinance requiring persons who loiter or wander the streets to provide a "credible and reliable" identification and to account for their presence when required by a police officer.

[An ordinance requiring a license for businesses selling any items "designed or marketed for use with illegal cannabis or drugs"—what are commonly known as "headshops"—was *not* considered unconstitutionally vague.]

[8]*Connally v. General Construction Co.*, 269 U.S. 385 (1976).

129

free men."[9] The property protected is a whole bundle of rights, which may include a job, various kinds of licenses, and other things of value conferred by state laws. The blurring of the distinctions between liberty rights and property rights and between rights and privileges means that public welfare, housing, education, employment, professional licenses, and so on are increasingly becoming matters of entitlement. Their denial involves some form of due process.

Nevertheless, "the range of interests protected by procedural due process is not indefinite." Not every "grievous loss visited upon a person by the State is sufficient to invoke the procedural protections of the due process clause."[10] Whether or not an interest is protected by due process depends on the nature of the interest, not its importance to the individual. Thus, faculty members are not entitled to procedural due process before being denied tenure, since they have no constitutional right to a teaching job. Public employees are not entitled to a hearing before being fired, since they have no constitutional right to a public job. (However, if there is any evidence they have been fired because of race or sex, or because they exercised First Amendment rights, or for any other reasons that threaten a constitutional right, they do have a right to procedural due process.)

"Once it is determined that due process applies, the question remains what process is due." What is due varies with the kind of interest involved, the reliability of the procedures used, and the governmental purposes to be served.[11] As applied in a federal courtroom, due process requires the careful observance of the provisions of the Bill of Rights as outlined in amendments Four through Eight.

For other kinds of proceedings, the question in each instance is what must be done to ensure *fundamental fairness*. It is hard to generalize because of the many kinds of proceedings involved, but at a minimum there must be adequate *notice* and an opportunity to be *heard*. The hearing required must be appropriate to the interest involved. Usually the hearing has to be held prior to the adverse governmental action. For example, juveniles cannot be declared delinquent without a hearing in which they have the right to confront and cross-examine hostile witnesses, to present evidence, and to be represented by counsel. The level of proof must show delinquency beyond any reasonable doubt, but juveniles are not entitled to have the decision made by a jury. Children are entitled to due process when their parents seek to send them to a mental hospital, but adversary proceedings that pit child against parents are not necessary, merely a personal interview and a review of the decision by a neutral health professional.

"What's so great about due process? Due process got me ten years." *Drawing by Handelsman; © 1970. The New Yorker, Magazine, Inc.*

Substantive due process

Procedural due process places limits on *how* governmental power may be exercised; substantive due process places limits on *why* that power may be exercised. Procedural due process has to do with the procedures of the law; substantive due process has to do with the content of the law. Procedural due process mainly limits the executive and judicial branches; substantive due process mainly limits the legislative branch. Substantive due process means that an "unreasonable" law, even if properly passed and properly applied, is unconstitutional.

In a recent decision involving substantive due process, it was held that school board regulations requiring teachers to cease teaching past the fourth month of pregnancy and barring them from returning to the classroom until

Substantive
due process-
place limits on
why a power
may be exercized
(unreasonable
Law is
un-const)

[9]*Meyer v. Nebraska*, 262 U.S. 390 (1923).
[10]*Meachum v. Fano*, 427 U.S. 215 (1976).
[11]*Morrissey v. Brewer*, 408 U.S. 471 (1972).

three months after the birth of a child are unreasonable interferences with the liberty of women teachers to bear children. Further, to confine against their wishes nondangerous mentally ill persons has been called an unreasonable deprivation of their liberty.

Perhaps the most celebrated—certainly the most controversial—illustration of the Court's recent use of substantive due process is *Roe* v. *Wade* (1973), in which the Court ruled: (1) During the first trimester of a woman's pregnancy (about the first three months), it is unreasonable and unconstitutional for a state to interfere with a woman's right to choose an abortion or with her doctor's medical judgments about how to carry it out. (2) During the second trimester the state's interest in protecting the health of women who undergo abortions becomes compelling, and a state may make reasonable regulations about how, where, and when abortions may be performed. (3) During the third trimester the state's interest in protecting the unborn child is so important that the state can proscribe abortions altogether, except when necessary to preserve the life or health of the mother.[12]

Four years later, in *Maher* v. *Roe*, the Court concluded that although a woman has the constitutional right to an abortion during the early months of pregnancy, she has no right to have the state pay for it, and a state may refuse to pay the nontherapeutic abortion-related medical expenses of poor women, even though it does cover such expenses related to childbirth.[13]

Several years later, in *Akron* v. *Akron Center for Reproductive Health*, the Court held that the state of medical science had so progressed that most abortions during the early part of the second trimester could now be performed safely in a doctor's office. Thus, a state regulation requiring all such abortions to be performed in a hospital, along with some other state regulations, unduly burden a woman's constitutional right to an abortion.[14]

Before 1937 substantive due process was used primarily to protect "liberty of contract"—that is, business liberty. Indeed, the adoption of the doctrine of substantive due process and the simultaneous expansion of the meaning of liberty and property made the Supreme Court, for a time, the final judge of our economic and industrial life. During this period the Supreme Court was dominated by conservative jurists who considered almost all social welfare legislation unreasonable. They used the due process clause to strike down laws regulating hours of labor, establishing minimum wages, regulating prices, and forbidding employers to fire workers for union membership. The Supreme Court vetoed laws adversely affecting property rights unless the judges could be persuaded that such laws were necessary to protect the public health or safety.

The trouble with the substantive interpretation of due process is that the reasonableness of a law depends on one's economic, social, and political views. In democracies elected officials are supposed to accommodate opposing notions of reasonableness and to decide what regulations of liberty and property are needed to promote the public welfare. When the Supreme Court substitutes its own ideas of reasonableness for those of the legislature, it acts like a superlegislature. But how competent are judges to say what the nation's economic (or other) policies should be?

Because of this criticism, the Supreme Court since 1937 has largely abandoned the doctrine of "liberty of contract" and in general has refused to apply the doctrine of substantive due process to laws regulating the economy. The Court now believes that deciding what constitutes reasonable regulations of the

The controversy over the Supreme Court's ruling on abortions is demonstrated by these two groups of marchers. *UPI.*

---

[12]410 U.S. 113 (1973).

[13]432 U.S. 464 (1977).

[14]76 L Ed 2d 687 (1983).

uses of property is a legislative, not a judicial, responsibility. As long as the justices see some connection between a law and the promotion of the public welfare, the Supreme Court will not interfere with it.

The abandonment of the doctrine of substantive due process as a limit on the government's power to regulate property rights has not meant a return to a narrow conception of liberty or the abandonment of substantive due process—quite the contrary. Since 1937 the word *liberty* in the Fifth and Fourteenth amendments has been expanded to include the basic civil liberties. Substantive due process has been given new life as a limitation on governmental power as regards these liberties. Further, since the 1950s the Supreme Court has developed a substantive interpretation of the equal protection clause to supplement the substantive interpretation of due process

Prior to 1937 liberal justices (in dissents) and liberal commentators used to accuse conservative justices in the majority of using substantive due process to impose their own ideas upon the nation. Today conservative judges, now in the minority, are contending that once again the Supreme Court justices in the majority are going beyond the bounds of their responsibilities.

Justices who support the majority position, of course, deny they are substituting their own values for those of the legislature. They argue that there is a fundamental difference between what they are doing in protecting civil liberties and what the conservative pre-1937 justices did to protect property rights. The earlier justices were writing into the Constitution the principles of laissez-faire economics, while the present justices are extracting from the Constitution its principles of civil liberties. Justice Powell, in behalf of the Court, conceded:

> Substantive due process has at times been a treacherous field for this Court. There are risks when the judicial branch gives enhanced protection to certain substantive liberties without the guidance of the more specific provisions of the Bill of Rights. . . . There is reason for concern lest the only limits to such judicial intervention become the predilections of those who happen at the time to be Members of this Court. . . . That history counsels caution and restraint. But it does not counsel abandonment [of substantive due process].[15]

The notion that laws must be reasonable has deep roots in natural law concepts and a long history in the American constitutional tradition. For most Americans most of the time, it is not enough merely to say that a law reflects the wishes of the popular or legislative majority. We also want our laws to be just, and we continue to rely heavily on judges to decide what is just. In Chapter 17 we will look again at the tensions between democratic procedures and judicial guardians.

FREEDOM FROM ARBITRARY ARREST, QUESTIONING, AND IMPRISONMENT

James Otis's address in 1761 protesting arbitrary searches and seizures by English customs officials was the signal for the American Revolution. As John Adams later said: "American independence was then and there born." The Fourth Amendment states: "The right of the people to be secure in their persons, houses, papers, and effects, against unreasonable searches and seizures, shall not be violated, and no Warrants shall issue, but upon probable cause, supported by Oath or affirmation, and particularly describing the place to be searched, and the persons or things to be seized."

4th
Right to be
secure in home
no search
without
authority

[15]*Moore v. City of East Cleveland*, 431 U.S. 494 (1977).

What is Unreasonable Search and Seizure?

Despite what we see in television police dramas and sometimes read about in the news, law enforcement officers have no general right to invade homes and break down doors. They are not supposed to search people except under certain conditions, and they have no right to arrest them except under certain circumstances. This is a highly technical area, and one in which the Supreme Court has had some difficulty in determining what the Constitution means.[16]

ARRESTS The Constitution does not forbid all searches and seizures, only "unreasonable" ones. "Seizures," or what we now call police detentions or arrests, are in fact given less protection than searches. Most arrests take place without an arrest warrant. Police may arrest persons in *public places* even without a warrant, provided they have probable cause to believe the persons have committed or are about to commit a crime. Immediately after making an arrest, especially one made without a warrant, the police must take those arrested to a magistrate so that the latter—not just the police—can decide whether probable cause existed to justify the warrantless arrest.

Police have no general right to stop people on the streets or in their automobiles merely to make random checks or to ask for identification. It is not enough that a person looks suspicious. (Police may set up roadblocks to check all drivers: What they cannot do is allow individual officers to pick and choose which cars or which persons to stop.) Not every encounter between police and citizens is a seizure. Persons are seized in a constitutional sense only when police—by means of physical force or a show of authority—restrain a person's freedom of movement such that a "reasonable person would have believed that he was not free to leave."[17]

Generally, arrests without warrants can take place only in public places. Except in emergencies—for example, when somebody's life is at stake or when police are in hot pursuit of someone they have seen commit a felony—police may not force their way into a suspect's home without a warrant to make an arrest. Even with a warrant, police may not break into a third party's home to arrest a suspect.

Edward Lawson, known as the California Walkman, who brought a suit for damages against San Diego police after they had arrested him fifteen times. Lawson had the practice of walking late at night, often in neighborhoods other than his own. Lawson won his case. *UPI.*

SEARCHES In general (see Box on next page for exceptions), a police search without proper consent is constitutionally unreasonable, unless it has been authorized by a valid search warrant, issued by a magistrate after the police indicate under oath that they have "probable cause" to justify its issuance. The magistrate must perform his or her function in a neutral and detached manner and not serve merely as a rubber stamp for the police. Thus, a search of an adult bookstore was held to violate the Fourth Amendment when the magistrate accompanied the police and made an on-the-spot determination of which items could be seized. The magistrate "was not acting as a judicial officer but as an adjunct law-enforcement officer."[18]

"The Court finds itself on the horns of a dilemma. On the one hand, wiretap evidence is inadmissible, and on the other hand I'm dying to hear it." *Drawing by Handelsman;* © *1972. The New Yorker Magazine, Inc.*

When a magistrate issues a warrant, the warrant must describe what places are to be searched and what things are to be seized. A general search warrant is outlawed by the Constitution. Also, a warrant to search a public place such as a tavern does not authorize the search of persons who happen to be in that place.

Places protected against warrantless searches include any place a person has a legitimate "expectation of privacy" for example, in a hotel room, in a rented home, while staying in the apartment of a friend, or even in a tele-

[16]The most comprehensive analysis of these complicated issues is Wayne R. LaFave, *Search and Seizure: A Treatise on the Fourth Amendment* (West Publishing, 1978, and 1984 supplement).

[17]*United States v. Mendenhall,* 446 U.S. 544 (1980).

[18]*Lo-Ji Sales, Inc. v. New York,* 442 U.S. 319 (1979).

phone booth. In short, the Fourth Amendment protects *people*, not places, from unreasonable governmental intrusions. However, once police have a valid search warrant, they may intrude into places of privacy and may even break and enter if such entry is the only means by which the warrant may be executed.

The Fourth Amendment protects against searches by government officers other than the police, such as internal revenue agents, health inspectors, and occupational and safety inspectors from the Department of Labor. However, there are less stringent conditions on nonpolice searches, especially of places of business.

The inventions of science have confronted judges with new problems in applying the Fourth Amendment. Obviously, the writers of the Fourth Amendment had in mind physical objects such as books, papers, letters, and other kinds of documents as the items that should not be seized by police except on the basis of limited search warrants issued by magistrates. But what of tapping phone wires, using electronic devices to eavesdrop, or using secret television cameras to make videotapes? In *Olmstead* v. *United States* (1928) a bare majority of the Supreme Court held that there was no unconstitutional search unless there was seizure of physical objects or actual physical entry into a premise. Justices Holmes and Brandeis, in dissent, argued that the Constitution should keep up with the times; the "dirty business" of wiretapping produced the same evil invasions of privacy the framers had in mind when they wrote the Fourteenth Amendment.[19]

Forty years later, in *Katz* v. *United States* (1967), the Supreme Court adopted the Holmes-Brandeis position: "The Fourth Amendment protects people—and not simply 'areas'—against unreasonable searches and seizures." The use by police officers of electronic devices to overhear a conversation in a public telephone booth is a search and seizure within the meaning of the Constitution. "Wherever a man may be" (subsequently modified and limited to those places where one has a "legitimate expectation of privacy")[20], "he is entitled to know that he will remain free from unreasonable searches and seizures."[21]

Since conversations are now constitutionally protected, legislatures and judges have had to develop rules to govern when and which conversations may be intercepted. The basic federal legislation is contained in a section of the Crime Control and Safe Streets Act of 1968, adopted over President Johnson's objection. Johnson felt it would lead to a "nation of snoopers bending through the keyholes of the homes and offices of America, spying on our neighbors."

The 1968 act makes it a crime for any unauthorized person to tap telephone wires or use or sell in interstate commerce electronic bugging devices. However, it empowers the attorney general to secure a warrant from a federal judge authorizing federal agents to engage in bugging in order to track down persons suspected of certain federal crimes. At the state level the act authorizes the principal prosecuting attorney of any state or political subdivision to apply to a state judge for a warrant approving wiretapping or oral intercepts for felonies. (Twenty-eight state and local jurisdictions allow such intercepts.) Judges may issue warrants only if they decide probable cause exists that a crime is being, has been, or is about to be committed, and that information relating to that crime may be obtained only by the intercept.

The act left unresolved the question of whether the president has the inherent constitutional authority to order electronic surveillance, without warrant, of agents of foreign powers or of persons suspected of subversion. The

[19]277 U.S. 438 (1928).
[20]*Rakas* v. *Illinois*, 439 U.S. 128 (1978).
[21]389 U.S. 347 (1967).

WHEN SEARCH
WARRANTS ARE
NOT REQUIRED

1. When searches are based on consent
2. In the case of automobiles, under certain conditions
3. To stop briefly and to frisk possibly armed and dangerous persons to remove weapons from them and to search the area under their immediate control, such as the passenger compartment of an automobile
4. When making a lawful arrest; police may search persons being arrested as well as the area under such persons' immediate control
5. When incriminating evidence or contraband is in "plain view" of where the officer has a right to be
6. As part of the routine procedure incident to incarcerating an arrested person; police may search any article in his or her possession in accordance with established inventory procedures
7. At international border crossings; this includes opening mail entering the country if officials have "reasonable cause" to suspect it contains merchandise imported contrary to the law
8. On ships on the waterways of the United States, including inland waterways that provide access to the open seas
9. When officers do not have time to secure a warrant before evidence is destroyed or where there is a need "to protect or preserve life and avoid serious injury"; for example, firefighters and police may break into a burning building

134

A specially-trained dog is used to sniff for narcotics. *UPI.*

Supreme Court in *United States* v. *United States District Court* has since decided that the president has no such power as regards surveillance of persons suspected of domestic subversion: "The danger to political dissent is acute where the government attempts to act under so vague a concept as the power to protect domestic security."[22] The Court pointedly did not rule on the scope of presidential authority to authorize surveillance of foreign agents.

In 1978, with the adoption of the Foreign Intelligence Surveillance Act, "Congress sent a message that it no longer recognized executive branch 'inherent power'" to order warrantless electronic surveillance of anybody for any purpose.[23] Congress itself, however, did authorize such searches, to be carried out by officials of the National Security Agency—the agency in charge of making and breaking codes. No other agency may "bug" foreign agents, unless it first secures a warrant from the United States Foreign Intelligence Surveillance Court, which consists of seven designated federal district judges. Meeting twice each month in secret, the court grants warrants for the "bugging" of agents of foreign powers, whether or not they are American citizens. It has refused, however, to authorize "black-bag" jobs—that is, surreptitious entry for the purpose of physical surveillance.[24]

It is important to note that as long as police officers do not make illegal entries or improper searches and seizures, there is nothing in the Constitution nor in any federal law preventing them from resorting to undercover tactics in their pursuit of wrongdoers. For example, they may use secret cameras or recording devices on their person or on their confederates'; they may use trained dogs to sniff luggage located in public places (to locate narcotics or bombs); and they can listen in to telephone conversations via extension phones, provided they have the consent of one of the parties to the conversation and are in a place where they have a right to be.

The Exclusionary Rule

Combining the Fourth Amendment prohibition against unreasonable searches with the Fifth Amendment injunction that persons shall not be compelled to be witnesses against themselves, the Supreme Court ruled in *Mapp* v. *Ohio* that evidence unconstitutionally obtained cannot be used in a criminal trial as part of the government's main case against persons from whom it was seized.[25] (The rule does not apply to grand juries.) The exclusionary rule was adopted mainly to prevent police misconduct. Since police are seldom prosecuted for making illegal searches and are often unable to pay civil damages, the justices felt that the exclusionary rule was the best—and maybe the only—sanction.

Critics of the exclusionary rule, including members of the Supreme Court, question why criminals should go free because of police misconduct. As a result, in *United States* v. *Leon* (1984) and *Massachusetts* v. *Sheppard* (1984), the Supreme Court made a limited good faith exception—evidence may be used if the police acted on the basis of what in good faith they thought to be a valid search warrant, even if it is ultimately found to be invalid.[26] Whether the Court will go further and make a good faith exception for all evidence obtained by the police, even without a warrant, "in a reasonable belief that they obtained it in a constitutional manner" remains to be seen.[27]

[22]407 U.S. 297 (1972).
[23]*Congressional Quarterly*, October 15, 1978, p. 2966.
[24]*The Washington Post*, June 24, 1981.
[25]367 U.S. 643 (1961).
[26]82 L Ed 2d 677 and 737 (1984).
[27]*Illinois* v. *Gates*.

In the meantime the Court has narrowed the exclusionary rule to cover only trials of those from whom the evidence was unconstitutionally seized, as one Jack Payner found out. Internal Revenue Agents, aided by a private investigator, operating in the best tradition of Charlie's Angels, broke into Payner's banker's hotel room while an undercover agent lured the banker out to dinner. The agents "borrowed" the banker's briefcase, photographed documents, put the original documents back, and returned the briefcase. This "caper" was clearly a deliberate intrusion into the banker's privacy and a violation of his Fourth Amendment rights. Nonetheless, the evidence was allowed to be used to convict Payner, one of the banker's customers, of income tax evasion. Payner had no expectation of privacy in his banker's briefcase or any ownership of the documents taken from it.[28]

The Right to Remain Silent

During the seventeenth century certain special courts in England forced confessions of heresy and sedition from religious dissenters. The British privilege against self-incrimination developed in response to these practices. Being familiar with this history, the framers of our Bill of Rights included in the Fifth Amendment the provision that persons shall not be compelled to testify against themselves in criminal prosecutions. The protection against self-incrimination is designed to strengthen a fundamental principle of Anglo-American justice—that no person has an obligation to prove innocence. Rather, the burden is on the government to prove guilt.

The privilege against self-incrimination applies literally only in criminal prosecutions, but it has always been interpreted to protect any person subject to questioning by any agency of government. A witness before a congressional committee, for example, may refuse to answer incriminating questions. However, to invoke the privilege, it is not enough that the witness's answers might be embarrassing or lead to loss of a job or even to civil suits; there must be a reasonable fear that the answers might support a criminal prosecution or "furnish a link in the chain of evidence needed to prosecute" a crime.[29] If defendants refuse to take the stand in their own defense, the judge must warn the jury not to be prejudiced by the defendants' silence. If defendants do choose to take the stand, they cannot claim the privilege against self-incrimination to prevent cross-examination by the prosecution.

Sometimes authorities would rather have answers from a witness than prosecute. Congress has established procedures so that prosecutors and congressional committees may secure from a federal judge a grant of immunity for a witness. After immunity has been granted, a witness may no longer claim a right to refuse to testify. However, the only immunity that Congress presently provides is that, except for perjury prosecution, the government cannot use the information directly derived from the testimony.

The Third Degree

The questioning of suspects by the police is a key procedure for solving crimes. It is also one that can easily be abused. Police officers sometimes forget or ignore the constitutional rights of suspects, especially of those who are frightened and ignorant. Torture, detention, and sustained interrogation to wring confessions from suspects are common practices in police states and are not unknown in the United States. What good is the presumption of innocence if, long before an accused is brought before the court, he or she is detained and forced to prove innocence to the police?

Judges, especially those on the Supreme Court, have done much to

[28]*United States* v. *Payner*, 447 U.S. 727 (1980).
[29]*Blau* v. *United States*, 340 U.S. 332 (1951).

stamp out police brutality. The Supreme Court has ruled that even though there may be sufficient evidence to support a conviction apart from a confession, the admission into evidence of a coerced confession violates the self-incrimination clause, deprives a person of the assistance of counsel guaranteed by the Sixth and Fourteenth amendments, deprives a person of due process, and undermines the entire proceeding.

The federal rules of criminal procedure and the laws of all our states require officers to take those whom they have arrested before a magistrate promptly. The magistrate must inform persons in custody of their constitutional rights and allow them to get in touch with friends and to seek legal advice. While the police have no right to hold persons for questioning prior to a hearing before the magistrate, they are often tempted to do so. Police may feel that if they can quiz suspects before the latter know their constitutional rights to remain silent, they can get them to confess.

Beginning in 1957 the Supreme Court handed down a series of decisions based on the self-incrimination clause of the Fifth Amendment, the right-to-counsel clause of the Sixth Amendment, and the due process clause of the Fifth and Fourteenth Amendments that began to cast doubt on the constitutional validity of any private questioning of persons suspected of crime by federal or state police. Then, in *Miranda* v. *Arizona* in 1966, the Supreme Court announced that no conviction—federal or state—could stand if evidence introduced at the trial had been obtained by the police as the result of "custodial interrogation," unless the following conditions were met. Suspects must have been (1) notified that they are free to remain silent; (2) warned that what they say may be used against them in court; (3) told that they have a right to have an attorney present during the questioning; (4) informed that if they cannot afford to hire their own lawyer, an attorney will be provided for them; and (5) permitted at any stage of the police interrogation to terminate it. If suspects answer questions in the absence of an attorney, the burden is on the prosecution to demonstrate that suspects knowingly and intelligently gave up their rights to remain silent and to have their own lawyer present. Failure to comply with these requirements will lead to reversal of a conviction even if other evidence is sufficient to establish guilt.[30]

Many critics of the *Miranda* decision believe the Court has unnecessarily and severely limited the ability of the police to bring criminals to justice. The importance of pretrial interrogations is underscored by the fact that roughly 90 percent of all criminal convictions result from pleas of guilty and never reach a full trial. Nevertheless, the Supreme Court has upheld *Miranda*, modified to some extent. Evidence obtained contrary to the *Miranda* guidelines is now allowed to be used to attack defendants' statements made at the trial if what defendants say is contrary to what they have previously told the police. Also, *Miranda* warnings are not required for casual questioning, but only when a person is deprived of freedom of action.

INTERROGATION WARNINGS TO PERSONS IN POLICE CUSTODY

THE FOLLOWING WARNINGS MUST BE GIVEN TO THE SUBJECT BEFORE THE INTERROGATION BEGINS:

1. "You have the right to remain silent and refuse to answer questions." Do you understand? Subject replied _____.
2. "Anything you do say may be used against you in a court of law." Do you understand? Subject replied _____.
3. "You have the right to consult an attorney before speaking to the police and to have an attorney present during any questioning now or in the future." Do you understand? Subject replied _____.
5. "If you do not have an attorney available, you have the right to remain silent until you have had an opportunity to consult with one." Do you understand? Subject replied _____.
6. "Now that I have advised you of your rights are you willing to answer questions without an attorney present?" Subject replied _____.

The Right of Privacy

While there is no mention of the right of privacy in the Constitution, the Supreme Court has put together some elements from the First, Fourth, Fifth, Ninth, and Fourteenth amendments recognizing that personal privacy is one of the rights protected by the Constitution. There appear to be three aspects of this right: (1) the right to be free from governmental surveillance and intrusion, especially in marital matters; (2) the right not to have private affairs made public

---

[30]384 U.S. 436 (1966). Liva Baker, *Miranda: Crime, Law and Politics* (Atheneum, 1983) explores every aspect of the decision, including subsequent controversy about its effects.

by the government; and (3) the right to be free in thought and belief from governmental compulsion.[31]

Congress began to show concern about privacy with the adoption of the Family Educational Rights Act of 1974 and the Privacy Act of 1974. These laws limit the record-keeping and record-disclosing activities of schools and universities that receive federal funds; place restraints on files kept by federal agencies; and under certain conditions give individuals access to government files in order to correct information about themselves. But privacy, although highly valued in the abstract, has often run afoul of other rights—for example, the rights of the press. When in conflict with these other rights, it has not fared well before either Congress or the courts. (The exception is the Supreme Court's protection of marital privacy from state regulation.)

The Writ of Habeas Corpus

Even though the framers did not think a Bill of Rights was necessary, they considered certain rights important enough to be included in the original Constitution. Foremost is the guarantee that the writ of habeas corpus will be available unless suspended in time of rebellion or invasion. Permission to suspend the writ is found in the article setting forth the powers of Congress, so, presumably, only Congress has the right to suspend it.

As originally used, the writ was merely an inquiry by a court to determine whether or not a person was being held in custody as the result of an act of a court with proper jurisdiction. But over the years it has developed into a remedy "available to effect discharge from any confinement contrary to the Constitution or fundamental law."[32] Simply stated, the writ is a court order to any person having another in custody directing the official to produce the prisoner in court and explain to the judge why the prisoner is being held. Those held in custody or subject to restraint apply under oath, usually through their attorney, and state why they believe they are being unlawfully held. The judge then orders the jailer to show cause why the writ should not be issued. If a judge finds a petitioner is being unlawfully detained, the judge may order the prisoner's immediate release.

The case of Messrs. Duncan and White is a good example of one use of the writ. Duncan, a civilian shipfitter, had been convicted two years after Pearl Harbor by military authorities for assaulting two marine sentries. White, a stockbroker, had been convicted by military authorities eight months after Pearl Harbor for embezzling stock from another civilian. They filed petitions for writs of habeas corpus in the district court of Hawaii, citing both statutory and constitutional reasons why the military had no right to try them and to keep them in prison. The court then asked the military to show cause why the petition should not be granted. The military replied that Hawaii had become part of an active theater of war; that the writ of habeas corpus had been suspended; that martial law had been established; and that consequently, the district court had no jurisdiction to issue the writs. Moreover, the writ of habeas corpus should not be issued in this case because the military trials of Duncan and White were valid. After hearing both sides, the district court, in an action eventually approved by the Supreme Court, agreed with Duncan and White and issued writs ordering their release.[33]

---

[31]Philip B. Kurland, "Some Reflections on Privacy and the Constitution" (The University of Chicago, Center for Policy Study, 1976), p. 9. A classic and influential article first raising the question is S. D. Warren and L. D. Brandeis, "The Right to Privacy," *Harvard Law Review*, Vol. 4 (December 15, 1890), pp. 193–220. David M. O'Brien, *Privacy, Law, and Public Policy* (Praeger, 1979) is the most comprehensive discussion of the privacy doctrine.

[32]*Preiser* v. *Rodriguez*, 411 U.S. 475 (1973).

[33]*Duncan* v. *Kahanamoku*, 327 U.S. 304 (1946).

State judges may not issue writs of habeas corpus to find out why persons are being held by national authorities, but federal judges may do so to find out why persons are being restrained by state and local officials. Sometimes a single federal judge will set aside a conviction even after it has been reviewed by the state supreme court. Partly as a result of criticism by state judges, partly because of a concern for the principles of federalism, and partly because of a growing overload on the federal courts, the Supreme Court has begun to restrict the use of habeas corpus by federal judges.[34] For example, if a state court has already provided an opportunity for a person to present the argument that he or she was unconstitutionally arrested or searched, a federal district judge may no longer review the matter in a habeas corpus hearing.

EX POST FACTO LAWS AND BILLS OF ATTAINDER

The Constitution forbids both the national and the state governments to pass ex post facto laws or enact bills of attainder (Article I, Sections 9 and 10).

An ex post facto law is a retroactive criminal law that works to the disadvantage of an individual. For example, it can be a law making a particular act a crime that was not a crime when committed. Or it can be a law that increases the punishment for a crime after it was committed or that changes the proof necessary to convict for a crime after it was committed. The prohibition does not prevent the passage of retroactive penal laws that work to the benefit of an accused—a law decreasing punishment or a procedural change making convictions more difficult or the imposition of more stringent sentences more unlikely. Nor does the prohibition against ex post facto laws prevent the passage of retroactive civil laws: Income tax rates as applied to income already earned may be increased.

A bill of attainder is a legislative act inflicting punishment without judicial trial on named individuals or members of a specified group. Although a law working to the disadvantage of an individual does not necessarily make it a bill of attainder, such bills are not limited to those imposing criminal sanctions. They also include laws depriving people of property or jobs. While bills of attainder have been rarely used throughout our history, Congress enacted two in the last three decades. One denied three named federal employees the right to be paid by the federal government, and the other denied members of the Communist Party the right to serve as trade union officers. Former President Richard Nixon has alleged Congress enacted yet a third such bill.

In 1974, four months after Nixon resigned, Congress directed the administrator of the General Services Administration to take custody of the Nixon papers and tapes. The administrator was instructed to return to Nixon his personal and private papers but to preserve in government custody—and eventually make public—those papers having historical value. Since every previous president had been given custody of his own papers, Nixon alleged that Congress had singled him out for punishment. The Supreme Court majority agreed that legislation which subjects a named individual to this humiliating treatment raises serious questions under the bill of attainder clause. Still, seven members held that Nixon was a "legitimate class of one" and that Congress was not motivated by a desire to punish. Pending study as to the disposition of future

[34]Neil D. McFeeley, "The Supreme Court and the Federal System: Federalism from Warren to Burger," *Publius* (Fall 1978), p. 13; William F. Duker, *A Constitutional History of Habeas Corpus* (Greenwood Press, 1980).

presidential papers, Congress could act to preserve the Nixon papers while accepting the fact that other presidential papers were already housed in special libraries under terms set by former presidents.[35]

RIGHTS OF PERSONS ACCUSED OF CRIME

Some feel that the rights of persons accused of a crime are less important than other civil liberties, but as Justice Frankfurter observed: "The history of liberty has largely been the history of observance of procedural safeguards." Further, these safeguards have frequently "been forged in controversies involving not very nice people."

The Federal Courts
The rights of persons accused of a crime by the national government can be found in the Fourth, Fifth, Sixth, and Eighth amendments. In order to gain some idea of the application of these constitutional safeguards, we will follow the fortunes and misfortunes of John T. Crook (a fictitious name).

Crook sent circulars through the mails soliciting purchases of stock in a nonexistent gold mine, an action contrary to at least three federal laws. When postal officers uncovered these activities, they went to the district court and secured from a United States magistrate a warrant to arrest Crook and another warrant to search his home for copies of the circulars. They found Crook at home and read the Miranda warning to him, emphasizing especially his *right to remain silent* and to *have the assistance of counsel*. They showed him the warrants, arrested him for using the mails to defraud, and found and seized some of the circulars mentioned in the search warrant.

Crook was promptly brought before a federal district judge. (He could have had his preliminaries handled by a United States magistrate—see Chapter 17.) The judge again emphasized that Crook had a constitutional right to assistance of counsel. Some years ago a judge merely had to allow a defendant to be represented by an attorney if the defendant showed up in the court with one. But ever since *Johnson* v. *Zerbst* (1938)[36] for federal judges and *Gideon* v. *Wainwright* (1963)[37] for state judges, judges have a positive obligation to ensure that all persons subject to any kind of custodial interrogation are represented by a lawyer.

Unless the record clearly shows that the accused were fully aware of what they were doing and gave up the right to counsel or intelligently exercised the right to represent themselves, the absence of such counsel will render criminal proceedings unconstitutional. The right extends to all trials, for all offenses for which an accused was in fact deprived of liberty, whether or not a jury trial is required. Trials in which fines are the only penalty are exempt from the assistance-of-counsel requirement. This assistance is required at every stage of a criminal proceeding—preliminary hearings, bail hearings, trial, sentence, and appeal.

The Supreme Court has repeatedly insisted on the assistance of counsel. Over the bitter dissent of four members, it reversed a conviction based on a confession made to a police officer after a prisoner had been arrested but while he was being driven to jail. Although his attorney had warned him not to talk and the police had promised not to question him on the ride, the defendant showed the police where the body of the little girl he had been accused of

---

[35]*Nixon v. Administrator of General Services, James M. Burns, et al.*, 433 U.S. 425 (1977).
[36]304 U.S. 458 (1938).
[37]373 U.S. 335 (1963). Anthony Lewis, *Gideon's Trumpet* (Random House, 1964 and 1972), has become a classic.

141

murdering was located; the officer asked him to do so "because her parents were entitled to a Christian burial for the girl."[38]

To return to Crook: When Crook told the judge he could not afford to hire his own counsel, the judge appointed an attorney to represent him, paid for by the federal government. The judge set bail at $2,500, and Crook was held over until the convening of the next federal grand jury. After hiring a professional bondsman who posted the bail and collected a 10 percent fee, Crook was free so long as he remained within the judicial district. The Eighth Amendment *forbids imposition of "excessive bail,"* for it is a basic principle of American justice that no person is guilty until pronounced so after a fair trial, and until declared guilty, no one should be deprived of freedom. To set bail higher than necessary to ensure the presence of a defendant at his or her trial is "excessive." The Bail Reform Act of 1966 allows federal judges to release persons without bail if, after taking into account such factors as past record and family and community ties, bail seems unnecessary. For capital crimes judges may refuse to release a person on bail: No amount of money may be sufficient to ensure that one who stands in jeopardy of losing his or her life will be around for the trial.

When the next grand jury was convened, the United States district attorney brought before the twenty-three jurors evidence to indicate that Crook had committed a federal crime. Grand jurors are concerned not with a person's guilt or innocence but merely with whether there is enough evidence to warrant a trial. No person has a right to appear before a grand jury, but one may be invited or ordered to do so. If a majority of the grand jurors agree that a trial is justified, they return what is known as a *true bill*, or indictment. Except in military cases involving service-connected crimes, the national government cannot force any person to stand trial for any serious crime except *on grand jury indictment*. In our particular case the grand jury was in agreement with the United States district attorney and returned a true bill against Crook.

After a copy of the indictment was served on Crook, he was again ordered to appear before a federal district judge. The Constitution guarantees the accused the *right to be informed of the nature and cause of the accusation* so that he or she can prepare a defense. Consequently, the federal prosecutor had seen to it that the indictment clearly stated the nature of the offense and that copies had been properly served on Crook and his lawyer.

Actually, Crook's attorney, prior to the hearing, had discussed with the United States attorney's office the possibility of Crook pleading guilty to a lesser offense. This kind of plea bargaining is often used. Faced with more charges than they can handle, prosecutors often prefer to accept a guilty plea to a reduced charge rather than to prosecute for the more serious offense. Likewise, defendants are often willing to "cop a plea" to a lesser offense to avoid the risk of more serious punishment.

When defendants plead guilty to a lesser offense, they give up their constitutional rights and under most circumstances are forever prevented from raising objections to their conviction. That is why a judge, before accepting a guilty plea, ordinarily will question a defendant to be sure the attorney has explained the alternatives and that the defendant knows what he or she is doing. It never came to this in Crook's case, however. After discussing the matter with his attorney, he elected to stand trial on the charge and entered a plea of not guilty.

After indictment Crook's bail was raised to $5,000. Now the federal government was obliged to give him *a speedy and a public trial*. The word *speedy*,

[38]*Brewer v. Williams*, 430 U.S. 387 (1977).

however, should not be taken too literally. Crook had to be given time to prepare his defense. Further, defendants often ask for delays, since these work to their advantage. Crowded court dockets often lead to delay, although federal courts have recently adopted a rule of procedure that requires them to state in advance the time limits in which the case must be brought to a hearing. If the government denies the accused a speedy trial in a constitutional sense, the remedy is drastic: Not only is the conviction reversed, but the case must be dismissed outright.

Crook's lawyer pointed out that under the Sixth Amendment, Crook had a right to *trial before an impartial jury* selected from the state and district where the alleged crime was committed, because he was being tried for a serious crime; that is, one punishable by more than six months in prison or a $500 fine. Although federal law requires juries of twelve, the Constitution requires only that juries consist of at least six persons. Conviction in federal courts must be by unanimous vote. (The Constitution permits state courts to render guilty verdicts by nonunanimous juries, provided the jury consists of six or more persons.) An impartial jury, and one that meets the requirements of due process and equal protection, consists of persons who represent a fair cross-section of the community. Although persons are not entitled to a jury on which there are members of their race, sex, religion, or national origin, they are entitled to be tried by a jury from which persons have not been excluded for these reasons. (Such action also violates the civil rights of those denied the opportunity to serve on juries.)

Although both the prosecution and defense have a right to question prospective jurors about their possible bias, there is no *per se*—that is, automatic—constitutional rule permitting defendants to question jurors about racial prejudice. The trial judge determines the need for such questions. However, in exercising general supervisory power over federal courts, the Supreme Court has adopted a rule requiring federal judges to permit such questioning when requested by a defendant accused of a violent crime, and where the defendant and victim are members of different racial or ethnic groups.

The Supreme Court has refused to give defendants with beards a constitutional right to interrogate potential jurors about the jurors' possible prejudice against bearded persons: This, too, is left to the discretion of trial judges. Of a more serious nature, at least to persons without beards, is the question of whether the Supreme Court should set aside, as some have argued, earlier decisions allowing prosecutors and defense attorneys to exercise their preemptory challenges (each side is allowed to exclude without explanation a limited number of persons from a jury) in such a fashion that all persons of one race, sex, or national origin are excluded from a jury.

In preparation for his defense, Crook told his lawyer that he had dinner with George Witness on the night on which he was charged with sending the damaging circulars. The attorney took advantage of Crook's constitutional right to obtain witnesses in his favor and had the judge subpoena Witness to appear at the trial and testify. While Witness could have refused to testify on the grounds that his testimony would tend to incriminate him, he nevertheless agreed to do so. Crook himself, however, chose to use his constitutional right not to be a witness against himself and refused to take the stand. He knew that if he did so, the prosecution would have a right to cross-examination, and he was fearful of what might be uncovered. The federal judge conducting the trial cautioned the jury against drawing any conclusions from Crook's reluctance to testify. All prosecution witnesses appeared in court and were available for defense cross-examination; the Constitution insists that accused persons have the right to be *confronted with the witnesses against them*.

At the conclusion of the trial, the jury brought in a verdict of guilty. The

"Considering the overwhelming case load in our nation's judiciary, Your Honor, may I suggest you dismiss the charges against me?" *Drawing by Stevenson; © The The New Yorker Magazine, Inc.*

judge then raised Crook's bail to $7,500 and announced that she would hand down a sentence on the following Monday. The Eighth Amendment forbids the *levying of excessive fines and the inflicting of cruel and unusual punishments*. The judge, in accordance with the law, gave Crook the maximum punishment of $7,500 and three years in the penitentiary; this could not be considered cruel and unusual.

The ban against cruel and unusual punishments limits government in three ways: (1) It limits the kinds of punishment that may be imposed—for example, it prohibits torture, intentionally denying medical care to prisoners, or holding prisoners in conditions that involve "the unnecessary and wanton infliction of pain."[39] (2) It prohibits punishments that are grossly disproportionate to the severity of the crime. However, "outside the context of capital punishment"—where the Court has limited the death penalty to crimes in which a life has been taken—the Court has been "reluctant to review legislatively mandated terms of imprisonment,"[40] and "successful challenges to the proportionality of particular sentences will be exceedingly rare."[41] The only noncapital punishment the Court has set aside—and that by a vote of five to four—was the sentence by a South Dakota court condemning a man to life in prison, without the possibility of parole, for passing a bad check for $100 after conviction for six previous nonviolent felonies. Justice Powell for the majority said the defendant's crimes were relatively minor; that the latter was being treated more severely than the South Dakota criminals who had committed far more serious

THOSE WHO FACE EXECUTION

Death-row inmates (and types of execution authorized)—

State	Count	Method	State	Count	Method
Alabama	64	Electrocution	Montana	4	Lethal injection or hanging
Arizona	50	Gas chamber			
Arkansas	21	Lethal injection or choice of electrocution if sentenced before 3/24/83.	Nebraska	12	Electrocution
			Nevada	18	Lethal injection
			New Jersey	1	Lethal injection
			New Mexico	5	Lethal injection
			New York	1	Electrocution
California	131	Gas chamber	North Carolina	35	Gas chamber or lethal injection
Colorado	1	Gas chamber			
Delaware	6	Lethal injection			
Florida	196	Electrocution	Ohio	7	Electrocution
Georgia	113	Electrocution	Oklahoma	36	Lethal injection
Idaho	7	Lethal injection or firing squad	Pennsylvania	50	Electrocution
			South Carolina	26	Electrocution
Illinois	53	Lethal injection	Tennessee	33	Electrocution
Indiana	17	Electrocution	Texas	159	Lethal injection
Kentucky	16	Electrocution	U.S. military	7	Hanging
Louisiana	33	Electrocution	Utah	4	Firing squad
Maryland	12	Gas chamber	Virginia	20	Electrocution
Mississippi	35	Gas chamber	Washington	3	Lethal injection or hanging
Missouri	23	Gas chamber			
			Wyoming	3	Gas chamber

Legal Defense and Educational Fund *Death Row, U.S.A.* report. Copyright 8/20/83.

[39]*Rhodes* v. *Chapman*, 452 U.S. 337 (1981).
[40]*Hutto* v. *Davis*, 454 U.S. 370 (1982).
[41]*Solem* v. *Helm*, 77 L Ed 2d 637 (1983).

crimes, and more severely than he would have been treated in any other state; and that therefore his punishment was "significantly disproportionate."

The ban against cruel and unusual punishments also limits the power of the government to decide what can be made a criminal offense: For example, the mere act of being a chronic alcoholic may not be made a crime, for it is an illness. However, being drunk in public may be made a criminal offense.

What of capital punishment? After much soul searching and a series of cases, the Supreme Court has ruled that the death penalty is not necessarily cruel and unusual punishment for the *crime of murder*. (These decisions are of more than passing interest to the well over 1000 persons now under death sentences in thirty-two states. For many years after the Supreme Court held in *Furman* v. *Georgia* (1972), that most death penalty statutes were unconstitutional because they left the juries with indirected discretion, no persons were executed in the United States.[42] A decade later most states have revised their statutes, and the executions have begun again).

However, the state must ensure that whoever imposes the penalty—judge or jury—does so only after careful consideration of the character and record of the person and the circumstances of the particular crime. The automatic use of the death sentence for every person convicted of a specified capital offense will not do: "It is essential that the capital sentencing decision allow for consideration of whatever mitigating circumstances may be relevant to either the particular offender or the particular offense."[43] The Court has suggested that the best procedure is first to have a jury determine guilt, and then in a subsequent proceeding to focus attention on whether the circumstances justify the death penalty. Although it has never ruled on crimes other than murder or rape, the Court has implied that "the death penalty may be properly imposed only as to crimes resulting in the death of the victim,"[44] perhaps only when death is inflicted in "aggravating circumstances."

The Nationalization of the Bill of Rights

While still in the federal penitentiary, Crook was taken by federal authorities before the state courts to answer charges that he had also committed a state crime. Since Crook was entitled to a speedy trial on these state charges, the state could not wait until he had been released by federal authorities before bringing him to justice.

Crook, through his state-appointed attorney, protested that he had already been tried by the federal government for using the mails to defraud. He pointed to the Fifth Amendment provision that no person shall be "subject for the same offense to be twice put in jeopardy of life or limb." This **double jeopardy** limitation, Crook's attorney pointed out, has been interpreted by the Supreme Court (*Benton* v. *Maryland*) to be part of the Fourteenth Amendment and therefore to be a limit on the power of a state.[45] The judge answered: "The Supreme Court has said that double jeopardy prevents two criminal trials by the *same* government for the same criminal offense." (Trial by a state and one of its municipalities is trial by the same government; trial in a juvenile proceeding precludes another trial for the same offense by the state in its regular courts.) It does not prevent punishment by the national and the state governments for the same offense. He pointed to a 1959 Supreme Court decision that

THE FOURTEENTH
AMENDMENT AND THE
NATIONALIZATION OF
THE BILL OF RIGHTS

A process of selective incorporation:

1925 Freedom of speech (*Gitlow* v. *New York*)

1931 Freedom of press (*Near* v. *Minnesota*)

1932 Fair trial (*Powell* v. *Alabama*)

[42]408 U.S. 238. See Raoul Berger, *Death Penalties: The Supreme Court's Obstacle Course* (Harvard University Press, 1982) for an attack on the Court for interfering with states' right to impose the death penalty. See also Hugo Adam Bedau, *The Death Penalty in America*, 3rd ed. (Oxford University Press, 1982) for a more balanced collection of readings by an opponent of the death penalty.

[43]*Roberts* v. *Louisiana*, 431 U.S. 633 (1977).

[44]Justice Stevens concurring in *Coker* v. *Georgia*; *Godfrey* v. *Georgia*.

[45]395 U.S. 784 (1969).

sustained a state conviction of a man for robbing a bank after he had previously been acquitted of the same offense by a federal court.

What constitutional rights can Crook claim in the state courts? First, every state constitution contains a bill of rights listing practically the same guarantees as those found in the Bill of Rights in the national Constitution. But, at least until recently, most state judges have been less inclined than federal judges to interpret the constitutional guarantees of their own state constitutions liberally in favor of those accused of a crime.

To what extent does the national Constitution protect courtroom procedures from state actions? The Bill of Rights does not apply to the states, but the Fourteenth Amendment does.

For some time a persistent minority on the Supreme Court argued that the due process clause of the Fourteenth Amendment should be interpreted to impose on states exactly the same limitations the Bill of Rights imposes on the national government: They favored "total incorporation" of the Bill of Rights into the Fourteenth Amendment.

Other justices argued that the due process clause does not prescribe any set procedures but does require states to provide "fundamental fairness." State actions contrary to a provision of the Bill of Rights should not be declared unconstitutional unless they deprive persons of fundamental fairness.

Still other justices argued that some provisions of the Bill of Rights should be incorporated into the due process clause, but not all of them. In fact, this doctrine of *selective incorporation* has prevailed.

In *Palko* v. *Connecticut* Justice Cardozo formulated the test for distinguishing between those provisions of the Bill of Rights that should be incorporated into the Fourteenth Amendment and those that should not. The rights to be incorporated are those "implicit in the concept of ordered liberty" and so important that neither "liberty nor justice would exist if they were sacrificed."[46] The rights not incorporated are those that while congenial to our system of justice, could be replaced by other procedures without necessarily resulting in a denial of justice or liberty.

Beginning in the 1930s, and at an accelerating pace after 1960, the Supreme Court selectively incorporated provision after provision of the Bill of Rights into the due process clause.[47] Today the Fourteenth Amendment imposes on the states all the provisions of the Bill of Rights except those of the Second, Third, Seventh, and Tenth amendments, and the grand jury requirements of the Fifth Amendment. (No Supreme Court decision applies the excessive bail and fine limitation of the Eighth Amendment to the states. However, almost by definition, if a bail or a fine is thought to be excessive, it is likely its imposition would be considered a denial of due process.)

The Supreme Court probably will not incorporate additional provisions; most lawyers, political scientists, and other observers believe states should be allowed to continue to indict persons for serious crimes by means other than grand juries. In eighteen states grand juries are no longer required for any crimes; in twenty-one, they are needed only for felonies. Only in eight are they required for all except minor offenses. Other provisions not yet incorporated are really not applicable to the states.

The late Justice Black, seeking to incorporate the whole Bill of Rights into the Fourteenth Amendment, argued that "the first section of the Fourteenth Amendment not only incorporates the specifics of the first eight amend-

[46]302 U.S. 319 (1937).

[47]Richard C. Cortner, *The Supreme Court and the Second Bill of Rights: The Fourteenth Amendment and the Nationalization of Civil Liberties* (University of Wisconsin Press, 1981) carefully traces these developments.

ments, but it is *confined to them*."[48] Justice Black would not have allowed members of the Court to impose on the country their own notions of fundamental rights, but only those specified in the Constitution. He quoted approvingly from Judge Learned Hand: "For myself it would be most irksome to be ruled by a bevy of Platonic Guardians, even if I know how to choose them, which I assuredly do not."[49]

But Justice Black has lost the argument to those who believe that in addition to incorporating all the specific provisions of the Bill of Rights, the due process clause protects other fundamental rights, too. "For example, the rights of association and of privacy, the right to be presumed innocent and the right to be judged by a standard of proof beyond a reasonable doubt in a criminal trial, as well as the right to travel, appear nowhere in the Constitution or Bill of Rights. Yet these important but unarticulated rights have nonetheless been found to share constitutional protection in common with explicit guarantees.[50] This view, now adhered to by a majority on the Supreme Court, sees the role of the Supreme Court in the words quoted approvingly by Justice Douglas of the late Edmond Cahn: "Be not reasonable with inquisitions, anonymous informers, and secret files that mock American justice. . . . Exercise the full judicial power of the United States; nullify them, forbid them, and make us proud again."[51]

HOW JUST IS OUR SYSTEM OF JUSTICE?

What are the major criticisms of the American system of justice? How have they been answered?

Too Many Loopholes

It is argued that to protect the innocent and place the burden of proof on the government, we have established so many procedures that justice is delayed, disrespect for the law is encouraged, and guilty persons go unpunished. Justice should be swift and sure without being arbitrary. But under our procedures criminals may go unpunished because (1) the police decide not to arrest them; (2) the judge decides not to hold them; (3) the prosecutor decides not to prosecute them; (4) the grand jury decides not to indict them; (5) the jury decides not to convict them; (6) the judge decides not to sentence them; (7) an appeals court decides to reverse the conviction; (8) a federal judge decides to release them on a habeas corpus writ; or (9) if retried and convicted, the executive decides to pardon, reprieve, or parole them. As a result, the public never knows whom to hold responsible when laws are not enforced. The police can blame the prosecutor, the prosecutor can blame the police, and they can all blame the judges.

Some argue that in our impossible pursuit of perfect justice, we are not achieving effective justice.[52] Many critics blame the Supreme Court for imposing its own notions of justice on the country and for placing so many disabilities on police and prosecutors that these officials are finding it increasingly difficult to bring any cases to conclusion. Others take a different view. They doubt the decisions of the Supreme Court have had that much impact on police and

[48]Henry J. Abraham, *Freedom and the Court: Civil Rights and Liberties in the United States* (Oxford University Press, 1967), p. 75. See also James J. Magee, *Mr. Justice Black: Absolutist on the Court* (Virginia Legal Studies, 1980).

[49]*Griswold* v. *Connecticut,* 381 U.S. 479 (1965).

[50]*Richmond Newspapers Inc.* v. *Virginia,* 448 U.S. 555 (1980).

[51]As quoted in Abraham, *Freedom and the Court.*

[52]Macklin Fleming, *The Price of Perfect Justice* (Basic Books, 1974).

prosecutors. They point out that there is more to justice than simply securing convictions. All the steps in the administration of criminal laws have been developed out of centuries of trial and error, and each has been constructed to provide protection against particular abuses. History warns against entrusting the instruments of criminal law enforcement to a single officer. For this reason, responsibility is vested in many officials.

Too Unreliable

Critics who complain that our system of justice is unreliable often point to trial by jury as the chief source of trouble. Trial by jury, they argue, leads to a theatrical combat between lawyers who base their appeals on the prejudice and sentiments of the jurors. "Mr. Prejudice and Miss Sympathy are the names of witnesses whose testimony is never recorded, but must nevertheless be reckoned with in trials by jury."[53] No other country relies as heavily on trial by jury as does the United States. Jury trials are also time consuming and costly.

Defenders of the jury system reply that trial by jury provides a check by nonprofessionals on the actions of judges and prosecutors. Also, there is no evidence to support the charge that juries are unreliable. On the contrary, decisions of juries do not systematically differ from those of judges.[54] Moreover, the jury system helps to educate citizens and enables them to participate in the application of their own law.

The grand jury system has also come under attack. In theory, the grand jury has two functions: to protect the innocent from having to stand trial by requiring prosecutors to demonstrate behind closed doors that they have evidence to justify trial; and to provide an independent agency, uncontrolled by those in power, to investigate wrongdoing. Critics charge, however, that the grand jury has become a tool of the prosecutor. Said Justice Douglas: "It is, indeed, common knowledge that the grand jury, having been conceived as a bulwark between the citizen and the Government, is now a tool of the Executive."[55]

Hartford police arrested forty picketers as a disturbance flared on the picket line at a nursing home. The employees' union charged that the police used unnecessary force in making arrests. *UPI.*

During the early 1970s critics from the left side of the political spectrum charged that grand juries had become instruments to intimidate radicals, blacks, and antiwar militants. However, by 1973 grand juries were being used to investigate the executive branch. It was through the use of the grand jury that the special prosecutor was able to get before the courts his contention that the president had no constitutional right to withhold information about wrongdoing. As the editors of the *Congressional Quarterly* have pointed out: "Liberals can applaud grand juries for investigating Watergate and denounce them for intimidating militants. Conservatives might just as easily reprove them for the former and commend them for the latter. The important question about grand juries is whether they are an effective instrument for protecting the innocent and bringing the guilty to trial. . . . On these questions, the jury is still out."[56]

Discrimination

The Supreme Court has worked particularly hard during the last several decades to give reality to the ideal of equal justice under the law. At the trial level persons accused of crime who cannot afford an attorney must be furnished one at government expense. If transcripts are required for appeals, such transcripts

[53]Jerome Frank, *Courts on Trial* (Princeton University Press, 1949), p. 122. See Harry Kalven, Jr., and Hans Zeisel, *The American Jury* (University of Chicago Press, 1971) for findings of the University of Chicago's massive study of the jury system. See also Rita James Simon (ed.), *The Jury System in America: A Critical Overview* (Sage Publications, 1975).

[54]Kalven and Zeisel, *The American Jury*, pp. 57ff.

[55]*United States v. Mara*, dissenting, 410 U.S. 19 (1973).

[56]"The Supreme Court; Justice and the Law," *Congressional Quarterly* (1973), p. 93. Leroy D. Clark, *The Grand Jury: The Use and Abuse of Political Power* (Quadrangle, 1975) is a critical account calling for reform of the grand jury.

must be made available to those who cannot afford to purchase them. If an appeal is permitted, the government must also provide an attorney for at least one legal appeal from the decision of the trial court. Once a poor person is sentenced, that person cannot be kept in jail beyond the term of the sentence because the person cannot afford to pay a fine. Poor people cannot be imprisoned because of inability to pay a fine. Even in the area of civil proceedings—divorce proceedings, for example—fees cannot be imposed that deny poor persons their fundamental rights such as the right to obtain a divorce. (A state has no obligation, however, to waive fees for those seeking to be declared bankrupt, the Court apparently believing that one has a constitutional right to be absolved of the ties that bind but not of one's debts.)

The major area of difficulty arises outside the courtroom, for one of the most acute problems of our society is the tension between the police and the black and Hispanic communities congregated in the ghettos and barrios of our large cities. Many members of minorities do not believe we have equal protection under the law: "Whether the stated belief is well founded or not is at least partly beside the point. The existence of the belief is damaging enough."[57] Blacks see the police as enforcers of white law. Studies of prejudice on the part of some white police officers and examples of undignified—if not brutal—police treatment of blacks are ample.

Still, if a sociological explanation is provided for the behavior of those who break the law—they are victims of poverty, prejudice, and other social factors—it is unfair to moralize about the misbehavior of those who enforce the law—they are brutal and without proper moral standards. For "the policeman," wrote a former attorney general, "is the most important American. . . . . He works in a highly flammable environment. A spark can cause an explosion. He must maintain order without provocation which will cause combustion."[58]

Police officers have a vital role in preserving (or restricting) civil liberties. They determine who shall be arrested; they give daily reality to the protections of our Constitution; and, as events in our large cities in the 1960s and in Miami in 1980 made clear, they have much to do with preventing or causing civil disorders. Yet these persons on whom we depend for so much, the only persons in our civil society whom we legally arm with deadly weapons, are often underpaid. In performing their tasks they often discover that the public is indifferent, even hostile. Little wonder that they are sometimes impatient with professors who talk about the complexities of the cycle of poverty or search and seizures laws. It is the officer, and not the scholars or judges, who at 2 A.M. must go into areas of high crime, often in the middle of hostile and crowded areas, to search a dark alley in response to a call about prowlers.

Until recently the role of police officers was generally ignored. Beginning in the late 1960s, for a variety of reasons, a sustained drive was begun to improve the quality of police services. Action was taken to recruit more blacks, Hispanics, and women. Community relations programs were established. Considerable progress was made, and tensions between police and minority communities appeared to be improving. However, after disorders in Miami in 1980 (sparked by the acquittal of white police officers who killed a black civilian during a high-speed chase for a minor traffic violation), tensions between police and many communities once again began to rise. Many blacks continue to feel that "the police force is racist whether officers are black or white," an attitude that adds to the difficulty of recruiting black officers.[59] "Within minority com-

A New York City policeman making his investigation at the scene of a crime. *Jim Anderson, Woodfin Camp.*

"How do I feel about being mugged? Well, naturally I didn't enjoy it and I certainly don't condone violence or threats of violence as a means toward social change. However, I can empathize with my assailant and realize that in his terms this is a valid response to the deteriorating socioeconomic situation in which we find ourselves." *Drawing by Lorenz; © 1972. The New Yorker Magazine, Inc.*

---

[57]George Edwards, *The Police on the Urban Frontier* (Institute of Human Relations Press and The American Jewish Committee, 1968), p. 28.

[58]Ramsey Clark, Foreword to Edwards, p. viii.

[59]John Herbers, "Minority Groups Distrust of Police Force Said to Be on the Rise around the Country," *The New York Times*, May 25, 1980, p. 16.

munities the perception that police abuse of authority is discriminatory is rein-forced by national statistics that show that disproportionately large numbers of minority civilians are victims of brutality and use of deadly force. This remains a potentially explosive issue which not only inhibits effective policing but in fact undermines the public security."[60] According to a member of the United States Commission on Civil Rights: "Although it would be cynical to conclude that there has been no progress in the last 20 years, serious problems persist in many cities."[61]

The Supreme Court and Civil Liberties

Plainly, judges—especially those on the Supreme Court—play a major role in enforcing constitutional guarantees. In fact, this combination of judicial en-forcement and written guarantees of enumerated liberties is one of the basic features of the American system of government. As Justice Jackson wrote: "The very purpose of a Bill of Rights was to withdraw certain subjects from the vicis-situdes of political controversy, to place them beyond the reach of majorities and officials and to establish them as legal principles to be applied by the courts. One's right to life, liberty, and property, to free speech, a free press, freedom of worship and assembly, and other fundamental rights may not be submitted to vote: they depend on the outcome of no elections."[62] Or as one political scientist put it: "One is reminded of Godfrey Cambridge's nightmare: A tele-phone rings and a voice announces: 'We've had a referendum on slavery in California and you lost. Report to the auction block in four hours.'"[63]

This emphasis on constitutional limitations and judicial enforcement is an example of the "auxiliary precautions" James Madison felt were necessary to prevent arbitrary governmental action. Other free nations rely more on elec-tions and political checks to protect their rights; in the United States we appeal to judges when we fear our freedoms are in danger.

In the United States our emphasis on judicial protection of civil liberties focuses attention on the Supreme Court. Yet only a small number of contro-versies are carried to the Court, and a Supreme Court decision is not the end of the policy-making process. Compliance with its rulings "does not necessar-ily, universally, or automatically follow. . . ."[64] It is the judges of lower courts as well as the police, the superintendents of schools, and the local prosecutors who translate the Court's doctrines and who do or do not apply them.

The Supreme Court can do little unless its decisions reflect a national consensus. Judges by themselves cannot guarantee anything: Neither can the First Amendment. As Justice Jackson once asked: "Must we first maintain a system of free political government to assure a free judiciary to guarantee free government? . . . [It] is my belief that the attitude of a society and of its orga-nized political forces, rather than its legal machinery, is the controlling force in the character of free institutions. . . . [Any] court which undertakes by its legal processes to enforce civil liberties needs the support of an enlightened and vigorous public opinion. . . ."[65]

Action has been recently taken to recruit more blacks, Hispanics, and women. *Sepp Sietz, Woodfin Camp.*

[60]United States Commission on Civil Rights, "Police Practices and the Preservation of Civil Rights" (statement issued July 9, 1980), p. 3.

[61]*The Washington Post*, July 10, 1980, p. A7.

[62]*West Virginia State Board of Education v. Barnette*, 319 U.S. 624 (1943).

[63]Samuel Krislov, *The Supreme Court and Political Freedom* (Free Press, 1968), p. 35.

[64]See Richard M. Johnson, *The Dynamics of Compliance: Supreme Court Decision-Making from a New Perspective* (Northwestern University Press, 1967), p. 3.

[65]Robert H. Jackson, *The Supreme Court in the American System of Government* (Harvard Uni-versity Press, 1955), pp. 81–82; Jonathan D. Casper, *The Politics of Civil Liberties* (Harper & Row, 1973).

SUMMARY

1. One of the basic distinctions between a free society and a police state is that there are *effective restraints* in a free society on the way public officials, especially law enforcement officials, perform their duties. In the United States these constitutional restraints are judicially enforceable.

2. The Constitution protects the acquisition and retention of citizenship. It protects the basic liberties of aliens as well as of citizens. It protects our property from arbitrary governmental interference, although debates as to which interferences are reasonable and which are arbitrary are not easily settled.

3. The Constitution imposes limits not only on the procedures government must follow but also on the *ends* it may pursue. Some things are out of bounds no matter what procedures are followed. In determining what is reasonable and what is unreasonable, legislatures have the primary role. However, the Supreme Court continues to exercise its own independent and final review of legislative determinations of reasonableness, especially on matters affecting civil liberties and civil rights.

4. The framers knew from their own experiences that in their zeal to maintain power and to enforce the laws, public officials are often tempted to infringe on the rights of those accused of crimes. To prevent such abuse, the Constitution imposes detailed *procedures* national officials must follow in order to make searches and arrests and to bring people to trial.

5. Recently the Supreme Court has interpreted the Constitution, especially the Fourteenth Amendment, to impose on state and local governments almost the same restraints in the administration of justice as those imposed on the national government.

6. The Supreme Court continues to play a prominent role in the development of public policy designed to protect the *rights of the accused,* to ensure that the innocent are not punished, and to ensure that the *public is protected* against those who break the laws. The Court's decisions influence what the public believes and how police officers and others involved in the administration of justice behave. But the Court cannot—and should not—alone insure fairness in the administration of justice.

FURTHER READING

Vincent Blasi (ed.). *The Burger Court: The Counter Revolution That Wasn't* (Yale University Press, 1983).

Abraham S. Blumberg. *Criminal Justice: Issues and Ironies,* 2nd ed. (New Viewpoints, 1979).

Alan M. Dershowitz. *The Best Defense* (Random House, 1982).

David Fellman. *The Defendant's Rights Today* (University of Wisconsin Press, 1976).

Macklin Fleming. *The Price of Perfect Justice* (Basic Books, 1974).

J. David Hirschel. *Fourth Amendment Rights* (Lexington Books, 1979)

Mary M. Kritz (ed.). *U.S. Immigration and Refugee Policy* (Heath, 1982).

James S. Kunen. *How Can You Defend Those People: The Making of a Criminal Lawyer* (Random House, 1983).

Stuart Nagel, Erika Fairchild, and Anthony Champagne. *The Political Science of Criminal Justice* (Chs. C Thomas, 1983).

David M. O'Brien. *Privacy, Law and Public Policy* (Praeger, 1979).

Charles E. Silberman. *Criminal Violence and Criminal Justice* (Random House, 1978).

Lloyd Weinreb. *Denial of Justice: Criminal Process in the United States,* 2nd ed. (Free Press, 1979).

GROUPS: THE POLITICS OF FACTION

7

What do the United States Catholic Conference, The United Church of Christ, the Lutheran Council in the U.S.A., the United Presbyterian Church, the Episcopal Church, and Bread for the World (a Christian citizens group against hunger) have in common with five former Secretaries of the United States Treasury and a former Secretary of Commerce? They all opposed President Reagan's 1984 budget.

Former secretaries—including John Connally, Douglas Dillon, and William Simon—headed the Bipartisan Budget Appeal. In full-page advertisements in *The New York Times*, these veteran officials argued for curbing the growth of federal spending, especially in the defense sector. Prominent ex-officials, educators, law firms, and executives signed the appeal, holding that military strength is grounded in economic strength, and that ever-ballooning budget deficits lead to a weakened economy.

The Catholic and Protestant churches, working together with Jewish organizations through the Washington Interreligious Staff Council, also opposed vast increases in military spending. Poor citizens, they contended, were "sacrificial lambs" in the budget. Cuts in social programs fall hardest on the elderly, women, and children—many of them already in soup lines or shelters. Further, a disproportionate number of those affected belong to racial and ethnic minorities.

The Bipartisan Budget Appeal and the Washington Interreligious Staff Council speak for factions—groups with particular interests that others see as adverse to their own interests or to the community good. Note how these groups, with their differing interests and perspectives, define the situation differently. The Bipartisan Budget Appeal sees the problem from the top down: Strong foreign policy needs a strong military, which needs a strong economy;

too rapid growth in the defense sector of the federal budget will put the rest of the economy out of kilter. The Interreligious Staff Council sees the problem from the bottom up. They define the common good in moral terms: The budget hurts those already down and thus tends to endanger social and political fabric. Both see the interrelationships of the federal budget and the economy, but each emphasizes different parts of the whole.

THE MAZE OF GROUP INTERESTS

Whether we see the economy in material or moral terms, issues and factions are at the heart of government and politics. James Madison argued in *The Federalist Number 10* that such factions are inherent in society. Persons by nature have diverse faculties, "from which the rights of property originate," and "the protection of these faculties is the first object of government. From the protection of different and unequal faculties of acquiring property, the possession of different degrees and kinds of property immediately results"; hence the "division of the society into different interests and parties." The principal task of government is to regulate the "various and interfering interests"—landed, manufacturing, mercantile, moneyed, creditor, and debtor.

Factions involved in *interest group politics*—commonly called *interest groups*—focus on concerns that most often are already well enmeshed in governmental institutions. We call this the politics of vested interests; throughout our history certain groups have written their concerns—principles, policies, or programs—into both the Constitution and statutory or case law through a process of bargaining and compromise.

Factions also take part in *movement politics*, focusing on concerns that have either been excluded from the government's agenda or insufficiently addressed. In one sense movements act for interests that have not yet found a niche in government. But movements also arise from group actions to change the structure of government itself—to change the arrangement of the niches themselves, so to speak. (We will examine movement politics in the next chapter.)

Madison's Fear of Factions

What does this kind of factional struggle mean for government by the people? When the young Virginian, James Madison, was writing what would become the famous *Federalist No. 10* (see Appendix) for the *New York Packet*, Dan Shays's desperate farmers were still on his mind. Madison had been almost as disturbed by the tumult and bloodshed as had his mentor, George Washington. In his small, precise handwriting Madison now warned of the tendency of popular government toward the "vice" of faction, toward "instability, injustice, and confusion" in the "public councils."

Madison favored the proposed new federal constitution because he believed it would control the effects of factionalism without suppressing liberty. He would have been disturbed by the violence surrounding women's struggle for the vote, and appalled by the many eruptions of violence in the nation's history: Northerners and Southerners slaughtering each other, whites brutalizing and lynching blacks, employers shooting strikers and strikers beating "scabs," protesting farmers seizing other farmers' milk and dumping it into the ditches. But Madison would also have noticed an enormous amount of peaceful conflict among factions, as interest groups bargained and compromised with one another within the federal system.

In the late eighteenth century Madison was concerned about religious, political, and economic factions. What are the key groups and issues today?

What are the sources of the groups' strengths and weaknesses? How do they seek to influence government? Are they as dangerous to the public interest now as Madison feared they were in his time? And if so, what has been done about it, and what else could be done?

Group Interests Today

For all their importance, the Bipartisan Budget Appeal and the Washington Interreligious Staff Council make up only a tiny part of American interest groups. The United States has often been called a nation of joiners. Europeans sometimes make fun of us for setting up all sorts of organizations, and we ourselves are often amused by the behavior of our groups—the noisy conventions of veterans' associations, the solemn rites of great fraternal organizations, the oratory of patriotic societies. Yet most of these groups are serious in their aims, and they play an enormous role in politics.

How many groups are there in America? There is no way of knowing accurately. Families are the most basic and important groups of all, and there are over 60 million families in the United States. We have a quarter of a million religious congregations; diverse farm groups and trade unions; and over two thousand trade associations. And all these are groups in the broadest sense of the term—that is, the members share some common outlook or attitude, and interact with one another in some way.[1] Nor can we measure the variety of groups in America, although we know it is tremendous—ranging from such well-known groups as the local Elks or the PTA or the controversial Moral Majority, to such exotic species as the Blizzard Men of 1888 (commemorating a devastating storm) or Friends of the Snail Darter.

One person may belong to a great variety of groups and organizations. At home he or she belongs to a family, neighborhood, religious congregation, and so on. But such a person may also be a member of the Rotary Club, the Masons, a law firm, the American Automobile Association, a taxpayers' association, the Republican party, a bowling league, the American Bar Association, or the state bar association. A person may be a member of all these groups but not *equally* so. Loyalty to family or law firm may greatly outweigh loyalty to all the other groups. Do the individual's allegiances to a wide variety of groups ever come into conflict with one another? Indeed yes. The AAA may demand better roads, while the taxpayers' association wants less governmental spending. The neighborhood may be largely made up of Democrats, while the individual in question is a Republican.

Organized interest groups raise questions very close to the central problems of this book. Do the organized groups fairly represent the great range and variety of interests in the United States? Do the leaders of specific associations—union presidents, for example—fairly represent the various interests of their own members?

Interest groups are of many types: Some are formal associations or organizations; others have no formal organization at all. Several interest groups may even exist within a single formal organization. Inside the American Bar Association there may be two or three interest groups in conflict over a particular issue. An interest group may be either broader or narrower than a particular organization. The American Federation of Labor and Congress of Industrial Organizations, for example, may be opposed to a specific labor reform measure. But not all members of the AFL-CIO are likely to oppose the bill, and some people who are not members will oppose it. The interest group working

[1]David B. Truman, *The Governmental Process* (Knopf, 1951), chap. 2. The basic approach of this chapter is drawn largely from Truman's book and from A. F. Bentley's pioneer work, *The Process of Government* (University of Chicago Press, 1908).

to oppose this measure, then, is composed of most members of the AFL-CIO, but not all, along with some people outside the formal labor organization.

Politics is largely a conflict among competing groups with conflicting ideas of what constitutes the general interest. In political arguments we inevitably talk about special interests versus the general welfare. But in political analysis it is better to talk about *this* group's idea of the general welfare as compared with *that* group's. We are all committed to particular values as persons, but as social scientists we cannot pretend to set up a clearly defined national interest. But how can we discover the general interest? Let us begin with the environment that surrounds interest groups, giving them meaning and impact—the local home setting and the broader community.

POLITICAL CULTURE: THE FEELING OF LASTING COMMUNITY

All Americans today are born or immigrate into a political community that shapes their sense of being an American, their relationship to their government, their sense of a common heritage and a collective purpose, and their faith in their nation, their community, and ultimately themselves. Anthropologists speak of the overall culture as the total way of life of a people, the social heritage persons acquire from their groups. Psychologists focus on the basic values, attitudes, myths, and traditions that are shared by a people and that endure generation after generation. Political scientists emphasize political culture—fundamental assumptions about nation, government, and citizenship and the purposes that nation, government, and citizens should serve.

Here we will focus on two key aspects of the American political community: the extent of our agreement over the proper *means* of collective political action (that is, over government), and the extent of our agreement over the *ends* of our political culture (that is, over the basic goals or purposes of government).

Common Means: Support of the Political System

A political system will tend to be vulnerable if people lack faith in their country and its organized political life. Like virtually all peoples, most Americans love their native land and strongly identify with their own country. Children in particular will assert flatly that "America is the best country in the world." They learn early about heroes like George Washington and Abe Lincoln (though less about heroes and heroines like Frederick Douglass and Sojourner Truth). They also learn about symbols like flags and national anthems and about famous battles won and lost. In contrast to people in some other countries, Americans have traditionally had pride in their governmental and political institutions.[2] Yet by 1976 a majority said they wanted change in the form of government, and a quarter of those questioned wanted "big changes," as Table 7–1 suggests.

During the 1960s Americans in general began to show less faith in government, and by the post-Watergate period almost two-thirds said they could trust the government only "some of the time"; less than four percent trusted it all the time.[3] By 1976 more people voiced the opinion that quite a few officials in government "don't seem to know what they are doing."[4] In that same year almost three times as many believed that the government was "pretty much run

---

[2]Gabriel Almond and Sidney Verba, *The Civic Culture: Political Attitudes and Democracy in Five Nations* (Princeton University Press, 1963), p. 102.

[3]Bruce A. Campbell, *The American Electorate* (Holt, Rinehart and Winston, 1979), p. 88; Arthur H. Miller, "Political Issues and Trust in Government: 1964-1970," *American Political Science Review* (September 1974), p. 953; ICPSR Archive: CPS Presidential Election Studies (1972 and 1976).

[4]Campbell, *The American Electorate*, p. 88.

	1972	1976
Pride in government		
I am proud of many things about our form of government	86%	80%
I can't find much about our form of government to be proud of	14	20
	100%	100%
Change our form of government?		
Keep our form of government as is	59%	47%
Some change needed	26	28
Big change needed	15	25
	100%	100%
N:	(1016)	(2673)

SOURCE: Bruce A. Campbell, *The American Electorate* (Holt, Rinehart and Winston, 1979). 1972 figures adapted from Jack Citrin, "Comment: The Political Relevance of Trust in Government," *American Political Science Review* (September 1974), p. 975; 1976 figures from ICPSR Archive: CPS 1976 Presidential Election Study.

Richard Viguerie, one of the noted leaders behind several right wing conservative groups. A businessman and conservative political activist, he is the king of direct mail fundraising. *UPI.*

by a *few big interests*" than felt it was run for the benefit of all the people.[5] Feelings of trust and confidence fell so low during the Carter administration that the president himself went on television to say that the nation was suffering a "crisis of confidence" that "threatens the very fabric of our society."[6] Black citizens, especially black women feeling the "double whammy" of race and sex discrimination, were the least trusting of all.[7]

What is to blame for this loss of trust, this failure of confidence? Presented with a list of possible causes, and allowed to offer several reasons if they wished, about half the persons questioned gave the following explanations:

- ☐ Letdown in moral values
- ☐ Lack of good leadership
- ☐ Permissiveness in the courts
- ☐ Wrongdoing in government
- ☐ Selfishness, people not thinking of others
- ☐ Too much commitment to other nations in the world

Somewhat fewer—about 40 percent of the respondents— said that "permissiveness of parents" was a cause of the problems, while about the same number listed "too much emphasis on money and materialism." Relatively few felt that radicalism or growing conservatism was at fault.

Over 50 percent blamed our problems on poor leadership, and this raises a major question about lack of faith in the political system as a common means to certain ends. Do people doubt the basic *system*, the current *leaders*, or both? On the whole, people seem more critical of their leaders than of their system. In recent years they have had less confidence in the leaders in other areas as well, such as medicine and the military. Confidence in people running the television news rose somewhat, and trust in the heads of organized labor, which had been low, remained that way.

The lack of faith in political leaders was especially interesting, because voters have the power to throw out bad leaders and put in good ones. But what if both parties nominate poor candidates? This was a major grievance about the

[5]Ibid., p. 90.

[6]For a sharp debate between "President Carter's pollster," Patrick H. Caddell, and political scientist Warren E. Miller, as to whether a crisis of confidence did exist in the summer of 1979, see *Public Opinion* (October-November 1979), pp. 2–16, 52–60.

[7]Sandra Baxter and Marjorie Lansing, *Women and Politics: The Invisible Majority* (University of Michigan Press, 1981), pp. 92–94.

1976, 1980, and 1984 campaigns. But what if the *system* tends to produce poor candidates and leaders? It is not easy to separate the leaders from the system in which they operate. Perhaps that is why so many people said they wanted "some" or "big" changes in government by the late 1970s.

Common Ends: Ideals Without Ideology

Every now and then you run into people who are absolutely set in their ideas, who have definite, clear attitudes about politics or religion or morality, who are quick to take a position on any issue that relates to those basic ideas, and who are slow and stubborn in changing to a different point of view. Some of these persons are ideologues—that is, they hold a unified, comprehensive, internally consistent, and continuing pattern of general ideas that readily determine the positions they take on specific issues and candidates.

Compared to other nations, and especially to dictatorships, the United States has rarely been given to ideology (or so some believe). We pride ourselves on being a "practical" people, calling the shots as we see them, happiest when we are improvising and experimenting. Others might counter that this is evidence that the founding fathers' attempts to mute the "mischiefs of faction" have been so successful that pragmatism itself should be seen as an ideology. Unlike certain parliamentary democracies, we do not have a neat array of parties representing ideological positions from Left to Right. When Americans were asked recently where they placed themselves on a scale running from "extremely liberal" to "extremely conservative," about one quarter put themselves at the center ("Moderate, middle of the road"), and roughly 10 percent in each of the designations: "Liberal," "Slightly liberal," "Slightly conservative," and "Conservative" (see chart). Only a few described themselves as "Extremely liberal" or "Extremely conservative." But—and this was the most important finding—over a third answered that they had "not thought much about it," or didn't know.

Most Americans, in short, do not think of themselves as liberal or conservative, unless pressed by pollsters or professors. "Vast numbers of the mass public (and for that matter some opinion leaders as well) have only the faintest notion of the meaning of terms like liberalism and conservatism, and when asked to apply the labels, often misclassify themselves."[8] Unlike ideologues, these people do not have internally consistent sets of ideas, and hence their position on one issue—such as level of government spending on health care for needy people—may not be an indication of their position on a wholly different issue—such as level of government spending on the problems of the central cities.

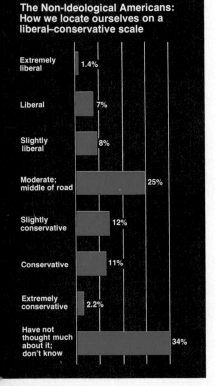

The Non-Ideological Americans:
How we locate ourselves on a liberal–conservative scale

Extremely liberal — 1.4%
Liberal — 7%
Slightly liberal — 8%
Moderate; middle of road — 25%
Slightly conservative — 12%
Conservative — 11%
Extremely conservative — 2.2%
Have not thought much about it; don't know — 34%

The Role of Values

That Americans tend not to be ideological does not mean they have no fundamental beliefs or principles or values—*ideals*, as we will call them here. In many respects Americans are a very believing, principled, even moralistic people. For example, they believe in their heritage of liberty and equality (see Chapter 1). Of course, the test of their belief in liberty is not simply whether they say they support it; virtually all Americans say they believe in *liberty*—but they define it in different ways in relation to different groups.

Thus, in recent years some students and teachers—most of whom doubtless cherish freedom of speech in the abstract—have stifled this liberty on campuses by drowning out speakers through heckling, or by intimidating them in advance so that the speakers declined to visit the campus. Plausible reasons are advanced, but the net result is an erosion of that competition of ideas that is at the heart of the learning process. Such mixed attitudes are nothing new.

Between the mid-1950s and the late 1970s, the percentage of Americans who said that they would be willing to allow an atheist to speak in their com-

Student group protests state budget cuts that will affect state colleges in New Jersey. *UPI*.

[8]Campbell, *passim*.

munity, or who would allow a communist to speak there, almost doubled. Only a minority, however, would still allow such persons to *teach*.[9] And doubtless many persons who believe in this kind of tolerance as an ideal might not be so tolerant when confronted with the actual prospect of having a person from another disliked group, or one with hated ideas, speak in their town.[10]

In certain ways the ideal of *equality* also seems to have grown stronger. During the past decade the number of persons favoring efforts to strengthen and change women's status in society increased from 42 to 65 percent, according to surveys. Approval of married women working rose sharply, and the number of persons stating that blacks had a right to live anywhere they could afford also rose significantly. Although many persons continued to oppose busing of schoolchildren from one district to another, the vast majority of white parents whose children had been bused said that the experience had worked out satisfactorily or partly satisfactorily.[11]

Still, ideals mask a good deal of mixed attitudes and inconsistent behavior. Americans have found it easier to express tolerant views to a middle-class pollster from outside their community than to *practice* tolerance in specific situations on their own street. While people may be more favorable to liberty and equality for women, by the late 1970s almost half the respondents still believed that "women's place is in the home." Over a third felt that blacks were trying to move too fast. Clearly, how people actually *behave* in specific situations depends not just on their ideals but on many other factors as well. Perhaps the most important of these is leadership, both in the community and in the nation. But many leaders at both levels are lacking in the kind of commitment and sense of purpose that would enable them truly to lead people toward observing their heritage of liberty and equality *in practice*. In the early 1980s a handful of state legislators kept the Equal Rights Amendment from being ratified. And civil rights groups expended much energy to convince Congress to extend the Voting Rights Act.

"Before I tell you who I'm for, perhaps you'd be interested to hear a little something about how my political thinking has evolved over the years." *Drawing by Stevenson;* © *1980 The New Yorker Magazine, Inc.*

HOW WE LEARN OUR POLITICAL BELIEFS

Our ideals and attitudes do not arise directly from some great "heritage." They come to us through parents and through many other "agents." No one is *born* with political values and attitudes. We *learn* them, and we have many teachers. Children in the United States typically show political interest by the age of ten, and by the early teens that interest is fairly high. Religious, sexual, racial, and ethnic identities usually develop even earlier, and these may have important political implications. These learning experiences slowly shape the values and attitudes we carry into adulthood. And even as adults we are subject to change in how we think and feel about government and politics. The process by which we develop our political values and attitudes is called political socialization. What each person develops in the way of political values and attitudes is both affected by and contributes to the total political culture.

The Influence of the Family

We begin to form our picture of the world listening to our parents talk at breakfast or absorbing the tales our older brothers and sisters bring home from school. We hear about the family past and about great events from the stories our grandmothers and grandfathers, aunts and uncles tell. What we learn in

[9]*Public Opinion* (December-January 1980), p. 39.

[10]John L. Sullivan, James Piereson, and George E. Marcus, "An Alternative Conceptualization of Political Tolerance: Illusory Increases 1950s–1970s," *American Political Science Review* (September 1979), pp. 781–94.

[11]*Public Opinion* (December-January 1980), pp. 33–34 and 37–38.

Basic attitudes that shape future opinions often originate in the family setting. *HUD.*

"I'm an Episcopalian on my mother's side and a supply-sider on my father's." *Drawing by Dana Fradon; © 1981 The New Yorker Magazine, Inc.*

Political Impact of the Schools

the family at the start are not so much specific political opinions but rather the basic attitudes that will shape our future opinions—attitudes toward our neighbors, toward other classes or types of people, and toward society in general. Some of us may rebel against the ways of the close little group in which we live, but most of us conform. The family is a link between the past and the present. It translates the world to us, but it does so on its own terms. And the terms are many and varied: families may be extended or nuclear, two-headed, female single-headed, male single-headed, or communal.

Studies of high school students, for example, indicate a high correlation between parents and children in the political party they support. And this relatively high degree of correspondence continues throughout life. Such a finding raises an interesting question: Is it the *direct* influence of parents that creates the correspondence? Or is it that most children grow up in the *same social situation* their parents did and that parents and children are equally influenced by their environment? The answer is *both*—and one influence often strengthens the other. A daughter of Democratic parents growing up in a small southern town of strong Democratic leanings will be affected by friends, by other parents, and perhaps by youngsters in a Sunday school group, all of whom may reinforce the attitudes of her parents.

Parents influence children's party identification, as suggested by a high degree of correspondence between the racial attitudes of parents and children, and moderate levels of agreement in political knowledge, political efficacy (the belief that one can influence government), and civic tolerance.[12] Again, we cannot say how much of the similarity between parents and children stems from direct family influence and how much results from parents and children living in the same social and political environment—but surely, both influences are important.

Who has the greater influence—the mother or the father—over children's political opinions? It used to be assumed that the father had the dominant impact, perhaps because it was assumed that "politics is a man's business." But the balance of influence between the two parents seems to be surprisingly level; it may even be tipped in the mother's favor.[13] What happens when mother and father disagree politically? The child is likely to favor the party of the parent with whom he or she has had closer ties.[14]

Still, older children sometimes do not share the views of their parents. What other forces are at work?

Schools also mold young citizens' values and attitudes. At an early age schoolchildren begin to pick up specific political values and to acquire basic attitudes toward our system of government. Even very small schoolchildren know the name of the president and the president's party affiliation and have strong feelings about the chief executive. Children as young as nine or ten begin to have fairly precise knowledge of what a president stands for, though this will vary with the personality of the president. For example, one researcher found that "the Kennedy image was rich, specific, and considerably more politicized than we had anticipated. He was particularly well remembered for his efforts on behalf of peace and civil rights."[15]

[12]Russell J. Dalton, "Reassessing Parental Socialization: Indicator Unreliability Versus Generational Transfer," *American Political Science Review* (June 1980), pp. 421–31.

[13]Richard G. Niemi, "Political Socialization," in Jeanne N. Knutson (ed.), *Handbook of Political Psychology* (Jossey-Bass, 1973), p. 128.

[14]M. Kent Jennings and Kenneth P. Langton, "Mothers versus Fathers: The Formation of Political Orientations among Young Americans," *Journal of Politics* (May 1969), p. 357.

[15]Roberta S. Sigel, "Image of a President: Some Insights into the Political Views of School Children," *American Political Science Review* (March 1968), pp. 216–26.

Do school influences tend to give young people a greater faith in political institutions? Yes and no. A classic study examined relationships between community leaders' attitudes, civics texts, and students' attitudes in three Boston communities—one upper middle class, one lower middle class, and one working class. The school texts in all communities stressed the right of citizens to try to influence government, but the texts used in the upper-middle-class community were the only ones to stress politics as a *conflict* process for settling differing group demands. Only the upper-class community leaders underscored politics as a conflict process, thus reinforcing the lessons in the texts. Edgar Litt concluded that the lower-class students were being brought up to view government as a process carried out by institutions in the students' behalf, while the upper-class students were learning to understand the political process in realistic terms and to take part in that process on their own behalf.[16]

In short, scholars are confirming what every high school student knows— that schools have a certain, usually rather Establishment, point of view. But here again the political scientist must look more closely at what shapes attitudes. Is it the teachers, the other students, the classes, or the fact that both teachers and students are subject to common stimuli? These are difficult factors to untangle. Another study found no evidence that the civics curriculum has a significant effect on the political orientations of the great majority of American high school students. Of course, students differed in their interest in politics, but this resulted not from taking (or not taking) civics or government courses, but from the students' backgrounds and life plans.

What about the influence of *college* on political opinions? One study suggested that students planning to attend college are more likely to be knowledgeable about politics, to be more interested in politics, to be more in favor of free speech, and to talk and read about politics. College students *in general* tend to become more tolerant and unprejudiced the longer they stay in college. Is this the influence of their professors, of the curriculum, or of other students? It is difficult to generalize. Parents sometimes fear that professors have too much influence on their offspring in school; the professors are likely to be skeptical about this.

But why talk in generalities when students reading this book can make their own judgments? What has influenced *you* the most—a teacher, a book (possibly even a *textbook?*), a particular course, bull sessions with other students, *60 Minutes?* And *how* have you been influenced?

Organizations such as the Girl Scouts are part of the socialization process of the young, instilling a sense of pride in the American political culture. *Stan Wakefield.*

Other Influences

Family and school are not the only sources of influence on the child and adolescent. Religious and ethnic attitudes may also be important, both within and outside the family. On the whole, Protestant families tend to be more conservative than Catholics on economic and welfare issues, while Jewish families tend to be more liberal on both economic and noneconomic issues than either Catholics or Protestants. But Protestants are quite variable on certain social issues, and all persons are subject to "cross pressures" (see p. 162). Evangelicals, who include a small percentage of Catholics but who are mainly made up of Baptists and many of the more fundamentalist sects, tend to be more socially conservative than nonevangelicals (see Table 7–2). Children in ethnic families learn of the heritage and customs of another country; they may also learn of

[16]Edgar Litt, "Civic Education, Community Norms, and Political Indoctrination," *American Sociological Review* (February 1963), pp. 69–75. See also Elizabeth Léonie Simpson, *Democracy's Stepchildren* (Jossey-Bass, 1971); M. Kent Jennings and Richard G. Niemi, *The Political Character of Adolescence* (Princeton University Press, 1974); Stanley Allen Renshon, "Personality and Family Dynamics in the Political Socialization Process," *American Journal of Political Science* (February 1975), pp. 63–80; and Frances Fitzgerald, *America Revised* (Atlantic-Little, Brown, 1979).

historical or current struggles in so vivid a way that their attitudes toward current American foreign policy may be affected.

What happens when a young person's parents and friends disagree? One study of high school students revealed that when the students were "cross-pressured" in this way, they tended to go along with their parents rather than their friends on party affiliations; with their friends rather than their parents on the issue of the vote for eighteen-year-olds; and somewhere in between on their actual vote in a presidential election.[17]

Adults are not simply the sum of all these early experiences. Analysts are becoming more and more interested in the ways in which adults keep modifying their views *after* completing school or college. Most people keep on growing as they move into new social situations and become exposed to new newspapers, television programs, and political leaders. A major factor may be harsh experience, as in a war or depression, that shocks people out of their existing attitudes. Many of Nixon's strongest admirers had to change their view about him after the Watergate revelations. Many did not, however, and rationalized their continued support by saying that while other presidents had been just as bad as Nixon, he happened to be the one who was caught.[18]

MAJOR INTERESTS: SIZE AND SCOPE

In some of the situations discussed above, the influencing person definitely intended to affect the behavior of another person. In other cases, however, the intention may be less clear and certain. Still, almost all these cases differ from those in which political leaders and propagandists approach potential followers with a definite message in order to influence opinion on *particular issues*. It is this latter function that is attempted by interest groups, of which the most numerous are the organizations representing the multitude of economic interests.

Major Economic Interests

The vast majority of gainfully employed Americans are members of at least one of the big occupational associations, which have much to say about income and working conditions for employers and professional people as well as for farmers and union workers. The typical large association is made up of a mosaic of local and state bodies, and is the product of slow and painful growth over a period of decades.

Probably the oldest "unions" in America are farm organizations. The earliest farm group—the South Carolina Agricultural Society—was founded even before the Constitution was written. In the late nineteenth century the National Grange, or Patrons of Husbandry, led farm rebellions against low farm prices,

[17]Suzanne Koprince Sebert, M. Kent Jennings, and Richard G. Niemi, "The Political Texture of Peer Groups," in Jennings and Niemi, *The Political Character of Adolescence*, p. 246.

[18]On the extent of the continuing support for Nixon, see Campbell, *The American Electorate*, pp. 287–88.

161

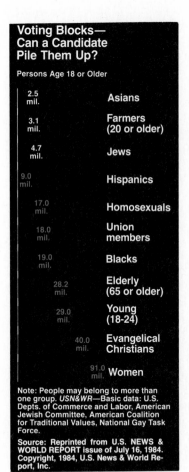

Voting Blocks—Can a Candidate Pile Them Up?

Persons Age 18 or Older

2.5 mil.	Asians
3.1 mil.	Farmers (20 or older)
4.7 mil.	Jews
9.0 mil.	Hispanics
17.0 mil.	Homosexuals
18.0 mil.	Union members
19.0 mil.	Blacks
28.2 mil.	Elderly (65 or older)
29.0 mil.	Young (18-24)
40.0 mil.	Evangelical Christians
91.0 mil.	Women

Note: People may belong to more than one group. *USN&WR*—Basic data: U.S. Depts. of Commerce and Labor, American Jewish Committee, American Coalition for Traditional Values, National Gay Task Force.

Source: Reprinted from U.S. NEWS & WORLD REPORT issue of July 16, 1984. Copyright, 1984, U.S. News & World Report, Inc.

railroad monopolies, and middlemen. The Grange, once a fighting organization with over a million members, is today smaller and more conservative than the other big farm groups. The largest farm group now is the American Farm Bureau Federation, which is especially strong in the corn belt. Organized originally around government agents who helped farmers in rural counties, the Federation today is almost a semigovernmental agency, but it retains full freedom to fight for such goals as price supports and expanded credit facilities. The most liberal (or radical) farm organization today is the Farmers Union, founded in 1902, which represents Plains States farmers to a marked extent and works for legislation that will protect the small farmer. A great number of other farm organizations are based on the interests of those who produce specific commodities, such as the American Soybean Association.

Workers, too, have long been organized—the earliest trade union locals were founded during Washington's first administration. Throughout the nineteenth century workers organized political parties and local unions. Their most ambitious effort at national organization, the Knights of Labor, claimed 700,000 members. By the beginning of this century, the American Federation of Labor, a confederation of strong and independent-minded national unions mainly representing craftworkers, was the dominant organization. During the ferment of the 1930s, unions more responsive to industrial workers broke away from the AFL and formed a rival national organization, the Congress of Industrial Organizations. Later the AFL and CIO reunited in the organization that exists today, but some industrial union leaders contend that the AFL-CIO has become too conservative, and some large unions, including those of the auto workers, remain outside the AFL-CIO.

Business "unions" are the most varied and numerous of all. The several thousand national trade associations and local groups are as diverse as the products and services they sell. The main general agency for business is the Chamber of Commerce of the United States, organized in 1912. The chamber is a federation of federations, composed of several thousand local chambers of commerce representing tens of thousands of business firms. Loosely allied with the chamber on most issues is the National Association of Manufacturers, which since its founding in the wake of the depression of 1893 has tended to speak for the more conservative elements of American business.

Some of the smaller and less well known business groups nevertheless have considerable influence. The Conference Board, founded in 1916, conducts research on practical problems and seeks to inform the public on the role of business in the economy. It does not take public stands on issues but emphasizes economic and policy analysis developed through a large staff, and frequently holds conferences, briefings, and seminars. The Business Roundtable, less than a decade old, is an association of the heads of major corporations, banks, and utilities. Founded in the belief that top business executives need to take unified public stands on issues such as taxation, government regulation, and energy, the Roundtable seeks to ensure that the views of big business are heard in public policy debates. It was reported to have had a major role in defeating a picketing bill strongly backed by the AFL-CIO.

Professional people have organized some of the strongest "unions" in the nation. Some are well known, such as the American Medical Association and the American Bar Association. Others are divided into many subgroups: Teachers are organized in the National Education Association, the American Association of University Professors, and also in particular subject groups, such as the Modern Language Association. Many professions are closely tied in with government, especially on the state level. Lawyers, for example, are licensed by the states, which have set up, often as a result of pressure from lawyers themselves, certain standards of admission to the state bar.

The Crisscross of Interests

John Gardner, founding chairman of Common Cause, "telling it like it is" to current chairman Archibald Cox, a well-known Harvard law professor who was also the celebrated Watergate Special Prosecutor fired by President Nixon prior to Nixon's forced removal from office. *UPI.*

Cutting across associations based on economic interest or occupation are other groups based on sex or national origin, or on religious, racial, ideological, recreational, and other ties. Not many Americans are members of more than one occupational group, but they have endless nonoccupational interests and often are more emotionally and financially involved in them—in a veterans' organization, such as the American Legion, Veterans of Foreign Wars, or Amvets; in a nationality group, such as the multitude of Irish, German, Polish, Scandinavian, Hispanic, and other organizations; or in religious organizations, such as the Knights of Columbus. The variety of such groups is remarkable; there are more than 150 nationwide organizations based on national origin alone.

Cutting across both economic and ethnic groups are interest group associations focused on issues and ideology. Virtually all interest groups convince themselves that they are devoted to the public welfare and not merely to their own self-interest; the issue and ideological groups usually present their case in terms of its value to the "public interest." Americans for Democratic Action campaigns for liberal candidates and issues while Young Americans for Freedom works for conservative ones. The YAF is especially active on university and college campuses, where it supported Ronald Reagan in 1976 and 1980, while the ADA endorsed Senator Edward M. Kennedy for the Democratic nomination. Countless groups have organized around specific issues, such as civil liberties, birth control, abortion, opposition to the Panama Canal treaty, environmental protection, nuclear energy, and nuclear arms. Some highly ideological groups are thriving in the otherwise pragmatic, pluralistic politics of the 1980s, but the John Birch Society, on the extreme Right, has survived with only a hard-core membership in the tens of thousands. The Libertarian party, more an interest group than a party, has also attracted a small but provocative following on the Right. The Moral Majority, on the other hand, has large numbers and apparently had a significant impact in recent elections.

Large associations themselves are often made up of alliances of many small associations. As Tocqueville observed long ago, Americans form and reform associations for every conceivable purpose and function. And as government has become more central to Americans' lives, these associations have turned their attention more and more to government. In Washington today the associations rival the federal bureaucracy itself in number, size, complexity, and resources.

Of special importance in recent years have been the "public action" groups that arose out of the political ferment of the 1960s. Common Cause, founded in 1970 by independent Republican John W. Gardner and later led by noted Watergate prosecutor Archibald Cox, campaigned effectively for electoral reform and for making the political process more open. Its Washington staff raises money through direct mail campaigns, oversees state chapters, issues a flood of research reports and press releases on current issues, and lobbies on Capitol Hill and in the major government departments. Ralph Nader started a conglomerate of consumer organizations that investigate and report on governmental and corporate action—or inaction—relating to consumer interests. These groups have had a direct impact on legislation—for example, on the passage of the National Traffic and Motor Vehicle Safety Act and the Highway Safety Act.

More and more, groups are organizing to promote or oppose certain foreign policies. For years one of the most powerful associations in Washington, the China Lobby, carried on an intensive campaign against United States recognition of "Red China." Perhaps the most prestigious—and most controversial—foreign affairs group is the Council on Foreign Relations in New York. Long denounced by critics as the center of conservative and corporate power, the Council is in fact a relatively tame association of mainly aging Establishment types who gather to hear speakers and to make use of an unusually good library of international affairs. The Trilateral Commission is a newer but equally prestigious and controversial organization with concern for the economic problems of industrialized nations. Both the Right and the Left see it as a conspiracy, the Right believing it will bring universal communism, the Left believing it will bring worldwide monopoly capitalism.

While political factions are not a new phenomenon, in recent years there has been a virtual explosion in the number and variety of interests and associations. This is especially true of "single-cause" groups. (Again, this is not new. The Anti-Saloon League of the 1890s was single-mindedly devoted to barring the sale and manufacture of alcoholic beverages. It was said that the League did not care whether a legislator was drunk or sober as long as he voted dry.) Today single-cause groups crusade tirelessly in regard to highly specialized, but politically "hot" questions—such as the National Rifle Association's opposition to the regulation of sale of firearms, or the Nuclear Freeze movement's dedication to that particular issue.

The number and intensity and specialized nature of these single-cause groups raise a basic question about our "government by the people": Can it represent some kind of general or majority interest at the same time as it responds to a welter of narrow and particular interests?

"I would guess, sir, by the look on your face, that you are a single-issue person." *Drawing by Dana Fradon; © 1981 The New Yorker Magazine, Inc.*

WEAPONS OF GROUP POWER

Some Americans tend to overreact to organized groups—especially to ones they oppose. They see such groups as vast, well organized, well financed, and all but irresistible in political action. They should remember that large and relatively well-organized groups have weaknesses as well as strengths. The larger the group, the greater the likelihood of crisscrossing interests that drain the group of unity, energy, money, and singleness of purpose.

Strengths and Weaknesses

Obviously, size is still a central test of political power; an organization representing 5 million voters will have more influence than one speaking for 50,000. Obviously, too, the unity of the membership is a key element. Unity, however, is easier to achieve in a small group that focuses on a relatively specific and concrete concern—one that does not affect others noticeably; for example, a tariff on steel pins. But these and other bases of group power need to be looked at more closely.

A fundamental factor in group impact is the attitude and makeup of the membership. Many people join an organization for reasons that have little to do with its political objectives. They may join to secure group insurance, to take advantage of travel benefits, to participate in professional meetings, or to get a job. When the leaders of an organization can depend on the political backing of their followers, the organization is able to put its full strength into pursuing its aims, and it will have an enormous advantage in the political arena. If they cannot, the organization will not be nearly so effective.

Most Americans are members of many groups; their loyalties are divided. It is this fact of *overlapping membership* that largely determines the cohesiveness of a group. Organization leaders run up against the problem time after time. A union official, for example, asks a dozen members to come to a meeting. Several say they will come. But two say they have to be with their bowling club that night. Two others have to stay home with their families. Another has a church supper. Even those who finally do show up are not 100 percent supporters. Perhaps they are asked to vote for a particular candidate in a coming election. Some will. But one may decide to vote for the other candidate because they are neighbors or because they are both Italian-Americans, or Republicans, or Legionnaires. Or perhaps one will not know what to do and will not vote at all.

Usually a mass membership organization is made up of three types of members. First, we find a relatively small number of formal leaders, who may hold full-time, paid positions or at least devote much of their extra time, effort, and money to the group's activities.[19] Second, there is a hard core of those who are involved in the group organizationally and psychologically: They identify with the group's aims, show up at meetings, cheerfully pay dues, and do a lot of the legwork. Third, groups contain people who are members in name only: They do not participate actively; they do not look on themselves as Teamsters or Rotarians or Legionnaires; and they cannot be depended on to vote in elections or otherwise act as the leadership wants. In a typical organization, for every top leader there might be a few hundred hardcore activists and 10,000 more or less inactive members.

A second factor in the cohesion of a group is its organizational structure. Some groups have no formal organization. Others consist of local organizations that have joined together in some sort of loose state or national federation. The local organizations retain a measure of separate power and independence, just as the states did when they entered the Union. A sort of separation of powers may be found as well. The national assembly of an organization establishes— or at least ratifies—policy. An executive committee meets more frequently. A president or director is elected to head and speak for the group. And permanent, paid officials form the organization's bureaucracy. Power may be further divided between the organization's main headquarters and its Washington office. An organization of this sort tends to be far less cohesive than a centralized, disciplined group such as the Army or some trade unions.

Closely related to cohesion is a third factor—the nature of the leadership. In a group that embraces many attitudes and interests, leaders may either weld the various elements together or sharpen their disunity. The leader of a national business association, for example, must tread cautiously between big business and little business, between exporters and importers, between chain stores and corner grocery stores, between the makers and the sellers of competing products. Yet leaders must not be mere punching bags for different interests, for above all they must lead. They must show how to achieve whatever goals can be agreed on. The group leader is in the same position as a president or a member of Congress. He or she must know when to lead followers and when to follow them.

We have been talking about the characteristics of groups; but the power of a group is also affected by the nature of the political and governmental system in which it operates. Because of our federal system, a group consisting of 3 million supporters but concentrated in a few states will usually have less influence than another group consisting of the same number of supporters spread out in a large number of states. A group whose goals are contrary to widely accepted values will have a more difficult time than another group that can clothe its demands in acceptable ideology. And, as we shall see in later chapters, governmental structures are significant, allowing some groups more direct access to decision makers, and other groups much less.

Our typical image of interest groups in action is that of powerful, hard-

Police take away protestor in nuclear disarmament protest. *Ken Karp.*

[19]V. O. Key, Jr., *Public Opinion and American Democracy* (Knopf, 1961), pp. 504–7.

nosed lobbyists skillfully employing a combination of knowledge, persuasiveness, personal influence, charm, and money to influence legislators and bureaucrats. Interest group representatives seeking to wield influence often can choose from a variety of political weapons and targets. These include persuasion, litigation, rule making, election activities, and lobbying.

TECHNIQUES

PERSUASION   All interest groups exploit the communications media—television, radio, newspapers, leaflets, signs, direct mail, and word of mouth—to influence voters during elections and to motivate constituents to contact their representatives between elections. Business enjoys a special advantage in this arena, and businesspeople have the money to hire propaganda machinery. Being advertisers on a large scale, they know how to deliver their message effectively. Most important, they generally have easy access to the means of propaganda, such as the press. Other groups have also become aware of the uses of propaganda. When a business organization places full-page messages in newspapers across the nation, unions often find the funds to hire similar space for an answer. Although labor has not yet matched the propaganda skills of business, it is devoting a good deal of money and attention to this technique. Other interest groups, such as doctors and teachers, are also making use of publicity methods.

How effective is group propaganda? It is impossible to measure precisely the impact of propaganda campaigns, for too many other factors are involved. But we know enough to be skeptical of some of the extravagant claims made for them. For example, organized labor strongly denounced the Taft-Hartley Act for years after its passage, but surveys have shown that the great majority of the public and of *union members* either wanted to keep the new law or had no opinion about it. Also, the more a group publicizes its position, the more it risks arousing the opposition and stimulating *its* propaganda potential.

An estimated 2,500 teachers, parents, and children stage a massive demonstration in downtown Los Angeles to protest cuts in schooling and teachers threatened by Proposition 13. *UPI.*

LITIGATION   When groups find the usual political channels closed to them, they may seek other ways to influence public policy.[20] The courts have increasingly become the center of such efforts. The NAACP, for example, has instituted and won numerous cases in its efforts to improve legal protection for blacks. The technique is not new, of course,[21] but in recent decades urban interests and environmental groups, feeling underrepresented in state and national legislatures, have turned to the courts. Also, women's groups—such as the National Organization for Women and the American Civil Liberties Union Women's Rights Project—have used the courts as one arena for pursuing their objectives.[22] Ralph Nader, too, has exploited this device.

Groups can gain a forum for presenting their points of view by seeking permission to file amicus curiae (friend of the court) briefs even in cases in which they are not direct parties. The American Civil Liberties Union, for example, files many such briefs with the Supreme Court in cases that raise questions of constitutional liberties.

The League of Women Voters, some of their members shown below, formed after women won the right to vote. It has been a very successful organization in getting women prepared to run for office and hold government officials accountable. *Image.*

RULE MAKING   Groups have ready access to the rule-making process, in which executive and regulatory agencies write the rules that implement laws. Agencies publish proposed rules in the *Federal Register* and invite responses

[20]Lucius J. Barker, "Third Parties in Litigation: A Systemic View of the Judicial Function," *Journal of Politics* (February 1967), pp. 41–69.

[21]See, for example, C. Peter Magrath, *Yazoo: Law and Politics in the New Republic* (Brown University Press, 1966).

[22]Karen O'Connor, *Women's Organizations' Use of the Courts* (Lexington Books, 1980).

and reactions from all interested persons before the rules are finalized. The *Federal Register* is published daily. Well-staffed associations and corporations peruse the *Register*, ever alert for proposed agency actions that will affect their interests. You can find the publication in your school or public libraries.

GROUPS IN ELECTIONS While almost all large organizations say they are nonpolitical, almost all organized groups are involved in politics in one way or another. What group leaders usually mean when they say they are nonpolitical is that they are *nonpartisan*. A distinguishing feature of organized interest groups is that they try to work through one or both parties. Usually this means working for individual candidates in either party. The policy labor has followed for years—helping friends and defeating enemies—is the policy of almost all interest groups.

This policy is put into action in different ways. Occasionally an organization openly endorses a candidate and actively works for that person's election. In 1924 many labor unions endorsed "Fighting Bob" La Follette for president; the CIO officially backed Roosevelt in 1944; and the AFL-CIO supported Humphrey in 1968, Carter in 1976, and Mondale in 1984. Some labor organizations formally stay neutral, but prominent officials take a partisan stand. Because of such factors as overlapping membership, an organization may set up a front organization to carry on its political activities; the Committee on Political Education of the AFL-CIO is a case in point.

Individual labor unions, with somewhat homogeneous memberships, can sometimes afford to take a rather firm position. Other organizations are handicapped by the diversity of their members. A local retailers group, for example, might be composed equally of Republicans and Democrats, and many of its members might refuse to take an open position on a candidate for fear of losing business. In such cases more subtle means may be equally effective. At meetings word is passed around that candidate X is sound from the organization's point of view. Perhaps the hat is passed around, too.

Ideological groups, on the other hand, may "target" candidates, seeking to change the candidates' position or to influence voters. The Christian Voter's Victory Fund, for example, publicizes congressional candidates' "scores"—based on their roll call votes—on abortion, sex education, school busing, school prayer, and the Equal Rights Amendment. Americans for Democratic Action and Americans for Constitutional Action publish ratings of incumbents on a number of liberal and conservative issues, respectively.

How effective is electioneering by interest groups? No generalization is possible, because everything depends on the kinds of factors we have been discussing—the group's size, unity, objectives, political resources, and leadership, and the political context in which it is operating. In general, though, it can be said that the power of the mass-membership organizations to mobilize their full strength in elections has been exaggerated in the press. Too many cross-pressures are operating in the pluralistic politics of America for any one group to assume a really commanding role. Some groups reach their maximum influence only by allying closely with one of the two major parties. They have placed their members on local, state, and national party committees and have helped send them to party conventions as delegates. But this means losing some of their independence and singleness of purpose.

Another interest group strategy is to form a political party with the intent less of winning *elections* than of publicizing a *cause*. The Free Soil party was formed in 1848 to propagandize against the spread of slavery, and the Prohibition party was organized twenty years later to ban the sale of liquor. Farmers have formed a variety of such parties.

POLITICAL ACTION COMMITTEES: SOME BIG CONTRIBUTORS—1982 ELECTIONS

CORPORATE PACs

Tenneco Inc.	$454,150
Winn-Dixie Stores Inc.	281,375
Harris Corp.	249,250
American Family Corp.	232,775
Fluor Corp.	223,200
Litton Industries Inc.	218,550

LABOR PACs

United Auto Workers	$1,623,947
International Association of Machinists	1,444,959
National Education Association	1,183,215
AFL-CIO	906,425
Seafarers International Union	821,081
United Food and Commercial Workers	728,213

ASSOCIATION PACs

National Association of Realtors	$2,115,135
American Medical Association	1,737,090
National Association of Home Builders	1,005,628
American Bankers Association	947,460
National Automobile Dealers Association	917,295
National Rifle Association	710,902

IDEOLOGICAL PACs

National PAC (Pro-Israel)	$542,500
Citizens for the Republic (conservative)	471,367
National Committee for an Effective Congress (liberal)	368,443
Democrats for the 80s	359,883
National Abortion Rights Action League	288,863
National Conservative Political Action Committee	263,171

PACS: INTEREST GROUPS IN COMBAT

YOU DECIDE !

Before 1970 there were only a handful of informal caucuses in Congress. These have grown ten fold in the past fifteen years, as many members of Congress find such groups offer useful alternative channels of information and voting cues that are tailored to a member's region, ethnic, or issue interests. Can you suggest what some of these caucuses might be—that is, name of few of those informal groups that have developed in recent years?

(Answer/Discussion on the next page.)

The last few years have witnessed an explosion in the number and impact of political action committees (PACs). Technically, a PAC is simply the political arm of a business, labor, professional, or other interest group, legally entitled to raise funds on a voluntary basis from members, stockholders, or employees in order to contribute funds to favored candidates or political parties.[23] Since PACs link two vital techniques of influence—giving money and other political aid to politicians and persuading officeholders to act or vote "the right way" on issues—we will look at PACs more broadly as the means by which interest groups seek to control "who gets what, when, and how" through electoral activity and lobbying.

Ironically, considering that the explosion of PACs has occurred mainly in the business world, it was organized labor that invented this device. In the 1930s John L. Lewis, chief of the United Mine Workers, set up the Non-Partisan Political League as the political arm of the newly formed CIO. When the CIO merged with the American Federation of Labor, the new labor group established COPE (Committee on Political Education). This unit came to be the model for most political action committees: "From the outset, national, state, and local units of COPE have not only raised and distributed funds, but have also served as the mechanism for organized and widespread union activity in the electoral process, for example, in voter registration, political education, and get-out-the-vote drives."[24] Some years later manufacturers formed the Business-Industry Political Action Committee, but this committee, and the small number of other PACs in the 1960s, had a limited role.

The 1970s brought a near-revolution in the role and influence of PACs. The number of PACs increased dramatically, growing from about 150 to over 4000 today. Corporations and trade associations contributed most to this growth; their PACs today comprise the majority of all PACs. Labor PACs, on the other hand, increased only slightly in number, representing less than 10 percent of all PACs. But the increase in the number of PACs is less important than the intensity of recent PAC participation in elections and in lobbying.

PAC Money in Elections

Although PACs are involved in the whole election process, their main influence lies in their capacity to contribute money to candidates. Candidates increasingly need big money to wage their election or reelection campaigns. In the 1982 Congressional elections five candidates for House seats spent over $1 million each.[25] Senators running campaigns in the larger states can easily spend double that amount. PACs increasingly are providing the money to these needy candidates. PACs contributed 35 percent of the campaign funds collected by 1982 Congressional winners; this was up from 31 percent in 1980, 28 percent in 1978, and 26 percent in 1976. One-fourth of the House members raised more than half of their campaign funds from PAC contributions.[26] As corporate and industrial PACs increase rapidly in number, their influence grows accord-

[23]Herbert E. Alexander, *PACs: What They Are, How They Are Changing Political Campaign Financing Patterns* (Grass Roots Guides, 1979), p. 3.

[24]Edwin M. Epstein, "Business and Labor under the Federal Election Campaign Act of 1971," in Michael J. Malbin (ed.), *Parties, Interest Groups, and Campaign Finance Laws* (American Enterprise Institute for Public Policy Research, 1980), p. 112. See also Gary Jacobson, *Money in Congressional Elections* (Yale University Press, 1980).

[25]Adam Clymer, "Will Congress Pass the Buck on Campaign Financing?" *The New York Times*, February 20, 1983, p. E3.

[26]Adam Clymer, "PAC Money's Role in Congress Raises Suspicions," *The New York Times*, January 19, 1983, p. 8. See also Elizabeth Drew, *Politics and Money* (Macmillan, 1983).

SCORE CARD: ENDORSEMENTS AND CLAIMED OUTCOMES, 1982	Interest Group	House Endorsements	Percentage Victories	Senate Endorsements	Percentage Victories
	Americans for Democratic Action (Liberal)	138	73%	18	44%
	AFL-CIO/COPE (Labor)	374	64	31	65
	Business-Industry Political Action Committee (Business)	103	37	17	47
	Americans for Constitutional Action (Conservative)	144	78	15	47
	National Conservative Political Action Committee (Conservative)	86	81	3	0

SOURCE: *Congressional Quarterly Weekly Report.* November 6, 1982, pp. 2811–16.

John T. Dolan, Chairman of the National Conservative Political Action Committee (NCPAC): "There is no question about it . . . we are a negative organization. We're not interested in respectability. We're going to beat them and send a shiver down the spine of every Senator and Congressman" ("Poor Ronald's Almanac," 1982, Foundation for National Progress, San Francisco, California). *UPI/Bettmann Archive.*

Answer/Discussion

By some counts there are almost 100 informal interest group caucuses in the Congress. Among these are:

Frost Belt Caucus
Populist Caucus
Textile Caucus
Hispanic Caucus
Women's Caucus
Black Caucus
Arts Caucus
Rural Caucus
Steel Caucus
Environmental Study Group
Military Reform Group

ingly. What counts is not so much the amounts they give but rather to whom they give: the more influential incumbents. Thus, in 1982 the House minority leader, Republican Robert H. Michel of Illinois, received 68 percent of his funds from more than 400 PACs, mainly in the oil, food, and insurance industries. The chairperson of the Appropriations Committee, Democratic Representative Jamie L. Whitten of Mississippi, gained 75 percent of his funds from corporate and agricultural PACs.[27]

Despite lurid reports of freewheeling spending by big corporations, most business PACs proceed rather cautiously. In deciding which candidates to help and with how much, PACs first consider the candidate's record and his or her likelihood of voting as the PAC wishes. But other factors must be considered too: the likelihood that the candidate will win; how much difference the money would make in the campaign; whether the candidate is an incumbent (and hence would reasonably have more chance of winning); and the PACs access to the candidate if elected. Party is not a major criterion for corporate-related PACs, though they contribute somewhat more to Republican candidates than to Democratic ones. Labor PACs, on the other hand, give overwhelmingly to Democrats.

How much influence does PAC money, especially corporate PAC money, have on election outcomes and ultimately on legislation? Obviously, in this political area, as in others, "money talks." But it is easy to exaggerate that influence. Corporations find that raising political money from a diverse group of stockholders and/or executives is a slow venture. Corporations usually do not wish to raise a great deal of political money for fear that they will be attacked in the press for their "huge slush funds." In addition, it is not clear that campaign contributions have much effect on election outcomes, that winning candidates will feel willing and able to "remember" their financial angels, and that the money in the end produces a real payoff in legislation. So even big corporate PACs have learned to be patient. Declared Bernadette A. Budde, political education director of the Business-Industry PAC: "You know you're not going to make 10 yards on the first down, so you try to make 2 or 3 or 4 yards at a time."[28]

Much depends, however, on the context within which money is given and received. Many campaigns—especially congressional and state and local campaigns—are "low-voltage" undertakings in which a sizable amount of money seems to make a difference. Amid all the "murk" of campaigning, a candidate may feel grateful for so tangible and convertible a contribution as money. But much depends on whether PACs can protect their financial investment with the exercise of influence *within* government—that is, whether they can lobby effectively.

[27]Ibid.
[28]Quoted in *National Journal*, November 24, 1979, p. 1983.

LOBBYING, OLD AND NEW

Lobbying is one of the best-known weapons of group influence. It is probably the oldest weapon, and certainly one of the most criticized. Generations of Americans have been stirred by exposés of an "invisible government." From the time of the Yazoo land frauds 185 years ago, when a whole legislature was bribed and the postmaster general was put on a private payroll as a lobbyist, to the latest logrolling scandal in Congress, Americans have enjoyed denouncing lobbyists. Some truly powerful lobbies flourished in the last century. One of these was the Anti-Saloon League, which after years of warring against "demon rum" actually managed to win passage of a constitutional amendment—the highest and most difficult achievement in American politics. These so-called "drys" included famous women leaders such as Frances Willard and Carry Nation, as well as the Women's Christian Temperance Union. An equally powerful lobby of "wets," all men except for Pauline Morton ("When It Rains It Pours") Sabin and her Women's Organization for National Prohibition Reform, won repeal of the Prohibition Amendment, which of course required another constitutional amendment.[29]

Today lobbying is far more extensive and sophisticated, though not necessarily more effective. Countless thousands of lobbyists are active in Washington today, but few of them are as glamorous or as unscrupulous as the media suggest, nor are they necessarily very influential. Most lobbying is a rather routine, day-to-day affair conducted by spokespersons for such organizations as the National Fertilizer Association, the Retired Officers Association, or the Institute of Shortening and Edible Oils. Lobbyists for these associations are usually Washington attorneys, many with long experience in the agencies and on "the Hill," who are retained to keep an eye on a handful of bills and to keep in touch with a few administrative officials and members of Congress. Because lawmaking today is a highly technical matter, these lobbyists—or legislative counsels, as they prefer to be called—play a large role in modern government. Busy administrators or legislators, threading their way through mountains of paper and among conflicting interests, often turn to them gladly for their views and information.

James G. Watt, former Secretary of the Interior, (1981–1983) discussed federal policies regarding hunting on government lands with members of the National Rifle Association's legislative affairs staff. *The National Rifle Association of America.*

All this is the traditional "stuff" of government, but with the rise of Big Government and of the huge stakes of business and other organizations in governmental decisions, lobbying has taken on a far greater importance. Lobbyists know that influence in Washington depends on influence in the "precincts" and that they must use techniques of public persuasion in order to create the right political "climate" for the governmental actions they want. Hence, they must also know how to mobilize their organizations back home so that a blizzard of letters, telegrams, and petitions descends on Washington. Lobbyists have to be experts in the arts of political influence and also in legislative technique, as they take part in drafting laws, testifying before committees, and helping to speed some bills through while slowing up others.

Legal and political skills, along with specialized knowledge, have become so crucial in executive and legislative policy making as to be a form of power in themselves. Elected representatives in particular increasingly depend on their staffs for guidance. These staffs in turn are linked with the staffs of executive departments and of the interest group associations. Issue specialists will know more about Section 504 or Title IX or the amendment of 1972, and who wrote

[29]See Ruth Bordin, *Woman and Temperance: The Quest for Power and Liberty, 1873–1900* (Temple University Press, 1981); David E. Kyvig, *Repealing National Prohibition* (University of Chicago Press, 1979); Carol S. Greenwald, *Group Power; Lobbying and Public Policy* (Praeger, 1977); Norman J. Ornstein and Shirley Elder, *Interest Groups, Lobbying and Policymaking* (Congressional Quarterly Press, 1978).

that amendment and why, than the political and administrative leaders, who are usually generalists. It is in this gray area of policy making that many interest groups play a vital role, as people move freely from congressional or agency staff to association staff and perhaps back again.

The recent growth of PACs has immensely expanded these traditional activities and sharpened the issue as to their rightful place in the battle of interest groups. More than ever before, interest groups through PACs can organize a "triple-threat" offensive: skillful mobilization of public opinion through large, well-financed public relations campaigns; direct assistance to candidates in the form of money, campaign propaganda, "education" of voters by mailings, advertisements, and the like; and direct influence on officeholders through lobbying. The National Rifle Association, one of the most powerful of the medium-sized interest groups, with a membership of more than a million and a staff of three hundred, "has become a master at mobilizing citizens who support its cause. . . . The NRA boasts that it can flood Congress with 500,000 pieces of mail virtually overnight in opposition to any gun control proposals."[30]

Labor's Political "Machine"

For some years labor's COPE has been one of the most respected—and most feared—political organizations in the country.[31] In the Kennedy-Johnson years it won a reputation as the strongest national political "machine"—the word the late George Meany, AFL-CIO chief, used to describe his political arm. In many respects COPE could boast of its political effectiveness: It encouraged and supervised grassroots political activity on the part of the tens of thousands of union locals at the base of the AFL-CIO. The national organization adopted a detailed, explicit "platform," running to fifty or sixty pages, spelling out labor's position on the issues. Labor contributed money to candidates, ran registration and get-out-the-vote campaigns, and supported its favorites with leaflets, picnics, motorcades, and television and radio programs. COPE granted, or withheld, endorsements of candidates. Finally, organized labor marshaled in Washington, and in many of the state capitals, one of the largest, most experienced, and most knowledgeable lobbies of all the interest groups.

Yet this political "machine" often sputtered and faltered. Since the AFL-CIO is a federation of powerful and independent national unions, state and local groups or federations of unions were often politically divided. The aging national leadership of the AFL-CIO had been in office so long that it lacked vigor and freshness of approach. When George Meany retired in 1979, he had been president of the national organization for twenty-seven years; William Green had headed it for twenty-eight years before Meany, and Samuel Gompers had been in control off and on for thirty-eight years before Green. The AFL-CIO by no means spoke for all labor: Union labor represented about 60 percent of the nation's work force, and AFL-CIO membership amounted to about 60 percent of the total number of those organized.[32] In 1982, 64 percent of the COPE-endorsed candidates for United States representative won their elections—only a fair record.

Labor's political and lobbying muscle is obviously limited, and the prospects for increased influence in the future are dim. Organized labor's membership is dwindling relative to the increase in the national work force; it has failed to unionize a large part of industry in the South and the Sunbelt generally; and the number of corporate PACs has increased greatly while the number of labor

[30]Dennis S. Ippolito and Thomas G. Walker, *Political Parties, Interest Groups, and Public Policy: Group Influence in American Politics* (Prentice-Hall 1980), p. 335.

[31]Harry Holloway, "Interest Groups in the Postpartisan Era: The Political Machine of the AFL-CIO," *Political Science Quarterly* (Spring 1979), pp. 117–33.

[32]Holloway, "Interest Groups," p. 120.

PACs has remained almost the same. Knowing that it must look for political allies, labor is working increasingly closely with the Democratic party. Still, labor is jealous of its political independence and hesitates to join a party that has its own problems and weaknesses. Another possibility is temporary coalitions with other groups that have certain interests similar to labor's. Labor often follows this tactic, working closely with consumer, public interest, liberal, and sometimes—especially when faced with the issue of foreign imports—even with industry groups. But labor pays a price for such collaboration: watering down or even giving up some of its own goals. "We do our best when we're part of a coalition," says a top labor lobbyist, "and you don't have a coalition on a pure labor issue."[33]

Cooperative Lobbying

Other groups besides labor need to work with like interests without sacrificing their own goals. Business groups have worked out day-to-day, informal, flexible alliances, and some of these have developed into organizations in their own right. The Food Group, a thirty-year-old informal conference group in Washington, has represented more than sixty business and trade associations. This group spawned an Information Committee on Federal Food Regulations to fight "truth-in-packaging" legislation. While the Food Group was fairly effective, it ran into the usual problem of differences over goals and priorities, so that strong and unified pressure on Congress and government agencies was hard to achieve.[34]

Other like-minded groups have also worked out cooperative arrangements. The Leadership Conference on Civil Rights brought together many black and other group interests in this area. Different types of environmentalists work together, as do consumers and ideological groups on the Right and on the Left. Women continue to be represented by a large variety of groups, reflecting their diverse interests, and many of these banded together as ERAmerica to support passage of the ERA. But the larger the coalition, the greater the chance that women, like other groups, may divide over issues such as abortion and equal rights.

Temporary, flexible coalitions have often been viewed as relatively ineffective, given the American political process. A recent study of women's organizations, however, challenges this view. In this case issue coalitions seem to have been both the most realistic and the most common way to organize diverse interests. Cooperative lobbying allows "a great deal of diversity of opinion among cooperating groups while still combining lobbying capabilities. This is very important for an interest as varied as that of American women. Groups only need to agree on a single issue to join an ad hoc issue coalition."[35] Analysts of other common group interests might, of course, reach a different conclusion.

CONTROLLING FACTIONS—200 YEARS LATER

If James Madison were to return today, nearly 200 years after writing the *Federalist*, he would not be surprised by the existence of interest groups. Nor would he be surprised by the variety of interest groups. He *would* be surprised by the intense modern expression of factionalism—the varied weapons of group influence, the deep involvement of interest groups in the electoral process, and

[33]*Congressional Quarterly Weekly Report*, July 19, 1975, p. 1533.

[34]Donald R. Hall, *Cooperative Lobbying: The Power of Pressure* (University of Arizona Press, 1969).

[35]Anne N. Costain, "The Struggle for a National Women's Lobby: Organizing a Diffuse Interest," *Western Political Quarterly* (December 1980), p. 490.

the vast number of lobbyists in Washington and the state capitals. And doubtless Madison, if he were alive today, would be more concerned than ever about the power of faction, especially its tendency toward instability and injustice.

Certainly, Americans today are worried about the power of faction, and for somewhat the same reasons. Specifically, they fear that (1) the struggle among factions is not a fair fight; the narrower, more highly organized and better-financed "single-issue" or "single-cause" groups hold a decided advantage over the more general groups; (2) the interest group battle leads to great inequities, because lower-income people are grossly underrepresented among interest groups as compared to richer, more highly organized people, many of whom are represented by a multitude of organizations and lobbyists; (3) the organization of hundreds of single-issue groups has reinforced the diffusion of power and fragmentation in government so desired by the founding fathers. The result is incoherent policies, waste and inefficiency, endless delays, and inability to plan ahead and anticipate crises.

What to do? For decades Americans have been trying to find ways to keep interest groups in check. They have agreed with Madison that the "remedy" of suppressing factions would be worse than the disease—that it would be stupid to abolish liberty simply because it nourished faction. Today the existence and activity of interest groups and lobbies is solidly protected by the Constitution. Yet by safeguarding the value of *liberty*, Americans have allowed interest groups to threaten *equality*, the second great value in our national heritage. So we are left with the question: How can interest groups be regulated in a way that (1) does not threaten their constitutional liberties but that (2) curbs their tendencies toward inequity?

Regulation of Interest Group Lobbying

On the whole, Americans have responded to this question by seeking to regulate lobbying in general and political money in particular. Concern over the use of money—especially corporate funds—to influence politicians goes back well over a century, to the Crédit Mobilier scandals. In 1877 Georgia simply wrote into its constitution the provision that lobbying is a crime—but that provision was unconstitutional. By the turn of the century the liberal press was charging that corporations were pouring millions into the presidential campaigns of candidates like Benjamin Harrison and William McKinley. During the "Progressive" first decade of this century, Congress passed legislation outlawing corporate contributions in federal elections and requiring disclosure as to the use of money. In 1925 Congress passed the Federal Corrupt Practices Act, requiring disclosure reports, both before and after elections, of receipts and expenditures by Senate and House candidates and by political committees seeking to influence federal elections in more than one state. Note that these were *federal* laws applying to *federal* elections; regulation of state lobbying and elections was left to the states, which often failed to act effectively or at all.

Indeed, the federal legislation, including the 1946 Federal Regulation of Lobbying Act, was not very effective either. It was largely unenforced. Many candidates filed incomplete reports or none at all. The reform mood of the 1960s brought basic changes, "nurtured by the ever-increasing costs of campaigning, the incidence of millionaire candidates, the large disparities in campaign spending between various candidates and political parties, some clear cases of undue influence on the decision-making process by large contributors and special interests, and the apparent disadvantages of incumbency in an age of mass communications with a constant focus on the lives and activities of office-holders."[36] The upshot was the Federal Election Campaign Act (FECA) of 1971, which supplanted the earlier legislation.

[36]Alexander, *PACs: What They Are*, p. 5.

The main significance of recent laws has been their impact on elections, so they will be discussed later in Chapter 12. Here we must note the major impact of the 1971 act on interest groups themselves, especially on their political arms. Ironically, that impact was not to decrease or restrict them, but to enlarge their number and importance. The main reason for this was the new strategy of the 1971 law—to authorize direct and open participation by both labor and corporate organizations in elections and lobbying, with the hope that allowing a proper role for interest group activity, in the clear light of day, with effective enforcement, would be constitutional under the First Amendment and effective in the world of practical politics. The 1971 act allowed unions and corporations to communicate on political matters to members or stockholders; to conduct registration and get-out-the-vote drives; and to spend union and company funds to set up "separated segregated funds" to be used for political purposes.

At last corporations could be sure that their open and regulated political activities were wholly legal—and they made the most of it. The explosion of corporate PACs followed. But organized labor, which had previously enjoyed the right to set up its PACs, had less need of the act (except to legitimate what it was already doing). There was little increase in the number of labor PACs. The result, labor leaders contend, is a greater imbalance than ever between the political action and organization of a relatively small number of corporation executives and stockholders, and the large membership, and potential membership, of labor unions.

Lobbyists: Defense and Attack

Lobbyists have been defended as providing a kind of "third house" of Congress. While the Senate and House are set up on a geographical basis, lobbyists represent people on the basis of their main interests—their job or other economic interests, their issue positions, and their ideological leanings. Small but important groups, such as professional associations, can sometimes get representation in the "third house" that they might be unable to gain in the other two. In a nation of vast and important interests, this kind of functional representation, if not abused, is most useful as a supplement to geographical representation. Should the former kind of representation supplant the latter? Most analysts say no, because legislative institutions are needed to represent people in the totality of their lives and needs.

There are other arguments for "hands off the lobbyists." PACs support both Democratic and Republican candidates and hence do not favor just one party; ideological groups, especially those of a conservative cast, usually contribute more money than either business or labor, and that money does not have as direct or marked an effect on actual policy making as many outsiders suppose.[37] It is also argued that the increase in PAC corporate spending is not as great as it appears, that much of the PAC money may be "old wine in new bottles"—that is, money given earlier in the form of legal or illegal personal campaign contributions by business chiefs.[38] Finally, we are reminded, in the spirit of Jeffersonian and Madisonian libertarianism, that whatever the evils, no action should be taken that even remotely threatens the liberties and autonomy of corporations or interest groups in general.

The usual response to this problem among the public depends on the

[37]Some of these arguments are summarized in Edwin M. Epstein, "Business and Labor under the Federal Election Campaign Act of 1971," in Michael J. Malbin (ed.), *Parties, Interest Groups, and Campaign Finance Laws* (American Enterprise Institute for Public Policy Research, 1980), pp. 107–51.

[38]Michael J. Malbin, "Campaign Financing and the 'Special Interest'," *The Public Interest* (Summer 1979), pp. 21–42. But for a somewhat different view, see David Cohen and Wendy Wolff, "Freeing Congress from the Special Interest State: A Public Interest Agenda for the 1980s," *Harvard Journal of Legislation*, Vol. 17, No. 2 (1980), pp. 253–93.

interest group to which one belongs. Union leaders believe that business PACs are allowed too much financial power, and business leaders hold that labor is allowed too much electoral power. Groups with insufficiently vested interests— those defined in terms of race and sex—argue that a system so grounded in economic interests discriminates against those with so little access to economic power. Is a more objective position possible?

Scholars analyzing PACs and campaign financing have concluded, on balance, that the situation is serious, though not desperate. A Harvard study group concluded, as summarized by a participant, that "PAC money is 'interested money'—that is, linked to a legislative lobby agenda; that reliance on PAC funds had led to a nationalization of the sources of money available to candidates, bringing in funds from outside a candidate's state or district (particularly Washington); and that the growing role of PACs has resulted in political money becoming bureaucratically organized—that is, detached from their source and aggregated in a fashion which renders them unaccountable."[39] Others argue that PAC money helps candidates challenge incumbents, leading to much-needed "new blood" in Congress—though, in fact, PACs overwhelmingly favor incumbents.

To Reform or Not Reform?

Some observers favor wider regulation of political money and publicly financed congressional elections. Others call for "deregulation" of the political arms of interest groups, assuming that the groups will find a natural and proper balance. Still others believe that the balance must be righted between the present wide and intensive activity of corporate PACs, and the far less influential role of PACs for consumer groups, women's groups, environmental groups, and civil rights groups.[40]

A quite different school of thought holds that none of these "solutions" will work; the problem lies more outside interest groups and PACs than within them or among them. This school notes that James Madison set a good example in concluding that the *causes* of faction could not be removed and that the *effects* could be controlled only by fundamental changes in the whole political system. His solutions (extending the sphere of government to take in "a greater variety of parties and interests" [establishing a stronger national government]; creating federal-state-local tiers of government [federalism]; and fragmenting the power of government so no majority or minority could control it [checks and balances]) worked to some degree but also aggravated the problems. Today the main proposal for controlling interest groups by reshaping the external political system is that of proponents of stronger political parties (see Chapter 10).

Finally, there are those who believe that the main problem lies not in interest groups but in the way public opinion is made, managed, and manipulated—above all, in the rise of the barons of the electronic media, in a new age of communications politics. These observers are urging Congress to limit what commercial television stations can charge for political advertising and to discourage so-called "negative targeting" of candidates in political advertising. We will turn to this subject in Chapter 11.

[39]The Institute of Politics, John F. Kennedy School of Government, Harvard University, *An Analysis of the Impact of the Federal Election Campaign Act, 1972–78: A Report by the Campaign Finance Study Group to the Committee on House Administration of the U.S. House of Representatives,* May 1979, based in part on analysis by Xandra Kayden; summarized by Epstein in Malbin (ed.), *Parties, Interest Groups,* p. 142.

[40]See David Jessup, "Can Political Influence Be Democratized? A Labor Perspective," in Malbin (ed.), *Parties, Interest Groups,* pp. 26–55.

SUMMARY ▰▰▰▰▰▰▰▰▰▰▰▰▰▰▰▰▰▰▰▰

1. The dominant interest groups are economic or occupational, but a variety of other groups—religious, racial, ideological, ethnic—have memberships that cut across the big economic groupings and both reduce and stabilize their influence.

2. Groups in the local setting—family, school, church, or temple—socialize citizens to some larger community identity and to values and attitudes about self and others in the political process. Interest groups influence citizens' and officeholders' opinions about what government should do.

3. The sources of group power are size, unity, singleness of purpose, organization, and leadership, but the actual power of an interest group stems from the manner in which these elements relate to the political, governmental environment in which the interest group is operating.

4. For many decades interest groups have engaged in lobbying, but these efforts have become far more pervasive and significant with the deep involvement of groups in the electoral process, especially through the expanded use of political action committees.

5. Concern about PACs centers on their ability to raise money and spend it on elections, in behalf of endorsed candidates. This concern has led to extensive regulation of interest group political spending.

6. The key issue today in "controlling factions" is whether to allow groups to find some kind of balance of their own, to try to regulate groups, or to seek reforms outside the groups by building up balancing power in political parties or elsewhere.

FURTHER READING ▰▰▰▰▰▰▰▰▰▰▰▰▰▰▰▰

ALLAN J. CIGLER AND BURDETT A. LOOMIS (eds.). *Interest Group Politics* (C. Q. Press, 1983).

R. W. CONNELL. *The Child's Construction of Politics* (Melbourne University Press, 1971).

CAROL S. GREENWALD. *Group Power: Lobbying and Public Policy* (Praeger, 1977).

MILDA K. HEDBLOM. *Women and American Politics: A Perspective on Organizations and Institutions* (American Political Science Association, test ed., 1983).

M. KENT JENNINGS and RICHARD G. NIEMI. *Generations and Politics: A Panel Study of Young Adults and Their Parents* (Princeton University Press, 1981).

MICHAEL J. MALBIN (ed). *Parties, Interest Groups, and Campaign Finance Laws* (American Enterprise Institute for Public Policy Research, 1980).

ANDREW S. McFARLAND. *Common Cause: Lobbying in the Public Interest* (Chatham House, 1984).

NORMAN J. ORNSTEIN and SHIRLEY ELDER. *Interest Groups, Lobbying and Policymaking* (Congressional Quarterly Press, 1978).

ROBERTA S. SIGEL and MARILYN B. HOSKIN. *The Political Involvement of Adolescents* (Rutgers University Press, 1981).

DAVID B. TRUMAN. *The Governmental Process* (Knopf, 1951).

MOVEMENTS: THE POLITICS OF CONFLICT

8

It was a strange sight, that January day in 1917 at the gates of the White House. A group of women—society ladies from the Washington area, eminent professionals, young college graduates, workers from a munitions plant—marched up and down, carrying banners: "MR. PRESIDENT! WHAT WILL YOU DO FOR WOMAN SUFFRAGE?" "HOW LONG MUST WOMEN WAIT FOR LIBERTY?" As the days passed, the banners became more militant. Hoodlums and self-styled patriots began to harass the picketers, heckling them and tearing down their banners. Then the police began to arrest the women. Over 200 were taken into custody; almost 100 were jailed. The picketers dramatized their plight by going on hunger strikes; prison authorities responded with brutal efforts at forced feeding. By now the whole country was aware of the women's ordeal; a small band of leaders had aroused the consciousness of a nation.

Clearly, suffragists comprised a "group" as described in the last chapter; yet they were much more than a group. Indeed, they can best be described as a political *movement*. They were heavily politicized—looking toward political action as the chief means of reaching their goals. They had a sense of being excluded by law and society from full political participation on the basis of their sex. Even more, they perceived themselves as subject to a more powerful group—men—and confined to the "private sphere" of motherhood while being excluded from the "public sphere."[1]

---

[1]For a discussion of women as a sex-class, see Zillah Eisenstein, *The Radical Future of Liberal Feminism* (Longman, 1981). On the suffragists see Ellen Carol DuBois, *Feminism and Suffrage: The Emergence of an Independent Women's Movement in America 1848–1869* (Cornell University Press, 1978).

Despite its tremendous gains, the women's movement is still struggling to achieve equal rights. Other groups as well, both on the left and the right, are seeking to achieve liberty and equality and justice within the American value system. In looking at all these movements, note the central role of movement leadership in raising movement consciousness. Note also the role of conflict as the "outsiders" in movements confront the "insiders" in authority—conflict that in turn arouses more movement consciousness and enhances the role of movement leaders.

AMERICAN INDIANS: THE OLDEST MOVEMENT?

Indian leaders seek change in U.S. policy. *George Tames/NYT Pictures.*

Background of the Movement

Completing a march from San Francisco, American Indians come across the George Washington Bridge into New York. They started cross country June, 1980 to Washington to protest uranium mining on Indian land, sterilization of Indian women, nuclear power. They came to carry their protest to the United Nations. *UPI.*

Centuries ago colonists sailed west looking for another India. Often holding grants of land from their own governments, they believed the land in the New World "belonged" to them. However, the land also belonged by long usage to "Indians"—for these tribal peoples had long inhabited the mountains and valleys, meadows and plains. As settlers moved west, colonial leaders dealt with Indian representatives to obtain land for colonists, to reserve certain lands to Indians, and to gain access for Indian hunters in the ceded areas. Much was settled by negotiation and agreement; in North America the British made treaties with the Creek Confederacy, the Cherokee Nation, Wyandot, the Iroquois Confederacy, and the Seneca Nation.[2] But as the white people aggressively pressed into Indian lands, conflicts arose—and the red people resisted through both violent and nonviolent means.

The early Indian resistance movements reflected a deep division between cultures. Early in this century a congressional committee chairperson reflected the white cultural bias: "As a race of people, the Indian is not much inclined to continuous work; he is not very ambitious; he specially enjoys fishing, hunting, racing and other sports rather than any kind of hard labor; governmentally he is naturally a tribalist; he is more inclined to tribalism than to individualism. . . ."[3] White leaders, reflecting their own patriarchal society, assumed Indian tribes were patriarchal as well and hence treated only with Indian men, but in some tribes the braves lacked full authority.[4] Thus, the political cultures of the white and red peoples clashed, especially with regard to patriarchy, private property, individualism, capitalism versus communalism, tribalism, nonprivate lands, and a nonprofit economy.

During much of its history the federal government has followed a dual policy toward native Americans. On the one hand, Congress did not propose to rule the tribes but simply to regulate trade with them. In fact, white settlers continued to move into tribal lands, often with backing from their local and state governments—in defiance of treaties made in Washington. According to Chief Justice Marshall, Indians were "domestic dependent nations." "They occupy a territory to which we assert a title independent of their will, which must take effect in point of possession when their right of possession ceases. Meanwhile they are in a state of pupilage. Their relationship to the United States resembles that of a ward to his guardian."[5] Many native Americans, however, preferred to cling to their own culture.

[2]Dorothy V. Jones, *License for Empire: Colonialism by Treaty in Early America* (University of Chicago Press, 1982).

[3]Quoted in Russel Lawrence Barsh and James Youngblood Henderson, *The Road: Indian Tribes and Political Liberty* (University of California Press, 1980).

[4]On the roles of American Indian women, see Rayna Green, "Native American Women," *Signs: Journal of Women in Culture and Society* (Winter 1980), pp. 248–67.

[5]*Cherokee Nation* v. *Georgia*, 30 U.S. (5 Pet.) 17 (1831).

Indian leaders in 1944 formed the National Congress of American Indians, with Ruth Muskrat Bronson as its first director. In some respects the NCAI operated as a typical interest group, working on legislation affecting Indian tribes and conducting litigation in behalf of Indian voting rights, welfare, and civil rights. But the NCAI was also militant in defense of Indian culture. "Tribalism is not an association of interest but a form of consciousness," according to two authorities; it is a feeling of being born "into a family, a territory, a spiritual world . . . the mental experience" of "a warm, deep and lasting communal bond among all things in nature in a common vision of their proper relationship."[6]

This sense of "movement militance" erupted in charges that the United States government had practiced genocide in the Indian wars from 1790 to 1915—beginning with wars against the Indian tribes in the Old Northwest Territory and ending with wars against the Paiute in Colorado. Indian leaders also charged that the government had destroyed rights supposedly guaranteed by treaties, such as rights to fishing and hunting, as well as to timber and other natural resources. Such charges coincided with movements for national liberation that were surfacing in the 1960s around the world, especially in third world nations in Asia and Africa. American Indian leaders even claimed a kind of fourth world status, as a "colony within a nation."

MOVEMENTS IN
AMERICA
(some examples)

Abolitionist
Suffragist
Prohibitionist
Populist
Progressives
Black Rights
Anti-Vietnam War
Tax Cutters
Moral Majority
Nuclear Freeze

8–1

EXAMPLES OF THE OSCILLATING POLICY OF THE UNITED STATES TOWARD AMERICAN INDIANS

1831—*Cherokee Nation* v. *Georgia:* Indian tribes are "wards" of the United States.

1832—*Worcester* v. *Georgia:* Treaties between Indian tribes and the United States assume tribal sovereignty, and the state of Georgia cannot interfere with internal tribal affairs.

1830–1836—Act of May 28, 1830, Act of July 2, 1836, and United States treaties with various tribes: Indian tribes east of the Mississippi River must move to territories west of the Mississippi River.

1884—*Elk* v. *Wilkins:* Indians are not citizens, the Fourteenth Amendment notwithstanding.

1887—Dawes Indian General Allotment Act: United States subdivides tribal territories and allots plots of land to individual Indians.

1924—Act of June 2, 1924: United States confers citizenship on Indians who leave reservations; includes Indian women who marry non-Indians.

1934—Indian Reorganization Act: Indian tribes on reservations may adopt constitutions, which must be approved by the Secretary of the Interior.

1953—Public Law 83-280 and various subsequent acts: United States terminates relations with and services to Indian tribes.

1968—Indian Civil Rights Act: United States provides a Bill of Rights for individual Indians in relation to their tribes.

1983—*Arizona* v. *California:* Five southwestern Indian tribes cannot relitigate an original 1952 case to increase tribal water rights, even though the United States failed to claim all the tribes' rights for them in the original case.

Recent Movement Militance

In the summer of 1961 ten young college-educated Indians, five men and five women—a Paiute, a Mohawk, a Ute, a Shoshone-Bannock, a Ponca, a Potawatomi, a Tuscarora, two Navajos, and a Crow—met in the Gallup, New Mexico, Indian Community Center. They came to decide how to carry out a Declaration of Indian Purpose adopted at a national gathering of Indian tribal leaders earlier in the summer. They formed the National Indian Youth Council (NIYC). "In the Indian way," they elected one another members of the council and chose Paiute Mel Thom as their first president. Their membership would grow large in the coming years. In Mel Thom's words: "The movement grew in the Indian way. We had decided what we needed was a movement. Not an organization, but a movement. *Organizations rearrange history. Movements make history.* . . . Long ago the Indians knew how to use direct action. You

---

[6]Barsh and Henderson, *The Road*, pp. vii–viii.

Fenton by Wiley. © News Group Chicago, Inc.—Courtesy of News America Syndicate.

might say that was the traditional way that Indians got things done. We were concerned with direct action: Indians moving out and doing something."[7]

NIYC's first venture was to challenge their alleged denial of the Indians' tribal fishing rights by the State of Washington. Beginning in 1964 the NIYC and the Northwest Indian tribes held "fish-ins" on the Quillayute, Puyallup, Yakima, Nisqually, Columbia, and Green rivers. Men, women, and children participated, and the police arrested and jailed many of them. The NIYC actions sparked a surge of Indian activism. Indians of All Tribes, first organized in the San Francisco Bay area, retook Alcatraz Island. The American Indian Movement occupation of Wounded Knee mobilized the Indians of many tribes, focusing attention on the issue of recovering sovereignty in Indian lands.

Whatever the differences among Indians, the tribe still seems to be a focal point of concern. And as long as native Indians cherish their culture, it can be expected that their movement—militant but nonviolent—will continue.

BLACKS: FREEDOM NOW

MOVEMENTS VERSUS GROUPS

Groups in American politics tend to operate within the framework of government and the existing two-party system, to use the political tactics of lobbying, to build policy coalitions within the legislature and executive, to strive for consensus outside of government, and to advance their goals as beneficial to all groups—not just their own.

Movements tend to feel "left out" of government, to conduct political action at the grass roots, to put pressure on government from the outside, to build coalitions among mobilized publics, to see their causes as morally right and the opposition as wrong—and even evil— and to thrive on social and political conflict.

(These two tendencies, which may merge into each other in practice, are described more fully at the end of this chapter.)

"Ain't gonna let nobody, Lawdy, turn me 'round, turn me 'round, turn me round. Ain't gonna let nobody turn me 'round, gonna keep on a-walkin', keep on a-talkin', marchin' up to Freedom Land. . . ."[8]

As American Indians sought to regain political liberty in the form of tribal self-government, black African-Americans struggled to rise from chattel slavery to full United States citizenship. African-American movements have followed several paths of development, from slave rebellions and underground escapes, to the more recent tactics of freedom rides, sit-ins, marches, and boycotts. As with other movements, intragroup disagreements over goals and strategies have always existed. Within the black community the central question has been whether to strive for equality of opportunity inside the present federal system or outside of it.

Even though free black men and women lived, worked, and voted in small numbers in the northern colonies, and in smaller numbers in the southern colonies, by the nineteenth century the great majority of black Africans and succeeding generations of African Americans lived in slavery mainly on southern farms and plantations. Europeans wrenched these African peoples from complex and sophisticated societies in West Africa—Ghana, Mali, Hausa—herded them into slave trading posts along the West African coast, and branded and packed them into the holds of ships for the treacherous six- to ten-

[7]Stan Steiner, *The New Indians* (Harper & Row, 1968), p. 40. (Emphasis added.)

[8]Adaptation of traditional song by members of the Albany Movement, 1961–1962, which Bernice Reagon, then an Albany State College student, called the "Singing Movement." See Clayborne Carson, *In Struggle: SNCC and the Black Awakening of the 1960s* (Harvard University Press, 1981), especially pp. 56–65. The song is recorded on *Sing For Freedom: Lest We Forget*, Vol. 3, produced by Guy and Candie Carawan of the Highlander Center, Newmarket, Tennessee, for Folkways Records, 1980. Printed in *We Shall Overcome*, songs of the Southern Freedom Movement, compiled by Guy and Candie Carawan. Oak Publications, 1963.

week Atlantic crossing. This trade in humans supplied the workers and "breeders" of workers required by the white man to develop the economic staples of tobacco and cotton in the South and the textile industry in the North and in England.[9]

Resistance and Revolt

Coming from communal societies in which women as well as men exercised recognized and important functions, the Africans held their own well-developed conceptions of life, liberty, and property. In the New World Africans and their descendants began to construct their own cultures and relations anew.[10] Strategies used by slaves to overcome suppression ranged from what their owners took to be docility and ignorance to outright revolt. Many times rebellions took the form of individual, spontaneous action; at other times small groups defied their masters. Others escaped, sometimes via the Underground Railroad, engineered by people such as Harriet Tubman and Frederick Douglass. At the northern ends of the lines, greeting the escapees as they emerged from southern forests under cover of night, were the Vigilance Committees—groups of free blacks who helped the escapees start new lives.

A series of slave revolts—desperate, isolated, and ill-fated—broke out during the eighteenth and early nineteenth centuries, headed most notably by Gabriel Prosser in Richmond in 1800; Denmark Vesey in Charleston in 1822; and Nat Turner in Virginia in 1831. These major revolts revealed communication networks and leaders who were able to calculate opportunities and organize human and material resources.[11] The white authorities harshly put down all these revolts. Still, knowledge of the uprisings has provided black citizens with the courage and historical perspective needed to overcome continuing discrimination.

While black slaves in the South continued to resist their oppression, their brothers and sisters in the North were joined by white men and women convinced that slavery must somehow be ended. At first antislavery activists aimed to free the slaves and colonize them outside the United States—as evidenced by the formation of the American Colonization Society. Nevertheless, the movement soon flagged. However, William Lloyd Garrison later reinvigorated the movement by calling for a new direction and goal: Emancipate the slaves and grant equal rights to black citizens in the United States. Publications such as Garrison's newspaper *Liberator* and Lydia Maria Child's *An Appeal in Favor of that Class of Americans Called Africans*, along with meetings of local and state antislavery societies, culminated in the formation of the American Anti-Slavery Society in 1833. By 1838 a quarter of a million persons belonged to the 1350 societies that made up the national organization.

Dissension grew within this organization because of Garrison's radical views. Not only did he castigate church ministers who did not support abolition, but he also advocated the right of women to speak in public—a "right" that Angelina Grimke, a member of an old South Carolina family, exercised in appealing to Northerners. Garrison and his group became convinced, ironically, that secession of the *nonslave* states from the Union was a necessity. They argued that to continue union with the South was to support a Constitution that legitimized slavery.[12] The American and Foreign Anti-Slavery Society

[9]See August Meier and Elliott M. Rudwick, *From Plantation to Ghetto* (Hill and Wang, 1966); and Lerone Bennett, Jr., *Before the Mayflower: A History of the Negro in America 1619–1964*, rev. ed. (Penguin, 1966).

[10]Herbert G. Gutman, *The Black Family in Slavery and Freedom 1750–1925* (Vintage Books, 1977).

[11]Eugene D. Genovese, *From Rebellion to Revolution: Afro-American Slave Revolts in The Making of The New World* (Vintage Books, 1981), pp. 4, 27.

[12]Louis Ruchames, *The Abolitionists: A Collection of Their Writings* (Capricorn Books, 1964), pp. 13–24.

formed in opposition to Garrison, to pursue a more gradualist approach to ending slavery. The abolition movement continued up to the Civil War, helping to spawn the Liberty, Free Soil, and Republican parties. It was finally the proslavery rather than the antislavery states that seceded from the Union, and the Civil War accomplished in part what the Abolitionists began.

KKK: Countermovement

Following the Civil War many movements arose in support of or in opposition to reform. But two movements in particular concerned newly "freed" black people directly: the Ku Klux Klan, whose local chapters lynched people and burned homes to keep blacks "in their place"; and the antilynching movement led by one black woman, Ida Bell Wells-Barnett, who eventually was joined by others in forming antilynching societies.

The KKK sought to preserve their version of the white southern way of life. On the one hand, Klan leaders wanted to maintain the cheap black labor pool and prevent black ownership of property. On the other hand, they wanted to protect the symbol of the white woman, whose value would be greatly diminished if she were "violated" through any kind of contact with black men. They gave no regard to black women, who literally had been violated by their white owners and masters,[13] or to white women who might not wish to be so used and protected that they were confined to a "pedestal."[14] A more complex intertwining of race, sex, and class issues can hardly be found. The black scholar and activist W. E. B. Du Bois pinpointed the very human basis of the Klan fear: "The method of force, which hides itself in secrecy, is a method as old as humanity. The kind of thing that men are afraid or ashamed to do openly, and by day, they accomplish secretly, masked, and at night."[15] Small and often violent Klan groups are still active today.

After writing antilynching editorials in her own Memphis weekly, Ida Bell Wells went on to launch a national, even international, crusade against lynching. Her investigations into lynching incidents took her into the forbidden and murky heart of sex-race relations. She found that though the rape of white women was popularly thought to be the reason for lynching, rape was actually charged in only a third of the over 700 lynchings reported for the ten-year period she studied. Her last *Free Speech* editorial hinted at a truth she would elaborate in a study of lynching entitled *A Red Record*.[16] Indeed, black men lynched for "rape" often were involved in mutually affectionate, though necessarily clandestine, relationships with white women.

Continued lynchings spurred the formation of antilynching societies and the antilynching committee of the National Association for the Advancement of Colored People (NAACP). The Anti-Lynching Crusaders, led by Mrs. Mary B. Talbert, was organized in 1922 as a national effort to draw women into the NAACP efforts. Finally, in 1930 white women formed the Association of Southern Women for the Prevention of Lynching and brought home their own "revolt against chivalry."[17] This group chose to work for state laws against lynching. Though President Truman's 1947 Committee on Civil Rights called for federal antilynching legislation—the goal of the movement—it was never passed.

[13]Gerda Lerner (ed.), *Black Women in White America: A Documentary History* (Vintage Books, 1973), especially pp. 150–93.

[14]Anne Firor Scott, *The Southern Lady: From Pedestal to Politics 1830–1930* (University of Chicago Press, 1970).

[15]W. E. B. Du Bois, *Black Reconstruction in America 1860–1880* (Meridian Books, 1964; first published by Harcourt, Brace and Company, 1935), pp. 677–78.

[16]Ida B. Wells, *A Red Record* (Donohue & Henneberry, n.d.; reprinted by Arno Press, 1969).

[17]Jacquelyn D. Hall, *Revolt Against Chivalry: Jessie Daniel Ames and the Women's Campaign Against Lynching* (Columbia University Press, 1979).

The Black Movement Today

The contemporary black freedom movement began to surface quietly during World War I in New York City with an NAACP-sponsored Silent Parade protesting racial segregation. The movement grew slowly as first one organization and then another formed, their leaders inspired by news of the nonviolent marches and other actions of Gandhi in India. As we saw in Part Two, by the 1950s the movement against racial segregation was becoming more and more public. To combat segregated public transportation, the Congress of Racial Equality (CORE) and later the Student Nonviolent Coordinating Committee (SNCC) went freedom riding through the South on Greyhound and Trailways buses. In Montgomery, Alabama, Mrs. Rosa Parks refused to give up her seat on a city bus to a white person. Her arrest sparked the formation of the Southern Christian Leadership Conference (SCLC) by the Reverends E. D. Nixon, Ralph Abernathy, and Martin Luther King, Jr. Black students and their parents challenged segregated schools and universities by enrolling in Little Rock High School, the University of Mississippi, and the University of Alabama, among other institutions. Federal troops had to be called in to ensure the black students' safety.

Beginning in the 1960s the movement accelerated. Black college students challenged segregated public accommodations by sitting in at lunch counters in the South. As more and more people sat in or went on freedom rides, an increasing number were arrested and jailed for their nonviolent civil disobedience. SNCC advocated "jail, not bond," and these jail-ins brought many people into contact with racism and poor conditions in many southern jails. Activists challenged the white electoral process through the Voter Education Project (VEP), sponsored by the NAACP, CORE, SCLC, and SNCC. Black voter registration was a revolutionary action in the deep South and drew countless violent reactions by white mobs and police.[18] Throughout the nation reaction took violent forms, including assassination of leaders in or associated with ideas of the movement: Medgar Evers in June 1963; President John F. Kennedy in November 1963; Malcolm X in February 1965; and Martin Luther King, Jr., in April 1968.

Through direct actions—both spontaneous and organized—labor leaders, workers, ministers, students, blacks and whites, and countless others brought about comprehensive changes in the laws of the United States. But laws do not operate in a vacuum. Their implementation tends to be slow, complicated by bureaucratic politics. Many blacks by the 1960s were living in poverty in large cities, without the economic and social resources to take advantage of the opportunities held out by the laws. Police incidents in black ghettoes in Los Angeles (Watts), Detroit, and Newark set off riots—or what many came to see as rebellions against continuing racism.[19]

The legacy of the African American movement is one of continuing conflict: a renewed consciousness of the African roots of black Americans; increasing numbers of blacks skilled in political organizing; and enlarged visions of what has yet to be accomplished. However, critical socio-economic obstacles remain: racism still exists; the KKK is still active. Black movements continue; witness the landmark electoral victories of Harold Washington in Chicago and Wilson Goode in Philadelphia; massive voter registration and black mobilization stimulated by Jesse Jackson's unprecedented success as a presidential candidate. In New York City, foes of Mayor Edward Koch searched for a black mayoral candidate to capitalize on Jackson's success.

Rev. Jesse Jackson. *UPI/Bettmann.*

Jesse Jackson debating Walter Mondale and Gary Hart. *AP/Wide World Photos.*

[18]Carson, *In Struggle*; see also Robert Cooney and Helen Michalowski (eds.), *The Power of the People: Active Nonviolence in the United States* (Peace Press, 1977).

[19]*Report of the National Advisory Commission on Civil Disorders* (Kerner Commission) (Bantam, 1968).

WOMEN: THE CONTINUING STRUGGLE

The story of womens' movements in the United States is the story of a group of persons—large in numbers but otherwise lacking in political power—who developed a sense of group consciousness, moved into politics despite countless frustrations and setbacks and after long struggles achieved some of their major political goals.

Independence for Americans in the 1770s brought little independence for women, who—like their sisters in Western Europe—were still dependents of fathers and husbands. Women could not make legal arrangements or contracts, could not earn wages separate from those of their husband, and could not vote. By marrying, they forfeited to their husbands legal custody of themselves as well as custody of all property and children.[20] "A wife is dead in law" was a commonly accepted doctrine. And lacking the right to vote, women could not turn to electoral politics to overcome this kind of discrimination. Rather, they "determined to foment a rebellion," in Abigail Adams's words, for they would "not hold ourselves bound by any laws in which we have no voice or representation."[21]

Women needed to become conscious of themselves as a group and to learn their rights. During the Revolution, and later during the War of 1812, many wives had to take over their husbands' work. Later, tens of thousands of women flocked to New England and other textile mill areas to become factory workers.[22] On the western frontier women were recognized as essential to the community, yoking cattle and pitching tents until their ankle-length skirts hung in tatters. These types of experiences prepared women to become conscious of their own abilities and resources, both as individuals and as a group.

Generally, however, women were politically active in only two areas. One was in the fight for literacy and for education. Female academies existed, but they were mainly for the daughters of the wealthy, who were taught embroidery and other "female arts." Some women also took part in the early campaigns against slavery, but even their male counterparts often kept their distance from the "female agitators."

Such forays into the world of politics helped lay the groundwork for the movements to come, and numerous leaders emerged to organize their sisters. Sarah Bagley, a young Lowell mill worker, organized women workers in the Massachusetts and New Hampshire textile mills and founded the Female Labor Reform Association. The latter, together with other labor groups, submitted a petition signed by 10,000 workers to the Massachusetts legislature in favor of the ten-hour day. Lucretia Mott, a Philadelphia Quaker, toured meetings of the Friends to speak on temperance, peace, antislavery, and women's rights. Elizabeth Cady Stanton, who as a child in her father's law office had heard women pour out their grievances about discrimination and oppression, devoted her life to denouncing discrimination against women. In 1821 Emma Willard founded Troy Seminary for Women, and the college offered higher mathematics as well as the more conventional arts. Most controversial of all was Frances Wright, advocate of more liberal divorce laws, birth control, equal rights, and free public education. "Fanny" was denounced for her belief in the equality of all, regardless of sex, color, and class. It was even rumored that she favored "free love."

The women's suffrage movement was a celebrated example of groups in action. *Culver.*

[20]Eleanor Flexner, *Century of Struggle* (Harvard University Press, 1975), pp. 7–8, 63–65.

[21]Letter of Abigail Adams to John Adams, March 31, 1776, in Miriam Schneir, *Feminism: The Essential Historical Writings* (Vintage Books, 1972), p. 3.

[22]Milton Cantor and Bruce Laurie (eds.), *Class, Sex, and the Woman Worker* (Greenwood Press, 1977).

At an international antislavery meeting in London in 1840, delegates Lucretia Mott and Elizabeth Cady Stanton suffered the humiliation of being refused seats as delegates; rather, they were sent off to the gallery to watch. Then and there they resolved to hold a women's rights convention on their return home. Eight years later such a convention—to discuss the "social, civil, and religious conditions and rights of woman"—was held in Seneca Falls, New York. The convention was a curious "mixture of womanly modesty and feminist militancy."[23] Since no woman would chair the meeting, they asked Lucretia Mott's husband to do so. Yet the women's demands were radical for the times. The convention adopted resolutions calling for equal rights in marriage, property, contracts, trades, professions, and universities. Even more radical was a resolution to secure woman suffrage. Pushed by Elizabeth Cady Stanton and supported by Frederick Douglass, the measure barely passed.[24] Other conventions followed, in the East and as far west as Akron, Ohio. Women were on the march.

A Century of Struggle

Between the 1850s and the 1950s, leaders of the women's movement fought their political campaigns on many fronts. They took part in the antislavery movement, organized woman suffrage associations, won the right to vote in several western states, collaborated with temperance and other reform movements, helped found the National Association of Colored Women in 1896, fought against sexist discrimination on a state-by-state basis, established their right to higher education and professional positions, cooperated with women trade union workers, encountered defeat after defeat in their efforts to win the vote state by state, and finally won the national suffrage in August 1920 after a hard campaign for the enactment of the Nineteenth Amendment.

Many believe the women's movement died after this victory. But in fact, women's organizations continued to work on "women's issues"—that is, issues directly affecting women's status as women—and on other women's concerns, such as voter education, prison reform, antilynching measures, child welfare, and peace. Two organizations in particular continued the fight on women's issues: the National Woman's Party (NWP) and the National Federation of Business and Professional Women (BPW). Founded by Alice Paul, the NWP believed the vote alone would not get rid of economic inequality in the workplace. They held instead that only a constitutional amendment could establish the *principle* of sex equality. The NWP was responsible for introducing the Equal Rights Amendment in Congress in 1923 and for keeping it alive there session after session until it was embraced by the "second wave" of the women's movement in the 1960s. The BPW supported the Equal Rights Amendment during this period and worked generally to improve employed women's educational and employment opportunities.

In contrast, during this period the Women's Bureau of the Department of Labor worked against the Equal Rights Amendment. Because working conditions associated with so many women's jobs were harsh and unhealthy, the Women's Bureau instead supported protective legislation for employed women.[25]

This century of struggle raised a number of questions of ends and means, of strategy and tactics—questions that also confront other major groups. What is the *goal* of the women's movement—to secure rights only for women, or to

"ERA YES" and "STOP ERA" buttons were in evidence as pro and anti-ERA proponents listened to opening speeches at the Republican platform committee hearings in 1980. Supporters and opponents battled for their views to be written into the Republican platform. *UPI.*

---

[23]DuBois, *Feminism and Suffrage*, p. 23.

[24]Ibid., pp. 40–41.

[25]Judith Hole and Ellen Levine, *Rebirth of Feminism* (Quadrangle/The New York Times Book Company, 1971), especially pp. 77–81.

YOU DECIDE !

As a leader in the women's movement today, you are serving on a planning group considering new political strategies, in the light of the failure of the Equal Rights Amendment to pass. A rank-and-file activist tells your group that movement politics has failed, that a *party* strategy is necessary—and that women must form their own party. What is your response?

(Answer/Discussion on the next page.)

A New Consciousness: ERA

This button of the early 1980s was worn to dramatize the fact that women commonly are paid 59 cents while men get $1.00 for the same or similar work.

win them also for other disadvantaged groups, such as blacks, low-paid labor, immigrants, and Indians? If women's rights is the essential goal, *which* rights—to vote, to have a good education, to enjoy legal protection, to have a decent job, or to receive equal pay? To what extent should women work with *other groups*, at the expense possibly of having to dilute their own efforts? Should women form their own *party*, work within the existing two-party system, emphasize nonparty action (such as education and lobbying), or build a mass protest movement, march, and demonstrate for their demands? Should the movement concentrate on influencing the *federal* government, focus more on *state* action, or stress *local*, day-to-day concerns, such as education or neighborhood improvement?

Like most groups, women experimented, shifting tactics to meet new goals and circumstances. The national leaders of the past century actually split over whether to fight for suffrage alone or for a broader program, whether men should be allowed in the movement and on what basis, and what specific tactics should be adopted.

In the end, using a variety of political tactics and operating at all governmental levels paid off in securing the right to vote. Since conventional political action had not worked without the right to vote, it took the arrests of picketers and the forced feeding of society women in jails to dramatize the issues. The fact that many women were organized for both national and state politics paid off when they fought the suffrage amendment through the House and Senate, and then through three-quarters of the state legislatures. In fact, the Senate passed the amendment by exactly the two-thirds required, and the last legislature to ratify (Tennessee's) did so by a majority of one!

Armed with the right to vote, many American women entered the 1920s with heightened self-confidence and political influence. Congress acted favorably on maternity and infancy legislation, consumer bills, and other issues of special interest to women. By the end of 1921 twenty states had granted women the right to serve on juries. A few states passed equal pay and equal rights laws. Soon came the first woman governor, woman senator, and woman cabinet member; and others followed. A new organization, the League of Women Voters, educated its members on issues and urged them to exercise their hard-won right to vote.

But if women had new political clout, they faced new handicaps. A reaction to feminist successes set in. The child labor constitutional amendment failed to make any headway; and conservative groups put down feminist groups and women leaders, calling them communists, antifamily, and deviant lesbians. Some women who had been active in or influenced by the women's movement veered off in other directions. Most pursued "lifestyle feminism," using the opportunities opened up by the women's movement for their own personal self-development, and leaving behind the group effort that made the opportunities possible. While fewer continued to pursue the political aspects of feminism, they kept the fire burning until it burst out again in the 1960s.[26]

Women's goals expanded immensely following World War II, during which women had taken on heavy responsibilities, including military service. In the late 1950s and early 1960s, the struggle for black rights involved hundreds of women leaders and precipitated a more militant political effort. In the course of the struggle for "freedom now," it began to occur to more and more women, black and white, that sex as well as race was a source of oppres-

[26]Rayna Rapp and Ellen Ross, " 'It Seems We've Stood and Talked Like This Before': Wisdom from the 1920s," *Ms.* (April 1983), pp. 54–56.

sion. Women in the anti-Vietnam war and draft resistance movements began to realize they were being relegated to nonpolicymaking roles in those efforts. Whether black, socialist, or radical feminist, they broke off and joined the women's movement.[27] Women in the labor movement likewise recognized sexism in the movement as well as in the workplace and formed the Coalition of Labor Union Women (CLUW). To many women—especially middle-class housewives or those destined for that role—the appeals of Betty Friedan and other feminist writers came like fire sirens in the night.[28]

In expanding women's consciousness of their real needs and aspirations, literary and political leaders also expanded women's political and legislative goals. No longer would women be content working for a small number of legislative enactments; now they took positions, lobbied, or marched, demonstrated, or "boycotted" for bills cutting across all their concerns—equal pay, discrimination on the job, legal equality, divorce and child care, welfare rights, health care, protection against brutality and rape, equal credit opportunities, and educational equity. This range of interests required women to create new general organizations such as NOW, the National Organization for Women, as well as multitudes of women's liberation groups backing specific proposals or providing particular services.[29]

The women's movement of the late 1970s became more and more conscious of its own diversity; it was not just a white middle-class phenomenon. Many began to work on coalition building within the movement as well as with other groups—consumers, trade unions, blacks, religious and educational groups—in order to push bills in Congress and the state legislatures. As in any movement, women were internally divided: Some women deserted NOW because it was too radical, others because it was too conservative.

As we saw in Chapter 2, the efforts of many groups came to a focus in the battle for the Equal Rights Amendment (ERA) in the 1970s. To this struggle pro-ERA leaders brought not only moral claims and raised consciousness but also potentially vast numbers of voters and a large coalition of organizations. By the mid-1970s an alliance of younger organizations such as NOW and older groups such as the League of Women Voters and the BPW had set up a national lobby, ERAmerica, with headquarters in Washington. Yet the battle for ERA, like that for the vote a century before, proceeded slowly. Even though they constituted a majority of the American people, women faced opposition from small but well-organized minorities. Many women flatly opposed ERA, and they formed their own organization: STOP ERA. Others favored ERA but feared that concentrating so much on this one general issue would divert efforts from more specific and practical goals. While many men supported ERA, others assailed it. And millions of Americans, both women and men, were apathetic.

By the mid-1980s supporters of the ERA were still unable to win majorities in both houses of enough of the 38 states needed to pass the amendment.[30] But a striking symbolic and practical victory occurred in 1984 when the Democrats chose Congresswoman Geraldine A. Ferraro of New York as their vice-presidential candidate. She proved to be a vigorous campaigner, capable of holding her own in debate with the experienced Republican vice-president, George Bush.

Geraldine A. Ferraro, 1984 Democratic Vice-Presidential nominee. *UPI/Bettmann Archive.*

---

[27]Sara Evans, *Personal Politics: The Roots of Women's Liberation in the Civil Rights Movement and the New Left* (Vintage Books, 1980).

[28]Betty Friedan, *The Feminine Mystique* (Norton, 1963).

[29]Jo Freeman, *The Politics of Women's Liberation* (David McKay Co., 1975).

[30]Janet K. Boles, *The Politics of the Equal Rights Amendment* (Longman, 1979).

The mid-1980s strikingly parallel the 1920s in reacting to feminism. A right-wing Republican occupies the White House, and many conservatives view the women's movement as radical and antifamily. Yet women in the movement during the 1980s have learned from the past. They are more politically conscious, capable of organizing around controversial issues, and they have more political and economic resources and experiences to draw upon. The manner in which Geraldine A. Ferraro's candidacy influences the women's movement, and the way the movement capitalizes upon Ferraro's candidacy, may well be pivotal in the coming decade. Women are aware that their struggle will be difficult and that history will not repeat itself if they remain active and organized.

MOVEMENTS: THE WHY AND HOW

These brief histories of three political movements illustrate how groups organize and act in attempting to bring about major changes in the political system. Other types of groups have formed to challenge or regain basic values—philosophical, moral, or material—that cut across race, sex, and economic lines. A classic example is peace movements.

Certain religious groups have long rejected the notion of a State possessed of the ultimate authority to use violence for its formation or preservation. Historically *nonresistants* did not resist the State's use of violence; rather, they withdrew from society and were allowed to pay fines for noncompliance. Other groups, rejecting the military aspects of government, sought through elections or through movements to prevent the use of armed violence to settle disputes. These *pacifists*, practitioners of what we in the twentieth century call "active nonviolence," had visions of a peaceful society guided by individual and collective conscience. In matters of conscience concerning the use of violence, they refused to cooperate with the State, even refusing to pay fines for noncompliance. Rather, they engaged in acts of civil disobedience, for which they were arrested, and often sent to jail.

For as long as the United States has drafted armed forces and engaged in wars, even defensive wars, there have been organized groups—religious as well as secular—resisting such governmental actions. Well-known groups include the Woman's Peace Party, Women's International League for Peace and Freedom, Women Strike for Peace, Fellowship of Reconciliation, War Resisters League, American Friends Service Committee, War Tax Resistance, and New Mobilization Committee to End the War in Vietnam, to name just a few.[31] The peace movement today manifests itself in the anti-nuclear arms and anti-nuclear energy protests. Pacifists and believers in active nonviolence have also brought their writings and tactics—mass civil disobedience, marches, demonstrations—to the abolitionist, woman suffrage, civil rights, and women's movements.

A demonstration at the White House. *UPI.*

The Antitaxers

The antitax movement—not to be confused with the war tax resistance—is an attempt to restore the basic conservative principle: "That government is best which governs—and taxes—least." Sparked by the "crusty charisma of Howard Jarvis," the tax revolt started in California in 1978. Jarvis was responsible for placing Proposition 13—to cut property taxes by more than half—on a California ballot in order to reduce "unneeded" government services and bureaucratic

---

[31]See Helen Michalowski, "The Roots of American Nonviolence 1650–1915," in Cooney and Michalowski (eds.), *The Power of the People: Active Nonviolence in the United States*, pp. 14–37.

California tax fighter Howard Jarvis stands in front of the Internal Revenue Service Headquarters and announces formation of the "American Tax Reduction Movement" to cut federal spending by $100 billion and federal taxes by $50 billion over the next four years. *UPI.*

Thunder on the Right

Reverend Jerry Falwell, one of the leaders of the "Moral Majority" movement. *Dennis Brack, Black Star.*

waste. The proposition received 65 percent of the vote in California and attracted nationwide media attention. Thirty-seven states in quick succession followed California's example with similar tax cut referenda.

The antitax movement arises in part from a general feeling of impotence in political decision making and distrust of political leadership.[32] The efforts of President Reagan and conservative senators and representatives to bring down federal spending in the nonmilitary sector of the federal budget and to institute income tax cuts were part of a continuing tax revolt, even after the conservative leaders themselves came to the helm of government. The new governor of Georgia, Joe Frank Harris, running on a simple platform of "No New Taxes," won handily in 1982. If the tax revolt continues, and if conservative presidents and legislators actually cut spending, those who felt left out of government because they thought their tax dollars were being spent wrongly may now feel they are the "insiders."

But what of the large numbers of people who do not own property, or who do not earn large enough incomes to benefit from lower taxes? Will they turn to electoral politics or party politics to stem the tide of decreasing governmental services? Or will they be unable to find a party or candidates willing to run against the tax revolt? Movements engender countermovements—but not necessarily of equal strength.

A host of probusiness organizations have risen to combat organized labor, consumers, and "antibusiness" government. Feeling excluded from Democratic and even from Republican administrations, these groups have created a political movement of their own outside the regular parties. One of the most powerful of these organizations is the National Right to Work Committee and its legal arm, the National Right to Work Legal Defense Foundation. Claiming to have more than a million influential members, this group poured out such a huge volume of mail, it was granted its own postal zip number. The committee concentrates on opposing "pro-union" legislation and in particular attacks "compulsory" unionism. Another business organization, the Consumer Alert Council, has denounced "proconsumer" legislation, claiming it is harmful to consumers because of the extensive governmental regulation involved.

The proliferation of probusiness organizations—along with allied groups favoring "law and order" and bigger defense programs—rendered the New Right movement in need of political coordination. This was provided by Howard Phillips and Richard A. Viguerie, founders of the Conservative Caucus. Viguerie pioneered in the massive and skillful use of computerized direct mail. By the election of 1980 he had amassed the names of 4.5 million conservatives, drawn from single-issue and multi-issue groups, including the Right to Work Committee and the National Rifle Association. Operating wholly apart from the major party organizations, he helped both Democrats and Republicans—as long as they were solid conservatives.

The right-wing movement attracted intense support from "social" and "moral" conservatives concerned less with economic issues than with abortion, prayer in the classroom, busing, and sexual freedom. One of the most effective groups in the "profamily" movement was STOP ERA, led by Phyllis Schlafly, mother of six children and author of nine books who won a law degree at the age of fifty-four. Schlafly took on the battle against ERA when the Equal Rights Amendment seemed almost certain to pass. In her book *The Power of the Posi-*

---

[32]David Lowery and Lee Sigelman, "Understanding the Tax Revolt: Eight Explanations," *American Political Science Review* (December 1981), pp. 963–74. See also Howard Jarvis, *I'm Mad as Hell!* (Times Books, 1979).

tive Woman, she urged women to "reject socialism" and defend "our Judeo-Christian civilization." Her national 50,000-member movement against ERA, which viewed the amendment as communist-inspired at worst and unnecessary at best, had a central role in defeating it.[33]

How does the New Right movement—or the Moral Majority, as it is sometimes called—relate to presidential and party politics? Although Reagan and the movement shared views on such issues as busing and school prayer, each side views the other with some suspicion. After Reagan told a friendly meeting of evangelicals in Florida, "Let our children pray," Richard Viguerie praised his speech, but added: "The President has always been very good at giving conservatives their rhetoric. It remains to be seen if the White House staff will stay the President's course and fight for these issues." When the Republican Party platform called for a "religious test" requiring all federal judicial nominees to subscribe to an anti-abortion perspective Jerry Falwell victoriously cried "Now we'll get to appoint three justices."

Movements arise when numbers of people become conscious of wide gaps between their own values and conditions and the dominant political culture and structure. Movement leaders bring mobilized followers into a critical mass for action. Organization opens up channels of communication for spreading consciousness as well as news of planned actions. A particular event or personal happening may raise consciousness further. Action and thought interact through organization to fuel further movement. The media of the time—whether pamphlets and mass meetings for the abolitionists or newspapers or radio or television broadcasts for the civil rights movement—publicize the actions and further spread movements.

Political Socialization

Political action is a socializing force. Joining the women's movement or the moral majority or the antitax movement—or reading particular analyses in books or pamphlets—can change a person's perspective and values irrevocably, inspiring new sets of attitudes and opinions. Some people may even be brought up to endorse values that run counter to dominant social values.

We have already seen that schools, for the most part, "educate" to the dominant political culture; so it should not be surprising that large, ongoing movements establish their own educational efforts. These "alternative schools" present material that normally is left out of "mainstream" education. The freedom schools of the civil rights movements, the consciousness-raising groups of the women's movement, and the Native Controlled Survival Schools of AIM are examples of such schools.

We can compare movement politics and group politics in terms of the following characteristics: position of the group relative to the political system, mode of approach to political decision makers, style of action, type of communication channels used, and type of outcome intended.

OUTSIDE VERSUS INSIDE Groups excluded by custom or by law from the opportunities and/or the resources to participate effectively in a political system are most likely to engage in movement politics. Such engagement has three

[33]On right-wing movements and their leaders see Alan Crawford, *Thunder on the Right* (Pantheon, 1980); Kevin P. Phillips, *Post-Conservative America: People, Politics and Ideology in a Time of Crisis* (Random House, 1982); Carol Felsenthal, *The Sweetheart of the Silent Majority: The Biography of Phyllis Schlafly* (Doubleday, 1981); Richard A. Viguerie, *The New Right: We're Ready to Lead* (Carolina House, 1981).

Puerto Rican independence activists. *UPI.*

August 1983 march in Washington, D.C., to mark the twentieth anniversary of the "I have a dream" march for peace, jobs, and justice. *Marc Anderson.*

aspects: (1) The "outside" group perceives its exclusion or forced incorporation, (2) organizes to change its condition, and (3) risks severe punishment from the authorities for its actions. Excluded groups include women and pacifists, among others.

CONFLICT VERSUS CONSENSUS   Groups outside a political system typically do not share certain basic values with the groups and authorities inside the system. Interaction between the outside group and the system will involve conflict—a clash of values and persons. Puerto Ricans, for example, consider themselves to be a multiracial, multiethnic group with a proud heritage; some want Puerto Rico to become an independent nation.

By definition, groups inside a political system hold the values of that system and perceive its interests to some extent as their own. Interaction within the system involves disagreement within the bounds of a basic consensus—or agreement to disagree. Exxon Corporation, for example, may disagree with the Department of the Interior over the dollar amount for leasing public lands for oil exploration. Still, both sides agree that leasing is a legitimate end, and they will negotiate many leases over the years.

DIRECT ACTION VERSUS LOBBYING   Movements in conflict with a political system confront the authorities with demands for change. Their nonviolent direct actions may range from short-term marches, demonstrations, or rallies, to long-term boycotts. Movements that accept violent means in accomplishing their goals may plan armed strategies or engage in sporadic guerrilla tactics, such as bombings. In fact, nonviolent groups may bring about changes every bit as profound as those prompted by violent groups. While slave rebellions found violence the only means open to them to defend themselves against the expected armed reprisals of the slaveowners, the Southern Christian Leadership Conference has always espoused active nonviolence as a means of change.

Groups, on the other hand, take part in a system of bargaining to realize their goals. They pursue their objectives by lobbying in legislatures and bureaucracies and by taking part in elections. Candidates expect to receive information and contributions from such groups; and decision makers expect to hear from groups' lawyers, research staffers, or members concerning their views on various issues. The groups expect to have access to candidates and decision makers so that, at the least, they can present their views. Thus, the National Education Association bombards presidents and presidential candidates with contributions and research, letters and telegrams from its members about the need to keep and fund the various programs of the Department of Education.

PUBLIC VERSUS PRIVATE COMMUNICATION   Movement leaders try to reach a larger public in the hope of mobilizing their own membership and attracting new adherents—while at the same time catching the attention of the decision makers themselves as well as that of the national news media. Of course, the news media do not always report the action in the ways the movement would like, but public and dramatic displays by large numbers of people may be the only way to widen the conflict and build mass support. When the news media brought to our television screens pictures of peaceful black people marching and then praying at the bridge in Selma, Alabama, just for the right to vote—only to be met by police with billy clubs and snarling dogs—many people, black and white, became enraged. The pressure intensified for Congress to pass the Voting Rights Act.

Typically interest groups already have the attention of decision makers. Private meetings or written communications ease negotiations and compromises. The fewer people involved in the final decision, the better (though the people involved are understood to *represent* larger numbers of people). If the chemical manufacturers were to mount a demonstration at the Environmental Protection Agency demanding that they be allowed to flush toxic waste products into drinking water sources, environmental groups could countermobilize thousands of citizens demanding an end to the poisoning of our water supplies. On the other hand, private negotiations would more likely result in compromises allowing chemical companies to feed varying levels of wastes into the water supplies.

COMPREHENSIVE VERSUS INCREMENTAL CHANGE   The greater the differences seen to exist between an outside group's position and that of the political system, the greater the change the movement will demand. Some degree of comprehensive, structural change may be necessary in the system if the movement's intended goals are to be accomplished. The extension of a right to a group previously designated as inferior and unworthy—for example, suffrage for black males and for women of all races—would be seen as a change in the structure of power. Movements usually spurn incremental—that is, gradual, step-by-step—tactics to bring about change.

Movements and the Constitution

It is obvious that organized groups can thrive under our constitutional system. But what about movements? Leaders of major movements in American history point to severe constitutional obstacles to their political involvement. For example, the Constitution is all but silent concerning women. It speaks of "we the people" and "persons" but also refers to "a President . . . He." The Fourteenth Amendment specifically mentions *male* voting rights. Thus, the basic law of the land excluded women from the public sphere of government until the ratification of the Nineteenth Amendment.

As for race, the Constitution barred Congress from stopping the trade in slaves prior to 1808 and allowed a tax of ten dollars on each slave so imported. It not only prohibited any amendment of this clause but provided for the return of fugitive persons "held to service or labor"—slaves—to their owners. Thus, the Constitution supported slavery until the Thirteenth Amendment was ratified—and it made any major movement against slavery appear to be unconstitutional.

Indians cannot complain of being ignored in the Constitution, for the charter specifically acknowledged the existence of Indian tribes. The population to be counted in determining representation in the House of Representatives was to exclude "Indians not taxed"; and Congress was to regulate commerce "with foreign nations . . . and with the Indian tribes." Politically, however, the Indians had scant hope of operating within the constitutional system—their scattered numbers, their divisions, and the overwhelming military weight of incoming settlers effectively precluded their participation.[34]

However, defenders of the Constitution contend that while the constitutional system as it operated in the eighteenth and nineteenth centuries excluded women and slaves from the political process, these "outside" groups worked their way into the Constitution during this century. Blacks and Indians, they assert, have won more through litigation and lobbying than through movement politics. The Constitution was not written for women, admittedly; but for an eighteenth-century charter it is alleged to be rather advanced. This is a vital question for discussion during the present bicentennial era of "rethinking our constitution."

[34]From Diane L. Fowlkes, *How Gender Politics Reconstructs American Government and Politics* (American Political Science Association, 1983); see also Sarah Slavin, *Women and the Politics of Constitutional Principles* (American Political Science Association, 1983).

SUMMARY

1. Major groups in the population have organized movements because—as groups—they have been classified as inferior and excluded from the political system. These groups include American Indians of both sexes, black African-Americans of both sexes, and women of all races and economic classes.

2. The focal point of American Indian movements is recovering tribal sovereignty, which was first established by treaties and then abrogated continuously as settlers violated treaties.

3. The focal point of black African-American movements is changing the original slave status of black Africans to freedom as persons and full-fledged citizens of the United States.

4. The focal point of women's movements is transcending the artificially imposed dichotomy of the public and private spheres.

5. The key components of movements are negative perceptions of the political system, group consciousness of mistreatment, organization and leadership, and direct actions involving large numbers of group members and supporters.

6. Individuals gain group consciousness through movements. They may experience direct action itself or participate in alternative educational experiences, or they may be encouraged by families or movement leaders.

7. Movement politics involves groups outside the political system who are in conflict with and confront the system in public, direct actions intended to achieve comprehensive change. In contrast, interest group politics involves groups inside the political system who bargain privately within a framework of consensus to bring about incremental change.

FURTHER READING

RUSSEL LAWRENCE BARSH and JAMES YOUNGBLOOD HENDERSON. *The Road: Indian Tribes and Political Liberty* (University of California Press, 1980).

DEE BROWN. *Bury My Heart At Wounded Knee* (Holt, Rinehart and Winston, 1971).

STOKELY CARMICHAEL and CHARLES V. HAMILTON. *Black Power: The Politics of Liberation in America* (Vintage Books, 1967).

CLAYBORNE CARSON. *In Struggle: SNCC and the Black Awakening of the 1960s* (Harvard University Press, 1981).

ROBERT COONEY and HELEN MICHALOWSKI (eds.). *The Power of the People: Active Nonviolence in the United States* (Peace Press, 1977).

ALAN CRAWFORD. *Thunder on the Right* (Pantheon, 1980).

JOYCE GELB and ETHEL KLEIN. *Women's Movements* (American Political Science Association, test ed. 1983).

GLORIA T. HULL, PATRICIA BELL SCOTT, and BARBARA SMITH, (eds.). *All the Women Are White, All the Blacks Are Men, But Some of Us Are Brave: Black Women's Studies* (Feminist Press, 1982).

HOWARD JARVIS. *I'm Mad as Hell* (Times Books, 1979).

MARY SHANLEY and SHELBY LEWIS. *Feminism: Ideology and Theory.* (American Political Science Association, test ed. 1983).

BARBARA DECKARD SINCLAIR. *The Women's Movement* (Harper & Row, 1983).

U.S. Commission on Civil Rights. *Indian Tribes: A Continuing Quest for Survival* (Government Printing Office, 1981).

RICHARD VIGUERIE. *The New Right* (Carolina House, 1981).

VOTING
AND PUBLIC
OPINION

9

If movement politics involves those who see themselves as "outside" government (Chapter 8), while interest group politics is for "insiders,"giving them a pipeline to the decision makers between and during elections (Chapter 7), electoral politics provides another vital "inside" connection between voters and leaders. In this chapter we will examine the grassroots end of the electoral connection—voting and public opinion. In Chapter 13 we will examine the leadership end of the connection.

The question of who takes part in electoral politics—how and why we participate or not—is first of all a practical one. Almost any day we may have to decide whether to picket city hall or demonstrate in the street, or whether to watch a candidate on television, write a letter to our senator, criticize the president, contact a local politician for a favor, complain to the mayor's office about trash collection, read the political news, or decide how or whether we will vote. But participation in electoral politics also goes to the heart of the issues we raised at the very start: What do Americans believe in? What does this country stand for? What is the essence of American democracy?

Historically Americans have supported two supreme values, though they have defined these lofty principles in such diverse ways as to raise key questions, especially for the conduct of a "government by the people":

1. *Liberty*. Who is allowed the freedom to participate in politics, the right to speak out in elections, the power to vote?

2. *Equality*. Do Americans take part in these political activities on more or less equal terms? Is the system biased against certain groups or classes, in favor of others? Does any inequality result not merely from the "system" but from the behavior of people themselves?

Throughout American history a major test of participation has been voting. But participation in the broader sense means more than voting; it may mean running for office or helping others run for office, working for a political party, reading or listening to political speeches and analyses, developing opinions on the issues, and voting in some or all elections; or it may involve direct action, such as strikes and demonstrations. Participation includes taking part in social and community and organizational activities, for these activities often affect government, and those who are active in social or community organizations tend to be active in political ones.[1] Participation even includes serving on a jury when called. *Intensity* of participation is also a factor: some devote almost all their waking hours to politics and hold strong opinions, while others are spectators or bystanders and don't think much about politics and issues.

Still, voting and expressing opinions are key aspects of electoral participation. They decide who gets office and who does not. They set the direction of government and policy. They symbolize and embody the lofty aims of liberty and equality. For both leaders and people as a whole, voting is the crux of the whole political struggle, the bottom line. For politicians, the ballot is the payoff.

THE STRUGGLE FOR THE BALLOT

Extending the suffrage in the United States has involved a long battle to broaden the right to vote from a small group of property-owning white males to virtually all persons eighteen and over. We have noted the struggle of women and of blacks (Chapters 5 and 8). The first great expansion of the right to vote was for white men without property. And in all these struggles the central issue has been whether all Americans, including poor people, white women, black men and women, should have the right to take part in the democratic process.

The Declaration of Independence states that all men are created equal but says nothing about the right to vote. Indeed, most of our Revolutionary forefathers would not have dreamed of giving the ballot to black men, to women of any race, or to people under twenty-one; and they were dubious about granting the vote to people without property. The colonies had restrictions on voting, based on property—and the framers of the new Constitution were not about to discard them. Yet powerful eighteenth-century doctrines of natural rights, both in England and America, held that the franchise must be considered a basic right of all men. If all men were naturally endowed with reason, on what grounds could some be excluded from the process of self-government?

The response of conservatives like Chancellor Kent of New York was ingenious. Only those men with a real and continuing economic stake in society should vote. The property-holding middle class would serve as a great stabilizing force in the young republic. And—their shrewdest point—withholding the ballot from the poor would really help the poor, because men without property—if granted the right to vote—would in effect "sell" that right to the unscrupulous rich, who would hence become more powerful than ever! Universal male suffrage, thundered Kent at the New York constitutional convention of 1821, would not only "jeopardize the rights of property" but also threaten the "principles of liberty."

[1] Ronald M. Mason, "Toward a Non-Liberal Perspective on Participation," paper prepared for the Midwest Political Science Association meeting, Chicago, April 1980, offers a different perspective and a useful bibliography.

One Man, One Vote

9–1
VOTING BY RACE AND SEX, 1980

Race/Sex	Percent Voted
White men	60.9
White women	60.9
Black men	47.5
Black women	52.8
Hispanic men	29.2
Hispanic women	30.4

SOURCE: U.S. Bureau of the Census, *Voting and Registration in the Election of November 1980* (Government Printing Office, 1982).

The radicals of the day ridiculed such "elitist" arguments. They liked to quote Tom Paine on ridiculous implications of property qualifications. "You require that a man shall have sixty dollars' worth of property, or he shall not vote," Paine had written. "Very well, take an illustration. Here is a man who today owns a jackass, and the jackass is worth sixty dollars. Today the man is a voter and goes to the polls and deposits his vote. Tomorrow the jackass dies. The next day the man comes to vote without his jackass and he cannot vote at all. Now tell, me, which was the voter, the man or the jackass?"

The first great expansion of the right to vote was for men without property. Economic and social changes, as well as philosophical arguments, helped broaden the suffrage. Since the framers of the Constitution had evaded the issue by providing that members of the new House of Representatives would be elected by voters eligible to elect the lower houses of the various state legislatures, the fight for reform was channeled into at least thirteen state arenas. But different forces operated in different states. In the East "mechanics" and other workingmen were eager to express themselves politically, and their numbers were constantly being enlarged by the flow of immigrants. Here was a tremendous pool of voters. Shrewd politicans figured they could gain office, or tighten their hold on it, by giving the ballot to groups likely to vote "right." And, of course, as property-holding widened, so did the right to vote.

The great historian of the frontier, Frederick Jackson Turner, argued that the "wind of Democracy blew so strongly from the west" that eastern states were pushed toward imitating western states in broadening the franchise.[2] Other historians have held that extending the vote really had to wait for the Jacksonian era of the 1830s and 1840s. Actually, it is not easy to find a pattern in the process. Some restrictions were removed during the Jeffersonian era, with its emphasis on equal rights, and during the War of 1812, when soldiers argued that "if they were good enough to fight, they were good enough to vote." Property requirements were replaced by taxpaying requirements, which in turn gradually were dropped.

By the mid-nineteenth century white adult male suffrage had been established almost everywhere. North Carolina, the last state to yield, abandoned its property test for voting in 1856. But if one phase of a long struggle had come to a happy end, another phase had already begun with the abolitionist and women's rights movements.

Who Votes? Who Does Not?

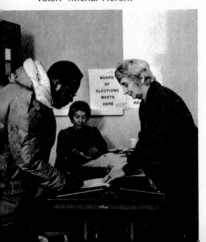

Registration official registering a voter. *Michal Heron.*

While you might expect a high rate of voting in the United States (after all, a lot of people: black men, black and white women fought for the right to vote) in fact, voting turnout in the United States is remarkably low. A few years ago over one hundred countries were ranked on voter turnout: Americans ranked twelfth from the *bottom*—a little above Barbados! And turnout has been falling, even in the presidential elections, from almost 63 percent in 1960 to about 56 percent in 1972 to less than 52.6 percent in 1980, and just 53 percent in 1984. Eighty and even 90 percent of the voters typically show up at the polls in the European democracies. In 1984, it is interesting to note that despite massive voter registration efforts by both the major political parties and from both the right (Moral Majority) and the left (Jesse Jackson), voter turnout increased less than 1 percent from the 1980 levels. Voter turnout, despite these efforts, may have been less than expected because virtually every poll indicated a lopsided win for the Reagan-Bush ticket.

[2]Frederick Jackson Turner, *The Frontier in American History* (Holt, 1920), p. 250. See also Chilton Williamson, *American Suffrage from Property to Democracy* (Princeton University Press, 1960).

How serious is low turnout? Certain factors should be noted. Americans conduct far more elections and types of elections than Europeans do. The student of voting behavior must be careful, too, to note whether turnout figures are based on the percentage of voters in the *total population*, which inflates the size of the "universe" by including aliens, people in penal and mental institutions and people under eighteen years of age, as opposed to those eligible to vote. And Americans, of course, have an absolute right *not* to vote. Still, we would expect a higher turnout.

Why is Turnout So Low?

The simplest answer to this question is: apathy. It is easy to criticize those who are just "too lazy" to vote. If people don't want to vote, a columnist wrote, "to hell with them—serves them right." The problem really is not that simple. Of course there are some people who just don't care. They would not go to the polls if King Kong were running against Snow White. But these persons are in a small minority. The main reasons for nonvoting are *institutional* and *political*. Let us consider both.

The institutional block is partly *registration* and *absentee ballot* requirements. People may forget to register in time (especially if the cutoff date is set far in advance of the election, as it often used to be). They may have moved too recently to reregister or they may be bedridden or away on long trips. Registration itself can be bothersome and time consuming. Getting an absentee ballot also can be difficult. One must also consider the ease and convenience of becoming registered. Is the registration office open on a regular basis? Is it available evenings and weekends? Can people register in their neighborhoods—in schools, firehouses, libraries? In some states registration is far easier than in others.

What effect do registration laws have on actual turnout? This has long been a subject of political science research. A study showed that the laws reduced turnout in the 1972 presidential election by about 9 percent; that the impact of the laws was most severe in the South and on less-educated people, both black and white; and that early deadlines for registration as well as inconvenient office hours were the main factors in lowering turnout. Many political conservatives and supporters of "states' rights" oppose federal efforts toward broadening registration, though there is little evidence that such broadening would produce a more liberal or Democratic vote than at present.[3]

Far more important than registration in nonvoting are *political* factors. Millions of Americans fail to show up at the polls because they feel it is not worth the trouble. They stay home on election day not because they lack concern but because their real interest, they feel, is not reflected in the "system." They feel there is no real choice between candidates or parties and they are less likely to identify strongly—or at all—with a major party. They believe politicians make promises they fail to carry out—that the government does not respond to their real needs and hopes. A few charge that the same groups run the government, no matter who wins the elections. Some are simply "disgusted" by politics. They are not apathetic toward politics, they contend—American politics are apathetic toward *them*.[4] These nonvoters are good candidates for movement politics.

WHY PEOPLE DON'T VOTE	
	Percent
Did not register	38%
Did not like the candidates	14
Not interested in politics	10
No particular reason	10
Were sick or disabled	7
Not U.S. citizens	4
New resident in area	4
Away from home	3
Could not leave job	2
No way to get to polls	2
Other reasons	6

Source: U.S. News & World Report Charts—Basic data U.S. Department of Commerce, Gallup Poll, 1980.

[3]Steven J. Rosenstone and Raymond E. Wolfinger, "The Effect of Registration Laws on Voter Turnout," *American Political Science Review* (March 1978), pp. 22–45; see Kevin P. Phillips and Paul H. Blackman, *Electoral Reform and Voter Participation* (American Enterprise Institute for Public Policy Research, 1975).

[4]See Arthur Hadley, *The Empty Polling Booth* (Prentice-Hall, 1978); Stephen D. Shaffer, "A Multivariate Explanation of Decreasing Turnout in Presidential Elections, 1960–1976," *American Journal of Political Science* (February 1981), pp. 68–95; Paul R. Abramson and John H. Aldrich, "The Decline of Electoral Participation in America," *American Political Science Review* (September 1982), pp. 502–21.

Who Fails to Vote Nonvoting might not be a serious problem if those who *do* vote were a cross section of those who do not. But this is not the case. The extent of voting varies widely among different types of *voters* and *elections* (see Table 9–2). Race and ethnicity help produce different levels of voting. Note the dropoff from white Anglos to blacks to Hispanics, whatever the other characteristics being examined. We should also note that lack of citizenship still accounts for some of the low Hispanic turnout.

Education seems by far the most important influence on voting, regardless of race and ethnicity: "Education increases one's capacity for understanding complex and intangible subjects such as politics," according to one study, "as well as encouraging the ethic of civic responsibility. Moreover, schools provide experience with a variety of bureaucratic problems, such as coping with requirements, filling out forms, and meeting deadlines."[5] The data are quite convincing: Those who finish grammar school are more likely to vote than those who do not; high school graduates tend to turn out more than grammar school graduates; college graduates more than high school graduates. Only black men and women with less than an eighth-grade education seem to contradict this finding. Also, the effects of college education are not so clear-cut for Hispanics.

9–2
GROUP CHARACTERISTICS OF VOTERS BY RACE AND SEX, 1980

Characteristics	White Women	White Men	Black Women	Black Men	Hispanic Women	Hispanic Men
			PERCENT VOTED			
Education						
Elementary 0 – 4	21.0%	31.3%	40.0%	42.3%	18.5%	21.5%
5–7	34.5	42.5	49.8	49.0	16.0	15.7
8	47.5	54.7	48.5	40.9	27.0	30.1
High school 1–3	45.7	47.2	47.3	37.7	24.5	21.4
4	62.0	57.7	51.9	48.2	37.9	33.2
College 1–3	71.6	66.4	59.1	51.6	49.1	40.7
4	80.8	79.3	74.8	71.1	44.6	53.1
5 +	84.0	83.3	82.8	78.7	B	52.4
Age						
18–20	39.1	36.2	24.7	25.9	14.6	11.7
21–24	46.5	43.5	36.5	30.9	21.6	14.7
25–34	57.7	55.0	49.8	43.8	28.3	26.7
35–44	67.2	64.3	62.6	54.1	35.6	33.3
45–54	68.9	69.3	62.4	54.2	38.3	44.5
55–64	70.8	74.1	68.0	60.1	45.0	44.8
65–74	67.2	73.9	66.1	63.2	35.9	45.2
75 +	53.9	67.2	44.7	54.6	21.0	41.4
Employed	64.3	62.3	59.9	51.1	35.3	30.2
Unemployed	45.3	38.6	45.6	37.2	27.4	21.3
Family Income*						
under $5,000	39.0		41.9		21.2	
5,000–9,999	50.3		45.2		24.1	
10,000–14,999	55.9		50.8		28.6	
15,000–19,999	61.5		54.6		34.3	
20,000–24,999	68.0		64.0		36.0	
25,000+	74.6		68.7		51.8	

*Includes those living in primary family.
SOURCE: U.S. Bureau of the Census, *Voting and Registration in the Election of November 1980* (Government Printing Office, 1982), Tables 10, 2, 11, 12, 13.

[5]Raymond E. Wolfinger and Steven J. Rosenstone, *Who Votes?* (Yale University Press, 1980), p. 102; see also Sandra Baxter and Marjorie Lansing, *Women and Politics: The Invisible Majority* (University of Michigan Press, 1980), pp. 35–37.

Income and age are also important factors. Those with higher family incomes are more likely to vote than those with lower incomes. Income, of course, goes along with type of occupation, and those with higher-status careers are more likely to vote than those with lower-status jobs. The older you are (unless you are *very* old and perhaps infirm), the more likely you are to vote. Persons eighteen to twenty-four years of age have a poor voting record; so do persons over seventy. Women's increased turnout generally is attributed to higher levels of education and employment, and black women in particular are influenced by their party identification and by feminism.[6]

But the most important fact remains: The poor, the uneducated, and members of racial minorities are still seriously underrepresented in the voting booth. More specifically, according to the conclusions of a recent study based on a wide sample, the "least educated, the very poor, Puerto Ricans, Chicanos, and people who moved in the year before the 1974 election all are underrepresented by between one-third and one-half. In addition, people without a high school diploma or below the median income, those who live in the South, the young, the elderly, the unemployed, the unmarried, and blacks show voting strength reduced by at least 15 per cent. On the other hand, college graduates are overrepresented by nearly one-third, as are people who earn more than $25,000."[7] The study added that the strength at the polls of government employees was 24 percent *greater* than their share of the population.

Why do low-income people vote in fewer numbers than the wealthy, especially when the poor would seem to have such a stake in government? For several reasons: They have less sense of involvement and confidence; they feel less of a sense of control over their political environment; they feel at a disadvantage in social contacts; and their social norms tend to deemphasize politics. Thus, nonvoting is not accidental—it is part of a larger political and psychological environment that discourages political activity.[8]

Black voting, especially in the South, shows another aspect of the voting-nonvoting equation. Since 1965 southern black voters have been turning out at higher and higher rates; but still they are not voting at the same rates as whites. Why not? For one thing, some fear reprisals for voting, though that restraint is declining in effect. It has also been found that apathy accounts for only a small part of nonvoting; strong black political organization increases black voter turnout; and perception of black electoral gain probably boosts turnout.[9] But a primary factor is the weakness of black political organizations. In the North the election of Harold Washington as mayor of Chicago and Wilson Goode as mayor of Philadelphia seem to be dramatic examples of the effects of organization and perceived stake on black voter turnout.

[6]See Baxter and Lansing, *Women and Politics*; also, Claire Knoche Fulenwider, *Feminism in American Politics: A Study of Ideological Influence* (Praeger, 1980).

[7]Wolfinger and Rosenstone, *Who Votes?*

[8]See Angus Campbell, Philip E. Converse, Warren E. Miller, and Donald E. Stokes, *The American Voter* (Wiley, 1960). This volume remains a foundation of modern voting analysis despite much new evidence and reinterpretation. See also Norman H. Nie, Sidney Verba, and John R. Petrocik, *The Changing American Voter* (Harvard University Press, 1976); and Warren E. Miller and Teresa E. Levitin, *Leadership and Change* (Winthrop, 1976).

[9]See Lester M. Salamon and Stephen Van Evera, "Fear, Apathy, and Discrimination: A Test of Three Explanations of Political Participation," *American Political Science Review* (December 1973), pp. 1288–1306; Douglas St. Angelo and Paul Puryear, "Fear, Apathy, and Other Dimensions of Black Voting," in Michael B. Preston, Lenneal J. Henderson, Jr., and Paul Puryear (eds.), *The New Black Politics: The Search for Political Power* (Longman, 1982), pp. 109–30; Philip L. Miller, "The Impact of Organizational Activity on Black Political Participation," *Social Science Quarterly* (March 1982), pp. 83–98.

Political institutions also have an impact on voting and nonvoting. You might think that the smaller the election district, the more closely involved people would feel with their elected officials, and hence the higher the voting turnout. You might also assume that people would tend to vote more heavily in elections for legislators than for executives, since the former are usually chosen in smaller districts. But note:

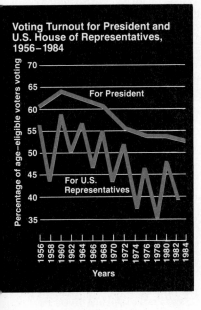

**Voting Turnout for President and
U.S. House of Representatives,
1956–1984**

For President

For U.S.
Representatives

Percentage of age-eligible voters voting

70 — 65 — 60 — 55 — 50 — 45 — 40 — 35

1956 1958 1960 1962 1964 1966 1968 1970 1972 1974 1976 1978 1980 1982 1984

Years

1. *National* elections bring out more voters than state or local campaigns. *Presidential* elections attract the greatest number of voters. Off-year congressional elections draw fewer persons to the polls. City and other local elections tend to attract an even smaller number. And participation is lowest in *party primaries*. Even when voters are marking a ballot that covers a variety of national and local contests, some voters will check their presidential choice but not bother with others.

2. Elections for *chief executives* attract more voters than elections for legislators. Turnout for representatives is considerably higher in years when a president is also elected, as the chart indicates. A somewhat similar difference exists at the state level between gubernatorial and legislative elections. The difference in executive and legislative turnout has major implications for governmental policy.

3. Voting is *lowest* in areas where there is little two-party competition. Thus, the lowest voting figures are likely to be found in states such as Mississippi, Alabama, and South Carolina, although recently there has been a marked increase in voting in the South.

Does this low rate of voting indicate that our democratic system is in danger? Some authorities see nonvoting as a sign of satisfaction with the state of affairs. Others believe that people are disgusted, cynical, and increasingly "turned off" and "tuned out" of the political system.

How can turnout be increased? Shorten the ballot by cutting down the number of unimportant elective positions. Simplify residence and registration requirements (permanent registration or registration by postcard are possibilities here; mail registration has worked well in the several states that have tried it). Make absentee voting easier. Make election day a big holiday and dramatize the importance of voting. Above all, make the parties more competitive in state and local as well as national elections, so that nonvoters will begin to see that they have a significant choice at the polls.

So much for the nonvoter. What about the people who *do* vote?

HOW WE VOTE: ELECTORAL PATTERNS

Sometimes Americans are called fickle voters—switching from party to party. Actually a majority of Americans stay with one party year after year, and their sons or granddaughters vote for the same party long after that. Politically, these voters are "set in their ways." Of course, there are still millions of so-called independent voters. They help make our elections the unpredictable affairs they so often are. Still, even in the variations from year to year, there are certain persistent elements:

1. A pattern of *sectional voting*. The South is the most famous example. The Democratic solidarity of the states that formed the Confederacy lasted over eighty years in presidential elections, and continues today in congressional

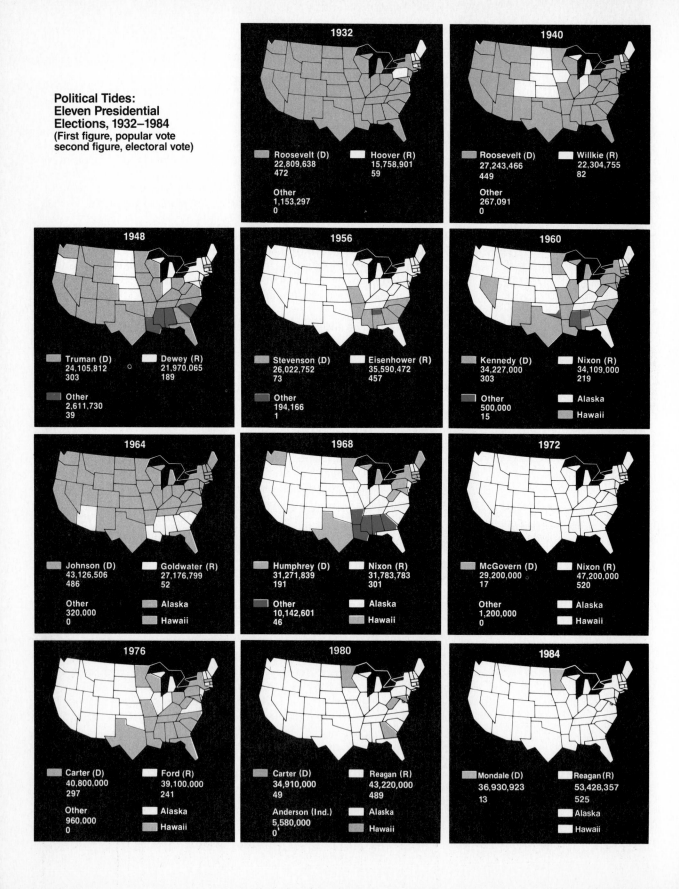

Political Tides: Eleven Presidential Elections, 1932–1984
(First figure, popular vote second figure, electoral vote)

1932

Roosevelt (D)
22,809,638
472

Hoover (R)
15,758,901
59

Other
1,153,297
0

1940

Roosevelt (D)
27,243,466
449

Willkie (R)
22,304,755
82

Other
267,091
0

1948

Truman (D)
24,105,812
303

Dewey (R)
21,970,065
189

Other
2,611,730
39

1956

Stevenson (D)
26,022,752
73

Eisenhower (R)
35,590,472
457

Other
194,166
1

1960

Kennedy (D)
34,227,000
303

Nixon (R)
34,109,000
219

Other
500,000
15

Alaska

Hawaii

1964

Johnson (D)
43,126,506
486

Goldwater (R)
27,176,799
52

Other
320,000
0

Alaska

Hawaii

1968

Humphrey (D)
31,271,839
191

Nixon (R)
31,783,783
301

Other
10,142,601
46

Alaska

Hawaii

1972

McGovern (D)
29,200,000
17

Nixon (R)
47,200,000
520

Other
1,200,000
0

Alaska

Hawaii

1976

Carter (D)
40,800,000
297

Ford (R)
39,100,000
241

Other
960,000
0

Alaska

Hawaii

1980

Carter (D)
34,910,000
49

Reagan (R)
43,220,000
489

Anderson (Ind.)
5,580,000
0

Alaska

Hawaii

1984

Mondale (D)
36,930,923
13

Reagan (R)
53,428,357
525

Alaska

Hawaii

elections. Republican sectionalism was not so clear-cut, but northern New England and parts of the Midwest have been dependable areas for the GOP. Vermont has given its electoral votes to the Democrats only once since the Civil War, and Maine only twice since 1912. More recently the South has become more Republican and the Northeast more Democratic, but Jimmy Carter partially reversed that Republican "trend" in the South in 1976.[10] Reagan won all of the South in 1984. Today the Republican "solid west" almost rivals the Democrats' "solid south" of old—at least for presidential elections.

Sectional patterns tend to be fuzzy and sometimes brief. Lately there has been much talk about the Sunbelt, the area from the southeastern states to California. This region was seen as the base of a rising American conservatism. But in many recent elections the divisions have tended to lie between the East and the West, and this pattern may not last long either. Sectional patterns often reflect very close election results within states, and those patterns can easily be changed by other influences.

2. A pattern of *national* voting. Traditional sectional alignments also give way to national trends. The Franklin Roosevelt administration, for example, ushered in a new age of Democratic popularity that affected even the most traditionally Republican areas, and Eisenhower's popularity accelerated the breakup of the solid south. States and sections are subject to a variety of local influences, but they cannot resist the great political tides that sweep the nation.

3. A pattern of *similar* voting for *different* offices. Sectional and national forces affect voting for different candidates and offices in the same election. A considerable number of voters usually vote a straight ticket—that is, they throw their support to every one of their party's candidates. If one candidate is an especially good vote getter, the party's whole slate may gain. This is the famous coattail effect, whose precise nature is one of the challenging problems in the study of political behavior. Evidently, popular presidential candidates like Roosevelt or Johnson have long coattails that help elect many other candidates on their party tickets. But congressional and state candidates may have helpful coattails too, and it is not easy to tell which candidates ride on whose coattails or just how important the relation is.[11]

4. A pattern of voting over *time*. Great political tides seem to flow back and forth across the generations. Most presidential elections are maintaining elections, in which the existing pattern of partisan support persists. Long periods of maintaining elections are occasionally interrupted by deviating elections, which the "out" party wins because it has an especially attractive presidential candidate or because the existing administration has lost the nation's confidence. In these elections the underlying division of party support is not long disturbed, and the next election result returns to the old pattern. Very occasionally, however, there occurs a realigning election that brings a basic and long-lasting transformation of party loyalties. A whole new balance of parties comes into being, as it did in the 1930s.[12] Some have predicted that we

Registering to vote can be made easy as this storefront setup shows. *Charles Gatewood, Magnum.*

New Jersey's Voter Registration Application: Your ticket to power.

---

[10] Important recent works on southern politics are Jack Bass and Walter DeVries, *The Transformation of Southern Politics* (Basic Books, 1976); and Louis Seagull, *Southern Republicanism* (Wiley, 1975). A provocative sectional theme is found in Kirkpatrick Sale, *Power Shift: The Rise of the Southern Rim and Its Challenge to the Eastern Establishment* (Vintage, 1976).

[11] For an example of some of the complex factors at work, see Barbara Hinckley, "Incumbency and the Presidential Vote in Senate Elections: Defining Parameters of Subpresidential Voting," *American Political Science Review* (September 1970), pp. 836–42. See also Gary C. Jacobson, "Presidential Coattails in 1972," *Public Opinion Quarterly* (Summer 1976), pp. 194–200; and Frank B. Feigert, "Illusions of Ticket-Splitting," *American Politics Quarterly* (October 1979), pp. 470–88.

[12] These three types of elections are defined and discussed in Angus Campbell, Philip E. Converse, Warren E. Miller, and Donald E. Stokes, *Elections and the Political Order* (Wiley, 1966). See also Walter Dean Burnham, *Critical Elections and the Mainsprings of American Politics* (Norton, 1970).

are on the eve of another series of realigning elections and a historic realignment of the parties. Others see mainly a pattern of confusion and dislocation.

Group Factors in Voting

Why do some voters stick with one party while others shift back and forth from election to election, and still others vote a split-party ticket in every election? In recent decades a vast amount of effort has been devoted to answering these questions.

A traditional explanation for the great political tides is that they reflect economic conditions. A drop in business activity has often preceded a loss of congressional seats and then a presidential defeat for the party in power. But we cannot be sure that business cycles *cause* political cycles. Psychological, political, traditional, sectional, international, and other forces may muddle the effect of economic factors.[13] It was not primarily economic issues but rather the sharply rising concern over slavery that precipitated the breakup of the Democratic-Whig party system in the 1850s. On the other hand, the Great Depression in the early 1930s was the main reason the GOP was toppled after its long period of supremacy. The Democrats won the elections of 1974 and 1976 in part because of public reaction against Watergate—a noneconomic issue. The GOP won in 1980 on high inflation and interest rates, and in 1984 on having "whipped inflation" and revived the economy.

Any patterns that do exist in American politics are rough and often blurred by unexplained variations. Indeed, patterns may exist for years and then disappear. Before the 1948 election a change in party control of Congress in an off-year election had regularly preceded a change in party fortunes in the following presidential election. But the Democrats, who lost control of Congress in 1946, won both houses and—to the surprise of everyone, especially Thomas Dewey and perhaps even Harry Truman—the presidency in 1948. And despite a 1954 congressional victory for the Democrats, the GOP won the presidential election of 1956.

Voting Patterns

Despite the murkiness of voting tendencies, analysis of massive amounts of voting data has uncovered some basic patterns:

1. Voting as members of *groups*. Most Americans vote the same way their families or friends or workmates vote. While on election day they mark their ballots or check off their voting machine levers in private, voting is largely a group experience. The most homogeneous of all groups in terms of molding party identification and ultimately the voting behavior of its members is the family. Members of the family shape one another's attitudes (often unintentionally); and members of the same family are naturally exposed to similar economic, religious, class, and geographical influences.[14]

As young adults move away from their families, they become members of many different groups. Some of their group memberships may mutually *reinforce* voting decisions. A young engineer who has grown up in a Democratically inclined family may marry a more conservatively inclined man, associate on her job with Republican executives, socialize a good deal with other members of a country club, and join a taxpayer's organization. The engineer will prob-

[13]For a noneconomic cyclical theory of presidential elections, see James David Barber, *The Pulse of Politics* (Norton, 1980).

[14]See Richard E. Dawson and Kenneth Prewitt, *Political Socialization* (Little, Brown, 1969); and for a specific example of an intrafamily relationship, M. Kent Jennings and Richard G. Niemi, "The Division of Political Labor between Mothers and Fathers," *American Political Science Review* (March 1971), pp. 69–82.

ably become a Republican, though she will long feel a Democratic tug from family years. Or group memberships may have conflicting impacts on a person's vote. Thus, a factory worker may associate with Democrats in his local union but with Republicans in his social group or ethnic organization. Such persons are said to be "cross-pressured" and sometimes take the easiest way out by not voting at all.

Group influences on voting may change over time. Blue-collar workers, blacks, and some urban ethnic groups tended to rally round FDR and the New Deal in the 1930s in part because they felt the Republican party had failed them, in part because the New Deal Democrats recognized them and gave them concrete social and economic benefits. Business and professional men and women tended to oppose New Deal "experimentation" and "waste." In the 1960s and 1970s newer issues—Vietnam, racial equality, law and order, Watergate—cut across group alignments, created new group allegiances to Republican candidates, and caused severe splits within the Democratic party coalition. Now, in the 1980s, economic, military, and social issues such as sexual equality, abortion, and gay/lesbian rights have come to the fore, with different impacts on groups.

2. Voting as members of *parties*. In this century most voters have identified with one or the other of the major parties. Many support their party almost automatically, no matter who the candidate or what the issues. Party identification was relatively stable during the 1950s and 1960s.[15] This traditional allegiance is not necessarily blind or irrational. People may vote for the same party over the years because they have thoughtfully concluded that that party serves their interests best.

Is party loyalty declining? A large number of Democrats ignored their long-time party identification in 1980, as did many Republicans in 1976. Democratic and Republican party self-identifiers (that is, persons who state that they are to some degree "Democrats" or "Republicans" when asked by pollsters) have dropped in recent years. Many voters identify with one of the major parties but vote for the opposition candidate. People usually do not openly and suddenly give up their party membership; rather, they talk more about voting "for the person and not the party." Whether the drop in party identification is a short-term or long-term development remains to be seen, but party feeling is still the best indicator of a person's vote.

3. Voting in terms of *class*, *occupation*, and *income*. Most studies of voting behavior confirm what everyday observation has already indicated. Most persons who prefer the Republican party are in the upper income brackets. But we cannot make too much of this factor, or indeed of any single factor. The relation of social class to party choice has declined since World War II. Older voters, with their memories of the Depression, still tend to vote on the basis of socioeconomic status, but younger voters seem less influenced by social and economic factors.

Still, whether you define social class on the basis of occupation, income, or self-identification, the higher the class, the stronger the tendency toward Republicanism. Much depends on the extent to which the candidates and the economic situation of the campaign year confront the voters with economic issues. After years of apparent decline in class voting—from a high point in the Truman-Dewey faceoff in 1948 to a low point in the Nixon-McGovern contest of 1972—class voting rose in 1976, when Jimmy Carter attacked President

[15]The Center for Political Studies, University of Michigan, periodically measures dimensions of party support. See also Philip E. Converse, *The Dynamics of Party Support: Cohort-Analyzing Party Identification* (Sage Library of Social Research, 1976).

Group Characteristic	1948		1960		1964	
	Dem.	Rep.	Dem.	Rep.	Dem.	Rep.
Religion						
Protestant	47%†	53%†	38%	62%	55%	45%
Catholic	66†	34†	78	22	76	24
Jewish	—	—	81	19	90	10
Race						
White	53†	47	49	51	59	41
Black	81†	19†	68	32	94	6
Union labor families	74‡	26	65	35	73	27
Young voters (age 21–29)	62‡	38	54	46	64	36
Sex						
Women	53†	47†	49	51	62	38
Men	56†	44†	52	48	60	40

Ford's economic policies.[16] In that year the Democrats gained most of the white working-class vote but only a minority of the white middle-class vote.

In 1980 and 1984 the income pattern held. People with family incomes of less than $12,500 voted for Mondale by clear though not heavy margins, while those earning over $35,000 voted for Reagan 2 to 1.[17] Mondale slimly won the union vote (see Table 9–3). Clearly, those with greater incomes perceived Reagan as their protector and Mondale as a threat, whereas those with lower incomes saw Reagan as a danger to their livelihood.

4. Voting by *religion* and *race*. In the 1960s "religion remained a potent source of political cleavage in the United States . . . the single most important of four predictors of political party identification, and was comparable to, if not more important than, the *combined* effects of education, occupation, and income."[18] John Kennedy's campaign for the presidency tended to align Catholics even more with the Democrats, and Protestants with the GOP. In 1984 religious issues experienced a political resurgence; emphasis on abortion and increased debate on religion in politics led Catholics and Protestants to vote Republican, by substantial margins. These results, heavily favoring Reagan, came despite opposition from minister's son Walter Mondale and Catholic Geraldine Ferraro. President Reagan, with help from the fundamentalist right, succeeded in portraying the GOP as a "Christian Party," thereby attracting much support.[19]

Racial voting has been a polarizing force. During the late nineteenth century northern blacks voted heavily Republican, and southern whites almost exclusively Democratic—a carry-over from the Civil War. During Roosevelt's New Deal and Truman's Fair Deal, blacks began shifting over to the Democratic party and to the civil rights policies that party was supporting. For the

[16]Paul R. Abramson, "Class Voting in the 1976 Presidential Election," *Journal of Politics* (November 1978), pp. 1066–72. See also David Knoke, "Stratification and the Dimensions of American Political Orientations," *American Journal of Political Science* (November 1979), pp. 772–91.

[17]*The New York Times*, Friday, November 9, 1984.

[18]David Knoke, "Religion, Stratification and Politics: America in the 1960s," *American Journal of Political Science* (May 1974), p. 344.

[19]See 1984 figures in Table 9–3.

Group Characteristic	1968 Dem.	1968 Rep.	1968 AIP*	1972 Dem.	1972 Rep.	1976 Dem.	1976 Rep.	1980 Dem.	1980 Rep.	1984 Dem.	1984 Rep.
Religion											
Protestant	35%	49%	16%	30%	70%	46%	53%	39%	54%	26%	73%
Catholic	59	33	8	48	52	57	42	46	47	44	55
Jewish	83	17	—	32	61	32	68	45	39	66	32
Race											
White	38	47	15	32	68	46	52	36	56	34	66
Black	85	12	3	87	13	85	15	86	10	90	09
Union labor families	56	29	15	46	54	63	36	50	43	53	45
Young voters (age 21–29)	47	38	15	48	52	53	45	47	41	41	58
Sex											
Women	45	43	12	38	62	48	51	44	49	37	61
Men	41	43	16	37	63	53	45	38	53	42	57

*The American Independent party, headed by George Wallace.
†Figures accompanied by a dagger are taken from Angus Campbell et al., *The Voter Decides* (New York: Harper & Row, 1954), pp. 70–71. Data given there were converted from a percentage of the total sample to a percentage of those voting, ignoring the "Other" column. Other data are taken from releases of the American Institute of Public Opinion (the Gallup Poll), and from NBC and CBS samples as reported in *Congressional Quarterly Weekly Reports*, November 11, 1972, p. 2949. 1976 data from *The New York Times*, November 4, 1976, p. 25, 1980 data from *National Journal*, November 8, 1980, p. 1878. 1984 figures derived from *New York Times* exit poll.
‡Includes Democratic, Progressive, and States' Rights votes.

same reason, southern whites began to move toward the Republican party. Blacks today are probably the most strongly Democratic of all groups. Blacks stuck with George McGovern in 1972 when other groups deserted him, and they were crucial to Carter's victory in 1976.

Some black leaders, notably presidential hopeful Jesse Jackson of Chicago, stressed the advantages of an independent black presidential candidate. Other black leaders, such as Atlanta mayor Andrew Young, President Carter's ambassador to the United Nations, argue for building a stronger base within the Democratic party.

5. Voting by *sex* or *gender*.[20] Women as a whole voted differently from men as a whole in 1980; women were more likely to vote for Carter, men for Reagan. Still, in absolute numbers more women *and* men voted for Reagan. The last time such a "gender gap" occurred was in the 1950s, when women voted for Ike at higher rates than men. In terms of values, women evaluate President Reagan more negatively than do men on issues of war and peace; and these negative evaluations are related to women's greater tendency to vote against Republicans and for Democrats.[21]

6. Voting by *age*. Traditionally, the younger you were the less chance you would vote Republican; young voters who had come to maturity after the Depression and the New Deal identified with Democrats. Today's youth, post-Vietnam, post-Watergate, remember instead the oil embargo, Democratic stagflation, and the Iranian hostage crisis. Although youth support tends to be transient, in 1984 it was Ronald Reagan's strongest age group.[22] Whether this will survive a popular president's passing, and whether the young voter's commitment is an emotional rather than an ideological one, will be tested in 1986 and 1988.

[20]On the difference between sex and gender, see Reesa M. Vaughter, "Review Essay: Psychology," *Signs: Journal of Women in Culture and Society* (Autumn 1976), pp. 122–23, note 14.
[21]Kathleen A. Frankovic, "Sex and Politics—New Alignments, Old Issues," *PS* (Summer 1982), pp. 439-48.
[22]*The New York Times*, October 16, 1984, p.1.

Partisans and Independents

Plainly, party affiliation is a key factor in how people vote, yet voting is also heavily influenced by opinions on major issues, evaluations of the candidates, and the impact of events at home and abroad. The stronger people's party feeling, however, the more likely they will look at issues and candidates through their "party lens"—that is, fit those factors into the overriding party factor. Those who are worried about party influence, however, can relax, because that influence seems to be declining. Moreover, parties do not reflect totally basic social, economic, geographical, or religious differences; thus there is no "party of the poor."

Is this desirable? Some favor a situation where neither major party can claim a monopoly of any group, since this keeps the parties from reinforcing and exaggerating differences.[23] Some party activists disagree. Parties with more clear-cut electoral support might supply national leaders with the kind of mandate they need to offer a firmer sense of direction to the American people.

In any event, while partisans are still important, independents are on the rise. Both groups are worth further examination.

WHO ARE THE PARTISANS? We measure party identification by asking people, "Generally speaking, do you usually think of yourself as a Republican, a Democrat, an Independent, or what?" Those who name one of the two major parties are then asked, "Would you call yourself a strong Republican/Democrat or a not very strong Republican/Democrat?" The others are asked, "Do you think of yourself as closer to the Republican or to the Democratic party?" Since 1952 strong and weak Democrats have declined from 47 percent to 43 percent of the sample, and Republicans from 28 percent to 24 percent; independents have increased from 23 percent to 34 percent.[24]

WHO ARE THE INDEPENDENTS? More than a third of the voters can be classified as independents—but "independent" is a tricky term. Some persons are called independent because they are party switchers; they cross and recross party lines from election to election. Some are ticket splitters; at the same election they vote for candidates of different parties.[25] Some are independents because they *feel* independent. Some call themselves independents because they think it is socially more respectable, but actually they vote for one party. One study indicates that younger voters with above-average incomes and college educations tend to be more independent than other groups, but that the independent vote otherwise is rather evenly distributed throughout the population.

Recently a study found that many who identify themselves as independents have made a conscious decision to be independent of either party; they are not merely apathetic. This category grew from almost 21 percent in 1964 to a peak of almost 29 percent in 1976, and dropped to about 24 percent in 1980. By 1984, the percentage was back up to 35 percent. On the other hand, some independents have no partisan preference. While they are aware of the party system, they are much more attuned to *individual candidates*. These nonpartisans have grown from 2 percent to almost 10 percent of the electorate.[26]

Is the independent voter the more informed voter? There has been heated debate over this question, but much of it is fruitless—everything depends on

"Me, I vote the man, not the party. Hoover, Landon, Dewey, Eisenhower, Goldwater, Nixon, Ford, Reagan. . ." © 1956 Crowell, Collier Publishing Company; reproduced by courtesy of Bill Mauldin.

[23]S. M. Lipset, *Political Man* (Doubleday, 1960), p. 31.

[24]Updated and adapted from Warren E. Miller, Arthur H. Miller, and Edward J. Schneider, *American National Election Studies Data Sourcebook, 1952–1978* (Harvard University Press, 1980), p. 81.

[25]Walter De Vries and V. Lance Tarrance, *The Ticket-Splitter: A New Force in American Politics* (Erdmans, 1972). See also Feigert, "Illusions of Ticket-Splitting."

[26]See Arthur H. Miller and Martin P. Wattenberg, "Measuring Party Identification: Independent or No Partisan Preference?" *American Journal of Political Science* (February 1983), pp. 106–21.

what kind of independent we are talking about. If independents are defined as those who fail to express a preference between parties, the independent voter tends to be less well informed and less likely to vote. But if we mean those who switch parties between elections, we find some who are highly informed and who carefully pick and choose at the polls. The independent is really not all that different from the partisan. Independents seem to be neither more nor less cynical about the "system" than party supporters. Most independents seem to vote as regularly for one or the other party as do those who identify with a party. Still, in a nation where parties seem to be losing many of their old-time supporters, candidates will seek to appeal to the "independent" voter, however defined.

BEHIND THE VOTES: PUBLIC OPINION

To understand voting behavior we must penetrate below surface factors and look at the more fundamental forces that, day in and day out, year in and year out, shape voters' attitudes and opinions. It is because journalists and pollsters so often look only at the surface manifestations that their analyses and predictions so often go awry. For example, they will speak of public opinion when in fact there are many publics, with differing sets of opinions.

Suppose a group of students invites a notorious criminal to speak on crime and punishment. Think of this incident in terms of the public opinion it creates. The "public" is actually made up of a number of publics—the rest of the student body (itself divided into subpublics), the administration, the faculty, the local townspeople, parents, and taxpayers. And all react in different ways. Some don't react at all; others shake their heads and promptly forget about it; others write to the governor or their state legislator. Many approve the invitation, but for conflicting reasons.

Translate the student episode into a national issue. A president's speech about labor legislation falls differently on the ears of union leaders and members, businesspeople, farmers, Democrats, and Republicans. When a senator calls for the end of government "handouts," many businesspeople applaud because they want lower taxes—but businesspeople *receiving* subsidies are critical. They may cry out that "the American public" wants a strong (that is, subsidized) merchant marine. Instead of one public opinion, we must think in terms of the diversity of opinion within a particular population. We must ask: What portion of the people is on one side of an issue, what portion on the other? Who feel strongly, who do not? What, in short, makes up the fabric of public opinion?

Heavy voter turnout in this Kansas City suburb forced long lines and a wait of up to an hour for some voters. *UPI*.

STABILITY Certain kinds of opinions change very little; they are part of one's personality. We may hang onto them all our lives. Other opinions may change slowly, even though the world is changing rapidly. This is especially true of loyalty toward one's own group and hostility toward competing groups. In general, people who remain in the same place, in the same occupation, and in the same income group throughout their lives are likely to have more stable opinions. But people can carry their attitudes with them. Families moving from cities to suburbs often retain their old big-city attitudes long after they have made their move.

FLUIDITY Certain kinds of public opinion, on the other hand, can change dramatically, and almost overnight. Thus, opposition to Roosevelt's foreign policies in 1941 practically disappeared following Japan's attack on Pearl Harbor. Change often comes about as a result of *events*—a depression, the nomination by a major party of a southerner for the first time in over a hundred years, a sharp increase in the crime rate, a natural event like a long drought in the Southwest, or the taking of hostages by Iran.

Sometimes even the strongest and most stable opinions are subject to change. One of the "sacred cows" of American politics twenty years ago was nonrecognition of the People's Republic of China. A powerful lobby, composed of leaders of both major parties, carried on a militant campaign against admitting "mainland China" to the United Nations. Then President Nixon, who had earlier been against the recognition of Peking, made his dramatic trip to the People's Republic. Soon he was following a policy of detente toward Peking. Many Americans, responding to Nixon's leadership, shifted their own position toward friendlier relations with China.

INTENSITY This factor produces the brightest and deepest hues in the fabric of public opinion. People vary greatly in the fervency of their beliefs. For example, some are mildly in favor of gun-control legislation while others are mildly opposed; still others are fanatically for or against. Some people may have no interest in the matter at all and may not even have heard of the issue.

LATENCY Political opinions may exist merely as a *potential*—they may not have crystallized. But they still can be very important, for they can be evoked by leaders and converted into action. Latent opinions set rough boundaries for leaders, who know that if they take certain actions, the opposition or support of millions of persons will be triggered. But latent opinions are also a great opportunity for leaders. If they have some understanding of people's real wants and needs and hopes, they will know how to activate those motives, mobilize people in groups or parties, and draw them to the polls on election day.

W. Wilson Goode speaks with a group of supporters on the steps of the Philadelphia Art Museum. Goode was elected Mayor of Philadelphia in 1983. *UPI.*

SALIENCE What causes opinions to be stable or fluid, intense or latent? A major factor is salience. Some people are deeply involved in certain issues and care little or nothing about others. By salient we mean that people feel the issue relates to their own lives; it *connects* with them. Your next-door neighbor may feel intensely about abortion or gun control, whereas you get excited about inflation or unemployment. Most people are more concerned about personal issues like health and jobs and families than about national issues. But connect their personal concerns with national issues, and salience rises sharply.

Salience may change over time. During the depression of the 1930s, Americans were mainly concerned about jobs and wages and economic security. In the late thirties and early forties, foreign issues came to the fore. In the sixties problems of race, poverty, and drugs aroused intense feeling, followed by Vietnam and then Watergate. Recently jobs and prices as well as nuclear arms and energy seem to top the agenda, along with continuing crises in the Middle East and in Central America.

CONSTRAINT Opinions tend to translate into votes more directly when they exhibit constraint; that is, when a person's opinion on one issue is related to that person's opinion on another issue. The relationships suggest that a person organizes his or her political thinking along a few dimensions rather than a single one.

CONSENSUS Looking at the electorate as a whole, we can find some opinions on which most people agree or disagree. When at least 75 percent of a sample agree that the schools should be racially integrated, we can say a consensus exists on that issue. In fact, as consensus is reached, the "issue" as such ceases to exist until people return to it—and perhaps divide over it—at some later time.

POLARIZATION   On most issues we find no consensus. Rather, we find divisions of various proportions. When we find a sample fairly evenly divided, say within a 60–40 split, and further, when we find some part of each side holding very intense feelings on the issue, we say the electorate is polarized on that issue. The war in Vietnam became such an issue. Abortion today is an example of a divisive issue.

TAKING THE PULSE OF THE PEOPLE ·

Public opinion polls attempt to serve as an accurate barometer of the pulse of the nation, but are sometimes hampered by error and inconsistency. *Paul Fusco, Magnum.*

"What I want," Abraham Lincoln once said, "is to get done what the people desire to have done, and the question for me is how to find that out exactly." This question faces every politician, in office or out. Another president, Woodrow Wilson, once complained to the newspapers that they had no business to say, as they often did, that all the people out their way thought so and so: "You do not know, and the worst of it is, since the responsibility is mine, I do not know, what they are thinking about. I have the most imperfect means of finding out, and yet I have got to act as if I knew . . . . "

How can the politician find out what the people are thinking? The usual way, of course, is to look at the election results. If Jane Brown wins over James Smith, presumably the people want what Jane Brown stands for. If Brown is an advocate of gun regulation and Smith is 100 percent against any form of control, evidently the majority of the people support some kind of firearms regulation. But we know that in practice, things do not work this way. Elections are rarely fought on single issues, and candidates rarely take clear-cut stands. It is impossible, moreover, to separate issues from candidates. Did Reagan win in 1980 because of Iran, crime, taxes, his personality, opposition to Carter, or shifts in party support? The answer is that he won for some of these reasons and for many others. Which brings us back to the question—what do the people want?

This is where public opinion polls come in. In this country public opinion polls are over a century old, but their main development has taken place in the last three decades. Today there are hundreds of polling organizations. We are usually aware of them because they constantly measure and report presidential popularity.

If a politician or a social scientist wants to measure opinion precisely, the first thing to be determined is the universe, the whole group whose opinion is being sought—every adult, all students on this campus, all students in the United States, all voters in city X. If the universe consists of only thirty units, the most precise way to find out what they think on a particular issue is to poll every one of them. But for most politically significant problems, this is impossible; so pollsters *sample* the universe they are interested in. The accuracy of the results depends largely on securing a sample representative of the total universe. If drawn properly, so that each unit in a universe has an equal chance to be included, a relatively small sample can provide accurate results. Beyond a certain point an increase in the size of the sample reduces only slightly the sampling error, the difference between the divisions found in the sample and those of the universe.

One way to develop a representative sample is to draw the sample completely at random. But this type of random sampling is impossible for most

"Would you say Attila is doing an excellent job, a good job, a fair job, or a poor job?" *Drawing by Chas. Addams;* © *1982. The New Yorker Magazine, Inc.*

Asking the Right Questions in the Right Way

political surveys. Instead, we use census tracts (where these are available), which give the number of residences and their locations. By shuffling census tracts, drawing out at random the required number, and then sending interviewers to every fifth or tenth or twentieth house, we get a random sample. A less complicated, but less reliable, method is quota sampling. Here an attempt is made to secure a sample which reflects those variables among the population that might affect opinion. In testing opinion thought to be affected by income status (for example, views on the income tax), a polling organization makes up a sample based on two wealthy persons, fourteen members of the upper-income class, fifty-two from the middle-income groups, and thirty-two from the poor. Interviewers are instructed to question people in each group until they have reached the quota for that group.

People are often suspicious of results based on what appears to be a small sample. Is it really possible, they wonder, to generalize about the opinions of 235 million persons on the basis of a few thousand interviews? Can such a small sample be truly representative? The answer is yes. In comparisons of demographic characteristics based on census results and those based on a carefully drawn sample, the differences in an exemplary study were very small. The census reported that 18.8 percent of the population were between the ages of twenty-one and twenty-nine, 23.5 percent were between thirty and thirty-nine, and 20.9 percent were between forty and forty-nine. The sample results were 18.4, 23.8, and 21.5, respectively.[27] Social scientists assume that if a sample chosen by modern techniques reproduces such characteristics of the population so precisely, it will reproduce the attitudes and opinions of the total population equally well.

Pollsters have a lot of leeway in choosing questions. The average man or woman may be concerned about problems that pollsters and political leaders know little about or have trouble defining. Another major difficulty is in phrasing questions. If you ask a question in a certain way, you can get the answer you want. Ask people if they favor labor unions and they may say no. Ask them if they favor organized efforts by workers to improve their well-being, and chances are more will answer yes. Also, trouble may arise in the alternatives a question presents. Clearly, asking a person "Do you favor the United States entering a world government, or do you prefer our traditional independence in determining our own affairs?" is loading the dice. Polling organizations go to great efforts to make their questions fair; some conduct trial runs with differently worded questions.[28]

One way to avoid this difficulty is to ask a multiple-choice question. For example, a Gallup poll asked, "How far do you, yourself, think the federal government should go in requiring employers to hire people without regard to race, religion, color, or nationality?" The respondent could answer: All the way; None of the way; Depends on type of work; Should be left to state governments; or Don't know. A variation of this type—the open-ended question—allows respondents to supply their own answer. They may be asked simply, "How do you think we should deal with the problem of air pollution by automobiles?" (The answers to this type of question are, of course, hard to tabulate accurately.)

Interviewing is a delicate task. The interviewer's appearance, clothes, language, and way of asking questions may influence the replies. Inaccurate find-

[27]Samuel A. Stouffer, *Communism, Conformity, and Civil Liberties* (Doubleday, 1955), p. 238.

[28]See Donald J. Devine, "The Problem of Question Form in Describing Public Opinion," *Polity* (Spring 1980), pp. 522–34.

Although the "election forecasting" of the opinion polls has been generally good, they have been known to miss the mark as in this now-classic 1948 presidential election forecast. *UPI.*

Interpreting the Results

ings may result from the bias of the interviewer or from failure to do the job fully and carefully. And the persons interviewed may be the source of error. Respondents suspicious of the interviewer's motives may give false or confused answers. Their memories may be poor. To cover up ignorance they may give neutral answers or appear undecided. Or they may give the answers they think the interviewer would like them to give.

Polls may give a false impression of the firmness and intensity of opinion; as we have seen, opinions may be volatile and fleeting. Moreover, polls do not differentiate among people—they give equal weight to a follower and to an opinion leader who may in the end influence other voters. Studies suggest that public opinion is not like an iceberg, where the movement of the top indicates the movement of the great mass under the water. The visible opinion among leaders and activists or among the more outspoken may be moving in a different direction—indeed it may even be differently located—from that of the great mass of less-visible opinion. In short, it is far easier to measure the surface of public opinion than to gauge its depth and intensity.

Election forecasting intrigues the average American; everyone likes to know in advance how an election will turn out. During the campaign pollsters submit regular "returns" on the standings of the candidates. On the whole, the record of the leading forecasters in "day-before" polling has been good, as Table 9–4 shows. The most sensational slip came in 1948, during the presidential battle between President Truman and Governor Dewey. The polls repeatedly indicated that Mr. Truman was running far behind. The president denounced the polls as unreliable, but the pollsters stood pat on their statistics. Early in September one of them actually announced that the race was over. Gallup gave the president 44.5 percent of the popular vote in his final forecast, and Roper's prediction was 37.1 percent. Mr. Truman won 49.4 percent of the popular vote, and the pollsters were subjected to general ridicule. Since then they have been more cautious in making predictions, and more careful in their methods.[29]

Political polls have taken on increasingly significant functions in our political system. Candidates use polls to determine where to campaign, how to campaign, and even whether to campaign. In the years and months preceding a national convention, politicians watch the polls to determine who among the hopefuls has political appeal. Questions have been raised about this use of polls. Should candidates run for office only when it seems safe to do so? If a candidate believes in a cause, should he or she not defend it publicly in order to present a meaningful choice to the voters?[30]

Surely the polls are no substitute for elections. Faced with a ballot, voters must translate opinions into concrete decisions between personalities and parties. They must decide what is important and what is not. For democracy is more than the expression of views, more than a simple mirror of opinion. It is also *choosing* among leaders taking sides on certain issues, and among the governmental actions that may follow. Democracy is the thoughtful participation of people in the political process; it means using heads as well as counting them. Elections, with all their failings, at least establish the link between the many voices of "We the People" and the decisions of their leaders.

[29]See Harold Mendelsohn and Irving Crespi, *Polls, Television, and the New Politics* (Chandler, 1970), chap. 2.

[30]Critical analyses of public opinion polling are C. W. Roll, Jr., and A. H. Cantril, *Polls: Their Use and Misuse in Politics* (Basic Books, 1972); and Leo Bogart, *Silent Politics: Polls and the Awareness of Public Opinion* (Wiley, 1972).

Year	Actual Dem. Vote	Roper Poll	Gallup Poll	Harris Poll
1936	60.2%	61.7%	53.8%	—
1940	54.7	55.2	55.0	—
1944	53.8	53.6	53.3	—
1948	49.4	37.1	44.5	—
1952	45.+	43.0	46.0	—
1956	42.0	40.0	40.5	—
1960	49.4	47.0	49.0	—
1964	61.4	—	61.0	—
1968	42.7	—	40.0	43.0
1972	37.7	—	35.0	34.8
1976	51.0	51.0	46.0*	46.0*
1980	41.0	—	44.0*	41.0
1984	41.0	45.0	41.0	44.0

*In 1976 both Gallup and Harris said it was a "tossup" and refused to make a prediction. They also reported that more people than usual had not made up their minds. In 1980 Harris predicted a Reagan win, while Gallup said it was too close to call.

From Opinions to Votes

How does public opinion translate into individual votes, which translate into elected officeholders? Let's look first at voting for presidents. Even the most sophisticated studies have concluded that the opinion most directly related to that decision is *which candidate the voter likes best*. The sophistication comes in explaining *how* voters come to like one candidate better than—or more than—another. As we have noted, the main influences are three-fold: party identification, attitudes on issues, and candidates' perceived integrity or competence as well as their past performance.

One's party identification has a lot to do with one's evaluation of the candidates—unless the favored party's candidate is assessed negatively on performance or on personal qualities. For example, in the 1980 election President Carter's loss appears to have resulted from the voters' negative assessments of his general competence as a leader and of his performance vis-á-vis inflation, interest rates, and the Iranian hostage situation. In the 1972 election Democratic voters defected in large numbers because they viewed George McGovern negatively both on the issues and on performance during the campaign. In that same election President Nixon gained votes on the basis of his own good marks in foreign policy leadership, including the perception that he was bringing the war in Vietnam to a slow but sure end. Generally we can say that voters tend to rely on their partisan identification when they see little or no difference between the candidates in terms of personal qualities or performance. When the voters have no party identification and/or when they do see differences between the candidates, they tend to vote for the candidate that comes out best in their assessment of personal qualities and/or issues.[31]

Voting in off-year congressional elections almost always results in losses of seats held by members of the president's party (the "in" party) and gains in seats by members of the "out" party. Voters in these elections appear to be influenced by the incumbency of the candidate (especially in House elections), their own party identification, and their opinions about presidential performance and the state of the economy.

Several studies have found a relationship between "out" party gains (and

THE POLLS VERSUS THE RESULTS
(In percent)

Source	Reagan	Mondale	Margin
Actual results	59%	41%	18
USA Today	60	35	25
NBC	58	34	24
NYT/CBS	58	36	22
Gallup	59	41	18
Wash. Post/ABC	54	40	14
Harris	56	44	12
Roper	55	45	10

(Figures reflect pollsters' allocation of undecided or leaning voters, where available. Where full allocation was unavailable, figures total less than 100%.)

Reagan's margin of victory ranged from 10 percent to 25 percent in these pre-election polls; with such discrepancies, it is becoming increasingly difficult to rely upon the predictive power of the polling process.

[31]Arthur H. Miller, Warren E. Miller, Alden S. Raine, and Thad A. Brown, "A Majority Party in Disarray: Policy Polarization in the 1972 Election," *American Political Science Review* (September 1976), pp. 753–78. But see also Samuel Popkin, John W. Gorman, Charles Phillips, and Jeffrey A. Smith, "Comment: What Have You Done for Me Lately? Toward An Investment Theory of Voting," *ibid.*, pp. 779–805; and further exchanges on this subject, *ibid.*, pp. 806–49; also of interest is Gregory B. Markus, "Political Attitudes during an Election Year: A Report on the 1980 NES Panel Study," *American Political Science Review* (September 1982), pp. 538–60.

"in" party losses) in congressional seats and the state of the economy,[32] but only recently have political scientists been able to locate the sources of this effect in individual voters' decision making. Voters tend to vote against candidates of the "in" party, including even incumbents (according to some studies), if the voters perceive that they (the voters) have experienced a decline or standstill in their own personal financial situations.[33] But a more recent study finds that this relationship is based on the voters' socioeconomic status. Lower-status voters tend to judge candidates on the basis of the voters' personal financial condition. Upper-status voters, who personally tend to suffer less when economic conditions decline, are more likely to watch the national performance of the economy through the newspapers and to judge candidates on that basis.[34]

Analysts of voting behavior have engaged in heated debates about the role of *issues* and *opinions* in voters' decisions. Whatever the outcome of these debates, we do have some idea from a recent survey about the status of issue voting—especially single-issue voting. Asked "Is there any *one* issue that is so important to you that you would change your vote because you disagreed with a candidate's position on that single issue?" 51 percent of the registered voters in a representative sample replied yes. Of these, 33 percent cited economic issues, including inflation and unemployment; 15 percent named abortion; and 13 percent mentioned social security. Four percent each were concerned most about nuclear war and the nuclear freeze, defense spending, foreign policy, or social programs.[35] In 1984, President Reagan was re-elected despite the fact that many of his supporters, when questioned on the issues, preferred Walter Mondale. Reagan's mandate was personal rather than conservative-ideological.

LIBERTY, EQUALITY, AND THE VOTE

We return now to the two questions posed at the start of this chapter: (1) Do Americans have the *liberty* to take part in American politics if they wish? (2) Do they have *equality* of influence on American politics and government?

The answer to the first question is relatively simple: Virtually all Americans have "freedom of the ballot box" and of other forms of participation. The answer to the second question is neither simple nor reassuring: Americans are sharply *unequal* in the actual influence they exert in electoral politics.

Part of the inequality stems from the structure of society, which is based on lingering inequalities of race and sex, socioeconomic status, organizational involvement, and attitudes of political competency or alienation. The late E. E. Schattschneider gives an apt example of the differences of place and viewpoint in our society when he talks about the bank clerk and the scrub woman. The bank clerk is underpaid but entertains realistic hopes of advancing his career in banking. He is likely to believe he has a real stake in exercising his vote in electoral politics. The scrub woman, who in all likelihood is a minority person, "may be demoralized and frustrated."[36] Not only is she underpaid but she is in a dead-end job without career possibilities. Why should she waste her

[32]See, for example, Gerald H. Kramer, "Short-Term Fluctuations in U.S. Voting Behavior, 1896–1964," *American Political Science Review* (March 1971), pp. 131–43, and the revision reprinted by Bobbs-Merrill (PS-498); and Edward R. Tufte, "Determinants of the Outcomes of Midterm Congressional Elections," *American Political Science Review* (September 1975), pp. 812–26.

[33]John R. Hibbing and John R. Alford, "The Electoral Impact of Economic Conditions: Who is Held Responsible?" *American Journal of Political Science* (August 1981), pp. 423–39; and Morris P. Fiorina, "Who is Held Responsible? Further Evidence on the Hibbing-Alford Thesis," *American Journal of Political Science* (February 1983), pp. 158–64.

[34]M. Stephen Weatherford, "Economic Voting and the 'Symbolic Politics' Argument: A Reinterpretation and Synthesis," *American Political Science Review* (March 1983), pp. 158–74.

[35]See "Election '82," *Public Opinion* (December /January 1983), p. 21.

[36]E. E. Schattschneider, *The Semisovereign People* (Dryden Press, 1960, 1975), p. 105.

precious time in electoral politics if she believes that neither party will carry through on the rhetoric of jobs or safety nets for the truly needy?

Still another part of the inequality stems from how politicians interpret election results. Here political scientists can provide some insights—though their own theories and methods are biased in certain ways by underlying philosophical assumptions about people and politics. The election of 1984 was characterized by a Republican presidential landslide without a clear policy mandate. New Progressive Senators were victorious and the Democrats maintained control of the House. *The New York Times* reported on November 11, 1984 that "President Reagan's lonely landslide is a personal victory with little precise policy mandate or clear ideological underpinning."

SUMMARY

1. Who is allowed to participate in American politics—especially to *vote*—and whether or not they participate on essentially equal terms, are questions involving the realization of liberty and equality in America.

2. White men without property, black men, and women of all races are the major groups that have had to fight for the right to vote in the United States.

3. Better-educated, middle-aged, and more party- and group-involved people tend to vote more; the poor tend to vote the least.

4. Voting tends to be higher for national elections than for state and local ones, and higher for executive than for legislative elections.

5. Sectional, cyclical, party, economic, and other patterns can be found in American voting behavior, but these patterns are cloudy and subject to change.

6. Public opinion is not a solid unit but a loose and complex combination of views and attitudes. It takes on qualities of stability, fluidity, intensity, latency, constraint, consensus, or polarization—all closely affected by persons' feelings of the salience of opinions to themselves.

7. We have fairly reliable methods for roughly measuring people's opinions at a given time, provided the polling is done carefully and responsibly, using tested procedures and safeguards.

8. People decide how to vote on the basis of complex calculations involving their party identification, as well as comparative assessments of the candidates on the issues, the candidates' past performance, and their personal qualities.

FURTHER READING

LUCIUS J. BARKER and JESSE J. McCORRY, JR. *Black Americans and the Political System* (Winthrop Publishers, 1976).

SANDRA BAXTER and MARJORIE LANSING. *Women and Politics: The Invisible Majority* (University of Michigan Press, 1980).

BRUCE A. CAMPBELL. *The American Electorate: Attitudes and Action* (Holt, Rinehart and Winston, 1979).

MORRIS P. FIORINA. *Retrospective Voting in American Elections* (Yale University Press, 1981).

CLAIRE KNOCHE FULENWIDER. *Feminism in American Politics: A Study of Ideological Influence* (Praeger, 1980).

V. O. KEY, JR. *Public Opinion and American Democracy* (Knopf, 1965).

EVERETT CARLL LADD, JR., with CHARLES D. HADLEY. *Transformations of the American Party System*, 2d. ed. (Norton, 1978).

MICHAEL B. PRESTON, LENNEAL J. HENDERSON JR., and PAUL PURYEAR (eds.). *The New Black Politics: The Search for Political Power* (Longman, 1982).

Public Opinion (a bimonthly).

Public Opinion Quarterly.

VIRGINIA SAPIRO. *Women, Political Action, and Political Participation* (American Political Science Association, test edition, 1983).

E. E. SCHATTSCHNEIDER. *The Semisovereign People* (Dryden Press, 1960, 1975).

ROBERT WEISSBERG. *Public Opinion and Popular Government* (Prentice-Hall, 1976).

PARTIES: DECLINE AND RENEWAL?

10

In the last three chapters we surveyed the immense variety of American political life. People belong to all kinds of groups—economic, religious, occupational. They join diverse movements, left and right, and hold all kinds of views. People vote in all kinds of patterns, some predictable, some not. But what holds the whole thing together? What produces enough political unity so that "government by the people" can actually govern? Look at an American coin, if you have one. *E pluribus unum*—these words are engraved there—but politically, how do we get the *unum* out of the *pluribus*?

In the "grand old days" of American politics, the answer was clear—through the major political parties. People were fiercely partisan. The party was part of your way of life, part of the eternal order of things, like the family and religion. It was part of your inheritance. Belonging to the "other" party was not quite respectable. *Which* party you belonged to was often a regional matter. If you were white and grew up in the South, Republicans were alien beings who opposed all you stood for. If you were black and grew up in the South, Republicans were the emancipators (except that they pulled their federal troops out too soon and you lost your rights to vote and hold office). If you were raised in Kansas, Democrats were people who frequented saloons and lived off a few patronage crumbs from Washington.

Things are different today. For twenty years or so parties have been declining in popular support and organizational strength. "Strong" Republicans and "strong" Democrats have dropped by about a third in the past quarter century. The number of independents has grown steadily during the same period. Party organization is feeble in most states. Where the party is strong locally, it is often ruled by a small group of "old timers." Americans have been losing faith in parties, as they have in most other institutions.[1]

The party as an organization no longer makes the single most crucial decision in national politics—choice of the presidential nominee. The two winning candidates are formally chosen in the Democratic and Republican national conventions; but in most cases they are *actually* chosen in a string of state presidential primaries. Independents as well as partisans voted their candidate preferences at the polls, while the party organizations stood by almost inactive. In 1976 Jimmy Carter won the nomination, even though he had little influence with the national Democratic party; and Ronald Reagan almost defeated President Ford, a long-time leader in the GOP.

Perhaps the most dramatic—and most tragic—example of party weakness was Watergate. President Nixon in his 1972 reelection campaign largely bypassed the Republican party organization and depended on his personal organization, the Committee for the Re-election of the President—the infamous CREEP. Watergate grew in part out of CREEP—its illegal actions, its secrecy, its financing, its excessive personal loyalty to Mr. Nixon. Ronald Reagan in the 1980s, like earlier presidents, converted his party's national committee into his own campaign vehicle, despite efforts of party leaders to work for all the party's nominees. Governors and mayors, whether Democratic or Republican, often control state and city party organizations, as in the case of the late Mayor Richard Daley of Chicago.

Most Americans have mixed feelings about the parties. Critics charge that the parties evade the issues; that they fail to deliver on their promises; that they have no new ideas; and that they follow public opinion rather than lead it. They are also sources of corruption and misgovernment. Others favor our party system and take part in it and while most Americans believe in voting for individual candidates regardless of party label, they want party labels on the ballot.[2]

Our parties are in deep trouble. Does it matter? Are parties relevant to "government by the people"? If so, can we breathe new life into them?

PARTIES: THEIR RISE AND THEIR ROLE

Before we begin, we need to make a crucial distinction between the *factions* we have discussed in earlier chapters and the *parties* we will now consider. If you find this question a bit baffling, you are in good company—it baffled the founding fathers too. In fact, they confused the issue; and we must try to clarify it.

The founders did understand the nature of faction; Madison's definition of it in the *Federalist No. 10* (see Appendix) is still the best we have. The factions Madison and others opposed they called "cliques," or "juntos," or even "parties" (by which they meant faction). Fearing the excesses of economic, social, and other highly organized groups, they devised a federal constitution that would moderate the power of faction, as we saw in Part One. And because they did not want to extinguish the freedom that stimulated faction, they provided for the fundamental liberties we examined in Chapters 4, 5, and 6.

To the leaders of the young Republic, parties usually meant bigger, better organized, and fiercer factions—and they did not want them. Benjamin Frank-

---

[1]On party decline and other aspects of party, see Gerald M. Pomper (ed.), *Party Renewal in America* (Praeger, 1980).

[2]These mixed attitudes toward parties are summarized in Austin Ranney, *Curing the Mischiefs of Faction* (University of California Press, 1975), pp. 53–56.

lin worried about the "infinite mutual abuse of parties, tearing to pieces the best of characters." In his farewell address, George Washington warned against the "baneful effects of the Spirit of Party." And Thomas Jefferson said: "If I could not go to heaven but with a party, I would not go there at all."[3]

How, then, did parties get started? Largely out of practical necessity. To get its measures passed through Congress and administered by the new government, the first administration (under Washington) had to build a kind of coalition among factions—that is, a rudimentary party. This job fell to Treasury Secretary Alexander Hamilton, who built an informal Federalist "team" while Washington stayed "above politics." Secretary of State Jefferson and other officials who hated Hamilton's aristocratic ways gravitated into their own political orbit, revolving around a more republican point of view. When Jefferson left Washington's cabinet at the end of 1793, his fellow Virginians remained in Congress, where they built a rudimentary party in opposition to Federalist fiscal and foreign policies. In 1800 Jefferson returned to the political wars and pieced together a coalition of groups and regions strong enough to defeat President John Adams and put himself into the newly built White House. Aaron Burr helped Jefferson in Manhattan by setting up a "party ticket" of Republican candidates, organizing rallies, and establishing get-out-the-vote committees in the wards.

Soon President Thomas Jefferson, the man who had denounced parties, became for a time one of the most successful party leaders the nation has known. Again, this was a matter of practical necessity. Jefferson wanted to get the Louisiana Purchase and other big bills and appropriations through Congress. He wanted to carry on the debate against the Federalists. He wanted to win reelection and keep the Republicans in power. So he had to maintain a coalition of group interests—southerners and northerners; farmers, laborers, and other economic interests; religious groups—and thus, in effect, he created a party.

But Jefferson as party leader turned out to be something of a flash in the pan: On the whole, the first Republicans never built a grassroots organization. Jefferson did not seem very clear as to his party role, nor did he understand the role of the minority party as the loyal opposition. His party as a strong national force hardly outlived him. His successor, James Madison, tried to act more as a broker among factions than as a national party leader. This resulted in a weak presidency. Following a period of partyless government, another great leader arose to knit together a winning combination of regions, group interests, and political doctrines. This was Andrew Jackson, brilliantly seconded by Martin Van Buren, who had had experience in party building in New York State. The Federalists, who never felt really comfortable appealing to the grass roots, faded as a party during the long period of Republican supremacy. They were succeeded by the Whigs, who developed as an opposition party to Jackson. By the time Van Buren succeeded Jackson in the White House in 1837, the Democrats had become a large, nationwide movement with national and state leadership, a clear party doctrine, and grassroots organization. The Whigs were almost as strong; and in 1840 they put their own man, General William Henry Harrison—"old Tippecanoe"—into the White House. A two-party system had been born.

We have had that two-party system ever since. The 1830s and 1840s saw the flowering of the party system. Whigs and Democrats competed strenuously. They reached out for supporters and helped broaden the franchise by gradually lifting property qualifications on voting. They fostered cooperation between

While the symbols of our major parties have remained the same, there have been major shifts in their positions and bases of support, making them fundamentally different from the parties of a century ago. *Courtesy of the Democratic and Republican National Committees.*

[3]Washington, Franklin, and Jefferson, as quoted in Richard Hofstadter, *The Idea of a Party System* (University of California Press, 1969), pp. 2, 123.

presidents and other partisans in Congress. They developed the national convention, party platforms, and strong party leadership in the House and Senate. Still, the Whigs never achieved as broad and durable a coalition as the Democrats. And neither party was strong enough to cope with the issue of slavery in the 1860s; Abraham Lincoln was elected in 1860 amid party disruption.

Out of this crisis evolved a new major party: the second Republican party—ultimately the "Grand Old Party." As the party of the Union, the Republicans won the support not only of financiers, industrialists, and merchants but also of large numbers of white and newly freed black male workers and farmers. For fifty years after 1860 this Republican coalition won every presidential race, except for Grover Cleveland's victories in 1884 and 1892. The Democratic party survived with its durable white male base in the South. For all their noisy battles during the century, both parties remained true to the rule that under a two-party system neither side can afford to be extremist. However, both parties contained liberal and conservative elements, and both appealed for support to all major economic interests, including business and labor. But the Democrats were less effective than the Republicans in building broad coalitions. They won (with Woodrow Wilson as their candidate) only in 1912 and 1916, when the Bull Moosers under Theodore Roosevelt rebelled against the party regulars. After 1920, the GOP was again dominant.

The Democrats were unable to build a durable winning coalition until the early 1930s, when the Hoover administration was overwhelmed by the Great Depression. Franklin Roosevelt strengthened the farm-labor-southern alliance that Woodrow Wilson had begun to build. He also put together a "grand coalition" of these groups plus unemployed middle-class persons, and national and racial minorities. This coalition reelected Roosevelt three times and brought presidential victories to the Democrats (except when Eisenhower ran) for two decades after Roosevelt died.

Still, the "Roosevelt coalition" was vulnerable to Dwight Eisenhower's personal popularity and to Richard Nixon's own coalition building. In 1968 Nixon brought together a coalition of predominantly white middle-class voters, "hard-hat" workers, southern conservatives, suburbanites, and business elements. Neither Hubert Humphrey in 1968 nor George McGovern in 1972 was able to overcome the Nixon organization, though the Democrats retained large majorities in Congress. In 1976 Jimmy Carter brought together just enough of the old coalition of union members, blacks, party regulars, and New Liberals to produce a razor-thin majority at the polls.[4] The key question facing Carter was whether he could convert his electoral coalition into a governing coalition. By 1980 his critics charged that he had failed to do so, and the way was open for the Grand Old Party to build a countercoalition big enough to vote the Democrats out of power.

This was what President Reagan accomplished in the early 1980s. On the one hand he succeeded in winning and holding the support of millions of conservatives while converting the "Grand Old Party" into the nation's right-wing party. On the other hand, through such tactics as choosing and keeping George Bush as his running mate and making occasional concessions to moderates in the party, he maintained a broad electoral coalition. But how much of Reagan's personal popularity had been converted into wide and stable *party* strength was still not clear after the 1984 election.

[4]Warren E. Miller and Teresa E. Levitin, *Leadership and Change*, 2nd ed. (Winthrop, 1977), chap. 7. See also Gerald M. Pomper et al., *The Election of 1976* (McKay, 1977).

Key Aspects of the Parties Today

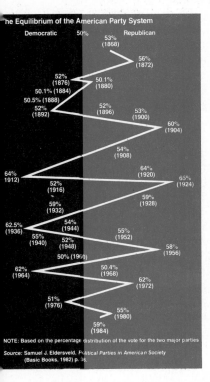

The Equilibrium of the American Party System

Democratic 50% Republican

53% (1868)
56% (1872)
52% (1876)
50.1% (1880)
50.1% (1884)
50.5% (1888)
52% (1892)
52% (1896)
53% (1900)
60% (1904)
54% (1908)
64% 1912
64% (1920)
52% (1916)
65% (1924)
59% (1928)
59% (1932)
54% (1944)
62.5% (1936)
55% (1940)
52% (1948)
55% (1952)
50% (1960)
58% (1956)
62% (1964)
50.4% (1968)
62% (1972)
51% (1976)
55% (1980)
59% (1984)

NOTE: Based on the percentage distribution of the vote for the two major parties

Source: Samuel J. Eldersveld, *Political Parties in American Society* (Basic Books, 1982) p. 34.

President Reagan's coattails served only President Reagan in 1984; veteran Senator Charles Percy suffered defeat at the hands of Illinois Democrat Paul Simon. *UPI/Bettmann Archive.*

Both parties are now middle-aged: The GOP has celebrated its centennial, and within a decade the Democrats will mark their bicentennial (they claim the present Democratic party grew directly out of the first Republican party, born when Jefferson departed from Washington's cabinet in 1793). The longevity of the two parties is remarkable, considering the depressions, wars, social changes, and political crises they have survived. But if the names and the symbols have stayed the same, what they represent has clearly changed. There have been extensive shifts in the positions of the major parties and in their social bases and electoral support.

Both parties are moderate in their policies and leadership. Successful party leaders must be group diplomats; to win presidential elections, they must find a middle ground among more or less hostile groups so that agreement can be reached on general principles. Each party takes its extremist supporters more or less for granted and seeks out the voters in the middle. This is one reason college students on the far Left or far Right are impatient with the leadership of the major parties. Both parties seem to such students to operate in the center—and in fact they do. (Some party analysts believe the major parties have become so weak and disorganized that they are not capable of following *any* strategy—Left, Right, or Center.)

The major parties are more complex today than in the last century. Like the government itself, they have national, state, and local organizations, and each level has executive, legislative, and other elements. Each party includes (1) a pyramid of national, state, and local organizations; (2) inner circles of leaders holding or seeking public office; (3) networks of leaders (sometimes called "bosses") who tend the organizational machinery around the clock, around the year; (4) party activists (usually called "party regulars") who give money, time, and enthusiasm to the party's candidates; and (5) voters who identify strongly with the party, almost always support its nominees, and desert it only as a result of disasters such as an unpopular war, a scandal like Watergate, or the soaring inflation and unemployment in the late 1970s.

Long after George Washington many Americans still feared parties: There was deep apprehension that a great popular majority—the kind led by a Jefferson or Jackson or Roosevelt—might be radical or extremist and thus threaten the liberties of free Americans. Before the Civil War the great South Carolina constitutional philosopher, John Calhoun, advanced the doctrine of "concurrent majority rule"—the idea that any large and significant region or interest should have the right to veto the actions of a numerical majority. Calhoun, of course, had a particular region and interest in mind—the South and its plantation slaveholders—but his reasoning has been used by countless minority leaders ever since.

But these fears were largely unrealized: In their own way, parties act as a check on governmental power. To win a party nomination, a candidate has to appear to be fairly moderate in order to appeal to a broad range of party interests. And to win the presidency itself, a candidate must appeal to an even broader and more varied range of interests across the country. Such a process tends to squeeze out the dogmatic or extremist group, as illustrated most recently by Ronald Reagan's defiance of the Republican right wing in some of his major appointments during 1983-1984. (Of course, this is not always the case: Witness the Republican choice in 1964 and the Democratic choice in 1972, when the presidential candidates were perceived as more extreme than usual.) In effect, then, parties serve as a kind of "second constitution," granting and limiting power in ways that both balance and support these principles enunciated in the Constitution.

The Republican presidential ticket of Ronald Reagan and George Bush share the jubilation with former President Gerald Ford at the 1980 Republican National Convention. *UPI.*

To the extent that parties *grant* power to a majority of the voters, they could even be called a "people's constitution."[5] Note, however, a crucial difference between the two constitutions. The Constitution of 1787 *disperses* power, as we have noted. The "second" constitution tends to *concentrate* power—that is, to unite a great variety of interests behind a program. The 1787 Constitution is based on the doctrines of the separation of power, checks and balances, federalism, pluralist conflict, and fragmented institutions. The "people's constitution" is based on the idea of men and women with common political attitudes coming together to forge a highly visible, articulate, national political organization that pulls the branches of government into some kind of team. We will return to the "two constitutions" later in the chapter; let us look now at the American experience with a very different type of party.

Third Parties: Persistence and Frustration

While we have been focusing on major parties, we must not lose sight of all the exotic third parties in American history—abolitionists, populists, anti-liquor, Bull Moose, Communist, the Citizens' Party of 1980, and John Anderson's Independent party. The crucial aspect about third parties is how often they charge into the national party arena and how they never win. To be sure, they have had a significant indirect influence. They have drawn attention to controversial issues the major parties wished to duck. And they have organized special interest or "cause" groups such as the antislavery and anti-civil rights movements. They boast, and sometimes correctly, that they are champions not of lost causes, but of causes yet to be won. But they have never won the presidency or more than a handful of congressional seats, unless one calls the Republican party of 1860 a third party: They have never shaped national policy from inside the government. And their influence on policy in general, and on the platforms of the two major parties, has been limited.[6]

Third parties have taken two forms. One type has been the *doctrinal* party, such as the small labor and socialist parties on the Left and the even smaller conservative movements on the Right. Most of these parties have lived on for decades publicizing their ideas but not expecting to win elections. The other type is the third party that arises over a particular issue and then dies as the issue is resolved or fades away. Several such third parties, such as the Free Soilers, rose and fell before the Civil War. The Progressive parties of Theodore Roosevelt in 1912 and of Robert La Follette in 1924 challenged the political power of big business. Most recently George Wallace's American Independent party (AIP) won about 13 million votes in 1968 over desegregation and other

Governor George Wallace of Alabama for a time created a third party, in the 1960s and early 1970s over the particular issues of desegregation and race. *UPI.*

			Presidential	Percentage	Electoral
	Year	Party	Candidate	of Vote	Vote
10-1 **THIRD PARTIES IN** **PRESIDENTIAL ELECTIONS**	1832	Anti-Masonic	William Wirt	7.8	7
	1856	American (Know Nothing)	Millard Fillmore	21.5	8
	1860	Democratic (Secessionist)	J. C. Breckinridge	18.1	72
	1860	Constitutional Union	John Bell	12.6	39
	1892	People's (Populist)	James B. Weaver	8.6	22
	1912	Progressive	Theodore Roosevelt	27.4	88
	1924	Progressive	Robert M. La Follette	16.6	13
	1948	States' Rights	Strom Thurmond	2.4	39
	1968	American Independent	George C. Wallace	13.5	46
	1980	National Unity Ticket	John B. Anderson	6.6	0

[5]James MacGregor Burns, in Pomper, *Party Renewal in America*, pp. 194–96.

[6]On the impact of third parties, see Howard R. Penniman, "Presidential Third Parties and the Modern American Two-Party System," in William Crotty (ed.), *The Party Symbol* (W. H. Freeman, 1980), pp. 101-17.

race issues. But the AIP was evidently fading even before Wallace was badly wounded in an assassination attempt in May 1972.

Why this pattern of failure? Why do we stick to a two-party system when most democracies have multiparty systems? The major reason is our electoral system.[7] Most of our election districts have a single incumbent, and the candidate with the most votes wins. Because only one candidate can win, the largest and second-largest parties have a near-monopoly. The system of electing the president operates in this way on a national scale. The presidency is the supreme prize in American politics: A party that cannot attain it, or show promise of attaining it, simply does not operate in the major league.

Congressman John Anderson's 1980 candidacy, which aroused much en-

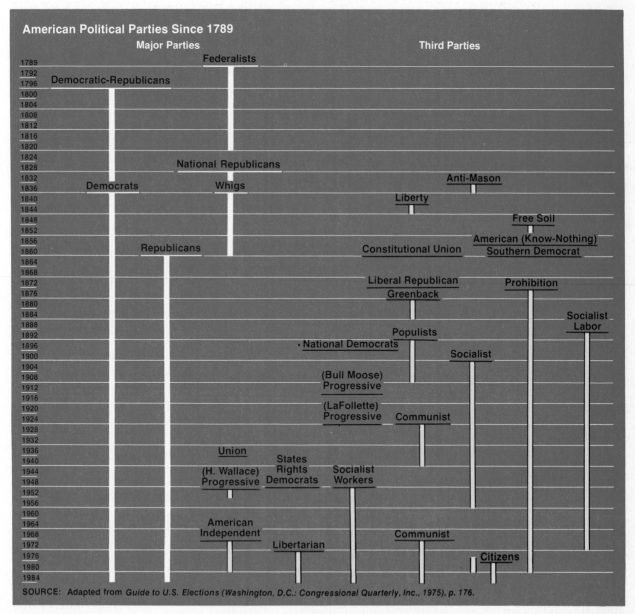

American Political Parties Since 1789

SOURCE: Adapted from *Guide to U.S. Elections* (Washington, D.C.: Congressional Quarterly, Inc., 1975), p. 176.

[7]William H. Riker, "The Two-Party System and Duverger's Law: An Essay on the History of Political Science," *American Political Science Review* (December 1982), pp. 753–66.

thusiasm on many college campuses, illustrates the handicaps third parties face. Anderson first tried to win the Republican presidential nomination and then decided to run as an independent. Significantly, John Anderson and Barry Commoner, of the Citizens Party, returned to two-party politics in 1984; Anderson rejected the Republicans entirely by endorsing Mondale and Commoner worked with Jackson. Thus, it is not surprising that the vast majority of American politicians operate within the two-party system, even though some of them admit that the two parties often fail to represent the interests and attitudes of significant numbers of people.

PARTY TASKS: THE HEAVY BURDEN

Our major parties are expected to take on many heavy tasks. As indicated, one of the key functions of our two-party system has been to unify the electorate and bring together groups, sections, and ideologies. The parties failed to bring the sections together in 1860 and broke up under the pressure of the North-South rupture. For over a century since that great break, however, the parties have managed to please various power groups and continue in operation.

The functions of the parties have also changed over time. Party activity used to be an important source of public welfare. To win votes, local party organizations provided jobs, loans, free coal, picnics, and recreation for the needy; and they helped those in trouble over pensions, taxes, and licenses. The boss of the Republican machine in Philadelphia bragged that his organization was "one of the greatest welfare organizations in the United States . . . without red tape, without class, religion, or color distinction." The takeover of welfare by the government during the New Deal removed this function from most city organizations, but not entirely.

Party Functions Today

To gain votes, parties simplify the choices. Usually they present the voters with two relatively different alternatives. But some people argue that parties confuse rather than simplify alternatives to get votes. On a popular issue the parties may try to appeal to such a wide electorate that there seems to be no difference between them. Parties also help to stimulate interest in public affairs. An election contest is exciting. It makes politics look like a big prizefight, or world series, and draws millions of people into controversy.

After a polite interval following the election, the opposition party begins to criticize the party in power. However, it often fails to perform this role very effectively. It tends to break up into opposing factions that take potshots at the government from all directions, or to mute its criticism on the grounds that some issues—foreign policy, religion, education, and so on—should be above politics.

Parties may recruit political leaders. In the past they were important channels of upward mobility for those "on the outside" of American public life (such as Irish Americans and Italian Americans). A few black men rose to leadership positions in the Republican party during the last century; in this century some black men and women have attained high offices within the Democratic party. Today there is a greater tendency for political leaders to be recruited—or self-recruited—outside the party organization.

For many Americans local parties are not only a ladder but a home. Local clubs provide a place to meet, talk about community and political affairs, have a social drink, work together on voting lists, and enjoy a sense of belonging. It is in part because the bosses of the big cities maintained these local associations—along with their glee clubs and athletic teams—that "bossism" flourished for so long. Since the parties are also nationally organized, local associations

---

FUNCTIONS—MAJOR
PARTIES*

Recruit candidates
Nominate candidates
Raise campaign funds
Register voters
Clarify issues
Unify diverse interests
Mobilize voters
Help run elections
Simplify voting choices
Provide some patronage
Write platforms
Oppose the incumbent party's policies
Help leaders to bridge the separation of powers
Link popular wishes and government action

*Parties are expected to perform most of these functions. Some are well performed, some not so well, and some hardly at all.

Formal and Actual Party Organization

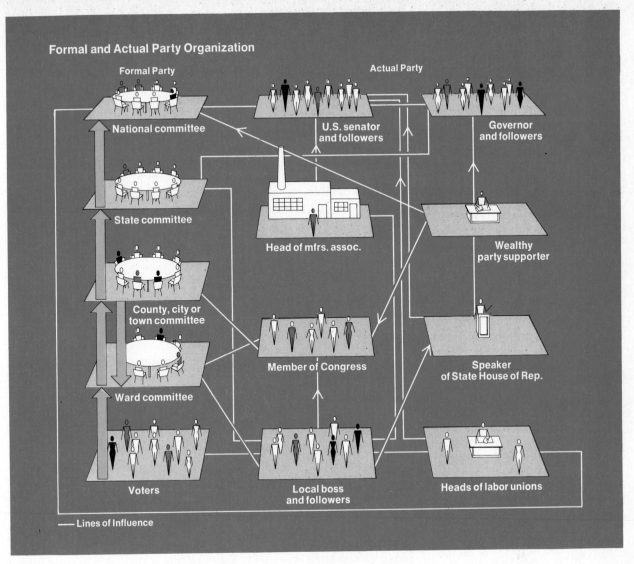

help build personal and political bonds between local communities and the national government.[8]

Parties, especially at the local level, have served as a kind of employment agency through their control of patronage. Leaders have long used their influence over government officials to obtain jobs for friends and party workers. They defended this practice on the ground that when a party wins an election, it should be able to put its own supporters into office in order to carry out the mandate of the election. Patronage has dwindled in importance in recent decades as a result of the rise of the civil service. It is estimated that of 2.8 million federal jobs, only a few thousand are patronage positions. The patronage system was delivered a heavy blow when the Supreme Court in 1980 ruled that public employees cannot ordinarily be fired solely on the basis of party affiliation.[9] The question, said Justice Stevens, speaking for the Court, "is not whether the label 'policy maker' or 'confidential' fits a particular position; rather the question is whether the hiring authority can demonstrate that party affiliation is an appropriate requirement for the effective performance of the public office involved." Justice Powell, speaking for a minority of three, pointed out that in

[8]See Wilson Carey McWilliams, "Parties as Civic Associations," in Pomper, *Party Renewal in America*, pp. 51–68.

[9]*Branti* v. *Finkel* 445 U.S. 507 (1980).

the view of many, patronage helps build strong political parties and helps keep the government responsive to the voters—and that in any case the issue of patronage versus civil service is one for the legislature, not the judiciary, to decide.

Parties sometimes serve as key instruments for uniting persons of different races, religions, and classes. Parties have an interest in playing down social conflict. Despite the fact that more Americans are white Protestants, party leaders and candidates for public office seek to please Hispanics, blacks, and Jews, if only because they represent a large number of votes. Of course, parties can be divisive as well, such as when Democrats play up issues, like civil rights or social welfare in order to win support; or when the GOP, as in 1980 and 1984, takes controversial positions on ERA and abortion. Just when parties should unite people and when they should divide them is a major tactical, strategic, and moral question for party leaders.

Parties can serve as the link between the wishes of the people and what government finally does. By choosing candidates in an open and democratic way, parties help legitimize our elected policy makers. They help organize the machinery of government and influence the men and women they have helped put into office. The president serves as party leader; Congress is organized on party lines; even bureaucrats are supposed to respond to new party leadership. Thus, parties partly bridge the separation of powers and prevent the constitutional checks and balances from fragmenting government. But the parties have only limited success in this role.[10]

Choosing Candidates

Certainly, the function that takes most of the party's energy is recruiting and selecting candidates for office. From the very beginning, parties have been the mechanism by which candidates for public office are selected. The earliest method was the caucus, a closed meeting of local leaders. It was the method used in Massachusetts only a few years after the *Mayflower* landed, and it played an important part in pre-Revolutionary politics. For several decades after the Union was established, party groups in the national and state legislatures served as the caucus. The legislators in each party simply met separately to nominate candidates. Our first presidential candidates were chosen by senators and representatives meeting as party delegates.

But the legislative caucus brought "secret deals" and "smoke-filled rooms." Moreover, it could not be representative of the people in areas where a party was in a minority, because only officeholders were members. There were efforts to make the caucus more representative: For example, the mixed caucus brought in delegates from districts where the party had no elected legislators. During the 1830s and 1840s a system of party conventions was instituted. Delegates, usually chosen directly by party members in towns and cities, chose the party standardbearers, debated and adopted a platform, and provided a chance to whip up party spirit and perhaps to celebrate a bit. But the convention method in turn came under criticism. It was charged that the convention was subject to control by the party bosses and their machines. Delegates were freely bought and sold, instructions from rank-and-file party members were ignored, and meetings got completely out of control.

To make party selections fairer and more democratic, and to cut down the power of party "bosses," the direct primary was used by Wisconsin on a statewide basis in 1903. It was adopted by state after state during the next fifteen years. This system gives every member of a party the right to vote on candidates in a primary election. The state supplies the ballots and supervises the election, which takes place sometime before the general election in November. The di-

---

[10]See Aage Clausen, "Party Voting in Congress," in Jeff Fishel (ed.), *Parties and Elections in an Anti-Party Age* (Indiana University Press, 1978), pp. 274–79.

PERSONAL CHOICE			REPUBLICAN Column 1	REPUBLICAN Column 2	REPUBLICAN Column 3	REPUBLICAN Column 4	REPUBLICAN Column 5
		Member of the House (VOTE FOR ONE)	Republicans for HOLLENBECK				
	2	Choice for President (VOTE FOR ONE)	RONALD REAGAN	GEORGE BUSH			HAROLD E. STASSEN
			Regular Republicans	George Bush	Moderate Republican	Wiley for Congress	Let's Fight

PERSONAL CHOICE			DEMOCRAT Column 1	DEMOCRAT Column 2	DEMOCRAT Column 3	DEMOCRAT Column 4	DEMOCRAT Column 5
		Member of the House	Bergen County Democratic	Regular Organization	Democrat		
	12	Choice for President (VOTE FOR ONE)	➡		EDWARD M. KENNEDY	LYNDON H. LA ROUCHE, Jr.	JIMMY CARTER

Today, the direct primary is the main method of selecting candidates, giving members the right to vote for the candidates of their choice.

Caucus night in Iowa, where the presidential candidates' popularity is first put to test. *UPI.*

rect primary was promoted as a major cure for party corruption. But it did not cure all the evils, and it led to some new ones. The rise of primaries has been an important development in American politics; we will return to this subject in the next chapter. Today the primary is the main method of picking party candidates, but the nominating convention is available in one form or another in a few states. The convention has also been retained nationally for picking presidential candidates.

Nor has the caucus disappeared from party life; it has been reborn in some states, but in a much more open, democratic, and participatory form. In these states party caucuses—open to all persons who profess themselves to be members of the party—choose delegates to higher party committees or conventions, which in turn select delegates to state and national conventions. The caucus system today is one of the most dynamic elements of party organization. In 1980 and 1984 the Iowa caucuses were the opening gun of the presidential nomination race. College students found they could enter these caucuses with no "hassle" such as absentee registration. Also, they had equal voice and vote with any of the local VIPs.[11]

THE CLANKING PARTY MACHINERY

If you look at an organizational chart of the Democratic or Republican party, everything seems neat and tidy. At the top is the presidential convention, which meets every four years and sets policy for the party. Below it is the national committee, then the pyramid widens out to state committees, hundreds of county and city committees, and thousands of ward, town, and precinct committees. But such a chart is deceptive. In fact, the national organizations have limited power over the state and local bodies; power typically flows up rather than down. Our parties have been essentially loose coalitions of state and local committees, with little national machinery, cohesion, or discipline.

Why have our parties been so decentralized? The main reason is the *federal* basis of our government. The Constitution has shaped our political system, just as the political system has shaped governmental structure. Parties are a prime example of this circular relation. They tend to be structured around elections and officeholders. Because our federal system sets up elections and offices on a national-state-local basis, our parties are organized on a similar basis.

[11]For an appraisal of key electoral criteria in Minnesota, another caucus state, in comparison with primaries, see Thomas R. Marshall, "Turnout and Representation: Caucuses Versus Primaries," *American Journal of Political Science* (February 1978), pp. 169–82.

Weakness at the Top

In both major parties the supreme authority is the *national presidential convention*. The convention meets every four years to nominate candidates for president and vice-president, to ratify the party platform, and to elect officers and adopt rules. But the convention in fact has limited power. The delegates have only three or four days in which to accomplish their business, and many key decisions have been made ahead of time. The convention usually ratifies the presidential aspirant already chosen in the presidential primaries and caucuses during the preceding months.

More directly in charge of the national party—at least on paper—is the *national committee*. In the past the national committee gave large states only a little more representation than small ones. Committee members were usually influential in their states but had little national standing, and the committees rarely met. The Republicans recently made their national committee more representative. The Democrats, largely as a result of the reform spirit of 1968, enlarged their national committee to make it more responsive to areas that tended to be more populous and more Democratic. Such changes, however, have not necessarily brought stronger leadership.

The main job of the national party committee *chairperson* is to manage the presidential campaign. Although this top officer is elected by the national committee, he or she is actually chosen by the party's presidential candidate at the close of the convention. Once that candidate enters the White House, the power of the chairperson dwindles. He or she is often described as a liaison person for the White House. Usually the national chairperson serves at the pleasure of the president. A *defeated* presidential candidate, on the other hand, may have little control over the national chairperson; or the national committee may elect a new head who responds to the balance of forces within the committee. The basic tasks of the national chairperson have been well summarized as image maker, fundraiser, campaign manager, administrator, and hell raiser.

Scenes from the 1984 Democratic (top) and Republican (bottom) national conventions. *Stan Wakefield.*

A retiring national chairman of the Republican party summed up the problems of running the party in competition with a Republican president: "It is a tough, tough job to be National Chairman when you have the White House. . . . The unique thing that always will exist—Democrats or Republicans—is that every clerk and secretary in the White House thinks that they can do your job better than you can, and they don't even know what you do. . . . Last year, you know why they wanted my job. Very simple. I had 40-million bucks and we could spend it any way we wanted to spend it."[12] The White House, of course, wanted to control that spending.

It is the national chairperson, backed by the president, who gives the party a little measure of unity and direction when it is in power. When the party loses a presidential race, it often has no real central leadership. The defeated nominee is the **titular leader,** who usually has little power over the organization without jobs or other rewards to hand out. As a result, the party out of power has no one who can really compete with congressional leaders in calling the signals. Who should speak for the "loyal opposition"—the party's leaders in the House and Senate, or the national chairperson? There is no agreement about this within either party. Congressional leaders have rarely been willing to take a back seat. At times party leaders have tried to assert themselves. William Brock was one of the more aggressive leaders of the Republican party when he took charge during Carter's first term. But other Republican leaders on Capitol Hill, such as Senator Howard Baker, also competed for the limelight.

[12]Richard Richards, interviewed in *Party Line* (February 1983), quoted at p. 7.

The *congressional* and *senatorial campaign committees* help members of Congress in their reelection campaigns. Today both the Republican and Democratic senatorial campaign committees are composed of senators chosen for two-year terms by party members in the Senate. The House campaign committees are chosen in the same way. After candidates have been nominated, the committees send them money, provide speakers, and supply campaign material. During presidential election years the activities of the national committee tend to overshadow the work of the congressional and senatorial committees. But during off-year elections these committees often provide the only national campaign.

Both a cause and a result of party disorganization is the manner in which candidates are nominated. Ordinarily politicians seeking nomination run on their own; the party remains "neutral." Lacking organized party support, each candidate builds a personal organization. And because dozens of candidates are running to become the party's nominee, the party becomes a confused arena. Rivalries developing at this time may carry over into the general election, even though the party should be unified in order to put up a strong fight. Thus, although a heated primary contest may seem democratic, it can also be damaging to party unity.[13]

Parties at the Grass Roots

At the next lower level in the hierarchy are the *state committees*. These are similar to the national committees but are filled by members chosen locally. Most state committees are dominated by governors, senators, or coalitions of strong local leaders. State chairpersons are sometimes chosen by governors or senators; occasionally, however, they are really the party bosses on the state level and are able to influence the nomination of governors, senators, and other key officials.

Below the state committees are *district and county committees*. These vary tremendously in functions and power. A few county chairpersons (they are still almost all men) are powerful bosses, as was the late Mayor Richard J. Daley.[14] Many county chairpersons decide the party slates for offices such as county commissioner, sheriff, and treasurer. Some, however, are just figureheads.

It is at the base of the party pyramid—at the city, town, ward, and precinct level—that we find the grass roots of the party in all their richness and variety. In a few places party politics is a round-the-clock, round-the-year occupation. The local ward and precinct leaders do countless favors for constituents, from fixing parking tickets to organizing clambakes. But such strong local organization is rare. Most local committees are small, poorly financed, and inactive except during the few weeks before election day.[15]

Our party systems are complex. For example, a state party organization may include a state committee, congressional district committees, county committees, state senatorial district committees, state judicial district committees, and precinct committees. Contemporary politics tends to be individualistic and personalized; in fact, it would be more nearly correct to say that we have *candidate* or *officeholder* politics rather than party politics. Also, our constitutional arrangements provide for many officeholders at many levels of govern-

Levels of Party Involvement

Leaders

Workers

Members

Primary voters

Party identifiers

General supporters

[13]Robert A. Bernstein, "Divisive Primaries Do Hurt," *American Political Science Review* (June 1977), pp. 540–45.

[14]For a fascinating account of Daley's chairmanship in Cook County, Illinois, see Milton Rakove, *Don't Make No Waves, Don't Back No Losers* (Indiana University Press, 1975).

[15]Local party effort is hard to measure, but it probably has significant influence; see Phillips Cutright, "Measuring the Impact of Local Party Activity on the General Election Vote," *Public Opinion Quarterly* (Fall 1963), pp. 372–86; Raymond E. Wolfinger, "The Influence of Precinct Work on Voting Behavior," *Public Opinion Quarterly* (Fall 1963), pp. 387–98; and William J. Crotty, "Party Effort and Its Impact on the Vote," *American Political Science Review* (June 1971), pp. 439–50.

ment. And the diversity of our country and the absence of strong national direction and control mean that party systems vary a good deal from state to state.

This complex situation opens a great gulf between national party headquarters and state and local parties. Deepening this gulf is the fact that elections—the main activity of parties—are actually regulated and run by the *states*, not by the national government. Some states hold their state and local elections in different years from national elections (mostly in an effort to insulate state politics from national). New York State, for example, elects its governors for four-year terms in even-numbered years between presidential elections, and New York City elects its mayors every four years in odd-numbered years. Most town and city elections are "nonpartisan" and often do not involve the parties as such.

DO WE REALLY NEED THE PARTIES?

The Democratic Rules Committee in session. *K. Jewell.*

Clearly, there is a big gap between what American parties *might* do and what they *actually* do. Ideally, parties build a bridge between the people and their government. They strengthen national unity by bringing conflicting groups together. They soften the impact of extremists at both ends of the political spectrum. They stimulate and channel public discussion. They find candidates for the voters and voters for the candidates. They help run elections. They both stimulate and moderate conflict. In short, parties should do much of the hard, day-to-day work of democracy. But in fact, parties do not perform these tasks very well. In many cases candidates' personal campaign organizations do a better job of raising money and electioneering than do the party organizations.

There are two main charges against the American party system: (1) The parties do not take meaningful and contrasting positions on issues, especially the issues of the 1980s. (2) Organizationally, they are in such a mess that they could not achieve their goals even if they wanted to, so they are not vehicles for popular expression and social progress. How valid are these charges?

Tweedledum and Tweedledee?

The typical party platform, it is said, seems designed to pick up every stray vote rather than speak out in a convincing manner on the vital questions of the day. Platforms are so vague, and candidates' statements so ambiguous, that voters have no basis on which to choose. This charge may once have been valid, but recent scholarship indicates that it overstates the problem. By the 1960s, at least, many voters *saw* their own party or the opposition party as standing for something. Thus, most business and professional people see the

By John Trevor. *Alburquerque Journal.* Courtesy of News America Syndicate.

"No Difference" Wins. Question: Do you feel that the Democratic party or the Republican party can do a better job in handling the issues below, or don't you think there is any real difference between them?

REGISTERED VOTERS	Can Do a Better Job		No Difference
	DEMOCRATIC PARTY	REPUBLICAN PARTY	
Handling inflation	19%	24%	58%
Handling Foreign Affairs and Relations Abroad	21	22	66
Reducing the Danger of Nuclear War	27	19	54
Making Sure Our Children Get a Better Education	36	11	52
Providing Leadership	23	28	49
Dealing with the Russians	17	33	49

Note: Sample Size = 1010 Registered Voters.
Source: Survey by *Time*/Yankelovich, Skelly and White, June 8–10, 1982. Reported in *Public Opinion* (August/September 1982), p. 32.

Republicans as the party that best serves their interests. Workers tend to look on the Democrats as the party most helpful to them. It is likely that the proportion seeing important differences increased sharply from 1964 to 1972, when parties seemed to become more polarized. Of course, there may be some *mis*perception involved. People who are strong Democrats or strong Republicans tend to look at events through the eyes of their party. This tendency is called selective perception or perceptual distortion.

After studying recent party platforms to see how similar they were, one scholar concluded: "Democrats and Republicans are not 'Tweedledee' and 'Tweedledum.'"[16] In 1984 the differences between the two parties are sharper than usual. Parties share a consensus on many matters, but their policies and supporters are hardly identical, as a reading of the 1984 Democratic and Republican platforms makes clear.[17]

Parties in Disarray?

The second general charge is that our national parties are badly led at the top, weakly structured in the middle, and disorganized at the foundations.

Some critics believe the root of all this trouble lies in the absence of big, solid, rank-and-file memberships. They note that anyone eighteen or over can "join" a party simply by registering as a party member or (in some states) by voting in a primary and asking for the ballot of a particular party (which automatically registers a person in that party), or by voting in a caucus. Critics point out that such party "members" pay no dues, do not work for the party, and rarely take part in discussions or activities. Some local party organizations do have active memberships. Active workers may be in the party mainly for personal and material reasons—jobs, favors, or access to government officials. Others belong mainly for social reasons—the local committee or club gives them a chance to meet other people. Still others use the party to advance public policies or candidates they support. The former types are the professionals or regulars; they stick with their party through thick and thin, support all its candidates, and keep the organization going between elections. The latter are the volunteers, who may be "issue purists" or "candidate loyalists." They see party

YOU
DECIDE
!

You have been hired by either the Democratic or the Republican national committee to plan grand strategy for the party for the late 1980s. You are given the data contained in the table above. What do you report to the national committee? (Pick your party, or try both.)

(Answer/Discussion on the next page.)

[16]Gerald M. Pomper, *Elections in America*, rev. ed. (Longman, 1980); see also Alan D. Monroe, "American Party Platforms and Public Opinion," *American Journal of Political Science* (February 1983), pp. 27–42.

[17]Students can address this question for themselves by consulting Donald Bruce Johnson (ed.), *National Party Platforms* (University of Illinois Press, 1978), Vol. 1, 1840–1956; Vol. 2, 1960–1976.

activity not as an end in itself but as a means to a greater good, such as changed governmental policies or new social programs.[18]

Tension and hostility sometimes develop between the two types of party members. The party pros often come from low-income backgrounds. The volunteers may be better educated and more ideological. Over a period of time, however, volunteers may gradually assume the political style and motive patterns of the professionals, with the result that the party becomes less concerned with ideology and programs. Some fear that the "defection" of the volunteers to the professional style may make the party less active as an agent of the public as a whole. But this view assumes that the well-educated, issue-oriented volunteer is more representative of the general population than is the professional.

All this reminds us that there are different kinds of party membership. The professional and the volunteer each offer certain strengths and weaknesses. The party base will have splits in it as long as the party appeals to a great range of people with very different motives. But different kinds of membership may also provide greater strength and durability.

Parties versus Progress?

American parties, some charge, are not vehicles for social reform. The fact that both major parties must be such inclusive and moderate organizations means that neither one can act boldly for the great mass of lower-class, low-income, and politically vulnerable people. Over the course of American history, some feel, this "party passiveness" has probably had a good effect, helping the parties to perform a peacemaking or reconciling function. But in a period of exceptionally rapid and extensive change, it may enfeeble the political system.[19] Since rapid social change seems continuous these days, it can be argued that parties were useful only in the past and are now outdated and should be scrapped.

According to this view, weak parties simply end up strengthening the status quo. The rich and powerful have plenty of political weapons of their own, such as lobbyists, money, and influence over the media; while the political party could be the vehicle of collective popular action. Ideally, it could be the "people's lobby." If the party is insipid in doctrine, ineffective both when in power and when in opposition, and disorganized from top to bottom, it blights the people's hopes instead of realizing them. Others contend that parties are more effective than critics admit, that pluralistic, decentralized parties are appropriate for a pluralistic, individualistic people.

"I'm not worried. The Democrats are always in disarray." *Drawing by Lorenz;* © 1975 The New Yorker Magazine, Inc.

SAVING THE PARTIES:
REFORM, RENEWAL, REALIGNMENT

ANSWER/DISCUSSION

You stall by asking for more information. For example, the table does not indicate how many voters are represented in each of those categories—a critical factor. However, you can still make some common-sense suggestions about reinforcing groups that lean in your direction, and you can point out the need to appeal to a wider variety of other groups to enlarge your party's ranks.

From the start, the very idea of political parties upset some Americans. George Washington's indictment of parties in his farewell address was remarkably broad and bitter for this man of rather moderate opinion. The spirit of party, he said, "serves always to distract the Public Councils and enfeeble the Public administration. It agitates the Community with ill-founded jealousies and false

---

[18]For further distinctions between volunteers and professionals, see Jeane Kirkpatrick, *The New Presidential Elite* (Russell Sage Foundation–Twentieth Century Fund, 1976); Robert T. Nakamura, "Beyond Purism and Professionalism: Styles of Convention Delegate Followership," *American Journal of Political Science* (May 1980), pp. 207–32; and E. Gene DeFelice, "Separating Professionalism from Pragmatism: A Research Note on the Study of Political Parties," *American Journal of Political Science* (November 1981), pp. 796–807.

[19]Everett Carll Ladd, Jr., *American Political Parties: Social Change and Political Response* (Norton, 1970), pp. 307–8. For the contention that mass membership organizations impede rather than facilitate political action by the poor, see Frances Fox Piven and Richard A. Cloward, *Poor People's Movements* (Pantheon, 1977).

alarms, kindles the animosities of one part against another, foments occasionally riot and insurrection. It opens the door to foreign influence and corruption . . . through the channels of party passions."[20] Most of the other political leaders of Washington's day strongly agreed.

These critics were really attacking big and powerful *factions*, since the party in the modern sense had not yet been born. But when sophisticated political parties developed during the Jacksonian era, they were equally controversial. Critics attacked them for granting the spoils of office to party henchmen, for exercising too much influence over the press (most of the newspapers of the day were violently partisan), and for turning lawmakers and other officials into robots hewing to the party line. But behind these criticisms was a deeper fear—the fear that one party might become the instrument for the great mass of people to take over the government and convert it to their own purposes. This was the fear of majority rule—or majority tyranny. Whigs accused the Democratic party under Jackson and Van Buren of truckling to the ignorant and unwashed. The "second" or "peoples' " constitution of the 1830s, in short, was even more controversial than the Constitution of 1787.

Much of this distrust has persisted into the present era. A politician is suspect if he or she is excessively partisan. And public officials are constantly urged by editorial writers to rise above party. On the other hand, most Americans think of themselves as Democrats or Republicans. They contribute a fair amount of money to parties. They look for the "R" or the "D" on the ballot. So far, at least, they have not given much support to presidential candidates who try to run as independents, outside of the party system. They believe, at least vaguely, that you cannot run a big democracy without parties.

Americans, in short, have a love-hate attitude toward parties. The practical result of this has been curious. On the one hand, we want our parties to stay—we even subsidize them a bit through our taxes. On the other hand, we keep trying to improve them. First we tried to reform our parties. Then we tried to reorganize or renew them. Currently some people are trying to realign them. Let us look at each of these efforts in turn.

George McGovern (center) headed a commission to propose a series of procedural reforms in the Democratic party structure after the debacle of the 1968 convention. He was the 1972 presidential candidate. *UPI.*

Party Reform

By 1900 party organizations had fastened their grip on countless American cities. These were not called organizations, however, but "machines" in the grip of party "bosses." Boss Tweed of New York City was long since dethroned and jailed, but his image lived on—the image of a crooked power wielder, in the midst of a vast web of influence, buying and selling legislators and councilors by the job lot, handing out spoils to party henchmen, bribing officials where he could not control them outright, making corrupt deals with business interests, living off kickbacks from contractors, and followed by a retinue of "toughs" and strong-arm men. The essence of the boss's power lay in his control of nominations. The party machine controlled nominations by packing conventions with its own people. By the dawn of the twentieth century, middle-class, white-collar people were becoming increasingly indignant. These reformers struck at the heart of bossism by taking the nominating process back to "the people" by means of the party primary. But many party experts hold the primary responsible for the downfall not only of the "bosses" but of parties as responsible and efficient organizations. For the conventions were not just a means of picking candidates; they were also the grass-roots leadership corps of the party. And in most cities and some states, the convention—and with it much of the leadership corps—simply disappeared.

The national party convention survived the onslaught, even though many reformers preferred a nationwide direct primary for choosing presidential can-

[20]John C. Fitzpatrick (ed.), *Writings of Washington*, Vol. 35 (United States George Washington Bicentennial Commission, 1940), p. 227.

didates. The next great wave of reform came in the 1960s, with a dramatic effort to change the way in which conventions were managed, convention delegates chosen, and other party affairs conducted. This was particularly the case in the Democratic party, but the GOP, too, was influenced by the political reforms of the 1960s and 1970s.

The critical year was 1968—and what a year that was! Amid rising tumult over Vietnam, Senator Eugene McCarthy of Minnesota challenged President Johnson for renomination, and soon Senator Robert Kennedy of New York plunged into the fray. After suffering an image (though not an electoral) defeat in the New Hampshire Democratic primary, Johnson suddenly announced he would not run again. As the temper of the country became more and more ugly, Martin Luther King, Jr., was assassinated, as was Robert Kennedy shortly after he won the California primary. The 1968 Democratic convention scene in Chicago dissolved into near-chaos, as outside the hall Yippies conducted love-ins, anti-Vietnam protestors demonstrated, thousands of outraged people ringed the Chicago hotels, and the police responded with clubbings and tear gas. Within the convention hall insurgents and regulars fought bitterly over the nomination, which had been made almost worthless as millions of television viewers watched the Democratic party bleed.

Hardly noticed in all the commotion was the appointment of a commission to study and improve the way in which convention delegates were chosen, for many years a bone of contention at Democratic conventions. Chaired by Senator George McGovern of South Dakota, the commission proposed a series of reforms.[21] A number of these guidelines, as they were called, were mainly procedural. State parties were to ensure that party meetings were held with proper advance notice, in public places, and at set times. Voting by proxy was to be forbidden. The **unit rule,** under which the vote of a whole delegation was cast as the majority voted, was prohibited. While such reforms might seem rather elementary, they were in fact a response to frequent violations of fair play.

Other guidelines were more substantive and involved efforts to broaden participation.[22] Just as proponents of party primaries at the turn of the century had charged that bosses restricted participation in conventions, the reformers of the 1960s held that countless Democrats were being excluded from party functions and decision making. Here the commission proposed three changes. One was not controversial: It ensured that party rules barred discrimination on the basis of race, color, creed, sex, or national origin. Another was a bit controversial: It allowed and encouraged all those eighteen or older to take part in party affairs (the Twenty-sixth Amendment had not yet been ratified). A third was *very* controversial: Specific steps must be taken to provide representation in party affairs (and especially in nomination decisions) of young people, women, and minorities "in reasonable relation to their presence in the state's population"—that is, enforced proportional representation. To some this seemed to imply a *quota.* Critics complained that a quota would determine the outcome in advance.

The commission's proposals were hotly opposed by some Democrats. Although they favored broadening the party, "centrists" feared that too much effort would be made to bring in young people and women, but not enough to

[21]These proposals are drawn mainly from the report of the McGovern Commission: *Mandate for Reform: A Report of the Commission on Party Structure and Delegate Selection to the Democratic National Committee* (Commission on Party Structure and Delegate Selection, Democratic National Committee, 1970).

[22]William J. Crotty, *Political Reform and the American Experiment* (Crowell, 1977), pp. 241–47, offers a full listing of the resolutions of the Democratic Charter conference. See also Crotty's *Party Reform* (Longman, 1983); and Austin Ranney, *Curing the Mischiefs of Faction* (University of California Press, 1975).

recruit working-class people, labor unionists, the elderly, and others. The emphasis on a participatory rank-and-file party, they declared, was really undemocratic: Those who would attend open grass-roots caucuses were the more educated and affluent—those who had the time and the stamina and interest to debate all night. Working and poor people lacked the leisure, energy, or self-confidence to express their interests at meetings or even to attend them. Critics especially opposed the quota system—"democracy by demography"—as arbitrary and basically unrepresentative. So heavy was the opposition to the quota system that it has been substantially eliminated.[23] However, it was clear that most of the essential reforms were here to stay. Party rules require nondiscrimination on the basis of "sex, race, age, religion, economic status, sexual orientation, ethnic identity, national origin, or color."[24]

Republicans have been more relaxed over the issue of party reform than the Democrats. For one thing, the pressure of minority elements in the GOP for recognition has not been as intense as within the Democratic Party; for another, Republicans are reluctant to give the national party too much authority over state and local parties. Still, Republican party rules prohibit discriminatory practices, and state committees are urged—though not required—to take positive action and to encourage broad participation in the delegate-selection process by young people, women, minority and ethnic groups, and senior persons.[25]

Party Renewal

Some politicians and scholars, both Republicans and Democrats, are far more concerned about party *renewal* than reform. In their view the party system needs to be saved and strengthened, not reformed. They may accept some of the proposed changes—especially those that fortify the party as an organization—but they would nurse both the elephant and the donkey back to health and vitality before they would teach either animal how to improve its ways.

So, while some Democrats at the 1968 and 1972 conventions were stressing the need for more participation, proper procedures, and fairer representation, other Democrats were focusing on the need to turn the party into a better-structured, more active, more effective, and more policy-oriented organization. This feeling came to a head at the 1972 convention in a successful movement to call a charter conference—a meeting that might revamp the Democratic party (just as a state constitutional convention might reorganize a state governmental system). Two years later more than 2000 delegates assembled in Kansas City for long sessions of debate on a proposed charter. Once again battles erupted between reformers and renewers, but most of the delegates were convinced that revitalization was crucial. In drawing up the first written "constitution" in American major-party history, the charter convention took the following steps:

1. It recognized the national convention as the supreme governing body of the party and required state parties to adapt their rules and practices to national party standards.

Senator Paul Laxalt (R-Nevada) Chairman of the Republican National Committee.

[23]Coalition for a Democratic Majority, Task Force on Democratic Party Rules and Structure, "Toward Fairness and Unity for '76," mimeographed (1974).

[24]*Delegate Selection Rules for the 1984 Democratic National Convention* (Democratic National Committee, 1982), p. 6; for a history of majority and minority women at the Democratic national conventions, see *Democratic Women Are Wonderful: A History of Women at Democratic National Conventions* (National Women's Political Caucus, 1980).

[25]Delegates and Organizations (DO) Committee, *The Delegate Selection Procedures for the Republican Party*, Part II of the DO Committee Progress Report (Republican National Committee, 1971); for a history of majority and minority women at the Republican national conventions, see *Republican Women Are Wonderful: A History of Women at Republican National Conventions* (National Women's Political Caucus, 1980).

2. It enlarged the Democratic National Committee to make it stronger and more representative.
3. It strengthened the national and financial agencies in the party.
4. It authorized midterm national party conferences for the discussion of national public policy, at a point halfway through the presidential term.

Potentially the most important of these changes was the creation of the midterm party conference. Following Jimmy Carter's election some doubted that the conference would even be called for 1978, since the White House might fear the delegates would "get out of hand" and criticize the administration for not living up to its 1976 campaign promises. But the conference did meet, delegates conducted a kind of dialogue with administration officials, and Senator Edward Kennedy and other critics of the president were allowed to speak. Further, delegates voted to divide national convention delegate spots equally between men and women and to remove all vestiges of "winner take all" from presidential primaries, "thereby settling two fights that have raged in the party for more than a decade.[26]

Bill Bradley. *UPI/Bettmann Archive.*

But the real test of the midterm conference idea came in 1982, when the party leader—the president—could not mediate disputes from the White House. Without a Democratic president, it fell to the national party chairperson, Charles Manatt, to guide the midterm conference: The priority was to urge officeholders and party professionals to prepare for the 1982 congressional elections and to continue developing state parties at the grass roots. The Democrats tried in vain to match the funding and organizational strength of the Republicans for the 1984 presidential election.[27]

Republicans, concerned about the health of their own party, were not idle during this period. The GOP, however, faced somewhat different problems. The national party had long been better organized and funded than the Democrats, with a larger, more professional staff in Washington. At the same time Republicans believed in a decentralized system and had no strong wish to nationalize the party. As a result, they have followed a middle road in efforts at reform and renewal. Committees have proposed giving the national committee more control over presidential campaigns in an effort to avoid Watergate-type excesses. Also, state parties have been urged to encourage broader participation by all groups, including women, minorities, youth, and the poor. As a result of its strenuous efforts at self-renewal, the Republican party entered the election of 1980 with a party organization far superior to that of Democrats. With Bill Brock as chairperson, the GOP emphasized grass-roots organization and membership recruitment. Seminars were held to teach Republican candidates how to make speeches and hold press conferences, and weekend conferences were organized for training young professionals. Candidates were taught how to "draw up a campaign plan, write and buy advertising, raise money, set up phone banks, recruit volunteers, and schedule [their] time.[28]

Gary Hart. *UPI/Bettmann Archive.*

A number of other forces may be strengthening the leadership of both parties. In this day of complex campaign laws, finance legislation, and election technology, it is likely that state and local parties, and candidates at every level, will increasingly turn to the national party for technical advice or assistance. While the GOP may remain just a federation of state parties, national headquarters will gain more visibility and perhaps influence from its expanded

Mario Cuomo. *UPI/Bettmann Archive.*

The future of the Democratic party?

[26]Ken Bode, "Miniconvention," *The New Republic,* December 23 and 30, 1978, p. 14.
[27]"Democrats Meet to Pump Life into Tired Idea," *Congressional Quarterly Weekly Report,* June 19, 1982, pp. 1467–69. "Democrats Develop Tactics; Laying Groundwork for 1984," *Congressional Quarterly Weekly Report,* July 3, 1982, pp. 1591–95.
[28]Morton Kondracke, "The G.O.P. Gets Its Act Together," *The New York Times Magazine,* July 13, 1980, p. 44.

services. In the Democratic party as well, the influence of federal campaign finance laws, expanded campaign advisory services, and bigger and more professional staffs may well favor centralization. One analyst predicts that both national parties "will become national bureaucracies with hierarchies, divisions of labor," and specialized experts.[29]

Must reform or renewal be alternatives, or even conflict with each other? Some party experts believe that parties can be open, representative, participatory, and fair in their procedures, *and* at the same time be well organized, competently led, politically effective, and highly competitive. The key to such a fusion, they feel, may lie at the base of the party, in the local caucus. Properly conducted, caucuses are open to all local-area persons. All present have the same vote, the same right to speak. Decisions are made by majority vote, but minorities may still have the right to some representation—for example, in the selection of delegates to higher party meetings. Caucuses can actively recruit and involve new members of the party; they can help finance party activities through the collection of dues; they can train people in party issues and administration; they can be an active party presence in the community; and they can identify talented persons and supply leadership to the higher echelons. In short, caucuses can be the building blocks of both participation and organization. Other state parties may follow the lead of Iowa and Minnesota. In 1979 Massachusetts Democrats adopted a party charter that requires local ward and town committees to convene open caucuses whenever candidates or public issues are voted on.[30]

Party Realignment

Some people contend that neither reform nor renewal is possible or even desirable today, because parties have simply become irrelevant to American politics. They have decomposed into weak collections of factions because they have not realigned themselves to meet changing political and governmental conditions in the United States.

The essence of party, in this view, is *coalition*. Parties, notes a recent study, "are flexible, loose coalitions of electoral supporters. It is expected, therefore, that changes in the composition of these coalitions will continue to occur. When the changes are of a magnitude sufficient to shift the balance of power between the parties, such alterations become critical to the political process."[31] To survive, coalitions may need to realign. The catalyst of coalition is party conflict. That is, the way in which two major parties line up to fight each other depends on the groups they can mobilize; at the same time their potential backing influences when, where, and how the parties battle each other. Parties may realign their group support to meet changing conditions, just as nations change their alliances with shifting circumstances.

We have noted the "grand coalitions" the Republicans put together in the last century and the Democrats under Franklin Roosevelt forged in the 1930s and 1940s. Although these coalitions were based to some degree on regional, religious, and racial groups, they were based even more on socioeconomic

PARTY PREFERENCES—1984

Several polling companies regularly ask people about their party preferences. As of early 1984, Democrats enjoyed most allegiance, Republicans least. When asked with which party they identified, this was the result:

Democrats 40%
Independents 35%
Republicans 25%

Note, however, that Republicans typically are more likely to register to vote and more likely to vote than are Democratic identifiers.

[29]Xandra Kayden, "The Nationalizing of the Party System," in Michael J. Malbin (ed.), *Parties, Interest Groups, and Campaign Finance Laws* (American Enterprise Institute for Public Policy Research, 1980), pp. 257–82, quoted at p. 276. Several conferences have gathered for bipartisan discussions of the serious state of the major political parties: Conference on the Parties and the Nominating Process, Institute of Politics, Harvard University, December 4–6, 1981; and Conference on the Future of American Political Parties, The American Assembly, Arden House (under Columbia University), April 15–18, 1982. Proceedings and papers of each were published respectively: *Commonsense* (A "Republican Journal of Thought and Opinion"), Vol. 4, No. 2, 1981 (papers); *ibid.*, Vol. 5, No. 1, 1982 (proceedings); and (American Assembly) Joel F. Fleishman (ed.), *The Future of American Political Parties* (Prentice-Hall, 1982) (papers).

[30]Jerome M. Mileur, "Massachusetts: The Democratic Party Charter Movement," in Pomper (ed.), *Party Renewal in America*, pp. 159–75.

[31]Robert H. Blank, *Political Parties: An Introduction* (Prentice-Hall, 1980), p. 292.

classes. In the 1880s and 1890s the GOP to a considerable extent was the party of big business, while the Democrats to a marked degree represented northern labor and southern poor whites (along with some upper-income groups). The core of Democratic party strength from the 1930s to the 1950s was the working class, although this of course included important ethnic and religious and black low-income groups.

How desirable is a party coalition of the less affluent arrayed against a coalition of the more affluent? Since the poor usually outnumber the rich, class voting might seem likely to produce exactly what the framers of the Constitution feared—a big faction consisting of poor people numerous enough to win election majorities and take control of the government. Some of the framers would have agreed with the cynic who defined politics as the art of extracting money from the rich and votes from the poor, both on the pretext of protecting the one against the other. In fact, low-income Americans have never achieved the kind of "naked majority rule" the framers—and many persons since—feared. To develop majority support, politicians have had to mobilize so many different groups and factions that straight working-class rule has been impossible. Majority rule had to be moderate in order to gain and keep the support of a great variety of factions.

In recent years the old New Deal Democratic party coalition has declined, but no new "grand coalition" has taken its place. And hopes of an emerging Republican majority collapsed in the era of Vietnam and Watergate.[32] There were high hopes for a new Democratic coalition, but these fell with George McGovern's overwhelming defeat in 1972. President Carter seemed unable to put together a winning Democratic coalition, at least in Congress; and Republicans seemed unable to maintain the majority coalition they developed in Congress after the 1980 elections.

What will replace class voting as the basis of party coalitions? Early in the 1980s party analysts could not answer that question. The Democratic party had become an uneasy alliance between diverse racial and ethnic groups, including low-income people, some working-class people, and some high-income government and professional people. The Republican party had made inroads into old Democratic enclaves in the South and among the skilled workers of the big cities, but it remained a minority in voter registration and lost most congressional, state, and local elections. Some people wondered if the age of powerful party coalitions was over for good. Groups had become so strong, political personalities had become so visible and dominant (compared with party officials), television had catered so much to the unique and the bizarre, party registration had fallen off so much, that they feared the parties might just disappear, like the dinosaur. Cutting across party lines were many single-interest, regional, foreign policy, and divisive social and lifestyle issues.[33]

On the other hand, political parties—despite all their weaknesses—continued to show considerable resilience and durability. The Republicans proved in 1980 that organizational development could deliver the ultimate payoff, and the Democrats laid plans to match this strength in the mid and late 1980s.[34]

We will look more closely at these developments in the chapter on elec-

[32]Kevin Phillips, *The Emerging Republican Majority* (Arlington, 1969).

[33]Major recent works on party coalition include Everett Carll Ladd, Jr., with Charles D. Hadley, *Transformations of the American Party System* (Norton, 1975); and Seymour Martin Lipset, *Emerging Coalitions in American Politics* (Institute for Contemporary Studies, 1978). See also a basic source, Walter Dean Burnham, *Critical Elections and the Mainsprings of American Politics* (Norton, 1970).

[34]For the forces working both in favor of and against fundamental party realignment, see Robert Harmel and Kenneth Janda, *Parties and Their Environments: Limits to Reform?* (Longman, 1982); and Walter Dean Burnham, *The Current Crisis in American Politics* (Oxford University Press, 1983).

tions. But we must not ignore the implications of the decline of effective party coalitions. Such coalitions enable majorities to be organized in the House and Senate. They help focus national debate and conflict. They supply both leadership, national and state, and they help pull the different parts of a fragmented system together. If parties decompose further, what will take their place? In fact, the media have moved into part of the vacuum left by the decaying parties, and it is to the media we now turn.

SUMMARY

1. Over the past generation American political parties have declined both in organizational strength and in the estimation of many Americans.

2. The major parties maintained their ascendancy in the past by bringing factions and interests together in coalitions broad enough to win the presidency and congressional elections.

3. Today the major parties are moderate and middle-aged, and they rest on weak foundations.

4. Throughout our history third parties—whether doctrinal or forming around current issues or personalities—have not been notably successful.

5. Parties have many functions, which they often perform inadequately: recruiting and nominating candidates, raising money, clarifying issues, mobilizing voters, providing patronage, uniting diverse interests, and serving as a link between government and the grass roots.

6. The two major parties have been criticized as being too much alike, but this criticism is overstated. They are also said to be poorly organized and financed, a criticism that has been quite true, especially for the Democrats.

7. Whether the major parties—or any parties—can survive depends on their capacity for effective reform, renewal, and realignment.[35]

FURTHER READING

SANDRA BAXTER AND MARJORIE LANSING. *Women and Politics: The Invisible Majority* (University of Michigan Press, 1980).

WILLIAM CROTTY. *Party Reform* (Longman, 1983).

SAMUEL J. ELDERSVELD. *Political Parties in American Society.* (Basic Books, 1982).

JOEL L. FLEISHMAN (ed.). *The Future of American Political Parties* (Prentice-Hall, 1982).

MILDA K. HEDBLOM. *Women and American Politics: A Perspective on Organizations and Institutions* (American Political Science Association, test ed., 1983).

RICHARD HOFSTADTER. *The Idea of a Party System* (University of California Press, 1969).

PAUL KLEPPNER, WALTER DEAN BURNHAM, RONALD P. FORMISANO, SAMUEL P. HAYS, RICHARD JENSEN, and WILLIAM G. SHADE. *The Evolution of American Electoral Systems* (Greenwood Press, 1981).

NELSON W. POLSBY. *Consequences of Party Reform* (Oxford University Press, 1983).

GERALD M. POMPER (ed.). *Party Renewal in America* (Praeger, 1980).

AUSTIN RANNEY. *Curing the Mischiefs of Faction* (University of California Press, 1975).

FRANK SMALLWOOD. *The Other Candidates: Third Parties in Presidential Elections* (University Press of New England, 1983).

JAMES SUNDQUIST. *Dynamics of the Party System*, rev. ed. (Brookings Institution, 1983).

HANES WALTON, JR. *Black Politics* (Lippincott, 1972).

See also *Party Line* (Eagleton Institute of Politics, Rutgers University), a quarterly newsletter of the Committee for Party Renewal; and *Vox Pop*, newsletter of Political Organizations and Parties (Department of Political Science, Northwestern University).

[35]On 1984 realignment developments, see Morton Kondracke, "Is 'Realignment' at Hand?," *The New Republic*, October 22, 1984, pp. 12-13; John Kenneth White and Dwight L. Morris, "Shifting Coalitions in American Politics: The Changing Partisans," paper prepared for delivery at the annual meeting of the American Political Science Association, Washington, D.C., September, 1984.

MEDIA POLITICS: THE BIG LENS

11

While your parents and grandparents tended to look at politics through a Democratic or Republican "party lens," today politics is filtered through a very different and a very real lens—that of a television camera. The mass media are powerful institutions in a society more and more involved in creating, processing, managing, and disseminating information. They have been called the "other government" or "the fourth branch of government."[1] Certainly they are big business. They live off high audience ratings and big advertising traffic, essential to the "bottom line" of big profits.

The president, it is said, commands the media. But the media also command the president, for chief executives have to be available to the media in order to reach and influence the public. Central to media politics are the persons who present the president to the public through the camera lens. Such a person is Judy Woodruff who is now with the "MacNeil-Lehrer Report" on PBS. She was formerly with NBC and covered the White House for the "NBC Nightly News."

Most of Judy Woodruff's working life was not glamorous—the hasty lunches; the sunrise "stand-ups" in subzero weather on the White House lawn for the TODAY show; the two-hour "stakeouts," waiting for a potential newsmaker who may have nothing to say. Most of the day she worked with her network colleagues in a cramped eight-by-six booth "like a deep closet" in the West Wing of the White House. Here three NBC correspondents shared a seven-foot counter, three typewriters, three chairs, three television sets (for viewing the competition), telephones, and reams of press releases. Next door

[1]William Rivers, *The Other Government* (Universe Books, 1982); Douglass Cater, *The Fourth Branch of Government* (Houghton Mifflin, 1959); Dom Bonafede, "The Washington Press—An Interpreter or a Participant in Policy Making?" *National Journal*, April 24, 1982, pp. 716–21.

was a small, soundproof booth for recording radio and television "voice-over" spots, and outside was a clacking teletype.

For Woodruff the daily press briefings were frustrating affairs—"the daily skirmish . . . a war of wills between the briefer, the presidential press secretary, who wants to give us information that suits the purposes of the White House, and the press, who always want more than they are told and usually more than there is to tell." There are also the "photo opportunities," when the press corps is herded into the Oval Office or elsewhere, and each reporter or photographer jockeys for the best position for a question or picture while the president is talking with someone or signing a bill into law.[2]

Presidents, Woodruff knew, seek to set the public agenda—whether with the press, with Congress, or with the voters. Similarly, television—always seeking more viewers—wishes to picture the issues through its own lens. Some presidents are more effective than others. During its first year (according to Jody Powell, who served as press secretary under President Carter) the Reagan administration "enjoyed a great deal of success in dealing with the press. For the most part, they've been successful in keeping the press focused on the issues they wanted it to deal with and away from questions and stories they didn't particularly want to tackle. That is one of the goals—if not *the* goal—in dealing with the press—setting the agenda, determining what the questions and answers are going to be."[3] Media-smart presidents make the most of their opportunities during their "honeymoon period" with the press, and know how to protect themselves later as they and the press move into a continuing tug of war.[4]

FDR made effective use of the radio; his "fireside chats" reached millions of homes. *UPI.*

Every now and then Judy Woodruff's day exploded into high drama. Such a day was March 30, 1981. The day began for Woodruff at 6:30 A.M. Three months pregnant, she looked forward to this "quiet Monday," for the only major event on President Reagan's schedule was a speech at the Washington Hilton Hotel. As the President emerged from the hotel's VIP door after the speech, she saw her chance to move in for a quick "question-and-answer" she could use for the evening news. But her camera and sound crew were not yet out of the hotel, and—so she later wrote—"this is the one time when technical difficulties, the bane of my job, may have saved my life. Instead of running over to the limousine, I stayed back." Just at that moment, a young man poured bullets into the President and the men around him.

In quick succession Woodruff had to grasp what had happened, deal with an inaccurate statement that the President had not been hit, race for a nearby telephone (which proved to be out of order), get back to the White House—which she found in pandemonium—and try to learn something from presidential aides who knew nothing. Above all, she felt a tremendous sense of responsibility to do a good job of reporting, "measuring every word in describing what had happened." Her description, she knew, "would be the first eyewitness account millions of viewers would hear of the attempt on the President's life. But above all, I sensed it was important to appear calm, so as not to convey an air

Judy Woodruff. *UPI.*

[2]Judy Woodruff, with Kathleen Maxa, *"This is Judy Woodruff at the White House"* (Addison-Wesley, 1982), pp. 27–33, quoted at p. 33.

[3]"Meeting the Press: A Conversation with David Gergen and Jody Powell," *Public Opinion* (December/January 1982), p. 10. On agenda setting as an approach to understanding the influence of the mass media, see Maxwell E. McCombs, "The Agenda-Setting Approach," in Dan D. Nimmo and Keith R. Sanders (eds.), *Handbook of Political Communication* (Sage Publications, 1981), pp. 121–40.

[4]Michael Jay Robinson and Margaret Sheehan, "Brief Encounters with the Fourth Kind: Reagan's Press Honeymoon," *Public Opinion* (December/January 1981), pp. 56–59. On the alliance, competition, and detachment phases of the president-press relationship, see Michael Grossman and Martha Kumar, "The White House and the News Media: The Phases of Their Relationship," *Political Science Quarterly* (Spring 1979), pp. 37–53.

of panic." Her calm outward appearance, she felt, was more reflexive than calculated—the result of years of experience and training.[5]

Judy Woodruff's day-to-day work, both dull and exciting, tells something about the people behind the "big lens." Her main interest is not in taking sides with or against a president, or in being proliberal or proconservative. Rather, her goal is to do a good job professionally, to act like a "real pro." Any bias or inaccuracy in her reporting results far less from political attitude than from White House control of news, technical problems, the pressure of deadlines, or lack of time for study and reflection. Within these constraints, however, Woodruff had a certain flexibility as to what she presented and how she presented it. Above all, she operated within a network, a television industry, and a political system filled with both political balance and conflict.

THE POWER OF THE MASS MEDIA

YOU DECIDE !

Do the mass media have a heavy impact on public opinion? Some years ago experts—and especially people in the media—saw the media as very influential. More recent and more systematic research indicated that the power of the media has been exaggerated. And very recent research throws new and different light on the question. But what about your own experience? How deeply do you believe your political views have been influenced by the mass media, as compared with parental influence, teachers in high school or college, siblings and friends, religious teachings? (Answer/Discussion on page 242.)

The media—mass media such as newspapers, radio, and television; and specialized media such as magazines, books, film, cable television, and audio-video tapes and disks—seem to be very powerful indeed. They envelop us in information, music, symbols, and images; provide vicarious experiences that contribute to our socialization; and serve as surrogate companions. Through advertising, a major part of their revenue, they suggest one product after another for our consumption. And yet combined, they had less revenue than General Motors in 1978. "Exxon receives more revenue in a week than *The New York Times* receives in a year."[6] Why are these private, nongiant companies and corporations nonetheless called "media giants?" Because they deal in "products" that permeate our environment and operate in the domain of free speech protected by the First Amendment.

A political system must have freedom of thought and speech, which is to say competition of ideas and symbols, if it is to be considered a democracy. How can a few media conglomerates support competition of ideas?[7] On the other hand, how can the local populations scattered around the country find out what is happening in the nation's capital if they depend only on local media companies? But why not have government-owned media carry out educational and information functions, as well as entertainment functions, as in Great Britain and France?[8] Americans are too suspicious of the government and too jealous of their rights ever to accept this. In this country the media are privately owned. They include almost 1800 daily newspapers and almost 10,000 other newspapers, about 18,000 radio and television stations, over 9000 magazines or serial publications, over 4300 film producers and distributors, over 10,000 movie theaters, and about 1300 book publishers.[9] Many are owned singly. Some are owned by groups who own, for example, more than one newspaper or more than one television station or combinations of media types. Some are owned by conglomerates (such as Gulf and Western or General Tire and Rubber) who deal in other than media products. According to veteran journalist

[5]Woodruff, pp. 14–25, quoted at pp. 14, 20.

[6]Benjamin M. Compaine (ed.), *Who Owns the Media? Concentration of Ownership in the Mass Communications Industry* (Knowledge Industry Publications, 1979), p. 1.

[7]Ben H. Bagdikian, *The Media Monopoly* (Beacon Press, 1983).

[8]On these media functions see Doris A. Graber, *Mass Media and American Politics* (Congressional Quarterly Press, 1980). On socialization see also M. Margaret Conway, Mikel L. Wyckoff, Eleanor Feldbaum, and David Ahern, "The News Media in Children's Political Socialization," *Public Opinion Quarterly* (Summer 1981), pp. 164–78; and U.S. Department of Health and Human Services, *Television and Behavior: Ten Years of Scientific Progress and Implications for the Eighties* (National Institute of Mental Health, 1982).

[9]Compaine, *Who Owns the Media?*

Ben Bagdikian, twenty newspaper chains now control more than half the daily newspaper sales in the United States; twenty corporations command just over half the annual magazine sales; and only 2 percent of the newspapers face competition from another newspaper in their community.[10]

It is estimated that about 60 million Americans watch some part of the weekday early evening news programs on the three major networks. Americans buy about 65 million newspapers a day, and there are countless foreign-language newspapers, thousands of weeklies, and a free-wheeling alternative press. Walter Lippmann called the newspaper the "bible of democracy, the book out of which a people determines its conduct." And radio continues to reach tens of millions of persons. What, then, is the ultimate impact of the media on public opinion? For many years observers of the media have been debating this issue, which is really two issues: How great is the influence, and is it beneficial or not?

For a long time analysts tended to play down the influence of the news media in American politics. Franklin D. Roosevelt's use of radio for his "fireside chats" seemed to symbolize the power of the politician as against that of the news editor. FDR spoke directly to his listeners over the radio in a way—and at a time—of his own choosing. No network official was able to block or influence that direct connection. President John Kennedy's use of the televised press conference represented the same kind of direct contact with the public. Yet most studies concluded that exposure to the media rarely changed people's minds, or that the media's effects were at best of secondary importance.[11] However, analysts were working from the false assumption that the media had "hypodermic" effects; that is, that the content sent through the various channels—newspapers, radio, television—was received at the other end by people who accepted it whole.

If the news media were relatively unimportant, what did influence people's opinions? First, the basic perceptions and ideas of the public. People are not empty vessels to be filled up with torrents of television talk or acres of newsprint. Rather, they tend to focus on those speeches and news stories that meet their interests or fit their bias; they buy the newspapers and magazines that tend to support their prejudices. The news media may present "new facts," but we have an enormous capacity to filter those "facts" and see what we want to see. This difference between exposure and effect is largely caused by *selective perception*.

A second powerful opinion-making force, and thus a check on the direct influence of the news media, is group affiliation. Authoritative members of groups who *do* consume the media act as *opinion leaders* in channeling and interpreting media content for others in the group.[12] In this way family and other primary groups that heavily influence the growing child also intervene between adults and the direct impact of the media. Direct face-to-face contacts often have far more impact on people than the more impersonal tube or newspaper. Belonging to a party also acts as a powerful filter.[13] A solid Reagan Republican may watch the "Eastern liberal networks" night after night and year after year and stick to his or her own opinions—perhaps even strengthen them.

More recent studies have found somewhat greater influence by the news media on public opinion in general. Also, analysts have begun to look at the

PRESS RIGHTS AND WARTIME

In late 1983 when the U.S. troops were sent into Grenada, the Reagan administration kept the press away for several days—insisting that the lives of citizens and the lives of military necessitated secrecy and quick actions. Some members of the press protested. Howard Simons, managing editor of *The Washington Post*, for example, said this was contrary to the First Amendment and the "people's right to know." But the Reagan administration was successful, at least for awhile. The debate about the "people's right to know," however, continued and doubtless will be raised anew anytime military activities take place. The Pentagon, which allowed direct news coverage of hostilities from World War I to Vietnam, is attempting to draw guidelines for press coverage of wartime events. Many in the media question the Pentagon's suggestions: Who will be chosen to cover the war? At whose expense? With what protection? Some challenge the authority of the Pentagon to decide such matters. What do you think? Where would you draw the line?

[10]Bagdikian, *The Media Monopoly*; Graeber, *Mass Media and American Politics*.

[11]See the classic works: Paul Lazarsfeld, Bernard Berelson, and Hazel Gaudet, *The People's Choice*, 3rd ed. (Columbia University Press, 1968); and Bernard Berelson, Paul Lazarsfeld, and William McPhee, *Voting* (University of Chicago Press, 1954).

[12]Elihu Katz and Paul Lazarsfeld, *Personal Influence: The Part Played by People in the Flow of Mass Communications* (Free Press, 1955).

[13]See another classic, Angus Campbell et al., *The American Voter* (Wiley, 1960).

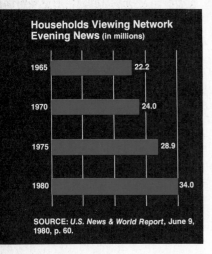

Households Viewing Network Evening News (in millions)

Year	Millions
1965	22.2
1970	24.0
1975	28.9
1980	34.0

SOURCE: *U.S. News & World Report*, June 9, 1980, p. 60.

What Kind of Impact?

ANSWER/DISCUSSION

According to a 1983 study, the media do make a significant difference. How much of course depends on the type of person or group being influenced, the nature of the issue, and the nature of the medium, especially newspapers versus television. "Reading a newspaper," this study concludes, "increases the ability to discriminate between the candidates in a presidential election." This study reminds us that we must deal with such questions in terms of specific influences, specific "targets," and whether the media influence helps foster a more rational or intelligent public opinion, including the ability to discriminate.

How about yourself—what media not only influence you more but help make you a more thoughtful observer of events?

Source: Joseph Wagner, "Media Do Make a Difference: The Differential Impact of Mass Media in the 1976 Presidential Race," *American Journal of Political Science* (August 1983), pp. 407-430, quoted on p. 426.

different reasons people have for using the media. One study of television viewers found people use the media to have something to talk about, to gain information with which to influence others, to get ideas for their own creative activities, to escape from problems and from boredom, to lift their own spirits and feel better about themselves, for intellectual stimulation and growth, and as a way of being with their family.[14]

While the reasons cited above are in themselves nonpolitical, political messages may be found in all types of programming. Every sports event begins with the national anthem, which exhorts people to be proud of their country. Many entertainment programs include jokes about political figures. Most media content, including ever-present advertising, still portrays mostly white men and women. The token black, Hispanic, and Asian men and women who *are* portrayed are often shown in stereotypic gender and race roles, thus subtly reinforcing the cultural values of sex and race inequality.[15]

A major part of the mass media's influence is their agenda-setting function: The media ultimately filter the events that become "the news." At the least, the mass media news determines to a large degree what issues people will be discussing during a particular period of time.[16]

Richard Nixon said, as the coils of Watergate tightened around him: "Basically, they're ultra-liberal and I am conservative. . . . The reasons for their attitudes toward the president go back many years, but they're basically ideological, and I respect that. If I would pander to their liberal views, I could be infinitely popular with some of our friends out there, and a lot of the heat would go out of Watergate. . . ." Nixon had long been battling with the press, and a year after entering the White House, had launched a campaign against the television networks. Now he was trying to shift responsibility for Watergate to the news media.

This was by no means the first time politicians had attacked the news media, or at least tried to turn them to their own uses. Jefferson was so upset by the influence of the Federalist press that he founded a Republican newspaper. During the nineteenth century most newspapers were proudly and openly partisan. In recent decades liberals contended that the newspapers were overwhelmingly biased toward conservative policies and candidates. It was because they felt that the press was mainly Republican or conservative that Franklin Roosevelt turned to radio and John Kennedy to television.

It is true that newspapers today still tend, sometimes by overwhelming margins, to endorse Republican over Democratic presidential candidates. Nixon had the support of 83 percent of the daily circulation in 1960, and of 78 percent in 1968. But the issue today is not so much partisanship (few newspapers support a party as such) as ideology or general point of view. President Lyndon B. Johnson believed the "big" media were controlled by a handful of persons in the Northeast who hated him because he was a Texan and an outlander. Moderates and conservatives like Irving Kristol and Kevin Phillips fear that the big newspapers, television networks, wire services, and many maga-

[14]Ronald E. Frank and Marshall G. Greenberg, *The Public's Use of Television* (Sage Publications, 1980).

[15]Matilda Butler and William Paisley, *Women and the Mass Media* (Human Sciences Press, 1980); Paula M. Poindexter and Carolyn A. Stroman, "Blacks and Television: A Review of the Research Literature," *Journal of Broadcasting* (Spring 1981), pp. 103–22.

[16]See generally Maxwell E. McCombs and Donald L. Shaw, "Setting the Political Agenda: Structuring the 'Unseen Environment,'" *Journal of Communication* (Spring 1976), pp. 18–22; Robert D. McClure and Thomas E. Patterson, "Setting the Political Agenda: Print vs. Network News," *Journal of Communication* (Spring 1976), pp. 23–28; and Shanto Iyengar, Mark D. Peters, and Donald R. Kinder, "Experimental Demonstrations of the 'Not-So-Minimal' Consequences of Television News Programs," *American Political Science Review* (December 1982), pp. 848–58.

At left, presidential candidates Walter Mondale and Ronald Reagan meet for 1984 debate *(UPI/Bettmann Archive).* At right, vice-presidential candidates George Bush and Geraldine Ferraro debate in October 1984 *(D. Goldberg-Sygma).*

zines are controlled by members of the "liberal establishment." Daniel P. Moynihan, long before he became senator from New York, saw a growing tendency for journalists to be recruited from among college graduates, and especially those graduates with hostile attitudes toward middle-class Americans.[17] Others contend that although reporters may tend to be liberal, publishers take conservative positions; like other businesspeople, they worry about sales and profits. According to a recent study, although journalists as a group are liberal and Democratic in opinion, their professional behavior as news reporters does not reflect their personal opinions and partisan identification.[18]

Certain newspapers, such as *The New York Times* and *The Washington Post*, have special influence because of the leaders they reach at home and abroad. They even serve as communications links among such leaders. Readers of these newspapers tend to be more affluent and more liberal than the rest of the nation. Moynihan contends that as a result, our most influential newspapers tend "to set a tone of pervasive dissatisfaction with the performance of the national government, whoever the presidential incumbent may be and whatever the substance of the policies.[19]

It is sometimes said that the editorial columns of newspapers do not affect opinion very much, because editors think one way and people vote the opposite. Franklin D. Roosevelt's four presidential victories in a row, against heavy editoral opposition, are cases in point; so to a lesser degree, is Kennedy's victory in 1960. Although it is significant that Roosevelt and Kennedy won despite heavy press opposition, we should also question the extent to which they had to modify their political views in order to minimize the effect of that opposition.

In discussing media influence we tend to focus attention on the national news—to talk about a Dan Rather versus a Ronald Reagan. But as Speaker Tip O'Neill has pointed out, congressional politics is local politics. Indeed, it is at the local level that the media may be more influential. Let us consider the case of a member of Congress from a district in which there is one key newspaper and one important radio station. If the newspaper editor or station manager asks the member to vote a certain way on a bill, the latter will think twice before offending that person, who is—a "big media frog in a small puddle."

Not only do editorials directly influence our political attitudes and voting decisions, but the press also shapes our political opinions through its overall news and editorial posture. Through its use of headlines and pictures, and by playing up some items while downplaying others, the press influences the "picture in our heads," the basic attitudes that predispose us to interpret news one way or another. The press has a long-term, continuous influence on opinions that may not be obvious in a particular election.

President Reagan meets the press at a news conference. He has had fewer press conferences than his predecessors (e.g., 26 to Jimmy Carter's 59); many critics contend that this has led to an isolated presidency. *Jack Kightlinger, The White House.*

[17]"The Presidency and the Press," *Commentary* (March 1971), p. 43.

[18]Michael Jay Robinson, "Just How Liberal Is the News? 1980 Revisited," *Public Opinion* (February/March 1983), pp. 55–60.

[19]"The Presidency and the Press," p. 44.

Criticism of newspapers has been abundant; practical remedies have been few. Some suggest that newspaper chains be broken up through antimonopoly legislation. Others propose that the government subsidize competing newspapers. Such proposals have received little support; many Americans oppose any action that might, in their view, threaten the freedom of the press. Better a biased, commercially oriented press, they feel, than a government-controlled one. As a result, the press has been allowed to "police" its own practices.

Television News: Electronic Throne?

Some observers believe television in general, and TV news in particular, is a much greater threat to popular government than all other media. Numerous newspapers that cross state lines provide considerable choice for the reader, but only a few networks dominate the American television scene, each with about 200 local affiliates. And people seem exceptionally vulnerable to the tube. They *trust* television far more than they do newspapers. Television news exposure cuts across age groups, educational levels, social classes, and races to an astonishing degree. The TV audience is often captive, compared to newspaper subscribers who can read selectively. And video, with all its concreteness, vividness, and drama, has an emotional impact print cannot hope to match.[20]

The "electronic throne" of television provides the presidency today with a potential power undreamed of by mighty kings and emperors. *Constantine Manos, Magnum.*

Some fear "big television" will become allied with "big government." Presidents can command the television networks at prime time, virtually at will. They can speak directly to the nation. They do not need to answer questions, and they can minimize their press conferences, as Nixon did. Thus, television has been called an "electronic throne." According to one observer: "No mighty king, no ambitious emperor, no pope, or prophet ever dreamt of such an awesome pulpit. . . ."[21]

Other observers have been less extravagant but still concerned. A close study of a controversial and much-touted CBS special evening news program, "The Selling of the Pentagon," showed it led viewers to believe the American military had taken part in national politics, and misled the public about Vietnam. Television journalism has a special importance, this study concluded, because it "disseminates news and information far more widely than does any other news source, bringing political information to people in the society who might never have bothered to obtain this information before television arrived, and who might still not bother, were it not for TV news." More broadly, the study suggested that reliance on television news fostered political cynicism, distrust, and negativism.[22] (The cynicism, however, may be caused by the unhappy reality investigative reporters often reveal.)

Another study—of the CBS and NBC evening news, and of the two newsmagazines *Time* and *Newsweek*—focused on the kind of people who control the news media. According to this study, the national news organizations are dominated by persons of privileged background and standing. The producers believe in individualism, moderation, social order, and the need for strong national leadership; and these ideas tend to be reflected in the news. In the long run the news media cater to, and uphold the actions of, "elite individuals and elite institutions." News, in short, has a major class bias that favors the

"All you lack for *my* vote, sir, is a little more media exposure." *Drawing by Dana Fradon:* © *1980 The New Yorker Magazine, Inc.*

---

[20]Gary L. Wamsley and Richard A. Pride, "Television Network News: Re-Thinking the Iceberg Problem," *Western Political Quarterly* (September 1972), pp. 434–50.

[21]Fred W. Friendly, foreword to Newton M. Minow, John Bartlow Martin, and Lee M. Mitchell, *Presidential Television* (Basic Books, 1973), pp. vii–viii. See also Harold Mendelsohn and Irving Crespi, *Polls, Television, and the New Politics* (Chandler, 1970); and James Aronson, *Deadline for the Media: Today's Challenges to the Press, TV, and Radio* (Bobbs-Merrill, 1974).

[22]Michael J. Robinson, "Public Affairs Television and the Growth of Political Malaise: The Case of 'The Selling of the Pentagon,'" *American Political Science Review* (June 1976), pp. 409–32, quoted at p. 430.

Television news personalities often command a great deal of trust among the viewers.

Stan Wakefield.

UPI/Bettmann Archive.

Stan Wakefield.

status quo.[23] This view has been extensively rebutted, of course, especially by the media.

Are these problems serious enough to warrant any action? Diverse proposals have been offered to deal with such problems as news media sensationalism, overemphasis on "theater" and spectacles, obsession with violence, lack of self-criticism within the media, lack of objectivity, superficial reporting, and so on. The news media have been urged to conduct more in-depth reporting, to deal effectively with complex issues like energy and ecology, to develop better staffs in local stations, and to try to educate readers, listeners, and viewers—not merely entertain them.[24] In 1973 a group of concerned persons established the National News Council to advance "accurate and fair reporting of the news." Composed of legal, journalistic, and political leaders, and of such artists as the creator of "Sesame Street" and "The Electric Company," the council reviewed a number of complaints against networks and newspapers, and upheld a few of them. The council, however, had no enforcement power.

Ten years later, in a speech to the American Society of Newspaper Editors, an editor admitted that the news media were guilty of "having missed some of the biggest stories of the last half century: the great migration of blacks from the South to the industrial cities of the North, something we didn't discover until there were riots in the streets of Detroit; the first mincing steps toward war in Vietnam, which we did not begin reporting seriously until our troops were involved; the women's liberation movement and the massive migration of women into the job market, a social revolution that we originally dismissed as an outbreak of bra burnings."[25] (The "bra burning" was a media concoction.)[26]

Critics hesitate to propose harsh or sweeping remedies for the failures of press, television, and radio, because they fear any threat to First Amendment liberties. But they are also uncertain as to how serious the problem really is and how improvement can best be brought about. Further, the seriousness of the problem varies widely with the situation. For example, in closely balanced election races, where media influence or bias might be large enough to tilt the outcome one way or the other, the influences of major press and networks might be crucial. Still, in a pluralistic nation, with the enormous variety of groups mentioned in Chapters 7 and 8, Americans have so many "filters" through which to observe events that it is extremely difficult to influence public opinion—as many a propagandist has discovered.

Our decentralized governmental system may also serve as a partial defense against undue media influence. Members of Congress may be far more concerned about what the local anchorperson reports about them than whether or not Dan Rather mentions them. Most congressional candidates are more dependent on local press coverage than on television, because even local channels, covering perhaps half a dozen congressional districts, cannot pay much attention to any one race. Thus, while the overall combined influence of the media is enormous, how it affects the president and several hundred members of Congress in their own political habitats is a matter for analysis, not overgeneralization.

[23]Herbert J. Gans, *Deciding What's News: A Study of CBS Evening News, NBC Nightly News, Newsweek, and Time* (Pantheon, 1979), p. 61. See also Sidney Kraus and Dennis Davis, *The Effects of Mass Communication on Political Behavior* (Pennsylvania State University Press, 1976).
[24]For some of these proposals see Bernard Rubin, *Media, Politics, and Democracy* (Oxford University Press, 1977).
[25]Michael J. O'Neill, "The Power of the Press: How It Can Be Used More Effectively," *Boston Globe*, May 17, 1982.
[26]Judith Hole and Ellen Levine, *Rebirth of Feminism* (Quadrangle/New York Times Book Company, 1971), pp. 229–30.

"IMAGE CAMPAIGN": THE MASS MEDIA ELECTION

"I must admit to a real frustration today," the usually cheerful George Bush admitted one morning a few weeks before the Republican presidential convention of 1980. Candidate Bush had just won a resounding victory in Michigan over Ronald Reagan, but when he watched the television news, all he heard were reports of how Reagan had sewn up the Republican presidential nomination. "If this kind of thing keeps up," Bush told reporters, "by 1984 Howard Cosell will be deciding the nomination during a commercial break on the 'LaVerne and Shirley' show."[27]

Late in 1979, about the time Edward Kennedy announced his candidacy for the Democratic presidential nomination, CBS aired an interview of the Massachusetts senator by Roger Mudd. Kennedy seemed strangely ambiguous as to why he was running for the presidency—so much so that the interview became a political event in itself, as people compared this vague Kennedy with the heroic figure they thought they knew. Actually, relatively few persons saw the Roger Mudd interview—most were watching *Jaws* on another network. Nevertheless, the interview got Kennedy's campaign off to a poor start, from which he never seemed to recover. Viewers did not know that Roger Mudd had actually conducted the interview much earlier, and that Kennedy was evasive about the presidency in part because he did not want to reveal his political plans prematurely.

It was clear to most Americans long before Ronald Reagan's 1980 campaign for the presidency that the former California governor was in his late sixties. But as the campaign began, the media kept beating this point to death. While his vigor was evident in his indefatigable campaigning, when it came time for Reagan to choose a running mate once again we were told that Reagan was choosing a likely "next president of the United States."

To describe the modern presidential campaign as just a matter of rules and strategies would be like portraying the Kentucky Derby as just a collection of riders racing around a track in accordance with certain rules. In both cases the event is dominated by celebrities, crowds of spectators, big money, and endless coverage by television, radio, and the "print media."[28] The "mass media campaign" aims to create certain images about the candidates. This campaign has two aspects: One is the intentional and unintentional impact of the mass media on the voters, especially in the primaries. The other is the effort of candidates to exploit the media in their own behalf.

11–1

MEDIA INFLUENCE: NEWS SOURCE USED MOST OFTEN, DEPENDING ON FREQUENCY OF EXPOSURE (PERCENT), 1976

Highest Level of Exposure to Either News Source	Network News	Newspaper	TV and Paper Equally
Regularly	11%	22%	18%
Somewhat often	12	9	6
Once in a while	10	2	3
Infrequently	4	0.4	2
Never	0	0	1
Total	37	33	30

NOTE: The table combines Erie and Los Angeles respondents. The pattern was similar in both locations.
SOURCE: Thomas E. Patterson, *The Mass Media Election* (Praeger, 1980), p. 60. Reprinted by permission.

[27]*The New York Times*, May 22, 1980, p. B11.

[28]Richard Stout, "The Pre-Pre-Campaign-Campaign," *Public Opinion* (December/January 1983), pp. 17–20, 60.

The News Media: Election Impact

Long ago there was much more concern about the way candidates exploited the media than about the electronic and print media themselves. But in recent decades network television, big-circulation newspapers and magazines, and large radio chains have become huge industries with their own identities, interests, internal politics, and political biases. Even when the media try to be neutral, some critics say, they bias the outcome of campaigns. They do this by focusing public attention on certain candidates or controversies rather than others, by playing up certain issues and ignoring or playing down others, and by openly editorializing about candidates and campaign issues. A key criticism of the media—especially television—is that it often treats campaigns more as games than as serious encounters over issues (see Table 11–2). Presidential primaries in particular are treated as "horse races." The news media award the victory to the candidate who wins the "beauty contest" rather than to the candidate who, tortoiselike, is slowly rolling up a large number of delegate votes.

"Many stories focus on who is ahead, who is behind, who is going to win, and who is going to lose, rather than examining how and why the race is as it is," according to one analysis.[29] The press "sees the electorate as a people influenced mostly by tactics and strategy," and "thus exaggerates seemingly dramatic forces such as 'momentum,'" according to another.[30] The media seem to alternate between a kind of "gee whiz" attitude toward their current hero and a tendency to pounce on a candidate's blunder and exploit it for days, as in the case of Jimmy Carter's comment about lust in his heart in the 1976 *Playboy* interview.

Sensationalizing or trivializing campaigns is serious enough, but even more serious is playing down the *substance* of the campaign, especially issues. A media advertising expert says the press spends too much time reporting why a candidate chooses a speech for a particular day and place, what the candidate's staff argued about in writing the speech, and so on: "What tends to get lost is what he *said*."[31] A featured "game" of recent presidential primary politics was raising false expectations about "winners" and "losers" on the basis of overreliance on inadequate polling. Again and again the news media erred in their predictions. After the results were in, instead of confessing their error,

11–2

SUBSTANCE AND GAME: NEWS COVERAGE DURING PRIMARY, CONVENTION, AND GENERAL ELECTION PERIODS (PERCENT), 1976

Period	Network Evening Newscasts	Erie Times/News	L.A. Herald-Examiner	L.A. Times	Time/Newsweek
Primaries					
Game	64%	64%	62%	59%	62%
Substance	24	26	24	28	24
Other	12	10	14	13	14
Total	100	100	100	100	100
Conventions					
Game	58	59	55	52	54
Substance	29	28	28	33	31
Other	13	13	17	15	15
Total	100	100	100	100	100
General Election					
Game	51	52	51	42	46
Substance	35	36	36	42	41
Other	14	12	13	16	13
Total	100	100	100	100	100

SOURCE: Patterson, *The Mass Media Election*, p. 29. Reprinted by permission of Praeger Publishers.

[29]John H. Aldrich, *Before the Convention* (University of Chicago Press, 1980), p. 65. This is a study of candidates' choices and strategies. See also Patterson, *The Mass Media Election*.
[30]John Foley et al., *Nominating a President: The Process and the Press* (Praeger, 1980), p. 39.
[31]Ibid., p. 78. Emphasis added.

the media made new headlines—and a whole pseudo-event—over the "surprise" results. Only the press won this election game.

Criticism of the news media increased during the 1970s. A study of television coverage of the Nixon-McGovern race of 1972 concluded:

> First, most election issues are mentioned so infrequently that viewers could not possibly learn about them. . . . Second, most issue references are so fleeting that they could not be expected to leave an impression on viewers. . . . Third, the candidates' issue positions generally were reported in ways guaranteed to make them elusive. Often, issue references were only part of the audio while the news film pictured the candidate getting off an airplane, wading through a crowd, or riding in a motorcade. . . .[32]

Poor polling predictions by the media during the Hart-Mondale confrontations of 1984 helped lead to Hart's "surprise" victories in Iowa and New Hampshire. *Dennis Brack, Gama-Liaison.*

Recent presidential races have brought a turning point in our understanding of the media and elections. According to Michael J. Robinson, though the media "dominate candidate schedules and campaign decisions,[33] they may not affect the outcome as much as is commonly believed. Or, at least, the media—especially news coverage—may have different influences on different subgroups of the electorate. Robinson's analysis suggests that while the news reporters and commentators were covering the "horse race," the voters were focusing on the perceived differences between the candidates' stands on the economic situation and national defense.[34]

Probably it is the early deciders—often strong party identifiers and activists—who most enjoy watching exciting campaign coverage. Swing voters—mainly the independents and weak party identifiers—tend to vote on the issues salient to them, not on whom the media see as winning.

Paid campaign advertising in the congressional elections may have more influence than presidential campaign advertising. But again there are conditions for greatest effectiveness. For example, advertising—especially negative advertising—must go unanswered if it is to be most effective. A rule of thumb in the "old politics" was to ignore the charges of the opposition, thus according one's rival no importance or standing; that practice may not have changed. Advertising is particularly effective for the candidate whose public image is vague, and who is taking on an incumbent thought to be on the "wrong" side of issues that are salient to the electorate during the time of the campaign.[35]

Building the Candidate's Image: Campaign Technology

There is nothing new in office seekers trying to improve their standing with the voters through various techniques of advertising and promotion. What is new is the rapidly expanding technology of image building, and the escalating financial and other costs. So complex and elaborate is this technology that candidates often hire media advisers and campaign consultants. These are typically experts in mass-mail promotion, "thirty-second spots" and other television advertising devices, intensive fundraising methods, improving relations with the press, "targeting" special audiences, staging campaign activities for maximum media impact, and much else.[36]

Polling is a key weapon in the arsenal of campaign technology. Campaign consultants use polls to assess the strengths and weaknesses in the present "image" of clients and of opposing candidates, to learn how voters feel about policy

---

[32]Thomas E. Patterson and Robert D. McClure, *The Unseeing Eye* (Putnam's, 1976), p. 58.

[33]Michael J. Robinson, "The Media in 1980: Was the Message the Message?" in Austin Ranney (ed.), *The American Elections of 1980* (American Enterprise Institute for Public Policy Research, 1981), p. 178.

[34]See also Jeff Greenfield, *The Real Campaign: The Media and the Battle for the White House* (Summit Books, 1982).

[35]Robinson, "The Media in 1980."

[36]See Larry J. Sabato, *The Rise of Political Consultants* (Basic Books, 1981).

issues and "character" issues, and to discover where candidates should make their main effort. When and where polls should be taken, when and how the results should be released, and whether to release disappointing poll results in order to "lower expectations" and thus make the final election outcome look better are some of the choices that make campaign polling both an art and a science. Patrick Caddell, Jimmy Carter's pollster in both 1976 and 1980, illustrates the influence such campaign technicians may have.[37] Like other major pollsters, he advised his client on major questions of strategy, the state of public opinion and the mood of the voters, and the relation between popular expectations and desires and government policy. Caddell advised Carter on the existence of the "national malaise" the President thought he found in the summer of 1979; and he advanced another idea that Carter seemed to adopt—"governing with public approval requires a continuing political campaign."[38]

President Reagan's 1980 campaign provides some good examples of how campaign strategy focuses polling, direct mail, and media and organizational resources on winning. (See Table 11-3 for campaign objectives.) "The most fundamental tenet of the strategy was that *Ronald Reagan was the best electronic media candidate in American history.* . . . the campaign was divided into three periods . . . . The general thrust of the first period was *to solidify the Republican base.* The second period was *to expand the coalitional base.* . . . The final period was designed *to turn out the vote,* and . . . *to attack aggressively* the performance of the Carter administration."[39] Reagan's strategists attribute his victory to the following factors:

1. The sheer mass of media resources brought to bear on targeted states and communities in the last ten days.
2. Reagan's excellent preparation and effectiveness in the October 1980 debate, [possibly with the help of "moles" who sent back information on Carter's campaign plans].
3. The organizational effort which was nearly twice as effective as the Carter organization in identifying and turning out the vote.
4. The skill of the tour and its tactical responses to a complex and volatile political environment.
5. The question "Are you better off today than four years ago?" which focused voter attention on the Carter record—his Achilles heel.[40]

Some critics charge that the consultants have taken the place of the old-time party leaders. Such leaders made their judgments about possible candidates on the basis of long observation of the candidates' performance under fire, decisiveness, conviction, political skill, and other "presidential" qualities. The consultants, according to the critics, think more in terms of the candidate's image, television technique, flexibility, "salability," and the like. Some critics even allege that campaign consultants have become a new "political elite" that can virtually choose candidates by determining in advance what men and women have the right image—or at least an image that can be restyled for the widest popularity.[41]

Campaign consultants say they are simply modernizing election techniques and adapting them to the electronic age. They also warn against exag-

"Damn media! You should know better than to report all the dopey things he says." © 1983 by Herblock in The Washington Post.

[37]Sidney Blumenthal, *Boston Globe Magazine*, April 20, 1980, p. 9.

[38]Ibid., p. 56.

[39]Richard Wirthlin, Vincent Breglio, and Richard Beal, "Campaign Chronicle," *Public Opinion* (February/March 1981), pp. 44–45.

[40]Ibid., p. 44.

[41]See in general Bernard Rubin, *Media, Politics, and Democracy* (Oxford University Press, 1977); and James David Barber, *The Pulse of Politics: Electing Presidents in the Media Age* (Norton, 1980).

Exhibit 1

11–3
REAGAN'S 1980 CAMPAIGN STRATEGY

EXCERPTS FROM THE *SEVEN CONDITIONS OF VICTORY* MEMORANDUM OF OCTOBER 9, 1980

(1) Without alienating the Reagan base, we can beat Jimmy Carter twenty-five days from now if we continue to expand it to include more
  • Independents
  • Anderson voters
  • Disaffected Democrats—union members, Catholics
  • Urban ethnics and Hispanics
  to offset Carter's larger Democratic base and the incumbency advantage.
  We should *not* break any major new issue ground except in the foreign policy and highly targeted "social" issue areas. The thrust of our speeches to accomplish this condition must be directed toward:
  • Inflation
  • Jobs
  • Economic growth and
  • A more responsible and more efficient federal government

(2) Allocate all campaign resources carefully against the target list of battleground states.
  We must remember that the successful outcome of many months of effort hinges on just the few percentage points we garner marginally in less than ten states.
  Sufficient media funds should be available to purchase heavy spot market exposure in a few key states during the final two weeks.
  The time commitments of Ronald Reagan and George Bush must be assessed and assigned against state target priorities.
  Event schedules should be kept free of low-mileage meetings or events and provide sufficient personal time to *recharge* during the closing days of the campaign.

(3) Focus campaign resources to reinforce the Governor's image strengths that embody the presidential values a majority of Americans think are important:
  • Leadership
  • Competence
  • Strength and
  • Decisiveness
  At the same time, we must minimize the perception that he is dangerous and uncaring.
  Ultimately the voters will choose the man they believe best suited to *lead* this country in the decade of the 80s. In addition to the above general "leader perceptions" we need to reinforce, we must give the voter the opportunity to get a glimpse of the quality, skill, and experience of the men and women that a Reagan Administration would attract.

(4) Reinforce through our media and spokespersons Carter's major weaknesses—that he is:
  • An ineffective and error-prone leader
  • Incapable of implementing policies
  • Mean-spirited and unpresidential
  • Too willing to use his presidential power politically, and
  • Vacillating in foreign policy, creating a climate of crisis
  A sharp contrast must be drawn between Carter's political promises and his performance. Given Carter's proclivity to mount personal and vindictive attacks, we have the opportunity to play it very cool and come out of those exchanges more "presidential" than "President" Carter. In sum, the voters do not want Carter, but are not yet quite sure of us. His outbursts help. They may be muted, but they will continue.

(5) Maintain control of the thrust of our campaign by refusing to let it become event-driven especially in the last two weeks. Be prepared to end the campaign either on a hard note or a high note depending on the momentum and level of support we achieve next week.

SOURCE: Reprinted by permission of Elsevier Science Publishing Co., Inc. from "Campaign Chronicle" by Wirthlin, Breglio, and Beal, in *Public Opinion*, (February/March, 1981), pp. 44 – 45.

gerating the impact of television advertising: In 1980 John Connally built his campaign around a heavily financed television advertising effort, and he ran well behind other candidates in the presidential primaries. However, the advertising consultant for Republican Howard H. Baker, Jr., sees the issue differently: "Television is more and more a dominant part of politics," he notes. "There's been an enormously dramatic increase in that dominance from 1976 to 1980."[42] Critics of television advertising fear this tendency might intensify.

[42]Douglas Bailey, quoted in William J. Lanouette, "You Can't Be Elected with TV Alone, But You Can't Win without It Either," *National Journal*, March 1, 1980, pp. 344–48.

While the media are definitely forces to be reckoned with, their political messages apparently do not have the mass effects attributed to them in the past. Rather, values and interests and group identities bend media messages to an individual's particular needs. The same message will turn one person on and another person off.

The mass media, as noted in the last chapter, have taken over some of the functions once performed by political parties. They provide information: Throughout the year they set the agenda on important issues, and during the campaign political advertising provides information on candidates and issues to those less involved in and identified with the parties. Also, during the campaign the news media appear to provide the excitement of the "horse race" that party-identified voters and activists need to stay enthusiastically involved in the campaign. Nevertheless, the media can never substitute for the organizational, program-building, leadership mobilizing, and sustaining role of parties—when parties do their job.

In the next chapter we will examine the formal and informal rules of the "electoral game" that help determine the best strategy for winning the final vote payoff—the bottom line in electoral politics.

SUMMARY

1. The president is the focal point of much mass media news coverage. The relationship between the press and the president sometimes breaks down in time of severe crisis, but otherwise the routine is a combination of consensus and conflict, a process of honeymoon, competition, and detachment.

2. The power of the mass media over public opinion is significant but not overwhelming. People may not pay much attention to the media, or believe what they read or see or hear. They may be critical or suspicious of the media and hence resistant to it. They live in groups or homes or neighborhoods that "filter" opinions coming in through the media.

3. A major effect of mass media news is agenda setting, that is, determining what problems will become salient issues for many people to discuss and about which to form opinions.

4. The mass media are big business, but their product is information, which is protected under the First Amendment.

5. The media are under attack for sensationalism, superficial reporting, biased coverage, and overemphasis on "theater." Any efforts at comprehensive reform will be frustrated, however, by at least two factors: Reformers are not agreed on what course to follow; and they, and virtually all other Americans, fear taking any action that might threaten the freedom of the press.

6. Presidential campaigns are dominated by the media during both the pre- and postconvention stages. One effect of media influence is that most people seem more interested in the contest as a "game" or "horse race," than as an occasion for serious discussion of issues and candidates.

FURTHER READING

BEN H. BAGDIKIAN. The Media Monopoly (Beacon Press, 1983).

EDWIN DIAMOND AND STEPHEN BATES. The Spot: The Rise of Political Advertising on Television (MIT Press, 1984).

DORIS A. GRABER. Mass Media and American Politics (Congressional Quarterly Press, 1980).

MICHAEL B. GROSSMAN AND MARTHA J. KUMAR. Portraying the President: The White House and the News Media (Johns Hopkins University Press, 1981).

STEPHEN HESS. The Washington Reporters (Brookings Institution, 1981).

SIDNEY KRAUS AND DENNIS DAVIS. The Effects of Mass Communication on Political Behavior (Pennsylvania State University Press, 1976).

M. J. MacKUEN AND S. L. COOMBS. More Than News: Media Power in Public Affairs (Sage Publications, 1981).

DAVID L. PALETZ AND ROBERT M. ENTMAN. Media Power Politics (Free Press, 1981).

THOMAS E. PATTERSON. The Mass Media Election (Praeger, 1980).

AUSTIN RANNEY. Channels of Power: The Impact of Television on American Politics (Basic Books, 1983).

MICHAEL J. ROBINSON and MARGARET A. SHEEHAN. Over the Wire and on TV: CBS and UPI in Campaign '80 (Russell Sage Foundation, 1983).

ELECTIONS: THE STRUGGLE FOR OFFICE

12

If you were not wholly carried away by recent presidential contests you might enjoy going back more than a hundred years to the campaign of 1880. The vast majority of the white male electorate seemed aroused to a fever pitch during much of that year, believing huge stakes were involved: the tariff, reconstruction, western policy, states' rights. The last shots of the Civil War had been fired only fifteen years before. White southerners attacked "centralized power in Washington," while northerners continued to "wave the bloody flag."

Electoral politics was exciting that year because it was fun and because it was filled with suspense. It was a time of political picnics, excursion trips on the Hudson and other rivers, torchlight parades, and dramatic speeches. A Republican parade in New York City took four hours to pass the reviewing stand. In a little Ohio town 40,000 people turned out to hear a silver-voiced senator. No one knew in advance who would win the presidential nominations. The Democrats surprised everyone by nominating General Winfield Scott Hancock, a Civil War hero. The Republicans balloted thirty-six times when, "in perhaps the most dramatic scene ever witnessed in a national political convention," the delegates began to "break" toward a congressman, James A. Garfield, who was not even an announced candidate.[1] Pandemonium broke loose as the delegations shifted, 10,000 delegates and spectators chanted Garfield's name, and cannons boomed outside.

The fall campaign was equally suspenseful. Four years before, the Republicans had won by one electoral vote in a disputed election, and now both parties strained to bring out every possible voter. Each party operated like an

---

[1]Quoted from Allan Peskin, "The Election of 1880," *The Wilson Quarterly* (Spring 1980), pp. 172–81. See also Leonard Dinnerstein, "Election of 1880," in Arthur M. Schlesinger, Jr. (ed.), *History of American Presidential Elections*, Vol. 2 (Chelsea House, 1971), pp. 1491–558.

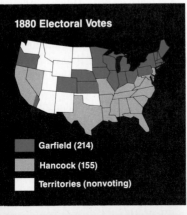

1880 Electoral Votes

■ Garfield (214)

■ Hancock (155)

□ Territories (nonvoting)

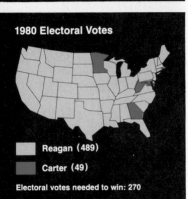

1980 Electoral Votes

■ Reagan (489)

■ Carter (49)

Electoral votes needed to win: 270

electoral team, with senatorial and congressional candidates tying in with the national platform and strategy. In the end every vote counted. Garfield's plurality over Hancock was less than 7500 votes—less than one-tenth of 1 percent of the total—and the Republicans won a majority in the House and an even division in the Senate. The electoral college magnified Garfield's victory, in part because one California elector broke ranks and voted for him even though Hancock had carried the state.

Now look back at recent elections. In almost all cases the winners of the two presidential nominations were known weeks before the conventions. The conclaves themselves were fairly tepid affairs, with most of the excitement whipped up by the news media. Many candidates for the House and Senate ran on their own rather than as part of a party team. While millions of voters in 1980 were turned off by both presidential candidates, they were not particularly aroused by the availability of John Anderson or other minor party candidates— or at least they felt such candidates had no chance. The major candidates did not come to grips with one another over political philosophy or political issues. Perhaps the following comparison best illustrates the difference between the two elections: In 1880, 78 percent of the eligible voters showed up at the polls. In recent elections barely half the voters showed up.

The 1880 election had a vitality, a sense of excitement, a degree of participation, and a popular and grassroots flavor that have all been sorely missing from some of our recent presidential contests. Yet in 1880 black and white women, eighteen- to twenty-year-olds, and Indians were still excluded from the electoral process. And Jim Crow was moving in to take the vote away from most black men in the South. Further, neither party faced up to the human problems of a rapidly industrializing and urbanizing nation. The election campaign was full of the usual blather and demagoguery. The sharply sectional outcome was both a poignant carry-over from civil conflict and a foretaste of the regional division that would plague the nation for decades. The man who was elected president would be dead within a year from a disappointed office seeker's bullet—the first of a score of peacetime assassinations over the next century.

In this chapter we will look more closely at modern campaigns for Congress and the presidency. We will note three problems—the role of primaries, the danger and distortion inherent in the electoral college, and the influence of money—that are entrenched in our electoral system.

GOAL "THE HILL": RUNNING FOR CONGRESS

Congressional candidate campaigning in a rural community, 1982.

How you run for Congress obviously depends largely on the nature of your district or state. Much also depends on who you are: a first-term senator or representative running for reelection, a veteran with a strong personal organization, or a novice who has never run for Congress before. But we can note certain similarities between and among Senate and House elections.

First, we find a relative lack of competitiveness in elections, as defined by closeness of the vote between the two major parties. The degree of competition in House elections has declined since 1896, even if we exclude elections in the South, though there was a flurry of competition from 1934 to 1942. But competition increased slightly beginning with the 1966 midterm elections.[2] The strength of incumbency in large part explains the lack of competition. Once a

[2]James C. Garand and Donald A. Gross, "Changes in the Vote Margins for Congressional Candidates: A Specification of Historical Trends," *American Political Science Review* (Forthcoming, 1984).

SEATS IN THE U.S.
HOUSE OF
REPRESENTATIVES
GAINED OR LOST BY
WHITE HOUSE PARTY
IN NATIONAL MIDTERM
ELECTIONS:

1930	− 49
34	+ 9
38	− 71
42	− 45
46	− 55
50	− 29
54	− 18
58	− 48
62	− 4
66	− 47
70	− 12
74	− 48
78	− 12
82	− 26
86	

person has gained a seat in the House or Senate, that officeholder can use the powers and privileges of office to maintain the support of the constituency.[3] If the recent trend toward more competitive elections continues, however, it may be due to two factors: (1) the efforts of first the Republicans and then the Democrats to recruit strong candidates to challenge incumbents; and (2) the availability of larger and larger amounts of PAC money for the campaigns of strong candidates to run against incumbents as well as in open seats.[4]

Less competition means more safe seats; and the existence of such seats affects the number and kinds of persons willing to compete for the House, as well as that body's policy-making process and output. While many Senate seats tend to be noncompetitive, the situation is less pronounced there than in the House. The population of a whole state is much more diverse than that of the usual congressional district, and diversity of population affects competitiveness of elections.

Presidential performance also affects both House and Senate elections. We have noted the coattail effect: Some presidential candidates affect voters' attitudes in ways that help determine who wins congressional races as well. There is some evidence that presidents affect congressional races even in midterm elections. To a considerable degree the votes cast in these elections seem to be a judgment or referendum on the performance of the president and especially on the latter's management of the economy. "Although the in-party's share of the nationwide congressional vote almost invariably declines in the midterm compared to the previous on-year election," according to a recent study, "the magnitude of that loss is substantially smaller if the President has a high level of popular approval, or if the economy is performing well, or both."[5]

Most campaigns for the House and Senate are increasingly influenced by the new technology of politics: the use of campaign managers, campaign agencies, opinion polling, consultants, fundraising, direct mail, heavy use of the media, "political packaging," basic information systems, and so on. Some fear this new technology emphasizes *personality* at the expense of issues and party. And consultants are often criticized for running "negative campaigns" that focus primarily on opponents' alleged failings.

Campaigning for the House

For a person with some political experience and contacts throughout the district, the first question is one of timing. Does the year look good for the candidate and the party? Is there any kind of groundswell against incumbents? If it is a presidential election year, will the party's ticket be headed by attractive national or state candidates? If so, can the would-be representative get a firm hold on their coattails? Should the candidate wait two or four years in order to broaden his or her own range of acquaintances? Or will it be too late by then?

After deciding to run, the candidate must first plan a primary race, unless there are no opponents for the party's nomination. (This piece of luck is more likely when a party has little chance of carrying the district.) The first step is to build a personal organization, because the party organization is supposed to

[3]See, for example, David Mayhew, "Congressional Elections: The Case of the Vanishing Marginals," *Polity* (Spring 1974), pp. 295–317; Morris P. Fiorina, "The Case of the Vanishing Marginals: The Bureaucracy Did It," *American Political Science Review* (March 1977), pp. 177–81; and the same author's *Congress: Keystone of the Washington Establishment* (Yale University Press, 1977).

[4]See Gary C. Jacobson and Samuel Kernell, "Strategy and Choice in the 1982 Congressional Elections," *PS* (Summer 1982), pp. 423–30.

[5]Edward R. Tufte, "Determinants of the Outcomes of Midterm Congressional Elections," *American Political Science Review* (September 1975), pp. 812–26, 824. See also Gary C. Jacobson, *The Politics of Congressional Elections* (Little, Brown, 1983), pp. 131–37; Randall L. Calvert and John A. Ferejohn, "Coattail Voting in Recent Presidential Elections," *American Political Science Review* (June 1983), pp. 407–19.

IMPORTANT FACTORS
IN WINNING A
CONTESTED ELECTION

Uncontrollable factors:
Incumbent rerunning or open
seat
Strength of party organization
National tides or landslide
possibility
Socioeconomic makeup of
district
Organizational factors:
Registration drives
Fundraising machinery
Campaign organization
Volunteers
Effective media campaign
Direct mail campaign efforts
Get-out-the-vote effort
Personal leadership factors:
Candidate's personal appeal
Candidate's knowledge of issues
Candidate's speaking and
debating ability
Candidate's commitment and
determination

stay neutral until the nomination is decided. A candidate can build an organization while holding a lesser office such as a seat in the state legislature, or by deliberately getting to know people, serving in civic causes, helping other candidates, and being conspicuous without being overly controversial. The next step is to raise funds to hire campaign managers and technicians, to buy television and other advertising, to conduct polls, and so on.

Once nominated, candidates come into an inheritance—the bloc of votes cast by the party faithful, most of whom (60 to 90 percent) automatically support their party's nominee—although with the decline of party loyalty, that inheritance is worth less than it was just a decade or so ago. They will also get some attention from the press and from state and national party leaders. Still, the party provides them with far less financial support than they need, though the 1980 elections seem to have been a turning point, with the Republicans leading the way in supplying more "in kind" contributions and money for coordinated expenditures than in the past.[6] Still, candidates find they must depend on a personal organization and contributions from individuals to provide the bulk of their financial support. Most campaigns cost under $500,000, but in recent years the top ten spenders laid out from over $800,000 to over $2 million (see Table 12–1). And even more for U.S. Senate races.

The main problem for a congressional candidate usually is one of *visibility*. In a large metropolitan area it is hard to get attention in the press and on television, and in rural areas the press may play down political news. As a result, congressional candidates often stress advertising and promotion. Especially for nonincumbents, candidates' spending on radio and television has a positive effect on the margin of victory.[7] But in congressional campaigning there is no substitute for personal contact—shaking hands, canvassing homes, emphasizing local problems, remembering peoples' names. A congressional election is usually a combination of national politics, congressional policy making, and grassroots politicking. "All politics is local," says U.S. House of Representatives Speaker Thomas (Tip) O'Neill.

Keeping a House seat is usually much easier than gaining it. Representatives over the years have provided themselves with a host of perquisites that help

12–1

"BIG SPENDERS" IN 1982 HOUSE AND SENATE ELECTIONS—AND HOW THEY FARED

House

Adam K. Levin (D–NJ/07)—lost	$2,337,537
Barney Frank (D–MA/04)—won	1,502,581
Cissy Baker (R–TN/04)—lost	1,225,458
Thomas P. Lantos (D–CA/11)—won	1,192,394
Johnnie Crean (R–CA/43)—lost	1,140,863
John H. Rousselot (R–CA/30)—lost	990,236
Margaret M. Heckler (R–MA/04)—lost	966,621
Tom Vandergriff (D–TX/26)—won	948,024
James Cooper (D–TN/04)—won	905,474
Ronald V. Dellums (D–CA/08)—won	868,705

Senate

Mark B. Dayton (D–MN)—lost	7,172,312
Pete Wilson (R–CA)—won	7,082,651
Frank R. Lautenberg (D–NJ)—won	6,435,743
Edmund G. Brown (D–CA)—lost	5,367,931
Lloyd Bentsen (D–TX)—won	4,971,342
James Collins (R–TX)—lost	4,139,736
David Durenberger (R–MN)—won	3,969,408
Orrin Hatch (R–UT)—won	3,735,671
Richard G. Lugar (R–IN)—won	2,973,791
Howard M. Metzenbaum (D–OH)—won	2,792,968

Source: Federal Election Commission.

[6]Jacobson, *The Politics of Congressional Elections*, pp. 51–59.
[7]Ibid.

them gain reelection. These "perks" include patronage (for example, census jobs in 1980), free mailings to constituents, free tapings that can be played over local radio stations, and much else, along with a large staff that can do countless favors, or "casework," in the member's name, and send a stream of press reports back to the district. Astute representatives also try to win committee posts that relate especially to the needs of their district, even if these are on relatively minor committees.[8] A high percentage of representatives who run for reelection retain office, if they work at it.[9] Representatives seeking reelection typically run on their own, relying on their own staff and campaign organization. Ironically, at the very time presidents need stable congressional support, congressional candidates are distancing themselves from the presidential candidates and taking the role of political long-distance "lonely runners."[10]

Running for Senator

Because state populations vary so widely, generalizing about Senate campaigns is difficult. But running for the Senate is big-time politics. The six-year term and the national exposure make a Senate seat a glittering prize, so competition is usually intense. The race may easily cost a million dollars. In 1982 two candidates spent over $7 million (see Table 12–1), and 1984 candidates planned to spend even more. Candidates for the Senate are far more visible than those for the House. They find it more important to take positions on national problems, and they cannot duck tough issues very easily.

Otherwise, Senate races tend to be much like those for the House. The essential tactics are to get others involved, use as much personal contact as possible, be brief in statements to the public, not publicize the opposition if you can help it, and have a simple campaign theme. Persuade people through the basic methods of *reinforcement* of present feelings, *activation* of latent attitudes, and *conversion* of opposing views to the extent possible. Facts do not speak for themselves—an intellectual and psychological framework must be provided. And Senate races usually call for even more campaign technology than those for the House.

All other things being equal, incumbency weighs heavily in Senate elections. The reason is not wholly clear. "It may simply be," says Barbara Hinckley, "that an incumbent is more widely known than his opponent—due to the publicity available as a member of the Senate, the franking privilege, etc.— and that with generally low levels of voter interest and information about Congress, voters will tend to vote for the more familiar (less unfamiliar) name."[11] But incumbents are not unbeatable. In 1974, for example, Senator William Fulbright, a national figure, a thirty-year veteran of the Senate, and probably its most distinguished spokesperson on foreign policy, was beaten in the primary in Arkansas by a young, vigorous, and popular governor, Dale Bumpers. In 1980 Jacob Javits of New York faced a similar threat from a much younger Republican opponent, Alphonse D'Amato, and the veteran senator lost.

Is there any place for rational planning in all this? Or is it simply a matter of following a few obvious rules of thumb like those listed above? Most politicians would argue that victory is nine-tenths perspiration and one-tenth inspi-

4-17

"And, unlike my opponent, I don't owe a thing to special interests . . . In fact, they still owe me two installments!" *Dunagin's People by Ralph Dunagin.* © *News Group Chicago, Inc.—Courtesy of News America Syndicate.*

[8]David R. Mayhew, *Congress: The Electoral Connection* (Yale University Press, 1975).

[9]Thomas E. Mann, *Unsafe at Any Margin: Interpreting Congressional Elections* (American Enterprise Institute, 1978); See also Seymour Martin Lipset, "The Congressional Candidate," *Journal of Contemporary Studies* (Summer, 1983), pp. 87–105.

[10]Tidmarch and Carpenter, "Congressmen and the Electorate," p. 487; George C. Edwards III, "Presidential Electoral Performance as a Source of Presidential Power," *American Journal of Political Science* (February 1978), pp. 152–68.

[11]Barbara Hinckley, "Incumbency and the Presidential Vote in Senate Elections: Defining Parameters of Subpresidential Voting," *American Political Science Review* (September 1970), pp. 841–42.

"Ned Appleton, of the 'Journal Post,' Senator. I think we'd all like to know what, in your opinion, makes you think you're so hot." *Drawing by H. Martin; © 1980. The New Yorker Magazine, Inc.*

ration. But careful calculation may pay off, especially in the tricky business of picking a good year to run and a good presidential candidate to run with or against.

In 1964 Republican candidates faced the difficult decision of whether to cling to the coattails of Barry Goldwater or conduct independent campaigns. Those who thought Goldwater a sure winner and climbed aboard his bandwagon fared worse at the polls than those who ran a somewhat separate campaign. A decade later, Republican candidates in most districts did their best to separate themselves from President Nixon, Watergate, and inflation, as did many Democrats from Walter Mondale in 1984. But the results in most elections are also affected by factors over which candidates have little control. These include ballots that emphasize the link between presidential and congressional candidates, national trends, party registration, and the influence of local candidates.[12]

We may be entering a period in which campaigns will become more significant in determining election outcomes. This may happen not merely because of the greater effectiveness of new political techniques but also because a growing number of young voters are not loyal to any one party. They enter the campaign periods ready to be persuaded. Although party loyalties will probably not disappear altogether, there are likely to be fewer voters to whom candidates can appeal in terms of party loyalty alone.

RUNNING FOR PRESIDENT: RULES AND STRATEGIES

There are really two campaigns for the presidency. One is the "mass media election,"[13] which we examined in Chapter 11. The other is the day-to-day efforts of campaigners to win delegates in a series of primaries and caucuses, gain a majority at the national convention, and win a majority in the electoral college on the first Tuesday after the first Monday in November. There are three stages in the "formal" campaign.

Stage One: Winning Delegates

Presidential hopefuls must make a series of tactical decisions, any one of which might be critical. The first is when to start campaigning. Some candidates begin almost two years before election day, as several Democratic hopefuls did in 1982. "Inactive" candidates are not really inactive; they can concentrate on quietly trying to line up key governmental and party leaders who might deliver delegate support at the convention. In either case, presidential nominating campaigns now begin so early that some analysts fear nominations are decided even before the first primary is held. The hardest job for the candidate, however, is calculating how to deal with the crazy-quilt system of presidential primaries and caucuses that makes up the delegate-choosing system. This complex system varies from state to state and often between the two parties in the same state: While the process is influenced somewhat by federal regulation and national party rules, within broad limits the states can set up the system they prefer. The result has been a smörgasbord.

---

[12]Robert A. Schoenberger, "Campaign Strategy and Party Loyalty: The Electoral Relevance of Candidate Decision-Making in the 1964 Congressional Elections," *American Political Science Review* (June 1969), pp. 515–20. See also Robert J. Huckshorn and Robert C. Spencer, *The Politics of Defeat* (University of Massachusetts Press, 1971), which emphasizes the difficulty of challenging incumbents in noncompetitive districts.

[13]The title of a recent major study: Thomas E. Patterson, *The Mass Media Election: How Americans Choose Their President* (Praeger, 1980).

PRESIDENTIAL PRIMARIES State presidential primaries for choosing convention delegates (unknown before this century) have become by far the main method of choosing such delegates. In 1984 around thirty-one states, including most of the larger states and hence the vast majority of voters, used presidential primaries. The rest used "old-fashioned" caucuses or conventions (see below). Presidential primaries have two main features: the "beauty contest," in which voters indicate their choice for president, usually from a list; and the actual selection of delegates to the convention. Different combinations of these two features have produced the following main systems:

1. *Proportional representation* of voters' presidential preference. Delegates to the national convention are allocated on the basis of the votes candidates win in the "beauty contest." This system has been used in most of the states, including several of the largest ones.[14]

2. *Winner-take-all.* The results of the presidential preference poll bind all the delegates, so that whoever wins the "popularity contest" wins *all* the delegates in that state or district. To win all the delegates of a state like California, of course, is an enormous bonus to a candidate. (Ronald Reagan won all of California's delegates in both 1976 and 1980.) Only the Republicans use this system; the Democrats banned it in 1976.

3. *Delegate selection*, no preference poll. In several states, large and small, voters choose delegate candidates who may or may not have indicated how they will vote in the presidential convention if victorious in the presidential primary. The names of the presidential hopefuls do not appear separately on the ballot; there is no presidential preference poll or "beauty contest." Under this arrangement delegates chosen are more likely to feel free to exercise their independent judgment at the convention.

4. *Delegate selection and separate presidential poll.* In several states, including New Hampshire (where in recent years the first primary has been held), voters decide twice: once to state their choice for president and once to choose delegates shown on the ballot to be pledged, or at least favorable, to a presidential candidate. This is one of the oldest types of presidential primary.[15]

Presidents for the past sixteen years. From the left, Ronald Reagan, Gerald Ford, Jimmy Carter, and Richard Nixon. *Bill Fitz-Patrick, The White House.*

CAUCUSES AND CONVENTIONS About twenty states do not use the presidential primary at all; they use a caucus and convention system for choosing delegates. This is the oldest method of choosing delegates and is fundamentally different from the primary system because it centers on the *party organization.* In principle the caucus-convention system is far simpler than the primary method. Delegates to national conventions are chosen by delegates to state or district conventions, the delegates to which are chosen earlier in county and precinct caucuses or at other local meetings. Thus, the process starts with precinct meetings open to all party members, who discuss and take positions on candidates and issues and elect delegates to the next higher caucus. This process is repeated until presidential convention delegates are chosen at the higher levels.

There are many varieties of the caucus-and-convention system, because they are regulated by different state parties and legislatures. The most important and significant type may be that of Iowa, if only because Iowa has held the first caucuses. Early in 1984 on a Sunday evening, Iowa held hundreds of Democratic and Republican precinct meetings. A large number of persons

---

[14]Paul T. David and James W. Ceaser, *Proportional Representation in Presidential Nominating Politics* (University of Virginia Press, 1980) assesses the influence of proportional representation on candidate support and convention balloting.

[15]These types are drawn from James W. Davis, *Presidential Primaries: Road to the White House* (Greenwood Press, Westport, Ct. 1980), chap. 3; see pp. 56–63 for specifics on each state (and Puerto Rico). This material is used with the permission of the publisher.

showed up at these small "party town meetings." Although an even larger number of Iowans doubtless would have voted in a primary had there been one, the thousands attending the caucuses at least had a chance to meet and to exchange views about issues and candidates. A special feature of the Iowa caucus was that college students could attend a local caucus in their college town or in their home town, as the students preferred, with a minimum of "hassle."

Stage Two: Capturing the Convention

Former Vice-President Walter Mondale previously served as Attorney General in Minnesota and as United States Senator from Minnesota. He ran for his party's presidential nomination briefly in 1974 (for 1976) and won it in 1984, only to suffer a major defeat in the November 1984 elections.

Vice-President George Bush previously served as a member of Congress from Texas, as Chairman of the Republican National Committee, Director of the CIA, and as Ambassador to China.

Presidential conventions compress into three or four days all the excitement of the preceding six months or so of preconvention politics. The first convention probably was held in 1808, when a few Federalist leaders met secretly in New York to nominate candidates for president and vice-president. In the early 1830s, under the leadership of Democrats Andrew Jackson and Martin Van Buren, the first real "open" convention was held by a major party. Today the national convention is a famous and unique political institution. For about four days every four years, each party enjoys world attention; covered by batteries of cameras and battalions of newspersons, selected incidents in the convention hall are carried to millions in this country and abroad. This is very much a *party* affair; even though nominating a president is the main event, the party has a chance to come together as a national institution, parade its leaders, adopt a platform, and indulge in oratory, hoopla, and high jinks.

For the presidential hopeful the object in either major party convention is simple: to win a straight majority of votes on the earliest ballot possible, preferably the first. A key factor is the makeup, as well as the presidential preferences, of the state delegations. Each party convention represents the states roughly in proportion to the number of voters in the state, but there is a bonus for states where the party is especially strong. The two parties have often changed their rules for dividing the votes among the states in an attempt to satisfy both criteria. Because Democrats grant some delegates only half a vote, and Republicans favor granting delegates a full vote each, Democratic conventions have more delegates.

Historically delegates have arrived at national conventions with all degrees of commitment, semicommitment, and noncommitment to presidential candidates. Some delegates were pledged to no candidate at all; others to a specific candidate for one or two ballots; others to their favorite "until hell freezes over." Recent conventions have seen two changes. Because of the adoption of "reforms" requiring delegates to pledge themselves to a definite presidential hopeful, and because a Nixon or a Reagan, a Carter or a Mondale has been able to amass the necessary amount of delegate support in advance, most recent conventions have merely ratified a decision already made in the primaries and caucuses. And because of "reforms" requiring delegates to stick to the person to whom they are pledged for at least two convention roll calls, there has been less room for maneuver at conventions, especially before the first ballot.

How tightly should delegates be bound in the convention to presidential candidates to whom they were pledged in the primaries? This question dominated the first day of proceedings at the 1980 Democratic convention. Delegates supporting President Carter, who had won most of the primaries, argued that primaries would be a farce, and conventions undemocratic and unrepresentative, if delegates could violate their "pledges." Delegates backing Senator Edward Kennedy contended that such a rule would make delegates into "pawns" and conventions into "rubber stamps." Why have a convention at all, they asked, if delegates could not act in a deliberative—rather than merely a representative—capacity, especially since months had gone by since many delegates had been selected, and conditions had changed. A majority of the convention supported the president's position, and party rules appeared to require that "delegates elected to the national convention pledged to a presidential candidate shall in all good conscience reflect the sentiments of those who elected them."[16]

Conventions have their own rules, routine, and ritual. Usually the first day is devoted to a keynote address as well as to other speeches touting the party and denouncing the opposition; the second day to committee reports; the third day to the start—and sometimes the finish—of presidential balloting; and the fourth to choosing a vice-presidential nominee.[17] Balloting for president is of course the highlight of the proceedings, but dramatic struggles can occur over the adoption of the rules and of the platform, if one or more candidates see some advantage in challenging a convention rule or a party plank. Not long ago sharp encounters occurred over credentials—that is, over which delegates should be seated when the matter was in dispute—but recently these have dwindled because of more nearly certain procedures in choosing delegates.

Conventions usually spend many hours debating their platforms. Why? Critics have long pointed out that the party platform is binding on no one. It has been compared to a train platform—something to get in on, not to stand on. But presidential politicians take the platform seriously. It gives a good indication of the general direction a party wants to take and provides rival candidates with a test of their convention strength.

The choice of the vice-presidential nominee has become increasingly important (see p. 341). For many years the just-elected presidential nominee has dictated the choice of a running mate; this practice is now taken for granted. Almost no one actually "runs" for the vice-presidential nomination, since only one vote counts. But there is a good deal of maneuvering in order to capture that one vote.

Traditionally the presidential nominee has chosen a running mate who would "balance the ticket." Walter Mondale raised this tradition to a dramatic new height in 1984 by selecting a woman, Representative Geraldine A. Ferraro, to run with him. Mondale's bold decision not only strengthened his appeal to women voters, it also created a precedent that was sure to influence the selection of vice-presidential nominees for years to come—and would hasten the day when one or both major parties would choose a woman for *president*.

Stage Three: The Fall Campaign

The convention adjourns immediately after the presidential and vice-presidential candidates deliver their acceptance speeches to the delegates. The presidential nominee may choose a new party chair, who usually serves as presidential campaign manager. After a rest the candidate spends the final days of the summer binding up party wounds, gearing the party for action, and planning campaign strategy. By early fall the presidential race is on.

Strategy differs from one election to another, but politicians, pollsters, and political scientists have collected enough information in recent decades to agree broadly that a number of basic factors affect election outcomes. The great bulk of the electorate votes on the basis of party, candidate appeal, and issues. Much depends on voter turnout as well as on party disposition. Nationally the Democrats have a great advantage in party registration and support. But the Republicans have an advantage because their partisans are more likely to turn out on election day, and they have better access to money and usually a somewhat more favorable press (at least in terms of editorial endorsements). Pledges on policy and program may not arouse the mass of the electorate, but they do help activate interest groups and party organizations, which in turn help get out a favorable vote.

The course of the presidential campaign has become familiar over time.

[16]*Delegate Selection Rules for the 1984 Democratic National Convention* (Democratic National Committee, 1982), p. 13.

[17]Stephen J. Wayne, *The Road to the White House* (St. Martin's Press, 1980), pp. 118–24.

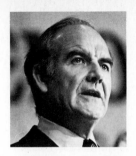

1984 Democratic Presidential candidates.

First there is a postconvention breathing spell, allowing the candidates and their entourages to plan strategy. For example, they must decide where to stump. Building group support calls for a major effort. Each candidate sets up veterans, farmers, and other campaign groups to operate within the big interest group organizations such as the American Legion, the AFL-CIO, and the American Medical Association. The question of offensive or defensive strategies plagues the tacticians: Do Americans vote for or against candidates? Should the opposition be attacked or ignored? Should the candidate campaign aggressively or seem to stay above the battle? And always there is the need to work on the image of the candidate. This was a major, and evidently highly effective, effort of the 1968 Nixon campaigners. They knew the Republican nominee must shed his old image of divisive campaigning and, indeed, of failure as a campaigner.[18]

No one has captured the spirit of presidential campaigning better than Adlai E. Stevenson, the unsuccessful Democratic candidate in 1952 and 1956:

> You must emerge, bright and bubbling with wisdom and well-being, every morning at 8 o'clock, just in time for a charming and profound breakfast talk, shake hands with hundreds, often literally thousands, of people, make several inspiring, "newsworthy" speeches during the day, confer with political leaders along the way and with your staff all the time, write at every chance, think if possible, read mail and newspapers, talk on the telephone, talk to everybody, dictate, receive delegations, eat, with decorum—and discretion!—and ride through city after city on the back of an open car, smiling until your mouth is dehydrated by the wind, waving until the blood runs out of your arm, and then bounce gaily, confidently, masterfully into great howling halls, shaved and all made up for television with the right color shirt and tie—I always forgot—and a manuscript so defaced with chicken tracks and last-minute jottings that you couldn't follow it, even if the spotlights weren't blinding and even if the still photographers didn't shoot you in the eye every time you looked at them. (I've often wondered what happened to all those pictures!) Then all you have to do is make a great, imperishable speech, get out through the pressing crowds with a few score autographs, your clothes intact, your hands bruised, and back to the hotel—in time to see a few important people.
>
> But the real work has just commenced—two or three, sometimes four hours of frenzied writing and editing of the next day's immortal mouthings so you can get something to the stenographers, so they can get something to the mimeograph machines, so they can get something to the reporters, so they can get something to their papers by deadline time. (And I quickly concluded that all deadlines were yesterday!) Finally sleep, sweet sleep, steals you away, unless you worry—which I do. . . .[19]

In recent years presidential debates have enlivened—or at least focused—the campaigns. In 1960 John Kennedy and Richard Nixon challenged each other to a series of debates. Kennedy's apparent "victory" in the first debate greatly boosted his campaign. In the following elections incumbent Presidents Johnson and Nixon did not deign to give their opponents equal billing in debates, but in 1976 President Ford had the courage to do so. He and Carter squared off in three debates sponsored by the League of Women Voters. Both contenders debated well, and the outcome was widely viewed as a standoff. A new feature in the 1976 campaign was a debate between the vice-presidential candidates. Again, both showed their debating skill, but Walter Mondale—according to many observers—gained some votes for his national ticket.[20] The

[18]On the key factor of personality in presidential campaigning, see Richard W. Boyd, "Presidential Elections: An Explanation of Voting Defection," *American Political Science Review* (June 1969), pp. 498–514. See also Herbert Asher, *Presidential Elections and American Politics*, rev. ed. (Dorsey Press, 1980), especially pp. 235–37.

[19]Adlai E. Stevenson, *Major Campaign Speeches, 1952* (Random House, 1953); pp. xi–xii. Copyright 1953 by Random House, Inc.

[20]See generally Austin Ranney (ed.), *The Past and Future of Presidential Debates* (American Enterprise Institute for Public Policy, 1979).

NUMBER OF ELECTORS
FOR EACH STATE: 1984

State	
Alabama	9
Alaska	3
Arizona	7
Arkansas	6
California	47
Colorado	8
Connecticut	8
Delaware	3
Florida	21
Georgia	12
Hawaii	4
Idaho	4
Illinois	24
Indiana	12
Iowa	8
Kansas	7
Kentucky	9
Louisiana	10
Maine	4
Maryland	10
Massachusetts	13
Michigan	20
Minnesota	10
Mississippi	7
Missouri	11
Montana	4
Nebraska	5
Nevada	4
New Hampshire	4
New Jersey	16
New Mexico	5
New York	36
North Carolina	13
North Dakota	3
Ohio	23
Oklahoma	8
Oregon	7
Pennsylvania	25
Rhode Island	4
South Carolina	8
South Dakota	3
Tennessee	11
Texas	29
Utah	5
Vermont	3
Virginia	12
Washington	10
West Virginia	6
Wisconsin	11
Wyoming	3

The District of Columbia, which has
no voting delegation in Congress, receives 3 votes.

Carter-Reagan debate in the last week of the 1980 campaign attracted a huge television audience, with Carter, some said, winning on issues and Reagan on style.

Even more enlivening are the inevitable mistakes that occur in presidential campaigns. In speaking for the "absolute and total separation of church and state," Jimmy Carter warned in a *Playboy* interview against the sin of pride. To illustrate his point, he went on: "I've looked on a lot of women with lust. I've committed adultery in my heart many times." This comment became a "nine-days' wonder" at the height of the campaign. President Ford matched this blunder by stating, in defending his record of negotiating with Russia over Eastern Europe, that each of these countries "is independent, autonomous, it has its own territorial integrity, and none was under Soviet domination." The Democrats exploited this for a full week.[21] Such blunders probably have only a little effect on the final vote. The major influences on election outcome are party affiliation, interest group membership, attitudes on issues, the candidates' personality, and how the nominees exploit these various factors.

One standard feature of presidential campaigns almost disappeared in 1976—the desperate search for money. President Harry Truman ran so short in 1948 that funds had to be raised from day to day to keep the campaign train moving. Presidential candidates have found the task of raising money a demeaning business, aside from the ever-present worry that donors are trying to buy special influence, or at least access. In 1976, for the first time, government funding was available for the fall campaign. Since 1976 the major party presidential candidates have each received a flat grant of about $30 million. In accepting these funds, they became ineligible to receive private donations, although groups sympathetic but independent of these candidates are allowed to raise and spend funds to help elect them. Each major party is allowed to raise for election expenses about $3 million more, from private donations. Aside from the federal grants to the parties for their conventions, the big subsidies go directly to the candidates' campaigns.

THE ELECTORAL COLLEGE SYSTEM: MECHANICS To win the presidency, candidates must put together a combination of electoral votes that will give them a majority in the **electoral college**. This unique institution never meets and serves only a limited electoral function. Yet it has an importance of its own. The framers of the Constitution devised the electoral college system because they wanted the president chosen by electors exercising independent judgment. Subsequent political changes have transformed the electors into straight party representatives who simply register the voters' decision.

In making a presidential choice on election day, the voter technically does not vote directly for a candidate but chooses between slates of presidential electors. Each slate is made up of persons selected by the state party (in most states in party conventions) to serve in this essentially honorary role. The slate that wins the most popular votes throughout the state gets to cast all the electoral votes for the state (a state has one electoral vote for every senator and representative).

The electors on the winning slate travel to their state capital the first Monday after the second Wednesday in December; go through the ceremony of casting their ballots for their party's candidates; perhaps hear some speeches; and go home. The ballots are sent from the state capitals to Washington, where early in January they are formally counted by the House and Senate. The name of the next president is then announced.

[21]Gerald Pomper et al., *The Election of 1976* (David McKay, 1977) deals with this and many other aspects of the Carter-Ford contest; the congressional, state, and local elections of 1976; and implications for the future. See also Jules Witcover, *Marathon, 1972–1976* (Viking, 1977).

The House and Senate also must act when no candidate secures a majority of the electoral votes. This is not likely so long as there are only two serious contending parties. Nevertheless, it has happened twice in the case of president and once in the case of vice-president. When this situation occurs, the House chooses the president from among the top three candidates. Each *state delegation has one vote*, and a majority is necessary for election. (A tied delegation has no vote.) If no person receives a majority of the electoral vote in the vice-presidential contest, the Senate picks from among the top two candidates. Each senator has one vote, and again a majority is required.

THE ELECTORAL COLLEGE SYSTEM: POLITICS The operation of the electoral college, with its statewide electoral slates, sharply influences the presidency and presidential politics. In order to win a presidential election, a candidate must appeal successfully to urban and suburban groups in states such as New York, California, Pennsylvania, and Illinois. Under the electoral college system, as we have seen, a candidate wins either *all* a state's electoral votes or *none*. So presidential candidates ordinarily will not waste time campaigning in states unless they have at least a fighting chance of carrying those states; nor will they waste time in states in which their parties will be sure winners. The fight usually narrows down to the medium-sized and big states where the balance between the parties tends to be fairly even.

Both the mechanics and politics of the electoral college can be unpredictable. In 1976 an elector in the state of Washington chosen on the Republican ticket refused to cast his vote for Ford and gave it to Ronald Reagan. Such departures from custom are rare and have never affected the outcome of an election. But many people agree it is dangerous to have a system that allows individual electors to vote for whomever they wish despite the results of the popular vote in their state. Although under the present system some states attempt by law to bind electors to vote for the presidential and vice-presidential candidates of their party, these laws may not be enforceable.

All states except Maine now provide for the selection of electors on a general, statewide, winner-take-all, straight-ticket basis. This makes it possible for a person to receive a majority of the national popular vote without receiving a majority of the electoral vote. This happened in 1824, when Andrew Jackson won 12 percent more of the vote than John Quincy Adams; in 1876, when Samuel Tilden received more popular votes but lost the electoral vote to Hayes; and again in 1888, when Grover Cleveland, despite his large popular vote, got fewer electoral votes than Harrison.

1984 New York City Columbus Day Parade. *UPI/Bettmann Archive.*

CAMPAIGN MONEY

Big, long campaigns—especially presidential campaigns—require big money. Compare elections in the United States to those in Great Britain, where each candidate for Parliament—including the prime minister—was limited to spending $6,633.72 in a three-week campaign in the 1983 general election.[22] Watergate, the resignations of President Nixon and Vice-President Agnew, "laundering" of money through secret bank accounts outside the country, the heavy presidential primary spending of 1980—these and much else have fueled American worries over the use of money in campaigns to buy influence in politics and government. But the world of political money still remains shadowy. How much does campaigning cost? Should it cost that much? Who gives the money?

[22]R. W. Apple, Jr., "Campaigning in Britain: No Frills and No Glamour, Just $6,633.72," *The New York Times,* June 4, 1983, p. 3.

Why? Where does it go? Is campaign money a serious problem? If so, what has been done about it? What can be done about it?

Presidential campaigns are expensive. Richard Nixon spent over $60 million in the general election alone in 1972, McGovern about half that. Carter and Ford each spent about $22 million in the 1976 fall election. The total cost of presidential primaries is even higher. The thirteen Democratic and two Republican contenders in 1976 spent over $66 million.[23] Big-time Senate campaigns can cost a lot too, as we have already seen. The total cost for all national races—presidential, senatorial, congressional—in 1976 was estimated at about $175 million. This figure is bound to rise, if only because of inflation. A chartered ninety-six-seat 727 jet, flown into a dozen or so states, cost $37.5 thousand in 1976, but $91 thousand in 1980 (up by 143 percent). A sixty-second television commercial in a top-rated, prime-time show in Boston cost $4800 in 1976, but $7400 in 1980 (up 63 percent). A batch of 50,000 one-page campaign flyers, triple-folded, rose from 3.8 cents each to 6.2 cents (63 percent). A thousand bumper stickers increased from $60 to $75 (25 percent). The cost of all national races in 1980 was $500 million.

These are big sums, but they must be put into perspective. The $500 million spent on national races in 1980 was but a fraction of a percent of the total cost of government. One Trident submarine, for example, costs hundreds of millions of dollars. Or compare the cost of political campaigns with the money spent on commercial advertising. One big soap company will budget in 1984 almost as much as the cost of all campaigning for that presidential year. Or compare political expenditure per voter in the United States with spending in other countries. Americans spent $1.12 per capita in a recent year, much less than that spent in most countries. In Israel, for contrast, the cost per voter was $21.20.

There are many reasons for giving political money. Most givers want something specific. Business, labor, and other groups want certain laws passed or repealed, certain funds appropriated, or certain administrative decisions rendered. Those holding government jobs want to stay in office (and in certain cities pay the party an assessment to do so). Some big donors want ambassadorships or other important posts. Some want recognition—an invitation to a White House dinner, a low license plate number, an honorific appointment. Others simply want *access* to officeholders. They neither expect nor get specific governmental rewards for their "cash on the barrelhead"; what they *do* expect

A TYPICAL BUDGET FOR A RECENT CONGRESSIONAL CAMPAIGN

Entertainment	$ 7,500.00
Travel	12,000.00
Hotels	1,500.00
Hq. equipment, furniture	10,000.00
Rent	13,000.00
Media consultant	35,000.00
Printing	46,000.00
Research	1,500.00
Television and radio advertising	180,000.00
Stamps	6,000.00
Telephone charges	14,000.00
Tickets for dinners, etc.	3,000.00
Staff payroll	80,000.00
Direct mail campaign	55,000.00
Polls	17,000.00
Voter surveys	20,000.00
Mail and vote list computerization	12,000.00
Videotape machines	2,000.00

12–2 SOURCES OF CONTRIBUTIONS IN THE 1980 ELECTIONS (IN %)— LEADING CANDIDATES

Office Sought/ Candidate	Individual Contributions	Personal Loans	Federal Matching	Parties	Nonparty Committees
House	67	—	NA	4	29 (100%)
Senate	78	—	NA	2	21 (101%)
Presidency					
Carter	66	0	26		8* (100%)
Kennedy	46	16	23		15 (100%)
Brown	53	12	28		7 (100%)
Reagan	49	19	26		6 (100%)
Bush	49	20	26		5 (100%)
Connally	86	8			6 (100%)

—Data not given   NA Not Applicable

Sources: House and Senate figures from Jacobson, *The Politics of Congressional Elections*, p. 53; Presidency figures from Gary R. Orren, "Fundraising in the Primaries: An Analysis of Contributions to Presidential Campaigns," in Campaign Finance Study Group, *Financing Presidential Campaigns: An Examination of the Ongoing Effects of the Federal Election Campaign Laws Upon the Conduct of Presidential Campaigns* (Institute of Politics, John F. Kennedy School of Government, Harvard University, 1982), pp. 2–13. *Note that the fourth column of the Presidency figures represents a category "Other" that includes "Party" and "Nonparty Committee" funds.

[23]Wayne, *The Road to the White House*, p. 28.

Governor James B. Hunt, Jr. (D.) from North Carolina ran unsuccessfully for the U.S. Senate in 1984 in one of the nation's most expensive campaigns. His opponent, Senator Jesse Helms (R.).

Regulating Campaign Money

Jesse Helms. *Office of Senator Jesse Helms.*

and usually get is the opportunity to see the officeholder after the election and present their case. Many givers are moved by higher motives. They believe their candidate or party will govern best for them and their country. Their motives range from the vaguest idealism to the hardheaded calculation that certain candidates, parties, or governmental actions would be best for the nation.

A recent study of contributors to 1972 presidential candidates found the following types of political activists: public and party officeholders who also have been involved in organizing groups to solve community problems; party workers and public office appointees who emphasize campaign work at all levels of government, mainly presidential campaign workers who are otherwise active in groups other than political parties; high-income contributors, with family incomes over $100,000, who are asked by others for help in dealing with all levels of government; predominantly Democratic lower-income contributors involved in community activities; campaign workers in nonleadership roles; and "contributing specialists," who do little else but contribute money.[24]

Is giving worthwhile? Is there a payoff? This question is unanswerable because the relation between giving money and the passage of an act, for example, is extremely obscure. Too many other factors are involved (including the giving of money by people on the other side of an issue). Perhaps it is enough to say that most politicians and most donors *think* that giving money brings results.

For many years the national and state governments have been trying to "sanitize" campaign finance, with very mixed results. Reformers have tried three basic strategies in trying to prevent abuse: *limitations* on the giving, receiving, and spending of political money; *disclosure* of the sources and uses of political money; and governmental *subsidies* of campaigns, including incentive arrangements. Recent campaign finance laws have tended to use all three in attempts to deal with a problem that sometimes seems insoluble.

Limiting campaign spending is one of the older methods. Under the 1925 Corrupt Practices Act, a candidate for the United States House of Representatives could not spend more than certain set sums. The act was utterly unrealistic and easily evaded. Reporting was inadequate; often reports were filed after the election was over. Policing was almost nonexistent. Much of the corrupt practice legislation did not cover primary elections. The 1925 act was "more loophole than law."

In 1971 Congress decided to emphasize disclosure. All political committees that anticipated receiving or spending more than $1000 on behalf of federal candidates in any year were required to register with the government; periodic reports had to be filed including full data on all major contributions and expenditures; and one person was not allowed to contribute in the name of another person. Candidates for federal office were also limited in the amounts they could spend on campaign advertising. The main thrust of the act was to throw the "pitiless light" of full publicity onto the sources and uses of political money. Its impact was limited.

In another act of 1971 Congress turned to a different strategy: subsidy tax incentives. The purpose was to draw into politics more money with no strings attached. The law provided that political donors might claim a tax credit against federal income tax for part of their contributions. The 1971 law also provided a tax checkoff that allowed taxpayers to direct $1 of general revenue to a fund to subsidize presidential campaigns.

Watergate gave a sharp push to further regulation of political money. Late in 1974, after prolonged debate, Congress passed and President Ford signed

[24]Clifford W. Brown, Jr., Roman B. Hedges, and Lynda W. Powell, "Modes of Elite Political Participation: Contributors to the 1972 Presidential Candidates," *American Journal of Political Science* (May 1980), pp. 259–90.

the most sweeping campaign reform measure in American history. The new act established more realistic limits on contributions and spending. For example, there would be a spending limit of $30 million for each presidential candidate in the general election. The act tightened disclosure, reporting, and accountability. But what made the new measure a breakthrough was a new set of provisions for public financing of presidential campaigns. Under the 1974 law:

- ☐ The Federal Election Commission appointed by the president with the consent of the Senate regulates the campaign financing of candidates for president, senator, and representative.

- ☐ All candidates must report contributions and expenditures. Originally congressional candidates were limited in personal spending, but a Supreme Court decision overturned that restriction.[25]

- ☐ Presidential candidates who wish to receive federal subsidies (most of which come out of the tax checkoff) are limited as to what they may spend. They are not required to accept federal subsidies, *but if they do:* They may spend in the preconvention stage about $15 million, half of which may be federal matching funds; and as a party nominee may spend $30 million in the general election campaign, all of it provided by the federal treasury.

- ☐ A national political party may receive a federal subsidy of $4.5 million for its national convention expenses.

- ☐ Each party may spend about $5 million in presidential and congressional elections, without federal subsidies.

- ☐ Minor parties, if they polled 5 percent of the total vote in the previous presidential election, are also eligible for subsidy, which they can receive after the current election if they poll at least 5 percent.

- ☐ Individuals and organizations can spend as much as they choose on independent activities, that is, activities not coordinated with a candidate's campaign.

- ☐ A person can give up to $1000 to a candidate in each primary and general election and no more than a total of $25,000 in all federal campaigns. Organizations can give up to $5000 per candidate per election.[26]

The Impact of Campaign Finance Laws

How has all this supervising, regulating, and subsidizing worked out? The 1974 law had a marked impact on the 1976 election. For the first time in American history, over half the cost of the presidential campaign was covered by public subsidy. The amount of private money invested in the national election dropped from $127 million in 1972 to less than half of that.[27] A number of presidential campaign committees, including that of Jimmy Carter himself, were fined by the Federal Election Commission for various violations. Carter's committee was fined $11,200 for use in campaign trips of a plane owned and operated by a Georgia bank. Reports on the 1980 presidential campaign, however, indicate that campaign spending has begun to climb again, especially through the independent expenditure loophole.[28]

Campaign finance legislation has been defended as having largely met the original goals of broadening the base of public support, reducing dependence on large donors, curtailing contributions, and equalizing the financial support of the Democratic and Republican parties. It has reduced the role of large contributors and boosted the role of small ones. Through stringent reporting requirements it has brought the whole world of political money out of the shadows and into the light of public scrutiny and debate.

YOU DECIDE

As a member of Congress who almost lost out to a heavily PAC-financed candidate in the last election, you are urged by constituents to take a bold and simple step—vote to abolish all PACs. A bill is introduced that would simply abolish all such political action committees on the grounds that through financial contributions to candidates they are gaining an excessive influence over politics and policy. How do you vote?

(Answer/Discussion on the next page.)

[25]*Buckley* v. *Valeo*, 424 U.S. 1 (1976).

[26]For an extensive discussion of recent legislation, see Herbert E. Alexander, *Financing Politics: Money, Elections and Political Reform*, 2nd ed. (Congressional Quarterly Press, 1980).

[27]Report of the Federal Election Commission, June 4, 1977, *The New York Times*, June 5, 1977, p. 25.

[28]Campaign Finance Study Group, *Financing Presidential Campaigns.*

The legislation has been roundly criticized as well. Some say it plays into the hands of rich candidates—such as Reagan, Kennedy, Bush, and Connally. These critics say big money makes a big difference, especially in the period before the primaries. Further, the act does little to curb the growing power and heavy spending of PACs (see Chapter 7). Some criticize the law for giving vast sums to candidates and relatively little—mainly for convention costs—to the national parties. Helping candidates at the expense of parties, it is said, intensifies the growing trend toward a more personalistic, fragmented, and individualistic politics. Some would favor greater subsidies to parties, until they can get on their feet and be self-supporting.

The severest criticism comes from those who supported John Anderson in the 1980 campaign, and independent candidates in general. It was bad enough, they said, that some states made it difficult for Anderson to get on the ballot. Even worse, as an independent candidate he received only a fraction of the subsidy Carter and Reagan each received. Another major criticism is that the independent expenditures loophole provides a channel for increasingly large contributions and expenditures for which there is no accountability.[29]

Many Democrats, Republicans, and independents agree also on a gaping hole in the subsidy law—its inapplicability to congressional campaigns. Money is considered a serious problem in the legislative branch, especially as the number of PACs and the amount of their contributions have skyrocketed. Although President Carter urged Congress to extend public financing to campaigns for the House and Senate, Congress has refused to "subsidize" itself. The result is that wealthier Senate and House candidates have a big advantage over poorer ones. Public financing of congressional campaigns, some argue, might help prevent the bribery that allegedly took place in the recent ABSCAM scandal.

There is skepticism that Congress ever will reform itself in this area. Members would fear that subsidies might encourage opponents to run against them, and equalize the battle of the "outs" versus the "ins." On the other hand, opposition might be discouraged because potential rivals might not accept subsidies if they also had to accept ceilings on their campaign spending—which they would have to do if they accepted public money. Some supporters of public funding of congressional races have urged that, if such a law is passed, government money be channeled to candidates through party organizations—not directly—in order to strengthen the role of the party. But most members of Congress operate quite independently of parties and would be little tempted by this proposal.

There is little doubt that PACs will continue to be the key financial contributors to congressional campaigns—and will continue to be controversial. In a "Declaration of War" on PACs, Common Cause declared that "unless we change our system for financing Congressional campaigns and change it soon, our representative system of government will be gone. We will be left with a government of, by and for the PACs." Common Cause would like to see rigid limits on PAC contributions. In response, the Mobil Corporation, in magazine ads, called PACs "truly the voice of the people—people who band together to make their electoral choices more emphatic by pooling their funds in support of one or more candidates." The alternative, Mobil said, might be public campaign financing, causing inequities and taxing voters without giving them the chance to name the candidate for whom their dollars were intended.[30]

---

[29]Xandra Kayden, "Independent Spending," in *Financing Presidential Campaigns*, pp. 7-31.

[30]See Herbert E. Alexander, "Public Financing of Congressional Campaigns," *Regulation* (January-February 1980), pp. 27–32. See, in general, Gary C. Jacobson, *Money In Congressional Elections* (Yale University Press, 1980). On the PAC controversy see *Campaign Practices Reports*, February 28, 1983, pp. 5–6; and an advertisement by Mobil, "PACs—Consider the Alternatives," *Time*, May 9, 1983, p. 4.

ANSWER/DISCUSSION

Since you "know your Constitution," you probably vote against the bill because it would threaten the right to form an association for political purposes—a right protected under the Bill of Rights. Instead, you might bring in a substitute bill—perhaps setting a limit of, say, $10,000 on the amount a PAC could contribute to any one candidate or party—without imparing the right of citizens to set up the PAC itself. But you would do so knowing that even this substitute bill might be declared unconstitutional some day by the Supreme Court.

Unsuccessful presidential candidate John Anderson had to win at least 5 percent of the popular vote in 1980 to qualify for federal campaign funds. He won 6.61 percent, but supported Walter Mondale rather than run again in 1984. *UPI.*

POLITICAL ACTION COMMITTEE CONTRIBUTIONS TO CANDIDATES

For 1981 and 1982, political action committees' receipts and contributions by them to candidates for Federal office, in millions of dollars. Ideological organizations are political action committees not connected with corporations, unions or other organizations that can legally absorb administrative costs.

Contributions to Federal Candidates

Total receipts: $64.7	
$11.1	$53.6 Ideological Organizations
Total receipts: $47.2	
$29.3	$17.9 Corporate
Total receipts: $43.2	
$22.8	$20.4 Trade Organizations (e.g. Health)
Total receipts: $37.4	
$20.8	$16.6 Labor

Source: © 1983 by The New York Times Company. Reprinted by permission.

IS THIS THE WAY TO PICK PRESIDENTS?

Concern over how we choose presidents now centers on two main issues: the rise in the number and power of presidential primaries, which now dominate the whole presidential selection process, and the continued threat that a presidential election might be thrown into Congress, with possibly dire results. While in recent years the American people have "lucked out" in the electoral college gamble, the threat remains.

Presidential Primaries: Pros and Cons

The main argument for presidential primaries is that they open up the nominating process to a larger number of voters than was previously the case. Today the media play up the primary in every important state, and voters follow the race in other states as well as their own. In doing so they can judge the candidates' political qualities—their ability to organize a campaign, to communicate through the media, to stand up under pressure, to avoid making mistakes (or to recover if they do make them), to adjust their appeals to shifting events and to different regions of the country, to control their staffs as well as to utilize them, to be decisive, articulate, resilient, informed, and ultimately successful in winning votes. In short, the primaries, it is said, test candidates on the very qualities they must exhibit in the presidency.

Reverend Jesse Jackson is shown addressing the Alabama legislature here. Jackson, the first black since reconstruction to address a joint session, was invited to speak because of his status as a potential Democratic presidential candidate. A few weeks later Jackson announced his candidacy for the Democratic nomination. *UPI.*

Presidential primaries, it is argued, are also open in another way—they are open to candidates who are rich or poor, from big states or small, or from North or South. A candidate from a small state, such as George McGovern of South Dakota, or a candidate from a southern state, such as Jimmy Carter of Georgia, now has a reasonable chance to win the big prize. Candidates with little money—and with few moneyed friends—can now run with some hope of success, in part because they can pick a limited number of states in which to "show their stuff," and in part because of federal campaign subsidies.

Finally, it is said, the primaries are not only the most participatory but also the most *representative* of methods. With millions of voters participating in nearly forty state primaries,[31] the public gets a good picture of the popular support for each candidate. As the primaries take place, some aspirants drop out, so that the number of entrants is narrowed down and the public learns who is the more popular among the remaining candidates, as in the case of Republicans Ronald Reagan and George Bush and of Democrats Jimmy Carter and Edward Kennedy. The primary results are then converted into delegate

[31]Estimate of Austin Ranney, *The New York Times*, June 8, 1980, p. E5.

votes at the presidential conventions, which in turn become more representative of party rank-and-file feeling than before.

Critics of primaries rebut these arguments and add some criticisms of their own. They grant that more voters take part in primaries than in the caucus and committee methods of choosing delegates—but they question the *quality* of the participation. For one thing, there is no chance for supporters of the different candidates to deliberate together in public. Voters in primaries, therefore, must depend largely on the news media and advertising for their information and basis for judgment. Voters in presidential primaries tend to be far more interested in candidates' personalities and media skills than in their positions on vital issues.[32]

Second, the primaries are badly scheduled and last too long. The first primary takes place in New Hampshire, a small, untypical state. Primaries in some of the larger states, such as Pennsylvania and Michigan, are held later in the spring. In 1984 California, New Jersey, and five other states did not hold their primaries until June 5—when the contests in both parties had been virtually decided, most of the people had become somewhat bored with the process, and the voters of those eight states felt rather miffed that the fight was over before they were able to participate. The length of the primary campaign exhausts the candidates and tries the patience of the voters. Victory may go to the candidates with the stronger physiques rather than the stronger brains.

The main criticism directed against primaries is that they test candidates for their ability to compete in the media "game" rather than in the qualities needed in the presidency (see Table 12–3). Granted that players in this "game" must demonstrate flexibility, resourcefulness, attractiveness, and articulateness, are these the key qualities required of a *president?* Thomas Jefferson, Abraham Lincoln, and Harry Truman were great presidents, critics say, but they would never have gained or retained their posts if they had had to pass the test of "media appeal." Critics point to Jimmy Carter as a candidate who was generally effective with the media but far less effective in governing the country. It is the gap between the qualities required to carry primary contests and qualities needed to organize an administration, get support on issues, and deal with congressional leaders, governors, and mayors that worries critics of the primary system.

Courtesy of Ben Blank.

Proposed Reforms

What would the critics substitute for state presidential primaries? Some argue in favor of the *national presidential primary.* This would take the form of a single nationwide election, probably held in May or September, or of separate

12–3 THE ELECTION AS A GAME: PERCEPTIONS OF MOST IMPORTANT ASPECT AT DIFFERENT TIMES DURING THE CAMPAIGN (PERCENT), 1976	Type of Aspect Mentioned	February	April	June	August	October
	Game	56	85	81	72	22
	Substance					
	Policy issues	24	7	9	6	10
	Campaign issues	2	3	1	1	13
	Candidate traits	3	2	2	2	3
	Subtotal	29	12	12	9	26
	Events (e.g., debates)	8	1	1	16	44
	Other	7	2	6	3	8
	Total	100	100	100	100	100
		(n = 212)	(n = 520)	(n = 585)	(n = 610)	(n = 550)

NOTE: The table is based on replies on the following question: "So far during the presidential campaign, what do you think is the most important thing that has happened?" Based on samples of voters in Erie, Pa., and Los Angeles.
SOURCE: From *The Mass Media Election* by Thomas E. Patterson. Copyright © 1980 Praeger Publishers. Reprinted by permission of Praeger Publishers.

[32]See John G. Geer, "Voting in Presidential Primaries," paper prepared for delivery at the annual meeting of the American Political Science Association, Washington, D.C., September 1984.

state primaries in all the states and all held on the same day. Supporters contend that a one-shot national presidential primary (though a runoff might be necessary) would be simple, direct, and representative; would cut down the wear and tear on candidates; and would attract a large turnout because of intensive media coverage. Opponents argue that this "reform" would make the present system even worse, would enhance the role of media showmanship and candidate gamesmanship, and would be enormously expensive and hence hurt the chances of candidates lacking strong financial backing.[33]

A more modest proposal is for *regional primaries*. These could be held at two- or three-week intervals across the country. The first regional primaries might take place in the South and then move north as the summer approached. Such a change might bring more coherence to the process, encourage more emphasis on issues of regional concern, and cut down a bit on wear and tear. But it would retain most of the disadvantages of the present system—especially the emphasis on money and media. And it might encourage regional candidates and polarization among sections of the country.

A quite different proposal is to cut down drastically on the number of state presidential primaries and make more use of the *caucus* system. The huge turnout of voters in the Iowa caucuses of 1980, it is said, demonstrates that participation can be high; and the fact that participants had to spend some hours discussing candidates and issues proves that such participation can be thoughtful and informed. In caucus states candidates are less dependent on the media and more dependent on their ability to reach political activists. The caucus system, by centering delegate selection in *party* meetings, would also enhance the role of the party.

Still another idea, used in Colorado *state* nominations since 1910, would turn the process around so that beginning in May, local caucuses and then state conventions would precede a national convention in July, which would precede a national primary in September, which would choose the party nominee to run in the November general election. In this *national preprimary convention plan*, all over the country participants in local party caucuses scheduled in early May would choose delegates to state conventions, which in turn would choose delegates to a national convention in which 25 percent of all delegates would be required to be unpledged. Deliberations at the national convention would result in the selection of two or three candidates who would appear on a September primary ballot. Voters registered by party would be allowed to vote in their respective party primary, and the winners of the primaries would be the parties' candidates in the November general election. The plan, though probably no less expensive than the present system, might provide incentives for presidential hopefuls to develop better relations with party activists in the grassroots organizations and shift the focus of the media from primary "horse races" to candidate and party substance. It would also shorten the formal campaign—at least from the voter's standpoint. And it would allow all sections of the country equal participation in the nomination of presidential candidates.[34]

Courtesy of Ben Blank.

Reforming the Electoral College

Americans have long been concerned about the nature and workings of the electoral college. Critics argue that (1) small states and large "swing" states are overrepresented; (2) the winner-take-all aspect distorts equal representation of all voters and can elect a candidate who receives fewer popular votes than an opponent; (3) electors can (and do) vote for a person other than the candidate

[33]Compare "A National Agenda for the Eighties," *Report of the President's Commission for National Agenda for the Eighties* (Washington, D.C.: Government Printing Office, 1980), p. 97, proposing only four presidential primaries, scheduled about one month apart.

[34]Thomas E. Cronin and Robert Loevy, "The Case for a National Preprimary Convention Plan," *Public Opinion* (December/January 1983), pp. 50–53.

they were pledged to vote for; (4) if no candidate wins a majority, the issue is thrown into the House of Representatives, where each state delegation, no matter how large or small, has one vote, thus distorting the representative process even more. The electoral college has been compared to the human appendix—useless, unpredictable, and possibly dangerous.

Defenders of the system say opponents exaggerate the possible dangers—the system has not broken down so far and probably never will. And if the electoral college is antipopular or antimajoritarian—so what? "The electoral college promotes unity and legitimacy by helping to generate majorities that are not narrow, geographically or ideologically, and by magnifying (as in 1960, 1968, 1976) narrow margins of victories in the popular vote," says George F. Will.[35]

The simplest and least drastic reform is to abolish the individual electors while retaining the winner-take-all method of counting the electoral vote. This proposal has never gotten very far, mainly because it does not deal with the main issue of "misrepresentation." Another reform proposal is the proportional plan, under which each candidate would receive the same proportion of the electoral vote of a state as he or she had won of its popular vote; actual electors would be abolished. Thus, a candidate who got one-third of the popular vote in a state having twelve electoral votes would win four electoral votes. Liberal Democrats fear this proposal would increase the influence of rural, small-town conservatives. Since the present system forces presidential candidates to fight especially hard for the big, urban states, many liberals feel the president must be especially responsive to the needs and hopes of working-class, black, ethnic, and lower-income groups who make up the urban electorate.

The most important and controversial reform is *direct popular election of the president.* Presidents would be elected directly by the voters just as governors are; the electoral college and individual electors would be abolished. This kind of plan usually provides that if no candidate receives at least 40 percent of the total popular vote, a runoff election would be held between the two contenders with the most votes. Supporters argue that this plan would give every voter the same weight in the presidential balloting, in accordance with the one person, one vote doctrine. Winners would take on more credibility or "legitimacy" because of their clear-cut popular victory. And, of course, the dangers and complications of the present electoral system would be replaced by a simple, visible, and decisive method. Opponents argue that the plan would require a national election system, thus further undermining federalism; that it would encourage naked, unrestrained majority rule and hence political extremism; and that the smaller states would be submerged and lose some of their present influence. Some fear also that the plan would make presidential campaigns more remote from the voters; candidates might stress television and give up their present forays into shopping centers and city malls.[36]

In 1977 President Carter recommended that Congress adopt a constitutional amendment to provide for direct popular election of the president. In July 1979 the Senate voted fifty-one to forty-eight in support of such an amendment—far short of the two-thirds vote needed. The proposal was opposed by conservatives and by liberals responsive to black and Jewish groups who feared they might lose their "swing" vote power under the present system.[37] Prospects for changing to direct election seem dim.

Courtesy of Ben Blank.

[35]George F. Will, "Don't Fool With the Electoral College," *Newsweek,* April 4, 1977, p. 96.

[36]Neal R. Peirce and Lawrence Longley, *The People's President,* 2nd ed. (Yale University Press, 1981) describes and advocates the direct-vote alternative. Nelson W. Polsby and Aaron B. Wildavsky, *Presidential Elections,* 6th ed. (Scribners, 1984) essentially favors the present system. Lawrence D. Longley and Alan G. Braun, *The Politics of Electoral College Reform* (Yale University Press, 1972) is a comprehensive treatment.

[37]Wayne, *The Road to the White House,* p. 21.

An ingenious proposal for a "national bonus plan" has been worked out by a group of scholars and politicians. Under this plan the electoral college would be retained, but it would be heavily weighted toward the winner of the popular vote. The plan would work like this: A pool of 102 electoral votes (two for each state and the District of Columbia) would automatically be granted to the candidate who gained the most popular votes, these bonus votes to be added to that candidate's electoral college vote gained in the election. He or she would be elected if these totaled a majority in the electoral college. If not, a runoff would be held between the two candidates winning the most popular votes. The position of elector would be eliminated. Proponents contend the plan would ensure that the popular vote winner would also be the electoral vote winner; that the chances of deadlock in the electoral college would be reduced; that it would encourage two-party competition in one-party states; and that it would do away with the elector who votes against the decision in his or her state. Opponents say minor parties and independent candidates would be discouraged by such a system. The plan has not enlisted much public support. Only a major electoral college crisis will bring about any significant reform.

INTERPRETING THE 1984 ELECTION—AND LOOKING TOWARD 1988

President Reagan's lopsided electoral college victory in 1984 raised key questions about American politics and government. Was this essentially a personal victory for Reagan—in which case how did he achieve it? Or was it primarily a victory for the Republican party or for conservative ideas—in which case what was its significance for the future, especially for the elections of 1988? What would these elections tell us about political movements and coalitions? About party realignment or de-alignment? About political leadership?

That Ronald Reagan had gained a huge presidential victory was clear almost as soon as the polls closed on November 6, 1984; his final margin was 53,428,357 votes, a lead of 16,497,434 over Walter Mondale. Because his strength was so uniform across the country (compare the contrasting state returns in the election map on page 200), the president carried the whole electoral college except for the District of Columbia and Mondale's own state of Minnesota. But the Republicans as a party did far less well. Democrats retained most of their governorships, held their clear majority in the House of Representatives, and gained two Senate seats. Reagan's "coattails" were short indeed.

The president won his personal victory in large part by stressing personal leadership qualities over party issues and philosophy. He countered the issues of taxation and the huge deficit, which Mondale raised early in the campaign, by attacking his opponent but offering no clear or believable program of his own. The president built a personal election coalition much broader than his party's. His coalition included, aside from stalwart Republicans and persons with high incomes (see pages 204–205), the following groups.

"Man, what an electoral score! It's as unbalanced as the budget."

Copyright © 1984 by *Herblock* in *The Washington Post*.

RELIGIOUS FUNDAMENTALISTS In 1980 the "Moral Majority," headed by the television evangelist Jerry Falwell, and other right-wing religious groups had brought great fervor and "big money" to Reagan's support. Largely satisfied with the new president's behavior in office, the "religious right" registered a host of new voters in 1984 and heavily supported Reagan over Mondale. "White born-again Christians" voted for the president by a ratio of 80 percent to 20 percent, according to a leading exit poll. They also triggered a debate over the old subject of religion-in-politics.

YOUNG VOTERS This was the surprise of the election of 1984. Voters 18 to 29 years old who had divided evenly between Carter and Reagan in 1980 split for the president by almost 3 to 2 four years later. This "constituency" gave him one of his best percentages. Why? Perhaps because this generation just plain "loves winners," columnist Ellen Goodman wrote, or because "every generation of young allies with grandpa," or—more likely, she thought—because young persons in this country are increasingly independent and liked Reagan's philosophy of individualism.[38] Others believe that youth support for Ronald Reagan came about because of Reagan's strong leadership on economic questions and in the area of military preparedness. But perhaps the student reader of this book can give a more authoritative answer! How did you and your friends vote—how *would* you have voted—for president in 1984, and why?

Walter Mondale did his best to muster the old Democratic Party coalition of union households, Catholics and Jews, and low-income voters, and to combine these with mobilized women and blacks. Despite his selection of Geraldine Ferraro as his running mate women split for Reagan 57 percent to 42 percent, almost as decisively as men (61–37). With the vital aid of Jesse Jackson the Democratic candidate won 90 percent of the black vote. Another Mondale "constituency" consisted of most of those who had voted for John Anderson in 1980. But Reagan carved into the old Democratic party coalition, winning almost half of low-income voters, over half of "blue-collar workers," over half of teachers and other government employees, and a clear majority of voters of Italian descent. The Jewish turnout, however, went for Mondale by more than two to one, as did the jobless and self-identified "liberals."

To understand which groups and kinds of people voted for Reagan and which for Mondale is important, but it does not explain why they did so. Much has been made about Reagan's personal popularity. But probably the most important factor to explain the 1984 outcome is that the economic conditions for most of the people were favorable and most people perceived the world position of the United States as improved. These conditions were probably more important than personalities or campaign tactics. No matter who the Democrats nominated or what tactics were used, it would have been unusual for an incumbent president to be turned out of office while the nation was prosperous and at peace.

A notable aspect of the election was the low voting turnout of about 53 percent. To be sure, the percentage of those voting rose three-tenths of 1 percent, reversing the steady decline in turnout over the past 20 years. But it was a disappointment in the light of high turnout expectations based on vigorous efforts of Democrats, state and local officials, poor peoples' groups and others to bring millions of new voters to the polls, and of the equally rigorous efforts of Republicans and religious fundamentalists to mobilize their own constituencies. After a two-year election campaign, tremendous media coverage, and frantic appeals by candidates and interest-group leaders, almost half the eligible voters did not show up at the polls.

What about 1988 and after? Reagan's failure to take clear positions on vital issues such as the deficit, his lame duck status, factional differences within both parties, and early jockeying of the 1988 starting line might produce guerrilla warfare in Washington, followed by perhaps the most wide-open presidential race of this century. How would the parties line up? During the 1984 campaign Reagan spoke of the "historical electoral realignment" ahead. Reagan and other conservative leaders helped produce a partial realignment, by attracting scores of conservative Democratic leaders into the "Reaganized" GOP.

[38]Ellen Goodman, "Reagan Optimism Brings Those Youthful Cheers," *The Boston Globe*, Oct. 25, 1984, p. 21.

WHY PEOPLE VOTED FOR REAGAN

"He is a strong leader"	41%
"he'd keep America prosperous"	20
"he'd keep America strong militarily"	20
"he's experienced in government"	9
"he's pro-religion"	5
"he would keep us out of war"	3

ABC election day exit poll, November 1984.

WHY REAGAN WON— ACCORDING TO THE POLITICAL ANALYSTS

Upturn in the economy

Ronald Reagan's personal appeal—"great communicator"

Ronald Reagan's image of being "tough"

Ronald Reagan's support by "moral majority" and Catholic middle class

Mondale tied too closely to "special interest"

Democratic party viewed as too much the party of minorities and the party of taxes

Analysts call the 1984 election the de-aligning election—meaning that although some Democrats are deserting their former party, they are not necessarily becoming Republicans. Partisan affiliations are becoming weaker in general. The ranks of the independents continue to grow—especially with young voters. If this trend continues in the coming years, we may become a nation of one-third Democrats, one-third Republicans, and the remaining third independents.

Still, the Democrats have lost four out of five of the last presidential elections, and they must rethink their general message. Unless they can win the middle-class vote and balance their ticket, they risk becoming a permanent minority party—at least in terms of the White House.

Will the support Reagan received in 1984 be available to his Republican successors? Much depended on the top leadership in both parties. Leadership had become the single key factor in the 1984 election, and Reagan, with his hearty optimism, his emphatic if fuzzy views, and his media appeal, had emerged looking like a "strong leader" compared with Mondale. But the president had shown little effectiveness as a *party* leader. To the rising cadre of Republican leaders he left the job of making the GOP truly the majority party in the Congress and in the states. Can they mobilize the full Republican voting potential, hold on to the rightward-looking "Baby Boomers" and "Yuppies," and continue to carve into the Democrats' old constituencies like union labor? We shall have to see.

ECONOMIC ATTITUDES AND THE REAGAN VOTE—1984

Attitudes about the Economy:	Voted for	
	Mondale	Reagan
Gotten better (41%)	81%	19%
Stayed the same (40%)	51	49
Gotten worse (19%)	27	73

Los Angeles Times exit poll, November 6, 1984.

SUMMARY

1. Candidates for the Senate and the House tend to campaign more on the basis of their personal organizations and access to the media than of party affiliation.

2. The race for the presidency actually consists of three campaigns—winning delegate support in presidential primaries and caucuses, gaining the actual party nomination at the presidential convention, and winning a majority of the electoral college.

3. Even though today presidential nominations are usually decided weeks or months before the convention, these conventions still have an important role in setting the party's direction, unifying its ranks, and adopting a platform.

4. Because large campaign contributions are suspected of improperly influencing public officials, Congress has long sought to regulate political money. Its main approaches

have been (1) limitations on receiving and spending money; (2) public disclosure of the sources and uses of political money; and (3) government subsidy of candidates, campaigns, and parties. Present regulation includes all three approaches.

5. The electoral college lends extra influence to the small and very large states. It could also throw a presidential election into the House of Representatives, where the influence of small states would be enhanced.

6. The present presidential selection system is under heavy criticism because of its length and expense and because it seems to test candidates for qualities that are less needed in the White House than certain others, such as the ability to govern. In short, many accuse our present system of failing to recruit presidential *leadership*.

FURTHER READING

WALTER DEAN BURNHAM. *Critical Elections and the Mainsprings of American Politics* (Norton, 1970).

JAMES CEASER. *Presidential Selection: Theory and Development* (Princeton University Press, 1979).

JAMES W. DAVIS. *Presidential Primaries*, rev.ed. (Greenwood Press, 1984).

BARBARA HINCKLEY. *Congressional Elections* (Congressional Quarterly Press, 1981).

GARY C. JACOBSON. *The Politics of Congressional Elections* (Little, Brown, 1983).

STANLEY KELLEY, JR. *Interpreting Elections* (Princeton University Press, 1983).

NEAL PEIRCE and LAWRENCE LONGLEY. *The People's President: The Electoral College in American History and the Direct-Vote Alternative* (Yale University Press, 1981).

LARRY J. SABATO. *The Rise of Political Consultants* (Basic Books, 1981).

THE AMERICAN POLITICIAN: LEADER OR BROKER?

13

Americans seem to have a love-hate attitude toward politicians. While we yearn for leadership, we also want to be left alone. Further, we suspect politicians of being ambitious, conniving, unprincipled, opportunistic, and even corrupt—"just into politics for what they can get out of it for themselves." Not long ago a board game similar to *Monopoly* was invented and marketed with the cynical title, *Lie, Cheat and Steal: The Game of Political Power*.

Newspaper cartoonists and television comedians mercilessly caricature politicians as unscrupulous and manipulative, or as naive and confused. Public opinion surveys report that at least one in three Americans rates politicians low or very low on honesty and ethical standards (see Table 13-1). Even politicians themselves often hold their profession in low esteem. A New York county chairman, after spending a lifetime in local and state politics, calls politics a "snakepit and a cesspool." Politics may be the only profession whose practitioners invoke the name of their profession as a term of derision. "You're just a politician!" Or "that's political!" one will shout at another. It is as if a gathering of doctors accused one another with shouts of "Medical! Medical!"

Yet we often find individual officeholders to be responsive, bright, hardworking, and friendly (even though we may suspect they are simply trying to get out the vote). And our liking often turns to reverence after these same politicians depart or die. Surely Washington, Lincoln, Eisenhower, and John F. Kennedy are widely acclaimed today. Harry Truman liked to say that a statesman is merely a politician who has been dead for about ten years. The past few years have witnessed several ceremonies marking the birthdays or deaths of notable American leaders: Franklin Roosevelt, Dwight Eisenhower, Martin Luther King Jr., Harry Truman, and John Kennedy, to mention just a few. We wonder: Will our politicians today be remembered as true leaders?

HONESTY AND ETHICAL STANDARDS—VARIOUS OCCUPATIONS

Percentages	High	Avg.	Low	No Opinion
Clergy	64%	27%	5%	4%
Pharmacists	61	33	4	2
Doctors	53	35	10	2
Dentists	51	41	5	3
College teachers	47	38	5	10
Engineers	46	39	3	12
Police	42	45	11	2
Bankers	38	49	9	4
TV reporters	33	47	15	5
Funeral directors	29	43	19	9
Newspaper reporters	26	52	16	6
Lawyers	24	43	27	6
Stockbrokers	19	45	11	25
Business executives	18	55	20	7
U.S. Senators	17	48	29	6
Building contractors	17	54	23	6
Local officeholders	16	49	29	6
U.S. Representatives	14	43	38	5
Realtors	13	52	28	7
State officeholders	13	49	31	7
Insurance sellers	13	49	34	4
Union leaders	12	35	44	9
Advertising people	8	43	39	10
Car salespeople	6	34	55	5

Source: Gallup Poll, August 1983. Question asked: "How would you rate the honesty and ethical standards of people in these different fields . . .?"

Of course, we must put the problem in perspective. In all democracies (and perhaps even more in democracies) the public may expect too much from politicians. Further, people naturally dislike those who wield power. Public officeholders, after all, tax us, regulate us and conscript us. We dislike political compromisers, bargainers, and ambitious opportunists—even though we may need such people to get things done.

Yet Americans seem to have a particular contempt for politicians.[1] Viewing ourselves as self-reliant and ruggedly individualistic, we mistrust their power. Like Thomas Paine, some of us view government and politics as "a badge of innocence lost." Moreover, demanding quick remedies, we have little patience with politicians who endlessly squabble and delay. Yet at the same time, being idealistic and even moralistic, we deplore the give-and-take, the wheeling and dealing, the sacrifice of principle (or at least campaign promises), and the influence of money.

Some Americans suspect that the opportunity to become a leader is unfairly restricted to a chosen few—that the rich have a big advantage, as do white Anglo-Saxon Protestants (WASPs), and that women and minorities do not have an equal opportunity to enter electoral politics and win office. Where, they ask, is the equivalent of "from rags to riches" in politics?

Since our attitude toward politicians may be described as somewhat confused, it may be helpful here to look at the "opportunity structure" in American politics—at the type of persons entering politics, the ideas that dominate our approach to leadership and politics, and the structural arrangements of our political system.

[1]This is not just a post-Watergate view. For an especially harsh treatment of American politicians after the Civil War, see Henry Adams, *Democracy: An American Novel* (Airmont Publishing Co., 1968).

HOW TO BECOME A STATESMAN—
OR AT LEAST A POLITICIAN

YOU DECIDE !

Please finish the following sentences. The typical American politician is _____

_____

_____

The ideal American politician is

_____

_____

_____

(Answer/Discussion on the next page.)

Many Americans have effectively been denied the chance to run for office in our political system, just as many Americans have been denied the vote (and the two facts are related). Yet to millions of other Americans, the system has been accessible. This was notably true of the immigrants who arrived late in the last century and early in this one. Arriving in this country bright with hope but often poor in worldly goods, eager to live in a free society but often uneducated and even illiterate, aspiring to be good citizens but often unable even to speak the language, the newcomers were sometimes greeted "at the dock" by politicians, party bosses, religious leaders, and charity officers, who helped them make a new start in the new land. To be sure, the politicians wanted their votes and the church officials their religious affiliation, but the result was to help integrate these immigrants into American politics and culture. Such political outreach efforts have decreased somewhat with more recent waves of immigrants.

The big-city party bosses in the Northeast were often immigrants themselves or were the sons of immigrants, and they knew how to extend a helping hand. They also learned to advance their own interests as well as those of their followers. Born in a shantytown called Nanny Goat Hill on New York City's upper west side, Boss Plunkitt of Tammany Hall—the famous "bootblack stand pundit"—received little schooling and had nothing but contempt for young people who thought they could learn about politics from books.

No, said Plunkitt, the best way to succeed was the way he himself had used to become district leader, "and so on up and up till I became a statesman." Did he offer his services as stump speaker to the then district leader? "Not much. The woods are always full of speakers. Did I get up a book on municipal government and show it to the leader? I wasn't such a fool. What I did was to get some marketable goods before goin' to the leaders." By "marketable goods," Plunkitt meant a group of young men he had personally organized, called—naturally—the "George Washington Plunkitt Association." His plan was to auction off himself and his followers to the highest bidders in Tammany. "You ought to have seen how I was courted and petted then by the

13–2
CONFIDENCE IN GOVERNMENT AND POLITICIANS, 1964–1982

QUESTION: I DON'T THINK PUBLIC OFFICIALS CARE MUCH WHAT PEOPLE LIKE ME THINK.

	1964	1968	1972	1976	1980	1982
Agree	35%	43%	49%	51%	52%	46%
Disagree	62	55	49	44	44	49
Don't know	2	2	2	4	4	5

QUESTION: WOULD YOU SAY THE GOVERNMENT IS PRETTY MUCH RUN BY A FEW BIG INTERESTS LOOKING OUT FOR THEMSELVES OR THAT IT IS RUN FOR THE BENEFIT OF ALL PEOPLE?

	1964	1968	1972	1976	1980	1982
Few big interests	29%	40%	53%	66%	69%	61%
Benefit of all	64	51	38	24	21	29
Don't know	8	9	9	10	10	10

Source: Surveys by the University of Michigan, Institute for Social Research, *Public Opinion*, June/July 1983, p. 17.

leaders of the rival organizations"—and offered jobs for himself and his henchmen.[2]

The Structure of Opportunity

To Plunkitt the system was wide open; but to others in New York at that time—a black man or woman, for example—the system often was closed. But there are factors other than race or sex that may open a political system to people's ambitions, or close it off. These factors constitute an elaborate system—*a structure of opportunity*. Three major structures stand between being potential leaders and becoming elected leaders.[3]

Social opportunity is based primarily on race and sex, with advantages going to white males; religion has played a role in the past, with Protestants being favored. *Party* opportunity is the advantage candidates receive by running in the dominant party. Obviously, a Republican candidate has a better chance in a Republican district—but he or she may have a tougher fight for the party nomination. *Office* opportunity is based on the number of elective positions on the ballot, the length of terms, and eligibility to run again for the same office. Aspiring politicians watch these office openings and "closures" carefully, as leaders move on through their office "boxes" in a vast game of political checkers.

A dramatic and tragic example of closure has been the long-time exclusion of blacks from Congress. During Reconstruction two black senators were sent to Washington from the South—both from Mississippi—along with twenty-four black congressmen, but this was a result of northern-enforced election regulation. After Reconstruction black representation in Congress slowly declined, and from 1900 to 1928 not a single black was elected to Congress from any part of the country. Starting in 1928 blacks began to be elected from the urban areas of the North, and their number grew steadily but slowly during the 1950s, 1960s, and 1970s. But it was not until Andrew Young won a congressional seat from Atlanta that a southern black again entered Congress—the first in seventy-two years.[4]

Our political system was also closed to women, who lacked even the right to vote until about 1920. But more recently black and women's political movements as well as Hispanics have begun to chip away at the social opportunity structure that has so overtly favored white males. After 1960 blacks and women in growing numbers began to seek and gain public office at local and state levels as well as in the United States Congress, as noted in Chapter 5. The more elected at the state and local levels, the larger the recruitment pool for national

ANSWER/DISCUSSION

In the past few years we have surveyed several hundred people of all ages on these questions. Plainly, a gap exists between our view of politicians in general and what we would like to see. The following are the responses we have been getting to these questions.

The typical American politician is: ambitious, power hungry, on an ego trip, outgoing, personable, glib/talkative, superficial, evasive, self-serving, an opportunist, preoccupied with getting reelected, promises too much, "male, middle-aged, and usually a lawyer."

The ideal American politician is: compassionate, sensitive to the needs of others, well-informed/competent, fair-minded, objective, intellectually honest, a good listener, candid, "a candidate of the people, not of the money," "does the job and gets out when finished," a good mediator, self-confident and has the ability to inspire others.

---

[2]William L. Riordon, *Plunkitt of Tammany Hall* (Dutton, 1963), pp. 7–9.

[3]Joseph A. Schlesinger, *Ambition and Politics: Political Careers in the United States* (Rand McNally, 1966).

[4]Lucius J. Barker and Jesse J. McCorry, Jr., *Black Americans and the Political System* (Winthrop Publishers, 1976), pp. 270–73.

Kentucky Governor Martha Layne Collins (right) shown here with former Governor John V. Brown and his wife Phyliss George Brown (left), was elected governor of Kentucky in late 1983. She became the first woman governor of that state. *UPI.*

office.[5] By 1984 there were about 5000 black elected officials (or about 1 percent of all elected officials in the United States.)[6]

A major obstacle for female candidates is lack of access to campaign funds. This is related to occupational status; female candidates are more likely to have been housewives or to have held certain sex-segregated jobs, such as secretary, elementary and secondary school teacher, nurse, and social worker. They are more likely to have gained their preelective political experience in community organizations and political parties.[7] Men are more likely to come into political leadership positions from law and business. As more women enter law and attend business schools, there will be more female leaders from these occupational groups.[8]

Today the "opportunity" shoe is occasionally on the other foot—politicians may court active minorities and their leaders instead of excluding them. Harold Washington, 1983 candidate for Chicago mayor and a black, appealed to Hispanics and won more than half their vote. Ronald Reagan campaigned actively for Hispanic support throughout Sunbelt states. Thus, he flew to San Antonio, which had its first Hispanic mayor, to celebrate a Hispanic festival; and he appointed a Hispanic attorney to a federal district court judgeship in Texas. Reagan also spoke to several national Hispanic conventions. Texas, Florida, and California have large Hispanic populations as well as big blocks of presidential electoral votes—a fact well appreciated by all aspirants to the White House. Still, two things need to be remembered: Politically active minorities are usually only a small percentage of the minority population as a whole; and being courted by those already in power does not necessarily give minorities the opportunity to share in that power.

RUNNING FOR OFFICE—AND LOSING: A DIALOGUE

White male Anglo-Saxon candidates may have their troubles with the opportunity structure too—especially if they run in areas dominated by the other party. Two of the authors of this book had this experience when they ran for Congress: Burns in 1958 in Massachusetts, and Cronin in 1982 in Colorado—both as Democrats. They were questioned by the third author, Peltason, during the writing of this chapter.[9]

Peltason: Why did you decide to run when the party voting patterns in your districts were so much against you?

Burns: The very fact that the congressional district was so Republican and there was a veteran Republican incumbent, made it more attractive to me to run because no other Democrat probably would run under such circum-

[5]Marilyn Johnson and Susan Carroll, *Profile of Women Holding Office II* (Center for the American Woman and Politics, 1978).

[6]Adapted from Eddie N. Williams, "Black Political Progress in the 1970s: The Electoral Arena," in Michael B. Preston, Lenneal J. Henderson, Jr., and Paul Puryear (eds.), *The New Black Politics: The Search for Political Power* (Longman, 1982), pp. 76, 78, 98.

[7]Ruth Mandel, *In the Running: The New Woman Candidate* (Ticknor and Fields, 1981).

[8]See also Susan Welch and Lee Sigelman, "Changes in Public Attitudes Toward Women in Politics," *Social Science Quarterly* (June 1982), pp. 312–22.

[9]For a more systematic treatment of unsuccessful campaigns for Congress, see Robert J. Huckshorn and Robert C. Spencer, *The Politics of Defeat* (University of Massachusetts Press, 1971). See also Louis Sandy Maisel, *From Obscurity to Oblivion: Running in the Congressional Primary* (University of Tennessee Press, 1982).

stances. Hence, I would not have a primary fight and would have a clean shot at taking on the incumbent. What happened, however, was that the incumbent dropped out, other opposition in both parties came in, and I had a very divisive primary fight after all. I believed I could have done very well in a one-on-one race against the aging Republican. Instead, I had to run against Democrats first, and then against a popular young Republican state senator.

Cronin: While the district I ran in had a decided Republican edge over Democrats, it actually had a plurality of independents. And I was guided, in part, by the old political saying: "If you run, you may lose. But if you don't run, you're guaranteed to lose!" I was motivated to run in large part because I disagreed with so many of the votes and policy views of the man I sought to defeat.

Peltason: It is often said that "money is the mother's milk of politics." Did you find money to be as important in a congressional race as many people say?

Cronin: There is an old joke in politics that it takes three things to win in politics: "Money, money, and money." There is some truth to this—especially in federal elections. Obviously, you need many other things too—a strong candidate, good party organization, plenty of volunteers, and so on. But money buys television and radio ads, and they are crucial to gaining name recognition and credibility. Money can also be used to purchase many of the elements of a good campaign organization: media advisors, a direct mail operation, an effective voter registration drive, useful polling, and so on. I raised almost $180,000 in four months. But my incumbent opponent raised twice that over a two-year period. A successful challenger has to raise somewhere near what an incumbent raises.

Burns: Money was not nearly so important in my race as it evidently was in Tom's. I could have spent about twice as much as I did—the campaign cost about forty or fifty thousand dollars—and I expect I would not have increased my vote more than 1 or 2 percentage points above the 45 percent I received. Perhaps the difference in Tom's and my situation reflects what has happened in American politics during the past twenty years.

Peltason: They say that nothing succeeds like success, and nothing teaches like defeat. What did you learn from your congressional bids?

Burns: The unpredictability of campaigning, that is, not knowing for sure who your opponent may be, the difficulty of planning strategy, and all the sudden crises and unforeseen events that can happen in a hard-fought contest. You have to learn to be ready for anything. I also learned what it's like to "run on the long ballot."

Peltason: What do you mean by that?

Burns: I was one of about sixty candidates running in the various primaries for all offices, and later one of twenty or so Democratic or Republican party nominees running for United States senator, state senator, state representative, district attorney, county offices, etc., etc., as well as for Congress. Toward the end it was awfully hard to get my message through when so many candidates were speaking out. My "priceless prose" often got cut down to one paragraph in the local newspaper!

Cronin: Well, I learned that coming in second is not that much fun. But I am glad I ran. It's an enormous "head-over-heels" learning experience. You learn a lot about yourself, a lot about people, and you learn to appreciate both the diversity of this country's problems and some of the possible remedies. I was struck by how many people might complain at

WHY PEOPLE RUN FOR POLITICAL OFFICE

To solve problems and promote the "American Dream"—enhancing liberty and justice

To advance fresh ideas and approaches

To "throw some rascal out" whose views you dislike

To gain a voice in policy making

To serve as a party spokesperson

To acquire political influence and a platform from which to influence public opinion

To gain prominence and power

To satisfy ego needs

To gain the opportunity to learn, grow, travel, and meet all kinds of people

To join in the "game of politics"—campaigning, debating, drafting laws, reconciling diverse views, and making the system responsive

To be where the "action is"—involved in the thick of government and political life

first about some aspect of government. Nearly everybody has a pet peeve or gripe. And yet if you have the chance to chat awhile, most of these same people become reasonable about what can be done and about what is best for the country. I came away with an optimism about the degree to which people want to solve our mutual problems and want to make government work and even are willing to make needed sacrifices for their country—so long as others are willing to do so too.

Peltason: Boss Plunkitt said that you can't win in politics by reading books and all that "college rot." Did your earlier work in political science help you in your campaign?

Cronin: Training in political science and in economics is helpful. But there is no substitute for experience gained by being active in community organizations and in grassroots party activities. Business and public speaking experience is also invaluable. Above all else, you've got to like and enjoy people. And have a sense of humor. It helps too to have thick skin.

Burns: At the time I ran, scholars were finding evidence that the media has less direct impact on voters than it has indirect effects through local or neighborhood leaders—the barber, the PTA head, the shop steward in a factory, the bartender, or someone else you know and trust. These persons in a sense reinterpret the message of the media in their face-to-face contacts with the voters. I tried to use this insight. Since I could not possibly do much door-to-door canvassing in a district of several hundred thousand voters, I had my young volunteers collect hundreds of names of shop stewards, PTA members, officers of veterans' groups and other societies, then organize the names on a geographical basis, plot out their locations on a street map, and then drive me during a morning to these "key activists" so I could meet them in their homes. This way I could really talk with them, and also plan a continuous follow-up of letters to them and campaign material until election day.

Peltason: Did it work?

Burns: I don't know! That's the trouble with campaigning (and political science!)—there are so many variables, you don't know what worked and what didn't.

Peltason: What was the biggest miscalculation or disappointment in your campaign?

Cronin: We began too late. Fundraising and recruitment of key campaign aides have to be done several months in advance of an effective fall campaign. We had plenty of enthusiasm, hundreds of volunteers, and ample excitement—but I underestimated the time and effort needed to build the foundation for a well-managed and adequately financed campaign. Ours was what we called "trickle-up politics"—but as in many other losing efforts, it was too little, too late and not effectively enough managed.

Burns: My biggest disappointment was in the non-"coattail" vote. I was a Democrat in Massachusetts on the same ticket as John F. Kennedy, who was running again for senator. He was, of course, very popular and drew big crowds and a big vote. Since I too was running for a seat in the national legislature, I hoped I would pick up some extra support by campaigning with Kennedy as much as possible. The voters showed they knew how to split their tickets.

My biggest miscalculation was a kind of calculated risk. I ran mainly on economic issues, because the "Eisenhower recession" was still on, and the whole textile industry in western Massachusetts was disappearing before our eyes. Even my billboards proclaimed "JOBS, HOMES,

---

WHY PEOPLE SHY
AWAY FROM RUNNING
FOR PUBLIC OFFICE

Loss of privacy for you and your family

Less time to spend with families or favorite pastimes

Less income than in many business or professional occupations

Exposure to partisan and media criticism

Campaigning involves many things most people would rather not do—like marching in countless parades, attending county fairs, going to endless political dinners, banquets, service club meetings, and so on

The image of politics is not high

Rewards of serving in office appear meager

Fear that one may have to compromise one's principles because of the complexity of our adversarial system

Campaigning can often be very expensive

Some people don't want to show their ambitions, and they don't like conflict and divisiveness

Some people think the constitutional structure and the party systems we now have make it nearly impossible to exercise meaningful leadership

SCHOOLS." But it was like the 1983 general election in Britain—many of the poor and even the jobless did not vote for me. I felt I might really be able to help the local economic situation if I went to Washington. We now have virtually no textile industry left in western Massachusetts.

It's a reminder that behind all the oratory and propaganda, politics can be pretty important!

WHAT KIND OF LEADERSHIP?

Can we generalize about the leadership abilities of those who are elected today? While the concept of leadership—like many other concepts in political science—is broad and hazy, we can break it down into meaningful types, distinguishing among *agitators*, *coalition builders*, and *officeholders*.

Types of Leaders   Agitators or people who often start movements, as noted in Chapter 8, arouse people's consciousness of their needs and problems, raise their hopes and expectations, organize or take leadership of movements, and mobilize grassroots pressure on government from the outside. Movement leaders are often considered crusaders or even prophets, whether they be abolitionists, women's suffrage leaders, anti-slavery leaders such as William Lloyd Garrison, or conservatives such as California's crusading tax cutter Howard Jarvis.[10]

Coalition builders are usually intent on winning elections, while movement founders are more concerned with mobilizing groups of people who may or may not take part in elections. (Women for decades had to work *outside* the electoral process in order to influence men to let them *into* that process.) Coalition builders must knit together a variety of groups and movements in order to build a majority that can carry elections. Hence, such leaders tend to be brokers, widening their political appeals as broadly as possible without becoming *too* thin or flabby, accommodating single-interest or single-cause groups or movements with intense concerns, and building compromise party platforms.

Officeholders are in a mixed position to exercise leadership—they have the authority that goes with their office, but they must try not to alienate elements of the electoral majority they will need at the next election. They dare not be too far in advance of their times. Their behavior under these circumstances may be closely affected by the political system. Thus, presidents may wish not to worry about their electoral majority until the last year of their term, but they have to consider the midterm elections for senators and representatives. The latter have to think about winning the next election in a year or two; thus, most almost constantly refurbish their electoral majority. Senators, with their six-year tenures, can think in somewhat longer terms.

The relationship between John F. Kennedy and Martin Luther King Jr. exemplifies these three types of leaders. While Kennedy raised civil rights issues during his campaign for the presidency in 1960, these were never accorded top priority in his program; rather, Kennedy held off making major civil rights proposals until he could get his economic program through Congress. In the meantime King and other black leaders were protesting, demonstrating, encountering violence, appealing to northern and southern public opinion, and putting intense pressure on Kennedy and other federal officials to protect their civil rights and especially to put through legislation that would protect their

MARTIN LUTHER KING, JR. OBSERVATIONS ON JOHN F. KENNEDY

"The basic thing about him—he had the ability to respond to creative pressure.

"I never wanted—and I told him this—to be in the position that I couldn't criticize him if I thought he was wrong.

"And Kennedy said, 'it often helps me to be pushed.'

"When he saw the power of the movement, he didn't stand there arguing about it. He had the vision and wisdom to see the problem in all of its dimensions and the courage to do something about it."

From T. George Harris, "The Competent American," *Look*, November 17, 1964.

[10]See, for example, Charles Madison, *Critics and Crusaders* (Holt, 1947); Saul Alinsky, *Rules for Radicals* (Random House, 1972); and Harvey Goldberg (ed.), *American Radicals: Some Problems and Personalities* (Monthly Review Press, 1957). On Howard Jarvis see Jarvis, *Mad As Hell!* (Times Books, 1979). See also Edward N. Kearney, *Mavericks in American Politics* (MIMIR Publishers, 1976).

right to vote. As a result of this kind of *movement* pressure, Kennedy by 1963 was appealing to Congress for civil rights legislation, working closely with King and other civil rights leaders through his brother Robert, the attorney general, and at the same time trying to maintain old-time Democratic party coalitions of northerners and white southerners. Movement leaders and coalition-builders like King put pressure on the government from the outside—while also working with the White House from the inside—and after JFK's assassination, office holders like President Lyndon B. Johnson together with congressional leaders built a broad coalition of blacks, liberals, and moderate whites that helped to put the Civil Rights Act of 1964 and the Voting Rights Act of 1965 into law.[11]

Politicians as Brokers

Two of America's effective politicians, President Eisenhower and his successor, John F. Kennedy, shown in high hats as they leave the White House for the Capitol where Kennedy was to take his oath of office on January 20, 1961. *UPI.*

Most American politicians hardly aspire to such grand leadership roles as movement founders or coalition builders. They work at the grass roots as city council members, sheriffs, state legislators, district attorneys, and county commissioners. As such they are popular targets for cartoonists and others who picture the politicians as ridiculous, confused, and addled—and above all as ignorant and incompetent. Most of these portraits, especially the last two, are caricatures. Talk to the average politician in office and you will find an alert, shrewd, calculating mind. Elected politicians, after all, have had to run a tough race, winning more votes than the opposition; and this is no easy feat.

The most serious charge leveled against American politicians is that they are mere horse-traders, bargainers, adjusters—in short, brokers. These "wheeler-dealers" are pictured as lacking strong convictions of their own, as opportunists willing to sell out to the highest bidder in money or votes, and as political entrepreneurs looking for the best deal. For most American officeholders, on the local as well as on the national level, this indictment is exaggerated—yet a kernel of truth remains. Politicians *have* to be brokers in order to make the system work. For the American political system has so much built-in conflict, is so adversarial in nature, is designed to have so many representatives of competing or warring constituencies, and has so many checks and balances that compromise and adjustment and "smoothing-over" is needed to get anything done. In short, politicians are needed to grease the rusty, creaking, clashing wheels and gears—and they sometimes look "greasy" after doing their jobs. The politician works out the acceptable compromise, and compromise is the heart of democratic politics. The principle of compromise is to democracy what imagination is to poetry, what precision is to physics, what empathy and compassion are to preaching.

THINKING ABOUT LEADERSHIP

It used to be said that leaders are born and not made—but the opposite is more likely to be true: Most leaders have learned their leadership ability. People can be trained for specific leadership positions, such as commanding an infantry company or quarterbacking a football team; but the more people are trained for specialized responsibilities, the less adaptable they may be to more general positions. Many a crack business leader, for example, has come to Washington to take over a major federal post or has been elected a member of the United States Senate—only to discover that leadership in government and politics calls for very different skills, styles, and qualities than those found most effective in business.

[11]See Herbert S. Parmet, *The Presidency of John F. Kennedy* (Dial Press, 1983). See also Stephen B. Oates, *Let the Trumpets Sound! The Life of Martin Luther King, Jr.* (Harper & Row, 1982); and Harris Wofford, *Of Kennedys & Kings* (Farrar, Straus & Giroux, 1980).

"We not only lack leadership. We also need someone to tell us what to do." © 1979 Universal Press Syndicate.

WHAT ARE THE MOST IMPORTANT QUALITIES OF A LEADER?

No one knows—so much depends on the context, the challenge, and the need. Still, the following qualities or skills are often cited as critically important. (But none of these guarantees leadership effectiveness.)

Self-knowledge

Self-confidence

Optimism/hope

Sensitivity/empathy

Stamina/energy

Tenacity/persistence

Integrity

Vision

Risk taking

Morale building

Coalition building

Negotiating/mediating

Communicating

Breadth/creativity

Sense of humor

Enjoying people

One of the most universal cravings of our time is a hunger for creative and compelling leadership (but defining creative leadership is a challenge in itself). A cartoon appeared in *The Wall Street Journal* showing two people talking about leadership. Finally, one said to the other: "We not only lack leadership. We also need someone to tell us what to do." Obviously, leadership is often a hazy, elusive abstraction.

Leadership can be understood only in the context of both leaders and followers—for a leader without followers is a contradiction in terms. Leadership is also situational and contextual. A person is often effective in only one kind of situation. Leadership is not necessarily transferable. Thus, James Madison was a brilliant political and constitutional theorist. He was also a superb founding politician. Still, he was not a particularly able presidential leader. The leadership required to lead a marine platoon up a hill in battle is different from the leadership needed to change racist, sexist attitudes in city or community governments. The leadership required of a campaign manager differs from that required of a candidate. Leaders of thought are not always effective as leaders of action.

While leaders are often skilled managers, they often have to have more than just managerial skills. Managers do things *the right way*, while leaders are more concerned, or perhaps more preoccupied, with doing *the right thing*—that is, they are more concerned with the longer range, with the purposes and ends of a society or an organization. Put another way, managers are concerned with efficiency, with keeping things going, especially as regards routines and standard operating procedures. Leaders, on the other hand—in addition to having certain managerial skills—also are inventors, risk takers, and entrepreneurs. Further, they are morale builders and can infuse values and purpose into the mission of their community or nation.

Leaders have those indispensable qualities of contagious self-confidence, unwarranted optimism, and incurable idealism that attract others, mobilizing them to undertake tasks they never dreamed they could accomplish. In short, transcending or transformational leaders empower others, enabling many of their followers to become leaders in their own right. Most of the significant breakthroughs in our nation (as well as in our communities) have been made (or shaped) by people who, while seeing all the complexities and obstacles ahead of them, believed in themselves and in their purposes so much that they refused to be overwhelmed and paralyzed by self-doubts. They were willing to gamble, to take risks, to look at things in a fresh way, and often to invent new rules.

Leaders must recognize the fundamental—unexpressed as well as felt—wants and needs of potential followers, bring followers to a fuller consciousness of their needs, and help convert the resulting hopes and aspirations into practical demands on other leaders (especially leaders in government). Leaders also must sense when people are ready for action. A leader in a democracy consults and listens while educating followers and attempting to renew the goals of an organization. Civic leaders often emerge when we are able to agree upon goals. Thus, if we are to have the leaders we need, we will first have to agree upon the course we wish to follow and the purposes we wish to achieve. In a sense, if we are to discover leaders to follow, we will often have to show them the way.

Leaders must also be ever-sensitive to the distinctions between *power* and *authority*. Power is the strength or raw force to exercise control or coerce someone to do something. Authority is power that is accepted as legitimate by subordinates or constituents. The whole issue of leadership raises countless questions about participation in and acceptance of power in superior-subordinate, or leader-led, relationships. How much participation is needed, or is desirable?

What is the impact of participation on effectiveness? How best can leaders earn and sustain moral and social acceptance for their authority? Americans generally prize participation in all kinds of organizations, most especially in civic and political life. Yet a part of us yearns for charismatic leaders—decisive, attractive leaders who will simplify problems and relieve us of the burdens of leadership. Ironically, however, savior figures and charismatic leaders often—indeed almost always—create distance, not participation.

Effective political leaders have practical leadership *skills* and often distinctive political *styles*. By skill, we mean the capacity to do something well. Most leaders need to have *technical skills*—the ability to speak well, write well, and negotiate; *human relations skills*—the capacity to supervise, inspire, and build coalitions; and *conceptual skills*—the ability to learn quickly, plan, seek advice, and forge grand strategy. However, skills alone can not ensure leadership success.

A politician's style may also be critical to leadership effectiveness. Style refers to how a person relates to people, to tasks, and to challenges. A style may be democratic or autocratic, centralizing or decentralizing, empathetic or detached, extroverted or introverted, assertive or passive, and so on. Different styles may or may not work equally well in different situations. A person's *behavioral style* refers to one's way of relating to other people—to peers, rivals, subordinates, bosses, advisers, the press, and so on. A person's *psychological style* is how one handles stress, tensions, challenges to the ego, and conflict. Political science and the field of leadership and organizational studies are just beginning to learn the consequences for leadership of differing skills and styles as well as personality differences.[12]

Ultimately there are two overriding kinds of political leadership: *transactional leadership* and *transformational leadership*. The transactional leader engages in an exchange, usually a short-term bargain—as in a *quid* for a *quo*. "I'll vote for your bill if you vote for mine." Or "You raise money for my campaign and I'll help get your daughter a state job after I'm elected." Most political officeholders practice transactional leadership as a practical necessity. It is the common means of doing business. The transforming leader is the person who, as we discussed above, so engages with followers as to bring them to heightened political consciousness and activity, and in the process converts many of these followers into leaders in their own right.[13]

The transforming leader is usually preoccupied with the longer term and is, as a rule, less interested in selfish gains than in community or societal improvements. The transforming leader is also in many ways an educator or teacher—pointing out the possibilities and the hopes and dreams of a people. Is it possible for most elected political officials to exercise transforming leadership? Does transforming leadership require a special set of circumstances, or a special set of personal qualities, or possibly certain kinds of constitutional and structural arrangements? We shall turn to these questions in the remaining sections of this chapter.

One of the few photographs that show four Presidents of the United States in one sitting. From the left, John F. Kennedy, Lyndon B. Johnson, Dwight D. Eisenhower, and Harry S Truman. *UPI.*

POLITICIANS AS ACT III LEADERS (OR BROKERS)

One reason we are often so skeptical or even cynical toward politicians is that we fail to appreciate the importance of politics and the limits or constraints within which politicians must work. Officeholding politicians are in many ways

[12]See, for example, the study by James David Barber, *Presidential Character*, rev. ed. (Prentice-Hall, 1977); and Margaret Hermann (ed.), *A Psychological Examination of Political Leaders* (Free Press, 1977).

[13]These distinctions are outlined in detail in James MacGregor Burns, *Leadership* (Harper & Row, 1978), chaps. 1 and 2.

Act III leaders. Most plays have three acts. In politics, different tasks or different periods often seem to require different kinds of political leaders.

Act I leaders are the *crowd gatherers* or *agitators*. They stir things up and thus are often viewed as cranks and troublemakers—Patrick Henry, Sam Adams, and Tom Paine, for example. Also in this category are John Brown (in the pre-Civil War days), Rap Brown (in the early civil rights protests of the 1960s), and Saul Alinsky (in urban protests).

Act II leaders are *coalition builders*. Often unelected and even unelectable, they galvanize movements and coalitions in such a way that politicians heed their message. Martin Luther King Jr., Susan B. Anthony, and the leaders of the contemporary balanced-budget amendment and nuclear freeze movements are illustrative.

Act III leaders typically are *the elected officials*. Some have highly publicized and sometimes even glamorous careers; but theirs are also often the hardest, least secure, and least rewarding careers. They have to be risk takers, ambitious, and willing to assume a frantic lifestyle. Yet they also have to be brokers, ever-sensitive to the policy views of pluralities and majorities. As elected representatives they cannot be too innovative. They usually have to be balancers and bargainers, trying to reconcile competing claims of what is in "the public interest." Act III types have to follow public opinion as well as mold or shape it. They are usually more constrained than other kinds of political leaders, and they are also dependent on Act I and II leaders for fresh ideas and novel approaches to public problems.

Carl Sandburg, one of America's legendary poets, once wrote:

Who shall speak for the people?
Who has the answers?
Where is the sure interpreter?
Who knows what to say?[14]

Saul Alinsky (right), who organized the poor and dispossessed for more than 20 years before he turned his attention to the middle class a few years ago, shakes hands with Black power advocate Stokely Carmichael after both shared the same platform in Detroit on January 18, 1967. *UPI.*

Our elected officials are bold enough to step forward in the midst of endless controversies and give it a try. This requires ambition—a trait often not much admired. Politicians are pretty much self-selected. Ambition, however, lies at the heart of politics. There is a widely held ethical position that politics ought not to revolve around personal ambition. Intellectuals insistently demand that political leaders be motivated by high principles or ideology. Shame to those who might run and win office to satisfy personal ambitions! But we ought to take another look at the role of ambition. Personal ambition sparks just about any person's efforts to do more than subsist. It motivates the great problem solvers just as it motivates the great runners and the great composers.[15]

Theodore Roosevelt tells a story in his autobiography about his early interest in politics. Some of his upper-class and cultured relatives warned him rather bluntly that "our kind" do not go into politics. Young Teddy replied that if this were so, it merely meant "that people I know did not belong to the governing class, and that other people did." He added: "I intend to be one of the governing class; that if they proved too hard-bit for me I supposed I would have to quit, but that I certainly would not quit until I had made the effort and found out whether I really was too weak to hold my own in the rough and tumble."[16]

If elected politicians often seem bewildered in dealing with controversial issues in these confusing times, so are the rest of us. If elected officials sometimes make mistakes, so do the rest of us. If they sometimes postpone things

President Reagan being greeted by Mayor Henry Cisneros at the Cinco de Mayo festival in San Antonio, Texas, 1983. Cisneros was carefully considered by Walter Mondale as his vice-presidential running mate in 1984. *AP.*

[14]Carl Sandburg, *The People Yes* (Harcourt Brace, 1936).

[15]We have adapted this paragraph from Joseph Schlesinger, *Ambition in Politics* (Rand McNally, 1965).

[16]Theodore Roosevelt, *Theodore Roosevelt: An Autobiography* (Charles Scribner's, 1920), p. 56.

rather than directly confront them, so do we. The late Senator Everett Dirksen of Illinois offered a helpful perspective on politicians:

> Politics is not something you can afford to leave to 'other people.' Since politics is the art of ordering the affairs of men through government, it should be the vocation of the very best in this Republic and the avocation of all.
>
> There have been many who seem to equate politics with that which is bad, that which is corrupt, that which is venal, and that which is corrosive of our moral fiber. I find that throughout history most such disparaging remarks are made by those who never dared seek elective office.
>
> To scorn all politicians and to decry their actions is to scorn those who elect them and support them—namely the citizen-elector.[17]

Susan B. Anthony. *UPI.*

The American people will never be completely satisfied with their politicians, nor should they be. The ideal politician is truly a fictional character. For the ideal politician would be able to please absolutely everyone. The person would also be able to make conflicts disappear. Such a person could exist only in an extremely small community where all the people shared the same ideas, ideals, and interests. But American liberties invite diversity, and therefore conflict. Politicians as well as the people they represent can and do have different ideas about what is best for the nation. After all, who is really to say what is good for anyone else—let alone for *everyone* else? That's why we have politicians and politics. To understand this is to better appreciate the delicate and crucial responsibilities entrusted to our elected Act III politicians.[18]

IMPEDIMENTS TO CREATIVE POLITICAL LEADERSHIP

Some observers of the American political system contend the problem with our system is not that it fails to make dumb ideas work—no government can do that—but that it does not allow good ideas and good people to have a chance. We elect good people—certainly people who want to do good—so why not give them the opportunity to rise above transactional leadership and exercise transforming leadership?

Critics often say our constitutional framework thwarts majority rule, programmatic leadership, and comprehensive planning: Only in rare moments of severe upheaval or crisis do we get any kind of effective leadership. The founding fathers, suspicious of tyranny above all other evils, provided for transactional leadership and gradual, incremental change. They were, and we remain, largely suspicious of any mechanism—such as a powerful leader, centralized planning, or strong national parties—that might supply too much leadership. Plainly, the system was designed to prevent swift bursts of activist leadership, but nowadays it seems (according to these writers) that the system has worked too well, for it has encouraged stalemate, deadlock, and often paralysis of government.[19]

Critics also charge that the founders built a great deal of friction and conflict into government: Ambitious politicians are so tied to their separate constituencies that they are bound to fight among themselves. The framers' strategy worked brilliantly for their own purposes—but it worked altogether too well. Today exercising positive leadership is almost impossible. Congress is adept at

[17]Quoted in Conrad Joyner, *The American Politician* (University of Arizona Press, 1971). See also many of the essays in Paul Tillett (ed.), *The Political Vocation* (Basic Books, 1965).

[18]See also Bernard Crick, *In Defense of Politics*, rev. ed. (Pelican Books, 1983); and Stimson Bullitt, *To Be a Politician*, rev. ed. (Yale University Press, 1977).

[19]Critics include Thomas K. Finletter, *Can Representative Government Do The Job?* (Reynal and Hitchcock, 1945); Charles Hardin, *Presidential Power and Accountability* (University of Chicago Press, 1974); and Lloyd N. Cutler, "To Form A Government," *Foreign Affairs* (Fall 1980), pp. 126–143.

checking presidents; and presidents can veto acts of Congress. Also, interest groups and political action committees can block policy ideas that might hurt their interests. Institutions check institutions—but the result is inaction.

Some critics say the framers' strategy must now be turned upside down. If the Constitution was drafted in such a way as to *divide* leaders among themselves, it must now be reframed or reconstituted in order to *unite* them—to provide teamwork, effectiveness, accountability, and responsibility in government. The most radical would-be reformers would opt for a parliamentary system on the European model. The immediate need is to knit together constitutionally what the framers took apart. They would have members of Congress and presidential nominees run on the same ticket, sharing the same platform ideas. They would also enable the president to choose leading members of Congress for cabinet positions in order to form a powerful president-cabinet-congressional linkage. They would renew and reinvigorate our party system.

Proposals for reframing the constitutional system are numerous. The following are some examples.

"I'd like to introduce the man who has become known as the lesser of two evils!" *From The Wall Street Journal. Permission, Cartoon Features Syndicate.*

☐ Through constitutional amendment create a "team ticket"; voters could cast a single party ballot for president, senator, and member of the House of Representatives (as voters now do for president and vice-president), thus creating electoral support for congressional-presidential collective leadership.

☐ Convert impeachment into a means of removing presidents not only when they have committed high crimes and misdemeanors but when they have dramatically and irretrievably lost the confidence of the nation.

☐ Through constitutional amendment adopt a proposal enabling the president to choose senators or representatives for cabinet membership without requiring these legislators to give up their seats in Congress.

☐ Realign the two-party system to establish a party of the liberal-Left to match the present (Republican) party of the Right. Make the parties more organized, disciplined, programmatic, and principled, so that they might offer meaningful alternatives to the voters, sustain their leadership in office, and pull the government together behind the winning platform.

In short, these reformers or reframers would establish majority rule more securely in the political system, at the expense of the present "coalition of minorities." Reminding us that the bicentennial of the framing of the Constitution lies just ahead (1987), the "reframers" contend that if we would really honor the framers, we might imitate their daring intellectual feat of standing back, criticizing, and restructuring the government. They like to quote Thomas Jefferson, who wrote: "I am not an advocate for frequent changes in laws and constitutions. But laws and institutions must go hand in hand with the progress of the human mind. As that becomes more developed, more enlightened, as new discoveries are made, new truths discovered and manners and opinions change, with the change of circumstances, institutions must advance able to keep pace with the times. . . ."

The views and proposals of these modern-day reframers are rejected by most political scientists, since such suggestions usually gloss over the difficulties of parliamentary systems and overstate the problems of modern American government. While our system of checks and balances has its defects, it nevertheless encourages deliberation and scrutiny of all policy changes. And by requiring coalition-building efforts among the diverse regions and interest groups of this vast nation, it has permitted a union to be created out of great diversity. It also provides separate constitutional institutions on which different individuals and groups can focus their loyalties. To be sure, ours is a patchwork system that often encourages inaction rather than swift, unified, collective action. But this is what most Americans seem to prefer. They want diverse opportunities "to peck and chip and constrain in order to moderate policy. If we compare American policy with that of most parliamentary democracies, its leading characteristic is moderation. . . . Taken as a whole . . . we tend to temper the enthusiasm of temporary majorities by the need constantly to reformulate that majority. . . ."[20]

Other observers suggest that our problem is less a crisis of constitutional structure or party system paralysis than it is a crisis of ideas. Leaders, according to this notion, are only as good as the ideas a society can invent and foster. Indeed, the most lasting and pervasive leadership is intangible and noninstitutional. It is the leadership fostered by ideas embodied in social, political, or artistic movements, in books, documents, and speeches, and in the memory of great lives greatly lived. Ideas are vital to a society. They give shape to, and express, visions. Intellectual leadership at its best is provided by those—who may or may not hold political office—who can clarify values as well as the implications of such values for public policy. Such leaders creatively theorize about linking ends and means in a way that will unite purpose, politics, and the practice of government.

Few elected leaders are intellectuals. They want to be seen as nonideological pragmatists, as people of action. They resist ideological commitment. They deal in the short-term and in the practical. They see themselves, in FDR's phrase, as quarterbacks in a football game. The quarterback cannot plan beyond the next play, because future plays will depend on how the preceding one works. Politicians move cautiously; they typically deal with insufficient information and have limited time in which to arrive at a correct decision. They seek to preserve all options and not get bogged down with any untenable positions.

We commonly have to look outside the normal political arena for new ideas, philosophies, beliefs, and arguments that can prod the nation to move in a certain direction, shape a vision, or give coherence to a program. Historically the programs and policies of most elected officials have been culled from a synthesis of ideas and opinions formulated by a host of lesser-known but significant creative renewers. Often these have been the Act I or Act II leaders discussed earlier in this chapter. By the time politicians adopt ideas as their own, the ideas have usually been discussed and debated for several years in the intellectual and grassroots communities of the nation.

Thus, writers like Upton Sinclair and Herbert Croly are as responsible for the lasting ideas of the Progressive movement as are politicians like Presidents Theodore Roosevelt and Woodrow Wilson. The publication of Rachel Carson's *Silent Spring* and Michael Harrington's *The Other America* did as much to spark the ecology movement and the War on Poverty as anything done in the Oval Office or the legislative cloakrooms. The supply side economic ideas preached and practiced by the Reagan administration in the 1980s owe their genesis to writers and economists such as Arthur Laffer, Jude Wanniski, and George Gilder, who passed their ideas along to officeholders like Congressman Jack Kemp and Governor Ronald Reagan, who, in turn, used their skills to try to get variations of these ideas embodied into law. This process illustrates a vital way in which the elected political leaders, the technicians and the brokers of our political system, are dependent upon intellectual leaders for the ideas that can give shape to their programs.

None of this is meant to deprecate the role of politicians, the elected leaders. We look to them to be brokers, to balance and reconcile competing

PROUD TO BE A POLITICIAN

Must a politician gain public office by denouncing his or her own profession? From the tone of many recent congressional races it would appear that this is a growing trend. Journalist Charles McDowell of the *Richmond Times-Dispatch* recently noted this trend on the new PBS series "The Lawmakers," and suggested that such a tactic . . . "demeans an honorable and essential profession—that of the politician." McDowell proposed that every member of Congress be required to take the following oath:

"I affirm that I am a politician. That I am willing to associate with other known politicians. That I have no moral reservations about committing acts of politics.

Under the Constitution, I insist that politicians have as much right to indulge in politics as preachers, single-issue zealots, generals, bird-watchers, labor leaders, big business lobbyists, and all other truth-givers.

I confess that, as a politician, I participate in negotiation, compromise, and tradeoffs in order to achieve something that seems reasonable to a majority.

And, although I try to be guided by principle, I confess that I often find people of principle on the other side, too.

So help me God."

---

[20]James Q. Wilson, "In Defense of Separation of Powers," in Thomas E. Cronin (ed.), *Rethinking the Presidency* (Little, Brown, 1982), p. 180.

interests. This responsibility should not be minimized—if social peace is the precondition of all other values, we should be pleased indeed to have leaders able to keep the peace and provide society with social and political cohesion. It is important that we be aware of what our elected leaders can and cannot do. We must be mindful of the constraints our representative system and our structural arrangements impose on politicians' ability to create fresh programmatic visions, mobilize the masses, and educate society for the future. This should hardly be an occasion to give up on either our politicians or our Constitution. Rather it may well be an opportunity to recognize the need of other leaders— the nonelected and nongovernmental leaders—in the public and private sectors, "out there" beyond Washington, D.C. and even our fifty state capitals to take up the "leadership slack," to play a part in inventing, creating, and mobilizing people for purposeful problem solving.

SUMMARY

1. Americans have ambivalent attitudes toward politics and politicians. We tend to dislike politicians in the abstract, but often like politicians we know, and sometimes even revere departed political leaders. We dislike politicians in part because they wield power over us. More important, however, we force politicians to be brokers and bargainers, to help achieve compromises—and then we turn around and condemn them for lack of principle or for "selling out."

2. The profession of politics in the past has often been restricted to upper- or upper-middle-class white male Americans. This is slowly changing—but the advantages still remain with those who are part of that dominant tradition in American politics.

3. There are all kinds of political officeholders and political leaders. Some are movement organizers or political agitators. Others are coalition builders who forge together disparate political interest groups to work for some common goal. Still others are "Act III political officeholders"—who

generally serve as brokers, reconciling different views and interests and translating various political demands into practical laws and regulations.

4. Leadership is not the same thing as officeholding and takes a variety of forms. Transactional leaders do perform various managerial and conflict-resolving leadership tasks. Uncommon officeholders sometimes exercise transformational leadership, raising expectations, galvanizing organizational strength, and liberating and educating constituents to become leaders in their own right.

5. In practice, many constraints limit the leadership capacities of those we elect to political office in America. Public opinion, constitutional arrangements, and sometimes the deficiency of new and fresh ideas can thwart those who seek to be effective political leaders. Our system is not designed to facilitate easy leadership; it is in many ways designed to ensure that the rights of individuals and the safeguards against tyranny always take precedence.

FURTHER READING

Saul Alinsky. *Rules for Radicals* (Random House, 1972).

Stimson Bullitt. *To Be a Politician*, rev. ed. (Yale University Press, 1977).

James MacGregor Burns. *Leadership* (Harper & Row, 1978).

Bernard Crick. *In Defense of Politics*, rev. and exp. ed. (Pelican Books, 1983).

Richard Hofstadter. *The American Political Tradition* (Vintage, 1948).

Michael Johnston. *Political Corruption and Public Policy in America* (Brooks-Cole, 1982).

Harold Lasswell. *Psychopathology and Politics* (University of Chicago Press, 1930).

Michael Maccoby. *The Leader* (Simon & Schuster, 1981).

Charles A. Madison. *Critics and Crusaders: A Century of American Protest* (Holt, 1947).

Louis Sandy Maisel. *From Obscurity to Oblivion: Running in the Congressional Primary* (University of Tennessee Press, 1983).

William K. Muir. *Legislature* (University of Chicago Press, 1983).

Robert Tucker. *Politics as Leadership* (University of Missouri Press, 1981).

CONGRESS: THE PEOPLE'S BRANCH?

14

In January 1983 a congressman in his early forties retired from his relatively safe seat in Michigan. An eight-year veteran, he was virtually assured of winning reelection by about a 60 percent margin. But he had had enough of Congress.

Why did he resign? A growing number of senators and representatives voluntarily retire. Some leave because of the attractive retirement benefits Congress has provided for its members. Others depart because the pace has greatly increased and because greater demands are now placed on members of Congress. Still others leave because they can make much more money—in a much less stressful way—in business or in the professions.

William Brodhead quit mainly for two other reasons. He was increasingly irritated by the growing pressure from lobbyists and big campaign contributors: "As the years went by, I began to see that most of the people I was dealing with didn't want me to work for the good of the country. Most of the people were trying to work for some selfish good." The growth of political action committees only made matters worse. "The major culprit is a segment of the business community actively engaged in trying to corrupt the Congress through campaign contributions and the rating systems that have become almost bribes."

Second, Brodhead yearned to spend more time with his family and to have some control over his own life. "I find that I no longer have enthusiasm for my work. I have a strong desire for more time with my family and more quiet goals in my life." He added: "It's a question of saving my health, my sense of perspective and my integrity. It's very hard to be a congressman nowadays and keep your integrity."

Brodhead didn't always feel this way. When he arrived in Congress back in 1975, he said it was so much fun he couldn't believe he got paid for working

Congress is not a perfect institution
Congressmen get re-elected because people like them & work

THE MANY MEANINGS OF REPRESENTATION

One of the more troublesome concepts in political science, and one of the most important, is that of representation. These definitions may be helpful:

1. *Formal Representation* is the authority to act in another's behalf, gained through an institutional process or arrangement such as free and open elections. The *formal* arrangement of selection, not the behavior of the representative, defines representation in this usage of the term.

2. *Descriptive or Demographic Representation* is the extent to which representatives reflect or mirror the characteristics of the people they formally represent. According to this usage of the term, a representative legislature should be an exact portrait, in miniature, of the people at large.

3. *Symbolic Representation* is the extent to which a legislator is accepted as believable and as "one of their own" by the folks back home. This usage of the term has a lot to do with the style of a legislator and the nonverbal signals a legislator gives off.

4. *Substantive Representation* is the type of responsiveness to constituents shown by a legislator. Here we are interested in whether the policy and voting views of a legislator match those of constituents, or whether the legislator relies primarily on his or her own judgment. The latter course is that of a guardian or trustee, as opposed to a direct delegate of the citizens.

there. He wanted to fight to make sure none of his constituents were unemployed. And he fought to make sure no handicapped child went without educational opportunities. He wanted very much to help people and to solve problems. But after working eighty- and ninety-hour weeks for eight years and coming under constant and growing pressure from lobbyists and special-interest groups, he says he became burnt out.

What did he think about Congress and its members? For the most part he considered his fellow legislators very self-sacrificing people: "I love the institution, my colleagues, and the job. . . ."[1] Congressman Brodhead's mixed feelings about Congress are similar to those of large numbers of Americans. Most Americans realize Congress is not a perfect institution, and we often characterize it as a bickering, timid, ignorant, selfish, or narrow-minded body. Yet we often admire the stamina and civic responsibility of members of Congress that we know. And incumbent members of Congress keep getting reelected—presumably because people like them and their work.

Several scholars have noted this seeming contradiction: Members of Congress are popular, while Congress is not. This is so because we expect Congress as an institution to solve most, or even all, our national ills. But we judge members of Congress primarily on how well they individually serve the interests of their states and districts, and on their personal appeal.[2] Much of the criticism of Congress as an institution is unjustified. Critics usually forget that our national legislature is particularly exposed. In the first place, Congress does nearly all its work directly in the public eye. Unfortunate incidents—quarrels, name calling, evasive actions, inaccurate statements—that might be hushed up in the executive or judicial branches are almost always observed by journalists. Second, Congress by its nature is controversial and argumentative. Its 535 members are found on both sides, sometimes on half a dozen sides, of every important question. The average citizen holding one opinion is likely to be intolerant of other views and of the legislators holding them. Also, there is a considerable difference between holding an opinion and writing legislation.

The chief complaints about Congress are that it is inefficient and unrepresentative, and is not accountable enough. Further, critics say it is paralyzed by personal bickering and interest group favoritism. Some critics contend that Congress is two "Houses of Misrepresentatives," with many members beholden to special interests. Legislators are described as being obsessed with staying elected—indeed as concentrating solely on winning reelection—often at the expense of dealing seriously with critical national issues such as the arms race, unemployment, foreign policy, and trade. Former House Republican leader John Rhodes was especially harsh when he wrote that "the majority of congressional actions are not aimed at producing results for the American people as much as perpetuating the longevity and comfort of the men who run Congress."[3]

Some of the paralysis in Congress is caused by the proliferation of subcommittees, the overlapping jurisdictions of these committees, and the great increase of congressional staff. A complicated and relatively new budget process also has caused problems. Better-educated and more independent-minded persons are coming to Congress, often with loose or weak ties to political parties. This has made it difficult for party leaders to build coalitions and to stick to an efficient agenda for Congress.

Congressmen only want to be re-elected not better govt

[1] "Why One Man Had Enough of Congress," *Newsweek*, May 31, 1982, p. 36. All quotations are from this source.

[2] Glenn R. Parker, "Can Congress Ever Be a Popular Institution?" in Joseph Cooper and G. Calvin MacKenzie (eds.), *The House at Work* (University of Texas Press, 1981), p. 48.

[3] John Rhodes, *The Futile System* (EPM Publications, 1976), p. 15.

Congress in public eye
Congressmen popular – Congress not

[handwritten margin notes: Congress elections cause Congress members to bow down to special Interest groups]

[handwritten margin notes: 2 congresses: 1st Lawmaking Institution 2nd Representative assembly Congress balances national issues w/ local concerns]

Many people allege that special interests and single-issue groups are stronger than ever, and they are able to fragment and often delay or block proceedings in Congress. The current system of financing congressional elections has been called a scandal. "It virtually forces members of Congress to go around hat in hand begging for money from Washington-based special interest, political action committees whose sole purpose for existing is to seek a quid pro quo," says Senator Eagleton of Missouri. "We see the degrading spectacle of elected representatives completing detailed questionnaires on their positions on special interest issues, knowing that the monetary reward of PAC support depends on the correct answers."[4]

Still others suggest that Congress really has such a split personality that one can even say there are two Congresses. The first Congress is *a lawmaking institution*. It is asked to write laws and make policy for the entire nation. In this capacity all the members are expected to set aside their personal ambitions and perhaps even their concerns about their own constituency. But Congress is also a *representative assembly*, and it is made up of 535 elected officials who are asked to serve as links between their constituents and the national government. The dual roles of *making laws* and *responding to constituents' demands* were very much bound together in the minds of the framers of the Constitution when they designed a legislature elected from states and geographical districts. "Since the first Congress formed in 1789, these two functions have forced members to balance great national issues with vital local concerns."[5]

In fact, pressures mount continuously on members of Congress to help constituents deal with an increasingly complicated government. Indeed, members must spend considerable time and effort helping constituents, especially if they want to stay elected. This notion of the "two Congresses" has important implications for how Congress works and how it is organized—a subject we shall consider later.

THE CAPITOL

Congress is the seat of legislative authority, the center of public debate, a carry-over of folksy political traditions from earlier days—and a collection of several hundred relatively independent politicians with separate but overlapping constituencies. The architecture of the capital bespeaks its ways—two chambers, endless corridors, ornate rotundas and galleries, and a rabbit warren of grand rooms, tiny offices, and winding passageways. There is no culminating point of authority but a multiplicity of decision centers.

[4]Thomas Eagleton, quoted in Norman C. Miller, "The Pernicious Influence of PACs on Congress." Reprinted by permission of *The Wall Street Journal*, February 17, 1983, editorial page. © Dow Jones & Company, Inc. 1983. All rights reserved.

[5]*How Congress Works* (Congressional Quarterly Press, 1983), p. 153.

HOUSE OF REPRESENTATIVES

Washington, D.C. 20515

1 Speaker's Office
2 Committee on Ways and Means
3 Parliamentarian
4 House Floor Library
5 Cloakrooms
6 Members' Retiring Room and Lobby
7 House Chamber
8 Committee on Appropriations
9 Minority Whip

10 House Reception Room
11 House Minority Conference Room
12 House Majority Conference Room
13 House Document Room
14 Committee Meeting Room
15 Representatives' Offices
16 Prayer Room
17 Minority Leader

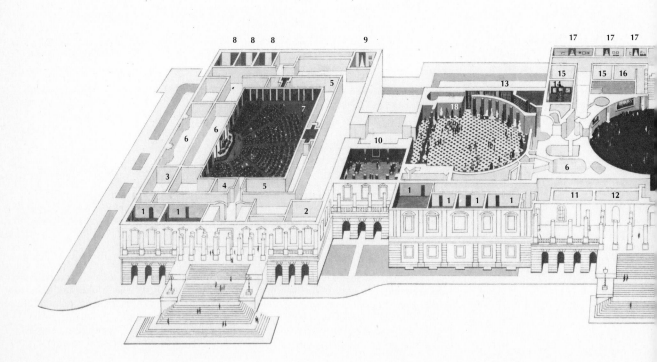

PUBLIC AREAS

18 Statuary Room
19 Rotunda
20 Senate Rotunda
21 Old Senate Chamber

SENATE

Washington, D.C. 20510

22 Senators' Office
23 Executive Clerk
24 Senate Conference Room
25 Majority Leader
26 Majority Leader
27 Minority Leader
28 Office of the Vice President
29 Senators' Reception Room

30 Cloakrooms
31 Senate Chamber
32 Marble Room
33 President's Room
34 Office of the Secretary
35 Chief Clerk
36 Bill Clerk and Journal Clerk
37 Official Reporters of Debates

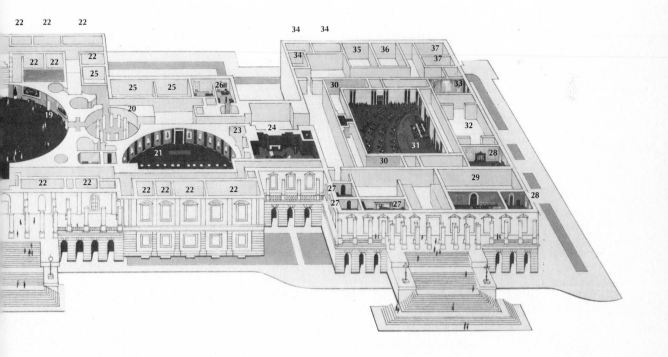

WHO ARE THE LEGISLATORS?

Nancy Landon Kassenbaum, one of two women senators, is the daughter of the 1936 GOP presidential candidate Alf Landon. *UPI*

All members of Congress are successful politicians, mostly between the ages of thirty-five and seventy, who have risen to national office through local processes in their home communities and states. The entire membership of the House of Representatives (435) is elected every second year. Elections for the six-year Senate terms are staggered, so that one-third of the Senate's 100 members are chosen every two years. The Constitution sets up no major barriers to holding office except age and citizenship. Members of the House of Representatives must be twenty-five years old and must have been citizens for seven years. Senators must be at least thirty and must have been citizens for nine years. Yet the composition of Congress does not reflect the socioeconomic makeup of the people as whole. The overwhelming number of national legislators are male (95 percent), well educated, middle-aged, and from middle- or upper-middle-income backgrounds. Until recently members were also mainly white Anglo-Saxon Protestants (WASPs). The greater numbers of Roman Catholics and Jews in recent Congresses—about 140 Catholics and 38 Jews—now bring the religious makeup of Congress closer in line with that of the general population. But there are far fewer blacks and women in Congress than in the general public (see Table 14–1). In the 99th Congress (1985–87) there are also four members of Oriental descent and ten with Spanish surnames.

About 45 percent of national legislators are lawyers. The 99th Congress also included one veterinarian, two former judges, a retired admiral, two clergymen, about two dozen farmers, and a large number of teachers, professors, and businesspeople. Plainly, Congress does not mirror the nation as a whole from an occupational standpoint. Rarely does a member of Congress emerge

14–1
PROFILE OF THE 99th CONGRESS (1985–87)

	House	Senate	
Party			
Democrats	253	Democrats	47
Republicans	182	Republicans	53
Age			
99th U.S. House	49.6	99th Senate	54.2
Sex			
Male	413	Male	98
Female	22	Female	2
Religion			
Protestant	59%	Protestant	69%
Catholic	29	Catholic	20
Other	12	Other	11
Race			
White	403	White	98
Minority	32	Minority	2
Percentage of Lawyers			
Lawyers	42%	Lawyers	60%

Congresswoman Patricia Shroeder of Denver, Colorado is currently the woman with greatest seniority in the U.S. Congress.

out of trade unions or from the so-called blue-collar occupations, although a dozen or so members of the House of Representatives have formed a "blue-collar caucus" composed of members with working-class backgrounds. Among these are a former longshoreman, a pipefitter, a warehouse worker, and an ex-riverboat captain. How important is this "misrepresentation"? Critics say it offers just one more instance of government of the elite by the elite and for the elite. Defenders point out that we would hardly expect to find the national percentage of high school dropouts mirrored in Congress. Whatever its makeup, an important question is whether a Congress composed of legislators drawn from a restricted segment of the population is biased in favor of certain points of view. The present makeup of Congress doubtless means that specific questions such as women's rights and antipoverty measures get somewhat less support than they would if Congress were representative in a literal sense. Still, just because most members are the products of middle- and upper-class families does not mean they are interested only in improving the position of that portion of the population.

GETTING TO AND REMAINING IN CONGRESS

Getting elected to Congress depends on a number of factors—as noted in Chapter 12—party strength in the area, personal character and appeal, whether or not you are an incumbent, occasional national tides (such as in the 1964, 1972, or 1974 elections), and campaign strategies and fundraising abilities. An overriding factor, however, is the type of district or state in which a candidate runs. Is it a safe seat—one that is predictably won by one party or the other or a highly competitive one? Congress has left control over the drawing of congressional districts to the state legislatures. Senators, of course, represent entire states, but House seats are distributed among the states according to population, with each state receiving at least one seat.

In many states the party in control of the state legislature openly engages in gerrymandering—that is, it tries to draw district boundaries in such a way as to secure for its party as many representatives as possible. This is why congressional districts take on weird shapes. The once rural-dominated legislatures used to arrange the districts so as to overrepresent rural areas. But this was modified both by the population shift to the cities and suburbs and by a notable Supreme Court decision, *Wesberry* v. *Sanders* (1964).[6] In this case the Court ruled the Constitution requires all congressional districts in a state to have precisely the same number of people (as nearly as possible), so that one person's vote is equal to that of every other person. How much difference did this and subsequent Supreme Court rulings make? Population inequalities have ended. The voice of suburban populations has been strengthened. But a certain amount of gerrymandering continues: State politicians still draw boundary lines—usually to protect incumbents. The Supreme Court continues to monitor state apportionment of congressional districts. They overruled New Jersey's plan in 1983 because that state had failed to make its districts mathematically equal in population.[7]

The Incumbency Advantage

Incumbents in Congress have a very good chance of remaining in Congress: About 80 percent of Senate incumbents and over 90 percent of House members who run again are reelected. Most House seats are "safe" in the sense that incumbents win by such majorities that the chances of challengers defeating them are minimal.

[6]376 U.S. 1(1964).
[7]*Karcher v. Daggett,* 77 L Ed 2nd 133 (1983).

297

[handwritten: Reps are not well known. Senators are known by 1/3 - 1/2]

As long as the members can keep "the folks and the interests back home" happy, they can remain reasonably independent from the president and from their party leadership. Of course, an incumbent can be voted out of office, especially if a legislator loses touch with constituents or national needs. But how would the voters know if this was the case? Few people know the name of their representative. Senators are better known, but one-third to one-half the public do not know their names. Still fewer citizens evaluate legislators on their stands or votes on issues. Unhappily (or happily, depending on your view), members of Congress are judged on service to their constituents, communications with the district, attendance records, "small favors done over the years," and other such nonlegislative matters.

Not surprisingly, most members of Congress pursue policies and assignments, and allocate their time and energy, in ways that increase their chances of getting reelected. A safe seat, however, permits a legislator to serve as a national leader without having to worry too much about constantly returning home. Senator Edward Kennedy, for example—as long as he does not take issue with sensitive domestic concerns of the people of Massachusetts—can count on the base from which he has become a national spokesman for certain economic and foreign policy points of view. Representatives from competitive states or districts, on the other hand, find it somewhat more difficult to ignore local concerns, and tend to concentrate their time and energies on narrower issues. Doubtless the rise in the number of safe seats has increased in large part because members of Congress have become much more skilled in servicing constituent requests.[8]

"Yes, I did promise to take care of the people in the district. Similarly, I'm sure that each of you has at one time or another said something rash in the heat of the moment." *Reprinted by permission.*

THE POWERS OF CONGRESS

[handwritten: Congress judged on service, popularity. ① Powers: spend & tax, borrow $, Regulate commerce w/ nations & States, declare war, raise army]

The Constitution is generous in its grant of powers to Congress. In the very first article the founding fathers outlined the structure, powers, and responsibilities of Congress, giving it "all legislative powers herein granted." Among these powers are the power to spend and tax in order to "provide for the common defense and general welfare of the United States"; the power to borrow money; the power to regulate commerce with foreign nations and among the states; the power to declare war, raise and support armies, and provide and maintain a navy; the power to establish post offices and postroads; and the power to set up the federal courts under the Supreme Court. As a final catch-all, the Constitution gave the Congress the right "to make all laws which shall be necessary and proper for carrying into execution" the powers set out. Several nonlegislative functions were also granted, such as participating in the process of constitutional amendment and impeachment (given to the House), and trying an impeached federal officer (given to the Senate).

[handwritten: Power to make laws necessary & proper to execute arms]

The Constitution confers special additional responsibilities on the Senate. The Senate has the power to confirm presidential nominations—sometimes as many as 500 key executive and judicial nominees a year. (In Chapter 16 we discuss how the Senate meets this responsibility.) The Senate also must give its consent, by a two-thirds vote of the senators present, before a president may ratify a treaty. This gives the Senate a special role in foreign policy.

The House also has some special responsibilities, but these have not proved to be as important as those given to the Senate. For example, all reve-

WHY INCUMBENT MEMBERS OF CONGRESS USUALLY WIN:

□ They enjoy *better name recognition,* and to be known at all is generally to be known favorably—challengers are almost always less well known, or unknown.

□ They enjoy *free mailings* (called the "franking privilege") to every household in the state or district, and these mailings—often looking almost like campaign brochures—are designed to make them known and to portray them as hard-working and influential.

□ They usually have had *more campaign experience,* and they can claim to have had *more experience in Congress* and in Washington.

□ They have a *large staff* to help do casework and constituency services for the folks back home.

□ They *take credit for federal monies* that get allocated to their regions.

[8]See A. D. Cover and David Mayhew, "Congressional Dynamics and the Decline of Competitive Congressional Elections," in Larry Dodd and Bruce Oppenheimer (eds.), *Congress Reconsidered,* 2nd ed. (Congressional Quarterly Press, 1981); J. L. Payne, "The Personal Electoral Advantages of House Incumbents, 1936–1976," *American Politics Quarterly,* Vol. 8 (1980), pp. 465–82; and Richard S. Beth, "Incumbency Advantage and Incumbency Resources: Recent Articles," *Congress and the Presidency* (Winter 1981/82), pp. 119–36.

□ They *raise more campaign money* and do so more easily than challengers, since lobbyists and political action committees seek their ear and their favor right now. In addition, many campaign contributors know incumbents stand a better chance of getting reelected than challengers, so they give to those they know will win.

□ They are in a better position than challengers to *take advantage of government research staffs,* new government studies, and even unclassified information that comes their way because of their current position.

Note: No one of these factors can guarantee a member's reelection, but skillful use of these and related resources makes it difficult to unseat a healthy incumbent.

nue bills must originate in the House. In fact, this has made little practical difference, since the Senate has freely amended bills that originate in the House, and changed everything except the title.

The framers had no intention of making Congress all-powerful: They reserved certain authority to the states and to the people and gave other powers to the executive and judicial branches of the national government. As time passed, Congress gained power in some respects and lost it in others. The power of Congress also changes depending on the times and on who is president. As the role and authority of the national government have expanded, so too have the policy-making and oversight responsibilities of Congress. Still, Congress has not kept pace with its great rival, the presidency, which in many respects today holds the place in our national government that most of the founding fathers apparently desired for Congress. This may be part of a worldwide trend. Legislative bodies have almost everywhere become subordinate to the executive at all levels of government.

Despite its secondary role in recent decades, Congress still performs at least these six important functions: *representation, lawmaking, consensus-building, overseeing, policy clarification,* and *legitimizing.* Representation is expressing the diversity and conflicting views of the economic, social, racial, religious, and other interests making up the United States. Lawmaking is enacting measures to help solve substantive problems. Consensus building is the bargaining process by which these interests are reconciled. Overseeing the bureaucracy means seeing that laws and policies approved by Congress are faithfully carried out and that they accomplish what was intended. Policy clarification, or "policy incubation," as it is sometimes called, is the identification and publicizing of issues. Legitimizing is the formal ratifying of policies through proper channels.

THE JOB OF THE LEGISLATOR

Legislators keep busy
Average stay elected 11 or 12 years

National legislators lead a hectic life. Congress now meets year round, whereas a hundred years ago it often met for just a few months each year. There is never enough time to digest all the information, letters, complaints, reports, and advice that pour in. Staying elected is a chief priority; some members seem to have few other interests. But most undertake the constantly demanding tasks of keeping on top of their committee responsibilities, staying in touch with key leaders and activists back home, and striving to understand national problems. Most legislators work extremely hard. They drive themselves at a pace far more strenuous than that of typical professional or business persons. Their travel commitments are almost as demanding as those of airline pilots or cross-country truck drivers. The average member stays elected about eleven or twelve years. Depending on the kind of district, the personality of the member, and the issues of the day, members of Congress emphasize representation, lawmaking and committee work, constituency casework, external relations with interest groups or the White House, or reelection tasks.

Senator Lawton Chiles (D-Florida) with students from Deltona Jr. High School. *Dev O'Neill.*

Legislators as Representatives

For whom does the representative speak? The geographical district and its immediate interests? the party? the nation? some special clientele? his or her conscience? How legislators define their representative role has been one of the major questions in political science—and for good reason. Congress was intended to serve as a forum for registering the interests and values that make up the nation. It was never intended that the legislative branch should represent views identical with those of the executive. But to whom does the individual representative listen?

Most legislators see role as trustee. They are to vote as they see fit for welfare of whole nation.

Some legislators believe they should act as delegates ob "Folks back home"

Burke: "Legislature is a place of deliberation and learning."

Most legislators shift back & forth in their role

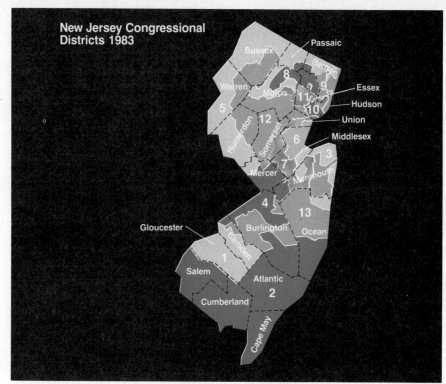

New Jersey Congressional
Districts 1983

Congressman Phil Gramm (R-Texas) made news in 1983 by resigning from Congress as a Democrat and running again for Congress as a Republican in a special election. Then in 1984 he won an impressive victory to become a U.S. Senator from Texas—also as a Republican.

While certain patterns are evident, their meaning is far from clear. For one thing members of Congress perceive their roles differently. Some believe they should serve as delegates from their districts; they should find out what the "folks back home" need or want and serve those needs as effectively as possible. In a sense they would simply *re-present* the views of the voters who sent them to Washington. This orientation, studies show, is often assumed by Republicans, nonleaders, nonsoutherners, or members with low seniority.

But most members see their role as that of trustee. Their constituents, they argue, did not send them to Congress to serve as agents. They are to vote independently, on the basis of their own, more complete information and greater experience for the welfare of the whole nation. As one member once put it: "This means that we must on occasion lead, inform, correct, and sometimes even ignore constituent opinion, if we are to exercise fully that judgment for which we were elected." This view echoes the stand once championed by the famed English legislator Edmund Burke, who said his judgment and conscience ought not to be sacrificed to the opinions of others. In his view a legislature was a place for deliberation and learning. It was not a mere gathering of ambassadors from localities. Interviews with members of the House of Representatives suggest that the trustee, or national, focus is more common among Democrats, House leaders, southerners, and high-seniority members.

Although the question of delegate versus trustee is an old one, it is somewhat misleading. Representatives cannot follow detailed instructions from their constituents, because such instructions seldom exist. On many important policy questions members hear nothing from their constituents. And they hear most often from those who agree with them. On the other hand, it is rather unrealistic to expect a legislator to be able to define the national interest if this means understanding the needs and aspirations of millions of people. Most legislators shift back and forth in their role, depending on their perception of the public interest, the electoral facts of life, and the pressures of the moment.

If issue involves home district, legislator listens to constituents, if not, he goes on own convictions

Legislators as Lawmakers

Congressman Timothy E. Wirth (D-Colorado) talking with a constituent at one of his many town meetings back in his district. *Rebecca Cantwell.*

In their major role as lawmakers, the members of Congress are influenced by how they perceive the nation's key problems and what can be done about them; how they respond to their constituents' interests; and how they follow suggestions from colleagues, staff, the White House, and lobbies.

How a member of Congress makes up his or her mind varies according to issues and to the contexts of decision making. No single factor determines how a member votes most of the time. Members cast more than 1200 votes on a wide variety of subjects in the span of a single Congress. Some issues are controversial and directly affect a member's district or state. On such occasions a national legislator will more often than not heed the interests of the folks back home. On issues that may be complicated and have little or no bearing on the home district, most members of Congress are more likely to rely on their own convictions and on the advice of colleagues and friends. Sometimes the president will single out an issue as crucial to the success of the administration, and this factor plus party considerations may weigh more heavily. Obviously, how a member decides to vote depends on many factors and contexts.[9] *(liberal) (conserv)*

A legislator usually follows the same ideology on all issues.

THE INFLUENCE OF A MEMBER'S POLICY AND PHILOSOPHICAL CONVICTIONS

Ideological or issue orientation is the best predictor of how members will vote on specific issues and on a wide variety of issues. If one is a liberal on social issues, one is likely also to be a liberal on tax and national security issues. The policy convictions of a Senator Edward Kennedy are reasonably consistent, as are those of a Representative Jack Kemp (R-N.Y.). Thus, on controversial issues such as national health insurance, gas and oil decontrol, or the MX mobile missile system, knowing the general philosophical leanings of individual members provides a helpful guide both to how they make up their minds and how they will vote. One study finds that an increasing and continuing ideological split has developed in Congress: A social and economic justice coalition is pitted against a growing coalition of free market economic conservatives.[10] In a watered down sense it is a Walter Mondale versus Ronald Reagan split. Or in economic terms it is a John Kenneth Galbraith "progressives" versus a Milton Friedman "free market" coalition. Other scholars detect flexible majorities of the moment and say ideology plays a less constant role.

Two coalitions in Congress: Social & Economic Justice vs. Free market Econ. Conserv.

THE INFLUENCE OF THE VOTERS

Much of the time a major influence on legislators is their perception of how their constituents feel. Party and executive branch pressures also play a role, but when all is said and done, the members' political future depends on how a majority of voters feel about their performance. It is the rare person who consistently and deliberately votes against the wishes of the people back home. *Most of time, legislators vote to please constituents*

This commonsense observation is supported by several studies. On domestic issues such as social welfare and civil rights, there usually is a great deal of agreement between legislators and their districts. Junior members from competitive seats, in particular, often vote their constituencies' attitudes as they perceive them. But even members who win by a substantial margin are not necessarily free to ignore the concerns of the voters. They may, in fact, have won easily precisely because people know these legislators will follow voters' wishes on issues important to them.[11] Of course, the extent to which members try to respond to their constituents' views also depends on the measure under consideration. Legislators might pay more attention to voter attitudes where

[9]See David C. Kozak, "Decisionmaking on Role Call Votes in the House of Representatives," *Congress and the Presidency,* Vol. 9 (1982), pp. 51–78.

[10]Jerrold E. Schneider, *Ideological Coalitions in Congress* (Greenwood Press, 1979).

[11]John W. Kingdon, *Congressmen's Voting Decisions* (Harper & Row, 1973), p. 31.

People don't really know that much of what Legislator does. They worry too much about change in vote

social and economic matters are involved than where mass opinion is not so well informed.

Something of a paradox is evident here. Members of Congress sometimes think their individual lawmaking actions may have considerable impact on constituents. Yet the constituents' general ignorance of how their representatives vote implies that the impact can be small. Members may think the folks back home like (or dislike) what they are doing, when actually the voters have little idea of what is going on in Congress. This is explained in part by the tendency of legislators to overestimate their visibility. Partly, too, members must constantly be concerned about how they will explain their votes. Also, some members are worried about small shifts in the vote on election day. Even if only a few voters are aware of their stand on a given issue, this group might make the difference between victory and defeat.

Legislators Rely on Colleagues for advice in voting, Colleagues are usually from same Background or area (Friends, Advisors)

THE INFLUENCE OF COLLEAGUES Voting decisions are also affected by the advice members obtain from other representatives. Severe time limitations and the frequent necessity to make decisions with only a few hours or even a few minutes notice force legislators to depend on others. Most members develop friendships with people who think as they do. They often ask one another what they think of a piece of pending legislation. In particular, they look to respected members of the committee working on the bill.

Unlike most of the voters back home, other members usually have detailed knowledge about many of the issues before Congress. Their views are often public. They may have voted on the matter in previous sessions, or in committee, and their public statements may have been placed in the *Congressional Record*. Sometimes members are influenced to vote one way merely because they know a colleague is on the other side of the issue. More often legislators find out how their friends stand on an issue, listen to the party leadership's advice, and take into account the various committee reports. If they are still in doubt, they consult additional friends and staff. The members most often consulted by their colleagues are those who represent similar districts or the same region or state, or like-minded members of the same party or faction—especially those who serve on the committee from which the legislation has come.

Congress has built Staff, Congressmen have enlarged Personal staffs

THE INFLUENCE OF CONGRESSIONAL STAFF Perhaps the fastest-growing bureaucracy in Washington is that attached to Congress. For years political scientists urged Congress to strengthen its staff. Without additional help, they said, representatives and senators were at a disadvantage in dealing with the executive branch and were overly dependent on information supplied them by the White House or lobbyists. Congress has responded—some would say with a vengeance. Every committee and subcommittee is now elaborately staffed. In addition, members of Congress have all enlarged the number of personal staff working for them in both their Washington and home district offices. Congress in recent years also added a Congressional Budget Office, an Office of Technology Assessment, and a Cost Accounting Standards Board to its already existing Library of Congress and General Accounting Office staffs.

Complexity of issues and increasingly demanding schedules have led to an explosion in congressional staffs. Nearly 32,000 staff members, researchers, budget analysts, and others now work for Congress (this figure excludes the U.S. Government Printing Office, which is nominally part of the legislative branch). This number has grown at least fourfold in the last twenty-five years. But numbers tell only part of the story of staff influence. Members of Congress have had to delegate all kinds of tasks to their staffs. It has reached the point where some members now ask whether they or their staffs are in charge. Much of the growth in congressional staffs occurred during the 1970s, when Congress believed the executive branch was failing to share needed information and studies. Congress is the only legislature in the world with a vast staff. This is one of its chief sources of power; without its staffs Congress would doubtless become too much the prisoner of the executive branch and interest groups.

Increasing numbers of congressional staff members now work in the home district or state offices. In the House of Representatives about one-third of all staff is home based; in the Senate, one-fourth. In part this is due to the increased attention focused on constituency services and casework. Doubtless, too, it helps members stay in close communication with the voters back home. Much of the work done in these district offices is akin to a continuous campaign effort—generating favorable publicity, arranging for local appearances and newspaper interviews, scheduling, and general contact with important civic and business leaders in the region.

One of the consequences both of the increasing congressional staff and of growing demands on members of Congress is that the latter sometimes become very dependent upon staff. This is especially so in the case of senators, who are more likely to have a wider range of subject matter specialties than are representatives. At congressional hearings it is the staff member who often tells the legislator what to ask. Congressional staff become very knowledgeable about special policy areas and deal on a day-to-day basis with their counterparts in the executive departments and interest groups. Indeed, many close observers say some of the most powerful people in Washington are congressional "staffers," as they are called. They draft bills, do the research, and often do much of the parliamentary negotiating and coalition building. No wonder an increasing number of lobbyists concentrate on influencing staffers.[12]

Yet we should not exaggerate the independent power base of a staffperson. He or she can be summarily fired at the whim of the person they serve. Staffers lack civil service protection—although they cannot be dismissed because of their race, sex, or national origin. And they know that if they wander too far from the views of the one person who can hire and fire them, they will quickly be called back into line. *Staffers can be fired easily*

THE INFLUENCE OF THE PARTY   Another source of influence on legislative behavior is the *political party*. Friendships tend to develop within the party. Of course, there is a fair amount of natural agreement among party colleagues. On some issues the pressure to conform to a party position is immediate and direct. Sometimes there is pressure to go along with the party even when a member does not believe in the party position.

The result of party pressures is a tendency, on major bills, for *most* Democrats to be arrayed against *most* Republicans. Members of Congress typically vote with their party majority about two-thirds of the time. However, senators are slightly more independent than representatives. Party influence also varies over time. It was stronger during the nineteenth century than it has been in this century, and it is somewhat stronger in recent years than it was in the post–World War II era. Party influence varies by issue. Party differences have been stronger over domestic, regulatory, and welfare measures than over foreign policy and civil liberty issues.[13] *Political Parties influence Congressmen Most Demo's against Most Repubs,*

[12]Michael J. Malbin, *Unelected Representatives* (Basic Books, 1980). See also Robert H. Salisbury and Kenneth A. Shepsle, "Congressional Staff Turnover and the Ties-That-Bind," *American Political Science Association*, Vol. 75 (1981), pp. 381–96.

[13]See, for example, Aage R. Clausen, *How Congressmen Decide* (St. Martin's, 1973).

CONGRESSIONAL PARTY SPLIT

The elections of 1980 and 1982 produced a Republican controlled Senate and a Democratic House. The last time the two houses were split was in the days of Herbert Hoover. The 72nd Congress (1931–33) had a Republican Senate and a Democratic House.

Members of Congress depend too much on staff. Staffers do much of the Legislators work

GROWING CONGRESSIONAL STAFFS

Congress had a staff of just a dozen in 1800. That doubled in the next thirty years. By 1935 the Senate had a staff of about 600, and the House had a staff of around 1000. Today the number of personnel employed by the whole congressional establishment is over 30,000.

	Number
House:	
Committee staff	2,073
Personal staff	7,067
Leadership staff	162
Others	1,487
Senate:	
Committee staff	1,217
Personal staff	3,612
Leadership staff	170
Others	1,351
Joint Committee staff	138
Support agencies:	
General Accounting Office	5,303
Library of Congress	5,390
(Congressional Research Service)	(847)
Congressional Budget Office	207
Office of Technology Assessment	145
Miscellaneous:	
Architect	2,296
Capitol Police	1,167
Total	31,783

Source: Charles O. Jones, *The United States Congress* (Dorsey Press, 1982), p. 59.

[handwritten margin notes: Coalitions can influence votes (Northern Demos vs South Demos & Rep'ubs)]

[handwritten margin notes: Congress sometimes yields too Power to Exec.]

PRESIDENTIAL AND OTHER INFLUENCES   Many forces—regional, local, ties of friendship—can override party influence. Members are sometimes influenced by informal groups (state delegations, ideological groups, ethnic caucuses, regional groupings, and even the class of colleagues with whom they were elected—for example, "the class of 1986"). Also, they are influenced by the more important interest groups and lobbyists—especially those who can help pay off past and future campaign debts. One voting pattern in Congress reflects a conservative coalition of Republicans and southern Democrats. In the 1950s and 1960s a majority of southern Democrats and a majority of Republicans voted against the majority of northern Democrats on about a quarter of the important roll call votes.[14] This was less the case in the 1970s, but it reappeared in the Reagan years. The conservative coalition is most likely to appear on domestic issues, especially on social welfare legislation. But its strength in Congress cannot be measured by voting decisions alone, because the many committee leaders who are members of this group are often able to prevent legislation they oppose from ever being voted on. The pattern is now changing, since Democrats elected from the South in recent years are more "national" than "sectional" in their voting patterns; and the Democrats, especially in the House, have strengthened party discipline.

Presidents and the executive branch can also influence how legislators vote. Some critics say Congress has yielded extensive policy initiation and budgetary planning to the administrative branch: They say no matter how hard the Congress may struggle on one issue, it is overwhelmed by the vastly greater forces of the presidency. Even today a fair number of legislators complain (as they have throughout our history) that as now organized and staffed, Congress cannot really come to grips with the enormously complex questions involved in making national policy.

Even if Congress were better organized or its members more expert, the growing significance of foreign policy and complicated economic issues would still make the role of the president vital. Presidents have the tools of foreign policy in their hands, and even those they share with Congress, such as the treaty-making power, are usually less significant than their overall negotiating and agenda-setting roles. Although presidents, like Lyndon Johnson and Ronald Reagan, through the full use of their emergency, constitutional, and political powers, have become serious, full-time partners in legislation, members of Congress are reluctant to admit they are influenced by pressures from the White House. Some studies suggest, moreover, presidential influence on congressional voting decisions may not be as significant as most observers believe.[15] While a president has more impact on votes in the area of national security policy than in other areas, even on these questions power is very much a shared responsibility.[16] On key domestic issues legislators are more likely to be influenced by what the constituents want (or what they think they want) and by their own policy convictions than by what the White House wants.

FACTORS THAT CAN INFLUENCE HOW A MEMBER OF CONGRESS VOTES

A member's policy and philosophical convictions

A member's perception of his or her state or district's needs

Constituent opinion and mail

Committee leaders

Other committee members

Members of one's state delegation

Other members of Congress

Congressional staff members

Interest groups and lobbyists

Ideological or ethnic caucuses

President's position

Party leaders

Campaign contributions

Political action committees

Congressional research publications

The Legislative Obstacle Course

[handwritten margin notes: Prez shares foriegn-policy power w/ Congress (Reagan, Johnson) President has influence on National Issues, Constituents have influence on domestic issues]

From the very beginning Congress has been a system of multiple vetoes. This was in part the intent of the framers, who wanted to disperse powers so these powers could not be accumulated by any would-be tyrant. In addition, Congress has developed an elaborate set of customs that distributes political influ-

[14]See John F. Manley, "The Conservative Coalition in Congress," *American Behavioral Scientist* (December 1973), pp. 223–47.

[15]George G. Edwards III, *Presidential Influence in Congress* (Freeman, 1980), chaps. 5, 6, and 7.

[16]See Cecil V. Crabb, Jr., and Pat M. Holt, *Invitation to Struggle* (Congressional Quarterly Press, 1980); and Thomas M. Franck and Edward Weisband, *Foreign Policy by Congress* (Oxford University Press, 1979).

[handwritten margin notes: Congress is series of vetoes so no one will have too much Power]

[handwritten marginalia: "95% of Bills die in Subcommittee" / "Congress has system to disperse power" / "Subcommittee & Committee revise & vote on bill, then whole house votes, is passed, sent to other house & voted on. If differences, sent to conference committee"]

ence in different ways to different people. To follow a bill through Congress is to see this *dispersion of power*. Procedures and rules in the two houses are somewhat different, but the basic distribution of power, in its effect on shaping legislation, is roughly the same.

Every bill, including those drawn up in the executive branch, must be introduced in either house by a member of that body. The vast bulk (more than 95 percent) of the 15,000 or so bills introduced every two years die in a subcommittee for lack of support. On major legislation that has significant backing, the committee or one of its subcommittees holds hearings to receive opinions. It then meets to "mark up" (discuss and revise) and vote on the bill. If the subcommittee and then the parent committee vote in favor of the bill, it is reported—or sent—to the full house, where it is debated and voted on. If passed, it goes to the other house, where the whole process is repeated. If there are differences between the bills as passed by the House and the Senate—and there often are—the two versions must go to a conference committee for reconciliation.

In 1789 through 1790, 142 bills were introduced in the House of Representatives, and only 85 reports were filed from committees. In recent sessions as many as 15,000 bills are introduced and sometimes as many as 2,500 committee reports are prepared. The 97th Congress has lower figures because it focused more on tax and budget matters.

14–2

THE AVERAGE HOUSE LEGISLATIVE WORKLOAD—80TH THROUGH 92ND AND 97TH CONGRESS (1946–72, 81–83)

Category	Average per Congress 1946–72	97th Congress 1981–83
Bills introduced	13,711	9,175
Committee reports	2,456	1,013
Public laws passed	790	210
Private laws passed	618	41
Total laws and resolutions	1,408	579
Presidential messages to Congress	185*	209
Presidential messages referred to committee	167	205
Executive branch communications	2,372	5,329

*Figures for 89th through 92nd Congress only (1965–72).
†Figure includes all bills and resolutions.
**Figure includes reports on bills and resolutions only.
‡In addition, 987 resolutions were passed by Congress.
***In most cases similar messages are sent to both the House and the Senate.
SOURCE: *Congressional Record*.

Multiple Opportunities For Delay

The complexity of the congressional system provides a tremendous built-in advantage for the opponents of any measure. Those who sponsor a bill must win at every step; opponents need to win only once. Multiple opportunities for vetoes exist because of the dispersion of influence and because at a dozen points in committee or in the house, a bill may be killed or allowed to die. Whether good or bad, a proposal can be delayed by any one of the following: (1) the chairperson of the House substantive subcommittee, (2) the House substantive committee, (3) the House Rules Committee, (4) the House, (5) the chairperson of the Senate subcommittee, (6) the Senate committee, (7) the majority of the Senate, (8) the floor leaders in both chambers, (9) a few members of the Senate in the case of a filibuster, (10) the House-Senate conference committee if the chambers disagree, and (11) the president. If the agreement of still other committees is required—appropriations, for example—the points of possible veto are multiplied.

Clearly, a controversial bill cannot get through without good legislative leadership and compromise. One tactical question at the start is whether to

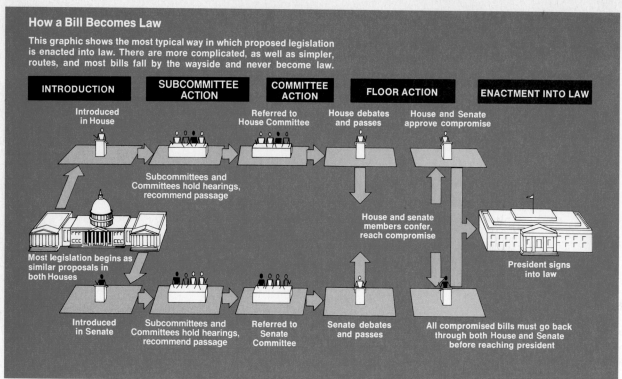

How a Bill Becomes Law

This graphic shows the most typical way in which proposed legislation is enacted into law. There are more complicated, as well as simpler, routes, and most bills fall by the wayside and never become law.

INTRODUCTION	SUBCOMMITTEE ACTION	COMMITTEE ACTION	FLOOR ACTION	ENACTMENT INTO LAW

Introduced in House

Referred to House Committee

House debates and passes

House and Senate approve compromise

Subcommittees and Committees hold hearings, recommend passage

Most legislation begins as similar proposals in both Houses

House and senate members confer, reach compromise

President signs into law

Introduced in Senate

Subcommittees and Committees hold hearings, recommend passage

Referred to Senate Committee

Senate debates and passes

All compromised bills must go back through both House and Senate before reaching president

[handwritten margin note: Bills referred to committees]

push for initial action in the Senate or in the House. If a bill is expected to have a rough time in the Senate, for example, its sponsors may seek passage in the House and hope that a sizable victory will spur the Senate into action. Another question concerns the committee to which the bill should be assigned. Normally referral to a committee is automatic. Sometimes, however, a bill cuts across more than one jurisdiction, but it can be written in such a way that it is bound to go to one committee rather than another.

Getting a bill through Congress requires more than a majority at any one time or place. Majorities must be mobilized over and over again—in subcommittee, in committee, and in chamber. These majorities shift and change, involving different legislators in different situations at different points in time. New coalitions must be built again and again.

[handwritten margin note: If bill passes, It must go through process again to secure appropriations]

These days, almost everything Congress wants to do by legislation requires dollars. So even if a bill passes, it must go through the process again to secure appropriations. Congress may go through the entire process of authorizing a program, and then fail to appropriate money to implement it; or it may appropriate so little money that what was authorized cannot be carried out.

THE HOUSES OF CONGRESS

[handwritten margin note: Senate & house have veto over each other]

The single most important fact about Congress is the dispersion of power between its two houses. The Senate and the House each have an absolute veto over the lawmaking of the other. Each house runs its own affairs, sets its own rules, and conducts its own investigations. The lawmaking role, however, is shared. Each house must be seen as a separate institution, even though they both reflect somewhat similar political forces and share organizational patterns.

[handwritten margin note: Procedure is different in house & senate]

The House of Representatives

Organization and procedure in the House are somewhat different from that in the Senate, if only because the House is over four times as large as the Senate. In recent years these two bodies have grown more similar. Still, *how* things are done usually affects *what* is done. The House assigns different types of bills to

[handwritten margin notes: House is informal, debate limits by majority vote, quorum of 100, Electronic Voting]

[handwritten margin notes: Speaker, presiding officer of house, Leader of Majority party]

different calendars. For example, finance measures—tax or appropriations bills—are put on a special calendar for quicker action. The House has worked out other ways of speeding up lawmaking, including an electronic voting device. Ordinary rules may be suspended by a two-thirds vote, or immediate action may be taken by unanimous consent of the members on the floor. By sitting as the *committee of the whole*, the House is able to operate more informally and more quickly than under its regular rules. A quorum in this committee is only one hundred members, rather than a majority of the whole chamber, and voting is quicker and simpler. Members are limited in how long they can speak. In contrast to the Senate, debate may be cut off simply by majority vote.

[handwritten: Speaker directs business of House]

THE SPEAKER   The **speaker** is the presiding officer in the House of Representatives. This officer is formally elected by the House but actually selected by the majority party. Throughout most of this century House members were unwilling to vest power in their party leaders. Revolts in 1910 by the rank-and-file progressives stripped speakers of most of their authority, which included control over who served on congressional committees. In the mid-1970s, however, several changes strengthened the speakership. The 1910 changes, designed to reduce the power of the speaker, were introduced as progressive reforms: Sixty years later, progressive reforms gave back to the speaker some of these powers.

The routine powers of the speaker include recognizing members who wish to speak, ruling on questions of parliamentary procedure, and appointing members to select and conference committees—that is, temporary committees, not standing committees. In general, the speaker directs the business on the floor of the House. More significant, of course, is a speaker's political and behind-the-scenes influence. (When Democrats are in the majority, the speaker chairs the influential Democratic Steering and Policy Committee. This committee consists of about twenty-four members: the speaker's lieutenants, four others appointed by the speaker, and twelve elected by regional caucuses within the House Democratic party. It devises and directs party strategy.) In 1975 the speaker was given the authority to refer legislation to the relevant committee and to select most members and the chair of the House Rules Committee.

The job of speaker goes to a member of the majority party, usually one with substantial seniority. Speaker Thomas "Tip" O'Neill, elected in January 1977, for example, had served in the House since 1953.[17] The speaker is assisted by a **majority floor leader**, who helps plan party strategy, confers with other party leaders, and tries to keep members of the party in line. The minority party elects a minority floor leader, who usually steps into the speakership when his or her party gains a majority in the House. Assisting each floor leader are the party **whips**. (The term comes from the whipper-in, who in fox hunts keeps the hounds bunched in the pack.) The whips serve as liaison between the House leadership of each party and the rank and file. They inform members when important bills will come up for a vote, and prepare summaries of the bills' contents; do nose counts for the leadership; exert mild pressure on members to support the leadership; and try to ensure maximum attendance on the floor for critical votes.

At the beginning of the session and occasionally afterward, each party holds a **caucus** of all its members (called a conference by Republicans) to elect party officers, approve committee assignments, elect committee leaders, discuss important legislation, and perhaps try to agree on party policy.

[handwritten: Plan strategy / confer]

[handwritten: Speaker assisted by majority floor Leader]

Presidents give their State of the Union address before a joint session of both houses of Congress. *Bill Fitz-Patrick, The White House.*

[handwritten margin note: 1910: Revolts took some of Speaker power]

House Speaker Thomas O'Neill (right) and House Minority leader Bob Michel (R-Ill.), talk during the opening of the 98th Congress on the House floor. *UPI.*

[17]For an analysis of how congressional leaders get selected, see Robert L. Peabody, *Leadership in Congress: Stability, Succession and Change* (Little, Brown, 1976). For a sympathetic biography of House Speaker Thomas P. O'Neill, see Paul Clancy and Shirley Elder, *Tip: A Biography of Thomas P. O'Neill* (Macmillan, 1980).

[handwritten: caucus - elect party officers, leaders discuss political policy]

[handwritten: Whips - liaison between house Leader and rank & file]

[handwritten margin notes: Power vested in Rules Committee. Rules Committee ways to kill bills. Can use Rules Committee the Arm of leadership]

THE HOUSE RULES COMMITTEE   One way in which the House differs from the Senate is in the procedure for deciding the flow of business. In the House this power is vested in the Rules Committee, one of the regular House standing committees. In the normal course of events, a bill does not come up for action on the floor without a rule from the Rules Committee. By failing to act or refusing to grant a rule, the committee can hold up a bill. The rule granted gives the conditions under which the bill will be discussed, and these conditions may seriously affect the chance of passage. The Rules Committee may grant a rule that makes it easy for a bill to be amended to death on the floor. A special rule may prohibit amendments altogether or provide that only members of the committee reporting the bill may offer amendments. The rule also sets the length of debate and specifies what can and cannot be amended.

Up to about the mid-1960s the Rules Committee was dominated by a coalition of Republicans and conservative Democrats. Liberals denounced it as being unrepresentative, unfair, and dictatorial. Today it seldom blocks legislation unless the House leadership prefers measures to be held up. Meanwhile the Rules Committee membership—due to deaths and new appointments—has come to reflect the views of the total membership of the majority party. Because the speaker can control its membership, the Rules Committee today is usually an arm of the leadership. And rather than blocking legislation, it offers what one analyst calls a "dress rehearsal" opportunity to those who are trying to press for new legislation.[18]

[handwritten: Senate: More time for debate, Less formal]

The Senate

Senate Majority leader Robert Dole (top, *UPI/Bettmann Archive)* and Senate Minority leader Robert Byrd (bottom, *UPI)* in the 99th Congress.

[handwritten: Majority Leader has most power]

In many respects the Senate resembles the House. There is the same basic committee structure, elected party leadership, and dispersion of power. But because the Senate is a smaller body, its procedures are considerably more informal, and it has more time for debate. *[handwritten: Pres Pro Tempore - Majority Party]*

The president of the Senate (the vice-president of the United States) has little influence. Such officials can vote only in case of a tie, and they are seldom consulted when important decisions are made. The Senate also elects from among the majority party a **president pro tempore**, who is the official chairperson in the absence of the vice-president. But presiding over the Senate is a thankless task and is generally carried out by a junior member of the chamber.

Party machinery in the Senate is somewhat similar to that of the House. There are party conferences (caucuses), majority and minority floor leaders, and party whips. Each party has a *policy committee*, composed of the leaders of the party, which is theoretically responsible for the party's overall legislative program. (In the Senate the party steering committees handle only committee assignments.) Unlike the House steering committees, the Senate's policy committees are formally provided for by law, and each has a regular staff and a budget. Although the Senate policy committees have some influence on legislation, they have not asserted strong legislative leadership or managed to coordinate policy. *[handwritten: Policy Committee - Party Leaders in Charge of Policy]*

The majority leader, however, is usually a person of influence within the Senate and sometimes nationally. The majority leader is the body's major power broker. He has the right to be the first senator heard on the floor. In consultation with the minority floor leader, the majority leader determines the Senate's agenda and has much to say about committee assignments for members of the majority party. But the position confers somewhat less authority than the speakership in the House, and its influence depends on the person's political and parliamentary skills and on the national political situation.

[18]Bruce I. Oppenheimer, "The Rules Committee: New Arm of Leadership in a Decentralized House," in Larry Dodd and Bruce Oppenheimer (eds.), *Congress Reconsidered* (Praeger, 1977), p. 113. For a perceptive analysis of the House rules committee since 1961, see Spark M. Matsunaga and Ping Chen, *Rulemakers of the House* (University of Illinois Press, 1976).

[handwritten marginalia: Reciprocity - I scratch your back...]

[handwritten marginalia: Senators have more room than Reps. by 6 yr terms. Members protect each other]

POLITICAL ENVIRONMENT Senators are a somewhat different breed from most House members, and some people feel the Senate has a character all its own. Senators have more political elbow room than representatives, if only because of the six-year-term. In addition, senators are more likely to wield power in their state parties. Average senators become visible and politically significant earlier in their careers. Part of this is due to the relative smallness of the Senate and to its easier access to the media; part is due, no doubt, to larger staffs. *[handwritten: Senators have unwritten rules of courtesy]*

To a degree the Senate is a mutual protection society. Members tend to guard the rights and privileges of other senators—so that their own rights and privileges will be protected in turn. Members learn to live together. Two senators may attack each other rather sharply on the floor, only to be seen a short time later strolling together in the corridors. Like many close-knit social or professional groups, the Senate has developed a set of informal folkways—standards of behavior to which new members are expected to conform. Courtesy in debate is a cardinal rule, for example, and debate takes place in the third person. By far the most important folkway is *reciprocity*. A senator requests and receives many favors and courtesies from colleagues, always with the understanding that he or she will repay the kindness in some form. A senator may be out of town and request that the vote on a particular bill be delayed. Or a senator may ask a committee chair how a given bill will affect constituents, and rely on the colleague's judgment. Reciprocity may involve trivial pleasantries—or millions of dollars in traded votes for public works appropriations.

In the mid-1950s liberal senators and freshmen used to complain of a conservative "Establishment" or "club" that dominated the Senate through the power of these folkways and through control of key committees and processes. But the Senate has changed. An activist and attractive senator, especially one representing a large state, often becomes a national political figure and is sometimes talked about as a possible candidate for the presidency. Indeed, presidential ambition in the Senate has also led to the decline of the Senate Establishment. What is notable about the Senate today is the dispersion of power among party leaders, more than a dozen committee leaders, several dozen subcommittee chairs, senators from the larger states, and young activists. The contemporary Senate is individualistic. Committee leaders have more power than regular members, but with the expanding role of subcommittee chairs and expanding staff, their influence has lessened. More and more key decisions are made on the Senate floor. The Senate is a more open and fluid and more decentralized body now than it was in the 1950s or early 1960s.[19] It also has a considerably increased workload. *[handwritten: Filibuster - Debate unlimited in Senate]*

THE FILIBUSTER RULE A major difference between the Senate and the House is that debate is almost unlimited in the Senate. Once a senator gains the floor, he or she has the right to go on talking until relinquishing it voluntarily or through exhaustion. This right to unlimited debate may be used by a small group of senators to filibuster—or delay the proceedings of the Senate in order to prevent a vote.

At one time the filibuster was a favorite weapon used by southern senators to block civil rights legislation. More recently the filibuster has been used less frequently. But at the end of any Senate session, when there is a fixed date for adjournment, threat of filibuster is a real danger for controversial legislation. The knowledge that a bill might be subject to a filibuster is often just enough to force a compromise satisfactory to its opponents. Of course, if there are enough votes, the objections can be overcome—if there is enough time. But at

DIFFERENCES BETWEEN HOUSE AND SENATE

HOUSE

Two-year term
435 members
Smaller constituencies
Less staff
Represents equal populations
Less flexible rules
Limited debate
More policy specialists
Less media coverage
Less prestige
Less reliance on staff
Rules Committee important
Committee leaders more powerful
Committees very important
22 major committees
Nongermaine amendments ("riders" not allowed)

SENATE

Six-year term
100 members
Larger constituencies
More staff
Represents states
More flexible rules
Unlimited debate
Policy generalists
More media coverage
More prestige
More reliance on staff
More equal distribution of power
Committees less important
16 major committees
Rules Committee less important
Special treaty ratification power
Special confirmation power
Nongermane amendments ("riders") allowed

---

[19]Norman Ornstein, Robert Peabody, and David Rohde, "The Changing Senate: From the 1950's to the 1970's," in Dodd and Oppenheimer (eds.), *Congress Reconsidered*, p. 16.

the end of a session, senators are anxious to go home and campaign. Sometimes the leadership, knowing that a filibuster would tie up the Senate and keep it from enacting other needed legislation, does not bother to bring a bill to the floor.

Can a filibuster be defeated? The majority can keep the Senate in continuous session so that a filibustering senator will have to give up the floor. But if two or more senators cooperate, they can keep on talking almost indefinitely. They merely ask one another long questions that permit their partners to take lengthy rests. As long as the senators who are doing the talking stay on their feet, debate can be shut off only by a cloture vote. Under the rule of cloture, if sixteen members sign a petition, two days later the question of curtailing debate is put to a vote. If three-fifths of the total number of elected senators vote for cloture, no senator may speak for more than one hour. Nowadays, too, a final vote must be taken after no more than a hundred hours of debate—including all delaying tactics such as quorum calls, roll call votes on procedure, and the like. After the hundred hours debate the motion before the Senate must be brought to a vote.

Until early 1975 it took a two-thirds vote of the senators present to close off debate. But in that year the Senate voted to modify its cloture rule to make it slightly easier to end debate. Most liberals argued for a simple majority of those present and voting to force an end to a filibuster. Most conservatives wanted to retain the two-thirds requirement. Requiring three-fifths of the entire membership (or sixty votes if there are no vacancies) was a compromise decision. Filibusters are rare. Still, the filibuster, *and the threat of it*, remains a delaying device available to Senate minorities, forcing the majority to compromise and water down their preferences.

Senator Pete Wilson (R-Calif.), former Mayor of San Diego, Ca.

COMMITTEES: THE LITTLE LEGISLATURES

It is sometimes said that Congress is a collection of committees that come together in a chamber every once in a while to approve one another's actions. There is much truth in this. The main struggle over legislation takes place in committees and especially in subcommittees, for this is where the basic work of Congress is done. The House of Representatives has twenty-two standing committees, each with an average membership of over thirty representatives. These committees have a total of about 135 subcommittees. The committees are "the eye, the ear, the hand, and very often the brain of the House."

Standing committees have great power, for all bills introduced in the House are referred to them. They can defeat bills, pigeonhole them for weeks, amend them beyond recognition, or speed them on their way. A committee reports out favorably only a small fraction of all the bills that come to it. Although a bill can be forced to the floor of the House through a discharge petition signed by a majority of the membership, legislators are reluctant to bypass committees. For one thing, they regard committee members as experts in their field. Sometimes, too, they are reluctant to risk the anger of committee leaders. And there is a strong sense of reciprocity—"You respect my committee's jurisdiction, and I will respect yours." It is not surprising that few discharge petitions gain the necessary number of signatures.

The Senate has sixteen standing committees, each composed of twelve to twenty-nine members. Whereas members of the House hold relatively few committee assignments, each senator normally serves on three committees and an average of eight subcommittees. Among the most important Senate committees are foreign relations, finance, and appropriations. Senate committees

Congressman Thomas S. Foley (D-Washington), asking questions at a House hearing.

have the same powers over the framing of legislation as do those of the House, but they do not have the same power to keep bills from reaching the floor.

On committee subject to interests

Partisanship shapes the control and staffing of standing committees. The chair and a majority of the members are elected from the majority party. The minority party is represented roughly in proportion to its membership in the entire chamber. Getting on a politically advantageous committee is important to members of Congress. A representative from Kansas, for example, would much rather serve on the agriculture committee than on the merchant marine and fisheries committee. Members usually stay on the same committee from one Congress to the next, although younger members who have had undesirable assignments often bid for a better committee when places become available.

Choosing Committee Members

Joint House and Senate Appropriations Committee. *K. Jewell.*

How are committee members chosen? In the House of Representatives a Committee on Committees of the Republican membership allots places to new Republican members. This committee is composed of one member from each state having Republican representation in the House; this member is almost always the senior member of the state's delegation. Because each member has as many votes in the committee as there are Republicans in the delegation, the group is dominated by senior members from the large-state delegations. On the Democratic side assignment to committees is handled by the Steering Committee of the Democratic caucus in negotiation with senior Democrats from the state delegations. In the Senate veterans also dominate the assignment process, with each party having a small steering committee for that purpose. In making assignments, leaders are guided by various considerations: how talented and cooperative a member is, whether his or her region is already well represented on a committee, and whether the assignment will aid in reelecting the member. Committees & sub-coms. specialize

Senator Paul Laxalt (R-Nevada), a frequent spokesman for Ronald Reagan and conservative issues positions in the U.S. Senate.

One reason Congress can cope with its huge workload is that its committees and subcommittees are organized around subject matter specialties. This allows members to develop technical expertise in specific areas and to recruit skilled staffs, so that Congress is often able to criticize and challenge experts from the bureaucracy. Interest groups and lobbyists realize the great power a specific committee has in certain areas and focus their attention on its members. Similarly, members of executive departments are careful to cultivate the committee and subcommittee chairs and members of "their" committees. One powerful Senate committee chairman reminded his constituents of the amount of federal tax money being spent in their state: "This does not happen by accident," the senator's campaign folder said. "It takes power and influence in Congress."

Committee Diversity and Persistence

Most committees are separate little centers of power, with rules, patterns of action, and internal processes of their own. Analyzing the House appropriations committee, students of Congress discovered it is characterized by a remarkable agreement among its members on key issues and on the role the committee should play. Leadership is stable, and members tend to remain a long time. They have worked out a way of life emphasizing conformity, give-and-take, and hard work. The subcommittee chairpersons of the House Appropriations Committee become specialists on the budgets and programs of the agencies within their jurisdiction, and often exercise more influence over administrative policy than any other single representative. For example, the chair of the Appropriations Subcommittee on Foreign Aid has more influence over that program than the chair of the House Committee on Foreign Affairs. The various appropriations subcommittees defer to one another's recommendations and back up the decisions of the parent committee.

[handwritten: Senate Foreign Relations committees more powerful than the House of]

[handwritten: House appropriation committee is more powerful than Senate]

Committees, however, differ. While some are powerful, others are much less important. Because of the Senate's special role in foreign policy, for example, the Senate Foreign Relations Committee is usually more influential than the House Committee on Foreign Affairs. For the two appropriations committees, however, the reverse is true: The House committee sometimes plays a more significant role than the Senate committee. However, these differences are less than they used to be. We should also note that committees differ not only for institutional reasons but also according to the goals and abilities of their members.[20]

How Congress uses committees is critical in its role as a partner in national policy making. Progress has been made in recent years to open hearings to the public and to improve the quality of committee staffs. But it is difficult to modernize jurisdictions, and jurisdictional overlap is common. For example, a dozen different committees deal with energy and education. Efforts to make the committee system more rational are often seen as a threat to the delicate balance of power within the chamber. In 1977, however, the Senate did streamline its committee structure. The new system prohibits any senator from chairing more than three committees and subcommittees, reduces the number of Senate committees, provides for somewhat more coherent committee jurisdiction, and establishes a computer system to schedule committee and subcommittee meetings, to avoid conflicts.

[handwritten: Reduce # of Senate Coms,]
[handwritten: New System: no senator can chair more than 3 subs & coms]

A conference committee composed of members from the Senate Finance and the House Ways and Means committees. *Rick Bloom.*

The Importance of Committee and Subcommittee Leaders

[handwritten: Com leaders Run the show]
[handwritten: younger members want more power]
[handwritten: Chairs given by seniority]

Committee and subcommittee leaders exercise influence over both the operations of their committees and the final output of Congress. Until the mid-1970s leaders determined the total workload of committees; hired and fired staff; and formed subcommittees and assigned them jurisdictions, members, and aides. Chairs also managed the most important bills assigned to their committees.

In recent years, however, as more activists and young members have been elected, they have insisted that they be given more authority, and have been impatient with their seniors. There has been a tendency to give subcommittee chairs more independence from the parent committee. It is not uncommon these days for a member of Congress of only one or two terms to be the chair of an important subcommittee, and indeed this is the tradition in the Senate.

Chairs are still usually awarded on the basis of *seniority*. The member of the majority party who has had the longest continuous service on the committee ordinarily becomes its head. The chair may be at odds with other members of the party, may oppose the party's national program, and may even be incompetent—still, he or she usually wins the chair position because of seniority.

Modifying Seniority

[handwritten: some elder committee heads got booted]

Committee leadership positions as well as assignments are the responsibility of the party caucuses in both chambers. The custom of seniority still prevails, but it is not a written rule, and other factors are beginning to be taken into account. In 1971, for example, the House Republican Conference decided that ranking Republicans on committees henceforth would be elected by the conference by a secret ballot. Soon afterwards Democrats authorized a secret ballot vote on chair positions if 20 percent of the caucus demanded it. In 1975 rank-and-file House Democrats, their ranks swollen and resolve stiffened by seventy-five mostly liberal newcomers, removed from their membership three elderly committee chairmen. In early 1979 younger members of the House successfully thwarted the seniority system in at least two subcommittee chair fights. Not only were House leaders surprised by these setbacks, but they let it

[20]Richard F. Fenno, Jr., *Congressmen in Committees* (Little, Brown, 1972.)

Suppose you are a moderate Republican representing a district in the U.S. House of Representatives from suburban Milwaukee. The president, who is also a Republican, is seeking your vote to help abolish the Department of Education. He claims it wastes money and that education is a state and local matter; hence, there is no need for a federal cabinet department.

You are not too involved in the issue and haven't heard much from your constituents back home. But all of a sudden you get hundreds of letters from teachers and educators back in your district urging you to vote against the president and help save the Department of Education. You hear hardly a word from people back home supporting the president's position. In your last election, which you won by a very narrow margin, the teachers associations endorsed you and donated both money and campaign help for your reelection.

What will you decide? What considerations will you weigh as you make your decision on this issue?

(Answer/Discussion on the next page.)

be known they believed the seniority system is still a valid means of moving members into committee leadership posts. A senior member, they said, should not be knocked off unless he or she is incompetent, autocratic, or has some other gross deficiency. However, younger, more independent-minded members of the House often favor a contest for committee leadership posts. And they especially want to know in advance of their support for a chair candidate whether or not the candidate will regularly consult with younger members of a committee.

When Republicans control the Senate, Republican members of the major committees choose each committee's chair. When their party loses control over the Senate, these same persons become the ranking minority members. As a regular practice, Republican members almost always elect the senior member to serve as their leader on a committee.

The Senate Democrats choose their nominees for ranking minority member or for chair positions by a secret ballot of the Democratic Conference whenever requested to do so by 20 percent of the Senate Democratic membership. The Senate Democrats almost always do elect the senior Democratic member of the Senate committee to serve as the ranking committee member, but the fact that the Democratic Conference could by secret ballot do otherwise has forced senior members to make concessions to ensure their reelection.

Many people think the system of seniority tends to give the most influence in Congress to those constituencies that are politically stable or even stagnant. These are the areas where party competition is low or where a particular interest group or machine influence may be greatest. It stacks the cards against areas where the two parties are more evenly matched, where interest in politics is high, and where competition is keen.

Seniority is defended on the grounds that elevating the most experienced members to leadership positions is automatic and impersonal and prevents disputes. Basically, the argument over seniority is about self-interest. Rural interests tend to favor the system. It is opposed by such groups as organized labor, advocates of civil rights legislation, and other urban-based interests, who feel it gives rural interest and their conservative representatives too much power in Congress. Yet liberal groups may also profit from the system. The passage of time may cause the seniority custom to increase the influence of suburban and urban-based northern interests.

The system of seniority remains because it supports the interests of congressional leaders. Many legislators conclude: "The longer I'm here, the better I like the system." Further, those who are most anxious to change the system have the least power to produce such changes. But as power has become dispersed, and as subcommittees have become increasingly important, the issue of seniority has diminished in importance. Subcommittee chairs tend to be members with less seniority, and they are likely to be more moderate than the committee chairs. In the Senate all but a handful of the majority party chair their own subcommittee; in the House more than a hundred Democrats are subcommittee chairs. In recent years there have also been moves to strengthen the powers of the party leaders and caucuses—again at the expense of the committee chairs.

Committee Investigations

One of the activities of Congress that is most likely to generate controversy is its investigations, especially such well-publicized open hearings as those of the Senate Foreign Relations Committee during the Vietnam war or those of various committees that investigated the Environmental Protection Agency in 1983. Why does Congress investigate? Hearings by standing committees, their subcommittees, or special select committees are an important source of infor-

hearings used for communication

mation and opinion. They provide an arena in which experts can submit their views and where statements and statistics can be entered in the record.

Public hearings are an important channel of communication and influence. A committee or its chair may use a hearing to address Congress. Hearings on the CIA and the FBI in 1976 were one way of impressing upon Congress the need for legislation to prevent the abuse of power in the intelligence agencies. Committee hearings may also be used to communicate with the public at large. The Senate's Watergate Committee's televised investigations into election practices and campaign finance abuses in 1973 were not intended merely to obtain new information. The senators involved were attempting to arouse citizens and to promote public support for election reforms, among other things.[21] Some investigations by regular committees involve overseeing administration. A committee can summon administration officials to testify in hearings. Some officials fear these inquiries; they dread the loaded questions of hostile members and the likelihood that some administrative error in their agency may be uncovered and publicized.[22] Former Senator Sam Ervin summed up the assets and the liabilities of congressional investigations as follows:

> A legislative inquiry can serve as the tool to pry open the barriers that hide corruption. It can be the catalyst that spurs Congress and the public to support vital reforms in our nation's laws. Or it can debase our principles, invade the privacy of our citizens, and afford a platform for demagogues and the rankest partisans.[23]

Congress can not get individuals question private citizens

Are there any constitutional limits to Congress's power to compel private citizens to answer questions? The Supreme Court in 1957 in *Watkins* v. *United States* cautioned Congress that the First Amendment limits its power to investigate, that no committee has the power "to expose for the sake of exposure," that Congress and its committees are not courts to try and punish individuals, and that "no inquiry is an end in itself; it must be related to, and in furtherance of, a legitimate task of Congress." But the Supreme Court has shown no inclination to set up a judicial check on legislative investigations in behalf of First Amendment rights. So far there are only two judicial checks.[24] The Fifth Amendment protection against self-incrimination has been construed broadly to protect congressional witnesses who are willing to risk public censure by invoking the amendment to refuse to answer questions. The Supreme Court has also narrowly construed the crime of contempt of Congress in order to avoid punishing witnesses for refusing to answer questions unless these questions are clearly important to the functions of an authorized committee investigation.

GETTING IT TOGETHER: CONFERENCE COMMITTEES AND SENATE-HOUSE COORDINATION

When the framers created a two-house national legislature, they anticipated that the two chambers would represent sharply different interests. The Senate was to be a small chamber of persons elected indirectly by the people and holding long, overlapping terms. As noted, it would have the sole power to confirm nominations. Proposed treaties required the approval of a two-thirds vote in the Senate. The Senate was to be a chamber of scrutiny, a gathering of "wise men" who would counsel and sanction a president—whether that president liked it or not.

[21]For a study of the role of congressional investigations, see James Hamilton, *The Power to Probe: A Study of Congressional Investigations* (Vintage, 1976).

[22]See Morris S. Ogul, *Congress Oversees the Bureaucracy* (University of Pittsburgh Press, 1976).

[23]Sam J. Ervin, Jr., in the introduction to Hamilton, *The Power to Probe*, p. xii.

[24]354 U.S. 178 (1957).

The House of Representatives, elected anew every two years, was to be a more direct instrument of the people. The Senate was a conservative check on the House, especially in the late nineteenth and early twentieth century, when it was extremely conservative and something of a rich man's club. But some factors—chiefly political—have altered the character of the House and Senate. Sometimes now the House serves as a conservative check on the Senate. Executive departments and agencies sometimes see the Senate as a court of appeals for appropriations that have been shot down by the House—although this was somewhat less the case in the Reagan years, when the Senate was controlled by Republicans.

How has this come about? A senator's constituency nearly always consists of a wider variety of interests than does that of a member of the House. But the Senate's behavior is also partly a result of the appropriations process and institutionalized rules. In the appropriations area the House completes its work before the Senate—and this has its consequences. Senate committee decisions often take the form of reactions to prior House decisions, adjusting the appropriation figures upwards or downwards depending on the issue.

Given the differences between the House and the Senate, it is not surprising that the version of a bill passed by one chamber may differ substantially from the version passed by the other. Only if both houses pass an absolutely identical measure can it become law. As a general rule, one house accepts the language of the other, but about 10 percent of all bills passed (usually major ones) must be referred to a conference committee.

If neither house will accept the other's bill, a conference committee—a special committee of members from each chamber—settles the differences. Both parties are represented, with the majority party having more members. The proceedings of this committee are usually an elaborate bargaining process. When it is brought back to the two houses, the conference report can be accepted or rejected (often with further negotiations ordered), but it cannot be amended. Each set of conference members must convince its colleagues that any concessions made to the other house were on unimportant points and that nothing basic in their own version of the bill was surrendered.

How much leeway does a conference committee have? Ordinarily the members are expected to stay somewhere between the different versions. On matters where there is no clear middle ground, members are sometimes accused of exceeding their instructions and producing a new bill. The conference committee has even been called a "third house" of Congress, one that arbitrarily revises policy. Conference committees are also criticized on the ground that they are not representative, even of the committees approving the bill, and that they disproportionately represent senior committee leaders. Critics also complain that little can be done about biases that may creep into the bill in the conference committee, since the houses are usually confronted with a take-it or leave-it situation. Despite such criticism, some kind of conference committee is needed for a two-house legislature to work. Conference committees integrate the houses, help resolve disputes, and make compromises.

Senate Watergate Committee Chairman Sam Ervin was a very strong force throughout those difficult but important hearings. *UPI.*

CONGRESSIONAL REFORM

There is so much criticism of Congress that here we can only briefly review the main charges against it.

1. Congress is *inefficient*. The House and Senate are simply not suited to the needs of an industrial nation. Bills require an endless amount of time to get through the complicated legislative process and are often blocked in the

middle. Members are not as well informed as they should be. The dispersion of power guarantees slowness, if not inertia.

Some of this criticism is exaggerated. Evaluating procedure and structure is difficult to separate from evaluating policy, where everyone has an individual preference. For example, from the White House vantage point, Congress is inefficient when it does not process the president's bills quickly.

Congress deals with an enormous number of complex measures. Many procedures in both houses expedite handling of bills, and the committee and subcommittee system is about the most reasonable device for hearing arguments and compiling information. Still, the question of efficiency remains. Many members themselves feel defeated by the system. Study groups inside and outside Congress have urged the houses to reduce the number of committee assignments, establish better information systems, and strengthen majority rule—and Congress has done many of these things—but the pace is worse than ever.

2. Congress is *unrepresentative*. The complaint is often made that Congress represents local interests over the national interest. Thus, it is said that the committee system often responds to organized regional or special interests. The seniority system, even with its modifications, biases both houses toward conservatism. Defenders of Congress contend there should be a strong institution to guarantee minority rights and to act as a check on mindless majority rule. Critics answer by arguing that minorities should have a right to publicize and delay what the majority proposes to do, but not to defeat it.

Both houses, critics hold, overrepresent well-organized economic power structures at the expense of the average citizen. Can the members of Congress, who are so much the products of upper- or upper-middle-class backgrounds, really speak for the needs of low-income groups? Can a Congress that has only 3 or 4 percent women and 3 or 4 percent black membership truly represent our female and minority population?

Recently Congress has tried to strengthen its representative character. Many observers say that in the 1980s the large middle class is better represented in Congress than ever.

In fact, we have a system of dual representation in which both Congress and president can and do claim to speak for the people. But since "the people" seldom if ever speak with a single voice, the structure and character of the two systems tend to give us a Congress that speaks for one majority and a president who often speaks for another. Between the two, we sometimes get a kind of balance—and sometimes a deadlock.

3. Congress is *unethical*. Many critics complain that some members of Congress are too tied to the economic interests they are asked to regulate. It is also charged that members of Congress get too many personal privileges and that there have been too many abuses of these so-called fringe benefits. To be sure, the misbehavior of Congress members is more frequently played up in the press than the misbehavior of others. Thus, the Elizabeth Ray sex scandal (she was the typist who could not type), the South Korean government's favors and contributions to several influential legislators, and ABSCAM (the FBI's staged bribery of several House members in 1979) became public matters, as indeed they should.

In response to these and other scandals, both houses have passed reasonably strong ethics codes and created ethics committees. These changes require full public disclosure of income and property holdings by legislators, key aides, and spouses. They also bar gifts of over $100 to a legislator, a staff member, or a legislator's family from a registered lobbyist, an organization with a political action committee, a foreign government, or a business with an interest in legislation before Congress.

"So far, my mail is running three to one in favor of my position." *Drawing by Robert Day.* © *1970 The New Yorker Magazine, Inc.*

4. *Congress is irresponsible.* The main problem in Congress is the dispersion of power among committee and subcommittee leaders, elected party officials, factional leaders, and other legislators. It's a "nobody's in charge" system. This dispersion of power means that to get things done, congressional leaders must bargain and negotiate. The result of this "brokerage" system is that laws may be watered down, defeated, delayed, or written in vague language. One result is that too much leeway, according to some critics, is given to unknown bureaucrats. Accountability is confused, responsibility is eroded, and well-organized special interests who know how to work the system are given an unfair advantage.

Critics worry that if Congress responds to so many single interests, it cannot speak for the great majority or for the nation as a whole. It cannot anticipate problems, plan ahead, and put together political coalitions to deal with critical problems. Those concerned about congressional irresponsibility do not blame a few conservative interests or elite elements. They recognize that brokerage is mainly the result of a constitutional system that divides authority, checks power with power, and disperses political leadership. Yet other factors making it difficult for Congress to act as a unified branch arise from the fact that each house is controlled by a different party. Also, we are now electing brighter and more independent-minded individuals.

5. *Congress delegates too much to the executive branch.* Another charge is that Congress fails to do its job, and tends to delegate too much authority to the executive branch. Because of the complexity of modern problems and an inability to work out coalitions and compromises, there is a tendency for Congress to say to the executive branch: "Do something" about affirmative action; or "Do something" about consumer product safety. Congress turns the matter over to an administrative agency, with the result that the rules and regulations issued by the administrators actually become the law.

These critics often disagree with the policy initiatives in question. Still, the complaint is valid, for we expect our *elected* officials to hammer out public policies. Congress is aware of this criticism, but sometimes escaping responsibility is a major consideration. If Congress passed specific legislation, affected persons or groups might then blame Congress rather than the administrative agencies—and perhaps even particular members of Congress, who then might lose their seats.

6. *Congress is too responsive to organized interests that through their political action committees make large campaign contributions.* This final charge suggests that while few members of Congress can be bought by campaign contributions, the way Congress conducts its business—and who gets heard at its hearings and in its corridors—is influenced to too great an extent by those who can raise and disburse large sums of money. Former Senator S. I. Hayakawa put it this way: "I'm not saying my colleagues are corrupted by the system. But it isn't hard for the recipient of a generous contribution from, let us say, the dairy industry to convince himself that what is in the interest of the dairy industry is indeed in the public interest."[25] Congressional campaign costs have skyrocketed in recent years; typical campaigns cost over $300,000 for the House, and often over a million dollars for the Senate. Money buys access, so it is claimed. The 1979 ABSCAM scandals, in which FBI agents posing as Arab sheiks successfully bought several promises of influence and favors from a handful of members of Congress, provide evidence for this criticism. It is small consolation that all these members were subsequently indicted and convicted by the federal courts.

[25]Quoted in *U.S. News & World Report*, December 20, 1982, p. 24.

Defenders of Congress say these charges are overstated. They say money would hardly influence the nearly three dozen millionaires who are members of the Senate and the nearly one hundred members of the House who are very well off financially. Defenders of Congress also point out that many members of Congress regularly turn down certain types of campaign contributions. Because of various campaign reform laws, candidates for Congress must now report all major campaign contributions to the Federal Elections Commission. Thus, who gives what to whom is at least part of the public record. Still, the criticism is valid, and a large number of Americans are perplexed or outraged about the degree of influence seemingly associated with campaign contributions.

In the mid-1980s the following questions remain: Can Congress create majorities? Can it have a long-range view, staying power, span of attention, and the ability to make sensible laws for the whole nation? While answers would differ, all would agree that a vital, responsive, and effective Congress is a must if we would make government by the people work.

SUMMARY

1. Senators and representatives come primarily from upper- and middle-class backgrounds. They are far better educated than Americans as a whole. The typical member of Congress is a middle-aged, white, male lawyer.

2. Most of the work in Congress gets done in committees and subcommittees. Congress has attempted in recent years to streamline its committee system and modify its methods of selecting committee chairs. Seniority practices are still generally followed, but the threat of removal forces committee chairs to consult with younger members of the majority party. Subcommittees are now more important in an increasingly decentralized Congress.

3. Congress performs these functions: representing, lawmaking, consensus building, overseeing, policy clarifying, and legitimizing.

4. The workload for Congress has never been greater. Much could be done to make our national legislature perform its functions more effectively. Some improvements have been made in recent years: Redistricting and reapportionment have shaped a Congress that more accurately reflects the population. The filibuster in the Senate and the Rules Committee in the House are less obstructive than they once were. The role of the speaker and of the party steering committee has been enhanced, and Congress is better staffed.

5. The negative image of Congress as a ponderous or sluggish institution is still common. Its greatest strengths—its diversity and deliberative character—also serve to weaken its capacity to be a match for the executive branch. Its members will rarely be fast on their 1,070 feet. The 535 members divided into two houses, two parties, dozens of committees, and hundreds of subcommittees will always have a difficult time arriving at a common strategy to combat a president determined to use executive powers to the full. How effectively can Congress assert itself, especially with respect to the presidency? We return to a consideration of this question in Chapter 16 after we have had a chance to examine the modern presidency and its responsibilities.

FURTHER READING

JOSEPH COOPER and G. CALVIN MACKENZIE (eds.). *The House at Work* (University of Texas Press, 1981).

ROGER H. DAVIDSON and WALTER J. OLESZEK. *Congress and Its Members* (Congressional Quarterly Press, 1981).

LAWRENCE C. DODD and BRUCE I. OPPENHEIMER (eds.). *Congress Reconsidered*, 2nd ed. (Congressional Quarterly Press, 1981).

RICHARD F. FENNO, JR. *Home Style: House Members in Their Districts* (Little, Brown, 1978).

MORRIS FIORINA. *Congress—The Keystone of the American Establishment* (Yale University Press, 1977).

CHARLES O. JONES. *The United States Congress* (Dorsey Press, 1982).

DAVID KOZAK and JOHN MACARTNEY (eds.). *Congress and Public Policy: A Source Book of Documents and Readings* (Dorsey Press, 1982).

MICHAEL MALBIN. *Unelected Representatives: Congressional Staff and the Future of Representation* (Basic Books, 1980).

THOMAS MANN and NORMAN J. ORNSTEIN (eds.). *The New Congress* (American Enterprise Institute, 1981).

DAVID R. MAYHEW. *Congress: The Electoral Connection* (Yale University Press, 1974).

WALTER J. OLESZEK. *Congressional Procedures and the Policy Process*, 2nd ed. (Congressional Quarterly Press, 1983).

RANDALL RIPLEY. *Congress*, 3rd ed. (Norton, 1983).

THE PRESIDENCY: LEADERSHIP BRANCH?

15

Prez must be 35 yrs, lived in U.S. 14 yrs. Natural Born Citizen

What does it take to be an effective president? Are the constitutional powers of the presidency adequate for carrying out modern presidential responsibilities? Can the modern presidency meet our high expectations of president? And can it survive the grinding pressures of crises abroad and human demands at home?

Our Constitution establishes only three qualifications for the office: A president must be at least thirty-five years of age, have lived in the United States for fourteen years, and be a natural-born citizen. On this last point the courts have never had to decide whether a person born abroad to American parents could serve as president, but many scholars believe such a person would qualify.

Our "unwritten presidential job description"—the one we carry around as images in our heads—says that a president has to be virtually all things to all people. Every four years Americans search the national landscape for a new superstar who is blessed with the mind of a Jefferson, the steadfastness of a Lincoln, the calm of an Eisenhower, and the grace of a John F. Kennedy. While the American presidency may not have been designed in 1787 as a leadership institution (certainly not as a party, legislative, or economic leadership post), the situation has certainly changed.

One of the decisive forces shaping American democracy, many analysts say, has been the capacity of the presidency to provide strong, able, and popular leadership. Others say what is needed are leaders who can grasp the real needs, wants, and higher aspirations of the American people and make our huge, fragmented system of government serve those needs and aspirations. In periods of crisis our so-called three-branch system seems to have worked best as a presidential system—that is, as a system in which the presidency has been dominant. Some writers suggest that only strong presidents have been able to overcome the tendency toward inertia inherent in a nation so beset with checks and balances and separated powers.

Voters put emphasis on character & integrity instead of policy (handwritten)

Three Presidents—Harry S Truman, Dwight D. Eisenhower, and John F. Kennedy—are shown together in this picture. They were attending the 1962 funeral of Speaker of the House, Sam Rayburn, in Texas. *UPI.*

WHO WERE THE BEST PRESIDENTS?

A. Surveys of *historians* (including a 1983 survey of 970 historians) have consistently obtained these results:

1. Lincoln
2. Washington
3. F. D. Roosevelt
4. Jefferson
   Wilson
   Theodore Roosevelt
   Jackson

B. But surveys of the public turn out differently: Gallup Poll (1975) of the American people: "What three presidents do you regard as the greatest?"

1. Kennedy 52%
2. Lincoln 49%
3. F. D. Roosevelt 45%
4. Truman 37%
5. Washington 25%
6. Eisenhower 24%

C. Gallup Poll (late 1983) of the American people: "Of all the Presidents we have ever had, who do you wish were President today?"

1. Kennedy (JFK) 30%
2. F. D. Roosevelt 10%
3. Truman 9%
4. Reagan 8%
5. Lincoln 5%
6. Carter 5%
7. Eisenhower 4%

But exactly what do the American people want of their president? They want strong leadership—an ability to work with Congress, to solve economic problems, to keep the peace, to gain the people's confidence, and to get things done. Opinion polls show that people yearn for an intellectually honest person in the White House. They also want someone who can provide a sense of vision and a sense of purpose—someone who can remind us of our basic aspirations as a democratic and generous nation, and as an innovative and experimenting people.

Voters often place more emphasis on a candidate's *character and integrity* than they do on the candidate's *policy* preferences. This is not as misguided an approach as some would believe. After all, presidents have enormous power, especially in emergencies. They also play an important role in making appointments, which in turn reflect their interest in upholding ethical standards of governmental performance. Thus, it is important to assess their character. Will they become rigid or dogmatic in dealing with crises, or with Congress, the press, advisers, and critics? Will they display vision, judgment, a grasp of history, a sense of proportion, and a sense of humor? To be sure, people prefer those candidates whose views on issues accord with their own; and if they like a person's personality, they sometimes judge that individual's policy ideas to be acceptable. Hence, a candidate's character and policy preferences sometimes get blurred—if not confused—in the voter's mind.

Still, the public also wants a president to be tough, decisive, and competent. Voters recognize the need, *even in a democracy*, for strong leadership. They yearn for a leader with foresight and personal strength. Moreover, people want someone who will personalize government and authority, simplify politics, symbolize the protective role of the state, and yet seem to be concerned with *them*. We want *effectiveness*, but also *fairness*. Do we ask too much? Novelist John Steinbeck thought so: "We give the President more work than a man can do, more responsibility than a man should take, more pressure than a man can bear. We abuse him often and rarely praise him. We wear him out, use him up, eat him up. . . . he is ours and we exercise the right to destroy him."[1]

people want a strong pres; we want effectiveness & fairness (handwritten)

[1]John Steinbeck, *America and Americans* (Bonanza Books, 1966), p. 46.

15-1
PERSONAL CHARACTERISTICS OR QUALITIES DESIRED IN A PRESIDENT

QUESTION: Here is a list of personal characteristics or qualities. Would you read off all of those which you feel are important for a president to have?

	TOTAL MENTIONS
Placing country's interest ahead of politics	83%
Sound judgment in crisis	82
Intelligence	82
Taking a firm stand on issues	75
Competence, ability to get job done	74
Compassion, concern for little man/average citizen	70
Experience in public office	69
Ability to anticipate the nation's needs	68

Reprinted by permission, from "Looking for Leadership" by Thomas E. Cronin in *Public Opinion*, February/March, 1980, p. 19.

[handwritten margin note: Pres gets blame for everything]

Americans applaud presidents when things go well and blame them when things go wrong. Disasters as well as triumphs are credited to presidents—Wilson's League of Nations, Hoover's Depression, Roosevelt's New Deal, Johnson's Vietnam war, Nixon's **Watergate**, Carter's Iranian crisis, Reagan's Lebanon problem. An exaggerated sense of presidential wisdom and power has caused us to forget that there are limits to what presidents can accomplish. While the tragedies of American involvement in Vietnam and of presidential involvement in the Watergate scandals deglamorized the presidency, the vitality of our democracy still depends in large measure on creative presidential leadership.

IS THE PRESIDENCY TOO STRONG— OR STRONG ENOUGH?

[handwritten margin note: critics charge pres as less accountable - manipulates and uses TV too much]

Some critics see the presidency as fast becoming inconsistent with democratic ideals. They view it as an institution that is often remote and autocratic, as the citadel of the status quo, as the center of the industrial-military-political complex—and as the very heart of the Establishment. They charge that presidents are less accountable today than ever before, with the ability to get around the formal checks and balances designed by the framers. Critics complain too that presidents now manipulate the public's sense of reality by relying on secrecy, emergency powers, and the "electronic throne" of television. Finally, some say the Reagan administration reversed some of the "open government" and accountability reforms passed in the wake of Watergate.

Many people care less about the extent of presidential authority than about the *purposes* for which it is used: Only when the president appears to represent interests which these people approve of do they say the power should be left unchecked. Other critics are more concerned about *process.* If the president's actions reflect the wishes of the majority of the people most of the time, the process is assumed to be working properly.

Progressives in both parties on the other hand look to the president as the potential spokesperson for the common person. Throughout our history active presidents have tended to bring about changes that have pleased the liberal-progressive forces. The Kennedy-Johnson initiatives on civil rights are examples. There is no guarantee, of course, that a strong president will please the progressives. Vietnam provides an example to the contrary. The Reagan tax and budget cuts are another, more recent example.

[handwritten margin note: strong pres pleases progressives]

"Harrison sat down and wrote—as the President requested, mind you—a long letter itemizing in detail what he felt was wrong with the country and outlining possible remedies for said wrongs. Ten pages, if you please. And to this date no response." *Drawing by Mulligan; © 1977 The New Yorker Magazine, Inc.*

THE WHITE HOUSE
1600 Pennsylvania Ave., N.W.
Washington, D.C. 20500

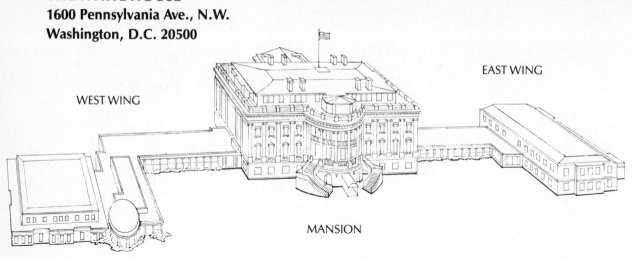

WEST WING

MANSION

EAST WING

The White House complex is an executive office, a ceremonial mansion, and a home. Several presidents have viewed it almost as a jail, preferring to spend as much time as possible at other presidential retreats outside of Washington. But most Americans view the White House as the center of political and social activity in the nation's capital. It is also something of a national shrine as millions of people from America as well as around the world visit it each year.

EAST WING

1 Theater
2 Tour Entrance
3 Official Visitors' Lobby
4 President's Military Aide
5 First Lady's Press Secretary
6 Social Secretary
7 Congressional Relations Staff
8 First Lady's Director of Special Projects

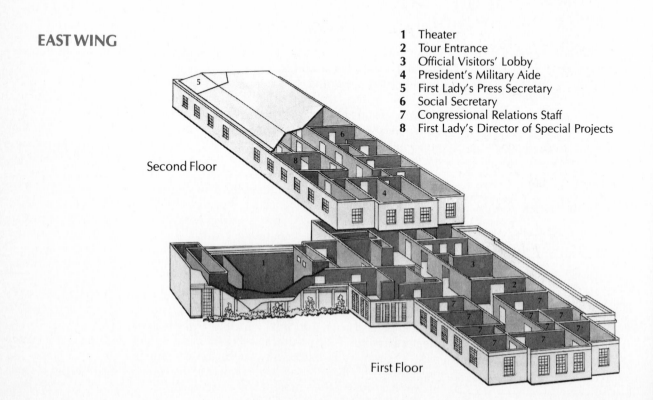

Second Floor

First Floor

WEST WING

 1 Situation Room
 2 National Security Council Staff
 3 Oval Office
 4 Cabinet Room
 5 West Lobby
 6 Roosevelt Room (Conference Room)
 7 Assistants to the President
 8 Presidential Press Secretary
 9 Press Briefing Room and Filing Center
10 Vice President's Office
11 Photo Office
12 Mini-Barber Shop (For the President
    and Vice President Only)
13 White House Staff Mess

Second Floor

Main Floor

Basement

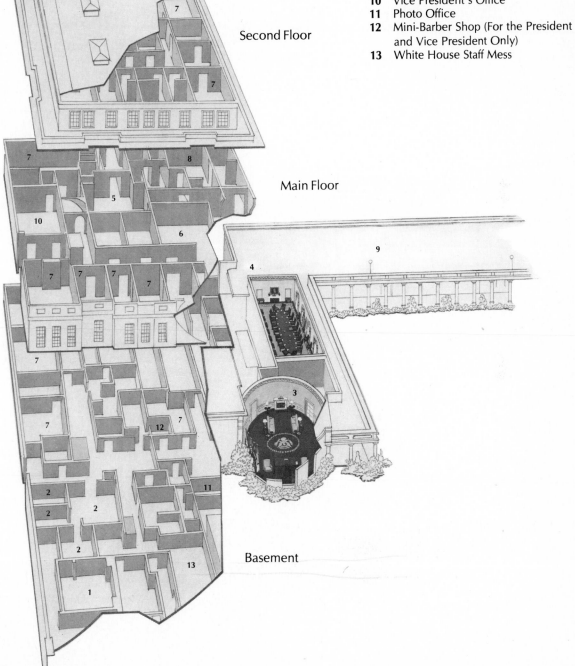

Ground Floor

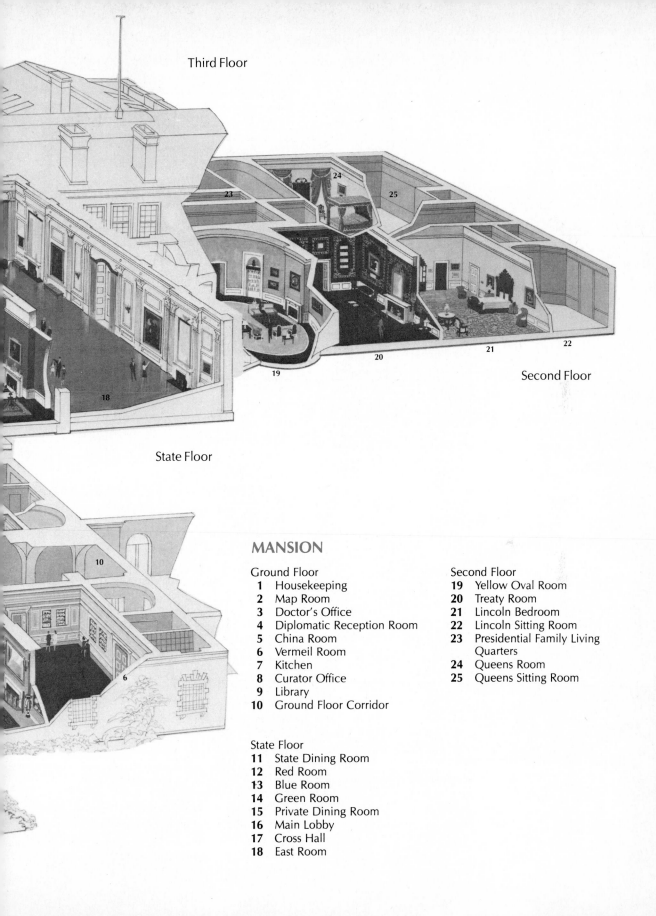

Third Floor

Second Floor

State Floor

MANSION

Ground Floor
 1 Housekeeping
 2 Map Room
 3 Doctor's Office
 4 Diplomatic Reception Room
 5 China Room
 6 Vermeil Room
 7 Kitchen
 8 Curator Office
 9 Library
10 Ground Floor Corridor

State Floor
11 State Dining Room
12 Red Room
13 Blue Room
14 Green Room
15 Private Dining Room
16 Main Lobby
17 Cross Hall
18 East Room

Second Floor
19 Yellow Oval Room
20 Treaty Room
21 Lincoln Bedroom
22 Lincoln Sitting Room
23 Presidential Family Living
    Quarters
24 Queens Room
25 Queens Sitting Room

[handwritten margin notes: Strong Pres [move] outside elite power structures to reach the masses? / people want strong leadership]

Many historians contend the great presidents have been the strong presidents who have moved outside elite power structures to reach the masses. That was how Jefferson and Jackson overcame the Adamses of their day; that is how the two Roosevelts overcame the "economic royalists" of their day. While presidents often have to compromise with existing elites, sometimes the chief executive has the power to defy the "establishment." Presidents like to quote Franklin Roosevelt who, after some businessmen had cursed him for his "radical" New Deal policies, cried out at the height of his 1936 reelection campaign: "I should like to have it said of my first Administration that in it the forces of selfishness and of lust for power met their match. I should like to have it said of my second Administration that in it these forces met their master!"

After the Watergate scandals of the Nixon administration, many argued persuasively that our system of checks and balances needed to be strengthened. But once Watergate had faded into the past and the nation was faced with inflation, unemployment, and countless other problems that nobody seemed able to solve—including Presidents Ford and Carter—the public seemed to demand stronger presidential leadership.

The public attitude toward the presidency is difficult to discover. Public opinion polls are not always clear. But at least in recent years, they do seem to indicate a public mood in favor of strong leadership.

THE JOB OF THE PRESIDENT

The nation's founders created a presidency of somewhat limited powers. They wanted a presidential office that would stay clear of parties and factions, enforce the laws passed by Congress, deal with foreign governments, and help states put down disorders. They wanted a presidency strong enough to match Congress, but not so strong that it would overpower Congress. They seemed to have in mind that the president should be an elected king with substantial personal authority, acting above factions. The delegates rejected a *plural* or *collegial* executive; there would be no ceremonial head separate from an administrative one. The term would be for four years, and presidents would be permitted to run for reelection. Independent from the legislature, presidents would still share considerable power with Congress. The essence of the arrangement would be an *intermingling* of powers with Congress. To achieve change, the separate branches would have to work in cooperation and consult with one another. A president's major appointments would have to be approved by the Senate; Congress could override the chief executive's veto by a two-thirds vote of each chamber; and the president could make treaties only with the advice and consent of two-thirds of the senators. And, of course, all appropriations (the power of the purse) would be legislated by Congress, not the president.

Even a presidency with such limited powers, hemmed in by the system of checks and balances, worried some Americans in 1787. But they were reassured by the fact that George Washington was to be the first chief executive. And they recognized that, at least on paper, Congress was truly the first branch. A relatively unified Congress could make life pretty miserable for a president. It could, for example, refuse to confirm a president's vital nominations, refuse to pass legislation suggested by a president, refuse funds for key programs, refuse to ratify treaties, and could override the chief executive's vetoes. But the historical record suggests most presidents have enjoyed far greater leeway than this implies.

Modern-day presidents are much more powerful than those of the last century, despite the fact that their constitutional powers have not changed. The

CONSTITUTIONAL RESPONSIBILITIES OF A PRESIDENT

Commander in chief
Conduct foreign policy
Negotiate treaties
Nominate top federal officials
Veto bills
Faithfully administer federal laws
Pardon for federal offenses
Address Congress and nation

framers deliberately gave to the president broadly outlined, as well as vaguely defined, powers. The president, they thought, should have discretionary power, so that this official could act when other governmental branches failed to meet their responsibilities or to respond to the urgencies of the day.

After nearly two centuries our presidential "track record" is good. Perhaps in no other nation have persons with such power at their command so carefully followed the restraints imposed on them by a written Constitution. But to describe presidential power is inadequate. The exact dimensions of executive power at any given moment are largely the consequence of the incumbent's character and energy, combined with the needs of the time and the challenges to our nation's survival. By and large, the history of the presidency is one of steady but uneven growth. Of the forty individuals who have filled the office, about a third have enlarged its powers. The Jacksons, Lincolns, and Roosevelts, for example, strengthened both the institution and its powers.

In this extension of the executive power Congress and the courts have often been willing partners. In emergencies Congress often rushes to delegate discretion to the executive branch; and the legislature sometimes seems incapable of dealing with matters that are highly technical or that require constant managment or consistent judgment. Some people think what Congress lacks most is the will to use the powers it already has. But this hardly seems to be a satisfactory explanation. For Congress is not unique among legislative bodies. During the last two centuries in all democracies, and at all levels, power has drifted from legislators to executives. The English prime minister, the French president, governors of our states, and mayors of our cities all play a more dominant role than they did, generally speaking, a hundred years ago.

The danger of war plainly increases a president's impact on the nation's affairs. The Cold War shattered most of the remaining nostalgia for isolation-ism. The combination of an enormous standing army, nuclear weapons, and the Cold War invited presidential dominance in national security matters. Television has also contributed to the growth of presidential influence. With access to prime time, presidents can take their case directly to the people. This invitation to bypass and sometimes to ignore Congress, the Washington press, and even party leaders weakens the checks once imposed on the presidency.

The great growth of the federal role in domestic and economic matters has also enlarged presidential responsibility and contributed to the swollen presidential establishment. Problems that are not easily delegated to any one department often get pulled into the White House. When new programs concern several federal agencies, someone near the president is often sought to fashion a consistent policy and reconcile conflicts. White House aides, with some justification, claim the presidency is the only place in government where it is possible to establish and coordinate national priorities. And presidents constantly set up central review and coordination units. These help formulate new policies, settle jurisdictional disputes among departments, and provide access for the well-organized interest groups who want their views to be given weight in decision making.

The swelling of the presidency has also been encouraged by the public's expectations. Although we may dislike or condemn individual presidents, popular attitudes toward the institution of the presidency remain positive. We want very much to believe in and trust our presidents. Perhaps this is because we have no royal family, no established church, and no common ceremonial leadership divorced from executive responsibilities. In an effort to live up to unrealistic expectations, some presidents overextend themselves. Maintaining the presidential image requires them to expand their power, thus creating a circle of rising expectations.

ADDITIONAL RESPONSIBILITIES AND INFORMAL ROLES

Morale builder
Party leader
Legislative leader
Coalition builder
Crisis manager
Personnel recruiter
World leader
Budget setter
Priority setter
Bargainer and persuader
Conflict resolver

Nowadays a president is asked to play countless roles that are not carefully spelled out in the Constitution. We want the chief executive to be an international peacemaker as well as a national morale builder, a politician-in-chief, and a unifying representative of all the people. We want every new president to be virtually everything all our great presidents have been. Rightly or wrongly, we believe our greatest presidents were models of talent, tenacity, and optimism; persons who could clarify the vital issues of the day and mobilize the nation for action. We like to think of our great presidents as leaders who could not only symbolize the best in the nation and move the enterprise forward, but who could summon the highest kinds of moral commitment from the American people. These storybook images of our great presidents often make it tough for modern presidents to do their job.

In addition to the obvious policy leadership responsibilities a president has in foreign policy, economics, and domestic policy, there are seven broad functional kinds of leadership expected of a president. These policy areas and functions, when examined together, permit us to develop a job profile of an American president (see Table 15–2).

15–2 A PRESIDENTIAL JOB DESCRIPTION

	Examples of Policy Responsibilities		
TYPES OF FUNCTIONAL LEADERSHIP:	FOREIGN POLICY	ECONOMICS	DOMESTIC POLICY
Crisis management	Grenada crisis, U.S. troops in Lebanon, 1983	FDR & the Depression, 1930s	Enforcing court orders on school desegregation
Symbolic and morale-building leadership	Nixon trip to China, 1971	Being bullish on American productivity	Visiting flood and disaster victims
Recruitment of top officials	Selecting chairpersons of the joint chiefs of staff	Hiring the wisest possible economic advisers	Appointing a Chief Justice
Priority setting and problem clarification	Defining our relations with the USSR	Outlining a tax cut program	Setting priorities in environmental protection
Legislative and political coalition building	Reagan's fight for aid for El Salvador, 1983	Reagan's campaign for tax cuts, 1981	Carter's efforts to pass civil service reform
Program implementation and administration	Making Middle East peace accords work	Shoring up the social security program	Seeing that the laws are faithfully executed
Oversight of government performance and early detection of possible problems	Evaluating our relations with Japan	Monitoring internal revenue service performance	Appraising the impact of federal welfare programs

PRESIDENTS AS CRISIS MANAGERS

"The President shall be Commander in Chief of the Army and the Navy of the United States," reads Section 2 of Article II of the Constitution. Even though this is the first of the president's powers listed in the Constitution, the framers intended the military role to be a limited one—far less than a king's. It was as if the president would be a sort of first general and first admiral. As it turns out, the military role has become much more important: The president has a finger on the nuclear button and appears to have sole authority over limited wars as well.

When crises and national emergencies occur, we instinctively turn to the chief executive, who is expected to provide not only executive and political leadership but also the appearance of a confident, "take-charge" leader who has a steady hand at the helm. Public necessity forces presidents to do what Lincoln and Franklin Roosevelt once did during the national emergencies of their day—namely, to protect the union and to safeguard vital American interests.

Nearly two centuries of national expansion and recurrent crises have increased the powers of the president beyond those specified by the Constitution. The complexity of Congress's decision-making procedures, its unwieldy numbers, and its constitutional tasks make it a more public, deliberative, and divided organization than the presidency. When major crises occur, Congress traditionally holds debates—but just as predictably delegates authority to a president, charging that official to take whatever actions are necessary.

The primary factor underlying this transformation in the president's function as commander in chief has been the changed role of the United States in the world, especially since World War II. In the postwar years every president argued for and won widespread support for the position that military strength, especially military superiority over the Soviet Union, was the primary route to national security. Nations willingly grew dependent on our assistance, which rapidly became translated into a multitude of treaties, pacts, and **executive agreements**. From then on, nearly every threat to the political stability of our far-flung network of allies became a test of whether we would honor our commitments in good faith. These commitments, plus the fear of nuclear war and the importance of deterrence, prompted Congress to give great flexibility to presidents in this area.

Presidents are expected to be crisis managers in the domestic sphere as well. Whenever things go wrong, we demand presidential-level planning and problem solving. When New York City and Chrysler were on the verge of bankruptcy, people turned to the White House for help. When Mt. St. Helens erupted, when the accident at Three Mile Island nuclear power plant occurred, and when nationwide strikes break out, people assume that the president will take care of the problem. In a crisis a president is often little more than the victim of fast-breaking events and environmental forces. Very often presidents are surprised, overtaken by developments beyond their control, and placed on the defensive.

PRESIDENTS AS MORALE-BUILDING LEADERS

Presidents are the nation's number-one celebrity; almost anything they do is news. Merely by going to church or to a sports event, presidents command attention. By their actions presidents can arouse a sense of hope or despair, honor or dishonor.

The framers did not fully anticipate the symbolic and morale-building functions a president must perform. Certain magisterial functions, such as the granting of pardons, were conferred. But the presidency over time has acquired enormous symbolic significance. No matter how enlightened or rational we consider ourselves, all of us respond in some way to symbols and rituals. The president often affects our images of authority, legitimacy, and confidence in our political system.

The Popular Need for Leadership

A president's personal conduct affects how millions of Americans view their political loyalties and civic responsibilities. Of course, the symbolic influence of presidents is not always evoked in favor of worthy causes, and sometimes presidents do not live up to our expectations of moral leadership. But even in this nation of hard-nosed pragmatists, we yearn for a sense of purpose, a vision of where the nation is going. "The Presidency is the focus for the most intense

"One thing I'll say for him. He does have a coherent foreign policy." *Drawing by Dana Fradon; © 1982. The New Yorker Magazine, Inc.*

A Presidential Dilemma

ANSWER/DISCUSSION

President John F. Kennedy was confronted with a similar situation in October 1962. Soviet offensive weapons were being shipped to and installed in Cuba. He reviewed several recommendations similar to those presented to you. Kennedy chose to impose a naval blockade on Cuba aimed at preventing further shipments of Soviet equipment, and he pressed Nikita Khrushchev, the Soviet leader, to have the Russians immediately withdraw all offensive weapons from Cuba. His initiatives succeeded, even though the two countries may have come close to nuclear war. Since then, Congress, fearful of unchecked presidential initiatives, has adopted several acts designed to limit presidential discretion in times of emergencies, most especially the War Powers Resolution of 1973 (see chapter 16).

and persistent emotions. . . .The President is . . . the one figure who draws together the people's hopes and fears for the political future. On top of all his routine duties, he has to carry that off—or fail."[2]

It would be much easier for everyone, some writers say, if our president were a prime minister, called on merely to manage the affairs of government in as efficient and practical a way as possible and not also our chief of state. But this is not the case.[3] Americans are not about to invent a head of state position separate from the presidency. That would be too much like England. Moreover it would weaken an already fragile institution.

Presidential head-of-state duties often seem trivial and unimportant. For example, pitching out the first baseball of the season, buying Christmas or Easter seals, pressing buttons that start big power projects, and visiting the scene of national disasters do not require executive talents. Yet our president is asked continuously to champion our common heritage, to help unify the nation, and also to create an improved climate within which the diverse interests of the nation can work together.

Under ordinary conditions the presidential claim to be "leader of all the people," or symbolic leader of the nation, conflicts with the reality of a president who tries to act for only part of the people. Some presidential functions are fundamentally inconsistent with one another. On the one hand, the president is a party leader—the spokesperson and representative of a segment of the population that is loosely identified with a particular party. As such the chief executive not only directs the national party organization but—as chief legislator—also affects the party program. On the other hand, as ceremonial leader and chief of state, the president attempts to act for all the people. A chief executive must faithfully administer the laws, whether passed by Democratic or Republican majorities in Congress. Yet in choosing subordinates and in applying the law, often presidents understandably think first of the interests of those who elected them.

The relationship between these presidential roles is uneasy. For example, the president may wish to address the nation about a problem—and usually the chief executive is granted free time on radio and TV. But if an election is close, the opposition often charges the president is really acting as party chief and that the party should pay for the radio or TV time. The same question comes up in connection with a president's inspection trips, especially when they are used as occasions for political talks and general politicking.

Most of the time a president manages to combine the offices of chief of state and party leader without too much difficulty. Most people understand that a president holds both roles, moving from one to the other as conditions demand. There is nothing wrong with the symbolic powers that come with the office. They become a problem only when they lead the public to believe symbolism equals accomplishment, or when ceremonial and symbolic responsibilities keep presidents from performing their more demanding duties.

The morale-building job of the president involves much more than just ceremonial, cheerleading, or quasi-chaplain duties. Presidential leadership, at its finest, radiates confidence and empowers people to give their best, to unleash the vast energies for good that are at large in the nation. Our best leaders have been able to provide this special and often intangible element. Perhaps it could be called morale revitalization or purposive renewal. While it may defy

[2]James David Barber, *The Presidential Character*, 2nd ed. (Prentice-Hall, 1977). See also George Edwards, *The Public Presidency* (St. Martin's Press, 1983).

[3]For a more extensive treatment of the symbolic implications of the presidency, see Michael Novak, *Choosing Our King* (Macmillan, 1974).

easy definition, we know Washington, Jefferson, Jackson, Lincoln, the Roosevelts, Eisenhower, and John F. Kennedy, each in his own way, provided it. Still, we know all too well that it is not something that the Constitution confers or something conveniently closeted in the White House for the use of each new occupant.

PRESIDENTS AS CHIEF RECRUITERS

George Washington. *Library of Congress.*

Abraham Lincoln. *Library of Congress.*

Often a single appointment may achieve more than scores of presidential policy initiatives. President Eisenhower's nomination and appointment of Earl Warren to be Chief Justice of the Supreme Court may have been the single most significant decision of that administration in the area of domestic policy. Warren served in that post for over fifteen years and presided over vast changes in civil rights and civil liberties. In a similar way selection of a secretary of state, of top economic advisers, of the secretary of the interior, or of top White House aides can have an enormous impact on national policy over a four-year period.

Effective presidents shrewdly use their appointment powers—presidents have control over 5,000 appointments, including hundreds of federal judgeships and top positions in the military and diplomatic service—not only to reward campaign supporters and enhance ties to Congress but also to communicate priorities and policy directions. (Note, however, that many appointments must be made with the approval of the Senate. This limits the appointment powers to some extent.) A president's top appointees are also a major link between the White House and the millions of people who serve in the career federal and military services; and the chief executive needs the best possible managers and motivators in these crucial positions. Besides identifying and recruiting them, the president must also try to keep the most talented of these officials in government as long as possible.[4]

The turnover problem is acute. Many able people come to top positions—say in the cabinet or subcabinet—and stay for only eighteen months or two years. Many of these top federal posts do not pay as much as comparable positions in the private sector. Also, living in Washington can be expensive.

A president must strengthen the hand of the ablest people working in the bureaucracy and often promote these people to higher positions at the senior reaches of the executive branch. In short, the personnel responsibilities of a president are far greater and require far more time than anyone, including presidents, expects.

PRESIDENTS AS PRIORITY SETTERS

Presidents, by custom, have become responsible for proposing new initiatives in the areas of foreign policy, economic growth and stability, and the quality of life in America. This was not always the case. But beginning with Woodrow Wilson, and especially since the New Deal, a president is expected to promote peace, prevent depressions, and propose reforms to ensure domestic progress. The trend in national policy making is toward greater centralization: Federal programs are conceived by a president searching for campaign issues or legislative program material, and they are planned by the executive office or by special task forces and commissions.

[4]See Calvin MacKenzie, *The Politics of Presidential Appointments* (Free Press, 1981).

National Security Policy

Presidents generally have more leeway in foreign and military affairs than they have in domestic matters. This is partly due to grants of authority stipulated in the Constitution, and partly due to the character of diplomatic and military activity. The framers foresaw a special need for speed and unity in our dealings with other nations. The Constitution vests in a president command of the two major instruments of foreign policy—the diplomatic corps and the armed services. It also gives the chief executive responsibility for negotiating treaties and commitments with other nations.

Congress has granted presidents wide discretion in initiating foreign policies, for diplomacy frequently requires quick action. A president can act swiftly; Congress usually does not. The Supreme Court has upheld strong presidential authority in this area. In the Curtiss-Wright case in 1936, the Court referred to the "exclusive power of the President as the sole organ of the Federal Government in the field of international relations—a power which does not require as a basis for its exercise an act of Congress, but which, of course, like every other governmental power, must be exercised in subordination to the applicable provisions of the Constitution."[5] These are sweeping words. Yet a determined Congress *that knows what it wants to do*, and can agree on it, does not lack power in foreign relations. It must authorize and appropriate the funds that back up our policies abroad. It is a forum for debate and criticism. And, as it at least tried to do after the Vietnam war, it can specify the conditions of war making (more on this in Chapter 16).

Theodore Roosevelt. *Library of Congress.*

Economic Policy

Pres is expected to promote economic success

Ever since the New Deal, presidents have been expected to initiate action to prevent unemployment, to fight inflation, to keep taxes down, to ensure economic growth and prosperity, and to do whatever they think necessary and proper to prevent depressions. The Constitution does not place these duties on the White House, but presidents know that if they fail to act, they will suffer the fate of Herbert Hoover, who was denounced for years by the Democrats for his alleged inaction during the Great Depression. Recent elections have turned largely on economics.

The chief advisers to the president on economic policy are the three members of the Council of Economic Advisers, the secretary of the treasury, and the director of the Office of Management and Budget. While presidents sometimes get their economic advice elsewhere, it is these persons who advise the president on what actions to take. The growth and complexity of economic problems have placed even more initiative in the hands of the president. The delicate balancing required to keep a modern economy operating means that the presidency must play a central role.

Dwight D. Eisenhower. *Library of Congress.*

Domestic Policy

A leader is one who knows where the followers are. Lincoln did not invent the antislavery movement. Kennedy and Johnson did not begin the civil rights movement. Reagan did not initiate the "cut the taxes" crusade. But they all, in their respective time, became embroiled in these controversies, for a president cannot ignore for long what divides or inspires a nation.

The essence of the modern presidency lies in its potential capability to resolve societal conflicts. To be sure, much of the time a president will avoid conflict where possible, seeking instead to defer, delegate, or otherwise delay controversial decisions. The effective president, however, will clarify the major issues of the day, define what is possible, and organize the governmental structure so that important goals can be realized.

A president—with the cooperation of Congress—can set national goals and propose legislation. Close inspection indicates, however, that in most in-

[5]*United States v. Curtiss-Wright Export Corp.*, 299 U.S. 304 (1936).

stances a president's "new initiatives" in domestic policy are measures that have been under consideration in previous sessions of Congress. Just as the celebrated New Deal legislation had a fairly well-defined history extending back several years before its embrace by Franklin Roosevelt, many of Reagan's initiatives were the fruits of long campaigns by congressional activists and special interests.

The president "shall from time to time give to the Congress information on the State of the Union, and recommend to their Consideration such Measures as he shall judge necessary and expedient," the Constitution provides. From the start strong presidents have exploited this power. Washington and Adams came in person to Congress to deliver information and recommendations. Jefferson and many presidents after him sent written messages, but Wilson restored the practice of delivering a personal, and often dramatic, message. Franklin Roosevelt used personal appearances (as have most presidents since then) to draw the attention of the whole nation to his program. Carter went to Congress to unveil his energy program. Reagan visited Congress the very week after he was elected—and went back on several additional occasions to give major reports to the nation.

Less obvious, but perhaps equally important, are the frequent written messages dispatched from the White House to Capitol Hill on a vast range of public problems. These messages may not create much stir, but they are important in defining the administration's position and in giving a lead to friendly legislators. Moreover, these messages are often accompanied by detailed drafts of legislation that members of Congress may sponsor with little or no change. These White House proposals, the products of bill-drafting experts on the president's own staff or in the executive departments and agencies, may be strengthened or diluted by Congress, but many of the original provisions survive.

"The question is, do we want to emphasize foreign policy to take the people's minds off domestic policy, or emphasize domestic policy to take the people's minds off foreign policy?" *Drawing by Dana Fradon; © 1979 The New Yorker Magazine, Inc.*

PRESIDENTS AS LEGISLATIVE AND POLITICAL COALITION BUILDERS

John F. Kennedy. *UPI.*

An effective president is an effective politician—the most visible and potentially the strongest mobilizer of influence in the American system of power. As discussed in Chapter 13, *politician* is a nasty word to many Americans; it denotes a scheming, evasive person out for his or her own self-interest. Little wonder many politicians claim they are "above politics." There is, however, a more constructive definition of *politician:* one who helps manage conflict; one who knows how to negotiate, bargain, and help reconcile different views in order to make the difficult and desirable become a reality. Presidents cannot escape political coalition-building tasks. As candidates, they have made promises to the people. To get things done, a president must work with many people and countless interest groups who have differing loyalties and responsibilities. Inevitably, a president is embroiled in legislative politics, bureaucratic politics, and lobbying for important programs.

Despite the available formal powers, presidents can rarely command; they spend most of their time *persuading* people. Potentially, presidents have enormous persuasive powers, but in the long run people think of their own self-interests, and presidential wishes often go unheeded. In a government of separated institutions that share powers, some congressional and bureaucratic and even military leaders are beyond the political reach of the president. They have their own constituencies—a House committee, for example, or a powerful interest group. Presidents cannot simply give orders like a first sergeant. Before Dwight Eisenhower became president, Harry Truman said of him: "He'll sit here, and he'll say, 'Do this! Do that!' And nothing will happen, Poor Ike—it

[handwritten margin notes: Pres is one person most in touch w/ Public. Pres uses Press Conference to stay In touch w/ Public]

won't be a bit like the Army. He'll find it very frustrating."[6] *All* presidents have found it frustrating.

Many students of the presidency think the power to persuade is the chief resource of a president and that the power to persuade comes through bargaining. Bargaining, in turn, comes primarily through getting others to feel that it is in their own self-interest to cooperate. Hence, the skill of a president in communicating and in winning others over is the necessary energizing factor in moving the institutions of the national government to action. This school of thought also holds that a president cannot be shy and above the battle, or above politics. Rather, a president must enjoy the give and take of congressional-presidential relations, and the give and take between the parties and between the White House and the press. Classic examples of effective presidential political coalition building are Franklin Roosevelt's building of public support around his New Deal programs, Lyndon Johnson's successful efforts to pass his civil rights and education legislation, and Ronald Reagan's mobilizing public and congressional support for his economic programs in the early 1980s.

The Prime-Time Presidency

No other politician (and few television or film stars) can achieve a closer contact with the people than can the president. Typically, the chief executive has been a prominent senator, a vice-president, or a governor, and has built up a host of followers. Having won a nomination and an election, the president has been in the public eye for years. But the White House is the finest platform of all. The president has a television studio right in the White House, which can be used for a direct appeal to the people. Presidents can summon the press when they wish, arrange fireside chats or radio call-in shows, choose a sympathetic audience, or undertake a "nonpolitical" speaking tour. And they can time all these moves for maximum advantage.[7]

The press conference is an example of how the president can employ the machinery of communication in a systematic manner. Years ago the conferences were rather casual affairs. Franklin Roosevelt ran his get-togethers informally and was a master at withholding information as well as giving it. Under Truman the conference became "an increasingly routinized, institutionalized part of the presidential communications apparatus. Preparation became elaborately formalized, as did the conduct of the meetings themselves."[8] Kennedy authorized the first live telecast of a press conference and used it frequently for direct communication with the people. Ronald Reagan regularly and effectively used five-minute Saturday afternoon radio chats to communicate his views, ask for support, and win Sunday morning media coverage.

Presidents commission private polls to gauge public opinion; they must be able to distinguish its petty whims, estimate its endurance, and respond to its impatience—and they must respect its potential impact. A president must know not only what to do but when to do it. Public opinion can be unstable and unpredictable. The public generally rejects government by public opinion; they do not want a president falling captive to the polls. President Johnson recognized that his wide popular support of the mid-1960s had melted away by 1968, when he decided not to run again. President Nixon's dramatic drop of nearly 45 percentage points in public opinion polls, a result of the Watergate

WHY PRESIDENTIAL APPROVAL (IN POLLS) USUALLY DECLINES THE LONGER PRESIDENTS ARE IN OFFICE

☐ Expectations that are raised in campaigns and by early promises get dashed as time forecloses resources and options.*

☐ Things that go wrong get blamed, rightly or wrongly, on presidents—whether or not a president has the power to deal with these matters.

☐ Inflation and unemployment increases often are linked with rising disapproval of incumbent presidents.

☐ Major negative events, such as Vietnam, Watergate scandals, Iranian hostage crisis, influence how people evaluate presidents.

☐ Press and media criticism accumulate over time and sharpen the public's dissatisfaction toward a president.

☐ Perhaps, too, just time in office wears out our welcome for a president.

*Note: Political scientists are not exactly sure of the precise relationships here; different studies produce different findings. The factors listed above, however, are plainly some of the more important ones—and some of these are doubtless interrelated.

[6]Richard E. Neustadt, *Presidential Power* (Wiley, 1980), p. 9.

[7]See Newton W. Minow, John B. Martin, and Lee M. Mitchell, *Presidential Television* (Basic Books, 1973); and George Edwards, *The Public Presidency* (St. Martin's Press, 1983).

[8]Elmer E. Cornwell, Jr., *Presidential Leadership of Public Opinion* (Indiana University Press, 1965), p. 175.

scandals, helped force his resignation. And nearly all presidents lose support the longer they are in office. Dissatisfaction sets in; interest groups grow impatient; unkept promises must be accounted for; and the president gets blamed for whatever goes wrong.

Party Leadership

Another potential source of influence for the president is the political party. Most presidents since Jefferson have been party leaders, and generally the more effective the presidents, the more use they have made of party support. Wilson and the two Roosevelts fortified their executive and legislative influence by mobilizing support within their party. Yet no president has ever fully led a party.

The president has no formal position in the party structure, but the chief executive's influence over national policies and over thousands of appointments commands respect from party leaders. Both president and party need each other. The president needs the party's backing in order to enact a legislative program. The party needs the president's direction and prestige—and the political "gravy" that flows from the White House.

The strings of the national organization all lie in a president's hands. Formally, the national party committee picks the national party chair; actually, the president lets the committee know the desired candidate and the members choose that person. Today presidents can hire or fire national party chairs much as they shift department heads or even their own staff. The president's pronouncements on national party policy are more authoritative than those of any party committee, even more significant than the party platform itself. Presidents can give a candidate a good deal of recognition and publicity in Washington. They can grant—or deny—campaign assistance and even financial assistance.

Ronald Reagan pictured delivering one of his Saturday radio talks to the public. *Karl H. Schumacher, The White House.*

Limits on Party Leadership

Yet the president's practical power over the party is sharply limited and often comes to an end precisely when it is needed most. Presidents rarely have influence over the selection of party candidates for Congress and for state and local office. Presidents also sometimes have trouble getting crucial votes from individuals in their own parties in Congress. This is due in part to the chief executive's limited control of state and local organizations. But also, party organizations themselves do not control their candidates in office: Most candidates win office less through the efforts of the organized party than through their own individual campaigning. Of course, the situation varies from place to place, but in most instances *personalized politics* emphasizing the candidate is more successful than *programmatic politics* emphasizing party and issues.

Franklin Roosevelt's "purge" of 1938 is a dramatic example of the limits of the president's power. Despite his own sweeping victory in the 1936 election and the lopsided Democratic majorities in Congress, Roosevelt ran into heavy opposition from many Democratic senators and representatives in 1937 and 1938. Angered by this opposition within the party, Roosevelt decided to use his influence to bar the nomination of anti-New Deal candidates in the 1938 congressional primaries. He announced that not as president but as "head of the Democratic party, charged with the responsibility of carrying out the definitely liberal" 1936 Democratic party platform, he would intervene where party principles were clearly at stake. Roosevelt won a significant victory in New York City when he repudiated the anti-New Deal chairman of the House Rules Committee and helped a proadministration Democrat win nomination. But elsewhere—mainly in the South—he was defeated.

Presidents must *bargain* and *negotiate* with the party leaders as they do with other independent power centers. Lacking full support from the whole

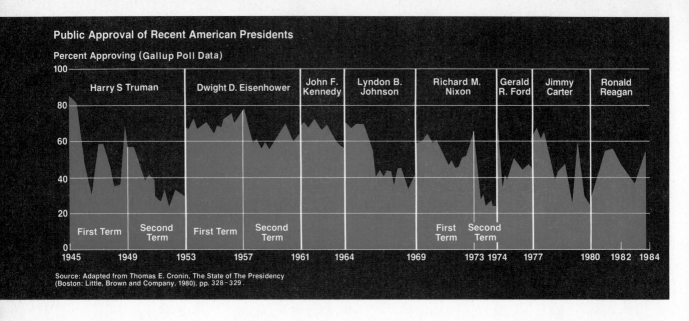

Public Approval of Recent American Presidents

Percent Approving (Gallup Poll Data)

Harry S Truman | Dwight D. Eisenhower | John F. Kennedy | Lyndon B. Johnson | Richard M. Nixon | Gerald R. Ford | Jimmy Carter | Ronald Reagan

First Term | Second Term | First Term | Second Term | First Term | Second Term

1945 1949 1953 1957 1961 1964 1969 1973 1974 1977 1980 1982 1984

Source: Adapted from Thomas E. Cronin, The State of The Presidency (Boston: Little, Brown and Company, 1980), pp. 328–329.

party, presidents usually fall back on the personal organizations that originally enabled them to gain the nomination.[9]

PRESIDENTS AS ADMINISTRATORS

presidential orders flow down an administrative line pres is assisted by staff

The Constitution charges the president to "take care that the laws be faithfully executed." Presidents, however, can be only part-time administrators, for they are forever overscheduled and other responsibilities demand most of their attention. They are, then, dependent on their dependents. Theoretically, at least, orders flow down an administrative *line*, from president to department heads, to bureau chiefs, and down to smaller offices. The president, like all top executives, is assisted by a *staff*, who advise the chief executive from the latter's point of view. This line and staff organization is inherent in any large administrative entity, whether it be the Army, General Motors, or the United Nations.

Presidents have come to rely heavily on their personal staffs. Nowhere else—not in Congress, not in the cabinet, not in the party—can presidents find the loyalty, the single-mindedness, and the team spirit that develops among their closest aides. Moreover, presidents come to view most cabinet heads as advocates, peddling ideas that benefit the particular friends and interest groups associated with their departments. Presidents apparently think their own aides will provide them with more neutral and objective advice. But there are substantial costs to listening only to one's closest aides. George Reedy, a former press secretary to President Johnson, depicts the White House as a palace court with strong presidents creating an environment in which any assistant who persists in presenting irritating thoughts is weeded out. "Palace-guard survivors learn early to camouflage themselves with a coating of battleship grey. . . . Inevitably in a battle between courtiers and advisers, the courtiers will win out. This represents the greatest of all barriers to presidential access to

President Reagan confers with economic advisers: Secretary of the Treasury Donald Regan (left), and Budget Director David Stockman (right). *Michael Evans, The White House.*

[9]For a more detailed treatment see Thomas E. Cronin, "The Presidency and The Parties," in Thomas E. Cronin (ed.), *Rethinking the Presidency* (Little, Brown, 1982), chap. 21; and Robert Harmel (ed.), *The President as Party Leader* (Praeger, 1984).

336

GROWTH OF WHITE HOUSE STAFF		
1943	FDR	50
1949	Truman	240
1953	Ike	250
1962	JFK	340
1965	LBJ	300
1971	Nixon	580
1975	Ford	525
1984	Reagan	575

reality. . . ."[10] And an astute British writer notes: ". . . if a president needs to be protected by his White House staff against the departments, he also needs to be kept on guard by the departments against his White House staff, who may all too easily begin to think only they know the purposes and the needs and the mind of their president, until *he* becomes *their* creature and believes that his interests are safe with them."[11]

The number of employees in the presidential entourage has grown steadily since the early 1900s, when only a few dozen people served a president at a cost of less than a few hundred thousand dollars annually. Today a White House staff of over 500 operates at the cost of several million dollars a year. The Executive Office of the President, approved by Congress in 1939, was the recommendation of President Franklin Roosevelt's Committee on Administrative Management. The Executive Office was to provide presidents help they obviously needed in carrying out the growing responsibilities imposed by the Depression and by the enlarged role of government.

Pres staff of 500 operates at several million annually

The Institutionalized Executive Office

Pres should not give advisor too much power

The Executive Office of the President consists of the Office of Management and Budget, the Council of Economic Advisers, and several other staff units. The most prominent and controversial presidential staff, of course, is the White House Office. A president's immediate staff, working out of the White House itself, does not have fixed form; indeed, part of its value lies in its flexibility and adaptability. Most presidents, however, have an appointments

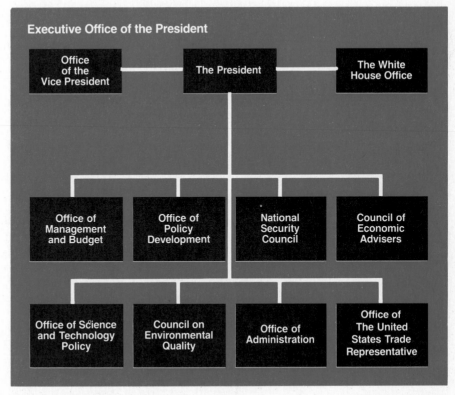

Executive Office of the President

[10]George Reedy, *The Twilight of the Presidency* (World, 1970), p. 98. For different points of view see Henry Kissinger, *The White House Years* (Little, Brown, 1979); and Zbigniew Brzezinski, *Power and Principle* (Farrar, Straus & Giroux, 1983).

[11]Henry Fairlie, *The Kennedy Promise* (Doubleday, 1973), pp. 167–68. See also Stephen Hess, *Organizing the Presidency* (Brookings Institution, 1976); and Edward Weisband and Thomas M. Franck, *Resignation as Protest* (Penguin, 1975).

Presidential Aides are too close to Pres

secretary, a press secretary, a correspondence secretary, a legal counsel, a national security advisor, military aides, and several other legislative, administrative, and political assistants. The staff of the White House office can be categorized by functions: (1) domestic policy, (2) economic policy, (3) national security or foreign policy, (4) administration and personnel matters (as well as personal paper work and scheduling for the president), (5) congressional relations, and (6) public relations.

Presidential aides sometimes insist that they are simply the eyes and ears of the president, that they make few important decisions, and that they never insert themselves between the chief executive and the heads of departments. But the burgeoning White House staff has made this traditional picture nearly obsolete. Some White House aides, impatient with bureaucratic and congressional bottlenecks or even political sabotage, come to view the presidency as if it alone were the whole government. Separation of powers means little to them, and they lose sight of their location within the larger constitutional system. Listen to a Nixon aide: "There shouldn't be a lot of leeway in following the President's policies. It should be like a corporation, where the executive vice-presidents [the cabinet officers] are tied closely to the Chief Executive, or to put it in extreme terms, when he says jump, they only ask how high."[12] And a Carter aide told one of the authors that giving so much power to the cabinet members "was probably President Carter's biggest mistake."

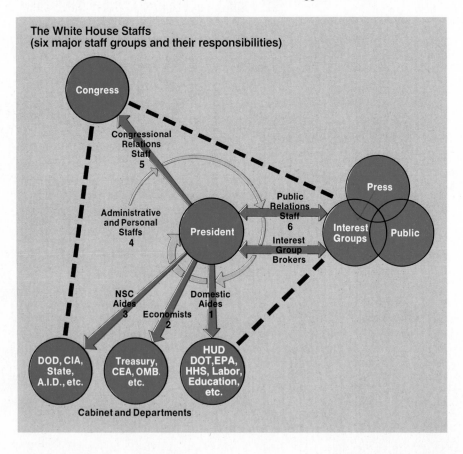

The White House Staffs
(six major staff groups and their responsibilities)

Congress

Congressional Relations Staff 5

Administrative and Personal Staffs 4

President

Public Relations Staff 6

Interest Group Brokers

Press

Interest Groups

Public

NSC Aides 3

Economists 2

Domestic Aides 1

DOD, CIA, State, A.I.D., etc.

Treasury, CEA, OMB. etc.

HUD DOT,EPA, HHS, Labor, Education, etc.

Cabinet and Departments

[12]John Ehrlichman, interview published in *The Washington Post*, August 24, 1972. See also Jeb Stuart Magruder's account of White House life in the Nixon administration, *An American Life: One Man's Road to Watergate* (Atheneum, 1974); and John Dean, *Blind Ambition* (Simon and Schuster, 1976).

*Office of
Mgmt & Budget
is central
presidential
staff agency*

The Office of Management and Budget continues to be the central presidential staff agency. Its director advises the president in detail about the hundreds of government agencies—how much money they should be allotted in the budget, and what kind of job they are doing. OMB seeks to improve the planning, management, and statistical work of the agencies. It makes a special effort to see that each agency conforms to presidential policies in its dealings with Congress; each agency has to clear its policy recommendations to Congress through OMB first.

A budget is not just a financial plan, for it reflects power struggles and indicates policy directions (and wishful thinking).[13] To the president the budget is a means of control over administrators who may be trying to join ranks with politicians or interest groups to thwart presidential priorities. Through the long budget-preparing process, presidents use the OMB as a way of conserving and centralizing their own influence.

The Cabinet

*Most Pres's
Just met w/
people concerned
not whole
cabinet*

*Cabinet
useless*

It is hard to find a more unusual institution than the cabinet. It is not specifically mentioned by name in the Constitution. Yet since George Washington's administration, every president has had a cabinet. Washington's consisted of his secretaries of state, treasury, and war, plus his attorney general. Today the cabinet consists of the president, the vice-president, the officers who head the thirteen executive departments, and a few others. The cabinet has always been a loosely designated body, and it is not always clear who belongs to it. In recent years, for example, certain executive branch administrators and White House counselors have been accorded cabinet rank.

Cabinet government as practiced in parliamentary systems simply does not exist in America. In fact, a president is not required by law to form a cabinet or to hold regular meetings. Kennedy, Johnson, and Nixon all preferred small conferences with those specifically involved in a problem. Kennedy saw no reason to discuss defense department matters with his secretaries of agriculture and labor, and he thought cabinet meetings wasted valuable time for too many already busy people. During his administration crucial decisions were often reached in informal conferences between the president, the heads of two or three major departments, and senior White House staff members. Both Carter and Reagan tried to revive the cabinet, and both met often with their cabinets during their first two years. But the longer they remained in office, the less frequently they met with their cabinets as a whole. Carter's Assistant for National Security, who by presidential designation held cabinet rank, remembers that the Carter cabinet meetings almost never dealt with foreign policy issues. "Moreover, they were almost useless. The discussions were desultory, there was no coherent theme to them, and after a while they were held less and less frequently."[14] This senior aide even admits he used the more boring cabinet meetings to catch up on reading the latest editions of *Time* and other newsweeklies "carefully hidden on my knees below the edge of the Cabinet table."[15]

Personal presidential advisers and the heads of various White House based cabinet councils or review units such as the National Security Council and the Office of Management and Budget have gained superior status over many of the department and cabinet secretaries. This has occurred in part because these people are located physically in or next door to the White House. Further,

Woodrow Wilson was one of the first presidents to set trends in national policy making. *UPI.*

[13]Howard E. Shuman, *Politics and the Budget* (Prentice-Hall, 1984); and Aaron Wildavsky, *The Politics of the Budgetary Process*, 4th ed. (Little, Brown, 1983).

[14]Zbigniew Brzezinski, *Power and Principle: Memoirs of the National Security Adviser, 1977–1981* (Farrar, Straus & Giroux, 1983), p. 67.

[15]Ibid.

THE REAGAN CABINET COUNCILS
PRESIDENT REAGAN INSTITUTED THE FOLLOWING PRESIDENTIAL CABINET COUNCILS. THESE ARE IN ADDITION TO THE NATIONAL SECURITY COUNCIL ESTABLISHED BY STATUTE.

Cabinet Council on Economic Affairs

* Secretary of the Treasury, chairman *pro tempore*
* Secretary of State
* Secretary of Commerce
* Secretary of Labor
* Secretary of Transportation
* Director, Office of Management & Budget
* U.S. Trade Representative
* Chairman, Council of Economic Advisers
(*Ex officio* members—The Vice President, Counsellor to the President, White House Chief of Staff, Assistant to the President for Policy Development.)

Cabinet Council on Natural Resources and Environment

* Secretary of the Interior, chairman *pro tempore*
* Attorney General
* Secretary of Agriculture
* Secretary of Transportation
* Secretary of Housing and Urban Development
* Secretary of Energy
* Chairman, Council of Environmental Quality
* Chairman, Council of Economic Advisers
(*Ex officio* members—The Vice President, Counsellor to the President, Chief of Staff, Assistant to the President for Policy Development.)

Cabinet Council on Human Resources

* Secretary of Health & Human Services, chairman *pro tempore*
* Attorney General
* Secretary of Agriculture
* Secretary of Labor
* Secretary of Housing and Urban Development
* Secretary of Education
(*Ex officio* members—The Vice President, Counsellor to the President, Chief of Staff, Assistant to the President for Policy Development.)

Cabinet Council on Food and Agriculture

* Secretary of Agriculture, chairman *pro tempore*
* Secretary of State
* Secretary of the Interior
* Secretary of Commerce
* Secretary of Transportation
* U.S. Trade Representative
(*Ex officio* members—The Vice President, Counsellor to the President, Chief of Staff, Assistant to the President for Policy Development.)

Cabinet Council on Legal Policy

* Attorney General, chairman *pro tempore*
* Secretary of State
* Secretary of Treasury
* Secretary of Interior
* Secretary of Commerce
* Secretary of Labor
* Secretary of Health and Human Services
* Secretary of Housing and Urban Development
* Secretary of Transportation
* Director of Office of Management & Budget
* White House Counsel
* Chairman of the Administrative Conference of the U.S.
(*Ex officio* members—The Vice President, Counsellor to the President, Chief of Staff, Assistant to the President for Policy Development.)

Cabinet Council on Commerce and Trade

* Secretary of Commerce, chairman *pro tempore*
* Secretary of State
* Secretary of the Treasury
* Attorney General
* Secretary of Agriculture
* Secretary of Labor
* Secretary of Transportation
* Secretary of Energy
* U.S. Trade Representative
* Chairman, Council of Economic Advisers
(*Ex officio* members—The Vice President, Counsellor to the President, Chief of Staff, Assistant to the President for Policy Development.)

Cabinet Council for Management and Administration

* Counsellor to the President, chairman *pro tempore*
* Secretary of Treasury
* Secretary of Defense
* Secretary of Commerce
* Secretary of Health and Human Services
* Secretary of Transportation
* Secretary of Energy
* Director of Office of Management & Budget
* Administrator of General Services Administration
* Director of the Office of Personnel Management
(*Ex officio* members—The Vice President, Chief of Staff, Assistant to the President for Policy Development.)

presidents believe their department heads adopt narrow "advocate" views: The agriculture cabinet officer is viewed as a strident advocate for the farmers; the Housing and Urban Development cabinet officer is seen as an ambassador for the housing industry and to some extent also for the mayors; and so it goes, through much of the cabinet—especially for those preoccupied with domestic policy matters. As good relations between presidents and these cabinet members weaken, the former, in frustration, turn more often to trusted senior White House staff aides to settle conflicts and coordinate policy. As a result, tension almost always builds between senior White House aides and their counterparts in the cabinet. Personal staff remains close to the president's ear, and more influential as a result.

Some recent presidents formed various cabinet councils to integrate key departmental and White House advisers around major policy matters. President Ford was pleased with this system, while President Reagan, with a notable penchant for delegating responsibility, relied heavily upon these cabinet councils—always having a senior White House or executive office aide in charge of the council. The councils were patterned after the National Security Council, which was established by law in 1947. The Reagan efforts were aimed at decentralizing policy discussions and collaborative efforts while giving the various cabinet members a genuine feeling they were being consulted and involved in important policy developments.[16]

Cabinet members, as individuals, are often important advisers and administrators. But the cabinet as a decision-making body is not as important as press accounts would have us believe. At present it would take a leap of the imagination to think of cabinet meetings as a place where the large outlines of policy are hammered out in common, or where the essential strategy is decided upon.

THE CABINET/1984

Secretary of State
Secretary of Treasury
Secretary of Defense
Attorney General
Secretary of Interior
Secretary of Agriculture
Secretary of Commerce
Secretary of Labor
Secretary of Health and Human Services
Secretary of Housing and Urban Development
Secretary of Transportation
Secretary of Energy
Secretary of Education
Ambassador to the UN
CIA Director
Director, Office of Management and Budget
White House Counselor

THE VICE-PRESIDENCY

Though the vice-presidency is now very much a part of the presidential establishment, it has not been that way for long. Most vice-presidents served mainly as president of the Senate. In most administrations the vice-president was at best a kind of fifth wheel and at worst a political rival who sometimes connived against the president. The office was often dismissed as a joke. The main reason for the vice-president's posture as outsider was that presidential nominees usually chose as running mates candidates who were geographically, ideologically, and in other ways likely to "balance the ticket."

In recent decades, however, presidential candidates have selected somewhat more like-minded persons for their running mates and have made more use of them. President Carter gave considerably more responsibilities to Vice-President Walter Mondale than most vice-presidents had received in the past. Mondale served as a senior adviser on a wide range of policy and political issues. George Bush was given a variety of responsibilities under Reagan—although he was always careful not to upstage the president.[17]

George Bush being sworn in as Vice-President. *Bill Fitz-Patrick, The White House.*

[16]See Edwin Meese III, "The Institutional Presidency: A View from the White House," *Presidential Studies Quarterly* (Spring 1983), pp. 191–97.

[17]For an analysis of the recent growth of the vice-presidency as a potential adviser to presidents, see Thomas E. Cronin, "Rethinking the Vice Presidency," in T. E. Cronin (ed.), *Rethinking the Presidency* (Little, Brown, 1982); and Paul Light, "The Institutional Vice Presidency," *Presidential Studies Quarterly* (Spring 1983), pp. 198–211.

342

Ideally, a vice-president serves several roles in addition to the largely ceremonial function of acting as president of the Senate. As successor to the president should the latter die, resign, or become incapacitated, the vice-president works as an understudy—assuming some of the president's party and ceremonial duties, and thereby easing some of the president's burden. A vice-president can also perform specialized assignments, such as chairing advisory councils, cabinet-level committees, or a White House conference, or undertaking good-will missions abroad.

Tensions usually develop between top presidential aides and vice-presidents and their staffs. Part of the problem arises because presidents prefer not to give up any ceremonial duties for which they themselves can win credit. Neither do cabinet members like to share their responsibilities with vice-presidents, which makes it very hard for vice-presidents to gain administrative experience. Then too, presidents often delegate unpleasant political chores to the vice-president.

The search for a better way to select and use vice-presidents is made more urgent by the fact that eight presidents have died in office—four by assassination, four by natural death—and one president has resigned. One-third of our presidents were once vice-presidents, including four of our last eight presidents.

Some people contend that a vice-presidency is no longer needed. They recommend that some officer, like the secretary of state or the speaker of the House of Representatives, serve as acting president in the event the office becomes vacant until ninety days later, when a special election for president could be held. These proposals reflect the belief that the president must, except for the briefest periods, be a person elected to that office by the people.

Most people feel the office should be continued, but this does not mean they are satisfied with it. Support exists for devising better ways to pick vice-presidential nominees as well as for making the vice-presidency a more significant office. Both major parties have considered practical means of making the selection procedure for the vice-presidency more democratic. Under the existing system presidential nominees have a free hand in choosing their running mates. Although there are some notable advantages to the present system—especially the possibility that the ticket will be ideologically compatible—drawbacks are also clearly present. Disadvantages of the present methods include the pressure of time (which contributed to the abortive choice of Senator Thomas F. Eagleton by George McGovern in 1972), the lack of formalized consultation within the party, the rubber-stamp role for convention delegates, and the absence of public scrutiny of prospective vice-presidential candidates before the nomination.

The vice-presidency has been significantly affected by two post World War II constitutional amendments. The *Twenty-second Amendment* imposes a two-term limit on the presidency, meaning vice-presidents have a better chance of moving up to the Oval Office. The *Twenty-fifth Amendment*, ratified in 1967, confirms the prior practice whereby on the death of a president, the vice-president becomes not acting president but president. Of greater significance, this amendment provides a procedure to determine whether an incumbent president is unable to discharge the powers and duties of the office, and it establishes procedures to fill a vacancy in the vice-presidency. In the event of a vacancy in the office of the vice-president, the president nominates a vice-president, who takes office upon confirmation by a majority vote of both houses of Congress. This procedure generally ensures the appointment of a vice-president in whom the president has confidence. Thus, vice-presidents who have to take over the presidency can be expected to reflect most of their predecessors' policies. President Nixon selected Gerald Ford, and President Ford selected Nelson Rockefeller, according to these new methods.

Walter Mondale, back in 1977, being sworn in as Vice-President. Former vice-presidents Hubert Humphrey (behind Carter on the left), and Nelson Rockefeller at right, watch. *UPI.*

Vice-President George Bush on podium at GOP National Convention. Because of Ronald Reagan's age, Vice-President George Bush may well play a vital role in the Reagan Administration. *UPI.*

The vice-presidency will doubtless remain attractive to aspiring politicians if only because it is one of the major paths to the presidency. Plainly, too, the policy-advising role of the vice-president was enhanced under Carter and Reagan. However, the tensions between a president and a vice-president are natural (after all, everybody else who works closely with presidents can be fired by them). It is almost certain the vice-president will continue to have an undefined role, subject more to the good will and moods of the president than to any fixed job description.[18]

CAN THE MODERN PRESIDENCY SURVIVE THE MODERN MEDIA?

John F. Kennedy once canceled over fifty White House subscriptions to the *New York Herald Tribune* because he was furious about how the paper was treating his decision making. Lyndon Johnson regularly planted "softball questions" (questions he knew he could easily answer) among friendly reporters at presidential press conferences. All recent presidents have complained both that the modern media have misrepresented them and that the media are too preoccupied with reporting only the bad news. Ronald Reagan once suggested that the media report some good news—"just for a change."

Enjoying enormous First Amendment rights in this country, the reporters go about their business of analyzing and criticizing presidents with a gusto that is striking. Dozens of media representatives are regularly stationed at the White House, and they travel everywhere the president goes, reporting on the president's every move. Presidential statements—even on the most trivial matter—get sent back to the newsrooms and usually get printed or aired. Major statements and policy initiatives are reported and subjected to interpretative analysis. Presidents, of course, want all their initiatives printed and praised as much as possible.

But the press and the media believe they should provide a context in which presidential statements can be understood. Hence, not only do they tell people what a president said, but they often try to explain what the statement means. This is done primarily by columnists, editorial writers, and commentators—who are expected to agree with or to criticize a president while providing their own reasons for doing so. Further, the management of most newspapers and radio and television stations in the country want to balance their stories about what presidents say—and especially coverage of presidential speeches—with an equal amount of time for the spokespersons of the opposition party or at least for persons who hold different points of view. Thus, when President Reagan spoke against a nuclear freeze proposal—as he often did in 1982 and 1983—the media frequently gave an almost equal amount of attention to the views of Senator Edward M. Kennedy, or to the statement by the Catholic Bishops endorsing the nuclear freeze, or to some of the vocal grass-roots organizations advocating a mutually verifiable freeze on nuclear weapons. On other issues as well—such as amending the Clean Air Act, military aid to El Salvador, CIA covert operations, Granada, abortion politics, and other matters—the media usually will attempt to give some if not equal attention to a president's critics.

In recent years this kind of adversarial media coverage has often left the impression that a president is a divisive figure in national politics rather than a

[18]Two recent books on the vice-presidency are Paul Light, *Vice Presidential Power* (Johns Hopkins University Press, 1984); and Joel Goldstein, *The Modern Vice Presidency* (Princeton University Press, 1982).

343

source of unifying leadership. Except when a president attends a baseball game or welcomes to the White House some noted sports or arts hero, media coverage seems always to be—at best—ambivalent. No reporter has ever won a Pulitzer or any other prize for writing a story favorable to the Administration. The entire journalism profession honors those who uncover wrongdoing.

What have presidents done about this? Typically they have been patient and respected the critical dialogue so essential in a democracy. However, presidents and their aides have also engaged in extensive public relations efforts. Reagan, for example, frequently invited friendly newspaper reporters for extensive interviews. Out-of-town editors were invited in for special briefings, and special efforts were made to get the president out of Washington for meetings with local and regional media representatives—who were generally viewed as less critical than Washington-based media. Special White House media experts regularly met to devise better ways to get the president's point of view out to the public and to get him on prime-time television, or to arrange for flattering action photos.[19]

Reagan's efforts were not novel; every recent president has tried similar public relations stratagems. Presidents and their aides often conclude that leadership, and especially unifying national leadership, is almost impossible to bring about in a country that encourages such a critical—even cynical—media. Some White House aides go so far as to say the media are badly hurting the nation. "They destroy every hero," said Reagan deputy chief of staff, Michael Deaver. "We don't have heros anymore, we don't have anyone to believe in because they strip them naked."[20]

Some would say the modern media are the number one adversary of the modern presidency. Some would go further and complain the American presidency is being brutally wounded and its capacity for leadership sapped—if not paralyzed—because of the excesses of media criticism. While defenders of the media admit occasional abuses by the press, they rally to cherished "free press" traditions. Defenders of the press also like to quote from Thomas Jefferson, who although angered by the press when he was president, once said: "Were it left to me to decide whether we should have a government without newspapers or newpapers without a government, I should not hesitate to prefer the latter." Finally, defenders of the media say that presidents have too often lied or manipulated the public's understanding of issues. The media, they contend, are obligated to stand up and speak out—especially when they think a president is wrong.

In sum, no matter who is in the White House, presidents and the media will often be in conflict. It is an ongoing struggle, inherent in a democracy. The Watergate scandals fortified the media in their independence—and many people credited the media with playing a very important role in bringing these scandals to the public's attention. Further, since the media—especially television—are·viewed as more trustworthy and believable than most other American institutions, most Americans, most of the time, believe that what they hear on television is as true as what presidents say. The goals of a president and of the media are often in conflict; and so long as this continues to be the case, presidents and the media will be adversaries. But the resources of the White

[19]Juan Williams, "Presidential Newsmaking: How Reagan's Staff Spreads His Message," *Washington Post*, February 13, 1983, pp. 1 and 18.

[20]Ibid., p. 18. For two books that examine Washington reporters and the White House press office, see Stephen Hess, *The Washington Reporters* (Brookings Institution, 1981); and Michael B. Grossman and Martha J. Kumar, *Portraying the President* (Johns Hopkins Press, 1981).

House, especially in the hands of savvy communicators such as FDR, John Kennedy, and Ronald Reagan, seem worthy combatants in taking on the so-called fourth branch of government.

MAKING THE PRESIDENCY SAFE FOR DEMOCRACY

The startling series of events of the Watergate scandals a decade ago sharpened the old question: How much executive power can a democracy afford? New questions also were raised: Was a bigger presidency necessarily better? Did presidential powers grow because they were usurped by presidents or handed over by Congress? Would we be better served by a six-year presidential term? Would some form of parliamentary government be better than our three-branch "presidential" system?

In the mid-1970s presidents were accused of: impounding billions of congressionally approved funds, obstructing justice, abusing the doctrine of executive privilege, lying about the conduct of the Vietnam war, and acting with excessive secrecy. People lost confidence first in Johnson's and then in Nixon's brand of leadership, and then, for different reasons, in Ford and Carter. The very legitimacy of the presidency was being tested.

Presidents Ford, Reagan, Nixon, and Carter came together in 1981. The three pre-Reagan presidents joined the U.S. delegation going to the funeral of President Anwar Sadat. *UPI.*

How much formal authority does and should a president have? The Constitution is vague. It seems to grant broad executive authority without defining boundaries. Some scholars hold that in emergencies the president has wide powers to protect the public interest, even at the cost of overriding existing laws. There seems to be a kind of *inherent* power in the presidency, vast but undefined, that an aggressive president can exploit in times of crisis. Unfortunately, crisis is now the rule rather than the exception.

Franklin Roosevelt's conception of his powers—sometimes called the **prerogative theory**—was that in the face of emergencies a president had the same power John Locke once claimed for kings—the power to act according to discretion for the public good, without the prescription of the law and sometimes even against it. The World War II destroyer-bases agreement, for example, in which Roosevelt on his own initiative traded naval destroyers to England in return for some military bases, conflicted with several laws—setting what some believe was a dangerous precedent which others (like Nixon) seem to have followed.

Presidential Character

What about presidential personality? If the presidency has too much power for the safety of the country (and the world), and yet not enough to solve some of the nation's toughest problems, what kind of person do we need in this office? Political scientist James David Barber writes that because the issues are always changing, we should be concerned somewhat less with the stands a candidate takes than with the candidate's *character*. The character, Barber claims, will stay pretty much the same.[21]

Barber says we can classify presidents and would-be presidents according to their *activism* on the one hand and their *enjoyment* of politics and public service on the other. With these two dimensions, he says, we can pretty well predict presidential performance. Table 15–3 shows Barber's classification

[21]Barber, *The Presidential Character*. See evaluations of this study by Alexander L. George, "Assessing Presidential Character," *World Politics* (January 1974), pp. 234–82, and by Alan C. Elms, *Personality in Politics* (Harcourt Brace Jovanovich, 1976), chap. 4. See also Michael Nelson, "James David Barber and The Psychological Presidency," *Virginia Quarterly Review* (Autumn 1980).

		Energy Level in Their Political Job	
		ACTIVE:	PASSIVE:
Emotional attitude toward politics and the job of the presidency	POSITIVE:	Franklin Roosevelt Harry Truman John F. Kennedy Gerald Ford Jimmy Carter	William H. Taft Warren Harding Ronald Reagan
	NEGATIVE:	Richard Nixon Lyndon Johnson Herbert Hoover Woodrow Wilson	Dwight Eisenhower Calvin Coolidge

scheme and how he assesses most twentieth-century presidents. Barber holds that the people best suited for the presidency are politicians who creatively shape their environment and savor the give-and-take exchanges of political life. He calls them "active-positives." Beware, he tells us, of the active-negative types. They are the driven personalities, compelled to feverish activity, yet doomed by rigidity and personal frustration in the way they approach their jobs. Wilson, Hoover, Johnson, and Nixon are illustrative cases. Barber said Ford was an active-positive type, but others think of Ford as somewhat more of a passive-positive. Some observers thought Carter was as much in the negative category as in the positive. Still others thought that the contradictory conclusions about where to put them merely demonstrated that this scheme was more confusing than helpful—more likely to tell us about the classifiers than the classified. Barber calls President Reagan a passive-positive. He worries that Reagan would be tempted to let things drift and that he will be overly deferential to his friends.

Our understanding of personality and character, however, is not yet developed to the stage where accurate predictions can be made about suitable presidential candidates. Moreover, some critics doubt Barber's generalizations are based on sufficient evidence. For example, many people judge Reagan to be an "active" and not a "passive," at least in Barber's terms. Still others, who are persuaded by Barber's analysis, doubt that we can really put it to work during most elections. What happens, for example, if most of the candidates are "active-positive"? Further, using strict character criteria to screen candidates probably would have prevented the moody and often depressed Abraham Lincoln from winning office. Nor can we be sure that a president's character will stay the same throughout an entire term or even over the life span of an issue. In addition to a presidential candidate's character, voters want and deserve to know the issue positions of the candidates. It would also help to know the kind of people a candidate seeks out as advisers.

President Ronald Reagan. *Reagan Committee.*

**New checks
and balances**

Presidential power is doubtless greater today than ever before. It is misleading, however, to infer from a president's capacity to drop an H-bomb that the chief executive has similar power to bring about positive change and solutions in most policy-making areas. Seldom are presidents free agents in bringing about basic social change. As priority setter, politician, and executive, a president must share power with members of Congress, bureaucrats, and interest group elites. The ability to set priorities, and even to pass laws, is not the same as being able to enforce and administer them properly. Presidents who want to be effective in implementing policy changes must know what they want to achieve and how to motivate and strengthen the bureaucracy to that end.

This is a tough assignment in a political system held together in such large measure by compromise and contradictory goals. Not only must presidents deal with key congressional leaders, cabinet members, important bureaucrats, a vice-president, party chiefs, and even leaders of the opposition party, but they must also cope with the political forces operating around the White House—public opinion, pressures from organized interests, demands from their own party. They must negotiate endlessly among individuals and among interests. They will constantly struggle with investigative reporters and muckrakers. And they must respond to public sentiment at the same time as they educate it. The fierce light of public opinion, magnified by the press and the electronic media, always beats down upon the White House.

A New Attitude Toward the Presidency?

Unrealistic expectations of the presidency have helped to weaken it. Part of the reason presidents have turned to secrecy and subordinated substance to style has been that we have overburdened the office with exaggerated expectations. We elect a politician and then insist on a super-human performance. As currently designed, the presidency is an institution that manipulates its occupants, and accentuates their *shortcomings* as well as their virtues.[22] It seems cruel to put people in a position where they may well fail and then condemn them for not succeeding—but this is usually what we do.

In one sense the best safeguard and restraint on presidential powers rest with the attitudes of the American people. Citizens have far more power than they generally realize. Presidents usually hear them when they are "sending a message." Citizens can also "vote" between elections in innumerable ways—by changing parties, by organizing protests, or by voting for the opposition party in off-year elections.

We need a healthy skepticism toward presidential decisions. A major lesson learned from the Watergate period, most scholars agree, is not that the powers of the presidency should be lessened, but that other institutions—parties, Congress, the courts—should grow in stature. Unless we can find ways to revitalize our political parties, to achieve some measure of reponsiveness to the electorate and party control over public policy, we may well be destined to continue the march toward an American version of the De Gaulle model of leadership in France.

A few former presidential advisers and scholars believe we need to rethink our constitutional system and our doctrine of separation of powers. Our old constitutional restraints, they fear, too severely constrain presidential leadership, especially the ability of a president to get a program enacted. To make the presidency more effective, these "reformers" would amend the Constitution so that Congress and the president would be elected at the same time, and perhaps on some type of ticket—where the voter would choose a package or unified party ticket rather than opt for a representative and senator from one party and a president from another. It has also been suggested that presidents serve a single, six-year term, and that they be able to ask a member of Congress to serve in the cabinet—as is done in parliamentary systems. Still more radical is the suggestion that presidents—failing to get support for their programs in Congress—be empowered to dissolve Congress and call for new elections as a test of strength and as a kind of referendum or vote of confidence for their programs.[23] These are radical steps, and they are not likely to win approval; yet

FACTORS THAT CONSTRAIN PRESIDENTS

Constitution
Federalism
Separation of powers
Congress
Federal courts
Investigative press and media
Public opinion
Opposing party
Opposing factions in president's party
Interest groups
Editorial opinion (and cartoonists)
Bureaucratic resistance
Opposing world powers
World public opinion and UN policies
Regularly fixed elections
Unrealistic expectations
Party platforms
The shape of the economy

[22]See Bruce Buchanan, *The Presidential Experience* (Prentice-Hall, 1978).

[23]See Lloyd Cutler, "To Form a Government—On the Defects of Separation of Powers," in T.E. Cronin (ed.), *Rethinking the Presidency* (Little, Brown, 1982).

SHOULD WE HAVE A
SIX-YEAR
NONRENEWABLE TERM
FOR PRESIDENTS?

Pro:
It might help take the politics
out of the presidency, and
thereby lessen the likelihood of
Watergate scandals.

Four years is too short a time to
get the job done.

Presidents could concentrate on
the job rather than on getting
reelected.

During wartime a president
wouldn't waste time on campaigning.

Budgets are already cast for
about two years ahead when a
president gets into office.

Six years is enough even for the
healthiest of presidents.

Con:
A six-year term would give us
two more years of the "clunk-
ers" and two less years of the
great ones.

Four years is long enough for
the voters to tell whether a president is doing the job and moving in the right direction.

The best way to be reelected is
to do the job well maintain majority support, and be an effective leader.

The four-year term forces presidents to be accountable—to try
to make good on their promises
and platforms.

Many of our great presidents
served ably for more than six
years—Washington, Jefferson,
Wilson, FDR, and Ike.

A healthy, democratic country
needs a politician in the White
House—one who can bargain,
persuade, and build crucial political coalitions—and get diverse political factions to work
together.

We should not surrender a
hard-won democratic right—to
kick a leader *out* of office.

students and scholars should at least think about them as we celebrate the two hundredth anniversary of the Constitution later in this decade.

One of the persisting paradoxes of the American presidency is that on the one hand, it is always too powerful, and on the other, it is too weak: It is always too strong, because in many ways it is contrary to our ideals of government by the people and decentralization of power; yet the office seems to have inadequate powers, because presidents seldom are able to keep the promises they make. Of course, the presidency is always too strong when we dislike the incumbent. And the presidency is always too constrained when we believe a president is striving to serve the public interest as we define it. For some people the presidency of Lyndon Johnson illustrates this paradox: Many felt he was too strong in his handling of the Vietnam war, with which they disagreed; but they also felt he was too weak in waging his war on poverty, with which they agreed.

The ultimate dilemma for concerned Americans is that curbing the powers of a president who abuses public trust will usually undermine the capacity of fair-minded presidents who would dedicate themselves to serving the public interest. In the nearly two centuries since Washington took office, we have multiplied the requirements for presidential leadership and yet made it increasingly difficult for presidents to lead.

The presidency will surely remain one of our nation's best sources for creative policy change. Americans will expect presidents to do more, not less, in the future. Our presidents will be more important and yet less popular than they have been in the past. The presidency will almost certainly continue to be a hard-pressed office, laden with the cumulative weight of contradictory expectations. Americans' mixed views of the job of the president often put our presidents in "no-win" situations.[24] Thus, we want our president to be

1. Gentle and decent but also forceful, cunning, and decisive
2. A common person who can give an uncommon performance
3. Above politics, yet a skilled political coalition builder
4. An inspirational leader who never promises more than can be achieved
5. A programmatic but also pragmatic and flexible leader
6. Innovative and inventive, ahead of the times, yet always responsive to popular majorities
7. A moral leader, yet not too preachy or moralizing
8. A leader of all the people, but also a leader of one political party

History suggests there is no foolproof way to guarantee that our presidents will possess the appropriate functional skills as well as the moral character the office requires. Voters have selected both wisely and mistakenly in the past. James Madison's advice remains useful: "A dependence on the people is, no doubt, the primary control of the government; but experience has taught mankind the necessity of auxiliary precautions."[25] We must maintain the effectiveness of these "auxiliary precautions"—Congress, parties, the courts, the press, and concerned citizens' groups—if we are to ensure a properly balanced and constitutional presidency.

---

[24]These and related paradoxes are discussed in Thomas E. Cronin, *The State of the Presidency*, 2nd ed. (Little, Brown, 1980), chap. 1. See also Godfrey Hodgson, *All Things To All Men* (Simon & Schuster, 1980).

[25]James Madison, *Federalist No. 51* (Modern Library, 1937), p. 337.

SUMMARY

1. Presidents must act as crisis-managing, morale-building, recruiting, priority-setting, coalition-building, and managerial leaders. No president can divide the job into tidy compartments. Ultimately, all the responsibilities mix with one another.

2. The office of the president is a combination of the huge presidential establishment, a president's personality and character, and the heavy demands and expectations on the chief executive. It is still being reshaped as new presidents with ideas and styles of their own move into the White House.

3. The expansion of presidential powers has been a continuous development during the past several decades. Crises, both foreign and economic, have enlarged the powers of the president. When there is a need for decisive action, presidents are asked to supply it. Congress, of course, is traditionally expected to share in the formulation of national policy. Yet Congress is often so fragmented that it has been a willing partner in the growth of the presidency—at the same time that it is constantly setting boundaries on how far presidents can extend their influence. Every president must learn anew the need to work closely with the members of Congress and to enlist their support before major policy changes can be made.

4. The overriding task of American citizens is to bind presidents to the majority will without shackling them. To expect too much of our presidents may be to weaken them in the leadership tasks we need them to perform. To require immediate accountability might paralyze the presidency. Presidential leadership, properly defined, must be more than the power to persuade and less than the power to coerce: It must be the power to achieve by democratic means results acceptable to the people.

FURTHER READING

HARRY A. BAILEY, JR. (ed.). *Classics of the American Presidency* (Moore Publishing, 1980).

JAMES DAVID BARBER. *The Presidential Character*, rev. ed. (Prentice-Hall, 1977).

COLIN CAMPBELL. *Governments Under Stress; Political Executives and Key Bureaucrats in Washington, London, and Ottawa* (University of Toronto Press, 1983).

THOMAS E. CRONIN. *The State of the Presidency*, 2nd ed. (Little, Brown, 1980).

THOMAS E. CRONIN (ed.). *Rethinking The Presidency* (Little, Brown, 1982).

ALEXANDER L. GEORGE. *Presidential Decisionmaking in Foreign Policy* (Westview, 1980).

GEORGE EDWARDS. *The Public Presidency* (St. Martin's Press, 1983).

GEORGE EDWARDS and STEPHEN WAYNE (eds.). *Studying The Presidency* (University of Tennessee Press, 1983).

MICHAEL NELSON (ed.). *The Presidency and the Political System* (Congressional Quarterly Press, 1984).

RICHARD E. NEUSTADT. *Presidential Power*, rev. ed. (Wiley, 1980).

RICHARD A. WATSON and NORMAN C. THOMAS. *The Politics of the Presidency* (Wiley, 1983).

CONGRESS VS. PRESIDENT: THE CONTINUING STRUGGLE

16

"Oh, if I could only be president and Congress too, for just ten minutes!" President Theodore Roosevelt once remarked. While most presidents share the same wish, our Constitution rules this out—and for good reason.

The United States is unique among major world powers because it is neither a parliamentary democracy nor a wholly executive-dominated government. Our Constitution invites both Congress and the president to set policy and govern the nation. Much of the time during our nation's history, the main role of Congress has been to respond to executive branch leadership, the president serving as policy promoter and the Congress as a policy adapter. But this has not always been the case, and in recent years Congress often has yearned to be an equal partner in national policy making.

Article I of the Constitution grants to Congress "all legislative powers" but limits them to those "herein granted." It then sets forth in some detail the powers vested in Congress. Article II, in contrast, grants to the president "the executive power," but describes these powers only in vague terms. Is this difference significant? Some scholars and most presidents have argued that a president has an undefined power to act to promote the well-being of the United States. Therefore, they contend, a president is not limited to the powers spelled out in the Constitution, as is Congress. Other scholars and most members of Congress have argued that the president has no such inherent power.

Whatever the language of the Constitution, powers not expressly defined in it have often been exercised by the president. These powers have a variety of names: implied or inherent powers or moral, residual, and emergency powers. Implied powers are often considered to be more restricted in scope than inherent or emergency powers. Clear distinctions, however, are hard to establish.[1]

[1]Louis Fisher, *President and Congress* (Free Press, 1972), pp. 31–32. See also his *The Constitution between Friends: Law and Politics in America* (St. Martin's Press, 1978).

[handwritten: Framers wanted Prez to be stronger in Foreign Policy than domestic]

[handwritten: Media increased Public opinion that we need stronger Prez & Congress don't always Trust...]

The framers never intended the president to be the dominant agent in domestic policy making. They did expect presidents to be a major influence in foreign policy. In the eighteenth century foreign affairs were generally thought to be an executive matter. But our framers did not want the president to be the only agent. Indeed, some of the powers specified in the Constitution as being vested in Congress were designed to bring Congress into foreign policy.

For much of the twentieth century, however, scholars held that we needed a strong, dynamic presidency to overcome the tremendous fragmentation of power in America. The creaky machinery of our government could be made to work only if we gave a president the proper amount of help and authority. The American people generally favored the expansion of presidential powers. With the development of radio and television, the visibility of the president increased. Indeed, considering the publicity given presidents, it is hardly surprising that citizens look to them to solve the nation's problems.

Tensions between Congress and the presidency are inevitable. They were not only anticipated but planned. Thus, the branches were designed with different constituencies, different-length terms, and different responsibilities. The branches are also organized differently, and they are jealous of their powers; with members of both branches often suspicious of the other.

Still, while the Constitution disperses power and invites a continuing struggle between these two branches, it also requires the two branches to integrate the fragmented parts of the system into a workable government. And usually these two branches do work together. Even when the relationship "is guarded or hostile, bills get passed and signed into law. Presidential appointments are approved by the Senate. Budgets are enacted and the government is kept afloat. This necessary cooperation goes on even when the White House and the Capitol are controlled by different parties."[2]

What are the sources of conflict and cooperation between these two branches? In dealing with this central question we look first at the legislative role of presidents and the efforts of Congress to fulfill its constitutional responsibilities.

[handwritten: Even though there are differences in Prez & Congress, They Cooperate]

GERALD FORD ON CONGRESS VERSUS THE PRESIDENCY

"When I was in the House for 25 years I almost always looked down Pennsylvania Avenue at the White House, regardless of whether Democrats or Republicans were there, and wondered why they were so arrogant.

Then, when I was in the White House myself, I looked up at the Congress and wondered how there could be 535 irresponsible members of Congress."

SOURCE: Talk at Hinckley Institute of Politics, University of Utah, February 1982.

PRESIDENTIAL INFLUENCE IN CONGRESS

[handwritten: Prez get most of their way except major initiatives. Checks & Balances]

The presidential record of dealing with Congress in recent years is a mixed one. *[handwritten: No Dictator]* Presidents enjoy considerable success in getting most of their nominations confirmed by the Senate. Few presidential vetoes have been overturned by Congress. And the vast bulk of their budget requests eventually win approval. On the other hand, presidents often have only a .500 batting average or less in gaining passage of their major policy initiatives.[3] Tax reform, energy development, the SALT II treaty, government reorganization, and other proposals often die somewhere in the congressional process.

Why are presidents in conflict with the Congress so often? In part, because the whole process was designed to maximize checks and balances and deliberation—rather than cooperation or subordination. And Americans by and large want it that way. They do not want presidents dictating policies and laws (see Table 16–1).

"Kingsley says if he were President he'd tell Congress to either put up or shut up." *Drawing by Stan Hunt; © 1978. The New Yorker Magazine, Inc.*

[2]Roger H. Davidson and Walter J. Oleszek, *Congress and Its Members* (Congressional Quarterly Press, 1981), p. 292.

[3]A recent work on this subject is George C. Edwards III, *Presidential Influence in Congress* (W. H. Freeman, 1980), from which we have drawn for some of this discussion. See also Douglas Rivers and Nancy Rose, "Passing the President's Program: Public Opinion and Presidential Influence in Congress." Paper delivered at Western Political Science Association Meeting, Seattle, Washington, March 1983.

Who Should Have the Major Responsibility?	Energy Policy	Economic Policy	Foreign Policy	General Responsibility
Congress	40%	40%	27%	36%
Equal	19	20	18	22
President	35	34	49	37
Don't know	6	6	6	5
	100	100	100	100

Question Asked: Now I would like to ask you some questions about the president and Congress. Some people think that the president ought to have the major responsibility for making policy, while other people think that Congress ought to have the major responsibility. In general, which do you think should have the major responsibility for setting policy?

SOURCE: Gallup Poll of a nationwide survey of over 1500 adults conducted by WHYY, Inc., Philadelphia–Wilmington, in connection with "Every Four Years," a three-part study of the American presidency produced for the Public Broadcasting Service (PBS), Fall 1979.

[handwritten: Prez & Congress from different backgrounds, different election times, etc.]

[handwritten: Opposite Control of Congress & White house causes tension]

Another reason for the conflict is that the presidency and Congress represent different constituencies. Not only do members of Congress represent state and local citizenry—and hence reflect somewhat different geographical interests than a president—but many in Congress are elected at different times. Some are elected two years earlier than a president, and some two years later; this no doubt makes them responsive to somewhat different moods and points of view. Moreover, many members of Congress may have been there for ten or twenty years, and look forward to serving perhaps another ten or so. Presidents, however, think in four-year cycles.

Still other factors are at work. Typically the opposition party in Congress tries to mount its own programs. It will, when possible, defeat a president's policy initiatives and substitute its own. Sometimes it will merely defeat White House measures. This becomes especially troublesome for a president if Congress is controlled by a majority of the opposition—as has been the case for ten years of the past generation (1953–1954 and 1969–1977). President Reagan was forced to deal with a Democratically controlled House.

What can and does a president do in working with Congress? What are the chief sources of influence? The greatest asset for presidents in working with Congress is having both houses populated by large numbers from their own political party. Presidents often try to enlarge their party's representation in Congress during the midterm elections, but they are seldom very successful in this effort.[4] Nowadays many members of Congress prefer to run their own campaigns. Even when a president's help is sought, it is not clear whether this aid is effective.

SOURCES OF CONGRESS-PRESIDENCY CONFLICT

Diverse geographical constituencies

Staggered terms of election

Conflicting responsibilities

Different partisan ties (often)

Constitutional provisions requiring extensive sharing of power

Presidents seeing Congress as disorganized and inefficient

Congress viewing the White House as arbitrary and insensitive

Little gets done unless they both cooperate—but each wants the credit for successes, and each seeks to blame the other when things go wrong

Presidential coattails, once thought to be a significant factor in helping to elect members of a president's party to Congress, have had little effect in recent years. Members of Congress usually get reelected because of the quality of their constituency services and because they can take advantage of incumbency.

From the president's vantage point it is seldom helpful to punish party mavericks. With power dispersed and decentralized in Congress there is just too much risk for a president to single out a few party "disloyalists" for retribution. White House congressional relations aides learn to abide by the motto of "no permanent allies, no permanent enemies." You may lose someone on a vote today, but his or her vote may be crucial on some other measure next week.

A president who wins widespread backing in the country—and in the states and congressional districts—can use this popularity to try to influence

[handwritten: Prez tries to get most of Congress his party in elections, Congress can do nothing about party disloyalty. Prez party disloyalty]

[4]See Randall L. Calvert and John A. Ferejohn, "Coattail Voting in Recent Presidential Elections," *American Political Science Review* June, 1983, pp. 407–419.

Congress expects Prez' favors; Prez must have Resources to be effective in Congress

certain members of Congress. In addition, presidents are now expected to be coalition builders with key interest groups. Lyndon Johnson and Ronald Reagan were effective in this regard. Presidents today are expected to meet regularly not only with the leadership within Congress but also with the members of key committees and subcommittees.

Members of Congress take it for granted that a president will meet with them socially, arrange visits to their districts by cabinet officers (or even by the president personally), send them autographed photos, and so on. The White House now employs a staff just to "service" these requests and favors. The granting or withholding of these favors, however, probably does not help a president in dealings with Congress, since members of Congress have come to expect these favors from the White House.

On balance, a president's position in dealing with Congress is relatively fragile. President Nixon may have misused and abused many presidential powers, but he was no more able to influence Congress than other presidents. In fact, he won passage of fewer key policy initiatives than did most recent presidents. To say a president is in a relatively weak position in dealing with Congress is to say the White House does not have a large number of resources with which to influence most members of Congress. True, presidents can make stirring appeals for party unity—if their party enjoys majorities in Congress. They can also try to educate and rally the public around their major programs. They can—as President Reagan did with his tax cut proposal—build effective public coalitions in support of a key measure.

FACTORS THAT SOMETIMES HELP A PRESIDENT WIN SUPPORT IN CONGRESS

- Publicity power (press conferences, addresses)
- Popularity (when it is high)
- Patronage powers (appointments, public works project support)
- Party leader role (sometimes)
- Personal lobbying and persuasiveness
- Informal social ties
- Political bargaining
- Threat of a presidential veto
- National emergencies

But much of the time a president must deal with a Congress that moves according to its own pace and that responds to a variety of interests above and beyond those coming from the White House. As we noted in Chapter 14, members of Congress are influenced more by their own philosophical and ideological convictions, by their colleagues in Congress, and by the interests of their districts back home than they are by instructions or pleas from the White House. These realities will remain one of the central features in presidential-congressional relations. *Before Seventies, Prez was gallant*

Congress listens to home, colleagues, more than to Prez

Until Vietnam and Watergate both citizens and scholars held that the presidency was "the great engine of democracy," the "American people's one authentic trumpet," and "the central instrument of democracy." A president was "a kind of magnificent lion who can roam widely and do great deeds." What was good for the presidency was good for the country.[5] But the feud that erupted between Congress and the president for control of national policy in the early seventies continues today. *Critics said Prez was 2 powerful during Nam & Wtrgate*

Reaction to Watergate and Vietnam took at least two forms. Critics said these events provided real evidence that the presidency was isolated, autocratic, and imperial. They charged that the deceptions during Vietnam and the corruptions of Watergate occurred because our checks and balances did not work. Too much power had been given to the presidency.

Watergate—and the first forced resignation of a president in our history—aroused public concern about the role of Congress. Most of the people called for Congress to be a more coequal branch of government, more assertive and alert, and more jealous of its own powers. The change in public attitudes is documented by polls taken before and after Vietnam and Watergate. Support for Congress soared in the mid-1970s, although public support for the two branches became more balanced by about 1980. But Congress was put on notice by the American people: Shape up and assert yourself!

What form has congressional reassertion taken? Could a vast new array of

A rare event. A president comes before a congressional committee. President Ford faces the House Judiciary subcommittee on Criminal Justice to explain why he pardoned former President Richard M. Nixon. *UPI.*

[5]See a critical discussion of the romanticized view of the presidency in Thomas E. Cronin, *The State of the Presidency*, 2nd ed. (Little, Brown, 1980), esp. chap. 3.

Support of Congress ↑ aft Nam & Wtrgate; Balanced now

THE IMPERIAL PRESIDENCY ARGUMENT

Many critics held that during the 1960s and early 1970s the presidency became an imperial institution. This came about because of abuse of power by presidents, especially abuse of the war powers and secrecy. Thus, in his book *The Imperial Presidency*, historian and former John Kennedy adviser Arthur M. Schlesinger, Jr., argues that presidential power was so expanded and misused by 1972 that it threatened our constitutional system.[6] He claims that an imperial presidency was created as a result of America's wartime experiences, particularly Vietnam.

Imperial presidency theorists argue that the difficulty stems in part from ambiguity concerning the president's power as commander in chief: It is an undefined *office*, not a *function*. Schlesinger and others acknowledge that Nixon and Johnson did not create the imperial presidency; they merely built on some of the more questionable practices of their predecessors. But observers contend there is a distinction between the *abuse* and the *usurpation* of power. Abraham Lincoln, FDR, and Harry Truman temporarily usurped power in wartime. Johnson and Nixon abused power, even in peacetime, by claiming absolute power to be a part of their office.

Secrecy has often been used to protect and preserve a president's national security power. It is argued that Nixon pushed the doctrine beyond acceptable limits. Before Eisenhower the presumption was that Congress would get the information it sought from the executive branch. Instances of secrecy and executive privilege were the rare exceptions. Today they are the rule. And a Congress that knows only what the president wants it to know is not an independent body.[7]

Those who are critical of Nixon contend that he made the presidency not only fully imperial but also revolutionary. For example, in authorizing the "plumbers," Nixon became the first president in our history to establish an extralegal investigative force, paid for by the taxpayers but unknown to Congress and accountable to no one but himself. Other misuses of intelligence agencies and of authorized breaking and entering meant that Nixon became the only American president who had supervised lawless actions in peacetime.

Schlesinger's book is a useful point of departure for discussing the alleged too-powerful presidency. The chief complaints include presidential war making, too many emergency powers, diplomacy by executive agreement, secrecy and executive privilege, impoundment, and government by veto.

President Franklin D. Roosevelt, surrounded by Congressional leaders, signs Declaration of War against Japan on December 8, 1941. *Wide World.*

Presidential War Making

The Constitution delegates to Congress the authority to *declare* the legal state of war (with the consent of the president), but in practice the commander in chief often starts or initiates war (or actions that lead to war). This power has been used by the chief executive time and time again. Polk in 1846 ordered American forces to advance into disputed territory; when Mexico resisted, Polk informed Congress that war existed by act of Mexico, and a formal declaration of war was soon forthcoming. McKinley's dispatch of a battleship to Havana, where it was blown up, helped precipitate war with Spain in 1898. The United

[6]Arthur M. Schlesinger, Jr., *The Imperial Presidency* (Houghton Mifflin, 1973).
[7]See Louis Henkin, *Foreign Affairs and the Constitution* (Norton, 1975).

States was not formally at war with Germany until late 1941, but prior to Pearl Harbor Roosevelt ordered the Navy to guard convoys to Great Britain and to open fire on submarines threatening the convoys. Truman had no specific authorization from Congress in 1950 when he ordered American forces to resist aggression in Korea. Nor did President Kennedy when he ordered a troop buildup during the Berlin crisis of 1961, when he sent forces into Southeast Asia in the spring of 1962, and when he ordered a naval quarantine of Cuba in the fall of 1962. Nor did President Johnson when he bolstered American forces in Vietnam from 1965 to 1968. Nor did Nixon in his invasion of Cambodia in 1970, or in his support for Saigon's invasion of Laos in 1971.[8]

Thus, from Washington's time on, by ordering the troops into battle, the president has often decided when Americans will fight, and when they will not. When the cause has had political support, the president's use of this authority has been approved. Abraham Lincoln called up troops, spent money, set up a blockade, and fought the first few months of the Civil War without even calling Congress into session. More recently it became obvious that the president needed the power to respond to sudden attacks and to protect the rights and property of American citizens. The State Department described this enlarged mandate as follows:

> In the twentieth century the world has grown much smaller. An attack on a country far from its shores can impinge directly on the nation's security. . . . The Constitution leaves to the President the judgment to determine whether the circumstances of a particular armed attack are so urgent and the potential consequences so threatening to the security of the U.S. that he should act without formally consulting the Congress.[9]

Many war acts w/o Congress knowing. Why Framers set up dec of war by congress

Lyndon Johnson's failure to end the use of U.S. ground forces in Vietnam led to Richard Nixon's election as president in 1968. *UPI.*

But Congress became upset when President Johnson in 1964 won approval of his Vietnam initiatives on the basis of misleading information. Later a secret air war was waged in Cambodia in 1969 and 1970 with no formal congressional knowledge or authorization. The military also operated in Laos without formally notifying Congress. It was to prevent just such acts as these that the framers of the Constitution gave Congress the power to declare war; and many members of Congress believe that what happened in Indochina was the result of the White House bypassing the constitutional requirements. But they also agree that presidential excesses came about because Congress either agreed with presidents or did nothing to stop them.

President Lyndon Johnson giving his state of the union address in 1965. *UPI.*

What the Johnson and Nixon war experiences also show is that at the beginning of hostilities, the country and Congress rally behind a president. As casualties mount and the fighting continues, support usually falls off. In both Korea and Vietnam presidential failure to end the use of American ground forces led to increased political trouble. Eisenhower swept into power in 1952 promising to bring the boys home; Nixon won in 1968 when Johnson was forced out over Vietnam. But while Congress may have been misled during the Vietnam war, it enthusiastically supported the president and went along with his actions. It was not until the war turned sour that senators and representatives began to charge misrepresentation. Why then were they so easily talked into approving funds for the war? They continued to pass appropriations for it right up to April 1975. The more general lesson appears to be that the country and Congress (and the courts) tend to go along with a president's judgments about military action overseas. Congress goes along w/ Pres judgment about military action

[8]See Thomas A. Bailey, *The Pugnacious Presidents: War Presidents on Parade* (Free Press, 1980.)

[9]Leonard C. Meeker, "The Legality of U.S. Participation in the Defense of Vietnam, *Department of State Bulletin* (March 28, 1966), pp. 484–85.

There are additional reasons why no formal congressional declarations of war have been issued in recent times. During a state of war the president assumes certain legal prerogatives that Congress might not always be willing to grant. There are also international legal consequences of a formal declaration of war regarding foreign assets, the rights of neutrals, and so on, which our allies would not always be willing to recognize and which would be difficult to insist upon. Moreover, there is the psychological consequence of declaring war, compounded by the fact that—according to Article 2, Section 2, of the United Nations Charter—war is illegal except in self-defense.

Too Many Emergency Powers

From the early 1930s to the mid-1970s, Congress passed about 500 federal statutes collectively giving a president extraordinary powers. Once a state of emergency was declared, for example, a president could seize property, organize and control the means of production, seize commodities, assign military forces abroad, declare martial law, and control all transportation and communications. A president might, in fact, control almost all aspects of citizens' lives. Abuses of presidential power under these emergency laws include the detention of American citizens of Japanese ancestry during World War II, the coverup of the bombings in Cambodia, and the directives to the FBI for illegal domestic surveillance and intelligence work.[10]

Too Much Diplomacy by Executive Agreement

As indicated in Table 16–2, the growing use of executive agreements shows their popularity with recent presidents. Prior to a president ratifying a treaty, two-thirds of the Senate must consent. But executive agreements permit a president to enter into formal agreements with a foreign nation without senatorial approval. These agreements have been recognized as distinct from treaties since George Washington's day. And their use by the executive has been upheld by the courts. What irked Congress in the 1960s and 1970s was that the Senate was being asked to ratify international accords only on trivial matters. Critically important mutual aid and military agreements were being arranged by the White House without its even informing Congress.

For example, while the Senate was ratifying treaties to preserve archeological artifacts in Mexico and maintain certain lights in the Red Sea, the president was using executive agreements to make vital decisions about United States presence in Vietnam, Laos, Korea, and Thailand. Walter F. Mondale, then a senator, and others argued that these practices violated the Constitution's intent that Congress share in making foreign policy. And so the members of Congress began to look for ways to limit a president's executive agreement authority.

16–2
TREATIES AND EXECUTIVE AGREEMENTS, (1789–1983)

Period	Treaties	Executive Agreements	Totals
1789–1839	60	27	87
1839–1889	215	238	453
1889–1939	524	917	1441
1940–1973	364	6395	6759
1974–1979	102	2233	2335
1980–1982	55	1063	1118
	1320	10,873	12,193

SOURCES: Congressional Research Service, Library of Congress.

[10]For a discussion of abuses of power in U.S. intelligence agencies during the Cold War years, see Morton H. Halperin, Jerry J. Berman, Robert L. Borosage, and Christine M. Marwick, *The Lawless State* (Penguin, 1976); and David Wise, *The American Police State: The Government against the People* (Random House, 1976).

Bricker; Amendment - approve all Exec Agreements

Pres has keep right to... i.e. D-Day secret

Nixon abused Exec Privilege

Privacy during H2O gate

Ironically, it was conservative members of Congress who tried during the 1940s and 1950s to check the president's power to make executive agreements. Senator John Bricker (R-Ohio) introduced a constitutional amendment in 1953 that would have required Congress to approve all executive agreements. He was opposed by liberals, especially liberal political scientists and historians, who feared the Bricker amendment would reintroduce a mindless isolationism. Bricker was opposed too by Eisenhower's secretary of state who called it dangerous to our peace and security. In the wake of Vietnam and especially during the Nixon administration, the shoe was on the other foot. The liberals, fearing an interventionist foreign policy, now wanted to limit executive agreements.

Secrecy and Executive Privilege

President Nixon resigning from office, August 9, 1974. *UPI.*

The founding fathers were aware of the saying that the person who controls the flow of information rules our destinies. They did not intend that the president should decide what information Congress and the American people should have. Without information Congress cannot oversee the administration of its laws; if it cannot do that, it is scarcely in a position to legislate at all. However, constitutional scholars, the courts, and Congress agree that a president *does* have the right to withhold information vital to national security. Thus, during World War II the time and place of the Normandy Beach invasion were properly kept secret.

In the 1960s and 1970s presidents invoked the doctrine of executive privilege to claim that a president may withhold information, even from Congress, whenever the White House thinks it is necessary to protect the public interest. It was not until the combination of Vietnam and Watergate that this doctrine became controversial. President Nixon and his lawyers claimed the president's decision to invoke executive privilege was not subject to review, either by Congress or the courts. Accordingly, Nixon refused to turn over to congressional committees documents and tapes they requested.

One legal historian argued that executive privilege is "a myth, without constitutional basis,"[11] but most people think the truth is somewhere in between. As we noted in Chapter 4, the Supreme Court ruled in 1974 that a president does have a limited power of executive privilege, but is subject to judicial scrutiny.

Impoundment

Nixon frequently impounded funds approp. by Congress

Impounding: Pres forbids spending of appropriated funds

Nixon abused impoundment

Some members of Congress used to joke during the Nixon period that ours was a system of checks and balances all right: Congress wrote the checks and the White House kept the balance. They were referring to President Nixon's frequent use of the power to impound funds appropriated by Congress.

By *impounding* funds a president forbids agencies to spend money even though it has been appropriated by Congress. Impoundment can take many forms. It may be necessary due to a change in events (a war ends) or for managerial reasons (a project can be carried out more efficiently). Before Nixon impoundments were infrequent and were usually temporary; generally they involved small amounts of money. Nixon stretched the use of impoundment to new lengths. Altogether he impounded about $18 billion of funds appropriated by Congress for water pollution control, urban aid, and other programs. Nixon claimed the Democratic Congress was spending too much and causing huge deficits. Congress claimed Nixon was using impoundment to set policy.

Congress responded to Nixon's impoundments by pointing to a clause in the Constitution reading: "No money shall be drawn from the Treasury, but in consequence of appropriations made by law." Congress took this to mean it had the final say in fiscal policy making. By refusing to spend appropriated funds,

[11]Raoul Berger, "The Grand Inquest of the Nation," *Harper's* (October 1973) p. 12. See also his *Executive Privilege: A Constitutional Myth* (Harvard University Press, 1974).

the executive was in effect exercising an item veto. He was destroying or delaying a program while avoiding a public veto message and the risk of a congressional override.

Government by Presidential Veto?

A president can veto a bill by returning it, together with specific objections, to the house in which it originated. Congress, by a two-thirds vote in each chamber, may then override the president's veto. Another variation of the veto is known as the pocket veto. In the ordinary course of events, if the president does not sign or veto a bill within ten weekdays after receiving it, it becomes law without the chief executive's signature. But if Congress adjourns within the ten days, the president—by taking no action—can kill the bill.

The veto's strength lies in the ordinary failure of Congress to get a two-thirds majority of both houses. Historically Congress has overridden only about 3 percent of the president's vetoes. Yet a Congress that can repeatedly mobilize such a majority against a president can almost take command of the government. Such was the fate of Andrew Johnson in the late 1860s.

In ordinary times Congress can manipulate legislation to reduce the chance of a presidential veto. It can attach irrelevant but controversial provisions, called *riders*, to vitally needed legislation. Presidents must either accept or reject the whole bill, for they do not have the power to delete individual items; that is, they do not have the item veto. In one appropriations bill, for example, lawmakers may combine badly needed funds for the armed forces with costly pork-barrel items. The president must take the bill as it is or not at all.

For their part, presidents can also use the veto power in a positive way. They can announce that a bill under consideration by Congress will be turned back unless certain changes are made. They can use the threat of a veto against some bill Congress wants badly in exchange for another bill that they want. But the veto is essentially a negative weapon of limited use to a president who has a positive program. For it is the *president* who usually is pressing for action.

The presidential veto power has stirred less controversy than the other changes we have discussed. Carter vetoed only 31 bills, Nixon vetoed 43, and Ford 66. Still, the occasional use of the *pocket* veto has stirred some criticism.

© 1980 King Features Syndicate, Inc. World rights reserved.

Handwritten margin notes:
Congress has overridden 3% of vetoes

Pocket veto
After 10 days if Prez doesn't sign or veto = Law unless Congress adjourns kills Bill

Congress can add riders they want to Important bills

PRESIDENTIAL VETOES—1789–1984

President	Vetoes	Vetoes Overridden	President	Vetoes	Vetoes Overridden	President	Vetoes	Vetoes Overridden
George Washington	2	—	James Buchanan	7	—	Warren G. Harding	6	—
John Adams	0	—	Abraham Lincoln	7	—	Calvin Coolidge	50	4
Thomas Jefferson	0	—	Andrew Johnson	29	15	Herbert Hoover	37	3
James Madison	7	—	Ulysses S. Grant	93	4	Franklin D. Roosevelt	635	9
James Monroe	1	—	Rutherford B. Hayes	13	1	Harry S Truman	250	12
John Q. Adams	0	—	James A. Garfield	0	—	Dwight D. Eisenhower	181	2
Andrew Jackson	12	—	Chester A. Arthur	12	1	John F. Kennedy	21	—
Martin Van Buren	1	—	Grover Cleveland	414	2	Lyndon B. Johnson	30	—
W. H. Harrison	0	—	Benjamin Harrison	44	1	Richard M. Nixon	43	7
John Tyler	10	1	Grover Cleveland	170	5	Gerald R. Ford	66	12
James K. Polk	3	—	William McKinley	42	—	Jimmy Carter	31	2
Zachary Taylor	0	—	Theodore Roosevelt	82	1	Ronald Reagan	18	2
Millard Fillmore	0	—	William H. Taft	39	1	Total	2809	96
Franklin Pierce	9	5	Woodrow Wilson	44	6			

Source: *Library of Congress and Congressional Quarterly.*

358

Some members of Congress said the founding fathers envisioned a more limited use of the veto. Other members of Congress, led by Senator Edward Kennedy, objected to Nixon's use of the pocket veto during short holiday recesses. The courts upheld Kennedy's contention that the pocket veto did not apply while Congress was in recess, but only when it had adjourned.

In fact, there is little that Congress can do when confronted with a presidential veto. It must either get enough votes to override the veto or modify the legislation and try again.

CONGRESS REASSERTS ITSELF: 1972–1980

The end of the war in Vietnam, the 1974 impeachment hearings, and the resignation of President Nixon gave Congress new life.[12] It set about to recover lost authority and discover new ways to participate more fully in making national policy. Some of Congress's more notable efforts to reassert itself are outlined below.

The War Over the War Powers

In 1973 Congress took the unprecedented step of overriding a presidential veto and enacting the War Powers Resolution. Congress declared that henceforth the president can commit the armed forces of the United States only (1) after a declaration of war by Congress, (2) by specific statutory authorization, or (3) in a national emergency created by an attack on the United States or its armed forces. After committing the armed forces under the third circumstance, the president is required to report within forty eight hours to Congress. Within sixty days, unless Congress has declared war, the troop commitment will be ended. The president is allowed another thirty days if the chief executive claims the safety of United States forces requires their continued use. A president is also obligated by this resolution to consult Congress "in every possible instance" before committing troops to battle. Moreover, Congress at any time, by concurrent resolution *not subject to presidential veto*, may direct the president to disengage such troops. Because of a 1983 court ruling, the question of whether Congress can remove the troops by concurrent resolution or legislative veto is now in doubt (see the discussion of the legislative veto later in this chapter).

Not everyone was pleased by the passage of the War Powers Resolution. Nixon called it an unconstitutional intrusion into the president's authority, an "action that seriously undermines this nation's ability to act decisively and convincingly in times of international crisis." Some felt this resolution granted presidents more power than they already had, and even encouraged short-term interventions.[13] But many experts believed the War Powers law to be of symbolic and institutional significance, reflecting a new determination in Congress. Any future president will know that commitment of American troops is subject to the approval of Congress. Presidents will have to persuade the nation that their actions are justified by the gravest of national emergencies. Since its adoption in 1973 the process spelled out in the War Powers Resolution has been used several times—most dramatically when Marines were sent in 1975 to free the merchant cargo ship *Mayaguez* which had been captured by the Cambodians. President Reagan in 1982 reported to Congress, along the lines of the resolution, after he sent troops into Lebanon although he insisted at first that the War Powers Resolution did not apply there or in Granada.

THE TROUBLED LIFE OF THE WAR POWERS RESOLUTION

When Congress passed the War Powers Resolution in 1973 it was hoped it would pave the way for improved White House-congressional cooperation when US troops had to be used in emergency situations. In the next twelve years, conflict and strain characterized these relations more than cooperation. Congress seldom believes it is properly consulted. Presidents Nixon, Ford, Carter, and Reagan all believed the War Powers Resolution was unconstitutional, impractical, or undesirable. All three branches have weakened the spirit of the War Powers Resolution. Presidents often ignored it or complied with it in a minimal way. The Burger Court ruled on another measure that implicitly suggested a major provision of the Resolution was unconstitutional. Congress sometimes failed to follow through and use the Resolution. In the Lebanon case, after a long struggle it ruled the President could keep troops there for up to 18 months. In the Grenada case, Congress seemed overwhelmed both by the President and public opinion and never put the War Powers Resolution into effect.

[12]See James Sundquist, *The Decline and Resurgence of Congress* (Brookings Institution, 1981).

[13]See, for example, Thomas F. Eagleton, *War and Presidential Power: A Chronicle of Congressional Surrender* (Liveright, 1974).

While Congress has the constitutional authority to intervene whenever it has the will to do so, the history of presidential actions when our troops are engaged in combat suggests that presidents in the future will not have much difficulty in doing pretty much what they please as was made clear in the 1983 "Grenada affair." The Constitution, as Chief Justice Hughes once said, is a "fighting Constitution."[14]

National Emergencies Acts Restricts power of Pres to declare emergency, Pres must notify Congress 1st 6 mo. Lmt

Curbing the Emergency Powers

The National Emergencies Act of 1976 terminated, as of September 1978, the extensive powers and authorities possessed by the president as a result of the continuing state of emergency the nation had been in since the mid-1930s. It also established authority for the declaration of future emergencies in a manner that will clearly define the powers of the president and provide for regular congressional review.

The act also calls upon presidents to inform Congress in advance and identify those laws they plan to use when declaring a national emergency. A state of emergency so declared would automatically end after six months, although a president could then declare it again for another six months. But Congress must review the declaration of emergency powers at least every six months.

Congress hopes this legislation will ensure that emergency powers can be utilized only when legitimate emergencies actually exist, and then only with the safeguard of legislative review. As one senator reported to Congress: "Reliance on emergency authority, intended for use in crisis situations, would no longer be available in non-crisis situations. At a time when governments throughout the world are turning with increasing desperation to an all-powerful executive, this legislation is designed to insure that the United States travels a road marked by carefully constructed legal safeguards."[15]

October, 1983. U.S. Marines patrol the streets in St. George's Grenada —shown here shortly after our military intervention. *UPI.*

CIA - not in U.S.

Congress and the Intelligence Agencies

Presidents have also been charged with abusing the intelligence and spying agencies. The Central Intelligence Agency (CIA) was established in 1947, when the threat of "world communism" led to a vast number of national security efforts. When the CIA was established, Congress recognized the dangers to a free society inherent in such a secret organization. Hence, it was stipulated that the CIA *was not to engage in any police work or to perform operations within the United States.* *Congress doesn't know about CIA activities*

President Reagan delivering a state of the union address to a joint session of Congress. Vice-President George Bush and House Speaker Thomas P. O'Neill watch from behind. *UPI.*

From 1947 to the mid-1970s, no area of national policy making was more removed from Congress than CIA operations. In many instances Congress acted as if it really didn't want to know what was going on. Said one senator: "It is not a question of reluctance on the part of CIA officials to speak to us. Instead it is a question of our reluctance, if you will, to seek information and knowledge on subjects which I personally, as a Member of Congress and as a citizen, would rather not have."[16] There is much evidence that Congress as well as the White House was lax in supervising intelligence activities.

In recent years Congress has tried to reassert control. In 1974 it enacted the Hughes-Ryan Amendment, which required the administration to advise

---

[14]Charles Evans Hughes, "War Powers under the Constitution," *American Bar Association Reports,* Vol. 42 (1917), p. 238. See also *Home Building and Loan Association* v. *Blaisdell,* 290 U.S. 398, 426 (1934). See also Bailey, *The Pugnacious Presidents.*

[15]Abraham Ribicoff, quoted in *National Emergencies Act, Report of the Committee on Government Operations, United States Senate* (U.S. Government Printing Office, 1976), p. 2.

[16]Statement of Senator Leverett Saltonstall (R-Mass.), quoted in Henry Howe Ransom, *The Intelligence Establishment* (Harvard University Press, 1970), p. 169.

Hughes Ryan Amendment - advise 8 congress committees of clandestine operations (Later changed to 2 comm.)

Select Committee of Intelligence legislative, Budget Control Over CIA

Congress wants more control over Intelligence

YOU DECIDE

You are president and the director of the CIA and chairman of the Joint Chiefs of Staff at the Pentagon advise you that a country in North Africa headed by a notoriously anti-American dictator has, with the help of the Soviet Union, assembled a team of scientists who are about to build an atomic bomb.

They also advise you that within the country a group of persons in opposition to the head of state believe that if they are given some weapons they can overthrow the government and would establish one that would be friendly to the United States, more democratic, and would pledge not to introduce atomic weapons into the Middle East.

Many members of Congress oppose covert actions by the CIA. Should you, would you, authorize the CIA to assist the rebels in a covert way?

(Answer/Discussion on the next page.)

eight congressional committees of plans for clandestine operations. Later, in 1980, this was changed to just two committees. This same measure forbids such clandestine operations unless they are specifically approved by the president. In 1975 the Senate established a temporary committee of inquiry chaired by Senator Frank Church. This committee found widespread abuses of power and violations of the rights of American citizens in the conduct of both foreign and domestic intelligence operations. The Church committee recommended that Congress bring all intelligence operations within the framework of congressional oversight.

The Senate then voted to create a permanent Select Committee on Intelligence, with legislative and budgetary authority over the CIA and other intelligence agencies. Subsequently, the House voted to set up a similar panel. But since we now know that even presidents have had difficulty getting a handle on the CIA, there is some doubt about whether Congress will have any better luck. Yet in an unprecedented exercise of its power over the intelligence budget, Congress in 1976 amended the Defense Appropriations Bill to terminate American covert intervention in Angola. "The inevitable public disclosure of a secret operation served, in this instance, the will of Congress; and in the short run the Angola controversy was a warning that the Executive should proceed with caution."[17]

How likely is it that Congress will be effective in regulating the CIA? One study concludes: "To date, only a few patchwork elements of reform have been put into effect. At every turn, the executive branch continues to fight any major changes and, instead, offers 'reforms' that end up authorizing for the future the abuses of the past."[18] Some critics say the Senate committee should spell out a charter that would limit the CIA to foreign operations, severely restrict and control all covert activities, require written approval for any major field operations, and shut down the political intelligence work of the FBI. Others feel full disclosure of the intelligence community's budget is necessary.

Presidents Ford, Carter, and Reagan criticized Congress for weakening the CIA. They felt Congress went too far and should ease the restrictions on covert operations. The Carter administration especially pressed this case in 1980, during the Iranian and Afghanistan crises. Officials in the Carter White House said the administration was deterred from going ahead on certain overseas operations for fear that their disclosure to the eight congressional committees might result in leaks to the press. The Carter and Reagan administrations also favored tightening provisions of the Freedom of Information Act, which gives individuals and foreign governments access to large amounts of official data that used to be classified.

A longer-range view suggests that the intensity and direction of congressional interest in these matters depend on the movement of larger political forces. That is, when a national consensus supports a president and that president's foreign policy initiatives—as it plainly did in the early part of the Cold War—Congress is likely to go along. But in the absence of such a consensus, Congress may try to find a more realistic system of accountability for the CIA and related activities as a substitute for the public scrutiny normally given major governmental operations. It is worth recalling that already-existing congressional committees designed to oversee the intelligence agencies did not do their job.

[17]John T. Elliff, "Congress and the Intelligence Community," in Lawrence C. Dodd and Bruce J. Oppenheimer (eds.), *Congress Reconsidered* (Praeger, 1977), pp. 193–206.

[18]Morton H. Halperin et al., *The Lawless State: The Crimes of the U.S. Intelligence Agencies* (Penguin Books, 1976), p. 279. For general background on this question, see Tyrus G. Gain et al. (eds.), *The Intelligence Community: History, Organization and Issues* (Bowker, 1977).

The Budget and Impoundment Control Act of 1974

ANSWER/DISCUSSION

The case for covert operations is that they are deemed necessary in order to protect America's vital national security interests. Defenders of covert operations say that the Soviet Union does not hesitate to operate in the "back alleys" of the world and that the U.S. puts itself at a serious disadvantage by ruling out all covert operations.

The case against covert action is that such actions have caused us more trouble than they have been helpful. Critics say the era of superpower interventionism has passed; its discovery causes an uproar in the third world. Further, covert operations are basically at odds with American democracy.

It turns out, of course, that Congress as a whole does not want to eliminate all covert actions. But it wants to support those covert actions that can be kept truly secret but requires they be reported to Congressional leaders. Reagan supported covert operations. Many leading Democrats have opposed them. You get to decide again!

Congressional Budget Of gives experts & computers to Congress in dealing w/ Pres proposals

Rep. James Jones (D-Okla.) served as chairman of the House Budget Committee in the 97th and 98th Congresses. *Rick Bloom.*

"Congress has seen its control over the federal purse-strings ebb away over the past 50 years because of its inability to get a grip on the overall budget, while the Office of Management and Budget in the executive branch has increased its power and influence," said then Senator Edmund S. Muskie (D-Maine) in 1974.[19] Congress became dependent on the president's budget proposals. It had no budget system of its own—only many separate actions and decisions coming at various intervals throughout the year. More and more members of Congress grew to appreciate the old saying: The one who controls the purse has the power. *Budget & Impoundment Control = Give Congress spending power*

Muskie was one of the chief authors of the 1974 Congressional Budget and Impoundment Control Act, which was designed to encourage Congress to evaluate the nation's fiscal situation and spending priorities in a comprehensive way. It was also hoped that in a period of high inflation, Congress could help put a lid on unnecessary spending. The act creates a permanent budget committee for each chamber. In the House it is now a thirty-member committee. The Senate has a twenty-two member committee picked in the regular fashion.

Under the law Congress also established a Congressional Budget Office (CBO). It provides budgetary and fiscal experts and computer services and gives Congress technical assistance in dealing with the president's proposals. Some members of Congress hoped the CBO would provide hard, practical data to guide the drafting of spending legislation. Others saw it as a potential "think tank" that might propose standards for spending and national priorities. In fact, CBO is most frequently used to provide routine cost estimates of spending and tax bills and to keep track of the overall budget level.

Optimists hoped the Budget Reform Act would force Congress into more systematic and timely action on budgetary legislation. They hoped, too, it would tie separate spending decisions in with fiscal policy objectives. The new budgetary timetable gives Congress three additional months to consider the president's recommendations (see Table 16–3). By May 15 of each year, Congress adopts a tentative budget that sets target totals for spending and taxes. This target serves as a guide for the committees considering detailed appropriation measures. By September 15 Congress adopts a second resolution that either affirms or revises the earlier targets. If necessary to meet the final budget totals, this resolution must also dictate any changes in expenditures and revenues.[20]

How did the reformed budget process work in its first decade? The quality of information produced by the Congressional Budget Office greatly improved congressional deliberation on the budget. The new budget committees in each house worked reasonably well. The budget resolutions provided a vehicle for certain helpful debates on key economic issues. But overall the new budgetary process did not diminish the budgetary powers of the president. In fact, in 1981 President Reagan—fresh from his impressive 1980 election victory—dramatically used the "reconciliation" aspect of the process to push through budget cuts of some $35 billion. While it was perfectly legal this presidential use of the act was unanticipated by those who wrote it. The effect was to give Reagan, backed by majorities in both houses of Congress, an initiative and domination over the budget process that no president had exercised before. And it was contrary to what the writers of the act intended; indeed it was the very kind of presidential assertiveness Congress had hoped to limit.[21] Reagan enjoyed less

[19]Quoted in *National Journal*, May 29, 1976, p. 742.

[20]Three books describing the origins and early years of the 1974 Budget Reform Act are Lance T. LeLoup, *The Fiscal Congress: Legislative Control of the Budget* (Greenwood Press, 1980); Allen Schick, *Congress and Money: Budgeting, Spending and Taxing* (Urban Institute, 1980), and Howard Shuman, *Politics and the Budget* (Prentice-Hall, 1984).

[21]Shuman, *Politics and the Budget.*

16-3
CONGRESSIONAL BUDGET TIMETABLE

On or Before	Action to be Completed
Between October and December	Congressional Budget Office (CBO) submits a five-year projection of current spending.
November 10	President submits the current services budget.
15th day after Congress meets	President submits budget.
Between January and March	Budget committees hold hearings and start work on the first budget resolution.
March 15	Legislative committees submit reports to the budget committees.
April 15	Budget Committees report the first concurrent resolution on the budget to their respective chambers.
May 15	Appropriate committees report bills and resolutions authorizing new budget authority, and Congress completes all action on the first concurrent budget resolution.
August	Budget committees prepare the second concurrent budget resolution and report to their houses.
September 15	Congress completes all action on the second concurrent budget resolution.
September 25	Congress completes action on a reconciliation bill or resolution containing provisions necessary to accomplish any change in budget authority, revenues, or the public debt directed by the second budget resolution.
October 1	The federal government's fiscal year begins.

Give Congress more power w/ Budget

success in controlling the budget after this remarkable first-year experience. Budget process politics became highly partisan in both houses of Congress, and legislative-executive budget relations often became very strained.

The jury is still out on the budgetary reforms of the 1970s. Some progress has been made, but surely the fondest hopes of the reformers have not been achieved. Congress still too often fails to apply intelligent cuts to welfare, subsidy and defense spending "sacred cows." Far too much confusion still surrounds the budgetary process. The whole point of having this new budget process was to force Congress to make choices, to put together in one place the spending claims and the revenues, and to decide what it wants. Many people believe the problem is structural and not due to the personal faults of members of Congress. Congress reflects local pressures, presidents reflect national interest group pressures. All this gets reflected in the budget process. Congress may well have to restructure itself to strengthen places where overall consensus can be built. This may mean weakening subcommittees and curbing the recent tendencies to disperse power. The central question is whether Congress is willing to do this. If it cannot do this, Congress will very likely have to respond to the choices and priorities set by presidents.

The impoundment control provisions of this new law have worked out fairly well—better, in fact, then the budgetary provisions. Congress has put the executive branch on the defensive, and presidents are restricted in their ability to impound funds. If presidents withhold funds temporarily, they must report it to Congress, and their impoundment decision can be overturned by a resolution of *either* chamber. But if presidents impound funds for some project permanently, their action is ineffective unless *both* houses approve within forty-five days. The comptroller general (in the General Accounting Office) who finds that impoundments have been made without proper reports to Congress may report them personally. Congress may then act to force release of the

Senate House conferees neared agreement on a 1984 budget opposed by President Reagan that would increase taxes $73 billion over three years, slash his military buildup, and produce a deficit of about $180 billion. *UPI.*

Impounding can be overturned by either chamber

Too much paper work—too vague

funds. Should a president fail to comply with action overruling an impoundment, Congress may ask for a court order requiring the funds to be spent.

There have been complaints that the new impoundment law creates too much paperwork. Reports need to be sent to Congress even when a few thousand dollars are not spent for simple managerial and efficiency purposes. Other complaints stem from the vagueness of the law. But the new impoundment procedure definitely reclaimed some power for Congress. In the future, however, this reform must be adapted to the Supreme Court's decision on the legislative veto.

Confirmation Politics

Pres has reasonable control of appointments of...

Since Watergate, Senate tough on appointments

The Senate and the president often struggle over control of top personnel in the executive and judicial branches. The Constitution leaves the question somewhat ambiguous: "The President . . . shall nominate, and by and with the advice and consent of the Senate, shall appoint Ambassadors, other public Ministers and Consuls, Judges of the Supreme Court, all other officers of the United States. . . ." Presidents, however, have never enjoyed exclusive control over hiring and firing in the executive branch. The Senate jealously guards its right to confirm or reject major appointments; during the period of congressional government after the Civil War, presidents had to struggle to keep their power to appoint and dismiss. But for most of the twentieth century, presidents have gained a reasonable amount of control over top appointments. This has happened in part because public administration experts warned that a chief executive cannot otherwise be held accountable.

Since Watergate, the Senate has taken a somewhat tougher stand on presidential appointments. Senators are especially concerned about potential conflicts of interest. "Our tolerance for mediocrity and lack of independence from economic interests is rapidly coming to an end," said one senator. Another summed it up this way: "Surely, we have learned that one item the government is short on is credibility." Screening is somewhat tighter now; Presidents Ford and Carter have had several high-level appointees turned down. Reagan lost some potential nominees because of conflict-of-interests problems; a few who joined his administration had to leave for the same reasons.

It is difficult to tell to what extent this trend toward greater congressional activity was the result of the normal antagonism that arises when one party controls Congress and the other the White House. Partisan factors must have contributed to this development in the 1969–1977 period. But the scandal of Watergate, in which so many appointees were indicted and convicted, also contributed. It is also true that members of the Senate often push their own favorites and encourage their quick confirmation of them.

senatorial courtesy

willingness of senate to confirm appointments if they R not personally obnoxious

When presidents appoint someone to a federal position in a *state* (a U.S. attorney for example), they need the approval of the senators from the state, especially if these senators are members of the president's party and that party controls the Senate. They need that approval because of a practice known as senatorial courtesy: the willingness of the Senate to confirm presidential appointments only if they are not "personally obnoxious," that is, politically objectionable, to the senators from the state. Thus, for nearly all district court judgeships, many appellate court judgeships, and a variety of other positions, senators exercise what is in fact a veto. It can be overriden only with the greatest difficulty. Further, it is usually exercised in secret and is subject to little accountability. But the patronage is so important to senators that senatorial courtesy is likely to continue.

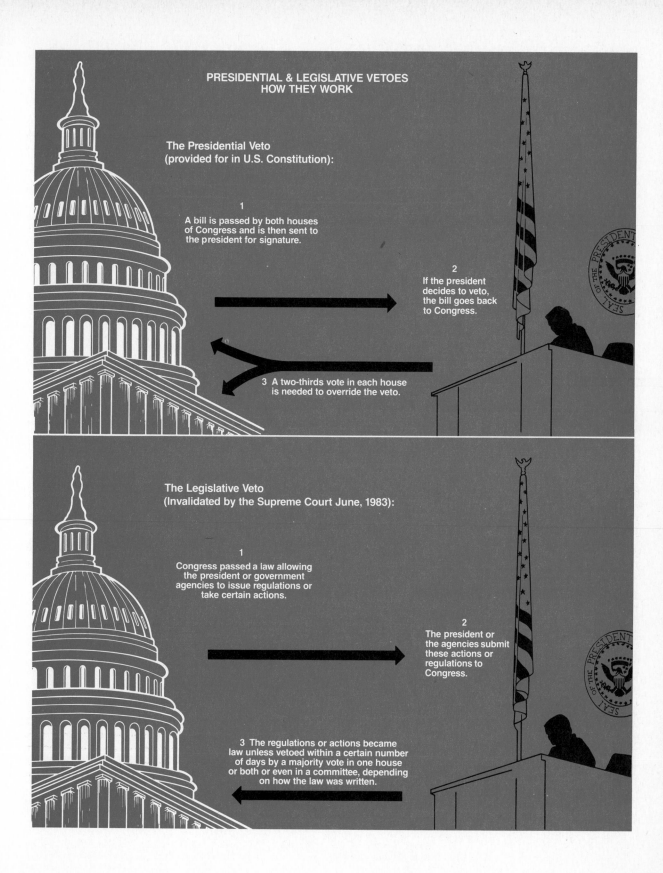

**PRESIDENTIAL & LEGISLATIVE VETOES
HOW THEY WORK**

The Presidential Veto
(provided for in U.S. Constitution):

1
A bill is passed by both houses of Congress and is then sent to the president for signature.

2
If the president decides to veto, the bill goes back to Congress.

3 A two-thirds vote in each house is needed to override the veto.

The Legislative Veto
(Invalidated by the Supreme Court June, 1983):

1
Congress passed a law allowing the president or government agencies to issue regulations or take certain actions.

2
The president or the agencies submit these actions or regulations to Congress.

3 The regulations or actions became law unless vetoed within a certain number of days by a majority vote in one house or both or even in a committee, depending on how the law was written.

365

The Legislative Veto

As yet another means of strengthening itself as it struggled with the presidency, Congress turned often in the 1970s and early 1980s to the **legislative veto**. Under this device Congress would draft a law broadly but incorporate a provision calling for review of the executive branch's implementation of the law. The legislative veto could be put into effect by a majority vote of one house, by both houses, or sometimes even a single congressional committee, depending on how the law was written.

Whatever the form, the legislative veto allowed Congress to delegate general power and then take it away without having to secure presidential approval. In effect, it permitted Congress to legislate without exposing its handiwork to a presidential veto, as the framers intended. The Constitution stipulates that every bill or resolution or vote to which the agreement of the Senate and the House of Representatives may be necessary shall be presented to the president for approval or veto. "Joint resolutions" were regularly submitted to the president. Not so with "concurrent resolutions"; in the past this made little difference, since concurrent or simple one-house resolutions were mainly used to express congressional opinion and had no force of law.

Then in 1932, Congress passed a resolution allowing President Hoover limited authority to reorganize the executive branch agencies. It stipulated that the president's proposals would not be put into effect for ninety days, during which time either house of Congress by a simple resolution could veto the proposal. For the next fifty-one years, the legislative veto became a standard practice.[22] Most frequently Congress required sixty to ninety days in which to consider a proposed regulation. During that time either house could veto the regulation by passing a resolution. However, Congress sometimes simply required legislative approval *before* a regulation took effect.

Between 1932 and mid-1983 at least 210 pieces of legislation carried some form of legislative veto. About half of these were enacted between 1973 and 1983. Major statutes bearing legislative veto provisions included the War Powers Resolution of 1973, the Budget and Impoundment Control Act of 1974, the International Security Assistance and Arms Control Act of 1976, the Federal Trade Commission Improvements Act of 1980.

The device was used to ensure that bureaucratic regulations conformed to congressional intentions. This was important to Congress because of the rapid increase of such regulations—often having the same or nearly the same force as laws. In any given year in the late 1970s or early 1980s, Congress might pass a few hundred public laws; but the administrators in about seventy executive branch agencies were responsible for twenty times as many regulations.

But the legislative veto was also used to keep presidents in check. Arms sales had to be submitted to Congress for its scrutiny. Presidential use of military troops abroad had to be reported to Congress and was subject to recall by unilateral congressional action. In short, upset by presidents who had either lied to or ignored Congress, a reassertive legislature used the legislative veto to recapture some of its authority.

Then in June 1983 Chief Justice Warren Burger—speaking for a Supreme Court majority in a 7–2 decision (*INS* v. *Chadha*)—said that to maintain the separation of powers, the carefully defined limits on the power of each branch must not be eroded. Thus, the legislative veto was found unconstitutional. Said Burger: "With all the obvious flaws . . . we have not yet found a better way to preserve freedom than by making the exercise of power subject to the carefully crafted restraints spelled out in the Constitution."[23] In effect, the Court told

---

CONSTRAINTS ON THE PRESIDENT: POST-WATERGATE CONGRESSIONAL ASSERTIVENESS

☐ War Powers Resolution of 1973

☐ Budget and Impoundment Act of 1974

☐ Frequent use of legislative vetoes (until Supreme Court ruled them unconstitutional in 1983)

☐ Curbs on CIA and FBI

☐ Redefinition of national emergency powers

☐ Growth of congressional staffs and research agencies

☐ Curbs on executive agreements

☐ Curbs (with the help of the courts) on executive privilege and secrecy

☐ Slightly better use of the confirmation hearing process

☐ Somewhat better oversight of executive branch program implementation

☐ Greater Congressional involvement in national security policy and arms trade deals

---

[22]Joseph Cooper and Patricia Hurley, "The Legislative Veto: A Policy Analysis," *Congress and The Presidency* (Spring 1983), pp. 25–46. See also Barbara Hinkson Craig, *The Legislative Veto* (Westview Press, 1983).

[23]77 L Ed 2d 317 (1983).

ITEM-VETO

Throughout the 1984 presidential campaign and in his second term President Reagan has called for an amendment to the Constitution that would permit him the power to veto or in effect to delete any subsection of an appropriations bill passed by Congress. He says it would give him a major tool to reduce deficits. Many in the Congress say, however, it would give too much power to the White House and violate the doctrine of separation of powers. Reagan counters by saying there is too much fat in the budget. Leaders in Congress say, well, why doesn't the President propose a balanced budget and use his general veto more vigorously. The debate continues.

Congress that to obtain more influence over an agency or the presidency, Congress should pass a law that accomplished this explicitly. In the words of dissenting Justice Byron White, the Court's decision "sounds the death knell for nearly 200 other statutory provisions in which Congress has reserved a 'legislative veto . . .' [It] strikes down in one fell swoop provisions in more laws enacted by Congress than the Court has cumulatively invalidated in its history." Ronald Reagan's attorney general immediately hailed this as a victory and said it would result in a "more effective Presidency."[24] Many members of Congress, as well as some students of the Congress, criticized the Court's decision as too sweeping; they feared it might set back the efforts of Congress to recapture and fulfill its functions.

In this historic decision the Court curbed a weapon that Congress had sometimes used effectively to intimidate executive branch officials. Clearly, the existence of the legislative veto stimulated compromise between executive and legislative officials. Some observers viewed the Burger ruling as just one in a long series of Supreme Court decisions that generally approve of and encourage an assertive and increasingly powerful presidency. But others saw it as a needed prod to make Congress more explicit about the policy directions it sets. While the legislative veto may have been a convenient shortcut in congressional-presidential dealings, as the chief justice reminded the nation in his opinion, it is obvious the framers ranked other values higher than efficiency. The legislative veto sometimes had helped Congress in the 1970s to get back into the center of things. Now, in the mid and late 1980s Congress would have to rely on other devices—such as explicit legislation, congressional oversight of the administration of programs, and perhaps other consultative arrangements it can work out with executive branch officialdom.

Other Actions

Maintaining democratic control over foreign and military policy has become increasingly difficult in the nuclear age. Secrecy has been at the heart of the problem. President Nixon argued: "You cannot in today's world have successful diplomacy without secrecy. It is impossible. . . . And it is particularly impossible when you are dealing not with your friends, but with your adversaries."

But executive secrecy is subject to abuses, as Watergate illustrated. People could understand the use of secrecy in negotiations with China or for diplomatic initiatives in the Middle East. But most people found it difficult to understand the use of secrecy in dealing with congressional leaders. Tapping telephones and breaking into offices may be appropriate ways to deal with enemies, but they are not appropriate ways to deal with domestic political opponents.

How can we prevent what may be a necessary evil—secrecy for diplomatic purposes—from becoming secrecy to cover up obstruction of justice? Many Americans believed that even at the risk of a less effective foreign policy, what was needed was greater power sharing with Congress.[25]

Congress has also become more involved in general foreign policy. Shaking off years of inertia, Congress imposed a cutoff of aid to Vietnam and a bombing halt in Cambodia. As of 1972 it required the secretary of state to submit to Congress the final texts of executive agreements. It also restrained the Ford administration from getting involved in Portugal and Angola. This was clearly a case of Congress imposing its goals on the executive. Congress has also demanded and won a greater role in arms sales abroad and in determining U.S. involvement in Lebanon, Central America, and in the Caribbean.

Some attempts by Congress to reassert itself did not succeed. One proposal was the notion of an American "question hour." Cabinet members or even the president would regularly go before Congress to answer questions on major

[24]William French Smith, quoted in *U.S. News and World Report*, July 4, 1983, p. 15.

[25]See John M. Orman, *Presidential Secrecy and Deception* (Greenwood Press, 1980).

policy decisions. Some members of Congress wanted to establish ceilings on how many White House aides there should be; they also wanted to involve Congress in overseeing the policy made by the White House staff. This measure failed, in part because of the president's claim of separation of powers. It also failed because congressional staffs have grown so much in recent years that Congress really cannot point a finger in this case.

RESTORING THE BALANCE OR OVERREACTION?

The 1970s were a decade of redressing the constitutional balance. Nowadays, however, politicians and political analysts differ about the results of congressional assertion. Did Congress overreact to Vietnam and Nixon, endangering the effectiveness of the presidency? Some experts think so. Some rebalancing may have been needed, but Congress was carried away, they contend. Others, however, think reassertion was not only much needed but has been achieved with due respect for an effective presidency. Still others don't believe Congress really gained many of its powers back, and they are skeptical of Congress's ability to match the advantages of the presidency.

Restrengthen the Presidency

Even as the presidency was being roundly criticized for abuses of power in the late 1960s and early 1970s, some felt it was alarmingly battered by the Vietnam war and Watergate. The ranks of the defenders of presidential government may have been temporarily thinned in 1973 and 1974, but at least by 1980 the support for a strong presidency was alive and well. Some people even yearned for "the good old days" of the imperial presidency.[26] As several analysts have observed, the Right worries about the imperial presidency at home, and the Left worries about the imperial presidency abroad. What is not pointed out is that the Right sometimes wants a near-imperial Teddy Roosevelt kind of presidency abroad, and the Left often wants something approaching an imperial superplanning presidency at home.

The American public may have lost confidence in its leaders, but it has not lost hope in the efficacy of strong, purposive leadership. One of the realities of the 1980 and 1984 elections was that while most people said "Public officials are not really interested in the problems of the average man," they nonetheless looked long and hard for stronger candidates who might reclaim more power for the White House. Ronald Reagan stressed the need for tougher stands and signaled often that if elected, he could make things work—that he could "make America great again." To many, Carter seemed afflicted with a case of terminal meekness; the American voters yearned instead for a new team and for a more muscular presidency. Fears of another Watergate presidency seemed to have disappeared. Perhaps all the revelations about the crimes of Watergate and the dramatic resignation of a president persuaded most people into believing that "the system worked"—that the checks checked and the balances balanced. Perhaps the very cataloguing of the misuses of presidential powers seemed to solve the problem.

In the wake of the wounded or imperiled presidency of the Watergate era, could Congress furnish the leadership necessary to govern the country? Most scholars and writers say no. The conventional answer heard in the 1980s is that the United States will need a presidency of substantial power if it is to get on top of the energy and economic problems and maintain its position in foreign

[26]Senator John G. Tower comes close to this position in his "Congress versus the President: The Formulation and Implementation of American Foreign Policy," *Foreign Affairs* (Winter 1981/1982), pp. 230–46.

affairs. Today the federal government has become committed to burdens of administration that demand vigorous, positive leadership. Further, we live in a continuous state of emergency, where instant nuclear warfare could destroy the country in a matter of minutes; and where global competition of almost every sort highlights the need for swiftness, efficiency, and unity in our government. Also, today's social, urban, and environmental problems require a persistent display of creative leadership. A weakening of the presidency may mean a strengthening of the bureaucracy more than a strengthening of Congress. Any reduction in the powers of the president might leave us naked to our enemies, to the forces of inflation and depression at home, and to forces of unrest and aggression abroad.

In 1977 former President Gerald Ford scoffed at the idea that Congress had improved things in recent years. Speaking for the repeal of the War Powers Resolution of 1973, Ford said: "When a crisis breaks out, it is impossible to draw the Congress into the decision-making process in an effective way." Ford cited these reasons for this claim:

Legislators have too many other concerns to be abreast of foreign policy situations.

It is impossible to wait for a consensus among scattered and perhaps disagreeing congressional leaders.

Sensitive information supplied to legislators, particularly via the telephone, might be disclosed.

Waiting for consultation could risk penalties for the President "as severe as impeachment."

Consultations with congressional leaders might not bind the rank and file, particularly independent younger members.[27]

Defenders of a powerful presidency wondered if the United States could afford to have two foreign policies. A nation cannot long retain a leadership role in the world unless its own leadership is both clear and decisive. They argued, too, that congressional decisions—including foreign policy decisions—are very often based almost entirely on domestic politics.

One critic of the impaired presidency, Professor Samuel Huntington of Harvard, urged people to recognize the legitimacy and the necessity "of hierarchy, coercion, discipline, secrecy, and deception—all of which are, in some measure, inescapable attributes of the process of government. . . . When the President is unable to exercise authority, no one else has been able to supply comparable purpose and initiative. To the extent that the United States has been governed on a national basis, it has been governed by the President."[28]

The same verdict is heard from those who yearn for strong creative leadership in domestic or economic matters. Thus, Arthur Schlesinger, Jr.—even as he condemns the imperial presidency—says that "history has shown the presidency to be the most effective instrumentality for justice and progress."[29] Supporters of a strong, powerful presidency worry that a president has too little power today to tackle economic and energy resource problems effectively. For example, a president has little influence over the Federal Reserve Board's pol-

[27]Ford, quoted in Don Oberdorfer, "Ford: War Powers Act Not Practical," *The Washington Post*, April 12, 1977. See also Gerald R. Ford, "The War Powers Resolution: Striking a Balance between the Executive and Legislative Branches." Speech delivered April 11, 1977, at the University of Kentucky, Louisville, and reprinted in David Abshire and Ralph Nurnberger (eds.), *The Growing Power of Congress* (Sage Publications, 1981).

[28]Samuel Huntington, "The Democratic Distemper," in Nathan Glazer and Irving Kristol (eds.), *The American Commonwealth* (Basic Books, 1976), p. 24.

[29]Schlesinger, *Imperial Presidency*, p. 404. See also a similar theme in Theodore Sorensen, *Watchmen in the Night: Presidential Accountability after Watergate* (MIT Press, 1975).

icies on credit and money. Presidents have few tools for effective, long-range economic planning. And their authority over government reorganization is puny compared to expectations of them as the official "chief executive."

Those who hold to the overreaction thesis say the White House today is enmeshed in a complex web of constraints—especially structural constraints—that hobbles presidents. Fears of presidential dictatorship, they say, are much exaggerated. It is unfortunate that people dwell so much on Richard Nixon and his abuse of office. The Nixon presidency, they contend, was one of a kind, and it was dealt with effectively by the impeachment provisions of the Constitution. The central challenge, then, is not to reduce the president's power to lead, to govern, or to persuade, but to check the president's power to mislead and corrupt. Defenders of the presidency call for repeal of the War Powers Resolution of 1973, restraints on the oversight of the intelligence agencies, and independence for the executive's use of executive agreements. These observers delight in the Court's 1983 outlawing of legislative vetoes.

The Case for an Even More Assertive Congress

Some want more congressional power

President Reagan and Domenica Prime Minister, Eugenia Charles (r) explain the invasion of Grenada involving U.S. troops. Reagan aides look on at left. Reagan acted to assist several Caribbean island nations, but he acted contrary to the wishes of several in Congress. Congress held hearings and sent their own task force to investigate. Reagan's actions won strong support in the country and this seemed to quiet congressional criticism. *UPI.*

There are, however, many who still insist that the reassertion of congressional power is a much-needed corrective that has not gone far enough. Supporters of a truly strong and tenacious Congress question the depth, sincerity, and staying power of congressional assertiveness. They point to the failures of Presidents Ford, Carter, and Reagan to comply in precise terms with the War Powers Resolution of 1973 when they ordered various military actions. They note that the Defense Department's budgets continue to grow and to pass through Congress with minimum changes. They contend, too, that despite all the talk about more and better program oversight, most members of Congress find this type of work unglamorous, unappealing, and unrewarding—especially in terms of winning reelection. Hence, they wonder whether Congress will really maintain its interest in this vital work. They suggest also that despite much talk about strengthening the confirmation process, Congress all too easily lapses into its traditional "rubber stamp" habits.

Those who want more reform point out that the imperial presidency was at least as much the product of an unassertive Congress as it was of power-hungry presidents. Although Congress may have asserted itself in response to the events of Watergate, the more distant those events become, the less motivated Congress will be to challenge the presidency. Thus, it is Congress after Watergate that bears watching, and it is Congress that needs to develop a leadership strength of its own.

By 1980 or so the period of post-Watergate reforming had just about run its course. Fears of another era of congressional government seem unfounded. The pendulum swung back in the other direction, although how far it will swing and what consequences will follow cannot yet be determined.

THE PRESIDENT AND CONGRESS IN THE 1980s

Nearly everyone agrees that Congress is likely to remain an important force in domestic, economic, and foreign policy making. If many of the reforms of the 1970s were symbolic in nature, others did have the effect of permitting Congress to gain the information it needs to play a more responsible role in policy making. Much of the effort at reassertion makes sense, and although it makes life more difficult for presidents and executive branch officials, it is clearly in keeping with our tradition of dispersed powers and checks and balances. How long will Congress remain an activist influence in policy making? How long will the American public support Congress in its more assertive activities? Much will depend, understandably, on how Congress exercises its regained and new influence.

However much the public may want Congress to be a major partner with the president and a major check on the president, the public's support for Congress is always subject to deterioration. Power is very much dispersed in Congress. Its deliberations and quarrels are very public. After a while, the public begins to view Congress as "the bickering branch," especially if there is a persuasive activist in the White House.

Polls show that people think Congress pays more attention to public views than does the president. Assuredly, Congress is a splendid forum that represents and registers the diversity of America. But that very virtue makes it difficult for Congress to provide leadership and difficult for it to challenge and bargain effectively with presidents. Not surprisingly, a wary public—dissatisfied with programs that do not work and policies that do not measure up to the urgencies of the moment—will look elsewhere—often to the president or to an aspiring presidential candidate.

Ronald Reagan time and again demonstrated that a president with a program and with shrewd political skills could shape the national agenda and win victories in Congress. Why was Reagan successful? He was able to rally the country and especially his party behind his program. He also concentrated on a few key measures (such as the tax cut and defense buildups), rather than going to Congress with scores of programs. Reagan skillfully exploited the first year of his administration—he obviously had learned the lessons of the Ford-Carter years, and he seized the opportunities his honeymoon period afforded. Above all, he gave the impression of strong commitment to a relatively coherent program.

Further, Reagan exploited the growing sentiment in favor of a stronger presidency. And he exploited some of the new opportunities presented by the so-called "reforms" of the 1970s. Political scientist Norman Ornstein puts it well: "Future Presidents will find Congress frustrating, confusing, capricious and challenging. Past Presidents found Congress frustrating, confusing, capricious and challenging. Enough has changed in the past decade or so to make the confusion different and the challenge more formidable, perhaps, but the changes also offer a President new opportunities and openings for influence in Congress. A combination of old political skills applied in new ways can make a future President at least as pleased with his relations with Congress as were past giants [such] as FDR and LBJ."[30]

A theory of cyclical relations between the president and Congress has long been fashionable. It holds that there will be periods of presidential ascendancy followed by periods of congressional ascendancy. Usually these periods last a decade or more, and sometimes they are a generation in length. Analysis suggests that a moderate but real congressional resurgence did take place in the immediate post-Watergate years. But the responsibilities of the presidency these days, coupled with the complexities of foreign and economic policy, do not really permit any serious weakening of the office. Congress has regained some of its own lost power, and it has very correctly tried to curb the misuse and abuse of power—but it has not really weakened the presidency.

Many will continue to worry about future imperial presidents and about the possible alienation of the people from their leaders as complex issues continue to centralize responsibilities in the hands of the national government and in the executive. Those who are concerned about these matters will not content themselves, nor should they, with the existing safeguards against the future misuse of presidential powers. It is not easy, however, to contrive devices that

President Reagan meeting with Congressional leaders Senator Paul Laxalt (R-Nv.) and Speaker of the House, Thomas P. O'Neill (D-Mass.). *UPI.*

[30]Norman Ornstein, "Something Old, Something New: Lessons for a President About Congress in the Eighties," in James S. Young, *Problems and Prospects of Presidential Leadership in the Nineteen Eighties,* Vol II (University Press of America, 1983), p. 29. See also Anthony King, ed., *Both Ends of the Avenue* (American Enterprise Institute, 1983).

will check the president who would misuse powers without hamstringing the president who would use those same powers for purposive and democratically acceptable ends.

Both president and Congress have to recognize they are not two sides out to "win" but two parts of the same government, both elected to pursue together the interests of the American people. Too much has been made by too many presidents and by too many scholars of that ancient but partial truth that only the president is the representative of all the people. Members of Congress do not represent the people exactly as a president does, but its two houses collectively represent them in ways a president cannot and does not.

In the end, it is not so much a matter of whether the presidency should be stronger than Congress, or vice versa. What matters is that Congress and the presidency must both be strengthened to do the pressing work required for the well-being of the nation.

SUMMARY

1. Congressional-presidential relations are not merely *constitutional* questions; they are also *political* struggles for the support of public opinion, as well as attempts to influence public policy. People may be far more attentive to presidents than to the operations of Congress, yet most Americans today believe that Congress should also have a major role in forming public policy.

2. The 1970s witnessed notable efforts by Congress to reassert itself as a coequal policy-making branch. Congressional self-confidence increased as Congress reformed some of its practices and redefined certain presidential practices. Whether or not Congress can sustain its more aggressive stance toward the executive branch is an open question.

3. We have a system of checks and balances that is de-

signed to be strong enough for effective leadership, but in which power is dispersed enough to ensure liberty. This delicate balance is constantly being readjusted.

4. Congressional reassertion took place in the immediate post-Watergate years. But the responsibilities of the presidency today, coupled with the complexities of foreign and economic policy, have not really permitted any serious weakening of the office. Congress has its work cut out for itself just strengthening and organizing itself to stay involved in national policy making. And presidents, as always, have their work cut our for them just trying to win influence in Congress and in the nation for the priorities and policies they think are best for the nation.

FURTHER READING

CECIL V. CRABB, JR., and PAT M. HOLT. *Invitation to Struggle: Congress, the President and Foreign Policy* (Congressional Quarterly Press, 1980).

GEORGE C. EDWARDS III. *Presidential Influence in Congress* (W. H. Freeman, 1980).

LOUIS FISHER. *The Politics of Shared Power: Congress and the Executive* (Congressional Quarterly Press, 1981).

THOMAS M. FRANCK (ed.). *The Tethered Presidency* (New York University Press, 1981).

ANTHONY KING, ed. *Both Ends of the Avenue: The Presidency, the Executive Branch, and Congress in the 1980s* (American Enterprise Institute, 1983).

ALLEN SCHICK. *Congress and Money: Budgeting, Spending and Taxing* (Urban Institute, 1980).

ARTHUR M. SCHLESINGER, JR. *The Imperial Presidency* (Houghton Mifflin, 1973).

JAMES SUNDQUIST. *The Decline and Resurgence of Congress* (Brookings Institution, 1981).

STEPHEN J. WAYNE. *The Legislative Presidency* (Harper & Row, 1978).

JUDGES:
THE BALANCING
BRANCH

17

Foreigners are often amazed at the great power Americans give their judges, especially federal judges. In 1848, after his visit to America, the French aristocrat Alexis de Tocqueville wrote: "If I were asked where I place the American aristocracy, I should reply without hesitation . . . that it occupies the judicial bench and bar. . . . Scarcely any political question arises in the United States that is not resolved, sooner or later, into a judicial question."[1] A century later the English laborite Harold Laski observed: "The respect in which federal courts and, above all, the Supreme Court are held is hardly surpassed by the influence they exert on the life of the United States."[2]

Should our judges play such a central role in our political life? Before answering, we must first understand *why* they have such great influence. One reason is the power of judicial review—that is, the power to make the authoritative interpretation of the Constitution. Only a constitutional amendment or a later High Court can modify the Court's doctrine. Justice Frankfurter once put it tersely: "The Supreme Court is the Constitution."

Besides exercising the power of judicial review, judges resolve disputes involving millions of dollars, decide conflicts between interests, supervise the criminal justice system, and make rules that affect the lives of millions of people. They have become not only "dispute solvers," but also "problem solvers," and they have "begun to command government agencies to undertake certain policies, sometimes in minute detail. Some courts in some instances have in effect taken over management of businesses, schools, prisons, hospitals."[3]

[1] Phillips Bradley (ed.), *Democracy in America*, Vol. I (Knopf, 1944), pp. 278–80.

[2] *The American Democracy* (Viking, 1948), p. 110.

[3] Colin S. Diver, "The Judges as Political Powerbrokers," *Virginia Law Review*, Vol. 65 (February 1979). Bradley C. Canon, "Defining the Dimensions Of Judicial Activism," *Judicature*, Vol. 66 (December–January 1983), p. 239.

Still, the role of our judges is limited by the scope and nature of judicial power.

THE SCOPE OF JUDICIAL POWER

American judiciary is based on adversary system.

Logic of adversary system puts restraints on judicial power

Courts are passive, cannot act till someone comes there

Political question is one that doesn't require use of constitution Asked to political branch by constitution

The American judicial process is based on the *adversary system*. A court of law is a neutral arena in which two parties argue their differences before an impartial arbiter, with each side striving as hard as it can to present its point of view. Whether or not the "fight theory" is an adequate way of arriving at the truth, the fact that it lies at the basis of our judicial system is crucial. First, the *logic* of the adversary system imposes formal restraints on the scope of judicial power. Second, the *rhetoric* of the adversary system leads us to conceive the role of the judge in a very special way.

Judicial power is essentially *passive*—that is, courts cannot act until someone comes to them. The judiciary has no self-starter. Further, not all disputes are within the scope of judicial power. Judges decide only *justiciable disputes*—those that grow out of actual cases and are capable of settlement by legal methods. Not all governmental questions or constitutional problems are justiciable. Some claims of unconstitutionality raise political questions. A "political" issue requires knowledge of a nonlegal character, requires the use of techniques not suitable for a court, and is addressed to the political branch of government by the Constitution. For example, Which of two competing state governments is the proper one, or, What is a republican form of state government?[4]

Judges are not supposed to use their power unless there is a real controversy. Two people cannot make up a suit merely to contest legislation. "It was never thought that, by means of a friendly suit, a party beaten in the legislature could transfer to the courts an inquiry as to the constitutionality of a legislative

TYPES OF LAW:

Statutory law—formulated primarily by a legislature, but also includes treaties and executive orders; law that comes from authoritative and specific lawmaking sources.

Common law—judge-made law that originated in England in the twelfth century, when royal judges traveled around the country settling disputes in each locality according to prevailing custom. The common law continues to develop according to the rule of *stare decisis*, which means "Let the decision stand." This is the rule of precedent, implying that once a rule has been established by a court, it shall be followed in all similar cases.

Equity—used whenever common law remedies are inadequate. For example, if an injury done to property may do irreparable harm for which money damages cannot provide compensation, under equity a person may ask the judge to issue an injunction ordering the offending person not to take the threatening action. If the wrongdoer persists, he or she may be punished for contempt of court.

Constitutional law—statements about the interpretation of the United States Constitution that have been given Supreme Court approval.

Admiralty and maritime law—law applicable to cases concerning shipping and water-way commerce on the high seas and on the navigable waters of the United States.

Administrative law—rules and decisions of administrators and of judges as they relate to the authority of administrators.

Criminal law—defines crimes against the public order and provides for punishment. Government is responsible for enforcing criminal law, the great body of which is enacted by states and enforced by state officials in state courts; however, the criminal caseload of federal judges is growing.

Civil law—governs the relations between individuals and defines their legal rights. However, the government can also be a party to a civil action: Under the Sherman Antitrust Act, for example, the federal government may initiate civil as well as criminal action to prevent violations of the law.

[4]*Luther v. Borden*, 7 Howard 1 (1849); *Coleman v. Miller*, 307 U.S. 433 (1939).

[handwritten margin notes: Must have good reason to sue (immediate danger or injury) Courts are busy because they are liberal about who they let sue]

act."[5] (This, of course, is exactly what is done in a nonfriendly suit. In such cases, however, the two parties have an interest in getting the full facts before the court.)

Not everyone may challenge a law. Litigants must have *standing to sue*; that is, they must have sustained or be in immediate danger of sustaining a direct and substantial injury. It is not enough merely to have a general interest in a subject or to believe that a law is unconstitutional.

Recently the Supreme Court and Congress have somewhat liberalized the doctrine of standing in order to permit a wider range of persons to use the courts to challenge the actions of governments or to attack corporate practices.[6] This explains in part the tremendous expansion in the business of the federal courts. Yet the Court has not gone as far as some of its members think it should—and certainly not as far as the late Justice Douglas wanted. He would have given standing to sue to trees "about to be despoiled, defaced, or invaded by roads and bulldozers."[7]

Do Judges Make Law?

[handwritten margin notes: Judge = referee. Judges do make laws. ? must make statutes to Apply statutes to concrete situations]

"Do judges make law? Course they do. Made some myself," remarked Jeremiah Smith, judge of the New Hampshire Supreme Court.[8] Although such statements are quite common, they are somehow disturbing. They do not conform to our notions of what a judge should do. Why do we think judges should not make law?

Many people equate a judge's role with that of a referee in a prizefight. What do we expect of referees? They must be impartial; they must be disinterested; and they must treat both parties as equals. Referees do not make rules; they apply the rules an athletic commission has established.

Laws are not made, however, in the same way as the rules of a sport, and herein lies the answer to our question. Not only *do* judges make law, but they *must*. Legislatures make law by enacting statutes, but judges apply statutes to concrete situations. There will be some cases to which general expressions are clearly applicable: "If anything is a vehicle, a motor-car is one."[9] But does the word *vehicle* in a statute include bicycles, airplanes, and roller skates? A judge is constantly faced with situations that possess some of the features of similar cases—but lack others. Statutes are drawn in broad terms: Drivers shall act with "reasonable care"; No one may make "excessive noise" in the vicinity of a hospital; Employers must maintain "safe working conditions." The reason broad terms must be used is that legislators cannot know exactly what will happen in the future.

Judge Learned Hand. *Wide World.*

These problems are intensified when judges are asked—as American judges are—to apply the Constitution, written nearly 200 years ago. If Congress passed a law extending the terms of senators beyond six years, the unconstitutionality of the statute would be apparent to everyone. But the Constitution is full of generalizations: "due process of law," "equal protection of the laws," "unreasonable searches and seizures," "commerce among the several states." It is not likely that recourse to the intent of the framers will help judges faced with cases involving electronic wiretaps, General Motors, or birth control pills. Because the rules by which society is governed cannot interpret themselves, judges cannot avoid making law. *[handwritten: Constitution is very general]*

The fact that judges make policy does not mean they are free to make it *[handwritten: Because of advancements, old const. may not cover everything]*

[5]*Chicago & Grand Trunk Railway Co.* v. *Wellman*, 143 U.S. 226 (1897).

[6]Karen Orren, "Standing to Sue, Interest Group Conflict in the Federal Courts," *The American Political Science Review* (September 1976), pp. 723–41.

[7]*Sierra Club* v. *Morton*, 405 U.S. 727 (1972).

[8]Quote in Paul E. Freund, *On Understanding the Supreme Court* (Little, Brown, 1949), p. 3.

[9]This discussion is based on H. L. A. Hart, *The Concept of Law* (Oxford University Press, 1961), chap. 7.

as they wish. They are subject to a variety of limits on what they decide—some imposed by the political system of which they are a part, some by their own professional obligations as lawyers. Among these constraints is the rule of stare decisis.

Adherence to Precedent

Stare decisis is the Rule of Precedence

Judges abide by previous decisions of theirs & higher courts. Judge can decide previous Laws apply.

Supreme Court are not very restricted by stare decisis

The rule of precedent, or stare decisis, pervades our judicial system. Judges are expected to abide by all previous decisions of their own court and all rulings of superior courts. Adherence to precedent is normally practiced as a rule of thumb, unless there is clear reason for change. Although the rule of precedent imposes restraints on the legal system, it is not nearly so restrictive as some people think.[10]

Consider, for example, the father who, removing his hat as he enters a church, says to his son: "This is the way to behave on such occasions. Do as I do."[11] The son, like the judge trying to follow a precedent, has a wide range of possibilities open to him: How much of the performance must be imitated? Does it matter if the hat is removed slowly or quickly? That the hat is put under the seat? That it is not replaced on the head inside the church? The judge can *distinguish* precedents by stating that a previous case does not control the immediate one because of differences in context. In addition, in many areas of law there are conflicting precedents, one of which can be chosen to support a decision for either party.

The doctrine of stare decisis is even less controlling in the field of constitutional law. Because the Constitution, rather than any one interpretation of it, is binding, the Court can reverse a previous decision it no longer wishes to follow. Supreme Court justices are therefore not seriously restricted by stare decisis. As the first Justice Harlan told a group of law students: "I want to say to you young gentlemen that if we don't like an act of Congress, we don't have too much trouble to find grounds for declaring it unconstitutional."[12]

FEDERAL JUSTICE

"It's nothing personal, Prescott. It's just that a higher court gets a kick out of overruling a lower court."
Copyright © 1967 by Sidney Harris.

Article III of the Constitution says: "The judicial Power of the United States, shall be vested in one supreme Court, and in such inferior Courts as the Congress may from time to time ordain and establish." Courts created to carry out this judicial power are called *Article III* or *constitutional courts*. In addition, Congress may also establish *legislative*, or *Article I courts* to carry out the legislative powers the Constitution has granted to Congress. The main difference between a legislative and a constitutional court is that the judges of the former need not be appointed "to hold their Offices during good Behavior" and may be assigned other than purely judicial duties.

A Supreme Court is a necessity if the national government is to have the power to frame and enforce laws superior to those of the states. The lack of such an agency to maintain national supremacy, to ensure uniform interpretation of national legislation, and to resolve conflicts among the states was one of the glaring deficiencies of the central government under the Articles of Confederation.

It is up to Congress to decide whether there shall be federal courts in addition to the one Supreme Court ordained by the Constitution. (The Constitution also allows Congress to determine the size of the Supreme Court.) The

[10]Benjamin Cardozo, *The Nature of the Judicial Process* (Yale University Press, 1921).

[11]This discussion is based on Hart, *The Concept of Law*, pp. 121, 122.

[12]Quoted by E. S. Corwin, *Constitutional Revolution* (Claremont and Associated Colleges, 1941), p. 38.

first Congress divided the nation into districts and created lower national courts for each district. That decision, though often supplemented, has never been seriously questioned. Today the hierarchy of national courts of general jurisdiction consists of *district courts*, *courts of appeals*, and one *Supreme Court*.

Federal Courts of General Jurisdiction

The workhorses of the federal judiciary are the district courts within the states, in the District of Columbia, and in the territories. Each state has at least one district court. The larger states have as many as the demands of judicial business and the pressure of politics require (though no state has more than four). Each district court is composed of at least one judge, but there may be as many as twenty-seven. District judges normally sit separately and hold court by themselves. There are 576 district judgeships, all filled by the president with the consent of the Senate. All district judges hold office for life.

District courts are trial courts of *original jurisdiction*. They are the only federal courts that regularly employ grand (indicting) and petit (trial) juries. Many of the cases tried before district judges involve citizens of different states, and the judges apply the appropriate state laws. Otherwise, district judges are concerned with federal laws. For example, they hear and decide cases involving crimes against the United States—suits under the national revenue, postal, patent, copyright, trademark, bankruptcy, and civil rights laws. District judges are assisted by clerks, bailiffs, stenographers, law clerks, court reporters, probation officers, and United States magistrates. All these persons are appointed by the judges.

The 260 full-time and 250 part-time magistrates are becoming increasingly important. These magistrates are appointed by the judges, after being screened by panels composed of residents of the judicial districts, for eight-year terms. Magistrates issue warrants for arrest, hold hearings to determine whether arrested persons should be held for action by the grand jury, and, if so, set

---

THE ROLE OF A FEDERAL JUDGE

What is it like to be a judge? Most of the time it is very satisfying. One enjoys the prestige. Courtrooms contain every symbol of authority that a set designer could imagine. Everyone stands up when you come in. You wear a costume identifying you as, if not quite divine, someone special. Attendants twitter all around. Most striking, at every sitting, at least two highly trained lawyers, whose job it is to talk, who *love* to talk, allow you to interrupt them whenever you want.

There are negatives, of course. We have been known to get frivolous cases, or splendidly prepared ones that are nevertheless boring and almost beyond belief. Also, the system is designed to maximize the judge's anxiety—that he has just made a mistake, or is about to. It is not just that (as the egg sorter complained about *his* job) it is "decisions, decisions, decisions all day long"; it is that the system is designed to ensure that the questions presented to us are the hardest to resolve.

Seeking a judicial solution to a problem is usually an act of last resort. The judicial system is the most expensive machine ever invented for finding out what happened and what to do about it. When we judges get a question, it is almost always (a) very important, and (b) a tough case that is close enough to drive one mad. Hence the craft is hard.

Much tension accompanies the job of deciding the questions that all the rest of the social matrix has found too hard to answer. But the effort is worth it. For the job of adjudication is to decide those questions according to particular rules and free of the influences that often affect decisions made outside the courtroom. We represent a third value that is not, and is trusted not to be, the prisoner of either wealth or popular prejudice. . .

.

Thus all the pleasing mummery in the courtroom, all our political insulation, indeed all our power, is designed to support a message: "Whichever side you're on, we are not on your side or your opponent's side; you must persuade us not that you've got money or that you've got votes, but that your cause is lawful and just." That is a role worth fulfilling.

SOURCE: From an address by Irving R. Kaufman, chief judge of the Manhattan based U.S. Court of Appeals for the Second Circuit, reprinted in *Time*, May 5, 1980, p. 70.

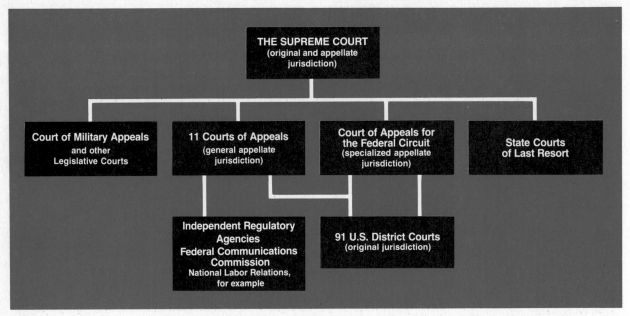

THE SUPREME COURT
(original and appellate jurisdiction)

Court of Military Appeals
and other
Legislative Courts

11 Courts of Appeals
(general appellate
jurisdiction)

Court of Appeals for
the Federal Circuit
(specialized appellate
jurisdiction)

State Courts
of Last Resort

Independent Regulatory
Agencies
Federal Communications
Commission
National Labor Relations,
for example

91 U.S. District Courts
(original jurisdiction)

bail. They preside over civil trials—jury and nonjury—with the consent of both parties, and nonjury trials for petty offenses with the consent of the defendant.[13]

A United States marshal, appointed by the president, is assigned to each district court. Although marshals no longer exercise general police jurisdiction, they maintain order in the courtroom, guard prisoners, make arrests, and carry out court orders, such as serving summonses for witnesses. At times they carry out orders of a federal court even in the face of violence.

Although a few kinds of district court decisions may be appealed directly to the Supreme Court, most decisions must first be appealed to a United States court of appeals. In fact, most district court decisions are not appealed. For those that are, the court of appeals is generally the court of last resort.

The United States courts of appeals are most important judicial policy makers. The United States is divided into twelve judicial circuits, with the District of Columbia counting as one. Each has a court of appeals consisting of from four to twenty-three permanent circuit judges, 156 in all.

SPECIAL ARTICLE III COURTS

In addition to Article III courts of general jurisdiction, Congress has created constitutional courts with special jurisdiction:

United States Court of Claims, consisting of sixteen judges, with jurisdiction over all property and contract damage suits against the United States.

United States Court of International Trade (formerly U.S. Customs Court), consisting of nine judges—with no more than five from the same political party—

with jurisdiction to review rulings of collectors of the customs and conflicts arising under various tariff and trade laws.

Foreign Intelligence Surveillance Court, consisting of seven district judges serving part time, to review applications for electronic surveillance by the government of foreign agents.

United States Court of Appeals for the Federal Circuit, consisting of twelve judges who sit in panels of three to hear appeals

from all federal courts of cases relating to patents, as well as to review decisions of the Patent Office and of the Court of International Trade.

Temporary Emergency Court of Appeals, consisting of eight district and circuit judges designated by the chief justice, who sit in panels of three and have exclusive jurisdiction of all appeals from the district courts in cases arising under economic stabilization laws.

---

[13]Steven Puro and Roger Goldman, "U.S. Magistrates: Changing Dimensions of First-Echelon Federal Judicial Officers," in Philip L. Dubois (ed.), *The Politics of Judicial Reform* (D.C. Heath, 1982).

379

Supreme is only fed court that special conditions) can review state

Circuit judges are appointed for life by the president with the consent of the Senate. The United States courts of appeals have only *appellate* jurisdiction. They review decisions of the district courts within their circuit and also some of the actions of the independent regulatory agencies, such as the Federal Trade Commission. Each court of appeals normally utilizes panels of three judges to hear cases, although for especially important and controversial cases, the whole court may sit *en banc*. Less than 1 percent of the cases from these courts are looked at carefully by the Supreme Court.

State and Federal Courts

In addition to this complex structure of federal courts, each of the fifty states maintains a complete judicial system of its own. (And many of the large municipalities have judicial systems as complex as those of the states.) This dual system of courts is not common—even among nations with federal systems of government.

The popular impression that all federal courts are superior to any state court is wrong. The two court systems are related, but they do not exist in a superior-inferior relationship. Except for the limited habeas corpus jurisdiction of the district courts, the Supreme Court is the only federal court that may review state court decisions—and it may do so only under special conditions.

State courts have sole jurisdiction to try all cases not within the judicial power of the United States, which the Constitution vests in "one supreme Court, and in such inferior Courts as the Congress may from time to time ordain and establish."

Congress determines whether the judicial power of the United States shall be exclusively exercised by federal courts, concurrently exercised by both federal and state courts, or (except for the original jurisdiction of the Supreme Court) denied to either or both federal and state courts. (The Supreme Court's original jursdiction is the only power the Constitution vests directly in any federal court.)

> ### JURISDICTION OF THE SUPREME COURT
>
> *Original*
> □ All cases affecting ambassadors, other public ministers, and consuls
> □ Cases in which a state is a party
>
> *Appellate*
> □ In all other cases arising under the judicial power of the United States, the Supreme Court shall have appellate jurisdiction—power to review decisions of other courts—with such exceptions and under such regulations as Congress shall make.

The "Hidden Judiciary"

1000 administrative law judges sit over benefit proceedings (ss?)

More than 1000 administrative law judges (or ALJs) preside over formal court-like proceedings to determine who is entitled to benefits under federal laws—social security, for example—or to enforce agency regulations. ALJs are employees of the various federal agencies, but they operate under the provisions and protections of the Administrative Procedures Act. They must be lawyers with at least ten years of experience as a judge or practitioner. They are evaluated, and their compensation is set, by the Office of Personnel Management—not by the agencies for which they work. In practice, their decisions become those of the agency they represent and are subject only to appeal to federal courts.[14]

OVERLOADED CIRCUITS: IMPROVING THE SYSTEM

1/3 of Chief Justices time is spent on administration

We do not have a ministry of justice with overall responsibility for the operation of our courts; such a centralized system is contrary to our traditions. Rather, each federal judge is an independent person over whom no one has much administrative authority. However, to provide some small measure of supervision, Congress has vested certain authority in the chief justice and in the Judicial Conference of the United States.

One-third of the chief justice's time is now spent on administrative duties. The "chief" presides over the Judicial Conference of the United States, which

---

[14]Daniel L. Skoler, "The Administrative Law Judiciary: Change, Challenge and Choices," *The Annals*, Vol. 462 (July 1982), pp. 34–47.

consists of the chief judge of each of the courts of appeals and one district judge from each circuit. The Judicial Conference, through its many committees, makes recommendations for rules to be followed by federal courts. The Supreme Court transmits these recommendations to Congress, and they become effective unless vetoed by either chamber. The conference is assisted by the Administrative Office of the United States Courts, whose director prepares budgets and makes reports about the flow of judicial business.

For each of the circuits there is a judicial council consisting of some judges from the court of appeals and some from the district court bench. The council may assign work among the several district courts. Moreover, with the Federal Judicial Discipline Act of 1980, the judicial council now has clear authority to investigate complaints against judges to determine if the latter have engaged in conduct inconsistent with their judicial roles, or to ascertain if judges are unable to discharge their duties because of physical or mental disabilities.

These administrative improvements have helped. Even so, judicial business has increased so dramatically that it takes longer and longer to get cases through the court system; many judges contend they lack the time to deal with issues as carefully as they should. In the past forty years the caseload for each district judge has doubled, and the issues before the bench have become more complex. The courts of appeals and the Supreme Court are also being overwhelmed. "We are," says Chief Justice Burger, "approaching a disaster area." The work of the Court, he argues, is more complicated than in the past, with the number of constitutional cases having doubled in a decade. If nothing is done and the cases increase at the same rate, by the end of the 1980s each justice will have to consider more than 6500 cases.[15] The chief justice's concern is shared by other members of the Court, most of whom have gone to the unusual extreme of making public speeches about the need for some changes if justice is to be properly served.

What should be done? The members of the Supreme Court, the legal profession, and the Congress—although generally agreeing that there are problems—do not agree as to their solution.

Some things have already been done. The number of federal judges has been substantially increased. Judges have been assigned more help in the form of law clerks and administrative assistants. (Some people do not consider this progress. They are concerned about the growth of a "faceless, semiautonomous bureaucracy" that will undermine the judges' unique function of being the only major actors of government who do their own work.)[16]

Further: Congress has eliminated the need for most three-judge federal courts. The Court of Appeals for the Federal Circuits was created to hear the highly technical and time-consuming cases having to do with patents. Magistrates have been given greater authority to dispose of some matters for the district judges. Six-person juries are being used more often in civil trials. And finally, laws and rules have been adopted to speed the hearing of criminal trials.

Yet despite these changes, the work increases faster than the judges' ability to dispose of it. What else might be done? Suggestions include: (1) Abolish diversity jurisdiction of the federal courts (cases between citizens of different states), thereby eliminating about 25 percent of their civil caseload. (2) Refer

---

MAJOR ARTICLE I OR LEGISLATIVE COURTS:

United States Court of Military Appeals, created by Congress under its grant of authority to make the rules and regulations for "land and naval Forces." It is composed of three civilian judges appointed for fifteen years by the president with the consent of the Senate. This court applies military law, which is separate from the body of law that governs the rest of the federal court system.

Bankruptcy judges, consisting of 232 judges appointed by the courts of appeals to serve as adjuncts to the federal district courts. These judges handle bankruptcy matters subject to review by federal district judges.

THE JUDICIAL POWER OF THE UNITED STATES

To hear and decide cases or controversies in law and equity if

1. They arise under the Constitution, a federal law, or a treaty
2. They arise under admiralty and maritime laws
3. They arise because of a dispute involving land claimed under titles granted by two or more states
4. The United States is a party to the case
5. A state is a party to the case (but not including suits begun or prosecuted against a state by an individual or a foreign nation)
6. They are between citizens of different states
7. They affect the accredited representatives of a foreign nation

---

[15]*The New York Times*, February 13, 1983.

[16]Phillip B. Kurland, *Watergate and the Constitution* (University of Chicago Press, 1978), p. 35; Richard B. Hoffman, "The Bureaucratic Spectre; Newest Challenge To the Courts," *Judicature*, Vol. 66 (August 1982), pp. 60–72.

"You have a pretty good case, Mr. Pitkin. How much justice can you afford?" *Drawing by Handlesman;* © *1973 The New Yorker Magazine, Inc.*

[handwritten margin note: Plan to add court of appeals to take load off Supreme court]

more conflicts to arbitration or mediation. (3) Reform the system of workmen's compensation for railroad workers, longshoremen, and seamen, and thus eliminate another 7 percent of the civil caseload. (4) Give the newly created Court of Appeals for the Circuits jurisdiction to take on antitrust and tax cases. (5) Persuade the judges, especially those on the Supreme Court, to write fewer concurring and dissenting opinions. (6) Persuade Congress to stop enacting legislation that imposes greater burdens on the courts. (7) Persuade the justices to make it more difficult for persons to bring lawsuits.

All these proposals are controversial, and there are costs as well as benefits associated with each of them. But the proposal that has generated the most attention and the most controversy is the idea of creating a new court of appeals to assist the Supreme Court. This idea—first put forward in 1972 by the Freund Study Group (appointed by the chief justice and named after its chairperson, a noted Harvard law professor)—called for a court of appeals to screen cases for the Supreme Court. In 1975 the Hruska Commission on Revision of the Federal Court Appellate System recommended that a court of appeals be created not just to screen cases but also to decide cases referred to it by the Supreme Court. In 1983 the chief justice once again urged Congress to create a new court of appeals to hear cases involving conflicts among the circuits, at least on an experimental basis. But many in Congress and on the bench are skeptical: They say another court will add as many burdens as it subtracts. Congress is considering the chief justice's proposal but it shows little disposition to act quickly.

PROSECUTION AND DEFENSE: FEDERAL LAWYERS

[handwritten margin note: are U.S. attorneys of Prez's party]

[handwritten margin note: Attorney General appoints assistant]

Judges decide cases; they do not prosecute persons. That job, on the federal level, falls to the Department of Justice: to the attorney general, the solicitor general, the 94 United States attorneys, and the 1200 assistant attorneys. The president, with the consent of the Senate, appoints a United States attorney for each district court. He or she serves a four-year term but may be dismissed by the president at any time. These appointments are of great interest to senators, who, through senatorial courtesy, exercise significant influence over the selection process. The U.S. attorneys are almost always members of the president's political party, and it is customary for them to resign when the opposition party wins the White House.[17]

The attorney general, in consultation with the U.S. attorney in each district, appoints assistant attorneys. In some districts there is only one. In the largest, the Southern District of New York, there are over sixty-five. Working with the U.S. attorney, assisted by the Federal Bureau of Investigation and other federal law enforcement agencies, these attorneys begin proceedings against those alleged to have broken federal laws. They also represent the United States in civil suits. In criminal cases the U.S. attorney or one of the assistants presents evidence to a grand jury that a national law has been violated by a particular person. If the grand jury agrees, it indicts, and the U.S. attorney's office prosecutes.

The Key Role of Prosecutors

[handwritten margin note: Prosecutors charge offenses]

Prosecutors decide whether to charge an offense and which offense to charge. They negotiate with defendants (usually through their lawyers) and work out plea bargains in which defendants often agree to plead guilty to one offense to avoid having to stand trial for a more serious one. Prosecutors make recommendations to judges about what sentence to recommend.

[17]James Eisenstein, *Counsel for the United States: U.S. Attorneys in the Political and Legal Systems* (The Johns Hopkins Press, 1978).

Attorneys from the department and from other federal agencies participate in well over half the cases on the Supreme Court's docket. Within the Department of Justice special divisions—such as the criminal division, civil division, antitrust division, and civil rights division—coordinate the work of the attorneys in the field, develop cases, and send out specialists to assist the attorneys. Of special importance is the solicitor general, who appears for and represents the government before the Supreme Court. Moreover, no appeal may be taken by the United States to any appellate court without the approval of the solicitor general.[18]

Federal Defense Lawyers

Criminal Justice Act provides Lawyers for the poor

Federal prosecutors are not the only lawyers provided by the national government. The Criminal Justice Act of 1970 provides funds for attorneys for poor defendants. Each district court has some discretion as to how to provide this assistance. Most districts have chosen to stay with the traditional system of assigning a private attorney to defend such people, but these attorneys are paid from public funds. Forty-one districts have opted to use the public defender system—most through a Federal Public Defender Organization, some through community defender organizations that are receiving federal grants. These salaried public defenders operate under the general supervision of the Administrative Office of the United States Courts.

In 1974 Congress created a Legal Services Corporation to take over the responsibility for the work of the lawyers previously employed in federally funded local legal aid offices. The corporation was formed after these offices were criticized for stretching their mandate to provide legal aid to the poor to using lawsuits and class actions to try to alter the distribution of political power. The Legal Services Corporation is limited to helping the poor with traditional problems such as back pay, bankruptcy, and divorce. It is not given authority to challenge the existing power structures in cities and states.

THE JUDGES

The Constitution places the selection of federal judges in the hands of the president, acting with the advice and consent of the Senate. But political reality imposes constraints on the president's power. The selection of a federal judge is actually a complex bargaining process. The principal figures involved are the candidates, the president, United States senators, the Department of Justice, the Standing Committee on the Federal Judiciary of the American Bar Association, and political party leaders.[19]

The Politics of Selection

The practice of senatorial courtesy gives a senator veto power over the appointment of a judge who is to sit in his or her state, if that senator is a member of the president's party. Even if he or she is from the opposition party, the senator must be consulted. When the Senate is controlled by political opponents of the president, the chief executive must still negotiate with both senators from the state, regardless of party affiliation. If negotiations between the senators and then between the senators and the Department of Justice deadlock, a seat may stay vacant for years.[20]

---

[18]Karen O'Connor, "The amicus curiae role of the U.S. solicitor general in Supreme Court litigation," *Judicature*, Vol. 66 (December-January 1983), pp. 256–64.

[19]Harold W. Chase, *Federal Judges: The Appointing Process* (University of Minnesota Press, 1972), pp. 3–47.

[20]See Chase, *Federal Judges*, and the more provocative journalistic account of Joseph C. Goulden, *The Benchwarmers: The Private World of the Powerful Federal Judges* (Ballantine, 1976), chap. 1.

The rule of senatorial courtesy does not apply to Supreme Court appointments and is less often applied to selection of judges for the courts of appeals, because these judges do not serve in any one senator's domain. So it is not surprising that judges in the district courts often reflect values different from those of persons appointed to the Supreme Court or to the courts of appeals. The American Bar Association's Committee on the Federal Judiciary plays an important role in the appointment process. Federal appointments are sent to the committee for evaluation. Although its ratings do not stop a president, any president is hesitant to submit to the Senate for confirmation a candidate rated unqualified by this group.

The Role of Party

Party considerations have always been important in the selection of judges. Presidents seldom choose a judge from the opposing party, and the use of judgeships as a form of political reward was, until recently, openly acknowledged by those involved.

President Carter ostensibly played down partisan considerations in appointing judges by screening his appointments to the courts of appeals through nominating commissions. Many senators also appointed nominating commissions to suggest candidates for the district bench. While disavowing the significance of partisan considerations, President Carter—like all presidents—appointed to the bench (with few exceptions) persons from his own party.

President Reagan has been more open about the importance of partisan affiliation, and his nominees have come overwhelmingly from his own party.

Race and Sex

While partisan considerations remain as significant as ever, presidents and newspeople are paying less attention to the party score cards and more to considerations of race and sex. President Carter appointed forty women, thirty-eight blacks, and sixteen Hispanics to the federal bench, more minority members and women than all other presidents combined. President Reagan, although the first to appoint a woman to the Supreme Court, has primarily appointed white males to judicial positions: decidedly fewer minority members or women have been selected by Reagan than by his predecessor.

The operation of the political process in the selection of judges may shock those who like to think judges are picked strictly in terms of legal merits and without regard for party, race, sex, or ideology. But as a former Justice De-

Women on the federal bench. *Judicature, Volume 65, Number 6, December-January, 1982.*

President	Party	Percentage
Cleveland	Democratic	97.3%
B. Harrison	Republican	87.9
McKinley	Republican	95.7
T. Roosevelt	Republican	95.8
Taft	Republican	82.2
Wilson	Democratic	98.6
Harding	Republican	97.7
Coolidge	Republican	94.1
Hoover	Republican	85.7
F. D. Roosevelt	Democratic	96.4
Truman	Democratic	93.1
Eisenhower	Republican	95.1
Kennedy	Democratic	90.9
L. B. Johnson	Democratic	95.2
Nixon	Republican	93.7
Ford	Republican	81.2
Carter	Democratic	94.1
Reagan	Republican	97.0 (as of 1983)

SOURCE: Henry J. Abraham, "Reflections on the Recruitment, Nomination, and Confirmation Process to the Federal Bench." Unpublished paper presented to Conference, The Federal Courts: 1980 American Enterprise Institute for Public Policy Research, October 1, 1980; Sheldon Goldman, "Carter's Judicial Appointments: A Lasting Legacy," *Judicature*, Vol. 64 (March 1981), p. 344; Sheldon Goldman, "Reagan's Judicial Appointments at Mid-term: Shaping The Bench in His Own Image," *Judicature*, Vol. 66 (March 1983), p. 334.

partment official has said: "When courts cease being an instrument for political change, then maybe the judges will stop being politically selected."[21]

The Role of Ideology

Justice Oliver Wendell Holmes.
Wide World.

Finding a party member is not enough. Presidents want to pick the "right" kind of Republican or "our" kind of Democrat. Especially when the appointment is to the Supreme Court, the policy orientation of the nominee is important. As President Lincoln told Congressman Boutewell when he appointed Salmon P. Chase to the Court: "We wish for a Chief Justice who will sustain what has been done in regard to emancipation and legal tender." (Lincoln guessed wrong on Chase and legal tender. Historical analysis suggests that presidents guess wrong about a fourth of the time—that is, the judges they appoint do not conform to their expectations.)[22] Theodore Roosevelt voiced this attitude in a letter to Senator Lodge about Judge Oliver Wendell Holmes of the Massachusetts Supreme Judicial Court, whom he was considering for the Supreme Court: "Now I should like to know that Judge Holmes was in entire sympathy with our views, that is with your views and mine. . . . I should hold myself guilty of an irreparable wrong to the nation if I should [appoint] any man who was not absolutely sane and sound on the great national policies for which we stand in public life."[23]

Roosevelt was even more specific in a letter to Lodge concerning the possible appointment of Horace Lurton: "[He] is right on the negro [*sic*] question; he is right on the power of the Federal Government; he is right on the insular business; he is right about corporations; and he is right about labor. On every

[21]Donald Santarelli, as quoted in Jerry Landauer, "Shaping the Bench," *The Wall Street Journal*, December 10, 1970, p. 1. See also J. W. Peltason, *Federal Courts in the Political Process* (Doubleday, 1955), p. 32.

[22]Quote from Lincoln in Peltason, *Federal Courts in the Political Process*: Robert Scigliano, *The Supreme Court and the Presidency* (Free Press, 1971), pp. 146–47.

[23]Henry Cabot Lodge, *Selections from the Correspondence of Theodore Roosevelt and Henry Cabot Lodge*, Vol. 1 (Scribner's, 1925), pp. 518–19.

384

question that would come before the bench he has so far shown himself to be in . . . touch with the policies in which you and I believe. . . ." Senator Lodge's reply is of equal interest: "I am glad that Lurton holds all the opinions that you say he does. . . . Those are the very questions on which I am just as anxious as you that judges should hold what we consider sound opinions, but I do not see why Republicans cannot be found who hold those opinions as well as Democrats."[24] The appointment went to a Republican, Attorney General William Moody.

President Carter, one of the few presidents never to have a chance to appoint a single Supreme Court justice, appointed 202 district judges and 56 judges to the courts of appeals—almost 40 percent of the federal judiciary. He put on the bench persons who, by and large, reflected his ideological persuasion. Because of Carter's willingness to defer to the recommendations of minority and women's organizations, the lower federal bench probably will remain for the next several decades more liberal than the Supreme Court.

President Reagan came to the office realizing that his predecessor had appointed people of a judicial philosophy quite different from his own. He set about trying to redress the balance and to appoint persons whose views of the role of the courts and of the doctrines they should espouse would be consistent with his own.[25]

Ideology affects not only who gets appointed to the federal courts but also when sitting judges decide to retire. Because federal judges serve for life, they may be able to schedule their retirements to allow a president whose views they approve to nominate their successors. Chief Justice Taney stayed on the bench long after his health began to fail to prevent Lincoln from nominating a Republican. In 1929 Chief Justice Taft wrote: "I am older and slower and less acute and more confused. However, as long as things continue as they are, and I am able to answer in my place, I must stay on the court in order to prevent the Bolsheviki [Hoover was in the White House] from getting control. . . ."[26]

With the Supreme Court currently so closely balanced between its conservative and liberal wings, it is highly probable that the older sitting justices are watching political events closely, trying to predict when the White House will be occupied by a president who will replace them with a person whose constitutional philosophy is similar to their own.

Associate Justice Sandra O'Connor, first woman on Supreme Court, was a former state legislator and state judge in Arizona and active in Republican party politics in Arizona. *The Supreme Court Historical Society.*

Senate Judiciary Committee

The Senate takes seriously its responsibility to confirm presidential nominations for the federal bench. Nominations are processed through the Senate Judiciary Committee. While it always seeks evaluations of each nominee from the ABA Standing Committee on the Federal Judiciary, the Senate makes its own investigations. The modern practice is to require each candidate to fill out an elaborate questionnaire about views, finances, and activities.

When the Democrats controlled the Senate during the Carter administration, Senator Kennedy was the chair of the Committee. Candidates were asked whether they belonged to clubs that discriminated against persons because of race and sex and if so, whether they had worked to change the rules. When the Republicans took control of the Senate during the Reagan administration, Senator Strom Thurmond assumed the chair. He had the questionnaire revised

[24]Quoted in Glendon A. Schubert, *Constitutional Politics* (Holt, Rinehart & Winston, 1960), pp. 40–41.

[25]Jonathan C. Roose, *Congressional Quarterly*, January 15, 1983, p. 83.

[26]Letter to Horace Taft, November 14, 1929, quoted in H. Pringle, *The Life and Times of William Howard Taft*, Vol. II (Farrar, 1939), p. 967.

to delete questions about equal justice and club memberships, and he substituted a set of questions having to do with **"judicial activism."** Nominees were asked to write essays not unlike those required from law and political science students; for example, "Please discuss your views on judicial activism." Professor Thurmond has not been bashful about letting the nominees know how he thinks the questions should be answered.[27]

Changing the Numbers

Party politics is also involved in decisions about the number of federal judges. One of the first actions of a political party after gaining control of the White House and Congress is to increase the number of federal judgeships. However, when one party controls Congress and the other holds the White House, there is likely to be a stalemate—relatively few new judicial positions will be created.

During Andrew Johnson's administration, Congress went so far as to reduce the size of the Supreme Court to prevent the president from filling two vacancies. After Johnson left the White House, Congress returned the Court to its prior size to permit Grant to fill the vacancies.

In 1937 President Roosevelt proposed an increase in the size of the Supreme Court of one additional justice for every member of the Court over seventy, up to a total of fifteen members. Ostensibly, the proposal aimed to make the Court more efficient. In fact, Roosevelt and his followers were frustrated because the Court had declared much of the New Deal unconstitutional. Despite Roosevelt's popularity, the "court-packing scheme" aroused intense opposition. In the midst of the congressional debate, Justice Roberts, who had previously voted with the conservative members of the Court against the New Deal, began to vote with the more liberal justices to sustain some important New Deal legislation—a famous "switch-in-time that saved nine." Since the Court was no longer an obstacle, Roosevelt's proposals to change its size failed. He lost the battle, but won the war.

Justice Felix Frankfurter. *Wide World.*

Changing Jurisdiction

Congressional control over the structure and jurisdiction of federal courts has been used to influence the course of judicial policy making. The Jeffersonians, although unable to get rid of Federalist judges by impeachment, abolished the circuit courts the Federalist Congress had created just prior to leaving office. In 1869 radical Republicans in Congress altered the Supreme Court's appellate jurisdiction in order to snatch from the Court a case it was about to review involving the constitutionality of some reconstruction legislation (*Ex parte McCardle*).[28]

The early years of the Reagan administration brought a dramatic increase in the number of bills introduced in Congress either to take from all federal courts their jurisdiction to deal with cases relating to abortion, school prayer, and school busing, or to eliminate the appellate jurisdiction of the Supreme Court over such matters. These bills sparked a major debate about whether the Constitution gives Congress authority to take these actions and whether Congress ought to do so. So far, persons angered by a particular line of decisions

[27]Sheldon Goldman, "Judicial Selection and the Qualities That Make a Good Judge," *The Annals,* Vol. 462 (July 1982), p. 117–18; Elliot E. Slotnick, "The ABA Standing Committee on Federal Judiciary: A Contemporary Assessment," *Judicature,* Vol. 66 (March-April 1983), pp. 348*ff* and 385*ff.*

[28]Wallace 506 (1869).

have not persuaded a majority of Congress to make what could be a fundamental shift in the nature of the relationship between Congress and the Supreme Court. Still, the knowledge that Congress can alter their jurisdiction may influence the actions of federal judges.

HOW THE SUPREME COURT OPERATES

Supreme Court justices are in session from the first Monday in October, through June. They listen to oral arguments for two weeks and then adjourn for two weeks to consider the cases and write their opinions. Six justices must participate in each decision. Cases are decided by a majority. In the event of a tie vote, the decision of the lower court is sustained, although the case may be reargued.

At 10 A.M. on the days when the Supreme Court sits, the eight associate justices and the Chief Justice, dressed in their robes, file into the Court. As they take their seats—arranged according to seniority, with the chief justice in the center—the clerk of the Court introduces them as the "Honorable Chief Justice and Associate Justices of the Supreme Court of the United States." Those present in the courtroom are seated, with counsel taking their places along tables in front of the bench. The attorneys for the Department of Justice,

Drawing by Richter, © 1983. The New Yorker Magazine, Inc.

DECISIONS, DECISIONS, DECISIONS

dressed in formal morning clothes, are at the right. The other attorneys are dressed conservatively; sport coats are not considered proper. This is all part of what has been called the " 'dramaturgy' of the Court—the majesty of its courtroom; the black robes of the justices; the ritual of its proceedings at oral argument and on decision day; the secrecy and isolation of its decision-making conferences; the formal opinions invoking the symbols of Constitution, precedent, and framers' intent; and all the other elements of setting and conduct that distinguish the Supreme Court, a body of constitutional guardians, from all other officials. . . ."[29]

What Cases Reach the Supreme Court?

When citizens vow they will take their case to the highest court of the land, even if it costs their last penny, they perhaps underestimate the difficulty of securing Supreme Court review, overestimate the cost (although it costs plenty), and reveal a basic misunderstanding of the role of the Court. The rules for appealing a case to the Supreme Court are established by act of Congress and are exceedingly complex. Certain types of cases are said to go to the Supreme Court on appeal; in theory, the Court is obligated to hear these cases. Other appellate cases come before the Court by means of a discretionary writ of certiorari. In addition, the Constitution stipulates that the Supreme Court has original jurisdiction in specified situations. But one basic fact lies behind all the technicalities—the Supreme Court has control of its agenda and decides which cases it wants to consider. The justices closely review fewer than two hundred of the thousands of cases annually presented to them.

It is not enough that Jones thinks he should have won his case against Smith. There has already been at least one appellate review of the trial, either in a federal court of appeals or in a state supreme court. The Supreme Court will review Jones's case only if his claim has broad public significance. It may be that there is a conflict between the rulings of two courts of appeals on a legal point. By deciding Jones's case, the Supreme Court can guarantee that one rule is followed throughout the judicial system. It may be that Jones's case raises a constitutional issue on which a state supreme court has presented an interpretation with which the Court disagrees. The crucial factor in determining whether the Supreme Court will hear a case is its importance not to Jones, but to the operation of the governmental system as a whole.

The court accepts cases under the rule of four. If four justices are sufficiently interested in a petition for a writ of certiorari, the petition will be granted and the case brought forward for review. Denial of a writ of certiorari does not mean that the justices agree with the decision of the lower court, and such denials do not necessarily establish precedents. Refusal to grant such a writ may indicate all kinds of things—the justices may not wish to become involved in a political "hot potato," or the Court may be so divided on an issue that it is not yet prepared to take a stand.

The rule of four also applies to cases presented to the Court on appeal, that is, under its mandatory obligation to review. Most appeals are dismissed "for want of a properly presented federal question," or "for want of a substantial federal question," or "for want of jurisdiction." Such dismissals, unlike those for a writ of certiorari, do have value as precedents. Lower court judges are supposed to take note that not even four members of the Supreme Court thought the issue raised any question of conflict with the Constitution or federal law or federal treaty.

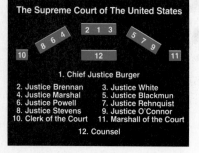

The Supreme Court of The United States

1. Chief Justice Burger
2. Justice Brennan
3. Justice White
4. Justice Marshal
5. Justice Blackmun
6. Justice Powell
7. Justice Rehnquist
8. Justice Stevens
9. Justice O'Connor
10. Clerk of the Court
11. Marshall of the Court
12. Counsel

Adapted from *The Judiciary: The Supreme Court in the Governmental Process*, Sixth Edition, by Henry J. Abraham. Copyright © 1983 by Allyn & Bacon, Inc. Used with permission.

[29]Richard Johnson, *The Dynamics of Compliance* (Wiley, 1967), pp. 33–41. This summary of Johnson's comment is taken from David Adamany, "Legitimacy, Realigning Elections, and the Supreme Court," *Wisconsin Law Review* (1973), p. 792.

U.S. Supreme Court Justices. *U.S. Supreme Court.*

THE SUPREME COURT

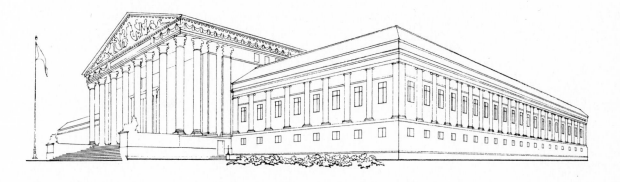

"We are very quiet there but it is the Quiet of a storm center. . . ."
—Oliver Wendell Holmes Jr.

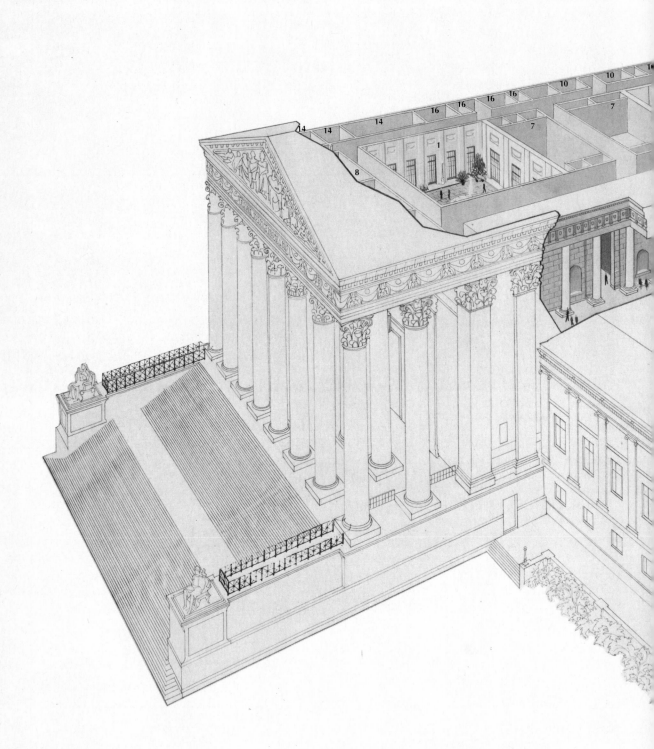

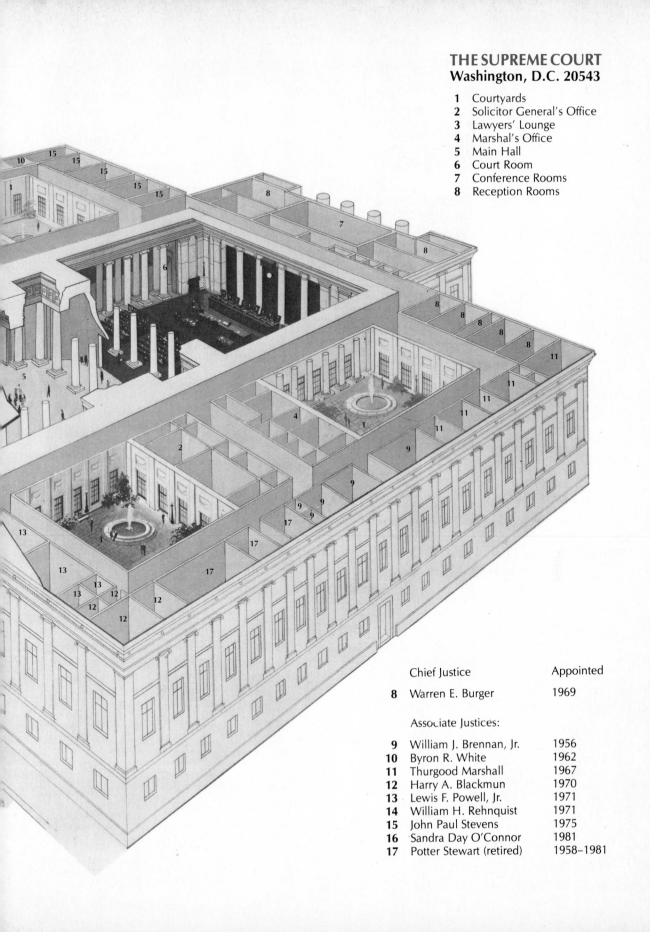

THE SUPREME COURT
Washington, D.C. 20543

1 Courtyards
2 Solicitor General's Office
3 Lawyers' Lounge
4 Marshal's Office
5 Main Hall
6 Court Room
7 Conference Rooms
8 Reception Rooms

Chief Justice	Appointed
8 Warren E. Burger	1969

Associate Justices:

9	William J. Brennan, Jr.	1956
10	Byron R. White	1962
11	Thurgood Marshall	1967
12	Harry A. Blackmun	1970
13	Lewis F. Powell, Jr.	1971
14	William H. Rehnquist	1971
15	John Paul Stevens	1975
16	Sandra Day O'Connor	1981
17	Potter Stewart (retired)	1958–1981

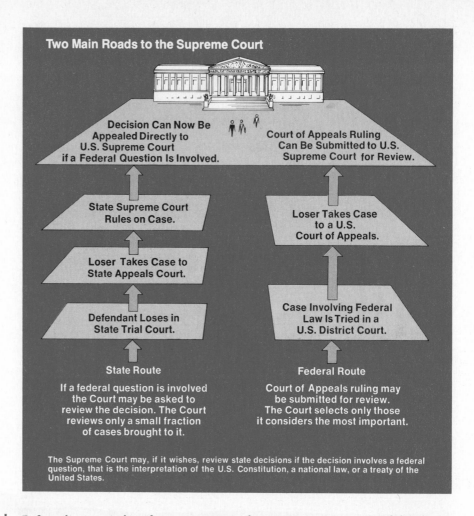

Two Main Roads to the Supreme Court

Decision Can Now Be Appealed Directly to U.S. Supreme Court if a Federal Question Is Involved.

Court of Appeals Ruling Can Be Submitted to U.S. Supreme Court for Review.

State Supreme Court Rules on Case.

Loser Takes Case to a U.S. Court of Appeals.

Loser Takes Case to State Appeals Court.

Defendant Loses in State Trial Court.

Case Involving Federal Law Is Tried in a U.S. District Court.

State Route

If a federal question is involved the Court may be asked to review the decision. The Court reviews only a small fraction of cases brought to it.

Federal Route

Court of Appeals ruling may be submitted for review. The Court selects only those it considers the most important.

The Supreme Court may, if it wishes, review state decisions if the decision involves a federal question, that is the interpretation of the U.S. Constitution, a national law, or a treaty of the United States.

The Briefs and Oral Argument

The "old" Supreme Court Chamber in the U.S. Capitol building. *Library of Congress.*

Before the case is heard in open court, the justices receive printed *briefs*, perhaps running into hundreds of pages, in which each side presents legal arguments, historical materials, and relevant precedents. In addition, the Supreme Court may receive briefs from amici curiae—friends of the court. These may be individuals, organizations, or government agencies who claim to have an interest in the case and information of value to the Court. This procedure guarantees the Department of Justice is represented if a suit between two private parties calls the constitutionality of an act of Congress into question. Although a brief brought by a private party or interest group may help the justices by presenting an argument or point of law that the parties to the case have not raised, often the briefs are filed as a means of "pressuring" the Court to reach a particular decision. In the 1954 school desegregation cases, twenty-four amicus briefs were filed. In the Bakke case thirty-seven amicus briefs were filed for the university, sixteen for Bakke, and five did not take sides.

Formal oratory before the Supreme Court, perhaps lasting for several days, is a thing of the past. As a rule, counsel for each side is limited to a thirty-minute argument—in some cases even less. Lawyers use a lectern to which two lights are attached; a white light flashes five minutes before time is up and when the red light goes on, the lawyer must stop, even in the middle of an "if."[30] The entire procedure is formally informal. Sometimes, to the annoyance of the attorneys, the justices talk among themselves or consult briefs

[30]Edwin McElwain, "The Business of the Supreme Court," *Harvard Law Review* (1959), pp. 5–26.

or legal volumes during the oral presentation. Justice Holmes occasionally napped during oral argument. When he found a presentation particularly bad, he would frequently and ostentatiously consult his watch.[31]

The justices freely interrupt the lawyers to ask questions and to request additional information. If a lawyer seems to be having a difficult time, they may try to help him present a better case. Occasionally the justices bounce arguments off a hapless attorney, at one another. During oral argument in the school desegregation cases, Justice Frankfurter was grilling an NAACP lawyer: "Are you saying that we can say that 'separate but equal' is not a doctrine that is relevant at the primary school level? Is that what you are saying?" he demanded. Justice Douglas tried to help the lawyer out. "I think you are saying," he ventured, "that segregation may be all right in streetcars and railroad cars and restaurants, but . . . education is different from that." The lawyer found the Douglas paraphrase to his liking. "Yes, sir," he replied. Douglas continued, "That is your argument, is it not? Isn't that your argument in this case?" Again a grateful "yes" from counsel. Frankfurter, however, was not even moderately impressed. "But how can that be your argument . . . ?" he cried, and the lawyer was once again on his own.[32]

The Conference

Each Wednesday and Friday the justices meet in conference. The justices have heard the oral arguments, read and studied the briefs, and examined the petitions. Before the conference each justice receives a list of the cases to be discussed. Each brings to the meeting a red leather book in which the cases and the votes of the justices are recorded.

These conferences are secret affairs, although in recent years the secrecy of the conference has been penetrated. They are marked by informality and vigorous give-and-take. The chief justice presides, usually opening the discussion by stating the facts, summarizing the questions of law, and making suggestions for disposing of the case. Each member of the Court is then asked, in order of seniority, to give his or her views and conclusions. In recent years the justices have not bothered with a formal vote, since they have already expressed their views at the discussion stage—but if they do vote, they do so in order of seniority.

The dynamics of the conference are illustrated by the maneuverings in the case of *National League of Cities* v. *Usery*, taken up by the Court at its Friday, March 5, 1976, session. The Court had asked that the case be reargued.[33] The chief justice opened the discussion. The question was whether the federal minimum wage law should be applied to municipal police and firefighters and other workers. In 1968, in *Maryland* v. *Wirtz*, the Court had upheld the application of this same law to state hospital workers and school employees. This would appear to be a binding precedent. Chief Justice Burger said for the time being he would pass, although the justices knew he really would like to see *Wirtz* overruled. Justice Brennan, next in seniority, argued that the Court was bound by the *Wirtz* precedent. Justice Stewart told his colleagues that although he had dissented in *Wirtz*, he would not vote to overrule it unless five other justices wanted to do so. In other words, he did not want to be the one to cause a reversal. Justices White and Marshall agreed that the *Wirtz* precedent controlled. As the discussion went around the table, the vote was three for

Associate Justice William J. Brennan, Jr., the leader of the progressive or liberal block on the Supreme Court in recent years. He was formerly a state judge in New Jersey. *The Supreme Court Historical Society.*

[31]Henry J. Abraham, *The Judicial Process*, 4th ed. *An Introductory Analysis of the Courts of the United States, England and France.* Copyright © 1980 by Oxford University Press, Inc. Reprinted by permission. See also Henry J. Abraham, *The Judiciary* (Allyn and Bacon, 1983), pp. 32–33.

[32]Daniel M. Berman, *It Is So Ordered: The Supreme Court Rules on School Segregation* (Norton, 1966), p. 69.

[33]Bob Woodward and Scott Armstrong, *The Brethren* (Simon and Schuster, 1979), p. 406. These materials are taken from pp. 406–10.

applying the federal law to city workers, with Justice Stewart prepared to go along, and the chief justice on the fence.

Justice Blackmun "wondered if there was some way to distinguish the case from *Wirtz* so that they could avoid the precedent."[34] Justices Powell and Rehnquist agreed with Blackmun that there was a way to make a distinction between the two types of employees, although they were quite ready to overrule *Wirtz* and hold that the federal law should not be applied to either state hospital workers or to city police and firefighters, if the rest of the justices would go along. Justice Stevens, the junior justice, said he thought *Wirtz* should prevail. Thus, there were five votes to uphold the law as applied to the additional state and municipal employees and to reinforce the *Wirtz* decision. But the discussion was not over. Justice White chided Justice Stewart for refusing to become the fifth vote to overturn a prior decision which they both thought was wrong. Justice Stewart responded: "I think you are right, I'll vote the other way." But he said he was not going to vote for some underhanded formula: He wanted a clear ruling that *Wirtz* was being overruled. The chief justice now declared he would vote to overrule, so the vote became five to four to do so. He assigned Justice Rehnquist the responsibility for drafting an opinion for the Court.

The Opinion

Opinion assigning is important. The justices want to work on opinions that deal with significant issues, and the justice to whom the opinion is assigned can influence the outcome. When voting with the majority, the chief justice decides who writes the first draft opinion. When the chief justice is in the minority, the senior justice among the majority makes the assignment. Justices are free to write dissenting opinions if they wish. If a justice agrees with the majority on how the case should be decided but differs on the reasoning, that justice may write a concurring opinion.

Circulating Drafts

The justice selected to write the Court's opinion is faced with an exacting task. The document must win the support of at least four—even more, if possible—intelligent, strong-willed persons, all of whom may have voted the same way but perhaps for very different reasons. Law clerks have in recent years taken on a more prominent role in opinion writing as the pressure of court business reduces the individual justice's time. Assisted by the law clerks, the justice writes a draft and sends it to colleagues for their comments. If the justice is lucky, the majority will accept the version, perhaps with only minor changes. But it may be that the draft is not satisfactory to the other justices. In that case the justice will redraft and recirculate the opinion until a majority can reach agreement.

If the initial version is not acceptable to a majority, an elaborate bargaining process occurs. The opinion ultimately published is not necessarily the opinion the author would have liked to write. Like a committee report, it represents the common denominator. Holmes bitterly complained to Laski that he had written an opinion "in terms to suit the majority of the brethren, although they didn't suit me. Years ago I did the same thing in the interest of getting a job done. I let the brethren put in a reason that I thought bad and cut out all that I thought good and I have squirmed ever since, and swore that never again—but again I yield and now comes a petition for rehearing pointing out all the horrors that will ensue from just what I didn't want to say."[35]

The two major weapons justices can use against their colleagues are their vote and their willingness to write a separate opinion that will attack a doctrine the majority wishes to see adopted. A dissenting opinion is often written and

[34]Ibid., p. 407.

[35]Mark De Wolfe Howe (ed.), *Holmes-Laski Letters*, Vol. II (Atheneum, 1963), pp. 124, 125.

circulated for the specific purpose of convincing the majority. If the opinion writer is persuaded by the logic of the dissenter, the dissenting opinion may never be published. Sometimes, however, an unpersuaded justice will be forced to give in to the demands of one colleague. Especially if the Court is closely divided, one justice may be in a position to demand that a given argument be included in—or removed from—the opinion as the price of his or her vote. Sometimes this can happen even if the Court is not closely divided. An opinion writer who anticipates that a decision will bring critical public reaction may very much wish to have it presented as the view of a unanimous Court and may be prepared to compromise to achieve unanimity.

The Internal Politics of Opinion Writing

The internal battling over the opinion in *National League of Cities* v. *Usery* is typical of what happens in many cases. After the first round of voting, it appeared that Justice Brennan would assign the opinion, since he was the senior justice in what appeared to be the majority. But when Justice Stewart switched his vote, it put the chief justice in the majority—so it now fell to him to assign the opinion, which he did, to Justice Rehnquist. As Justice Rehnquist circulated his draft, Justices Stevens and Brennan each sent around strong dissents. Justice Stewart's clerks hoped that they might be able to persuade him to change his mind, so they presented him with their own critical analysis of the Rehnquist draft.

Despite the pressures, Justice Stewart stood fast with Rehnquist. Justice Blackmun was wavering, and how he would go would determine the outcome. Justice Rehnquist modified his draft to take Blackmun's views into account, to be sure that he kept Blackmun's vote. Justice Brennan was also working on Blackmun. In his dissent he had written: "I cannot recall another instance in the Court's history when the reasoning of so many decisions covering so long a span of time has been discarded in such a roughshod manner."[36] On the draft he sent to Justice Blackmun he wrote a personal note, "asking if there was anything that he could do to get his vote."[37]

While Justice Blackmun was disturbed by the sarcastic tone of Brennan's opinion, he still had not made up his mind to stay with Rehnquist. He "toyed with concurring in the result only,"[38] which would have meant that Rehnquist would have been denied the fifth vote for his opinion, which was necessary to make it a controlling precedent. Finally he decided merely to write a single-paragraph concurring opinion explaining that in future cases—for example, those involving environmental law, where the federal government has a greater interest—federal intervention into the affairs of state and local governments might be justified. Since his concurrence did endorse the Rehnquist opinion, it became the opinion of the Court and thus a controlling precedent.

As a general rule, Supreme Court opinions that accompany decisions state the facts, present the issues, announce the decision, and—most important—attempt to justify the reasoning of the Court. These opinions are the Court's principal method of expressing itself to the outside world, and the justices address these opinions to various audiences. Perhaps the most important function of opinions is to instruct the lower courts how to decide similar cases in the future.

Judicial opinions may be directed at Congress or at the president. If the Court regrets that "in the absence of action by the Congress, we have no choice but to . . ." or insists that "relief of the sort that petitioner demands can only come from the political branches of government," it is clearly asking Congress

Associate Justice William H. Rehnquist, the leader of the Conservative block on the current Supreme Court. *The Supreme Court Historical Society.*

[36]426 U.S. 833 (1976).
[37]Woodward and Armstrong, *The Brethren*, p. 409.
[38]Ibid., p. 410.

to act. Sometimes the Court will interpret existing statutes so narrowly as to render them ineffective, in the hope of forcing fresh legislative action. Such a hope once prompted the following dissent from Justice Clark: "Unless the Congress changes the rule announced by the Court today, those intelligence agencies of our government engaged in law enforcement may as well close up shop. . . ."[39]

Finally, the justices use published opinions to communicate with the public. A well-handled opinion may increase support among specialized publics—especially lawyers and judges—and among the general population for a policy the Court is stressing. For this reason, the Court delayed declaring school segregation unconstitutional until unanimity could be secured. The justices understood that any sign of dissension on the bench on this major social issue would be an invitation to evade the Court's ruling.

The Powers of the Chief Justice

The ability of the chief justice to influence the Court has varied considerably. Chief Justice Hughes ran the conferences like a stern schoolmaster, keeping the justices talking to the point, moving the discussion along, and doing his best to work out compromises. He tried to achieve a unanimous vote in order to give decisions greater weight. Chief Justice Stone, on the other hand, encouraged justices to state their own point of view and let the discussion wander as it would. Chief Justice Burger has devoted much of his time to judicial reform, speaking to bar and lay groups and trying to build political support for modernizing the judicial structure. As one scholar reminds us: "The Chief Justiceship does not guarantee leadership. It only offers its incumbent an opportunity to lead. Optimum leadership inheres in the combination of the office and an able, persuasive, personable judge."[40]

After the Lawsuit Is Over

Victory in the Supreme Court does not necessarily mean that persons will get what they want. As a rule, the Court does not implement its own decision, but "remands" the case to the lower court with instructions to act in accordance with the Supreme Court's opinion. The lower courts have considerable leeway in interpreting the Court's mandates.

Chief Justice Warren Burger. *Library of Congress.*

The impact of a particular ruling announced by the Supreme Court on the behavior of those who are not immediate parties to a lawsuit is even more uncertain. Many of the more important decisions require further action by administrative and elected officials before they become the effective law of the land. Sometimes Supreme Court decisions are simply ignored: Despite the Supreme Court's holding that it is unconstitutional for school boards to require prayers within the schools, many school boards have continued their previous practices.[41] For years after the Supreme Court held public school segregation unconstitutional, a great number of school districts remained segregated. The Constitution may be what the Supreme Court says it is, but a Supreme Court opinion, for the moment at least, is what a trial judge or police officer or a prosecutor says it is.

The most difficult Supreme Court decisions to implement are those that require the cooperation of large numbers of officials. For example, a Supreme Court decision announcing a new standard for police arrest procedures is not likely to have an impact on the way police make arrests for some time. Not many police officers subscribe to the *United States Supreme Court Reports.*

[39]Berman, *It Is So Ordered,* p. 114; Walter F. Murphy, *Elements of Judicial Strategy* (University of Chicago Press, 1964), p. 66.

[40]David Danelski, "The Influence of the Chief Justice in the Decisional Process of the Supreme Court," in Thomas P. Jahnige and Sheldon Goldman (ed.), *The Federal Judicial System: Readings in Process and Behavior* (Holt, Rinehard & Winston, 1968), p. 148.

[41]Stephen L. Wasby, *The Impact of the United States Supreme Court* (Dorsey Press, 1970), and the literature cited therein.

During his tenure as Chief Justice, efforts were made to impeach Earl Warren. *Danny Lyon, Magnum.*

The process is more complex: Local prosecutors, state attorneys general, chiefs of police, and state and federal trial court judges must all participate in giving "meaning" to Supreme Court decisions.

Although Congress or a president has occasionally "ignored" or "construed" a Supreme Court ruling to avoid its impact, by and large, decisions whose implementation requires only the action of a central governmental agency become effective immediately. Thus, when the Supreme Court held that President Truman lacked constitutional authority to seize steel companies temporarily to avoid a shutdown during the Korean war, the president promptly complied. Of course, other presidents can use discretion in determining how that particular precedent should be applied to their own behavior.

JUDICIAL POWER IN A DEMOCRACY

An independent judiciary is one of the hallmarks of a free society. As impartial dispensers of equal justice under the law, judges should not be dependent on the executive, the legislature, the parties to the case, the electorate, or a mob outside the courtroom. But this very independence, essential to protect judges in their roles as legal umpires, raises basic problems when a democratic society decides—as has ours—also to make judges key policy makers. Perhaps in no other society do interests and individuals resort to litigation as much as they do here as a means of making public policy. The involvement of our courts, especially the Supreme Court, in choosing among competing values has historically opened up the judiciary to political criticism.

Since 1937, and especially since the end of World War II, federal courts under the Supreme Court's leadership generally have reversed their conservative policy direction. While judges have removed most of the constitutional restraints on government regulation of business, they have imposed many more restraints in order to protect civil liberties and civil rights, especially for the poor and the black. Since 1943 the Supreme Court has declared unconstitutional more than thirty-five provisions of acts of Congress as well as more than 500 acts of state legislatures and city councils. (Overall, the Supreme Court has struck down over 125 acts of Congress and almost 1000 pieces of state legislation and state constitutional provisions.)

The Great Society brought a major expansion of governmental programs. In subsequent years, however, there was a deadlock of democracy. Congress, presidents, state legislatures, and governors were often unable to deal with pressing issues. Faced with this inaction by the other branches, pressures mounted on judges in general and federal judges in particular "to do something." They responded positively.

President Nixon came to office with the avowed purpose of curtailing government by the judiciary. He was unsuccessful. True, the federal courts under Chief Justice Burger's leadership have been somewhat less activist in some areas than they were during the tenure of Chief Justice Warren—but in other areas they have been more so.

Judges must decide disputes—and when they do, they make policy. They have always done so. They cannot help it; it is not a matter of choice but of their role. But nowadays *they govern.* "The causes of the explosion are complex and imperfectly understood, but the effects are plain. Both in volume of litigation and in tasks undertaken there have been quantum leaps of judicial power . . . Courts have become surrogate lawmakers . . . (and) administrators of greater enterprises . . . Courts have become ombudsmen of bureaucratic mistakes."[42]

[42]J. Woodford Howard, Jr., "Are Heavy Caseloads Changing the Nature of Appellate Justice?" *Judicature,* Vol. 66 (August 1982), p. 57.

Naturally, those who like what the judges have done tend to defend their right to do it. Judges should do what is right, they say, even if such actions are not politically popular. They contend that courts have a duty to protect the long-range interests of the public, even against the short-range wishes of the voters. Defenders of judicial activism argue that in view of the inability of Congress, the White House, and the state legislatures to deal with pressing issues, the courts *must* do so, because there is no other spokesperson for the public (or national) interest—for the national consensus. Because of this vacuum, the Supreme Court should be "a leader in a vital national seminar that leads to the formulation of values for the American people," they contend.[43]

There have always been critics of judicial activism, especially among those who do not like the decisions the judges are making. But even among those who agree with the judges, there are those who argue that just as it was wrong for conservative justices prior to 1937 to strike down laws they did not like, so is it wrong for today's more liberal justices to strike down laws they dislike. These critics contend that even if courts make the "right" decisions, it is not right for courts to take over the legislative responsibilities of the people's elected representatives.

Many scholars and judges, however, believe in an active judicial role in some areas but a restrained role in others. They take their stand with Justice Harlan Stone, who in his famous Footnote Four in his opinion in *Carolene Products* argued that courts have a special duty to intervene (1) whenever legislation restricts the political process by which decisions are made or (2) whenever legislation restricts the rights of "discrete and insular minorities." In all other areas the political process should be allowed to work, and judges should not set aside legislation or interfere with administrative agencies merely because the judges would prefer some other policy or even some other interpretation of the Constitution.[44]

The People and the Court

The Supreme Court has always been involved in making policy. And throughout our history the Supreme Court has been attacked for engaging in "judicial legislation." Its recent more active and open role has returned these issues to the forefront of public discussion. Why should the branch of government least accountable to the people have a right to veto the actions of the people's elected representatives?

We no longer find acceptable the explanation that it is right to give the power of judicial review to politically independent judges because their own policy views are irrelevant to the decisions they make. The absurdity of the assumption that all they are doing is carrying out the clear commands of the Constitution is indicated by the fact that the justices divide so frequently over the question of what the Constitution means. More acceptable is the explanation that although judges do choose between competing values, they are not free to adopt whatever policies they wish. They are restricted by procedural limitations. The doctrine of *stare decisis* imposes some constraints, but the most significant restrictions are those of the political system of which the judges are a part.

[43]Arthur S. Miller, "In Defense of Judicial Activism," in Halpern and Lamb (eds.), *Supreme Court Activism and Restraint* (Heath, 1982), p. 177; and by the Chief Justice of the West Virginia Supreme Court, Richard Neely, *How Courts Govern America* (Yale University Press, 1981).

[44]*United States* v. *Carolene Products*, 304 U.S. 144 (1938). Variations in this basic position have been restated in influential books by John Hart Ely, *Democracy and Distrust: A Theory of Judicial Review* (Harvard University Press, 1980), and Jessee Choper, *Judicial Review and the National Political Process: A Functional Reconsideration of the Role of the Supreme Court* (University of Chicago Press, 1980). Stephen C. Halpern and Charles M. Lamb (eds.), *Supreme Court Activism and Restraint*, is a comprehensive treatment from all perspectives.

YOU DECIDE !

A few years ago the Texas state legislature decided Texas tax-payers should no longer provide a *free* public education for the children of undocumented aliens, that is, persons illegally in the United States and subject to deportation by the Federal government. The legislature acted after it estimated that there were tens of thousands of such children attending Texas public schools at no cost.

Setting aside for a moment whether or not you think such a policy is desirable, in your judgment is there anything in the United States Constitution that should prevent the Texas legislature from making such a choice?

(*Answer/ Discussion on the next page.*)

In the first place, the president and the Senate are likely to appoint to the bench justices whose decisions will reflect contemporary values. In the second place, as we have noted, judges have neither armies nor police to execute their rulings. Their policies are effective only to the extent that they are supported by a considerable portion of the electorate. To win a favorable Supreme Court decision is to win something of considerable political value, but the policies reflected by that decision may or may not alter the way people behave. If the Court's policies are too far out of step with the values of the country, the Court is likely to get "reversed" by Congress. It is also limited by the necessity of maintaining the allegiance of the judicial bureaucracy.

This connection between the public and the Supreme Court does not come about because of Mr. Dooley's celebrated charge, "The Supreme Court follows the illiction returns."[45] On the contrary, after major realigning elections when a new political coalition takes over the White House and Congress, the old regime stays on in the federal courts. Or as one unknown wit put it: "The good presidents do dies with them, the bad lives on after them on the Supreme Court." But despite initial clashes, the new electoral coalitions eventually also "take over" the federal courts. Before too long, new interpretations of the Constitution reflect the dominant political ideology.

Even if there is no realigning election, voters still have an impact on the course of constitutional development. Although his views about the Supreme Court probably had little to do with his victory, in 1980 Ronald Reagan made it clear that if elected, he would select judges of a more conservative bent than those chosen by Carter. And Carter made an issue of whether the voters wanted Ronald Reagan to be the man who, if elected, might well have the chance to pick several Supreme Court justices. Once elected, President Reagan lived up to his promise and made appointments to the bench that reflected his views.

Because five of the present members of the Court are in their mid-seventies, the 1984 election results are likely to have important consequences for constitutional development during the next several decades. The voters will select the person who probably will select at least two new Supreme Court justices—enough to alter the present court balance.

The Guardian Ethic under Attack[46]

Recently a variety of critics have challenged the rather comforting explanation that we have just given to reconcile the major policy-making role of the judiciary with its independence from direct political controls. These critics fall into two general camps.

First, there are those who say the Supreme Court, in its zeal to protect the people, especially the poor, has become unhinged from its political moorings in the system. It is running wild, imposing the judges' policy preferences on the nation. Second, some say the Supreme Court has never been, and never will be, very effective in protecting the poor and the dispossessed, because the judges will always reflect the wishes of the ruling coalition in Congress and the White House. The judges manipulate symbols, but they never really cause any major realignment of political values or economic goods.[47] Plainly, the contentions of these two groups are contradictory.

---

[45]Finley Peter Dunne, "Mr. Dooley's Opinions," in *Bartlett's Familiar Quotations*, 14th ed. (Little, Brown, 1968), p. 890.

[46]From Ward E. Y. Elliott, *The Rise of Guardian Democracy* (Harvard University Press, 1974).

[47]Stuart A. Scheingold, *The Politics of Rights* (Yale University Press, 1974); and Joan Roelofs, "Judicial Activism as Social Engineering: A Marxist Interpretation of the Warren Court," in Halpern and Lamb (eds.), *Supreme Court Activism and Restraint*, pp. 249–75. Lino A. Graglia, "In Defense of Judicial Restraint," in Halpern and Lamb (eds.), *Supreme Court Activism and Restraint*, pp. 249–75. Lino A. Graglia, "In Defense of Judicial Restraint," in Halpern and Lamb (eds.), *Supreme Court Activism and Restraint*, pp. 135–66.

First let us look at the arguments of those who charge that the Court is running wild and interfering too much and too often in our political life. According to these critics, although in earlier times the Supreme Court occasionally told other parts of government what could not be done, the most "distinctive characteristic" of the modern-day court has been to "*extend* the role of what the government could do, even when the government did not want to do it."[48] Thus, the Supreme Court has told Congress and state legislatures that they must provide attorneys for the poor, and adequate care to mental patients; modernize the prisons; reapportion legislative bodies; and do whatever is necessary and proper to bring about racial integration in the public schools, including busing of pupils. The "highly activist and intrusive judiciary is now a permanent part of the American Commonwealth," it is argued. No longer can we anticipate a cycle of liberal and activist judges, to be followed by conservative and restrained ones. The Burger Court is still more involved in policy making than any Court in our history, except perhaps the Warren Court.

What has happened to change the relations between the Court and the political system? According to these critics, three factors explain why the Court has become unhinged from the political restraints of the past: (1) Once the Court takes a stand on an issue, it starts a motion which is hard to reverse. (2) The role of government has expanded, bringing with it a more active role for courts in all kinds of areas—from measuring the validity of employment tests to determining which books are obscene. (3) The Court is no longer a reflection of public sentiments but a cause of them. The Court, of course, must have political support. But the present-day Court has created its own new and powerful constituency. Today public interest law firms, professional organizations, and trade unions are engaged in constitutional litigation. These groups, which work to expand the scope and power of government, have replaced the "powerful business interests of the 1930's and 1940's that engaged in constitutional litigation to *restrict* the power of government."[49] And surrounding this entire array of groups are "action-minded intellectuals," believers in the "guardian ethic."

The "guardian ethic" assumes "anything new must be better than anything old, that action must be better than inaction, expert better than amateur, standard better than special, and administered better than unadministered."[50] The guardian ethic is "democratic in its stress on equality, but it is antidemocratic in its stress on administration and intellectual elitism."[51] The "action-minded intellectuals" who are now the Court's powerful constituency, so it is charged, write most of the newspaper editorials and law reviews, teach in the universities, and dominate the bench. They urge judges not to wait for legislative action or for the political process but to do what must be done—to strike down segregation, get rid of capital punishment, secure better-apportioned legislatures, place restraints on the police, outlaw segregation in private schools, get rid of prayer in public schools, and strike down state abortion laws. These are desirable changes. No matter that they cannot be carried out through the electoral and legislative processes. No matter that most voters would be against some of these actions. No matter that the legislatures, which more directly reflect immediate public views, are unwilling to undertake these actions. The Supreme Court should be the people's guardian.

[48]Nathan Glazer, "Towards an Imperial Judiciary," *The Public Interest* (Fall 1976), p. 109. See also Raoul Berger, *Government by Judiciary* (Harvard University Press, 1977).

[49]Ibid., p. 120.

[50]Elliott, *The Rise of Guardian Democracy*, p. 2.

[51]Ibid.

U.S. SUPREME COURT DECLARATIONS OF UNCONSTITUTIONALITY OF FEDERAL STATUTES (IN WHOLE OR IN PART)

(Arranged chronologically in accordance with tenure of Chief Justices.)*

TIME SPAN	CHIEF JUSTICE	NUMBER OF DECLARATIONS OF UNCONSTITUTIONALITY	COMMENTARY
1798–1801	Jay	0	
	J. Rutledge	0	Weak, placid Court
	Ellsworth	0	
1801–1834	Marshall		1803: *Marbury* v. *Madison*
1836–1864	Taney	1	1857: *Dred Scott* v. *Sandford*
1864–1873	Chase	7	1870: *Legal Tender Cases*
1874–1888	Waite	9	1883: *Civil Rights Cases*†
1888–1910	Fuller	15	1895: *Income Tax Cases*
1910–1921	White	10	1918: *Child Labor Case*
1921–1930	Taft	10	1923: *Minimum Wage Case*
1930–1936	Hughes	14	Of these, 13 came in 1934–36!
1936–1941	Hughes	0	The New Deal Court emerges following the "switch-in-time that saved nine" in 1937.
1941–1946	Stone	1	New Libertarian emphasis
1946–1953	Vinson	1	Abstemious Court
1953–1969	Warren	21	High watermark of Libertarianism
1969–Present	Burger	24**	First Amendment, Equal Protection and Separation of Powers concerns
Total		125	

*As of October, 1983.
SOURCE: Adapted from Henry J. Abraham, *The Judicial Process* (Oxford University Press, 1980), p. 304; Congressional Research Service.
**One of these decisions calls into question the constitutionality of provisions in another variously estimated as 60 to 200 laws.

FACTORS CONSTRAINING FEDERAL JUDGES*

The Constitution

Precedent—*stare decisis*

Statutory law

Legal thought as found in books and law reviews

Opinions of other courts

Interest groups

Public opinion

Media opinion

Views of colleagues

Contemporary events and general social environment

Traditions of the law

Actions of the legislature, past and future

Actions of executives, past and future

*Not listed in any particular order. Some weigh more heavily at one time than at another, and on some judges more than others.

Now let us take up the arguments of the second set of critics, who argue that the Supreme Court is not now and probably never has been very effective in serving as a guardian of the rights of minorities, and that all it does is legitimize the status quo. According to these critics, the Court provides symbolic satisfactions, but it really does not have much to do with who gets what, where, when, and how much. The Supreme Court may declare prayers in public schools unconstitutional, but in many districts prayers are still being said. The Supreme Court may declare segregation unconstitutional, but many schools are still segregated. The Supreme Court may declare third-degree police methods unconstitutional, but such methods are still being used by many police departments. In other words, while litigation brings about symbolic changes, it does not cause a major shift in the distribution of public goods.[52]

Both sets of commentators are persuasive, but we remain unconvinced by either view. We remember that the most informed student of the Supreme Court, E. S. Corwin, predicted in 1934 that the Court's role in American politics was about to be limited, just a year before the Court entered one of its most prominent periods in our history.[53] This reminds us that we tend to exaggerate the trends in the particular historical cycle in which we live and write. It is an oversimplification to say the Court is nothing but part of a ruling "elite" that controls Congress and the White House. It is equally simplistic to say the Court's policies are irreversible and uncontrollable, that there are no effective checks on what the Court does. The policy-making process is complex. What Congress and the White House and state legislatures and police officers do has an effect on what the Supreme Court does, and what the Supreme Court does

[52]See, for example, Scheingold, *The Politics of Rights*.
[53]Edward S. Corwin, *The Twilight of the the Supreme Court* (Yale University Press, 1934).

Associate Justice Thurgood Marshall, first black to serve on the Supreme Court. He served as Solicitor General of the U.S. under President Lyndon Johnson. *The Supreme Court Historical Society.*

has an effect on what Congress and the White House and the state legislatures and the police do. Most important of all, what all these agencies do is related to what the various segments of "the people" want done. Take for example the chain of developments that made the Constitution more reflective of the values of equal rights under the law. Changing economic and social conditions led to the growth of a black leadership that in turn generated political power for blacks, which led to presidents who began to care about what blacks wanted, which led in turn to the appointment of judges who reflected the values of civil rights advocates. And this action led to action and reaction in city councils, school boards, and state legislatures.

"The people" speak in many ways and with many voices. The Supreme Court—and the other courts—represent and reflect the values of some of these people. And although the Court is not the defenseless, weak institution portrayed by some commentators, and although it is as much a cause of public opinion as a reflection of it, ultimately the power of the Court rests on retaining the support of most of the people most of the time. No better standard for determining the legitimacy of a governmental institution has ever been discovered.

SUMMARY

1. Judges in America play a more active role in our political life than they do in other democracies. Federal courts receive their jurisdiction immediately from Congress, which must decide the constitutional division of responsibilities among federal and state courts.

2. Federal judges apply statutory law, common law, equity, admiralty and maritime law, and administrative law. They apply federal, criminal, and civil law. Although bound by procedural requirements, including *stare decisis,* they have to exercise discretion.

3. Improvement in the administration of federal courts has become a major political issue.

4. Partisanship and ideology are important factors in the selection of federal judges at all levels, and they ensure a linkage between the courts and the rest of the political system.

5. The Supreme Court, with almost complete control over the cases it reviews as they come up from the state courts and from the courts of appeals and district courts, is a revered but somewhat mysterious branch of our government. Its nine justices annually dispose of thousands of cases, but they concentrate most of their time on about two hundred cases per year which establish guidelines for lower courts and the country.

6. A continuing question of major importance is the reconciliation of the role of judges—especially those on the Supreme Court—as independent and fair dispensers of justice for the parties before them, with their vital role as interpreters of the Constitution. This is an especially complex problem in our democracy because of the power of judicial review and the significant role courts play in the making of public policy.

FURTHER READING

HENRY J. ABRAHAM. *The Judiciary: The Supreme Court in the Governmental Process,* 6th ed. (Allyn and Bacon, 1983).

LAWRENCE BAUM. *The Supreme Court* (Congressional Quarterly Press, 1981).

BENJAMIN N. CARDOZO. *The Nature of the Judicial Process* (Yale University Press, 1921).

ARCHIBALD COX. *The Role of the Supreme Court in American Government* (Oxford University Press, 1976).

JOHN HART ELY. *Democracy and Distrust: A Theory of Judicial Review* (Harvard University Press, 1980).

SHELDON GOLDMAN and THOMAS P. JAHNIGE. *The Federal Courts As a Political System* (Harper & Row, 1976).

STEPHEN C. HALPERN and CHARLES M. LAMB (eds.). *Supreme Court Activism and Restraint* (Heath, 1982).

WALTER F. MURPHY and C. HERMAN PRICHETT. *Courts, Judges and Politics: An Introduction to the Judicial Process* (Random House, 1979).

JACK W. PELTASON. *Federal Courts in the Political Process* (Doubleday, 1955).

BERNARD SCHWARTZ. *Super Chief: Earl Warren and His Supreme Court—A Judicial Biography* (New York University Press, 1983).

MARTIN SHAPIRO. *Courts: A Comparative and Political Analysis* (The University of Chicago Press, 1981).

ELDER WITT (ed.). *Congressional Quarterly's Guide to the United States Supreme Court* (Congressional Quarterly, 1979).

BUREAUCRATS: THE REAL POWER?

18

Campaign on getting Rid of Beurocraut

President Reagan came to Washington vowing to tame the federal bureaucracy. He didn't mince words: "We need to get the bureaucracy off of our backs and out of our pocketbooks." In his 1981 inaugural address Reagan put it very simply: "Government is not the solution to our problem, government *is* the problem." And Reagan followed through on this pledge: The single largest budget cut early in his administration was federal civilian workers' pay and fringe benefits.

Reagan's complaint is a familiar one. Attacking the bureaucracy is as traditional as kissing babies and marching in Fourth of July parades. Candidates for public office frequently take aim at the federal bureaucracy and speak about it as an alien force or a foreign power. "Our government . . . is a horrible bureaucratic mess," said Jimmy Carter. "It is disorganized, wasteful, has no purpose and its policies are incomprehensible or devised by special interest groups with little regard for the welfare of the average citizen."

Members of Congress like to joke with the folks back home that there is a new parlor game being played in the nation's capital. "It's called 'Bureaucracy,'" they say. "And there is only one rule. The first one to move loses."

The public at large also dislikes or fears bureaucracy. Liberals say the federal bureaucracy is an overzealous guardian of the status quo and is too lazy or unimaginative to innovate or experiment. Conservatives fear a powerful national bureaucracy could bring about a social revolution of some kind. They also think the federal bureaucracy is too large, too powerful, and too unaccountable. People in the ideological center often fear the bureaucracy isn't working at all.

Such stereotypes may be as old as the nation (and probably a lot older,

Everyone hates Bureaucracy

for bureaucracies have never been popular), but the deep cultural hostility toward public bureaucracies seems greater today than ever before.[1]

The federal bureaucracy is an inviting target: There is hardly a citizen who has not been irritated, defeated, or offended at one time or another in dealing with the Internal Revenue Service, the Postal Service, the U.S. Army, the Department of Health and Human Services, or one of the dozens of national regulatory agencies such as the Food and Drug Administration or the Occupational Health and Safety Administration. Moreover, career public servants really have no press secretary who can tell their side of the story. But as with much of the oversimplified campaign talk in American politics, the "bureaucrats-are-bums" speeches are often misleading. Of course, we have a lot of red tape and overlap in our bureaucratic process—too much. And it is quite proper to ask whether bureaucracy and its methods have in some way stifled productivity. The real question is less the size or the existence of bureaucracy than whether the bureaucracy is responsive to the real needs and best interests of the country. We also want to know whether the bureaucracy is accountable to the president, to Congress, and ultimately to the citizens.

Bureaucrat at work with files. *Ellis Herwig, Stock, Boston.*

Is Bureaucracy accountable to citizens?

WHO ARE THE BUREAUCRATS?

YOU DECIDE !

TO WHOM SHOULD BUREAUCRATS BE ACCOUNTABLE?

To the Constitution
To the laws and statutes
To Congress
To the president
To their administrative superiors—bureau chiefs, cabinet officer, and so on
To their own view of "the public interest"
To court rulings
To public opinion
To interest groups
To the media
To their profession
To public employee unions
To political parties and their platforms
To intellectual opinion
To their coworkers and colleagues
(Answer/Discussion on the next page.)

In this chapter we are mainly interested in the nearly 5 million people (2.9 million civilians and about 2.1 million in uniform) who make up the executive branch of the federal government. Certain facts about these people need to be emphasized:

1. Only about 12 percent of the career civilian employees work in the Washington area. The vast majority are employed in regional, field, and local offices scattered throughout the country and around the world. California alone has almost 300,000 federal employees.

2. About 37 percent of the civilian employees work for the Army, the Navy, or the Air Force, or for some other defense agency.

3. The welfare state may consume a sizable portion of our budget, but the size of the federal bureaucracy that administers it is relatively small. Only about 15 percent of the bureaucracy works for welfare agencies (such as the Social Security Administration or the Rural Electrification Administration), and about half of these work for the Veterans Administration. A still smaller proportion of government employees work in regulatory agencies.

4. Federal employees are not of one type. Indeed, in terms of social origin, education, religion, and other background factors, bureaucrats are more broadly representative of the nation than are legislators or politically appointed executives.

5. Federal employment per 1000 people in the United States' population has decreased steadily over the past generation.

6. Bureaucrats work at an endless variety of jobs. Over 15,000 different personnel skills are represented in the federal government. Unlike Americans as a whole, however, most federal employees are white-collar workers—secretaries, clerks, lawyers, inspectors.

[1]See Herbert Kaufman, "Fear of Bureaucracy: A Raging Pandemic," *Public Administration Review* (January–February 1981), pp. 1–9; and Charles T. Goodsell, *The Case for Bureaucracy* (Chatham House, 1983).

The vast number of bureaucrats are honest professionals, expert at their business. The bureaucrats may often be criticized, but presidents and Congress ignore their advice at considerable risk. A compelling example is provided by the CIA's perceptive memos (many of them later published in the celebrated *Pentagon Papers*) arguing that the Vietnam war as President Johnson was intending to conduct it would be a disastrous failure. This was good advice, from an expert bureaucracy, that Johnson simply disregarded. The Nixon White House similarly chose to ignore or bypass the advice of the bureaucracy on matters of civil liberties—a move Nixon and his aides later regretted.

Bureaucrats, or career government employees, work in the executive branch, in the thirteen cabinet-level departments and more than fifty independent agencies embracing about 2000 bureaus, divisions, branches, offices, services, and other subunits. In size, five big agencies—the Departments of the Army, Navy, and Air Force, the Postal Service, and the Veterans Administration—tower over all the others. Most of the agencies are responsible to the president, but some are partly independent. Virtually all the agencies exist by act of Congress; legislators could abolish them either by passing a new law or by withholding funds.

Formal Organization

The cabinet departments are headed by cabinet members called secretaries (except Justice, which is headed by the attorney general). The secretaries are directly responsible to the president. Although the departments vary greatly in size, they have certain features in common: A deputy or an undersecretary takes part of the administrative load off the secretary's shoulders, and several assistant secretaries direct major programs. Like the president, the secretaries have various assistants who help them in planning, budget, personnel, legal services, public relations, and other staff functions. The departments are, of course, subdivided into bureaus and smaller units, but the basis for their division may differ. The most common basis is function. For example, the Commerce Department is divided into the Bureau of the Census, the Patent and Trademark Office, the Office of Minority Business Enterprise, and so on. The basis may also be clientele (for example, the Bureau of Indian Affairs of the Interior Department), or work processes (for example, the Economic Research Service of the Agriculture Department), or geography (for example, the Alaskan Air Command of the Department of the Air Force).

The score or more of government corporations, such as the Tennessee Valley Authority and the Federal Deposit Insurance Corporation, may be described as a sort of cross between a business corporation and a regular government agency. Government corporations were designed to make possible a freedom of action and flexibility not always found in the regular agencies. These corporations have been freed from certain regulations of the Office of Management and Budget and the comptroller general. They also have had more leeway in using their own earnings as they please. Still, the fact that the government owns the corporations means that it retains basic control over their activities.

The independent agencies have many types of organization and many degrees of independence. Broadly speaking, all agencies that are not corporations and that do not fall under the departments are called independent agencies. Many of these agencies, however, are no more independent of the president and Congress than the departments themselves. The huge Veterans Administration is usually not represented in the cabinet, for example, but its chief is directly responsible to the president, and its actions are closely watched by Congress.

Another type of independent agency is the independent regulatory board

CABINET DEPARTMENTS*

1. State
2. Treasury
3. Defense
4. Interior
5. Justice
6. Agriculture
7. Commerce
8. Labor
9. Health and Human Services
10. Housing and Urban Development
11. Transportation
12. Energy
13. Education

*In order of age

405

Bureaucrats at work at U.S. Bureau of Census (top) and Internal Revenue Service (bottom). One group is storing data; the other is disposing of excess mailing debris. *Wide World.*

[handwritten margin notes:] Regulatory Board or Commission's Free-from White house quasi-legislative - quasi-judicial

[handwritten margin notes:] Bureaus - units of Federal Gov't

or commission—agencies like the Securities and Exchange Commission, the National Labor Relations Board, and the Interstate Commerce Commission. Congress deliberately set up these boards to keep them somewhat free from White House influence; they exercise quasi-legislative and quasi-judicial functions. Congress has protected their independence in several ways: The boards are headed by three or more commissioners with overlapping terms; they often have to be bipartisan in membership; and the president's power to remove members is curbed.

Within the departments, corporations, and independent agencies are many subordinate units. The standard name for the largest subunit is the bureau, although sometimes it is called an office, administration, or service. Bureaus are the working agencies of the federal government. In contrast to the big departments, which are often holding companies for a variety of agencies, the bureaus usually have fairly definite and clearcut duties, as their names show: the Bureau of the Census in the Commerce Department, the Bureau of the Mint in the Treasury Department, the Bureau of Indian Affairs in the Interior Department, and the Bureau of Prisons in the Justice Department. Note that the U.S. Forest Service in Agriculture, the Social Security Administration in the Department of Health and Human Services, the Drug Enforcement Administration in Justice, and the National Park Service in Interior are also examples of what we here call a "bureau."

All this elaborate organization gives order to the business of administration. It assigns certain functions to certain units, places officials at the head of each unit and makes them responsible for performance, allows both specializa-

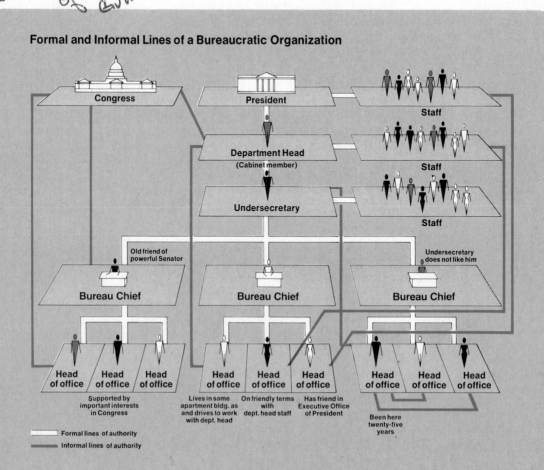

Formal and Informal Lines of a Bureaucratic Organization

tion and coordination, permits ready communication, and in general makes our far-flung administration somewhat controllable and manageable. But this formal organization can be somewhat misleading. Informal ties are sometimes equally important.

Informal Organization

Bureaucrats, like all people, differ—in attitude, motive, ability, experience, and political influence. Their very diversity leads to all kinds of complications. Relationships among officials in an agency may be based on influence rather than on formal authority, on expertise, or political clout with constituency interest groups. Leadership may be lodged not at the top but in a variety of places. A certain group of officials may have considerable influence, whereas another group, with the same formal status, may have much less. Further, the loyalties of some officials may cut across the formal aims of the agency.

Informal organization can have a substantial effect on administration. A subordinate official in an agency might be especially close to the chief simply because they went to the same college or played poker together, or because the subordinate knows how to ingratiate himself with the chief. A staff official may have tremendous influence not because of formal authority but because experience, fairness, common sense, and personality make people turn to him or her for advice. In an agency headed by a chief who is weak or unimaginative, a vacuum may develop, encouraging others to try to take over. Such informal organization and communication, cutting across regular channels, is inevitable in any organization—public or private, civilian or military.

THE UNITED STATES CIVIL SERVICE:
A BRIEF HISTORY

Until the middle of the nineteenth century, the federal civil service was based mainly on the spoils system. To ensure responsive government, it was believed new presidents should be free to put their own followers into office. Besides, it was thought government should not be that complicated—almost anybody should be able to do the job. Later in the nineteenth century, however, a sharp reaction set in against this system. In response to a series of events, including the assassination of President James Garfield in 1881 by a disappointed office seeker, Congress passed the Pendleton Act. This set up a merit system under a three-person bipartisan board called the Civil Service Commission (which functioned from 1893 to 1978).

The Civil Service Reform Act of 1978 abolished the Civil Service Commission and split its functions between two new agencies. The Office of Personnel Management (OPM) performs the functions of administering and enforcing the civil service laws, rules, and regulations. An independent Merit Systems Protection Board and its staff were created to protect the integrity of the federal merit system and the rights of federal employees. It conducts special studies of the merit system, hears and decides charges of wrongdoing, considers employee appeals against adverse agency actions, and orders corrective and disciplinary actions against an executive agency or employee when appropriate. The independent special counsel of this Merit Systems Protection Board investigates prohibited personnel practices and prosecutes officials who violate civil service rules and regulations.

Senior government administrators work with the Office of Personnel Management in staffing their agencies. OPM acts as a central clearing house for recruiting, examining, and appointing government workers. It advertises for

Applicants lined up to apply for Civil Service jobs. *UPI.*

Handwritten annotation at top: Procedures are intended to uphold merit procedures

new employees, prepares and administers oral and written examinations throughout the country, and makes up a register of names of those who pass the tests. OPM has a policy of delegating to individual agencies the responsibility for hiring new personnel, subject to its standards. Individual agencies may promote people from within or transfer a civil servant already in the government. If, however, they wish to consider an "outsider," they request OPM to certify possible candidates from its roster of applicants. OPM typically certifies the three top names of the appropriate applicants. Normally the agency would then select one of these. However, the agency can decide to make no appointment or to request other applicants if it feels none of the three is qualified. These procedures are intended to protect the merit principle and to meet agencies' needs for qualified personnel. But "in practice, the two objectives are not the same. Tradeoffs have to be made, particularly between central control by OPM and delegation of discretionary authority to the agencies. Furthermore, pursuit of both objectives is enfeebled by introduction of yet additional and often incompatible objectives"—for example, the veteran preference system.[2]

The Hatch Act

Handwritten annotation in left margin: Hatch act - bars civil service employee from getting too involved in elections. Cannot fire nonpolicymakers Fed officials for partisan reasons

In 1939 Congress passed an "Act to Prevent Pernicious Political Activities," usually called the Hatch Act after its chief sponsor, Senator Carl Hatch of New Mexico. In essence, this law bars federal civil service employees from getting overly involved in elections. With an ever-increasing portion of the nation's workforce on the government payroll, some people in the late 1930s saw a real danger that civil servants would be able to shape, if not dictate, the election of presidents and members of Congress. Thus, the Hatch Act was designed to neutralize the federal civil service. Federal employees may vote but may not take an active part in partisan politics. The Supreme Court has ruled that such limitations are constitutional. The Hatch Act also makes it illegal to dismiss nonpolicymaking federal officials (those below cabinet and subcabinet rank) for partisan reasons. The Supreme Court has ruled that even absent the Hatch Act it is unconstitutional to dismiss most public employees for partisan reasons.

The Hatch Act, say detractors, is an outmoded ban that denies millions of federal employees the political rights all other Americans enjoy, and discourages political participation among the kinds of people who would otherwise

---

WHAT FEDERAL EMPLOYEES MAY AND MAY NOT DO: HATCH ACT RULES

Prohibited activities:

May not be a candidate for nomination or for election to a national or state political office

May not campaign for or against a political party or party candidate

May not serve as an officer of a political party

May not serve as a delegate to party conventions

May not circulate partisan nominating petitions

May not raise funds for party candidates

Permissible activities:

May register and vote in any election

May join a political party or other political organization

May make campaign contributions to candidates or party of choice

May wear political buttons (off duty) and display bumper stickers on private car

May take part in nonpartisan activities, such as running for the school board or local nonpartisan office (about three-fourths of local elections are nonpartisan)

May express opinions on all political subjects and on all candidates

May attend political rallies and join political movements but not lead such activities

NOTE: Rules are even somewhat stricter for military personnel.

---

[2]James Fesler, *Public Administration: Theory and Practice* (Prentice-Hall, 1980), p. 100.

be vigorous activists in party and election activities. Supporters of the Hatch Act like to quote Thomas Jefferson, who said the best way to achieve an impartial government and protect the rights of all federal workers is through a politically neutral civil service. Jefferson held that a government employee's attempts to influence the votes of others is inconsistent with the spirit of the Constitution. Supporters say the Hatch Act was passed to ensure impartiality and integrity, and to protect federal workers from coercion or threats by superiors. Other defenders, fearing the growing influence of government employee unions, contend that a weakened Hatch Act could encourage these unions to extort from Congress both the right to strike and even greater pay raises and fringe benefits.[3] Democrats tend to favor modifying these limits, because more federal employees appear to be Democrats than Republicans. Republicans tend to oppose modifications.

Thus far efforts to modify the Hatch Act have failed.

BUREAUCRACY IN ACTION: THE CLASSICAL OR TEXTBOOK MODEL

Professor Woodrow Wilson of Princeton University. *Bettmann Archive.*

Early in this century, several scholars developed a formal model of administration from which they derived certain principles: (1) *Unity of command.* Every officer should have a superior to whom to report and from whom to take orders. (2) *Chain of command.* There should be a firm line of authority running from the top down, and responsibility running from the bottom up. (3) *Line and staff.* The staff advises the executive but gives no commands, whereas the line has operating duties. (4) *Span of control.* A hierarchical structure should be established so that no individuals supervise more agencies directly than they can effectively handle. (5) *Decentralization.* Administrators when possible should delegate decisions and responsibilities to lower levels.

Woodrow Wilson, while still a professor, adopted many of these views and argued too that *politics* and *policy administration* should be carefully separated: Leave politics to Congress and management to administrators who adhere to the laws as passed by Congress. Followers of the noted German sociologist Max Weber argued that a properly run bureaucracy could be a model of efficiency. Together with Weber's ideas, various textbook principles of public administration were thought to promote rational and impartial management.

According to the textbook model, bureaucrats should not have much discretion in making independent judgments. They should be closely controlled by established rules and regulations. And this is generally true in reality: Administrators are not free to make any rules they wish or to decide disputes any way they please. Limitations are of several kinds:

1. The basic legislative power of Congress compels the agencies to identify the will of Congress and to interpret and apply laws as Congress would wish. Congress can amend a law to make its intent clearer, or conduct oversight hearings and investigations, or restrict appropriations.

2. Congress has closely regulated the procedures to be followed by regulatory agencies. Under the Administrative Procedures Act of 1946, agencies must publicize their machinery and organization, must give advance information of proposed rules to interested persons, must allow such persons to present information and arguments, and must allow parties appearing before the agency to be accompanied by counsel and to cross-examine witnesses.

[3]On the general subject of federal pay, see Robert W. Hartman and Arnold R. Weber (eds.), *The Rewards of Public Service: Compensating Top Federal Officials* (Brookings Institution, 1980).

3. Under certain conditions final actions of agencies may be appealed to the courts.

4. Other federal agencies place limits on the administrators' activities, for example, the Office of Management and Budget (OMB) and the General Accounting Office (GAO). In addition to reviewing an agency's budget requests annually in the name of the president, the OMB has a management section to review management, organization, and administrative practices on a more or less continuous basis. The GAO conducts audits of agency spending, and in recent years it has begun to investigate the effectiveness of alternative programs designed for similar ends.

5. Administrators are also surrounded by informal political checks. They must keep in mind the demands of professional ethics, the advice and criticism of experts, and the attitudes of Congress, the president, interest groups, political parties, private persons, and so on. In the long run, these safeguards are the most important of all.

The textbook or classical model (sometimes also called "the rational person" approach) remains an influential ideal for those engaged in government administration. It describes a part of the reality of bureaucracy—*but only a part.* We need to emphasize here, however, that laws passed by Congress are not just important, they are central. Most scholars and practitioners agree that the more they see of the bureaucracy, the more impressed they become with the fact that the agencies and the career public servants are very much the creatures of the enabling laws they work under. So this textbook model is also, in part, the reality.

Max Weber (1864–1920) was a noted German sociologist who was a leading student of bureaucracy and organizational behavior. *Culver Pictures.*

BUREAUCRATS AS ADMINISTRATORS— SOME REALITIES

Bureaucrats are involved in National Policy Making

Today we know we cannot separate the administration of policy from political conflicts over what the policy should be. Congress cannot possibly spell out exactly what needs to be done in every instance. Our political system is, as we have noted in earlier chapters, always marked by a fair amount of compromise and ambiguity. Put another way, often we can agree on something only by leaving the matter a little vague. Since this is so often the case, a considerable amount of discretion is frequently left to the thousands of senior bureaucrats who administer federal programs and enforce government regulations.

Bureaucrats are heavily involved in the politics of national policy. Public employees are always called upon for advice and policy judgments during the policy-making process. Suppose Congress passes a law setting federal standards for automobile safety and designates the Department of Transportation to carry out the program. Conflicts over standards—or politics—do not stop with the adoption of the law. Or a president announces that we are about to become "energy self-sufficient," and Congress designates the Department of Energy to carry out certain programs, and appropriates funds. Politics—conflicts over who is to get what and who is to do what—still need to be considered as the policy is applied to changing economic or environmental conditions. Hence, certain political decisions are merely transferred or delegated from the legislators to the bureaucrats.

Pressures and Problems

A federal administrator must anticipate and understand what is expected by his or her superiors, by fellow professionals, by Congress, by the courts, and by the dictates of conscience. Career administrators are in a good position to know

Administrators try to increase the size and scope of agency (handwritten margin note)

when a program is not operating properly and what action is needed. But one of the major complaints about bureaucrats is that they do not go out of their way to make things better. The problem is that many bureaucrats often learn by hard experience that they are more likely to get into trouble by attempting to improve or change programs than they are if they just do nothing. Hardening of administrative arteries is more likely than administrative aggressiveness.

In those cases where administrators *are* aggressive, they usually seek to increase the size and scope of their agency. Often the fiercest battles in Washington are not over principles or programs but over territorial boundaries, personnel cuts, and fringe benefits: Career employees inevitably come to believe the health of their organization is vital to the public interest. Administrators sometimes become more skillful at building political alliances to protect their own organization than at building alliances to protect the programs the organization is supposed to administer.

Career government workers, like all those who work in complex organizations, tend to use the resources at their command on flashy programs, and to give priority to issues that help focus attention on their activities. For example, we hear much of the Defense Department's efforts to "sell the Pentagon," but except for the sheer size of its efforts, it is not exceptional. All organizations, public and private, work to promote a favorable image.

Organizations, again both public and private, also tend to resist change and to resent "outside" direction whether by a president or by other external central controls. A department head in the government, in a large corporation, or in a university is likely to consider the president to be an outsider whose authority in matters affecting his or her bureau is always suspect.

Administrators as Political Alliance Builders

In the real bureaucracy career administrators often become intricately involved in politics. They often have more bargaining and alliance-building skills than the elected and appointed officials to whom they report. In one sense, agency leaders are at the center of action in Washington. Over time many administrative agencies come to resemble entrenched pressure groups in that they continually operate to advance *their own* interests.

Most career bureaucrats develop a keen sensitivity to the political pressures on their bureaus. It is impossible for them not to get caught up in a network of issue specialists and policy politicians that make up the thousand and one policy subgovernments in Washington. With the growth of federal programs has come an explosion in the number of policy aides on Capitol Hill, of Washington law firms that specialize in assisting clients who are interested in policy developments, and of the lobbyists (some say as many as 15,000) that work with Congress and the federal bureaucracy to advance various economic and professional interests.[4] Plainly, groups that perceive real or potential harm to their interests cultivate the bureau chiefs and agency staffs of concern to their programs. They also work very closely with the specific committees or subcommittees of Congress that authorize, appropriate, and oversee programs run by these key bureaucracies. One former cabinet member, testifying before a congressional committee, described the process this way:

It is a fact, unknown to the general public, that some elements in Congress and some special interest lobbies have never really wanted the departmental Secretaries [cabinet members] to be strong. As everyone in this room knows but few people outside of Washington understand, questions of public policy nominally lodged with the Secre-

[4]See the useful discussion of this in Hugh Heclo, "Issue Networks and the Executive Establishment," in Anthony King (ed.), *The New American Political System* (American Enterprise Institute, 1978), pp. 87–124.

tary are often decided far beyond the Secretary's reach by a trinity—not exactly a holy trinity—consisting of (1) representatives of an outside lobby, (2) middle-level bureaucrats, and (3) selected Members of Congress, particularly concerned with appropriations.

In a given field these people may have collaborated for years. They may have formed deep personal and family friendships. They have traded innumerable favors. They have seen Secretaries come and go. . . . They have a durable alliance that cranks out legislation and appropriations in behalf of their special interest.[5]

Some bureaucrats become more entangled than others with these external coalitions. On the one hand, bureau chiefs are logical targets for the efforts of concerned interest groups. On the other hand, bureau chiefs, often recognizing the power of interest groups, frequently recruit them as allies in pursuing common goals. Sometimes the bureau chiefs will try to co-opt potential adversaries among the interest groups by getting them appointed to governmental advisory committees or by arranging for certain contracts for that particular interest. The main point is that bureau leaders seldom ignore powerful interest groups. Pragmatic alliances are usually sought and established.

What are the consequences of all this? First, it illustrates once again that the political system is composed of a wide variety of power centers. More specifically, it suggests that the executive branch of government is a many splintered as well as a many splendored branch of government. Cabinet members

Note: As this diagram suggests, bureau chiefs have to respond to a number of power centers in addition to cabinet members and the White House. Bureau chiefs are very much in the center of the action in Washington. Nearly everyone seeks to influence them, especially their strategies of policy and program implementation. Note especially the "iron-triangle" linking senior bureaucrats with interest groups and congressional officials.

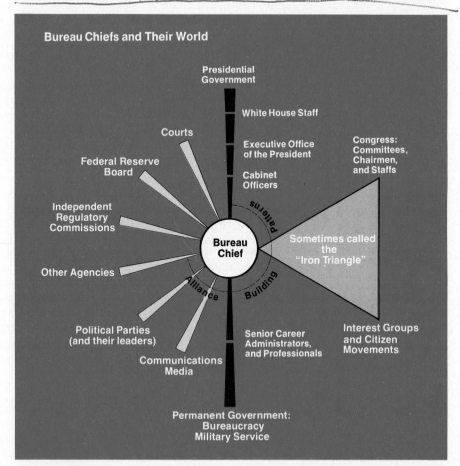

[5]John W. Gardner, testimony before the U.S. Senate Committee on Government Operations, *Executive Reorganization Proposals, Hearings* (U.S. Government Office, 1971), pp. 57–58. See also R. Douglas Arnold, *Congress and the Bureaucracy* (Yale University Press, 1979).

and the White House have their work cut out for them, for it is such alliances that cause the bureaucracy to resist change and direction from their appointed or elected political "superiors." Some view these external relations as a kind of administrative guerrilla warfare—and as a serious roadblock in the way of fulfilling electoral or party responsibility or of holding elected leaders to account. Others see merely an inevitable clash over values in a system that should provide ample opportunities for such clashes. After all, the bureaus themselves are merely one more forum for registering the many demands that make up the people's will.

Members of Congress pressure and cultivate bureau officials just as special interests nurture close ties with both Congress and bureau heads. Congress controls agency budgets and has the power to approve or deny requests for needed legislation. A bureau is especially careful to develop good relations with the members of the congressional committees and subcommittees handling its legislation and appropriations, as is seen from the following exchanges at hearings:

OFFICIAL OF THE FISH
AND WILDLIFE SERVICE: Last year at the hearings . . . you were quite interested in the aquarium there [the Senator's state], particularly in view of the centennial coming up. . . .

SENATOR MUNDT: That is right.

OFFICIAL: Rest assured we will try our best to have everything in order for the opening of that centennial.

SUBCOMMITTEE CHAIRMAN: I wrote you gentlemen . . a polite letter about it . . . and no action was taken. . . . Now, Savannah may be unimportant to the Weather Bureau but it is important to me. . . .

WEATHER BUREAU OFFICIAL: I can almost commit ourselves to seeing to it that the Savannah weather report gets distribution in the northeastern United States [source of tourists for the subcommittee chairman's district].[6]

ADMINISTRATORS IN ACTION: CASE STUDIES

We have discussed the pressures and loyalties amid which bureaucrats must work. We have seen how bureaucrats build alliances; sometimes they become so powerful that they defy presidents and Congress and seem to be little empires unto themselves.

The late J. Edgar Hoover, as chief of the FBI, was nominally subject to direction from the attorney general and the president of the United States. In fact, he was so popular with Congress and the public that he was practically immune from control. That immunity served the country poorly at times, such as when Hoover was able to wiretap Dr. Martin Luther King or others he disliked, but it served the country well when Hoover was able to thwart President Nixon in his effort to cover up Watergate. But how safe is a democracy when the administrative head of a major agency can defy even the elected president?

Of course, bureaucrats come in all shapes and sizes, with all kinds of political clout and alliances. Let's look at two case studies. One is real; the other is fictionalized but realistic.

Rickover of the Navy   The career of Admiral Hyman G. Rickover points up the sharp limits on the authority of presidents and cabinet members over some bureaucrats. For over thirty years Admiral Rickover worked with powerful members of Congress to build a nuclear-powered navy, often in complete and open defiance of the

[6]Quoted in Aaron Wildavsky, *The Politics of the Budgetary Process*, 2nd ed. (Little, Brown, 1974), pp. 80, 81. See also Lawrence Dodd and Richard Schott, *Congress and the Administrative State* (Wiley, 1979).

*Rickover
powerful
Bureaucrat
Successful*

President Carter and Admiral Rickover talk over the quality and condition of the navy fleet. Rickover retired at age 81 in 1982. *The White House.*

**Bureau Chief
George Brown**

chief of naval operations, the secretary of defense, and the president. In fact, he outlasted fourteen secretaries of defense, fourteen secretaries of the navy, and at least ten chiefs of naval operations. He lasted so long that one of his protégés became president of the United States. Time and again Congress chose to listen to Rickover rather than to Rickover's bureaucratic superiors, even when they had vigorous backing from various presidents. Yet Rickover was an admiral in the U.S. Navy and as such was presumably subject to the authority of many of those whom he defied:

> On the face of it, there is something extraordinary about an engineer who is essentially an expert in nuclear propulsion playing such an important role in defense policy. Rickover, who has never held a major Navy command, has risen from captain to four-star admiral in two decades of doing exactly what he does now. On paper he is a bureaucrat whose two offices are so obscure that they are hard to find on government organization tables. As deputy commander of the nuclear power directorate in the Naval Sea Systems Command, and director of naval reactors in the Energy Research and Development Administration, Rickover has only about 250 employees in Washington plus another 100 or so in the field.
>
> Through these two posts, Rickover, backed by a loyal band of powerful congressmen, has wrought an astounding transformation of our naval forces. Since the *Nautilus* sent its epic message ("Under way on nuclear power") . . . Congress has entrusted Rickover with $27 billion to build what some Senators like to call "Rickover's Navy."[7]

Part of Rickover's success was also due to the fact that his ships worked better than he promised. But his success also stemmed from the unwavering support he had from the members of the Armed Services Committees of both the House and the Senate and from members of the Joint Committee on Atomic Energy. "Rickover's skill at cultivating Congress—he works the hallways of congressional office buildings as assiduously as any lobbyist for a cause—has given his supporters on the Hill a sense that they also played a key role in creating the nuclear fleet."[8] He was a frequent expert witness at congressional hearings and a notoriously tough manager with his employees.

The following case is fictional but based on actual experiences of a typical bureaucrat. (Readers should be warned that not only is our main character George Brown fictitious, but there also is no Bureau of Erosion or Department of Conservation. Other agencies mentioned do exist.) It illustrates some of the painful choices bureaucrats have to make, whether they are in Washington or in the field.

George Brown is chief of the Bureau of Erosion in the Department of Conservation. He is still in his early forties; his appointment to the post was a result of both ability and luck. When the old bureau chief retired, the president wanted to bring in a new chief from outside the agency, but influential members of Congress pressed for the selection of a former senator who had represented a farm state. As a compromise, Brown, then a division head in the Bureau of Erosion, was promoted to bureau chief. A graduate of a midwestern agricultural college, Brown is a career official in the federal service and a member of the Senior Executive Service.

Early in March of Brown's second year in his new post, his boss, the secretary of conservation, summoned him and the other bureau heads to an important conference. The secretary informed the group that he had just attended a cabinet meeting in which the president, in order to fight inflation, had called on each department to make at least a 10 percent cut in spending in the coming fiscal year. The president, the secretary reported, was convinced that there was a great popular demand for federal fiscal restraint.

Brown quickly calculated what this cutback would mean for his agency. For several years the Bureau of Erosion had been spending about $600 million a year to help farmers protect their farmland. Could it get along on about $530 million, and where could savings be made? Returning to his office, Brown called a meeting of his personnel, budget, and management officials and his four division chiefs. After several hours of discussion it was agreed that savings could be effected only by decreasing the scope of the program—which would involve ending the jobs of about 1500 of the bureau's employees. He asked his subordinates to prepare a list of employees who were the least useful to the bureau. He would decide which to drop after checking with the affected members of Congress.

A few weeks later Mr. Brown presented a $530 million budget to Secretary Jones, who approved it and passed it along to the White House. The president then went over the figures in a conference with the director of the Office of Management and Budget, and a few weeks later the White House transmitted the budget for the whole executive department, incorporating the Erosion Bureau's $530 million, to Congress.

Meanwhile Brown was running into trouble. News of the proposed budget cut had leaked immediately to the bureau's personnel in the field. Nobody knew who would be dropped if the cut went through, and some officials were already looking around for other positions. Morale fell. Hearing of the cut, farmers' representatives in Washington notifed local farm organizations throughout the country. Soon Brown began to receive letters asking that certain services be maintained. Members of the farm bloc in Congress were also becoming restless.

Shortly after the president's budget went to Congress, Representative Smith of Kansas asked Brown to meet with him. Smith was chairman of the Subcommittee on Agriculture and related agencies of the House Appropriations Committee and thus was a powerful factor in congressional treatment of the budget. Brown immediately went up to the Hill. Smith began talking in an urgent tone. He said that he had consulted his fellow subcommittee members, both Democrat and Republican, and they all agreed that the Erosion Bureau's cut must not go through. The farmers needed the usual $600 million and even more. They would practically rise up in arms if the program were reduced. Members of Congress from agricultural areas, Smith went on, were under tremendous pressure. Leaders of farm groups in Washington were mobilizing the farmers everywhere. Besides, Smith said, the president was unfair in cracking down on the farm program; he did not understand agricultural problems, and he failed to understand that programs designed to increase agricultural output were the best way to fight inflation. Besides, the cuts in federal programs should be made elsewhere.

Then Smith came to the point. Brown, he said, must vigorously oppose the budget cut. Hearings on appropriations would begin in a few days, and Brown as bureau chief would of course testify. At that time he must state that the cut would hurt the bureau and undermine its whole program. Brown would not have to volunteer this statement, Smith said. He could just respond to leading questions put by committee members. Brown's testimony, he felt sure, would help clinch the argument against the cut, because the committee would respect the judgment of the administrator closest to the problem.

Smith informed Brown that other bureaucrats were fighting to save their appropriations. Obviously, said Smith, they are counting on public reaction to get them an exemption from the 10 percent cutback. Brown would be foolish not to do the same.

Brown was in an embarrassing position. He had submitted his estimates to the secretary of conservation and to the president and it was his duty to back them up. The rules of the game demanded, moreover, that agency heads defend budget estimates submitted to Congress, whatever their personal feelings might be. The president had appointed him to his position, and had a right to expect loyalty. On the other hand, he was on the spot with his own agency. The employees all expected their chief to look out for them. Brown had developed happy relations with "the field," and he squirmed at the thought of having to let more than a thousand employees go. What would they think when they heard him defend the cut? More important, he wanted to maintain friendly relations with the farmers, the farm organizations, and the farm bloc in Congress. Finally, Brown was committed to his program. He grasped its true importance, whereas the president's budget advisers were less likely to understand it. And he knew that his pet project—aid to rural poverty areas in Appalachia—would probably be sacrificed, because it was not supported by a powerful constituency.

Brown turned for advice to an old friend in the Office of Management and Budget. This friend urged him to defend the president's budget. He appealed to Brown's professional pride as an administrator and career public servant. He reminded him that the chief executive must have control of the budget, and that agency heads must subordinate their own interests to the executive program. He said the only way to stop inflation would be for all agencies to make program cuts. As for the employees to be dropped—well, that was part of the game. A lot of them could get jobs in defense agencies; civil service would protect their status. Anyway, they would understand Brown's position. In a parting shot he mentioned the president had Brown in mind for bigger things.

The next day Brown had lunch with the senator, wise and experienced in Washington ways, who had helped him get his start in government. The senator was sympathetic. He understood Brown's problem, for many similar cases had arisen in the past. But there was no doubt about what Brown should do, the senator said. He should follow Representative Smith's plan, of course, being as diplomatic as possible about it. This way he would protect his position with those who would be most important in the long run.

"After all," the senator said, "presidents come and go, parties rise and fall, but Smith and those other members of Congress will be here a long time, and so will these farm organizations. They can do a lot for you in future years. And remember one other thing—these people are elected representatives of the people. Constitutionally, Congress has the power to spend money as it sees fit. Why should you object if they want to spend an extra thirty or fifty million?"

Leaving the Senate Office Building, Brown realized that his dilemma was worse than ever. The arguments on both sides were persuasive. He felt hopelessly divided in his loyalties and responsibilities. The president expected one thing of him. Congress (he was sure Smith reflected widespread feeling on Capitol Hill) expected another. As a career man and professional administrator, he sided with the president; as head of an agency, however, he wanted to protect his team and his programs. His future? Whatever decision he made, he was bound to upset important people and interests.

In the last analysis, Brown realized the arguments in a sense canceled one another out, and this helped him make his decision. He decided finally that the issue involved more than loyalties, ambitions, and programs. Ultimately it boiled down to two questions. First, to whom was he, Brown, legally and administratively responsible? Formally, of course, to the chief executive who appointed him and who was accountable to the people for the actions of the administration. And second, which course of action did he think was better for the welfare of all the people? Looking at the question this way, he felt the president was right in asking for fiscal restraint. As a taxpayer and consumer himself, Brown knew of the strong sentiment for doing something about the federal budget deficits and inflation. To be sure, Congress must make the final decision. But to make the decision, Brown reflected, Congress had to know the attitude of the administration, and the administration should speak with one voice for the majority of the people, or it should not be speaking out at all. With mixed feelings Brown decided to support the president. Being a seasoned alliance builder, however, he hedged his bets somewhat. He came out strongly for the president's budget, but at the same time he sent to friendly congressmen some questions to be asked of himself in future hearings, so that he might be able to give some hints of the impact of the cutbacks. He also circulated to some of these same members of Congress an analysis of the impact of personnel and funding cuts in their states and districts.

The case studies we have just considered lead to three important generalizations:

1. Bureaucrats are people, not robots, and as people they are subject to many influences.
2. Bureaucrats do not respond merely to orders from the top but to a variety of motives stemming from their own personalities, formal and informal organization and communication, their political attitudes, their educational and professional background, and the political context in which they operate.
3. Bureaucrats are important in government. Some of them have tremendous discretion and make decisions of great significance. The cumulative effect of all their policies and actions on our daily lives is enormous.

WHAT THE PUBLIC THINKS OF BUREAUCRATS

Let's return to a central problem of bureaucracy—the public attitude toward officialdom. Cynical citizens think "government employees have got it made, and they know it." In general, the American people think federal bureaucrats are paid too much to do too little and that too many people are on the payroll. More than two-thirds believe government wastes a lot of their tax money. Further, a 1983 survey of the public at large indicates that most Americans believe federal employees do not work as hard as those who hold nongovernmental jobs of a similar kind. Also, public surveys often rank the federal bureaucracy dead last or pretty near the bottom among major institutions (about two dozen or so) in ability to get things done.

These findings are not too surprising. Big bureaucracy in the abstract—especially when it is out of sight in some remote capital—is unpopular; it engages in so many activities that almost everyone finds offensive something it does (like taxing you, inspecting you, conscripting you, and so on). Big bureaucracy has been defined as that part of the government you dislike. If you are not directly concerned about a program one way or the other, it is easy to say the national government should stay in Washington and mind its own business!

The Public View of Whether Government Wastes Money

	1964	1968	1972	1974	1978	1982
A Lot	47%	59%	66%	74%	78%	66%
Some	44	34	30	22	17	29
Not Very Much	6	4	2	1	2	2
No Opinion	3	3	2	3	3	3

SOURCE: Survey Research Center
University of Michigan, 1982

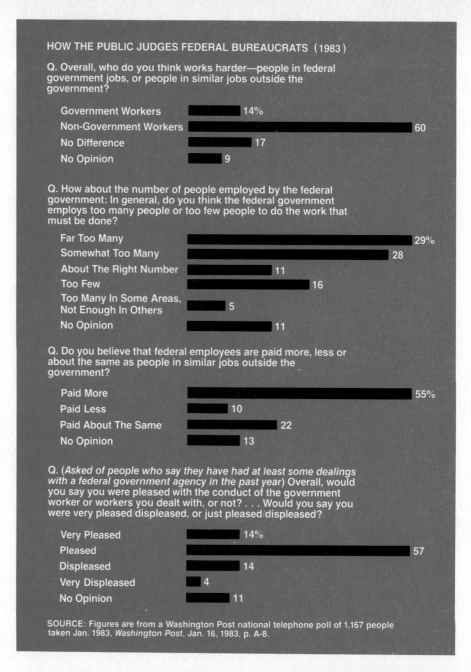

HOW THE PUBLIC JUDGES FEDERAL BUREAUCRATS (1983)

Q. Overall, who do you think works harder—people in federal government jobs, or people in similar jobs outside the government?

Government Workers — 14%
Non-Government Workers — 60
No Difference — 17
No Opinion — 9

Q. How about the number of people employed by the federal government: In general, do you think the federal government employs too many people or too few people to do the work that must be done?

Far Too Many — 29%
Somewhat Too Many — 28
About The Right Number — 11
Too Few — 16
Too Many In Some Areas, Not Enough In Others — 5
No Opinion — 11

Q. Do you believe that federal employees are paid more, less or about the same as people in similar jobs outside the government?

Paid More — 55%
Paid Less — 10
Paid About The Same — 22
No Opinion — 13

Q. (Asked of people who say they have had at least some dealings with a federal government agency in the past year) Overall, would you say you were pleased with the conduct of the government worker or workers you dealt with, or not? . . . Would you say you were very pleased/displeased, or just pleased/displeased?

Very Pleased — 14%
Pleased — 57
Displeased — 14
Very Displeased — 4
No Opinion — 11

SOURCE: Figures are from a Washington Post national telephone poll of 1,167 people taken Jan. 1983, *Washington Post*, Jan. 16, 1983, p. A-8.

But a poll by the *The Washington Post* has some good news for bureaucrats. The public actually likes and approves of the general conduct of most of the federal employees with whom it comes in contact.[9] An impressive 71 percent of the public who have had dealings with the government said they were pleased or very pleased by the performance of those federal employees they actually met and dealt with on a face-to-face basis. Only 4 percent were *very displeased;* another 14 percent said they were just *displeased* by their contact with federal workers. This suggests that in contrast to public scorn for bureaucrats and bureaucracy in the abstract, the typical American actually appreciates

[9]See *The Washington Post*, July 16, 1983, p. A8. Similar positive findings are discussed in Charles Goodsell, *The Case for Bureaucracy*, ch. 2.

[handwritten: most people like most Bureacrats]

and approves of the conduct of people such as their postal service delivery person, forest rangers they met last summer on a camping trip, Veterans Administration officials who helped their ailing uncle, or the U.S. Department of Agriculture county field agent who helps with the local 4-H program. And people also admire astronauts—who are also federal government workers.

One of the ironies of public attitudes toward bureaucrats is that some of the time we criticize federal employees for working too little, for laziness or lack of initiative—for failing to abide by the so-called work ethic. But at the very same time federal workers are viewed as too powerful, intervening in or regulating our lives far too much.

18–1

CONTRASTING CRITICISMS OF FEDERAL WORKERS

At one and the same time we condemn the nation's civil servants for being ineffective clerks *and* for being too powerful. Below are two lists of the time-honored criticisms or stereotypes aimed at the federal bureaucracy:

Bureaucrats as Paper-shuffling Clerks:	Bureaucrats as the Real Power in Washington:
1. Timid and indecisive	1. A self-anointed elite in our nation's capital
2. Flabby, overpaid, and lazy	2. An oppressive foreign power
3. Ruled by inertia	3. The fourth branch of government
4. Unimaginative	4. Intolerably meddlesome
5. Devoted to rigid procedures	5. A demanding giant
6. Slow to accept new ideas	6. The permanent government
7. Slow to abandon unsuccessful policies	7. The Super-Bureaucrats wield vast power
8. Impersonal and lacking individuality	8. They have enormous power to do great injury
9. Red tape artists	9. Intrusive, arrogant empire-builders
10. On "one long coffee break"	

[handwritten margin note: Bureaucrats R both timid & empire builders]

Can bureaucrats in reality be both timid and empire builders? In fact, there are enough bureaucrats to fulfill all kinds of contrasting stereotypes—so perhaps it is possible to hold both views about them—despite the seeming contradiction.

[handwritten margin note: Works like Job but dislike rigidity]

Even federal employees themselves gripe about the system. While top federal employees say they *like* the challenge of their work, the opportunity to participate in forming and managing important policies, and the quality of people they work with, as indicated in the Box on page 420, these workers *dislike* the rigidity, the red tape, and many of the frustrations of dealing with interest groups and politicians. About a third have joined unions or associations that represent them in seeking to improve government personnel policies. The right to form these unions dates back to 1962. Today some of the more important unions representing federal employees are the American Federation of Government Employees, the National Treasury Employees Union, the National Association of Government Employees, and the National Federation of Federal Employees. Unlike unions in the private sector, these groups lack the right to strike and are not able to bargain militantly over pay and benefits. What can they do? They attempt to negotiate better personnel policies and practices for federal workers, and they also represent federal bureaucrats during grievance and disciplinary proceedings. Further, they testify before Congress on measures affecting personnel changes.

[handwritten margin note: Federal Unions of employees, cannot to strike Attempt to Negotiate better policies]

Federal bureaucrats are painfully aware that the public isn't fond of them. However, this might improve if more people took the time to learn about what the federal bureaucracy does, and if more politicians resisted giving those "bureaucrats-are-bums" talks that win such easy applause. Still, the public will probably go on blaming the bureaucracy for rising taxes and for all the waste or crazy regulations they read about in the newspapers.

Americans have never been fond of big government. We still like to think of ourselves as a nation of rugged individualists, and we cherish the dream of

[handwritten bottom note: Public blames Bureacracy for taxes & waste]

a self-reliant, self-help society where government looms small, rather than large. Bureaucrats—especially Washington bureaucrats—are an emblem or symbol of losing that dream—of what Thomas Paine once called "a badge of innocence lost." To think of the bureaucracy is to think of our dependence on others, our inability to solve things at the neighborhood or family levels, and our impersonal way of trying to solve so many of today's complicated problems.

Government regulates more activities, offers more services and benefits, runs a more complex tax system, and imposes greater burdens on a larger number of citizens than ever before. Despite the fact that most of this growth is at the local and state levels of government, federal public workers get most of the publicity.

Further, "the administrative machinery of government has become so large and complex that modifying its procedures and outputs truly does require herculean efforts and great perseverance."[10] A simple command or a single new law or initiative often has little effect, causing much frustration for both those elected to high office and citizen reformers. "There is such a large body of existing law and practice, and such a strongly established set of rights and privileges and obligations that it is not possible for government officers and employees to respond to the latest instructions without violating others and without infringing on the legitimate interests of a good many people."[11]

Finally, bureaucrats have become the favorite punching bag for members of Congress or for reporters who have to place the blame on someone for things that go wrong in government. An irreverent and influential journal in the nation's capital, *The Washington Monthly*, rails against clumsy bureaucracy in every issue. *Fortune* magazine and *The Wall Street Journal* also often have banner stories critical of the federal bureaucracy. Senator William Proxmire, Democrat of Wisconsin, gives a monthly "Golden Fleece" award to some governmental entity that has wasted money or deceived the American taxpayer—and federal bureaucrats are the most frequent recipients of these unwelcome public awards. Thus, bureaucrats are a credible and convenient scapegoat for politicians whose policies do not succeed and for journalists who can always uncover some instance of stupidity or incompetence to file a story on an otherwise slow news day.

Plainly, the "organization man" or "bureaucratic man" has never been a hero in America. The lone cowboy or rugged individualist remains the cultural hero for most of us. Some of the hostility toward bureaucrats is part of the larger anti-Washington sentiment that developed in the wake of the Vietnam war and Watergate. Citizens have lost some of their confidence in the national government. Public opinion polls taken not long ago suggest the public is tired of waiting for solutions: Nearly 60 percent say they believe the national government is unresponsive. An even higher percentage say the people in Washington can be trusted only some of the time.

WHAT TOP FEDERAL CAREER EMPLOYEES LIKE LEAST AND MOST ABOUT THEIR WORK

Like Least:

☐ Inability to take personnel actions which should be a manager's prerogative (e.g., hiring and discipline) — 49%

☐ Inadequate resources (for example, personnel, budget) — 40

☐ Personal financial sacrifice — 38

☐ "Red tape" — 36

☐ Frustrations in dealing with interest groups, Congress, etc. . . . — 30

Like Most:

☐ Challenging assignments — 75%

☐ Opportunity to have an impact on policy or management of a particular program — 66

☐ Opportunity for public service — 53

☐ Opportunity to use and expand one's knowledge and occupational skills — 42

☐ Caliber of person worked with — 35

SOURCE: Government survey of 300 recently retired federal career executives; Annette Gaul, "Why do Executives Leave the Federal Service?" *Management* (Fall, 1981), and the Office of Personnel Management.

THE CASE AGAINST BIG BUREAUCRACY

Big government is generally viewed as bad. Bigness is equated with remoteness, injustice, incompetence, and unresponsiveness. It is also assumed that the bigger you get, the more you waste.

Perhaps the most criticized aspect of the federal bureaucracy is the fact that career public employees seem to enjoy the closest thing to permanent tenure—almost as good as getting confirmed for the Supreme Court. Critics say

[10]Herbert Kaufman,"Fear of Bureaucracy," p. 7.
[11]*Ibid.*

that for all practical purposes, federal workers can neither be fairly punished nor justly rewarded for performing well. Hence, most of them perform the bare minimum.

Few ever get fired. The government's rate of discharge for inefficiency is said to be less than one-seventh of 1 percent. Even the occasional reductions-in-force (known as RIFs) during the Reagan years involved few people, about 1 out of every 25,000 federal employees—and this was mostly done by encouraging a few people to retire a bit earlier than they otherwise would have.

Then there is the issue of waste and inefficiency. In the abstract, everyone is against waste, but one person's waste is another's means of survival. There is little agreement on precisely what is wasteful or unnecessary. Whether or not one concludes that aid to the farmers, Head Start programs, welfare assistance, aid for the arts and humanities, or funds for the MX missile system are a waste *or* ought to be top national priorities depends on differences in values.

When Jefferson was president, the federal government employed 2120 persons—Indian commissioners, postmasters, collectors of customs, tax collectors, marshals, lighthouse keepers, and clerks. Today the president heads an executive branch of about 2.9 million civilians and well over 2 million military employees, who work in at least 2000 units of federal administration.

Critics say the federal bureaucracy is growing at an alarming rate and that by the year 2000 it will control nearly every aspect of our lives. Figures can be presented that make the federal establishment look like a mushrooming giant. For example:

1. In 1929 federal spending amounted to about 2.5 percent of the gross national product. Today the federal share is over 24 percent of the GNP.
2. The estimated annual cost of federally mandated paperwork is at least $40 billion.
3. In the last fifteen years or so, nearly 250 new federal agencies or bureaus have sprung into being, while less than two dozen have been disbanded.
4. The national government owns one-third of the nation's land—and nearly 50 percent of the land west of Denver, Colorado. The Department of Defense alone owns land equivalent to the size of the state of Virginia. The government holds title to more than 400,000 buildings that cost well over $100 billion. It pays well over $800 million a year for rent for another 54,000 buildings.

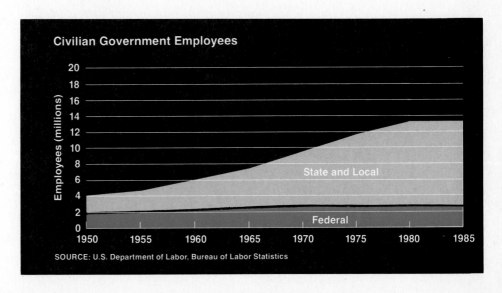

Civilian Government Employees

SOURCE: U.S. Department of Labor, Bureau of Labor Statistics

5. President Kennedy in 1961 was the first president to have a budget of over $100 billion. By 1986 the federal budget will be over $1000 billion.

6. Several studies today find that for every worker on the federal civilian payroll there may be as many as four workers who earn their living indirectly from the federal government (as consultants and contractors) for every one on the federal civilian payroll. That is, there may be about 8 to 10 million "invisible federal employees" as the government contracts out more of its work in order to keep its employment levels steady.

7. Another way the federal government conceals its growth is by shifting its work to the state and local governments. The federal government provides for well over one-fourth of total spending at the state and local level, and although no one knows exactly how many jobs this creates at those levels, estimates run as high as 5 million (of the 12 million state and local government jobs).

No wonder people often conclude the government is trying to do too many things, to make too many decisions, in too great detail, on too many subjects, for too many separate purposes. Some have advocated "birth control" for bureaucracy and federal programs. Or, as one person suggested, Congress should adopt the procedure that before a new law can be enacted, two existing ones must be repealed. The central problem with the bureaucracy, critics add, is not that it exists, but that we have failed to subject it to the control and discipline alleged to operate in the private sector. In private business "the workings of self-interest are tempered and channeled by market disciplines, such as competition and consumer choice, and by public restraints, such as antitrust laws."[12] A corporation president who served as President Carter's first secretary of the treasury said one of the lessons he learned about working in government was "that the tests of efficiency and cost-effectiveness which are the basic standards of business, are in government not the only—and frequently not even the major—criteria."[13] Former President Ford put it this way: "One of the enduring truths of the nation's capital is that bureaucrats *survive*. Agencies don't fold their tents and quietly fade away after their work is done. They find Something New to Do. Invariably, that Something New involves more people with more power and more paperwork—all involving more expenditures."[14]

Critics say too that the incentive system in the national bureaucracy seems to promote growth and inefficiency. Growth improves chances for promotion and higher salaries. Growth thus triggers growth. After a while a very significant portion of time in a bureaucracy is devoted to its own expansion. In short, one of the most frequently heard complaints is that our national civil servants seldom have any incentive to save taxpayers money. On the contrary, everything seems to tempt them in the opposite direction.

Another charge leveled against the bureaucrats is that they extend the authority granted to them beyond the intention of Congress. However, they do so not because they are interested in "power" but because once a program is established, the people assigned to it tend to be very much committed to the "cause." Thus, in the Office of Civil Rights in the Department of Education, appointments go to those concerned about protecting the rights of women and

"This is brief, clear, concise and to the point. Try again and remember this is a U.S. government office."
Reprinted from Federal Times, with permission.

[12]Tom Alexander, "Why Bureaucracy Keeps Growing," *Fortune*, May 7, 1979, p. 164. See also Frederic V. Malek, *Washington's Hidden Tragedy: The Failure to Make Government Work* (Free Press, 1978).

[13]W. Michael Blumenthal, "Candid Reflections of a Businessman in Washington," *Fortune*, January 29, 1979, p. 41.

[14]Gerald R. Ford, *A Time to Heal: The Autobiography of Gerald R. Ford* (Harper & Row/ Readers's Digest, 1979), p. 272.

18–2 HOW PUBLIC/PRIVATE SECTOR WAGES COMPARE	Average Federal Worker	Average Private Worker
Beginning file clerk	$ 9,831	$ 9,018
Beginning accounting clerk	10,703	10,478
Experienced typist	12,065	13,723
Computer operator	16,889	15,804
Senior stenographer	13,541	18,094
Top secretary	20,783	21,546
Beginning engineer	15,153	23,622
Computer programmer/analyst	22,956	25,192
Starting personnel director	27,776	31,136
Top auditor	27,776	32,004
Top buyer	27,776	33,409
Experienced engineer	27,776	34,443
Experienced attorney	39,586	49,818
Chief chemist	46,781	53,658
Chief accountant	46,781	61,255

SOURCE: U.S. Department of Labor, U.S. Office of Personnel Management, 1983.
Note: The federal government rejects eight applicants for every person it hires, so despite public criticism of federal bureaucrats, countless people seek government jobs.

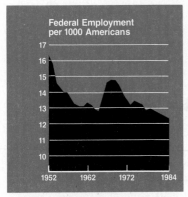

Federal Employment per 1000 Americans

Source: Census Bureau and Office of Personnel Management.

minorities. That is their assigned task, and in their zeal to get these things done, they strengthen their authority as far as they possibly can. Those assigned to the Bureau of Narcotics are likely to be persons convinced that enforcement of the federal tax laws against narcotics is of supreme importance; and in carrying out their duties, they sometimes go beyond their vested authority. Further, and perhaps most to the point, those groups outside the government who want to see the laws enforced and their program carried forward will place a great deal of pressure on the agency. Thus, women's groups and minority advocacy groups watch carefully the Office of Civil Rights, and so on.

Defenders of the federal bureaucracy—and there are some—point out that despite all the talk of a bloated bureaucracy, the federal workforce has grown very slowly in the past thirty years. In 1946 there were nineteen federal civil servants for every 1000 Americans; now there are only twelve point five. Those who defend the size of the government also like to say the proportion of our economic output consumed or distributed by the national government has increased only slightly during the past thirty years.

Are Government Bureaucracies Immortal?

We have all heard stories about government agencies being created, but we virtually never hear of any being abolished. Unlike old soldiers, they seldom die or fade away.

Herbert Kaufman, a political scientist at the Brookings Institution, set out a few years ago to study whether any old government agencies ever do die. He began by looking at 175 agencies in selected areas of the national government that existed in 1923, and then traced them for the next fifty years. All but twenty-seven were alive and well in 1973. In the meantime 246 new agencies had been created to work in these same areas, for a new total of 394. Kaufman found that death of a bureaucracy is the exception rather than the rule. Further, he discovered the birth of new units continued regardless of whether a Democrat or a Republican occupied the White House. New bureaucracies seem to be encouraged either by sudden shifts in economic conditions or international tensions or by a "built-in thrust that . . . assists the even finer division of labor in organizations."[15] Excessive workloads in existing agencies, pressure by groups who believe a new agency will be more sympathetic to their point of view, and a variety of societal change factors all work in the direction of creating more units of government.

THE CASE FOR BUREAUCRACY

Doubtless we often ask too much of our government; and sometimes we give it problems that are impossible to solve. One senator suggests our problem with big bureaucracy is not simply size or spending or taxes: "The central problem of big government springs from our attitudes and expectations. The problem of big government is big promises that cannot be backed up by performance. The problem of big government is inflated expectations that generate disillusionment rather than hope and progress. The problem of big government is the myth that it can solve every problem and meet every challenge. The problem of big government, frankly, is the demand placed upon it by every interest group in our society."[16] Bureaucracy is not a function only of governments, but corporations have them, universities have them, they are a fact of life. The size of the federal bureaucracy has remained fairly stable for at least the past generation despite population growth and despite the expansion of federal programs.

What about red tape? One person's red tape is another's proper procedures. Red tape may be viewed as a hopeless tangle of rules and regulations that keep public servants from doing anything but stamping and shuffling papers. Or these same rules and regulations may be said to require public servants to act impartially. A student who is told by her dean that she cannot drop a course after eight weeks without a penalty may complain about "red tape" and unfeeling bureaucrats. But the rule was adopted so that all students would be treated alike, so the dean would not be able to allow only students he or she likes to drop the course. In other words, red tape stems in large part from our desire not to give public servants too much discretion, and to hold them accountable. After all, they are spending other people's money.

A comparison of our bureaucracy with most bureaucracies in the world suggests we should be grateful for the service we do get from our public employees. The U.S. Postal Service provides a good example. It is faster, more efficient, and less costly than just about any comparable service in the world. Another less popular example is the United States tax system: It is plainly the most effective such system in the world.

Further, not all bureaucracies keep getting bigger. Some get bigger, some remain stable, and others actually shrink. "Much of the growth that occurs is due to population or workload expansion rather than Parkinson's Law or similar imperatives, whether jocular or not."[17] Also: "Regardless of changes in size, no evidence is available to support contentions that bigness creates 'badnesses' of inefficiency and rigidity. In fact, some empirical studies come to the opposite conclusion."[18] Surely the success of IBM in the private sector suggests some virtues of bigness.

[15]Herbert Kaufman, *Are Government Organizations Immortal?* (The Brookings Institution, 1976), p. 67. See also Carl Grafton, "The Creation of Federal Agencies," *Administration and Society* (November 1975), pp. 328–65.

[16]U.S. Senator Gary Hart, "Big Government: Real or Imaginary?" *Civil Service Journal* (July–September 1976), p. 19.

[17]Charles T. Goodsell, *The Case For Bureaucracy*, p. 143.

[18]Ibid.

Still, what is probably the best-equipped, best-trained and possibly the most efficient national bureaucracy in the world, operating in one of the most technologically advanced societies, remains the target of public criticism. And perhaps the skepticism is healthy. In a way, it is yet another check and balance in our system of constraints on those who wield public power.

BIG BUREAUCRACY—HOW RESPONSIVE?

One of the most complex questions concerning public bureaucracies is whether they are responsive enough to the citizens. *Responsive* means being answerable as well as being quick to respond or treating someone sympathetically. How responsive an agency is, depends on the perceptions of the person involved. If a person has to stand in a long line, whether at the post office or at a welfare agency, he or she often starts complaining about unresponsive bureaucrats. Or if one has a new or novel problem and the federal bureaucrat "goes by the book" rather than providing personalized service, again a critical view develops.

Bureaucracies necessarily have to develop routines and standard operating procedures. They do so in order to increase efficiency and productivity. They also do so because they are striving to achieve fairness and evenhandedness. But on occasion such "red tape" reduces flexibility. Just about everyone has at one time or another been turned away from the local post office because a package to be mailed was too large, or too small, or in the wrong kind of container. It is hard on such occasions to hold in our anger. Why can't they be flexible? Why can't they be reasonable? Why can't they be helpful and deal with me in a personal way?

The very procedures that allow the post office, or the army, or the IRS, or the Veterans Administration to perform efficiently for large numbers—and to do so in an impressively nondiscriminating way—sometimes also diminish the ability of these organizations to respond to the personalized needs of individuals. Plainly, routines help to prevent chaos and allow government behavior to be consistent, uniform, and just.

The inevitable and necessary result of big bureaucracy is often a tradeoff: Responsiveness—if we mean quick, personalized, individualized and sympathetic service—often must be sacrificed for the sake of orderly and impersonal routines.

A related question is whether certain problems ought to be handled by mechanisms other than bureaucracies. Political leaders of all persuasions now recognize that sometimes we have turned problems over to government bureaucracies when perhaps there was a more effective way to solve them. For example, can the government effectively allocate gasoline or regulate health care costs through bureaucracies, or should we allow the economic market mechanism to handle such policy matters? Perhaps something inherent in bureaucratic procedures makes bureaucracy less appropriate for certain types of activities. Thus, some programs or policies are best left to the private sector, or to state and local governments, or to the market system. This may be especially true as regards international trade policies, the role the government should play in encouraging high-technology industries, and various energy policies.

In the final analysis, the question of *bureaucratic responsiveness* is extremely difficult to disentangle from the question of *bureaucratic accountability*. In determining the responsiveness of the Navy, or of the FBI, we must also ask to whom they should be most responsive—which is very similar to the question of who should oversee and control them. Let's look now at the question of who controls, and who should control, the federal bureaucrats.

CONTROLLING THE BUREAUCRATS: WHO AND HOW?

To whom *should* the bureaucrats (sometimes called the "powercrats") be accountable—themselves, organized interest groups, the majority who elected the president, or the majority as reflected by Congress? Plainly, most Americans would like the bureaucracy to be responsive to the public interest. *But defining the public interest is the crucial problem.* Both the president and Congress claim to speak in behalf of the public interest. Here are some of the realities and some of the recent suggestions for making bureaucrats more responsive and accountable.

Presidents and Bureaucrats

One school of thought says the president should clearly be in charge, for the chief executive is responsive to the broadest constituency. The president, it is argued, must see that popular needs and expectations are converted into administrative action. When the nation elects a conservative president, such as Ronald Reagan, who favors major cutbacks in federal programs and restricted governmental intervention in the economy, these policies can be carried out only if the bureaucracy responds. The majority's wishes can be translated into action only if the bureaucrats support presidential policies.

Yet, as we have seen, under the American system of checks and balances a single political majority winning a presidential election does not acquire control of the national government, or even of the executive branch itself. For under our Constitution the president is not the undisputed master of the executive structure. Congress sets up the agencies, broadly determines their organization, provides money, and establishes the ground rules under which they operate. Congress constantly reviews the activities of the bureaucrats by appropriation hearings, special investigations, or informal inquiries. And, as we have also seen, the Senate must confirm most of the important cabinet-level leaders. In fact, it can be said that presidents come into an ongoing system over which they have relatively little control—or relatively little leeway to shape the bureaucracy and make it responsive to their view of the public interest. Still, some presidential control over the bureaucracy may be exercised through the powers of *appointment, reorganization,* and *budgeting.*

Presidents are allowed about 4000 political appointments to top positions within the executive branch. However, many of these apply to confidential assistants or highly specialized aides to cabinet officers. Moreover, many require confirmation by the Senate and thus are not exclusively a president's choice. Some reformers suggest that a president's hand could be strengthened if the chief executive were able to make two or three times as many political appointments.

President Carter did succeed in making some alterations in the higher reaches of the civil service. One of the changes brought about by the Civil Service Reform Act of 1978 was the creation of a Senior Executive Service. This service, or pool of about 8000 career (plus some noncareer) officials, can be filled without senatorial confirmation, and its individual members are subject to transfer from one agency to another according to an administration's wishes. The creation of the Senior Executive Service was intended to alleviate the feeling on the part of several recent presidents that the senior career bureaucrats—especially those enmeshed in outside networks—are not responsive to the goals and policy preferences of the White House. With this new service presidents and their political appointees can have greater flexibility in selecting,

"Think of it! Presidents come and go, but WE go on forever!" © 1976 by NEA, Inc. Reprinted by permission.

cific—the specifics may upset the already-established balance of power in the Washington power system.

Office of Management and Budget

Ever since Franklin Roosevelt strengthened the staffs of the presidency, the president's budget bureau, currently called the Office of Management and Budget, has been a key resource in helping to manage the executive branch. The OMB's primary task is to prepare the president's annual budget. A budget usually becomes the major vehicle for shaping a president's policy priorities. It is the place (and the process) that determines which programs will get more funds, which will be cut, and which will remain the same. Departments and agencies all over Washington fight to win larger chunks of the president's budget projections. The OMB supervises the preparation of the budget and hence assists very directly in the formulation of policy. The OMB is the closest thing a president has to an interest-free perspective on weighing and evaluating the merits of the countless proposals and pleas that constantly pour in upon the White House.

Ninety-six percent of the OMB's staff are career officials trained to evaluate ongoing projects and new spending requests. OMB's top officials, of course, are presidential appointees, and they are often among a president's most important advisers. Together OMB officials help a president make critical decisions not only about the budget but also about management practices, collaborative efforts among government agencies, and legislative planning. The OMB and its predecessor organization (the old Bureau of the Budget) have been actively involved in making sure that both the departments and Congress are informed of the president's legislative preferences.[23] All in all, the OMB plays an important role in expanding the policy and administrative options open to a president.

"H.U.D. called the F.A.A. The F.A.A. called the S.E.C. The S.E.C. called G.S.A. G.S.A. called O.M.B. O.M.B called Y-O-U." *Drawing by Vietor; © 1981. The New Yorker Magazine, Inc.*

Congressional Control Over the Bureaucracy

Congress has a number of means of exercising control over the bureaucracy: the budget, appropriations, investigations, reorganization authority, confirmation of personnel, and the ever-present possibility that it can hold hearings on any particular agency of government. Many students of Congress believe Congress should improve its capacity to oversee and control federal agencies. But congressional oversight is more easily talked about than put into effect.

Some people question whether we can approach problems with definite objectives in mind and with a good sense of alternative ways of reaching those objectives. Individuals simply do not know enough about the alternatives, they say. Their own goals and values are not clear enough, and the situations they face are too complex for systematic oversight. Rather, they are likely to go one step at a time, to feel their way, to cling to one familiar method rather than to consider all other methods. "Incrementalists" say they are merely being realistic, and that it is better to adjust to and compromise with institutions than to overhaul or overturn them. Not only is this the way people *do* act, but this so-called muddling-through approach is the way people *should* act, they say, if they wish to go about their affairs in a sensible and effective manner.

Still, Congress is under fire these days, at least in some quarters, for actually encouraging the growth of bureaucracy and for deliberately allowing it to remain somewhat out of control. Members of Congress, so this reasoning goes, profit from the growth and complexity of the bureaucracy: It is to the

[23]For useful studies of these functions of the OMB, see Larry Berman, *The Office of Budget and Management and the Presidency, 1921–1979* (Princeton University Press, 1979); and Howard Shuman, *Politics and the Budget* (Prentice-Hall, 1984).

local member of Congress that most constituents turn for help as they battle red tape and complications. Hence, as the federal bureaucracy and its programs grow, so too does the influence of members of Congress. One political scientist describes this trend as follows:

> The brutal fact is that only a small minority of our 535 congressmen would trade the present bureaucratic structure for one which was an efficient, effective agent of the general interest—the political payoffs of the latter are lower than those of the former. Congressional talk of inefficient, irresponsible, out-of-control bureaucracy is typically just that—talk—and when it is not, it usually refers to agencies under the jurisdiction of other congressmen's committees. Why do reformers continually ignore the fact that Congress has all the power necessary to enforce the "people's will" on the bureaucracy? The Congress can abolish or reorganize an agency. The Congress can limit or expand an agency's jurisdiction, or allow its authority to lapse entirely. The Congress can slash an agency's appropriations. The Congress can investigate. The Congress can do all these things, but individual congressmen generally find reasons not to do so.[24]

Basic to this point of view is the complaint that Congress does not pay enough attention to how its laws are administered, and that it delegates too much authority to bureaucrats. Congress, it is charged, anxious whenever possible to avoid conflict, adopts such sweeping legislation and delegates so much authority to the bureaucracy that bureaucrats, in effect, have become the nation's lawgivers.

But could Congress pass laws with very precise wording all the time? It would get too bogged down in the necessary details to complete its work. For example, imagine Congress is concerned that there be enough truck lines in operation to ensure prompt transportation service for shippers, but not so many as to lead to ruinous competition. If it should attempt to specify the exact circumstances under which a new truck route should be licensed, the statute would have to read as follows:

> Keokuk, Iowa, needs four truck lines unless the new superhighway that they have been talking about for ten years gets built. Then they will need five unless, of course, Uncle Charlie's Speedy Express gets rid of its Model T and gets two tractors and vans. Then they will only need three as long as two freight trains a day also stop there.
> On the other hand, Smithville, Tennessee, needs eight truck lines unless. . . .[25]

Of course, Congress seldom writes laws like these. Instead, it declares its policy in general terms and empowers the Interstate Commerce Commission to license new truck lines when such action would be warranted by "public convenience and necessity." The regulatory commissioners then judge the situation in Keokuk and Smithville and make specific rules.

But how can we get rid of obsolete programs? Many people agree too many federal programs are allowed to continue indefinitely, whether or not they are accomplishing what they were meant to do. If the country's needs and priorities change, programs should be adjusted or abolished accordingly. One proposed reform, already adopted in most state governments, is a sunset process. Sunset laws place government agencies or programs on limited life cycles, forcing them to justify their existence every six or seven years. Sunset review processes have been set up in more than two-thirds of the states. Their chief purpose, of course, is to weed out ineffective programs and make room for new ones. The technique gets its name from a group in Colorado which proposed

---

[24]Morris P. Fiorina, "Flagellating the Federal Bureaucracy," *Society*, March/April 1983, p. 73.
[25]Martin Shapiro, *The Supreme Court and Administrative Agencies* (Free Press, 1968), p. 4.

Congressional hearing on astronauts' program. *K. Jewell.*

that "the sun should set" on programs that have outlived their original purpose or whose benefits are outweighed by other considerations. The burden would be on the bureaucrats to perform well, so that in six or seven years they can prove themselves worthy of staying in business.

Sunset legislation is opposed by those who say it is too simple for the complicated and subtle evaluation work that needs to be done. Still others argue that sunset laws require enormous amounts of time and paperwork from bureaucrats who will have to justify their existence every few years.

It must be remembered it is not Congress as a whole that shares the direction over the bureaucracy with the president. More accurately, it is individual members to whom Congress has delegated its authority. These people, primarily committee and subcommittee chairs, usually specialize in the appropriations and policies of a particular cluster of agencies—often the agencies serving constituents in their own districts. Some legislators stake out a claim over more general policies. Members of Congress, who see presidents come and go, come to think they know more about agencies than the president does (and sometimes this is the case). Although Congress as an institution may prefer to have presidents in charge of the executive branch, so that it can hold them responsible for its operation, some congressional leaders often prefer to seal off "their" agencies from presidential direction in order to maintain their own influence over public policy.[26] Sometimes this is institutionalized—the Army chief of engineers, for example, is given authority by law to plan public works and report to Congress without going through the president. And, as already discussed in Chapter 16, until it was declared unconstitutional by the Supreme Court in 1983, the legislative veto was frequently used to keep a variety of agencies close to the wishes of Congress.

Another factor works in favor of the Congress. Every day thousands of bureaucrats are involved in making thousands of decisions. A president has limited time, limited resources, and limited political influence over many of these agencies. Presidents and their staffs can become involved only in matters of significant political interest. Members of Congress, with staffs of over 30,000, however, can operate in areas far from the presidential spotlight.[27]

So who controls the bureaucrats? Presidents and members of Congress strive to do so, each in their own way. Interest groups also influence the way

[26]See R. Douglas Arnold, *Congress and The Bureaucracy: A Theory of Influence* (Yale University Press, 1979).

[27]Herbert Kaufman, *The Administrative Behavior of Federal Bureau Chiefs* (Brookings Institution, 1981).

the bureaucracy operates. For their part career bureaucrats say they are responsive to the laws and statutes they work under and to their own standards of professionalism and responsibility. Plainly, there is no one answer to the question of who or what controls the bureaucracy. And because of this, there is a never-ending search for improved means of ensuring bureaucratic accountability. This search, and experiments with countless instruments—such as reorganizations, sunset practices, budgetary planning, and oversight hearings—will always be with us—as they should.

SUMMARY

1. We regularly condemn our bureaucracy and our bureaucrats, but we continue to turn to them to solve our toughest problems and to render more and better services. A survey of our bureaucratic agencies, then, is also a survey of how our political system has tried to identify many of our most important national goals.

2. The American bureaucracy is not strictly organized according to the textbook model of management organization. This is because our bureaucracy is not fully subordinate to any branch of government. It has at least two immediate bosses—Congress and the president—and it must pay considerable attention as well to the courts and their rulings, and of course to the views of well-organized interest groups. In many ways the bureaucracy is a semi-independent force—a fourth branch of government—in Washington politics.

3. The debate and controversy over big government and big bureaucracy and how to reorganize it is likely to continue. Meanwhile, most experts agree that the range and importance of the bureaucracy will expand in the years ahead. However, compared with many other nations and their centralized bureaucracies, the hand of the bureaucracy probably rests more gently and less oppressively on Americans than on other peoples.

4. Who and how the government hires and what discretion or powers it grants its employees will always be controversial topics. Still, to work in the career public service is often to have the opportunity to serve people, to solve problems, and to try to bring about a better society. Efforts to make the bureaucracy more responsive and more accountable are enduring struggles, and they are issues raised in every presidential election. But there are never any final answers or quick fixes.

FURTHER READING

R. Douglas Arnold. *Congress and the Bureaucracy* (Yale University Press, 1979).

Lawrence Dodd and Richard Schott. *Congress and the Administrative State* (Wiley, 1979).

Anthony Downs. *Inside Bureaucracy* (Little, Brown, 1967).

James Eccles. *The Hatch Act and the American Bureaucracy* (Vantage Press, 1981).

James W. Fesler. *Public Administration: Theory and Practice* (Prentice-Hall, 1980).

Charles T. Goodsell. *The Case For Bureaucracy* (Chatham House, 1983).

Robert Hartman. *Pay and Pensions for Federal Workers* (Brookings Institution, 1983).

Hugh Heclo. *A Government of Strangers* (Brookings Institution, 1977).

Herbert Kaufman. *The Administrative Behavior of Federal Bureau Chiefs* (Brookings Institution, 1981).

Guy Peters. *The Politics of Bureaucracy: A Comparative Perspective* (Longmans, 1978).

Francis E. Rourke (ed.). *Bureaucratic Power in National Politics*, 3rd ed. (Little, Brown, 1978).

MAKING PUBLIC POLICY

19

The Irish-English playwright George Bernard Shaw suggested progress comes about because of unreasonable people. Reasonable people, he said, adjust themselves to reality and cope with what they find. But unreasonable people dream dreams of a different and better world and try to adapt the world to themselves. This discontent or unreasonableness is often the first step in the progress of a person as well as a nation. Thus, many major policy changes in the U.S. have been begun by those unwilling to adjust themselves to the old ways of doing things—by impatient outsiders. Often these policy changes are then carried through by gifted coalition-building politicians, and by reasonable insiders.

Public policy is the substance of what government does. More specifically, it is the set of declared intentions and corresponding actions our elected officials take to meet human needs and to resolve conflicts within society. This chapter will examine some distinctive features and models of the national policy-making process. Five chapters that follow examine the most important policy functions of the national government—foreign policy, defense policy, government regulation, and domestic and economic policy.

GETTING THINGS DONE IN WASHINGTON

If we follow national policy making as it is reported in the newspapers or on television, we rarely see behind bill-signing ceremonies, press conferences, or formal statements. And very often we hear mainly about conflicts between the branches, or struggles within a branch. Congress refuses to go along with the president on an oil import tax. The Republican Senate is feuding with the Democratic-dominated House. The Supreme Court overrules congressional use

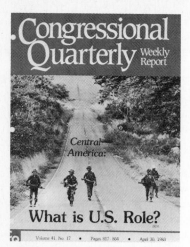

Congressional Quarterly.

of the legislative veto. Or the president vetoes a bill passed by Congress. These contests capture our interest much like sporting events.

Washington journalism feeds on such contests because they make for more interesting copy than the numerous small cooperative and collaborative efforts to make policy. But box scores indicating how many of the president's legislative measures pass Congress often conceal as much as they reveal. They do not really tell us why a president has or has not been successful. Nor do they tell us much about the quality of measures proposed, passed, and rejected. A president with an eye solely on the box score, for example, can avoid endorsing measures that are unlikely to pass. Moreover, a higher success rate may be due more to rapidly increasing federal revenues than to presidential leadership.

Beneath and behind "the governing class," thousands of individuals are at work in the Washington policy-making process. They help resolve conflicts and facilitate cooperation across institutions. Only by understanding these people can we appreciate the patterns of national policy making.

Sometimes just being in the right place at the right time enables an individual to contribute to policy decisions. Usually, however, people who make a difference have formal positions or needed knowledge, or both.[1] Specialists from various professional communities are often looked to for advice in the early stages, when policy makers are assigning relative importance to various competing issues. Of course, one must also be familiar with the rules of the Washington game.

Senior congressional committee staff positions, which before 1946 were filled on a patronage basis, are increasingly filled on the basis of professionalism. The ability of these professional staffs to analyze information for hearings and legislation gives them considerable impact on policy making. They become a kind of "shadow government" linking Congress, the executive branch, interest groups, and different constituencies around the nation.[2] Federal biomedical policy was remade in the 1960s by a small group of medical researchers, philanthropists, and members of Congress assisted by staffers in Congress and the White House. Writers, academics, and professional entrepreneurs are often the catalysts for policy change.

Representatives of state and local governments are increasingly present in Washington to get a hearing for their points of view. These governments send an official or hire consultants to represent their interests and to ensure that issues of great concern to them are not ignored. From a total of five in 1970, the number of offices representing individual governors or state legislatures in Washington has grown to over thirty—even though there already are lobbying offices working for the National Governors Association and the National Conference of State Legislators.

Washington is full of staff specialists who have served long periods within a given policy area and in a variety of governmental as well as nongovernmental positions. The career ladders of these specialists are neither tidy nor predictable. An economist at the OMB moves to the nongovernmental Brookings Institution and a few years later is back in government service within the Congressional Research Service. An aide to a senator goes to HUD and then back to elective state government positions. Later the aide returns to cabinet posts at HUD, Defense, and Justice, then becomes ambassador to Great Britain, again becomes a cabinet officer, and then once again becomes an ambassador. A young

---

[1] David S. Broder, *Changing of the Guard* (Simon and Schuster, 1980).
[2] Michael J. Malbin, *Unelected Representatives* (Basic Books, 1980).

lawyer works in the office of the secretary at the Department of Defense, then joins the White House National Security Council Staff, leaves to become counsel for the Senate Armed Services Committee, three years later enters private practice in Washington, D.C., and three years later becomes undersecretary of the navy.

These illustrations are by no means unusual. Mobility in Washington is extensive, and career ladders diverse. As a result, complex networks of friendships, influence, and loyalties characterize the policy-making process.[3]

One of the more fascinating aspects of Washington politics is the way in which policy activists in different branches of government, or associated with various nongovernmental organizations (such as research institutes, foundations, lobbyist units, or media), join forces in working alliances. Policy subsystems grow up around a set of interrelated issues—as much a response to the process of getting things done as to the issues themselves. Age and formal position are less important than information, imagination, energy, and persistence. Policy activists learn how to capture support from members of Congress and senior White House aides. This is not difficult, for certain members of Congress, as well as White House aides, are always looking for new ideas with which to promote their careers.

Then, too, there is usually some newspaper or journal willing to provide a forum for debate on a new issue. There are countless opportunities for testifying at hearings, bringing suits in court, or convincing staff people who serve cabinet or high executive office officials.

POLICY-MAKING MODELS

There are almost as many approaches used to study public policy making as there are persons who study our policy processes. Much depends on which policies are being considered and on the observer's political values. Differences may also come about because of the researcher's focus on only one stage of the policy process. There is a certain amount of agreement, however, as to how an issue gets attention and later becomes the subject of debate, deliberation, and action:

1. *Problem identification:* What is the problem? How does the problem fit into existing specifications and rankings of goals? Does the government need to help out, intervene, regulate, or make some kind of decision? Should the issue or problem be placed on the agenda of government? For example, if air pollution somewhere is making people sick, is this a matter for governmental attention?

2. *Policy formulation:* What should be done? How can we best assess the alternatives, including benefits, costs, and equity? Who should be involved in the planning and design of the policy? For example, if air pollution required government action, what action is preferable? Policy analysts need to consider all the alternatives, but have to remember always that alternatives have to be those that can realistically be implemented in our country.

3. *Policy adoption:* Who needs to act? What branch of government should get involved? What constitutional, legal, or political requirements must be met? How specific or how general must the decision be? For example, should Congress pass a clean air act, or should some regulatory body like the Envi-

[3]See Hugh Heclo, "Issue Networks and the Executive Establishment," in Anthony King (ed.), *The New American Political System* (American Enterprise Institute, 1978), chap. 3.

ronmental Protection Agency be asked to hold hearings on the matter and come up with recommendations? Or should this matter be one for presidential leadership—requiring an executive order and major addresses to the public?

4. *Policy implementation:* Once it is adopted, how should the policy be carried out? How much is to be spent where, and how? How will the process of administration affect the policy?

5. *Policy evaluation:* Is the policy working? How is the effectiveness or impact of the policy measured? Who evaluates the policy? What are the consequences of policy evaluation and congressional oversight? For example, are antipollution laws really improving air quality?

Policy making can occur in any branch of government. It is made by a series of political participants, not just lawmakers. Note, too, policy making cannot be separated entirely from administration, and as we saw in the chapter on bureaucrats, appointed public officials can often have just as much influence as elected officials. Policy making is influenced by the values of people participating in each of the policy stages listed above. Also, it is clearly influenced by interest groups of all kinds, especially by highly organized and well-financed groups and associations that can afford to maintain lobbyists in Washington, D.C.

Among the variety of approaches used to study policy making in the United States are the "rational person" model, the power elite model, the bureaucratic politics model, the policy systems model, and the incremental, or gradualist, approach. These are not all the ways various people think the system operates, but by examining them briefly we gain useful perspectives on how policy is shaped and made in the United States.

The Rational Person Model

While the rational person model is a textbook abstraction, it is still a helpful model to analyze public policy. Rational policy makers try to protect or maximize their own personal interests or what they think is in the public interest. They may be trying to improve the slums, for example. This could also be said of a rational group. Groups are out to protect their interests and advance only those policies from which they think they or society will profit. Rationality is also the basic assumption in capitalist theory. The rational approach suggests a calculating strategy, with participants constantly asking how much they or their values will gain or lose from government action or inaction and how much effort and time they should spend lobbying and building a constituency.

Faced with an issue, rational participants will first clarify their goals or objectives and rank them. They will then list all the important possible solutions and investigate the likely results of each. After considering each likely outcome, they then choose the policy with consequences most closely matching their goals.

Rational decision making in the policy process usually fails or achieves only moderate success—due to the inevitability of incomplete information and uncertainty.

The Power Elite Model

The power elite approach generally interprets what happens in the policy arena as the product of the political influence of powerful economic interests. The idea is that we have a government of the rich, by the friends of the rich, and for the rich. If 5 percent of U.S. families control 30 percent of the wealth, this is because our public policies favor the wealthy. If poverty programs seldom succeed in achieving their objectives, it is because the wealthy interests in the nation prefer these programs to be more symbolic than real.

The power elite school holds that we should study government *inaction* as much as government action, since powerful business interests often are able to keep certain issues *off* the agenda of government. And these powerful interests generally do not want any kind of governmental interference in the economy unless they stand to gain from it. In short, the power elite school believes there is a "ruling class" in America and that its influence and power are based upon the national corporate economy and the institutions that economy nourishes. Congress, presidents, and regulatory agencies are generally viewed as serving the interests of the powerful, monied class.[4]

The power elite model, although often described as one that visualizes the rich being the powerful, is somewhat compatible with the concept that many conservatives have of the way things get done in the United States. They sometimes think of the power elite as being the big unions, the big media, big bureaucracy, and others who in alliance with the "Eastern Establishment" force upon common people programs and goals contrary to what the majority wish. This might be called a "populist-conservative" school and it has been represented in part by George Wallace of Alabama, the Moral Majority, and others who are also persuaded that there is a "ruling class" that determines how policies get made and administered.

Another version—an extreme version—of the power elite approach is a Marxist model. Marxists argue that policy development and outcomes, especially for the working and poor classes, occur only as placating devices to lessen the likelihood of unrest and preserve the stability of a basically unfair system.[5]

Critics of the power elite approach say if researchers start with the assumption that elites account for policy change or lack of change, they are likely to find evidence to support it. But if they start with the assumption that the policy process is far more complicated, they will find evidence of a more complicated and subtle set of influences.

The Bureaucratic Politics Model

There is an older theory of American politics which holds that our politics and public policies are the product of the struggle among competing interest groups. As groups gain and lose power, public policy will be changed in favor of those who are on top at the moment. But more recently scholars have concluded that this theory overstates the role of outside interest groups and underestimates the role of public bureaucracies. They now suggest that what needs to be studied is the relative power and political strategies of the large bureaucracies in Washington. What bureaucracy one belongs to will determine one's policy views, they claim. This approach contends that concern for larger budgets and expanding mission all affect the information a bureaucracy will present to a president and to Congress. These same factors will also affect the way policies are implemented.

Adherents of this view recommend that students of public policy pay very close attention to the way the bureaucracy functions and the way bureaucrats become involved in the various stages of the policy-making process.

The Policy Systems Approach

A more ambitious but more general approach is offered by those who want to place all the factors and all the stages of the process into a systems framework. They claim that everything is interrelated and that a full understanding of how policies are made or changed can come only from a comprehensive look at

---

[4] The classic statement of this view was by C. Wright Mills, *The Power Elite* (Oxford University Press, 1956). For another look at elite influence, see Thomas R. Dye, *Who's Running America? The Reagan Years* (Prentice-Hall, 1983). Also see John Manley, "Neo-Pluralism: A Class Analysis of Pluralism I and Pluralism II," *American Political Science Review* (June, 1983), pp. 368–83.

[5] See, for example, some of the interpretation in Edward S. Greenberg, *The American Political System: A Radical Approach*, 3rd ed. (Little, Brown, 1983); and Robert Heilbroner, *Marxism: For and Against* (Norton, 1980).

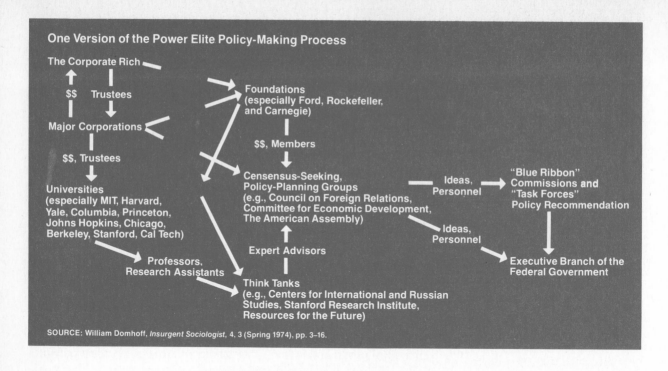

One Version of the Power Elite Policy-Making Process

The Corporate Rich

$$ Trustees

Major Corporations

$$, Trustees

Universities (especially MIT, Harvard, Yale, Columbia, Princeton, Johns Hopkins, Chicago, Berkeley, Stanford, Cal Tech)

Professors, Research Assistants

Foundations (especially Ford, Rockefeller, and Carnegie)

$$, Members

Censensus-Seeking, Policy-Planning Groups (e.g., Council on Foreign Relations, Committee for Economic Development, The American Assembly)

Expert Advisors

Think Tanks (e.g., Centers for International and Russian Studies, Stanford Research Institute, Resources for the Future)

Ideas, Personnel

Ideas, Personnel

"Blue Ribbon" Commissions and "Task Forces" Policy Recommendation

Executive Branch of the Federal Government

SOURCE: William Domhoff, *Insurgent Sociologist*, 4, 3 (Spring 1974), pp. 3–16.

these relationships. Borrowing from engineering and biological models, these researchers examine the inputs of the policy system and stress the way the process translates inputs into outputs, and then how the outputs—the laws—get converted into policy outcomes, or improvements in the lives of people. The diagram at the top of page 439 conveys much of the policy systems approach. Note that the feedback loop linking policy outcomes with the other aspects of the system implies that policy results, and how the public reacts to the results, will in turn affect other policies.

The Incrementalist Model

Incrementalism is an approach suggesting that problems can be solved only through gradual adjustments. Incrementalism is a result of the complexity of modern society. Does incrementalism mean there is no single, right, comprehensive answer to a problem? No. Incrementalism sometimes can allow for a single answer, but it must be arrived at gradually, rather than in a single, swift step.

Unlike the rational person model, the incrementalist model suggests that only some of the alternatives are examined. More attention is devoted to seeking mutual agreement about what small steps can be taken than to finding a single, comprehensive answer. Our system of separation of powers and dispersed authority promotes piecemeal policy change. Planning comprehensively is difficult in a system such as ours, which is glued together with alliance politics, majorities of the moment, and constant compromising.

Thinking comprehensively, however, is not impossible in our system. The problem is that in order to get something done and enforced, many different and often differing people must reach a consensus—with much compromising and bargaining. We have to get by so many potential veto groups that the resulting policy proposals are almost always different from what the sponsors desired.

Policy makers bend over backward to design programs to cultivate interest group support and to neutralize possible opponents. This results, not surprisingly, in watered-down objectives and laws that are extremely general and vague. To be sure, laws often are complex and detailed; yet they are deliberately written to permit a diversity of interpretations.

Drawing by Dedini; © 1980. The New Yorker Magazine, Inc.

438

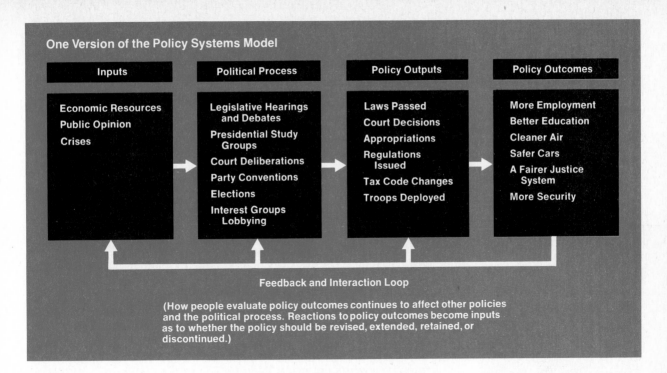

One Version of the Policy Systems Model

Inputs	Political Process	Policy Outputs	Policy Outcomes
Economic Resources Public Opinion Crises	Legislative Hearings and Debates Presidential Study Groups Court Deliberations Party Conventions Elections Interest Groups Lobbying	Laws Passed Court Decisions Appropriations Regulations Issued Tax Code Changes Troops Deployed	More Employment Better Education Cleaner Air Safer Cars A Fairer Justice System More Security

Feedback and Interaction Loop

(How people evaluate policy outcomes continues to affect other policies and the political process. Reactions to policy outcomes become inputs as to whether the policy should be revised, extended, retained, or discontinued.)

"Should we live miserably or die comfortably?" *By permission of Bill Mauldin and Wil-Jo Associates, Inc.*

Also, in a democracy political leaders are not likely to be risk takers, or to call on the people to sacrifice today in order to avoid some problem that will arise decades from now. We do not do much about a fuel crisis until we actually run out of gasoline; we do not do much about air pollution until people start coughing, choking, and dying of cancer.

In recent years there has been a growing recognition that direct governmental intervention in the form of a command and control approach is not the only or best way to intervene, and that the market approach may often be more effective. Thus, to control pollution, either the Environmental Protection Agency can enforce regulations for hundreds of thousands of different businesses, or we can make adjustments in the tax system to give industries an economic incentive to avoid pollution.

The move to transfer authority to states and localities also fosters incrementalism. With such strategies Washington officials are in effect saying: "Let local elites decide what is proper policy in their locality. Let us not interfere." Some people argue, and they are partly correct, that efficiency and a smaller federal bureaucracy should be a prime concern. But decentralization and "disaggregation" (dividing up policy making into fragmented, functional units) are also a means of getting Congress and federal bureaucrats to give up their power over federal funds. Thus, local policy making is still another way for Washington officials to make people happy. Yet it is often at the expense of national objectives, comprehensive planning, and swift action.

Policy-making processes in democratic countries are, except in matters of foreign relations, rarely insulated from local politics. Our party system and popular values concentrate power at the state and local levels. Numerous case studies document how the structural arrangements of our government are better suited to protect the local status quo than to force unpopular controls on local governments. Even when the national government is quite unified in its views, localities are often able to delay or modify federal policies by local administrative manipulations.

Most of the above models have some evidence to back them up, but it seems obvious that no single approach will explain everything. By and large, policies are shaped by a combination of events, the availability of resources, past experience, and the ideas of concerned public officials and activist citizens. Elections, public opinion, and the competition among groups and bureaucracies, as well as the struggles among the branches of government, all influence the way policies are defined and settled. We now turn to a more detailed examination of what takes place in some of the key stages of the policy-making process.

POLICY FORMULATION

Senator Daniel P. Moynihan, former adviser to Presidents Kennedy, Johnson, and Nixon, is a key force in the U.S. Senate. *Rick Bloom.*

Who sets the agenda for national policy making? Who raises issues? Policy is certainly not formed in a vacuum. Organized interests representing varied points of view press claims and counterclaims. Some groups and persons clearly enjoy more access, more opportunities to get their cases heard, and more possibilities for vetoing measures than others. Still, we cannot explain with certainty why some issues become national controversies and others do not.[6]

According to some critics: "The most significant fact about the distribution of power in America is not who makes such decisions as are made, but rather how many matters of the greatest social importance are not the objects of anyone's decision at all."[7] That is, matters of great importance to some people sometimes do not get on the public agenda.

However, government inactivity in some area does not mean the government is without a policy in that area: *Inaction is still a policy.* Inattention to issues can be as important as decisive action. Indifference to racial or sexual discrimination clearly was policy—very important policy for those affected by it. A former White House domestic advisor (currently a U.S. senator from New York), Daniel P. Moynihan, once called for a policy of "benign neglect" toward minority problems, not because he was indifferent to racial discrimination but because he felt less governmental assertiveness was a better way to handle discrimination. In short, everything has political consequences—including doing nothing.

Shared Leadership

Inaction by some policy makers often forces an issue to another part of the political system. All branches of the national government—as well as the bureaucracy, media, and interest groups—seem to take turns initiating policy changes: The Supreme Court's holding in *Brown* v. *Board of Education*[8] (1954) is a classic example of a landmark civil rights and education policy decision with implications for the other components of the political system. This same court decision was itself the result of a variety of economic, social, and political changes in the country; and it, in turn, triggered actions and reactions that ricocheted back on the Court.

Separation of powers ensures that when things get clogged in one part of the system, a safety valve can often be found elsewhere—sometimes in the courts, sometimes in a president, sometimes in regulatory agencies. Groups pressing for policy changes will seek to exert influence where they are most likely to succeed. If one has large sums of money to contribute to a political campaign, one is more likely to have influence with Congress and the presi-

[6]See, for example, T. R. Reid, *Congressional Odyssey: The Saga of a Senate Bill* (W. H. Freeman, 1980).

[7]Robert Paul Wolff, *The Poverty of Liberalism* (Beacon Press, 1968), p. 118. See also M. A. Crensen, *The Un-Politics of Air Pollution* (Johns Hopkins Press, 1971); and Peter Bachrach and Morton S. Baratz, "Decisions and Nondecisions: An Analytical Framework," *American Political Science Review* (September 1963), pp. 632–42.

[8]347 U.S. 483 (1954).

dency than with the courts. If persons lack funds and a large political base, they may find it more effective to resort to litigation. The Legal Defense Fund of the NAACP, for example, has won numerous cases in its long-term efforts to improve the legal protection of blacks. Litigation is also now a standard weapon in the arsenal of consumer and community groups working for reform. Public interest groups have gone to court seeking to gain compliance with laws already on the books.

Just as Congress delegates extensive legislative power to the president, so the chief executive delegates policy-making power to administrators. Obviously, a secretary of state can have a distinct influence on policy, as do other department heads and bureau, division, and section chiefs. In a sense, there is no level in the administrative hierarchy at which discretion ends. At any time the most routine matter may be called to the public's attention by a newspaper columnist or a member of Congress. The matter will then be given consideration by a bureau or department chief—perhaps even by the White House. In short, there are thousands of people throughout the government (and millions more outside, such as editors, lobbyists, and activist citizens) who exert direct pressure on legislators, legislation, and policy.

The extent to which presidents wield legislative power turns not only on their formal constitutional powers but also on their political powers. How good is their timing? How active and articulate are their lieutenants—their cabinet members and key agency heads? How close are their relations with congressional leaders? Can they mobilize public opinion? Does their influence reach into states and districts throughout the country? Does their party control Congress? A president's effectiveness turns also on that official's professional reputation as a politician. Presidents' words and actions are closely watched. Do they reward those who help them and punish those who do not? How well do they bargain with other power centers? Are they on top of the struggle for power, submerged in it, or remote from it? Presidents' political skill and political power are interrelated. Their influence over others derives from what the latter think of them and their power.[9]

John W. Gardener, founder of Common Cause and veteran citizen activist as well as former cabinet member under LBJ. *Rick Bloom.*

The Issue-Attention Cycle

The public's attention span is short. Shifting public moods and the need for publicity encourage elected officials to adopt new policies rather than restructure old ones. To rally support for a new program is easier than cutting back ongoing programs. Too many beneficiaries—those who receive money from the programs and those who administer the programs—will fight any changes in programs already on the books. Thus, reworking or even rethinking old programs becomes subordinate to what might be called an "add-on" approach to policy making. In other words: "Each of these new problems suddenly leaps into prominence, remains there for a short time, and then—though still largely unresolved—generally fades from the center of public attention."[10] Public boredom often sets in when large numbers of people realize the cost of solving the problem would be very high indeed. (Perhaps boredom is the most underrated force in history.)

Policy makers, especially those in a democracy, do not like to make anybody mad if they can help it. They would rather enlarge the size of the national economic pie and give new groups funds rather than redistribute what is currently there.[11] Like fathers and mothers—and university administrators—any-

---

[9]Richard E. Neustadt, *Presidential Power,* rev. ed. (Wiley, 1980), chap. 3.

[10]Anthony Downs, "Up and Down with Ecology—The Issue-Attention Cycle," *The Public Interest* (Summer 1972), p. 38.

[11]For a discussion of some of the implications of interest group and logrolling special claims, see Mancur Olson, *The Rise and Decline of Nations* (Yale University Press, 1982).

body who has the responsibility for allocating scarce resources would rather make everybody happy than take an allowance back from one child and give it to another, or take funds from one university department and redistribute them to another. If a group that is presently getting "the short end of the stick" lacks political clout, it is likely *not* to get its fair share of the economic goods of the society.

POLICY IMPLEMENTATION

Once a policy is adopted, how should it be carried out? Even if we know what to do, can get political leaders to agree to it, and can devise an appropriate strategy, we may still not be able to ensure that the strategy is implemented.[12] After the president has signed a bill into law or a regulatory agency has made its rules, the government must act. Money must be spent and rules enforced if goals are to be met.

Although the other parts of the policy process are well publicized, implementation is often hidden within the vast bureaucracy. A great number of federal programs fail to accomplish the desired goals because of problems that show up during the implementation phase. The Kennedy administration's economic reform programs in Latin America, the Johnson administration's Model Cities program, the Nixon-Ford programs in crime control, the Carter human rights initiatives in foreign policy, and Reagan's cutback of state and local aid all illustrate programs whose problems were not fully understood until long after they had been put into operation. When such failures occur, it is relatively easy to blame the original legislation rather than examine what happened after the bill became law. Of course, poorly written legislation and badly conceived policy yield poor results. But policy analysts have begun to realize that even the best legislation can fail because of problems encountered during implementation.[13] Sometimes these problems can lead to the outright failure of a program, but more often they mean excessive delay, watering down of original goals, or costs far above those originally expected.

Why Is It so Hard to Implement Federal Policies?

The coalition of supporters that comes together to get a bill through Congress often does not stay together after the bill has been enacted. Further, Congress often passes ambiguous legislation that conceals serious policy differences. Rather than set clear goals, Congress—reflecting differences among the supporters of the policies—sets general or vague goals, and then passes on the responsibility for interpretation to the bureaucrats. Bureaucrats get the blame, but they are merely trying to carry out deliberately unclear policies, and they must act in a political atmosphere of conflict and competing groups.

Take civil rights legislation, for example. Often the differences among women's groups, black groups, Hispanic groups, employer groups, and trade unions are momentarily resolved and a bill becomes law. But after the bill has been enacted, the coalition falls apart, and the resulting pressures are felt on

[12]See Eugene Bardach, *The Implementation Game: What Happens after a Bill Becomes a Law* (MIT Press, 1977).

[13]Many political scientists and economists who study policy implementation publish their articles and findings in the following quarterly publications: *The Public Interest*, *Policy Sciences*, and *The Journal of Policy Analysis and Management*. The Brookings Institution and the American Enterprise Institute for Public Policy Research, which are both nonprofit, nongovernmental research organizations located in Washington, D.C., also publish books and reports on policy implementation and evaluation.

the agencies trying to implement the policies. Conflicts arise and increase. Employers insist, for example, that the agency's regulations are unrealistic and interfere with their rights; women's groups argue that the agencies are failing to enforce the law vigorously; black groups claim that the agencies favor the women's groups but ignore the wishes of the blacks, and so on. The more controversial the issue, the greater the chance of delay, as powerful interest groups clash over a program and force bureaucrats charged with implementation to move cautiously.

The implementation process involves a long chain of decision points that must be cleared before a program can be successfully carried out. At each decision point is a public official or community leader who has the power to advance—or delay—the program. According to two students of implementation, the more decision points a program needs to clear, the greater the chance of failure or delay.[14] Special problems result if the successful implementation of a national program depends on the cooperation of state and local officials. One state or community may be eager to help; another may be opposed to a program and try to stop it.

Clearly, policy makers must consider the problems of implementation when they propose legislative solutions to national problems. One technique is to design policies and programs that can withstand buffeting by a constantly shifting set of political and social pressures. Another is to have public officials or consultants of some kind ready to serve as "fixers" to repair damage as it is detected. Still another plan is to write legislation that does not depend for its success on the need to persuade people to help with it. For example, changes in the tax code are sometimes favored over complex public jobs programs by those seeking to stimulate the economy. In the one case the apparatus for accomplishing a goal is already in place (the tax structure); in the other a large new administrative structure would have to be established, staffed, and supervised.

"Then we agree! We're doing the best job that can be done considering that the country's ungovernable." *Drawing by Dana Fradon;* © *1978. The New Yorker Magazine, Inc.*

Policy Evaluation

Is the policy working? As noted, the adoption of a policy is only the beginning of the process. After Congress passes a law and the president signs it, implementation takes place. But what happens next? Who decides whether it is working or not? The answer—or so it often seems—is everybody and nobody.

Program supporters and those who administer the programs tend to exaggerate the success of their favorite programs in order to justify the funds allocated to them. Bureaus and agencies often cast their proposals in such a way as to persuade, not to evaluate. Program "evaluation" reports coming into the White House or Congress from the bureaucracy have long been suspect. In this sense, evaluation is never entirely nonpolitical: It will be used by one party or branch of government against another. Evaluation will also be used by one department or agency against another.[15] Some bureaus become so involved with activities that enhance their prestige that they neglect the work for which they were created. Or delays and deficiencies in evaluation may occur because an agency wants to hide the real cost of its operations. Still, it is difficult and expensive to develop outcome or impact measures. It is hard to relate expenditures to outcomes, or to be precise about what has caused social change, even

Ralph Nader, perhaps the best known consumer advocate in America. *Rick Bloom.*

[14]Jeffrey Pressman and Aaron Wildavsky, *Implementation* (University of California Press, 1973). Other studies of policy execution include George C. Edwards III, *Implementing Public Policy* (Congressional Quarterly Press, 1980); and Robert T. Nakumura and Frank Smallwood, *The Politics of Policy Implementation* (St. Martin's Press, 1980).

[15]Aaron Wildavsky, *Speaking Truth to Power: The Art and Craft of Policy Analysis* (Little, Brown, 1979), chap. 9.

if change can be noticed or measured. The problem is one of social measurement.[16]

Political and social scientists have recently turned their attention to the product side of public policy. Instead of being concerned only with what affects government, or with what goes on inside government, they are now paying attention to what social or economic change comes out of the policy. The test of a program is not input but *outcome:* "It is interesting, and at times important, to know how much money is spent on schools in a particular neighborhood or city. But the crucial question is how much do the children learn. Programs are for people, not for bureaucracies."[17]

Why have Congress and the White House not insisted on more systematic planning and evaluation? Short-term political incentives seem to propel their energies in the opposite direction: *Pass now, plan later!* Presidents, especially, are always eager for fast results. They say they were elected not to study policies but to get things done and to put ideas into operation. Analysis, testing, small-scale experiments, and systematic reappraisal of ongoing programs are sometimes shoved aside. As Congress has been eclipsed by the executive in more and more policy formulation areas, there has been a move to strengthen it as a focus for program oversight. However, even its staunchest defenders readily admit Congress performs this responsibility with only modest success.

The Legislative Reorganization Act of 1946 assigned to each standing committee the responsibility to "exercise continuous watchfulness" over how agencies administer laws. Oversight is neither constant nor systematic, however. Comprehensive oversight of all federal programs would demand all the time of the staff and members of Congress. Members of Congress exercise the oversight function when they are particularly upset with the way they are being treated by executive branch officials and when it serves their constituents in a direct way. Certain standing committees have created specific oversight subcommittees, but it is unclear whether such subcommittees make any difference in the quality of policy making. What is frustrating, of course, is not that oversight is performed only selectively, but that too often it comes only after some mishap or tragedy, such as when the Air Force C-5A had its motor fall off and its landing gear collapse. Some within and outside Congress believe Congress should not perform oversight functions; instead, Congress should strenghthen itself in other ways. Yet oversight, properly conducted, can be a major means for Congress to retain its role in policy making. For the present, however, there are only modest incentives for conducting comprehensive program oversight.

Evaluation of programs, however, is not primarily a technical problem, but a political one. Of course, everyone will agree that something is wrong with Defense Department procurement when the cost of buying a weapons system is much more than Congress anticipated. But many evaluations involve choices between costs and benefits, a problem for which there is no expert answer. Is the welfare program worth the expenditure? Should we abolish subsidies to farmers? Has the interstate highway program produced good or bad results in the nation? Are grants for students to attend medical schools worthwhile? No experts can tell us whether or not these programs are "successful," because the answers depend on political values. This is why we rely on the democratic system and on politicians chosen by popular vote, and why policy making and implementation are so complex and frustrating.

"Remember, son, if at first you don't succeed, re-evaluate the situation, draw up various hypotheses for your failure, choose reasonable corrective measures, and try, try again." *Copyright © 1974. Saturday Review Magazine Co. Reprinted by permission.*

---

[16]A number of books on this topic have been written. See Laurence E. Lynn, Jr., *Designing Public Policy: A Casebook on the Role of Policy Analysis* (Goodyear, 1980); and Jerome T. Murphy, *Getting the Facts: A Fieldwork Guide for Evaluators and Policy Analysts* (Goodyear, 1980).

[17]Daniel P. Moynihan, "Policy vs. Program in the '70's," *The Public Interest* (Summer 1970), p. 100.

Debates over what is "right" public policy seldom occur in a complete vacuum. Such debates are at least partially shaped by a person's ideology—that is, a person's set of attitudes and beliefs about freedom and equality, humankind, and the desired role of the state and government. We have discussed ideology in Chapter 9, but briefly put, an ideology is a simplified picture of the world. Phrased yet another way, an ideology refers to a somewhat integrated belief system that has a "world view," an image of the relationship of people to their government and of how power should be used in society.

Some students of American politics say most of us cannot be classifed as ideologues. Our attitudes about politicians and public policies are not held in a highly systematic fashion. For instance, a voter may want increased spending for defense, but vote for the party that is for reducing defense spending, because he or she has always voted for that party. Or a person may be for the adoption of the Equal Rights Amendment and in favor of government-financed abortions but still vote for Ronald Reagan. For most people the consistency among various attitudes and opinions is relatively low. Most people, most of the time "view political issues as discrete, isolated matters and do not apply a general standard of performance in evaluating parties and candidates. More important, they have difficulty relating what happens in one situation to what happens in another."[18] And this problem becomes worse as government gets into more and more policy areas. Hence, people not surprisingly have difficulty finding candidates that reflect their preferences across a range of issues.

The absence of widespread, hardened ideologies in the United States makes for markedly different kinds of politics and policy-making processes than in most European or Third World nations. Our policy making is characterized more by coalitions of the moment than by fixed alignments pitting one set of warring ideologues against another. And our politics are more a politics of moderation and accommodation than a prolonged and strained battle between two, three, or more competing philosophies of government. Elsewhere things are different, as in countries where a strong communist or Christian-Democratic party exists.

By no means, however, does this mean that policies or ideas are not taken into account in our politics. As a result of better and more education and better and more sources of information about political activities, we have witnessed a slight increase in ideological thinking and issue voting. Issues such as affirmative action, welfare assistance programs, and the escalating nuclear arms race have aroused countless persons who previously were relatively passive about politics and political ideas. Evidently, a certain kind of modified ideology is playing an important role in our system.

Two major—but rather broad and hazy—schools of political thinking dominate American politics: *liberalism* and *conservatism*. However, two lesser—but more defined—schools of thought, *socialism* and *libertarianism*, also help define the spectrum of ideology in America.

SOCIALISM Socialism is an economic and governmental system based on public ownership of the means of production and exchange. Karl Marx once described socialism as a transitional stage of society between capitalism and communism. In a capitalist system the means of production and most of the property are privately owned, whereas in a communist or socialist system the property is "owned" by the state in common for all the people. In the ultimate socialist country justice is achieved by having participants determine their own

[18]H. T. Reynolds, *Politics and the Common Man* (Dorsey Press, 1974), p. 14.

needs, taking what is appropriate from the common product of society. Hence, Marx's dictum: "From each according to his ability, to each according to his needs."

American socialists, and there are probably a few million of them, favor a greatly expanded role for the government. They would nationalize certain industries. They would institute a public jobs program so that all who want work would be put to work. They would change the tax system to place a much steeper tax burden on the wealthy and eliminate tax preferences for the rich. In short, the American socialist favors policies to help the underdog and the common person by means of government redistribution programs. Economic justice and stepped-up efforts toward greater equality are favored over property rights. American socialists would also drastically cut defense spending.

Critics of socialism here say the last thing we need is more governmental interference in the economy. Do we want more operations like the U.S. Postal Service? They complain that already there are few incentives for efficiency in our bureaucracies. Further, socialism places too much faith in the state at the expense of individual rights and liberties. They generally add that the right to own private property and skepticism toward centralized government are key factors that have made America great—factors that would be vastly less important in a socialist scheme of things.

Senate hearing. *K. Jewell.*

LIBERALISM   In its modern American usage liberalism refers to a belief in the positive uses of government to bring about justice and equality of opportunity. Modern-day liberals wish to preserve the rights of the individual and the right to own private property, but they are very willing to have the government intervene in the economy to remedy the defects of capitalism and a market economy. Contemporary American liberalism has its roots in Franklin Roosevelt's New Deal programs, designed to aid the poor and to protect people against the possibilities of unemployment, inadequate or unavailable medical assistance, and inadequate or unavailable housing and education. Liberals believe in affirmative action programs and in progressive taxation measures and regulatory efforts that help protect the average worker's health and safety. American liberals have also favored the right of unions to organize as well as to strike.

On a more philosophical level, liberals generally believe in the near-perfectability of humans, the possibility of progress. They believe things can be made to work, that the future will be better, that obstacles can be overcome. This positive set of beliefs may explain some of their willingness to believe in the potential benefits of governmental action, a willingness to alter or even to negate the old Jeffersonian notion that "government governs best when it governs least." Liberals contend that the character of modern technology and the side effects of industrialization cry out for at least limited governmental programs that will offset the loss of liberties suffered by the less well-to-do and the weak. Hence, liberals frequently stress the need for a politics of compassion, a politics of affirmative government.

A brief historical note will be helpful here. Back in the seventeenth and eighteenth centuries, liberals stressed individual rights, but they perceived the central government as a prime threat to these rights and liberties. Thus, they favored a small government and sought ample guarantees of protection from governmental harassment. Modern liberals view government as protecting individuals from being abused by a variety of nongovernmental forces (market vagaries, business decisions, and so on). The emphasis on individualism has remained constant; it is the perception of government that has changed.

After the liberal setbacks of the late 1970s and early 1980s some moderate liberals acknowledged that they must come up with new ideas.[19] Critics of lib-

---

[19]See Gary Hart, *The New Democracy* (Quill, 1983).

eralism say it places too much reliance on government bureaucrats. They say liberalism may sound good, but its costs are greater than its benefits. Liberalism taken too far leads to a welfare state and a dependence on central government that is against the American grain. When you get too much government, there is a tendency for government to start dictating to the people, and then our rights and liberties are jeopardized. Moreover, too many governmental controls or regulations and too much taxation undermine the ethic of self-help or self-reliance in our society. Critics of liberalism favor doing things as much as possible in the private sector and according to the market economy. And they would revitalize wherever possible our nongovernmental and volunteer sectors.

CONSERVATISM   In America conservatism has its roots in the political thinking of John Adams and many of his contemporaries. They believed in limited government and had great faith in encouraging individual excellence and personal achievement. Private property rights and belief in free enterprise have been cardinal attributes of contemporary conservatism. In contrast to liberals, conservatives want to do as much as possible to keep government small, except in the area of national defense.

Most conservatives opposed New Deal programs and the War on Poverty in the 1960s, and they have seldom favored aggressive civil rights and affirmative action programs. Much of this, they say, could be done by charities or by encouraging citizens to be more tolerant. The conservative places considerable faith in the private sector and considers social justice to be essentially an economic question. Conservatives dislike the tendency of turning to the national government for the solutions to societal problems. Government activism, they say, has been highly inflationary and counterproductive. Conservatives also prize stability—stability of the dollar, stability in international affairs, and political and economic stability.

Critics of conservatism from the Left say it ignores the hardships of those who are not born into wealth or born with considerable talents. Critics on the Right say that conservatives have too often gone along with the liberals and have allowed government to grow too much. Critics on the Right also attack the contradiction in conservatism that encourages the buildup of huge defense budgets and CIAs. The so-called "New Right" conservatives are especially concerned with social issues such as abortion, prayer in schools, and lifestyle issues, and put intense pressure on Reagan on these issues.

LIBERTARIANISM   Libertarianism is an ideology that cherishes individual liberty and insists on a sharply limited state and government. It carries some overtones of anarchism, of the English liberalism of the past, and of a 1930-style conservatism. A Libertarian Party has gained a following in recent years, especially among those who feel that both liberals and conservatives lack consistency in their attitude toward the power of the national government. The libertarians preach opposition to government and just about all its programs. They favor massive cuts in government spending, an end to the FBI and CIA and most regulatory commissions, a minimal defense establishment (one that would defend America only if we were directly attacked), and complete disengagement of American troops from overseas missions. Libertarians favor eliminating welfare programs, but at the same time they favor getting rid of programs that subsidize business, farmers, and the rich. They opposed government-backed guaranteed loans for Chrysler and would turn the functions of the Postal Service over to private companies. Unlike most conservatives, libertarians would repeal laws regulating personal morality, such as antiprostitution or antimarijuana laws.

In 1980 and again in 1984 a Libertarian Party candidate for president was on the ballot in all fifty states (winning about 1 percent of the vote in 1980). A few books on libertarianism have become best sellers in recent years.[20] But critics dismiss libertarianism as hopelessly naive, and as ignoring the failure of the market and the at least occasional need for certain public goods and services. Critics on the Left say advocates of libertarianism would indeed return us to the good old days—but it would be more like the days of serfdom.

SUMMARY

1. Public policy is the *substance* of what government does. It is a process. Public policy is never made in any fixed or final way, but is always in the process of being made. Public policy is often expressed only in part by a law, then by a court decision interpreting that law, then by a law modifying the court decision, then by an agency regulation implementing that law, then by a presidential executive order, and then by another law of Congress, and so on.

2. Policy making in the United States is neither simple nor tidy. There is not a "top down" structure of authority, so policy is not made "on high." Rather, policy takes form gradually, with large numbers of persons helping to formulate a new response to a public problem. Policies change slowly, reflecting gradual changes in public opinion. Each shift in policy is a conscious action, as reflected in a new election, law, or court decision.

3. Policy outcomes are the consequences for society, the "so-what" or "bottom line" of what the government is doing and how it affects citizens. Policy making can be studied through five stages—the identification of a problem, the for-

mulation of solutions, the adoption or enactment of a new policy response, the implementation or application of the policy, and the evaluation of the policy.

4. Our policy-making processes permit large numbers of groups and individuals to battle both to protect their own private interests and to enhance the public interest. Our political system, like all large systems, is weighted in favor of the status quo and against swift or sweeping change. But those who know better ways of doing things and are willing to take part in the pulling and hauling of the policy-making process can make a difference. Knowledge, political skills, and the ability to build coalitions of like-minded supporters and to attract extensive press coverage are preconditions for changing public policy.

5. Making public policy cannot be easily described in the abstract. For how policies change depends very much on what kinds of policies are being discussed and who and how many persons they affect. The five chapters that follow describe and analyze foreign, military, regulatory, subsidy and entitlements, taxing and spending policies.

FURTHER READING

DAVID S. BRODER. *Changing of the Guard: Power and Leadership in America* (Simon and Schuster, 1980).

DAVID CAPUTO. *The Politics of Policy Making: Five Case Studies* (W. H. Freeman, 1977).

CARL P. CHELF. *Public Policymaking in America* (Scott Foresman, 1982).

GEORGE C. EDWARDS III. *Implementing Public Policy* (Congressional Quarterly Press, 1980).

ROBERT T. NAKAMURA and FRANK SMALLWOOD. *The Politics of Policy Implementation* (St. Martin's Press, 1980).

MANCUR OLSON. *The Rise and Decline of Nations* (Yale University Press, 1982).

GUY PETERS. *American Public Policy* (Franklin Watts, 1982).

LEONARD SILK and MARK SILK. *The American Establishment* (Basic Books, 1980).

ALLAN P. SINDLER (ed.). *American Politics and Public Policy* (Congressional Quarterly Press, 1982).

AARON WILDAVKSY. *Speaking Truth to Power: The Art and Craft of Policy Analysis* (Little, Brown, 1979).

[20]See, for example, Robert Ringer, *Restoring the American Dream* (QED, 1979), and Ed Clark, *A New Beginning* (Caroline House, 1980).

MAKING FOREIGN POLICY

20

Since World War II the United States has become involved in world affairs in a way and to a degree almost unprecedented in our history. Whether we like it or not, that involvement is increasing, primarily because we must pursue our security interests in an increasingly interlocked "global" world. Further, as the world's principal economic trader, we need markets for our products, and we depend heavily on imported raw materials—especially oil.

Our political values and interests are also a factor: We have a keen interest in encouraging peace and human rights and preventing terrorism, anarchy, and repression. We have a special relationship with those nations that share our commitment to representative democracy, or at least our common Western heritage of liberty and equality.

Our foreign policy leaders whether Democratic or Republican see American power as a vital means of shaping not only a more decent but also a more secure world. At the very heart of our national security policy has been a recognition of the reality of Soviet power, and of the fact that the Soviets see the world differently than we do. But relationships with China and the "third world" hold a central place on the foreign policy agenda.

DEFENDING AND DEFINING OUR VITAL INTERESTS

The chief objective of American foreign policy has been to protect and promote the national security and economic well-being of the United States. But promoting our vital interests provides only hazy guidelines for those who must make foreign policy on a day-to-day basis. Further, Americans differ on what constitutes our national interest (note the differing views in Table 20–1).

20–1
FOREIGN POLICY GOALS FOR THE UNITED STATES—SOME SURVEY POLL RESULTS—1982

		Public	Leaders
		"SAYING VERY IMPORTANT"	
1.	Protecting American jobs	77%	43%
2.	Keeping up the value of the dollar	71	38
3.	Securing adequate energy	70	72
4.	Worldwide arms control	64	86
5.	Containing communism	59	44
6.	Combating world hunger	58	64
7.	Defending our allies	50	82
8.	Matching Soviet military power	49	52
9.	Strengthening the United Nations	48	25
10.	Protecting our business interests abroad	44	25
11.	Promoting human rights abroad	43	41
12.	Helping to improve standards of living abroad	35	55
13.	Protecting weaker nations from foreign aggression	34	43
14.	Promoting democratic forms of government	29	23

Note: Public = national sample of 1546 persons; Leaders = 341 knowledgeable officials or business and professional executives.

Source: Gallup poll for Chicago Council on Foreign Relations, late 1982. Table adapted from John E. Rielly (ed.), *American Public Opinion and U.S. Foreign Policy 1983* (Chicago Council on Foreign Relations, 1983), p. 13.

Participants in the ninth annual summit of industrialized nations in Williamsburg, Va. Representatives are from Canada, the president of The European communities, W. Germany, France, United States, Japan, Britain, and Italy. *Wide World Photos.*

President Woodrow Wilson. *Library of Congress.*

Few would question the need to defend our country, to survive, to protect our institutions and our values. Controversy arises, however, over the means to these ends. For example, to what extent should we intervene in the affairs of other nations in order to maintain international stability or the flow of resources to our economy? At the same time we are deeply concerned about the status of human rights and democratic institutions in foreign lands—a concern that enhances both the challenge and complexities facing our foreign policy makers.

In the early nineteenth century, the Monroe Doctrine defined the Western Hemisphere as an area of vital interest to our country, and we have often used force to prevent any threats to our security in this hemisphere.[1] During and after World War I we began to be involved elsewhere. President Woodrow Wilson wanted the United States to take a more active role in the world in order to champion the cause of freedom and to encourage the rise of democratic nations. Wilsonian "internationalism"—sometimes also called idealism, globalism, or moralism—has been a powerful recurring strain in our foreign policy ever since. Jimmy Carter's human rights initiatives were in this tradition. So was President Harry Truman's Truman Doctrine. It promised our support to all free peoples who faced totalitarian aggression. Truman doubtless had Europe in mind, but some supporters of this *internationalist* brand of foreign policy were willing to intervene nearly anywhere in the world in order to create an international order congruent with American values.

Realists contend that it is just such broad, sweeping definitions of our vital interests that lead us to overextend ourselves and involve us in conflicts such as Korea, Vietnam, and Lebanon. Policy makers, they say, should disregard ideology and shape foreign policy on rational, "realistic" calculations: What are our national interests? and are we able to defend them? The *realists* say we should intervene in world affairs only if *our* vital interests are at stake, and if the other country is the victim of overt, outside aggression, not just an internal rebellion. Still, realists would generally have the U.S. work with any ally, regardless of that country's internal politics, whereas idealists prefer that we work only with "good" governments.

[1]Cecil V. Crabb, Jr., *The Doctrine of American Foreign Policy* (Louisiana State University Press, 1982).

The limits of a unilateral American role in reforming the world and defending freedom against aggressors are plain: There are limits to what a single country can or should do. But old questions remain and new ones arise. Thus, is the Persian Gulf oil vital to our national interests, and if it is can we effectively intervene to ensure its continued flow? Is the stability of Central American nations vital to the interests of the United States? Should the Monroe Doctrine be applied to oppose the intervention by foreign nations into the internal affairs of these countries? Military intervention in Grenada in 1983 sharpened the debate over these questions.

THE COLD WAR AND ITS LEGACY

Joseph Stalin, Nikita Khrushchev, and Leonid Brezhnev. *UPI.*

Basic to any understanding of our contemporary foreign and defense policies is a recognition of the impact of the Cold War. For a time in the 1970s the policy of detente—an easing of strained relations between nations—between the U.S. and the USSR was seen as heralding the beginning of a new era of Soviet-American relations. But, in fact, the Cold War left a legacy that continues to be the dominant factor in our foreign policy formulation.[2]

Although many people think the Cold War began after the Second World War, some scholars believe its roots lie in the troubled course of Soviet-American relations after the Russian Revolution of 1917. Americans saw the Bolsheviks as immoral anarchists and believed communism threatened both civilization and the world order envisioned by Woodrow Wilson after World War I. Great Britain and France joined the United States in open hostility to the new Soviet leaders, intervening briefly in that country's affairs. (The United States sent a few troops into Russia in 1918 soon after the revolution—a fact most Americans forget but Soviet officials never forget.) American leaders followed a policy of diplomatic nonrecognition toward the Soviet government.

Although there was a slight warming of relations between the East and the West by the 1930s, the Soviet Union still felt isolated. The Soviets worried especially about Germany; they could not forget the 20 million casualties of World War I. Moscow's warnings about the dangers of Hitler's Germany went mostly unheeded by Western leaders. The inaction, and even appeasement, by some Western nations further isolated the Soviet Union, leaving it once again feeling vulnerable to German attack. Appeasement is a term used to describe concessions made to a potential enemy in the hope of preventing aggression. Britain's 1938 Munich agreement with Adolf Hitler to accept the partition of Czechoslovakia in exchange for a vague guarantee of peace was an example. Soviet leader Joseph Stalin, fearing he and his military would be unable to repulse a Nazi attack, knowing he would have little assistance from the West, and not caring what happened to other countries, signed a non-aggression pact with Hitler in August 1939. But Hitler soon attacked Poland, and World War II erupted in full force.

The West was outraged, and with reason, by this Soviet sellout. But in less than two years, Hitler also turned his military machine against the Russians, and the West and the Soviets faced Hitler as a common enemy. The wartime alliance between the United States and the USSR was an uneasy one. Although Stalin had advocated a European invasion by the Allies in 1941, this second front did not begin until 1944, after the Russians had sustained tremendous losses and had become bitter toward the West. To understand the origins

[2]Useful treatments of the Cold War and its legacy are Paul Y. Hammond, *The Cold War Years: American Foreign Policy since 1945* (Harcourt Brace Jovanovich, 1969); and Daniel Yergin, *Shattered Peace: The Origins of the Cold War and the National Security State* (Houghton Mifflin, 1978); Robert Dallek, *The American Style of Foreign Policy* (Alfred A. Knopf, 1983), esp. chaps. 6–9.

of the Cold War, one must understand the aims of the United States and the Soviet Union as they emerged as superpowers at the end of World War II. Europe's economies had been crushed, and there was a power vacuum that had to be filled. President Franklin D. Roosevelt saw a world based on the dominance of these two great nations, and therefore saw the necessity of maintaining an uneasy alliance with Stalin. Stalin's postwar priorities were to establish several pro-Soviet nations along its borders and to keep Germany divided and weak.

After World War II

Franklin Delano Roosevelt, Harry S Truman, and John F. Kennedy. *Library of Congress.*

In early 1945, with Hitler's defeat inevitable, Roosevelt, Stalin, and Winston Churchill met at Yalta to decide on Europe's future. The agreement that emerged from these meetings has been subject to different interpretations. On the surface it appeared the three powers had agreed on a set of democratic principles that would govern Europe's recovery. Many analysts now think, however, that the Yalta meetings were a verbal screen to allow a Soviet sphere of influence in Eastern Europe in exchange for Soviet cooperation in pursuing the war against Japan and in furthering Roosevelt's vision of the postwar world. Roosevelt's death two months after Yalta signaled the death of world order as well. His successor, Harry Truman, soon embarked on a very different path. Truman and his advisers did not trust Soviet intentions. Truman increasingly came to see Soviet-American competition as a conflict between two diametrically opposed ways of life. Possibilities for cooperation diminished or vanished.

Soviet intervention in Eastern Europe, Iran, and Turkey reinforced U.S. views. Truman and his advisers developed the Truman Doctrine, mentioned earlier. The Marshall Plan, named after Secretary of State George C. Marshall, sought to rebuild Europe's economies with American economic assistance. NATO—the North Atlantic Treaty Organization—was created as a military alliance between the United States and Western Europe. This was the strategy of containment, aimed at maintaining the international status quo and preventing any further Soviet territorial gains. Some of Truman's policies have been criticized as overextending the United States and as portraying Soviet-American relations as a simplistic struggle between good and evil rather than as traditional superpower competition. On the other hand, one must remember that the appeasement of Hitler remained fresh in policy-makers' minds—"No More Munich!" was a fashionable saying—and they did not want to make the same mistakes with Stalin. The result of Truman's policies was a military buildup and a state of constant readiness for war, coupled with a strong commitment to use American military force almost anywhere in the world. This was a notable departure from previous foreign policy.

Soon the United States was involved in the Korean war, and our overall foreign policy was set for the next twenty years. We believed we had no choice but to respond: Not to respond in Korea would have meant that our will and our commitments could be doubted, and that we might be challenged everywhere—or so our chief policy makers believed. With Eisenhower in the White House in the 1950s, our foreign policy changed somewhat, but the basic idea of containment remained. He relied extensively on economic and military assistance and on covert operations by an expanded CIA to help overthrow unwanted governments, such as in Guatemala. World order was still defined by the status quo and the domino theory, the idea that if one of our allies falls, a series of others may soon fall.

President John F. Kennedy, elected in late 1960, brought a fresh and youthful spirit to the country. He extended aid to newly independent nations and spoke boldly of a new and different world. Still, he was sharply anticommunist, building up nuclear weapons and military forces; and he confronted the Soviets and their extending influence in Cuba (1961), Berlin (1961), and

Vietnam. He also acted decisively to oppose the Russians during the October 1962 Cuban Missile Crisis. It was only in his third and last year that he hinted at a possible detente with the Soviets.

Vietnam

Lyndon Johnson's foreign policy became dominated by the Vietnam war, a conflict that must be viewed as a logical outgrowth of Cold War containment policy. Most American policy makers saw in Vietnam a case of Soviet-controlled communist aggression. Critics charge it was primarily a revolutionary war deeply rooted in Vietnamese history.[3] Democratic institutions had few if any roots in Vietnam, and yet we became enmeshed in a war to prevent aggression and make the country safe for democracy. According to the domino theory, if Vietnam fell, so would the rest of Indo-China, Thailand, and then maybe the Philippines, and so on. The United States had to make a stand in Vietnam so that it need not fight communists closer to home. President Johnson—very much in the Truman tradition—said in 1965 that if we failed to come to the aid of the South Vietnamese, we would be saying to the world that we "don't live up to our treaties and don't stand by our friends." No matter that South Vietnamese leaders might be corrupt, they were still our allies. Thus began our ever-escalating involvement in a war we hardly understood.

This is not the place to retell the story of the Vietnam war. It is enough to know that as the war grew more costly and the chances for victory grew more remote, the American people began to express growing discontent with inflation, the draft that accompanied the war, and the rising number of American deaths (over 50,000). Massive bombing of North Vietnam failed to contain the opposition forces. The war divided the government, the Democratic Party, the whole nation. It became a central issue in the 1968 election as Nixon promised to end the war—but refused to say how.

Secretary of Defense Robert S. McNamara at a September 1967 news conference discussing our involvement in Vietnam. *UPI.*

Nixon and Detente

The Vietnam War Memorial in Washington, D.C. with the names of all those killed in Vietnam. *Marc Anderson.*

Once in office, Nixon continued to act on the same assumptions as his predecessors. He and his chief national security adviser, Henry Kissinger, believed the way to end the war was to increase the costs of the war to the Soviets and Chinese. But they also realized Americans would not continue to back further escalation. Thus were born the two principles of the Nixon-Kissinger foreign policy: *Vietnamization*, which sought to let the South Vietnamese shoulder more and more of the fighting while the American troops disengaged; and *detente* with the Soviet Union, a downplaying of the threat of force and a new emphasis on cooperation, trade, and mutual arms limitations. This policy (letting others fight in order to prevent the spread of communism) became known as the Nixon Doctrine.

The Nixon Doctrine specifically held that the United States would keep its treaty commitments. Moreover, we would provide a shield if a nuclear power threatened the freedom of a nation allied with us, or a nation whose survival we considered vital to our security and the security of the region as a whole. Finally, in cases involving other types of aggression, the United States would furnish military and economic assistance when requested and as appropriate. But the nation directly threatened must assume the primary responsibility of providing the manpower for its own defense.[4]

Nixon presided over our exit from Vietnam; not long afterward, our former allies there fell to the opposition forces. Despite the reevaluation of our commitment to Vietnam, foreign policy makers in the 1970s continued to see

[3]See especially Frances Fitzgerald, *Fire in the Lake* (Atlantic-Little, Brown, 1972).

[4]For Nixon's and Kissinger's own views, see Richard Nixon, *RN: The Memoirs of Richard Nixon* (Grosset and Dunlap, 1978); and Henry Kissinger, *White House Years* (Little, Brown, 1979), pp. 223–25; see also Seymour M. Hersh, *The Price of Power: Kissinger in the Nixon White House* (Summit Books, 1983).

the international system in the context of Soviet-American competition. Nationalist movements in the Third World (developing nations outside the traditional influence of the superpowers, such as in Africa or Latin America) were largely discounted as Soviet-inspired rabble-rousing.

In the late 1970s Japan, Western Europe, and the OPEC countries began to play a far greater role in economic matters, but relations with the Soviet Union still dominated our foreign policy.

Reagan and the New Cold War

Ronald Reagan, having campaigned on a pledge to counter the massive Soviet military buildup, once in office took a much harder line toward Russia than had his immediate predecessors. He also helped win major increases in military spending. Accused by Democrats of rekindling the Cold War, Reagan answered that it was the Soviets who were to blame. As he put it in 1983: "The ultimate Soviet goal in Europe is to force the nations to accommodate themselves to Soviet interests on Soviet terms. We should all know just what those terms are. We need look no further than the Berlin Wall and the Iron Curtain. The truth is something that we and our NATO allies must not hesitate to use to counter the slurs and threats made against us."[5] Reagan also charged that Soviet influence was our major threat in both Central America and the Middle East. Hence, the central thrust of Reagan's foreign policies was to talk tough to the Soviets and to counter their military buildup with one of our own.

Throughout 1984, Reagan's critics said his foreign policy was based more on paranoia than on reality. Walter F. Mondale chided Reagan and his foreign policy team for failing to negotiate any arms control agreements. Mondale also faulted the Reagan administration for escalating American military involvement in the internal affairs of several Central American nations. Mondale said about Nicaragua: "In 100 days, I will end the illegal war." Said George Bush: "Mondale does not understand the nature of the problem."

In any event, American foreign policy still seeks to preserve the international status quo. Most threats to this status quo are seen as a threat to our vital interests. This outlook views the world as a hostile place, and the Soviet Union as a particularly hostile country, with which no real peace is possible. Our concern with the Soviets is also based on distrust of their economic and political values, especially the repression of individual rights and liberties. But how are these important concerns to be balanced against considerations such as world peace, the need to prevent nuclear war, the need to combat world hunger, and the preservation of resources?

Konstantin Chernenko took over as General Secretary of the Communist Party after Yuri Andropov died in February 1984. *AP/Wide World Photos.*

The United States in a Changing World

The world continues to grow smaller. Technology alone makes this inevitable, with its introduction of nuclear weapons, long-range delivery missiles, and virtually instant communications. Intensifying food, fuel, and mineral shortages have profoundly changed international relations. Common interests and mutual problems are forcing some traditional conflicts and rivalries aside, and resource scarcities are creating new ties.

In the nineteenth century stability was maintained by a balance of power, characterized by shifting alliances among five relatively equal countries: Great Britain, France, Austria, Prussia, and Russia. By the middle of the twentieth century, the international system was characterized by a balance of power—or a "balance of terror" as Winston Churchill once called it—between the two superpowers, the USSR and the U.S. The dominance of the international system by these two countries has been referred to as a condition of bipolar world politics, or bipolarity. There is growing evidence, however, that this concept no longer defines the international system, although militarily the USSR and

OPEC MEMBER
NATIONS

Algeria	Libya
Ecuador	Nigeria
Gabon	Qatar
Indonesia	Saudi Arabia
Iran	United Arab
Iraq	Emirates
Kuwait	Venezuela

[5]Ronald Reagan, speech before the American Legion, February 22, 1983.

the U.S are still the dominant forces. Other powerful forces have emerged—Japan, China, the Common Market (officially called the European Economic Community), and OPEC (officially the Organization of Petroleum Exporting Countries), as well as nations such as Brazil and India, which are becoming increasingly important in their regions of the world. The rise of these regional and transnational powers has resulted in a more diffuse distribution of power, especially economic power, in the last ten to fifteen years.

Another important feature in the international system has been the growing demands of the Third World nations for a greater say in their own development and in world affairs. These nations, largely found in the Southern Hemisphere, feel they have been exploited in the past by the industrialized countries. Their problems, especially population growth and food and fuel shortages, threaten to grow worse. Some observers predict that competition for resources could be one of the most pressing problems of the next few decades. Others see a problem in what is sometimes called the Fourth World, countries so poor they cannot provide for themselves and must live off the charity of other nations. But what will happen when the providers themselves are faced with shortages?

Still another crisis that faces the world is arms proliferation. The arms race between the Soviet Union and the United States continues, but competition for military superiority over one's enemies is no longer confined to the superpowers. By the year 2000 we probably will see the emergence of many new nuclear powers, many of them in the Third World. The rise in military power and the spread of nuclear weapons is almost sure to contribute to instability in the world.

Although it would probably be in the best interests of both the U.S. and the USSR to cooperate in facing these problems, the legacy of the Cold War seems to prevent this. Or at least thus far it has limited the number of cooperative ventures. Further, solutions to our global problems would require many nations to redefine rather radically their traditional views of national security and perhaps also their ways of life. All this suggests that the world will become increasingly multipolar in the future, and perhaps increasingly unstable. An optimist these days, said one wag, is someone who thinks the future is uncertain.

THE USSR'S MILITARY-OUTREACH

Where Russia stations troops or advisers—

Afghanistan	Laos
Algeria	Libya
Angola	Madagascar
Bulgaria	Mali
Cape Verde	Mozambique
Congo	Nicaragua
Cuba	Peru
Czechoslovakia	Poland
East Germany	Romania
Ethiopia	South Yemen
Guinea	Syria
Guinea-Bissau	Tanzania
Hungary	Vietnam
Iraq	Zambia

Where Russia has access to air and naval facilities—

Afghanistan	Ethiopia
Angola	South Yemen
Cuba	Syria
Eastern Europe	Vietnam

Source: U.S. News & World Report. Copyright 1983, U. S. News & World Report.

THE POLITICS OF MAKING FOREIGN POLICY

Foreign policy flows through much the same institutional and constitutional structures as domestic policy. Public opinion, interest groups, members of Congress, elections, separation of powers, and federalism all affect the politics of making foreign policy. But they operate somewhat differently from the way they do in internal affairs.

Public Opinion and Foreign Policy

Different foreign policy issues evoke different degrees of public involvement. In crisis situations—such as the Cuban Missile Crisis or the use of troops in Grenada in 1983—decisions are made by a small group of persons. Yet even in these situations presidents and their advisers make decisions with the knowledge that what they decide will ultimately require support from the public and its institutions, especially Congress.

In noncrisis situations the public appears to consist of three subcategories. The largest, comprising perhaps as much as 75 percent of the adult population, is the mass public. This group knows little about foreign affairs, despite the importance of the subject. The mass public concerns itself with foreign affairs mainly in conflict situations, especially those involving the actual or possible use of American troops abroad. The second public is the **attentive public**. Comprising perhaps 15 to 20 percent of the population, it maintains an active interest in foreign policy. The **opinion makers** are the third and smallest public. They transmit information and judgments on foreign affairs and mobilize support in the other two publics. To illustrate the relationship between these three publics, one analyst has developed this instructive analogy of a huge theater with a tense drama being played out on the stage:

> The mass public, occupying the many seats in the balcony, is so far removed from the scene of action that its members can hardly grasp the plot, much less hear all the lines or distinguish between the actors. Thus, they may sit in stony silence or applaud impetuously, if not so vigorously as to shake the foundations of the theater. Usually, however, they get thoroughly bored and leave. . . . The attentive public, on the other hand, is located in the few choice orchestra seats. Its members can not only hear every line clearly, but can also see the facial expressions of the actors. Thus they become absorbed in the drama, applauding its high spots and disparaging its flaws. Indeed, their involvement is such that during the intermission they make their views known to any occupants of the balcony who may have wandered into the lobby. As for the members of the opinion-making public, they are the actors on the stage, performing their parts with gusto and intensity, not infrequently in an effort to upstage each other. Many are directing their performance at some specific portion of the orchestra audience. Others, those with especially strong vocal cords, try to make themselves heard as far as the balcony. All are keenly aware that the quality of their performance will greatly affect their bargaining power when they seek higher salaries or better parts in future productions.[6]

Why are so many people indifferent or uninformed? First, foreign affairs are usually more remote than domestic issues. People have more firsthand information about unemployment or inflation than about Zimbabwean land reform or Turkish political problems. The worker in the factory and the boss in the front office know what labor-management relations are about, and they have strong opinions on the subject. They are likely to be less concerned about the internal struggles for power within Ethiopia or our policy on Cambodia— or to feel that they could not do much about it anyway. Only when American soldiers, especially drafted soldiers, are being killed does the mass public become directly concerned with foreign affairs.

Lack of widespread concern, knowledge, and involvement in the politics of foreign policy should not be confused with lack of intense feelings about aspects of the international scene. Since World War II questions about our relations with other nations have been high on the list of public concerns. And when issues such as the Vietnam conflict or El Salvador and Nicaragua become domesticated—that is, when they visibly, directly, and immediately affect the people of the United States—the debate over such policies produces demonstrations, campaigns, and hearings: in other words, all the trappings of the ordinary political process.

Public Moods: An Unstable Base?

Fluctuating from no interest at all to intense feeling, the public reaction to foreign policy is sometimes based on moods.[7] It is said the mass public oversimplifies the problems of foreign politics. It tends to reduce all issues to the one that is most urgent at the moment. It often thinks of the participants in terms

---

[6]James N. Rosenau (ed.), *Public Opinion and Foreign Policy* (Random House, 1961), pp. 34–35. See also Bernard C. Cohen, *The Public's Impact on Foreign Policy* (Little, Brown, 1973); and Charles W. Kegley, Jr., and Eugene R. Wittkopf, *American Foreign Policy*, 2nd ed. (St. Martin's Press, 1982), chap. 8.

[7]See, for example, I. M. Destler, *Making Foreign Economic Policy* (Brookings Institution, 1980). See also Jacob Javits, "Congress and Foreign Relations: The Taiwan Relations Act," *Foreign Affairs* (Fall, 1981), pp. 54–62.

President Reagan stated that "defense of the Caribbean and Central America against Marxist-Leninist takeovers is vital to our national security." Hence he sent military advisers to El Salvador. Here a U.S. adviser instructs a Salvadorean air force cadet in the use of an M-60 mortar. The advisers have been in the country since mid-1981 to give instruction in country-insurgency tactics to regular army troops, air force cadets, and sailors. *UPI.*

of heroes and villains. It favors quick and easy remedies—fire the secretary of state, or raise trade barriers and all will be well. Although this "mood" theory has been challenged, it is conceded that Americans are extremely permissive with American foreign policy makers on international issues. However, while members of the attentive public and the decision makers are also subject to mood responses and oversimplification, their responses tend to be more sophisticated.

Popular indifference means that policy makers often have to dramatize issues in order to arouse support. On the other hand, in periods of public excitement, fear of rash public opinion causes policy makers to be overcautious. To secure American participation in the United Nations, for example, the State Department carried on an intensive publicity campaign. But in so doing, it gave many people the impression that the United Nations would ensure peace and order in the world.

Too much has been made, however, of the American people's ignorance about foreign policy when contrasted to their knowledge of domestic issues. The instability of public moods, to the extent that it does exist, probably does not affect policy makers all that much. Most do not consider the public mood unless it is likely to be hostile to a foreign policy decision. Moreover, issues are usually defined by policy makers; the public generally reacts to them. Policy makers, and events, shape the agenda. Still, public opinion determines the broad limits within which others make decisions. Clearly the public's support or antagonism toward a country shapes how our public officials treat that nation (see Box on opposite page).

The State Department makes an effort to keep people informed about those areas of policy it thinks should be talked about publicly, and makes an effort to keep itself informed about public opinion. Nevertheless, almost all negotiations in which our government has a major role are conducted in secret, and both the public and Congress are frequently kept at a distance.

Special Interests and Foreign Policy

Interest groups and opinion leaders throughout society form an attentive public whose support is actively sought by official policy makers. They have an influential voice in shaping foreign policy and serve as a national pulse for our decision makers.

The mass media are sometimes powerful in shaping public opinion, a fact reflected in frequent disputes between the media and government. Tension between the press and the Department of State is an issue of long standing. The press gets especially upset when the government uses classification or secrecy to bury its mistakes. On the other hand, Foreign Service officers sometimes think members of the press are arrogant and irresponsible.

Another segment of the attentive public consists of citizens' organizations dedicated to increasing public awareness of foreign policy. The Foreign Policy Association designs community and media programs to encourage citizens to study and discuss major controversies. The Council on Foreign Relations, sometimes called the cornerstone of the Eastern Establishment, publishes *Foreign Affairs* magazine and several books a year; it also provides a forum for bringing business leaders and government elites together for talks on new directions in foreign policy. Groups like the World Federalists argue for world government. Defense contractors also sometimes try to promote certain kinds of foreign policies. Religious and ethnic groups are particularly interested in certain phases of foreign policy. Anti-nuclear war activists and those opposed to our involvement in Central America have been very active in the mid-1980s. These groups sometimes have intense feelings about issues, and they are often strategically located to affect the outcome of the elections.

A group of about forty demonstrators sings peace songs and displays banners in front of the U.S. State Department, while protesting U.S. involvement in El Salvador. *UPI.*

It is difficult to generalize about the impact of special interest groups on American foreign policies. At moments of international crisis a president is usually able to mobilize so much public support that special groups find it difficult to exert much influence. Investigations into some areas of policy, outside the crisis areas, such as trade, find that special groups rarely have had a decisive role in the formulation of foreign policy. Of course, what is more difficult to determine is the impact on policy caused by policy-makers' *anticipations* of group reactions.

Ethnic interest groups sometimes play a role in foreign policy making. For example, Greece might sometimes be favored over Turkey in part because of the number of Greek Americans and the strategic location in Congress of legislators especially attuned to them—as well as because of the strategic location of Greece. The same is sometimes true for Israel and Jewish Americans.

Parties and Foreign Policy

Political parties do not usually play a major role in shaping foreign policy, for two reasons: First, many Americans would still prefer to keep foreign policy out of politics. Second, parties usually take less clear and candid stands on foreign policy than they do on domestic policy. All the party weaknesses discussed in Chapter 10 operate in full measure in foreign policy. Party platforms often obscure the issues instead of highlighting them and many members of Congress fail to follow even a very general party line.

Should parties be concerned with foreign policy? At the end of World War II, sentiment grew stronger for a bipartisan approach to foreign policy. An ambiguous term, *bipartisanship* seems to mean (1) collaboration between the executive and the congressional foreign policy leaders of both parties; (2) support of presidential foreign policies by both parties in Congress; and (3) downplaying of foreign policy issues in national elections and especially in presidential debates. In general, bipartisanship is an attempt to remove the issues of foreign policy from partisan politics.

Drawing by Ed Fisher; © 1980. The New Yorker Magazine, Inc.

Bipartisanship has appeal. In this era of chronic crisis, it seems to symbolize people standing shoulder to shoulder as they face an uncertain and potentially hostile world. It provides more continuity of policy, and it ensures that a wider variety of leaders and interests are consulted in policy making. Psychologically, it helps to satisfy the instinct of people to turn to one another for reassurance. Its motto—partisan politics stops at the water's edge—is comforting to the many Americans worried about disunity.

But the idea of bipartisanship sometimes comes under sharp attack. Some believe bipartisanship is merely a smokescreen for presidential domination in foreign policy. They suggest it obscures the fact that foreign policy is made by a relatively small, self-perpetuating elite of national security managers who are essentially nonpartisan *and* unelected. Other critics charge that it denies a basic tenet of democracy—the right of a people to choose between alternative lines of action. According to this argument, in a free society people should be allowed and even encouraged to differ. The need in a democracy is not to stifle differences or to ignore them. The need is to express the differences in a meaningful way, to find the will of the majority, to permit the government to act and the opposition to oppose.

Major divisions have also developed *within* the parties. Debates over our role in Vietnam, when they finally did take place, occurred primarily within the Democratic party, not between Democrats and Republicans.

Congress and Foreign Policy

It may seem strange to discuss our national legislative body as part of the attentive public rather than as part of the formal foreign policy establishment. But despite the importance of foreign policy, and despite the fact that Congress can block the president's policy and undermine the chief executive's decisions,

Congress as an institution seldom directly *makes* foreign policy. The power of Congress is mainly *consultative*, although increasingly the legislature has taken many initiatives in trade and in foreign economic and military assistance questions. As we discussed in Chapter 16, Congress has taken steps to curb presidential warmaking powers. It is also a link between the policy makers and the public. Like many of us, however, Congress wants a meaningful relationship—especially "meaningful consultation" with the president in matters of foreign relations.

Individual members of Congress are sometimes included within the circle of those who make the decisions. For example, the chairs of the Senate Committee on Foreign Relations have been involved at times, though usually their main role is helping to educate the public, or educating the president on what will or will not run into congressional opposition. When out of sympathy with the policies of the president, as was former Senator Fulbright regarding Vietnam, the chair may use the committee to focus attention on the differences.

During the 1930s and after World War II, the almost unanimous opinion of academics and the attentive public favored strengthening the hand of the president and limiting the role of Congress in the foreign policy area. It was generally thought that only the president had the knowledge, the political base, and the broad, global perspective from which to develop coherent foreign policies. Congress was thought to be too responsive to the parochial and uninformed attitudes of the public. When conservative leaders tried to alter constitutional arrangements in order to limit the president's power to make executive agreements and to implement treaties, they ran into solid opposition from the intellectual and academic elites. This sentiment was challenged in the 1970s, when there was so much opposition to the Vietnam policies of Presidents Johnson and Nixon that Congress, especially the Senate, became more assertive: The 1973 vote to cut off funds for bombing in Cambodia, the War Powers Resolution of 1973, and countless amendments restricting arms sales and economic and military aid in the late 1970s were signs of a growing restiveness over presidential supremacy. By the 1980s the public again yearned for strong presidential leadership; but it also wanted Congress and even public opinion to be consulted (see Tables 20–2 and 20–3).[8]

20–2 WHO SHAPES U.S. FOREIGN POLICY?	"How important a role do you think the following currently play in determining the foreign policy of the United States—a very important role, a somewhat important role, or hardly an important role at all?" Percent "Very Important"	
	PUBLIC 1982	LEADERS 1982
The President	70%	91%
Secretary of State	64	83
State Department	47	38
Congress	46	34
National Security Advisor	35	46
American Business	35	22
The Military	40	36
United Nations	29	2
The CIA	28	20
Public Opinion	23	15
Labor Unions	17	3

Source: John E. Rielly, ed., *American Public Opinion and U.S. Foreign Policy 1983* (Chicago Council on Foreign Relations, 1983), p. 33.

[8]See Thomas E. Cronin, "A Resurgent Congress and the Imperial Presidency," *Political Science Quarterly* (Summer 1980), pp. 209–38.

20–3
WHO SHOULD SHAPE U.S. FOREIGN POLICY?

"Do you feel the roles of the following should be more important than they are now, should be less important than they are now, or should be about as important as they are now?"

Percent "More Important"

	PUBLIC 1982	LEADERS 1982
The President	39%	17%
Secretary of State	33	22
State Department	34	34
Congress	44	34
National Security Advisor	31	13
American Business	23	22
The Military	26	3
United Nations	37	33
The CIA	16	9
Public Opinion	54	36
Labor Unions	17	14

Source: Ibid. p. 34

Can We Have a Democratic Foreign Policy?

A great paradox exists in conducting the foreign relations of a modern democracy. In the last century Tocqueville wrote that foreign relations "demand scarcely any of the qualities which are peculiar to a democracy; they require, on the contrary, the perfect use of all those in which it is deficient."[9] One leading scholar observed more directly that policy makers in our democracy "either . . . must sacrifice what they consider good policy upon the altar of public opinion, or they must by devious means gain support for policies whose true nature is concealed from the public."[10] Critics have charged our leaders with misleading the people, the experts with misleading our leaders, and ideologies with blinding all of us, especially in Vietnam.

Where shall we draw the line? How *do* our policy makers reconcile public rights with political realities? A democratic foreign policy is one in which policy makers are known and held accountable to the people. That is a tough test for any policy, but there are special liabilities in foreign policy: secrecy, the need to act with speed, a generally lower level of information among the general public, and of course the complexity of issues and options. Still, the American public wants to be consulted and informed—and ultimately it wants to be in charge.

In Vietnam our apparent policy was to stop communist expansion. Our policy makers guessed wrong in thinking gradual military pressure would deter the North. They miscalculated the character of the war as well as the commitment of those who opposed the Saigon government.[11] Finally, they tried to get out with some face-saving gestures. And because they recognized mistakes or believed the American people and Congress might not support them in what they thought necessary, they sought to conceal difficulties.

Perhaps our biggest disappointment was that our institutions did not make up for these failings or at least did not warn us of them sooner. Students of government must ask themselves: How can we organize our institutions and processes to prevent these human failings from exacting such a large toll again?

Vice-President George Bush wearing a Marine jacket and helmet listens to the commander of the U.S. Marines in Beirut, Lebanon in late 1983, near the devastated battalion landing team building where about 240 marines were instantly killed when a truck packed with explosives was detonated as it rammed into the building. In 1984 the U.S. withdrew all its troops from Lebanon. *UPI.*

[9]Alexis de Tocqueville, *Democracy in America*, Vol. I (Knopf, 1945), pp. 224–35.

[10]Hans Morgenthau, "The Conduct of American Foreign Policy," *Parliamentary Affairs* (Winter 1949), p. 147.

[11]For an excellent on-the-scene account of this miscalculation by a young Marine officer who fought there, see Philip Caputo, *A Rumor of War* (Holt, Rinehart and Winston, 1977). See also Leslie Gelb and Richard K. Betts, *The Irony of Vietnam: The System Worked* (Brookings Institution, 1979); and Harry G. Summers, Jr., *On Strategy: A Critical Analysis of the Vietnam War* (Presidio Press, 1983).

If one believes the American people were kept in the dark, then one ignores the fact that no group of citizens has ever had access to more information about a war than we had about Vietnam. We did not have all the information, but—because of a free press and independent judiciary—more was shown, written, and said about Vietnam than about any other war from the Revolution to Korea.

THE POLICY MACHINERY

It is the responsibility of those who formulate our foreign policies to determine the basic objectives vital to our national interests and to devise programs to achieve those objectives. To the best of their ability and resources, these people must decide how to use (or not use) the instruments available to them: bargaining or negotiation, persuasion, or propaganda, economic assistance or pressures, and the threat or actual use of armed force.

The responsibility for foreign policy was fixed in the Constitution at the national level. However, the powers over foreign relations are not divided cleanly or evenly. In England control over foreign relations had been given to the king and his ministers. The framers tried to redress the balance a bit. Many of the powers given to Congress by the Constitution reflect the decision to take them away from the executive branch; the framers wanted to make what had been a prerogative of the executive into a more shared relationship with the legislature. Congress was given the power to declare war, to appropriate funds, and to make rules for the armed forces. But the president was left as commander in chief of the armed forces and was expected to negotiate treaties and receive and send ambassadors—that is, to recognize or refuse to recognize other governments. The courts have the power to interpret treaties, but by and large they have ruled that our relations with other nations are matters for the executive to negotiate. Executive domination of foreign policy is a fact of the political life of all nations, including democratic ones. To appreciate this phenomenon, we will look at the people within the executive departments who make up the foreign policy establishment.

President Reagan with Secretary Shultz and former National Security Adviser William Clark. *Michael Evans, The White House.*

Presidential Decision Making and Foreign Policy

The president's chief foreign policy adviser, according to what presidents say and according to formal statutes, is supposed to be the secretary of state. In recent years, however, the secretary of state has had to compete with the president's national security adviser. Just how much influence the secretary has depends largely on the president's personal desires. Presidents Harding, Coolidge, Hoover, Eisenhower, and Ford turned over to their secretaries of state almost full responsibility for making important decisions. Other presidents—for example, Wilson, both Roosevelts, Kennedy, Nixon, Carter, and Reagan took a more active part themselves. Indeed, at times they were their own secretaries of state. Even so, important decisions on foreign policy are so numerous that both president and secretary of state play important roles.

Secretaries of state administer the Department of State and fill multiple roles. They receive many visits from foreign diplomats, attend international conferences, and usually head our delegation in the General Assembly of the United Nations. They also attempt to serve as the administration's chief coordinator of all governmental actions that affect our relations with foreign nations. Twice in this century secretaries of state have resigned because of policy differences with the presidents they served—William Jennings Bryan quit the Wilson administration, and Cyrus Vance resigned in mid-1980 over differences with Jimmy Carter. In 1982 Reagan requested that Secretary of State Alexander Haig resign, due to policy and style differences with the White House.

461

President Roosevelt at the Yalta Conference in 1945, with Winston Churchill (l) and Josef Stalin (r). *UPI.*

There was a time when *only* the secretary of state was called upon for advice in formulating and implementing foreign policies. Today, because of the interdependence of foreign, economic, and domestic policies, a president calls on an increasing number of civilian and economic advisers. The day-to-day conduct of foreign affairs is now the business of several major departments and agencies—State, Defense, Treasury, Agriculture, Commerce, Labor, Energy, the Central Intelligence Agency, and others. The need for immediate reaction and preparedness has transferred more responsibilities directly to the president—and to a great extent to the senior White House aides who assist in coordinating information and advice. White House staff members help identify issues likely to require immediate presidential attention, preside over an extensive information-gathering system, monitor the implementation of presidential decisions, and assess the results of decisions taken.[12] The quality of a president's advisory process is of paramount importance, but good organization does not necessarily ensure wise or successful policy.[13] Still, organizational and structural factors can influence the overall effectiveness of government policy making, especially in foreign affairs.[14]

In recent years the national security adviser to the president has become a key—and often the most important—adviser. John Kennedy had McGeorge Bundy, Richard Nixon had Henry Kissinger, Jimmy Carter had Zbigniew Brzezinski, and Ronald Reagan had Robert McFarlane as White House assistants for national security, and all of them became powerful—the more so the longer they held office. Presidents grow to rely on these White House aides because of the latter's proximity and because—or at least presidents believe—they owe their prime loyalties to the president, and not to any department or program.

John F. Kennedy with Walter Hallstein, then President of the European Economic Community, at the White House in 1963. *UPI.*

The nature of international communications now makes it possible for presidents and their national security advisers to communicate directly with foreign ministers and heads of state all around the globe. No longer do they have to conduct diplomacy through the Foreign Service or be dependent on overseas ambassadors. This reality has transformed the way in which foreign policy is conducted and has undercut and sometimes even threatened a prime role and mission of the State Department. It is plain that several of our recent secretaries of state have been annoyed with this development, and in turn these developments regularly cause strain between the White House and the State Department and between presidents and their secretaries of state.

The President's Foreign Policy Staff

Secretaries, agency chiefs, and their senior subordinates are chosen by the president and are expected to support and carry out the latter's decisions. Yet at the same time they retain a measure of independence; they naturally tend to reflect and defend the views of the departments and agencies they head.[15] As a result, our presidents have found a need to appoint personal advisers whose loyalties lie solely with the chief executive. Since each president views responsibility in a personal way, the special adviser has played a loosely defined role.

Heading a staff of about ninety, the national security policy assistant is assigned advisory, coordination, and sometimes negotiation duties. Originally this assistant to the president merely kept the president informed of important

President Nixon meeting with Chinese Communist Party Chairman Mao Tse-tung, February 21, 1972. *UPI.*

[12]See the useful analysis in Alexander L. George, *Presidential Decisionmaking in Foreign Policy: The Effective Use of Information and Advice* (Westview Press, 1980).

[13]*Report of the Commission on the Organization of the Government for the Conduct of Foreign Policy* (U.S. Government Printing Office, 1975). See also Kissinger, *The White House Years.*

[14]See Kissinger, *The White House Years*; and the equally self-flattering Zbigniew Brzezinski, *Power and Principle: Memoirs of the National Security Adviser,1977–1981* (Farrar, Straus & Giroux, 1983).

[15]See Morton Halperin, *Bureaucratic Politics and Foreign Policy* (Brookings Institution, 1974).

developments within the government and around the world. President Nixon gave Henry Kissinger much more responsibility while he served in this post; he indeed, served as a kind of deputy president for foreign affairs. More often, however, the national security aide serves as a top staff person helping to keep the president constantly briefed and assisting in frequent communications with the secretaries of state and defense, the CIA director, and others.

Coordinating the Foreign Policy Establishment—the NSC

With so many officials and agencies involved in foreign policy, the problem of coordination is immense. The key coordinating agency for the president is the National Security Council (NSC). Created by Congress in 1947 to help the president integrate foreign, military, and economic policies that affect national security, the council consists of the vice-president, secretary of state, secretary of defense, and such other officers as the president shall appoint. The chair of the Joint Chiefs of Staff usually attends meetings of the council, as does the CIA director (on organizational charts the CIA is an agency of the National Security Council). The assistant to the president for national security affairs serves as the executive secretary for the council.

The history of the National Security Council suggests that it has been built more around people than around organizational principles. Each president has shaped its structure and adapted its staff procedures to suit personal preferences. The NSC has been less important for the subjects it has treated than as an arena where options are lined up, opinions expressed, and predictions made. Under different administrations since 1947, and often within the same administration, the NSC has been the center for foreign policy deliberations, or relegated to the wings, or tolerated as an "educational" forum to which issues were brought after decisions had already been made.

Intelligence and the CIA

Policy makers must have some idea of the direction in which other nations are going to move in order to be able to assess and, if necessary, to counter those moves. In other words, they need high-level foreign policy intelligence. Therefore, those who gather and analyze material are among the most important assistants to the policy makers. They often become policy makers themselves.

What is the balance of government and rebel forces in El Salvador or Nicaragua? How many trained infantrymen are there in Czechoslovakia? What are the weapons and air strength of the North Korean military? Before policy makers can answer such questions, they have to know a great deal about other countries—their probable reactions to a particular policy, their strengths and weaknesses, and, if possible, their strategic plans and intentions. Moreover, the makers of foreign policy must be familiar with the geographical and physical structure of the nations of the world; with the people—their number, skills, age distribution; the status of their arts, technology, engineering, and sciences; and their political and social systems.

Although most of the information comes from open sources, the term *intelligence work* conjures up visions of spies and undercover agents. Secret intelligence occasionally does supply crucial data. Intelligence work involves three operations—reporting, research, and transmission. *Reporting* is based on the close and systematic observation of developments the world over; *research* is the attempt "to establish meaningful patterns out of what was observed in the past and attempts to get meaning out of what appears to be going on now,"[16] and *transmission* is getting the right information to the right people at the right time.

NATIONAL SECURITY COUNCIL

Origin: Established under President Truman in 1947.

Duties: To coordinate the policies of the Department of State, the Department of Defense, and the Central Intelligence Agency, assess national security needs, and make recommendations to the president.

Members: The president, vice-president, secretary of state, secretary of defense, director of the Central Intelligence Agency, chair of the Pentagon's Joint Chiefs of Staff, counselor to the president, White House chief of staff and deputy chief of staff, and the national security adviser.

Staff: About 90 persons, including 30 professionals with a variety of geographic and policy specialties.

[16]Sherman Kent, *Strategic Intelligence for American Policy* (Princeton University Press, 1949), esp. p. 4. On the limits of intelligence activities, see Richard K. Betts, "Analysis, War, and Decision: Why Intelligence Failures Are Inevitable," *World Politics* (October 1978).

Many agencies engage in intelligence work, among them the State Department's Bureau of Intelligence and Research, the Defense Intelligence Agency, the supersecret National Security Agency (which works on code breaking and electronic communications systems), the FBI, and the Central Intelligence Agency. These agencies form the United States Intelligence Board, which prepares intelligence surveys on most countries of the world.

The CIA was created in 1947 to coordinate the gathering and analysis of information that flows into the various parts of our government from all over the world. Yet organization alone cannot ensure that our policy makers will know all they need to know. As an expert on intelligence operations has pointed out:

> In both the Pearl Harbor and Cuban crises there was plenty of information. But in both cases, regardless of what the Monday morning quarterbacks have to say, the data was ambiguous and incomplete. There was never a single, definitive signal that said, "Get ready, get set, go!" but rather, a number of signals that, when put together, tended to crystallize suspicion. The true signals were always embedded in the noise or irrelevance of the false ones.[17]

Employing more than 15,000 persons, the CIA spends over a billion dollars annually. The CIA director, as head of our foreign intelligence community, oversees research, military intelligence operations, spy satellites, and U-2 and SR-71 exercises that may cost several billion dollars annually. Critics charge, with reason, that CIA operations amount to a secret foreign policy insulated from public control and public scrutiny. In a few nations the local CIA station chief has more staff, more agents, a larger budget, and more influence than the U.S. ambassador.

Since its creation in 1947, the CIA has left a trail of covert activities and deposed governments, such as those in Iran (1953) and Guatemala. The ill-fated 1961 Bay of Pigs invasion of Cuba was CIA directed. Later the CIA organized and trained anticommunist forces in Laos, and contributed considerable support to the anti-Allende forces in Chile. Because of its past record and because it must act when our government cannot officially intervene in another nation's affairs, there has been a growing tendency to credit (or blame) the CIA for all coups, purges, and revolts, whether or not it was actually involved.

In 1967 several CIA "front groups" were discovered supporting a variety of research and political action programs, both domestic and foreign. In the mid-1970s it was revealed that the CIA had kept illegal files on 10,000 domestic dissidents within the U.S. In the 1980s the CIA played an important role in U.S. involvement in Central American nations. Some observers think these activities represent an "integral part of our diplomacy and preparedness." Others have denounced them as "jeopardizing the very values we are resolved to defend."[18]

The CIA's political leverage, its information, its secrecy, its speed in communication, its ability to act, and its enormous size make it a potent force. Nevertheless, Congress has now resolved that this power will be used only by publicly accountable decision makers, and will not itself become a source of politically unaccountable decision making. There are now committees in both the Senate and the House whose primary purpose is to hold the CIA accountable to Congress, although it is important to remember that earlier versions of these committees seldom did their job well.

Former CIA Director Admiral Stansifield Turner. *U.S. Central Intelligence Agency.*

CIA Director William J. Casey. *U.S. Central Intelligence Agency.*

[17]Roberta Wohlstetter, *Cuba and Pearl Harbor: Hindsight and Foresight* (Rand, 1965), p. 36.

[18]Christopher Felix, "Secret Operations Are an Integral Part of Our Diplomacy," and J. William Fulbright, "We Must Not Fight Fire with Fire," in Young Hum Kim (ed.), *The Central Intelligence Agency: Problems of Secrecy in a Democracy* (Heath, 1968), pp. 36–46, 96–108. See also T. M. Franck and E. Weisband (eds.), *Secrecy and Foreign Policy* (Oxford University Press, 1974); and Thomas Powers, *The Man Who Kept the Secrets* (Knopf, 1979).

The Role of the State Department

The U.S. Department of State has been variously called "a fudge factory," a "machine that fails," and "a bowl of jelly." Yet it is also the central agency in the day-to-day management of foreign affairs. This executive department has six duties:

1. To negotiate with other nations and international organizations
2. To protect American citizens and interests abroad
3. To promote American commercial interests and enterprises
4. To collect and interpret intelligence
5. To represent an American "presence" abroad
6. To promote peace and human rights

As the diplomatic arm of a superpower, the State Department has responded to our new global concerns with continuous reorganization. Some critics insist, however, that the more it changes, the more it stays the same.[19] Among the cabinet departments, State's annual budget is the lowest—less than 2 percent of that of the Department of Defense. Considering the State Department's role and prestige, its staff of 23,000 worldwide is small, especially when compared with the nearly 3 million civilian and military officers in the Department of Defense.

But even though the State Department is relatively small, critics allege it is oversized. According to one former State Department employee: "There are too many people chasing too few jobs in a system where there is no job tenure. The result is massive insecurity and an attempt to define even the most pathetic job as earthshakingly important as well as finding meaningful work for high level people where none really exists."

Secretary of State George P. Shultz, appointed by President Reagan in mid-1982. A noted economist, he had previously served President Nixion as Secretary of Labor and later as Secretary of the Treasury.

The Role of the Foreign Service

The American Foreign Service is the eyes and ears of the United States in other countries. Although part of the State Department, the service represents the entire government and performs jobs for many other agencies. Its main duties are to carry out foreign policy as expressed in the directives of the secretary of state, gather data for American policy makers, protect Americans and American interests in foreign countries, and cultivate friendly relations with host governments and foreign peoples.

The Foreign Service is composed of Foreign Service officers, Foreign Service reserve officers, and Foreign Service staff officers. At the core of the service are the Foreign Service officers, comparable to the officers of the regular army in the military services. They are a select, specially trained body who are expected to take an assignment any place in the world on short notice. There are approximately 3500 such officers; in recent years less than 100 junior officers won appointment.[20]

The Foreign Service is one of the most prestigious and most criticized career services of the national government. Back in the 1950s criticism seemed to outweigh respect, and morale suffered accordingly. In loyalty-security hearings officers were asked to justify remarks sometimes taken out of context from confidential reports made years before to superiors. Critics accused the service of being infiltrated by communist sympathizers; others charged that it was dominated by a high-society elite still under the impression that diplomacy was the near monopoly of "gentlemen." The charges about communist infiltration were obviously overdrawn.

[19]See John Franklin Campbell, *The Foreign Affairs Fudge Factory* (Basic Books, 1971); and Graham Allison and Peter Szanton, *Remaking Foreign Policy* (Basic Books, 1976).

[20]See the assessment by James Fallows, "The Foreign Service as Mirror of America," *Washington Monthly* (April 1973), pp. 5–14. See also *Report of the Commission on the Organization of the Conduct of Foreign Policy*, chap. 12.

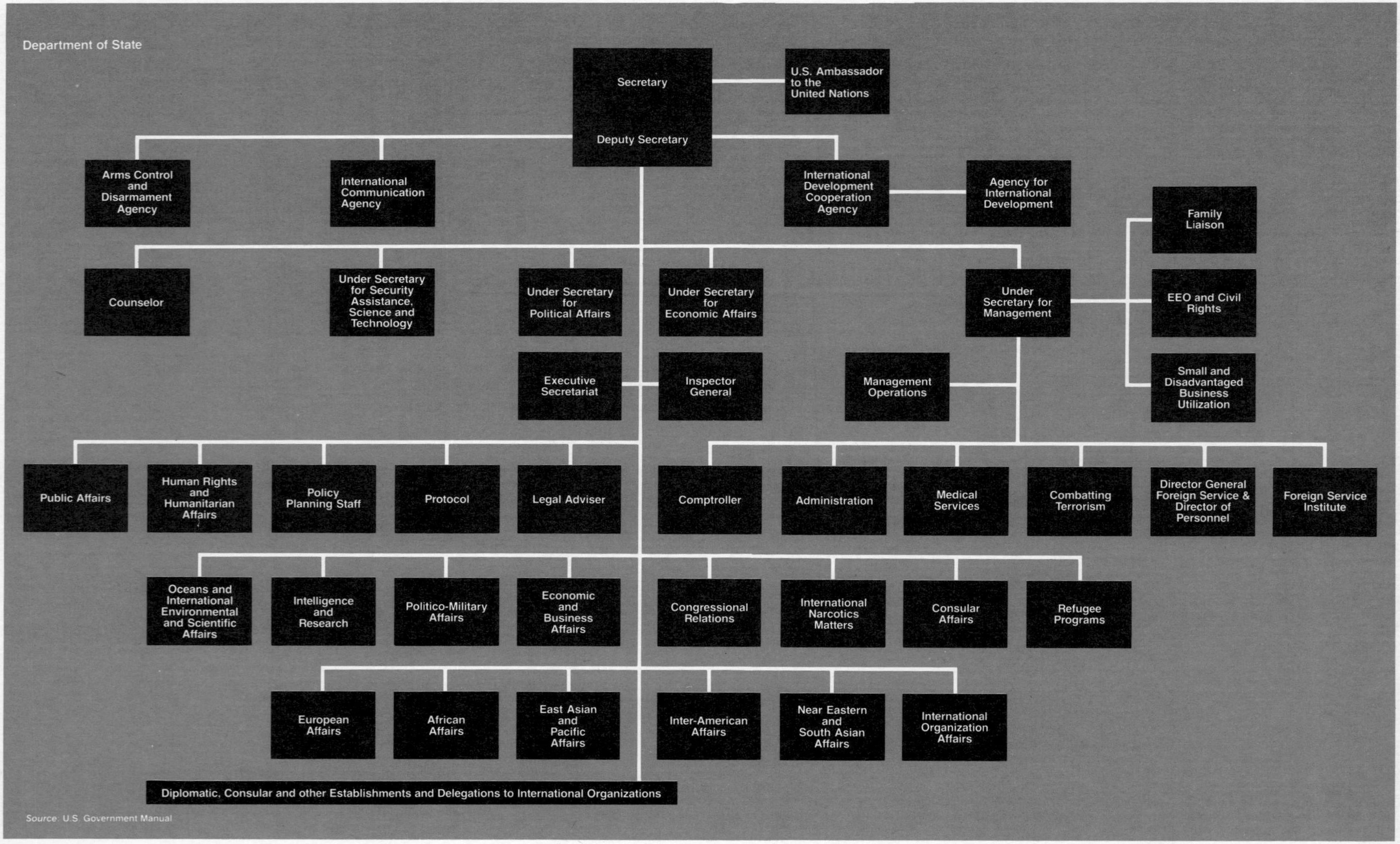

Department of State

Secretary

Deputy Secretary

U.S. Ambassador to the United Nations

Agency for International Development

International Development Cooperation Agency

Arms Control and Disarmament Agency

International Communication Agency

Counselor

Under Secretary for Security Assistance, Science and Technology

Under Secretary for Political Affairs

Under Secretary for Economic Affairs

Under Secretary for Management

Family Liaison

EEO and Civil Rights

Small and Disadvantaged Business Utilization

Inspector General

Executive Secretariat

Management Operations

Legal Adviser

Protocol

Policy Planning Staff

Human Rights and Humanitarian Affairs

Public Affairs

Combatting Terrorism

Director General Foreign Service & Director of Personnel

Foreign Service Institute

Medical Services

Refugee Programs

Administration

Comptroller

Congressional Relations

International Narcotics Matters

Consular Affairs

Economic and Business Affairs

Politico-Military Affairs

Intelligence and Research

Oceans and International Environmental and Scientific Affairs

European Affairs

African Affairs

East Asian and Pacific Affairs

Inter-American Affairs

Near Eastern and South Asian Affairs

International Organization Affairs

Diplomatic, Consular and other Establishments and Delegations to International Organizations

Drawing by Engleman, Federal Times, August 16, 1976.

In more recent years criticism of the Foreign Service has come as much from within as from outside. Most of the criticism claims the Foreign Service (1) stifles creativity; (2) attracts officers who are, or at least become, concerned more about *being* or *becoming* somebody than *doing* something; and (3) requires new recruits to wait fifteen to twenty years before being considered for positions of responsibility. The problems are recognized in Washington, and the task of improving the service continues. More women and minorities have been recruited in recent years. Certain managerial innovations have been tried. But the career service features of the Foreign Service—entry at the bottom, rank in the person rather than in the position, resistance to lateral entry, advancement through grades as determined by senior officers' evaluations, and the tendency toward self-government—make it resistant to change.[21]

Criticism of the Foreign Service because of social-class homogeneity is probably overstated. Some of the best congressional staff in recent years are former Foreign Service officers. More likely it is the structural characteristics of the State Department that prevent independent reporting and creativity. There is an old saying in the Foreign Service that there are old Foreign Service officers and there are bold Foreign Service officers, but there are no old bold Foreign Service officers. So we can expect the Foreign Service exposés to keep coming. Its problems of overstaffing, empty jobs, and tedious apprenticeships are in fact common in most bureaucracies.

International Organizations and the UN

The United States belongs to most important world organizations, and its representatives attend most major international conferences. These organizations and conferences are instruments of American diplomacy. In addition to the United Nations and its related agencies, the United States is a member of more than two hundred international organizations of various types. For example, in its own hemisphere the United States is a member of the Organization of American States (OAS), a regional agency of twenty-four Western Hemisphere republics. We also belong to the sixteen nation North Atlantic Treaty Organization (NATO).

The United Nations was set up by the victorious superpowers immediately after World War II in an effort to shape the postwar world and to promote peace. But when the superpowers, which of course included both the U.S. and the USSR, ceased to be friendly, the UN was doomed to political impotence. The liberal or idealist school of international relations believed the United Nations was destined to bring nations together, to maintain international peace and security, to achieve international cooperation in solving world problems, and to promote and encourage respect for human rights.

The United Nations' failure to solve each and every dispute among nations and its inability to end global problems such as famines or the arms race have caused some Americans to become disillusioned with it. The organization suffers also from "creeping irrelevance" and a rigid international civil service that makes our Foreign Service look healthy. We witness the "defeat of an ideal," says one critic—the members pay lip service to the organization's original goals while at the same time pursuing their short-term interests at its expense. Containing three times as many nations in the mid-1980s as belonged when it was founded in 1945, the UN is characterized by timidity, bureaucracy, and "geographical" appeasement. According to one former ambassador to the UN: "The United Nations has become an assembly line of mass produc-

NATO MEMBER NATIONS

Belgium
Canada
Denmark
France*
Great Britain
Greece
Iceland
Italy
Luxembourg
The Netherlands
Norway
Portugal
Spain
Turkey
United States
West Germany

*France withdrew from NATO's military committee in the mid-1960s. But otherwise France is an active member of NATO.

[21]For a critical exposé see Bill Keller and Ann Cooper, "Make-work in Morocco: Diplomatic Featherbedding," *The Washington Monthly* (November 1979), pp. 45–56.

Presidents Kennedy, Johnson, and Nixon addressing the UN during their terms in office. *UN, UPI, UN.*

tion of resolutions which have little relevance to the substance of the problem under discussion."[22]

The United Nations, like every other agency of international politics, is dominated by the fact the world is divided into separate nations acting, most of the time, in their own self-interest. The United States, like most nations, cites the UN Charter when it suits its short-term interest and ignores it when it does not. The U.S. has usually found that in important matters it is easier to deal with involved nations directly. The United Nations, with 159 member nations, can only do *what the member nations want it to do*. Rarely can it move fast. And rarely can it achieve solutions if there is no broad consensus.

Certain conservatives have long opposed our involvement in the UN, fearing we risk being trapped or outvoted by the communists or by Third World nations. Some of our disillusionment has come about because the UN is so large and unwieldy and because it seems to accomplish so little. Some critics ask too: Does it make sense to give every UN member nation a vote in the General Assembly regardless of its size, population, and contribution to the UN budget? There are many who feel the UN fails because we have had so little faith in it. They counsel us to expect more: *Try to make it work*. Meanwhile, the UN remains a sometimes helpful forum for working out joint programs on the law of the sea, economic development, world population problems, global energy supplies, and the protection of the international environment. Moreover, its peacekeeping record in international conflict spots remains helpful; about 15,000 troops have been serving in the Middle East, Cyprus, and elsewhere. On balance, while almost a majority of Americans say the UN has done a poor job, about 80 percent of Americans say we should remain in the UN. Most Americans appear to believe we are better with it than without it.

President Ronald Reagan addresses the UN General Assembly during its debate on disarmament. Reagan denounced Soviet backing of violence around the globe and puts forth his arms reduction proposals. *UPI.*

SUMMARY

1. American foreign policy during the past fifty years or more has been greatly influenced, and at times completely shaped, by our relations with the Soviet Union. To understand our foreign policy, one must first understand the continuing competition between these two major powers. The past fifteen years have witnessed the rise of other economic and nuclear powers, thus complicating even more the challenge of formulating wise and effective foreign policies.

2. Foreign policy is not made according to any set formula, but represents various traditions, organized interests, and constitutional processes. Our democracy has given the primary responsibility for making foreign policy to the chief executive. But presidents in turn are dependent on accidents of history, on advisers, and in the long run, on the American people. When there are no obvious solutions to international problems, our decision makers must predict,

[22]Personal interview. See also Shirley Hazzard, *Defeat of an Ideal: A Study of the Self-Destruction of the United Nations* (Little, Brown, 1973); and Mahdi Elmandjra, *The United Nations System: An Analysis* (Faber and Faber, 1973). For other views see the diary by William F. Buckley, Jr., *United Nations Journal* (Putnam, 1974); and the personal memoir by Daniel P. Moynihan with Suzanne Weaver, *A Dangerous Place* (Little, Brown, 1978).

act, and wait—sometimes successfully, but sometimes with unforeseeable and catastrophic consequences.

3. Presidents can act swiftly and decisively. They are often in a good position to see the nation's long-run interests above the tugging of bureaucratic and special interests. They must face the people in elections, but not so often that they must follow public opinion instead of leading it. Yet the desired presidential accountability between elections can only be achieved if the people are willing to inform themselves and demand answers, explanations, and honest reporting from their leaders.

4. War is merely an extension of diplomacy. Perhaps future generations will be able to eliminate this alternative entirely, but in our own time our leaders must deal with realities, not dreams; with the world as they see it, not as they wish it. Greater restraints upon decision makers might undermine our security, and fewer restraints might endanger our freedom. In the end, we have to be aware of the limits of our power to assist nations threatened by totalitarian systems and of the need to reappraise the balance of power among our institutions.

FURTHER READING

STEPHEN E. AMBROSE. *Rise to Globalism: American Foreign Policy, 1938–1980*, 2nd ed. (Penguin, 1980).

CECEL V. CRABB, Jr. *The Doctrines of American Foreign Policy* (Louisiana State University Press, 1982).

GORDON A. CRAIG and ALEXANDER L. GEORGE. *Force and Statecraft: Diplomatic Problems of Our Time* (Oxford University Press, 1983).

DARRELL DELAMAIDE, *Debt Shock: The Full Story of the World Credit Crisis* (Doubleday & Co., 1984).

I. M. DESTLER. *Making Foreign Economic Policy* (Brookings Institution, 1980).

ALEXANDER L. GEORGE. *Presidential Decision Making in Foreign Policy: The Effective Use of Information and Advice* (Westview, 1980).

JAMES A. NATHAN and JAMES K. OLIVER. *Foreign Policymaking and the American Political System* (Little, Brown, 1983).

AARON WILDAVSKY (ed.). *Beyond Containment: Alternative American Policies Toward the Soviet Union* (Institute for Contemporary Studies, 1983).

DANIEL YERGEN. *Shattered Peace: The Origins of the Cold War and the National Security State* (Houghton Mifflin, 1978).

Foreign Affairs and *Foreign Policy*, two excellent journals published quarterly.

PROVIDING FOR THE COMMON DEFENSE

21

The first concern of American presidents is the security and survival of the nation. Presidents and public alike hope, work, and pray for a world in which weapons and military forces may no longer be necessary, but our policy-makers must deal with the world as it is. Our security rests on several factors: an overall military balance with the Soviet Union, as well as our economic vitality, energy supplies, and our heritage of human rights and justice as a foundation for our national and international posture.

Both president and Congress are responsible for the common defense, and both have constitutional authority to discharge that responsibility. Congress appropriates the money and determines the size, structure, and organization of the fighting forces; the president is the commander in chief of these forces and initially determines how military power will be deployed. In defense as in foreign policy emergencies the president is often the key decision maker.

Heated debates continue over what constitutes an adequate national defense. Liberals usually want to reduce defense spending to make added funds available for social programs. Conservatives usually want to increase defense spending, either to ensure parity with the Soviets in weapon production, or to ensure adequate supplies of vital raw materials we have needed to keep strategic water and trade routes secure. Libertarians favor major cuts in military spending and sharply reduced commitments abroad, saying if we want others to stay out of our affairs, we should stay out of the internal affairs of other nations. The average American, often acting out of patriotic instinct, wants the country to remain as strong as it can. But we are rather confused about exactly what our national security goals are and how much money, personnel, and weapons are needed to provide for an effective national defense system.

The basic issues in defense policy are the following: (1) How much should we spend on defense? (2) How should we spend it? (3) What are the dynamics of the arms race and the possibilities for arms control?

THE NATION'S DEFENSE GOALS

The overriding mission of America's defense program is to defend the United States against possible nuclear blackmail as well as invasion or bombardment from the sea or the air. We are also committed to defend Western Europe, Japan, and several other nations and to protect our vital interests, such as our oil supplies. Americans expect the president, Congress, and the military to do everything in their power to prevent war and to protect the U.S. and its allies from attack.

Our military and defense policies are intertwined with foreign policy goals. At present they include the following:

1. To preserve the United States as an independent nation
2. To safeguard our institutions and values
3. To maintain our ability to deter aggression

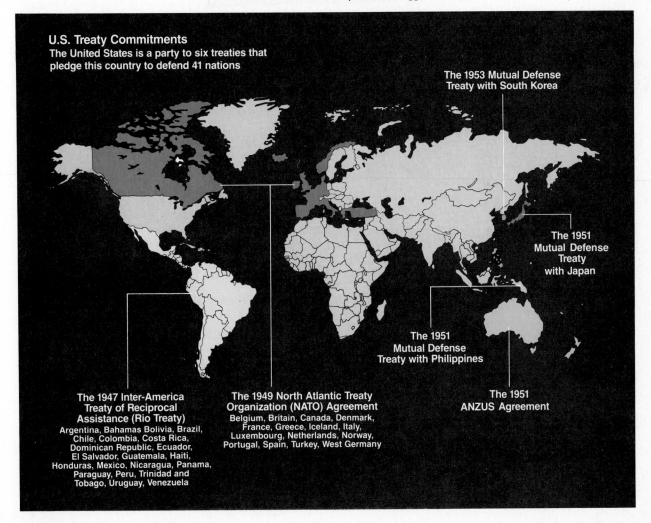

U.S. Treaty Commitments
The United States is a party to six treaties that pledge this country to defend 41 nations

The 1953 Mutual Defense Treaty with South Korea

The 1951 Mutual Defense Treaty with Japan

The 1951 Mutual Defense Treaty with Philippines

The 1947 Inter-America Treaty of Reciprocal Assistance (Rio Treaty)
Argentina, Bahamas Bolivia, Brazil, Chile, Colombia, Costa Rica, Dominican Republic, Ecuador, El Salvador, Guatemala, Haiti, Honduras, Mexico, Nicaragua, Panama, Paraguay, Peru, Trinidad and Tobago, Uruguay, Venezuela

The 1949 North Atlantic Treaty Organization (NATO) Agreement
Belgium, Britain, Canada, Denmark, France, Greece, Iceland, Italy, Luxembourg, Netherlands, Norway, Portugal, Spain, Turkey, West Germany

The 1951 ANZUS Agreement

U.S. Military advisor in El Salvador. *UPI.*

4. To reduce the perils of nuclear war
5. To protect as best we can our supplies of energy, strategic resources, and food
6. To help resolve regional conflicts that threaten global peace
7. To revitalize our bond with allies who share our traditions, values, and interests
8. To build more rational relationships with potential adversaries

The U.S. has been involved in military intervention of one kind or another about 150 times, although only about 6 of these occasions have been declared wars. American leaders often use military forces for ends other than war. Since World War II alone we have alerted or deployed military units on more than two hundred occasions to achieve specific goals that seemed important enough to warrant some show of military power.[1]

Controlling the Defense Budget

During the peak of the Vietnam war effort, almost half the American people thought we were spending too much on defense. However, by 1980 there was a marked increase in those who thought we were spending too little (Table 21–1). After Vietnam expenditures for health, welfare, and education went way up. Those for national defense—at least as a proportion of the budget—went down. During the Reagan presidency these trends were reversed, and once again many people began to think we were spending too much on defense.

21–1
PUBLIC OPINION AND DEFENSE SPENDING: *QUESTION:* IS THE U.S. SPENDING TOO MUCH, ABOUT RIGHT, OR TOO LITTLE ON DEFENSE?

	DEFENSE SPENDING			
Year	Too Much	About Right	Too Little	No Opinion
1983	45%	31%	14%	10%
1980	14	24	49	13
1976	36	32	22	10
1974	44	32	12	12
1971	49	31	11	9
1969	52	31	8	9

SOURCE: Gallup Poll Index.

President Reagan dramatically increased defense spending even as he cut the federal budget in some other areas. But soon public concern over waste and purchasing practices in the defense department sharply increased. Critics of the Reagan approach pointed out that our investments must be carefully targeted to those areas most vital to national security—especially in strengthening our conventional forces, improving troop readiness, upgrading the recruiting and training of military personnel.

Critics of the Reagan increases doubted the wisdom of funding every new system on the Pentagon's shopping list—especially the "star wars" space-defense program. They noted that historically the most important factor in winning wars has been people; strategy and tactics come second, and expensive equipment often comes third.

Constant Pressures to Increase Defense Spending

One of the chief reasons presidents and Congress have such difficulty controlling the defense budget is that so many people oppose any bold program of military base closings or the consolidation of military operations. Base closings anger politicians, as well as local economic interests; and the Defense Depart-

[1]Barry M. Blechman and Stephen S. Kaplan, *Force without War: U.S. Armed Forces as a Political Instrument* (Brookings Institution, 1978).

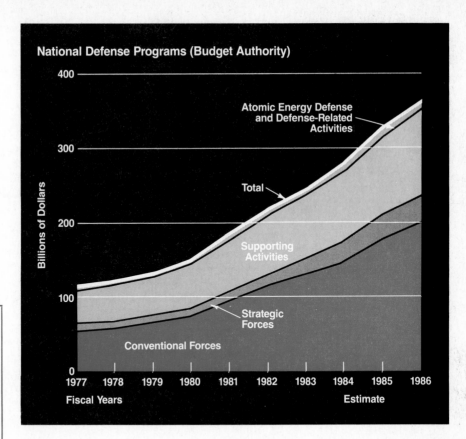

National Defense Programs (Budget Authority)

Billions of Dollars

Atomic Energy Defense and Defense-Related Activities

Total

Supporting Activities

Strategic Forces

Conventional Forces

Fiscal Years — Estimate

1977 1978 1979 1980 1981 1982 1983 1984 1985 1986

"Let's roll up our sleeves and get to it, gentlemen—we have to spend billions and billions and billions!" *Drawings by B. Tobey; © 1981. The New Yorker Magazine, Inc.*

PENTAGON SPENDING

News accounts in 1984 of the Pentagon being charged more than $400 for ordinary $16 carpenter's hammers, $9000 for a 15¢ wrench, and more than $1000 for a plastic cap on the leg of a stool used by navigators in B-52 bombers received widespread publicity. Even some Pentagon officials agreed the procurement process lacked proper safeguards and accountability. The response of one taxpayer was to send ten hammers to the Internal Revenue Service for his $4000 tax liability for 1983. Needless to say, the IRS politely rejected this in-kind exchange.

ment must hold extensive public hearings before it can actually close a base. Further, weapons are a major American industry—and the industry and the members of Congress from their areas work hard to promote their products. Representatives from shipyard districts push for more submarines; those from Texas or Seattle push for new planes. Then too, the logrolling arrangements that operate in other porkbarrel areas work here as well: You fatten my district, and I'll fatten yours. Even the fiercest antiwar doves in Congress often shout the loudest when a base closing or contract termination is suggested for their district or state.

Government is the sole purchaser or consumer of most military hardware. And wherever competition is limited to either one or a few consumers, prices tend to rise because of the absence of competition. The high technological levels of defense systems create high research and development costs that often lead to high initial sunk costs.

How much defense spending is enough? A nation can never tell if defense expenditures are adequate until they aren't—and then it is too late. Hence, when in doubt, the tendency is to spend more. Further, some of the best technical minds in the nation have been enticed into defense research and development work, and good minds can almost always come up with better, more expensive systems. The contracting structure of defense projects further escalates costs. It used to be that defense contracts operated on a cost-plus basis: A percentage of costs was designated as profits, providing a direct incentive to increase costs. Today (sometimes, but not always) contracts involve all costs plus a fixed fee, providing little incentive to hold defense costs down.

The Department of Defense will spend well over $300 billion a year in the late 1980s. More than half the people employed by the national government work in the Department of Defense. Nearly three-quarters of federal purchases of goods and services originate in the defense budget. Moreover, there are about 4000 defense installations scattered across the country. Contracts in excess of $85 billion result in defense-related non-governmental civilian employment of over 2 million. There are more than 1.5 million retired defense department personnel drawing pensions and other fringe benefits. Clearly, the Defense Department's size and impact on our society raise questions about how it can be controlled.

According to foreign policy expert George Kennan, this vast flow of "military spending comes to constitute a vested interest on the part of all those who participate in it and benefit from it." The number of people who have a stake in the continuation of high defense spending is enormous, and their political punch is usually very powerful. "This includes not just the industrialists who get the money and the Pentagon purchasers who get the hardware and services," says Kennan, "but also all those who benefit from the arrangement in other ways: not only the uniformed personnel of the armed services but those who serve the Pentagon directly as civilian workers, and beyond them the many more who, as workers in defense plants or in other capacities, share in the spin-off from these vast expenditures."[2]

The Military-Industrial Complex

By its nature the defense industry is different from most other large industries in America. National defense is what economists call a "public good"—there is no way to exclude citizens from "consuming" national defense, whether they wish to pay for it or not. Thus, the government must provide for defense by taxing citizens. If it did not, most people would not pay, since they would figure they would receive the benefits anyway. Because the government is really the sole purchaser of defense, the defense industries—aerospace, electronics, and shipbuilding—rely heavily on government contracts for a large part of their

The USS New Jersey Surface Action Group transits in the vicinity of Pearl Harbor enroute to Central America. *UPI.*

TOP DEFENSE CONTRACTORS—1982

Company	Value of Contracts
Gen. Dyn. . . .	$5,891,101,000
McD. Doug.	$5,630,104,000
U. Tech.	$4,208,293,000
Gen. Elec. . . .	$3,654,097,000
Lockheed	$3,498,550,000
Boeing.	$3,238,796,000
Hughes Air. . .	$3,140,735,000
Rock. Intl. . . .	$2,690,518,000
Raytheon	$2,262,290,000
Mart. Mar. . . .	$2,008,354,000
Grumman	$1,900,489,000
Northrop.	$1,598,194,000
West. El.	$1,491,700,000
FMC	$1,370,675,000
Litton Ind.	$1,316,603,000

Reprinted from *U.S. News & World Report.* Copyright, 1983, U.S. News & World Report, Inc.

[2]George F. Kennan, *The Cloud of Danger* (Atlantic-Little Brown, 1977), p. 13. See also Adam Yarmolinsky, *The Military Establishment* (Harper & Row, 1971).

"This is the multiple appropriation retention vehicle. It's to hold extra congressional funds till we figure out how to spend them." *From Herblock on All Fronts. New American Library, 1980.*

business. In turn, the localities in which these industries are located, especially in the Sunbelt areas (Charleston, San Antonio, Colorado Springs, and San Diego, for example), rely heavily on defense spending for economic growth and stability. The defense industry is intertwined in the American economy; yet it responds to a different set of demands than other industries, and remains largely independent of private consumption and investment trends.

More than 30 cents of every dollar spent by the military is used to purchase, construct, or develop weapons: At least $95 billion in recent defense budgets went for procurement of tanks, planes, and other weapons. There has been at least a 7 percent increase in defense budgets for each of the past few years, and the Joint Chiefs of Staff have urged even greater increases: They estimate that the USSR's defense program absorbs at least 12 percent of that nation's total output of goods and services.

Critics sometimes charge that the military conspires with defense contractors and other strategic elites to maintain a vast network of bases and fleets around the world. They contend that the military-industrial establishment has a life of its own, is too big to be managed or controlled, spends too large a share of our national wealth, and is dedicated to exaggerating the "Soviet menace."

President Eisenhower once asked Nikita Khrushchev how he decided the question of funds for military expenses in his nation. Eisenhower began by saying:

> Perhaps first I should tell you how it is with us. It's like this: My military leaders say, "Mr. President, we need such and such a sum for such and such a program." I say, "Sorry, we don't have the funds." They say, "We have reliable information that the Soviet Union has already allocated funds for their own such program." So I give in. That's how they wring the money out of me. Now tell me, how is it with you?

Khrushchev responded:

> It's just the same. They say, "Comrade Khrushchev, look at this! The Americans are developing such and such a system." I tell them there's no money. So we discuss it some more, and I end up giving them the money they asked for.[3]

Military leaders and many others generally deny the existence of a military-industrial establishment. They point to the reduced size of the military and note that since its wartime peak in 1968, the American defense budget has decreased in real dollars by more than one-third. The number of military personnel has dropped from 3.5 million to about 2.1 million. There are fewer people in uniform now, they add, than at any time since 1950, and fewer U.S. troops abroad than at any time since 1940. Further, our active fleet has dropped by more than half.

While we hear much about the military-industrial complex, it is not all-powerful, and it is not the only elite that operates in our democracy. There is also a scientific-intellectual elite, an agribusiness elite, a public employees elite, and a trade union elite. In short, our government is built on interest group-public agency-immediate benefit coalitions, all seeking to define the public interest.

In determining how much defense spending is enough, most U.S. leaders would agree that in addition to the general objectives outlined above, our major defense programs must ensure we have the military strength (1) to maintain a strategic balance with the USSR, (2) to maintain naval forces adequate to deter attacks and keep essential sea lanes open, and (3) to maintain conventional combat forces that enable us to defend against likely threats to our security and that of our allies, especially in Europe.

[3]Quoted by Clayton Fritchey, June 16, 1973, syndicated column, cited in Robert Sherrill, *Why They Call It Politics,* 2nd ed. (Harcourt Brace Jovanovich, 1974), pp. 58–59.

SELECTIVE SERVICE SYSTEM
Registration Form
READ PRIVACY ACT STATEMENT ON REVERSE
PLEASE PRINT CLEARLY

–DO NOT WRITE IN THE ABOVE SPACE–

1 DATE OF BIRTH

Name of Month   Day   Year

2 SEX
☐ MALE
☐ FEMALE

3 SOCIAL SECURITY NUMBER

4 PRINT FULL NAME

Last   First   Middle

5 CURRENT MAILING ADDRESS

Number and Street   City   State or Foreign Country   Zip Code

6 PERMANENT RESIDENCE

Number and Street   City   State or Foreign Country   Zip Code

7 CURRENT PHONE NUMBER

Area Code   Number

8 ☐ Check here if we may give your name, address and telephone number to Armed Forces recruiters.

9 I AFFIRM THE FOREGOING STATEMENTS ARE TRUE

Today's Date   Signature of Registrant

Postal Date Stamp & Clerk Initials
☐ ID
☐ NO ID
☐ OTHER

SSS Form 1 (Feb 80)   ☐   (Previous Editions Will Not Be Used)   OMB Approval 194-R0002

WILL U.S. CONVENTIONAL FORCES BE STRONG ENOUGH TO FIGHT?

Much of the debate over defense spending revolves around the question of *people* versus *weapons*. And central to this question is the question of military personnel and their preparedness. We have to ask: If the country's army of volunteers has to go to war, could it fight and win, or would it be outnumbered and outfought?

The All Volunteer Force

The means of maintaining our military forces have been debated since the beginning of the Republic. As early as 1814 Daniel Webster asked his colleagues in Congress: "Where is it written in the Constitution . . . that you may take children from their parents, and parents from their children, and compel them to fight battles of any war in which the folly or the wickedness of government may engage it[self]?" The Constitution authorizes Congress to do what is "necessary and proper" in order to "raise and support armies," "to provide and maintain a navy," and "to provide for calling forth the militia." The problem is that America's role in the world has changed dramatically since 1789, as have our military needs. While our boundaries once defined our national interest, those interests now reach around the globe.

Military conscription, or draft, was first instituted in 1862, during the Civil War. It was next used during World War I, when Congress passed the Selective Service Act. This act called for a draft of males between the ages of twenty-one and thirty, although exemptions were allowed for certain public officials and for clergy. In both instances conscription ended when the conflicts

HOW TO COMPLETE THIS FORM

- Read the Privacy Act Statement.

- Print all entries except your signature clearly in ink.

- Do not sign or date the form until asked to do so.

- Complete Blocks 1 thru 8 and take your form to the clerk.

- Print your date of birth in Block 1. Use a three letter abbreviation for the month and numerals for the day and year (Example: OCT 29 1960).

- Check the correct box in Block 2.

- Print your Social Security Number in Block 3.

- Print your full legal name in Block 4 in the order listed.

- Print your current mailing address in Block 5.

- Print your permanent residence address in Block 6, include ZIP code. If it is the same as your current mailing address (Block 5), leave this block blank.

- Print your telephone number in Block 7.

- Check the box in Block 8 if we may furnish the listed information to Armed Forces Recruiters.

- When you have completed your form to this point, recheck it and take it to the clerk.

PRIVACY ACT STATEMENT

The Military Selective Service Act, Selective Service Regulations, and the President's Proclamation on Registration require that you provide the indicated information, including your Social Security Account Number.

The principal purpose of the required information is to establish your registration with the Selective Service System. This information may be furnished to the following agencies for the purposes stated:

Department of Defense—for exchange of information concerning registration, classification, enlistment, examination and induction of individuals, availability of Standby Reservists, and if Block 8 is checked, identification of prospects for recruiting.

Alternate service employers—for exchange of information with employers regarding a registrant who is a conscientious objector for the purpose of placement and supervision of performance of alternate service in lieu of induction into military service.

Department of Justice—for review and processing of suspected violations of the Military Selective Service Act, or for perjury, and for defense of a civil action arising from administrative processing under such Act.

Federal Bureau of Investigation—for location of an individual when suspected of violation of the Military Selective Service Act.

Immigration and Naturalization Service—to provide information for use in determining an individual's eligibility for re-entry into the United States.

Department of State—for determination of an alien's eligibility for possible entry into the United States and United States citizenship.

Office of Veterans' Reemployment Rights, United States Department of Labor—to assist veterans in need of information concerning reemployment rights.

General Public—Registrant's Name, Selective Service Number, Date of Birth and Classification, Military Selective Service Act Section 6, 50 U.S.C. App. 456.

Your failure to provide the required information may violate the Military Selective Service Act. Conviction of such violation may result in imprisonment for not more than five years or a fine of not more than $10,000 or both imprisonment and fine.

MILITARY PERSONNEL	
Army	780,000
Air Force	583,000
Navy	553,000
Marine Corps	192,000
Total	2,108,000

NONACTIVE DUTY RESERVES		
Army National Guard		407,600
Army Reserves		256,000
Naval Reserve		93,000
Air National Guard		100,700
Air Force Reserve		64,000
Marine Corps Reserve		40,500
	Total	963,800

Source: Department of Defense, 1984.

ended. The first peacetime draft began in 1940, with the Selective Service and Training Act. By the time of Pearl Harbor in late 1941, men between the ages of eighteen and thirty-five were eligible for the draft. When World War II ended, however, the draft continued, in various forms, for almost three decades. Soon after Vietnam, in 1973, the all-volunteer force (AVF) was established by Congress. This force is to provide for our peacetime military personnel needs, although a draft is to be reinstituted in time of war. Draft registration ended in 1975—to the great delight of most young men.

The United States is the first and only world power to maintain large-scale armed forces without some form of conscription.

Since its beginning, the all-volunteer force has been the center of controversy. Some experts contend the AVF has worked, that the quality and quantity of recruits are as good or better than under the draft, and that the social costs are much lower. Other experts say quantity and quality have dropped; that the force is more and more made up of minorities or the disadvantaged, and that the AVF would be largely unable to defend our vital interests abroad.

In the early 1980s, the military had problems attracting the desired number of recruits. All four services reported serious shortfalls; and active reserves were at only 80 percent strength. Further, experienced personnel, physicians, technicians, and even pilots were in short supply in certain areas of the military. In the mid-1980s the nation was running short of eighteen-year-olds: The World War II baby boom was over; potential recruits in proportion to the total population will in the late 1980s be fewer than ever.

Still, in 1984 the all-volunteer force was thriving: Total personnel in all services was over 2.1 million. Reserve enlistments were also up. Today minorities are overrepresented in the armed services, notably in the Army, where blacks comprise over 32 percent of the enlisted ranks. Women are underrepresented, although the proportion of women to men in the armed forces is growing.

The combat readiness of the AVF is the subject, quite rightly, of heated debate. Preparedness may be judged in part by the educational level of new recruits. By 1984 about 89 percent of all new enlisted troops graduated from high school, the highest percentage ever. Another barometer of overall troop quality, reenlistment, is also increasing. Both trends may in part be attributed to economic conditions, and may thus be short-lived. High unemployment makes military service more attractive as compared to civilian employment; and for many individuals it may be the only economically viable alternative. Without long-term improvements such as higher pay for all ranks and increased educational benefits, the general strength and quality of the AVF may be only temporary.

Perhaps the most serious concern about the all-volunteer force is whether or not it is prepared for military combat. If there were a conflict requiring call-up of reserves and conscription, would we be able to produce enough combat-ready forces in time? Although some observers contend that conventional forces are obsolete in any large-scale conflict, such as a Soviet invasion of Europe, most insist we need conventional forces as a deterrent. The danger lies in becoming too reliant on "massive retaliation" and missiles, so that we would be forced to respond with nuclear weapons. That is why Presidents Carter and Reagan both supported a draft registration system although not a draft.

I WANT YOU
FOR U.S. ARMY
NEAREST RECRUITING STATION

The Return of Draft Registration

The all-volunteer force was set up as a peacetime measure: If emergencies came, so would the draft. In early 1980, however, President Jimmy Carter won approval for the resumption of draft registration. Carter's original plan called for the registration of men and women born in 1960 and 1961. Thereafter individuals would be required to register within thirty days of their eighteenth birthday. However, Congress refused to appropriate funds for the registration of women. Later the Supreme Court ruled Congress could, if it wished, call for the registration of men and not of women.

Carter based his advocacy for registration on two grounds. First, in the wake of the Soviet invasion of Afghanistan, registration would send a message to Russia demonstrating our resolve in resisting Soviet aggression. Second, this new process would enable us to mobilize more quickly in wartime emergencies, shortening the time period between initiation of conscription and full mobilization by as many as ninety days.

Many Americans oppose the draft registration process, believing it will inevitably lead to a draft. A report by a former director of the Selective Service suggests that registration would save less than two weeks in the event of mobilization. One political figure who spoke out against Carter's draft registration effort said it "destroys the very values that our society is committed to defending"—namely our freedom.[4] That critic, Ronald Reagan, changed his mind once he got to the White House. In 1984 the Supreme Court upheld a law passed by Congress that makes male college students ineligible for federal scholarship aid if they have not registered for the draft.

The Case for Reviving the Draft

About 60 percent of Americans favored substituting the draft for the present combination of volunteer enlistments and draft registration according to public opinion polls in the early 1980s. Supporters of the draft generally include some conservatives and some members of the military establishment, among others.[5]

---

[4]Reagan, quoted in Stuart Taylor, Jr., "Draft Registration: Snags Emerge in Prosecutions," *The New York Times*, December 8, 1982, p. 10.

[5]But some liberals and progressives also favor the draft. See, for example, James Fallows, *National Defense* (Random House, 1981), Ch. 5.

Doonesbury by Gary Trudeau.

They claim the armed services have not been able to attract an adequate number of recruits; those who do enlist, critics charge, are not sufficiently qualified to handle the modern, highly sophisticated weapons systems of today's armed forces. Further, supporters add, a draft would be much more equitable than the present system, correcting the disproportionately large minority membership in the services. Finally, many draft advocates think the privilege of being an American justifies compulsory national service.

Many Americans dispute the need for a draft—particularly the younger people most likely to be conscripted. President Reagan also opposed the draft. Those opposed to the draft claim the all-volunteer force is working well: Not only can it fill its quotas, but the overall mental capability of its personnel is significantly higher than that of conscripts. Also, draft opponents believe a peacetime draft contradicts the basic principles of liberty upon which America was founded.[6] By casting aside even the option of forced conscription, opponents say, we would affirm the notion that Americans are free men and women who will defend our country when needed, without the force of our government compelling us to do so.

Some support a form of universal national service, such as former Congressman Paul McCloskey's proposed National Youth Service Act. Under such a plan all eighteen-year-olds would be faced with choosing among four alternatives: (1) to serve in the active forces for two years at a subsistence wage and then receive four years of college benefits. (2) to volunteer for six months in the active forces and then serve five and half years in the reserves. (3) to volunteer for one year of active civilian service, such as in VISTA. (4) to choose none of these, but then be eligible for the draft between the ages of eighteen and twenty-four if the military fell short of personnel. Some observers think this would restore a sense of national duty to American youth, and that it would be fairer than a selective draft. Others argue that such a system would be very costly to fund and organize, and might utilize human resources poorly. Not only would it create yet another vast bureaucracy, but the government rather than the market would decide the allocation of youth labor. Says economist Milton Friedman: "No. However appealing at first sight, universal national service is a monstrosity utterly inconsistent with a free society. It should be shunned like the plague it is."[7]

The Role of Women in the Military

One of the more controversial questions in the 1980s is whether women should join men in military combat. Women now comprise 9 percent of the total enlistment in the armed forces, and this is expected to rise to about 12 percent in the late 1980s. Women are now regularly admitted to, and graduated from,

---

[6]The issues concerning the draft and the all-volunteer force are discussed in Brent Scowcroft (ed.), *Military Service in the United States* (Spectrum, 1982).

[7]Milton Friedman, *Newsweek*, May 14, 1979, p. 101. For a contrasting analysis see *Youth and the Needs of the Nation*, Report of the Committee for the Study of National Service (The Potomac Institute, 1979). Also see Charles S. Moskos, "Social Considerations of the All-Volunteer Force," in Brent Scowcroft (ed.), *Military Service in the United States*, pp. 129–150.

military academies; they have also moved into many military jobs once reserved for men. And as the military becomes more mechanized and technical, the role of women will increase. As one woman member of Congress put it, it doesn't take much muscle to launch an ICBM.

The rise of women in the military has not occurred without some problems. Some males have refused to take orders from women officers. Some have refused to assign females to certain hazardous duties. In addition, at any given time over 5 percent of women in the military are pregnant. However, by far the biggest problem is the question of women's role in combat. Women are currently excluded by law from combat duty in the Navy and Air Force. The Army and Marine Corps forbid the use of women in combat as a matter of established policy. Despite the legal and traditional barriers to the use of women in combat, some analysts say their large numbers and the fact that they increasingly fill important positions makes them destined to fight in any future war involving our military forces.

Should there be draft registration for women if there is one for men? In *Rostker* v. *Goldberg*, the Supreme Court ruled by a vote of six to three that Congress could legally limit registration to men.[8] Writing for the majority, Justice William Rehnquist held that actions by Congress in the area of national defense should be shown "great deference" by the judicial branch; and that the primary purpose of registration was and is to identify citizens for combat duty. Since women are not eligible for combat duty, it is not discriminatory to exclude them from registration.

Rostker firmly established the constitutionality of the legislation calling for registration of males. Some women's and civil rights groups objected to the decision, claiming it perpetuated the myth that women are inferior to men. Others suggested that many women could be drafted to fill noncombat positions.

Despite the Court's ruling, women are destined to remain an integral part of the country's national defense. As long as the armed services continue to rely on volunteers to fill their personnel needs, they cannot afford to overlook such a major—indeed majority—demographic group. Women may face combat simply because it will be inescapable in wartime situations. Still, the country may well have to undergo major changes in attitudes before large numbers of women routinely are used in combat situations. Meanwhile, the key to determining a proper role for women in the armed forces, a former secretary of defense has written, "is to move gradually toward expansion of the number of functions available to women, on a voluntary basis, and to insist that women accepted for such positions meet the same standards as the men who serve in them.[9]

Women are taking a more active role in the armed services. *U.S. Navy.*

PRESIDENTIAL POLITICS AND THE B-1 BOMBER

The fate of the B-1 bomber has been at the center of defense politics debates for the past ten years. As a major weapon system it is directly involved in the debate over what we should spend and what we can afford. Presidents Ford and Reagan supported it, and President Carter opposed it. Congress has shifted back and forth on the issue.

The B-1 is a 147-foot swing-wing aircraft whose prime mission is to penetrate to targets at high subsonic speed while presenting a very small radar im-

[8]453 U.S. 57 (1981).
[9]Harold Brown, *Thinking About National Security* (Westview, 1983), p. 253.

The U.S. B-1 bomber. *U.S. Air Force.*

age. Its wings can change position and thus allow it to fly both at supersonic speeds at high altitudes and just under the sound barrier at treetop altitudes. Traveling with a crew of four, the B-1 was built to carry a payload of twenty-four short-range attack missiles (SRAMs).

Supporters of the B-1 claim the bomber force is an important part of our nuclear deterrent; opponents contend bombers are the outmoded "battleships of the airforce" and no longer serve a useful purpose in a world of intercontinental rocket-fired missiles. Opponents also claim the Soviets' apparent disinterest in developing a long-range manned air bomber proves it is no longer a necessary weapon. Proponents point to its importance as part of the so-called triad of (1) land-based missiles, (2) sea-based missiles, and (3) manned bombers with missiles. In this scheme any Soviet action to destroy one arm of the triad will allow the United States to retain the capacity to retaliate. Defenders of the B-1 point out that the bombers are controlled by humans and, once sent to their targets, can be recalled and can thus be used as a threat.

In the 1976 presidential campaign candidate Carter said he opposed the production of the B-1 bomber "at this time." He added, however: "I believe that research and development should continue." Congress voted, by large majorities in both houses, to continue research and development of the B-1. The Air Force wanted 244 B-1 bombers. Production costs alone were expected to run to about $24 billion, or nearly $100 million for each plane. Over a twenty-year period the B-1 program would cost about $100 billion to build, maintain, and operate.

These were the arguments Carter had to weigh in early 1977. The Air Force claimed that by the late 1980s, when the B-1 force would be ready to operate, the B-52 fleet would be twenty-five years old and in need of replacement. It was argued, too, that by the mid-1980s Soviet air defenses would be developed to the point where the B-52 would not be able to penetrate to targets. The B-52 also does not have the ability to fly at very low altitudes; it may not be able to take off and escape an enemy attack fast enough and may also be vulnerable to certain effects of nearby nuclear blasts.

Critics of the B-1 argued this way: It costs too much. It is an environmental threat. It would need a fuel tanker to help it fly to and from the USSR. But by far the most telling criticism comes from those who feel there are more cost-effective alternatives to the B-1. A noted physicist who had served for many years on the president's science advisory committee summed it up as follows: "The B-1 is a superexpensive way to obtain a particular capability. It costs more to buy, it costs more to operate, and it provides less-certain results than an achievable alternative."[10] A Brookings Institution team came to the conclusion

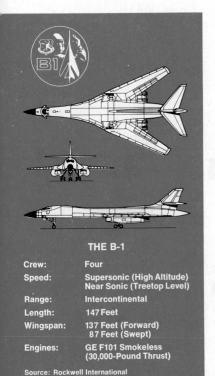

THE B-1

Crew:	Four
Speed:	Supersonic (High Altitude) Near Sonic (Treetop Level)
Range:	Intercontinental
Length:	147 Feet
Wingspan:	137 Feet (Forward) 87 Feet (Swept)
Engines:	GE F101 Smokeless (30,000-Pound Thrust)

Source: Rockwell International

[10]Richard L. Garwin, "You Can Do the Job Better and for Less Money," interview, *U.S. News & World Report*, April 26, 1976, p. 63.

that while a bomber force is needed, our current force will be "more than adequate" in the foreseeable future. They saw a marked economic advantage in studying a standoff missile system.[11] Such a system would involve an airplane like the 747 flying to the Soviet borders and launching missiles that would penetrate to their targets.

What was Carter to do? Most expected him to take the easy way out and compromise with the B-1 proponents by approving production of perhaps 100 of the 244 planes requested. Moreover, Carter was a military man himself, and the weight of military opinion favored the B-1. But he had also been a candidate who promised he would balance the budget. Carter collected information and consulted all sides. The Defense Department provided a steady flow of reports and briefing books for his appraisal. Three options emerged:

1. Build between 150 and 244 B-1s.
2. Refit the newest models of the fifteen-year-old B-52s to carry cruise missiles.
3. Modify the wide-bodied C-55 Galaxies or Boeing 747s to carry cruise missiles.

Carter retired to Camp David, a presidential vacation retreat in western Maryland, to go over the options one last time during the final weekend before his decision. Carter called the decision "one of the most difficult" he made.

As it turned out, President Carter decided to kill the Air Force's request for the B-1s and move ahead with option 2 outlined above. Washington was surprised over Carter's decision; officials had become accustomed to pragmatic presidents who were inclined to opt for some simple "split-the-difference" solution. Carter had had such an option open. Instead, by killing the B-1 program, he upset conservatives and won praise from liberals.

Candidate Reagan vowed to revise the B-1 program or to come up with something very similar. Once in office, he did just that. He took the issue to the public; he lobbied Congress about as hard as a president can; and he put the prestige of the White House on the line. Eventually he won congressional support for a revived B-1 production program.

However, the cost of the B-1s—to be ready by the late 1980s—jumped from the earlier estimates of nearly 100 million, and now run to about $200 million a plane. Defenders of the B-1 say if Carter hadn't cancelled the project, we would already have the B-1—at about half the cost. Critics of the B-1 say it is too costly; defense investments should be made in the more promising and advanced STEALTH system—still in the developing stages. Further, they charge that the B-1 will be obsolete before it is deployed. The STEALTH system, on the other hand, makes obsolete what the Soviets have, and what they will have, and forces them into a defensive mode that requires an enormous capital investment. Nonetheless, the B-1s are now being produced.

The Strategic Air Command monitors the movement of a Navy Cruise Missile during a test. *UPI.*

The Odyssey of the MX Missile

The history of the MX missile illustrates how defense weapons policy is made. Decisions made in the process of gaining approval for the MX were often as much the result of political considerations as national security needs.

An MX missile is a large, ten-warhead, extremely accurate nuclear weapon. The idea for an MX-type ICBM (Inter-Continental Ballistic Missile) arose back in 1965. The original purpose of the MX was to fill a perceived need on the part of the United States to maintain a land-based missile capable of surviving an attack by the Soviet Union. In addition, the MX was meant to give the U.S. for the first time the ability to threaten large numbers of Soviet

[11]Alton H. Quanbeck and Archie L. Wood, *Modernizing the Strategic Bomber Force* (Brookings Institution, 1976).

Military installations and defense contractors in eight states got 51 cents of every defense dollar spent in the U.S.

Ranking of 1982 defense spending on a state-population basis—

	Defense Spending	Per Capital
D. C. ..	$1.8 bil.	$2.791
Va.	$12.1 bil.	$2,234
Alaska	$0.9 bil.	$2,091
Conn. ..	$6.3 bil.	$2,013
Hawaii	$1.9 bil.	$1,969
Calif. ...	$32.3 bil.	$1,336
Mo.	$6.3 bil.	$1,283
Md.	$5.1 bil.	$1,197
Wash. ..	$5.0 bil.	$1,179
Mass. ..	$6.0 bil.	$1,036
N. H. ..	$0.9 bil.	$980
Me.	$1.1 bil.	$936
Kans. ..	$2.2 bil.	$910
N. Mex.	$1.2 bil.	$887
Ariz. ...	$2.4 bil.	$876
Miss. ...	$2.2 bil.	$851
Utah ...	$1.2 bil.	$819
Col.	$2.4 bil.	$816
Texas ..	$11.7 bil.	$792

Source: Reprinted from U.S. News & World Report. Copyright 1983, U. S. News & World Report.

land-based missiles. The combination of these two factors, it was expected, would deter the USSR from launching a nuclear invasion.

Carter's MX plan called for deployment of the missiles on a so-called "race track" in Utah and Nevada. Each missile was to have its own fifteen-mile roadway loop connecting twenty-three separate concrete launching points. The missiles were to be intermittently shuffled from one launching point to another in order to keep the Soviets guessing as to their whereabouts. The plan was later abandoned by the Reagan administration, in part due to widespread political opposition in Utah and Nevada. (One wag suggested that we merely put the MX on Amtrak trains. That way neither the USSR nor the U.S. would know where the MX missiles were—even with a schedule!)

President Reagan proposed his own deployment scheme. Known as "dense pack," this plan called for placing a hundred missiles in rows of two and three stretching in a fourteen-mile column. The theory behind dense pack, called "fratricide," is that a Soviet weapon detonating above an MX silo would destroy other incoming nuclear weapons before they reached their targets. The United States would then be able to launch the remaining MX missiles in retaliation. The dense pack proposal was rejected by Congress in late 1982.

In early 1983 Reagan appointed a blue-ribbon panel to try to break the political deadlock caused by congressional opposition to the various MX plans. By drawing on four former secretaries of defense, two former secretaries of state, two former national security advisers, and other high officials of four administrations, the White House hoped to develop a package of recommendations that would gain political appeal among Democrats as well as Republicans.

The Scowcroft Commission, named after its chairman, retired Air Force general and former White House aide Brent Scowcroft, released its findings in the spring of 1983. It recommended among other things that the United States temporarily deploy a hundred MX missiles in currently existing Minutemen missile silos. The commission also advised that the U.S. develop an unspecified number of smaller, single-warhead missiles to anchor America's long-term land-based defense.

Many of its recommendations were far-reaching in their implications. For example, it meant the entire complexion of U.S.-USSR arms control talks would have to be changed. Currently the two countries count missiles and missile launchers in determining each nation's relative strength for arms control purposes. This system encourages both nations to build multiple-warhead mis-

President Reagan appointed a Commission on the MX missile, shown here, comprised of several top State, Defense, and CIA officials from previous administrations. *Michael Evans, The White House.*

siles. The Scowcroft Commission suggested the U.S. eventually abandon large, multiple-warhead weapons in favor of small-warhead weapons. Should the proposal be accepted, new arms control agreements would have to be negotiated redefining the strength of nuclear forces.

President Reagan quickly endorsed the panel's findings, while his commission members reported to Congress and lobbied for the new version of the MX program. Predictably, the new MX plan generated opposition. Several senators and two former CIA directors said it would mean an escalation of the arms race. Former CIA director William Colby added that the MX would be seen by the Soviets as a first-strike weapon, and hence it would send a very dangerous message. These critics also pointed out that the MX is designed not for deterrence but as an offensive weapon. Others claim that deploying the MX in existing Minutemen silos would render the missiles too vulnerable.

While the MX won congressional approval, it did so by only slender majorities. And opponents of the MX did win commitments from Reagan to adjust his arms control negotiating strategy and to deploy a single-warhead missile system. Opposition to the costly MX program reappeared in the 1984 appropriations process, and the 1984 Democratic platform called for ending its production.

ORGANIZING FOR DEFENSE

The president, Congress, the National Security Council, and the State Department make overall policy and attempt to integrate our national security programs. But the day-to-day work of organizing for defense is the job of the Department of Defense. The Pentagon, its headquarters, houses within its miles of corridors nearly 23,000 top military and civilian personnel. The offices of several hundred generals and admirals are there, as is the office of the secretary of defense, symbolizing civilian control of the armed services.

Prior to 1947 there were two separate military departments, War and Navy. The difficulty of coordinating them during World War II led to demands for unification. In 1947 the Air Force, already an autonomous unit within the War Department, was made an independent unit. The three military departments—Army, Navy, and Air Force—were placed under the general supervision of the secretary of defense. The Unification Act of 1947 was a bundle of compromises between the Army, which favored a tightly integrated department, and the Navy, which wanted a loosely federated structure. It also reflected compromises between members of Congress who felt that disunity and interservice rivalries were undermining our defense efforts, and those who

The Pentagon—headquarters for the Department of Defense and the Joint Chiefs of Staff. Built during World War II, the Pentagon is the world's largest office building. Constructed on swamps and landfill on the west bank of the Potomac River in Northern Virginia, it has 20 miles of corridors. The Pentagon houses nearly 23,000 workers who tell time by 4200 clocks, drink water from 685 fountains, consume 30,000 cups of coffee daily, place 200,000 phone calls a day on 87,000 phones connected by 100,000 miles of cable. *UPI.*

Secretary of Defense Caspar Weinberger briefs reporters at a Pentagon Press Conference. *Frank Hall, Dept. of Defense.*

feared that a unified defense establishment would defy civilian control and smother dissenting views. Unfortunately, all the act really accomplished was to bring the military services under a common organizational chart. Instead of moving from two military departments to one, we ended up with three.

President Eisenhower felt strongly about the need to strengthen and centralize the Department of Defense. Using his prestige as the victorious commander of the Allied Forces in World War II, he secured from Congress the Defense Department Reorganization Act. The act gave additional authority to the secretary of defense and the joint chiefs of staff, especially its chair. Congress, however, refused to approve the appropriation of funds to the secretary of defense. Further, at the prompting of the Naval Air Force, Marine Corps, and National Guard, Congress insisted that the secretary of defense notify the House and Senate armed services committees when contemplating any major changes in combat functions. Congress also refused to repeal a provision, which Eisenhower called legalized insubordination, authorizing secretaries of a military department or members of the joint chiefs to make any recommendations they wish to Congress about Defense Department matters, even if their recommendations are contrary to department policy.

The Department of Defense, 1960s–1980s

Under Presidents Kennedy and Johnson, Secretary of Defense Robert McNamara proceeded to coordinate the supply and intelligence activities of the services, create unified military commands, and bring more unification to the department than Congress had been willing to provide by legislation. McNamara and his "Whiz kids," young economists and systems analysts, had their own ideas about strategic policies. Unlike many past civilian leaders of the department, they raised questions about military strategy and overruled military leaders when they felt the "top brass" lacked sound reasons.[12]

Nixon and Ford and their defense secretaries gave the military chiefs a stronger voice in budget and weapon decisions. Yet for much of their eight years, Nixon and Ford imposed Henry Kissinger between themselves and the Pentagon. Some people think Kissinger did an extraordinary job of balancing interests and serving the presidents; others think he did not.[13] President Carter appointed as his secretary of defense Harold Brown, a physicist who had served as secretary of the Air Force under McNamara in the 1960s. Brown restored some of the McNamara innovations and was one of the strongest persons in the Carter cabinet. Reagan had Caspar Weinberger as his Secretary of Defense. Together they presided over one of the biggest defense spending buildups of recent times.

The Joint Chiefs of Staff

The Joint Chiefs of Staff (JCS) serve as the principal military advisers to the president, the National Security Council, and the secretary of defense. They include the military heads of the three armed services, the commandant of the Marine Corps, and a chairman. The service chiefs are all appointed by the president with the consent of the Senate for four-year, nonrenewable terms. The chair of the JCS is appointed by the president with the consent of the Senate for a two-year term which may be renewed once.

The joint chiefs shape strategic plans, work out supply programs, review major supply and personnel requirements, formulate programs for training,

[12]Two of the best accounts of the McNamara period are William W. Kaufmann, *The McNamara Strategy* (Harper & Row, 1964); and Alan C. Enthoven and K. Wayne Smith, *How Much Is Enough? Shaping the Defense Program, 1961–1969* (Harper & Row, 1971).

[13]Elmo R. Zumwalt, Jr., *On Watch* (Quadrangle, 1976), p. 397. For a lengthier and more favorable treatment, see Marvin Kalb and Bernard Kalb, *Kissinger* (Little, Brown, 1974). Kissinger's views can be found in Henry Kissinger, *White House Years* (Little, Brown, 1979).

make recommendations to the secretary of defense on the establishment of un-ified commands in strategic areas, and provide American representation on the military commissions of the United Nations, NATO, and the OAS.

The chair of the joint chiefs takes precedence over all other military offi-cers. The chair presides over the meetings of the joint chiefs, prepares the agenda, directs the staff of some 400 officers in an overall JCS organization of about 2000 people, and informs the secretary of defense and the president of issues on which the joint chiefs have been unable to reach agreement.[14]

There is more to disputes among military services than professional jeal-ousies. The technological revolution in warfare has rendered obsolete existing concepts about military missions. In the past it made sense to divide command among land, sea, and air forces. Today technology makes a mockery of such distinctions. Defense research and development are constantly altering formerly established roles and missions. Yet the individual services are reluctant to give up their traditional functions. Each branch supports weapons that bring it pres-tige. This often leads to interservice rivalries such as the Army and Air Force quarrel over who should provide air support for ground troops, and the Air Force and Navy dispute over land- versus sea-based missiles.[15]

Sometimes interservice rivalries break out in Congress and the press. Or-ganizations such as the Association of the United States Army, the Navy League, and the Air Force Association lobby openly in behalf of their particu-lar service. Behind the scenes the military themselves are active. The president tries to keep interservice disputes inside the administration, but military com-manders who feel that administration policy threatens the national security have a problem. They are taught to respect civilian supremacy and to obey civilian superiors. But which civilian superiors? The president as commander in chief? Or should they—as they have a legal right to do—report to Congress, which is also a civilian superior? A few officers resolve the dilemma of conflicting loy-

The Joint Chiefs of Staff, from left: Gen. John A. Wickham Jr., Army; Gen. Charles A. Gabriel, Air Force; Adm. James D. Watkins, Navy; Gen. P. X. Kelley, Marine Comman-dant; and Gen. John W. Vessey Jr., Chairman. *D. Gorton. The New York Times.*

[14]One of the best studies of the operations of the JCS is found in Lawrence J. Korb, *The Joint Chiefs of Staff: The First Twenty-five Years* (Indiana University Press, 1976).

[15]Bruce M. Russett, *What Price Vigilance? The Burdens of National Defense* (Yale University Press, 1970). A study of interservice rivalries as well as of bureaucratic caution is Edmund Beard, *Developing the ICBM: A Study of Bureaucratic Politics* (Columbia University Press, 1976).

alties by resigning, so that they will be free to carry their views to the nation. Sometimes military personnel who wish to dissent from official policy get their views to Congress by resorting to the Washington practice of "leaking" information to the press. And when testifying before congressional committees, it is not difficult for officers to allow their views to come across.

The continuation of interservice differences has led some people to advocate the replacement of the joint chiefs by a single chief of staff, the complete integration of the military into a single branch, and the reassignment of forces in terms of strategic missions. Although such a system has had the support of some high-ranking Army and Air Force officers, it is opposed by most Navy officers, members of Congress, and respected students of the joint chiefs structure.[16]

In 1982 former Chairman of the Joint Chiefs, General David Jones, called for strengthening the role of the chair of the JCS and increasing the organization's staff capability, with correspondingly reduced service involvement in joint actions. He also urged broadened training, experience, and rewards for officers assigned to JCS staff. His view was that the service chairmen are too often immobilized by their statesman-spokesman dilemma. That is, they are expected both to take the overall national view and also to remain advocates of their respective services. Jones believed the service chiefs are just too imbued with their service's tradition, doctrine, and discipline to be objective about innovative proposals and needed military change. The Reagan administration and Jones's successor, General John W. Vessey, Jr., endorsed a watered-down version of this plan.

Strategic defense policy, much like policy in any other area, is the result not of a collective process of rational inquiry but of a mutual process of give and take. Whether strategic policies are worked out within the Defense Department, the White House, or Congress, the decisions result from a political process in which some measure of consensus is essential. And some conflict among the participants is not necessarily evil. The joint chiefs engage in the same type of logrolling tactics used in Congress. On budget issues they tend to endorse all the programs desired by each service. "When forced to choose on an issue of policy, the Chiefs compromise among the different service positions rather than attempting to develop a position based on a unified military point of view."[17]

ARMS CONTROL AND THE NUCLEAR FREEZE

President John F. Kennedy once said: "We have the power to make this the best generation in the history of mankind, or to make it the last." *United Nations.*

People have dreamed for centuries of a world in which conflicts would be resolved without force. But in reality, as long as the United States exists in a world of sovereign, independent nations, it will look to its own defenses. The policy of deterrence suggests that a strategic equilibrium between the U.S. and the USSR, or mutual deterrence, is the best realistic safeguard. (Effective deterrence is commonly measured by the usable strength of the survivable second-strike force.) The policy of deterrence is based on the idea that a conflict in values is the root cause of the East-West confrontation, and that military force is a reflection of that basic conflict. Moreover, proponents argue, we need to have a reserve military strength to back up our position in arms control negotiations.

[16]See *The Joint Chiefs of Staff: A Better System?* A report in the *AEI Foreign Policy and Defense Review* (American Enterprise Institute, 1980); and *The Role of the Joint Chiefs of Staff in National Policy* (American Enterprise Institute, 1978).

[17]Morton H. Halperin, "President and Military," *Foreign Affairs* (January 1972), p. 321.

Proponents of arms control say armaments themselves are a fundamental cause of international tension. They warn of the immense risks of the deterrence system: human error, a failure in the warning network, a misguided missile, and the inevitable increase in the number of nations with nuclear weapons. But they paint an even grimmer picture of a future without arms control: heightened tension as the result of the development of more devastating nuclear warheads and longer-ranged, more accurate delivery vehicles; the threat of biological, chemical, and neutron-radiation weapons; the constant surveillance of spy satellites; and ever-increasing defense budgets and commitments of human resources to weapons technology.[18]

There are already some substantial arms control agreements among the major world powers. As outlined below, several treaties have been negotiated—some among several nations and several between the U.S. and the USSR. *Disarmament* refers to some actual reductions in arms. *Arms control* refers to monitoring, mutual exclusion of certain weapons, notification, common ceilings that require no reduction, and similar agreements. Arms control strives to reduce the likelihood of war, to reduce the cost of defense, and to reduce the damage if war should occur.

The Committee on Disarmament hears statements by George Bush. *UN Photo.*

In the mid-1980s we are involved in two kinds of arms control negotiations. The START talks, begun by President Reagan, seek to achieve actual arms reductions. These talks have been going on in Geneva for the past few years. Second, negotiations are pending at what is called the Intermediate Nuclear Force Reduction Talks.

A brief look at some past negotiations suggests the kinds of arms control efforts that may be possible in the future. After looking at the recent past, we shall examine the contemporary debate over the nuclear freeze proposal.

In 1963 the United Kingdom, the Soviet Union, and the United States agreed on a treaty to ban nuclear explosions in the atmosphere or in any other place where there was danger of radioactive debris. The treaty permits nations to test underground and has an escape clause allowing any signer to withdraw on three months' notice. Its ratification by the United States and the Soviet Union, and the subsequent adherence to it by more than one hundred nations, was viewed as a first step toward nuclear disarmament.

President Jimmy Carter and Soviet leader Leonid Brezhnev exchange signed copies of the SALT II treaty in Vienna, June 18, 1979. *UPI.*

The test-ban treaty was followed in 1967 by the International Treaty on the Peaceful Uses of Outer Space, banning the use of satellites as vehicles or platforms for the launching of nuclear weapons. In 1968 came the Nonproliferation Treaty, which pledges the nuclear powers not to disseminate nuclear devices to nonnuclear powers for at least twenty-five years, and the nonnuclear nations not to seek to acquire such devices.

The first SALT (Strategic Arms Limitations Treaty) agreement was signed by President Nixon and Leonid Brezhnev in May 1972. In this treaty the U.S. sought to place a freeze on the Soviets for five years, the time needed for the U.S. to catch up by developing the Trident submarine, MX missile, cruise missile, and B-1 bomber. SALT I was criticized by some people for giving the Soviets a considerable advantage both in numbers and megatonnage, but Henry Kissinger defended the treaty as freezing an inequality we inherited in order to gain time to reverse the situation.

In October 1974 President Gerald Ford met with Brezhnev in Vladivostok to decide in principle the general outline of SALT II accords. Under these accords a limit was set on the number of offensive delivery vehicles (2400), with a sublimit on the number of launchers of strategic missiles equipped with

[18]Ralph E. Lapp, *Arms Beyond Doubt: The Tyranny of Weapons Technology* (Cowles, 1970). See also Alva Myrdal, *The Game of Disarmament, How the United States and Russia Run the Arms Race* (Pantheon, 1977).

multiple independently targetable reentry vehicles (MIRVs). No limits were to be placed on other weapons such as the cruise missiles, backfire planes, or strategic air defense. However, both sides soon decided that SALT II should place further limits on the other's new weapons, while not hindering their own weapons development. American cruise missiles and the Soviet backfire plane became the center of this controversy.

The Carter administration proposed that SALT II also put limits on "throw-weight" (the weight of the useful payload of the missile) and MIRVs, but this was met with strong Soviet opposition. As the SALT II agreements eventually took shape, it became apparent that they would have only a minimal effect on curbing the arms race. Carter was unsuccessful in winning Senate approval for SALT II. In any event, debate on SALT II was abruptly suspended in 1980 because of the Soviet intervention in Afghanistan.

THE NUCLEAR FREEZE DEBATE

A nuclear freeze is an immediate, bilateral, verifiable halt to the development, production, and deployment of nuclear weapons. And the nuclear freeze movement is one of the most volatile issues of the 1980s.

The freeze movement generated notable popular support and debate. In recent elections nuclear freeze resolutions have been placed on the ballot in several states and the District of Columbia. The resolutions have passed everywhere except in Arizona. Gallup polls have found that seven in ten Americans favor the general idea of a freeze. In 1983 the House of Representatives passed a nuclear freeze resolution. In 1984 the Democratic platform endorsed the freeze approach.

Because of the potentially cataclysmic nature of nuclear war, the freeze issue is like no other issue. And passionate arguments on both sides of the issue have presented convincing, logical, and compelling cases. Opponents and proponents of a freeze present arguments that can be divided into five categories: *The Prevention of Nuclear War*, *The Strategic Balance*, *The Economics of the Nuclear Freeze*, *The Morality of the Nuclear Freeze*, and *The Nuclear Freeze and Arms Control*. The following, is an outline, using these categories, of the main arguments for and against a nuclear freeze.

U. S. Senator Edward Kennedy (D-Mass.) and Senator Mark Hatfield (R-Oregon) in discussion. They were co-sponsors of the Nuclear Freeze Resolution. *UPI.*

I. THE PREVENTION OF NUCLEAR WAR Supporters of a nuclear freeze believe the continued development, production, and deployment of nuclear weapons greatly increases the likelihood of a nuclear holocaust. Senator Alan Cranston of California, who based much of his campaign for the 1984 Democratic presidential nomination on his support for a freeze, said that "without a freeze, sooner or later a nuclear war will happen."[19] Ever-increasing numbers of nuclear weapons only serve to increase the odds of an accident involving nuclear weapons, terrorist acquisition of atomic weapons, or the unnecessary use of nukes by a trigger-happy government leader.

Opponents of a nuclear freeze directly refute this contention, arguing that a freeze would increase rather than decrease the likelihood of nuclear war. Those who oppose a nuclear freeze claim it is the doctrine of deterrence which has prevented nuclear war thus far. A freeze would endanger this doctrine. Under the strategy of deterrence each side refrains from attacking the other because it fears retaliation in kind. Each side knows that nuclear aggression is tantamount to suicide.

[19]*Time*, March 29, 1982, p. 14.

Those against a nuclear freeze point out that deterrence has been successful in preventing nuclear war. Despite the outbreak of more than a hundred military conflicts since World War II, the general peace has been preserved. Nuclear weapons have not been used since the United States dropped atom bombs on Hiroshima and Nagasaki, Japan. Opponents of a freeze claim that modernization and strengthening of U.S. nuclear forces is essential to the continued success of deterrence. A freeze would prohibit the improvement of the American defense arsenal.

II. THE STRATEGIC BALANCE Freeze advocates believe a moratorium on nuclear weapons would enhance, not reduce, our overall national security. "It will halt the development of more powerful Soviet rockets and block their further deployment of existing weapons," according to Senator Edward Kennedy (D-Mass.), a leading freeze advocate and coauthor of the Senate version of the freeze resolution.[20] This argument assumes the United States and the Soviet Union are at "rough parity" in their nuclear arsenals. Each nation possesses relatively equal levels of destructive capability. Moreover, the arsenals of each nation are more than sufficient to achieve any deterrent, or first- or second-strike purpose. Each nation is unnecessarily and dangerously capable of overkill.

Detractors of a freeze say the Soviet Union currently enjoys strategic superiority over the United States. A freeze would lock the U.S. into this unequal position and provide an enticing target for Soviet aggression. The most prominent supporter of this viewpoint is President Reagan, who claims a freeze would "preserve today's high, unequal, and unstable levels of nuclear forces."[21]

III. THE ECONOMICS OF THE NUCLEAR FREEZE Continued production of nuclear weapons, freeze backers say, will increase inflation, produce fewer jobs, and force further cutbacks in services. They point to the futility of wasting vast sums of money on nonproductive goods such as nuclear weapons. Further, large savings would result from the reduction in arms that would immediately follow a freeze.

Opponents of a freeze hold that strategic nuclear weapons make up a relatively small share of the defense budget. Further, the protection provided by nuclear weapons is much cheaper than the same amount of protection provided by conventional weapons. Opponents of a freeze argue that reliance on nuclear weapons results in large part from a desire to *reduce* government spending.[22]

IV. THE MORALITY OF THE NUCLEAR FREEZE Many religious leaders call for a freeze on moral grounds. The National Conference of Catholic Bishops issued a widely publicized position paper expressing its disapproval of nuclear weapons. The bishops question the morality of the indiscriminate killing of innocent civilians that would inevitably result from the use of nuclear weapons.

[20]Testimony of Senator Edward M. Kennedy before the U.S. Senate Foreign Relations Committee, May 11, 1982. See also Edward Kennedy and Mark Hatfield, *Freeze! How You Can Help Prevent Nuclear War* (Bantam Books, 1982).

[21]Stephen R. Weisman; "Reagan Calls Nuclear Freeze Dangerous," *The New York Times*, April 1, 1983, p. 4.

[22]See, for example, Charles Krauthammer, "The Real Way to Prevent Nuclear War," *The New Republic*, April 28, 1982, p. 19.

According to critics of the freeze, the moral questions raised by totalitarian communist regimes are more important than the moral questions raised by nuclear war and weapons. Father Philip M. Hannan, Archbishop of New Orleans, claims "the deprivation of the human rights of hundreds of millions of people behind the Iron Curtain should be of primary concern."[23]

V. THE NUCLEAR FREEZE AND ARMS CONTROL Finally, supporters of a nuclear freeze claim that a halt to the development, production, and deployment of nuclear weapons is a necessary first step toward arms control and reduction. Senator Mark Hatfield (R-Oregon), coauthor of the Senate freeze resolution with Senator Kennedy, equates the arms race with a speeding locomotive. "You can't throw a freight train coming down the track into reverse," he says, "until you first stop it." Supporters of a comprehensive freeze claim it would also facilitate verification of arms control agreements. *Any* testing or production activity would suggest a violation. Piecemeal arms control agreements such as SALT I and II and the proposed START are concerned with detecting subtle deviations in arms activity, verification of which is far more difficult.

Those opposed to a freeze say it would eliminate the Soviet incentive to negotiate seriously in arms control talks. Soviet leaders participate in arms talks (they say) solely to stop the development, production, and deployment of new American weapons systems. A freeze would accomplish this for them, thereby ending all hope for future arms reductions. Those against a freeze claim a comprehensive freeze would be impossible to verify: The production, stockpiling, and qualitative upgrading of nuclear weapons cannot be detected by satellite, and the Soviets have always objected to on-site inspection.

The nuclear freeze issue is complex as well as controversial. Opposing sides in the debate interpret the same facts in different ways. Each side is committed to peace and genuinely feels its position represents the safest course. As with many other issues, public opinion and other political considerations may ultimately determine the outcome. What separates the nuclear freeze issue from all other political issues is that the stakes are far higher.[24]

SECURITY AND LIBERTY: NOT BY POWER ALONE

What should be the role of the military in a democratic society? A fear of the military is deeply rooted in the American tradition. And the unpopularity of the Vietnam war, together with the belief that vast military expenditures are giving undue influence to the military and their allies in the industrial community, arouses concern about how to ensure civilian control over the so-called military-industrial complex.[25]

The framers, recognizing that military domination is incompatible with free government, wove into the Constitution several precautions. The president, an elected official, is the commander in chief of the armed forces; with the Senate's consent the chief executive commissions all officers. Congress

[23]"Should The Church Oppose Nuclear Arms," *U.S. News & World Report*, December 20, 1982, p. 48.
[24]See, Paul M. Cole and William J. Taylor, Jr., eds., *The Nuclear Freeze Debate* (Westview Press, 1983).
[25]James Clotfelter, *The Military in American Politics* (Harper & Row, 1973), p. 234.

makes the rules for the governance of the military services; and appropriations for the army are limited to a two-year period. Congress has supplemented these precautions by requiring that the secretary of defense and the heads of the military departments be civilians, and by devising elaborate procedures to prevent the military from controlling the selection of men and women for West Point, Annapolis, and the Air Force Academy.

Maintaining civilian control over the military today is harder than it has ever been before. There is no longer a clear separation between military and civilian spheres of activity. In many cases it is the military who decide what information must remain top secret. Members of Congress and the general public are thus sometimes at a disadvantage. When a nation maintains a large military establishment, there tends to be an increase in centralization and in executive power, and a corresponding reduction in judicial and legislative control. A nation preoccupied with defense is also more likely to suppress dissent and to label critics as unpatriotic or subversive. Further, while Congress has the power to control defense policy and defense spending, it has apparently encouraged the tremendous growth in military responsibilities. By and large, members of Congress have followed the line of reasoning of the military leaders.

Defenders of the defense budget say those who want to reduce it are naive. They point out that with the help of more analytical audits, military procurement has been improved. They argue that defense programs in recent fiscal years have exacted the smallest percentage of the gross national product and the smallest percentage of the federal budget since 1950. They explain that the military budget must include the increasing expenditures necessary to maintain an all-volunteer army.

National debates about the military budget, weapons systems, arms control, and force levels are commonplace in American politics, as they should be. The objectives of an ever more effective, yet ever more efficient, military preparedness effort will guide these debates. In the final analysis, everyone recognizes true national security lies in something considerably more than troops and weapons. Still, providing for the nation's defense is recognized by almost everyone as a basic condition or first requirement that must be satisfied before the nation can go about its other business or begin to achieve its other aspirations.

Former Secretary of State Henry Kissinger. *U.S. State Department.*

SUMMARY

1. Providing for the nation's defense is one of the fundamental functions of the national government. But it is also one of the most costly and controversial functions. Nearly everything the nation's military does becomes enmeshed in politics—as it should.

2. Americans are often bewildered by the complicated weapons systems and the almost foreign language of the military appropriations debates. The prevailing attitude of Americans toward defense spending and the military establishment is one of modified support. But we want to deter war. We want military strength that will help achieve our foreign policy objectives. We are also concerned about the high cost of arms and the possibility of either a nuclear war or nuclear proliferation that some day will lead to war.

3. Our system is designed to provide for civilian control over the military. This is always a challenge; Presidents,

Congress, and the secretaries of defense must weigh national security against competing claims. This inevitably causes a certain amount of strain. While the military in any society has enormous potential for direct political involvement, this has not occurred in the United States.

4. Americans in the 1980s are concerned about military preparedness and strength. But they are equally concerned with arms control and reducing the threat of a nuclear war. We have had extensive debates about the draft, SALT II, and a nuclear freeze. We know we are now more dependent on the outside world than ever—especially for oil. The capacity for conflict and violence in the Middle East, Korea, Cuba, Central America, and elsewhere is well recognized. While military power alone may not guarantee international stability, it is generally viewed as a necessary condition.

BARRY BLECHMAN (ed.). *Rethinking the U.S. Strategic Posture* (Ballinger, 1982).

HAROLD BROWN. *Thinking About National Security* (Westview Press, 1983).

JAMES CLOTFELTER. *The Military in American Politics* (Harper & Row, 1973).

PAUL M. COLE and WILLIAM J. TAYLOR, Jr. (eds.). *The Nuclear Freeze Debate* (Westview Press, 1983).

JOHN M. COLLINS. *U.S. Defense Planning: A Critique* (Westview Press, 1982).

JAMES FALLOWS. *National Defense* (Random House, 1981).

ROBERT JERVIS. *The Illogic of American Nuclear Strategy* (Cornell University Press, 1984).

LAWRENCE J. KORB. *The Fall and Rise of the Pentagon: American Defense Policies in the 1970s* (Greenwood Press, 1979).

JOHN REICHART and STEVEN STURM (eds.). *American Defense Policy*, 5th ed. (Johns Hopkins University Press, 1982).

ROBERT SCHEER. *With Enough Shovels: Reagan, Bush and Nuclear War* (Random House, 1982).

BRENT SCOWCROFT (ed.). *Military Service in the United States* (Spectrum, 1982).

R. JAMES WOOLSEY (ed.). *Nuclear Arms: Ethics, Strategy and Politics* (Institute for Contemporary Studies, 1984).

THE POLITICS
OF REGULATION

22

What do lawn mowers, automobiles, telephones, smoke detectors, cereal ads, banks, natural gas companies, nuclear power plants, and workers' wages all have in common? They are all regulated in some way by the federal government. Virtually every activity in the United States is regulated in one form or another. Regulation has become a vast enterprise. And any activity as pervasive as regulation is bound to generate controversy.

If just the basic federal regulations were compiled, a shelf over fifteen feet long would be needed to hold the more than 60,000 pages of fine print. Federal agencies send out over 10,000 different forms a year, and businesses spend an estimated $20 billion or more completing them. The total cost to consumers of all regulatory activity is an estimated $100 billion a year.

Our regulatory arrangements were not arbitrarily created. They came into existence to clean up meatpacking conditions such as those exposed in Upton Sinclair's *The Jungle,* to prevent the kind of pesticide contamination described in Rachel Carson's *Silent Spring,* and to respond to the lack of auto safety concern documented in Ralph Nader's *Unsafe at Any Speed.* Regulations exist both to encourage competition and to achieve valued social objectives. More recently regulations have been enacted to protect us from raw sewage in rivers, lead in paint and gasoline, toxic wastes in the air, asbestos, cotton dust, and hazardous substances in toys and furniture.

Many of the new regulations have generated fierce resentment. Can we afford all these regulations? Are they driving people out of business? Do the costs outweigh the benefits? President Reagan sided with business in saying the United States has become overregulated. Labor, consumers, and environmentalists often disagree and say that in certain areas we need more—not less—regulation. Who is right? This chapter analyzes the goals of regulation, discusses some of the costs and consequences, and provides some examples of government regulation and the more recent efforts to deregulate.

WHAT IS REGULATION?

Regulation means the government steps in and alters the natural procedures of the open market to achieve some desired goal. The main regulatory role of government is to improve or supplant markets when they do not or cannot function effectively. In this sense regulation is a middle ground between socialism, or government ownership, and a "laissez faire," or "hands off," policy. The open market is characterized by self-adjustment, or natural regulation. Regulation by government interjects political goals and values into the economy in the form of rules that direct behavior in the marketplace.

All economies are sets of rules and regulations; there simply are no unregulated economies. The United States operates with a competitive market economy: Wages, prices, the allocation of goods and services, and the employment of resources are generally regulated by the laws of supply and demand. Put another way, we rely on private enterprise and market incentives to carry out most of our production and distribution.

A regulation is a limitation imposed on the discretion of a person or an organization—and it is backed up by government's use of police power. It means setting restraints on persons or groups, directly compelling them to take, or not take, certain actions. Perhaps as many as 100,000 people in about 100 federal agencies work on implementing and enforcing federal regulations.[1]

The Case for Regulation

The philosophy behind regulation is relatively simple: The marketplace too often fails to provide the necessary protection for the personal achievement of certain valued goals such as personal safety and environmental health. Through government supervision of or intervention in potentially hazardous or abusive situations, all of society will benefit.

The costs of regulation are exaggerated, according to some observers. The gross national product (GNP) measures growth in goods and services but not the worth of a cleaner environment, a slower rate of natural resource depletion, or increased recreational opportunities. We too often overlook the advantages of clean air, a clear view, and so on.

Supporters of regulation also say it is necessary to protect specific groups as well as society as a whole. Thus consumers often lack sufficient power to act as a check on business, and minorities sometimes need assistance in wiping out discriminatory practices. Since business is unlikely to regulate itself, government regulation is needed to prevent pollution of the environment, unfair practices, discrimination, or exorbitant pricing. The same protection must be provided for innocent third parties. Supporters of regulation say residents of areas near industrial waste sites, for example, need government help to ensure the reasonable safety of their neighborhoods.

Advocates of regulation do not necessarily oppose the free enterprise system. On the contrary, many believe regulation is the best instrument available for correcting the abuses of the system and thereby ensuring its survival. Some say the basic purpose of regulation is to ensure the continuation of a competitive atmosphere. If the government can prevent abuses by monopolies or correct market imperfections, economic competition will be enhanced for the benefit of all.

"All those in favor of establishing government regulatory agencies say 'Aye.'" *Drawing by H. Martin;* © *1983 The New Yorker Magazine, Inc.*

[1] See Alan Stone, *Regulation and Its Alternatives* (Congressional Quarterly Press, 1982).

| The Case Against Regulation | Opponents of extensive government regulation say in most cases government regulation is not needed; market forces compel business to work for the benefit of consumers. Their basic objectives are the same, they say—a clean, safe environment and an equitable and efficient economy—but differences arise over how best to achieve these objectives. Critics of regulation say the best mechanisms for attaining both economic and social goals are the free market forces and the forces of competition. Competition is the basis of the free market economy. With meaningful competition the consumer gets the most goods at the best price, and overall system output and efficiency are maximized. |

Critics of regulation also say it is inefficient. The labyrinth of federal rules dampens productivity, fuels inflation, and blunts our competitive strength abroad. Further, public officials cannot know as much about the intricacies of any particular economic pursuit as do those engaged in the business on a daily basis. This lack of knowledge results in regulations that unduly hamper production and cost much more than the benefits they provide.

Government regulation also is often counterproductive, critics say. Many times, they claim, government regulations hurt the very people they are intended to help, and vice versa. Thus, some believe government actions often protect monopolies and cartels. Removing restrictions would make markets more equitable, to the benefit of consumers. Moreover, opponents of regulation suggest that some federal regulations penalize consumers, to whom the costs of regulations are usually passed along. For example, the extra costs of automobile safety and auto emission devices (sometimes as much as $1000) become part of the price paid by the purchaser for a car.

The regulation debate is not as clear-cut as it may appear. Very few people call for unlimited government intervention in economic and social activity. Similarly, few people advocate absolute removal of government participation from the marketplace. Indeed, some people call for more regulation in some areas and less in others. It is important to appreciate that the diversity of regulations makes generalization difficult.

Increased Regulation

Just a generation ago the national government had major regulatory responsibility in only a handful of policy areas—**antitrust,** financial institutions, transportation, and communications. But in the 1980s nearly a hundred commissions, agencies, services, and administrations limit or control what we can produce or do. About twenty of these are called independent regulatory agencies. They are outside the regular executive departments, enjoy a certain independence from White House influence, and are headed by a group usually composed of seven members. Most of the other regulatory organizations are located within the executive departments.

New regulatory mechanisms established in recent years—for pollution control, employee pensions, consumer product safety, industrial health and safety, discrimination in hiring, and so on—have generated intense political controversy.

There have been four major waves of regulatory legislation in American history: at the turn of the century, in the 1910s, in the 1930s, and in the late 1960s through 1980. In each case changing political intentions and forces have given rise to such legislation. Primary reasons for regulation have included: controlling monopoly and oligopoly, compensating for market imperfections, and defending the economically weak.

CONTROLLING MONOPOLY AND OLIGOPOLY To achieve many economic goals, including the best allocation of resources, it is necessary to encourage competition. In a monopoly or oligopoly, power is concentrated in the hands of a few and there is no competition. Through antitrust regulation the government works to ensure competition. When monopoly and oligopoly exist, as in the case of power companies, for example, government regulation prevents these industries from taking advantage of their position. Thus, government regulates prices and sets standards of performance in some markets.

COMPENSATING FOR MARKET IMPERFECTIONS   The market does not always work to solve every problem, especially the problem of *externalities*, or side effects. Consider the example of pollution. For a long time there was no price imposed on a business for using air and water to store or discharge toxic wastes. Therefore, market forces did not consider what it cost society to have its air and water polluted. Or take the case of commuters who use their cars to go to work. The more who do so, the more difficult it is for commuters to get to work. (That is why commuters frequently favor mass transportation—so that *other* people will use it and thus open the roadways for *them*.) Still, present market forces do not encourage using the bus as against taking a car to work.

When the market fails to set appropriate costs and benefits, pressures develop for the government to step in. The government can pass regulations that impose costs on air pollution or gasoline.

Another market imperfection involves the case of natural monopoly. A natural monopoly exists when it would be grossly inefficient to have competition in a particular industry. If competition existed in electric utilities, the price of power might be higher to the public than if just one company supplied all the power, saving money because of the vast capital investment needed and the size of its operation. When such a natural monopoly exists, the government regulates it.

DEFENDING THE ECONOMICALLY WEAK   The government has involved itself directly in the economy to protect those who lack economic power. Thus, the government has worked to establish a minimum wage and to prevent abuses such as child labor. The government has also sought to control the conflict between labor and management and to protect workers' right to organize. In its role as protector of the weak, the government has sought especially to ensure equal opportunity (a topic discussed at length in Chapter 5).

Government Regulation: A Finger in Every Pie?

Although regulation has traditionally been defended as intervention to ensure more socially beneficial outcomes, it is sometimes criticized as imposing more costs on society than its benefits warrant. While we have many desired objectives—economic, social, and political—our resources are limited. A critical task of modern democratic government is to make wise, balanced choices among courses of action and competing objectives. Increasingly regulation is coming into conflict with other economic objectives: Critics charge that it is contributing to higher inflation, lower productivity, and economic stagnation.[2] Proponents argue that government regulation, though not perfect, has brought improvements in the areas of pollution, worker safety, and consumer protection.[3]

[2]See, for example, Milton Friedman and Rose Friedman, *Free to Choose* (Harcourt Brace Jovanovich, 1980); Murray L. Weidenbaum, *Business, Government and the Public* (Prentice-Hall, 1977); and Murray L. Weidenbaum and Robert DeFina, *The Cost of Federal Regulation of Economic Activity* (American Enterprise Institute Reprint, May 1978).

[3]See, for example, *Benefits of Environmental, Health and Safety Regulation* (Committee on Governmental Affairs, U.S. Senate, 1980); Steven Kelman, "Regulation That Works," *The New Republic*, November 25, 1978, pp. 16–19; and Timothy B. Clark, "The Costs and Benefits of Regulation," *National Journal*, December 1, 1979, pp. 2023–27.

In addition, we now have two very different types of regulation: traditional, or economic, regulation; and new, or *social regulation*. *Traditional* regulation is industry-specific—that is, it regulates prices and conditions of entry in a certain industry. Such regulation began in the nineteenth century when the Interstate Commerce Commission was established, and it has continued with the Federal Communications Commission and the Civil Aeronautics Board. Recently these regulatory agencies have drawn heavy fire; critics contend they help maintain artificially high prices and barriers to entry in the industries they regulate and are therefore very costly to consumers and to the economy as a whole.

Social regulation, however, draws the hottest fire. Such regulation cuts across industry lines and aims at providing goods such as clean air, worker safety, and consumer safety. In other words, producers must now pay for the "external" costs that once were free, such as using the atmosphere for waste disposal. These costs are then passed along to the consumer, and the true cost of the product is more accurately reflected in its price. Some goods may become too costly, and demand for them will drop. Others will become more popular (for instance, small cars). In the end a socially more beneficial allocation of resources will result.

How desirable is it to have *absolutely* clean air or *absolutely* safe workplaces? True, it is relatively inexpensive to remove a large amount of air pollution, and therefore socially desirable, but it becomes increasingly expensive to remove all of it. To do so would require an allocation of resources that, from a taxpayer's point of view, might be better used for something else—whether new missiles or hot tubs. Is there a socially optimal point of pollution

22–1
SOME REGULATORY AGENCIES AND THEIR MISSIONS*

Organization	Year Established	Primary Function
Interstate Commerce Commission (ICC)	1887	Regulates rates, routes, and practices of railroads, trucks, bus lines, etc.
Federal Trade Commission (FTC)	1914	Administers certain antitrust laws concerning advertising, labeling, and packaging to protect consumers from unfair business practices
Food and Drug Administration (FDA)	1931	Establishes regulations concerning purity, safety, and labeling accuracy of certain foods and drugs; issues licenses for manufacture and distribution
Federal Communications Commission (FCC)	1934	Licenses civilian radio and television communication; licenses and sets rates for interstate and international communication
Civil Aeronautics Board (CAB)	1938	Regulates airline routes, passenger fares, and freight fares
Animal and Plant Health Inspection Service	1953	Sets standards; inspects and enforces laws relating to meat, poultry, and plant safety
Environmental Protection Agency (EPA)	1970	Develops environmental quality standards, approves state environmental plans
Occupational Safety and Health Administration (OSHA)	1971	Develops and enforces worker safety and health regulations
Bureau of Alcohol, Tobacco and Firearms	1972	Enforces laws and regulates legal flow of these materials
Consumer Product Safety Commission (CPSC)	1972	Establishes mandatory product safety standards and bans sales of products that do not comply

*Examples of the nearly 100 services, commissions, agencies, or administrations that have a significant national regulatory function. Note that some of these are independent (not in the cabinet departments), and some are located within the regular executive departments. Note too that some of these, such as the ICC and FCC, are of the older, traditional type, and some, such as OSHA and the CPSC, are of the newer social type.
Source: Center for the Study of American Business.

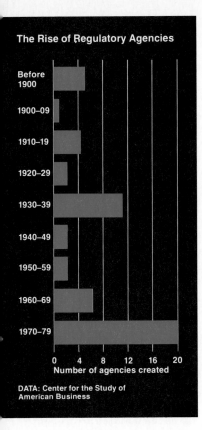

The Rise of Regulatory Agencies

Before 1900

1900–09

1910–19

1920–29

1930–39

1940–49

1950–59

1960–69

1970–79

0   4   8   12   16   20
Number of agencies created

DATA: Center for the Study of
American Business

control or worker safety beyond which it is too costly to go? The challenge for policy makers is to determine what this point is. In our political system, with its many competing interest groups, there is much difference of opinion on this matter.

Faced with this problem, Congress often legislates broad objectives for the regulatory agencies, which then set specific rules for meeting these goals. Thus far agency regulations have been largely in the form of specific rules that a firm may not violate without being punished. Usually of the "command-control" type, they have been criticized as being arbitrary, costly, and inflexible. The Carter administration made some attempts at reform. And the Reagan administration went even further. OSHA has trimmed over a thousand "nit-picking" regulations that governed such things as the shape of toilet seats.

Economists have proposed various types of regulations that would make it less expensive for industries to meet requirements. The concept behind such ideas as performance standards or effluent fees is that the government should set requirements for pollution control or worker safety but that the means of reaching these goals should be left to the market. Thus, for example, rather than installing expensive noise control facilities in factories, workers could wear hearing protectors.

The new regulatory techniques can be put into four categories: (1) *market approaches*—reliance on the economic incentives of the free market to nudge industry in the direction of the public interest; (2) *performance standards*—replacement of regulations spelling out exactly how industry must meet a particular goal with broader statements that allow industry to choose the means; (3) *informational approaches*—requirements that manufacturers disclose complete information about their products, on the theory that consumers can then make intelligent choices; and (4) *self-regulation*—a government decision to do little more than help industry set its own voluntary standards.[4]

The Costs of Regulation

Although it is difficult to measure the costs and benefits of regulation, some attempts have been made. Two such efforts are those of the Business Round-table and of economist Murray Weidenbaum at Washington University in St. Louis.[5] The Business Roundtable studied the impact of regulation by six federal agencies and programs (EPA, OSHA, Department of Energy, FTC, Equal Employment Opportunity Commission, and the Employee Retirement Income Security Act) on forty-eight companies. It found that *direct* annual costs (no indirect costs such as delays, losses in productivity, or misallocation of resources were included) were $2.6 billion. Weidenbaum sought to find the administrative and compliance costs of regulation to the U.S. economy as a whole. He concluded that regulation cost $102 billion in 1979. In a similar study for 1976, Weidenbaum found that 49.6 percent of regulatory costs were for industry-specific regulations (traditional type), while 50.4 percent were for consumer and worker safety, environmental, and financial regulation (social type).[6]

Congress Watch, a Ralph Nader group, disputes Weidenbaum's figures and argues that the benefits are greater than Weidenbaum's costs. For instance, Congress Watch estimates the benefits of OSHA regulations at $6.4 billion, compared to a cost of $4.3 billion.[7] The President's Council on Environmental

---

[4]Timothy Clark, "New Approaches to Regulatory Reform—Letting the Market Do the Job," *National Journal*, August 11, 1979, p. 1316.

[5]See Arthur Anderson & Co., *Cost of Government Regulation Study* (Business Roundtable, 1979); and Murray L. Weidenbaum, *The Future of Business Regulation* (AMACON, 1979).

[6]Weidenbaum and DeFina, *The Cost of Federal Regulation*.

[7]*The New York Times*, October 10, 1979, p. A24.

499

Quality contends that in a recent year air pollution regulations yielded $21.4 billion in benefits, compared to a cost of $16 billion. Quantifying the costs and benefits of regulation, however, is difficult: How can we put a dollar value on clean air or on a life saved as a result of regulation?

However, it is generally agreed that regulation could be less costly to society. Deregulation of traditionally regulated industries has already begun in airlines, trucking, and railroads. The communications industry will doubtless be next. Prehaps, the costs of social regulation could be greatly reduced by using more market incentives and streamlining rules, without a decrease in benefits.

REGULATION TO PROTECT THE ENVIRONMENT

Pollution is an issue that vividly illustrates this regulatory dilemma. Critics of strict controls on air, water, and noise pollution say our pursuit of a clean environment has damaged the economy and will continue to cause high unemployment. They call attention, for example, to the disastrous consequences of the shutdown of an industry (or even of one large company). Proponents of tough antipollution laws have argued that we must now pay the price for decades of environmental abuse. They further contend that the longer we delay, the greater the costs to society—both in dollars and in lives.

By its very nature the private sector of the economy tends to ignore pollution. Since everyone benefits from a pollution cleanup, whether they pay for it or not, it is not in any one party's interest to pay the cost. Consequently, the government steps in to control environmental damage. While people usually agree that the government should do something about pollution, there is far less agreement about what it should do, how much it should do, to whom it should be done, and who should pay the cost. These questions take on increased importance because of the special nature of the pollution issue.

Three House subcommittee chairmen investigating the Environmental Protection Agency tell a Capitol Hill news conference that two of the documents withheld by the administration from Congress had been turned over to a polluter. The chairmen, from left: Reps. James Scheter (D-N.Y.), Mike Synar (D-Okla.), and Elliott Levitas (D-Ga.), said the Justice Dept. released the court documents during a court case involving a toxic waste dump site in Hamilton, Ohio. *Wide World Photos.*

500

Nowadays the cost of pollution control tends to fall on the polluter, so we would expect opposition from industry. The benefits, on the other hand, go to everyone. Thus, the issue evokes concentrated opposition but diffuse or weak support.

Historically environmental issues were discussed by local and state governments. In a study of the pollution question, one political scientist found that municipal *in*action has been a regular response to the air pollution problem in communities throughout the nation: "The federal government has taken on new responsibilities in the field of pollution abatement not so much because these local officials demand it, but because these lower levels of government have often failed to take action themselves."[8]

Using its power as a promoter, the federal government finances research into control devices and assists states both in maintaining their own pollution control programs and in building waste treatment facilities. The primary federal agencies concerned with the environment are the Council of Environmental Quality and the Environmental Protection Agency. Other federal agencies also regulate the environment, including the Interior Department, the Food and Drug Administration, and the Departments of Energy and Transportation. The Council on Environmental Quality, in the executive office of the president, develops and recommends policy options to the president and Congress. The Environmental Protection Agency is responsible for the enforcement of federal environmental laws and regulations.

The federal government today administers rules and regulations covering many forms of pollution—air, water, and noise, as well as dangers to the environment from harmful chemicals. Arguments about pollution control rarely concern the question of whether to act or not; rather, they ask *what price* we are willing and able to pay for a clean environment and how best to do it.[9] The Council on Environmental Quality estimates that the cost of cleaning up the environment could be about $300 billion over the next ten years. The bulk of this spending would have to come from private sources. Laws already on the books will cost the average homeowner an extra $15 a month in electricity costs by the year 1985. Some private interests, including the automotive industry and the chemical industry, have been hit hard by pollution control laws.

Is pollution control too costly? Environmentalists point to the high costs of pollution itself. Dirty air and water and hazardous chemicals affect society in the form of health care costs and lost worker productivity. In the asbestos industry it is estimated that one out of five workers may develop cancer, and certain other job situations pose similar dangers.

Legislative progress in environmental control has been swift in the past ten years. The National Environmental Policy Act of 1969 set up the controversial requirement of environmental impact statements. The law requires the filing of statements assessing the potential effect of a federal action on the environment. This has been interpreted to require the filing of a statement for any project utilizing federal funds. Since 1970 thousands of statements have been filed. Critics claim environmental impact statements simply represent more government interference in the private sector. Supporters argue that the statements have pointed out major flaws in projects and have led to cost savings along with greater environmental awareness.

EPA workers in protective suits pour a chemical absorbent on a toxic waste site in Phoenixville, Pa. This former paint manufacturer is being cleaned up as part of the federal superfund for toxic waste sites. *UPI.*

[8]Matthew A. Crenson, *The Un-Politics of Air Pollution* (Johns Hopkins University Press, 1971), p. 10.

[9]See John C. Whitaker, *Striking a Balance* (American Enterprise Institute/Hoover Institution, 1976); Walter A. Rosenbaum, *The Politics of Environmental Concern*, 2nd ed. (Praeger, 1977); and Michael Brown, *Laying Waste: The Poisoning of America by Toxic Chemicals* (Pantheon, 1980).

A MAYOR'S REVENGE

Businessmen, local officials, and other victims seething over the burdens and insults of federal paperwork may find balm for their spirits in a nonfederal document that is floating around. It's a letter from Ernest Angelo Jr., mayor of Midland, Texas. Some time ago, Mayor Angelo went through the ordeal of applying for a grant from the U.S. Department of Housing and Urban Development, a process that lasted over ten months and turned into a red-tape nightmare. Not long afterward, he received from the Dallas regional office of HUD a request for a reserved parking space at Midland's municipal airport. Seizing the opportunity to give the feds a taste of their own medicine, he replied in a letter that read, in part, as follows:

1. You must obtain from the U.S. Government Printing Office, or the National Archives, or the Library of Congress, or someplace, a supply of application form COM-1975. You must submit three executed and fourteen conformed copies of this application . . .

2. With the application submit the make and model of the proposed vehicle together with certified assurances that everyone connected with the manufacture, servicing, and operation of same [was] paid according to a wage scale that complies with the requirements of the Davis-Bacon Act.

3. Submit a genealogical table for everyone who will operate said vehicle

so that we can ascertain that there will be a precisely exact equal percentage of whites, blacks, and other minorities, as well as women and the elderly.

4. Submit certified assurances that this plan has been discussed at length with the EEOC and submit that commission's certification that requirement 3 above has been fully complied with.

5. Submit certified assurances that all operators of said vehicle and any filling station personnel that service same will be equipped with steel-toed boots, safety goggles, and crash helmets and that the vehicle will be equipped with at least safety belts and an air bag to show compliance with the Occupational Safety and Health Act.

6. Submit an Environmental Impact Statement . . . The statement should show the number of times the vehicle will be operated, times of day, the name of the operator of the vehicle, the number of other vehicles that might be coming into or leaving the parking lot at the same time, as well as the number and type of aircraft that might be landing or taking off at the airport at the same time and an exact conclusion as to the effect this will have on

the atmosphere in West Texas.

7. In order to obtain approval of a negative Environmental Impact Statement, you will not be able to:
(a) operate the car on gasoline produced from domestic oil because that would require that someone discover it, process it, and deliver it, and it is possible that some private person, firm or corporation might realize a profit as a result of such activities . . .
(b) operate the car from energy produced by coal because this might require digging a hole in the ground . . .

8. Submit a certificate from the Attorney General of the United States that all of the certifiers of the above assurances are duly and legally authorized by Congress to make such certificates . . . and that the United States of America is a duly organized and legally existing independent nation with the full right, power, and authority to operate automobiles in the first place.

Upon receipt of the foregoing, rest assured that the application will be promptly referred to someone for approval. We cannot state at this time who that someone will be because whatever department he or she is in will be undergoing . . . reorganization. . . .

Reprinted by permission of *Fortune*, November 1976.

The Clean Air Act   One of the most significant pieces of environmental legislation in recent years is the 1970 amendment to the Clean Air Act of 1967.[10] The act establishes national quality standards for states, strict pollution guidelines for automobiles, and regulations concerning stationary sources of pollution. The Clean Air Act

[10]Charles O. Jones, *Clean Air: The Policies and Politics of Pollution* (University of Pittsburgh Press, 1975) offers a detailed analysis of national and local clean air legislation.

has been harshly criticized by business and industry, who contend substantial changes are needed to ease its economic and regulatory burden. Environmentalists claim the act, even with its admitted weaknesses, has substantially improved the quality of the air. Further, the American public supports such a tough law. In a recent Harris poll an overwhelming majority of Americans opposed changes that would make the antipollution law less strict.

The Reagan administration favored relaxation of the Clean Air Act, claiming excessive pollution standards have contributed to the difficulties of the auto industry. President Reagan and his aides hoped in vain to loosen the provisions of the Clean Air Act when it came up for renewal in 1982.

The EPA: Agency in a Crossfire

The Environmental Protection Agency (EPA) is the primary center of federal environmental regulation. Its jurisdiction extends from agricultural pesticides to toxic waste. The Reagan administration, in keeping with its philosophy of cutting back on regulation, cut the EPA's budget by as much as 48 percent in real dollars. Faced with this reduction in revenue, the EPA was forced to cut back on its operations.

Corporations that produce dangerous chemicals as byproducts of manufacturing processes must follow strict guidelines concerning the disposal of these potentially hazardous wastes. The EPA is responsible for enforcing these guidelines. As a result of budget cutbacks and agency policy, the EPA reduced its activity in the area of toxic waste disposal supervision.

EPA directors chose to slow down utilization of a $1.6 billion "superfund" established by Congress in 1980 to finance cleanup of hazardous waste dumps. Critics charged that the EPA cleaned up dumps in selected states in order to help Republican candidates in the 1982 elections. More dangerously, according to critics, the EPA deliberately neglected to clean up many potentially hazardous dumps in order to avoid helping Democratic candidates.

EPA officials were also accused of conflicts of interest. One superfund administrator had been previously employed by a corporation that had polluted one of the toxic waste dumps the superfund was supposed to clean up. She and other EPA officials, counselors, and advisers were accused of providing their former employers and other business interests with favorable treatment in their dealings with the agency.

Several congressional committees and subcommittees began investigating these and other charges. The panels subpoenaed many EPA documents. The president ordered director of the EPA, Anne Burford to refuse the documents on the grounds that congressional access to them might jeopardize ongoing enforcement efforts. He claimed the documents were protected by executive privilege. Burford was cited for contempt of Congress for her lack of compliance. She later resigned under heavy pressure.

The scandal at the EPA raised questions concerning the proper amount of direct political control over regulatory decisions. It also demonstrated the difficulty of implementing the Reagan administration's regulatory policies. Many observers think the EPA too often favored industrial development over environmental protection.

A health physics technician gives a report to engineers from inside the airlock leading to the reactor building at the Three Mile Island nuclear plant. For the first time in almost a year, workers entered the airlock on March 13, 1980. *UPI.*

Disposing of Toxic Waste

The EPA "sewergate" scandal focused American attention on a uniquely modern problem: disposing of toxic waste. The United States produces 255 million to 275 million metric tons of hazardous waste a year. Much of this waste is deposited in landfills, from where it seeps into and contaminates ground water. Toxic wastes create other types of health hazards as well: "Love Canal" and "Times Beach" have now joined Three Mile Island on the list of least desirable addresses in the United States.

Three Mile Island, Pennsylvania, site of a nuclear power plant. *UPI.*

Love Canal, a residential community in Niagara Falls, New York, was evacuated in 1979 when health officials linked unusually high death rates and illness there to chemicals leaking from an old industrial dump. Times Beach, Missouri, suffered a similar fate. Officials discovered that unpaved roads there had been sprayed with Dioxin, one of the most toxic man-made substances and a suspected cause of cancer. The beleaguered EPA took the unprecedented move of buying the town of Times Beach in order to save its residents. In the spring of 1983 the agency paid out $36.7 million and evacuated the residents of the community.

Toxic waste disposal is rapidly replacing nuclear energy as the dominant environmental issue of the 1980s. The apparent move away from the construction of nuclear power plants—and increased public awareness—may help to solve the separate problem of disposal of nuclear wastes. For example, a referendum passed in Massachusetts in 1982 placed limitations on the establishment of nuclear waste dump sites in that state. The Nuclear Regulatory Commission (NRC) has also become more active in overseeing potential hazards of nuclear power plants.

The Saga of James Watt (1981–1983)

Many environmentalists in the early 1980s thought there was a hazard to the environment even greater than toxic and nuclear waste. That hazard, they said, was James Watt. Watt served for nearly three years as Secretary of the Department of the Interior in the Reagan administration. Among other responsibilities, the department oversees lands owned by the federal government. Secretary Watt generated considerable protest with his plan to accelerate the utilization of public land for resource development. His goal was to sell more rights to mine coal or drill for oil on public land in order to make the U.S. less dependent on foreign energy supplies. Watt said he was also in favor of clean air and an enhanced environment, but he wanted to help create jobs and enhance the nation's economy and security. Watt contended we could encourage

William Clark, President Reagan's national security adviser, succeeded James Watt as Interior Secretary in late 1983. *UPI.*

increased mining and energy exploration and protect the environment as well. He accused the environmentalists of exaggeration. Opponents of Watt's policies, and they were many, said in addition to ruining aesthetically valuable wilderness lands, Watt was so eager to develop them that he sold mining and drilling rights for far less than market value. Watt was forced to resign in late 1983 for use of insensitve language.

Each of the issues discussed above represents the fundamental problem at the heart of environmental regulation: the problem of priorities. In a system such as ours, that aspires to one of free enterprise, the government tries to balance economic and environmental concerns. It attempts to guarantee the health and safety of its citizens and preserve the natural beauty of America for future generations. At the same time regulators try not to inhibit developments vital to improving the standard of living for all Americans.

REGULATING BUSINESS

Business has never been free of restrictive legislation, but during much of the latter part of the nineteenth century, our national policy was to leave business pretty much alone. With considerable freedom business leaders set about developing (as well as exploiting) a nation that was enormously rich in natural resources. The heroes of the 1870s and 1880s were not politicians but business magnates—the Rockefellers, Morgans, Carnegies, and Fricks. "From rags to riches" became the nation's motto.

Yet many businessmen in the late nineteenth century were not just given freedom; they often were given prime sections of land to subsidize expansion of rail systems, tariffs to protect infant industries, and implicit—if not explicit—police assistance to prevent rapid unionization. Government actually helped to *promote* many of these businesses.

Toward the end of the century sharp depressions rocked the economy and threw people out of work. Millions labored long hours in factories and fields for meager wages. Muckrakers revealed that some of the most famous business leaders had indulged in shoddy practices and corrupt deals. A demand for government regulation sprang up, and a series of national and state laws were passed in an attempt to correct the worst abuses. Such laws were adopted on the pragmatic assumption that each problem could be handled as it arose. On balance, however, these laws still reflected a commitment to competitive markets. The government intervened only for the purpose of remedying the defects of the marketplace.

Antitrust Policy   Social critics and reformers in the late nineteenth century believed consumers were being cheated where monopolies controlled goods and services, especially in the oil, sugar, whiskey, and steel industries. At the same time people began to have mixed feelings about big business. Americans, who have always been impressed by bigness—the tallest skyscraper, the largest football stadium, the biggest steel mill—and the efficiency that often goes with it, have also been skeptical about the power and side effects of giant enterprises. We believe our economic system functions best under conditions of fair competition among many businesses. We would like to believe, too, that enterprising individuals can set themselves up in virtually any business. These mixed views have long been reflected in our attempts to prevent monopoly and the restraint of competition through antitrust policy. ("Trusts" are collusions or arrangements to reduce competition.)

In 1890 Congress responded to this new mood by passing the Sherman

Pat Boone with one of his daughters. *UPI.*

Antitrust Act. Designed to foster competition and stop the growth of private monopolies, the act made clear its intention "to protect trade and commerce against unlawful restraints and monopolies." Henceforth, persons making contracts, combinations, or conspiracies in restraint of trade in interstate and foreign commerce could be sued for damages, required to stop their illegal practices, and subjected to criminal penalties. The Sherman Antitrust Act had little immediate impact. Presidents made little attempt to enforce it, and the Supreme Court's early construction of the act limited its scope.[11]

During Wilson's administration Congress added the Clayton Act to the antitrust arsenal. This act outlawed specific abuses such as charging different prices to different buyers in order to destroy a weaker competitor, granting rebates, making false statements about competitors and their products, buying up supplies to stifle competition, bribing competitor's employees, and so on. In addition, interlocking directorates (where an officer or director in one corporation serves on the board of another, especially a competitor) in large corporations were banned, and corporations were prohibited from acquiring stock (amended in 1950 to include assets) in competing concerns if such acquisitions substantially lessened interstate competition. Also in 1914 Congress established a five-person federal trade commission (FTC) to enforce the Clayton Act and to prevent unfair competitive practices. The FTC was to be the "traffic cop" for competition.

Still, antitrust activity continued to be weak during the 1920s. Times were prosperous: Republican administrations were actively probusiness. The FTC consisted of men who opposed government regulation of business. The Department of Justice, charged with enforcing the Sherman Act, paid little attention to it. During the Depression popular resentment mounted against big business as abuses were revealed. At first the Roosevelt administration tried to fight the Depression by setting aside the antitrust laws. But by the late 1930s a period of trustbusting began in earnest. Since then the Supreme Court has shown a more sympathetic attitude toward the purposes of the Sherman Act, and the FTC has sometimes acted with more vigor. The "beefed-up" Antitrust Division of the Department of Justice has won some notable victories.

But how effective has all this activity been? Have antitrust suits, FTC proceedings, and the fear of such reprisals kept our system competitive? It is difficult to tell. Some people think antitrust laws are out of date, in part because such laws were written in an era when the major economic competitors in any industry were from this country alone. That has markedly changed in recent years.

Americans tend to think issues of domestic economic policy are solely within the jurisdiction of this government. But in recent years we have discovered that the economic fate of this nation and of its industries is tied closely to what happens elsewhere. For years we thought the automobile market in the United States was dominated by the Big Three (GM, Ford, and Chrysler), and that they could pretty much control the market and set the prices. But after they set the prices "too high," we discovered that firms located in Japan, Germany, and elsewhere can also make and sell cars: As a result, Big Three look less Big.

Foreign corporations have captured increasing shares of U.S. markets, and American corporations have moved more of their production facilities overseas. More corporations have become multinational, seeking to benefit from the overlapping of national regulatory jurisdictions. Sometimes companies move operations to locations where regulations are less strict or even nonexis-

[11]*United States v. E. C. Knight Co.,* 156 U.S. 1 (1895).

"It so happens, Gregory, that your Grandfather Sloan was detained by an agency of our government over an honest misunderstanding concerning certain anti-trust matters! He was not 'busted by the Feds'!" *Drawing by W. Miller; © 1971 The New Yorker Magazine, Inc.*

Antitrust Enforcement and the Phone Company

tent. Today about one-third of the nation's manufacturing capacity is controlled by fifty companies, and well over two-thirds of all manufacturing assets are owned by only five hundred corporations.[12] But monopolies as such have virtually disappeared from the economic arena. In place of monopolies two new threats have emerged: the oligopoly, where a few firms dominate a market, as in the automobile industry or the food processing industry; and the conglomerate, where a firm owns businesses in many unrelated industries, such as ITT.

Antitrust tools have been seriously tested by these developments. Formerly federal prosecutors generally believed the Sherman Act and the Clayton Act could be applied only to the traditional single-firm monopoly. But in recent years the FTC and the Department of Justice have begun to expand the interpretation of existing legislation to attack oligopolies. They have moved against the major breakfast cereal producers and large oil companies, for example. Some critics view these actions as political "potshots" attacking the "economic royalists" because it is good politics. Others view these actions as cosmetic. They believe the goal of breaking up large concentrations of economic power can be accomplished only if Congress enacts new legislation.

The Reagan administration, ushering in a new attitude toward antitrust policy, maintained that bigness is not necessarily badness. Increased competition from foreign firms, rapid technological innovations, slow growth of the domestic economy, and stagnating productivity all combine to create a situation in which larger enterprises may be necessary to enable businesses to remain competitive. Accordingly, the Reagan administration relaxed its antitrust prosecution and enforcement activity.[13]

However, Justice Department officials in the Reagan administration continued the government's antitrust case against American Telephone and Telegraph (AT&T). In 1975 the giant communications firm had been charged with monopolizing the telephone service and telephone equipment industry. The Justice Department claimed AT&T was using control of its twenty-two local phone companies to shut out competition in the long-distance and phone equipment sales markets. Anti-trust laws were used in this instance by other business firms to break up AT&T. Pressures were not so much to protect consumers as to give other businesses an opportunity to sell telephones and long distance services.

The huge antitrust case was settled in 1983, after costing AT&T over $360 million in legal fees over a seven-year period. Under the terms of the settlement, the twenty-two local phone companies owned by AT&T became reorganized into seven independent companies. AT&T was allowed to keep its long-distance operations, its equipment manufacturing and sales arms, and its research facilities. All other phone services, however, were divided among the local companies.

The precise effects on telephone service and phone bills remain uncertain. Some analysts (including the president of AT&T) think rates for local service will increase as smaller phone companies are forced to pass on increased costs to consumers. Critics of the AT&T "break-up" think this is government regulation at its worst. Taking the world's best telephone service and altering it and weakening it just doesn't make sense, they say. The only people who will

[12]John Blair, *Economic Concentration: Structure, Behavior and Public Policy* (Harcourt Brace Jovanovich, 1972).

[13]See Fred L. Smith, "Why Not Abolish Antitrust?" *Regulation* (January/February, 1983), pp. 23–28, 33; and Joe Sims and William Blumenthal, "The New Era in Antitrust," *Regulation* (July/August, 1982), pp. 25–28.

profit will be lawyers, bankers, stock brokers, and those who print stock certificates. Others think increased competition in the long-distance market will result in savings which will more than offset local rate increases. The long-term effects of reorganizing the telephone industry may not be known until the late 1980s.[14]

While antitrust enforcement is sometimes necessary, enforcement often loses sight of its major objective: making the United States a more efficient and productive economy. In this context bigness is not always something to be avoided, and mergers by large corporations are not necessarily anticompetitive.

Controlling Big Business

What should the government do about big business? Few policy makers agree on an answer. Some say we are doing too much—and even those who think we are doing too little do not agree on the solutions. Some economists, for example, see no need for new initiatives. They say the alleged damage done by big business is vastly overestimated, and that even the extent of concentration is exaggerated. They reject as pure myth the view that the United States has become a corporate state. They see the increasing size of business as an indication of increased economies of scale. While the market is still as competitive as before, the companies are bigger. And we, as consumers, benefit from the technology provided by the large modern corporation.[15]

Economist John Kenneth Galbraith, among others, agrees that bigness contributes to efficiency, provides the capital necessary for innovation, and spurs economic growth. But he also recognizes the abuses that can occur when economic power is concentrated in the hands of a few corporate managers. Galbraith suggests three new tasks for government:

1. Provide assistance to the segment of our economy that is still considered to be competitive—for example, the corner grocery store or the independent TV repair shop.

2. Manage the economy directly by implementing wage-price controls in all the industries that are dominated by big business and big unions.

3. Control the direction of big business by restricting the use of resources in areas that are already overdeveloped; by setting limits on the use of technology; and by establishing stringent standards on the byproducts of industry—for example, pollution—*and* enforcing the standards once set.[16]

"But this would be socialism!" exclaim many economists and policy makers. No, says Galbraith; government already plays a major role in the development of individual firms and in the distribution of economic rewards among different industries. All Galbraith calls for, or so he claims, is the *redirection* of government subsidies. "If these proposals are socialism," he would reply to his critics, "socialism already exists."

Still other reformers want to break up large corporations, not just regulate them. These individuals believe the market can work; all it needs is a chance. They are against bigness, charging that bigness leads to irresponsibility and misconduct.[17] Are the nation's antitrust laws, drawn up several decades ago, still practical for a 1980s economy? This question evokes markedly different responses. At the Justice Department's Antitrust Division, about 320 lawyers

---

[14]See Michael Wines, "Transition to a New Era of Telephone Service Could be a Painful Passage," *National Journal*, January 15, 1983, pp. 104–10.

[15]Neil H. Jacoby, *Corporate Power and Social Responsibility* (Macmillan, 1973), pp. 138, 145, 249.

[16]John Kenneth Galbraith, *Economics and the Public Purpose* (Houghton Mifflin, 1973), pp. 221–22.

[17]See, for example, Ralph Nader et al., *Taming the Giant Corporation* (Norton, 1976).

work on such cases in an overall effort to protect the free enterprise system. In one recent four-and-a-half-year period, this division brought nearly 350 civil and criminal cases. Corporate conduct that may be illegal comes to their attention through complaints by a competitor, customer, or supplier.[18]

Veteran observers say the Antitrust Division does a reasonably fair and adequate job. Many think it is understaffed and, considering its responsibility, that it must work with an exceedingly small budget. In recent years the Federal Trade Commission also has been active in investigating the structure of concentrated industries. Many of the FTC's important cases, such as the Goodyear Tire and Rubber Company case in 1973, are settled during consent negotiations. Consent decrees are orders to cease anticompetitive conduct (although things other than anticompetitive conduct are sometimes specified in consent decrees).

Antitrust politics, like most economic controversies, resembles a tug of war. Major new battles in this arena are inevitable. Leading participants include private antitrust lawyers, the FTC, the Justice Department, Senate and House antitrust and monopoly subcommittees, the courts, lawyers representing corporate interests, and various public interest and consumer advocate lawyers. Each participant has a different idea of what should—or should not—be done to deal with the problem.

REGULATING LABOR-MANAGEMENT RELATIONS

Government regulation of business is essentially restrictive. Most governmental laws and rules have curbed certain business practices and steered private enterprise into socially useful channels. But regulation cuts two ways. In the case of American workers, most laws in recent decades have tended not to restrict but rather to confer rights and opportunities. Actually, many labor laws do not touch labor directly; instead, they regulate its relations with employers.

Labor and the Government

Labor leaders generally favor federal regulation. They fear labor would fare less well if regulation did not exist. Moreover, the federal government since FDR and prior to Reagan was usually a major ally in the campaign to improve job safety and working conditions.

During the first half of this century, governmental protection and promotion were gradually extended over the whole range of labor activity and organization. This was the result of two basic developments: labor's growing political power, and the awareness of millions of Americans that a healthy and secure nation depends in large measure on a healthy and secure labor force.

Labor's basic struggle was for the right to organize. For many decades trade unions had been held lawful by acts of state legislatures, but the courts had chipped away at their status by legalizing certain antiunion devices. The most notorious was the yellow-dog contract, by which employers made new workers promise not to join a labor organization. If labor organizers later tried to unionize the worker, the employer, on the basis of the yellow-dog contract, could apply for court orders to stop the organizers. In 1932 labor secured the passage of the Norris–La Guardia Act, which made yellow-dog contracts unenforceable and granted labor the right to organize. By 1932 unions had won other kinds of protection from the federal government, especially over conditions of labor. But progress was slow. With the New Deal, Congress began to enact a series of laws to protect workers and their right to form trade unions.

[18]Suzanne Weaver, *Decision to Prosecute: Organization and Public Policy in the Antitrust Division* (MIT Press, 1977) is one of the best books on the government's legal activities.

Protecting Workers

Among the more important areas of federal regulation designed to protect workers are the following:

1. *Public contracts.* The Walsh-Healey Act of 1936, as amended, requires that all contracts with the national government in excess of $10,000 provide that no worker employed under such contracts be paid less than the prevailing wage; and that he or she be paid overtime for all work in excess of eight hours per day or forty hours per week. One of the contested questions of the 1980s is how to determine what the prevailing wage is and whether or not this provision inserted in the mid-1930s should be retained in the 1980s. Skilled craftworkers and union officials insist that the Davis-Bacon provision, as it is known, is still necessary to protect their standard of living and to insure quality work on government projects. Others argue that in the present day context the prevailing wage requirement makes public work unreasonably expensive and that the provision merely gives craftworkers a special privilege at the expense of the taxpayers.

2. *Wages and hours.* The Fair Labor Standards Act of 1938 set a maximum work week of forty hours for all employers engaged in interstate commerce or in the production of goods for interstate commerce (with certain exemptions). Work beyond that amount must be paid for at one and one-half times the regular rate. Minimum wages, first set at 25 cents an hour, were progressively increased, reaching $3.35 in 1983.

3. *Child labor.* The Federal Labor Standards Act prohibits child labor (under sixteen years of age, or under eighteen in hazardous occupations) in industries that engage in, or that produce goods for, interstate commerce.

4. *Industrial safety and occupational health.* The Occupational Safety and Health Act of 1970 created the first comprehensive federal industrial safety program. It gives the secretary of labor broad authority to set safety and health standards for workers of companies in interstate commerce.

Protecting Unions

United Autoworkers President Douglas Fraser (l) with Chrysler Corporation Vice-President William O'Brien (r) signing an agreement. *UPI.*

Do unions need federal laws to protect their right to organize? The history of union efforts before 1933 suggests that organizing without federal protection was extremely difficult. Indeed, union membership and strength were waning fast until New Deal measures granted workers the right to organize and bargain collectively. The National Labor Relations Act of 1935 (usually called the Wagner Act) made these guarantees permanent. The preamble declared that workers in industries affecting interstate commerce (with certain exemptions) should have the right to organize and bargain collectively, and that inequality in bargaining power between employers and workers led to industrial strife and economic instability. The act made five types of action unfair for employers: (1) interfering with workers in their attempt to organize unions or bargain collectively; (2) supporting company unions (unions set up and dominated by the employer); (3) discriminating against members of unions; (4) firing or otherwise victimizing an employee for having taken action under the act; and (5) refusing to bargain with union representatives. The act was intended to prevent employers from using violence, espionage, propaganda, and community pressure to resist unionization.

To administer the act, a board of three (now five) members, holding overlapping terms of five years each, was set up. Under the act the National Labor Relations Board (NLRB), a regulatory commission, has the ticklish job of determining the appropriate bargaining unit—that is, whether the employees may organize by plant, by craft, or on some other basis. The board operates largely through regional officers, who investigate charges of unfair labor practices and issue formal complaints; and through trial examiners, who hold hearings and submit reports to the board in Washington.

Striking a Balance   From the start the Wagner Act was controversial. It strengthened the unions and helped them seize greater economic and political power. In 1936 a committee of noted attorneys declared it unconstitutional. In 1937 the Supreme Court, by a vote of five to four, upheld the constitutionality of the act.[19] The fight then shifted to Congress, where senators and representatives attacked the NLRB through denunciations, investigations, and slashes in appropriations.

What caused all this uproar? First, from the outset the board vigorously applied the prolabor provisions of the act. Second, the board got caught in the struggle between the AFL and the CIO. Whichever way it decided certain cases, it was bound to antagonize one labor faction or the other. Third, the purpose of the act was widely misunderstood. Employers and editorial writers solemnly charged that the act was biased in favor of labor, when the very aim of the act had been to improve the workers' bargaining power.

Most unions were run honestly and responsively. Nevertheless, public opinion seemed to swing against labor after World War II. Both labor excesses and a wave of great industrywide strikes intensified demands that Congress equalize the obligations of labor and management. In 1946 the Republicans won majorities in both the House and the Senate, paving the way for modification of the Wagner Act.

The Taft-Hartley Act   The result was the Labor-Management Relations Act of 1947, commonly called the Taft-Hartley Act. This act applies (with certain exceptions) to industries dealing in interstate commerce. The act

1. Outlaws the closed shop and permits the union shop only under certain conditions. (A closed shop requires an employer to hire and retain only union members in good standing. A union shop is one in which new employees must join the union within a stated period of time.)
2. Outlaws jurisdictional strikes (strikes arising from disputes between unions over whose members should perform a particular task); secondary boycotts

A special meeting of the AFL-CIO Public Employee Department's executive board in Washington with air traffic controllers. *AFL-CIO News.*

[19]*National Labor Relations Board v. Jones & Laughton Steel Corp.,* 301 U.S. 1 (1937).

(an effort by a union involved in a dispute with an employer to encourage another union to boycott a fourth party—usually their employer—who, in response to such pressure, might put pressure on the original offending employer); excessive union dues or fees; and strikes by federal employees.

3. Makes it an unfair labor practice for unions to refuse to bargain with employers.

4. Permits employers and unions to sue each other in federal court for violation of contracts.

5. Allows the use of the labor injunction on a limited scale. (Such an injunction is a court order forbidding specific individuals or groups to perform acts the court considers harmful to the rights or property of an employer or community.)

Organized labor called the new measure a "slave-labor" act and vowed to use its political power to wipe the act from the books. Senator Taft saw the bill as "an extraordinary reversal along the right lines toward equalizing the power of labor unions and employers." Since 1947 organized labor has kept up its drive to repeal the Taft-Hartley Act, especially the section that permits states to outlaw union shops. Union leaders contend these laws undermine their organizing efforts, especially in the South, where most states have passed so-called right to work laws. Right to work laws typically make it illegal for collective bargaining agreements to contain closed shop, union shop, preferential hiring, or any other clauses calling for compulsory union membership. The Taft-Hartley Act also set up machinery for handling disputes affecting an entire industry or a major part of it, where a stoppage would threaten national health or safety. When such a strike breaks out, the following steps are authorized:

1. The president appoints a special board to investigate and report the facts.

2. The president may then instruct the attorney general to seek in a federal court an eighty-day injunction against the strike.

3. If the court agrees that the national health or safety is endangered, it grants this injunction.

4. If the parties have not settled the strike within the eighty days, the board informs the president of the employer's last offer of settlement.

5. The NLRB takes a secret vote among the employees to see if they will accept the employer's last offer.

6. If no settlement is reached, the injunction expires, and the president reports to Congress with such recommendations as the chief executive may wish to make.

The Taft-Hartley Act has been frequently invoked against strikes in vital sectors of the economy, such as atomic energy, coal, shipping, steel, and telephone service. Sometimes a president and the secretary of labor attempt to mediate strikes without resorting to the act. The effectiveness of this act is difficult to assess because legislation is only one of the many factors that affect industrial peace. Still, the basic issue remains unresolved. Strikes are part of the price we pay for the system of collective bargaining. But under what conditions does the price become so high that the federal government should intervene, stop the strike, and force a settlement? The country will be dealing with the issue for a long time.

The policies of collective bargaining are part of a broader set of issues. Labor is deeply concerned not only with the traditional conditions of work—such as hours, wages, and pensions—but it must also deal with the issue of job security, which is now threatened by technological change and automation.

Business faces not only rising costs but intense foreign competition. The public is directly affected by altered patterns of competition, quality of goods, prices, and unemployment.

One major development in labor relations has been the considerable growth of public sector unionization. Our previously industrial economy has become service oriented, with a notable growth in government services. Unionization in the public sector is especially controversial, in part because of the essential nature of public services. Many states have laws prohibiting unionization and collective bargaining over economic benefits for public sector employees. Also, the Hatch Act at the federal level defines public sector (federal) employment as a privilege, not a right, and limits political participation by public employees. Unions, of course, often become highly political. Unlike the private sector, where there are two major adversarial parties—labor and management—the public sector has three—labor, management, and the taxpayer.[20]

REGULATING OCCUPATIONAL SAFETY AND HEALTH: A CASE STUDY

One of the most criticized federal regulatory agencies in recent years has been the Occupational Safety and Health Administration (OSHA), a unit in the Department of Labor created in 1970. If you have read about it in the newspapers, you have doubtless come across some report of its endless rules or its allegedly arrogant or patronizing warnings to business operators. OSHA has approximately 4000 rules on about 800 pages of the Code of Federal Regulations. It employs 2300 persons, about half of whom are safety and health inspectors.

OSHA was set up because the public perceived too many people were becoming disabled, or were dying, from work-related accidents. As of 1970 over 14,000 people were dying each year in industrial accidents, and an estimated 100,000 a year were being permanently disabled in workplace injuries. The mandate of OSHA is nothing less than to protect the health and safety of more than 60 million workers in about 5 million workplaces. It is also asked to issue compulsory safety and health standards and to monitor compliance. To achieve these objectives, OSHA is empowered to inspect businesses and to issue notices of violation and fines.

Criticism of OSHA   In business circles OSHA quickly became a four-letter word. Many business executives criticize OSHA's standards as having only nuisance value. They also contend that inspectors are not familiar enough with their operations to make criticisms. Further, they believe many of the OSHA regulations do not protect the workers. There is a widely held view that the costs of many OSHA changes have had an inflationary effect. General Motors, for example, claims to have spent nearly $100 million to meet OSHA standards.

In the first years of OSHA, small businesses (55 percent of industrial fatalities occur in businesses employing twenty-five or fewer workers) complained that OSHA made rules that were too numerous, too complex, and too technical. Further, the costs of compliance are prohibitive for small business operators and raise the costs of production to an unacceptable level. Some busi-

---

[20]See Alan Edward Bent and T. Zane Reeves, *Collective Bargaining in the Public Sector* (Benjamin/Cumming Publishing Co., 1978).

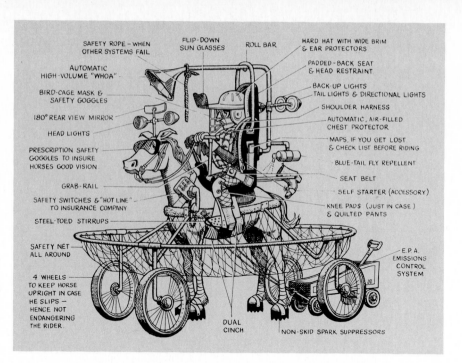

SAFETY ROPE – WHEN OTHER SYSTEMS FAIL

FLIP-DOWN SUN GLASSES

ROLL BAR

HARD HAT WITH WIDE BRIM & EAR PROTECTORS

AUTOMATIC HIGH-VOLUME "WHOA"

PADDED-BACK SEAT & HEAD RESTRAINT

BIRD-CAGE MASK & SAFETY GOGGLES

BACK-UP LIGHTS TAIL LIGHTS & DIRECTIONAL LIGHTS

SHOULDER HARNESS

180° REAR VIEW MIRROR

AUTOMATIC, AIR-FILLED CHEST PROTECTOR

HEAD LIGHTS

MAPS, IF YOU GET LOST & CHECK LIST BEFORE RIDING

PRESCRIPTION SAFETY GOGGLES TO INSURE HORSES GOOD VISION

BLUE-TAIL FLY REPELLENT

SEAT BELT

GRAB-RAIL

SELF STARTER (ACCESSORY)

SAFETY SWITCHES & "HOT LINE" TO INSURANCE COMPANY

KNEE PADS (JUST IN CASE) & QUILTED PANTS

STEEL-TOED STIRRUPS

SAFETY NET ALL AROUND

E.P.A. EMISSIONS CONTROL SYSTEM

4 WHEELS TO KEEP HORSE UPRIGHT IN CASE HE SLIPS – HENCE NOT ENDANGERING THE RIDER.

DUAL CINCH

NON-SKID SPARK SUPPRESSORS

Cowboy after OSHA. Mythical supersafe cowboy illustrates what many business people think of the practicality of federal health and safety rules. Union leaders, however, complain regulation is lax. *J. N. Devin in National Safety News.*

nesses even said they had to close down; others said they might have to close down because of OSHA and similar governmental regulations.

Labor groups have been OSHA's major source of support, especially in the 1970s. But even labor officials criticized it for being not strict enough with industry. Too much attention was given to trivial violations, and fines were too small. Still, labor believed workers could use OSHA to force an employer to correct unsafe conditions.

Nevertheless, the backlash from business interests was intense. Proposals sprang up in Congress to exempt small businesses from OSHA's provisions. President Ford repeatedly condemned OSHA, saying at one point he'd like to throw OSHA "into the ocean." Some of President Carter's economic advisers also suggested abolishing it. President Reagan campaigned for office saying he would curb OSHA's tendency to harass businesses—and Reagan did just that. He made it clear he wanted OSHA to be more conciliatory and to concentrate on major industries and major workplace hazards. After 1980 the whole tone of OSHA changed. It streamlined its restrictions and modified its enforcement policies. Critics in the labor and environmental movements believe Reagan virtually dismantled the agency.[21] Even the Supreme Court worked to modify OSHA; it held that OSHA's practices of making unannounced inspections of all businesses for violations, even though authorized by Congress, violated the Constitution.

OSHA has not been as bad as its critics maintain, but neither has it been as effective as it should be. It deserves credit for its energetic action against polyvinyl chloride and other serious threats to workers' health. OSHA has tried to concentrate its limited energies on severe health hazards and make more use of an emergency power to restrict use of dangerous substances. It has dropped many trivial safety rules and focused on four major industries (construction, heavy manufacturing, transportation, and petrochemicals) that are considered especially hazardous. It keeps pressure on a few industries it considers poten-

[21]See James Crawford, "The Dismantling of OSHA," *The Nation*, September 12, 1981.

tially dangerous, such as auto repair, dry cleaning, and building materials. Nowadays more simply written guidelines are used, and some paperwork has been simplified.

As the OSHA overhaul proceeds, more controversies are bound to arise. They cannot be avoided as the government faces up to some tough issues of industrial health in a world of complex technology. Workers are exposed to a host of substances whose effects on human health are not fully understood. Even when something is known to be toxic, the precise degree of risk—or an acceptable amount of exposure—is hard to calculate, and the costs of full protection can run very high. Often the harmful effects of many substances (such as asbestos and cotton dust) do not appear until years later, making proof of causation more difficult and the establishment of regulations more tenuous.

OSHA's problems stem from the fact that it is an attempt by government to intervene in the private sector by command-control types of devices rather than by economic incentives. Liberals as well as conservatives now hold that while it should be costly for businesses not to adopt safety standards, the details of administration should be worked out by the businesses themselves rather than by a government agency.

REGULATORY OUTCOMES AND ISSUES

Positive accomplishments of regulation usually get overlooked. Considerable progress has been made in air pollution control. Lead paint poisonings and accidental aspirin poisonings have markedly decreased as a result of new regulatory efforts. Childproof bottle tops, automobile seat belts, and federally insured bank accounts are all byproducts of federal regulation. The prevention of thalidomide babies can be credited to regulatory activity, as can the safety of airline travel. The decrease in airplane hijackings and the banning of many cancer-producing pesticides is a direct result of national regulation.

Positive accomplishments are, of course, somewhat offset by the costs. Thus, there has been a lower rate of new drug development and introduction of new drugs since the 1962 amendments to the Food and Drug Act were passed. There is also little doubt that get-tough pollution regulations have had an inflationary impact. Other studies argue that the Interstate Commerce Commission killed the railroad industry and that Federal Communications Commission regulations have caused drab uniformity in television programming.

The major problems and criticisms of regulation are as follows:

REGULATION DISTORTS AND DISRUPTS THE OPERATION OF THE MARKET Sometimes governmental intervention upsets the normal adjustment processes of the market and thus encourages higher prices, misallocation of resources, and inefficiency.

REGULATION CAN DISCOURAGE COMPETITION Some forms of regulation (often the kind desired by industry) actually have the reverse of their desired effect. This is especially true where the government grants operating licenses and charters and seeks to maintain a certain level of quality or stability in the market. (This used to exist in trucking and air travel, where the federal government exerted control over entry into markets.) Regulatory red tape has also been charged with discouraging entry into industries and driving small businesses out.

REGULATION MAY DISCOURAGE TECHNOLOGICAL DEVELOPMENT
It is argued that if the reward for an innovation is a new set of rules and a struggle for permission to use a new product, it may not be worth the effort.

REGULATORY AGENCIES ARE OFTEN "CAPTURED" BY THE INDUSTRIES THEY REGULATE It is suggested, especially by those on the political Left, that some regulatory bodies are controlled by the big businesses they are supposed to be regulating. This is a popular view among those who see big business as a great power in our society. This view may describe a few of the older regulatory bodies, but it has been discredited by several scholars. One student of regulation explains:

> An agency is established, sometimes with industry support and sometimes over industry objections, and then gradually creates a regulatory climate that acquires a life of its own. Certain firms will be helped by some of the specific regulatory decisions making up this climate, others will be hurt. But the industry as a whole will adjust to the climate and decide that the costs of shifting from the known hazards of regulation to the unknown ones of competition are too great; it thus will come to defend the system.[22]

The newer regulatory bodies are probably less "captured" because they deal with many industries and have intentionally been made harder to capture. Also public interest groups are increasingly on the lookout for potential conflicts of interest in nominees to regulatory boards. A number of presidential nominees to regulatory positions have been defeated, or their names have been withdrawn, because of opposition of this kind. General standards have been suggested against which to measure these nominees. These include the following:

1. Nominees should be persons of integrity, whose past records demonstrate they have conducted their affairs honestly and have conscientiously complied with the law.

2. Nominees should be committed to basic principles of accountability in the executive branch, such as strong conflict of interest regulations, financial disclosure, open meetings, and checks on inordinate influence by regulated interests over agency policy.

3. Nominees should be knowledgeable about the industries they will regulate.

Still, some evidence of the capture thesis does exist in the "revolving door" situation, where federal regulators leave their jobs to take high-paying posts with the industries they previously regulated. There is evidence too that some people see jobs in regulatory agencies as stepping stones to lucrative careers in private industry—and the industries obviously benefit in several ways from hiring some of the abler regulators.

REGULATION INCREASES COSTS TO INDUSTRY AND TO THE CONSUMER Federal regulations, as noted earlier, are costly. Probusiness estimates claim that overall federal regulations cost well over $500 for every man, woman, and child in the United States. Such figures are disputed by many labor and consumer advocates who say health and safety standards are the best investment we can make. Every life and every limb we save, and every disease we prevent, represents not only a human achievement but also a reduction in the nation's enormous hospital and medical bills. The cost of neglecting health and safety requirements can be calculated in terms of loss of worker productivity and in insurance costs such as workmen's compensation. Further, regulation provides new jobs in industry—perhaps as many as a million jobs in just the

---

[22]James Q. Wilson, "The Dead Hand of Regulation," *The Public Interest* (Fall 1971), p. 47; Paul Quirk, *Industry Influence in Federal Regulatory Agencies* (Princeton University Press, 1981).

last few years. Plainly, however, the debate over the costliness of federal regulations depends very much on where you sit—that is, on whether you favor labor or management, producer or consumer, energy developer or ecologist.

REGULATION HAS OFTEN BEEN INTRODUCED WITHOUT COST-BENEFIT ANALYSIS Many critics say too little attention is given to the question of whether the benefits of a particular piece of regulation are great enough to justify its cost. Is it worth it to clean up automobile emissions 95 percent if the cost is many times that of an 85 percent cleanup? The answer to this question may be yes, but regulatory agencies are criticized for failing to ask, let alone to answer, questions such as these.

REGULATORY AGENCIES LACK QUALIFIED PERSONNEL Critics of regulation, and the heads of regulatory agencies themselves, say regulators lack the expertise to do their jobs properly. Regulatory agencies complain they need larger budgets to attract more qualified staff. Critics argue, too, that government should not meddle in complex chemical or technological industries it knows little about.

THE DEREGULATION DEBATE

For the last thirty years every president has proposed a program for regulatory reform. Economists from the conservative "University of Chicago school" on the one side to the most liberal pro-Ted Kennedy and pro-Walter Mondale school on the other are all but unanimous in their view that much regulation is unnecessary and that some of it uses the wrong strategy. Although deregulation and regulatory reform have different meanings to different people, the terms are generally used to describe a cutback in the amount of regulation attempted by the federal government. While there is agreement that reform is needed, it is more difficult to find agreement on specific actions.

Deregulating Transportation

No industry has undergone as extensive deregulation as has the transportation industry. Airlines, trucking, and railroads have all recently been granted more freedom in conducting their operations. Enough time has now elapsed so that we may analyze the reasons behind transportation deregulation, the key provisions of each particular deregulation act, and the effects on each specific industry.

FAA inspectors check inside the cockpit of a DC–9 that crashed during a violent storm. Most airline crashes are thoroughly investigated by the FAA. *UPI.*

AIRLINE DEREGULATION The Civil Aeronautics Board (CAB) was established by the federal government in 1938 to protect airlines from unreasonable competition by controlling rates and fares. Critics of CAB regulation charged that airlines were competing only in the frequency and convenience of flights and in the services they offered on flights. Since there was no competition over price, consumers were being forced to pay high rates for services they may not have desired. Others claimed CAB regulation of fares may have been keeping them higher than they would be under more competitive conditions. It was also charged that new routes were being opened up very slowly under CAB supervision.

In light of these and other considerations, Congress passed the Airline Deregulation Act in the fall of 1978.[23] The act sought to gradually phase out

[23]See the public document that helped pave the way for this act: *Civil Aeronautics Board Practices and Procedures, Report of the Subcommittee on Administrative Practice and Procedure of the Committee on the Judiciary, U.S. Senate* (U.S. Government Printing Office, 1975).

the CAB, relax restrictions on airline fares and routes, and authorize federal subsidies to airlines serving certain unprofitable markets.

In the early years of airline deregulation, the industry faced difficult economic conditions. Also one of the first results of deregulation was that many medium sized cities lost service as larger carriers found it more profitable to use their aircraft in other markets. In time many of these cities had service restored by smaller airlines using smaller planes. But in the meantime, this shift caused scheduling problems at major airports—problems that were compounded by the strike and firing of the federal air traffic controllers in 1981. Also, airlines raised fares on routes over which they had monopolies in order to subsidize lower fares on more competitive routes. Finally, critics of airline deregulation charge that safety precautions and maintenance suffered as a result of cutthroat competition.

Supporters of airline deregulation think these developments are only temporary and are not the result of deregulation. They point to the recession of 1981 and 1982 as a major factor in the difficulties faced by the airline industry. Also, supporters of airline deregulation say the doubling of jet fuel prices was the main cause of higher air fares. Some say the economic problems facing the airline industry in the early years would have been much more severe if the deregulation act hadn't facilitated greater decisionmaking by management. Overall, airline deregulation has resulted in generally lower fares, greater choice of routes and fares in most markets, and more efficient use of assets by the industry.

The long-term effects of airline deregulation are generally expected to be positive. Eventually, analysts hope, the marketplace will determine the level of service. If an airline is overcharging passengers on a route, a competitor will eventually steal those travelers away by offering better or lower-priced service. Whether this occurs in practice is another matter. Some people remain skeptical. For it takes a while to set up a competitive airline and then the big airlines can temporarily cut rates. "Bring back regulation" may become the cry of customers who feel cheated. Nevertheless, in the long run, deregulation should strengthen the industry by forcing companies to streamline operations in order to survive in a competitive market.

TRUCKING AND RAILROAD DEREGULATION   Deregulation of the trucking and railroad industries soon followed airline deregulation. In 1980 the railroad industry (the first industry to be regulated back in the 1890s) was in poor condition—as it had been for several decades, especially in the East. Many railroads were in serious financial trouble; two went bankrupt. In addition, many observers believed the Interstate Commerce Commission (ICC), which had regulated the railroads since 1887, was being too rigid in interpreting and enforcing federal regulations. Moreover, a growing body of evidence suggested that regulation was causing great inefficiencies and that market forces could generate better service to shippers and travelers at lower prices.[24]

The trucking industry was much healthier. In fact, many observers said the industry was too healthy. ICC regulations had limited the entry of new competitors into trucking and kept rates high. Competition was generally low, allowing trucking companies to charge relatively high rates for hauling cargo. Both the trucking industry itself and the Teamsters Union opposed deregulation, fearing it would alter this mutually beneficial situation. Calls for deregulation came primarily from business leaders who were forced to pay high rates to have their goods transported.

[24]See, for example, Theodore E. Keeler, *Railroads, Freight, and Public Policy* (Brookings Institution, 1983), p. 97.

Truck trailers in "Piggy-Back" service. *Courtesy Dow Chemical Co.*

In 1980 Congress passed the Staggers Rail Act to deregulate railroads and the Motor Carrier Act to relax supervision of trucking. Both acts loosened restrictions on entry into their respective industries, made it easier for railroads and trucking companies to abandon unprofitable activities, and allowed each industry more freedom in setting fares.

The effects of deregulation on both industries have been broadly similar. In the case of trucking, the primary benefit of deregulation has been to increase profitability. New firms are entering the industry. Railroad deregulation has led to discounted rates, more competition, improved service, and service innovations. By most accounts deregulation of the railroad and trucking industries has been successful.

The deregulation of the transportation industry is an excellent example of the practical application of abstract economic theory. In the words of one observer:

> The airline, trucking and rail deregulation bills had several features in common. They represented attempts to eliminate what had come to be considered needless and damaging regulation. They signaled a return to relying on mechanisms of market competition to achieve what regulation was intended to do in the first place. They were designed to promote the well-being of the industry as a whole and to improve its services to the general public, the same goals that regulation initially was intended to achieve.[25]

Deregulating Other Industries

The relatively successful deregulation of airlines, railroads, and trucking has led to calls for relaxing federal supervision over other industries as well. Two such industries are banking and natural gas.

BANKING DEREGULATION   The banking industry has long been protected by the federal government. The trauma caused by the numerous bank failures during the Great Depression led to controls and regulations designed to ensure that such a shock would never recur. In addition, many economists point out the banking industry performs a special role in the economy and therefore warrants special treatment. Because banks and other financial institutions control the flow of money, the lifeblood of the economy, some observers believe the federal government must supervise the industry in order to guarantee that the flow is uninterrupted.[26]

[25]Martha V. Gottron (ed.), *Regulation: Process and Politics* (Congressional Quarterly Press, 1982), p. 90. Reprinted with the permission of Congressional Quarterly, Inc.

[26]Alan Stone, *Regulation and its Alternatives* (Congressional Quarterly Press, 1982), p. 46.

Regulation of the banking industry has consisted mainly of protective devices. The federal government established the Federal Deposit Insurance Corporation (FDIC) to insure bank deposits up to a specified amount. The Federal Savings and Loan Insurance Corporation (FSLIC) was set up to perform a similar function for savings and loans institutions. In addition, financial institutions were barred from performing certain financial services. Banks and savings and loans institutions have been prevented from offering speculative investment services, for fear they would cover bad investments with the deposits of innocent third-party customers.

As a result of the deregulation movement, the directors of the FDIC and the FSLIC now seek to shift responsibility for insurance of bank and savings and loan deposits to private companies. Also, the distinctions between financial institutions and securities firms are beginning to diminish. Investment firms such as Merrill Lynch now offer certain banking services. Even retailers such as Sears now compete with banks for deposits. Banking officials say deregulation is needed so that banks can compete with these new adversaries. And they are now allowed to compete in many areas.

Further banking deregulation is likely in the near future. Constant innovations in the now-crowded financial industry will increase pressure on federal regulators to allow banks and savings and loans institutions more freedom.

However, even the most ardent advocates of deregulation think we need to proceed carefully when it comes to deregulation of financial institutions, especially banks. The effects of failure in the banking industry on the entire economy are such that the federal government will in all likelihood always play a greater role here than elsewhere. It is one thing to let a railroad company go bankrupt, but quite another when it happens to large financial institutions.

NATURAL GAS DEREGULATION The natural gas industry has a long history of government regulation: The federal government has set price ceilings on natural gas for the last thirty years. The government also has mandated separate prices for gas sold in the state in which it is produced and gas which is transported across state lines.[27]

Recently efforts have been made to remove government-imposed price levels. In 1977 Congress passed the Natural Gas Policy Act. The act gradually phases out price controls on all categories of natural gas. Some economists and legislators wish to speed up the process and remove all controls immediately. They think prices will fall if government regulation of the natural gas industry is removed. Opponents of this plan claim the price of gas will rise sharply if controls are removed all at once.

EVALUATING DEREGULATION

Deregulation has taken place in several industries and is being anticipated in yet others. But the debate still continues as to whether it works. Like other complicated issues there is no clear or simple answer. Much depends on the particular industry.

Deregulation appears to be working better in some areas than others. In the area of mine safety a relaxation of federal regulations was followed by an increase in the death of coal miners. In the area of drug deregulation, the results are more mixed. The Food and Drug Administration, most especially

---

[27]See M. Elizabeth Sanders, *The Regulation of Natural Gas: Policy and Politics, 1938–1978* (Temple University Press, 1981).

under Reagan, has relaxed the requirements for the introduction of new medicines. Those in the drug industry applaud these efforts. They urge that as a result of deregulation the public gets better medicines faster and cheaper. Opponents contend, however, and with some growing evidence that the accelerated approval process is endangering public health by prematurely allowing potentially hazardous drugs on the market.[28]

When it comes to deregulation in general its advocates argue that consumers are capable of making intelligent choices and are profiting from the lower prices and expanded services brought about by deregulation. Opponents contend that deregulation results in such confusion in the marketplace that consumers cannot make sensible choices. Thus in the airline business, even experienced travel agents often cannot figure out the cheapest way to go "from here to there."

One other point: in our federal system the mere fact that the national government stops regulating an industry does not mean that that particular industry will be unregulated. On the contrary, when the national government ceases regulating it sometimes results in fifty different state regulations making it sometimes even more difficult to do business on a large scale. (This is why sometimes business people themselves call for more, not less national regulation. They would much prefer, for example, one set of national regulations for automobile safety than fifty different state ones.)

In the debate about deregulation it is desirable to separate out those problems associated with transition from regulation to deregulation. There are always problems of getting adjusted to new ways. Every change hurts some and benefits others. The question is whether in the long run deregulation benefits more people than does regulation and which people does it benefit and which does it hurt.

The picture is mixed, but in general the overall effects of the deregulation trends of the past few years appear to be positive. Deregulation has forced some industries to become more efficient. Consumers have had better services at less cost. Also, and not insignificantly, in a democracy such as ours, deregulation has made transfers of wealth visible rather than hidden. Under government regulation, transfers of wealth (that is benefits or profits from certain arrangements that get established and protected) are often the result of hidden subsidies. Prices of unregulated goods are kept artificially high in order to finance losses on goods whose prices are kept artificially low due to government controls. Under deregulation, prices are more in accord with cost. Any subsidies must be authorized by Congress and are therefore subject to public scrutiny. Subsidies are examined in detail in the following chapter.

SUMMARY

1. Regulation in America is neither socialism nor laissez-faire policy but rather a kind of pervasive intervention into the private sector built upon a commitment to a market economy. While we often think of politics as the pursuit of private power and private interests, it is plainly also an effort to define the public interest. We set up regulatory agencies in an effort to interpret the public interest and to achieve various goals.

2. Even though their members are nominated by the president, their powers derived from legislative delegation, and their decisions subject to review by the courts, independent regulatory agencies have a scope of responsibility in the American economy that sometimes exceeds that of the three regular branches of government.

3. While few people have a kind word to say about regulation, we will doubtless have a good deal more of it in the

[28]See Martin Tolchin and Susan J. Tolchin, "The Rush to Reregulate" in *The New York Times Magazine* (August 21, 1983), and by the same authors, *Dismantling America: The Rush to Deregulate* (Houghton Mifflin, 1983).

future. Regulation is a means of controlling or eliminating some of the abuses and problems generated by the private economy while avoiding government ownership and the risks of too much centralization. Increasing regulation is an inevitable byproduct of a complex, industrialized, high-technology society.

4. A deregulation movement designed to get the government out of the regulation of certain businesses has achieved victories in recent years, especially in the transportation industries. Liberals generally favor deregulation to encourage more competition. Conservatives generally favor deregulation that will get federal regulators off their backs in areas such as affirmative action, safety and health, and environmental and consumer protection standards. The late 1980s will see even more pressure from both the Left and the Right to deregulate where possible. But deregulation efforts will have a tough time matching the constantly increasing number of federal regulations approved each year. Of one thing we can be sure: Controversies in regulatory politics will always be with us.

FURTHER READING

Benefits of Environmental, Health, and Safety Regulation. Report prepared for the Committee on Governmental Affairs, United States Senate, by the Center for Policy Alternatives at M.I.T. U.S. Government Document, 96th Cong., 2nd Sess., 1980.

JULES BACKMAN. *Regulation and Deregulation* (Bobbs Merrill, 1981).

STEPHEN BREYER. *Regulation and Its Reforms* (Harvard University Press, 1982).

ROBERT A. KATZMANN. *Regulatory Bureaucracy: The Federal Trade Commission and Antitrust Policy* (MIT Press, 1980).

JOHN MENDELOFF. *Regulating Safety: An Economic and Political Analysis of Occupational Safety and Health Policy* (MIT Press, 1980).

ROGER NOLL and BRUCE M. OWEN (eds.). *The Political Economy of Deregulation: Interest Groups in the Regulatory Process* (American Enterprise Institute, 1983).

ROBERT W. POOLE (ed.). *Instead of Regulation: Alternatives to Federal Regulatory Agencies* (Heath, 1982).

PAUL QUIRK. *Industry Influence in Federal Regulatory Agencies* (Princeton University Press, 1981).

Regulation. A journal published bimonthly by the American Enterprise Institute for Public Policy in Washington, D.C.

Regulation: Process and Politics (Congressional Quarterly Press, 1982).

ALAN STONE. *Regulation and Its Alternatives* (Congressional Quarterly Press, 1982).

MARTIN TOLCHIN and SUSAN J. TOLCHIN. *Dismantling America: The Rush to Deregulate* (Houghton Mifflin, 1983).

MURRAY L. WEIDENBAUM. *The Future of Business Regulation* (AMACON, 1979).

JAMES Q. WILSON (ed.). *The Politics of Regulation* (Basic Books, 1980).

THE POLITICS OF SUBSIDIES AND ENTITLEMENTS

23

The federal government, now responsible for about 24 percent of the nation's gross national product, has a huge impact on the economic life of the country. Indeed, it is no longer clear where the public sector ends and the private sector begins. Close to half the federal budget goes to what economists call transfer programs, or programs that provide direct support or subsidies to individuals, families, and households. Much of this money is explicitly directed toward people with low incomes, the disabled and handicapped, and persons who are not working because of unemployment or retirement. Transfer programs can provide cash payments, as in social security; in-kind benefits, as in hospital care through Medicare; vouchers, as in food payments; or various kinds of tax credits or tax deductions.

All kinds of individuals and corporations benefit from government subsidies. Welfare programs for the poor may be the most publicized government assistance efforts, but "it is probably safe to assume that the preponderance of the benefits of many programs is garnered by profitable corporations and citizens in the top half of the nation's income distribution."[1]

Subsidies and welfare assistance reflect the use of public funds to accomplish what are thought to be public purposes—but considerable disagreement exists as to what is or is not in the public interest. Politics in a democracy is a continuous process of defining what is in the public interest. Conservatives say we need more economy in government and less government in the economy. Others say governmental "giveaway" programs are undermining the values that

---

[1]Robert D. Reischauer, "The Federal Budget: Subsidies for the Rich," in Michael J. Boskin and Aaron Wildavsky (eds.), *The Federal Budget: Economics and Politics* (Institute for Contemporary Studies, 1982), p. 236.

made this nation great. Conservative economic advisors believe if we could only cut back drastically on the role of the government in the economy, we could make major strides in solving our inflation and federal deficit problems. Critics on the Left condemn subsidies to industry and tax shelters for the wealthy as "welfare for the rich." Critics on the far Left charge that the so-called welfare state is merely a symbolic gesture by which the powerful hand out a few crumbs to keep the powerless quiet.

SUBSIDIES: WHY AND HOW

Government subsidies provide economic assistance to certain targeted producers or consumers at the expense of others in the economy. Magazine and book publishers enjoy reduced postal rates on the grounds that this will enhance public knowledge and democratic discussion. Oil companies get certain tax write-offs on the grounds that we vitally need more oil to free ourselves of dependence on the OPEC nations. Farmers and ranchers, much beloved as the contemporary examples of old-fashioned rugged individualism, are protected by a dizzying array of federal assistance programs. The Chrysler Corporation and the U.S. Postal Service have received special treatment as well, because we place special value on their services and continued existence. College students are the beneficiaries of subsidies both directly and indirectly because of the widespread conviction that all of us benefit from their education.

Government promotion, or subsidies, are not a new creation. In his first annual address to Congress, George Washington called for a tariff to protect business. Alexander Hamilton, Washington's secretary of the treasury, proposed that government give financial assistance to new business ventures. In the 1790s the new government promoted commerce in numerous ways: by establishing a money system and a postal service, granting charters, enforcing contracts in court, and subsidizing roads and waterways. Significant public purposes can be and are achieved—such as energy conservation and development; preserving vital nongovernmental sectors that fund and operate private hospitals, colleges, and charitable institutions; encouraging small businesses; and so on.

Some subsidies have outlived their purpose and today create unnecessary costs for taxpayers and consumers. They benefit narrow, well-organized interests, while their costs are spread out among unorganized taxpayers. Many of the subsidies are hard to see because they take the form of tax preferences, loans, or inflationary protective regulations. Subsidies that have outlived their usefulness are often continued primarily because of effective lobbying. Beneficiaries make strategic campaign contributions during elections and fight ruthlessly in other ways to hold on to their special advantages.

Computing how much is spent on subsidy programs is difficult because many federal subsidy programs are called something else. They may be called grant-in-aid, price support, tax incentive, stabilization program, and loan guarantee. Government subsidy programs include:

1. *Cash benefits.* The government pays the sugar beet and cane growers to protect the welfare of the domestic sugar industry, and pays sheep raisers to improve the quality of American wool. Cash payments also help to support artists as well as to support the privately owned U.S. merchant marine.

2. *Tax incentives.* The recipients of these subsidies receive no cash; they are permitted to pay lower taxes than would normally be required. Tax incentives to business to encourage oil exploration and production are examples. So too are the lower taxes on capital gains (profits made on stock or real estate or

President Reagan (c) and Mayor Ed Koch of New York City hold U.S. government check for help in New York City's Westway Highway Project. *UPI.*

other things of value) and the tax deductibility of interest on homes occupied by their owners. While the government makes no expenditure, it loses revenue.

3. *Credit subsidies.* These involve government participation in loan transactions that give lower rates of interest than prevailing market conditions would allow. Credit subsidies range from loans to finance a student through college, to the financing of a major public works project at a fraction of prevailing interest rates, to the financing of New York City.

4. *Benefit-in-kind subsidies.* Recipients receive a product or service paid for by the government. Food stamps for the poor or Medicare for the elderly are examples.

There are other ways in which the federal government has a direct impact on the economy. The government sometimes sets tariffs on imports that allow domestic producers to earn higher profits than free markets would bring. In fact, almost all groups at one time or another have benefited from government help. Many economic conservatives openly seek government aid to fund an SST, to bail out Lockheed Aircraft and Chrysler, to support government-backed loans to railroads, to subsidize the merchant marine industry, and so on. Similarly, spokespersons for the poor seek a larger government role in providing health services, establishing a floor below which incomes are not allowed to fall, and subsidizing improved housing and employment opportunities. Governmental promotion can be used to help any group. But who shall be aided in what way, and with what consequences, are important questions.

HELPING BUSINESS

A government that protects and enforces contracts enables owners of businesses to operate in a stable situation. A government that promotes a prosperous economy enables businesses to enjoy a large volume of sales and good profits. The kind of monetary policy established by government—for example, tight or easy money—is of direct interest to business. But the national government also supplies a number of specific services and assists individual sectors of the business community.

The Department of Commerce The Department of Commerce is the nation's "service center" for businesses. Its secretary is nearly always a person with an extensive business background. The department assists business in many ways. Its Social and Economic Statistics Administration reports on business activity and prospects at home and around the world. The National Bureau of Standards makes scientific investigations and standardizes units of weight and measure. The Bureau of the Census has been called the greatest fact-finding and figure-counting agency in the world. The Constitution requires that a national census be taken every ten years; the results supply valuable information on business and agricultural activity, incomes, occupations, employment, housing and home ownership, and governmental finances.

The Patent Office is also in the Commerce Department. A patent, conferring the right of exclusive use of an invention for seventeen years, is a valuable property right. On receiving an application for a patent, the Patent Office must study its records to see if any prior patent will be infringed upon and if the invention is sufficiently original and useful to be patentable.

Through the Maritime Administration the government subsidizes the American merchant marine by several hundred million dollars a year. For financial and security reasons Congress has determined we must have a domestic merchant marine capable of carrying a sizable part of our oceangoing trade. It is generally agreed that without these special arrangements there would be virtually *no* U.S. fleet and *no* U.S. shipbuilding industry. There are few industries in whose affairs the government has played so active a role.[2] Thus, the national government has been paying operating subsidies to selected U.S. flag steamship companies since 1936. By the early 1980s this program had cost well over $4 billion. The government also subsidizes the construction side of the maritime industry, and since 1936 this has cost $3 billion.

Critics say such subsidies discourage competition and raise the cost of ships to more than double the price of those built in foreign shipyards. They contend this government promotion causes more problems than it solves. The maritime industry, of course, denies these charges and maintains that we need these capabilities, especially during wartime. The maritime workers also fight, through their unions, to retain these subsidies. They, as much as the shippers and shipbuilders, are beneficiaries of this program.

Other Help for Business In addition to the activities of the Department of Commerce, the government assists business through agencies such as the Small Business Administration (SBA), an independent agency headed by an administrator appointed by the president. The SBA, with nearly 4000 full-time employees across the country, is designed to aid small companies through such services as financial counseling, research, and loans to victims of natural disasters such as floods and hurricanes.

The SBA provides assistance to those businesses for which it is argued that market imperfections may exist. Handicapped, minority, and first-time borrowers usually get priority consideration. For example, about 17 percent of SBA's 1984 guaranteed business loans were made to minority-owned firms.

The government also aids business through research and experimentation carried on by a variety of agencies. Examples include new commercial wood products resulting from work done in the laboratories of the U.S. Forest Service, and diversified uses of bituminous coal arising from research in the Department of the Interior.

[2]This promotional program is explained in Gerald R. Jantscher, *Bread upon the Waters: Federal Aids to the Maritime Industries* (Brookings Institution, 1975), p. 10.

Through a wide range of tax benefits for certain segments of the population, government encourages certain types of activity and investment. The money given up by the government through provisions in the tax code is now called a **tax expenditure**. The government defines a tax expenditure as a loss of tax revenue, "attributable to provisions of the federal tax law that allow a special exclusion, exemption or deduction from gross income or provide a special credit, preferential rate of tax, or a deferral of tax liability."

Tax expenditures are one means by which the government pursues public policy objectives. Nearly all tax expenditures are meant to encourage certain economic activities—investment, exporting, petroleum exploration and development, spending by state and local governments, or support of charitable institutions. Every nation's tax laws are in part a reflection of economic and social policy. They create incentives and disincentives for the use of capital and for the allocation of wealth between current consumption and investment (future consumption).

The notion of tax expenditures is resented by some business officials and a few economists who contend it wrongly suggests that the lost revenue belongs to the national government. But most members of Congress, as well as budget experts, now agree that these tax write-offs and deductions are indeed giving government money away. The Congressional Budget Act of 1974 requires a listing of these kinds of tax expenditures in the budget. Critics claim tax expenditures remain a hidden form of subsidy, because Congress exercises little fiscal control over them. Indeed, many of these tax exemptions and exclusions "tumble into the law without supporting studies, being propelled instead by clichés, debating points, and scraps of data and tables that are passed off as serious evidence."[3] Tax expenditures generally result in an upside-down welfare program; the richer the taxpayer, the greater the benefit. About 75 percent of these tax breaks go to individuals, the remaining 25 percent to corporations. The Congressional Budget Office estimates that tax expenditures will rise and will amount to over $400 billion by 1985.[4]

The Chrysler Story— Free Enterprise with a Little Help from the Government

YOU DECIDE !

Chrysler Corporation was successfully rescued with federally guaranteed loans in 1979. Most people think the risk was well taken and that the results prove the government made a good investment. But some people still say it was a bad idea. What, in your view, is the best case against the Chrysler bailout and similar governmental loans or aid?

(Answer/Discussion on page 529.)

Should the federal government intervene in the economic system to save a failing and presumably mismanaged enterprise? If so, when? One of the fundamental precepts of our system is the freedom to succeed—but along with this comes the possibility of failure.

The Chrysler Corporation is about the tenth largest manufacturer in the United States. Between 1978 and 1981 Chrysler lost $3.5 billion, the largest loss by any company in the history of the country. In 1979 its financial difficulties were so severe it was virtually bankrupt. It had not realized a profit since 1977, largely due to its failure to read market trends correctly. It was slow to respond to the demand for smaller, more fuel-efficient cars. It also continued operations that had become outdated and costly.

Officials at Chrysler said increased governmental regulations of the kind discussed in Chapter 22 (safety, workplace, and environmental standards in particular) hit Chrysler harder than Ford or General Motors, because Chrysler sells fewer cars and cannot spread the costs as easily.

In 1979 the corporation appealed to the federal government for assistance. At first it merely asked the government to relax its regulations. But soon it was forced to ask for aid and for various kinds of loans. Chrysler and officials of the

[3]Harvard law professor Stanley Surrey, quoted in *The Government Subsidy Squeeze* (Common Cause Report, 1980), p. 30.

[4]See John Karl Scholz, "Tax Expenditures," in Joseph Pechman (ed.), *Setting National Priorities: The 1984 Budget* (Brookings Institution, 1983), pp. 243–48.

Lee A. Iacocca, Chairman of Chrysler Corporation, presents $813,487,500 check to Edwin (Tony) Heard, Vice Chairman of the U.S. Trust Company, in New York City at a formal ceremony for repayment of the last two-thirds of the federally guaranteed notes Chrysler borrowed from private investors in 1980. Chrysler's repayment, on August 15, 1983, was seven years ahead of the 1990 redemption deadline for the notes and completed a dramatic three-year recovery period underwritten by the Loan Guarantee Act of 1979 at no cost to taxpayers. *Chrysler Corporation.*

United Auto Workers (UAW) argued it was in the best interests of the government to "bail out" Chrysler. If Chrysler went under, they said, as many as 600,000 jobs would be lost. Chrysler workers, 4800 dealers, and about 20,000 Chrysler suppliers would be badly hurt, if not thrown out of business altogether. In addition, if Chrysler shut down, its employees would swell the welfare rolls, and national revenue would decrease. Cities in which Chrysler plants are located would be seriously injured.

Critics claimed bailing out Chrysler would set a bad precedent; and they questioned the propriety of government interference in a competitive market economy such as that of the United States. Opponents also said Chrysler's misfortunes were mainly due to its own lack of leadership and lack of management. Why should businesses that do not respond to the demands of consumers get protection? Thousands of companies fail every year, and the government does not ordinarily help them. Moreover, bailing out failed businesses as a matter of course would create an unworkable system, rewarding mismanagement and inefficiency.

Advocates of giving aid to Chrysler triumphed. In late 1979 Congress passed a measure guaranteeing $1.2 billion worth of private loans to Chrysler. In order to receive this, Chrysler was required to come up with an equivalent amount of unsupported loans from banks and elsewhere. The company was also required to sell off $300 million worth of its assets.

Management agreed to defer dividends, to issue $500 million worth of new stock and to subject its operations to periodic government review. Chrysler was not alone in initiating austerity measures. The UAW had to swallow nearly $500 million worth of blue-collar employee wage concessions. White-collar workers suffered benefit cutbacks totaling $125 million. Chrysler suppliers were directed to pay $180 million. Finally, cities and states with Chrysler plants were required to supply $250 million in loan aid to the ailing firm.

The national government did not give Chrysler any money directly; instead, it guaranteed $1.5 billion in loans for the company. Chrysler was obliged to find an equal amount from its dealers, from the cities and states where it was located, and from other sources. It was able to do so.

With the aid of the federal government and other friendly interests, Chrysler survived. Many credited the spirited leadership and shrewd public relations efforts of Chrysler Chairman Lee Iacocca. Whatever the reasons, there are signs that the nation's third largest automaker may even become more competitive than it was before its decline. Indeed, Chrysler realized a small profit in 1982 and 1983. As a result of its financial difficulties, Chrysler streamlined its operations; it also paid back the entire $1.2 billion in government backed loans in mid-1983, seven years ahead of schedule.

As an unexpected bonus from the Chrysler aid package, the federal government will realize a profit. Part of the loan agreement gave the government the right to purchase 14.4 million shares of Chrysler stock at about $13 a share, at a time when it was selling for about twice that. The federal government probably made close to $200 million on the sale of its purchase rights.

The Chrysler revival was not achieved without some notable corporate dieting. Its 1984 personnel stands at about 68,000, compared to 131,000 back in 1979. Its productive capacity dwindled to about 1.7 million cars a year, down from nearly 2.4 million. Of the 5800 dealers around the country operating in 1979, only 3700 were still in business in the mid-1980s. Moreover, Chrysler had to cut back on some of its research and design operations—which may put it in a less effective position in the late 1980s—since it must continue to compete with General Motors, Ford, Toyota, and other companies. Workers, suppliers, and middle managers all want to be cut in on the growing profits—so Chrysler faces a considerable challenge. While most people are optimistic, some sober analysts suggest that Chrysler still has a long way to go to prove itself as a corporation back on its own feet—without government assistance.

The resurrection or rescue of the Chrysler Corporation is an intriguing example of governmental assistance or subsidy arrangements. It is also in part a tale of the ideological conflict between economic "survival of the fittest" theories and government promotion and protection strategies. It suggests that some circumstances may justify modifying the rule that government should stay out

---

ANSWER/DISCUSSION

Here are comments by a few people who opposed the Chrysler bailout back in 1979 and still oppose it:

□ **Milton Friedman,** Nobel-prize-winning economist: "Obviously, it's a good thing for Chrysler and the country that the company seems to be surviving, but one bad byproduct is that it will lead people to believe bailouts are a good thing. A free-enterprise system is one of profit and loss. If you guarantee against losses by bailing out losing companies, you remove the major monitoring device of a free market."

□ **Alan Greenspan,** economic consultant and former chairman of the Council of Economic Advisers: "Propping up failing companies with Government loans delays the shift of resources into more productive ventures. Policies focused on protecting jobs in moribund industries must eventually fail and, in the end, destroy more jobs than they save."

□ **Thomas Murphy,** former chairman of General Motors: "The Government should not be owning and running businesses. When it gives federal guarantees, it is in effect embarking on a course that could lead to Government ownership. The marketplace should determine success or failure."

□ **William Proxmire,** Democratic Senator from Wisconsin: "We'll have far better business management in the long run if we allow the tough, cold, cruel system of free enterprise to work. It's served us very well. In the year that Chrysler came to us, there were 6,000 business failures. But because Chrysler was big, with a lot of employees, and because it was a presidential election year, we bailed them out. Where do you draw the line? You could make a much better case for helping little firms than big ones. When you start bailing out obsolete industries, you keep us in the horse-and-buggy stage."

of the economic system. Nevertheless, rigid adherents of a rugged free enterprise system are not persuaded by the Chrysler story. Others see a different lesson. U.S. Senator Paul Tsongas (D-Mass.) wrote that as a result of the Chrysler episode, he believed there may be circumstances when a bailout is in the national interest. "Chrysler is such a case . . . The challenge is going beyond ideological posturing and looking at the particular situation. 'Will it work?' should be the test. Happily, in Chrysler's case, it did."[5]

Delivering the Mail: A Case Study

The government assumed the responsibility for delivering the mail even before the Revolution. For many years postmasters general were more important for their political than for their administrative responsibilities. Presidents often appointed to this post the national chair of their own party or one of their key campaign managers. The reason was obvious: The Post Office Department had thousands of patronage jobs to give to local party workers. Over the years postal employees were gradually brought under the civil service, and there have been continuing efforts to restructure the Post Office as a self-supporting business enterprise. Yet the Post Office is still subsidized, and many people believe it always will be.

In 1970, in response to the recommendations of a presidential commission, and after two years of debate in Congress in which postal workers and their unions bargained hard to protect their positions, Congress abolished the Post Office Department and created a new independent agency, the United States Postal Service.

The Postal Service is governed by an eleven-member board of governors, nine of whom are appointed by the president with the consent of the Senate. No more than five may be from the same political party. These nine members in turn appoint a postmaster general, who joins them in selecting a deputy postmaster general. These two administrative officers also serve on the board of governors. The appointed members serve for staggered nine-year terms, but the postmaster general and the deputy serve at the board's direction.

Although postal employees retain their civil service status, the board has authority to set salaries and determine fringe benefits. Employees are permitted to engage in collective bargaining, but they may not legally strike. In the event of a deadlock between the board and its employees, there is to be compulsory arbitration.

The United States Postal Service is the biggest nonmilitary department of the national government. It handles over 120 billion pieces of mail every year, and has about 650,000 permanent employees, 38,000 offices, and 168,000 routes.

In recent years the Postal Service has become self-supporting, even turning a slight profit. Like a business, the Postal Service is permitted to sell bonds to purchase capital equipment. Unlike a business, however, it may set its charges only after a recommendation from the presidentially appointed, five-member Postal Rate Commission. But the Postal Service still gets a "revenue foregone" subsidy of nearly $800 million for services it performs below cost. Congress explicitly intends this subsidy to provide for free mailing for the blind and the handicapped to provide lower rates for nonprofit organizations, and so on. However, this subsidy makes up only 3 percent of the Postal Service's more than $25 billion budget.

The new business organization reflects the fact that the decisions made by the Postal Service have a major impact on our economy and our political system. Its structure is designed to promote proper consideration of these political

---

[5]Paul E. Tsongas, "Did the Chrysler Bailout Work?" © 1983 by *The New York Times Company*. Reprinted by permission.

Postal workers sorting and collecting the mail. *U.S. Postal Service and Laimute E. Druskis.*

factors, and to avoid decisions made solely for profit. Has the experiment worked? Some say it works remarkably well. They point to the fact that the U.S. Postal Service provides the cheapest first-class rate of any nation in the world. It handles more pieces of mail per employee than any nation in the world. Moreover, it has made substantial cost savings through employee cutbacks and has eliminated patronage in the appointment of postmasters and carriers. The purpose of the Post Office is not to make money but to perform a service, and the USPS is doing that more efficiently than ever before.

Others disagree—and usually with fervor. Since its creation, they complain, costs of providing mail service have soared. Labor costs have risen greatly, as has the cost of fuel to run the USPS's massive fleet of vehicles. Critics also say postal workers are sometimes rude, and lines at the post office grow longer every year. Could it be, they ask, that public enterprises such as the Postal Service don't have the incentives to innovate and please the consumer that private enterprises do? The Postal Service is increasingly suffering from competition from private carriers of second- and third-class mail and parcel post. Some utilities are now delivering their own bills to save postage costs; several newspapers and magazines are experimenting with private carriers. A major legal obstacle to private mail delivery is that only a uniformed U.S. postal carrier is allowed by law to open a private mailbox.

Technological changes are also affecting the postal service. Instant communications via computers along with new competitors such as Western Union, Federal Express, and others are a challenge to the traditional ways of doing business through the mail. Some people think it is just a matter of years before most of us will be communicating and sending messages to one another via telex and other electronic devices. This is yet another example of how the world never stays the same and how technological developments alter the nature of the marketplace.

The major policy questions facing Congress are (1) Should the USPS continue to strive to break even at the expense of service? (2) Should federal subsidies be increased? (3) Should the USPS be abolished and responsibility for postal service returned to Congress or the president? Some, including the Postal Service management, believe that while the present system will work, subsidies will be needed for the foreseeable future. They also suggest that small rural post offices be closed down, that postage rates be increased, and that Saturday service be dropped. Many members of Congress oppose these suggestions, for their constituents complain when services are curtailed.

Protectionism vs. Free Trade

Tariffs are used by all governments to aid their nation's businesses. Over the years, when our businesses have been threatened by foreign competition, they and their employees have often successfully petitioned Congress to curb competitive imports. By imposing tariffs or negotiating agreements with other nations to restrict the quantities of cars or shoes or motorcycles that are imported into the U.S., the federal government maintains higher prices for these products—a situation that benefits domestic companies and their workers. Economists and diplomats usually favor free trade and dislike protectionism. The latter raises prices for American consumers and prevents efficient use of resources. It also invites retaliation from foreign countries.

Americans have usually favored free trade. Two hundred years ago Thomas Jefferson traveled to France to request that American whale oil, tobacco, and fish be allowed into that country without being subject to the intolerable tariff burdens the French had imposed. And over the years Americans have usually discovered that foreign trade is a two-way street: If you want people in a foreign market to buy your goods, you must be willing to buy theirs.

Back in the 1930s many nations experienced high unemployment, low production, and general economic misery. The United States was no exception. In an effort to aid ailing American industries, Congress passed the Smoot-Hawley tariff act. The act established the highest general tariff the U.S. had ever had. Supporters hoped high tariffs on imported goods would increase the demand for goods produced in the United States and thus help get the country out of the Depression. The exact opposite occurred. Other nations retaliated with high tariffs on American goods. Demand fell, aggravating the Depression. In 1934 Congress gave the president power to negotiate mutual tariff reductions with other nations, subject to certain restrictions. By the early 1970s tariffs on industrial products had been substantially reduced. But restrictions on agricultural commodities remain, along with nontariff limitations such as quotas, minimum import prices, and prohibitions on the sale of certain products.

The 1980s have seen a marked revival of the protectionist movement. Worldwide recession and widespread unemployment—especially in basic industries such as steel, mining, and automobiles—have led many nations to adopt measures protecting their industries from foreign competition. The European Economic Community subsidizes steel imported from Europe to other parts of the world. Japan virtually excludes American automobiles and limits many U.S. agricultural imports. Other nations have erected nontariff trade barriers such as lengthy inspection procedures for imported goods. The U.S. also conducts protectionist practices. We have imposed "voluntary" limits in recent years on Japanese automobiles and European steel imports. Further, the federal government subsidizes agricultural exports in the form of price supports and inexpensive credit.

Countless companies and industries seek help from Congress, especially against the difficulties of competiton with the Japanese. The Harley-Davidson motorcycle company is an example. The sight of so many Yamahas on the road drove the company to urge tariff or protectionist measures as a way to "solve" their problem.

In the mid-1980s Congress is considering a "domestic content" bill. This would require a significant percentage of the components in specified products imported from foreign countries to be made in the United States. Supporters of this legislation claim it would save and even create jobs in this country since foreign producers would be forced either to use American parts or to establish their own plants in the U.S. using American labor.

Opponents of a domestic content bill and other protectionist devices claim they cost the U.S. jobs rather than save them, and lead to higher prices. Pro-

'Buy American' rally in New York City. *Martin A. Levick, Black Star.*

Drawing by D. Reilly; © 1983. The New Yorker Magazine, Inc.

tected U.S. firms facing reduced competition from foreign firms are free to raise their prices. As demand falls, American manufacturers sell fewer products and are forced to lay off workers. Also, imposition of import restrictions invites almost immediate retaliation from other nations.

In the final analysis, protectionist measures are merely another kind of subsidy—and very often a subsidy that protects some industries at the expense of others. Thus, our attempt to cut down on imports of Japanese motorcycles and autos will very likely increase our imports of Japanese tires and porcelain products. U.S. workers in these industries will lose their jobs. Policies with huge, but invisible, costs are difficult to resist.

Energy Conservation and Development: Hard Choices

Energy research and development have been a major responsibility of the national government, especially since World War II. Since the Arab oil embargo of 1973, however, this involvement has grown dramatically. Not everyone applauds this kind of government promotion. Some Republicans, such as President Reagan, believe government involvement in energy matters has gone too far. Some say government interference in the market, together with the government's environmental and land policies, has resulted in the misallocation of capital resources and the overconsumption of scarce fuels. Government regulation of the interstate price of oil and natural gas produced in the United States has often kept the price of these commodities below the market level, especially after the OPEC nations raised their prices. The effect of price regulation was therefore to encourage consumption (in demand) while discouraging production (supply) with low prices. To fill the gap left by falling domestic production, which peaked in 1970, the United States began to import oil. The oil embargo resulted in much higher world prices, but the price for domestically produced oil was not allowed to reach those levels. Our reliance on imported oil grew from 35 percent in 1973 to about 40 percent (or about 20 percent of our total energy needs) in recent years.

U.S. Senator James A. McClure (R-Idaho) Chairman, Committee on Energy and Natural Resources.

To stem the increase of oil imports from the politically unstable Middle East, former President Carter, together with Congress, shaped an energy policy that relied partly on conservation and even more heavily on increased supply from unconventional sources. Some of the major features of the nation's energy policies, as of the early 1980s, were the following:

1. Eliminating the twin markets for natural gas (intra- and interstate) and gradually deregulating prices.

2. Gradual deregulation of domestic oil prices, accompanied by a "windfall profits" tax.

3. Use of the windfall profits tax, as enacted by Congress in 1980, to help the poor pay higher fuel bills, to promote the development of solar and other new energy sources, and to reduce taxes and the federal deficit.

4. Establishment of a synthetic fuels corporation to stimulate the development of a new American industry devoted to making fuels from nontraditional energy sources.

Deregulation of energy prices, it is hoped, will reduce energy waste, increase domestic production, and make previously uneconomical sources look more attractive. Certainly, energy prices must reflect the true cost of an energy source if production is to be increased and waste discouraged. Some people think, however, that the potential contributions of traditional sources (oil, natural gas, nuclear power, and coal) are limited; if we are to avoid growing reliance on imported oil, we must switch to newer sources of energy. Although coal was once thought to be the answer to our problems, there are restrictions to its large-scale use, such as environmental hazards and high transportation costs. Oil shale has been tested on an experimental scale, but its technology remains unproved on a commercial scale. Synthetic fuels from coal are still much more expensive than regular petroleum or natural gas. Nuclear power is still plagued by nagging questions about safety and waste disposal. As a study by the Harvard Business School concludes: "It is clear that domestic oil, gas, coal, and nuclear cannot deliver vastly increased supplies, although it is equally clear they cannot be ignored. Broadly speaking, however, the nation has only two major alternatives for the rest of this century—to import more oil or accelerate the development of conservation and solar energy."[6]

For many years the common attitude toward solar power was: "It's great for the future, but it's too costly now" and conservation implied freezing in the dark. Increasingly, however, the potential of these two sources is being recognized. Technological advances have made solar heating somewhat more affordable. There is growing evidence that dramatic cuts could be made in energy demand through more efficient use and through cutting waste, without any major changes in our lifestyle. Several recent estimates contend that the U.S., by making a serious commitment to conservation as an energy "source," could cut energy use by 30 percent "and still enjoy the same or an even higher standard of living."[7] Both solar and conservation strategies have been subsidized by the federal government through tax credits, research assistance, and related investment-incentive programs.

WELFARE: PROVIDING FOR THE POOR

Until the Great Depression the national government had no responsibility for taking care of persons in need, except for veterans and a few special groups. America was thought to be a land of unlimited opportunities. When persons failed to get ahead, people said, it was their own fault. The "worthy poor," widows and orphans, were taken care of through private or county relief. During the early twentieth century state governments extended relief to needy old people, the blind, and orphans, but the programs were limited. No work, no food was the ruling ethic.

Then came the Great Depression. In the early 1930s nearly 15 million people were without jobs. Breadlines, soup kitchens, private charity, and meager state and local programs were pitifully inadequate gestures. The Roosevelt administration created an elaborate series of emergency relief programs. But what started as an emergency response to a temporary condition has become a permanent feature of our system. During the past forty-five years the national government has become progressively and deeply involved in welfare activities. Most programs are administered by state and local governments but funded by the national government and thus subject to Washington's control. The complex tangle of programs has produced an administrative maze. Even after three decades of national economic expansion, there are between 25 and 30 million Americans receiving some kind of welfare. At least 15 percent of the population (34.4 million Americans) fell below the poverty line in 1983. And the numbers falling below the poverty line and the costs of the programs are increasing.[8]

While it is generally accepted that the national government should do something about poverty, few agree on *what* it should do. There is not even agreement about the dimensions of the problem—how many poor exist, who

"You don't look truly needy to me. . . . Needy, perhaps, but not truly needy!" *The Los Angeles Times, 1981.*

[6]Robert Stobaugh and Daniel Yergen, *Energy Future* (Random House, 1979), p. 216.

[7]See, for example, Stobaugh and Yergen, *Energy Future*, p. 136.

[8]See Gibert Y. Steiner, *The State of Welfare* (Brookings Institution, 1971), a dated but still useful analysis of welfare programs.

they are, and why they are poor. But it is clear that a substantial number of Americans, perhaps 40 million, do not have access to a "comfortable" life style. These are often the hidden poor. They remain invisible to the majority of Americans because they exist in the dark slums of the city and in the mountains and valleys of rural America.

A third of the poor are from families in which the breadwinner has been without a job for a long time. (A record 12 million people were unemployed in 1983.) Some of these are headed by a father or a mother whose skills are so meager that he or she cannot support the family. A large portion of the poor live in families headed by a person at least sixty-five years of age or someone with little or no education. Because black Americans have been subject to discrimination and denied opportunites for education, a greater percentage of blacks than whites are poor. Nevertheless, 70 percent of the poor are white.

Almost everybody is unhappy about the present state of national welfare policies, especially the largest of the so-called categorical relief programs, Aid to Families with Dependent Children. (There is little criticism of programs providing help for the aged, the blind, or the disabled.) Conservatives argue that the drain on the taxpayer is beyond endurance, and that welfare creates and perpetuates dependency. Liberals argue that it is immoral for a rich nation to spend billions for defense, to put people on the moon, to build highways, to subsidize wealthy farmers, and to assist business when millions are in want. Liberals argue too that welfare will in many cases improve opportunities for the poor and compensate for disadvantages imposed by society. Radicals argue that the poor are in poverty because of the deliberate design of the powerful or the natural workings of capitalism.

The famous exchange between F. Scott Fitzgerald and Ernest Hemingway continues to set the framework within which we debate welfare policies. Fitzgerald is reported to have said: "The rich are different from the poor." Hemingway responded: "Yes, they have more money." On the Fitzgerald side of the argument are some social scientists who believe we must make a distinction between those without money and the poor. A student at college from a middle-class background, or a space scientist out of work may be without much money, but he or she is not poor. To be poor is to be part of the "culture of poverty." This subculture, with its own system of values and behaviors, makes it possible for those living in poverty to exist but difficult for them to succeed in the larger society. "There is . . . a language of the poor, a psychology of the poor, a world view of the poor. To be impoverished is to be an internal alien, to grow up in a culture that is radically different from one that dominates the society."[9] Although modern-day Fitzgeralds vary in their political views, they tend to emphasize that welfare is unlikely to be reduced unless people are given the education, training, and skill they need to break out of the culture of poverty. They also tend to favor measures to increase the political power of the poor so that they can secure their share of society's resources. Those who take the Hemingway position say what the poor need most is money. With more money they will be able to provide decent housing, secure education for their children, and in time become capable of taking care of themselves.

During the last several decades we have had several waves of welfare reform. In broad terms, these reforms have had the following purposes:

1. *Trying to substitute work for welfare.* In November 1934 President Roosevelt wrote: "What I am seeking is the abolition of relief altogether. I cannot say so out loud yet but I hope to be able to substitute work for relief."[10] He hoped

[9]Michael Harrington, *The Other America* (Penguin, 1963), pp. 23–24.
[10]Quoted in Steiner, *The State of Welfare*, p. 1.

that with economic recovery and full employment, people would move from relief to employment—and many did. But five presidents later, Richard Nixon announced: "What America needs now is not more welfare but more work-fare."[11] Recent administrations also tried this. More jobs would benefit the temporarily unemployed. But the problem is that many of those on welfare are unemployable or unskilled.

2. *Trying to substitute social services.* In the early 1960s the major aim of reform was to provide professional help for those on welfare. It was believed that with this kind of assistance, those in need could learn to take care of themselves. Thus, if the problem appeared to be illness, a social worker or caseworker was to see to it that adequate health care was provided. If a family was about to lose its breadwinner because of a marital dispute, a caseworker would be assigned to see if the family could be kept together. The difficulty, however, is that there are not enough trained caseworkers to provide help for all those on welfare. In any event, experiments in which one group received services and another group merely received welfare payments demonstrated that the former group was not any less dependent on welfare than the latter.

This welfare recipient uses food stamps at a local supermarket. *UPI.*

3. *Trying to increase the political influence of the poor.* "As the political power and the political resources of the affected public in the area of poverty and ghetto problems are minimal, likewise their success in generating remedial action is minimal. . . . Those who need to use government the most so as to regulate the environment, are the least able to do so.[12]

A primary aim of Johnson's War on Poverty was to mobilize the poor for political action, to involve the poor in community action programs, and to create structures outside the regular channels the poor could use to claim a more adequate share of services.

4. *Trying to increase the cash income available to the very poor.* These reforms, the most recent, involve some kind of income maintenance program such as a family allowance, a negative income tax, or a guaranteed minimum annual income. Here the emphasis is on providing those in need with more dollars.

5. *Ronald Reagan and his supporters in Congress argued that a rising tide lifts all boats* and that their policies of stimulating private enterprise would, after a while, do more to help the poor than most of the social strategies programs promoted by liberals or Democrats. Thus the Reagan program cut food stamps and similar programs and emphasized tax cut programs that would, they hoped, stimulate investment and business expansion—which, in turn, would create a healthy economy, lower inflation, and lower interest rates, and create more jobs.

Fifty years of experimentation, tinkering, and development have resulted in a system that reflects all these approaches and more. What is the national government doing now?

Unemployment Insurance

This income maintenance system is operated jointly by the national and the state governments. All employers pay a payroll tax. These funds are paid out to the states for workers who are not covered by other unemployment compensation programs. It is estimated that an average 3.5 million persons received benefits each week in 1984.

[11]Quoted in Daniel P. Moynihan, *The Politics of a Guaranteed Income: The Nixon Administration and the Family Assistance Plan* (Random House, 1973), p. 225.

[12]John Adrian Strayer, "The American Policy Process and the Problems of the Ghetto," *Western Political Quarterly* (March 1971), pp. 50–51.

Social Security: A Case Analysis

Social security, the world's largest "insurance" program for retirees, survivors, and the disabled, covers over 90 percent of the American workforce and will cost well over $200 billion by 1985. The program pays 36 million Americans every month, while 115 million people contribute to it. As of early 1984, social security provided an estimated average payment of over $400 per month to a retired worker without dependents. Full benefits are paid between the ages of sixty-five and seventy only to those not presently earning wages of more than a certain amount. After age seventy people are entitled to retirement benefits regardless of wage earnings. Since the Social Security Act was passed in 1935, the history of social security programs has largely been one of steady growth. The purpose of the program was to provide support for the aged in American society, and it has grown to include disability payments and Medicare. It has been financed through compulsory "contributions" by workers and employers in the form of a payroll tax.

The growth of the social security program was gradual and incremental. This growth is largely due to the successful attempts of the program's executives to separate social security from other government expenditures and programs, and the successful—but inaccurate—portrayal of the program as an insurance program. Allied with labor and key congressional leaders, social security executives have had relatively clear sailing.

Until the 1970s growth was relatively noncontroversial, largely because, in Martha Derthick's words, "the costs were initially deceptively low," while benefits were steadily increasing, making it politically painless.[13] The liberalization and expansion of benefits was made possible by the steady economic growth of the fifties and sixties. "The nature of the program in the short run has been such as to disguise the true cost of it, the true relation between costs and benefits, and the true principles by which benefits and costs have been distributed. The nature of policy making did little to correct, but instead reinforced, a complacent, poorly informed acceptance of the program.[14]

Few people really understand how the social security system works. Most Americans, for example, believe their payroll taxes go into some type of insurance investment pool to be held and invested until the day they retire and benefits begin. Many people believe the social security system accumulates a large trust fund filled with reserves in order to pay out benefits according to the contributions.

The reality is different. Payroll taxes are not calculated to cover the costs of future pensions for today's wage earners. Rather, current benefits are paid out of current receipts. In addition, a large percentage of social security benefits are disproportionate to contributions. The working poor, for example, receive a larger portion of their contributions in the form of benefits than does the working middle class. The social security system is so structured that almost all retirees can expect to receive more in benefits than they and their employers ever paid into the system.

In the 1930s, when the system was created, the life expectancy of Americans was about fifty-nine years. That figure has since risen to almost seventy-four years. Most Americans now live longer and hence collect significantly more in social security benefits. A steadily declining birthrate has placed the burden of supporting the social security system on fewer and fewer workers. Currently, for every three beneficiaries, ten employees contribute to the sys-

---

[13]"No More Easy Votes for Social Security," *The Brookings Bulletin* (Fall 1979), p. 2.

[14]Martha Derthick, *Policymaking for Social Security* (Brookings Institution, 1979), p. 413.

FINANCING SOCIAL SECURITY (1983)

The National Commission on Social Security Reform was created by President Reagan to recommend ways to save the social security system. Its suggestions, adopted by Congress, were the result of compromise among many political leaders. Among the most important of the commission's twenty-two suggestions were the following:

☐ A six-month delay in the cost-of-living adjustment from July 1983 to January 1984. This provision saved the social security system an estimated $40 billion.

☐ A rescheduling of previously approved increases in social security payroll taxes. Increases will take place sooner than legislated in existing law. This provision will save the system an estimated $40 billion.

☐ A gradual increase in the retirement age. An increase in the benefit bonus for early retirement will be phased in gradually until 2010.

☐ An extension of coverage to all newly hired federal workers. New federal employees will contribute to the social security system rather than to their own pension plans. Also, all employees of nonprofit organizations not covered at present will come under the social security system. Further, state and local governments now in the system will be prohibited from withdrawing.

These steps will save $23 billion.

☐ Subjecting for the first time benefits to income tax. One-half of all social security benefits of individuals with other income over $20,000 and families with earnings over $25,000 will be taxed. The expected $30 billion yield will be credited to the social security system.

tem. But by the year 2030 or so, the same ten employees will have to support about five social security recipients.

By 1983 this pay-as-you-go structure had plunged the system into a state of considerable financial uncertainty. Benefits, and especially the annual cost-of-living increases, were rapidly outstripping its reserves. Politicians in both parties skirted the issue of cutbacks or modifications in the system—fearing the wrath of the 36 million or more social security recipients. Meanwhile senior Americans were growing very anxious about the system.

In early 1983 the system was said to be losing $20,000 every minute—and estimates of projected shortages ranged as high as $1.5 trillion. The pending crisis forced President Reagan and Congress to take action. Reagan created the bipartisan National Commission on Social Security Reform. This fifteen-member group was charged with suggesting ways to solve and improve the system's financial problems.

The commission released its findings in early 1983. (See box.) Among other things, it recommended delaying for six months a cost-of-living benefit increase, increasing payroll taxes, and gradually raising the retirement age. The commission also suggested (and Congress approved) that new federal employees be required to join the social security system and that benefits of some higher-income retired people be subject to federal income taxes. The commission's recommendations were quickly acted upon by Congress and signed into law by Reagan. While these changes will mean more taxes and more money withheld from our monthly paychecks, it reassured most people that the financial solvency of this highly visible federal program would be guaranteed for at least the next decade.

The Guaranteed Income Debate

When social security began in 1935, there were millions of people for whom the insurance benefits were of little help. Thus, the national government also made substantial grants to the states for welfare payments to certain needy persons. That there would always be some who would need welfare—those too handicapped to work, for example—was anticipated. But it was expected that with the return of prosperity and the buildup of social security insurance benefits, the federal government could eventually leave to the states the burden of providing assistance to the blind, the handicapped, and orphans. This has never happened.

In good times as well as bad, one out of every nineteen Americans receives some kind of public assistance. Unemployment insurance is of little help to someone too unskilled to get a job or earn enough for a family to live on; old-age insurance is not enough for those who have no other resources. And a mother with small children finds it difficult to support her family when her husband dies or deserts her.

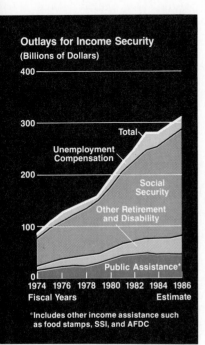

AID FOR FAMILIES WITH DEPENDENT CHILDREN The fastest-growing, most costly, and most controversial public assistance program is Aid for Families with Dependent Children. A dependent child is one under eighteen who has been deprived of parental support but who is living with a parent or with a close relative. AFDC helps over 11 million persons, most of whom are children. The program's aim is to keep families with children together. Many critics charge that because families with fathers are not eligible for assistance, AFDC encourages fathers to desert. The program has also been charged with encouraging immorality and making welfare a way of life. Some states have tried to deny assistance to families where the mother is unwed, where there is a man living in the house, where a family has just moved to the state, or where the family is headed by an alien. But Congress and the Supreme Court have ruled against such restrictions. The Court has even ruled that a recipient may not have welfare taken away without first being provided with a hearing. The state must show why the recipient is ineligible and give him or her an opportunity to confront any adverse witnesses.

Congress requires mothers of children over six years old to participate in job-training or work programs to qualify for federally assisted welfare. It has exempted from taxation a certain percentage of a mother's income so that she is not penalized because of earning a salary. The trouble is that nearly half of AFDC mothers have gone no further than the eighth grade in school. Even if AFDC children under six years of age were given a place in every licensed day-care facility in the country, there would still be 1 million such children left over.

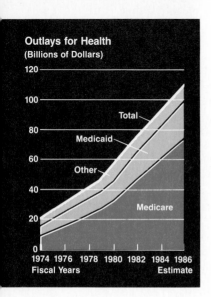

A MINIMUM INCOME Effective in 1974 the federal government guaranteed a minimum income to Americans at least sixty-five years old, and to the blind and disabled of any age. This guarantee is an "absolute right." The program replaces state-administered programs of assistance to the aged, blind, and disabled. Over 4 million people are covered. This program, called the Supplemental Security Income Program, is administered by the Social Security Administration. Its money, however, comes not from the Social Security Trust Fund but from general funds of the U.S. Treasury.

Is this income guarantee a major step toward a universal cash income guarantee? Some people think so. Supplemental Security Income makes the cash income of millions of Americans—the aged, the blind, the disabled—a legal obligation of the federal government. For a bewildering and unfair variety of state rules to decide who is 'needy' enough to be helped, SSI substitutes national standards of income and resources.

Welfare assistance line, New York
City. *UPI.*

PROMOTING EQUALITY

Welfare politics and welfare policies have remained on the public agenda for about twenty years. Some improvements have been realized. The number of substandard housing units has been lowered. More minority persons have entered and graduated from colleges. But welfare and antipoverty offensives have always been controversial. Many measures once proposed have been allowed to die, or were later scuttled, or are still under consideration. The beleaguered War on Poverty, the unsuccessful battle to pass a family assistance program, and the campaign for national health insurance are illustrative. Further, declining dollar value and a shrinking gross national product make upward mobility for all an almost impossible goal.[15]

The War on Poverty

The Economic Opportunity Act of 1964 created the Office of Economic Opportunity, within the executive office of the president, as a command post to distribute federal funds to other agencies and to operate a variety of programs through its own staff. Each program was aimed at a specific condition or group. Among the more important of these programs were the following:

1. *Operation Headstart.* Designed to get preschool children into school before the impact of a disadvantaged environment so disabled them that they would be unable to profit from formal instruction.
2. *Neighborhood Youth Corps.* For teenagers who dropped out or were in danger of dropping out of high school. Operated by the Department of Labor, the corps provided work experiences after school and during the summer.
3. *Community Action Programs.* This was an attempt to overcome what the drafters of the act thought to be the basic weaknesses of welfare programs—

[15]See Paul Blumberg, *Inequality in an Age of Decline* (Oxford University Press, 1980).

Wee Pals by Morrie Turner. © News Group Chicago, Inc.—Courtesy of News America Syndicate.

fragmentation and middle-class bias. The federal government made grants to local community action groups covering most of the costs for coordinated programs "that are developed and administered with maximum feasible participation of the residents of the areas and members of the group for whose benefit the Act was passed."

In its first ten years the Economic Opportunity Act was subjected to intense criticism from many quarters. Some charged that the programs did not call for enough participation by the poor and provided inadequate funds for a serious attack on the overwhelming problems of chronic poverty. Some said the act was used to support unsavory "rip-offs." Others contended that much of the federal money never really benefited those for whom it was intended.[16]

President Reagan's alleged attack on the war on poverty programs was a rallying point for those who believed Reagan favored the rich over the poor. Reagan's critics said his reductions in social service programs and his emphasis on tighter definitions of need demonstrate his indifference to the less needy in America. On the other side, Reagan and his supporters argued that too many federal programs had become *"entitlement programs"*—programs such as Social Security, Aid to Families with Dependent Children, Medicare, and unemployment insurance, that qualified citizens are "entitled" to by law. The problem raised by all these programs is that our federal budget is now set up so that certain subsidies are built into the system. Once Congress defines who gets benefits, these benefits get passed out no matter what. Moreover, it is increasingly difficult for Congress to reduce or redirect these entitlements for senior citizens, for students, for government employees because of the political pressures raised by these groups.

Many of the entitlement programs benefit middle income groups. And these groups are politically alert and organized. A growing number of analysts of several different political persuasions are now worried that the federal budget is "out of control." Congress is unlikely to curtail entitlement programs. The federal deficit continues to grow, and the debate over providing assistance to the poor intensifies.

Helping Farmers   The impressive success and competitiveness of American agriculture owes almost as much to the federal government and its subsidies as to fertile soil and hard work. Agriculture is a $150 billion-a-year enterprise and as such our nation's largest industry—bigger than steel, automobiles, computers, and even arcade game machines. Agriculture and food-related businesses generate one out of every five jobs in our private sector and account for about 20 percent of the GNP and one-fourth of our exports. It is also the industry with the highest rate of growth of productivity. Since the 1940s productivity has increased at a rate of more than 6 percent a year.

[16]For a contrary view, see Sar A. Levitan and Robert Taggart, *The Promise of Greatness: The Social Programs of the Last Decade and Their Major Achievements* (Harvard University Press, 1976).

While the success of agriculture has many causes, government cooperation, subsidies, and loans are key factors. The federal government has invested major sums in basic food research at our federally subsidized state agricultural universities. The resulting new seeds and techniques are further tested and refined at subsidized experimental farms. Local county agents funded by the U.S. Agriculture Department helped to spread the word to farmers.

Major federal initiatives in irrigation and rural electrification fostered great strides in productivity after World War II. Numerous loans and credit programs were established both to help farmers get through the tough years and to help them purchase needed equipment. Some of these programs have become self-financing, but usually they were begun with public money. Other federal initiatives have been enacted to stabilize incomes and output with price supports and acreage controls.

The federal government in recent years has been paying farmers more than $22 billion in direct subsidies and loans. By and large, the wealthier farmers benefit most. "The federal government still dispenses assistance to farmers with a blindfold, treating an extensive agrifactory as if it were a bedraggled operation with a hand-crank tractor and a cow. As a result, 1 percent of the nation's farmers receive 29 percent of all benefits."[17] This happens because many federal subsidy programs pay farmers for *not* planting crops. It is the biggest farmers who are able *not* to grow the greatest quantity of food, and who have lots of land *not* to grow it on. Hence, they get the lion's share of farm welfare.

The federal government attempts to stabilize farm prices and provide a floor under farmer's earnings on wheat, corn, rice, and cotton. Dairy products are covered also. A number of programs help to achieve these goals:

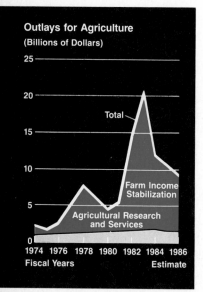

Outlays for Agriculture
(Billions of Dollars)

Martin A. Levick, Black Star.

☐ *Price support loans:* Loans made at Treasury interest rates with a farmer's crop put up as collateral. The per bushel loan rate is set by the secretary of agriculture. These loans, plus interest, may be repaid after nine months. Or they may be forfeited, without interest, by transferring the collateral crops to the Agriculture Department, which may not sell them until the market rises to 100 percent of the loan rate.

☐ *Subsidies:* Called "deficiency payments." The per bushel rate at which these are paid is the difference between the "target price" set by Congress and the average free-market price in the first five months after harvest. Eligible farmers receive these automatically, whether they sell their crop, take a loan on it, or store it.

☐ *Reserve:* Eligible farmers may designate part of their crops for the reserve, holding them on their own farms or at local elevators. When they do, they receive a loan at the bank rate. When the market reaches a "trigger price" set by Congress, these reserves may be sold and the loan, plus interest, paid off. When the market reaches a "release price," the farmer must pay off the loan and is no longer given storage payments if he or she holds reserves.

☐ *Paid diversion:* When the secretary offers a "diversion," a farmer who idles a percentage of the land normally planted in these crops is paid in cash, based on the average per acre yield on the land he or she diverted. The farmer may not plant another controlled crop on that land.

☐ *Payment-in-kind (PIK):* Farmers who leave idle additional land are given crops from government stores in proportion to the average yield from the land idled.

☐ *Milk price supports:* The support level for a hundred pounds of milk is set by Congress. Any amount of milk that is not bottled as fluid milk is "manufac-

[17]Congressman Bryan Dorgan, "America's Real Farm Problem," *Washington Monthly* (April 1983), pp. 12–18.

tured" into butter, cheese, or dried milk. Any of these dairy products not sold by the processors is bought by the Agriculture Department at the price support level. The department stores these products. It may not sell them in the open market but may use them in government food programs or for charity, both at home and abroad. They may also be sold in foreign markets at any price.[18]

Plainly, the vast array of subsidies, loans, credits, and related programs of research and investment have helped the American farmer increase productivity and enjoy a more stable income. Certain economists point out, however, that not only do the big farmers gain the most from federal programs, but various federal government income transfers to farmers often hurt poor people by driving up the price of food. Thus, although helping farmers encourages productivity, it also increases poverty. Why do we do this? Farmers vote in very large numbers. Further, not only are they organized, but just like senior citizens and unions and Chrysler and its friends, farmers know how to present their case to Congress. Caravans of farm equipment rolling back and forth in front of Congress can be rather intimidating.

SUMMARY

1. An entire book would be necessary just to describe all the subsidy and welfare efforts now being run by the federal government. We especially regret that we do not have space to talk about the complex ways government aids hospitals, homeowners, higher-education institutions, the airline industry, and others.

2. The role of government as promoter is not new. It is as old as the Republic itself. We have recently witnessed the latest surge of intense governmental concern with energy development, support of businesses such as Chrysler, and human resource assistance programs.

3. Many disagree with efforts by the national government to improve the quality of life, to focus resources and attention on the problems of the poor, and to improve the cities. They view with distaste the bureaucracy required for these programs, allege that the programs cost far more than they might cost if administered at the local level, and claim that many of these programs create a dependency that undermines our traditional ethic of self-reliance. On the other hand, most of these problems developed because local, private, and voluntary sectors were overwhelmed by them and were unable to respond in a meaningful way.

4. The pressures are usually for more, not less, involvement by the national government. In one way or another the government subsidizes nearly every segment of our population. Which of these programs are justified and which are not is the very heart of American politics. One person's subsidy is often viewed as the next person's boondoggle. Once a subsidy or entitlement program is established, it is hard to get rid of it. Sometimes they do not accomplish what Congress intended; hence all of these programs need to be constantly reviewed.

FURTHER READING

PAUL BLUMBERG. *Inequality in an Age of Decline* (Oxford University Press, 1980).

MARTIN CARNOY and DEREK SHEARER. *Economic Democracy: The Challenge of the 1980s* (M. E. Sharpe, 1980).

MARTHA DERTHICK. *Policymaking for Social Security* (Brookings Institution, 1979).

AMORY and HUNTER LOVINS. *Brittle Power: Energy Strategy for National Security* (Brick House, 1982).

BENJAMIN PAGE. *Who Gets What From Government.* (University of California Press, 1983).

JOSEPH PECHMAN (ed.). *Setting National Priorities: The Budget for 1984.* (Brookings Institution, 1983).

ROBERT RINGER. *Restoring the American Dream* (QED, 1979).

ROBERT STOBAUGH and DANIEL YERGEN. *Energy Future* (Random House, 1979).

[18]Adapted from *The New York Times*, August 8, 1983, p. 9. © 1983 by the New York Times Company. Reprinted by permission.

THE POLITICS OF TAXING AND SPENDING

24

We have looked at two of the main methods by which government influences society—regulation and subsidies. Through regulation government lays down the rules that control what people may and may not do. Through subsidies, government directly or indirectly advances the interests of certain groups or organizations. We have also looked at a·third method, the direct management of certain enterprises such as delivering the mail and developing energy.

But the most important influence the federal government has on the economy is the way in which it taxes and spends money. Enormous sums are involved. With a national budget of about $1000 billion by 1986, our national government spends 24 percent of the gross national product, or nearly one dollar out of every four. Government has come to intervene in the economy in so many ways that political leaders are to a very real extent economic leaders as well. Tax and budgetary decisions are especially important because they determine the division of resources between public and private goods and the distribution of private resources among different families and individuals. Tax and budget choices determine the government's priorities. The politics of taxing and spending centers on the questions of what we want to accomplish as a nation and who will actually pay for it.

RAISING MONEY

Big government is expensive. Federal, state, and local governments spend money equal to about a third of the income of all Americans. The national government is the biggest spender of all. In recent years Washington has disbursed more than all state and local governments combined.

Where does all this money come from? The federal government gets most of its funds from taxes. Other monies come from loans, income from special fees and fines, and grants and gifts. A third source of federal funds is administrative and commercial revenues. The fee paid to the State Department for a passport and the fine paid by a criminal are administrative revenues that account for a small portion of federal income. More important are the funds paid to the federal government in exchange for direct services—payments to the Post Office for stamps, to the Park Service for recreation, and to the Government Printing Office for pamphlets.

Levying Taxes

U.S. TAX MILESTONES	
1983	Collection reaches about $600 billion.
1981	Inflation boosts collections to $407 billion; tax per capita $2,687.
1950	Collections at $28 billion; tax per capita at $256.
1945	Wartime collections passed $43 billion.
1943	Withholding introduced.
1918	First $1 billion income tax collection.
1913	Income tax legalized by the 16th Amendment.
1895	Income tax declared unconstitutional.
1894	Income tax revived.
1872	Tax discontinued. Most revenue raised by taxing liquor and tobacco.
1862	First income tax to support Civil War.
Prior to 1862	The government only taxed imports, slaves, and certain manufactured goods.

© InfoGraphics 1983

© 1983 by Taylor.

TAX MAN

"In this world," Benjamin Franklin once said, "nothing is certain but death and taxes." Tax collecting is one of the oldest activities of government. Putting power over taxation into the hands of the people was a landmark in the rise of self-government. "No taxation without representation" has been the war cry of people the world over.

The Constitution clearly provides that Congress "shall have power to lay and collect taxes, duties, imposts, and excises." But duties and excise taxes have to be levied uniformly throughout the United States; direct taxes have to be apportioned among the states according to population; and no tax can be levied on articles exported from any state. Except during the Civil War, the federal government for a century relied on the tariff for most of its revenue. This hidden tax—which many people mistakenly thought to be a tax on foreigners—fluctuated with the rise and fall of trade and tariff levels. Congress supplemented these taxes with excise taxes on the manufacture or sale of certain goods. In 1894 an income tax law was enacted (such a tax had been used during the Civil War but given up shortly afterward). The 1894 tax was not drastic—only 2 percent on all income over $4,000. One opponent of the bill scorned it on the floor of the Senate as "an attempt to array the rich against the poor, the poor against the rich . . . Socialism, communism, *devilism.*" The next year, in *Pollock* v. *Farmers' Loan and Trust Co.,* the Supreme Court declared the tax unconstitutional on the grounds that it was a direct tax and therefore had to be apportioned among the states according to population.[1] About twenty years later, in 1915, the Sixteenth Amendment was adopted, authorizing Congress "to lay and collect taxes on incomes, from whatever source derived, without apportionment among the several States, and without regard to any census or enumeration."

Raising money is only one important objective of taxation. Regulating and, more recently, promoting economic growth, as well as controlling inflation, are others. Taxation as a device to promote economic growth will be discussed later. In a broad sense all taxation regulates human behavior. For example, a graduated income tax has a leveling tendency on incomes, and a tariff act affects foreign trade. Congress has used its taxing power to prevent or regulate certain practices. Years ago Congress laid a 10 percent tax on the circulation of notes by state banks, immediately putting an end to such issues. Today federal taxes include the following:

1. *Income taxes on individuals.* Taxes on the income of individuals account for about 44 percent of the federal government's tax revenue. Originally set at a low rate, the income tax was greatly increased during World War I and went to new heights during World War II and the Korean conflict. Over the years the income tax has grown increasingly complex, as Congress has responded to claims for differing kinds of exemptions and rates. But the tax has one great advantage in its flexibility. The schedule of rates can be raised or lowered in

[1]158 U.S. 601 (1895).

order to stimulate or restrain economic activity. The income tax is moderately progressive. People with high incomes generally pay larger fractions of their income than lower-income people, though many of the wealthy benefit from tax loopholes.[2]

2. *Income taxes on corporations.* These account for about 8 or 9 percent of the national government's tax revenues. As late as 1942 corporate income taxes amounted to more than individual income taxes, but returns from the latter increased more rapidly during World War II.

3. *Social insurance or payroll taxes.* This is the second largest and most rapidly rising source of federal revenue. From a mere $4 billion in 1950, this tax will raise nearly $280 billion in fiscal year 1985. These are the monies collected mainly from payroll deductions to finance social security and other insurance programs. They are, economists point out, highly regressive. Low-income people generally pay larger fractions of their income than do high-income people.

4. *Excise taxes.* Federal taxes on liquor, tobacco, gasoline, telephones, air travel, and other so-called luxury items will total about $40 billion in 1985.

5. *Customs duties.* Though no longer the main source of federal income, these taxes provided in recent years an annual yield of more than $9 billion.

The Politics and Machinery of Taxation

Most of us complain that our tax load is too heavy and that someone else is not carrying a fair share. People with large incomes naturally grumble about income taxes as high as 50 percent of their net income. Low-income people point out that even a low tax may deprive them of the necessities of life. People in the middle-income brackets feel their situation is the worst of all—their incomes are not high, but their taxes are.

What is the best type of tax? Some say the graduated income tax: It is relatively easy to collect, hits hardest those who are most able to pay, and hardly touches those at the bottom of the income ladder. Others argue that   are the fairest, because they are paid by people who are spending money for luxury goods and who thus obviously have money to spare. Further, by discouraging people from buying expensive goods, excise taxes sometimes have a deflationary effect in times of rising prices. On the other hand, excise taxes are more expensive to collect than income taxes; and in some cases, such as with the tax on tobacco, they may hit the poor the hardest. Excise taxes also face strong resistance from affected industries such as tobacco, liquor, airlines, and so on.

Most controversial is the general   which is levied against the sales of all goods. Labor and liberal organizations call this form of tax   —that is, causing lower-income citizens to pay a higher proportion of their income in tax revenues than is paid by higher-income citizens. The sales tax is regressive because the poor spend a larger proportion of their income than do the wealthy. Proponents of the sales tax stress its potential anti-inflationary effect and point to its successful use in a number of states.

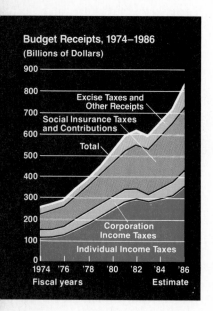

Budget Receipts, 1974–1986
(Billions of Dollars)

Excise Taxes and Other Receipts

Social Insurance Taxes and Contributions

Total

Corporation Income Taxes

Individual Income Taxes

1974 '76 '78 '80 '82 '84 '86
Fiscal years   Estimate

Flat Tax—Fair Tax Proposals

From time to time we are urged to overhaul the tax system and strive for greater efficiency and fairness in the tax process. One of the many suggestions gaining attention in recent years has been the so-called "flat tax" idea. Most flat tax proposals have two main elements. First, to tax incomes at the same rate, no matter what the income level of the taxpayer. Under the present, modestly progressive tax system, tax rates begin at 12 percent and increase to 50 percent. The second element of most flat tax plans is the elimination of all, or most, tax deductions. A *tax deduction* is any form of tax credit, exclusion, or "tax write-off" that allows taxpayers the right to lessen their tax burdens. For exam-

[2]See Joseph Pechman, *Federal Tax Policy*, 3rd ed. (Brookings Institution, 1977).

Senator Bill Bradley (D-New Jersey) an advocate for tax reform in the U.S. Senate.

ple, a contribution to a charity is tax deductible, as is the interest payment on a home mortgage.

Most flat tax plans would generate about as much revenue as the current tax system. Even though overall tax rates would be lower, the taxable income base would be increased. This would occur primarily through the elimination of tax deductions, or what is technically called "tax expenditures." **Tax expenditures** are government revenue losses due to provisions of the federal tax laws that provide special tax breaks to individuals and businesses. In 1986 tax expenditures are expected to total over $550 billion.

Flat tax advocates come from all political persuasions. They unite in believing that our tax code is currently too complicated. They believe the current system has lost its claim to being a progressive tax in that people of wealth can significantly lower their tax bracket by taking advantage of so many tax deductions or tax shelters. Further, many of these tax reformers believe taxes are just too high.

Economist Milton Friedman has proposed we slash the tax rates down to something like a straight 10 percent tax for everyone. The average person would pay 10 percent—as would David Rockefeller—on their annual income. Friedman would do away with all tax deductions.

Specific flat tax proposals before the Congress in the mid-1980s differ in the tax deductions or exemptions they would permit. The flat tax proposal generating the most political support is that put forward by Senator Bill Bradley (D-N.J.) and Congressman Richard Gephardt (D-Missouri) (see Box on this page), which envisions a flat tax within three tiers. The Bradley-Gephardt plan retains only the most politically sensitive deductions: Major medical expenses, state and local property taxes, interest on home mortgages, charitable contributions, as well as the standard personal exemption.

Proponents of the flat tax say it would (1) simplify the tax process, (2) be more equitable than the present system (which many claim is so full of loopholes that it is no longer progressive), (3) increase government revenues by increasing compliance with tax laws (since taxpayers might feel somewhat better about a system in which everyone is paying their fair share and where the wealthy cannot hire tax lawyers and accountants to "hide" their income from the taxation), and (4) make the economy more efficient. Flat tax advocates point out that a considerable amount of money increasingly is being diverted to nonproductive tax shelters. Also, additional monies are being diverted into an underground economy of bartering and trading of goods and services for the primary purpose of avoiding taxes of any kind.

Opponents of a flat rate tax claim the current system is more progressive than a flat tax would be. It is very fair, they say, to ask the well-off to contribute a larger share of their incomes than to increase the burden on those with lower income. Opponents also say elimination of many tax deductions might prove harmful to the health of the economy—especially the housing and building industries (if the interest on mortgages is ever affected). Finally, opponents suggest the tax code can be simplified and its abuses corrected without overhauling the entire system.

The flat tax plan will be difficult to pass; those who benefit from existing deductions present a very large obstacle. Still, the idea is likely to be debated for some time.

Levying and Collecting Taxes

Although the Constitution provides that all revenue bills must be initiated in the House of Representatives, it is usually the president who originates tax legislation. With the help of tax experts at the White House and in the Treasury Department, a president draws up a tax program designed to meet the government's revenue needs for the coming fiscal year. The program also takes into consideration the current and projected state of the economy. Often representatives of interest groups are consulted while the bill is being drawn up. Then the president submits the tax program to Congress, often along with the budget message. The powerful House Ways and Means Committee next holds hearings on the bill. Administration representatives, headed by the secretary of the treasury, usually lead the parade of witnesses, followed by representatives of interested groups, tax experts, and others. Then tax measures go through Congress in much the same way as other bills. Although the Senate cannot initiate tax legislation, it is active in tax matters. It often differs with the House and forces extensive changes in bills. Sometimes Congress refuses to follow the president's recommendations and works out a tax measure largely on its own.[3]

A recent tax bill illustrates the impact of taxes on a variety of individuals and groups. Testifying on proposed tax changes before a congressional committee, 138 witnesses expressed their views. The printed testimony covered more than 1600 pages. Business representatives opposed new taxes on corporations. Small businesspeople complained that existing taxes favored big business. Representative of tobacco growers, transportation interests, the wine and spirits industry, movies and legitimate theater, candymakers, telephone companies, and bowling alleys argued that the proposed tax would discriminate against them. Labor demanded a lighter burden for low-income groups and higher taxes on business. Unorganized workers and consumers, however, were not represented.

The Treasury Department has the job of collecting taxes. It employs almost 116,000 people. The actual tax-collecting job falls mainly to the Department's Internal Revenue Service, which employs nearly 83,000 people. Fifty-eight district directors are located throughout the country, and taxes are paid into district offices rather than directly to Washington. Customs duties are collected by the Treasury Department's Bureau of Customs, which maintains ports of entry, inspects cargo, assesses the value of merchandise, and—with the United States Coast Guard—prevents smuggling.

Uncle Sam, Borrower

When we are suddenly faced with expenses too heavy to meet out of regular income, we often have to borrow money. The same is true of government. During military and economic crises the federal government has gone heavily into debt. (See Box on this page) It borrowed $23 billion during World War I, about $13 billion more during the 1930s, and over $200 billion more during World War II. By 1985 the gross federal debt will be above $1,600 billion.

Borrowing costs money. The federal government can borrow at a relatively low rate. Nevertheless the interest on the federal debt is over $120 billion a year. The size of the debt and of the interest payments alarms many Americans. How long can we allow the debt to grow at this rate? Two considerations must be kept in mind. In the first place, the government owes most of the money to its own people rather than to foreign governments or persons. Second, the economic strength and resources of the country are more significant than the size of the public debt. Still, the interest we pay to service the debt is a real cause for concern. It sometimes threatens our credit markets and keeps interest rates high. Both political parties are now pledged to reduce the debt but they are not doing so with any speed.

How does the government borrow money? The Constitution says Congress may "borrow money on the credit of the United States"; it puts no limit on the extent or method of borrowing. Under congressional authorization the Treasury Department sells securities to banks, corporations, and individuals.

[3]See John F. Manley, *The Politics of Finance* (Little, Brown, 1970); and Lawrence C. Pierce, *The Politics of Fiscal Policy Formation* (Goodyear, 1971).

Usually these securities take the form of long-term bonds or short-term Treasury notes. Some bonds may be cashed in at any time, others not until maturity. Because the United States government guarantees these bonds, they are in demand, especially by banks and investment companies.

SPENDING THE MONEY

PRESIDENTS AND TOTAL DEFICITS—1934–1984	
Roosevelt	$197 billion
Truman	4.4
Eisenhower	15.8
Kennedy	11.9
Johnson	42
Nixon	68.7
Ford	124.6
Carter	181.0
Reagan (through 1984)	570 (est.)

Source: U.S. Department of Commerce, and Office of Management and Budget.

Nothing reflects the rise of big government more clearly than the change in the amounts and methods of its spending. As recently as 1933 the federal government spent only $4 billion, about $30 per capita. By 1985 the respective figures will be about $1000 billion and about $4400. The machinery for spending has changed, too. At one time spending was loosely administered. Records show, for example, that in the early Republic one Nicholas Johnson, a Navy agent of Newburyport, Massachusetts, was handed several thousands dollars to supply "Cpt. Brown for recruiting his Crew."[4] Today Mr. Johnson would have to make out detailed forms and wait for a check.

Where does the money go? Much of it, of course, is for national defense. In recent years about 30 percent has gone to national security; 13 percent to interest on the national debt; and more than 40 percent to social insurance, education, and other major social programs. Much of the federal debt is for payments for past wars. Defense-related expenditures such as veterans' pensions and benefits are sometimes buried in categories other than national security.

Years ago federal revenues and outlays were so small, national taxing and spending had little impact on the overall economy. Today the federal government cannot drain billions of dollars from certain areas of the economy and pump them back into others without having a profound effect on the economy of the nation and of the world. This problem will be considered later in the chapter; first we must see how the federal budget is drawn up and made into law.

Formulating the Budget

As we have seen, Congress must authorize the spending of funds, but the initiation of appropriations is a responsibility of the president. The first step in preparing a federal budget is for the various departments and agencies to estimate their needs.[5] This process starts early. While Congress is debating the budget for the fiscal year immediately ahead, the agencies are making estimates for the year following. The estimating job is handled largely by officers under the direction of agency chiefs. Agency officials must take into account not only their needs as they see them but also the overall presidential program and the probable reactions of Congress. Departmental budgets are detailed; they include estimates on expected needs for personnel, supplies, office space, and the like.

The **Office of Management and Budget** (OMB) handles the next phase. A staff agency of the president, the OMB examines each agency budget to see if it is in accord with the president's plans. This job is done by budget examiners. Hearings are then held to give agency people a chance to clarify and defend their estimates. The OMB director and OMB aides, who make the final decision, sometimes prune the agencies' requests rather severely.

Finally, the director goes to the White House with a single consolidated set of estimates of both revenue and expenditures, the product of perhaps a year's work. The president takes a few days to review these figures. The budget

Ronald Reagan's OMB Director, David Stockman. Stockman was a former member of Congress from Michigan. *UPI.*

[4]L. D. White, *The Federalists* (Macmillan, 1948), p. 341.

[5]For a discussion of the budgetary cycle, see Aaron Wildavsky, *The Politics of the Budgetary Process*, 4th ed. (Little, Brown, 1983). See also Allen Schick, *Congress and Money* (Urban Institute, 1980); and Howard Shuman, *Politics and The Budget* (Prentice-Hall, 1984).

director also helps the president prepare a budget message that will stress key aspects of the budget and tie it in with broad national plans. By January, soon after Congress convenes, the budget and the message are ready for the legislature and the public.

Processing Budget Proposals

Under the Constitution only Congress can appropriate funds. In 1974 Congress adopted the Budget Reform Act, which was intended to give it a more effective role in the budget process. The act specifies that when submitting proposals, the president include proposed changes in tax laws, estimates of amounts of revenue lost through existing preferential tax treatments, and five-year estimates of the costs of new and continuing federal programs. The act also calls on the president to seek authorizing legislation for a program a year before asking Congress for the funds to fund it. Preparing budget proposals is only the beginning. For as we saw in Chapter 16, the Budget Reform Act of 1974 also called for Congress to make important changes in the way it appropriates funds.

Checking up on Expenditures

After Congress has appropriated money, it reserves the right to check up on the way the money is being spent. Under the Budget and Accounting Act of 1921, the General Accounting Office (GAO) does the national government's accounting job. The GAO is headed by a comptroller general, who is appointed by the president with the approval of the Senate for a term of fifteen years. The comptroller general was originally intended to be an independent auditor serving as an arm of Congress to guard against improper and unauthorized expenditures. But as time went on the office was swamped by a gigantic accounting job that forced the auditor to handle administrative matters in the executive branch even though the office is not responsible to the chief executive. At the same time, overall management in the executive branch suffered, because daily accounting, an important instrument of administrative control, had been placed in a separate agency.

"Remember, son, we are a government of loopholes, and not of men!" *Drawing by Dana Fradon;* © *1976. The New Yorker Magazine, Inc.*

The GAO, with over 5100 employees, now uses spot sampling methods to check vouchers, and makes its audits in the field rather than in Washington. Although the comptroller general still has the authority to disallow expenditures, approval is no longer needed for the disbursement of funds. The General Accounting Office, as a result of the Legislative Reorganization Act of 1970, has taken on broader responsibilities in investigating and even evaluating programs. GAO is increasingly checking up on the adequacy and effectiveness of a program's performance as well as the honesty of it.

MANAGING THE MONEY

Today's economy is a money economy: We exchange commodities through a vast system of money and credit. Aside from its role as the biggest buyer and seller of goods and services, the national government has a more direct impact on our money economy. It regulates the value of money; it controls the nation's credit system.

Manufacturing money is relatively easy. The Bureau of Engraving and Printing in the Treasury Department turns out millions of dollars in the form of bills, bonds, and postage stamps every week. This money is fed into general circulation through the Treasury and the Federal Reserve banks. But in itself, this money is only so much paper. How does the government maintain its value?

The Currency System

The Constitution gives the national government the right to manage the nation's monetary system. Under the Articles of Confederation the national currency had consisted mainly of almost worthless paper money, and the individual states had maintained separate currencies. To correct this, the Constitution gave Congress authority to coin money and to regulate its value, carefully withholding this power from the states. Thanks partly to Alexander Hamilton, our first secretary of the treasury, Americans scrapped the confusing British system of guineas, pounds, shillings, and pence and adopted a decimal system.

Today the United States is on a highly modified gold standard. The unit of monetary value is defined in terms of gold. But all the currency of the United States is legal tender and cannot be freely exchanged for gold or silver. In short, the money of the United States is redeemable only for other money of the United States.

Money makes up only a part of the circulating medium and is less important to our economy than credit. In the expansion and contraction of credit the most important institutions are the banks and the Federal Reserve system.

The Federal Reserve System

In many nations a central bank owned and operated by the national government makes monetary policy. The Constitution does not specifically authorize the national government to create such a bank—indeed, it says nothing at all about banking. But Alexander Hamilton believed that some such institution was necessary. In 1791 the United States Bank was incorporated by the national government and given a twenty-year charter. This bank was partly private and partly public; the national government owned a minority of the shares and had only a minority voice in its management. Jefferson and his supporters opposed the bank and refused to renew the charter in 1812. But Madison found it necessary to have the bank rechartered for another twenty years in 1816. In 1819 the Supreme Court in *McCulloch* v. *Maryland*[6] (see Chapter 3) upheld the constitutionality of the bank as a necessary and proper way for the national government to establish a uniform currency and to care for the property of the United States.

The Governors of the Federal Reserve Board in Washington in session. *Rick Bloom.*

After the United States Bank closed its doors in 1836, state banks, which had previously been restrained by the federal bank, began issuing notes that often could not be redeemed. A military crisis forced a housecleaning. To stabilize a war economy, Congress in 1863 authorized the chartering of national banks. (These are privately owned corporations, not central banks or an institution like the United States Bank.) State banks were permitted to continue in business, but a 10 percent federal tax on their notes quickly drove state bank notes out of existence.

The national bank system created during the Civil War was stable—so stable that it was inflexible. Financial crises during the late nineteenth century and in 1907 revealed a tendency to restrict loans and to contract the issuance of notes just when an expansion of money was needed. In order to furnish an elastic currency, and for other reasons, Congress in 1913 established the Federal Reserve system.

The Federal Reserve Act of 1913 was a compromise. While some wanted a strong central bank, others feared this would centralize control over currency in too few hands. Thus, a mechanism was established combining a modified central banking system with considerable decentralization.

A seven-member Board of Governors sits atop the Federal Reserve System (the Fed). Governors are appointed by the president to fourteen-year nonrenewable terms and must be confirmed by the Senate. From these seven governors

[6] 4 Wheaton 316 (1819).

the president appoints a chair and a vice-chair, who also must be confirmed by the Senate. The chair and vice-chair serve for four years and may be reappointed. The chair of the Board of Governors of the Federal Reserve System is a highly visible member of the financial community. Paul A. Volcker, chair during the Carter and Reagan years, enjoyed as much visibility and notoriety as a leading member of the cabinet or United States Senate.

The chair, vice-chair, and remaining members of the Board of Governors oversee the Federal Reserve System. The system is divided into twelve Federal Reserve districts, each containing a Federal Reserve bank. Most Federal Reserve banks have branches. Each Federal Reserve bank is owned by banks which are members of the Federal Reserve System. Membership in the Federal Reserve System is mandatory for national banks but voluntary for state banks which meet certain standards. The Depository Institutions Deregulation and Monetary Control Act of 1980 has considerably reduced the distinction between member and nonmember banks. Among other provisions, the act extended the Fed's power over reserves in nonmember banks. Today approximately 5800 of the 15,000 banks in the United States are members of the system; these are the nation's largest banks and hold over 80 percent of total deposits.

Each Federal Reserve district is headed by a nineteen-member board of directors. The Federal Reserve Act of 1913 intended that the district bank directors have considerable autonomy. Over time, however, their power has eroded. Most of the major policy decisions are made by the Board of Governors in Washington, D.C. While some district bank directors sit on important Federal Reserve committees, most notably the federal open market committee, the district banks are now primarily reponsible only for carrying out the day-to-day operations of the Federal Reserve System. The district banks keep in close contact with member banks in order to implement the policies of the board of governors.

The Federal Reserve System uses four major devices to control economic activity:

1. *Reserve requirements:* The Fed can increase or decrease within legal limits the reserves member banks must maintain against their deposits in Federal Reserve banks.
2. *Discount rates:* The Fed can raise or lower the discount rate charged by Federal Reserve banks to member banks. The discount rate is the price member banks must pay to get cash from the Federal Reserve banks for acceptable commercial notes the banks hold.
3. *Open market operations:* Through its federal open market committee, the Fed can buy and sell government securities and certain other bills of exchange, bank acceptances, and so on.
4. *Margin requirements:* The Fed can exercise direct control over credit extended in order to purchase securities. From time to time Congress has given the board of governors temporary authority to fix terms of consumer credit.

Of these four tools, open market operations is the device most commonly used. The Fed can be more precise in conducting open market operations than it can in manipulating reserve requirements, the discount rate, or margin requirements. However, each device can have a direct effect on the economy.

Thus, if inflation is threatening, the board of governors can raise reserve requirements. Such a move cuts down on the cash banks have to lend, takes money out of circulation, and reduces inflation by making dollars already in circulation more valuable relative to goods. Or the Fed can raise the discount rate, making it expensive for member banks to borrow money. This encourages banks to reduce their lending. This also takes money out of circulation and thereby reduces inflation. The Fed can also take money out of circulation by

Paul Volcker, appointed by Jimmy Carter to a four-year term as chairman of the Fed. Ronald Reagan reappointed him and Congress reconfirmed him. Volcker won great praise and criticism for his role in responding to inflation in the early 1980s. *UPI.*

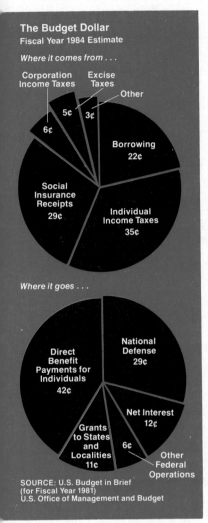

The Budget Dollar
Fiscal Year 1984 Estimate

Where it comes from . . .

Corporation Income Taxes 6¢
Excise Taxes 5¢
Other 3¢
Borrowing 22¢
Social Insurance Receipts 29¢
Individual Income Taxes 35¢

Where it goes . . .

Direct Benefit Payments for Individuals 42¢
National Defense 29¢
Net Interest 12¢
Grants to States and Localities 11¢
Other Federal Operations 6¢

SOURCE: U.S. Budget in Brief
(for Fiscal Year 1981)
U.S. Office of Management and Budget

selling government securities. Banks pay for these securities out of their reserves, thereby reducing the money supply. Finally, the Fed might raise margin requirements. This would reduce the credit available to bid up the prices of stocks and bonds.

Still, due to certain irregularities in financial markets, external factors beyond the control of the Fed, and the unpredictability of human behavior, the Fed has difficulty exerting rigorous control over the money supply. Moreover, the money supply itself is difficult to define precisely, due to the advent of new and different types of accounts in banks and savings institutions.

In addition to its money management duties, the Federal Reserve System also performs other functions. Federal Reserve banks serve as depositories for government funds, clear checks, and transfer funds among member banks, and may, in case of economic emergency, lend money directly to businesses.

The Federal Reserve System is not under the control of the Treasury Department or any other executive agency. It finances its activities through internally generated funds and fees, so it is not subject to the customary congressional appropriations process. By statute the Fed is independent. Devised as a service agency for banking and commerce—to achieve a semiautomatic adjustment of the money supply—today the Federal Reserve is also an influential policy-making institution with major responsibility for national economic stabilization.

Many oberservers think it is somehow improper to give this important responsibility to an agency seemingly so divorced from public accountability. The board of governors, for example, often has to make a choice between fighting inflation that may cause unemployment and promoting employment at the expense of increasing inflation. Chairman Paul Volcker, for example, was accused of being responsible for the 1982 recession precisely because he chose to tighten money supplies to fight inflation. Still, most bankers and political leaders want to preserve the system's independence. Only an agency insulated from political pressures, they believe, can take the unpopular steps needed to prevent severe inflation.[7]

In practice, the Fed is not entirely independent. The Federal Reserve is a political institution, directed by policy makers who live and work in a highly charged and highly constrained political environment.[8] In addition to the intangible political pressures from within and without government, the Fed is responsive in a variety of ways to both the executive and legislative branches. Members of the Board of Governors are appointed by a president (with the approval of the Senate) and are thus encouraged to lean somewhat toward the administration's beliefs. Most board members have served in the executive branch at one time or another. The Fed's chair regularly meets with the president's top economic and financial advisers. Also, the chair must give an annual report to Congress and occasionally testifies before key congressional committees.

Under recent chairs, the Fed has grown both in power and independence. Almost all recent leaders of the Federal Reserve have made a strong case that a major source of inflation is government deficits. While to some degree the Fed has the ability to aid or counter any attempts by a president or Congress to stimulate the economy, what are called the Fed's **monetary policy** strategies are only one weapon to combat depression, control inflation, foster full employment, and encourage economic growth.

[7]For a detailed analysis of the present structure and policy implications of the Federal Reserve system, see *The Federal Reserve System: Purpose and Functions* (Government Printing Office, 1979). For a critical view of the Federal Reserve system and some of its myths, see John Kenneth Galbraith, *Money* (Houghton Mifflin, 1975), chap. 10. For a critical view from the right, see Maxwell Newton, *The Fed* (Times Books, 1983).

[8]Peter Quick and Robert Shapiro, "The Myth of the Fed," *The New York Times*, March 17, 1982, p. 27.

Does the government have the same direct control over the national economy that it has, say, over the military or national forests? No. Only if we had a socialized economy administered from Washington would we have a managed economy in that sense. In our economy a great deal of power is left to private individuals and enterprises. Yet the government keeps a firm hand on many of the gears and levers that control the economy's general direction and the rate at which it moves. These gears and levers are taxes, spending, and credit.

Lessons of the Great Depression

Depression is a hard teacher, and the 1930s had a tremendous impact on American thinking about the role of government in the economy. While we had had long, severe depressions before—for example, in the 1870s and 1890s—the Great Depression of 1929 brought mass misery. "One vivid, gruesome moment of those dark days we shall never forget," wrote one observer. "We saw a crowd of some fifty men fighting over a barrel of garbage which had been set outside the back door of a restaurant. American citizens fighting for scraps of food like animals!"[9]

Despite the efforts of the Roosevelt administration to cope with the Depression, it hung on. Faint signs of recovery could be seen in the mid-1930s; but the recession of 1937–1938 indicated that we were by no means out of the woods. Eight or nine million people were jobless in 1939. Then came the war, and unemployment seemed cured. Millions of people had more income, more security, and a higher standard of living. Lord Beveridge in England posed a question that bothered many thoughtful Americans: "Unemployment has been practically abolished twice in the lives of most of us—in the last war and in this war. Why does war solve the problem of unemployment which is so insoluble in peace?"[10] Worried that the economy might collapse after the war, thousands of people came up with plans to ensure jobs for all.

Some people think the Great Depression was caused by the Federal Reserve and its mismanagement of the money supply. These people claim that had the Fed expanded the money supply in the early 1930s instead of keeping it constant and even reducing it, many of the bank failures and much of the misery of the Depression could have been avoided.

Others think the Depression lasted so long because the New Deal was hostile to business. Government intruded too long and too much into the economic life of the nation. Proponents of this theory urged the government to reduce spending, lower taxes, curb the power of labor, and generally leave business and economy alone. Another large group said that the trouble with the New Deal was not that it had done too much but that it had done too little. The thinking of this group was deeply influenced by the work of John Maynard Keynes the English economist.[11] In visits to the United States during the 1930s, Keynes warned that if people did not consume enough or invest enough, national income would fall. The way to increase national income is to spend money on consumption goods (such as clothes or food or automobiles), or on investment goods (steel mills and dock facilities), or on both. Finally, *in a recession government must do the spending and investing if private enterprise by itself will not or cannot.* Congress, through the passage of the Employment Act of 1946, accepted the Keynesian approach.

Reagan's tax cuts were widely applauded, especially by businessmen, and widely criticized by workers and the unemployed. *Jean-Louis Atlan/Sygma.*

[9]Quoted in F. L. Allen, *Since Yesterday* (Harper, 1940), p. 64.

[10]W. H. Beveridge, *The Pillars of Security* (Macmillan, 1943) p. 51.

[11]The debate over Keynes and his economic theories still takes place in the United States. See, for example, Robert Lekachman, "A Keynes for All Seasons," *The New Republic*, June 20, 1983, pp. 21–25; and the special issues on Keynes in *The Economist* (American Enterprise Institute, June, 1983).

Passing a law specifically recognizing the major role of the national government in maintaining full employment was bound to be difficult.[12] The bill as presented by the Truman administration had the support of organized labor, many senators, and members of several Senate committee staffs. Against the bill were such organizations as the National Association of Manufacturers, chambers of commerce, the American Farm Bureau Federation, and a number of key conservatives in Congress. Although the bill easily passed the Senate in close to its original form, the conservative House Rules Committee ensured that only a much weaker version would pass the House. Enacted in February 1946, the act declared:

> It is the continuing policy and responsibility of the Federal Government to use all practicable means consistent with its needs and obligations and other essential considerations of national policy, with the assistance and cooperation of industry, agriculture, labor, and state and local governments, to coordinate and utilize all its plans, functions, and resources for the purpose of creating and maintaining, in a manner calculated to foster and promote free competitive enterprise and the general welfare, conditions under which there will be afforded useful employment, for those able, willing, and seeking to work, and to promote maximum employment, production, and purchasing power.

If this sounds like double talk, it is because the bill was a medley of compromises. In effect, the bill made the government responsible for maintaining high employment. Equally important, the act established machinery to carry out that responsibility:

1. *The Council of Economic Advisers (CEA).* This body of three members appointed by the president with the consent of the Senate is located in the executive office of the president. It studies and forecasts economic trends, assesses the contribution of federal programs to maximum employment, and recommends to the president "national economic policies to foster and promote free competition, to avoid economic fluctuations or to diminish the effects thereof, and to maintain employment, production, and purchasing power."

2. *The Economic Report of the President.* Every January the president must submit to Congress an economic report based on the data and forecasts of the council. The report must include a program for carrying out the policy of the act; it can also include recommendations for legislation.

3. *Joint Economic Committee (JEC).* This committee of Congress composed of senators and representatives reports its findings and proposals in response to annual presidential recommendations. Aside from publishing various reports, the JEC tries to give Congress an overview of the economy. In this sense it is a planning and theory group in a legislature otherwise fiercely devoted to short-term, practical matters. The new Senate and House Budget Committees created in the mid-1970s are now also trying to provide this kind of overview.

Senator Lloyd Bentsen (left) and Special Trade Representative William Brock discuss U.S. trade problems. *UPI.*

How has the Employment Act worked in practice? The CEA has emerged as a high-level presidential advisory body. Its chair serves both as an adviser to the president and as a spokesperson for the president before Congress and the country. The annual economic report and the budget message are major presidential statements on the role governmental fiscal policies will play in the economy. The JEC has played a useful role in developing information on important economic problems. The various mechanisms of the act work reasonably well, but concern over inflation, trade, and budget deficits have prompted

---

[12]For the full history of the bill, see Stephen K. Bailey, *Congress Makes a Law* (Columbia University Press, 1950). For a history of national efforts at economic planning since the 1930s, see Otis L. Graham, *Toward a Planned Society* (Oxford University Press, 1976).

recent presidents to set up their own economic policy boards. These cabinet-level coordinating units seek to provide policy options to the president and to coordinate the actions that result from economic decisions.[13] Most of these mechanisms work, while the policies generated by them often fail.

FISCAL POLICY

Nowadays the national government unquestionably has tremendous economic power. But soaring government spending and soaring deficits have raised a number of questions about how effectively the government is doing its job. Through two types of policy—*monetary* (control of the money supply) and *fiscal* (taxing and spending)—the government attempts to manage the economy's ups and downs, moderating both while allowing steady economic growth. This management power emerged fairly recently with such developments as the Federal Reserve System, the income tax, and the great growth of government spending.

Government management of the economy is still based to a large degree on the theories of John Maynard Keynes—increasing aggregate demand by government spending during business slumps, and curbing spending during booms. Politically, however, there is a problem: It is much easier to increase

YOU DECIDE !

Here is the actual wording of a proposed amendment to the U.S. Constitution. It has the backing of several senators and members of Congress. Would you support it? If so, why? If not, why not? And what do you think are some of the reasons why people favor it or oppose it?

TEXT OF A PROPOSED AMENDMENT

ARTICLE
Resolved by the Senate and House of Representatives of the United States of America in Congress assembled (two-thirds of each House concurring therein), That the following article is proposed as an amendment to the Constitution of the United States, which shall be valid to all intents and purposes as part of the Constitution if ratified by the legislatures of three-fourths of the several states within seven years after its submission to the states for ratification:
Section 1. Prior to each fiscal year, the Congress shall adopt a statement of receipts and outlays for that year in which

total outlays are not greater than total receipts. The Congress may amend such statement provided revised outlays are no greater than revised receipts. Whenever three-fifths of the whole number of both Houses shall deem it necessary, Congress in such statement may provide for a specific excess of outlays over receipts by a vote directed solely to the subject. The Congress and the President shall, pursuant to legislation or through the exercise of their powers under the first and second articles, ensure that actual outlays do not exceed the outlays set forth in such statement.
Section 2. Total receipts for any fiscal year set forth in the statement adopted pursuant to this article shall not increase by a rate greater than the rate of increase in national income in the year or years ending not less than six months nor more than twelve months before such fiscal year, unless a majority of the whole number of both Houses of Congress have passed a bill directed solely to approving specific additional receipts and

such bill has become law.
Section 3. The Congress may waive the provisions of this article for any fiscal year in which a declaration of war is in effect.
Section 4. Total receipts shall include all receipts of the United States except those derived from borrowing and total outlays shall include all outlays of the United States except those for repayment of debt principal.
Section 5. The Congress shall enforce and implement this article by appropriate legislation.
Section 6. On and after the day this article takes effect, the amount of federal public limit as of such date shall become permanent and there shall be no increase in such amount unless three-fifths of the whole number of both Houses of Congress shall have passed a bill approving such increase and such bill has become law.
Section 7. This article shall take effect for the second fiscal year beginning after its ratification.

(Answer/Discussion on page 558.)

---

[13]See Roger B. Porter, *Presidential Decision-Making: The Economic Policy Board* (Cambridge University Press, 1980).

spending and government programs than it is to curb them. As a result, deficit spending has become increasingly common. To stimulate demand, the government spends more money than it takes in. For many years this policy was thought to be beneficial to the economy—and it was very convenient politically. But during the 1970s deficits grew rapidly, and there were no surpluses, even during upswings. In fact, there has been only one year of surpluses in over twenty-five years. Economists found that such policies, when accompanied by a loose-money policy by the Federal Reserve, resulted in a hidden cost—inflation. Even though taxpayers did not pay the entire cost of national programs, consumers did, as the pumped-up economy had too many dollars chasing too few goods. Although government spending is not responsible for all inflation, it has been a major contributor; and as a result, more and more people have begun to look for new economic remedies.

Supply Side Economics

Ronald Reagan came to the White House preaching an alternative to Keynesian economics. He pledged to balance the budget by cutting taxes and cutting government spending. He advocated supply side economics. In simple terms, supply side economics holds that large cuts in taxes will inspire productive investment so that the initial loss of federal revenues will be offset by the taxes generated from expanded private economic activity. Reagan maintained that by creating favorable conditions for businesses, investments would increase, companies would expand their operations, and more jobs would be created.

Once in office, President Reagan discovered that it was easier to cut taxes than federal spending and he pushed through Congress in 1981, the largest tax cuts in our history. Critics of supply side economics said the Reagan tax cuts would be inflationary. They also claimed Reagan's brand of tax cuts would increase corporate profits and that these profits would mainly go toward stock dividends or into the pockets of corporate directors. That is, the money would not necessarily be reinvested in company expansion to create more jobs.

The lag between Reagan's tax cuts and the expected economic recovery took longer than Reagan and his advisers expected. Unemployment continued at a higher rate than they expected or wanted. Whether or not supply side economics will work remains an open question, and is surely to be debated for some time to come.[14]

The Balanced Budget Amendment

Alan Greenspan, an economic adviser to Presidents Ford and Reagan, is one of the leading Republican advocates of tax cuts, a reduction of federal expenditures, and reduced federal regulations. *Rick Bloom.*

The apparent inability of the federal government to balance its budget has led some politicians and economists to propose that it be constitutionally required to do so. The proposed balanced budget amendment would require Congress to adopt a budget in which projected spending is no larger than projected tax receipts. In addition, the amendment would limit the increase in taxes (and/or spending) in any fiscal year to the percentage increase in the gross national product (GNP) during the previous calendar year. The amendment has two escape clauses. Congress could waive the requirements of the amendment by a vote of two-thirds of all members of both houses. Also, the provisions of the amendment would not apply in any year in which a war had been declared.

Advocates of a balanced budget amendment (and these include Ronald Reagan and George Bush) claim that such an amendment is necessary to correct what they call the "spending bias" that currently exists in government decision making. Senators such as Orrin Hatch (R-Utah), Strom Thurmond (R-S.C.), and Dennis DeConcini (D-Ariz.), and Congressman Barber Conable (R-N.Y.), claim there is a structural deficiency within our political system that causes higher levels of spending than is desired by the citizenry. Well-organized, powerful, and heavily financed special interest groups sometimes

[14]For an early criticism of supply side economics by one prominent economist, see Lester Thurow, *Dangerous Currents* (Random House, 1983).

"How do I spell 'relief'? T-A-X-C-U-T!" *Reprinted by permission.* © 1979 NEA, Inc.

overwhelm relatively weak taxpayer lobbies and regularly win on spending measures in Congress.[15]

Opponents of a balanced budget amendment say that such an amendment would reduce the flexibility of economic policy makers. It would virtually eliminate fiscal policy as a tool for managing the economy. Political leaders such as Senators Alan Cranston (D-Calif.) and Daniel Patrick Moynihan (D-N.Y.) say that often a federal budget deficit is an effective means of boosting the economy. In times of economic downturn, they say, government spending in excess of revenues can increase employment, generate investment, stimulate demand, and prevent a recession from deepening into a depression.

Opponents also say it is unwise to place an economic theory into the Constitution. The Constitution, they contend, should be a broad charter dealing with fundamental principles of governance not a document that gets specific about theories of economic management. Further, they contend, balancing the budget is a legislative—not constitutional—matter.

The balanced budget amendment is either a "fraud" or a "disaster," argue many opponents. It is a fraud in the sense that there are countless variables as to how much it will cost to run our national government and how much it will collect. Such changes as a drought in the middle west, a flood in California affect both sides of the budget—so much so it would be only an educated guess as to what federal revenues would be. If the balanced budget is adopted, Congress may very well have to resort to subterfuges to "pretend" it has balanced the books.

If the above twisting of the intent is not accurate, and the amendment is actually used to cut back on federal expenditures to the level that one can be sure that tax revenues will cover them, it will force such alterations as to cause major social upheavals. Social security entitlements, military pay, veterans benefits, and a whole host of federal aid and educational benefits would have to be reduced.

Perhaps more likely, the balanced budget amendment would change the "rules of the game" making it easier for social and economic conservatives to win more of the legislative battles. More votes would be required to adopt new programs and some of these would require a two-thirds vote to appropriate money.

What are the chances that such an amendment will be passed and adopted? Reasonably good—especially if one looks at public opinion polls, and recent votes in Congress. Polls show that between 70 and 80 percent of Americans favor a required balanced budget. President Reagan repeatedly fought for the measure. The proposal passed the Senate in 1982 by the required two-thirds majority. Moreover, a majority of the state legislatures have approved some version of the balanced budget measure and have urged a national constitutional convention be held to consider ratifying it. The 1984 and 1986 elections may determine the fate of this measure.

A Constitutional Amendment to Limit Government Spending

A similar measure to fight inflation—also often supported by majorities in public opinion surveys—would tie the percentage of increased annual government spending to increases in the nation's economic growth. Initially backed primarily by conservatives, this measure has won more and more support from moderates as well. Advocates of this amendment do not want to tamper with the Constitution—except, they say, when all else fails—and attempts to curb reckless spending have so far failed. Government is growing so fast and becoming such a dominant force in so many aspects of the economy that we risk crushing

[15]See the debate on the amendment in *Congressional Digest*, October 1982. See also Edward Cowan, "Congress Ponders a Constitutional Amendment to Requiring a Balanced Budget," *The New York Times*, April 2, 1982, p. 12 Y.

Rep. Jack Kemp (R-N.Y.) was a major influence on the tax cuts in the Reagan first term, and he is a key leader of the conservative wing of the Republican party, both in Congress and around the country. *Rick Bloom.*

Income Policy and Wage and Price Controls

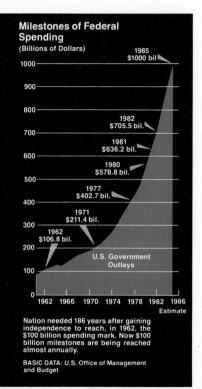

Milestones of Federal Spending
(Billions of Dollars)

1985
$1000 bil

1982
$705.5 bil.

1981
$636.2 bil.

1980
$578.8 bil.

1977
$402.7 bil.

1971
$211.4 bil.

1962
$106.8 bil.

U.S. Government Outlays

1962 1966 1970 1974 1978 1982 1986
Estimate

Nation needed 186 years after gaining independence to reach, in 1962, the $100 billion spending mark. Now $100 billion milestones are being reached almost annually.

BASIC DATA: U.S. Office of Management and Budget

what is left of the so-called private sector: "Disciplines that were once unnecessary because big government had not yet arrived must now be invented."[16]

With a mandatory spending limitation, they add, perhaps the incentive to improve internal efficiency will be greatly increased. Writes one close student of the budgetary process:

> Knowing that they [government bureaucrats] are unlikely to get more and may well get less (depending on the state of the economy . . .), agencies will try to get the most out of what they have. Efficiency will no longer be a secondary consideration, to be satisfied if nothing else is pressing, or be no consideration at all if evidence that they can do less would reduce their future income: efficiency will be the primary path of the steady state in which they find themselves.[17]

Critics of this proposed amendment, say it is too drastic a step: They would prefer to make the relatively new congressional budget processes work more effectively. They say too that a spending limitation would be a vote of no confidence in Congress—it would signify that Congress cannot handle its taxing and spending and power of the purse responsibilities. Further, critics contend the losers under such a new scheme would surely be the poor and less well-organized people, who cannot afford wealthy lobbyists to protect their interests in Congress. Besides, if we really need a spending limitation to discipline Congress and help bring some rationality to spending levels, why not do it by law rather than by constitutional amendment? This could be done, for example, by having Congress establish some kind of spending ceiling each year that is tied to a percentage of the past year's economic growth. To break this ceiling later in the year—when individual appropriations come up—Congress would have to vote by two-thirds or even by 70 percent to break the prearranged limit.

Stagflation—a combination of high unemployment and high inflation—has baffled modern policy makers. Traditional thought holds that to decrease one will necessarily increase the other. One solution to the problem has been suggested by some liberal economists: A tax-based incomes policy would focus on breaking the inflationary wage-price spiral by using a carrot and stick approach to wage and price increases. There would be penalties for excessive increases and benefits for moderate increases. Some argue that such a policy, when coupled with monetary and fiscal restraint, could effectively cure the present stagflation problem.[18]

From time to time liberals also urge some form of wage and price controls. Back in 1980, for example, Senator Edward Kennedy supported a freeze on prices, wages, interest rates, profits, dividends, and rents, to be followed by a period of controls, "to ensure that the psychology of inflation is broken." Most economists, and most business and labor leaders, oppose wage and price controls, saying they might be needed in an emergency situation, *but not now.* Critics say wage and price controls rudely interfere with market transactions that generate prices and wage rates consistent with the intensity of consumer demand and the eagerness of sellers to fill it. If there is too much supply, prices fall. If there is high demand, suppliers will produce more. Further, critics say wage and price controls are an administrative nightmare—and thus to be used only as a last resort.

Those who support controls complain that while the case against them is based mainly on the model of a free marketplace, this situation does not prevail

---

[16]Aaron Wildavsky, *How to Limit Government Spending* (University of California Press, 1980), p. 57.

[17]Ibid., p. 36. See also Robert Lubar, "Making Democracy Less Inflation-Prone," *Fortune,* September 22, 1980, pp. 78–85. For somewhat different views on the same topic, see Lester Thurow, *The Zero-Sum Society: Distribution and the Possibilities for Economic Change* (Basic Books, 1980).

[18]Arthur Okun and George Perry (eds.), *Curing Chronic Inflation* (Brookings Institution, 1978).

in many cases, especially where giant corporations control production. "Who believes," writes one economist, "that General Motors, Ford and Chrysler engage in classic price competition? . . . Over a broad expanse of the American economy, price competition is a myth."[19] Advocates of wage and price controls admit universal controls would be hard to administer, but they suggest that selective controls be applied to the sectors in which large bureaucracies operate major industries. Thus far, the concept of wage and price controls has won little support from public officials.

The problem of controlling inflation and trying to curb government spending is not unique to the United States; it remains a serious issue for all market-oriented democratic economies. In the old days factions were pitted against factions. Separation of powers and federalism were supposed to work against organized narrow interests. Later, parties sometimes played the mediating role. But modern technology has undermined many of the old premises. Groups now form more easily than ever, and they have previously unheard of means to press their case and punish uncooperative legislators or public officials. We live in an interest group state—as discussed in part in Chapter 7. The challenge today is to invent new institutions and revitalize processes that can help discipline the natural selfish instincts of individuals and groups.

SUMMARY

1. In the last three chapters we have seen how economic and political life in our society are interwoven. The once easily defined boundaries between private and public life are now irretrievably blurred. A few still insist that government and the economy must be strictly separated. Whatever its theoretical merits, this view is unrealistic. In modern American society we have a political economy in which a decision in one area inevitably affects decisions in others. The political economy is a mixed economy: It blends private and public enterprise, individual initiative and government promotion, personal responsibility and public regulation, and federal and state governments.

2. Government regulation, subsidies, and economic management are not really distinct. Promotion may be used for regulatory purposes and regulation for promotional; government taxing and spending in the broadest sense always entail both.

3. A central concern of the past two presidential elections, and one that will be with us throughout the 1980s, is how

to limit government spending, curb inflation, avoid unreasonable unemployment, balance the budget, and keep our economy productive and competitive—all at the same time. Strategies to achieve these purposes are now being widely debated. But there are limits to all these strategies, and everything we do has consequences we never intend. Moreover, we are often limited in what we can do, because we must carry out new policies by democratic procedures.

4. One of the greatest challenges in a democracy is how to mobilize the government so that it can respond to changing economic conditions, but in a way that keeps government accountable to the people. The problem in part is whether a system such as ours can act effectively when action is needed. But the problem is also one of knowing what to do and when to do it. Further, we no longer have a domestic economy autonomous from an international economy; and we have only just begun to understand the ramifications of this new reality.

FURTHER READING

MICHAEL BOSKINS and AARON WILDAVSKY (eds.). *The Federal Budget: Economics and Politics* (Institute for Contemporary Studies, 1982).

BILL BRADLEY. *The Fair Tax* (Pocket Books, 1984).

RICHARD E. BROWN. *The GAO: Untapped Source of Congressional Power* (University of Tennessee Press, 1970).

MILTON and ROSE FRIEDMAN. *Free to Choose* (Harcourt Brace Jovanovich, 1980).

ROGER B. PORTER. *Presidential Decision-Making: The Economic Policy Board* (Cambridge University Press, 1980).

ALICE RIVLIN. *Economic Choices—1984* (Brookings Institution, 1984).

HOWARD SHUMAN. *Politics and the Budget* (Prentice-Hall, 1984).

LESTER C. THUROW. *Dangerous Currents: The State of Economics* (Random House, 1983)

AARON WILDAVSKY. *How to Limit Government Spending* (University of California Press, 1980).

AARON WILDAVSKY. *The Politics of the Budgetary Process*, 4th ed. (Little, Brown, 1983).

[19]Robert Lekachman, "The Case for Controls," *New Republic*, October 14, 1978, p. 20.

THE DEMOCRATIC FAITH

25

More than any other form of government, democracy requires a certain kind of faith—and a certain kind of skepticism. It requires faith and optimism concerning the common human enterprise; a belief that if the people are informed and caring, they can be trusted with their own self-government; and a belief that when things begin to go wrong, the people may be relied on to set them right. At bottom the democratic faith holds that the will of the people is the only legitimate foundation of any government.

A healthy skepticism is needed as well. Democracy requires us to be questioning of our leaders and not too trusting of any group with too much power. While we prize majority rule, we are skeptical enough to ask whether a majority is always right. Democracy requires us to be constantly concerned about whether we really tolerate and protect the rights and opinions of others, and about whether democratic processes are in fact serving the principles of liberty, equality, and justice. In short, the democratic faith rests upon a peculiar blend of faith in the people and skepticism of them.

Thomas Jefferson, our best-known champion of the democratic faith, believed in the common sense of humankind and in the flowering of the human spirit. Jefferson believed deeply that every government degenerates when it is trusted to rulers alone. The people themselves, he wrote, are the only safe depositories of government. His was a robust commitment to popular control, to representative processes, and to accountable leadership. But he was no believer in the simple participatory democratic system of ancient Greece or revolutionary France: The people, too, must have their power checked and balanced.

Thomas Jefferson. *Library of Congress.*

The customary government of humankind has been authoritarian, or tyrannical. Throughout most of history, including the present, most people have lived in societies where a small group at the top imposed their will on the others. Today some of these authoritarian governments justify their actions by saying people are too weak to govern themselves; they need to be ruled. Others claim to be true representatives of all the people. But whether in Castro's Cuba or in a military regime of Chile, whether in the People's Republic of China or South Africa, ordinary people have little voice in the types of decisions Americans routinely make—who should go to college, or work in the fields, or serve in the army; or how much money should be spent for schools or to protect the environment.

It is only by intense thought, great commitment, countless sacrifices, and an enduring faith in democracy that liberty and equality have prevailed—at least to the extent they have—in the United States. The celebrated efforts and faith that were necessary to create this democratic republic are fully as necessary to sustain it in our own time. Ben Franklin's question, raised in the very first chapter of this book, is as pertinent today as ever. In contrast to much of the factual material presented earlier in this book, the democratic faith may seem a hazy or elusive idea. Yet we believe that in addition to knowing the facts of American political life, understanding this idea is crucial to any appraisal of our government by the people.

THE AMERICAN DREAM

"It's about the American Dream. . ." © 1979 by NEA Inc.

The beliefs people hold most dear are often called myths or dreams. These help hold societies together, and they can be very powerful. Sometimes they are more powerful than logic, because usually they cannot be refuted. Is it any wonder that shrewd political leaders have seen the importance of myths and dreams and have often used them as a means to get power? Plato argued that rulers should invent myths even when they know them to be wrong. Machiavelli, the brilliant observer of politics in Renaissance Italy, advised princes to use religion and myth as an aid to power. Dreams and myths have a different look today than in former times, but they are no less important.

It is the official philosophy in America, of course, that America has no official philosophy. But we do have a rather general body of ideas and values that serve as rough but persisting guides to our civic and political actions. These ideas and values help to define us as a people and as a nation. But there is no one unified, consistent, and well-defined ideology. Indeed, many of the myths and dreams by which Americans live contradict one another. In part, this is because values from one era have been carried over uncritically into new situations. Also, it is part of American pragmatism to hold contradictory beliefs simultaneously without bothering to resolve the potential conflicts between them.

We do not mean to stress the uniqueness of the American people, as if America were isolated from the rest of the world. For example, a few years ago something known as the "democracy wall" sprang into being in downtown Peking, China. Democracy wall was a place where posters could be pasted up and where students, poets, writers, factory workers, critics of the government, and foreign visitors could come together for discussions about political ideas and personal grievances. Sharply worded essays demanded more freedom. Poems and commentary asked about human rights and liberties. But above all else, people raised searching questions about forms of government and political rights. Just what is democracy? Just how could they arrange for more freedom of expression, for free newspapers, for free elections? Democracy wall flourished for scarcely a year before Chinese authorities moved it to a less conspicuous and more controlled location. But no authorities in China, no authorities anywhere, have been able to stamp out the dream of democratic self-government.

The American Dream has much in common with the aspirations of most peoples: peace, prosperity, personal ownership of property, personal liberty, and the overriding belief that one is free to achieve any goal, to accumulate material wealth, to live any lifestyle. Ralph Waldo Emerson wrote: "The office of America is to liberate, to abolish kingcraft, priestcraft, castle, monopoly, to pull down the gallows, to burn up the bloody statute-book, to take in the immigrant, to open the doors of the sea and the fields of the earth." All should have the chance to grow, to chart their own course, to become rich or to become president, to mold their own destinies—to go as far as their abilities permit.

For some, the American Dream is a misleading term used by the middle and upper classes to fool the poor and unemployed into thinking their lives can be improved. Others point out that while the dream has become a reality for some white Anglo-Saxon males, it has not been fulfilled for millions who suffer discrimination, unemployment, and substandard housing and medical care. For the latter the dream has often been a nightmare: Equality of opportunity is a bitter myth for those who cannot get a decent education, who are generally unorganized and unrepresented politically, and who do not know how to make the system work for them. These people have understandably become disillusioned and embittered. But however contradictory and paradoxical our dream may be, it nonetheless exists—helping to shape how most Americans conduct their lives and respond to government and its policies.

Central to the American Dream is the notion that this is the land of opportunity for the enterprising. Here the competitive, practical go-getter can make a fortune, or build a dream home. Our large homes and automobiles are symbolic. The achievement, self-help, or success ethic is so strong here—and always has been—that many people believe the prime function of the state is to assist private individuals in the production of wealth and the protection of property.

This part of the American Dream has doubtless shaped the American national character in several ways. Its focus is primarily self-centered, materialistic, pragmatic, and individualistic; and rugged individualism and resourcefulness are the traits celebrated in our folklore and ballads. One byproduct of this aspect of the American Dream has been the continuous quest for liberty and freedom—the leave-me-alone, let-me-do-my-thing ethic. Often the hero is the lone cowboy—unrestrained, unregulated, and self-reliant. Often the villain is the bureaucrat, the government regulator, the tax collector, or (indeed) any restrictions. Henry David Thoreau's retreat to the woods is illustrative of this desire for reality, for the natural: ". . .to live deep and suck out all the marrow of life, to live so sturdily and Spartan-like as to put to rout all that was not life." America as a practical experiment is part and parcel of this concern for self-reliance.

Still another element of the American Dream is faith in the common sense of the ordinary person. The tradition of Abraham Lincoln and Harry Truman, that anyone can become president, has been a bold one. We prefer action to reflection; we are antitheoretical, antiexpert, and indeed anti-intellectual. Stressing practicality and immediacy, the ethic of the marketplace—

Peking residents read posters chastizing "Gang of Four" on "Democracy wall." *UPI.*

BASIC AMERICAN VALUES (as noted in Chapter 1)

GOALS
Personal independence
Dignity of the individual
Liberty, civil rights
Property rights
Equality before the law
Equality of opportunity
An open society
Justice

MEANS
Constitutionalism
Representative processes
Free and frequent elections
Majority rule, minority rights
Checks and balances
Bill of rights
Federalism
Separation of powers
Due process
Judicial review

the notion of "street sense," has become part of our image. Poets like Walt Whitman, Stephen Vincent Benet, and Carl Sandburg, and story-tellers such as Mark Twain and Will Rogers, helped make this idea into tradition. This reverence for the common person helps in part to explain Americans' ambivalence toward power, politics, and government authority. Although we aspire, in Lincoln's words, to be a government of and by the people, in practice, government leadership almost always is provided by the few. In America government has always been viewed as a necessary *evil* (with a certain stress on evil).

Paradoxically, however, just as we are able to criticize our government as inept, corrupt, and something to be feared, it is equally American to be deeply convinced that ours is the best system in the world. Some of us would even like to impose our brand of political theories and practices on everyone else. Understanding this paradox is basic to understanding the most confusing aspect of the national character. Americans seem to live and breathe and function by paradox. We cherish our pragmatic, experimental, predominantly individualistic tradition, and yet there has always been a sense of moral superiority, manifest destiny, and collective nationalism in America.

We are told that all great nations often have identified their mission with a divine purpose. Perhaps, then, it is not surprising that a streak of messianic spirit runs through our history: America as the symbol of the future, as a quasi-sacred mission. Even a Herman Melville could write that "we Americans are the peculiar chosen people . . . the Israel of our time." Woodrow Wilson claimed that "the heart of the people is pure" and talked often of the spiritual energy in this nation. Wilson rallied the nation by stressing that America came into existence not to vindicate the rights of property or of wealth but to vindicate the rights of people, "to show the way to mankind in every part of the world to justice and freedom and liberty." "America must be ready," Wilson insisted, "to exert her whole force, moral and physical, to the assertion of those rights throughout the round globe."

The Lincoln Memorial. *Stan Wakefield.*

There remains a remarkable belief that America is better, stronger, and more virtuous than other nations. Doubtless this sense of mission is a source of discipline, an obvious builder of morale, and a fortifier of nationalism. But an excessive or wrongheaded sense of mission can also be a source of problems. The Wilsonian notion that "America is the most unselfish of nations" is an example of a romanticized and inflated sense of mission. Our dealings with native Americans, our era of Manifest Destiny, and our intrusion into the affairs of others in the post-World War II period are all illustrative. Leaders from John Foster Dulles in the 1950s to Jimmy Carter and Ronald Reagan in the 1980s have committed the United States to protect, assist, and rescue people all around the globe—presumably because we have the answers to the world's problems.

The Statue of Liberty. *N.Y. Convention & Visitors Bureau.*

There are those among us, of course, who deride this righteousness, this false purity, this notion of the United States as an elect or redeemer nation. Some critics say this messianism or providential destiny is an illusion. No nation is sacred. America, like every country, has interests and motives that are generous as well as selfish. We have motives that are idealistic as well as squalid. We, too, are part of human history.

Still, there is a persistent idealism and moralism that at times looms large as part of the promise of America. Our efforts in the human rights area today, our food relief, financial support for the International Red Cross and the United Nations, and countless other humanitarian contributions provide some evidence. America, for many of us, may not be the only hope for the world—but it is still one of the prime hopes.

CONTENDING AMERICAN DREAMS

THE AMERICAN WAY	THE AMERICAN TESTAMENT
Liberty	Equality
Freedom	Liberation from discrimination
Rugged individualism	*E pluribus unum*—commonwealth
Private property rights	Community
Survival of the fittest	Pro-underdog, pro-yeoman farmer
Success to the best	Affirmative action
Achievement, merit, excellence	Help for those who can't help themselves
Leave me alone	Generosity
Don't fence me in	Fairness
"Life is unfair"	"We can do better"
People are not angels—government by the best	Government by the people
Emphasis on our Republic	Emphasis on participatory democracy and the common sense of the common person
"This land became great not by what government did for the people but what the people did for themselves."	"America must educate every individual to his or her capacity, eliminate ignorance, prejudice, hate and the squalor in which crime is bred. We must also protect against the economic catastrophes of illness, disability, and unemployment."

NOTE: Both lists of values are part of the American Dream. Most of us have grown up being introduced and somewhat conditioned by both American Dreams. The first list (on the left) has doubtless been the primary American Dream for most Americans—as most of it was for the founders of this nation in the 1770s and 1780s. Over the years, however, elements of the list on the right have evolved to take an important place in our lives. Many of our major national public documents, and the most memorable addresses of various American leaders, are associated with the list on the right: Jefferson, Lincoln, Susan B. Anthony, Franklin and Eleanor Roosevelt, Martin Luther King, Jr., John F. Kennedy. On the other hand, many of our distinguished leaders and politicians are plainly associated with the list on the left: John Adams, Madison, Hamilton, Teddy Roosevelt, and Ronald Reagan, to name just a few. How about you? Which set of values and aspirations most define your views? Are you a partisan of one list to the exclusion of the other—or do you, like most modern Americans, subscribe to a mixture of the two?

RESTORING THE AMERICAN DREAM?

Many people believe the American Dream is in trouble because we have become too democratic and have lost our commitment to truly limited government. Some of these critics view American history as a series of betrayals of the true American Dream. They say it is time for Big Brother to get out of our private lives and let us fend for ourselves. They point to the idea of majority rule—that one group of people, simply by outnumbering another group, can do what it wishes to that group—as a chief culprit. One best-selling "libertarian" tract concludes that precisely because of this excess of democracy, we have become a welfare state and have thereby undermined not only the American Dream but nearly everything that was so vital about liberty. The author would end welfare, affirmative action, busing, compulsory education, and the draft, and markedly reduce taxation:

> The American Dream was not about government's taking huge sums of money from citizens by force. The American Dream was not about "using all its power and resources to meet new social problems with new social controls."
>
> The American Dream was about people, not government. It was about people who, for the first time in history, declared that they were *above* government. It was about

individualism and the *opportunity* to achieve success without interference from others. Most of all, the American Dream was about *freedom*.

. . .the last thing in the world that the American Dream was about was taxation![1]

Other, usually more moderate, voices have warned that the very governability of America is threatened these days because of intense commitment to democratic and egalitarian ideals. They say, for example, that the effective operation of our political system requires some measure of apathy and noninvolvement. They point out that government needs to operate with a measure of secrecy, deception, and even manipulation; for in times of crisis government must have the political authority to impose upon its peoples certain necessary sacrifices. They quote John Adams, who said a democracy never lasts long: "It soon wastes, exhausts, and murders itself. There never was a democracy yet that did not commit suicide." In short, we must beware the excesses of democracy. Just as we have come to recognize that there are potentially desirable limits to economic growth, we must realize "there are also potentially desirable limits to the indefinite extension of political democracy."[2]

Another challenge to Americans was sharply put in Alexander Solzhenitsyn's 1978 Harvard University commencement speech. The famed Russian exile roundly criticized America's unchecked materialism, timid leadership, irresponsible press, and legalism in the face of a spiritual and moral vacuum. Further, he said Americans had taken freedom too far; leading to a permissiveness that in turn encouraged crime, violence, pornography, and a tasteless, third-rate culture. He plainly thought we had lost our way—that America needed some kind of moral revitalization and more central direction to overcome its softness, its decadence, its drift.[3]

Alexander Solzhenitsyn, the Nobel Prize-winning novelist and political dissident, now living in the United States. *UPI.*

Critics on the Left have a different set of charges. They say the rich get richer, the poor get poorer. The rich are better treated before the law than the poor. Further, our tax system is deeply regressive and becoming more so, and most federal laws and regulations actually benefit the more prosperous in the nation.[4] The rich are also better represented in political decision-making bodies, such as legislatures or courts. Money alone may not buy elections, they say, but it buys just about all the political resources needed to gain information, influence voters, and shape the outcomes of public policy. Like money, freedom of expression is available to all, but in widely varying quantities. The rich have the time, the organizational knowhow, and the ability to hire experts (lobbyists, speechwriters, public relations firms) that allow them more access, more say, and hence more influence. The rich are more represented than the poor. A true democracy, say some of these critics, would necessitate a more equal distribution of the basic resources needed for real participation and valid representation.

THE CASE FOR GOVERNMENT BY THE PEOPLE

The challenges outlined above are not frivolous. They pose fundamental questions about the health and direction of our political system. How faithfully does our democratic republic reflect the American Dream? Is that Dream still appropriate to the modern world? Is government of, by, and for the people a real-

[1]Robert J. Ringer, *Restoring the American Dream* (QED/Harper & Row, 1979), p. 198. See also Ed Clark, *A New Beginning* (Caroline House, 1980).

[2]Samuel Huntington, in Michel J. Crozier, Samuel P. Huntington, and Joji Wantanuki, *The Crisis of Democracy* (New York University Press, 1975), p. 115.

[3]See Alexander Solzhenitsyn, "The West Has Lost Its Courage," *The Washington Post*, June 11, 1978, p. C1.

[4]See Benjamin Page, *Who Gets What From Government* (University of California Press, 1983).

ity—or just another part of the myth? What follows are some summary considerations as well as some personal views the authors want to leave you with.

The essence of our Constitution is that it both grants power to and withholds power from the national government. Fearing national weakness and popular disorder, the framers wanted to grant the government enough power to do its basic jobs, such as maintaining national defense and financial stability. Yet valuing above all the principle of individual liberty, the framers also wanted to protect the people from too much government. They wanted a limited government—but one that would work. The solution was to make government responsive to the people—but not too responsive.

The first step was to distribute power among the three branches of government—legislative, executive, and judicial. The second step was to leave extensive authority with state and local governments. Then the framers took a third step, the most brilliant and successful of all. Public officials were provided with different and competing constituencies to satisfy. The framers also assumed that the constituents themselves would be divided—northerners versus southerners, rich versus poor, city people versus country people. By their arrangement of offices, powers, and elections, the framers guaranteed that officials would compete and conflict with one another as they sought to please the voters.

This was not, of course, a very efficient system. But efficiency was not the main goal; the framers wanted a government that was safe. As the decades passed, the national government came under greater and greater pressure to perform effectively. The twentieth century in particular brought American involvement in vast global wars, depressions, and huge migrations of Europeans from abroad. There were also migrations of blacks and other rural people into northern cities, industrialization, and technological changes in transportation, communications, medicine, and education. Divided governments always have trouble pulling themselves together, but the American experiment had even more trouble. It was too easy for leaders to "pass the buck." Certain arrangements also increased minority power: The filibuster in the Senate, for example, or the power of the Supreme Court to declare national or state laws unconstitutional. The power of organized minorities to obstruct sharpened the whole question of a representative republic. If leaders acting for a majority of the people could not act—could not pass a gun control law, for example, or obtain a constitutional amendment protecting the rights of women—was this really government by the people?

The pressure on government to act also produced changes, formal and informal, in our constitutional system. Americans tended to turn to whichever branch or level of government could act. Sometimes this was state government; more often it was national. Years ago Congress was the main seat of action, as in the great compromises between North and South over slavery before the Civil War. In this century people have tended to turn to the presidency for action. More recently the Supreme Court—the least democratic or "representative" of the three branches—has moved into the vacuum that surrounded such touchy issues as segregation, busing, abortion, and separation of church and state.

Through all these changes one great beacon has continued to shine—Americans' commitment to *liberty*. Sometimes the beacon has flickered or even seemed to go out, as in the long tolerance of slavery; the suppression of the rights of blacks, women, and others; and the inquisitions of Joe McCarthy. But always the light was renewed. Today our commitment to liberty is perhaps stronger than ever. But we define it somewhat differently. The framers believed individual liberty was above all to be protected against government; today many believe vital liberties or freedoms must be gained with the help of government, in order to move in the direction of another great goal, *equality*. Most Ameri-

The Liberty Bell. *Independence National Historical Park Collection.*

cans today believe not only in equality before the law and in equal political suffrage, but also in equality of opportunity and economic justice. Put in baseball terms: We may not all hit home runs, but every person should at least have a chance at bat and perhaps more than this—to get to first base. Liberty (or freedom) today means the right to a job, to a good education, and to decent housing and medical care—not merely the ancient and basic liberties of speech and press and religion. As Franklin D. Roosevelt said, an economic bill of rights must supplement—and strengthen—the original ten amendments. This idea puts enormous burdens on government and makes it harder to sustain traditional notions of rugged individualism.

Americans now want a government that is efficient and effective—that gets things done. We want to maintain our commitment to liberty and freedom. Yet some measure of equality is needed in order to enjoy liberty. We want a government that acts for the majority but also protects minorities. We want to safeguard our nation in a world full of change and violence. We live in an era of rising demands on resources and declining supply, of widening concepts of the rights of the poor, the elderly, and others. Do we expect too much from government? Of course we do!

Democracy is a system of checks and balances. It is a system that continually balances values and competing dreams. We have to balance all individual liberties against the collective security and needs of society; we must also balance certain individual liberties against other individual liberties. The question is always which rights of which people are to be protected by what means and at what price. We must also balance traditional rights against other rights that have become increasingly important in a crowded urban society. The right of privacy as such is not mentioned in the Bill of Rights, but many city dwellers today might consider it as important as freedom of expression.

Drawing by Richter © 1982. The New Yorker Magazine, Inc.

PARTICIPATION AND REPRESENTATION

In essence, the challenge to the future of democracy is whether we can make our representative process work. No political problem is more complicated than this. For one thing, exact representation is impossible in the literal sense. Every man and woman has a host of conflicting desires, fears, hopes, and expectations; and no government can represent them all. Moreover, even if millions of voters could be represented in their billions of interests, the question would remain as to how they were to be represented. Through direct representation, such as a New England town meeting? Through economic or professional associations, such as labor unions or political action committees? Through a coalition of minority groups? Through a direct popular majority? All these, and other alternatives, can be defended as proper forms of representation in a pluralist democracy.

Some propose to bypass this thorny problem of representation by vastly increasing the role of direct popular participation in decision making. What many people would regard as the most perfect form of democracy exists when every person within a given group has a full and equal opportunity to participate in all decisions and in all the processes of influence, persuasion, and discussion that bear on that decision. Direct participation in decision making, its advocates contend, will serve two major purposes. It will enhance the dignity, self-respect, and understanding of the individual by giving him or her responsibility for the decisions that shape his or her life. And it will act as a safeguard against antidemocratic and undemocratic forms of government and prevent the replacement of democracy by dictatorship or tyranny. This idea rests on a the-

UPI.

ory of self-protection that says interests can be represented, furthered, and protected best by those whom they concern directly.

Experience with many forms of participatory democracy, however, suggests that it has limitations as a form of decision making. In an age of burgeoning population, increasingly complex economic and social systems, and enormously wide-ranging decision-making units of government, direct participation can work only in smaller communities or at the neighborhood level. As a practical matter, people simply cannot put in endless hours taking part in every decision that affects their lives.

Participatory democracy still has a great role in smaller units—in the running of colleges, communes, poverty organizations, local party committees, and the like. And perhaps the idea of participation should be greatly extended—for example, to greater control by workers over the running of factories. But we must distinguish between democracy as participation and a greater role for participation in a democracy. One course of action is to enlarge the role of participation in representation—that is, to broaden the power of all people to take part in local decision making and in choosing their representatives in larger units of government. And this brings us back to the hard questions of indirect representation.

If we must have representatives, who shall represent whom? While this question can be answered in countless ways, in practice there are two basic ways to organize representation. By electing representatives in a multitude of local districts, it is possible to build into representative institutions—the American Congress, for example—most minority interests and attitudes found throughout the nation. The other way is through an election system that emphasizes majority representation. This can be achieved by creating a nationwide electorate that elects one representative (the American president, for example) or by developing a strong two-party system that knits all the local constituencies into coalitions that can elect and sustain national majorities. A nation does not have to choose between these alternatives. It can have both, as does the United States.

Which is better: a government that represents coalitions of minorities, or a government that represents a relatively clear-cut majority and has no obligation to the minority? The answer depends on one's basic values—especially on what one expects from government. A system that represents coalitions of minorities usually reflects the trading, competition, and compromising that must take place in order to reach agreement among the various groups. Such a government has been called "broker rule"; the government acts essentially as a go-between, as a mediator among organized groups that have definite policy goals. Under broker rule leaders cannot get too far ahead of the groups; they must tack back and forth, shifting in response to changing group pressures. Instead of acting for a united popular majority with a fairly definite program, either liberal or conservative, the government tries to satisfy all major interests by giving them a voice in decisions and sometimes a veto over actions. In the pushing and hauling of political groups, the government is continually involved in delicate balancing acts.

Some critics believe in full representation of minority groups—in broker rule—but point out that fair representation has not been achieved in the American system. They point to the extent of nonvoting and other forms of nonparticipation in politics; the fact that low-income persons are less well organized in groups than upper-income persons; the bias of the stronger organized groups toward the status quo; the lack of competition among much of the news and opinion media, combined with the domination of television and the press by a few corporations; and the virtual monopoly of party politics by the two major parties, which do not always offer the voters meaningful alternatives. In the

TO PROTECT THE DISSENTER

☐ When one element in a pluralistic system becomes very powerful in relation to the others, the pluralism of the system itself is in danger. Even with the best of intentions, the dominant element is likely to squeeze out the other elements or render them impotent. . . .

☐ So we have devised a variety of ways to protect the dissenter. Our civil liberties are a part of that system, and so are Robert's Rules of Order, and grievance procedures and the commonly held view that we should hear both sides of an argument. In short, we have a tradition, a set of attitudes and specific social arrangements designed to ensure that points of view at odds with prevailing doctrine will not be rejected out of hand.

☐ But why be so considerate of dissent and criticism? To answer this question is to state one of the strongest tenets of our political philosophy. We do not expect organizations or societies to be above criticism nor do we trust the men who run them to be adequately self-critical. We believe that even those aspects of society that are healthy today may deteriorate tomorrow. We believe that power wielded justly today may be wielded corruptly tomorrow. We know that from the ranks of the critics come cranks and troublemakers, but from the same ranks come the saviors and innovators. And since the spirit that welcomes nonconformity is a fragile thing, we have not depended on that spirit alone. We have devised explicit legal and constitutional arrangements to protect the dissenter.

John W. Gardner, *Self-Renewal* (Perennial Library edition, 1971), pp. 88–89.

governmental system itself, critics note the devices in Congress to block majority will and overrepresent certain minorities; the distortion of representation embodied in the electoral college; and the power of the Supreme Court to invalidate laws demanded by popular majorities acting through the legislative and executive branches.

These charges may be exaggerated, but they cannot be denied, as the material in this book shows. Those who believe in fairer representation, however, can point to fairly steady improvement in recent years: for example, changes in election laws to simplify and extend voting, to enforce one person-one vote standards, and to renew political parties, especially in the conduct of presidential nominating conventions; efforts to regulate campaign finance; and some progress in Congress to strengthen majority rule. Further, the Supreme Court rarely imposes a substantive veto in economic and social areas; but it does impose its veto in the area where most democrats welcome a restraining hand—namely civil liberties.

THE DEMOCRATIC PROMISE

The ultimate test of a democratic system is the legal existence of an officially recognized opposition. A cardinal characteristic of a democracy is that it not only recognizes the need for the free organization of opposing views but even positively encourages this organization. Freedom for political expression and dissent is basic—even freedom for nonsense to be spoken so that good sense not yet recognized gets a chance to be heard.

Crucial to the democratic faith is the belief that a democracy cherishes the free play of ideas. Only where the safety valve of public discussion is available and where almost any policy is subject to perpetual questioning and challenge can there be the assurance that both minority and majority rights will be served. To be afraid of public debate is to be afraid of self-government.

Americans have always been somewhat irreverent and disrespectful toward political leaders and established or conventional thinking. Our political values have always exalted the individual—the common person—over the state. Experimentation and pragmatism rather than dogma or preconceived theories have been the animating spirit of American progress. We have long recognized that people who raise new ideas have often been the bane of the politicians' existence—and we have sought to protect and even encourage the right to raise precisely those ideas that may be troublesome.

We hold with Jefferson that there is nothing in the country so radically wrong that it cannot be cured by good newspapers and sound schoolmasters. Inform and educate the citizenry, and a major hurdle is overcome. Jefferson had boundless faith in education. He believed that people are rationally endowed by nature with an innate sense of justice; the average person has only to be informed to act wisely. In the long run, said Jefferson, only an educated and enlightened democracy can hope to endure. A striking difference between a democracy and every other form of government is that

James Madison. *Library of Congress.*

> . . . a democracy educates for continuous and active citizenship whereas other forms of government only for passive obedience—and technical skills. The *sine qua non* [the that without which] of a successful democracy is that all citizens think for themselves about all issues that may arise; the requirement of successful totalitarianism is that citizens obey those who think for them.[5]

[5]Henry Steele Commager, *Majority Rule and Minority Rights* (Oxford University Press, 1943), p. 76.

MAKING THE DEMOCRATIC EXPERIMENT WORK

It was James Bryce, an Englishman who visited our nation a hundred years ago, who observed that America represents an experiment in the rule of the multitude, tried on an unprecedently vast scale. Yet, he added, it is something more than just an American experiment, for the rest of the world is watching.

But America is nonetheless an experiment. Every institution and policy is at best a reasonable approximation of what might work. Americans must constantly check their experience to see how well or how badly our experiment is working. Experience, said James Madison, is the guide that ought always to be followed whenever it can be found. We must stand ready to preserve what is working and change what is not.

What is the function of leadership in a democracy? Leadership is an elusive term. We think of national leadership as the ability to mobilize human and economic resources in pursuit of desired social goals. But progress seldom follows a fixed route. Change often occurs through a long and disorderly process, in a way similar to an infant learning to walk—we try, fail, learn a bit more, have partial success, bump our nose, cry, try again—and after a while, learning by doing, we find our way. Effective leadership usually comes from those who banish their self-doubts and believe failure is impossible. Leaders, as noted in Chapter 13, often have some combination of contagious self-confidence, unwarranted optimism, and incurable idealism. They believe in themselves and are willing to gamble—and sometimes to invent or write new rules. We need these types. We need all the problem clarifiers, agenda setters, morale builders, coalition builders, crisis managers, political organizers, and persuasive educators we can get.

We need responsible and effective leadership in the White House. Still, a nation such as ours believes in the dispersal of power, which should be able to do reasonably well with *good* rather than *great* leaders. Leadership in a society such as ours should not be a top-down proposition. We need several hundred thousand middle-level leaders who operate not only in local and state government but in business, unions, universities, and communities—in nongovernmental America. Too many Americans for too long have not only yearned for stronger presidential leadership but have secretly felt such a terror of assuming responsibility themselves that they have sought a leader who will somehow make their decisions for them.

The American Dream that lured so many millions to our shores is not just a dream of material plenty. It is a dream of self-government, of tolerance of diverse races and ethnic backgrounds, and of individual freedom and opportunity. The framers embarked upon a great gamble—whether a more perfect union of peoples could develop trusting relations and institutions of governance they could hold to account. The American Dream welcomed diversity and encouraged inclusiveness. The triumph of America is the triumph of a coalescing federal system. Unity and disunity, uniformity and diversity, cooperation and conflict, these are basic elements in American society. The democratic faith cherishes the diversity in unity; it looks for the unity in diversity.

We are a restless, dissatisfied, and searching people. We are our own toughest critics. Our political system is far from perfect, but it still is an open system. People can fight city hall. People who disagree with policies in the nation can band together and be heard. We know only too well that the American Dream is never something fully attained, and it is certainly not something inherited; it is always something to be achieved. Ultimately, we the people will determine whether we can make a government by the people work. Enormous stamina and democratic faith are needed.

Our future will be shaped by those who care about making and preserving our political rights and freedoms. Our individual liberties will never be assured unless there are people willing to take considerable personal responsibility for the progress of the whole community, and people willing to exercise their determination and democratic faith. On one of the long corridors in a building on the Harvard College campus, are carved in granite these words of the U.S. poet Archibald MacLeish:

> How shall freedom be defended? By arms when it is attacked by arms; by truth when it is attacked by lies, by democratic faith when it is attacked by authoritarian dogma. Always, in the final act, by determination and faith.

Millions of Americans tour through the great monuments in our nation's capitol each year. They admire the beauty and are always impressed by the memorials to Washington, Jefferson and Lincoln, the Capitol, the Supreme Court and the White House. The strength of the nation, however, does not reside in these official buildings. It lies rather in the hearts and minds of citizens. If they lose faith, stop caring, and stop believing in the possibilities of self-government, the monuments "will be meaningless piles of stone, and the venture that began with the Declaration of Independence, the venture familiarly known as America will be as lifeless as the stone."[6]

One thing is certain amid all the murk. The celebrations and the traumas, the advances and failures, the processes and institutions of "a government by the people"—as contrasted with something called the state in other lands—are inseparable from the daily lives and hopes and needs of 240 million Americans. No one has made this argument more eloquently than Walt Whitman, in his "By Blue Ontario's Shore":

> O I see flashing that this America is only you and me,
> Its power, weapons, testimony, are you and me.
> Its crimes, lies, thefts, defections, are you and me,
> Its Congress is you and me, the officers, capitols, armies, ships are you and me.
> Its endless gestation of new states are you and me,
> The war (that war so bloody and grim, the war I will henceforth forget),
>   was you and me,
> Freedom, language, poems, employments, are you and me,
> Past, present, future, are you and me,
> I dare not shirk any part of myself,
> Nor any part of America good or bad. . . .

Walt Whitman. *UPI.*

[6]John W. Gardner, preface, *Self-Renewal* (Norton, 1981), p. xiv.

APPENDIX
GETTING INVOLVED: STRATEGIES AND SUGGESTIONS

Government by the people is just about the most exacting venture any nation can undertake. Exhilarating, demanding, and sometimes frustrating, the burden falls on a very large number of us if we would make democracy work.

At the beginning of our Republic, in simpler times, those who were allowed to participate in politics (mostly white males) could see the results of their participation, especially in small communities. Today we have eighty times as many people, political participation has been opened to all citizens over eighteen, and the issues are complex and interrelated. It is more difficult to see how what one does has any consequences. Yet we need, perhaps more than ever, large numbers of citizen-politicians to help make government and political processes work. Those who want to help can find plenty of opportunities.

RUNNING FOR OFFICE

There are several hundred thousand elective offices in the United States. One of the difficulties in our democracy is finding talented people of integrity to run for office. Most Americans have little or no interest in running for any elective post. Some are willing to serve but not to run. The personal sacrifices political life demands—less privacy, less time spent with families or in relaxation, dangers to health, and often lower income—are far more than most people are willing to make.

What makes for success? Certainly, chance plays a role in determining whether one succeeds in a political career. This, along with the obvious lack of job security, often stops able people from even considering electoral politics. People who enter politics must realize that they will have to live dangerously. In business the line between the red and the black di-

vides anxiety and comfort, but a businessperson can survive a bad year; in politics 0.1 percent on one's gross vote can mean the difference between prosperity and ruin. Before entering politics, prospective candidates would be wise to reflect on their personal strengths and weaknesses. If they are sensitive to criticism, shy, and short-tempered, and if they prefer to lead a quiet, peaceful life, the chances are strong that they will neither be happy in politics nor able to develop the kind of temperament essential for elective public service today.

What can the citizen-activists do who choose to seek political office? They can work actively in the campaigns of others to see at first hand the challenge of winning a nomination and then an election. The would-be politician should also read widely in history, politics, economics, and philosophy, know how to use parables, develop an excellent memory, study the major issues of the day, cultivate the leadership of major organizations in the region, and develop as fully as possible the capacity to listen and to learn.

Former politicians view the following personality traits as especially helpful for those who would like to be active in politics:

1. Being politically informed.
2. Integrity. Despite the prevailing cynicism about politics, a dishonest politician is almost always exposed sooner or later.
3. Patience.
4. Courtesy. "On Ballot Boulevard there's no market at all for the sour stuff."
5. Gregariousness.
6. Hard work. "To know your district and to help your neighbors is a 365-day-a-year job."
7. Don't burn too many bridges; today's foe may be tomorrow's

ally. Politics requires continual coalition-building.
8. A sense of humor. Freshman members of legislatures are warned by their elders, "Don't violate Rule Six." And what is Rule Six? "Don't take yourself too seriously." And Rules One to Five? "Don't take yourself too seriously." Have a sense of proportion, a sense of humor.
9. Courage.

An important lesson learned time and again is that by finding out the rules and simply getting enough people to the right caucuses, preconvention meetings, party gatherings, and to the polls, newcomers to politics can get themselves elected to important posts. But the rules are often difficult to figure out. Rarely is a candidacy successfully launched and brought to fruition in a few weeks. There is a long list of celebrated, successful politicians who won office only after losing election bids one or several times.

A candidate for office should also learn how to use several different advisers and should know the danger of listening to only one set of counselors. Many younger politicians can find themselves surrounded by people who act more like cheerleaders than candid advisers.

ADVISING ON PUBLIC POLICIES

For many, elective politics will not be the best way to contribute to government by the people. Those who have specialized knowledge that might improve governmental performance may prefer other alternatives.

Public officials and career public servants at all levels of government usually welcome advice on public policy. In practice, most officials conduct hearings, appoint study groups, establish advisory committees, and frequently have small sums of money available for consultant studies. For the citizen-activist who wants to change existing policies or help pass and establish new policies, there are many opportunities to obtain a hearing and press one's arguments.

It is important to remember, however, that especially in a democracy the academically well-researched argument may carry less weight than the political argument. That is, whether an adviser believes that a policy is "right" may be less important to many officials than how the policy will affect career or reelection chances. Politicians fear being too much out in front or out of line with those who elect them.

Every community needs a loose coalition of people willing to work together, often on a nonpartisan basis, to examine and offer policy advice on urgent local problems. What is needed are citizen-advisers who will apply their professional skills as well as their common sense to such issues. Help is also needed in assisting those in office to promote equitable and effective programs in areas such as tax reform, consumer protection, jobs for those who want to work, and so on.

Citizen-advisers, to be sure, will often be disillusioned by the clumsiness with which politicians and bureaucrats use advice; but the adviser will also learn that knowledge is power. Most people holding public office are receptive to constructive ideas. Anyone who is willing to undertake systematic policy and program evaluations and who can present convincing rationales for dealing with the realities will find a ready audience. Those who can design cars that will cause less smog, or invent better ways to produce energy and conserve natural resources, or formulate better foreign policies will find politicians knocking at their door.

Citizen-advisers learn too that once they have gained recognition and visibility in their field, their ability to influence officials and make governments more responsible is that much greater. They can help organize opposition coalitions of experts. They can use their positions of acknowledged expertise to educate other citizens to support or oppose government programs.

Citizen-advisers should be concerned with the often inadequate means of putting programs into action. In the best of situations they will not only come up with new ideas but also develop new ways of turning these ideas into successful programs.

MOVEMENT POLITICS

The best insurance system for honest government is an alert citizenry, watchful of its leaders, and increasingly imaginative in developing new means to keep public officials and party leaders accountable and within the Constitution. Government by the people need not be a utopia unrelated to present-day processes and politics.

The difficulty with pressure politics is that not all the pressures are represented. The American political system is often biased in favor of producer interests and against the concerns of consumers, and it often favors the wealthy and educated against the poor and ignorant. While this has become well recognized, it does not have to be accepted.

To choose pressure politics, means to try to influence those people who already hold power, who sit in official seats. Here again there are few established rules. Tactics differ markedly—from the nuclear freeze sit-ins and Saul Alinsky kind of militance on the one hand, to the less militant techniques of a Ralph Nader study report and of the League of Women Voters on the other. Certain general strategies are similar. Do not assume that all officials, media people, and outsiders will be hostile. Alliances and coalitions with other related groups should be explored. Every effort should be made to increase the membership's understanding of how government works and what the issues are.

PARTY POLITICS

Though many people may have little interest in seeking political or career jobs in government, they can and should consider taking an active role in a political party. As we have seen, our parties badly need strengthening at every level. The country needs more party politicians to hunt out quality candidates and help elect them, and

then to remind those elected of their responsibilities to the people.

Jeffersonian Republicans and Democrats dreamed a great dream—that a party system could be effective, could raise issues for rational deliberation, and could build coalitions to achieve a more just and decent society. Seldom have our parties lived up to the Jeffersonian Dream. Seldom have they served to discipline the whims of those in public office who have lost touch with the people. But if we have not lived up to the Jeffersonian hopes, this does not mean that parties are unimportant. We can still build a healthy, competitive party system that will recruit able public servants, spur provocative debate over national priorities, and inspire honesty in government.

The first step for citizen-activists is to call local party officials and find out their views, objectives, and organizational routines. If you disagree with their views, your initial work is clear. If you agree with their views and intentions, they will doubtless welcome you and sign you up for some subcommittee or future campaign assignment.

One important job in party politics is enlarging the number of the party faithful. The task of getting people out to vote is equally important. Identification systems have to be devised. Names and addresses of those not registered must be obtained. Records of those who have moved away and of those who have moved into the community must be continually updated. Registration laws vary from state to state. The unregistered voter is sometimes apathetic, but in most states our complex system of registration also discourages many people who are interested in voting. They often don't know when or where they can register, what the registration deadlines are, and when and how they must affiliate with a particular party in order to participate directly in party caucuses and primaries. The shrewd party activist will know the answers to these questions.

The heart of registration and voting drives lies in approaching the individual voter in person, but the approach is much more effective if it comes as part of a general effort. Often the best procedure is a nonpartisan communitywide program. Much of this work would be simple drudgery under any other circumstances. In the heat of a campaign, however, it often takes on an aura of drama. Volunteers are part of a team engaged in a struggle. Party headquarters is always crowded; the phone seems always to be ringing. Crisis follows crisis. Candidates dash in to make arrangements for television spots and rush out to speak at the Kiwanis Club's annual barbecue. Rumors flow thick and fast.

Taking part in party politics can be a rewarding business, especially if, ideally, the names on the ballot are those of persons you have helped to nominate and elect. However, new activists should go into party politics with a realistic view of how parties operate. On the local level organizations are often stagnant. Committees rarely meet, and attendance is typically low. By and large, the parties are run by small groups of people. Often the power over crucial matters such as candidate selection, allocation of convention delegates, and campaign finances becomes centralized in the hands of a few state and county party insiders.

Party veterans often try to run campaigns by offering something for everyone, while at the same time saying nothing that will offend anyone. Typically they have tried to capture as many differing viewpoints and fence-sitting independents as they can. If parties today are often not very democratic in their internal activities, this can be changed. If corruption and the influence of wealthy individuals or organized groups are excessive, this too can be changed.

Old-line leaders may try to close out newcomers to keep the organization as a kind of private preserve. They should not be allowed to succeed without a struggle. Turnover in local and state party posts is higher than most people think. Affirmative action rules are helping to open the parties up. And in many states there are a variety of factions within the two major parties. If necessary, one can often work with another part of the organization or join or form auxiliary groups.

VOLUNTEER SERVICE OPPORTUNITIES

The Peace Corps recruits from a wide range of skilled Americans for overseas work. After screening and training, volunteers are assigned to countries that request Peace Crops services. Applicants must be eighteen years of age or older. Volunteers receive no regular salaries but get allowances to cover the cost of clothing, housing, food, and incidental expenses. Typically they live at an economic level equivalent to their clients in the host country. Upon completion of service, Peace Corps volunteers receive a separation allotment based on time spent overseas.

Volunteers in Service to America (VISTA) is the domestic counterpart of the Peace Corps. Volunteers lend their talents for a year to communities that are striving to solve pressing economic and social problems. After a training period that stresses supervised field experience, volunteers are sent to work in communities of migrant workers, Indian reservations, rural and urban community action programs, hospitals, schools, and mental health facilities. In short, workers may be sent wherever poverty exists. VISTA volunteers are paid only subsistence expenses and a modest monthly stipend and personal allowance.

The several federal volunteer programs are consolidated in a national agency called ACTION. ACTION administers the Peace Corps, VISTA, the National Student Volunteer Program, Foster Grandparents, the Retired Senior Volunteer Program, and the Service Corps of Retired Executives. Inquiries about these programs should be addressed to ACTION Recruiting Office, Washington, D.C. 20525.

CAREERS IN PUBLIC SERVICE

Public employment is the segment of the American workforce that has grown most rapidly. More than one out of every seven people in the workforce serve as employees of the 83,000 governmental agencies at the national, state, county, or municipal level. Most positions in government service are open to qualified people, regardless of their political persuasions. The career services at every level constantly need to recruit able newcomers.

Over 90 percent of the positions in the federal executive branch are open to qualified citizens by appointment. Most of these positions are filled through civil service examinations.

Positions calling for professional training are filled through interviews and questionnaires that enable the U.S. Office of Personnel Management and the appointing agencies to examine the competence and experience of the individual.

Several federal agencies have their own personnel systems and are not covered by regular civil service rules. The TVA, FBI, National Security Agency, International Communications Agency, CIA, and Foreign Service Officer Corps, for example, recruit and hire their own employees.

The Foreign Service Officer Corps deserves special mention because of its more specialized testing and its important diplomatic responsibilities. Written, oral, and language tests are required, and intensive interviews are used. Persons who wish to take the examinations may receive application forms from the Board of Examiners for the Foreign Service, Department of State, Washington, D.C. 20520.

Those who seek work in the federal career services should do so without illusions. Despite valiant efforts to make the merit system work, a seniority system often takes root. Departments and bureaus do develop a political life of their own—as well as a passion for size, growth, and an independent mission.

One of the fastest-growing segments of public employment is in state and local governments. The positions of city manager and city planning director are especially challenging and demand talented executives with well-developed political and managerial skills.

Young people interested in sampling public service may participate in a variety of government internship programs. Such programs provide people with short-term government experience and a firsthand look at the process. Many members of Congress take on college students as summer interns. Most states and many cities operate intern programs. Information about intern opportunities can usually be obtained from your department of political science or from local student government officers.

LAST WORD

Citizen-activists can have an impact on governmental and political processes. Progress in civil rights, consumerism, ecology, the women's movement, campaign finance reform, and countless other areas came about only when concerned groups grew too large and too strong to be ignored. To have impact, however, people must be willing to concentrate their energies, enlarge the number of those sharing their views, and work hard to channel their activities into effective political action. The essence of democracy is participatory and advocacy politics. Politics without parties, and without partisan politics, is really not democratic and open politics at all. Beware of those who try to remove critical policy issues from politics.

For those who believe that the common human enterprise can best progress under a government of, by, and for the people, there is plenty to be done. For those who would make democracy work, the 1980s cry out for better ways to keep the peace, manage our economy, and revitalize our productivity while protecting our liberties and enhancing human rights. We must also provide

- □ Better ways for the individual to participate in government and see that participation count
- □ Better ways to make government open, responsive, and effective
- □ Better ways to make government serve the common interests of us all rather than the narrow interests of the few.

FURTHER READING

Stimson Bullitt, *To Be A Politician*, rev. ed. (Yale University Press, 1977).

Jeff Greenfield, *Playing to Win: An Insider's Guide to Politics* (Simon and Schuster, 1980).

Stuart Langton, ed., *Citizen Participation in America* (Lexington Books, 1978).

Louis Sandy Maisel, *From Obscurity to Oblivion: Running in the Congressional Primary* (University of Tennessee Press, 1982).

Michael Walzer, *Political Action: A Practical Guide to Movement Politics* (Quadrangle Books, 1971).

KEEPING INFORMED:
READING AND RESEARCH SOURCES

Newspaper, radio, and television are important sources of information, but the person who depends solely on these sources will have an imperfect picture of the world. They provide only part of the story, usually the sensational—newsworthy—events. They tell little of the whys and wherefores.

Magazines of general circulation contain useful material, but they do not go deeply into particular questions. Where do you find a law? How do you look up a court decision? Where can you find information on the United Nations? How do you find out how your representative in Congress has voted? What are some good books on the USSR? Many aids and services have been designed to make such information readily available. An excellent place to begin is Clement Vose, *A Guide to Library Sources in Political Science: American Government* (1975), published by the American Political Science Association.

Among the important information-dispensing centers are the more than 7,500 public libraries and the many hundreds of private libraries that are open to the public. These libraries contain, in addition to magazines of general interest, many specialized journals, such as *The American Political Science Review*. There are also a number of periodical indexes, of which the *Public Affairs Information Service* is particularly useful because it indexes books, pamphlets, and reports—as well as articles from hundreds of periodicals—for a broad range of current public interest topics. Major political science journals are included in the *Social Science and Humanities Index* and also in the *Social Sciences Citation Index*. The *International Political Science Abstracts*, edited by the International Political Science Association, provides summaries of articles from major political science journals throughout the world. The *Reader's Guide to Periodical Literature* includes mainly popular magazines with mass or family circulation. The *Index to Legal Periodicals*, *Business Periodicals Index*, the *Index of Economic Articles*, *Index to U.S. Govern-* *ment Periodicals*, *Urban Affairs Abstracts*, and *Energy Abstracts for Policy Analysis* are also useful.

The *Universal Reference System* is the most comprehensive reference to books, papers, journals, and reviews. Most of these indexes are published monthly and indexed cumulatively at the end of the year. They can help you locate materials on most subjects. In addition, see Robert Harmon's *Political Science: A Bibliographical Guide to the Literature* (1965), which is kept up to date by supplements—no. 2 (1972), no. 3 (1974). See also, by the same author, *Political Science Bibliographies*, vol. 1 (1973), and vol. 2 (1976). The ABS *Guide to Recent Publications in the Social and Behavioral Sciences* (1965), also kept up to date with annual supplements, is useful.

Other bibliographies you might consult are Federick Holler's five-volume *The Information Sources of Political Science*, 3rd ed. (1981) and *ABC Pol Sci; Advance Bibliography of Contents: Political Science and Government*, a monthly service which reproduces the tables of contents of periodicals in the field of political science. The card catalog in the library will reveal the books that are available there. You may be able to learn something about an author's reputation or a particular book in the *Book Review Digest*; but reviews in this digest are taken from a limited group of publications. You will also find the *Current Book Review Index* helpful; it complements the *Book Review Digest* but is more current and complete. It lists sources of all reviews in the periodicals indexed, and it comes in monthly and quarterly issues with annual cumulations. Most larger libraries also subscribe to *Perspective*, a thoughtful monthly journal that carries reviews of new books on government, politics, and international affairs.

Useful for foreign policy research are Richard D. Burns's *Guide to American Foreign Relations Since 1700* (ABC Clio Press, 1983) and Alexander DeConde, ed., *Encyclopedia of American Foreign Policy*, 3 vols. (Scribners, 1978).

One of the most useful volumes is the *United States Government Manual*, an annual publication. This manual, which can be obtained from the Superintendent of Documents, U.S. Government Printing Office, Washington, D.C. 20402, covers the authority, organization, and functions of all branches of the government. It has up-to-date organizational charts, tells who holds the higher executive positions, and gives a brief description of the work of each unit of government. The *Congressional Directory*, also published annually, has some of the materials found in the *Manual*, and it includes autobiographical sketches of members of Congress, lists of congressional committees and committee assignments, election statistics for the last several congressional elections, and maps of congressional districts. The *Directory* is the place to find out the name of your representative, a short sketch of his or her life, what committees he or she is on, and the boundaries of his or her district. The *Almanac of American Politics*, published by Gambit, contains current biographies, voting records, lobbying interests, as well as political and economic profiles of a member's district.

Of special interest to persons interested in social sciences is the *Encyclopedia of the Social Sciences*, published in 1930 under the editorship of Edwin Seligman and Alvin Johnson; it contains articles on various topics—for example, political parties, sovereignty, representation, John Locke,— that are among the best short treatments to be found. The *International Encyclopedia of the Social Sciences*, edited by David Sills and published in 1968, complements its predecessor and brings the information up to date. Valuable review and survey articles can be found in the eight-volume series *Handbook of Political Science* (1975, 1976), edited by Fred Greenstein and Nelson Polsby.

Although both encyclopedias contain a great many biographies, the *Dictionary of National Biography* and the *Dictionary of American Biography* are the prime sources for this type of data. Included are some outstanding articles; one by Carl Becker on Benjamin Franklin, for example, is found in the *Dictionary of American Biography*. In *Current Biography* you can find materials and background information on people in the news, and there is a companion set, *Biography Index*, in case specific information has not been written up fully in *Current Biography* for ten years or so. Also of help will be *Who's Who in American Politics*, *Who's Who in Government*, and *Biographical Directory of the American Congress, 1774–1971* (U.S. Government Printing Office).

Certain important tools are available for quick reference to current events, such as *Facts on File*, the *New York Times Index*, the *Wall Street Journal Index*, and *Keesing's Contemporary Archives*.

If you want raw figures, consult the *Statistical Abstract of the United States*, another yearly publication of the Government Printing Office. The reference librarian will be able to point out other useful tools of this nature, such as the *Historical Statistics of the United States*, the *Congressional District Data Book*, and the many publications from the Bureau of the Census. The *American Statistical Index* is a comprehensive guide to the statistical publications of the U.S. government. It is useful in helping students locate particular statistical publications issued by the government. Phyllis Carter's *U.S. Census Data for Political and Social Research: A Resource Guide*, published in 1976 by the American Political Science Association, is also helpful.

Where can you find the actual text of a law? The laws of the United States as passed by Congress are first printed individually and are known as slip laws. Each law has a number; in recent years public laws have been numbered according to the term of Congress in which they were enacted. At the end of each year, the laws are collected and published by the Government Printing Office under the title of *United States Statutes at Large*. Each year's collection is separately numbered, though there are two separate parts of each number. Part One contains *public laws*—that is, laws affecting the people generally or having to do with governmental organization. Part Two contains *private laws*, those having to do with particular groups or individuals. The laws in the *Statutes at Large* are listed chronologically, each law constituting a separate chapter. The Taft–Hartley Act, for example, is chapter 120 of volume 61, on page 136; it is cited as 61 Stat. 136.

The volumes of *Statutes at Large* are useful for research, but they include many laws of only specialized interest. Further, many of the measures modify earlier legislation and are themselves modified by later legislation. To find *current* laws on a topic, it is best to go to the *United States Code*, which contains the public laws of the United States that are in force at the present time. The official edition of the *United States Code* is published every six years. Supplements are issued annually between editions. The laws are arranged according to fifty titles; each title is divided into sections, and each section is broken down into paragraphs that are consecutively numbered for each title. The fifty titles cover subjects such as Congress, Title 2; Armed Forces, Title 10; Bankruptcy, Title 11; Labor, Title 29; and so on. The Code is cited by title and paragraph. The citation of the Taft–Hartley Act, for example, is 29 U.S.C. 141 ff.

The *Code*, like the *Statutes at Large*, is printed by the Government Printing Office, but there are also commercially published editions, known as *United States Code Annotated* (USCA) and the *Federal Code Annotated* (FCA). These annotated editions include notes on judicial interpretations of the law as well as the law itself. If available, they are more useful than the *Code*.

The series *Treaties in Force* is the best source of information about treaties and executive agreements. These volumes are published annually and are organized chronologically.

Where does one find the rules and regulations issued by the president and the executive agencies? Every day except Sunday and Monday the government publishes the *Federal Register*, which contains executive orders, regulations, and proclamations issued by the president, as well as the orders and regulations promulgated by the executive agencies (including the independent regulatory commissions). These administrative rules and regulations are collected, codified, and kept up to date in the *Code of Federal Regulations*, organized on the same plan as the *United States Code*. The *Code of Federal Regulations*, the *Federal Register*, along with the *United States Government Manual* previously mentioned and the annual publication *Public Papers of the Presidents*, are part of what is known as the Federal Register System. The *Weekly Compilation of Presidential Documents*, which contains public messages, speeches, and statements of the president, is published every Monday. Students doing research work on the presidency should definitely consult Fred Greenstein et al., *Evolution of the Modern Presidency: A Bibliographical Survey* (American Enterprise Institute, 1977), George Edwards and Stephen Wayne, eds., *Studying The Presidency* (University of Tennessee Press, 1983), and Kenneth Davison's helpful *The American Presidency: A Guide to Information Sources* (Gale Research Company, 1983).

Still, the laws as they finally appear on the statute books give only part of the story. Where do you find out what went on before the laws were passed or why certain laws were not passed? This information can, in part, be found in one of the most interesting items of American letters—the *Congressional Record*. The *Record* is issued every day Congress is in session and is bound and indexed at the end of each session. It contains everything

that is said on the floors of the two chambers, plus a lot that is not said. Congress freely gives its consent to requests of its members "to revise and extend their remarks," which is a polite way of saying that members are permitted to include in the *Record* statements they did not make before Congress. Each day's *Record* is now accompanied by a *Daily Digest* that highlights the events both on the floor of Congress and in committees. Action on specific items can be traced by searching through the index. An easier method is to use the *Digest of Public General Bills*, which gives a brief summary of all the public bills and traces their progress. *Major Legislation of the United States Congress*, published by the Congressional Research Service, The Library of Congress, is a monthly that gives a broad overview of legislation in various subject areas. It includes background information on topics as well as a survey of current bills under consideration.

Helpful general guides for students of the congressional process are Robert Goehlert, *Congress and Law-Making: Researching the Legislative Process* (Clio Books, 1979) and Robert Goehlert and John Sayre's *The United States Congress: A Bibliography* (Free Press, 1982). Another helpful reference work is Jerrold Zwirn, *Congressional Publications: A Research Guide to Legislation, Budgets, and Treaties* (Libraries Unlimited, 1983).

Several commercial services provide convenient references to congressional activities. The *Congressional Quarterly Weekly Report* contains voting records, legislative action, reports on lobbying, and other materials about Congress in action. This is the best source for materials on lobbying activity. The materials are indexed and collected in the *Congressional Quarterly Almanac*, an annual publication. The *United States Code: Congressional and Administrative News* and the *Congressional Index* also provide ready reference to congressional activity. Another helpful way to monitor congressional activity is through the *CIS/Index*, an index to publications of Congress that is issued monthly with annual compilations by the Congressional Information Service. It indexes and abstracts committee

hearings, prints chamber reports and other congressional documents, and contains a brief summary of the statement of each witness in a hearing, including page numbers on which particular testimonies appear.

Because most of the real work of Congress is done in committees, the reports of these committees and the printed records of hearings are important sources of information. The hearings and reports may be found in any of the more than one thousand depository libraries in the United States. (A depository library receives regular publications issued by the Government Printing Office.)

Congress is not the only branch of the federal government that keeps a record of its work. All the other agencies have their own publications, which describe their work and supply the citizen with general and specialized information. These publications can be obtained from the Superintendent of Documents, Government Printing Office, Washington, D.C. 20402, at a nominal price. They are indexed in the *Monthly Catalog of United States Government Publications*. One of the several general guides to government publications is Joe Morehead, *Introduction to United States Public Documents*, 2nd ed. (Libraries Unlimited, 1978).

Activities of the executive branch of the federal government as well as those of Congress and the courts are analyzed in the *National Journal*, a weekly publication. This is the best single source on developments within the federal executive branch. Congressional Quarterly, Inc., publishes two excellent annual sources, the *Federal Regulatory Directory* and the *Washington Information Directory*. The *Washington Monthly* and *The Public Interest* provide critical essays on policy politics and bureaucracy in Washington. Two publications, *Public Opinion* and *Regulation*, published by the American Enterprise Institute, are also helpful in following national politics and policy developments.

A quarterly journal of research, *Women and Politics*, offers an interdisciplinary approach to the growing field of women in politics and the political behavior of women.

Where can you find the reports

and rulings of the federal judiciary? The decisions of the Supreme Court are published by the government in numbered volumes known as the *United States Reports*. Cases are cited by volume and page number. *Regents of the University of California v. Bakke*, 438 U.S. 265 (1979), means that this case can be found in the 438th volume of the United States Reports, on page 265, and that the opinion was handed down in 1979. Decisions of the Court prior to 1875 are cited by the name of the Supreme Court Reporter. Thus, *Marbury v. Madison*, 1 Cranch 137 (1803), can be found in the first volume of Cranch's Supreme Court reports, on page 137; the opinion was announced in 1803.

It now takes months before the official Supreme Court reports are available, so to review recent opinions it is necessary to consult *United States Law Week*—a comprehensive and promptly published review. Also available are the *Supreme Court Reporter*, published by West Publishing Company, and *United States Supreme Court Reports, Lawyers Edition*, published by the Lawyers Co-operative Publishing Company. An excellent general survey of the history, decisions, and procedures of the Supreme Court is the *Guide to the U.S. Supreme Court* (Congressional Quarterly, Inc., 1979). *The National Law Journal* and *The Legal Times of Washington* are two other weeklies that might be helpful.

Students doing research on the United Nations and its politics and policies might best start with *Basic Facts about the United Nations* (1977, and regularly revised), published by the UN Office of Public Information, and with *Reference Guide to the United Nations* (1979), published by the UN Association of the United States of America. More specialized research guides are Peter Hajnal, *United Nations Handbook for Students, Researchers and Librarians* (Oceana Publishers, 1978) and Mary K. Fetzer, *United Nations Document and Publications: A Research Guide* (Rutgers University Graduate School of Library Service, 1978). Since 1980 many libraries have the *UNDOC* guide, an up-to-date, comprehensive description of all United Nations documents, with subject, author, and title indexes.

You will also get excellent assistance from your college and university professional librarians, who will gladly direct you to the newest reference and document sources.

THE DECLARATION OF INDEPENDENCE

IN CONGRESS, JULY 4, 1776
(The unanimous Declaration of
the Thirteen United States of America)

PREAMBLE

When, in the course of human events, it becomes necessary for one people to dissolve the political bands which have connected them with another, and to assume, among the powers of the earth, the separate and equal station to which the laws of nature and of nature's God entitle them, a decent respect to the opinions of mankind requires that they should declare the causes which impel them to the separation.

NEW PRINCIPLES OF GOVERNMENT

We hold these truths to be self-evident; that all men are created equal, that they are endowed by their Creator with certain unalienable rights, that among these are life, liberty, and the pursuit of happiness.

That, to secure these rights, governments are instituted among men, deriving their just powers from the consent of the governed;

That whenever any form of government becomes destructive of these ends, it is the right of the people to alter or to abolish it, and to institute new government, laying its foundation on such principles, and organizing its powers in such form, as to them shall seem most likely to effect their safety and happiness. Prudence, indeed, will dictate that governments long established should not be changed for light and transient causes; and accordingly all experience hath shown that mankind are more disposed to suffer while evils are sufferable, than to right themselves by abolishing the forms to which they are accustomed. But when a long train of abuses and usurpations, pursuing invariably the same object, evinces a design to reduce them under absolute despotism, it is their right, it is their duty, to throw off such government, and to provide new guards for their future security.

REASONS FOR SEPARATION

Such has been the patient sufferance of these colonies; and such is now the necessity which constrains them to alter their former systems of government. The history of the present king of Great Britain is a history of repeated injuries and usurpations, all having in direct object the establishment of an absolute tyranny over these states. To prove this, let facts be submitted to a candid world.

He has refused his assent to laws the most wholesome and necessary for the public good.

He has forbidden his governors to pass laws of immediate and pressing importance unless suspended in their operation till his assent should be obtained; and when so supended, he has utterly neglected to attend to them.

He has refused to pass other laws for the accommodation of large districts of people, unless those people would relinquish the right of representation in the legislature, a right inestimable to them, and formidable to tyrants only.

He has called together legislative bodies at places unusual, uncomfortable, and distant from the depository of their public records, for the sole purpose of fatiguing them into compliance with his measures.

He has dissolved representative houses repeatedly, for opposing, with manly firmness, his invasions on the rights of people.

He has refused, for a long time after such dissolutions, to cause others to be elected; whereby the legislative powers, incapable of annihilation, have returned to the people at large for their exercise; the state remaining, in the mean time, exposed to all the dangers of invasion from without and convulsions within.

He has endeavored to prevent the population of these states; for that purpose obstructing the laws of naturalization of foreigners, refusing to pass others to encourage their migration hither, and raising the conditions of new appropriations of lands.

He has obstructed the administration of justice, by refusing his assent to laws for establishing judiciary powers.

He has made judges dependent on his will alone for the tenure of their offices, and the amount and payment of their salaries.

He has erected a multitude of new offices, and sent hither swarms of officers to harass our people and eat out their substance.

He has kept among us, in times of peace, standing armies, without the consent of our legislature.

He has affected to render the military independent of, and superior to, the civil power.

He has combined with others to subject us to a jurisdiction foreign to our constitution and unacknowledged by our laws, giving his assent to their acts of pretended legislation:

For quartering large bodies of armed troops among us;

For protecting them, by a mock trial, from punishment for any murders which they should commit on the inhabitants of these states;

For cutting off our trade with all parts of the world;

For imposing taxes on us without our consent;

For depriving us, in many cases, of the benefits of trial by jury;

For transporting us beyond seas, to be tried for pretended offenses;

For abolishing the free system of English laws in a neighboring province, establishing therein an arbitrary government, and enlarging its boundaries, so as to render it at once an example and fit instrument for introducing the same absolute rule into these colonies;

For taking away our charters, abolishing our most valuable laws, and altering, fundamentally, the forms of our governments;

For suspending our own legislatures, and declaring themselves invested with power to legislate for us in all cases whatsoever.

He has abdicated government here, by declaring us out of his protection and waging war against us.

He has plundered our seas, ravaged our coasts, burned our towns, and destroyed the lives of our people.

He is at this time transporting large armies of foreign mercenaries to complete the works of death, desolation, and tyranny already begun with circumstances of cruelty and perfidy scarcely paralleled in the most barbarous ages and totally unworthy the head of a civilized nation.

He has constrained our fellow-citizens, taken captive on the high seas, to bear arms against their country, to become the executioners of their friends and brethren, or to fall themselves by their hands.

He has excited domestic insur-rections among us, and has endeavored to bring on the inhabitants of our frontiers the merciless Indian savages, whose known rule of warfare is an undistinguished destruction of all ages, sexes, and conditions.

In every stage of these oppressions we have petitioned for redress in the most humble terms; our repeated petitions have been answered only by repeated injury. A prince whose character is thus marked by every act which may define a tyrant is unfit to be the ruler of a free people.

Nor have we been wanting in attention to our British brethren. We have warned them, from time to time, of attempts by their legislature to extend an unwarrantable jurisdiction over us. We have reminded them of the circumstances of our emigration and settlement here. We have appealed to their native justice and magnanimity; and we have conjured them, by the ties of our common kindred, to disavow these usurpations, which would inevitably interrupt our connections and correspondence. They, too, have been deaf to the voice of justice and of consanguinity. We must, therefore, acquiesce in the ne-cessity which denounces our separation, and hold them, as we hold the rest of mankind, enemies in war, in peace, friends.

We, therefore, the representatives of the United States of America, in General Congress assembled, appealing to the Supreme Judge of the world for the rectitude of our intentions, do, in the name and by authority of the good people of these colonies, solemnly publish and declare, that these united colonies are, and of right ought to be, free and independent states; that they are absolved from all allegiance to the British crown, and that all political connection between them and the state of Great Britain is, and ought to be, totally dissolved; and that, as free and independent states, they have full power to levy war, conclude peace, contract alliances, establish commerce, and do all other acts and things which independent states may of a right do. And, for the support of this declaration, with a firm reliance on the protection of Divine Providence, we mutually pledge to each other our lives, our fortunes, and our sacred honor.

Note: Drafted mainly by Thomas Jefferson, this document adopted by the Second Continental Congress outlines the rights of man and the rights to rebellion and self-government. It declared the independence of the colonies from Great Britain, justified rebellion, and listed the grievances against George the III and his government. Today it is considered a basic statement of the American democratic faith.

THE FEDERALIST, NO. 10 (1787) JAMES MADISON

To the People of the State of New York:
Among the numerous advantages promised by a well-constructed union, none deserves to be more accurately developed than its tendency to break and control the violence of faction. The friend of popular governments, never finds himself so much alarmed for their character and fate, as when he contemplates their propensity to this dangerous vice. He will not fail, therefore, to set a due value on any plan which, without violating the principles to which he is attached, provides a proper cure for it. The instability, injustice, and confusion introduced into the public councils, have, in truth, been the mortal diseases under which popular governments have everywhere perished; as they continue to be the favourite and fruitful topics from which the adversaries to liberty derive their most specious declamations. The valuable improvements made by the American constitutions on the popular models, both ancient and modern, cannot certainly be too much admired; but it would be an unwarrantable partiality, to contend that they have as effectually obviated the danger on this side, as was wished and expected. Complaints are everywhere heard from our most considerate and virtuous citizens, equally the friends of public and private faith, and of public and personal liberty, that our governments are too unstable; that the public good is disregarded in the conflicts of rival parties; and that measures are too often decided, not according to the rules of justice, and the rights of the minor party, but by the superior force of an interested and overbearing majority. However anxiously we may wish that these complaints had no foundation, the evidence of known facts will not permit us to deny that they are in some degree true. It will be found, indeed, on a candid review of our situation, that some of the distresses under which we labour have been erroneously charged on the operation of our governments; but it will be found, at the same time, that other causes will not alone account for many of our heaviest misfortunes; and, particularly, for that prevailing and increasing distrust of public engagements, and alarm for private rights, which are echoed from one end of the continent to the other. These must be chiefly, if not wholly, effects of the unsteadiness and injustice, with which a factious spirit has tainted our public administrations.

By a faction, I understand a number of citizens, whether amounting to a majority or minority of the whole, who are united and actuated by some common impulse of passion, or of interest, adverse to the rights of other citizens, or to the permanent and aggregate interests of the community.

There are two methods of curing the mischiefs of faction: The one, by removing its causes; the other, by controlling its effects.

There are again two methods of removing the causes of faction: The one, by destroying the liberty which is essential to its existence; the other, by giving to every citizen the same opinions, the same passions, and the same interests.

It could never be more truly said, than of the first remedy, that it was worse than the disease. Liberty is to faction what air is to fire, an aliment without which it instantly expires. But it could not be a less folly to abolish liberty, which is essential to political life, because it nourishes faction, than it would be to wish the annihilation of air, which is essential to animal life, because it imparts to fire its destructive agency.

The second expedient is as impracticable, as the first would be unwise. As long as the reason of man continues fallible, and he is at liberty to exercise it, different opinions will be formed. As long as the connection subsists between his reason and his self-love, his opinions and his passions will have a reciprocal influence on each other; and the former will be objects to which the latter will attach themselves. The diversity in the faculties of men, from which the rights of property originate, is not less an insuperable obstacle to an uniformity of interests. The protection of these faculties is the first object of government. From the protection of different and unequal faculties of acquiring property, the possession of different degrees and kinds of property immediately results; and from the influence of these on the sentiments and views of the respective proprietors, ensues a division of the society into different interests and parties.

The latent causes of action are thus sown in the nature of man; and we see them everywhere brought into different degrees of activity, according to the different circumstances of civil society. A zeal for different opinions concerning religion, concerning government, and many other points, as well of speculation as of practice; an attachment to different leaders ambitiously contending for preeminence and power; or to persons of other descriptions whose fortunes have been interesting to the human passions, have, in turn, divided mankind into parties, inflamed them with mutual animosity, and rendered them much more disposed to vex and oppress each other, than to cooperate for their common good. So strong is this propensity of mankind, to fall into mutual animosities, that where no substantial occasion presents itself, the most frivolous and fanciful distinctions have been sufficient to kindle their unfriendly passions and excite their most violent conflicts. But the most common and durable source of factions, has been the various and unequal distribution of property. Those who hold, and those who are without property, have ever formed distinct interests in society. Those who are creditors, and those who are debtors, fall under a like discrimination. A landed interest, a manufacturing interest, a mercantile interest, a moneyed interest, with many lesser interests, grow up of necessity in civilized nations, and divide them into different classes, actuated by different sentiments and views. The regulation of these various and interfering interests forms the principal task of modern legislation, and involves the spirit of the party and faction in the necessary and ordinary operations of the government

No man is allowed to be a judge in his own cause; because his interest will certainly bias his judgment, and, not improbably, corrupt his integrity. With equal, nay, with greater reason, a body of men are unfit to be both judges and parties at the same time; yet what are many of the most important acts of legislation, but so many judicial determinations, not indeed concerning the right of single persons, but concerning the rights of large bodies of citizens? And what are the different classes of legislators, but advocates and parties to the causes which they determine? Is a law proposed concerning private debts? It is a question to which the creditors are parties on one side, and the debtors on the other. Justice ought to hold the balance between them. Yet the parties are, and must be, themselves the judges; and the most numerous party, or, in other words, the most powerful faction, must be expected to prevail. Shall domestic manufactures be encouraged, and in what degree, by restrictions on foreign manufactures? are questions which would be differently decided by the landed and the manufacturing classes; and probably by neither with a sole regard to justice and the public good. The apportionment of taxes, on the various descriptions of property, is an act which seems to require the most exact impartiality; yet there is, perhaps, no legislative act, in which greater opportunity and temptation are given to a predominant party to trample on the rules of justice. Every shilling, with which they overburden the inferior number, is a shilling saved to their own pockets.

It is in vain to say, that enlightened statesmen will be able to adjust these clashing interests, and render them all subservient to the public good. Enlightened statesmen will not always be at the helm: nor, in many cases, can such an adjustment be made at all, without taking into view indirect and remote considerations, which will rarely prevail over the immediate interest which one party may find in disregarding the rights of another, or the good of the whole.

The inference to which we are brought is, that the *causes* of faction cannot be removed; and that relief is only to be sought in the means of controlling its *effects*.

If a faction consists of less than a majority, relief is supplied by the republican principle, which enables the majority to defeat its sinister views, by regular vote. It may clog the administration, it may convulse the society; but it will be unable to execute and mask its violence under the forms of the constitution. When a majority is included in a faction, the form of popular government, on the other hand, enables it to sacrifice to its ruling passion or interest, both the public good and the rights of other citizens. To secure the public good, and private rights, against the danger of such a faction, and at the same time to preserve the spirit and the form of popular government, is then the great object to which our inquiries are directed. Let me add, that it is the great desideratum, by which alone this form of government can be rescued from the opprobrium under which it has so long laboured, and be recommended to the esteem and adoption of mankind.

By what means is this object attainable? Evidently by one of two only. Either the existence of the same passion or interest in a majority, at the same time, must be prevented; or the majority, having such coexistent passion or interest, must be rendered, by their number and local situation, unable to concert and carry into effect schemes of oppression. If the impulse and the opportunity be suffered to coincide, we well know that neither moral nor religious motives can be relied on as an adequate control. They are not found to be such on the injustice and violence of individuals, and lose their efficacy in proportion to the number combined together; that is, in proportion as their efficacy becomes needful.

From this view of the subject, it may be concluded, that a pure democracy, by which I mean a society consisting of a small number of citizens, who assemble and administer the government in person, can admit of no cure for the mischiefs of faction. A common passion or interest will, in almost every case, be felt by a majority of the whole; a communication and concert, results from the form of government itself; and there is nothing to check the inducements to sacrifice the weaker party, or an obnoxious individual. Hence, it is, that such democracies have ever been spectacles of turbulence and contention; have ever been found incompatible with personal security, or the rights of property; and have in general been as short in their lives, as they have been violent in their deaths. Theoretic politicians, who have patronized this species of government, have erroneously supposed, that by reducing mankind to a perfect equality in their political rights, they would, at the same time, be perfectly equalized and assimilated in their possessions, their opinions, and their passions.

A republic, by which I mean a government in which the scheme of representation takes place, opens a different prospect, and promises the cure for which we are seeking. Let us examine the points in which it varies from pure democracy, and we shall comprehend both the nature of the cure and the efficacy which it must derive from the union.

The two great points of difference, between a democracy and a republic, are, first, the delegation of the government, in the latter, to a small number of citizens, elected by the rest; secondly, the greater number of citizens, and greater sphere of country, over which the latter may be extended.

The effect of the first difference is, on the one hand, to refine and enlarge the public views, by passing them through the medium of a chosen body of citizens, whose wisdom may best discern the true interest of their country, and whose patriotism and love of justice, will be least likely to sacrifice it to temporary or partial considerations. Under such a regulation, it may well happen, that the public voice, pronounced by the representatives of the people, will be more consonant to the public good, than if pronounced by the people themselves, convened for the purpose. On the other hand the effect may be inverted. Men of factious tempers, of local prejudices, or of sinister designs, may by intrigue, by corruption, or by other means, first obtain the suffrages, and then betray the interest of the people. The question resulting is, whether small or extensive republics are most favourable to the election of proper guardians of the public weal; and it is clearly decided in favour of the latter by two obvious considerations.

In the first place, it is to be remarked that, however small the republic may be, the representatives must be raised to a certain number, in order to guard against the cabals of a few; and that however large it may be, they must be limited to a certain number, in order to guard against the confusion of a multitude. Hence, the number of representatives in the two cases not being in proportion to that of the constituents, and being proportionally greatest in the small republic, it follows, that if the proportion of fit characters be not less in the large than in the small republic, the former will present a greater option, and consequently a greater probability of a fit choice.

In the next place, as each representative will be chosen by a greater number of citizens in the large than in the small republic, it will be more difficult for unworthy candidates to practise with success the vicious arts, by which elections are too often carried; and the suffrages of the people being more free, will be more likely to centre in men who possess the most attractive merit, and the most diffusive and established characters.

It must be confessed, that in this, as in most other cases, there is a mean, on both sides of which inconveniences will be found to lie. By enlarging too much the number of electors, you render the representatives too little acquainted with all their local circumstances and lesser interests; as by reducing it too much, you render him unduly attached to these, and too little fit to comprehend and pursue great and national objects. The federal constitution forms a happy combination in this respect; the great and aggregate interests being referred to the national, the local and particular to the state legislatures.

The other point of difference is, the greater number of citizens, and extent of territory, which may be brought within the compass of republican, than of democratic government; and it is this circumstance principally which renders factious combinations less to be dreaded in the former, than in the latter. The smaller the society, the fewer probably will be the distinct parties and interests composing it; the fewer the distinct parties and interests, the more frequently will a majority be found of the same party; and the smaller the number of individuals composing a majority, and the smaller the compass within which they are placed, the more easily will they concert and execute their plans of oppression. Extend the sphere, and you take in a greater variety of parties and interests; you make it less probable that a majority of the whole will have a common motive to invade the rights of other citizens; or if such a common motive exists, it will be more difficult for all who feel it to discover their own strength, and to act in unison with each other. Besides other impediments, it may be remarked, that where there is a consciousness of unjust or dishonourable purposes, communication is always checked by distrust, in proportion to the number whose concurrence is necessary.

Hence, it clearly appears, that the same advantage, which a republic has over a democracy, in controlling the effects of faction, is enjoyed by a large over a small republic,—is enjoyed by the union over the states composing it. Does this advantage consist in the substitution of representatives, whose enlightened views and virtuous sentiments render them superior to local prejudices, and to schemes of injustice? It will not be denied that the representation of the union will be most likely to possess these requisite endowments. Does it consist in the greater security afforded by a greater variety of parties, against the event of any one party being able to outnumber and oppress the rest? In an equal degree does the increased variety of parties, comprised within the union, increase the security? Does it, in fine, consist in the greater obstacles opposed to the concert and accomplishment of the secret wishes of an unjust and interested majority? Here, again, the extent of the union gives it the most palpable advantage.

The influence of factious leaders may kindle a flame within their particular states, but will be unable to spread a general conflagration through the other states; a religious sect may degenerate into a political faction in a part of the confederacy; but the variety of sects dispersed over the entire face of it, must secure the national councils against any danger from that source: a rage for paper money, for an abolition of debts, for an equal division of property, or for any other improper or wicked project, will be less apt to pervade the whole body of the union than a particular member of it; in the same proportion as such a malady is more likely to taint a particular county or district, than an entire state.

In the extent and proper structure of the union, therefore, we behold a republican remedy for the diseases most incident to republican government. And according to the degree of pleasure and pride we feel in being republicans, ought to be our zeal in cherishing the spirit, and supporting the character of federalists.

Note: *Federalist 10*, written by James Madison soon after the Constitutional Convention, was prepared as one of several dozen newspaper essays aimed at persuading New Yorkers to ratify the proposed constitution. One of the most important basic documents in American political history, it outlines the need for and the general principles of a democratic republic. It also provides a political and economic analysis of the realities of interest group or faction politics. Students should, if at all possible, read the entire collection of the Federalist papers; collectively they constitute one of the more notable contributions made in the United States to the development of political theory.

THE CONSTITUTION OF THE UNITED STATES

THE PREAMBLE

We the People of the United States, in Order to form a more perfect Union, establish Justice, insure domestic Tranquility, provide for the common defence, promote the general Welfare, and secure the Blessings of Liberty to ourselves and our Posterity, do ordain and establish this Constitution for the United States of America.

ARTICLE 1—THE LEGISLATIVE ARTICLE

Legislative Power

Section 1. All Legislative Powers herein granted shall be vested in a Congress of the United States, which shall consist of a Senate and House of Representatives.

House of Representatives: Composition; Qualifications; Apportionment; Impeachment Power

Section 2. The House of Representatives shall be composed of Members chosen every second Year by the People of the several States, and the Electors in each state shall have the Qualifications requisite for Electors of the most numerous Branch of the State Legislature.

No Person shall be a Representative who shall not have attained to the Age of twenty five Years, and been seven Years a Citizen of the United States, and who shall not, when elected, be an Inhabitant of that State in which he shall be chosen.

Representatives and direct [Taxes][1] shall be apportioned among the several States which may be included within this Union, according to their respective Numbers, [which shall be determined by adding to the whole Number of free Persons, including those bound to Service for a Term of Years, and excluding Indians not taxed, three fifths of all other Persons].[2] The actual Enumeration shall be made within three Years after the first Meeting of the Congress of the United States, and within every subsequent Term of ten Years, in such Manner as they shall by Law direct. The Number of Representatives shall not exceed one for every thirty Thousand, but each State shall have at Least one Representative; and until such enumeration shall be made, the State of New Hampshire shall be entitled to chuse three, Maryland six, Virginia ten, North Carolina five, Massachusetts eight, Rhode-Island and Providence Plantations one, Connecticut five, New-York six, New Jersey four, Pennsylvania eight, Delaware one, South Carolina five, and Georgia three.

When vacancies happen in the Representation from any State, the Executive Authority thereof shall issue Writs of Election to fill such Vacancies.

The House of Representatives shall chuse their speaker and other Officers; and shall have the sole Power of Impeachment.

Senate: Composition; Qualifications, Impeachment Trials

Section 3. The Senate of the United States shall be composed of Two Senators from each State, (chosen by the Legislature thereof,)[3] for six Years; and each Senator shall have one Vote.

Immediately after they shall be assembled in Consequence of the first Election, they shall be divided as equally as may be into three Classes. The Seats of the Senators of the first Class shall be vacated at the Expiration of the second Year, of the second Class at the Expiration of the fourth year, and of the third Class at the Expiration of the sixth year, so that one third may be chosen every second Year; (and if Vacancies happen by Resignation, or otherwise, during the Recess of the Legislature of any State, the Executive thereof may make temporary Appointments until the next Meeting of the Legislature, which shall then fill such Vacancies.)[4]

No Person shall be a Senator who shall not have attained to the Age of thirty Years, and been nine Years a Citizen of the United States, and who shall not, when elected, be an Inhabitant of that State for which he shall be chosen.

The Vice President of the United States shall be President of the Senate, but shall have no Vote, unless they be equally divided.

The Senate shall chuse their other Officers, and also a President pro tempore, in the Absence of the Vice President, or when he shall exercise the Office of the President of the United States.

The Senate shall have the sole Power to try all Impeachments. When sitting for that Purpose, they shall be on Oath or Affirmation. When the President of the United States is tried, the Chief Justice shall preside; And no Person shall be convicted without the Concurrence of two thirds of the Members present.

Judgment in Cases of Impeachment shall not extend further than to removal from Office, and disqualification to hold and enjoy any Office of honor, Trust or Profit under the United States: but the Party convicted shall nevertheless be liable and subject to Indictment, Trial, Judgment and Punishment, according to law.

Congressional Elections: Time; Place; Manner

Section 4. The Times, Places and Manner of holding Elections for Senators and Representatives, shall be prescribed in each State by the legislature thereof; but the Congress may at any

---

[1]Modified by the 16th Amendment

[2]"Other Persons" refers to black slaves. Replaced by Section 2, 14th Amendment

[3]Repealed by the 17th Amendment

[4]Modified by the 17th Amendment

time by Law make or alter such Regulations, except as to the Places of chusing Senators.

[The Congress shall assemble at least once in every Year, and such Meeting shall be on the first Monday in December, unless they shall by Law appoint a different Day.][5]

Powers and Duties of the Houses

Section 5. Each House shall be the Judge of the Elections, Returns and Qualifications of its own Members, and a Majority of each shall constitute a Quorum to do Business; but a smaller Number may adjourn from day to day, and may be authorized to compel the Attendance of absent Members, in such Manner, and under such Penalties as each House may provide.

Each House may determine the Rules of its Proceedings, punish its Members for disorderly Behaviour, and, with the Concurrence of two thirds, expel a Member.

Each House shall keep a Journal of its Proceedings, and from time to time publish the same, excepting such Parts as may in their Judgment require Secrecy; and the Yeas and Nays of the Members of either House on any question shall, at the Desire of one fifth of those Present, be entered on the Journal.

Neither House, during the Session of Congress, shall, without the Consent of the other, adjourn for more than three days, nor to any other Place than that in which the two Houses shall be sitting.

Rights of Members

Section 6. The Senators and Representatives shall receive a Compensation for their Services, to be ascertained by Law, and paid out of the Treasury of the United States. They shall in all Cases, except Treason, Felony and Breach of the Peace, be privileged from Arrest during their Attendance at the Session of their respective Houses, and in going to and returning from the same; and for any Speech or Debate in either House, they shall not be questioned in any other Place.

No Senator or Representative

shall, during the Time for which he was elected, be appointed to any civil Office under the Authority of the United States, which shall have been created, or the Emoluments whereof shall have been increased during such time; and no Person holding any Office under the United States, shall be a Member of either House during his Continuance in Office.

Legislative Powers: Bills and Resolutions

Section 7. All Bills for raising Revenue shall originate in the House of Representatives; but the Senate may propose or concur with Amendments as on other Bills.

Every Bill which shall have passed the House of Representatives and the Senate, shall, before it become a Law, be presented to the President of the United States; If he approve he shall sign it, but if not he shall return it, with his Objections to that House in which it shall have originated, who shall enter the Objections at large on their Journal, and proceed to reconsider it. If after such Reconsideration two thirds of that House shall agree to pass the Bill, it shall be sent, together with the Objections, to the other House, by which it shall likewise be reconsidered, and if approved by two thirds of that House, it shall become a Law. But in all such Cases the Votes of both the Houses shall be determined by Yeas and Nays, and the Names of the Persons voting for and against the Bill shall be entered on the Journal of Each House respectively. If any Bill shall not be returned by the President within the ten Days (Sunday excepted) after it shall have been presented to him, the Same shall be a Law, in like Manner as if he had signed it, unless the Congress by their Adjournment prevent its Return, in which Case it shall not be a Law.

Every Order, Resolution, or Vote to which the Concurrence of the Senate and House of Representatives may be necessary (except on a question of Adjournment) shall be presented to the President of the United States; and before the Same shall take Effect, shall be approved by him, or being disapproved by him, shall be repassed by two thirds of the Senate and House of Representatives, according to the

Rules and Limitations prescribed in the Case of a Bill.

Powers of Congress

Section 8. The Congress shall have Power to lay and collect Taxes, Duties, Imposts and Excises, to pay the Debts and provide for the common Defence and general Welfare of the United States; but all Duties, Imposts and Excises shall be uniform throughout the United States;

To Borrow Money on the credit of the United States;

To regulate Commerce with foreign Nations, and among the several States, and with the Indian Tribes;

To establish an uniform Rule of Naturalization, and uniform Laws on the subject of Bankruptcies throughout the United States;

To coin Money, regulate the Value thereof, and of foreign Coin, and fix the Standard of Weights and Measures;

To provide for the Punishment of counterfeiting the Securities and current Coin of the United States;

To establish Post Offices and post Roads;

To promote the Progress of Science and useful Arts, by securing for limited Times to Authors and Inventors the exclusive Right to their respective Writings and Discoveries;

To constitute Tribunals inferior to the supreme Court;

To define and punish Piracies and Felonies committed on the high Seas, and Offences against the Law of Nations;

To declare War, grant Letters of Marque and Reprisal, and make Rules concerning Captures on Land and Water;

To raise and support Armies, but no Appropriation of Money to that Use shall be for a longer Term than two years;

To provide and maintain a Navy;

To make Rules for the Government and Regulation of the land and naval Forces;

To provide for calling forth the Militia to execute the Laws of the Union, suppress Insurrections and repel Invasions;

To provide for organizing, arming, and disciplining, the Militia, and for governing such Part of them as may be employed in the Service of the United States, reserving to the States respectively, the Appointment of the Officers, and the Authority of training the Militia according to the discipline prescribed by Congress;

To exercise exclusive Legislation in all Cases whatsoever, over such District (not exceeding ten Miles square) as may, by Cession of particular States, and the Acceptance of Congress, become the Seat of the Government of the United States, and to exercise like Authority over all Places purchased by the Consent of the Legislature of the State in which the Same shall be for the Erection of Forts, Magazines, Arsenals, dockYards, and other needful Buildings;-And

To make all Laws which shall be necessary and proper for carrying into Execution for foregoing Powers, and all other Powers vested by this Constitution in the Government of the United States, or in any Department or Officer thereof.

Powers Denied to Congress

Section 9. The Migration or Importation of such Persons as any of the States now existing shall think proper to admit, shall not be prohibited by the Congress prior to the Year one thousand eight hundred and eight, but a Tax or duty may be imposed on such Importation, not exceeding ten dollars for each Person.

The Privilege of the Writ of Habeas Corpus shall not be suspended, unless when in Cases of Rebellion or Invasion the public Safety may require it.

No Bill of Attainder or ex post facto Law shall be passed.

(No Capitation, or other direct, Tax shall be laid, unless in Proportion to the Census or Enumeration herein before directed to be taken.)[6]

No Tax or Duty shall be laid on Articles exported from any State.

No Preference shall be given by any Regulation of Commerce or Revenue to the Ports of one State over those of another: nor shall Vessels bound to, or from, one State be obliged to enter, clear, or pay Duties in another.

No Money shall be drawn from

[6]Modified by the 16th Amendment

the Treasury, but in Consequence of Appropriations made by Law; and a regular Statement and Account of the Receipts and Expenditures of all public Money shall be published from time to time.

No Title of Nobility shall be granted by the United States: And no Person holding any Office of Profit or Trust under them, shall, without the Consent of the Congress, accept of any present, Emolument, Office, or Title, of any kind whatever, from any King, Prince, or foreign States.

Powers Denied to the States

Section 10. No States shall enter into any Treaty, Alliance, or Confederation; grant Letters of Marque and Reprisal; coin Money; emit Bills of Credit; make any Thing but gold and silver Coin a Tender in Payment of Debts; pass any Bill of Attainder, ex post facto Law, or Law impairing the Obligation of Contracts, or grant any Title of Nobility.

No State shall, without the Consent of the Congress, lay any Imposts or Duties on Imports or or Exports, except what may be absolutely necessary for executing its inspection Laws: and the net Produce of all Duties and Imposts, laid by any State on Imports or Exports, shall be for the Use of the Treasury of the United States; and all such Laws shall be subject to the Revision and Control of the Congress.

No State shall, without the Consent of Congress, lay any Duty of Tonnage, keep Troops, or Ships of War in time of Peace, enter into any Agreement or Compact with another State, or with a foreign Power, or engage in War, unless actually invaded, or in such imminent Danger as will not admit of delay.

ARTICLE II—THE EXECUTIVE ARTICLE

Nature and Scope of Presidential Power

Section 1. The executive Power shall be vested in a President of the United States of America. He shall hold his Office during the Term of four Years, and, together with the Vice President, chosen for the same term, be elected, as follows.

Each State shall appoint, in such Manner as the Legislature thereof may direct, a Number of Electors, Equal to the whole Number of Senators and Representatives to which the State may be entitled in the Congress: but no Senator or Representative, or Person holding an Office of Trust or Profit under the United States, shall be appointed an Elector.

[The Electors shall meet in their respective States, and vote by Ballot for two Persons, of whom one at least shall not be an Inhabitant of the same State with themselves. And they shall make a List of all the Persons voted for, and the Number of Votes for each; which List they shall sign and certify, and transmit sealed to the Seat of the Government of the United States, directed to the President of the Senate. The President of the Senate shall, in the Presence of the Senate and House of Representatives, open all the Certificates, and the Votes shall then be counted. The Person having the greatest Number of votes shall be the President, if such Number be a Majority of the whole Number of Electors appointed; and if there be more than one who have such Majority, and have an equal Number of Votes, then the House of Representatives shall immediately chuse by Ballot one of them for President: and if no Person have a Majority, then from the five highest on the List the said House shall in like Manner chuse the President. But in chusing the President, the Votes shall be taken by States, the Representation from each State having one Vote; A quorum for this purpose shall consist of a Member or Members from two thirds of the States, and a Majority of all the States shall be necessary to a Choice. In every Case, after the Choice of the President, the Person having the greatest Number of Votes of the Electors shall be the Vice President. But if there should remain two or more who have equal Votes, the Senate shall chuse from them by Ballot the Vice President.][7]

The Congress may determine the Time of chusing the Electors and the Day on which they shall give their Votes; which Day shall be the same throughout the United States.

No Person except a natural born

[7]Changed by the 12th and 20th Amendments

Citizen, or a Citizen of the United States, at the time of the Adoption of this Constitution, shall be eligible to the Office of President; neither shall any Person be eligible to that Office who shall not have attained the Age of thirty five Years, and been fourteen Years a Resident within the United States.

[In Case of the Removal of the President from Office, or of his Death, Resignation, or Inability to discharge the Powers and Duties of the said Office, the Same shall devolve on the Vice President, and the Congress may by Law provide for the Case of Removal, Death, Resignation, or Inability, both of the President and Vice President, declaring what Officer shall then act as President, and such Officer shall act accordingly, until the Disability be removed, or a President shall be elected.][8]

The President shall, at stated Times, receive for his Services a Compensation, which shall neither be increased nor diminished during the Period for which he shall have been elected, and he shall not receive within that Period any other Emolument from the United States, or any of them.

Before he enter the Execution of his Office, he shall take the following Oath or Affirmation:-"I do solemnly swear (or affirm) that I will faithfully execute the Office of President of the United States, and will to the best of my Ability, preserve, protect and defend the Constitution of the United States."

Powers and Duties of the President

Section 2. The President shall be Commander in Chief of the Army and Navy of the United States, and of the Militia of the several States, when called into the actual Service of the United States; he may require the Opinion, in writing, of the principal Officer in each of the executive Departments, upon any Subject relating to the Duties of their respective Offices, and he shall have power to grant Reprieves and Pardons for Offences against the United States, except in Cases of Impeachment.

He shall have Power, by and

with the Advice and Consent of the Senate, to make Treaties, provided two thirds of the Senators present concur; and he shall nominate, and by and with the Advice and Consent of the Senate, shall appoint Ambassadors, other public Ministers and Consuls, Judges of the supreme Court, and all other Officers of the United States, whose Appointments are not herein otherwise provided for, and which shall be established by Law; but the Congress may by Law vest the Appointment of such inferior Officers, as they think proper, in the President alone, in the Courts of Law, or in the Heads of Departments.

The President shall have Power to fill up all Vacancies that may happen during the Recess of the Senate, by granting Commissions which shall expire at the End of their next Session.

Section 3. He shall from time to time give to the Congress Information of the State of the Union, and recommend to their Consideration such Measures as he shall judge necessary and expedient; he may, on extraordinary Occasions, convene both Houses, or either of them, and in Case of Disagreement between them, with Respect to the Time of Adjournment, he may adjourn them to such Time as he shall think proper; he shall receive Ambassadors and other public ministers; he shall take Care that the Laws be faithfully executed, and shall Commission all the Officers of the United States.

Impeachment

Section 4. The President, Vice President and all civil Officers of the United States, shall be removed from Office on Impeachment for, and Conviction of, Treason, Bribery, or other High Crimes and Misdemeanors.

ARTICLE III—THE JUDICIAL ARTICLE

Judicial Power, Courts, Judges

Section 1. The judicial Power of the United States, shall be vested in one supreme Court, and in such inferior Courts as the Congress may from time to time ordain and establish. The Judges, both of the supreme and inferior Courts, shall hold their Offices

during good Behaviour, and shall, at stated Times, receive for their Services, a Compensation, which shall not be diminished during their Continuance in Office.

Jurisdiction

Section 2. The judicial Power shall extend to all Cases, in Law and Equity, arising under this Constitution, the Laws of the United States, and Treaties made, or which shall be made, under their Authority;-to all Cases affecting Ambassadors, other public Ministers and Consuls;-to all Cases of admiralty and maritime Jurisdiction;-to Controversies to which the United States shall be a Party;-to Controversies between two or more States; [between a State and Citizens of another State][9] between Citizens of different States;-between Citizens of the same State claiming Lands under Grants of different States, [and between a State or the Citizens thereof, and foreign States, Citizens or Subjects.][9]

In all Cases affecting Ambassadors, other public Ministers and Consuls, and those in which a State shall be Party, the supreme Court shall have original Jurisdiction. In all the other Cases before mentioned, the supreme Court shall have appellate Jurisdiction, both as to Law and Fact, with such Exceptions, and under such Regulations as the Congress shall make.

The Trial of all Crimes, except in Cases of Impeachment, shall be by Jury; and such Trial shall be held in the State where the said Crimes shall have been committed; but when not committed within any State, the Trial shall be at such Place or Places as the Congress may by Law have directed.

Treason

Section 3. Treason against the United States, shall consist only in levying War against them, or in adhering to their Enemies, giving them Aid and Comfort. No Person shall be convicted of Treason unless on the Testimony of two Witnesses to the same overt Act, or on Confession in open Court.

The Congress shall have Power to declare the Punishment of Treason, but no Attainder of Treason shall work

[8]Modified by the 25th Amendment

[9]Modified by the 11th Amendment

Corruption of Blood, or Forfeiture except during the Life of the Person attainted.

ARTICLE IV—INTERSTATE RELATIONS

Full Faith and Credit Clause

Section 1. Full Faith and Credit shall be given in each State to the public Acts, Records, and judicial Proceedings of every other State. And the Congress may by general Laws prescribe the Manner in which such Acts, Records and Proceedings shall be proved, and the Effect thereof.

Privileges and Immunities; Interstate Extradition

Section 2. The citizens of each State shall be entitled to all Privileges and Immunities of Citizens in the several States.

A Person charged in any State with Treason, Felony, or other Crime, who shall flee from Justice, and be found in another State, shall on Demand of the executive Authority of the State from which he fled, be delivered up, to be removed to the State having Jurisdiction of the Crime.

[No Person held to Service or Labour in one State, under the Laws thereof, escaping into another, shall, in Consequence of any Law or Regulation therein, be discharged from such Service or Labour, but shall be delivered up on Claim of the Party to whom such Service or labour may be due].[10]

Admission of States

Section 3. New States may be admitted by the Congress into this Union; but no new State shall be formed or erected within the Jurisdiction of any other State; nor any State be formed by the Junction of two or more States, or Parts of States, without the Consent of the Legislatures of the States concerned as well as of the Congress.

The Congress shall have Power to dispose of and make all needful Rules and Regulations respecting the Territory or other Property belonging to the United States; and nothing in this Constitution shall be so construed

[10]Repealed by the 13th Amendment

as to Prejudice any Claims of the United States, or of any particular State.

Republican Form of Government

Section 4. The United States shall guarantee to every State in this Union a Republican Form of Government, and shall protect each of them against Invasion; and on Application of the Legislature, or of the Executive (when the Legislature cannot be convened) against domestic Violence.

ARTICLE V—THE AMENDING POWER

The Congress, whenever two thirds of both Houses shall deem it necessary, shall propose Amendments to this Constitution, or, on the Application of the Legislatures of two thirds of the several States, shall call a Convention for proposing Amendments, which, in either Case, shall be valid to all Intents and Purposes, as Part of this Constitution, when ratified by the Legislatures of three fourths of the several States, or by Conventions in three fourths thereof as the one or the other Mode of Ratification may be proposed by the Congress; Provided that no Amendment which may be made prior to the Year One thousand eight hundred and eight shall in any Manner affect the first and fourth Clauses in the Ninth Section of the first Article; and that no State, without its Consent, shall be deprived of its equal Suffrage in the Senate.

ARTICLE VI—THE SUPREMACY ARTICLE

All Debts contracted and Engagements entered into, before the Adoption of this Constitution, shall be as valid against the United States under this Constitution, as under the Confederation.

This Constitution, and the Laws of the United States which shall be made in Pursuance thereof; and all Treaties made, or which shall be made, under the Authority of the United States, shall be the supreme Law of the Land; and the Judges in every State shall be bound thereby,

any Thing in the Constitution or Laws of any State to the Contrary notwithstanding.

The Senators and Representatives before mentioned, and the Members of the several State Legislatures, and all executive and judicial Officers, both of the United States and of the several States, shall be bound by Oath or Affirmation, to support this Constitution; but no religious Test shall ever be required as a Qualification to any Office or public Trust under the United States.

ARTICLE VII—RATIFICATION

The Ratification of the Conventions of nine States, shall be sufficient for the Establishment of this Constitution between the States so ratifying the Same.

Done in Convention by the Unanimous Consent of the States present the Seventeenth day in September in the Year of our Lord one thousand seven hundred and Eighty seven and of the Independence of the United States of America the Twelfth. In witness whereof We have hereunto subscribed our Names.

THE BILL OF RIGHTS

[The first 10 Amendments were ratified December 15, 1791, and form what is known as the Bill of Rights]

AMENDMENT 1—RELIGION, SPEECH, ASSEMBLY, AND POLITICS

Congress shall make no law respecting an establishment of religion, or prohibiting the free exercise thereof; or abridging the freedom of speech, or of the press; or the right of the people peaceably to assemble, and to petition the Government for a redress of grievances.

AMENDMENT 2—MILITIA AND THE RIGHT TO BEAR ARMS

A well regulated Militia, being necessary to the security of a free State, the right of the people to keep and bear Arms, shall not be infringed.

AMENDMENT 3— QUARTERING OF SOLDIERS

No Soldier shall, in time of peace, be quartered in any house, without the consent of the Owner, nor in time of war, but in a manner to be prescribed by law.

AMENDMENT 4—SEARCHES AND SEIZURES

The right of the people to be secure in their persons, houses, papers, and effects, against unreasonable searches and seizures, shall not be violated, and no Warrants shall issue, but upon probable cause, supported by Oath or affirmation, and particularly describing the place to be searched and the persons or things to be seized.

AMENDMENT 5—GRAND JURIES, SELF-INCRIMINATION, DOUBLE JEOPARDY, DUE PROCESS, AND EMINENT DOMAIN

No person shall be held to answer for a capital, or otherwise infamous crime, unless on a presentment or indictment of a Grand Jury, except in cases arising in the land or naval forces, or in the Militia, when in actual service in time of War or public danger, nor shall any person be subject for the same offence to be twice put in jeopardy of life or limb; nor shall be compelled in any criminal case to be a witness against himself, nor be deprived of life, liberty, or property, without due process of law; nor shall private property be taken for public use, without just compensation.

AMENDMENT 6—CRIMINAL COURT PROCEDURES

In all criminal prosecutions, the accused shall enjoy the right to a speedy and public trial, by an impartial jury of the State and district wherein the crime shall have been committed, which district shall have been previously ascertained by law, and to be informed of the nature and cause of the accusation; to be confronted with the witnesses against him; to have compul-

sory process for obtaining witnesses in his favor, and to have the Assistance of Counsel for his defence.

AMENDMENT 7—TRIAL BY JURY IN COMMON LAW CASES

In Suits at common law, where the value in controversy shall exceed twenty dollars, the right of trial by jury shall be preserved, and no fact tried by a jury, shall be otherwise reexamined in any Court of the United States, than according to the rules of the common law.

AMENDMENT 8—BAIL, CRUEL AND UNUSUAL PUNISHMENT

Excessive bail shall not be required, nor excessive fines imposed, nor cruel and unusual punishments inflicted.

AMENDMENT 9—RIGHTS RETAINED BY THE PEOPLE

The enumeration in the Constitution, of certain rights, shall not be construed to deny or disparage others retained by the people.

AMENDMENT 10—RESERVED POWERS OF THE STATES

The powers not delegated to the United States by the Constitution, nor prohibited by it to the States, are reserved to the States respectively, or to the people.

PRE-CIVIL WAR AMENDMENTS

AMENDMENT 11—SUITS AGAINST THE STATES

[Ratified February 7, 1795]

The Judicial power of the United States shall not be construed to extend to any suit in law or equity, commenced or prosecuted against one of the United States by Citizens of another State, or by Citizens or Subjects of any Foreign State.

AMENDMENT 12—ELECTION OF THE PRESIDENT

[Ratified July 27, 1804]

The Electors shall meet in their respective states and vote by ballot for President and Vice-President, one of whom, at least, shall not be an inhabitant of the same state with themselves; they shall name in their ballots the person voted for as President, and in distinct ballots the person voted for as Vice-President, and they shall make distinct lists of all persons voted for as President, and of all persons voted for as Vice-President, and of the number of votes for each, which lists they shall sign and certify, and transmit sealed to the seat of the government of the United States, directed to the President of the Senate;-The President of the Senate shall, in the presence of the Senate and House of Representatives, open all the certificates and the votes shall then be counted;-The person having the greatest number of votes for President, shall be the President, if such number be a majority of the whole number of Electors appointed; and if no person have such majority, then from the persons having the highest numbers not exceeding three on the list of those voted for as President, the House of Representatives shall choose immediately, by ballot, the President. But in choosing the President, the votes shall be taken by states, the representation from each state having one vote; a quorum for this purpose shall consist of a member or members from two-thirds of the states, and a majority of all the states shall be necessary to a choice. [And if the House of Representatives shall not choose a President whenever the right of the choice shall devolve upon them, before the fourth day of March next following, then the Vice-President shall act as President, as in the case of the death or other constitutional disability of the President].[11] The person having the greatest number of votes as Vice-President, shall be the Vice-President, if such number be a majority of the whole number of Electors appointed, and if no person have a majority, then from the two highest numbers on the list, the Senate shall choose the Vice-President; a quorum for the purpose shall

[11]Changed by the 20th Amendment

consist of two-thirds of the whole number of Senators, and a majority of the whole number shall be necessary to a choice. But no person constitutionally ineligible to the office of President shall be eligible to that of Vice-President of the United States.

CIVIL WAR AMENDMENTS

AMENDMENT 13— PROHIBITION OF SLAVERY

[Ratified December 6, 1865]

Section 1. Neither slavery nor involuntary servitude, except as a punishment for crime whereof the party shall have been duly convicted, shall exist within the United States, or any place subject to their jurisdiction.

Section 2. Congress shall have power to enforce this article by appropriate legislation.

AMENDMENT 14— CITIZENSHIP, DUE PROCESS, AND EQUAL PROTECTION OF THE LAWS

[Ratified July 9, 1868]

Section 1. All persons born or naturalized in the United States, and subject to the jurisdiction thereof, are citizens of the United States and of the State wherein they reside. No State shall make or enforce any law which shall abridge the privileges or immunities of citizens of the United States; nor shall any State deprive any person of life, liberty, or property, without due process of law; nor deny to any person within its jurisdiction the equal protection of the laws.

Section 2. Representatives shall be apportioned among the several States according to their respective numbers, counting the whole number of persons in each State, excluding Indians not taxed. But when the right to vote at any election for the choice of electors for President and Vice President of the United States, Representatives in Congress, the Executive and Judicial Officers of a State, or the members of the Legislature thereof, is denied to any of the male inhabitants of such state, being [twenty-one][12] years of age, and citizens of the United States, or in any way abridged, except for participation in rebellion, or other crime, the basis of representation therein shall be reduced in the proportion which the number of such male citizens shall bear to the whole number of male citizens twenty-one years of age in such State.

Section 3. No person shall be a Senator or Representative in Congress, or elector of President and Vice President, or hold any office, civil or military, under the United States, or under any State, who having previously taken an oath, as member of Congress, or as an officer of the United States, or as a member of any State legislature, or as an executive or judicial officer of any State, to support the Constitution of the United States, shall have engaged in insurrection or rebellion against the same, or given aid or comfort to the enemies thereof. But Congress may by a vote of two-thirds of each House, remove such disability.

Section 4. The validity of the public debt of the United States, authorized by law, including debts incurred for payment of pensions and bounties for services in suppressing insurrection or rebellion, shall not be questioned. But neither the United States nor any State shall assume or pay any debt or obligation incurred in aid of insurrection or rebellion against the United States, or any claim for the loss or emancipation of any slave; but all such debts, obligations and claims shall be held illegal and void.

Section 5. The Congress shall have power to enforce, by appropriate legislation, the provisions of this article.

AMENDMENT 15—THE RIGHT TO VOTE

[Ratified February 3, 1870]

Section 1. The right of citizens of the United States to vote shall not be denied or abridged by the United States or by any State on account of race, color, or previous condition of servitude.

Section 2. The Congress shall have power to enforce this article by appropriate legislation.

[12]Changed by the 26th Amendment

TWENTIETH-CENTURY AMENDMENTS

AMENDMENT 16—INCOME TAXES

[Ratified February 3, 1913]

The Congress shall have power to lay and collect taxes on incomes, from whatever source derived, without apportionment among the several States, and without regard to any census or enumeration.

AMENDMENT 17—DIRECT ELECTION OF SENATORS

[Ratified April 8, 1913]

The Senate of the United States shall be composed of two Senators from each State, elected by the people thereof for six years; and each Senator shall have one vote. The electors in each State shall have the qualifications requisite for electors of the most numerous branch of the State legislatures.

When vacancies happen in the representation of any State in the Senate, the executive authority of such State shall issue writs of election to fill such vacancies: *Provided,* That the legislature of any State may empower the executive thereof to make temporary appointments until the people fill the vacancies by election as the legislature may direct.

This amendment shall not be so construed as to affect the election or term of any Senator chosen before it becomes valid as part of the Constitution.

AMENDMENT 18— PROHIBITION

[Ratified January 16, 1919]

Section 1. After one year from the ratification of this article the manufacture, sale, or transportation of intoxicating liquors within, the importation thereof into, or the exportation thereof from the United States and all territory subject to the jurisdiction thereof for beverage purposes is hereby prohibited.

Section 2. The Congress and the several States shall have concurrent power to enforce this article by appropriate legislation.

Section 3. This article shall be inoperative unless it shall have been ratified as an amendment to the Constitution by the legislatures of the several States, as provided in the Constitution, within seven years from the date of the submission hereof to the States by the Congress.[13]

AMENDMENT 19—FOR WOMEN'S SUFFRAGE

[Ratified August 18, 1920]

The right of citizens of the United States to vote shall not be denied or abridged by the United States or by any State on account of sex. Congress shall have power to enforce this article by appropriate legislation.

AMENDMENT 20—THE LAME DUCK AMENDMENT

[Ratified January 23, 1933]

Section 1. The terms of the President and Vice President shall end at noon on the 20th day of January, and the terms of Senators and Representatives at noon on the 3d of January, of the years in which such terms would have ended if this article had not been ratified; and the terms of their successors shall then begin.
Section 2. The Congress shall assemble at least once in every year, and such meeting shall begin at noon on the 3d day of January, unless they shall by law appoint a different day.
Section 3. If, at the time fixed for the beginning of the term of the President, the President elect shall have died, the Vice President elect shall become President. If a President shall not have been chosen before the time fixed for the beginning of his term, or if the President elect shall have failed to qualify, then the Vice President elect shall act as President until a President shall have qualified; and the Congress may by law provide for the case wherein neither a President elect nor a Vice President elect shall have qualified, declaring who shall then act as President, or the manner in which one who is to act shall be selected, and such person shall act accordingly until

[13]Repealed by the 21st Amendment

a President or Vice President shall have qualified.
Section 4. The Congress may by law provide for the case of death of any of the persons from whom the House of Representatives may choose a President whenever the right of choice shall have devolved upon them, and for the case of the death of any of the persons from whom the Senate may choose a Vice President whenever the right of choice shall have devolved upon them.
Section 5. Sections 1 and 2 shall take effect on the 15th day of October following the ratification of this article.
Section 6. This article shall be inoperative unless it shall have been ratified as an amendment to the Constitution by the legislatures of three-fourths of the several States within seven years from the date of its submission.

AMENDMENT 21—REPEAL OF PROHIBITION

[Ratified December 5, 1933]

Section 1. The eighteenth article of amendment to the Constitution of the United States is hereby repealed.
Section 2. The transportation or importation into any State, Territory, or possession of the United States for delivery or use therein of intoxicating liquors, in violation of the laws thereof, is hereby prohibited.
Section 3. This article shall be inoperative unless it shall have been ratified by conventions in the several States, as provided in the Constitution, within seven years from the date of the submission hereof to the States by the Congress.

AMENDMENT 22—NUMBER OF PRESIDENTIAL TERMS

[Ratified February 27, 1951]

Section 1. No person shall be elected to the office of the President more than twice, and no person who has held the office of President, or acted as President for more two years of a term to which some other person was elected President shall be elected to the office of the President more than once. But this Article shall not apply to any person holding the office of President when this Article was proposed by the Con-

gress, and shall not prevent any person who may be holding the office of President, or acting as President, during the term within which this Article becomes operative from holding office of President, or acting as President, during the remainder of such term.
Section 2. This article shall be inoperative unless it shall have been ratified as an amendment to the Constitution by the legislatures of three-fourths of the several States within seven years from the date of its submission to the States by the Congress.

AMENDMENT 23— PRESIDENTIAL ELECTORS FOR THE DISTRICT OF COLUMBIA

[Ratified March 29, 1961]

Section 1. The District constituting the seat of Government of the United States shall appoint in such manner as the Congress may direct:
    A number of electors of President and Vice President equal to the whole number of Senators and Representatives in Congress to which the District would be entitled if it were a State, but in no event more than the least populous State; they shall be in addition to those appointed by the States, but they shall be considered, for the purposes of the election of President and Vice President, to be electors appointed by a State; and they shall meet in the District and perform such duties as provided by the twelfth article of amendment.
Section 2. The Congress shall have power to enforce this article by appropriate legislation.

AMENDMENT 24—THE ANTI-POLL TAX AMENDMENT

[Ratified January 23, 1964]

Section 1. The right of citizens of the United States to vote in any primary or other election for President or Vice President, for electors for President or Vice President, or for Senator or Representative in Congress, shall not be denied or abridged by the United States or any State by reason of failure to pay any poll tax or other tax.
Section 2. The Congress shall have power to enforce this article by appropriate legislation.

592

AMENDMENT 25— PRESIDENTIAL DISABILITY, VICE PRESIDENTIAL VACANCIES

[Ratified February 10, 1967]

Section 1. In case of the removal of the President from office or of his death or resignation, the Vice President shall become President.

Section 2. Whenever there is a vacancy in the office of the Vice President, the President shall nominate a Vice President, who shall take office upon confirmation by a majority vote of both Houses of Congress.

Section 3. Whenever the President transmits to the President pro tempore of the Senate and the Speaker of the House of Representatives his written declaration that he is unable to discharge the powers and duties of his office, and until he transmits to them a written declaration to the contrary, such powers and duties shall be discharged by the Vice President as Acting President.

Section 4. Whenever the Vice President and a majority of either the principal officers of the executive departments or of such other body as Congress may by law provide, transmit to the President pro tempore of the Senate and the Speaker of the House of Representatives their written declaration that the President is unable to discharge the powers and duties of his office, the Vice President shall immediately assume the powers and duties of the office as Acting President.

Thereafter, when the President transmits to the President pro tempore of the Senate and the Speaker of the House of Representatives his written declaration that no inability exists, he shall resume the powers and duties of his office unless the Vice President and a majority of either the principal officers of the executive department or of such other body as Congress may by law provide, transmit within four days to the President pro tempore of the Senate and the Speaker of the House of Representatives their written declaration that the President is unable to discharge the powers and duties of his office. Thereupon Congress shall decide the issue, assembling within forty-eight hours for that purpose if not in session. If the Congress, within twenty-one days after receipt of the latter written declaration, or, if Congress is not in session, within twenty-one days after Congress is required to assemble, determines by two-thirds vote of both Houses that the President is unable to discharge the powers and duties of his office, the Vice President shall continue to discharge the same as Acting President; otherwise, the President shall resume the powers and duties of his office.

AMENDMENT 26—EIGHTEEN-YEAR-OLD VOTE

[Ratified June 30, 1971]

Section 1. The right of citizens of the United States, who are eighteen years of age or older, to vote shall not be denied or abridged by the United States or by any State on account of age.

Section 2. The Congress shall have the power to enforce this article by appropriate legislation.

PROPOSED AMENDMENT— DISTRICT OF COLUMBIA FULL VOTING REPRESENTATION IN THE U.S. CONGRESS

[Proposed August 22, 1978]

Section 1. For purposes of representation in Congress, election of the President and Vice President and Article V of this Constitution, the District constituting the seat of government of the United States shall be treated as though it were a state.

Section 2. The exercise of the rights and powers conferred under this article shall be by the people of the District constituting the seat of government, and as shall be provided by the Congress.

Section 3. The twenty-third article of amendment to the Constitution is hereby repealed.

Section 4. This article shall be inoperative unless it shall have been ratified as an amendment to the Constitution by legislatures of three-fourths of the several states within seven years from the date of its submission.

Year	Candidates	Party	Popular Vote	Electoral Vote
1789	**George Washington**			69
	John Adams			34
	Others			35
1792	**George Washington**			132
	John Adams			77
	George Clinton			50
	Others			5
1796	**John Adams**	Federalist		71
	Thomas Jefferson	Democratic-Republican		68
	Thomas Pinckney	Federalist		59
	Aaron Burr	Democratic-Republican		30
	Others			48
1800	**Thomas Jefferson**	Democratic-Republican		73
	Aaron Burr	Democratic-Republican		73
	John Adams	Federalist		65
	Charles C. Pinckney	Federalist		64
1804	**Thomas Jefferson**	Democratic-Republican		162
	Charles C. Pinckney	Federalist		14
1808	**James Madison**	Democratic-Republican		122
	Charles C. Pinckney	Federalist		47
	George Clinton	Independent-Republican		6
1812	**James Madison**	Democratic-Republican		128
	DeWitt Clinton	Federalist		89
1816	**James Monroe**	Democratic-Republican		183
	Rufus King	Federalist		34
1820	**James Monroe**	Democratic-Republican		231
	John Quincy Adams	Independent-Republican		1
1824	**John Quincy Adams**	Democratic-Republican	108,740 (30.5%)	84
	Andrew Jackson	Democratic-Republican	153,544 (43.1%)	99
	Henry Clay	Democratic-Republican	47,136 (13.2%)	37
	William H. Crawford	Democratic-Republican	46,618 (13.1%)	41
1828	**Andrew Jackson**	Democratic	647,231 (56.0%)	178
	John Quincy Adams	National Republican	509,097 (44.0%)	83
1832	**Andrew Jackson**	Democratic	687,502 (55.0%)	219
	Henry Clay	National Republican	530,189 (42.4%)	49
	William Wirt	Anti-Masonic		7
	John Floyd	National Republican	33,108 (2.6%)	11
1836	**Martin Van Buren**	Democratic	761,549 (50.9%)	170
	William H. Harrison	Whig	549,567 (36.7%)	73
	Hugh L. White	Whig	145,396 (9.7%)	26
	Daniel Webster	Whig	41,287 (2.7%)	14
1840	**William H. Harrison**	Whig	1,275,017 (53.1%)	234
	Martin Van Buren	Democratic	1,128,702 (46.9%)	60
1844	**James K. Polk**	Democratic	1,337,243 (49.6%)	170
	Henry Clay	Whig	1,299,068 (48.1%)	105
	James G. Birney	Liberty	63,300 (2.3%)	
1848	**Zachary Taylor**	Whig	1,360,101 (47.4%)	163
	Lewis Cass	democratic	1,220,544 (42.5%)	127
	Martin Van Buren	Free Soil	291,163 (10.1%)	
1852	**Franklin Pierce**	Democratic	1,601,474 (50.9%)	254
	Winfield Scott	Whig	1,386,578 (44,1%)	42
1856	**James Buchanan**	Democratic	1,838,169 (45.4%)	174
	John C. Fremont	Republican	1,335,264 (33.0%)	114
	Millard Fillmore	American	874,534 (21.6%)	8
1860	**Abraham Lincoln**	Republican	1,865,593 (39.8%)	180
	Stephen A. Douglas	Democratic	1,381,713 (29.5%)	12
	John C. Breckinridge	Democratic	848,356 (18.1%)	72
	John Bell	Constitutional Union	592,906 (12.6%)	79
1864	**Abraham Lincoln**	Republican	2,206,938 (55.0%)	212
	George B. McClellan	Democratic	1,803,787 (45.0%)	21
1868	**Ulysses S. Grant**	Republican	3,013,421 (52.7%)	214
	Horatio Seymour	Democratic	2,706,829 (47.3%)	80
1872	**Ulysses S. Grant**	Republican	3,596,745 (55.6%)	286
	Horace Greeley	Democratic	2,843,446 (43.9%)	66
1876	**Rutherford B. Hayes**	Republican	4,036,571 (48.0%)	185
	Samuel J. Tilden	Democratic	4,284,020 (51.0%)	184
1880	**James A. Garfield**	Republican	4,449,053 (48.3%)	214
	Winfield S. Hancock	Democratic	4,442,035 (48.2%)	155
	James B. Weaver	Greenback-Labor	308,578 (3.4%)	

Year	Candidates	Party	Popular Vote	Electoral Vote
1884	**Grover Cleveland**	Democratic	4,874,986 (48.5%)	219
	James G. Blaine	Republican	4,851,931 (48.2%)	182
	Benjamin F. Butler	Greenback-Labor	175,370 (1.8%)	
1888	**Benjamin Harrison**	Republican	5,444,337 (47.8%)	233
	Grover Cleveland	Democratic	5,540,050 (48.6%)	168
1892	**Grover Cleveland**	Democratic	5,554,414 (46.0%)	277
	Benjamin Harrison	Republican	5,190,802 (43.0%)	145
	James B. Weaver	People's	1,027,329 (8.5%)	22
1896	**William McKinley**	Republican	7,035,638 (50.8%)	271
	William J. Bryan	Democratic; Populist	6,467,946 (46.7%)	176
1900	**William McKinley**	Republican	7,219,530 (51.7%)	292
	William J. Bryan	Democratic; Populist	6,356,734 (45.5%)	155
1904	**Theodore Roosevelt**	Republican	7,628,834 (56.4%)	336
	Alton B. Parker	Democratic	5,084,401 (37.6%)	140
	Eugene V. Debs	Socialist	402,460 (3.0%)	
1908	**William H. Taft**	Republican	7,679,006 (51.6%)	321
	William J. Bryan	Democratic	6,409,106 (43.1%)	162
	Eugene V. Debs	Socialist	420,820 (2.8%)	
1912	**Woodrow Wilson**	Democratic	6,286,820 (41.8%)	435
	Theodore Roosevelt	Progressive	4,126,020 (27.4%)	88
	William H. Taft	Republican	3,483,922 (23.2%)	8
	Eugene V. Debs	Socialist	897,011 (6.0%)	
1916	**Woodrow Wilson**	Democratic	9,129,606 (49.3%)	277
	Charles E. Hughes	Republican	8,538,211 (46.1%)	254
1920	**Warren G. Harding**	Republican	16,152,200 (61.0%)	404
	James M. Cox	Democratic	9,147,353 (34.6%)	127
	Eugene V. Debs	Socialist	919,799 (3.5%)	
1924	**Calvin Coolidge**	Republican	15,725,016 (54.1%)	382
	John W. Davis	Democratic	8,385,586 (28.8%)	136
	Robert M. La Follette	Progressive	4,822,856 (16.6%)	13
1928	**Herbert C. Hoover**	Republican	21,392,190 (58.2%)	444
	Alfred E. Smith	Democratic	15,016,443 (40.8%)	87
1932	**Franklin D. Roosevelt**	Democratic	22,809,638 (57.3%)	472
	Herbert C. Hoover	Republican	15,758,901 (39.6%)	59
	Norman Thomas	Socialist	881,951 (2.2%)	
1936	**Franklin D. Roosevelt**	Democratic	27,751,612 (60.7%)	523
	Alfred M. Landon	Republican	16,681,913 (36.4%)	8
	William Lemke	Union	891,858 (1.9%)	
1940	**Franklin D. Roosevelt**	Democratic	27,243,466 (54.7%)	449
	Wendell L. Willkie	Republican	22,304,755 (44.8%)	82
1944	**Franklin D. Roosevelt**	Democratic	25,602,505 (52.8%)	432
	Thomas E. Dewey	Republican	22,006,278 (44.5%)	99
1948	**Harry S Truman**	Democratic	24,105,812 (49.5%)	303
	Thomas E. Dewey	Republican	21,970,065 (45.1%)	189
	J. Strom Thurmond	States' Rights	1,169,063 (2.4%)	39
	Henry A. Wallace	Progressive	1,157,172 (2.4%)	
1952	**Dwight D. Eisenhower**	Republican	33,936,234 (55.2%)	442
	Adlai E. Stevenson	Democratic	27,314,992 (44.5%)	89
1956	**Dwight D. Eisenhower**	Republican	35,590,472 (57.4%)	457
	Adlai E. Stevenson	Democratic	26,022,752 (42.0%)	73
1960	**John F. Kennedy**	Democratic	34,227,096 (49.9%)	303
	Richard M. Nixon	Republican	34,108,546 (49.6%)	219
1964	**Lyndon B. Johnson**	Democratic	43,126,233 (61.1%)	486
	Barry M. Goldwater	Republican	27,174,989 (38.5%)	52
1968	**Richard M. Nixon**	Republican	31,783,783 (43.4%)	301
	Hubert H. Humphrey	Democratic	31,271,839 (42.7%)	191
	George C. Wallace	American Independent	9,899,557 (13.5%)	46
1972	**Richard M. Nixon**	Republican	46,632,189 (61.3%)	521
	George McGovern	Democratic	28,422,015 (37.3%)	17
1976	**Jimmy Carter**	Democratic	40,828,587 (50.1%)	297
	Gerald R. Ford	Republican	39,147,613 (48.0%)	240
1980	**Ronald Reagan**	Republican	42,951,145 (51.0%)	489
	Jimmy Carter	Democrat	34,663,037 (41.0%)	49
	John B. Anderson	Independent	5,551,551 (6.6%)	
1984	**Ronald Reagan**	Republican	53,428,357 (59%)	525
	Walter F. Mondale	Democrat	36,930,923 (41%)	13

GLOSSARY OF KEY TERMS

We have tried to write a highly readable book about American politics and government. We realize, however, that certain legal terms and political science phrases may not be familiar. To make such words more understandable, we have compiled this glossary. Words or phrases in the text in boldface color are defined here. We welcome suggestions for additions to the glossary.

Act III leaders. Typically, officeholders and elected politicians who are skilled in the art of bargaining and brokerage politics—of reconciling competing conceptions of the public interest and making the necessary compromises so that government can work. The notion of Act III implies that they are often dependent on other kinds of leaders to set the agenda and to mobilize public opinion and to begin the movements and even the early stages of coalition-building that precede law making and policy making.

Administrative law. Law relating to the authority and procedures of administrative agencies as well as the rules and regulations issued by the administrative agencies.

Admiralty and maritime law. Law derived from the general maritime law of nations, modified by Congress; applicable not only on the high seas but also on all navigable waterways in the United States.

Advisory Commission on Intergovernmental Relations. Created by Congress in 1959 to monitor the operation of the U.S. federal system and recommend improvements, ACIR is a permanent national bipartisan board composed of representatives from the executive and legislative branches of federal, state, and local government, and as well as members of the public.

Amendment. Addition to or deletions from a constitution or law.

Amicus curiae brief. Literally, a "friend of the court" brief, filed by an individual or organization with the permission of the court; provides arguments in addition to those presented by the immediate parties to the case.

Antifederalists. Persons opposed to more nationally centralized government in general, and to the 1787 Philadelphia Constitution in particular.

Antitrust policy. The several federal laws (of which the Sherman Antitrust Act of 1890 is most prominent), supplemented by state laws, that try to prevent one or a few business firms from dominating a particular market.

Appeasement. Term used to describe concessions made to a potential military opponent.

Articles of Confederation. The first constitution of the newly independent American states—drafted in 1777, ratified in 1781, and replaced by the present Constitution in 1789.

Assigned counsel system. Arrangement whereby attorneys are provided for persons accused of crime who are unable to hire their own lawyers. The judge assigns a member of the bar to provide counsel to a particular defendant.

Attentive public. Those who follow public affairs fairly carefully; who read newspapers and magazines to keep informed.

Autocracy. Government in which all power is concentrated in one person.

Bad tendency doctrine. Interpretation of the First Amendment that would permit legislatures to make illegal speech that can reasonably be said to have a tendency to cause people to engage in illegal action.

Baker v. Carr (1962). Supreme Court ruling that legislative apportionment could be challenged and reviewed by federal courts.

Bicameral legislature. Two-house legislature; form for forty-nine of the states, as well as for the U.S. Congress.

Bill of attainder. Legislative act inflicting punishment on either named individuals or on a readily identifiable group.

Binding arbitration. See *Compulsory and binding arbitration*.

Bipartisanship. Policy that emphasizes cooperation and a united front between the major political parties.

Bipolarity. Refers to a world in which two major superpowers dominate world politics.

Block grant. Broad grant of funds made by one level of government to another for specific program areas—for example, health programs or fighting crime.

Bureau. Generally, the largest subunit of a government department or agency.

Bureaucrat. Government official; normally, one who gains office by appointment rather than election.

Categorical formula grant. Grant of funds made by one level of government to another, to be used for specified purposes and in specified ways.

Caucus (local party). Meetings of party members in wards and towns to choose party officials and/or candidates for public office and to decide questions of policy (e.g., platforms).

Caucus (legislative) or conference. Meetings of the members of a party in a chamber of legislature to select the party leadership in that chamber and to take party positions on pending legislative issues.

Checks and balances. Constitutional grant of powers to each of the three branches of government that ensures a sufficient role in the actions of the others so that no one branch may dominate the others; they must work together if governmental business is to be performed.

City manager plan. Same as council manager plan. Cities hire a professional manager to administer city departments and agencies. The city manager reports directly to the city council in most cities.

Class action. Lawsuit brought by a person or group of persons in behalf of all persons similarly situated. The class may consist of a few persons or of thousands of persons. An example of a class action would be a suit by one black student denied admission to a school in behalf of all black students denied admission to that school.

Clear and present danger doctrine. Interpretation of the First Amendment first announced by Justice Holmes. This doctrine would not let laws that directly or indirectly restrict freedom of speech be applied unless the particular speech or article or book in question is made or published under such circumstances that there is a clear and present danger that the speech will lead to acts which the government may make illegal.

Closed shop. Labor arrangement in which an employer must hire only those people who are continuing union members.

Cloture (closure). Procedure for terminating debate (especially filibusters) in the U.S. Senate.

Coattail effect. Influence a popular or unpopular candidate has on the electoral success or failure of other candidates on the same party ticket.

Collective bargaining. Method whereby representatives of the union and the employer determine wages, hours, and other conditions of employment through direct negotiation.

Commission charter. Form of city government in which a group of commissioners (usually five) serve as the city council and act as heads of departments in the municipal administration.

Common law. Judge-made law developed as judges decided cases; part of the English and American systems of justice.

Compulsory and binding arbitration Process whereby a dispute between mangement and union is settled by an impartial third party. When the law dictates that a stalemated labor dispute must be turned over to an outside arbitrator, the process is called *compulsory arbitration*. When union and management are required by law to accept the decision of the arbitrator, it is called *binding arbitration*.

Concurrent powers. Powers the Constitution gives to both the national and state governments.

Confederation. Government created by nation-states when by compact they create a new government and delegate certain powers to it; but in contrast to a federation, they do not give it power to regulate the conduct of individuals directly.

Conference committee. Committee appointed by the presiding officers of each house of the legislature to adjust differences on a particular bill. The report of the conference committee back to each chamber cannot be amended but must be accepted or rejected as it stands.

Conglomerate. Firm that owns businesses in many unrelated industries.

Connecticut Compromise. Agreement by delegates to the Constitutional Convention to give each state two senators, regardless of population. This would offset the decision to allocate representatives in the House of Representatives among the states according to population. This compromise between the less and more populous states was the price required by the less populous states for agreeing to the new Constitution.

Consent decree. Order issued by either a regulatory commission or a court in which a party, while not conceding guilt, agrees to modify future behavior. It is often used by the Federal Trade Commission to require business firms to cease alleged anticompetitive or illegal practices.

Conservatism. Philosophical approach to the role of government that generally opposes governmental regulation of the economy and favors local or state governmental action over federal governmental action. Both Barry Goldwater in 1964 and Ronald Reagan in the 1980s were major proponents of this approach.

Conspiracy. Combination between two or more persons for the purpose of committing an unlawful act or an act which is lawful by itself but unlawful when done by the concerted action of two or more persons.

Constitution. The fundamental rules that determine how those who govern are selected, the procedures by which they operate, and the limits to their powers.

Constitutional government. Government in which there are recognized and regularly enforced limits on the powers of those who govern.

Constitutional home rule. State constitutional authorization for local governmental units to conduct their own affairs.

Constitutional law. In an American context, the authoritative interpretations of the meaning of the Constitution of the United States; such interpretations are chiefly found in the opinions of the U.S. Supreme Court.

Containment. Foreign policy strategy pursued to some extent by all post-World War II presidential administrations—but especially by the Truman administration. Its basic aim was to prevent the industrial or emerging powers of Europe or the Middle East from falling under the control of the Soviet Union.

Council-manager plan. Form of city government in which the city council hires a professional administrator to manage city affairs; also known as the city-manager plan.

Curtiss-Wright case (U.S. v. Curtiss-Wright, 1936). Supreme Court case upholding the sovereignty of the national government in foreign affairs and declaring the president to be its prime agent.

De facto segregation. Racial segregation that results from nongovernmental practices.

Defendant. In a civil action, the party defending himself or herself against charges brought by the plaintiff. In a criminal action, the person charged with the offense.

De jure segregation. Racial segregation that results from governmental actions; see also *Jim Crow laws*.

Delegate role. Concept used to describe the role of a member of a legislature. It holds that the legislator should represent the views of constituents even when the legislator may personally hold different views.

Demagogue. Leader who gains power by means of impassioned appeals to the prejudices and emotions of the masses.

Democracy. Government by the people, either directly or indirectly, with free and frequent elections.

Deregulation. Efforts to reduce or eliminate governmental controls, rules, or regulation of economic activity. Typically deregulation implies allowing more of a market or "hands off" approach as opposed to detailed federal rules or specifications to guide some industrial operations.

Detente. Relaxation of tension with another nation; conciliation or settlement with another nation.

Deviating election. Election in which the party out of power wins, but underlying voting patterns remain unchanged.

Direct primary. Election open to all members of the party, in which voters choose the persons who will be the party's nominees in the general election.

Direct transmission satellite. Communications satellite that transmits messages to individual receiving sets in homes or offices.

Discharge petition. Petition if signed by a majority of the members of the House of Representatives will pry a bill from committee and bring it to the floor for consideration.

Domino theory. Doctrine that assumes if some key nation or region falls into Communist control, a string of other nations will subsequently fall. President Eisenhower and later presidents used this theory to describe the situation in Indochina.

Double jeopardy. Trial for the *same* crime by the *same* government. Such a practice is forbidden by the Constitution.

Due process clauses. In the Fifth and Fourteenth amendments, these clauses state that the national (Fifth) and the state (Fourteenth) governments shall not deprive any person of life, liberty, or property without due process of law.

Economic Opportunity Act of 1964. Law that mapped out a many-faceted attack on American poverty.

Economies of scale. The assumption that larger size makes possible lower per unit costs and thus more efficiency.

Electoral college. In general, the procedures established by the Constitution for the election of the president and vice-president. More specifically, the gathering in each state of electors from that state who formally cast their ballots for their party's candidates for president and vice-president; largely a formality.

Eminent domain. Power of governments to take private property for public use. The Constitution requires governments to provide just compensation for property so taken.

Entitlement programs. Programs such as Social Security, Aid to Families with Dependent Children, Medicare, and unemployment insurance that qualified citizens are "entitled" to by definitions in national legislation.

Environmental impact statement. A statement required by federal law from all agencies for any project using federal funds that assesses the potential effect of a federal action on the environment.

Equal protection clause. Clause in the Fourteenth Amendment that forbids any state (by interpretation, the Fifth Amendment imposes the same limitation on the national government) to deny to any person within its jurisdiction the equal protection of the laws. This is the major constitutional restraint on the power of governments to discriminate against persons because of race, national origin, or sex.

Equal Rights Amendment (ERA). Constitutional amendment proposed by Congress in 1972, designed to guarantee women equality of rights under the law. Although ratified by thirty-five states, the additional three states necessary for ratification failed to approve it by the June 30, 1982, deadline. An ERA-type amendment is likely to be proposed again by Congress.

Equity. Judicial remedy used whenever suits for money damages do not provide adequate justice.

Establishment clause. Clause in the First Amendment which states that Congress (by interpretation the Fourteenth Amendment imposes the same limitation on state legislatures) shall make no law respecting an establishment of religion. It has been interpreted by the Supreme Court to forbid governmental support to any or all religions.

Ethnocentrism. Belief in the superiority of one's nation or ethnic society; an overriding concern or preoccupation with one's own group.

Excise tax. Consumer tax on a specific kind of merchandise, such as tobacco.

Executive agreement. International agreement made by a president that has the force of a treaty. It does not need the approval of the Senate.

Executive Office of the President. Cluster of staff agencies created by the Reorganization Act of 1939 to help the president. Currently the Executive Office includes an Office of Management and Budget, the Council of Economic Advisers, the National Security Council, and a number of specialized offices.

Executive privilege. The claim by presidents that they have the discretion to decide that the national interest will be better served if certain information in the custody of the executive departments is withheld from the public, including the courts and Congress. The Supreme Court in *United States* v. *Nixon* ruled that while presidents are entitled to the privilege, it is not unlimited, and its extent is subject to judicial determination.

Ex post facto law. Retroactive criminal law.

Express powers. Powers specifically granted to one of the branches of the national government by the Constitution.

Extradition. Legal process whereby an alleged criminal offender is surrendered by the officials of one state to officials of the state where the crime is alleged to have been committed.

Faction. Organized group of politically active persons, usually less than a majority, seeking to realize group goals in competition with other groups.

Fairness doctrine. Doctrine written into law and interpreted by the Federal Communications Commission that imposes on radio and television licensees an obligation to ensure that differing viewpoints are presented about controversial issues or persons.

Federal Reserve System. The private-public banking regulatory system, created by Congress in 1913, to establish banking practices and regulate currency in circulation and the amount of credit available. Comprised of twelve regional banks, its major responsibilities are supervised by a seven-member presidentially appointed Federal Reserve Board of Governors in Washington, D.C.

Federal system. Governmental arrangement whereby power is divided by a constitution between a national government and constituent governments, called states in the U.S., with the national and the constitutent governments both exercising direct authority over individuals.

Federalism. Same as *Federal system*.

The Federalist. Series of essays favoring the new Constitution, written by Alexander Hamilton, John Jay, and James Madison in 1787 and 1788, during the debate over ratification.

Federalists. Persons who supported the Constitution before its ratification in 1787–1788. After ratification a Federalist party developed under the leadership of Alexander Hamilton, Washington's first secretary of the treasury. Federalists like John Adams and John Marshall generally favored a strong central government and a fiscal policy of assuming state debts and establishing a national bank.

Fighting words. Words that by their very nature inflict injury upon those to whom they are addressed.

Filibuster. Holding the floor of the U.S. Senate to delay proceedings and thereby prevent a vote on a controversial issue.

Floating debt. Short-term government loans, in the form of bank notes or tax-anticipation warrants, that are paid out of current revenues.

Four Freedoms. American goals proclaimed by Franklin D. Roosevelt in his annual message to Congress, January 6, 1941: freedom of speech and expression, freedom of worship, freedom from want, and freedom from fear.

Fourth World. Those nations that are among the poorest in the world and whose per capita standard of living are among the lowest of any nations.

Franchise. The right to vote.

Full faith and credit. Clause in the Constitution requiring each state to recognize the civil judgments rendered by the courts of the other states.

General property tax. Tax levied by local (and some state) governments on real or personal, tangible property—the major portion of which is on the estimated value of one's home and land.

Gerrymandering. Drawing an election district in such a way that one party of group has a distinct advantage; the strategy is to provide a close but safe margin in numerous districts while concentrating (and hence wasting) the opposition's vote in a few districts.

Government corporation. Cross between a business corporation and a government agency, created to secure greater freedom of action for a particular program.

Grand jury. Twelve to twenty-three persons who in private hear evidence presented by the government to determine whether persons shall be required to stand trial.

Gross national product (GNP). The monetary value of all goods and services produced in the nation in a given year.

Habeas corpus. See *Writ of habeas corpus*.

Hatch Act. Federal statute barring federal employees from active participation in certain kinds of politics and protecting them from being fired on partisan grounds.

Ideology. Interrelated or integrated set of attitudes and beliefs about political values and the role of power and government.

Ideologue. Person who has a relatively fixed and highly integrated set of attitudes and beliefs about the role of government as it affects individuals and public policy.

Immunity. Exemption from prosecution based on evidence secured as the result of testimony compelled by a government agency.

Implied limitations. Doctrine regarding constitutional construction of state constitutions. It holds that powers not granted to municipal corporations are denied to such corporations.

Implied powers. Powers given to Congress by the Constitution, allowing Congress to do whatever is necessary and proper in order to carry out one of the express powers or any combination of them.

Impoundment. Presidential refusal to allow an agency to spend funds authorized and appropriated by Congress.

Incrementalism. Theory of public policy and public administration that deemphasizes comprehensiveness and insists that administrative decisions are and should be made piecemeal.

Independent agency. Sometimes used interchangeably with "independent regulatory agency" to refer to an agency that is not part of the legislative, executive, or judicial branch, such as the Interstate Commerce Commission. The term also refers to an agency that is not part of a cabinet department, such as the Veterans Administration.

Indiana ballot. See *Party column ballot*.

Inflation. Rise in the general level of prices, which is the same thing as a fall in the value of money.

Inherent powers. Those powers of the national government in the field of foreign affairs that the Supreme Court has declared do not depend upon constitutional grants but rather grow out of the very existence of the national government.

Initiative petition. Procedure whereby a certain number of voters may, by petition, propose a law and get it submitted to the people for a vote. Initiative may be direct (the proposed law is voted on directly by the people) or indirect (the proposal is submitted first to the legislature and then to the people, if the legislature rejects it).

Intangible property. Wealth indicated by cash, stocks, bonds, savings accounts, partnerships, money funds, and so on, in contrast to wealth in the form of physical objects such as land, houses, automobiles, and jewels.

Interest groups. Collections of persons who share some common interest or attitude, who interact with one another directly or indirectly, and who ordinarily make demands on other groups.

Interlocking directorate. Situation where the same persons serve as members of the board of directors of competing companies.

Interstate compacts. Agreements among the states. The Constitution requires that most such agreements be approved by Congress.

Isolationism. The attitude (somewhat in fashion in the 1930s) that the U.S. should retreat from world affairs and curb the tendency to intervene abroad—especially in military conflicts.

Item veto. Authority of the executive (usually the governor of a state) to veto parts of a legislative bill without having to veto the entire bill. Presidents do not have the power of the item veto.

Jim Crow laws. Laws that require public facilities and places of public accommodation, including those privately owned and operated, to be segregated by race.

Joint committee. Committee composed of members of both houses of a legislature; such committees are intended to speed legislative action.

Judicial activism. Variously defined, one of which is the belief that judges cannot decide cases merely by applying the literal words of the Constitution or by discerning the intention of the framers, but they must and should openly recognize that judicial decision making is choosing among conflicting values. Judges should so interpret the Constitution as to keep it reflecting the current values of the American people. Judicial activism is used in contrast with judicial restraint.

Judicial restraint. Variously defined, one of which is the belief that judges in deciding cases should declare unconstitutional only those legislative actions and executive actions that clearly violate the words of the Constitution or the intent of the framers, and that constitutional changes should be left to the formal amendatory process.

Judicial review. The authority, spelled out by Chief Justice Marshall in *Marbury* v. *Madison* (1803), of judges when deciding cases to examine statutes and the action of executive officials in order to determine their validity, according to the judges' interpretation of the Constitution.

Jus sanguinis. Citizenship acquired through citizenship of parents.

Jus soli. Citizenship acquired through place of birth.

Keynes, John Maynard. English economist whose views have dominated economic thinking in recent decades.

Labor injunction. Court order forbidding specific individuals or groups from performing certain acts, such as striking, that the court considers harmful to the rights and property of others.

Lame duck. Official serving out a term of office after defeat for reelection and before the inauguration of a successor.

Legislative home rule. Power given by the legislature to local governments that eliminates the need for local governments to go back to the legislature for additional grants of power. However, state law still takes precedence over local ordinances, and powers given to the local government by the legislature may be rescinded.

Legislative veto. Until it was declared unconstitutional by the Supreme Court in 1983, it was a provision in a law reserving to Congress, or to a chamber or committee of Congress, the power to reject by majority vote an act or regulation of a department or agency of the national government.

Libel. Written defamation of another person. Especially in the case of public officials and public figures, the constitutional tests designed to restrict libel actions are very rigid.

Liberalism. Philosophical approach to the role of government that generally favors governmental action, especially to help the underdog and achieve equal opportunity for all.

Libertarianism. Philosophical approach to the role of government that favors as limited a government as possible and believes in free-market economics and a noninterventionist foreign policy.

Lobby. To conduct activities aimed at influencing public officials and the policies they enact. This is, of course, part of the citizen's right to petition the government.

Lobbyist. Person who acts for an organized interest group or association or corporation in seeking to influence policy decisions and positions in the executive and—especially—legislative branches.

Long ballot. Ballot that came into general use in the late 1820s; based on the belief that voters should elect all, or nearly all, the people who governed them. It is criticized as being unwieldy and confusing because it contains too many offices and candidates.

Maintaining election. Election that shows a continuation of a pattern of partisan support.

Majority floor leader. Legislative position held by an important party member selected by the majority party in caucus or conference. The majority floor leader helps frame party strategy and tries to keep the membership in line. In the U.S. Senate the majority leader (in consultation with the minority floor leader) determines the agenda and has strong influence in committee selection.

Marshall Plan. The American program to assist European economic recovery following World War II.

Massachusetts ballot. See *Office group ballot*.

Mass public. The general public, including a large segment of the population that is often uninformed about the details of political controversy and policy debates.

Mayor-council charter. The oldest and most common form of city government, consisting of either a weak mayor and city council or a strong mayor and council.

McCulloch v. Maryland (1819). Celebrated Supreme Court decision that established the doctrine of national supremacy and the principle that the implied powers of the national government are to be generously interpreted.

Messianic spirit. Belief in the future deliverance or saving of a people or a nation; the notion that a people are select, singled out for a special destiny.

Metropolis. City regarded as the center or central community of a particular area; generally an important city with a population of over 500,000.

Midterm party conference. National meeting, presently of Democratic party members, held halfway through a presidential term, designed to activate the party and bring its platform up to date.

Military-industrial complex. Alleged alliance between top military and industrial leaders, who have a common interest in arms production and utilization.

Minority floor leader. Party leader in each house of a legislature, elected by the minority party as spokesperson for the opposition.

Misdemeanor. Offense of lesser gravity than a felony, for which punishment may be a fine or imprisonment for a relatively brief time, usually less than a year.

Missouri Plan. System for the selection of judges which combines features of the appointive and elective methods. The governor makes an initial appointment from a list of persons—usually three—presented by a panel of lawyers and laypersons, the panel usually being appointed by the chief judge of the state court of last resort. After the judge has served for a year, the electorate is asked at the next general election whether or not the judge should be retained in office. If a majority vote yes, the judge serves the rest of the term. At the end of the term, if a judge wishes to serve again, his or her name is once again presented to the electorate.

Monetary policy. National government policy that seeks to change the interest, credit, or stock market rates. The Federal Reserve Board, for example, uses "tight money" policies to restrain and prolong boom periods and to fight inflation. "Loose money" policies—making credit and money more freely—are used to fight recessions or a depression.

Multipolar. Refers to a world in which many nations share in shaping world political developments and enjoy an influence in world affairs.

National Security Council. Planning and advisory board that confers with the president on matters relating to national security. Permanent members include the president, vice-president, secretary of state, secretary of defense, and the chairman of the joint chiefs of staff.

National supremacy. Constitutional doctrine that whenever there is a conflict between the constitutionally authorized actions of the national government and those of a state or local government, the actions of the national government take priority.

Naturalization. Process by which persons acquire citizenship in a country other than the nation of their birth.

Natural monopoly. Condition that exists when it would be inefficient to have competition in a particular industry, as in the case of a power company.

Necessary and proper clause. Clause of the Constitution setting forth the implied powers of Congress. It states that Congress, in addition to its enumerated powers, has the power to make all laws necessary and proper for carrying out all powers vested by the Constitution in the national government.

New Jersey Plan. Plan presented by Paterson of New Jersey at the Constitutional Convention as a counterproposal to the Virginia Plan. The New Jersey Plan proposed only modifications in the Articles of Confederation and provided for a confederation built around powerful state governments.

Nixon Doctrine. Policy suggested by President Nixon in the early 1970s that would have the U.S. come to the assistance of allies and friendly nations, but only if they themselves would do the main fighting.

Nonproliferation Treaty. International agreement under which nuclear powers pledge not to distribute nuclear devices to nonnuclear powers.

Obscenity. Work that taken as a whole appeals to a prurient interest in sex by depicting sexual conduct as specifically defined by legislation or judicial interpretation in a patently offensive way, and that lacks serious literary, artistic, political, or scientific value.

Office group ballot. Method of voting in which all candidates are listed under the office for which they are running; sometimes called the Massachusetts ballot or the office-block ballot.

Office of Management and Budget (OMB). Presidential staff agency that serves as a clearinghouse for budgetary requests and management improvements.

Oligarchy. Government controlled by a small segment of the people, who are chosen on the basis of wealth or power.

Oligopoly. Situation where a few firms dominate an industry.

Ombudsman. Office in Sweden and elsewhere that handles citizen complaints against the government.

On appeal. Order issued by the Supreme Court to review those decisions of the lower courts, federal and state, which Congress has stipulated the Supreme Court is required to review.

Opinion maker. Person who influences how the general public views policy problems—for example, elected officials, editors, writers, and teachers.

Override. Congress may override a presidential veto (a veto by the president of legislation) by means of a two-thirds vote in both chambers of the Congress. Veto overrides are rare—successful only about 3 percent of the time.

Palko Test. In the case of *Palko* v. *Connecticut* (1937), the Supreme Court established a test to determine which provisions of the Bill of Rights should be "incorporated" into the Fourteenth Amendment as a limitation on state and local governments: namely, those provisions that relate to rights that are so important that neither "liberty nor justice would exist if they were sacrificed."

Party column ballot. Method of voting in which all candidates are listed under their party designation, making it easy for the voter to cast votes for all the candidates of one party; sometimes called the Indiana ballot.

Party convention. See *Convention.*

Party primary. Election for choosing party nominees; open to members and supporters of the party making the nomination.

Party realignment. Fundamental change in the economic, racial, and social, sectional, and other electoral foundations of a party as it seeks to maintain its competitive position in elections.

Patronage. Dispensing government jobs to persons who belong to the winning political party.

Personal property. As opposed to real estate—houses and land—this refers to household goods, jewelery, stocks, and bonds.

Petit jury. The ordinary jury for the trial of a civil or criminal action; so called to distinguish it from the grand jury.

Plaintiff. Party who brings a civil action or sues to obtain a legal remedy from a court for injury to his or her rights.

Plea bargaining. Negotiations between prosecutor and defendant aimed at getting the defendant to plead guilty in return for prosecutor's agreement to reduce the seriousness of the crime for which the defendant will be convicted.

Pluralistic power structure. The notion that while some people do have more influence than others, that influence is shared among many people and tends to be limited to particular issues and policy areas.

Pocket veto. Special veto power exercised by a chief executive after a legislative body has adjourned. Bills that a chief executive refuses to sign at this time do not become law; it is as if the governor or the president "put the bill in his or her pocket," and the bill thus dies.

Police powers. Powers of a government to regulate persons and property in order to promote the public health, welfare, and safety. The states, but not the national government, in the United States have such general police power.

Political Action Committee (PAC). The political arms of organized interests. PACs have become major agencies through which to finance congressional campaigns.

Political machine. Organized subgroup within a party, consisting of a political boss and supporting ward and precinct workers who get out the vote and perform a variety of "services" for local constituents between elections.

Political questions. Constitutional questions that judges refuse to answer because to do so would involve judicial encroachment upon the authority of Congress or the president. For example: Congress determines if a sufficient number of states have ratified a constitutional amendment within a reasonable time; Congress determines which states have the required republican form of government; and the president determines which foreign governments are to be recognized by the United States. Since the Supreme Court determines which constitutional questions are political and which are justiciable, this limitation on the authority of the courts is self-defined.

Political socialization. Processes by which we develop our political attitudes, values, and behavior.

Poll tax. Payment by a person; formerly required in some states as a condition for voting.

Populists. Movement and political party of the 1880s and 1890s. Its geographical base was rural-Midwest, South, and Southwest especially. Waging "reformist" efforts against the banks, railroads, and other establishments, it raised issues that influenced the Progressive movement and the Democratic Party after 1892.

Power elite. Term originally used by the sociologist C. Wright Mills to describe the small group of people who he believed rule the country because of their socioeconomic status.

Preferred-position doctrine. Interpretation of the First Amendment which holds that no law restricting expression is constitutional unless the government can demonstrate convincingly to a court that the law is absolutely necessary to prevent serious injury to the public well-being.

Presidential primaries. Statewide primaries in which rank-and-file party members choose the delegates to the national party convention and may indicate their choice as to whom the party shall nominate for president.

President pro tempore. Officer of the U.S. Senate chosen from the ranks—usually the senior member of the majority party; serves as president of the Senate in the absence of the vice-president.

Principle democrats. Persons more concerned with the goals and values of "government by the people" than with the procedures used to reach those goals.

Prior restraint. Restraint imposed prior to a speech being made, a newspaper being published, or a motion picture being shown. The restraint may be of various kinds—for example, a requirement that a license be granted or that the approval of a censorship board be given.

Pro bono work. The work lawyers (or other professionals) do to serve the public good and for which they receive no fees—or decline fees.

Procedural due process. Constitutional requirement that governments proceed by proper means.

Process democrats. Persons who believe if proper procedures are followed in running the government, the more likelihood there is that sound and democratic policy will result. (All democrats believe in both good processes and principles—they differ over the balance between the two.)

Program oversight. Process of monitoring and evaluating the details of how a program is being, or has been, carried out.

Progressives. "Good government" movement in the first two decades of this century—advocating measures that would open up the system and weaken party bosses. Its adherents favored nonpartisan elections, participatory primaries, and direct elections of senators. The Progressive Party, especially active from 1912 through the mid-1920s, emerged as a visible part of this movement.

Progressive tax. A tax where upper-income citizens pay a higher proportion of their incomes in tax revenues than is paid by lower-income citizens.

Project grant. Federal funds given for specified purposes and based on the merits of applications.

Public defender. Public officer whose job is to provide legal assistance to those persons accused of crimes who are unable to hire their own attorney.

Public opinion. Cluster of views and attitudes held by people on a significant issue. Since any complex society has many groups, it is more precise to talk about publics, subpublics, and public opinions than about a single public opinion.

Public policy. The substance of what government does—more generally, the intentions of a government and the subsequent follow-up actions that seek to implement laws and other decisions of governmental bodies.

Public/special authority. Special government agencies frequently found in metropolitan areas, set up to undertake highly specialized functions such as overseeing mass transit, an interstate harbor complex, or a regional airport.

Quasi-legislative and quasi-judicial. Phrase coined by the Supreme Court to permit noncourt and nonlegislative bodies to decide disputes and make rules; however, decisions must be subject to court review and rules must be within the general guidelines established by the legislature.

Quota sampling. Accounting for the variables in the population and assigning a quota for each variable to produce a representative cross-section.

Random sampling. Creating a representative sample through random selection; for example, shuffling housing tracts and interviewing individuals in every fifth, tenth, or fifteenth house.

Rational basis test. Test used to measure laws for compliance with the requirements of the equal protection clause. This test is applied to laws that do *not* affect a suspect classification of fundamental rights. Such laws need only a rational basis in fact.

Realigning election. Election in which the basic partisan commitments of a significant segment of the electorate change, as in 1932.

Real property. Land and buildings.

Reapportionment. Redrawing of legislative district lines to recognize the existing population distribution.

Recall. Election held to determine whether or not an official should be removed from office before the end of his or her term. A certain number of voters must petition for the holding of a recall election.

Redistributive policy. Governmental policy that seeks to use tax revenues in such a way as to help those who have less. In effect, tax monies from the upper and middle classes are channeled into programs that assist lower income or truly needy by redistributing some of society's wealth.

Red tape. Procedures and forms used in carrying out policies and governmental functions; a term often used to express dissatisfaction with especially slow and formal rules and procedures.

Reduction veto. The power of a governor in a few states to reduce a particular money-providing measure approved by the state legislature.

Referendum. Practice of submitting to popular vote measures passed by the legislature or proposed by initiative. Use of the referendum may be required or optional.

Registration. Process of appearing before an official during a certain period of time before an election, to establish eligibility to vote.

Regressive tax. Tax that weighs most heavily on those least able to pay.

Regulation. Governmental order having the force of law and designed to control or govern the behavior of a business, union, or of similar organizations and individuals.

Regulatory board or **commission.** Agency responsible for enforcing particular statutes; generally these agencies have quasi-legislative and quasi-judicial functions as well as executive powers.

Representative democracy. See *Republic*.

Republic. Form of government that derives its powers directly or indirectly from the people; those chosen to govern are accountable, directly or indirectly, to those whom they govern. In contrast to a direct democracy, where the people make rules directly, in a republic the people select representatives who make the rules.

Republican form of government. See *Republic*.

Revenue sharing. Program where federal funds are provided to state and local governments to be spent largely at the discretion of the receiving governments.

Right to work law. Provision in state laws that prohibits arrangements between a union and an employer requiring membership in a union as a condition for getting or keeping a job.

Runoff election. Election held when no candidate receives a required percentage of the vote in an earlier election; usually held between the two candidates who received the most votes in the first election.

Safe seat. Electoral office, usually in legislature, where the party or the incumbent is so strong that reelection is almost taken for granted.

Sales tax. General tax on sales transactions.

Salience. Significance of an event or issue.

SALT. Strategic arms limitation talks between the U.S. and Soviet governments to limit both defensive and offensive weapons systems.

Sampling error. The degree to which a sample is distorted and does not represent the "polling universe" to be measured.

Secondary boycott. Concerted effort by a union involved in a dispute with an employer to place pressure on a third party, who—in response to such pressure—might put pressure on the workers' employer. Such boycotts are forbidden by the 1947 Taft-Hartley Act.

Sedition. Attempting to overthrow the government by force or to interrupt its activities by violence.

Seditious speech. Advocating the forceful overthrow of the government. The Supreme Court has ruled that Congress may make seditious speech a crime, but no one may be punished for seditious speech unless it can be shown that he or she specifically urged people to engage in concrete acts of violence.

Senatorial courtesy. Custom in the U.S. Senate of (1) referring the names of prospective appointees, especially federal judges, to senators from the states in which the appointees reside and (2) withdrawing any nominees these senators deem objectionable, especially if senators are from the same party as the nominating president.

Separation of powers. Constitutional division of power among legislative, executive, and judicial branches: The legislative branch is assigned the power to make laws; the executive is charged with the power to apply the laws; and the judiciary receives the power to interpret laws.

Severance tax. Tax on the privilege of "severing" natural resources such as coal, oil, and timber, charged to the companies doing the extracting or severing.

Shays's Rebellion. Rural rebellion of 1786–87 in western Massachusetts protesting mortgage foreclosures; led by Daniel Shays, it brought conservative support for a stronger national government.

Shield law. Law establishing a legal right for reporters and other representatives of the media under certain circumstances to refuse to respond to orders of legislative committees or court subpoenas to reveal sources of information.

Socialism. Philosophical approach to the role of government that favors national planning and public ownership of business.

Social stratification. Sociological theory suggesting that the upper class, or the wealthy, wield extensive influence over the decisions and policies made by governments at all levels.

Speaker. Presiding officer in the House of Representatives, formally elected by the House but actually selected by the majority party. The Speaker's powers include referring legislation to committees, making appointments to the House Rules Committee, recognizing members who wish to speak, ruling on questions of parliamentary procedure, and appointing special conference committees.

603

Stagflation. Combination of sustained high inflation and high unemployment.

Standard Metropolitan Statistical Area (SMSA). A central city—or twin cities—of at least 50,000 people, along with the surrounding counties that are economically and socially dependent upon the city.

Stare decisis. The rule of precedent, whereby a rule of law contained in a judicial decision is commonly viewed as binding on judges whenever the same question is presented.

Statism. Belief in the rights of the state over those of the individual—the opposite of the American tradition that the individual is exalted above the state.

Statutory law. Law enacted by a legislature.

Strong mayor–council. Form of local government in which the public directly elects the mayor as well as the city council. However, the mayor appoints the department heads with the approval of the council, and in effect serves as the chief executive officer for the city and its administration.

Subsidy. Governmental support that can take many forms—reduction of taxes, government loans, special protections, outright cash or credit assistance—designed to encourage a particular type of private sector action.

Substantive due process. Constitutional requirement that governments act reasonably and that the substance of the laws themselves be reasonable.

Subpoena. Court order to present oneself before an official agency. A subpoena duces tecum is a court order to present specific documents.

Suburbs. Residential areas or communities in the outlying regions around a city.

Sunset process. Legislative review process that calls for the termination of a program after a certain number of years, often six or seven, unless it is carefully examined, certified to be doing what it was intended to do, and repassed by the legislature. Many states have adopted this practice. The word comes from the expression that "the sun should set" on programs that have outlived their usefulness.

Sunshine law. Law requiring governmental agencies, under certain circumstances and usually subject to certain exceptions, to operate in public.

Supply side economics. Economic strategy of stimulating production through tax cuts or reduced governmental regulation.

Suspect classifications. Racial or national origin classifications created by law and subject to careful judicial scrutiny; likely to be declared unconstitutional unless they can be justified by overwhelmingly desirable state purposes that can be achieved in no other way.

Taft-Hartley Act. Passed by Congress in 1947, this act elaborates the terms of labor-management bargaining, the conditions under which strikes can occur, and related aspects of union organization.

Tariff. Tax levied on imports in order to help protect a nation's industries, labor, or farmers from foreign competition. It can also be used merely to raise additional revenue.

Tax expenditure. Loss of tax revenue due to provisions of the federal tax laws that allow a special exclusion, exemption, or deduction or that provide a special credit, preferential rate of tax, or deferral of tax liability.

Third World. Those nations that are relatively poor but that are seeking to modernize and develop.

Three-Fifths Compromise. North-South agreement at the Constitutional Convention of 1787 to count only three-fifths of the slave population in determining representation in the House of Representatives.

Ticket splitting. Practice of voting for candidates at the ballot box with little or no regard to their parties, with the result that the voter may vote for a Democrat for governor and a Republican for Congress, or vice versa.

Transactional leader. A leader who deals in the short term and generally for self-interest. One who engages in exchanges and bargains as in a quid pro quo fashion.

Transforming leader. A leader who helps liberate followers so they can achieve higher aspirations and longer range goals. A leader who so engages with followers as to heighten their political awareness and their own abilities for leadership.

Treason. Carefully defined by the Constitution so that treason against the United States consists only of levying war against the United States, adhering to its enemies, or giving the latter aid and comfort. Moreover, no person can be convicted of treason unless the accused confesses in open court or unless there are two witnesses who will testify in court that they saw the acts of treason being committed.

Truman Doctrine. Policy, sponsored by President Harry Truman in 1947, aimed at halting Communist expansion in southeastern Europe. It called for American support and funds for all free peoples so that they might resist being taken over by outside forces of repression.

Trustee role. Concept used to describe the function of a member of a legislature. It holds that legislators may believe that they were sent to Washington or the state capital to think and vote independently for the general welfare—and not as their constituents—determine.

Unicameral legislature. One-house legislature; Nebraska and almost all cities use this form.

Union shop. "Union-security" provision found in some collective bargaining agreements requiring all employees to become members of the union within a short period—usually thirty days after being hired—and to remain members as a condition of employment.

Unitary system. Government with power concentrated by the constitution in the central government.

Unit rule. Requirement that the whole delegation to a party convention cast its vote as the majority decides.

Universe. The entire population of a group about which information is sought.

User charges. Fees charged directly to individuals who use certain public services on the basis of service consumed; sometimes called a user fee or user tax.

Virginia Plan. Proposal at the Constitutional Convention that provided for a strong legislature with representation in each house determined by population—thus favoring the large states.

Voter registration. See *Registration*.

Watergate. The general name given to a set of both major and minor violations of the law committed by Nixon Administration officials and their "friends" that occurred in 1972—including obstruction of justice or covering up of crimes that took place when the National Democratic Committee headquarters was broken into in 1972. The Committee was then located in the Watergate Office Building adjacent to the fashionable Watergate Hotel in Washington DC. Other incidents involved misuse of the Internal Revenue Service, the Central Intelligence Agency, and the FBI, the breaking in and entering of a psychiatrist's office, and various "dirty tricks" perpetrated on some of President Nixon's election opponents in the 1972 presidential election. Nixon was eventually forced out of office because of these events, and several of his advisors were indicted and served jail sentences.

Weak mayor–council. Form of local government in which the mayor must share most of the executive powers of a city with other elected or appointed boards and commissions. The mayor in weak-mayor cities is often mainly a ceremonial leader.

Whip. Party leader who is the liaison between the leadership and the rank and file in the legislature.

White Primary. Under the pretense that it was not governmental action, officials of the Democratic Party in the South used to admit to its primaries only white persons. Since in those days in the South candidates of the Democratic Party were the only ones with any chance of winning in the following general election, blacks were excluded from the only election that counted. The White Primary in all its various forms was declared unconstitutional by the Supreme Court in *Smith* v. *Allwright* (1944).

Writ of certiorari. Writ used by the Supreme Court to review decisions of lower courts, federal and state, that are within the discretionary appellate jurisdiction of the Supreme Court. It is a formal device regularly used to bring a case up to the Court.

Writ of habeas corpus. Court order requiring jailers to explain to a judge why they are holding a prisoner in custody.

Writ of mandamus. Court order directing an official to perform a nondiscretionary, or ministerial, act as required by law.

Yellow-dog contract. Contract by an antiunion employer which forces prospective workers to promise they will not join a union after employment.

Zero-based budgeting (ZBB). A budgeting procedure popularized by former President Carter that forces an agency or department to reevaluate its existing programs and performance. According to this procedure, agencies must specify alternative levels of service and rank their highest priorities.

Zoning. The use of city laws to classify land uses and assign land to certain uses—for example, residential, commercial, or industrial.

ABOUT THE AUTHORS

James MacGregor Burns

James MacGregor Burns, a native and lifelong resident of Massachusetts, is Woodrow Wilson Professor of Political Science at Williams College, where he has taught for the past thirty years. He has written several books, including *The Vineyard of Liberty* (1982); *Leadership* (1979); *The Deadlock of Democracy: Four Party Politics in America* (1963); *Roosevelt: The Lion and The Fox* (1956); *Roosevelt: The Soldier of Freedom* (1970); and *Uncommon Sense* (1972). Active in professional and civic life, Burns is a past president of the American Political Science Association and a former congressional candidate. He has also served as delegate to several national political conventions. Although his major loves are writing (for which he has won numerous prizes, including the Pulitzer Prize and the National Book Award) and undergraduate teaching, he can sometimes be found chopping wood, running, skiing, or playing tennis in his own cherished Berkshire community of Williamstown.

J. W. Peltason

J. W. Peltason is one of the country's leading scholars on courts, judicial process, and public law. Educated at Missouri and Princeton, he has taught political science at Princeton, Midwestern Univ., Smith College, and the Univ. of Illinois. He is at present an administrator and professor of Political Science at the Univ. of California, Irvine; he has served as an administrator at the Univ. of Illinois, Urbana-Champaign; and was president of the American Council on Education. He has been the spokesperson for higher education before Congress and state legislatures, and his writings include *Federal Courts in the Political Process* (1955); *Fifty-Eight Lonely Men: Southern Federal Judges and School Desegregation* (1961); and *Understanding the Constitution* (1981). Peltason recently completed a two-year term as president of Phi Sigma Alpha, the national political science honor society. His work on behalf of higher education takes him to many college and university campuses. Dr. Peltason received the American Political Science Association's Charles E. Merriam Award in 1983 to "the person whose published work and career represents a significant contribution to the art of government. . . ."

Thomas E. Cronin

Thomas E. Cronin earned his PhD in political science from Stanford University. A former White House Fellow and White House aide (in the mid-1960s), he has served on the staffs of the Brookings Institution, the Center for the Study of Democratic Institutions, and the Aspen Institute. Cronin has taught at the Universities of North Carolina and Delaware and is now on the faculty at Colorado College. He is the author or coauthor of *The Presidential Advisory System* (1969); *The State of the Presidency* (1980); *U.S.* v. *Crime in the Streets* (1981); and *Rethinking the Presidency* (1982). Cronin serves on the editorial boards of the *Presidential Studies Quarterly*, the *Western Political Quarterly*, and *Congress and the Presidency*. He has been active in partisan politics, serving as a delegate to several national conventions, and he was a candidate for the U.S. Congress in 1982. A hiker and skier, Cronin has lectured at over 150 colleges and is a frequent contributor to national journals.

INDEX

Blacks (African Americans)
  in the Constitution, 191
  and the law, 148–49
  militants, 90
  movement politics of, 179–82, 191
  political opportunity of, 278–79
  rights of, 97–101, 105–6, 107
  voting power of, 115, 198
Blockbusting techniques, 120
Block grants, 57
Blue laws, 70
B-1 bomber, 480–82
Boone, Pat, 507
Borah, Frank, 96
Borough (see County government)
Bossism, 222, 231
Boycott, secondary, 511–12
Bradley, Bill, 547
Bradley-Gephardt plan, 546–47
Branches of government (see also Checks and balances), 2
Brandeis, Louis, 45, 74, 134
Branzburg v. Hayes, 79
Bricker, John 357
Briefs (court procedure), 392
British system of government (parliamentary), 3, 30–31, 288
Brock, William, 226, 234
Brodhead, William, 291–92
Broker rule, 569
Bronson, Ruth Muskrat, 178
Brown, John, 286
Brown, Minnie Jean, 112
Brown, Rap, 286
Brown v. Board of Education, 105, 110, 440
Bryan, William Jennings, 461
Bryce, James, 7, 571
Brzezinski, Zbigniew, 462
Buckley v. Valeo, 89
Budde, Bernadette A., 168
Budget
  balanced budget amendment, 35, 36, 557–59
  congress and, 362–64, 548
  preparing, 429, 548–50
Budget and Accounting Act of 1921, 550
Budget Reform Act of 1974, 550
Bumpers, Dale, 256
Bundy, McGeorge, 462
Bureaucracy, federal, 404–32
  civil service, 407–9
  control over, 426–32
  criticism of, 420–23
  model of administration of, 409–10
  organization of, 405–7
  politics and, 410–13, 414–17
  proponents of, 424–25
  public opinion of, 417–19
  responsiveness and accountability of, 425
  statistics on, 404–5
Bureaucratic politics model (for studying policy-making), 437
Bureaucrats, federal, 404–32
  hiring of, 407–9
  politics of, 410–17
  public opinion of, 407–20
  as scapegoats, 420
  unions of, 419
Bureaus, federal, 406
Burford, Anne, 503
Burger, Warren, 77–78, 82, 83, 366
Burke, Edmund, 300
Bush, George, 186, 246
Business
  government regulation of, 505–9
  and "liberty of contract," 131–32
  subsidies to, 525–34
  "unions" of, 161
Business-Industry Political Action Committee, 167

Business Roundtable, 161, 499
Busing, 112–13
By Blue Ontario's Shore, 572

Cabinet, presidential, 339–41, 405
Caddell, Patrick, 249
Cahn, Edmond, 146
Calhoun, John C., 51, 219
California Walkman, 133
Cameras, hidden, 134–35
Campaign Finance Law (1974), 266–67
Campaigns, political
  committees, 226–28
  contributions, 167–68, 172, 264–67
  criticism of, 155–56
  funds, 89, 167–68, 172, 262, 263–68
  the media and, 82, 245–50
  regulation of, 89, 172
  for various offices, 254–68, 297–98
Candidates, political, 254–68
  funding of, 155–56, 167–68, 172, 263–68
  and media, 246–50
  selection of, 224–25
  for various offices, 254–63
Capital punishment, 143–44
Capitol, the, 293
Cardozo, Benjamin, 145
Carey, Hugh, 63
Carnal Knowledge case, 85
Career, political (see Politics, career ladder in)
Carson, Rachel, 290, 494
Carter, Jimmy, 61, 218
  appointments, 385
  and B-1 bomber debate, 480–82
  and cabinet, 339–41
  and energy issues, 533
Categorical formula grants, 56–57
Caucus, congressional, 307
Caucus system, 224–25, 235, 258–59, 270
CBS, 244–45
Censorship, 76, 81, 86
Census, Bureau of the, 526
Census tracts, 210
Central government (see Federal government)
Central Intelligence Agency (CIA), 360–61, 464
Certiorari, writ of, 388
Chada decision, 126
Chamber of Commerce of the United States, 161
Checks and balances, 2–4, 24–25, 28–30, 224
Chicago National Convention (Democratic, 1968), 232
Chicanos, 102
Chief Justice(s), 379–96
  and Congress, 386
  influence of, 396
  procedures of, 387–96
  selection of, 382–86
Child Labor Amendment, 37, 39
China, People's Republic of, 208, 455
China Lobby, 162
Christian Scientists, 72
Chrysler Corporation, 527–30
Churchill, Winston, 452
Cinema, censorship of, 81, 85–86
Circuit court, 378–79
Citizen, private, and libel, 84
Citizens party, 222
Citizenship
  American, 124–28
  dual, 125
  obligations of, 123
  rights of, 125–28
  state, 125
Civil Aeronautics Board (CAB), 517–18
Civil disobedience, 88, 187

WASHINGTON
Centers of Decision and Landmarks

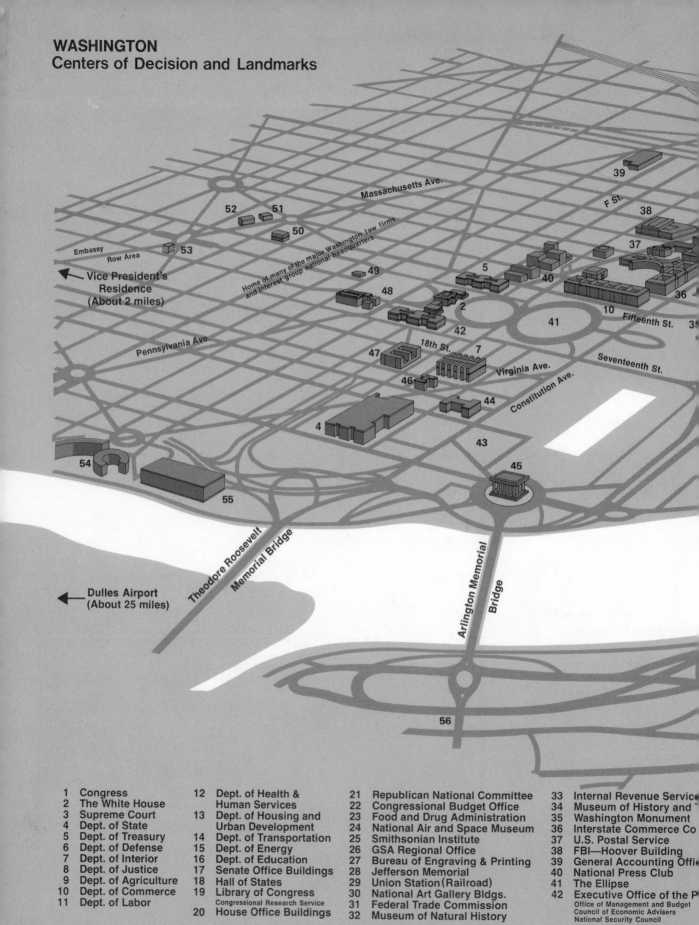

Massachusetts Ave.

F St.

39

38

52 51

50

37

Embassy
Row Area   53

Home of many of the major Washington law firms
and interest group national headquarters

5

49

40

36

← Vice President's
Residence
(About 2 miles)

48

2

10

Pennsylvania Ave.

42

41

Fifteenth St.

47   18th St.   7

Virginia Ave.

46   44   Constitution Ave.

Seventeenth St.

4

43

54

45

55

Theodore Roosevelt
Memorial Bridge

Arlington Memorial
Bridge

← Dulles Airport
(About 25 miles)

56

1	Congress	12	Dept. of Health &	21	Republican National Committee	33	Internal Revenue Service
2	The White House		Human Services	22	Congressional Budget Office	34	Museum of History and
3	Supreme Court	13	Dept. of Housing and	23	Food and Drug Administration	35	Washington Monument
4	Dept. of State		Urban Development	24	National Air and Space Museum	36	Interstate Commerce Co
5	Dept. of Treasury	14	Dept. of Transportation	25	Smithsonian Institute	37	U.S. Postal Service
6	Dept. of Defense	15	Dept. of Energy	26	GSA Regional Office	38	FBI—Hoover Building
7	Dept. of Interior	16	Dept. of Education	27	Bureau of Engraving & Printing	39	General Accounting Offi
8	Dept. of Justice	17	Senate Office Buildings	28	Jefferson Memorial	40	National Press Club
9	Dept. of Agriculture	18	Hall of States	29	Union Station (Railroad)	41	The Ellipse
10	Dept. of Commerce	19	Library of Congress	30	National Art Gallery Bldgs.	42	Executive Office of the P
11	Dept. of Labor		Congressional Research Service	31	Federal Trade Commission		Office of Management and Budget
		20	House Office Buildings	32	Museum of Natural History		Council of Economic Advisers
							National Security Council